The Papers of Dwight David Eisenhower

THE PAPERS OF DWIGHT DAVID EISENHOWER

THE PRESIDENCY: THE MIDDLE WAY
XVII

EDITORS

LOUIS GALAMBOS   DAUN VAN EE

EXECUTIVE EDITOR
ELIZABETH S. HUGHES

ASSOCIATE EDITORS
ROBIN D. COBLENTZ   ROBERT J. BRUGGER

PRODUCTION EDITOR
JANET L. SERAPHINE

ASSISTANT EDITOR
JILL A. FRIEDMAN

THE JOHNS HOPKINS UNIVERSITY PRESS

BALTIMORE AND LONDON

This book has been brought to publication with the generous assistance of the National Endowment for the Humanities, the National Historical Publications and Records Commission, and the Eisenhower World Affairs Institute.

The Johns Hopkins University Press, 2715 North Charles Street,
Baltimore, Maryland 21218-4139
The Johns Hopkins Press Ltd., London

All illustrations in this volume are from the
Dwight D. Eisenhower Library, Abilene,
Kansas, unless indicated otherwise.

Library of Congress Cataloging-in-Publication Data

Eisenhower, Dwight D. (Dwight David), 1890–1969.
The papers of Dwight D. Eisenhower.

Vol. 6 edited by A. D. Chandler and L. Galambos;
v. 7–   , by L. Galambos.
Includes bibliographies and index.
Contents: v. 1–5. The war years.—[etc.]—
v. 10–11. Columbia University.—v. 12–13. NATO and the
Campaign of 1952.
1. World War, 1939–1945—United States.   2. World War,
1939–1945—Campaigns.   3. United States—Politics and
government—1953–1961.   4. Presidents—United States—
Election—1952.   5. Eisenhower, Dwight D. (Dwight David),
1890–1969.   6. Presidents—United States—Archives.
I. Chandler, Alfred Dupont, ed.   II. Galambos, Louis, ed.
III. United States. President (1953–1961 : Eisenhower)
IV. Title.
E742.E37   1970   973.921′092′4[B]   65-27672
ISBN 0-8018-1078-7 (v. 1–5)
ISBN 0-8018-2061-8 (v. 6–9)
ISBN 0-8018-2720-5 (v. 10–11)
ISBN 0-8018-3726-x (v. 12–13)
ISBN 0-8018-4752-4 (v. 14–17)

Contents

The Papers of Dwight David Eisenhower

The Presidency: The Middle Way

Cracks in the Alliance

MAY 1956 TO SEPTEMBER 1956

20

Confronting "great risks"

To Herbert Clark Hoover, Jr.   *May 2, 1956*
Eyes Only for the Acting Secretary of State.
Personal and secret

During the course of the day, a number of matters have come to my attention affecting our international situation. I present them to you below, for your informal comment at a convenient time.

(*a*). You will recall that when we once invited Magsaysay to the United States, he let us know that he could not come unless the visit could be made the occasion of some kind of financial present. To this we could not agree, if for no other reason than the impossible precedent it would establish.[1]

But there is another outstanding question between the Philippines and ourselves, involving certain of the property to which we have retained title in that country.[2] It is possible that the Defense Department has at last come to see that not all of these would be necessary to our interests in the region, and it might be that a return of title to the Philippines would offer to Ma[g]saysay a real reason for coming and might bring both him and his country closer to us. I realize that such places as Olongapo and Clark Field cannot be given up, but I have no doubt that we have other holdings that we are retaining more because of their need in a hypothetical case than because of any established requirement.[3]

(*b*). With respect to the military disadvantages we are suffering in Korea because of the Armistice and of our failure to have the Armistice Commission removed from Korea, I wonder whether the time has not come when we should not publicly announce our intention of keeping our forces there equipped with the newest types of weapons, because of the impossibility of supplying spare parts and maintenance for the older types.[4]

(*c*). A good many weeks ago we made a firm offer to Egypt to help in the construction of the Aswan Dam.[5] I see no reason to change the opinion we then held that the intervention of the Soviets in this proposition would be more or less disastrous. If this is true, I would assume we are attempting to make progress with the Egyptians in the arrangement that we proposed.

What has happened?[6]

(*d*). In connection with our secret preparations for the meeting that has been suggested for June 25th and 26th, I should like to make certain that no long formal speeches will be expected of anyone, especially of me.[7]

(*e*). After reading a New York Times editorial on the ILO proposition, I am not so sure as I was that a convention would violate our concepts of the proper purposes of an international instrument.[8] The editorial implied the convention was nothing but a condemnation of the theory of forced labor, with a commitment on the part of each participating nation to use *its own constitutional processes* to see that forced labor was not in practice within the confines of that country.

I realize that when our conference on this matter broke up the other morning, that State, Justice and Labor Departments had all agreed to study the matter further. My feeling is that while we must be particularly careful to avoid including improper subjects in international instruments, we must likewise be careful not to discourage the abolition of forced labor and so thereby incur a very bad propaganda defeat.

There is no rush about replying to any of these matters, but I do hope that at your convenience you will take the occasion to discuss them with me further.

¹ On the invitation to Philippine President Ramon Magsaysay see no. 1250.

² The Military Bases Agreement of 1947 provided the United States with ninety-nine year leases on twenty-three sites to be used as military bases. This agreement covered three significant installations: the Air Force base at Clark Field in Central Luzon, a major Fleet and Fleet Air Base at Subic Bay, and a Naval Air Station at Sangley Point on Manila Bay. For background on base negotiations see no. 319; see also Galambos, *Chief of Staff*, no. 1210; State, *Foreign Relations, 1952–1954*, vol. XII, *East Asia and the Pacific*, pt. 2, pp. 543, 552–54, 569–70, 586–89, 600–603, 643–44; and State, *Foreign Relations, 1955–1957*, vol. XXII, *Southeast Asia*, pp. 579–87, 592–97, 625–28.

³ Acting Secretary Hoover would tell Eisenhower that negotiations regarding the bases would begin shortly after the newly-appointed ambassador arrived in Manila in July. "We hope to obtain from the Filipinos the right to use certain new land areas which the Defense Department regards as necessary to permit optimum development of the bases," Hoover wrote. "We plan to return to the Philippines a number of bases which we no longer need, and to withdraw our claim to title to all the lands which we now own." President Magsaysay already knew that the United States intended to return title to the properties, Hoover said, and would probably not consider it an incentive to come to the United States (Hoover to Eisenhower, May 3, 1956, AWF/I: Philippines; on the progress of negotiations see State, *Foreign Relations, 1955–1957*, vol. XXII, *Southeast Asia*, pp. 649–51, 662–90). Eisenhower would write Magasaysay in October to express his hope that a mutually satisfactory agreement could be reached. Resolution of the issue, however, would not occur during Eisenhower's term in office (Oct. 5, 1956, AWF/I: Philippines).

⁴ Although the armistice prohibited the reinforcement of troops and the introduction of additional materiel, the Chinese Communists had moved increasing numbers of modern weapons and aircraft into North Korea. The Neutral Nations Supervisory Commission (NNSC), charged with the investigation of alleged violations of the armistice, had been unable to prevent this buildup. The Administration had revised its official Korean policy to reflect these infractions (NSC 5514) and had participated in discussions to abolish the commission.

Hoover would tell Eisenhower that although the time was near for the United States to supply new weapons for its forces, the problem of the NNSC and its inspection teams had to be solved. The State Department planned to tell the governments of the United Nations Command that the UNC was planning to suspend provisionally the terms of the armistice relating to the operations of the commission because of "flagrant Communist violations." Some important allies were not pleased with the decision, Hoover said, and their support would be necessary when the action was considered by the United Nations. Negotiations with other nations and disagreements between the departments of State and Defense would delay the modernization program until June 1957 (see State, *Foreign Relations, 1952–1954*, vol. XV, *Korea*, pt. 1, pp. 256, 1790–91, 1806–8, 1868, 1875, 1910–11, 1924–26, 1946; State, *Foreign Relations, 1955–1957*, vol. XXIII, pt. 2, *Korea* [1993], pp. 71, 179, 198–202, 204–9, 228–33, 237–39; Condit, *The Joint Chiefs of Staff and National Policy, 1955–1956*, pp. 211–20; and NSC meeting minutes, Mar. 11, 1955, AWF/NSC).

[5] For background see nos. 1759 and 1811.

[6] Hoover would reply that the Egyptians had made counter proposals "which basically alter the premise on which the original . . . offer was made." Egypt wanted firmer guarantees of U.S. aid for the whole project and Sudanese agreement on the division of the Nile River waters before construction could begin. Once the United States reached agreement with the British on their response to the proposals, discussions would be held with the World Bank, Hoover said (Hoover to Eisenhower, May 3, 1956, AWF/I: Egypt; see also State, *Foreign Relations, 1955–1957*, vol. XV, *Arab-Israeli Dispute January 1–July 26, 1956*, pp. 450–51, 588–89). For developments see no. 1932.

[7] Eisenhower was scheduled to visit Panama for the meeting of the Presidents of the American Republics. Hoover assured him that no formal speeches would be expected of any of the visiting presidents (Hoover to Eisenhower, May 3, 1956, AWF/D-H). For more on the trip see no. 1925.

[8] For background on the International Labor Organization, its proposed convention opposing forced labor, and the State Department's position on the issue, see no. 1855. The editorial had appeared on April 29.

1860   *EM, AWF, DDE Diaries Series*

To Bernard Law Montgomery   *May 2, 1956*
Secret

Dear Monty: I have read your CPX address with the greatest interest. I was particularly intrigued by the way you approached the subject— looking back rather than forward to a conflict.[1]

I agree with much you have to say about the need for planning, for approaching our problems of today realistically.[2] However, you have one thesis in your paper to which I take exception. It is that the Russians undertook this war knowing that they were going to lose, and that they did this in order to promote Communism. I think this is an unrealistic assumption. These Communists are not early Christian martyrs. The men in the Kremlin are avid for power and are ruthlessly ambitious. I cannot see them starting a war merely for the opportunity that such a conflict might offer their successors to spread their doctrine.[3]

Another point I raise about your study is that you made no attempt to visualize the true nature of the holocaust that would result from the exchange of "eight thousand nuclear weapons." Presumably the warheads on a good number of these would be hydrogen bombs, and I believe you have far underestimated the degree of destruction that would result.[4] I think also that you give more credit than I do to the estimated accuracy with which guided missiles of an intercontinental variety will be operating in another ten years. I believe the main part of the blow in any such hypothetical war would be delivered by the manned airplane, supplemented by guided missiles, rather than the reverse. For our side, this would be almost mandatory because of the great difficulty in getting the exact locations of interior targets in the Soviet Union.

Now with respect to the degree of damage, entirely aside from the material destruction you visualize, I believe there would be literally millions of dead after any such nuclear attack. In such circumstances what does a nation do; what can it do? I realize that the side suffering the lesser damage—in this case the allies—could achieve some restored capacity for action earlier than would the other, and so I do not quarrel with your description of later events.

All of this of course is just by way of giving you some observations that occurred to me immediately after going through your document. I do applaud you for your imagination in tackling the problem and for bringing into focus some of the great needs of our times; that is, intelligence, scientific development, plans and, so far as we can achieve it, central control of some of our forces.

As for next May—please write to me about the turn of the year. It's impossible at this moment to say, on a scheduled basis, where we shall be or what we shall be doing at any given time. But, of course, we'll work something out; and we'll be truly glad to see you.[5]

With warm regard, *As ever*

[1] Deputy Supreme Allied Commander, Europe, Montgomery had written the President and had enclosed a copy of his address to the sixth annual NATO command post exercises, CPX SIX (Apr. 27, 1956, AWF/N). Montgomery had written the lengthy address as if he were a NATO general in 1969, discussing a three-year war that had occurred in 1966. He expected the West to win the war through the use of sophisticated systems of nuclear power. Nuclear reactors might be fueled, Montgomery suggested, by transport missiles filled with nuclear fuel and fired at Europe from uranium mines in Africa. He also grappled with the problem of transporting adequate food to the Allied armies in Europe: "Pills instead of normal food I am told are not a scientific possibility except for very short periods; the human body needs the bulk." Despite this difficulty, he believed that the problem would "partially solve itself" as the nuclear-powered armies of the future diminished in size ("CPX SIX, Final Address by D/SACEUR," Apr. 27, 1956, AWF/N, Montgomery Corr.).

[2] Montgomery had called for more realistic planning to make statesmen and scientists aware of what the military would need to reconstruct the world after a global war. The need, he observed, was immediate and would "require all the wisdom and energies of our politicians, economists and military leaders." In particular, Montgomery believed that NATO needed better intelligence, a centrally-controlled air and missile force, powerful, self-sufficient fighting divisions armed with nuclear weapons and powered with "special fuels of high energy." Another key to Montgomery's strategy was sea power—the ability to track submarines at long range combined with allied fleets of

surface and underwater missile-firing ships. He had argued that after widespread destruction of land forces, Western naval superiority would be decisive (*ibid.*).

³ Montgomery had written that the Soviet Union planned to start nuclear war in order to create chaos and misery so that it could conquer the West by subversion. The Soviets, he said, expected to have enough resources to pull through after the war was over (*ibid.*). For more on Eisenhower's views on Soviet intentions see NSC meeting minutes, May 10, 1956, AWF/NSC.

⁴ Montgomery would reply: "As regards the frightful results of some 8000 nuclear weapons, I did indeed paint a very unpleasant picture. But Al [Gruenther] asked me to play it down because he thought it would upset the Germans, and other continental nations!!" (May 7, 1956, AWF/N). Eisenhower would forward a copy of his correspondence with Montgomery to General Gruenther (May 8, 1956, Gruenther Papers).

⁵ Montgomery had asked if he could spend a weekend with the Eisenhowers at Gettysburg during a visit planned for May 1957 (Montgomery to Eisenhower, Apr. 27, 1956, AWF/N).

1861   *EM, AWF, Name Series*

To Edgar Newton Eisenhower   *May 2, 1956*
Personal and confidential

Dear Ed: Contrary to your assumption, I had not seen the clipping that carried the story on your visit to Senator Bridges.¹ The fact is that it is so tame or pale as compared to some things that are said about me, my family or Administration that the staff was not impressed sufficiently to call it to my attention.

I am interested in your statement, "I do think and have said so to you, that the Government is rapidly drifting into a socialistic state." A statement such as this seems indication to me that you are not studying the march of events with as clear an eye as you should; you are talking from impressions and prejudices without giving the important factors serious examination.²

In 1948, '49, '50, '51 and early '52, many hundreds of people were urging me to go into politics. Scores of different reasons were advanced as to why I should do so, but in general they all boiled down to something as follows: "The country is going socialistic so rapidly that, unless Republicans can get in immediately and defeat this trend, our country is gone. Four more years of New Dealism and there will be no turning back. This is our last chance."³

To all of these people I made the same reply time and time again: (*a*) It is silly to believe that any individual in the world—or, indeed, any party—can actually turn a whole population back from a course it has pursued in the belief that that course is assisting the majority of the population. (Naturally, I am now speaking of a self-governing country.)

Neither I nor anyone else can bring about the abandonment of projects supported by the government that are generally believed to help the social or economic welfare of vast portions of our population. (*b*) The most that anyone—even if he is supported by a good majority in the Congress—could do would be gradually to stop the trend in this direction, slowly to bend the rising curve toward greater socialism and eventually to flatten it out so that further advance in this dangerous direction would be prevented.

(*c*) To bring about this result would not only take persistence and patience by the government, but it would require a maximum degree of understanding on the part of the so-called "standpatters." These people will have to recognize the truth of the statements made in (*a*) and (*b*), and must devote their efforts *to helping stabilize the situation rather than criticizing efforts which recognize that you cannot return to the days of 1860.*[4]

Now just one or two more general comments. Shortly after I was elected, former President Hoover visited me in my office. He said something to me which I quote roughly as follows: "You have, from an economic viewpoint, the most difficult task that has ever faced any of our Presidents. All of us believe that there is great danger lying ahead in the direction we are now travelling. Yet you cannot go back. Your accomplishments will necessarily be confined to a gradual halting of that movement. As a result, the reactionaries will snarl at you, as well, of course, as the people that join the ADA and other so-called 'liberal' groups. Education of the entire people will be a task of the Party, and since so many people will misunderstand what is going on, that education will be a slow and laborious process."[5]

My only other point is really a suggestion. Stevenson has lately been speaking in Oregon. Why don't you get copies of his talks and read them over? You will find that he is complaining bitterly because the Republican Party, under my leadership, is guided only by its devotion to the monopoly of money, to the service of the rich, and to the exploitation of the masses. Of course he makes different speeches in different States, but in Oregon he is applying these generalizations to my attitude about power development. Since I believe that the responsibility for power development should not reside exclusively in the Federal Government, he asserts that I am giving away to the rich the assets of the whole people. In other States he is quite capable of saying something entirely different.[6]

Even the big fight in the TVA region came about because I refused to build more *steam* plants at Federal expense to produce power for that area. All of the hydroelectric capacity has been developed in the area and so many steam plants have been built by the Federal Government that already one-half of the power for that region is produced in that way. Yet I am called a reactionary because I believe that the Federal Government should not be building more steam plants in that region.[7]

I am a little amused about this word "real" that in your clipping modifies the word "Republican." I assume that Lincoln was a *real* Republican—in fact, I think we should have to assume that every President, being the elected leader of the Party, is a *real* Republican.[8] Therefore, the President's branch of the Party requires, for its description, no adjective whatsoever. I should think that the splinter groups, which oppose the leader, would be the ones requiring the descriptive adjectives. In any event, please look up sometime what Lincoln had to say about the proper *functions* of government.[9] *As ever*

[1] Edgar had written on April 30 (AWF/N) to complain about a newspaper article which had quoted him as having said, "You know, my brother is a little bit socialistic. As a matter of fact, I'm the only real Republican in the family." The article had further stated that while "right-wing" Republicans probably had recognized that the President's brother had been joking, they also believed that "many a bit of truth comes out in a jest." An infuriated Edgar had written, "If this is a privilege of free speech and free press, then I think we should amend the Constitution to muzzle fellows like this reporter. If I were young and strong like I used to be, I would make a trip to Washington just to punch this fellow in the nose." A draft of this letter, with Eisenhower's handwritten changes, is in AWF/Drafts.

[2] The President's brother had written that he never had "thought you were socialistic, although I do think and have said so to you, that the Government is rapidly drifting into a socialistic state."

[3] See *Eisenhower Papers*, vols. X–XIII.

[4] See also Galambos, *NATO and the Campaign of 1952*, no. 562.

[5] Hoover had written in September 1953 that he had taken the job of chairman of the second Hoover Commission in the hope that he could "keep the ADA from running the United States" (see Best, *Herbert Hoover: The Postpresidential Years*, p. 376).

[6] Stevenson had scored the Adminstration for the "infamous Dixon-Yates deal to give away a big profit at little or no risk to a private utility company, while at the same time striking a blow at the T.V.A." (for background see no. 1515). See *New York Times*, April 30, May 1, 2.

[7] See, for example, no. 1132.

[8] See also no. 977.

[9] Lincoln had written that the object of government was to do for people what needed to be done, but which they could not, by individual effort, do at all or do so well. "There are many such things—some of them exist independently of the injustice in the world. Making and maintaining roads, bridges, and the like; providing for the helpless young and afflicted; common schools; and disposing of deceased men's property, are instances" (Abraham Lincoln, *The Collected Works of Abraham Lincoln*, ed. Roy P. Basler, 8 vols. [New Brunswick, N. J., 1953], vol. II, *1848–1858*, p. 221).

1862   *EM, AWF, Dulles-Herter Series*

To Robert Anthony Eden   *May 2, 1956*
Telegram. Top secret

Dear Anthony: Thank you very much for your interesting report on your recent visitors.[1] Comparison of their conduct in Britain with the deportment of these same two individuals in Yugoslavia a couple of years ago does at least show that these men are capable of learning from experience.[2]

I am delighted that you made your views so utterly plain to them. At least in some areas we should be able to avoid emergencies that could arise out of misunderstanding or miscalculation on their part.

Foster left for Europe last evening, but I believe that on this trip he is not counting on stopping in London, so he will not get to see you.[3] With warm regard, *As ever*

[1] Soviet Premier Nikolai Bulganin and Party Secretary Nikita Khrushchev had completed a nine-day visit to London on April 27 (see no. 1828). Eden had described the discussions as "tough" but "useful and instructive." Khrushchev had told Eden that although Soviet influence in the Eastern European bloc was considerable, the countries "could be touchy and the Russians could not just order them about." During discussions regarding the Middle East, Eden said, he had made plain to the Soviet officials that Great Britain had to have oil and was "prepared to fight for it." "They accepted this and though they continued to inveigh against the Baghdad Pact (or the Eden Pact, as Bulganin told me they call it in Moscow) I think that they may have begun to understand that it is a protective pad for our vital interests and not a dagger pointing at their guts" (Eden to Eisenhower, n.d., AWF/I: Eden; see also State, *Foreign Relations, 1955–1957*, vol. XXVII, *Western Europe and Canada*, pp. 657–58).

[2] Eisenhower may have been referring to a verbal confrontation between Khrushchev and the U.S. ambassador to Yugoslavia during the visit of Soviet officials to that country in May 1955 (see State, *Foreign Relations, 1955–1957*, vol. XXVI, *Central and Southeastern Europe*, pp. 650–58; see also no. 1593). The words "a couple of years ago" were changed to "about a year" by State Department officials in the final draft of this letter (TEDUL 5).

[3] Secretary Dulles was in Paris for the North Atlantic Council meeting, held on May 4 and 5.

1863   *EM, AWF, Dulles-Herter Series*

To Robert Anthony Eden   *May 2, 1956*
Telegram. Secret

Dear Anthony: I regret that the copper wire items offers for you such a problem. There is no question in our minds that this is the most important thing that the Bears and their Associates now get from us.[1]

As to the rest of your telegram, I think that Foster will be able to propose something that will ease the situation for you. I do hope that he and Selwyn Lloyd can work out something that will be satisfactory.[2] *As ever*

[1] For background see no. 1854. In an undated letter that Eisenhower received on this day, Eden had told the President that adding copper wire to the list of items embargoed

from Russia and its Communist allies would present "serious difficulties" for Great Britain. "I do not see how we could agree to this now," he wrote (State, *Foreign Relations, 1955–1957*, vol. X, *Foreign Aid and Economic Defense Policy*, p. 359).

2 Eden had asked for "appreciable relaxation" of the embargo list, "particularly because of progress toward self-government in our colonial territories. A country like Malaya simply does not understand why it has to accept restrictions which are not in operation in, for example, Ceylon."

Dulles would arrive in Paris on May 2 for a North Atlantic Council meeting, which British Foreign Secretary Lloyd also attended. After Dulles realized that the British would not accept restrictions on the sale of copper, he wrote the President that there was "room for an honest difference of opinion as to the strategic importance of the copper wire." Lloyd would eventually inform Dulles that the British intended to expand exports to the East unilaterally (*Foreign Relations, 1955–1957*, vol. X, *Foreign Aid and Economic Defense Policy*, pp. 360–66). For developments see no. 1868.

1864   *EM, AWF, Dulles-Herter Series*

To HERBERT CLARK HOOVER, JR.   *May 3, 1956*
Personal

Dear Herbert: Herewith a brief file that you may find interesting.[1] I would like to have your opinion on the paragraph of the press release that I have marked in ink.[2] When I talked to Foster about the theory of multi-lateral aid, he said that in his opinion it would open up to Russia greater opportunities to propagandize than she now has.[3] By that he meant that by participating in all international aid wherever extended, the Russians would have greater opportunities for political penetration. Cabot seems to have discounted this idea.[4] *As ever*

[1] Eisenhower had sent Acting Secretary of State Hoover a copy of a statement made by U.N. Ambassador Henry Cabot Lodge, Jr., endorsing the concept of multilateral economic aid under the auspices of the United Nations. In his covering letter Lodge had told Eisenhower that after the President had expressed general approval of such aid, the press had asked the ambassador for a follow-up explanation (see Lodge to Eisenhower, May 1, 1956; and Statement by Ambassador Henry Cabot Lodge, Jr., Apr. 30, 1956, both in AWF/A; see also State, *Foreign Relations, 1955–1957*, vol. IX, *Foreign Economic Policy; Foreign Information Program*, pp. 359–80 for background; Eisenhower's statement is in *Public Papers of the Presidents: Eisenhower, 1956*, pp. 430–31).

[2] The paragraph read: "A multilateral program supplies no cover for engaging in political penetration, which is what the communists do and which we are unjustly suspected of wanting to do. We thus get credit for unselfish motives in contributing to such a fund; yet we can influence it constructively."

[3] In his conversation with Dulles, Eisenhower had said that he personally favored aid through the United Nations if the Soviet Union were to participate on a matching basis; he believed that the procedure would "sterilize" Soviet money. The theory was true in principle, Dulles said, but in fact the fund would be administered by "human beings who have to be picked." Since the Soviets would have an equal voice in selecting the administering officials, "agents might get into neutral countries under conditions more

dangerous than if they went directly as Soviet technicians. . ." (Memorandum of Conversation, May 1, 1956, Dulles Papers, White House Memoranda Series).
[4] Hoover's response in not in AWF. For developments see no. 1883.

1865

To HERBERT CLARK HOOVER, JR.

May 3, 1956

Memorandum for the Acting Secretary of State: Mr. Ward Canaday is one of the Americans who is active in the building of the new American School of Classical Studies in Athens.[1] The building, which is supposed to be a replica of an ancient Athenic structure, will be dedicated on September 2nd.

Mr. Canaday asked me whether I would be disposed to send a special representative to be present at the ceremony.[2] It is the kind of thing I would like to do if we don't twist up too many diplomatic wires in the attempt.

Would it be all right for me to tell him that he might notify the School authorities that I would accept their invitation to send such representative provided the Greek Government concurred?

My thought would be that the School authorities could go to our Ambassador in Athens, seeking such concurrence on the part of the Government, and then I could select some individual to represent me at the ceremony.

I believe that some 75 American universities are back of the project and have been supporting it for some 75 years.

Please let me know what you think.[3]

[1] For background on Ward Murphey Canaday, president of Overland Corporation, see Galambos, *NATO and the Campaign of 1952*, no. 687. Canaday was chairman of the board of trustees of the American School of Classical Studies.

[2] Eisenhower had met with Canaday earlier on this same day.

[3] Hoover would support Eisenhower's proposal. "This would be an effective way of showing American admiration for Greek civilization and I am sure that such a gesture would be received very sympathetically in Greece," he wrote (May 3, 1956; see also Eisenhower to Canaday, May 8, 1956; and Canaday to Eisenhower, May 15, 1956). The State Department would receive the invitation through appropriate channels, and the President would ask Canaday to serve as his personal representative (see Dulles to Eisenhower, June 27, 1956; Eisenhower to Canaday, July 20, 1956; and Canaday to Eisenhower, July 25, 1956). On September 2 Canaday would read a message from Eisenhower commemorating the seventy-fifth anniversary of the American School of Classical Studies and the dedication of the reconstruction of the Stoa of Attalos as the Museum of the Athenian Agora. All papers, including the President's message and other supporting material, are in the same file as the document.

To Katherine Graham Howard   *May 3, 1956*

Dear Katherine: Thank you for your note of the thirtieth and for sending
me your article on NATO, as it appeared in the State Department
Bulletin of March fifth.[1] I tried it out on my ill-informed secretary,
who informs me that she found it more informative than any of the
official bulletins on the purposes of NATO that have gone through
this office in the past years.[2] I agree that it's an excellent piece.

With warm regard, *Sincerely*

P.S. With or without your prettiest hat, I am sure you captivated
Pug Ismay![3]

---

[1] Katherine Graham Howard, former secretary of the Republican National Committee,
was Special Advisor, Federal Civil Defense Administration, and Permanent U.S. Alter-
nate Delegate to the NATO Civil Defense Committee (Howard to Eisenhower, Apr. 30,
1956, AWF/N). Her article was titled "Peace Through Strength: A Look at the North
Atlantic Treaty Organization" (*U.S. Department of State Bulletin* 34, no. 871 [March 5,
1956], 375–78).

[2] In the original text, this sentence was followed by an asterisk with a note "Insert by
same secretary!"—presumably Ann Whitman.

[3] Lord Ismay, Secretary General of NATO.

1867   *EM, AWF, Name Series:*
                                        Mamie Eisenhower Corr.

To Mamie Doud Eisenhower   *May 3, 1956*

I see nothing wrong with the letter, except that I have a suggestion
with respect to the final sentence of the first paragraph.[1] I would say
something as follows:

"As a resident of Adams County, I sincerely congratulate all of
you on your banding together to discharge more effectively the
duties and responsibilities of citizenship devolving upon every citizen in our country."

It is my thought that such a sentence as this would take your letter
a little bit more out of the partisan and put it a little more in the
"public service" level.

---

[1] Eisenhower was referring to a draft of a letter that his wife planned to send to Mrs. A.
W. Butterfield, a Gettysburg, Pennsylvania, resident and president of the Adams County Women's Republican Council. The Eisenhowers had met Mrs. Butterfield on February 3 at the Adams County Courthouse while registering to vote in the state of Pennsylvania (see correspondence in WHCF/PPF 1-A-15). We have been unable to find Mrs.

Eisenhower's letter to Mrs. Butterfield in EM. On October 29 the First Lady would thank Mrs. Butterfield for her "tireless, selfless" efforts. And, she would add, "our victory on November 6 will depend upon the continued loyalty and devotion of friends like you" (WHO/SO: BUTTER). Presidential secretary Ann Whitman sent the President's dictated message to Mary Jane McCaffree, Mamie Eisenhower's social secretary.

1868   *EM, AWF, DDE Diaries Series*

To John Foster Dulles   *May 4, 1956*

Dear Foster: Thanks for your message. I appreciate what you are up against and sympathize with your trials and troubles.[1] But I know that in your negotiations your performance, as always, will be superb.

I have asked Hollister to get busy on the quid pro quo of the trade affair, and to get in touch with you at the earliest possible moment.[2]

[1] Dulles had written the President that British Foreign Secretary Selwyn Lloyd had refused to embargo exports of copper wire to the Eastern Bloc. The British might, however, have been willing to consider quantitative controls on copper if other items were taken off the prohibited list (State, *Foreign Relations, 1955–1957*, vol. X, *Foreign Aid and Economic Defense Policy*, pp. 361–63; Dulles to Eisenhower, May 3, 1956, AWF/D-H; see also no. 1854). Ultimately, the British would refuse to limit their profitable exports of copper (State, *Foreign Relations, 1955–1957*, vol. X, *Foreign Aid and Economic Defense Policy*, pp. 363–66).
[2] John B. Hollister was director of the International Cooperation Administration of the Department of State.

1869   *EM, AWF, Administration Series*

To Henry Cabot Lodge, Jr.   *May 7, 1956*

Dear Cabot: The first part of the suggestions from your farmer friend may be very helpful.[1]

As to the second part, I don't understand it very well except for items #1 and #6.[2] If we are to assist—by which I assume he means the Federal government is to pay part of the cost—in the purchase of feed, fertilizer, farm machinery, insurance and livestock, we are actually running the farmers' business. It looks very cumbersome to me.

However, I shall ask Ezra Benson to study the matter.[3] *Sincerely*

¹ Lodge had written Eisenhower on May 1 (AWF/A) to offer the ideas of a farmer friend who had suggested that "skillful public relations" could convince farmers that rigid price supports would aggravate the surplus problem and would not prevent farm income from dropping if worldwide agricultural prices fell.
² Lodge's friend had also suggested six ways in which the farmer could be helped. Items 1 and 6 included the Soil Bank and special tax exemptions. Items 2–5 advocated assistance in purchasing feed, seed, fertilizer, farm machinery, livestock, and insurance. Such assistance would give money to the farmer that "he *must spend in acquiring the things he needs to run his business,* and this is a source of purchasing power which will dry up rapidly if the slide is allowed to continue."
³ For background on the Agricultural Act of 1956 see no. 1841.

1870   *EM, AWF, Administration Series*

To Paul Gray Hoffman   *May 8, 1956*

Dear Paul: I don't believe I adequately acknowledged your letter regarding the necessity for a bipartisan committee for reappraising our foreign economic policy and the memorandum that accompanied it.¹ As I told you, I deleted all references that might point to you as the author, and sent it to some of the people around here.² The consensus of reaction that I received was that it was a "penetrating" analysis of the problem.³

At any rate, I do want you to know of my appreciation of the time and trouble you took to set down so lucidly your thoughts on the matter. The document has been most helpful and I am very grateful.⁴

With warm regard, *As ever*

¹ Hoffman had told Eisenhower that the Soviet program of increased economic aid and expanded trade with uncommitted nations was designed to "soften" those countries for their acceptance of Communism. The United States must help destroy the plan, Hoffman said, "if we are to have the climate in which an enduring peace can be negotiated." The uncommitted nations needed a "bold, resolute, untimid program," one that was not just sharing U.S. wealth. Hoffman recommended the establishment of a bipartisan committee of nongovernment experts to assess the needs of the newly independent nations and their capacities for administering economic programs; the committee could then recommend programs for legislative action (Hoffman to Eisenhower, Apr. 24, 1956, AWF/A; see also Memorandum on Foreign Economic Policy, Apr. 24, 1956, *ibid.*
² Hoffman's letter, bearing Eisenhower's handwritten emendations, is in *ibid.*
³ Eisenhower had discussed the letter with Secretary Dulles on April 27. After identifying the author, the President had told Dulles that "he had been surprised at the sobriety of the remarks" (Memorandum of Conversation, Dulles Papers, White House Memoranda Series).
⁴ On the establishment of the President's Citizen Advisors Commission on the Mutual Security Program see no. 1849. For developments see no. 1883.

1871 EM, AWF, Administration Series

To HENRY CABOT LODGE, JR. May 8, 1956

Dear Cabot: While I would not want any serious matter coming before the United Nations to be delayed by a local United States election, nevertheless I suspect you are right in thinking that some of the issues might be "bothersome."[1]

With warm regard, *As ever*

[1] Lodge had told Eisenhower that after "a prolonged effort" by him to avoid having the General Assembly in session during the presidential campaign, Secretary General Hammarskjöld had announced that the Eleventh Session would open on November 12, after the election. "There are several issues in the U.N. which would be bothersome," Lodge said. "This would not be good for us—or for the United Nations" (Lodge to Eisenhower, May 3, 1956, AWF/A). Among the items on the U.N. agenda would be Chinese Communist representation and issues concerning Cyprus, Algeria, and Korea (State, *Foreign Relations, 1955–1957,* vol. XI, *United Nations and General International Matters,* pp. 118–28).

1872 EM, AWF, Name Series

To WALTER FRANKLIN GEORGE May 9, 1956

Dear Walter: I know that your present term in the Senate expires this year. In view of that fact, I should like to say two things to you:

It has been my great hope that you would continue on in the Senate where you have been able to make so great a contribution to peace through helping to develop and sustain a non-partisan foreign policy. Your contribution in that respect has been incalculable and I believe it was the overwhelming desire of the American people that you would have found yourself able to continue in the Senate.

I can, however, realize that you may desire to concentrate more exclusively on the great problems of war and peace which confront our nation, free of the other responsibilities which inevitably go with the Senatorship. If that is your preference, I earnestly hope that you will be willing to act for this nation with reference to the development of the North Atlantic Community so that it will in greater unity and greater effectiveness serve the cause of international peace and the preservation of those ideals of human liberty and freedom which are so deeply rooted in the Community.[1]

As you know, at the latest meeting of the North Atlantic Treaty Council, it was decided to explore ways and means by which the North Atlantic Community, through the NATO Council or otherwise, might more fully realize its potential for peace and human welfare.[2] I regard the contribution which the United States can make to this project as of the utmost importance and feel that it may indeed play a decisive role in the achievement of a just and durable peace and the preservation of the great values inherent in our Western civilization.

It would be a great service to the nation and, indeed in a broader sense, to the whole world if you would be willing, for as long as I may hold my present office, to act as my Personal Representative and Special Ambassador in the development of this new evolutionary step within the North Atlantic Community. In case you do feel impelled to lay down the responsibilities of your present office, I can think of no way where you could better serve our nation and more fittingly crown your great career as a statesman.

I may say that Foster Dulles has asked me to express his warm concurrence in what I say and that he greatly hopes that you will favorably consider this important mission.[3]

With warm personal regard. *Sincerely*

[1] For background see no. 1701. George would announce the same day that he had accepted the President's offer but would not run for reelection to the Senate (*New York Times*, May 10, 1956).

[2] Senator George would discuss this letter with the President on May 14. He would be charged with finding ways to improve NATO cooperation in nonmilitary fields and to foster greater unity within the Atlantic community (Statement, May 14, 1956, AWF/N, George Corr.). For Dulles's ideas on expanding nonmilitary cooperation within NATO see *Foreign Relations, 1955–1957*, vol. IV, *Western European Security and Integration*, pp. 63–76; NSC meeting minutes, May 11, 1956, AWF/NSC).

[3] For developments see no. 1964.

1873   *EM, AWF, Name Series*

To Edgar Newton Eisenhower   *May 10, 1956*

Dear Edgar: Don't worry about the matter you bring up in your letter of May seventh. If anyone asks you about it further, just tell them you were sick and that I was concerned and sent my doctor to see you. You might further want to say that you certainly did not call for help.

I shall query General Snyder about any costs being involved, and if there were any, I will pay them. So just forget that part of it.

In other words, please relieve your mind of any worry in connection with the whole business.[1]

I am a little alarmed to note that you are getting more pugnacious![2]

As ever

[1] Embarrassed over charges that he had received "free medical service" by presidential physician Howard Snyder, Edgar had asked the President for advice (AWF/N). Snyder had treated the President's brother when Edgar had become ill while visiting Washington. Later while lunching with some senators (see no. 1861), one asked who had treated his illness. When Edgar replied that Snyder had administered to him, the Senator asked if the President's personal physician tended "all the President's family?" Edgar said he had "replied to the effect that I always pay my own way." Now he needed to know how he could repay Snyder without offending him, and at the same time avoid "having some two-bit politician make an issue of it?"

[2] Edgar had concluded: "I have almost entirely recovered from my ailment and therefore getting more pugnacious."

1874

TO JOHN FOSTER DULLES

EM, AWF, Dulles-Herter Series

May 11, 1956

Dear Foster: I am enclosing, for State Department comment, a copy of a letter from Spyros Skouras.

Mr. Skouras came to see me personally and outlined his proposal in considerably greater detail than is set forth in his letter.[1]

He is, of course, of Greek blood, but is a devoted and dedicated American citizen. He believes he is close enough to the governments of Greece and Turkey to do some good as a private citizen, providing he is assured that he is not crossing up any wires either for our State Department or for the British Foreign Office. Incidentally, he has a very fine standing with the British Government because of the help he gave in the early part of World War II to publicize, in America, the British position in that war.[2] *As ever*

[1] Skouras, president of Twentieth Century-Fox Films, had met with Eisenhower on May 9. He offered to ask the president of the Turkish Republic, whom he knew personally, to withdraw from Cyprus and leave the future of the island in the hands of the Greeks and the British (for background see nos. 1031 and 1785). Greece and Turkey could then return to the "cordial relationship" they had before the Cyprus question became acute—a relationship that would benefit the NATO alliance and the free world. "Before Cyprus became a provocative issue, the people of Turkey had resigned themselves to the abandonment of any claim to Cyprus in the same manner that they did not claim any other area in the old Turkish Empire," Skouras wrote. Skouras asked the State Department to make arrangements for him to see Prime Minister Eden regarding his proposal (Skouras to Eisenhower, May 9, 1956, Dulles Papers, White House Memoranda Series; see also Eisenhower to Skouras, May 11, 1956; and Eisenhower to Skouras, May 12, 1956, both in AWF/D-H).

[2] Dulles would tell Eisenhower that he and other State Department officials had agreed to place no obstacles in Skouras's way. Dulles and his colleagues thought, however, that Skouras seriously underestimated "the intensity and scope of the Turkish feeling on the Cyprus matter" and that knowing the Turkish president would not surmount the obstacles. "Nevertheless," he said, "it may be helpful for Skouras to learn the Turkish attitude first hand" (Dulles to Eisenhower, May 12, 1956, AWF/D-H).

The film executive would see Prime Minister Eden on June 20 and Prime Minister Karamanlis of Greece early in July. On September 10 Skouras would tell Secretary Dulles that he had been unable to see the Turkish president or the prime minister and had found "the Turkish attitude extremely stiff." His attempt to convice Turkish officials that good relations between Greece and Turkey were more important than the Cyprus question had apparently failed, Skouras said. His trip had convinced him that the solution to the Cyprus question was for the British to give the island commonwealth status (see Eisenhower to Skouras, Sept. 17, 1956, AWF/D; and State, *Foreign Relations, 1955–1957*, vol. XXIV, *Soviet Union; Eastern Mediterranean*, pp. 381–83, 405–6).

1875   *EM, AWF, International Series:*
                                                                   Saudi Arabia

To Ibn Abd al-Aziz Saud   *May 14, 1956*
Secret

Your Majesty:[1] I am taking the opportunity to send to you by Ambassador Wadsworth my acknowledgement of your recent messages.[2] Both the one which you gave the Ambassador orally during his farewell audience and your subsequent letter of April third are new milestones in the long history of the relations between the United States and Saudi Arabia.[3] I am most appreciative of the sincere expressions of friendship which these convey.

We greatly value the close relationship which has existed between our two countries and especially the basis of mutual trust and cooperation which has characterized that friendship. In recent months I have been impressed by the understanding and statesmanlike patience with which you have faced the numerous problems and pressures upon you and by your resolute determination to shun the temptations of precipitate action.

We are encouraged by the word which Ambassador Wadsworth brings on the Dhahran Airfield.[4] We are gratified that it is your intention to continue our cooperation in this matter. I welcome the opportunity to reiterate my desire to continue to cooperate in the strengthening of your Kingdom. Ambassador Wadsworth is now in a position to discuss fully with you how, in our view, this objective may best be implemented and how the United States may be of assistance to you in the strengthening of your defense force.

I thank you for that portion of your message concerning Buraimi. We are hopeful that it may soon be possible for your Government and that of the United Kingdom to bring your discussions of the issues between you to a satisfactory conclusion. We will continue to exercise our good offices to the end that your discussions may be fruitful.[5]

The United States continues to be deeply interested in the territorial integrity, prosperous development and independence of Saudi Arabia. I look forward to a continued period of close and mutually beneficial friendship between us and our peoples.[6] *Sincerely*

[1] State Department officials drafted this letter.

[2] George E. Wadsworth was U.S. Ambassador to Saudi Arabia.

[3] King Saud's April 3 letter (not in AWF) had expressed the Saudi Arabian monarch's desire for continued close cooperation between the two countries. In his oral message King Saud told Eisenhower that he had not purchased arms from the Soviet bloc and hoped to receive more military aid from the United States (Dulles to Eisenhower, May 12, 1956, AWF/I: Saudi Arabia).

[4] In August 1945 Saudi Arabia had granted the United States permission to build an airfield at Dhahran—an agreement renewed for five years in 1951. Although King Saud wished to continue the relationship, he would, in subsequent negotiations, ask for "justifications"—initially $250 million yearly for five years—to extend the agreement. The amount was subsequently reduced, and the two countries negotiated an extension of the agreement into 1957 (State, *Foreign Relations, 1955–1957*, vol. XII, *Near East Region; Iran; Iraq*, pp. 238, 423, and 427; State, *Foreign Relations, 1955–1957*, vol. XIII, *Near East: Jordan-Yemen*, pp. 368–74, 383–87, 397–98, 469).

[5] For background on the Buraimi controversy see no. 1744; see also Frauke Heard-Bey, *From Trucial States to United Arab Emirates* (London, 1982), pp. 304–5, 368; and Abdullah Omran Taryam, *The Establishment of the United Arab Emirates 1950–85* (London, 1987), pp. 22–25; 218–21. King Saud had expressed his appreciation for U.S. support in the controversy, but the dispute would not be settled during Eisenhower's Administration.

[6] On U.S. intentions to strengthen cooperation with Saudi Arabia see no. 1811. Ambassador Wadsworth would deliver this letter during an audience with King Saud on May 28.

1876   *EM, AWF, Name Series*

To WILLIAM EDWARD ROBINSON   *May 14, 1956*

Dear Bill: I hear by the grapevine that on Wednesday the doctors are going to whack out that spot they have been examining to make certain, once and for all, that it creates no further trouble.[1] The report reaching me is that they are completely confident that you will come through with flags flying, guns blazing, and with a full head of steam.

Of course I am sorry that you have to go through the discomfort of an operation, but I do applaud the decision to get this thing cleared up without taking chances that it could develop into something worse.

The bridge that we planned for next Monday and Tuesday will not be the same without your presence, but I shall do my very best to punish George severely so that he will regret the times that he has implied a lack of confidence in your bidding ability and will look forward with renewed pleasure to your early return to the first team.[2]

Mamie and I both send you our warm wishes for a quick and

relatively painless recovery—we will be thinking of you every moment.[3] *As ever*

[1] For background see no. 1834. On May 16 the right lower lobe of Robinson's right lung would be removed. A pathological examination would reveal no malignant tissue (see Robinson to Eisenhower, May 14, 1956, AWF/N; and Snyder's report, May 16, AWF/N, Robinson Corr.).

[2] Robinson's usual bridge partner was George E. Allen. On this same day (AWF/N) Robinson would write, "My gravest worry at the moment is what will happen to my partner, George, when I can't be on hand for the bridge contest with Al Gruenther on the 21st and 22nd" (see no. 1837).

[3] Robinson would remain in the hospital until May 28. On the day of his discharge he would thank the President for his "concern" and "constant attention to every development" (AWF/N; see also Eisenhower to Robinson, May 21, 23, June 4, 1956, all in AWF/N; Eisenhower to Crocker, May 23, 1956, *ibid.*, Robinson Corr.; and Robinson to the Eisenhowers, May 21, 1956, AWF/D).

1877   *EM, AWF, Administration Series*

To Harold Edward Stassen   *May 16, 1956*
Personal and confidential

Dear Harold: At least in a general sense I agree with your memorandum of May fourteenth.[1] When we knew that the Federal Reserve Board was considering the raising of the rediscount rate, the Secretary of the Treasury and Arthur Burns argued against it long and earnestly—but, as you know, unsuccessfully.[2] I had a number of conferences with the Secretary of the Treasury and authorized him to tell the Board of my conviction that they were making a mistake.

Since that time we have been doing our best to urge the Board toward making more money available to small banks and throughout the nation so that even at the higher rate, there would be no dearth of money for expansion purposes.

It is something with which the Board, the Secretary of the Treasury, and the Council of Economic Advisers are constantly in touch.[3]

Thank you for your note. *As ever*

[1] Stassen had written to express his grave concern over the Federal Reserve's "tight money" policy, which was aimed at slowing economic growth in order to prevent inflation. Stassen advocated a relaxation of credit for long-term investment, particularly for housing and small business, and a tightening of consumer credit (May 14, 1956, AWF/A; see also Cabinet meeting minutes, June 1, 1956, AWF/Cabinet; and Stassen to Eisenhower, June 1, 1956, AWF/A).

[2] As early as January, Burns and Humphrey had warned the President that the economy was poised between inflation and recession. While they believed recession was the more likely danger, the Federal Reserve was more concerned about potential inflation

(see no. 1692; Arthur F. Burns, *Prosperity Without Inflation* [New York, 1957]). On April 13 the Federal Reserve had boosted its discount rate; later, Secretary Humphrey and Chairman Burns of the Council of Economic Advisers would publicly confirm their opposition to the rate rise (*Wall Street Journal*, May 18, 1956; see also Humphrey's statement to the President on April 23 that he wanted "to begin to make credit and money easier." Telephone conversation, AWF/D).

[3] For Eisenhower's general view of the role of government in the economy see nos. 449 and 728. The Eisenhower Administration frequently disagreed with the Federal Reserve, as had other postwar administrations; see nos. 464, 650, and 822. For background see Nathaniel R. Howard, ed., *The Basic Papers of George M. Humphrey*, and Raymond J. Saulnier, *Constructive Years*, pp. 75–116. For developments see no. 2005.

1878

EM, AWF, International Series:
Formosa (China)

To Chiang Kai-Shek

May 17, 1956

Dear Mr. President:[1] I am indeed grateful for your solicitude and your warm remarks concerning my health, which prefaced your letter of April 16th. Secretary of State Dulles has told me of the cordial hospitality which you so generously showed him on his recent visit.[2] I was glad to hear from him that you are well and in good spirits.

I have studied your thoughtful analysis of the world situation contained in your letter. In this period of change and ferment in the Far East, it is very helpful to have the candid views of Asian leaders, particularly those of our staunch allies in the struggle against Communist aggression.[3] As you know from your recent conversations with Secretary Dulles, there are many points at which our views coincide with yours.[4]

Your Government has a unique role in Asia as the only government which can contest with the Chinese Communists the allegiance of the Chinese people, both those on the mainland and overseas. The American people recognize the importance of that role and have contributed in various ways to assure that the Government of the Republic of China remains strong and independent. I am convinced that the opportunity may arise for your Government to provide leadership to people on the China mainland seeking to free themselves from the yoke of Communism. In the meantime, I feel sure that the close and fruitful cooperation of the past few years between our two Governments will continue. You can rely upon my intention to do what I appropriately can to safeguard the international position of your Government and to ensure that it remains economically and militarily strong.

I do not believe that it would be in the best interests of our two countries to espouse the use of force to solve the difficult problem of Communist control of the China mainland. We do not consider that to invoke military force is an appropriate means of freeing Communist-dominated peoples and we are opposed to initiating action which might expose the world to a conflagration which could spread beyond control.

I have been greatly encouraged by the growing strength of the Free World. The shift in Communist tactics which this has brought about must be met with carefully planned actions, vigorously applied.[5] If we preserve our faith in the ideals of freedom and apply ourselves with energy and fortitude, I am confident we can surmount the challenge implicit in the new Soviet posture. *Sincerely*

[1] State Department officials drafted this letter (see Dulles to Eisenhower, Apr. 30 and May 16, 1956, AWF/I: Formosa [China]).

[2] Dulles had visited Taipei on March 16, following the SEATO council meeting in Karachi.

[3] Chiang had told Eisenhower that the best way to counter the Soviet policy of world conquest was to induce anti-Communist revolutions in countries behind the Iron Curtain. Specifically, he proposed that Nationalist China should establish beachheads on the mainland coast to encourage revolt throughout the country, and he asked for logistical support from the United States (Chiang Kai-shek to Eisenhower, Apr. 16, 1956, AWF/I: Formosa [China]; see also Dulles to Eisenhower, Apr. 30, 1956, *ibid.*). In a covering memo Dulles told Eisenhower that "President Chiang must be aware from the repeated expression of our views on this point that we are unlikely to accept his proposal." The Chinese leader was probably hoping to receive Eisenhower's personal assurances that the United States continued to support his government, the Secretary said, and "at least tacit acceptance" of his desire to return to the mainland by force at some future time (Dulles to Eisenhower, May 16, 1956, *ibid.*).

[4] On Dulles's meetings with Chiang see State, *Foreign Relations, 1955–1957*, vol. III, *China*, pp. 323–30.

[5] On the Soviet policy of offering economic aid to underdeveloped countries see no. 1652.

1879   *EM, AWF, Administration Series*

To Percival Flack Brundage   *May 17, 1956*

Memorandum for the Director, Bureau of the Budget: The attached memorandum, dated April 30th and signed by Mr. Wilson, appears to me to represent a satisfactory policy in respect to the housing problem of the services.

The other attachment to your memorandum of May 14th (a draft dated May 10th, but without signature) contains one statement I do not fully understand.[1] It is in paragraph #3d, "Under all circumstances, Wherry projects will be included in the tabulation of existing satisfactory government assets." It is my impression that this state-

ment will have to be somewhat amplified for the reason that I understand it to be one of the grave complaints of junior officers that
Wherry housing is entirely inadequate and unsatisfactory in many
instances.[2]

When you have satisfied yourself on this point, you are authorized
to approve the regulations in my name.

[1] Neither memorandum is in AWF. Secretary of Defense Charles E. Wilson apparently
wrote the earlier paper.
[2] For background on Eisenhower's efforts to improve military housing see no. 1775.
Eisenhower was referring to the Military Housing Act of 1949; this measure provided
for private construction of rental housing for military and civilian personnel at military
installations (see *Congressional Quarterly Almanac*, vol. V, *1949*, p. 486). The act was
named for former Senator Kenneth S. Wherry (Rep., Nebraska).

1880   *EM, AWF, Administration Series: OTC*

DIARY   *May 18, 1956*

I talked to Joe Martin about the foreign aid program and the chances
of enacting the bill on OTC (Organization for Trade Cooperation).[1]

The foreign aid bill is having pretty rough sledding, mostly because
of the hope on the part of a lot of opponents that their opposition will
make them popular in their districts this fall. Actually the amount of
money we are devoting to our mutual security program this year is
very modest as compared to the huge sums we are spending for security and protection in other directions. The Congressmen are fully
aware of the fact that we cannot live alone in the world, but slogans
such as "I am against giveaways" are so effective in stirring up prejudices and misunderstanding that it is difficult for the ordinary Congressman (normally not a very big person in any event) to resist.[2]

However, I asked Joe to come in to see me primarily because of my
concern as to the general attitude toward OTC. There is a very great
deal of misunderstanding concerning OTC.[3] Attached is a memorandum that shows what OTC is.[4]

Joe understands this, as do the other Congressional leaders. However, since the popular concept is that OTC is a device for lowering
tariffs, the project is disliked in manufacturing districts such as Joe's.
Consequently, he himself is very lukewarm.[5]

I insisted that there be a conference called of Republican Congressmen (immediately after action on the foreign aid bill is completed) to
make certain that each of them understands exactly what OTC is.
Moreover, I insisted that each understand how intensely interested I
am in having it favorably considered. I pointed out to Joe that many of
these people would, this coming fall, be asking for my blessing in races

for reelection. I told him that, as always, I would stand for principles and important measures, and of the measures I would [insist] was needed by our country was this OTC. This would create a very difficult situation if we found a majority of House Republicans opposing me on this point; any request of mine under the circumstances for a Republican House would be greeted with a considerable amount of justifiable ridicule.

I think that Mr. Martin got the point; he promised faithfully to get the group together and allow any Congressman to present the case to the Congress whom I might consider capable of doing well.[6]

I told Bryce Harlow to keep in touch with the matter, and expressed the opinion that Charlie Halleck would probably do the best job of anyone.

[1] House Minority Leader Joseph W. Martin, Jr., had met with the President for twenty minutes on this same day.

[2] See also nos. 1891 and 1893.

[3] For background on the Organization for Trade Cooperation see no. 1142. Eisenhower had called for U.S. membership in the OTC in April, saying that membership would demonstrate American commitment to cooperate with the free world "in the struggle against Communist domination" (*Public Papers of the Presidents: Eisenhower, 1955*, pp. 393–98).

[4] See *Important Facts on OTC*, May 18, 1956 and *The Truth About the Organization for Trade Cooperation (H.R. 5550)* both in AWF/D.

[5] Although H.R. 5550, a bill to authorize U.S. membership in OTC, had been introduced in Congress in April 1955, action had been postponed until 1956. Despite repeated calls by the President for passage, Congress would again fail to act (see, for example, *Public Papers of the Presidents: Eisenhower, 1956*, pp. 7–8, 181, 420). Opposition to the bill had been led by the oil, agricultural, textile and synthetic material industries, all of which feared the "continuing sacrifice of our living industries to the brutal gods of the foreign market places. . ." (*Congressional Quarterly Almanac*, vol. XII, *1956*, p. 485–86). Congressional opponents also feared the infringement of their jurisdiction in tariff and trade legislation (see Kaufman, *Trade and Aid*, p. 75). Although the House Ways and Means Committee had reported the bill on April 18, House Majority Leader John W. McCormack would refuse in July to bring H.R. 5550 to the floor, saying that it was opposed by many Democrats and by a two-to-one majority among Republicans.

[6] In light of the opposition in the House, Eisenhower would ultimately drop his request for membership in OTC from his legislative priorities list for 1956. Although the Administration would renew its request for legislation in 1957, no further action would be taken (see *Congressional Quarterly Almanac*, vol. XIII, *1957*, p. 90, and Kaufman, *Trade and Aid*, p. 75–76). For more on Eisenhower's efforts on behalf of OTC see, for example, Persons, Memorandum for record, Feb. 2, 1956, AWF/A: OTC.

1881   *EM, AWF, Gettysburg Series*

To Herman R. Purdy   *May 21, 1956*

Dear Dr. Purdy: There are a number of questions I have wanted to ask you and now I put them down on paper with the request that when you get the opportunity, you give me such answers as you can. I know this is an imposition, but in the past you have been so extremely kind in helping me out that I am presuming further on your friendship.

The questions are:

1. You remarked to me that when your bull was returned from Michigan State, you could probably breed one or two of our best heifers. I have tentatively hoped to select the Moles Hill Kirstie and the Mallardine heifer when the time comes. My question is: When do you expect the bull to come back to Penn State?[1]

2. You also mentioned that occasionally you sell off from your herd some of your good heifers, bred to your own bull. You said that when next you had any available to dispose of this way, you would make to me some kind of an offer. Under this heading I am curious about two points.

   a. When do you think that you may have one or two that you will consider selling?

   b. To what families will they probably belong?[2]

3. My next question involves exclusively the matter of families. Mr. Allen is setting about accumulating some fifteen or twenty more very good heifers to bring to the farm. The question is as to what are the best families to try to get hold of. In some instances, I am unsure from examination of our registration papers the exact name of the families to which our present cows belong.[3]

   a. For example, is "Jilt" a family name or, as actually carried on one set of papers I have, is the family name a particular "Jilt"—for example, "Whitney Jilt?"

   b. Is there a book that contains all family names?[4]

   c. Can an individual start a family name just from the progeny of some particularly good producing cow?

   d. If so, does he register that family name with the Angus Association?[5]

4. I told Mr. Allen that if any of the heifers he now plans to purchase are to be bred before being brought to the farm, he should look for a bull that features the Eileenmere, Bandolier and Bardolier blood lines, or any combination of these. At the moment I wouldn't know anything else to suggest. So my question is: What other blood lines would fit in well with this kind of combination?[6]

When you have read this far, you will be reminded of how little I really know about this whole Angus business, but at least I am trying to learn enough to be classed as a rank amateur.[7]

A week ago I visited the farm and of course the regular spring transformation has taken place. Everything looked splendid. The cattle seemed to be in particularly good condition. I am sincerely appreciative of your offer to be helpful and I apologize again for asking you to undertake the burden of answering all these questions.[8]

With warm personal regard, *Sincerely*

[1] Purdy would reply (May 29, 1956, AWF/Gettysburg) that the bull was expected to return to Pennsylvania State University between June 15 and July 1.

[2] Heifers representing the Pride of Aberdeen, Blackbirds, Fannie Bess, Barbara and other lines would be available in the fall or winter, Purdy reported.

[3] Eisenhower's partner, George E. Allen and his partner, Billy G. Byars, had given Arthur Nevins permission to purchase Black Angus cattle (Byars to Nevins, May 16, 1956; Eisenhower to Byars, May 21, 28, 1956; Byars to Eisenhower, May 29, 1956; and Eisenhower to Byars, June 1, 1956, all in AWF/N). For background on the Eisenhower-Allen partnership see no. 1661; on the Allen-Byars partnership see no. 1155.

Purdy would emphasize the necessity of checking background. Many buyers, he would write, will buy a cow "that traces in the 6th or 7th generation to a famous . . . cow and forget all about the immediate ancestors." With his letter he included a table showing the average percentage of inheritance contributed by each ancestor for five generations.

[4] Purdy would explain that "Jilt . . . has many branches; Whitney Jilt simply means that Whitney Farm bred the heifer." He also said he would send Eisenhower a book on families.

[5] Regarding registration of a family name with the Angus Association, Purdy said, "An individual can start a family from a good producing cow."

[6] Purdy said that Eisenhower's advice to Allen "would be very satisfactory." For developments see no. 1906.

[7] "I am convinced that the longer a person is in the cattle business," Purdy would write, "the more he comes to realize how little knowledge he actually has and how much there is to be learned."

[8] For developments see no. 1888.

1882

To PHILIP STANLEY HITCHCOCK
Personal

EM, AWF, DDE Diaries Series

May 22, 1956

Dear Mr. Hitchcock:[1] When Secretary McKay left the Cabinet, I wrote him a letter expressing the hope that he could win the Oregon Senatorial seat now held by our opponent.[2] At the moment of writing the letter, I mistakenly assumed that he was to be without opposition in the primary. Otherwise, I would not have written the letter at that time, for the simple reason that, in spite of my liking and admiration for Douglas McKay, I never take sides in any contest between good Republicans.

I am delighted that the campaign in your State was, according to all reports made to me, conducted in the cleanest possible fashion, with no personalities and no crimination or recrimination.[3] As a consequence, I think we have every right to hope that the Republicans in Oregon will be a truly united group this fall and should succeed in winning to our side a great portion of the independent voters. The Independents cannot fail to be impressed by the character of the campaign through which you and Secretary McKay have just passed, and by the exemplary conduct which distinguished both candidates.[4]

May I request that if you should at any time in the future make a visit to this city, you give my secretary a ring with a view to setting up a personal visit in my office. I should like much to see you.[5] With best wishes, *Sincerely*

[1] Hitchcock (A.B. Washington State University 1926) was director of public relations at Lewis and Clark College in Portland, Oregon. He was a Republican candidate in the Oregon senatorial primary on May 18, 1956.

[2] See Eisenhower's letter to Douglas McKay, March 28, 1956, WHCF/OF 4, accepting his resignation as Secretary of the Interior (see also [Ann Whitman], memorandum of conversation, Mar. 13, 1956, AWF/D). At the time of his resignation, McKay had been assured that he would not face a primary (see no. 1987). McKay had served as governor of Oregon from 1948 to 1952.

[3] Howard Pyle had written the President that the campaign between McKay and Hitchcock continued to be directed at Senator Wayne Morse, "meaning that our two primary candidates are letting each other alone" (memorandum for the President, May 3, 1956, AWF/A). See also no. 1886.

[4] McKay had defeated Hitchcock by a vote of 123,281 to 99,296, with 26,695 votes for two minor candidates. Eisenhower wrote McKay a note of congratulations and sent him a $25 campaign contribution. Eisenhower had saved the money for the contribution in a piggy bank (Eisenhower to McKay, May 22, 1956, AWF/A).

[5] Hitchcock would meet with the President and Howard Pyle on May 28, 1956 (President's daily appointments). Hitchcock would express his support for McKay, and Eisenhower would encourage Hitchcock to run for office in the future, noting the need to encourage younger candidates (memorandum, May 29, 1956, AWF/A).

1883   *EM, AWF, Administration Series*

To HENRY CABOT LODGE, JR.   *May 24, 1956*

Dear Cabot: I have just had a talk with Foster on the subject matter of your letters of May eleventh and seventeenth.[1] He agrees that a meeting of the minds on this subject must be achieved through some kind of conference such as you suggest.[2]

He does point out, however, that such a discussion, if fruitful, would be carried on under such circumstances and at such length that it could not possibly be kept secret. Therefore, it could have an adverse effect, at this moment, on the bill we are trying to fight through Congress.[3] He believes under the circumstances that such a conference should take place soon after Congress adjourns.

I should like for you to keep this matter in mind and when Congress adjourns, or possibly even after the Mutual Security bill is out of the way, that you ask Foster to invite in for a talk all the men named in your letter.[4] With warm regard, *As ever*

¹ Lodge's May 11 letter (AWF/A) expressed his reaction to a letter Treasury Secretary George Humphrey had sent to Eisenhower (with a copy to Lodge) regarding the concept of multilateral economic aid under the auspices of the United Nations (see no. 1864 for background). Humphrey had argued that the framework for the dissemination of multilateral aid already existed in the World Bank, whose funds were supplied by the participating countries. The United States also contributed to the International Finance Corporation and the International Monetary Fund, which also provided multilateral aid. Humphrey was opposed to the establishment of additional agencies for dispensing aid, particularly the Special United Nations Fund for Economic Development (SUNFED). Humphrey feared that the United States would provide "the great bulk of controvertible dollars" to these new agencies, while other countries would "supply the majority of the board of directors to dispense it" (see Humphrey to Eisenhower, May 7, 1956; and Eisenhower to Humphrey, May 8, 1956, both in AWF/A).

"The subject of economic aid to underdeveloped countries cannot be dealt with adequately soley from the standpoint of so-called 'orthodox' financing," Lodge told Eisenhower, "but must be viewed from the standpoint of the Soviet threat." Lodge's proposal was "markedly dissimilar" from the SUNFED program, he said, and in no way competed with the established agencies Humphrey had mentioned; it was "designed entirely to fill the gaps" for such infrastructure projects as highways and harbors. Eisenhower had asked Lodge to send a copy of his letter to Humphrey. "I think he should have your thinking on this matter," he wrote, "and I would prefer it come directly from you" (Eisenhower to Lodge, May 14, 1956, AWF/A; see also State, *Foreign Relations, 1955–1957*, vol. IX, *Foreign Economic Policy; Foreign Information Program*, pp. 359–61, 364–66, 370–78).

² In his letter of May 17 Lodge had suggested a meeting with Secretaries Dulles and Humphrey, Under Secretary of State Herbert Hoover, Jr., International Cooperation Administration Director John Hollister, and Special Presidential Assistant William Jackson. "I am sure that once this idea gets 'on the table' we can really settle things," he said (AWF/A).

³ On the Mutual Security bill see no. 1893; see also Memorandum of Conversation, May 24, 1956, Dulles Papers, White House Memoranda Series; and *Congressional Quarterly Almanac*, vol. XII, *1956*, pp. 418–27).

⁴ Ambassador Lodge would meet with the members of the President's Citizen Advisers on the Mutual Security Program to discuss U.S. participation in SUNFED on November 30 (see State, *Foreign Relations, 1955–1957*, vol. IX, *Foreign Economic Policy; Foreign Information Program*, pp. 395–401; see also no. 1849). For developments see no. 2141.

1884   *EM, WHCF, Official File 133*

To GEORGE FIELDING ELIOT   *May 30, 1956*
Personal

Dear Major Eliot: From your letter of the twenty-fourth, it is evident that for some time you and I have been preoccupied with the same concern—and as you will recall, I have touched on the subject recently at several press conferences. Moreover, I agree that due both to the complexities of the subject and to the constantly changing factors in it, we should have a better method for keeping the fundamentals before the public.[1]

One difficulty with the method you suggest is that, regardless of the sincerity of my personal effort to keep this subject on a non-partisan basis, election year tensions and ambitions make any purely educational effort almost an impossibility. Since this particular subject is so delicate, with the slightest mishandling apt to create complacency on one side or incipient hysteria on the other, the basic problem is truly a difficult one to solve.

Nevertheless, I am grateful to you for writing and more than glad to have your thoughts in the matter. Moreover, I have not dismissed from my mind the possibility that you suggest.

With warm regard, *Sincerely*

[1] Eliot, the military editor of *Collier's* magazine, had written Eisenhower suggesting that he give a "fireside chat" on defense policy (same file as document). The President's May 23 news conference had dealt almost exclusively with military affairs (see *Public Papers of the Presidents: Eisenhower, 1956*, pp. 511–26).

1885   *EM, AWF, Gettysburg Series*

To N. David Keefer, Jr.   *May 30, 1956*

Dear David: Answering your letter in backward fashion, I first take up the item of the painting. Recently I have seemed to lack almost any time to go to my easel, but I have been fooling with one or two landscapes, neither of which is coming along as well as I could wish— but I have my promise in mind and one of these days I will turn up with one that I would be willing to send to you. Even at that it will be in the amateur class normally known as "rank."[1]

As for the geese, I think they did not produce any eggs this year, possibly because someone sent us two swans. These swans seem to have particularly bad dispositions and are constantly annoying all the other birds in the pond. At least we have noted that in recent weeks the geese have been visiting around in the area. They have not attempted to fly away, but simply sauntered over to a neighboring farm and camped there. I have been anxious to get them back but I have not succeeded so far. I am sure that at no place else do they get so much feed and are bothered so little.[2]

I have come to the conclusion that if we are to keep the swans—and I do not even know that they are a pair, because they look to be identical—we must build another small pond for them.

The additional quail that came from Indiana have been scattered around in lots of ten.[3] Of the quail you brought down I know of one very large covey and have occasionally seen another. The large one ranges along the stream line on which the pond is located. This spring they have been scattered while mating, and Chief West saw one quail with seventeen little chicks following it.[4]

Some of the ducklings hatched out. Strangely enough, one of the ducks made her nest right up near the house, under a pine tree, well hidden and camouflaged. However, after nesting there about a week, she apparently got discouraged and deserted the nest. A few days back I saw altogether about nine young ducklings. One hen had one with her, another three, and another five. The hen with the five ducklings was in the creek and not in the pond. However, I saw the swans chasing the ducks, and Chief West tells me he knows the swans killed two of the ducklings so I have another peeve against these particular birds.

At least the season seems to be far enough advanced to show that we will scarcely have replacements for natural wastage this fall, so if you should hatch about a dozen for me and pinion them at the proper time, I would be very grateful. I think that some three or four in number have flown away, although it is possible I have just seen them take off and that they have later come back, but on two occasions I saw a pair start out like they were really going to the North Pole. Incidentally, would it not be possible, when a duckling is quite small—something like five or six weeks old—that one wing tip could be clipped, taking off, say, about a quarter of an inch. Then if on this tip were placed iodine or something of the sort, it would seem to me the scar would heal and the flying feathers on that wing tip would never again appear. This may be completely impractical, but it just occurred to me.[5]

I should think that we could watch the quail through the summer— and I am certain there should be some fair shooting this fall and if we can succeed in giving them sufficient water, feed and cover, I think we will have a good quail stand started.[6] Even if I shoot this fall, it will be only for a day or two just to make sure that they don't get too tame.

I doubt that there is enough cover on the farm at present for pheasant, but I did see one the other day over at the farm we have across the road. It was a cock wandering around alone.[7]

I think this brings you up to date on the birds at the farm. Again my thanks for all the help you have given me.

With warm regard, *Sincerely*

P.S. My warm greetings to Mrs. Keefer.

---

[1] For background on Keefer's generosity in placing game birds on Eisenhower's farm see no. 1678. With that service in mind, Keefer had expressed his "sincere desire . . . to someday be worthy and deserving" of a painting by Eisenhower (May 26, 1956,

AWF/Gettysburg). The President would agree to send Keefer an autographed picture (Oct. 28) in his reply to Keefer's second request (Oct. 21, both in *ibid.*).

[2] Keefer had wanted to know whether the Canada geese would decide "to set up housekeeping this year." He would reply that he would study the geese and their camping grounds in early June (Keefer to Eisenhower, June 2, 1956, AWF/Gettysburg).

[3] Indiana Governor George N. Craig had sent the quail (see Eisenhower's letters to Craig, Aug. 11, 1955, and May 10, 1956, AWF/Gettysburg).

[4] Keefer had suggested "that there should be an abundance of these birds about the farm this Autumn." He went on to offer more quail if the coveys did not propagate well over the summer.

[5] Keefer had inquired about the number of hatchlings and had offered to hatch more if needed. He would reply that he would be "happy to hatch, rear and pinion about a dozen ducklings for release" on the pond this summer. He went on to explain his method for impairing flight of the ducks, a technique which, he said, was "not unlike" Eisenhower's suggestion. The ducklings would be delivered to the farm on July 23 (see Nevins to Whitman, July 19, 1956, and Eisenhower to Keefer, July 25, 1956, both in AWF/Gettysburg).

[6] On June 2 Keefer would reply that he thought "the prospects look good for many large coveys this Autumn" (AWF/Gettysburg).

[7] Keefer said that since local pheasant breeders had offered to place the birds on Eisenhower's farm, he had not hatched any for the President (Keefer to Eisenhower, May 26, 1956, *ibid.*).

1886   *EM, AWF, Administration Series*

To DOUGLAS MCKAY   *June 4, 1956*
Personal

Dear Doug: I hasten to answer your letter of June first because my interest in your Senatorial candidacy is keen and continuous.[1] I assure you that all your old friends here will be pulling for you and have no doubt that you will be successful.[2]

When Mr. Hitchcock was here, he stressed that the membership of the organization he had developed in the primary campaign was, on the average, quite young. He felt that if you could incorporate it in some way into your own organization, you would extend your appeal, particularly to the youth of Oregon. You know of my deep-set conviction that we must constantly find new ways and means of appealing to the young. Not only must we convince them that the Republicans are the party of the future and of progress; we must be ready to use them in positions of party and governmental responsibility.

Several times Mr. Hitchcock assured me that he *wanted* to be of maximum assistance to you. From your letter I gain the impression that you have already taken advantage of his cooperative attitude and that the two of you will work strongly together during the campaign.

Please give my affectionate greetings to Mabel.[3] Mamie and I miss you both very much indeed and assure you that our reasons for wanting you back here are personal as well as official.[4]

With warm regard, *As ever*

[1] McKay had written Eisenhower thanking him for his support and for receiving at the White House Philip S. Hitchcock (whom McKay had defeated in the primary), thereby cementing Hitchcock's active support in the general election campaign. See no. 1882.

[2] Incumbent Democratic Senator Wayne Morse would defeat McKay in the general election by a vote of 396,849 (54.2%) to 335,405 (45.8%).

[3] McKay's wife, the former Mabel Hill.

[4] McKay had resigned as Secretary of the Interior on March 27, 1956, in order to return to Oregon to run for the Senate (see Eisenhower to McKay, Mar. 28, 1956, WHCF/OF 4).

1887   *EM, WHCF, Official File 126-A-2*

To Harley Cope   *June 4, 1956*

Dear Admiral Cope: I read with great interest the memorandum that you left with me, entitled, "A Simple, Practical, Effective Plan for Curbing Juvenile Delinquency."[1]

There are several points in which my agreement is very emphatic. The first of these is that the suggested program should be carried out unobtrusively and should contain no hint that it is for the purpose of curbing juvenile delinquency.[2] I really believe the words "juvenile delinquency" are doing as much as any other that I can think of to defeat our purposes in this regard. What we should be talking about is something positive; namely, the sane, healthy development of our children morally, intellectually and physically.

Your memorandum attacks one phase of the effort—and it may well be the most important—the relationship of the child to his home.

In any event, I am going to send your memorandum to the Department of Health, Education and Welfare with the request that they study it earnestly. It is easily possible that you may hear from them with a request that you go into further detail as to the organization and implementation of your idea.[3]

It was a pleasure to see you, and I thank you once more for the delivery of your World War message to me.[4]

With personal regard, *Sincerely*

[1] Rear Admiral (Ret.) Harley Francis Cope (USNA 1919), a member of the staff of the Naval Command in London during 1944, had been responsible for the establishment of the naval commands in Nantes and Paris. Cope, who was active in children's charitable

organizations, had met with the President on June 4 to suggest that juvenile delinquency be curbed through subliminal advertising aimed at influencing parents to find
activities for their children at home (Cope's memorandum, dated June 4, 1956, is in the
same file as the document).
[2] Cope had written that "The parents who have potential delinquents simply don't
comprise the seeing, listening or reading audience. Therefore the message must be
gotten to them in such a manner that they will not realize that it is being directed at
them."
[3] On June 20 HEW Secretary Folsom would write Cope to say that his program would
contribute to HEW's ongoing efforts to develop appropriate policies for preventing and
treating juvenile delinquency (same file as document). For more on Eisenhower's concern about juvenile delinquency and the establishment of the President's Council on
Youth Fitness see *Public Papers of the Presidents: Eisenhower, 1956*, pp. 478–79, 577–79.
[4] The "message" was one that in 1944 USMA Cadet John S. D. Eisenhower had tried
to send to his father; John had asked Cope to say hello to his father, should the two men
see each other in London (see Cope to Eisenhower, May 23, 1956, WHCF/PPF 1524).

1888   *EM, AWF, Gettysburg Series*

To HERMAN R. PURDY   *June 4, 1956*

Dear Dr. Purdy: Thank you for your recent letter. It is indeed helpful.

Please enter my name now as one of the prospective purchasers, at
the proper time, of a couple of Penn State heifers bred to that outstanding bull of yours. I gather from your letter that it may be a
considerable time before you can offer these animals for sale.[1]

Upon receipt of your letter I telephoned to the farm to direct the
Kirstie and Mallardine heifers be held, without breeding, until we
could send them to you. I discovered the following:

(*a*) the Kirstie heifer was bred by artificial insemination to Slater's
Eva Bandolier Lad.[2]

(*b*) the Mallardine heifer is still too young; I believe she is just
slightly over a year old.

However, I have two or three of the very good ones still unbred and
there is a great possibility that the Kirstie may yet prove to be not
settled (we have had very poor luck with artificial insemination). I
have the Mignonne heifer and Tacaro Pride II. Moreover, I believe
that my Bosta Blackbird (from Mr. Gall) showed another failure in
artificial insemination.[3] From this group, if you would indicate the
two you might prefer to mate with your bull, I will continue to hold
them out.

General Nevins will be in communication with Allan Ryan, and I
think will make some arrangements for this summer's breeding of our
cows. However, I do appreciate your offer to be of help in this regard
and if anything turns up, I shall let you know instantly.[4]

I was particularly impressed by what you had to say about the people who forget all about the immediate ancestors of an individual merely to get a name like Cherry Blossom or Barbarosa or so on. I brought up this point when I wrote to Mr. Byars and said it was important to look through the entire background of a heifer he was buying.[5] It is clear that a name can be completely nullified by some undesirable blood introduced along the line.

Please write to me whenever you think you have hold of something in which I might be interested—and it is hard to think of anything connected with the Angus industry in which I am not interested.

Thank you again for your letter, and with warm regard, *Sincerely*

P.S. The book on families arrived late this afternoon.[6] I shall study it with the greatest interest—many thanks!

[1] Purdy's May 29 letter is in AWF/Gettysburg (see no. 1881).
[2] On the bull belonging to Ellis D. Slater see no. 1714.
[3] John C. Gall owned Amandale Farm in Upperville, Virginia.
[4] Purdy said he had spoken to Allan A. Ryan, owner of Ankony Farms in Rhinebeck, New York, regarding arrangements for use of a bull. For developments see nos. 1892, 1906, and 1929.
[5] Eisenhower had written to Billy G. Byars of Tyler, Texas, on May 21, 28, and June 1 (AWF/N). For developments see no. 1892.
[6] See no. 1881.

1889   *EM, AWF, Name Series*

To Roy Wilson Howard   *June 6, 1956*
Personal

Dear Roy: Not only have I read your letter, I am sending it for study to two or three of my most experienced men in this field. After they have read it, I should like to make a date for them to come to see you. If you could spare a couple of hours, I should like you to present your side of the thing from beginning to end.[1]

Possibly the picture is exactly as you paint it, but I am sure that these people can give you one instance where inexcusably bad reporting on the part of a news service created consternation in Formosa—so much so that we had to issue a corrected statement as rapidly as possible.[2]

This is human—I am not complaining. I am merely trying to say that the picture cannot be totally black, just as it is most certainly not completely white.

Many thanks for all the trouble you took in writing.

With warm personal regard, *As ever*

P.S. Won't you please let me know whether you will be willing to see my boys?[3]

[1] Scripps Howard President Roy Howard had answered the President's request for a detailed report on his assessment of the activities of the United States Information Agency (see no. 1838). Howard had criticized the USIA's dissemination of American news abroad. Compared to the three U.S. owned and operated news agencies, whose "reputation for honesty, integrity and freedom from government pressure and propaganda taint" was unchallenged, Howard said, the USIA was "not only a total loss, but is actually a liability insofar as its bumbling in the field of news dissemination is concerned. Its efforts are not only fantastically wasteful and hopelessly inept, but they constitute an actual menace . . . to the priceless reputation . . . of the three American press associations" (Howard to Eisenhower, June 2, 1956, AWF/N). Eisenhower would send a copy of Howard's letter to Secretary of State Dulles, USIA Director Theodore Streibert, and Press Secretary James Hagerty (see Whitman to Dulles, Streibert, and Hagerty, June 7, 1956, AWF/D).

[2] We have been unable to identify this incident.

[3] Howard would tell Presidential Assistant Bernard Shanley that he would make time to see anyone that the President chose. "I don't mind telling you personally, however, that I sure hope that one of them is not Mr. Streibert," he wrote. "I feel that my talking to that man about world news and its distribution would be just about as profitable as somebody talking to me about Aztec grammar" (Howard to Shanley, June 11, 1956, AWF/N, Howard Corr.; see also Jackson to Whitman, June 27, 1956, *ibid.*). Howard would meet with Eisenhower on October 10.

1890   *EM, AWF, Gettysburg Series*

To LESTER GOODSON   *June 6, 1956*

Dear Mr. Goodson: This letter is just to make a record of my very deep gratitude to you and all the members of the American Quarter Horse Association for the gift of Doodle De Doo and Sporty Miss.[1]

My appreciation to you covers so many items that I find it difficult to enumerate them all. I know you spent a great deal of your own time in finding animals that you judged to be exactly right for David and for me; additionally I am conscious of the time you took from your own business in order that you could deliver them in person to the Gettysburg farm. There is also the matter of the accessories that you brought along, and the fact that before the horses were delivered you had them bred to your outstanding stallion.

I suspect I have neglected to mention a number of other things that you did in the entirely successful effort to please David and me. I know that we will enjoy to the fullest the distinction of owning such fine horses and the pleasure they will give us now and in the future.

Mrs. Whitman is collecting all the photographs and will send you a set as soon as possible, and I understood from her, too, that you will give me a list of the Quarter Horse officials to whom you want to give autographed photographs.

I am afraid that I have neglected to mention some of the thoughtful things you did in connection with the gift; if so, I hope you will forgive me and know that I am truly appreciative and personally most grateful to you.

With warm regard, *Sincerely*

¹ Goodson was president of the American Quarter Horse Association. The presentation had taken place on June 2. A list of the participants is in AWF/Gettysburg (see also *New York Times*, June 3, 1956). For background on the gift see no. 1507.

1891   *EM, WHCF,*
                                      President's Personal File 825

To Barbara Bates Gunderson   *June 7, 1956*

Dear Barbara: It is always refreshing to hear from you, and it doesn't do me a bit of harm personally to have now and then a nod of approval from you on some particular talk or speech. Particularly I appreciate your kind words about the Baylor speech.¹ I worked over it what seemed like endless hours, and at the end I was afraid I had tried to jam too much into too short a period of time.

If there is any way you can tell me how to convince people that our entire domestic life is based upon what we do in the foreign field and that, therefore, the current foreign aid bill is an absolute necessity and absolute minimum, I would welcome your thoughts. I have talked— endlessly it seems to me—on the subject—and you know the mediocre success I have had, even with some of the Republican members of the Congress.²

As one of your part time projects, why don't you put your idea for a radio serial into concrete form and see if you can't sell it commercially?³

Thank you for writing and for giving me the chance to reply—at least in part—to the many interesting ideas I find in your letter.

With warm regard to you and Mr. Gunderson, *Sincerely*

¹ In his address at the Baylor University commencement, on May 25, 1956, Eisenhower had discussed nationalism, trade, and various forms of international cooperation (*Public Papers of the Presidents: Eisenhower, 1956*, pp. 526–37).
² See no. 1893.
³ Gunderson had hoped that "a soap company would sponsor a daytime radio serial involving a likable young couple in Foreign Service with a homespun but authentic background" to get "the official line delivered from the back door." Perhaps, she

suggested, "the breathless, unctuous announcer" could tempt people with teasers such as "How will Jane make out with her protocol tomorrow when the king of Siam drops in for fudgey-bites and goat milk[?]" (Gunderson to Eisenhower, May 31, 1956, AWF/N; see also Gunderson to Adams, May 31, 1956, and Adams to Gunderson, June 4, 1956, same file as document).

1892   *EM, AWF, Name Series*

To Billy G. Byars   *June 7, 1956*

Dear Billy: I personally do not believe that just to get some "name" family, you should go overboard in the matter of expense. I agree with you that conformation must go along with a good background pedigree.[1]

I notice that almost every good herd has quite a number of Blackbirds, Blackcaps, Ericas, Miss Burgess and Prides. Consequently, on the average those families must be producing as well as some of the more fancy priced ones.[2]

So far as breeding is concerned, we have made a very good arrangement with a friend of mine for a splendid bull.[3] If everything works smoothly, we will have him for the remainder of this entire year. Therefore, I suggest that as you accumulate these animals, you send them on without breeding. In this way the entire crop of calves for next year, except in the case of those heifers already bred, should show a desirable uniformity in conformation and should be top flight. By the time those calves are ready for breeding, we should have been able to raise one or two very fine bulls of our own.

I know you keep in touch with General Nevins on all these things. But I was afraid by writing down the names of Barbarosa and Primose and so on, you might think I was advising investing heavily in those particular—and usually—high priced animals.[4] I would rather trust Tommie Stuart's and your judgment on conformation than I would a family name carried by a cow which may be removed by as much as six generations from the foundation cow.[5]

Give my love to your charming bride, and I would like it if you would also give my warm greetings to Tommie Stuart.

With personal regard, *Sincerely*

[1] For background on Eisenhower's efforts to procure fifteen or twenty Black Angus cattle for his Gettysburg farm see no. 1888. On June 5 Byars had sent Eisenhower a list of families from which the cattle could be secured (AWF/N).
[2] See no. 1881.
[3] See no. 1888.
[4] Eisenhower had suggested the Barbarosa and Prim*r*ose families in his May 28 (AWF/N) letter to Byars (see nos. 1881 and 1888).
[5] Tommie Stuart was probably the herdsman on Byars's Royal Oaks Farm. On June 29

Eisenhower would tell Byars that "the new animals . . . are due to arrive today" (AWF/N). By early July Eisenhower's Black Angus herd would number twenty (see *New York Times*, July 3, 1956).

1893   *EM, AWF, Administration Series*

To Joseph William Martin, Jr.   *June 7, 1956*

Dear Joe: No doubt you and other House leaders on both sides of the aisle realize full well, from our discussions in the White House and from my remarks yesterday to the press, the importance I attach to the pending mutual security legislation.[1] Nevertheless, to remove any possible doubt as to my feelings I am sending you this letter. You may, if you wish, bring it to the attention of the entire House membership, so strongly do I believe that the pending issue concerns the security of our country.[2]

Great consequences are involved in this legislation. In the present international situation, the free world can ill afford to move hesitatingly and uncertainly. The United States—the most powerful of the free nations—can afford least of all to take a backward step in this constant battle all of us are waging for a just and enduring peace.

I am deeply convinced that our nation's security and our partnership with like minded nations in the world will be seriously impaired by the extent of the proposed cut in the funds requested this year for the mutual security program. I therefore hope most earnestly that the large majority of these funds can be restored. If we fail to do so, we must either eliminate essential programs or so reduce them as to cripple our entire effort.[3]

I know that many conscientious people are of the opinion that there will be no serious results if a severe reduction in mutual security funds is made at this time. Yet, I personally, the Secretary of State, the Director of the International Cooperation Administration, and the Joint Chiefs of Staff are united in the conviction that the proposed cut will be hurtful to the best interests of our own people and to the well being of our friends throughout the world. I do therefore urge that you and your colleagues in the Congress vigorously carry forward your efforts to restore to this legislation the funds needed to maintain the pace of our battle to win a lasting peace throughout the world.

With warm regard, *Sincerely*

[1] On May 25 the House Committee on Foreign Affairs had reported a Mutual Security bill that cut $1.1 billion dollars from the Administration's request. The President had met with Minority Leader Martin and other legislative leaders on June 5 in an effort to

persuade them to restore the cut. Martin had said, however, that it would not be possible to secure approval for the entire amount requested (Minnich to Brundage, June 5, 1956, AWF/D). During a news conference on June 6 the President urged the full House to restore the cuts made by its committee (*Public Papers of the Presidents: Eisenhower, 1956*, pp. 553–56). On June 11 the House would pass the bill without restoring the funds cut by the Foreign Affairs Committee (*Congressional Quarterly Almanac*, vol. XII, *1956*, p.420).

[2] The White House would continue its campaign to rescue the funds. On June 12, during the President's hospitalization for ileitis, Governor Adams, Secretary Dulles, Admiral Radford, and others would meet with a bipartisan group of senators to make the case for a fully-funded mutual security program (Minutes of Conference on Mutual Security Program, June 12, 1956, AWF/LM). On June 19 the President would follow with letters to several other House leaders to thank them for their help (see letters to Carl Albert, John McCormack, Leslie C. Arends and Sam Rayburn, WHCF/OF 99-V).

[3] On June 29 the Senate would vote to restore $742 million to the bill. On July 9 Congress would pass a House-Senate conference report which restored $360 million, and the President would sign P.L. 84–726 on July 18 (*Congressional Quarterly Almanac*, vol. XII, *1956*, pp. 418–27).

1894

TO PAUL HOY HELMS

EM, AWF, Name Series

[*June 15, 1956*]

Dear Paul: At this point I feel that I owe an apology to my friends for causing them so much concern. I think you know how much your prayers and good wishes mean to me.[1]

For the first two or three days after this unfortunate business, I not only mistrusted the doctors' prognosis, but I doubted seriously that I would ever feel like myself again. Now, however, most of the discomfort has passed, and I am told that with reasonable care on my part the remainder of my convalescence will be rapid.

I had had you on my mind for days before this thing happened, and had meant to write you a long letter. My good intentions went astray, as they have a habit of doing, and now the doctors allow me only a limited amount of time for dictation.[2]

At any rate I do want you to know that Mamie and I think of you and Pearl often, and send you our affectionate regard. *As always*

[1] Helms had sent a get-well telegram on June 11 (AWF/N). On June 9 the President had had an ileotransverse colostomy performed at Walter Reed Hospital. The preceding day he had been diagnosed as having ileitis—inflamation in the lowest portion of the small intestine (the ileum) where it meets the large intestine. Due to increasing discomfort, tenderness, and swelling in his abdomen throughout the day, Eisenhower had been admitted to the hospital. After midnight, following several hours of consultation, a team of thirteen doctors had agreed that surgery was necessary (see Memorandum, June 8–11, 1956, AWF/AWD; Eisenhower, *Waging Peace*, p. 9; Adams, *Firsthand*

Report, pp. 193–94; Gilbert, *The Mortal Presidency*, pp. 99–104; and *New York Times*, June 9, 1956).
² According to a memorandum in AWF/D, Eisenhower signed twenty thank-you letters to well-wishers from the United States and all over the world on this date.

1895   *EM, AWF, Name Series*

To Benjamin Franklin Caffey, Jr.   *June 18, 1956*

Dear Frank: Just before this latest difficulty hit me, your letter of June sixth reached my desk.¹ I know you understand fully the delay in replying.

Your ideas go perhaps a little further than some of the approaches Governor Stassen has gone into. I think serious thought ought to be given to the things you suggest, and I am passing your outline along to Governor Stassen for earnest consideration.²

With affectionate regard to Louise, and, as always, the best to yourself, *Sincerely*

P.S. Thank you, too, for your note of the thirteenth.³ I appreciate your comments and your good wishes.

¹ Eisenhower was referring to his hospitalization for ileitis on June 9. See no. 1894. Caffey had sent Eisenhower a lengthy memo urging the Administration to begin preliminary planning for disarmament inspection teams and to outline now a training program for these teams (June 6, 1956, AWF/N).
² Stassen would write Caffey that many of the problems he raised had been "flagged and some planning has been done on a few of them." Further planning, he said, would be "premature" until basic disarmament agreements were reached (July 2, 1956, AWF/N, Stassen Corr.).
³ On June 13 Caffey had sent Eisenhower a letter expressing his sympathy and urging him to continue his presidential campaign (AWF/N).

1896   *EM, WHCF,*
                                       President's Personal File 1052

To William Franklin Graham   *June 21, 1956*

Dear Billy: I believe my secretary wrote you, immediately after my latest mishap, to tell you that your letter of the fourth did not arrive at the White House until the day that I was taken to the hospital.¹

Despite the fact that even yet the doctors will not allow me much time for dictation, I do want to acknowledge briefly your note and to tell you that I appreciate very much all you are doing toward our mutual goal of improving race relations.[2] I have taken the liberty of sharing with some of my associates the views expressed in your third paragraph.[3]

With warm regard, *Sincerely*

[1] On Eisenhower's illness see no. 1894. On June 11 Ann Whitman had written Graham to acknowledge his June 4 letter to the President (AWF/N, Graham Corr).

[2] Graham had written that since meeting with Eisenhower in March, he had had several private meetings with "religious leaders of both races" and had spoken at "Protestant religious conferences" and "Negro universities." His "sensible program for bettering race relations" had been, he believed, well received. He wrote, "I believe the Lord is helping us, and if the Supreme Court will go slowly and the extremists on both sides will quiet down, we can have a peaceful social readjustment over the next ten-year period" (see no. 1816).

[3] Graham had written that he was disturbed by the "rumors" that the Republicans were planning to "go all out" in an attempt to win the "Negro vote in the North regardless of the South's feelings." Graham cautioned Eisenhower against jeopardizing the "amazing degree [to which] you have the confidence of white and Negro leaders" by yielding to any pressure groups. Graham suggested that the President's "complete sincerity, honesty, fairness and religious conviction are going to carry you overwhelmingly back to the White House with a greater majority than in 1952." (See Morrow to Adams, Dec. 16, 1955, WHCF/OF 138-A-6, and Morrow to Hauge, Mar. 21, 1956 [AWF/D] for an analysis of African American support for the Democratic party. For background on Republican campaign strategy see Burk, *The Eisenhower Administration and Black Civil Rights*, pp. 165–66, and Duram, *A Moderate Among Extremists*, pp. 130–37).

1897   *EM, AWF, Name Series,*
                                David Eisenhower II Corr.

To Dan Gilmer   *June 21, 1956*

Dear Dan: Nothing could please me more than Michael's spontaneous evaluation of young David. Of course I agree that my grandson is one of the "nicest little boys" I know—but I have a distinct prejudice in that respect.[1]

Won't you please tell Michael that his words have done more to speed my recovery than any medicine the doctors could possibly provide?[2]

With warm regard to you and Mrs. Gilmer, *Sincerely*

[1] Gilmer, a U.S. Army colonel stationed at Fort Belvoir, Virginia, had served Eisenhower at SHAEF. He had written on June 12 (AWF/N, David Eisenhower II Corr.), explaining that his ten-year-old son, Michael, occasionally played with David (on John Eisenhower's assignment to Fort Belvoir see no. 1465).

[2] On Eisenhower's recent surgery see no. 1894. A notation in this file indicates that John Eisenhower had delivered Gilmer's letter to Eisenhower's hospital room (McCaffree to Whitman, n.d., AWF/N).

To Floyd Bostwick Odlum and   *June 21, 1956*
Jacqueline Cochran Odlum

Dear Jacqueline and Floyd: Your two letters of the tenth and the fifteenth
pleased me greatly, and despite the fact that the doctors are still
curtailing the time I have for personal affairs, I want to answer them,
if briefly and jointly.[1]
   Most importantly—when this last mishap hit me I had in mind a
note to Jacqueline regarding her primary victory. My sincere, if belated, congratulations come with this note, along with my good wishes
to her for success as the Republican nominee in the campaign this fall.[2]
   I know both of you understand only too well from your personal
experiences how miserably uncomfortable the first few days after the
operation were. However, at last I am beginning to feel human—and
if I can ever recover as Jacqueline did from a similar operation, I shall
consider the operation a great success.[3] I am by nature optimistic, and
I hope that before long I shall be able to resume the major part of my
duties.
   With gratitude to both of you for writing, and warm personal regard, *Sincerely*
   P.S. Poor Rosebloom![4]

[1] The get-well letters, written by Floyd and Jacqueline respectively, are in AWF/N (see
also Whitman to Floyd Odlum, June 15, 1956, AWF/N, Odlum Corr.). On
Eisenhower's June 9 ileotransverse colostomy see no. 1894.
[2] See no. 1729.
[3] The Odlums had described their similar experiences and positive outcomes.
[4] Rosebloom of Dalmeny was an Aberdeen Angus heifer which had been purchased in
Scotland. Odlum had written (June 10, AWF/Gettysburg) that Rosebloom's quarantine had been delayed because of a slight case of mange. On June 25 (*ibid.*) Odlum
would tell farm manager Arthur Nevins that another heifer would be substituted for
Rosebloom (see also Carruthers to Wiltshire, June 14, 1956; Hobson to Odlum, June
19, 1956; and Eisenhower to Odlum, June 29, 1956, all in *ibid.*). The substitute, Janessa
11th of Dalmeny, would be shipped from Scotland on July 12 (see Odlum to Whitman,
July 25, 1956, and related correspondence in *ibid.*). For developments see no. 2049.

1899   *EM, AWF, Name Series*

To William Alton Jones   *June 22, 1956*

Dear Pete: I understand from Art Nevins that the skeet and trap
shooting range is completely installed and in good working order.[1]
That's just one more incentive for me to hurry this convalescence
business and get up to Gettysburg as soon as possible.[2]

Of course it is understood that when I see you we have a controversy to settle (and I shall undoubtedly win).[3] At the same time, I shall try more adequately to tell you how much I appreciate all that you have done in connection with the skeet and trap range. Meantime, this is just a note to say the barest kind of "thank you" and to tell you that I hope soon to be released from this latest bad dream.

With warm regard to Nettie, and, as always, the best to yourself, *As ever*

P.S. The doctors say your scar is unquestionably *longer* than mine— but mine is *wider*!

---

[1] The range was a gift from Jones (see Eisenhower to Jones, Dec. 23, 1955, AWF/N; and Nevins to Eisenhower, Dec. 28, 1955, and Jan. 11, 1956, both in AWF/Gettysburg; see also Nevins, *Five-Star Farmer*, p. 111).
[2] On the President's surgery see no. 1894. On June 30 Eisenhower would be discharged from Walter Reed Hospital to convalesce at his Gettysburg farm (see Eisenhower to Jones, June 29, 1956, AWF/N; see also Whitman to Jones, June 27, 1956, AWF/N, Jones Corr.).
[3] Jones would reply, "I would be glad to match scars with you" (June 25, 1956, AWF/N).

1900   *EM, AWF, International Series: Eden*

To ROBERT ANTHONY EDEN   *June 23, 1956*
Secret

Dear Anthony:[1] Thank you very much for your letter of June seventh concerning Cyprus. Despite my present physical difficulty, I have studied it with much interest. I know your deep concern with this problem and it is a concern which I, too, share.[2]

Foster has told me of the statement which you propose to make on the Cyprus question.[3] He has, I think, some questions which he has raised with Roger Makins.[4] Is it wise, I wonder, for you to dilute your own authority by giving both Greece and Turkey what amounts to an indefinite veto power over any future change in the international status of Cyprus? Might that not further complicate a problem already complicated enough? Of course, they have legitimate interests which should be taken into account. But it seems to me important that the United Kingdom should retain a sufficient initiative and flexibility in its own hands to meet the changing circumstances which are bound to occur in a situation as complicated and as charged with emotion as is this one. Could you not therefore avoid giving an inflexible veto power to anybody?

I know it is much easier to put questions than to answer them. But I want you to know of my interest and our desire, as far as I properly can, to help at the right moment and in the right way to achieve some acceptable solution which will relieve NATO of the great risks which have developed around the present situation.[5]

At last I can report that I seem steadily to regain my strength. With warm personal regard, *As ever*

[1] Secretary of State Dulles drafted this message to the British Prime Minister (see State, *Foreign Relations, 1955–1957*, vol. XXIV, *Soviet Union; Eastern Mediterranean*, p. 376; see also Telephone conversation, Eisenhower and Dulles, June 23, 1956, Dulles Papers, Telephone Conversations).

[2] Eden had told the President—who was recovering from surgery—that the British had broken up two bands of guerillas and had captured the leaders of two other bands on Cyprus. He feared that Greek and Turkish rioting would place a burden upon British forces to restore order (see no. 1785 for background). Eden emphasized the importance of Cyprus as a base of operations to protect the supply of Middle Eastern oil going to Western Europe (AWF/I: Eden).

Eisenhower and Secretary Dulles agreed that Eden's letter "was not very informative." During their discussions the President suggested "that possibly the island could be split between Greece and Turkey, particularly if it were feasible to shift the Turkish population to a Turkish portion of the island which would be nearest Turkey" (Memorandum of Conversation, June 7, 1956, Dulles Papers, White House Memoranda Series).

[3] Dulles had told Eisenhower on the preceding day that the British had proposed a constitution for Cyprus that would provide a bicameral legislature—one house to be determined proportionately by population and the second divided equally between Greeks and Turks. A security treaty, negotiated among the British, Greeks, and Turks, would spell out the manner in which Cyprus could be used for military purposes and would ensure the responsibility of Great Britain for the external defense of the island. After ten years a plebiscite would be held to determine the island's future status. Both Greece and Turkey would have to agree to the treaty before the issue of self-determination could be resolved (Dulles to Eisenhower, Jan. 22, 1956, AWF/D-H; Text of Statement, June 19, 1956, AWF/I: Eden; State, *Foreign Relations, 1955–1957*, vol. XXIV, *Soviet Union; Eastern Mediterranean*, pp. 366–71).

[4] Dulles's discussions with the British ambassador are in *ibid.*, pp. 371–74.

[5] On June 26 Eden would tell Eisenhower that the Turkish government had rejected the British proposals. "Our formula has much to recommend it to the Greeks," Eden wrote. "No doubt they will always ask for more. But, all else apart, I am sure that we cannot go further in placating them without disaster in our relations with the Turks" (*ibid.*, pp. 377–78).

1901   *EM, WHCF, Official File 133-L*

To James Prioleau Richards   *June 29, 1956*
Personal

Dear Dick:[1] I have just read your recent letter to me, with its 1944 clipping, and also your letter to Chalmers Roberts and his printed retraction. For both of these items I am most grateful. Just to see the 1944 clipping brings back clearly our enjoyable conversation during your visit to France at that time.[2] I find it very touching that Mrs. Richards should have saved this item.

I want to use this opportunity to express a personal comment or two on our differing convictions on the mutual security program. First, I want to say once again, as I said during our meeting at the White House, that I harbor no personal feelings about this situation. As a matter of fact, the deep respect I have for your judgment on these matters is certainly no less today than it has always been. Of course, it has disappointed me a great deal that for the first time we have reached differing conclusions of any major consequence as to the amount of funds needed to advance our national interest through this program.

You know perhaps better than I that the situation on this bill in the Senate is unpredictable at the moment. There is possibility that some $750 million will be restored, but the chances are at least equal that the House figure will be sustained. However, should the Senate restore a good part of the funds reduced by the House, I do hope that when the matter reaches you in conference, you can find your way clear to accept at least a reasonable increase over the House figure.[3] I venture to suggest this only because I am so profoundly convinced that in the present state of world affairs a sharp cut in the figure originally recommended will have extremely serious and far-reaching consequences for our country. I am gravely apprehensive lest such a cut will have a dissolving effect on our bonds throughout the world with nations—especially of NATO—which have long been joined with us in our struggle to maintain peace in the world.

I want to add this final comment: So deeply do I value your judgment and integrity in these matters, whatever action you do decide to take on this legislation will in no way affect my warm regard for you personally or my deep appreciation of the exemplary public service you have so long rendered our country in this crucial field. *Sincerely*

---

[1] Richards, a Democratic congressman from South Carolina, was chairman of the House Foreign Affairs Committee. White House aide Bryce Harlow drafted this letter for the President.

[2] Richards had sent Eisenhower a newspaper clipping from September 1944 praising Eisenhower for his diplomatic skills. He also sent a 1956 clipping in which journalist Chalmers Roberts had retracted a misquotation of Richards. Richards had *not* commented, as reported, that the size of the request for mutual security funding was based upon the President's "whim" (Richards to Eisenhower, n.d., and Richards to Roberts, June 21, 1956, same file as document).

[3] Richards had met with Eisenhower and other legislative leaders to discuss the Mutual Security bill on June 5. For the result of the House-Senate conference report, which would restore some of the funds requested by the Administration see no. 1893.

To SINCLAIR WEEKS   *June 29, 1956*

Dear Sinny: I ignore the "P.S." to your longhand letter of the twenty-third.[1]
These last weeks have been anything but pleasant, but since the doctors have promised definitely that I may go to Gettysburg tomorrow, I consider them already behind me.[2] I shall hope to see you soon; meantime, I assure you that both Mamie and I appreciate greatly the good wishes of you and Jane.[3]

With warm regard, *As ever*

[1] The postscript on Weeks's get-well letter had read: "And please do not ans. this" (AWF/N).
[2] On Eisenhower's recent surgery see no. 1894. On this same day Eisenhower would write similar thank-you letters to friends who had sent him get-well messages (see Eisenhower to Odlum, Roberts, Robinson, Slater, and Woodruff, all in AWF/N).
[3] Weeks's wife was the former Jane Tompkins Rankin.

To HERBERT CLARK HOOVER   *July 2, 1956*

Dear Mr. Hoover: Len Hall has told me of your letter of June fifteenth.[1] I hope very much that you will be able to arrange your plans so that you can attend the Republican National Convention.[2]

You exemplify in more ways than I am sure you realize the dignity and the spirit of the Republican Party, and I know that every delegate to the Convention would be keenly disappointed, as would I, if you were not there to lend your counsel and advice.

With warm regard, *Sincerely*

[1] Hoover's letter of June 15 (AWF/A, Hoover Corr.) was in response to Hall's request that he be available for the convention (see Hall to Adams, June 28, 1956, *ibid.*). Hoover replied that if the President wished him to appear at the convention, he would try to rearrange his other plans, although he had previously said that his last appearance was the final one (he had last appeared at a Republican National Convention in 1952 [*New York Times*, Aug. 22, 1956]).
[2] Hoover would agree to Eisenhower's request (Hoover to Eisenhower, July 5, 1956, AWF/A; Hoover to Hall, July 5, 1956, AWF/A, Hoover Corr.). The convention would be held August 20–23, 1956, in San Francisco, and Hoover would speak on August 21 to a standing ovation (*New York Times*, Aug. 22, 1956).

To Earl Dewey Eisenhower and
Kathryn McIntyre Eisenhower   *July 3, 1955*

Dear Earl and Kathryn: Mamie and I got a great kick out of the card and note you sent us on our wedding anniversary.[1] Actually I have reformed, or been forced to reform, in a number of ways lately.[2] The hospital routine being what it is, I found I had practically no time to myself during the last few weeks—and it is a great relief to be here at Gettysburg and comparatively free of the supervision I had constantly at Walter Reed.[3] Many thanks for thinking of us, and our affectionate regard, *As ever*

[1] Earl and Kathryn had congratulated the Eisenhowers on forty years of marriage (the handwritten note and card, dated June 27, 1956, are in AWF/N).
[2] Reminiscing about the first time he had met Mamie as a bride in Abilene, Earl observed "Dwight has reformed: he has changed from all night poker to 12 o'clock bridge" (*ibid.*). On Mrs. Eisenhower's reaction as a newlywed (July 1, 1916) to her husband's poker playing see Ambrose, *Eisenhower*, vol. I, *Soldier, General of the Army, President-Elect*, p. 59.
[3] Eisenhower was convalescing at his Gettysburg farm following an ileotransverse colostomy (see nos. 1894 and 1899).

To Milton Stover Eisenhower   *July 9, 1956*

Dear Milton: Slowly but steadily I am regaining some strength, and I feel there is no doubt that I shall be able to make the trip to Panama. As we get closer to departure time, I will be in touch with you. In fact, I have not recently examined my exact schedule, and therefore I am not sure just what time we should leave and when we can expect to return. Having you along will be a great thing for me; for example, if I should get unexpectedly tired, you could always do a little substituting job for me.[1]

I am glad that the announcement is soon to be made of your new position. The announcement will eliminate the danger of leaks and consequent embarrassment.[2]

Give my best to Mr. Eakin, to the Tilts, the Lamberts, Howard Young, Willard Cox, and anyone else in the region that I happen to know. This includes particularly Eddie, the man who always guides for Howard Young.[3] *As ever*

[1] Milton had written from Wisconsin regarding their trip to Panama. It had been set for

June 25–26, but had been rescheduled due to the President's surgery (see nos. 1894 and 1899). The President and Milton would attend a meeting of the Presidents of the Americas on July 21–23 (for developments see Eisenhower, *Waging Peace*, p. 533n; and Milton Eisenhower, *The Wine is Bitter*, pp. 10–11). The record of the President's daily appointments indicates the presidents who attended and Eisenhower's official party; for Eisenhower's summation of the trip see no. 1924.

[2] Milton would be named to the presidency of The Johns Hopkins University on July 23, 1956. He had submitted his resignation as president of Pennsylvania State University in May 1956, but he had asked that no offical announcement of his plans be made at that time (Milton Eisenhower to Eisenhower, May 14, 1956, AWF/N; Ambrose and Immerman, *Educational Statesman*, pp. 164–65, 170–227; and *New York Times*, June 9, 30, and July 24, 1956).

[3] LeRoy Eakin was Milton's father-in-law. Agnes J. (Morgan) and Charles Arthur Tilt (who would die in the fall of 1956), Marion L. J. ("Mick") and Mary Lambert, Willard Cox, and Howard Young were old friends with whom the Eisenhowers and Milton often vacationed in Wisconsin. Young had invited Eisenhower to visit Minocqua, Wisconsin, this summer (Howard to Eisenhower, Mar. 26, 1956, and Eisenhower to Howard, May 2, 1956, both in AWF/N). For background on these relationships see *Eisenhower Papers*, vols. VI–XVII.

1906   *EM, AWF, Gettysburg Series*

To Allan A. Ryan   *July 9, 1956*

Dear Allan: I feel I should apologize for my failure to write sooner to tell you how proud we all are of Ankonian 3551.[1] My excuse is a lack of vim and vigor that I think is understandable, to say nothing of a regime of treatment, exercise and rest that really keeps me pretty busy.[2]

John Gall was up Saturday afternoon to see Ankonian and to look over our little herd. I had hoped to see him, but it happened that Saturday morning was a very busy period for me and I really had to rest the entire afternoon. Mr. Gall and General Nevins made arrangements for weekly shipments of semen to Mr. Gall, and from the reports I have, he seemed very pleased with what he saw here.[3]

Incidentally, you may have been told that there was some early trouble about Pennsylvania clearances for Ankonian, but the difficulty was quickly cleared up.

George Allen has brought in a new group of heifers, which are now on our quarantine farm, although the certificates that came with them show that they have had the tuberculosis and Bangs tests, and all are negative and healthy. Among them is one Barbarosa and one Ballindalloch Jilt. I have had only a brief glimpse of the group, but they all look to me to be splendid.[4]

It is useless for me to attempt to express my true appreciation of your kindly generosity in making Ankonian available to me. I feel that he transforms what was otherwise a good little herd into almost an outstanding one.

Please remember me kindly to Mrs. Ryan and, of course, my warm greetings to Mr. Leachman.[5]

With personal regard, *Sincerely*

[1] On the herd sire see no. 1888 (see also Eisenhower to Theodore S. Ryan and Eisenhower to Adams, both July 9, 1956; and Ryan to Eisenhower, July 13, 1956; AWF/Gettysburg).
[2] See no. 1894.
[3] For background see no. 1888; for developments see no. 1929.
[4] See no. 1881 on Eisenhower's directions to Allen.
[5] Mrs. Ryan was the former Grace M. Amory. Lee Leachman was Ryan's partner.

1907   *EM, AWF, Name Series*

To CLIFFORD ROBERTS   *July 9, 1956*

Dear Cliff: In some round-about fashion I have heard that you are coming along very well, but that your throat is still quite sore.[1] Until I had my current operation, I thought that my second tonsillectomy (when I was about 47) was the most annoying thing I had experienced.[2] At any event, I know that such things are bad—and you have had my complete sympathy, even though I have not been able to communicate with you often.

I earnestly hope that by now you are back again into your old habits and are starting to pick up your golf.

I am certainly looking forward to seeing you before too long. *As ever*

[1] Roberts had had a tonsillectomy. On June 30 Roberts's nurse had telephoned the White House with an anniversary greeting from Roberts to the Eisenhowers. Presidential Secretary Ann Whitman had noted Roberts's condition at the bottom of the message (AWF/N, Roberts Corr.; see also Eisenhower to Roberts, July 3, 1956, AWF/N).
[2] On Eisenhower's recent transverse colostomy see no. 1894. The President's tonsils were removed in 1919 and again in 1936, when he was forty-six (Gilbert, *Mortal Presidency*, p. 80).

1908   *EM, AWF, Name Series*

To SID WILLIAMS RICHARDSON   *July 10, 1956*
Confidential

Dear Sid: My comparative silence during the past four weeks does not mean that I have not been thinking of you. But—especially since we came up here to Gettysburg—I have been subject to such a full regime of treatment, exercise and rest that I have had little time for other matters.[1]

Among the things that have been on my mind has been the desire to tell you how wonderful Lyndon was to me while I was ill. His solicitude really touched me deeply. Also, during the past year when I have had to call on him for help on non-partisan issues, he has always done his best.[2] I just wanted you to know what a great assistance he has been, and how appreciative I am.

Of course I have to write this on a confidential basis, because no individual of one party is ever supposed to say a nice word about a member of another party, but I did want you to know of my gratitude.

Gradually my strength seems to be returning, and I think that in another week or so I shall be almost up to par.[3]

With warm regard, *As ever*

[1] Eisenhower was recovering from his June ninth ileitis surgery (see no. 1894) and had gone to the farm from Walter Reed Hospital on June 30 for convalescence (President's daily appointments, June 30, 1956).

[2] Senate Majority Leader Lyndon B. Johnson was among the well-wishers who had sent Eisenhower flowers (see name list for senders of flowers and get-well wishes, June 15, 1956, AWF/D). Eisenhower may have been referring to Lyndon Johnson's rejection of partisan action on tax policy (see no. 1314).

[3] Eisenhower would return to Washington, D.C., on July 14.

1909   *Gruenther Papers*

TO ALFRED MAXIMILIAN GRUENTHER   *July 10, 1956*

Dear Al: I realize that I have not been very communicative of late, but I blame that upon the regime that Howard Snyder and Leonard Heaton had inflicted on me.[1] What with treatment, exercise and rest the hours pass all too quickly. I do seem to be regaining my strength, and I think that I shall be able to make the trip to Panama all right.[2]

Incidentally, George has vested in himself your position as physician-in-chief, and gives me hourly, if professionally questionable, advice.[3]

We had David and Anne here for four days, and the rest of the family for the weekend.[4] David's current preoccupation is with the Battle of Gettysburg, and I admit, rather fondly, that he is an apt pupil.

Give my love to Grace and, of course, the best to yourself. *As ever*

P.S. I have heard splendid reports about your speech before the Governors' Conference.[5]

[1] On Eisenhower's recent surgery see no. 1894. Snyder was Eisenhower's personal physician (see no. 1919). Major General Leonard Dudley Heaton (M.S. University of Louisiana 1926) was the commanding officer at the Walter Reed Army Medical Center.

² Gruenther had written that he hoped Eisenhower would be "in the pink" or if not, would "have wisdom enough to cancel the trip not later than July 10th" (June 27, 1956, AWF/A). As it turned out, the President would attend the conferences (see no. 1925).
³ This was mutual friend George E. Allen. Gruenther had written several times since Eisenhower's surgery. In addition to sending humorous advice to the President, he sent gifts to the resident staff of Ward 8 at Walter Reed Army Medical Center (June 13, 20, 27 and July 8, 1956, all in AWF/A; and Whitman to Gruenther, June 18, 1956, AWF/A, Gruenther Corr.).
⁴ These were the Eisenhowers' oldest grandchildren.
⁵ The forty-eighth annual conference had been held in Atlantic City, New Jersey, the week of June 25 (see *New York Times*, July 1, 1956).

1910

EM, WHCF,
Official File 99-V

To Samuel Kerns McConnell, Jr.

July 11, 1956

Dear Sam: I share your deep disappointment that the House rejected a workable education bill. I believe that failure to enact this key measure is a serious mistake, for it needlessly and hurtfully perpetuates classroom shortages throughout our country.[1]

But despite this unfortunate outcome I am most appreciative of the great deal of time and effort you expended to get a good bill passed.[2] I feel that you have reason for much satisfaction in the service you rendered. I, for one, am personally grateful to you for all that you did. With warm regard, *Sincerely*

[1] On July 5 the House of Representatives had rejected a bill that authorized federal aid for local school construction. Opposition to H.R. 7535 had focused on the issues of federal *vs.* local control of schools, and on an amendment by Adam Clayton Powell, Jr., that barred federal aid to school districts practicing discrimination (see nos. 1483 and 1719). White House aide Bryce Harlow drafted this letter for Eisenhower.
[2] In his July 20 response to the President, McConnell would say that he was disappointed because it had seemed possible that the bill would pass had the Powell amendment been dropped, or had McConnell's amendment, requiring states to match federal grants and limiting the federal share in school construction, been accepted (same file as document).

1911

EM, AWF, Name Series

To Edward Everett Hazlett, Jr.

July 12, 1956

Dear Swede: Your letter to me in the hospital (which reached me promptly, despite my long delay in acknowledging it personally) really gave me a lift at the time it was most needed.[1] I don't want to complain unduly, but the first days after the operation were really uncomfortable. But your reassurances, coupled with those of the doctors, buoyed my flagging spirits and got me through three very difficult weeks.[2]

Now that I am here at Gettysburg and can detect a daily increase in strength and vitality, I am ready to put the whole nasty business behind me. The announcement which filtered out Tuesday through Senator Knowland was an attempt to do just that.[3]

The farm has never looked better, mainly by virtue of the frequent gentle rains we have had since we have been here, and I have been happily renewing my acquaintance with my tiny Angus herd.[4] Official business, a small amount of "farming," and a strict regime of treatment, mild exercise and rest, more than occupy my days.

I want to write you again when I have more time to myself, but meantime I did want to tell you, before another day passed, how greatly [appreciated were] the thoughts and prayers of Ibby and yourself.[5]

With warm regard, *As ever*

---

[1] On Eisenhower's recent ileotransverse colostomy see no. 1894. Hazlett's get-well letter (date obscured) is in AWF/N; see also Whitman to Hazlett, June 15, 1956; Hazlett to Whitman, June 24, 1956; and Whitman to Hazlett, June 28, 1956; all in AWF/N, Hazlett Corr.).

[2] See also no. 1898.

[3] Eisenhower had been convalescing at his Gettysburg farm since June 30. Knowland had announced Eisenhower's plans to seek reelection on July 10 (*New York Times,* July 11, 1956).

[4] On the President's recent efforts to improve the herd see no. 1892.

[5] This was Elizabeth ("Ibby") Hazlett.

1912   *EM, AWF, Administration Series*

To Isidor Schwaner Ravdin   *July 12, 1956*

Dear Rav: Of course I shall not try, in a letter, to express to you my deep sense of obligation for all you did for me through these past weeks. I know that from the very beginning of my illness, when you had to rush from your meeting in Chicago, to Washington, to participate in the early consultations, until this moment, you have given to me the ultimate in professional aid and in friendly understanding.[1]

I suppose that the old saw, "Every cloud has a silver lining," is roughly true. At least this particular cloud of sickness brought to me the silver lining of your friendship, something that I shall always highly value.

Leonard tells me that we can look forward to seeing you in a couple of days, so I will wait until then to give you all the news about my sore stomach.[2]

I wrote to Mrs. Ravdin to thank her for the tea; I must say that when she sends such a prize by the case, she is certain to make of me a confirmed tea drinker.[3]

I understand that Leonard is calling you to extend from Mamie and me an invitation to Mrs. Ravdin to accompany you to Gettysburg when next you come, with the hope that you can spend the night with us.[4] It would be fun to have you both.

With warm regard, *Sincerely*

[1] Ravdin (M.D. University of Pennsylvania 1918) was a professor of surgery at the University of Pennsylvania School of Medicine. He had been one of the physicians who consulted throughout the night and early morning of June 8 and 9 regarding the necessity to operate on the President (see no. 1894).

[2] Dr. Leonard Heaton and Ravdin would examine Eisenhower at the Gettysburg farm on July 15.

[3] Ravdin's wife was the former Elizabeth Glenn. Eisenhower's July 10 letter to her is in AWF/A.

[4] Mrs. Ravdin would not accompany her husband to Gettysburg, where Eisenhower had been convalescing since June 30.

1913   *EM, AWF, Administration Series*

To Arthur Frank Burns   *July 14, 1956*

Dear Arthur: Many thanks for your letter of July tenth.[1] Of course I have daily talked with Sherman Adams and others about the steel strike, and I am glad to have your thoughts as to possible future action.[2]

I'll be back in Washington the early part of the week, and when we see each other I suspect that the matter will be the main item on the agenda.[3]

With warm regard, *As ever*

[1] Burns had written the President on July 10 (AWF/A), noting that the economic picture (with the exception of the steel strike) had improved: credit was more plentiful; interest rates had eased; employment had risen faster than unemployment; and retail trade had picked up.

[2] On July 1 650,000 steel workers had walked out on strike, seeking a three-year contract with a sixty-cents-an-hour wage increase and a package of improved benefits (see *New York Times*, July 1–10, 1956). Concerned about the potential for an extended strike, Burns had discussed the various courses of action open to the President: the

establishment of a fact finding board; the application of "moral pressure"; and invocation of the Taft-Hartley Act, which Burns believed had the disadvantage of being seen by some working people as a symbol of injustice. "More important still is the consideration that if the Taft-Hartley Act were applied in the near future, the 80-day cooling-off period would expire shortly before the election and we might then have another strike." Burns believed that continuing the efforts of the Federal Mediation Service was all that should be done for the time being. For background see no. 1564.

[3] Eisenhower would return on this same date from Gettysburg, where he had been recuperating from his ileitis attack (see no. 1894). On July 18 he would meet with Burns as well as with Sherman Adams, the Secretaries of Labor, Commerce, and the Treasury, and Joseph Finnegan, Director of the Federal Mediation and Conciliation Service. On July 19 *The New York Times* would report that industry and union leaders had received a "blunt warning" that the President expected them to end the steel strike within a week or face White House action that "neither side would like" (*New York Times*, July 19, 1956). The strike would be settled on July 27, with a contract calling for wage increases of 45.6 cents an hour over three years as well as liberalized benefits (*ibid.*, July 28, 1956). Eisenhower hailed the agreement reached by "free collective bargaining" as "good news" and commended the Secretary of Labor and the Director of the Federal Mediation and Conciliation Service for their help in bringing about the settlement (*Public Papers of the Presidents: Eisenhower, 1956*, p. 617). See also Tiffany, *The Decline of American Steel*, pp. 149–52. On the steel industry's subsequent price hike see *New York Times*, August 7, 1956.

1914   *EM, AWF, DDE Diaries Series*

To DWIGHT DAVID EISENHOWER II   *July 14, 1956*

Dear David: I am sure you want to know that Sporty Miss is getting along fine.[1] Her lameness has practically disappeared.

The farm has been beautiful.[2] We have had cool, somewhat cloudy weather, and all the fields are green and the crops are growing rapidly.

I get stronger every day, and yesterday walked all the way to the gate and back, a distance of a mile.

I am sure that you are having a fine time at camp and I am sorry that I cannot be up at Byers Peak Ranch to have a party for all the boys again this year.[3]

Please remember me to your Uncle Jack, and to any of the boys who came up last year for the picnic at the camp. I am looking forward to seeing you when you come back. I shall probably be in the White House then.

In the meantime, best of luck and of course love from, *Your granddad*

[1] Sporty Miss was David's horse (see no. 1890).
[2] The President had had surgery on June 9 (see no. 1894), and had been convalescing at his Gettysburg farm since June 30.
[3] For background see no. 1574.

To ALFRED MAXIMILIAN GRUENTHER   *July 16, 1956*
Cable. Confidential

Dear Al: Preparatory to conversations with the British concerning future NATO policy, I plan to hold some informal talks with State and Defense beginning August 13 and possibly running through parts of the next two days.[1] I want to hold these talks only when you can be present and so I am sending you this cable in order to determine whether the dates mentioned would be convenient to you. Would you please let me have a prompt answer?[2]

[1] On Eisenhower's conversations with the British regarding the possible reduction of American troops in Europe see no. 1931. For Gruenther's meetings with Dulles, Wilson, Radford and other officials to discuss a proposed reduction in troop levels without the withdrawal of any divisions see State, *Foreign Relations, 1955–1957*, vol. IV, *Western European Security and Integration*, pp. 90–102.

[2] Gruenther would reply that the dates that Eisenhower had selected were fine with him. They would meet on August 12 and 13 (Gruenther to Eisenhower, July 16, 1956, AWF/A; President's daily appointments). For developments see no. 1944.

To ELLIS DWINNELL SLATER   *July 16, 1956*

Dear Slats: I am in a dilemma as to how to answer your query regarding San Francisco.[1] My plans are still quite indefinite, but it looks as though Mamie and I would fly out there just in time to do my chore, and then stay somewhere in the vicinity for a day or so, or longer. My principal reason for not returning immediately is that at best Mamie is always somewhat disturbed by such a long plane trip, and it would be too much to ask her to return immediately.

Of course I would like to have my close personal friends there; at the same time there will inevitably be a lot of politicking to do, and I don't know how much free time I would have. I think I shall just have to leave the whole matter to your superior judgment!

Incidentally, though I can't officially go on record with this, I think Tom Stephens has a number of hotel rooms at the St. Francis reserved for just such a purpose.[2]

With warm regard, *As ever*

[1] Ann Whitman had passed on Slater's inquiry about the plans for the Republican National Convention (Whitman to Slater, July 12, 1956, AWF/N, Slater Corr.).

² This was Eisenhower's former appointments secretary Thomas E. Stephens (see no. 1571). As it turned out, the Slaters and a number of friends would stay at the hotel with the Eisenhowers and would accompany them to the Monterey Peninsula of California for some post-convention golf at the Cypress Point Club (see Slater, *The Ike I Knew*, pp. 133–37; and *New York Times*, Aug. 20–26, 1956). See no. 1970 for developments.

1917   *EM, AWF, Administration Series*

TO ISIDOR SCHWANER RAVDIN   *July 17, 1956*

Dear Rav: This noon when I went home to luncheon, the butler confronted me with an extensive array of choice meat cuts and demanded that from them I choose one for my dinner tonight.[1] In one way or another, there is always one more difficult decision for me to make in this office, but at least this one didn't wear me down.

For tonight I chose a sweetbread, and since I have learned that my son is coming up to have dinner with me tomorrow night (and possibly Mamie will be home), I picked on a couple of those beautiful steaks.

This morning we had one of the usual blood samples, with the "horse syringe" instrument. They are going to take cholesterol along with the other things.

Howard and Leonard are both becoming internists.[2] They are now calculating that one meal a day of yogurt and carrots is what I need to make me absorb my proteins. They have some complicated theory which they will explain to you—it is beyond me. Frankly, I have more faith in that Tyson's Elixir that you are sending down than I do in carrots. Howard tells me the bottle is already in the mail.

Yesterday afternoon and evening I was somewhat more uncomfortable than I have been for several days. Today I seem to be better. It is now almost 4:30.

Of course my great ambition is to gain back some strength so that a short walk does not make me feel so completely useless. In this effort the hams, steaks, roast beef, bacon and other delicacies should be a great help. At least I am going to give them a complete trial. I am more than grateful for your thoughtfulness (and I am also writing a note to Mr. Wagenheim to thank him).[3]

Please remember me warmly to Mrs. Ravdin and, of course, all the best to your good self, *Sincerely*

2 These were Eisenhower's personal physician, Howard Snyder, and the commanding officer at Walter Reed Army Medical Center, Leonard Heaton.
3 We have been unable to identify Mr. Wagenheim.

1918   *EM, AWF, Name Series*

To Chester Bowles   *July 18, 1956*
Personal

Dear Governor:[1] Your book has just come to my desk. I thank you for it and its inscription to me.[2]

As yet, I have had no opportunity to read it; but a hasty glance through it gives me a feeling of satisfaction in knowing that informed individuals are facing up to the fact that our country is confronted with crucial problems in a strange new international world and are striving to establish guideposts leading to reasonable answers. Possibly, at one time, America's foreign policy was largely a tail to the domestic political or business kite. If so, the situation is now reversed.[3]

I thought that with the initiation of the Marshall Plan a few years ago, we were definitely embarked on a long-term world policy and program that would find the vast majority of Americans in vigorous support. I took great satisfaction—in view of my political sympathies—in the fact that Arthur Vandenberg championed that program earnestly and effectively.[4] When writing the World War II book that I published in 1948, I tried to grapple with elements of this problem in the final chapter.[5] Because of my beliefs, I consented to give up my Columbia post and return to active duty in Europe, late in 1950.[6]

My rambling on in this rather loose way is merely to convince you that I shall read your book very earnestly and thoughtfully. But I tell you in advance that if it suggests an answer that depends upon the kind of political argument that presently engages the attention of our press and other publicity media, I shall disagree with you heartily.[7]

With personal regard, *Sincerely*

1 Two drafts of this letter, with Eisenhower's extensive emendations, are in AWF/Drafts.
2 Bowles, formerly governor of Connecticut and U.S. ambassador to India, had sent Eisenhower his recently published *American Politics in a Revolutionary World*. Bowles said the book described "the inevitable coming realignment in our political system under the weight of new problems" (Bowles to Eisenhower, July 24, 1956, AWF/N).

[3] Eisenhower had originally included two paragraphs at this point regarding the difficulties of adapting U.S. political parties, business enterprises, and the "whole governmental organism" to problems that demanded "prompt and decisive action." Public opinion, he said, was slow to support governmental acts that involve "present sacrifice as the cost of securing future peace and prosperity."

[4] Republican Senator Vandenberg had been chairman of the Senate Foreign Relations Committee (see Galambos, *Columbia University*, no. 537).

[5] In *Crusade in Europe* Eisenhower concluded that democracies must learn that the world was too small for the traditional, "rigid concepts of national sovereignty." Without surrendering sovereignty, countries needed to establish a central agency that could resolve disputes by examining the facts, by deciding "the justice of the case by majority vote," and by enforcing "its decision" (p. 477).

[6] Eisenhower deleted from the final version of his letter a paragraph at this point that said he doubted the matter would be settled through any election. "Even if the issues were clearly enough crystallized in our people's minds to permit them to register an emphatic approval or disapproval of any particular proposal, I think the politicians would succeed in beclouding the questions to the point of complete confusion. Moreover, to the extent of my ability I shall keep it out of the 'partisan' turmoil" (AWF/Drafts).

[7] Bowles would reply that although he was a member of the opposition party, he hoped the President would agree that "only through such a political coalition cutting across existing party lines can we preserve our free society at home and seize the initiative overseas in behalf of our traditional democratic principles of individual growth and opportunity" (Bowles to Eisenhower, July 24, 1956, AWF/N).

1919   *EM, AWF, Name Series*

To Howard McCrum Snyder, Sr.   *July 18, 1956*

Dear Howard: Because you have so long been my friend and physician, I am afraid that sometimes I overlook telling you, as best I can, the true measure of my gratitude to you.[1] I have, unwittingly to be sure, imposed a responsibility on you twice within the last year that would have staggered a lesser man; but you have responded brilliantly, with all the great skill and warm compassion at your command.[2] All I can say is a simple "thank you"—but you will, with your understanding and devotion, know what those two words really mean.
As ever

[1] Snyder had been Eisenhower's personal physician since his assignment to the Army Ground Forces (AGF) in December 1945 (see Galambos, *Chief of Staff*, no. 511).

[2] On the President's September 1955 heart attack see no. 1595; on his recent ileotransverse colostomy see no. 1894.

To JOHN FOSTER DULLES   *July 19, 1956*

Dear Foster:[1] One thesis developed herein is one concerning which I've often spoken to you—weakening Nasser.[2]

Please return to my file.

(Record of conversation with Cardinal Tisserant attached).[3]

[1] Eisenhower wrote this note at the bottom of a letter regarding U.S. policy in the Middle East sent to him by Columbia University Professor Eli Ginzberg (Ginzberg to Eisenhower, July 17, 1956, AWF/D-H).

[2] The United States had "failed to produce a clear and strong policy" regarding the Middle East, Ginzberg had written, yet had given Nasser enough support to weaken the forces against him in Egypt and the rest of the world. "Nasser represents the focal center for the undermining of Western influence," he said, "and a constructive American policy must be aimed at weakening, and if necessary toppling, him" (Ginzberg, U.S. Policy in the Middle East, n.d., *ibid.*). For Eisenhower's opinions regarding the destabilization of Nasser's regime see nos. 1784 and 1811.

[3] Eugene, Cardinal Tisserant, Dean of the Sacred College of Cardinals and a Prefect of the Sacred Congregation for the Oriental Church, had met with Ginsberg in early June. The Cardinal, who had travelled widely in the Middle East, believed that the religion of Islam was communism's natural ally and urged the United States to toughen its stand against Soviet attempts to extend its influence in the region. He supported Ginzberg's opinion that Nasser was a major threat to the West (Memorandum for Record, June 6, 1956, AWF/D-H).

To EUGENE HOLMAN   *July 19, 1956*

Dear Gene:[1] As you know, the Free Europe Committee, the Crusade for Freedom, and Radio Free Europe constitute a group of activities that I have enthusiastically supported since their inception some years ago. I have just heard that you have indicated a possible willingness to head up the Crusade for Freedom Drive for another year. I sincerely hope you will find your way clear to do so.

Just at this moment, when developments on the other side of the Iron Curtain clearly show that the yearning for freedom remains alive and vibrant, it is particularly important that the Crusade continue its effective work.[2] For maximum usefulness, wide contributions by American citizens and American enterprise are essential in this work.

The list of those whom you would propose to associate with you in this work has been shown me. In inviting them to do so, I trust that you will tell them of the deep and continuing interest I take in the

Crusade for Freedom because of its proven value to this country and the free world.[3]

With my grateful thanks and warm personal regard, *Sincerely*

[1] Eugene Holman (M.A. University of Texas 1917) had been Chairman of the Board and Chief Executive Officer of the Standard Oil Company of New Jersey since 1954. CIA Director Allen Dulles drafted this letter for the President. A note at the bottom of a copy said that the President had done "considerable editing" on the first draft of the letter and that Mr. Dulles had "asked permission to give that draft, along with [the] signed final version to Mr. Holman. The President consented."

[2] Eisenhower may have been referring to the seizure of a Hungarian airliner by seven students who forced the pilot at gunpoint to fly them to West Germany (*New York Times*, July 14, 1956).

[3] During a meeting on this day Dulles had shown Eisenhower a list of those who would serve on the Crusade's board (see Memorandum of Conference, July 19, 1956, AWF/D).

1922 · *EM, AWF, Administration Series*

To HENRY CABOT LODGE, JR. · · · · · · · · · · *July 20, 1956*
Personal

Dear Cabot: I suppose politicians would consider me a little less than bright, but for the life of me I cannot bring myself to make the word "Platform" mean an over-embellished account of what has happened in the past. I had always thought that a Platform meant a pledge, a promise, or, if you will, a political plan and program.

It happens that of all the parts now included in the document you sent me, I had previously seen only the one submitted by the State Department. Part of my comments on that document were that the whole paper up to "Future Foreign Policy," on your page thirteen, belonged in someone's speech, not in a Platform.

I find the highlights very interesting and to the point.

In view of the bright hope you expressed to me of writing a Platform on one page, I suspect you feel somewhat as I do about the whole thing. But I find there is very much about this political business with which I never seem to be quite in step.

Anyway, for every word that you cut out of the original script, my profound thanks.[1]

With warm regard, *As ever*

P.S. It just occurs to me that it might still be a good Platform if you put the highlights first, called them the Platform, and called all the remainder Appendix or Amplification.

[1] Lodge had secretly edited the proposed Republican platform (see no. 1799; Lodge to Eisenhower, July 20, 1956, AWF/A). For the text of the 1956 Republican platform see Schlesinger, ed., *History of American Presidential Elections*, vol. IV, *1940–1968*, pp. 3385–3411. For a copy of Lodge's draft, and his editorial objectives see Lodge to Adams, July 17, 1956, WHCF/OF 138-C-3.

1923   *EM, AWF, Name Series*

To Mamie Doud Eisenhower   *July 21, 1956*
Telegram

Darling: Trip down very pleasant and I have rested well both nights. Steady improvement continues. No distress of any kind. Schedule fairly strenuous but my hosts and associates very kind and help see that I avoid fatigue. Many have inquired for you and I have a small commemorative medal for you as a gift from Panamanian Government.[1]

Still expect to be in Washington early Tuesday weather permitting. Remember me to Min and friends and all my love to you.[2]

[1] Eisenhower had traveled to Panama on this same day for a conference with various Latin American leaders (see nos. 1905 and 1925). His handwritten telegram is in AWF/Drafts. On his recent surgery for ileitis see no. 1894.

[2] Eisenhower would return on July 24. Elivera Carlson Doud, Mrs. Eisenhower's mother, was nicknamed "Min."

1924   *EM, AWF, Name Series*

To Mamie Doud Eisenhower   *July 23, 1956*
Telegram

Yesterday was crowded but feel well this morning. Have a full schedule of appointments today but due to reach Washington at eight Tuesday morning your time.[1]

If you still expect to be at White House tomorrow hope you can spend Tuesday night before returning to farm. Believe I can come to farm Friday afternoon and stay through Monday.[2] Best to Min and my love to you.[3]

[1] Eisenhower had spent July 22 touring the Panama Canal Zone. On the trip, the meetings and the President's return see the preceding document and nos. 1905 and 1925. The handwritten original of this telegram is in AWF/Drafts.

2 The President would spend July 28–31 at his Gettysburg farm (President's daily appointments).
3 Elivera Carlson Doud.

1925   *EM, AWF, DDE Diaries Series*

Diary   *July 25, 1956*

So far as I am concerned, the meeting just concluded at Panama gave me a chance to pay my respects, in a single conference, to each of the Republics lying to the south of us.[1] From time to time I had entertained the idea of a tour of that region, but all such plans were always wrecked on the obstacle of time. No President could ever leave the country for a sufficient length of time to pay a meaningful visit to each of twenty countries.

The opportunity to make the trip came about in a rather odd way. A new Secretary General of the Organization of American States, Senor Mora, was appointed and promptly requested permission to come to my office to pay his respects. He was accompanied by Mr. Holland. During the conversation at my desk, he told about the forth-coming meeting in Panama in celebration of the 130th anniversary of the signing of the Bolivar Agreement. He happened to remark, "It would be wonderful if you personally could come." I instantly replied that if other heads of state would show any interest in the matter, I thought I could come.[2]

When the idea was suggested to the President of Panama, he picked it up and issued invitations to the heads of state and we were soon assured that most of the heads of state would attend.[3]

The date of the meeting was June 20th, but when I was taken sick and had to undergo an operation, the other Presidents agreed to postpone the meeting in the hope that I could come later.[4]

It was a great success from the standpoint of public relations. Each of the Presidents that I met seemed to consider my visit to Panama practically as a personal visit to his particular country. It had, of course, been my hope to inspire this feeling. Press stories from some of these countries more or less reflected the same view.

The official parts of the meeting were completed within two days. I stayed over a third day because so many of the other Presidents had asked permission to make a personal call on me at the American Embassy. I had an opportunity either that day or the evening before to talk privately to each, with the exception of the President of Uruguay.

As individuals I thought the President of Paraguay (Stroessner) and Nicaragua (Somoza) stood out. I was also quite taken with old General Ibanez of Chile. Kubitschek of Brazil is smart, quick, but I am a little uncertain as to his stamina if he gets into a real battle.[5] All in all, I would class the meeting as a very successful affair in the promotion of good will.

[1] Eisenhower had spent July 21–23 in Panama (State, *Foreign Relations, 1955–57*, vol. VI, *American Republics: Multilateral; Mexico; Caribbean*, pp. 437–96; and no. 1905).

[2] José A. Mora, secretary general of the Organization of American States and former ambassador of Uruguay to the United States. For the memorandum of this conversation see *ibid.*, pp. 438–39.

[3] *Ibid.*, p. 443.

[4] For background on Eisenhower's ileitis attack see no. 1894.

[5] The references are to General Alfredo Stroessner, president of Paraguay, General Carlos Ibañez del Campo, president of Chile, and Juscelino Kubitschek de Oliveira, president of Brazil. For minutes of these meetings and Eisenhower's sessions with fifteen other American presidents see AWF/I: Panama, July 1956 or State, *Foreign Relations, 1955–1957*, vol. VII, *American Republics: Central and South America*. For evaluation of Eisenhower's conversations with Stroessner and Somoza see Rabe, *Eisenhower and Latin America*, pp. 86–87. The American presidents who met at Panama would sign a declaration calling for democracy, liberty and economic cooperation; they would denounce "totalitarian forces" (see Embassy in Panama to Department of State, July 30, 1956, AWF/I: Panama Chronology; *U.S. Department of State Bulletin* 35, no. 893 [August 6, 1956], 220). See also State, *Foreign Relations, 1955–1957*, vol. VI, *American Republics: Multilateral; Mexico; Caribbean*, pp. 450–51. For the text of Eisenhower's speeches in Panama see *Public Papers of the Presidents: 1956, Eisenhower*, pp. 608–12.

1926   *EM, AWF, Administration Series*

To CHARLES ERWIN WILSON   *July 25, 1956*

Memorandum for the Secretary of Defense: While I was in Panama, the President of that country told me that in certain instances the arrangements between the Canal authorities and his country were not, in his opinion, working fairly, or were tending in such a way that he foresaw future trouble.[1]

I recall instances that he mentioned specifically. The first had to do with the tax on liquor. It being manifestly impossible to establish custom guards or any kind of surveillance on the numerous roads leading from the Zone into Panamanian territory, it is clear that if an article can be purchased much more cheaply in the Zone than in Panama, smuggling will occur. He said that this was the case in the matter of liquor. As I understand it, Zone personnel, whether in the civil or military service, are able to purchase liquor at such a low rate of taxation that the total price in the Zone is little more than one-third what it is in Panama. He pointed out that the liquor tax was an item on which they had to depend for considerable revenue and that the existing situation was working great hardship on them.

Another point of complaint was what he termed the "slowness" in securing action on any Panamanian complaint or protest. He said that while the Ambassador was always readily available for hearing a complaint and forwarding it promptly to Washington, when a matter got into the hands of the Defense Department and the Canal authorities, seemingly endless delays ensued. With respect to this one, I told him that I would ask you to keep as close touch with such matters as possible so that you could personally determine that no unwarranted delays occurred.

He then referred to a difficulty that he foresaw as arising out of the recently concluded treaty. One article of that treaty provides for equal pay for equal work. But the President said that a system of work classification was being developed which the Panamanians were fearful was designed to place all the Panamanians in the lowest of pay categories. He asked assurance that entry into any grade would be strictly on merit, conducted by fair examination. To this I replied that the United States was in the habit of maintaining the spirit as well as the letter of its treaties.[2]

I bring these matters to your attention because, first of all, I know that you would want to know of them. My more important reason is, however, that we must be exceedingly careful that the future years do not bring about for us, in Panama, the situation that Britain has to face in the Suez.[3]

Local politics can feed on resentments brought about by real or imagined injustices to the native population. I think it behooves us to be *scrupulously fair and considerate of Panamanian problems, and more than ready to meet them halfway*, in any matter that seems to require adjustment between us, but *without* incurring the risk of divided control or beclouding our clear title to ownership.

---

[1] Ricardo M. Arias Espinosa was president of Panama. Eisenhower also met with the president-elect of Panama, Ernesto de la Guardia, Jr., on July 23. (See also Memorandum of Conversation, Aug. 17, 1956, AWF/I: Panama [Meetings of Presidents]; State, *Foreign Relations*, vol. VII, *American Republics: Central and South America*, pp. 276–81. For background see nos. 437, 533, 740, and 753.)

[2] Wilson's August 1 response would maintain that the United States had "acted fairly and with consideration of Panamanian problems." Reports prepared at Wilson's request had concluded that legislation pending before Congress would solve the equal pay problem, even though disparities between most American and Panamanian workers in the Zone would continue to exist. Army reports also claimed that liquor sales were well regulated, despite a smuggling problem, and that the United States had "gone beyond [the] letter of [the] treaty in [a] number of instances." Moreover, Wilson assured the President that it was his understanding that the Defense Department had expedited rather than delayed negotiations over problems between the United States and Panama. While further investigations were continuing, the Department of Defense

"will continue to bear in mind all of the points in your memorandum in our relationship with the Panamanian authorities" (Wilson to Eisenhower, Aug. 1, 1956; and Summary of Memorandum, n.d., AWF/A, Wilson Corr.). Eisenhower would write on the bottom "Send memo—including my letter of inquiry—to State Dept.—and return." The memorandums were forwarded to Secretary Dulles and the Assistant Secretary for Inter-American Affairs (Whitman to Bernau, Aug. 3, 1956, AWF/D-H).

[3] On the relation between the Suez crisis and U.S. relations with Panama see State, *Foreign Relations, 1955–1957*, vol. VII, *American Republics: Central and South America*, pp. 243–349; Telephone conversation, Eisenhower and Dulles, Aug. 31, 1956, AWF/D. Eisenhower would differentiate the Suez and Panamanian situations, contending that Suez was built as a result of an international treaty and Panama a bilateral agreement (Telephone coversation, Eisenhower and Dulles, Aug. 8, 1956, AWF/D). For developments see nos. 2013, 2019, and 2020. See also Michael L. Conniff, *Panama and the United States: The Forced Alliance* (Athens, Ga., 1992), pp. 98–115; Walter La Feber, *The Panama Canal: The Crisis in Historical Perspective* (New York, 1989).

1927   *EM, AWF, Administration Series*

To Frederick Andrew Seaton   *July 25, 1956*

Memorandum for the Secretary of the Interior: While in Panama, it was reported to me that there has been discovered and partially restored an old Spanish Fort within the limits of the Canal Zone.[1] The name of the site is Fort Lorenzo. I believe its exact location is at the mouth of the Chagres River on the North Coast.[2]

General Harrison said that to date the Army has done all of the work in refurbishing the Fort and that thousands of American travellers visit the location annually.[3] Harrison further said that maintenance was getting to be quite a problem and wondered whether the Park Service could not take over a small acreage designating it as a National Park.

This note is to discharge my promise to Harrison that I would bring the matter to your attention.[4]

[1] On Eisenhower's Panama trip see no. 1925.

[2] Fort San Lorenzo, which was built by the Spanish to defend the harbor at Portobelo, had been destroyed by the pirate Henry Morgan in 1668. For a description of the ruins of the fort see A. Hyatt Verrill, *Panama: Past and Present* (New York, 1921), pp. 94–99.

[3] For background on Lieutenant General William K. Harrison, Jr., see Chandler, *War Years*, no. 263. Harrison had been the Army's Commander in Chief, Caribbean, since 1954.

[4] In September Seaton would report back to the President that the National Park Service had scheduled studies to determine the advisability of including the fort in the National Park system. No action would be taken during Eisenhower's first Administration (see WHCF/OF 4-Q).

To Edward John Bermingham *July 25, 1956*
Personal

Dear Ed: I know that it is difficult for you to realize how little time I have to give to the detailed study and thinking that are required to evaluate properly the kind of ideas that Mr. Makinsky presents.[1] I always read his letters, and in nine out of ten cases then forward them to the State Department, usually removing any identification marks. In this way I get his ideas into circulation among people who are working hard on the matters he discusses, with a minimum of my time and energy.[2]

I think that his writing does do some real good, because while we frequently disagree with him violently, the mere fact of his presentation compels a closer study of the indicated subjects than otherwise might take place.

When I knew him in Europe, I liked him. Consequently, should he come through here, I would have no objection to seeing him, but I would want him to know in advance that there would be no use in expecting to give me an hour's lecture or so on Europe and the Mediterranean. On the other hand, I could put him in touch with people in the State Department who would be more than delighted to hear his views—even though, as I say, there would be many of his thoughts with which they would not agree.[3]

With warm regard, *Sincerely*

---

[1] Bermingham had sent Eisenhower a long communication he had received from Coca-Cola executive Alexander Makinsky, who was concerned about U.S. policy in the Soviet Union and the Middle East. Makinsky had criticized the U.S. stance regarding Soviet repudiation of the Stalin regime. By supporting the denunciation, he argued, the United States had actually consolidated Communist parties abroad. He also wrote about the "complete lack" of a Middle-Eastern policy "which, if continued, is the surest way to get us involved in a Middle-Eastern war. . ." (Makinsky memorandum, n.d., AWF/D-H; see also Eisenhower to Bermingham, July 12, 1956, *ibid.*). On July 23 Bermingham had sent an addendum from Makinsky. "He is bursting with news and ideas for the Middle East," Bermingham had written, "and is anxious to unburden his thinking to you" (AWF/N). The addendum is in Dulles Papers, White House Memoranda Series.

[2] See, for example, nos. 1038 and 1039; see also Eisenhower to Dulles and Whitman to Adams, July 12, 1956, AWF/D-H; Eisenhower to Hoover, July 25, AWF/N, Bermingham Corr.; Hoover to Eisenhower, July 26, 1956, AWF/D-H; and Hoover to Dulles, July 27, 1956, Dulles Papers, White House Memoranda Series).

[3] Bermingham would not pursue a presidential meeting with Makinsky. "I can at any time ask [him] to fly over, without attaching undue importance to the suggestion, should you ever want him to talk with State," he wrote (Bermingham to Eisenhower, July 28, 1956, AWF/N).

To HERMAN R. PURDY   *July 25, 1956*

Dear Herman: Thank you very much for your letter and for your good wishes for my improvement in health.[1]
It would appear that we should forget, for the moment, the possibility of mating any of our animals to O. Bardoliermere 32nd. Since you breed by artificial insemination, we would be unable to do anything about the matter. If however, the time should arrive when he returns to Penn State and we should have a couple of our better heifers ready for breeding, I will get in touch with you.[2]
As you know, up until this time George Allen is running the Gettysburg farms without my participation. Consequently, he should be the one to interview Mr. Hartley.[3] While Mr. Allen is temporarily on the West Coast, he will be back soon, I am sure. I shall see that he gets the information you sent on, and know that he will be anxious to make agreeable arrangements with Mr. Hartley in the event that he should like our setup. I am certain that you will be hearing from Mr. Allen within a very few days.
With my grateful thanks for the trouble you have taken in behalf of both of us, *Sincerely*

[1] Beef cattle specialist Purdy had written on July 23 (AWF/Gettysburg).
[2] Purdy had offered the bull's services. For background on the bull and Eisenhower's efforts to improve his Black Angus herd see no. 1881.
[3] On the Eisenhower-Allen partnership see no. 1661. Eisenhower would write to Allen and send him a copy of Purdy's letter on this same day (AWF/D). Purdy had recommended a former student, Robert S. Hartley, for the job of herdsman on Eisenhower's farm. On November 1 Hartley would begin his duties (see Nevins to Eisenhower, Oct. 15, 1956 and Jan. 11, 1957, both in AWF/Gettysburg; and Nevins, *Five-Star Farmer*, p. 126).

1930   *EM, WHCF, Confidential File:*
                                             Atlantic Community

To CLARENCE KIRSHMAN STREIT   *July 26, 1956*

Dear Mr. Streit: Thank you for your letter of July twenty-fourth referring to the Resolution for an Atlantic Exploratory Convention.[1] I am aware of your deep interest in furthering a closer unity among the members of the Atlantic Community. Because I share that interest, I have given your letter earnest study.[2]
As the Secretary of State has, I believe, explained to you, the Ad-

ministration has in recent months given considerable thought to the strengthening of the Atlantic Community and is currently cooperating with the Committee of Three Ministers appointed by the North Atlantic Council in May of this year to study this subject.[3] The study now being made by the Committee of Three Ministers, which this government supports, is in the context of at least a fifteen-nation Community. The Convention, on the other hand, would be concerned with a seven-nation Community, or, if amended as suggested by some of the sponsors, with a nine- or ten-nation Community.[4]

Under the circumstances, you will understand the concern I have felt over the possibility of seeming simultaneously to support two different concepts of Atlantic unity, and thus creating confusion.[5]

It was to avoid such a possibility that the Administration decided not to take, at this moment, a position in affirmative support of Senate Concurrent Resolution 12.[6] This by no means forecloses future consideration of the alternative you support. I am most deeply appreciative of your continuing interest in this subject.[7]

With personal regard, *Sincerely*

[1] Streit was author of *Union Now* (New York, 1940), which called for a federation of the Atlantic democracies to replace national governments. He was also editor of the periodical *Federal Union*. He had written Eisenhower to advocate a convention of representatives from the nations bordering the Atlantic—patterned on the 1787 Constitutional Convention—to start such a federation. Streit's ambitious plans differed greatly from the Administration's more limited proposals for using NATO to promote a modest increase in nonmilitary cooperation among its fifteen member nations (Streit to Eisenhower, July 24, 1956; "Why Congress Should Adopt *Now* The Amended Atlantic Convention Resolution," condensed statement by Clarence K. Streit at the Senate Foreign Relations Committee hearing, July 11, 1956, same file as document; on NATO cooperation see no. 1964).

[2] A State Department draft of Eisenhower's reply (originally intended for signature by Sherman Adams) is in the same file as the document (see Howe to Goodpaster, July 20, 1956, same file as document; Hoover to Eisenhower, July 26, 1956, *ibid.*). This sentence was added at the White House. The President had already declined to meet with Streit (Shanley to Roper, July 25, 1956, *ibid.*).

[3] The Committee of Three—comprised of three foreign ministers: Lester B. Pearson of Canada, Halvard M. Lange of Norway, and Gaetano Martino of Italy—would study ways of improving cooperation within NATO (State, *Foreign Relations, 1955–1957*, vol. IV, *Western European Security and Integration*, p. 75). See also no. 1964; for developments see no. 2122.

[4] The President was referring to the fact that Streit's scheme excluded several NATO member countries (see Dulles to Streit, July 20, 1956, same file as document; Dulles declined to support Streit's proposal). For background see no. 1872.

[5] Ignoring the fact that Administration policy was to work within NATO, Streit would urge the President to name a commission to further Atlantic union (Streit to Eisenhower, Aug. 11, 1956, same file as document).

[6] On Resolution 12, which supported a meeting to create a stronger Atlantic Union, see Streit's testimony before the Senate Foreign Relations Committee, July 11, 1956; and other papers in the same file as the document.

[7] The final two sentences were added to the draft at the White House.

To ROBERT ANTHONY EDEN   *July 27, 1956*
Top secret

Dear Anthony: Thank you for your recent message concerning the future of NATO, which reached me as I was about to leave for the meeting in Panama. I greatly appreciate your letting me know your thoughts on this matter. As you know, it is a subject in which I have the deepest personal interest.[1]

I know that you are aware of the profound and far-reaching political and military implications of the question of NATO defense policy, which must be considered most carefully in terms of their effect on the continuing unity and strength of our NATO alliance. We have to think about the effect on Germany and on our friend Adenauer.[2]

As Foster has told Roger Makins, we are giving our urgent attention to these matters and we hope to be ready about the middle of August to give you our views.[3] I am confident that our exchange of views will help us to find the right solution.

With warm regard, *As ever*

---

[1] Eden had written Eisenhower to advocate a reformulation of NATO strategy. The Prime Minister believed that the Soviets had accepted thermonuclear deterrence—the idea that an attack on Western Europe would result in unacceptable damage to both sides. Eden also suggested that the public in the democracies recognized that the threat of war had receded because of the strength of deterrence. He anticipated "a growing reluctance" to maintain high levels of military spending.

Nuclear deterrence, Eden argued, had fundamentally changed the purpose of NATO ground forces. These units should be reoriented, he said, and the troop levels in Germany reduced. The reductions should not be allowed to lead West Germans to question the Anglo-American commitment to their defense. But NATO's new military strategy should be "to deal with any local infiltration, to prevent external intimidation and to enable aggression to be identified as such." The forces should be able to impose "some delay on the progress of a Soviet land invasion," while that nation was being destroyed by thermonuclear weapons. In these regards, Eden's position was compatible with the basic strategies of Eisenhower's New Look defense policy (State, *Foreign Relations, 1955–1957*, vol. IV, *Western European Security and Integration*, pp. 90–92). For developments see no. 1944; on Eisenhower's trip to Panama see no. 1925; on the New Look see no. 1233 and Soffer, "Matthew Bunker Ridgway."

[2] Eisenhower added this sentence to the State Department draft (Hoover to Eisenhower, July 26, 1956, AWF/I: Eden). Eisenhower would continue to fear that German Chancellor Adenauer would interpret American and British troop reductions as a lessening of their commitment to defend the Federal Republic (State, *Foreign Relations, 1955–1957*, vol. IV, *Western European Security and Integration*, p. 101). See also no. 1944.

Senator Walter George would meet with Adenauer on September 28 to assure him that the United States did not anticipate any troop withdrawals from Germany (State, *Foreign Relations, 1955–1957*, vol. IV, *Western European Security and Integration*, pp. 96–97). He had previously informed several NATO foreign ministers that the Administration would not withdraw any forces from Germany, though divisions might be streamlined

in ways that permitted a reduction in manpower. Eisenhower endorsed this position (Dulles to Eisenhower, Oct. 1, 1956, Dulles Papers, White House Memoranda Series).
[3] State, *Foreign Relations, 1955–1957*, vol. IV, *Western European Security and Integration*, pp. 89–90.

1932   *EM, AWF, International Series: Eden*

To ROBERT ANTHONY EDEN   *July 27, 1956*
Cable. Top secret

Your cable just received.[1] To meet immediate situation we are sending Robert Murphy to London to arrive there Sunday or very early Monday.[2] In view of Foster's long trip, I doubt that he will be able to join in these talks, particularly since he could scarcely reach there Monday in any event.[3]

I shall not take time in this cable to outline for you the trend of our own thinking. While we agree with much that you have to say, we rather think there are one or two additional thoughts that you and we might profitably consider.[4] Murphy will be prepared to talk these over with Selwyn Lloyd.

We are of the earnest opinion that the maximum number of maritime nations affected by the Nasser action should be consulted quickly in the hope of obtaining an agreed basis of understanding.[5]

[1] Eden's July 27 cable is in AWF/I: Eden. Eisenhower dictated this message after a meeting with Acting Secretary of State Hoover; Andrew Goodpaster telephoned it to the State Department for transmittal at 5:30 P.M. on this same day (Goodpaster, Memorandum of Conference, July 30, 1956, AWF/D; and State, *Foreign Relations, 1955–1957*, vol. XVI, *Suez Crisis July 26–December 31, 1956* [1990], pp. 9–12).
[2] Reacting to a U.S. decision (July 19) to withdraw its offer to help finance the Aswan Dam, Egyptian President Nasser had announced the nationalization of the Suez Canal on July 26. In his speech, which he described as an answer to American and British conspiracies against Egypt, Nasser said that an autonomous government agency under the Egyptian Ministry of Commerce would operate the canal. All company assets in Egypt and abroad would be frozen. All employees would continue to discharge their duties under penalty of imprisonment, Nasser said, and shareholders would be compensated. Yearly net income from the canal would finance the Aswan Dam construction, although discussions with the Soviet Union regarding that country's offer of financial assistance would continue (for background see nos. 1759, 1859, and 1946; State, *Foreign Relations, 1955–1957*, vol. XV, *Arab-Israeli Dispute January 1–July 26, 1956*, pp. 754–56, 848–53, 861–62, 906–7; NSC meeting minutes, June 29, 1956, AWF/NSC; Memorandum of Conversation, July 13, 1956, Dulles Papers, White House Memoranda Series; *U.S. Department of State Bulletin* 35, no. 892 [July 30, 1956], 188; Eisenhower, *Waging Peace*, pp. 30–33; Evelyn Shuckburgh, *Descent to Suez: Diaries 1951–56* [London, 1986]; Steven Z. Freiberger, *Dawn Over Suez: The Rise of American Power in the Middle East, 1953–1957* [Chicago, 1992]; Keith Kyle, *Suez* [New York, 1991]; and Diane B. Kunz, *The Economic Diplomacy of the Suez Crisis* [Chapel Hill, N.C., 1991], pp. 36–76; see also

State, *Foreign Relations, 1955–1957*, vol. XVI, *Suez Crisis July 26–December 31, 1956*, pp. 1–3).

Citing the immediate threat to the oil supplies of Western Europe and the long-term consequences of Nasser's action, Eden had cabled Eisenhower that he and his colleagues were convinced that economic pressures alone would not resolve the crisis. Great Britain "must be ready, in the last resort, to use force to bring Nasser to his senses." He had, he said, instructed his chiefs of staff to prepare an appropriate military plan. The first step was to meet with the United States and France "to exchange views, align our policies and concert together how we can best bring the maximum pressure to bear on the Egyptian Government." Eden asked that Eisenhower send to London someone "at a high level" who could begin discussions no later than July 30. Murphy was Deputy Under Secretary of State for Political Affairs (Eden, *Full Circle*, pp. 467–80; Selwyn Lloyd, *Suez 1956: A Personal Account* [New York, 1978], pp. 82–87; Harold Macmillan, *Riding the Storm, 1956–1959* [London, 1971], pp. 103–5; and Murphy, *Diplomat Among Warriors*, pp. 375–81; see also Goodpaster, Notes on Conversation, July 28, 1956; and Goodpaster, Supplementary Note, July 30, 1956, AWF/D).

[3] Secretary Dulles had arrived in Lima, Peru, on this same day, after attending the meeting of the American presidents in Panama.

[4] Eisenhower had met with CIA Director Allen Dulles and Acting Secretary of State Hoover earlier this same day regarding the canal takeover and the Administration's response. After Hoover had expressed concern that the British would want to "move very drastically," Eisenhower, referring to Egypt and colonialism, said that no nation was likely to permit its people to be held in what amounted to slavery. The United States and many other countries, however, could suffer as a result of Nasser's actions. All three men agreed that NATO should discuss the issue (Goodpaster, Memorandum of Conference, July 27, 1956, AWF/D; see also *U.S. Department of State Bulletin* 35, no. 893 [August 6, 1956], 221–22).

[5] For developments see no. 1935.

1933   *EM, AWF, International Series: Mollet*

To Guy Mollet   *July 31, 1956*

Secret

Dear Mr. President: I have received your letter of July thirty-first regarding the Suez Canal situation which at this moment is being studied and discussed by representatives of our Governments in London.[1] I am glad to have this frank expression of your thoughts on a matter which we all view with grave concern. As you are already aware, I have today asked Secretary Dulles to fly to London to confer with the French and British representatives there.[2]

While I recognize that events may ultimately make forceful action necessary, I feel that the present situation demands that we act moderately, but firmly, to bring about a dependable administration of the Canal. I feel that the utmost calm is required in charting the course of the Western nations at this time and it is for this reason that we propose that a meeting of interested states be held promptly. I believe that our efforts now should be directed toward the holding of such an international conference which would have an educational effect on public opinion throughout the world. If the Egyptian Government defies such a conference, or rejects reasonable proposals, then there should result a broader basis than now exists for other affirmative action.

I am convinced that the Western nations must show the world that every effective peaceful means to resolve this difficulty has been exhausted and I sincerely hope that precipitate action can be avoided.[3] With assurances of my highest esteem, *Sincerely*

[1] See the preceding document. Mollet had recommended "a rapid and energetic riposte" to demonstrate Western solidarity. The position of the free world was in danger, he said, and only positive action could "forestall the rapid deterioration of the situation and prevent the Soviet Union from exercising shortly a determining influence in the region concerned" (State, *Foreign Relations, 1955–1957*, vol. XVI, *Suez Crisis July 26–December 31, 1956*, p. 74).
[2] See Goodpaster, Memorandum of Conference, July 31, 1956, AWF/D.
[3] For developments see no. 1935.

1934   *EM, AWF, Name Series*

To Edwin Palmer Hoyt   *July 31, 1956*

Dear Ep: Many thanks for your note of the twenty-first.[1] Since you wrote, of course, the Colorado picture has changed, and I hope the Post will support Dan's candidacy with enthusiasm.[2]

Howard Snyder has me on a daily dose of yogurt, which is certainly a relative of the buttermilk family.[3] Since I started taking it I have had noticeably less trouble, so I guess there is something to the theory. At any rate I have the advantage over you in that I don't dislike the stuff.

Please give all my friends at Cherry Hills my best, and to you, of course, warm personal regard.[4] *Sincerely*

P.S. I doubt that I'll make it to Denver this summer—which saddens me greatly.[5]

[1] Hoyt was editor and publisher of *The Denver Post*.
[2] Former Colorado Governor Dan Thornton had announced his candidacy for a seat in the U.S. Senate (*New York Times*, July 30, 1956). Hoyt would reply that "we hope to support him enthusiastically" (Aug. 3, 1956, AWF/N; see also Pexton to Thornton, Aug. 1, 1956, AWF/N, Hoyt Corr.). For developments see no. 2110.
[3] Hoyt had successfully used buttermilk to deal with his bowel problems. On Eisenhower's recent ileotransverse colostomy see no. 1894.
[4] The President had played golf for years at Cherry Hills Country Club in Denver, Colorado.

Campaign obligations would preclude the Eisenhowers' traditional Denver vacation.

1935   *EM, AWF, International Series: Eden*

To ROBERT ANTHONY EDEN   *July 31, 1956*
Top secret

Dear Anthony: From the moment that Nasser announced nationalization of the Suez Canal Company, my thoughts have been constantly with you.[1] Grave problems are placed before both our governments, although for each of us they naturally differ in type and character. Until this morning, I was happy to feel that we were approaching decisions as to applicable procedures somewhat along parallel lines, even though there were, as would be expected, important differences as to detail. But early this morning I received the messages, communicated to me through Murphy from you and Harold Macmillan, telling me on a most secret basis of your decision to employ force without delay or attempting any intermediate and less drastic steps.[2]

We recognize the transcendent worth of the Canal to the free world and the possibility that eventually the use of force might become necessary in order to protect international rights. But we have been hopeful that through a Conference in which would be represented the signatories to the Convention of 1888, as well as other maritime nations, there would be brought about such pressures on the Egyptian government that the efficient operation of the Canal could be assured for the future.

For my part, I cannot over-emphasize the strength of my conviction that some such method must be attempted before action such as you contemplate should be undertaken. If unfortunately the situation can finally be resolved only by drastic means, there should be no grounds for belief anywhere that corrective measures were undertaken merely to protect national or individual investors, or the legal rights of a sovereign nation were ruthlessly flouted. A conference, at the very least, should have a great educational effect throughout the world. Public opinion here and, I am convinced, in most of the world, would be outraged should there be a failure to make such efforts. Moreover, initial military successes might be easy, but the eventual price might become far too heavy.

I have given you my own personal conviction, as well as that of my associates, as to the unwisdom even of contemplating the use of military force at this moment.[3] Assuming, however, that the whole situation continued to deteriorate to the point where such action would seem the only recourse, there are certain political facts to remember. As you realize employment of United States forces is possible only through positive action on the part of the Congress, which is now adjourned but can be reconvened on my call for special reasons. If those reasons should involve the issue of employing United States military strength abroad, there would have to be a showing that every peaceful means of resolving the difficulty had previously been exhausted. Without such a showing, there would be a reaction that could very seriously affect our peoples' feeling toward our Western Allies. I do not want to exaggerate, but I assure you that this could grow to such an intensity as to have the most far reaching consequences.

I realize that the messages from both you and Harold stressed that the decision taken was already approved by the government and was firm and irrevocable. But I personally feel sure that the American reaction would be severe and that the great areas of the world would share that reaction. On the other hand, I believe we can marshal that opinion in support of a reasonable and conciliatory, but absolutely firm, position. So I hope that you will consent to reviewing this matter once more in its broadest aspects. It is for this reason that I have asked Foster to leave this afternoon to meet with your people tomorrow in London.

I have given you here only a few highlights in the chain of reasoning that compels us to conclude that the step you contemplate should not be undertaken until every peaceful means of protecting the rights and the livelihood of great portions of the world had been thoroughly explored and exhausted. Should these means fail, and I think it is erroneous to assume in advance that they needs must fail, then world opinion would understand how earnestly all of us had attempted to be just, fair and considerate, but that we simply could not accept a situation that would in the long run prove disastrous to the prosperity and living standards of every nation whose economy depends directly or indirectly upon East-West shipping.[4]

With warm personal regard—and with earnest assurances of my continuing respect and friendship, *As ever*

---

[1] See no. 1932.

[2] Eisenhower directed Secretary of State Dulles to take this letter to London and give it to Prime Minister Eden (Telephone conversation, July 31, 1956, AWF/D). Eden and Chancellor of the Exchequer Macmillan had told Robert Murphy that they wanted the President to know "in utter secrecy" that the British government had made a firm decision "to drive Nasser out of Egypt." Both ardently hoped that the United States would support them in a decision that had the support, they said, of Parliament and the British people (State, *Foreign Relations, 1955–1957*, vol. XVI, *Suez Crisis July 26–December 31, 1956*, pp. 60–61; see also Murphy, *Diplomat Among Warriors*, pp. 380–81; and Tele-

phone conversation, Eisenhower and Dulles, July 30, 1956, Dulles Papers, Telephone Conversations).

[3] For a summary of Eisenhower's meeting with Administration officials regarding the British decision see Goodpaster, Memorandum of Conference, July 31, 1956, AWF/D; see also Dulles to Murphy, July 30, 1956, AWF/D-H.

[4] For developments see no. 1948.

21

"Grave difficulties in the Suez crisis"

To Edward Everett Hazlett, Jr.   *August 3, 1956*

Dear Swede: From a personal viewpoint, the past year has been notable mainly because of unaccustomed illness.[1] It is scarcely useful, however, to make this a subject of a letter to you because my "innards" have been pictured, described and discussed in the papers, to say nothing of on the television and radio, until you, along with many others, must be heartily sick of the whole business.

Of course, the two illnesses taken together provide for partisan political opponents a very fine platform from which to "view with alarm." Such people pretend to be astonished that I have not rebounded, within seven weeks, from a major operation, to my preoperational level of weight, strength and physical activity.

I notice that one man has gone to the trouble of figuring out that, due to my heart attack, I was 143 days absent from duty, while in the second instance he figured I added another 42, at least. Nothing is said about the fact that in Denver, within five days of my initial attack, staff officers were in my room asking for decisions, while in my latest operation I had to be functioning again in the space of three days.[2] Actually, after an operation on Saturday morning, I sat up to receive and talk to Chancellor Adenauer for quite a visit on the following Thursday.[3]

I am, of course, disappointed that no other Republican has come sufficiently to the fore in public opinion as to make of himself a possible Presidential candidate satisfactory to the Party. But this was true before I thought of being sick; I still believe that, had I not suffered a heart attack in September, I could have taken much more dramatic steps than I did to force the Republican Party to consider and accept someone else.[4]

All that is in the past.

Today the difficult things for me are political, both in the domestic and in the international fields. Nasser and the Suez Canal are foremost in my thoughts.[5] Whether or not we can get a satisfactory solution for this problem and one that tends to restore rather than further to damage the prestige of the Western powers, particularly of Britain and France, is something that is not yet resolved. In the kind of world that we are trying to establish, we frequently find ourselves victims of the tyrannies of the weak. In the effort to promote the rights of all, and observe the equality of sovereignty as between the great and the small, we unavoidably give to the little nations opportunities to embarrass us greatly. Faithfulness to the underlying concepts of freedom is frequently costly. Yet there can be no doubt that in the long run such faithfulness will produce real rewards.

One of the frustrating facts of my daily existence is the seeming inability of our people to understand our position and role in the world and what our own best interests demand of us.

The other day I happened onto a copy of McKinley's last speech, delivered the day before he was shot.[6] In it he argued for more and freer trade, for reciprocal trade treaties—and made the flat assertion, "Isolation is no longer possible or desirable." What he discerned 55 years ago has grown more true with every passing year, especially as we became more and more a creditor nation. Yet an astonishing number of people today believe that our welfare lies in higher tariffs, meaning greater isolation and a refusal to buy goods from others. They fail to see that no matter what we do in providing, through loans, for the urgent needs of other countries in investment capital, unless we simultaneously pursue a policy that permits them to make a living, we are doomed to eventual isolation and to the disappearance of our form of government.[7]

Now I do not expect the trend of which I speak to go that far. Before a final disaster of this kind came upon us, there would be greater understanding of the facts and corrective action gradually applied. But I do greatly fear that this trend could continue until we might have lost certain important segments of the remaining free world—a loss which will make our future existence more difficult, and possibly even more dangerous.

Many years ago someone wrote a little novel or story, the central theme of which was that the rich owner of a factory could not forever live on top of the hill in luxury and serenity, while all around him at the bottom of the hill his workmen lived in misery, privation and resentment. In comparatively recent years we learned this lesson nationally. As a result, we have the greatest middle class in the world because there is practically nobody in the lowest or "edge of starvation" group.[8] Now we must learn the same lesson internationally— and once having learned the lesson we must study the best ways to bring about better standards for the underdeveloped nations. It cannot be done by grants, it will not be the result of any one specific action.

We must pursue a broad and intelligent program of loans, trade, technical assistance and, under current conditions, mutual guarantees of security. We must stop talking about "give aways." We must understand that our foreign expenditures are investments in America's future.[9] A simple example: No other nation is exhausting its irreplaceable resources so rapidly as is ours. Unless we are careful to build up and maintain a great group of international friends ready to trade with us, where do we hope to get all the materials that we will one day need as our rate of consumption continues and accelerates? Possibly the future chemist will make all the materials we need out of crops grown annually, but, if he does, that day will probably come long after our minerals of various kinds are fairly well exhausted.

It just occurs to me that I seem to be thrusting off on to you some of my problems and troubles. I didn't mean to do so, but at least you will see that in the approach to such grave difficulties as the Suez crisis, there is a great need for keeping in the back of the mind the understanding of these broader, long-term issues in the international world.

Give my love to Ibby. *As ever*

[1] On Eisenhower's heart attack, see nos. 1595 and 1596; for background on Eisenhower's June 9 operation for ileitis see nos. 1894 and 1895.

[2] On Eisenhower's decision-making process after his heart attack see no. 1766.

[3] Chancellor Adenauer had met secretly with the President on June 14 (President's daily appointments; State, *Foreign Relations, 1955–1957*, vol. XXVI, *Central and Southeastern Europe*, pp. 106–7).

[4] On Eisenhower's attempts to groom a successor see no. 1192.

[5] For background on the Suez crisis see no. 1932.

[6] President William McKinley delivered his final speech on September 5, 1901, in Buffalo, New York (James D. Richardson, *A Supplement to a Compilation of the Messages and Papers of the Presidents 1789–1902* [Washington, D.C., 1903], pp. 292–96). An assassin shot McKinley on September 6, 1901, and the President died on September 14. See Eisenhower to Hauge, July 26, 1956, AWF/A.

[7] For background on Eisenhower's tariff policy see nos. 293, 985 and 1123.

[8] A few years later Michael Harrington would publish a different conclusion in *The Other America: Poverty in the United States* (New York, 1962).

[9] On Eisenhower's problems in persuading Congress of the necessity for such "foreign expenditures" see no. 1893.

1937
                                                              EM, AWF,
                                                      International Series:
                                                                Bulganin

To Nikolai Aleksandrovich Bulganin   *August 4, 1956*
Secret

Dear Mr. Chairman: I refer to your letter of June sixth to which I have given a great deal of thought.[1]

It confirmed your announcement of last May that you plan to reduce somewhat the manpower level of your armed forces.[2] Such a reduction I welcome. That would correspond with the action of the United States Government in steadily reducing the size of its armed forces ever since the end of World War II, with an exception only for the Korean war period.[3]

However, I doubt that such reductions of this particular kind as our governments may make in their respective national interests will contribute effectively to eliminate the fear, and the vast cost, generated by national armaments.[4] There is obvious need of international supervisory mechanisms and controls which will encourage greater reductions. I regret that we have made so little progress in this respect.[5]

Some time ago I agreed to your proposal for ground inspection on the assumption that you would also agree to my proposal for aerial inspection, and exchange of military information, made at Geneva a year ago.[6] So far, I understand that you reject this on the ground that it would be an intelligence operation. What I proposed was to be preceded by an exchange of complete military blueprint information, and was designed to make known to each other that neither of us is preparing a sudden massive attack against the other, and that each of us is fulfilling such agreements as I trust we shall be able to reach in the field of disarmament. Surely that kind of intelligence is desirable and necessary, and in the interest of peace and international confidence. Can we not make progress on this?

And also I recall my letter to you of March 1, 1956, [in] which I proposed that, after a date to be agreed upon, production of fissionable materials anywhere in the world would no longer be used to increase the stockpiles of explosive weapons. I had hoped that this proposal, which seemed to me to be of considerable significance, would appeal to you as an important step toward bringing the nuclear threat under control. However, you have never responded to that proposal, and your letter of June sixth makes no reference to the control of nuclear weapons. May I again urge careful consideration of the matter, and especially my proposal of last March?

You refer in your letter to a possible reduction of our respective forces in Germany. Obviously the problem of forces in Germany cannot be dealt with as an isolated matter. In this respect, I must confess that I am greatly disturbed by the developments which have occurred since we met at Geneva last year. We there agreed that the reunification of Germany was a common responsibility of the four Governments at Geneva, and we also agreed that Germany should be reunified by means of free elections carried out in conformity with the national interests of the German people and the interests of European security. Not only has this not happened, but I hear of statements from your side which seem to imply that your Government is determined to maintain indefinitely the division of Germany.[7]

I must confess that I am perplexed as to how we can work together constructively if agreements which are negotiated at the highest level after the most thorough exploration do not seem dependable.

Nevertheless, it is my earnest hope that we will find ways to make progress toward a meaningful control of armaments, a hope shared, I believe, not only by ourselves but by the peoples of the world.

I and my associates have never ceased to give the most intensive study to this whole matter of limitation of armaments and above all the elimination of the growing threat of nuclear weapons and new means of delivery. If this study develops further possibilities of international action, as I trust it will, I shall communicate them to you, either directly or through the appropriate organs of the United Nations. In this connection, I must say that I do not share your view about the activities of the United Nations Disarmament Subcommittee.[8] Discussions there have done much to shed light on this difficult problem and, I hope, to narrow somewhat the gap between our points of view.

May we not, Mr. Chairman, do more to realize the hopes which were born of our meeting at Geneva? We then made promises, notably about Germany, which desperately need to be fulfilled. We pledged ourselves to disarmament efforts which could be fruitful of good for all the world if only we could agree on measures of supervision and control which should be attainable if neither of us has anything hostile to hide. We sought to find the way to develop contacts which would enable our peoples, through better knowledge of each other, to strengthen their friendship, which can be a precious bulwark of peace.

We realize that efforts are being made in your country to eradicate some of the evils of an earlier period.[9] This we welcome. But I hope that you and your associates will not confine those efforts to those evils as manifested within your Party and nation. Those evils were also projected into the international field. Even today they constitute a grievous obstacle to doing those things which we both agreed ought to be done. This situation needs also to be remedied by a new spirit for which I earnestly appeal.

I am, *Sincerely*

---

[1] Chairman of the Soviet Council of Ministers Nikolai A. Bulganin had informed Eisenhower of a unilateral cut in Soviet forces in 1956 of one million two hundred thousand men. He asked for a reciprocal reduction of NATO forces stationed in Germany (Bulganin to Eisenhower, June 6, 1956, AWF/I: Bulganin).

[2] An August 4 State Department draft of this letter, with Eisenhower's approval and emendations is in AWF/I: Bulganin. Eisenhower had added the word "manpower."

[3] Consistent with his emphasis on firepower, rather than manpower, Eisenhower thought that arms reduction should be achieved by cutting armaments instead of troop levels (see nos. 1744 and 1765). Some scholars have suggested that Soviet troop cuts after World War II may have been deeper than Eisenhower suggests here (Matthew Evangelista, "Stalin's Postwar Army Reappraised," *International Security*, 7 [Winter 1982–1983], pp. 110–38). See also State, *Foreign Relations, 1955–1957*, vol. XX, *Regulation of Armaments; Atomic Energy*, pp. 402–11.

[4] Eisenhower added the words "of this particular kind" to the State Department draft.

[5] For background see nos. 1709 and 1765.

[6] See no. 1523; see also Eisenhower, *Mandate for Change*, pp. 503–31.

[7] Eisenhower had used similar language regarding the division of Germany in an earlier letter to Bulganin. See no. 1723. For background on Eisenhower's views on this issue see nos. 1535, 1618, and 1633.

[8] Bulganin had written Eisenhower that the U.N. subcommittee's activities were "retarding progress" in the disarmament negotiations (Bulganin to Eisenhower, June 6, 1956, AWF/I: Bulganin).

⁹ Eisenhower was probably referring to Nikita Khrushchev's speech to the Twentieth Communist Party Congress denouncing Josef Stalin (see no. 1813).

1938

EM, AWF,
International Series:
Bulganin

To Nikolai Aleksandrovich Bulganin   *August 6, 1956*
Personal and confidential

Dear Mr. Chairman: I understand that Ambassador Bohlen may be seeing you within the next few hours to deliver my reply to your letter of June sixth on disarmament.¹ I have asked Ambassador Bohlen in this connection to let you know personally how seriously I regard the situation precipitated by the Egyptian Government's effort to seize the operations of the Suez Canal.² The United States is strongly exerting itself in favor of a solution by the peaceful conference method, as has been proposed, and I hope that you will do the same.³ I also greatly hope that the Egyptian Government will not reject this approach.

The prospect of any good progress in the field of disarmament would indeed be dimmed unless those primarily concerned with the Suez international waterways can meet, as proposed, to seek peacefully an acceptable solution.

With assurance of my best wishes,⁴ *Sincerely*

¹ See no. 1937; see also State, *Foreign Relations, 1955–1957*, vol. XVI, *Suez Crisis July 26–December 31, 1956*, pp. 149–50.
² See no. 1932.
³ On the conference, which would begin in London on August 16, see no. 1948. Although Egypt would not attend, the chief of Nasser's political cabinet, Ali Sabri, would be in London during this period as an unofficial observer.
⁴ Eisenhower added these six words to Dulles's draft of this letter (see Telephone conversation, Eisenhower and Dulles, Aug. 6, 1956, Dulles Papers, Telephone Conversations).

1939

EM, AWF, Name Series

To Norman Cousins   *August 6, 1956*¹
Personal and confidential

Dear Mr. Cousins:² Up to this moment I have had only the time to read your editorial most sketchily. Because of its meaningful character I shall, later, ponder it seriously.³

But, even so, I see that you have expressed in powerful and persuasive terms some of the great dangers facing the individual—which means civilization—and the need for that same individual to do something about it. I started thinking along these lines when I learned that the first atomic bomb had been successfully tested in 1945 and that the United States planned to use it against a Japanese city. Never has the matter ceased troubling me. As early as 1947 I put into a book I wrote a germ or two of the ideas you express so eloquently.[4]

There is one human habit or trait that you have not brought to the fore. It seems to be an historical fact that when a people become strong, prosperous, and on the whole contented with their lot, it becomes very difficult to reach them with an idea that requires them to think of unpleasant possibilities or to undertake the work and effort required to eliminate such possibilities.

There is, moreover, one other disturbing fact that you do not mention, even though you are possibly aware of it. This fact is that there is no presently known method by which could be uncovered, and counted, even sizeable numbers of hydrogen and other bombs already manufactured and deliberately concealed. It is possible, with the consent of the manufacturing country for rigid inspection, to keep rather close track of new fissionable material produced, as well as its use. Here you find the reason why certain of my disarmament proposals have talked about uses of fissionable material produced in the future rather than about that already manufactured into bombs. I am sure you would agree that a disarmament agreement with the Soviets, with which we would strictly comply and which they could easily evade, would be worse than none at all. This would be true of either a bilateral or a collective treaty.[5]

To me it is especially encouraging to see that intelligent people are studying this problem so seriously. Thank you very much for bringing your article to my attention. I am going to circulate it among some of my close associates here.[6]

With warm personal regard, *Sincerely*

---

[1] This was the eleventh anniversary of the bombing of Hiroshima.

[2] Cousins was editor of *The Saturday Review*; for background see Galambos, *NATO and the Campaign of 1952*, no. 97.

[3] Cousins had sent Eisenhower a forthcoming editorial which, he said, reflected "the general affirmative philosophy underlying your own thought and work" (July 26, 1956, AWF/N). Cousins's editorial, entitled "Think of a Man," which appeared in *The Saturday Review* on August 4, 1956, discussed the effects of the hydrogen bomb and called for disarmament.

[4] See Eisenhower, *Crusade in Europe*, p. 456.

[5] For background on Eisenhower's disarmament proposals, see nos. 1523 and 1937.

[6] Cousins would reply that he was "profoundly impressed" by Eisenhower's observations concerning the difficulty of controlling nuclear weapons. He warned that "the verdict of history" might not be in America's favor for dropping the bomb and noted that recently released papers from the Yalta conference seemed to indicate that the

primary reason for dropping it was political rather than military. In any case, he feared that "the sensitivities of the Asians being what they are, especially on matters involving color or status, it is not unnatural perhaps that they should have mistakenly viewed our decision to drop the atomic bomb in the context of the old East-West relationship rather than in terms of military necessity" (Aug. 22, 1956, AWF/N).

1940   *EM, AWF, DDE Diaries Series*

DIARY   *August 6, 1956*

Today I signed a letter directing Admiral Strauss as to the estimated amounts of fissionable material to be produced in '57.[1] The letter was of six pages. I initialled each one and signed the last one. It was reported to me orally the number of weapons of various sizes we now have in our possession.

[1] We were unable to find this document in AWF. The Eisenhower Administration had greatly increased the production of fissionable material; see Eisenhower to Anderson, June 13, 1956, WHCF/OF 108; and Hewlett and Holl, *Atoms for Peace and War*, pp. 159–63, 166–68, 580.

1941   *EM, AWF, Administration Series*

TO LEWIS WILLIAMS DOUGLAS   *August 6, 1956*

Dear Lew: I delayed an answer to your letter of the twelfth until I was sure that you and Peggy were back in this country.[1] Nevertheless, I do want you to know that on two scores I found your comments highly gratifying. Certainly I am reassured by your long record of good health after an operation similar to the one I recently had.[2]

Perhaps more importantly, I appreciated your comments regarding NATO. Although I do not believe official announcement has been made, we are currently planning a series of meetings to reappraise NATO, to be held within the next month.[3]

If you come to Washington, I am sure we can set up a convenient appointment. I am always glad to see you.[4]

With affectionate regard to Peggy, and all the best, as always, to yourself, *Sincerely*

[1] Douglas's wife, Peggy Zinnser Douglas.
[2] Douglas had written Eisenhower from London that he had had surgery for ileitis twenty years before (Douglas to Eisenhower, July 12, 1956, AWF/A).

³ Douglas, a former ambassador, had claimed partial credit for devising NATO. He had recently toured several European countries and reported that though there was strong support for NATO, there was also a "growing view" that its strategy and tactics should be updated to respond to the possibility of thermonuclear war (*ibid.*; for background see no. 1931). Eisenhower marked the paragraphs of Douglas's letter that concerned NATO and sent a copy to Secretary Dulles (Eisenhower to Dulles, July 16, 1956, AWF/A, Douglas Corr.).
⁴ Though Douglas had wanted to talk to the President about "a whole variety of other matters to which my antennae are sensitive," he and Eisenhower would not meet in 1956 (President's daily appointments).

1942   *EM, AWF, DDE Diaries Series*

To ADELAIDE O'MARA   *August 6, 1956*
Personal and confidential

Dear Miss O'Mara: With a real sense of personal uplift I read about the card containing The Ten Commandments that you placed in the BMT subway trains serving your area of New York City.[1] The newspaper account reported you as saying that sometimes a small thing can change the world.

How right you are.

The world can well use an accumulation of good thoughts and good deeds, such as yours, which can call forth what Lincoln described as "the better angels of our nature."[2] Despite the massive forces in motion in the world, it is still the individual person, believing in the right and doing good, that counts for most.

Certainly it is better to try to light a light than to bewail the darkness. For what you did, a personal "thank you." *Sincerely*

¹ O'Mara, a forty-eight-year-old stenographer, had paid $400 for the month-long advertisement on the Brooklyn-Manhattan Transit System (*New York Times*, Aug. 5, 1956). Drafts of this letter containing Eisenhower's extensive handwritten emendations are in AWF/Drafts.
² The quotation is from Lincoln's First Inaugural Address (see Lincoln, *Collected Works*, vol. IV, p. 271).

1943   *EM, AWF, Administration Series*

To PAUL GRAY HOFFMAN   *August 6, 1956*

Dear Paul: At this moment I don't see any possibility of a return visit to Southern California after the San Francisco affair. It is a possibility

I may spend a few days on the Monterey Peninsula, but even that is not completely definite.[1]

Don't worry about your "enemies;" I have learned, the hard way to be sure, to ignore them.[2]

With warm regard, *As ever*

[1] On the arrangements for the Republican National Convention and the week following see no. 1916.

[2] "I would settle for one or two fewer enemies," Hoffman had written on August 3 (AWF/A), "although I am enormously proud of the 64 fine Senators who did vote for me." On July 13 Eisenhower had sent to the Senate Hoffman's nomination as a delegate to the United Nations General Assembly. Despite objections voiced by Senator Joseph R. McCarthy, the Senate Foreign Relations Committee unanimously approved the nomination on July 17 (*New York Times*, July 14, 18, 1956).

1944   *Gruenther Papers*

To ALFRED MAXIMILIAN GRUENTHER   *August 7, 1956*
Confidential

I realize you have been told that our conference scheduled from the 10th to the 14th has gone into the doubtful stage because of preoccupation with other matters—and because we rather think that the British view may have undergone some alterations.[1] In spite of this I believe you should come on to spend with us roughly the time that was planned, unless, of course, you sense some compelling reason for staying at your headquarters.[2] By carrying out the original plan we can hold the proposed conference if that should prove feasible, but if not, we could have a series of very profitable talks. I am particularly anxious to get your personal views on some of the NATO affairs, and of course I feel a great need for checking up on some of your personal practices in other fields.[3]

[1] The "other matters" Eisenhower mentions stem from the nationalization of the Suez Canal, which had taken place on July 26 (State, *Foreign Relations, 1955–1957*, vol. IV, *Western European Security and Integration*, p. 95). For background see nos. 1932 and 1935. On Eisenhower's scheduled meetings with the State and Defense departments see no. 1915.

The President would meet with Gruenther on August 12 and 13 (President's daily appointments). In the August 12 meeting, Gruenther would brief the President and others on West German Chancellor Konrad Adenauer's displeasure at recent press reports about the Administration's intentions to reduce NATO manpower requirements by increasing each division's firepower with atomic weapons (see no. 1931). In his presentation, Gruenther remarked that the streamlining of divisions was "beyond his province" and that he was not sure whether the increased atomic firepower would allow a reduction of the standard 17,000 man division. Although British plans for nuclear armed divisions called for an increase to 19,000 men, he understood that the U.S. Army was working on a plan for a 12,000 man division of five battalions. See A. J. Bacevich, *The Pentomic Era: The U.S. Army Between Korea and Vietnam* (Washington, 1986). Eisenhower remarked that with a force of thirty divisions, each division could be reduced in size and overhead to as little as 9,000 men; atomic weapons would still increase divisional firepower. He also observed that the Germans could do more for their own defense (Memorandum for Record, Aug. 13, 1956, AWF/D).

[2] Gruenther would reply that he intended to return to Washington on August 10 even if the official meeting should be cancelled (Gruenther to Eisenhower, Aug. 8, 1956, AWF/D).

[3] Gruenther, concerned that his heavy schedule of meetings might force him to miss out on a bridge game with the President, had jokingly asked Eisenhower to tell the Secretary of State to shorten his meeting schedule. He had suggested that the President say the following to Dulles: "'Knowing Gruenther as I do, I am positive that you will have extracted from him any ideas which he may have within the first 30 minutes of play. The rest of the day will be devoted, with all of his stubborn insistence, to his reiteration of the same cliches, with nary a new thought.'" Gruenther further suggested that Eisenhower should tell Dulles that the bridge game "'might be able to help me dissipate any lingering gas which may still be in my [Eisenhower's] abdomen. Confidentially, we have a couple of ripe pigeons on the hook for that evening, and if we could take them over the jumps it would help us both very much. Moreover, I get damned tired of eating ground carrots and yoghurt, and a variation of that pigeon meat will really do me a world of good.'" As it turned out, the two would indeed be able to play bridge during Gruenther's visit (Gruenther to Eisenhower, Aug. 1, 1956; Whitman to Gruenther, Aug. 3, 1956, Eisenhower to Gruenther, Aug. 14, 1956, AWF/A, Gruenther Corr.).

1945   *EM, AWF, Administration Series*

To Lorraine P. Knox   *August 7, 1956*

Dear Lorraine: This is a belated but very sincere "thank you" for your two nice letters of early June.[1] I know you follow the newspapers so you will understand that I have been fairly busy for these many weeks.

Following my operation, the doctors gave me a brand new set of rules to follow, some of which did not fit very well with those that I was given when I left Fitzsimons.[2] However, I do have laid down for me a daily schedule of work, exercise, rest and diet. Colonel Mattingly has been watching me all the time and says that my heart has withstood this latest affair in splendid fashion.

In any event, I seem to grow a little stronger each day, and while I would not want to play eighteen holes of golf on a hot day, I am confident that soon I will be very much better than I was before this latest sojourn in the hospital.

I am delighted that you and your friend were able to take a motor trip over our Western States.[3] I have had that experience two or three times, and I must say it is one that I look forward to repeating if ever I again get the opportunity. I know you must have had a very good time. I think the two things I always recall with the greatest pleasure are the Grand Canyon and the Redwood Forest.

I think it is quite possible that I owe both Colonel Turner and Captain Koger letters. Should you see either one, tell her that I will soon find time to drop her a note. It is high time, also, that I write to Colonel Pollock, although I suppose that Colonel Mattingly keeps him informed of my progress on the cardiac front.[4]

By this time I suppose that you are a veteran in your new work; probably you are conducting classes in the logistics of hospital operations![5]

With affectionate regard, *Sincerely*

P.S. Under present plans I shall not visit Denver this summer, even briefly, so I shall not have the pleasure of calling on you and the other people who were so wonderful to me last year.[6]

[1] Lieutenant Colonel Knox had written on June 6 and again on June 9 after hearing about Eisenhower's ileotransverse colostomy (both in AWF/A; see also Knox to Whitman, June 9, 1956, AWF/A, Knox Corr.). On the surgery see no. 1894.

[2] On the President's September 1955 heart attack see no. 1595.

[3] Knox had written (June 6) that she planned to visit the West throughout the month of June.

[4] All of these officers, and Knox, had helped care for the President following his heart attack. For developments see no. 2002 (see also Eisenhower to Griffin, Aug. 7, 1956, AWF/A: Fitzsimons).

[5] On Knox's recent promotion see no. 1767.

[6] Campaign obligations would preclude the Eisenhowers' traditional Denver vacation.

1946   *EM, AWF, DDE Diaries Series*

DIARY   *August 8, 1956*

The current Suez crisis.

The Suez affair has a long and intricate background and at this moment the outcome of the quarrel is so undetermined that it would be difficult indeed to predict what will probably happen.[1]

Unlike the Panama Canal, which was built as a national undertaking by the United States under the terms of a bilateral treaty with Panama, the Suez Canal was built by an international group. There seems to have been felt the need for clarifying rights and privileges of the several nations in the use of the Canal, and so in 1888 a Convention or Treaty was signed, among a group of nations (about 10, I think) and which was left open for the purpose of permitting other nations to sign later should they so choose. That Treaty, among other things, made the waterway an international one forever, open to the shipping of all countries both in peace and war.

The Canal was originally constructed under a concession from Egypt, which expires in 1968, but the 1888 Convention specifically provided that the international character will continue no matter what the future ownership or concession arrangements might be.

Originally, I believe the stock was held largely by Egypt and by Frenchmen, but during the course of the years Egyptian rulers sold theirs. In any event a large block was acquired by the British Government. I am not certain, but it is possible that the British Government may have owned some of the original stock. In any event, as of today the British own about 400,000 shares.

On the morning of July 27th, Gamal Abdel Nasser, the President of Egypt, made a very inflammatory speech, in which he announced the nationalizing of the Canal Company.[2] This meant that the Egyptian Government took over the entire resources of the Suez Canal Company wherever they might be located. He also issued an extraordinary order to the effect that all people working for the Canal would be required to continue in their present employment under penalty of imprisonment. A further statement indicated that he expected to realize something on the order of one hundred million dollars profit a year out of the Canal and this undoubtedly meant a steep increase in Canal tolls since today after the payment to Egypt of the normal ground rental of some seventeen million dollars, there is only about thirty-five million dollars' profit. Another point in this connection is that the volume of traffic and the size of vessels is increasing so rapidly that very soon an extra three-quarters of a billion dollars must be spent to deepen and widen the Canal.

Nasser said he was doing these things because of the refusal of the United States to help him build the Aswan Dam.[3]

When we made our first offer, I think more than a year ago, to help build the Aswan Dam, it was conceived of as a joint venture of ourselves and the British, which, once accomplished, would enable the World Bank to go in and help Nasser to completion of the work.[4] It was felt that under this basis, the project would be feasible but would require all the resources that Egypt could donate to public affairs.

Egypt at once did two things:

(1) They sent back to us a whole list of conditions that would have to be met before they would go along with this plan and some of these conditions were unacceptable.

(2) They began to build up their military forces by taking over equipment provided by the Soviets, and they went to such an extent that we did not believe they would have a sufficient balance of resources left to do their part in building the Dam.[5]

We lost interest and said nothing more about the matter.

Suddenly, about a month ago, Nasser sent us a message to the effect that he had withdrawn all of the conditions that he had laid down, and was ready to proceed under our original offer. Since conditions had changed markedly and we had thought the whole project dead, we merely replied we were no longer interested.[6]

[1] On Egyptian President Nasser's nationalization of the Suez Canal see no. 1932.

[2] Nasser's speech was delivered in Alexandria on July 26.

[3] See nos. 1759 and 1859.

[4] On December 16, 1955, the United States had presented the financing proposal to the Egyptian government (State, *Foreign Relations, 1955–1957*, vol. XIV, *Arab-Israeli Dispute 1955*, pp. 849–51, 860–65, 868–70).

[5] See no. 1859 and *U.S. Department of State Bulletin* 35, no. 892 (July 30, 1956), p. 188; see also Eisenhower, *Waging Peace*, pp. 30–33.

[6] On July 19 Secretary Dulles had told Eisenhower that internal economic conditions in Egypt had changed markedly since the initial offer and that the problem of the division of the Nile waters was far from a solution. An additional problem, he said, was the increasing difficulty of close cooperation with the Nasser regime—a necessity for the successful completion of the project. Eisenhower agreed that the United States should withdraw the offer (State, *Foreign Relations, 1955–1957*, vol. XV, *Arab-Israeli Dispute January 1–July 26, 1956*, pp. 861–64, 867–74; see also Telephone conversation, Dulles and Allen Dulles, July 19, 1956, Dulles Papers, Telephone Conversations).

1947   *EM, AWF, DDE Diaries Series*

To William Rudolph Gruber   *August 8, 1956*

Dear Bill: Many thanks for your letter of July twenty-ninth and the one of August first.[1]

As far as my visit to Cypress Point is concerned—if it goes through (and everything is problematical these days)—I believe that Mamie and I will stay at the Cypress Point Club, since the matter has already been tentatively set up that way.[2] However, I am grateful to Mr. Griffin for his kind suggestion, and I am writing him a note to thank him.[3]

While I deny that any one man is "indispensable," I find interesting your list of "indispensable qualities" needed in a President.

With warm regard, *Sincerely*

[1] Gruber's letters are not in AWF.

[2] See no. 1916.

[3] Eisenhower's August 8 letter to Allen Griffin, Governor of the Cypress Point Club, is in AWF/D.

To Michael Joseph Mansfield   *August 9, 1956*

Dear Senator Mansfield:[1] I venture to urge that you attend with Secretary of State Dulles the forthcoming Suez Canal Conference in London.[2]

The issues before that Conference, or which may emerge from it, are of great importance from the standpoint of the United States. I know that, as a member of the Foreign Relations Committee, you have been studying the problems of this area and I am confident that you can make a valuable contribution to our goal of a peaceful outcome which will assure a dependable administration and operation of the Canal, as contemplated by the 1888 Treaty.

I consider that senatorial participation is particularly useful because out of the present talks may come a new Suez Canal Treaty or Convention, to which the United States may desire to become a party.

Secretary Dulles heartily joins me in this request and I understand that Senator George, the Chairman of the Foreign Relations Committee, agrees as to the desirability of your attendance.[3]

With warm regard, *Sincerely*

[1] Secretary Dulles sent Mansfield, a member of the Senate Foreign Relations Committee, a copy of this letter, saying that the original would follow when it was "convenient for the Senator to receive it." The letter was probably not sent (see n. 3; Bernau to Whitman, Aug. 10, 1956, AWF/N, Mansfield Corr.; and Telephone conversation, Dulles and O'Connor, Aug. 9, 1956, Dulles Papers, Telephone Conversations).

[2] See no. 1932. At meetings with British and French officials in London beginning on August 1, Secretary Dulles had proposed a conference of the signatories of the 1888 convention as well as those with vital interests in trade through the canal. The conference would seek a treaty incorporating the principles of the original convention and providing for the internationalization of the canal. Dulles told British and French officials that although the United States did not exclude military action if all other methods to resolve the problem failed, "the use of force, if not backed by public opinion, would have disastrous results." The Suez Canal Conference, with twenty-two nations participating, would meet in London from August 16–23 (State, *Foreign Relations, 1955–1957*, vol. XVI, *Suez Crisis July 26–December 31, 1956*, pp. 94–116; see also Eisenhower to Dulles, and Dulles to Eisenhower, Aug. 2, 1956, AWF/D-H).

Dulles had asked Senator Mansfield on August 6 to attend the conference. Mansfield had indicated his willingness to attend but suggested that a leading Republican also be invited (Memorandums of Conversation, Aug. 6 and 8, 1956, Dulles Papers, White House Memoranda Series; Telephone conversation, Dulles and Mansfield, Aug. 8, 1956, Dulles Papers, Telephone Conversations).

[3] Mansfield would tell Dulles on this same day that for personal reasons he was unable to attend the conference (Telephone conversations, Dulles and Mansfield, and Dulles and Adams, Aug. 9, 1956, Dulles Papers, Telephone Conversations; see also Memorandum of Conversation, Aug. 11, 1956, Dulles Papers, White House Memoranda Series). For developments see no. 1958.

To CHARLES ABRAHAM HALLECK   *August 9, 1956*

Dear Charlie: I suppose I need hardly to say any of this to you as you know it already; and yet, I deeply feel that I must express my warmest personal appreciation of your extraordinarily fine work throughout this past session. Time and again I have known of your help and guidance on key measures in which I have had personal interest.[1] I know too that on many occasions you have willingly taken the lead in behalf of measures which for various reasons were especially difficult for you to manage.[2]

This pattern of loyalty to our combined efforts to advance the public good has been unbroken throughout the past four years, and I want to tell you once again, as I have occasion to after each session, how deeply grateful I am. You, no doubt, have some appreciation of how heartening it is to me to have the continuing awareness of your presence in the House and your constant desire to make our program succeed.

It is a matter of great personal satisfaction to me that you will place my name in nomination at the convention.[3] From my standpoint, it is only right and proper that this assignment should go to you. I assure you that I will watch and listen with the greatest interest when you present that speech!

With warm personal regard, *Sincerely*

[1] Former Majority Leader Halleck (Rep., Ind.) had strongly supported the Administration's legislative agendas, and Eisenhower had praised Halleck's congressional performance on several occasions (see nos. 627 and 669). Eisenhower had been particularly pleased with Halleck's work on the tax bill in 1954 (see nos. 784 and 799). White House aide Bryce Harlow drafted this letter for the President.

[2] Eisenhower may have been referring to Halleck's support in the Eighty-fourth Congress for the Administration's position on agricultural and civil rights legislation (see Scheele, *Halleck*, pp. 165–71; for background on the 1956 Agricultural Act see *Congressional Quarterly Almanac*, vol. XII, *1956*, pp. 375ff.

[3] Eisenhower had selected Halleck to nominate him for a second term (Halleck to Eisenhower, Aug. 16, 1956, WHCF/OF 99-V; Eisenhower, *Waging Peace*, p. 13), and Halleck would do so on August 22 at the Republican National Convention in San Francisco (*New York Times*, Aug. 23, 1956; see also Scheele, *Halleck*, pp. 171–72).

To ROBERT DANIEL MURPHY   *August 10, 1956*

Dear Bob: I heard indirectly and inadvertently that Mrs. Arias was quite disturbed because apparently no one had met her and no attention had been paid to her since she has been in the city.[1] I see very little use of my going to Panama and making friends with the people of those countries if such things occur.[2]

Mrs. Eisenhower is trying to arrange to see her for a short visit, and I shall do my best to join them. I would like to know what the State Department plans to do. I believe Mrs. Arias has been in Washington since Tuesday, and leaves within a day or two.[3] *As ever*

[1] Olga de Arias, the wife of Panamanian President Ricardo M. Arias Espinosa, had visited Washington to expedite shipment of the Salk polio vaccine to Panama (*New York Times*, Aug. 3, 1956).

[2] For background on the President's recent visit to Panama see nos. 1925 and 1926.

[3] Deputy Under Secretary of State for Political Affairs, Robert D. Murphy would report that Mrs. Arias had been met at the airport by State Department officials and had been in contact with the Department daily. Murphy added: "Unfortunately, I fear that on the social side we have not been as diligent perhaps as we should have." Mrs. Eisenhower would meet with Mrs. Arias on the afternoon of August 10 (Murphy to Eisenhower, Aug. 10, 1956, AWF/I: Panama). The President would approve the shipment of 45,000 ccs. of Salk vaccine to Panama several weeks before permission was given for shipments to other countries (Minnich to Whitman, Aug. 13, 1956, *ibid.*). Murphy would write Eisenhower that Mrs. Arias had telegraphed from Miami her "sincere gratitude for your great cooperation" (Aug. 11, 1956, AWF/D-H).

1951   *EM, AWF, Administration Series*

To Arthur Sherwood Flemming   *August 13, 1956*

Dear Arthur: The Suez Canal crisis has made all of us give more than the normal amount of attention to oil supplies, present and potential.[1]

The other day someone mentioned to me that it was almost a crime that the American pipe line had not been authorized and built from somewhere in Louisiana or Texas (I have forgotten which) up through Pittsburgh and on to Newark.

I know nothing about the need of such a pipe line, and I send this note merely to inquire whether it is something that has come to your personal attention and whether you believe that whatever decisions the government may have taken in the matter are still correct and applicable.[2] *As ever*

[1] For background see no. 1932.

[2] Director of Defense Mobilization Flemming would respond to Eisenhower's letter on August 20 (AWF/A). As he explained, the government agencies involved had determined in early 1953 that American defense required the capacity to deliver 1,000,000 barrels of crude oil per day by pipeline to East Coast refineries. The point of assembly was to be the Ohio-Pittsburgh area. The United States currently had the capacity to move 665,000 barrels of crude oil a day from Canada, the American Southwest and

Midwest. Still needed was the capacity to move an additional 335,000 barrels of crude from the Gulf Coast. Two companies, the American Pipeline Corporation and the Texas Eastern Transmission Corporation, had presented proposals to the government to build a new line from the Gulf to the Ohio-Pittsburgh area using federal financing. The Department of the Interior, however, believed that the construction of a private pipeline was unnecessary due to the existence of the "Big Inch," a twenty-four inch pipeline running from Longview, Texas, through the Pittsburgh area. The Big Inch had been constructed by the government during World War II as a substitute for tanker movement of crude oil from the Gulf Coast. It had been sold in 1947 and converted to the shipment of natural gas, with a recapture provision included in the contract. This provision provided that the government had the right for a period of twenty years, should national defense so require, to take full possession of the pipeline and to have it restored by the purchaser to the transportation of petroleum. With that in mind, the Department of the Interior had concluded that "the Government is not justified in obligating funds either in the form of direct loans or guarantees of private loans for the development of capacity above that which is already potentially available" (AWF/A, Flemming Corr.). For further background see George S. Wolbert, Jr., *U.S. Oil Pipelines: An Examination of How Oil Pipe Lines Operate and the Current Public Policy Issues Concerning Their Ownership* (Washington, D.C., 1979), pp. 20–26, 250–52; see also Christopher J. Castaneda and Joseph A. Pratt, *From Texas to the East: A Strategic History of Texas Eastern Corporation* (College Station, Tex., 1993), pp. 13–76, 101–29.

1952   *EM, AWF, Name Series*

To Edward John Bermingham   *August 13, 1956*

Dear Ed: There seems to be some confusion about the rate at which Mexican oil production could be increased. After you were here the other day, I spoke to one of my assistants about the "million barrels a day" figure you suggested. He got in touch with some experts, who challenged the figure.[1] Do you have a copy of the geological report that substantiates your understanding in the matter?[2] *As ever*

[1] Egyptian President Nasser's nationalization of the Suez Canal on July 26 (see no. 1932) had prompted Administration discussion of alternative ways to supply Western Europe with oil (see NSC meeting minutes, Aug. 10, 1956, AWF/NSC; and no. 1951). At a meeting on August 9 Bermingham had told Eisenhower that Mexico produced three hundred thousand barrels of oil per day, with home consumption of two hundred twenty-five thousand. "With increased and adequate facilities," Bermingham had said, "present production could be stepped up to one million barrels daily from its already proven fields" (Bermingham to Eisenhower, Aug. 10, 1956, AWF/N). Eisenhower had discussed this issue with ODM Director Arthur Flemming (NSC meeting minutes, Aug. 10, 1956, AWF/NSC; see also Dillon Anderson to Eisenhower, Aug. 20, 1956, AWF/A).

[2] Bermingham would write that the figures he had given Eisenhower were the correct estimates. "Naturally, and this I should have emphasized," he wrote, "daily production

cannot be stepped up to 1,000,000 barrels from producing wells; additional drilling *in proven fields* would be required, and perhaps that caused the confusion of which you spoke" (Bermingham to Eisenhower, Aug. 15, 1956, AWF/A, Dillon Anderson Corr.). Bermingham would later tell Eisenhower that Antonio Bermudez, Director General of Pemex, had confirmed the one million barrel estimate but "was hesitant to be too specific." The geological reports were available to Bermingham or his designate, Bermudez had said, but "he was reluctant to have them out of his keeping" (Bermingham to Eisenhower, Aug. 18, 1956, AWF/A, Anderson Corr.; see also Bermudez to Bermingham, Aug. 16, 1956, *ibid.*).

1953   *EM, AWF, DDE Diaries Series*

TO HILDA GLEASON   *August 14, 1956*

Dear Sister Hilda Gleason: Some time back when my friend Charles Tompkins was making a visit to your College, I asked him to express to you the gratitude I felt for the compliment paid me by the students and faculty of your school when I returned to Gettysburg following my illness in Denver, last year.[1] The sight of your student body and the faculty lined up along the road is one that will always be fresh in my memory, and I assure you that I was deeply touched.

When I next saw Mr. Tompkins after he carried that message to you, he told me that you were then conducting a summer school for teachers, and that each night the entire three hundred fifty of them included in their prayers a plea for my health and return to strength.[2] While I have been hoping that I could drop in at St. Joseph's to thank you personally for this further evidence of your concern, I have recently been disappointed in my efforts to come to that region for a weekend.

The purpose of this note is just to say "Thank you," and to express the hope that I yet may have the opportunity of meeting you personally to repeat that simple message. *Sincerely*

[1] Sister Hilda Gleason was Mother Superior of St. Joseph's College for Women in Emmitsburg, Maryland. The group from St. Joseph's were among an estimated 7,000 persons who had welcomed the President and Mrs. Eisenhower (see *New York Times,* Nov. 15, 1955). On Eisenhower's September 1955 heart attack see no. 1595.

[2] On July 11 Tompkins had visited Eisenhower while he was convalescing at his Gettysburg farm. On the President's ileotransverse colostomy in June see no. 1894.

To Sinclair Weeks   *August 15, 1956*

Dear Sinclair: I realize that it is not my responsibility to select members for your Business Advisory Council. However, I venture to suggest an individual who is both a warm friend of mine and a broadly experienced business man.[1]

His name is:

> William E. Robinson,
> President,
> Coca Cola Company,
> 515 Madison Avenue,
> New York, New York.

As ever

[1] Weeks would respond with a quotation from Shakespeare's *The Tempest*: "I will be correspondent to command and do my spiriting gently" (Weeks to Eisenhower, Aug. 15, 1956, AWF/A). On December 26 Weeks would write the President that he had invited Robinson to become a member of the Council (AWF/A).

To Wilton Burton Persons   *August 16, 1956*
Memorandum

If ever we need a man with considerable experience in the Caribbean, Central or South American area, for a diplomatic or similar post, we might consider a retired Vice Admiral, by name Frank George Fahrion.[1] I believe he is about 62, but I understand he looks much younger, and I know he has had an excellent Naval record.

This is merely a suggestion in case we find ourselves looking for a man with his qualifications.

[1] On August 10 Eisenhower's close friend, Swede Hazlett, had written the President (AWF/N; see also no. 1963) to recommend his brother-in-law, "Spike" Fahrion (USNA 1917), who had retired from the U.S. Navy in May (for further background see Chandler and Galambos, *Occupation, 1945*, no. 493). Hazlett had written that he took "it for granted that you are always glad to know of able, self-effacing men with built-in integrity, so you can consider this paragraph as purely informational. . . . But I think that Spike could handle a diplomatic post in the Carribean, Central-South American area, which he knows well, with credit." On August 20 Persons would forward Eisenhower's memorandum with a covering memo to a White House special assistant requesting that it be passed along to the State Department (see also Bea to Mr. Gray, Aug. 22, 1956; and Biographical Information in same file as document).

To EMMET JOHN HUGHES   *August 17, 1956*
Personal

Dear Emmet: I hasten to reply to your latest letter. My only negative reaction—if any—is that you felt it necessary to make such a long explanation to me as to why you believed that you could best deliver the talk.[1] Both your dedication and your abilities are things that I count on so completely as to take them for granted.

The second that I saw your letter, I told Jim Hagerty to begin telephoning to people in charge of the Convention to see what might be done.[2] One difficulty arose because of the rule we had made to limit "seconding speeches" to three, or maybe it was four, minutes. Therefore the speech would have to be given as a special event.

Now to me this seemed all to the good. I should think that the Chairman could merely announce that the Convention had been anxious to hear from some young Independent, who had announced his purpose of voting to continue the present Administration in office. He could frankly say that you had always been an Independent, but had been a member of the White House staff for the first nine or ten months following the '53 inauguration.[3]

When your first note to me arrived, I merely assumed that the fact that you had been so closely associated with me at one time disqualified you from delivering the speech, but after some sober second thinking, I decided that might prove to be an asset rather than otherwise.

In any event, we should know very quickly what they can arrange in San Francisco.[4] Certainly I am grateful to you for the frank expression of your feelings, and I am proud indeed that they include such a high estimate of my current value to the country.

My warm greetings to your lovely bride.[5] *As ever*

P.S. I have one thought to add. If by any chance this speech is not delivered, as written, to the Convention, I am most certainly going to plagiarize the parts that are not quotes from former talks. In the half dozen or so speeches that I have to make this fall, I can already see dreariness developing that will make my blood pressure rise to astronomical heights. To lift out the "We believe" portion of your talk and insert it at the end of a foreign policy talk or another I have that is entitled "The Government and the People" would raise either far beyond the ordinary.

---

[1] Hughes, an editor on leave from *Fortune* to write for the 1956 Republican campaign (*New York Times*, Aug. 23, 1956), had sent a draft of a speech meant for a political independent. He hinted that he would like to deliver the speech himself (Aug. 13, 1956,

AWF/A). Before the President sent this response, Hughes had written again, this time arguing that he would be a strategic choice to give the speech as it would seem authentic if given by a "politically unknown" ([n.d.], AWF/A).

[2] On August 17 Eisenhower called the Attorney General regarding the possibility of the journalist delivering the convention speech as an independent (Telephone conversation, Aug. 17, 1956, AWF/D). The next day Eisenhower would discuss this idea with Governor Adams (AWF/AWD); see also no. 1960.

[3] Hughes had drafted speeches for the 1952 race and had served briefly in 1953 as an administrative assistant to Eisenhower (see nos. 974 and 1003).

[4] On August 22 at the Republican National Convention, Hughes would deliver a speech similar to the draft giving support to Eisenhower while disclaiming any party affiliation (*New York Times*, Aug. 23, 1956; *Proceedings of the Twenty-sixth Republican National Convention*, pp. 246–51). Eisenhower would afterwards write Hughes that his speech had "almost single-handedly raised the plane of ideals that, otherwise, might have been nothing but standard political pyrotechnics" (Aug. 29, 1956, AWF/A).

[5] The former Eileen Lanouette.

1957   *EM, AWF, Administration Series*

To Arthur Frank Burns   *August 17, 1956*

Dear Arthur: You must have been very persuasive in your talk with Bill Martin. Thank you for telling me about the outcome.[1]

Incidentally, I think that your success in getting such unanimity of agreement on your "Small Business" Report was one of the leadership triumphs of my past three and a half years in the White House. My conviction that no one else could have done it measures the debt of my gratitude to you.[2]

With warm regard, *As ever*

[1] Burns had written the President on August 16 (AWF/A) to inform him that Federal Reserve Board Chairman William McChesney Martin, Jr., had agreed to postpone raising the discount rate until early September, when the economic situation could be reevaluated. The Fed would, however, raise the discount rate on August 23 from 2 3/4 to 3 percent in a move to curb inflationary forces (see *New York Times*, Aug. 24, 26, 1956). For background see no. 1877; Saulnier, *Constructive Years*, pp. 90–92; and John W. Sloan, *Eisenhower and the Management of Prosperity* [Kansas, 1991], pp. 119–22. For developments see no. 2005.

[2] On August 17 Burns had sent the President a copy of the Report of the Cabinet Committee on Small Business (AWF/A). Burns had recommended the establishment of the committee during the Cabinet meeting of May 16 (see Cabinet meeting minutes, May 16, 1956, AWF/Cabinet; see also Cabinet meeting minutes, July 27, 1956). The committee recommended providing tax relief for small business—through accelerated and extended depreciation on property and machinery—and facilitating the participation of small business in government contracts. The Committee also called for legislation to enable closer federal scrutiny of mergers, procedural changes in the antitrust laws to facilitate enforcement, and measures to reduce paperwork for the small businessman (see First Progress Report of the Cabinet Committee on Small Business, Sept.

24, 1956, AWF/Cabinet; see also Saulnier, *Constructive Years*, pp. 188–94). For more on the plight of small business as a campaign issue see Arthur M. Schlesinger, Jr., *History of American Presidential Elections*, vol. IV, *1940–1968*, pp. 3365–66, 3390–91. For developments see no. 2154.

1958   *EM, AWF, Dulles-Herter Series*

To John Foster Dulles   *August 18, 1956*
Cable TEDUL 9. Secret

Dear Foster:[1] From all reports you seem to be surpassing even your own unique capacity for bringing some order and sanity to confused situations.[2] We here follow with great confidence and interest your cables and the news through collateral sources.

Good luck and warm regard.[3]

[1] Eisenhower's handwritten draft of this message is in AWF/Drafts.
[2] Dulles had left for London on August 14 to attend the Suez Canal Conference (see no. 1948; on Eisenhower's meeting with Dulles regarding their objectives for the conference see Memorandum of Conversation, Aug. 14, 1956, Dulles Papers, White House Memoranda Series; and Eisenhower, *Waging Peace*, pp. 43–44). After the first day of meetings Dulles had told Eisenhower that there was "increasing evidence that the British and French, as they study the logistics of their planned operation, are feeling the need for time for preparation" (Dulles to Eisenhower, DULTE 4, Aug. 16, 1956, AWF/D-H). Dulles reported on August 17 that he was ready to propose that operation of the canal should be controlled by a nonpolitical, international entity. Of the twenty-two countries participating in the conference, he said, twelve could be counted on to support the plan. The danger was that the ultimate line-up would be the West against Asia and the Soviet Union. Iran and Pakistan were also reluctant to commit themselves to a plan that seemed anti-Egyptian (Dulles to Eisenhower, DULTE 7, Aug. 17, 1956, *ibid.*; see also State, *Foreign Relations, 1955–1957*, vol. XVI, *Suez Crisis July 26–December 31, 1956*, pp. 213–26).
[3] For developments see no. 1961.

1959   *EM, AWF, Administration Series*

To Arthur Frank Burns   *August 18, 1956*

Dear Arthur: I have never been one to "point with pride to" any accomplishments with which I have been associated, but I assure you that I am full of that commodity as I look over the tables you have put together to indicate the extraordinary improvement in the economic welfare of the American people over the past few years.[1] (Incidentally,

I think we might in the months to come stress that economic welfare aspect to the fullest).[2] At any rate, you give me a provocative and exciting document—and I am grateful to you not only for initiating the project, but for the large part you have played in guiding our economic policies toward the results that you now demonstrate.

You have more than earned a long and enjoyable vacation.[3] I shall hope to see you soon after we settle down once again to routine (if such a thing is going to be at all possible in the next two months).

With warm regard, *As ever*

---

[1] Burns had sent the President (August 17, AWF/A) a statistical history of the "diffusion of economic well-being." Burns said "the past three and a half years have been a period of great and widely shared prosperity." He had analyzed, he said, what had "really happened in the sphere of economic *welfare*, rather than economic activity." In thirty tables Burns presented data covering a wide range of subjects, from comparisons of gross national product and average gross weekly earnings in selected industries to statistics on vacations, families owning automobiles, and homes with selected electrical appliances (Aug. 16, 1956, AWF/A, Burns Corr.). For background see Sloan, *Eisenhower and the Management of Prosperity*, pp. 49–52, and Saulnier, *Constructive Years*, pp. 75–97.
[2] Eisenhower had written on Ann Whitman's cover memorandum "We must use these" (AWF/A, Burns Corr.).
[3] Burns had said that he was planning on vacationing at his farm. "I hope that you, too, will get some vacation before the campaign gets actively under way."

1960   *EM, AWF, Administration Series*

To Leonard Wood Hall   *August 18, 1956*

Dear Len: I give you herewith some completely gratuitous advice, which may possibly be worth nothing more than such advice usually is. It is based on reactions from typical television viewers and my own limited experience in the political world.[1]

(*a*) Allow no, repeat no, long and dreary speeches from anyone.

(*b*) While a National Convention has a serious purpose and should be conducted with dignity, there is no reason why the tremendous television audience should become so weary as to turn the dials in search of relief, even to finding a good commercial. Every speech should have some intellectual content.

(*c*) Change of pace is desirable. A succession of speakers that continually repeat the same unchanging story can become just as monotonous as a Clement and bore the public just as much as he.[2]

(*d*) Don't be afraid of a suggestion merely because "it has never been done before." A dedicated and genuine "independent" on your program for a few minutes should be really helpful.[3]

(*e*) By all means get *some* speakers to mention the welcome that we extend to all independents and all "straight-thinking" or intelligent Democrats.

(*f*) Be firm in enforcing the rules you lay down so that events happen as scheduled.

(*g*) Allow no "steam-rollering" on any proposition whatsoever.

(*h*) Lastly, I repeat the first: *No long and dreary speeches.*[4]

[1] This message was dictated by Ann Whitman from Washington to Republican National Committee Chairman Hall at the Republican Convention in San Francisco. On Eisenhower's interest in preparations for the convention see, for example, nos. 1818 and 1903. A draft of this letter, showing Eisenhower's handwritten emendations, is in AWF/Drafts.

[2] Tennessee Governor Frank Goad Clement had delivered the keynote speech at the Democratic National Convention in Chicago on August 14 (see *New York Times*, Aug. 15, 1956).

[3] See no. 1956.

[4] For developments see no. 1967.

1961   *EM, AWF, Dulles-Herter Series*

To JOHN FOSTER DULLES   *August 19, 1956*
Secret

Dear Foster: I have just received your personal telegram to me, dispatched this morning, and your cabled copy of the text of the agreement.[1] I should think that if Nasser has any disposition whatsoever to negotiate this difficulty, you will find your paper fairly acceptable except possibly for that part in 3A which prescribes the duties of the Board.[2] The paper apparently contemplates that the Board shall do the actual "operating, maintaining and developing of the Canal." Nasser may find it impossible to swallow the whole of this as now specified. On the other hand, I realize that you may have already written into the draft the minimum position that our British and French friends feel they can take.

So far as we are concerned, I see no objection to agreeing to a Board with supervisory rather than operating authority. Of course the authority for supervision would have to be clear, and the contention could be made, therefore, that there is no real difference between the two concepts. I think, however, that if we should get something like one of our corporate board of directors, with operating responsibility residing in some one appointed by Nasser, subject to Board approval, we should be establishing an organization which could achieve the ends we seek.

Under such a system I realize that your "Arbitral Commission" might become very busy in settling disputes between Nasser and the Board, but as long as the Canal operated effectively this would be a detail.[3]

Other than expressing the hope that the results of the conference will not be wrecked on the rigidity of the positions of the two sides on this particular point, I have no other comments to submit. Your document looks extraordinarily good to me.[4]

With warm regard, *As ever*

---

[1] See no. 1958 for background. Dulles had told Eisenhower that the United States, Britain, and France had worked out the draft of a proposal that would be presented as a U.S. rather than a tripartite plan. "I felt it wiser to have the control of the situation which goes with it being a U.S. paper," Dulles said. He also told the President that he believed that the Soviets would be interested in an agreement with the United States that they could "impose" upon Egypt "if on the one hand it were couched in a way which would not gravely prejudice the Soviet Union with the Arab world and if on the other hand we would make it a two-party affair with some downgrading of the British and the French." Dulles doubted whether such a proposal was worth having at that price but said he would "do everything possible short of disloyalty to the British and the French to get Soviet agreement" (Dulles to Eisenhower, DULTE 10, Aug. 18, 1956, AWF/D-H).

The declaration reaffirmed the purpose of the Convention of 1888 "to guarantee at all times, and for all the powers, the free use of the Suez Maritime Canal." While purporting to respect Egyptian sovereignty, it called for insulating the operation of the canal from the politics of any nation (Dulles to Eisenhower, DULTE 20, Aug. 18, 1956, *ibid.*; see also State, *Foreign Relations, 1955–1957*, vol. XVI, *Suez Crisis July 26–December 31, 1956*, pp. 228–29; *U.S. Department of State Bulletin* 35, no. 896 [August 27, 1956], 335–39; Eisenhower, *Waging Peace*, pp. 45–46; and Lloyd, *Suez 1956*, pp. 113–17).

[2] The declaration stated that an international board would operate, maintain, and develop the canal, and that Egypt would grant the board all rights and facilities appropriate to its functioning. The board, whose members would represent the geographic distribution of the countries using the canal, would make periodic reports to the United Nations.

[3] Section 3B would establish an arbitral commission to settle disputes regarding the financial return to Egypt, compensation to the Universal Suez Canal Company, and other matters regarding the operation of the canal.

[4] The State Department sent this message to Dulles as TEDUL 13 on this same date (AWF/D-H). For developments see the following document.

1962   *EM, AWF, Dulles-Herter Series*

To JOHN FOSTER DULLES   *August 20, 1956*
Secret

Dear Foster:[1] I have just received both your personal cables to me dispatched this morning.

With respect to the suggestion I made to you yesterday, I tried to make clear in my original message that I understood the difficult position you were probably in, and I was merely expressing the hope that we would not permit negotiations to come to an eventual point of collapse over the details of the operating arrangement proposed.[2] As a minimum, I am sure that any international Board should have the unquestioned right to appoint the general manager of the operation, or at least, to have a veto over the appointment of anyone unsatisfactory to the Board. If that authority should include also the dismissal of a general manager who proved incapable of handling the affairs of the Canal, I believe that the hiring and firing of all lesser officials would tend to become an administrative detail. I repeat, however, that I understand the box you are in.

With respect to your second message, I have to give you my opinion under the handicap of ignorance respecting your own confidence in anybody of another nationality who might do the job in your stead. In addition, I am unaware of the timing and duration of the negotiations visualized with Nasser.[3]

By no means should you become involved in a long wearisome negotiation, especially with an anticipated probability of negative results in the end. On the other hand, if there were some advance evidence that Nasser might prove reasonable and agreement as to principle could be achieved in a very short time, I could see certain advantages of your doing the thing personally. In this way, there would be no chance for erroneous interpretation of our intentions and understanding, and I cannot help but believe that there would be more chance of success with you in a situation where you deal with Nasser than if some lesser individual should undertake the work.

Our Government has expressed the opinion that in this problem, the peaceful processes of a negotiation should prove equal to the development of a satisfactory solution. We cannot afford to do less than our best to assure success, and yet I repeat that it would be worse than embarrassing if you should get tied into drawn-out conversations which would in the long run prove unsuccessful.

I realize that this is very little help in your present problem, but I am a long ways from the individuals who are primarily concerned and the only feel I have of their temper and attitudes is as you have described to me in your cables.

I need scarcely add that I will approve your decision and support you in whatever action you finally decide you must take.[4] *As ever*

[1] A draft of this letter, with Eisenhower's handwritten emendations, is in AWF/Drafts.
[2] See the previous document for background. Regarding the concept of supervisory, rather than operating, authority for the canal board, Dulles had told Eisenhower that most of the countries felt strongly "that if all of the hiring and firing of pilots, traffic directors and other technicians and engineers is made by the Egyptians with only some

right of appeal, then in fact Egypt will be able to use the Canal as an instrument of its national policy." Great Britain and France would not agree to the abandonment of operating authority, Dulles said, and he doubted that concessions to Egypt should be made before presenting the proposal to President Nasser. "It may be possible to soften up somewhat the sentence to which you refer," Dulles added, "but with your approval I shall at this stage defer use of your suggestion" (see the preceding document; and Dulles to Eisenhower, DULTE 13, Aug. 20, 1956, AWF/D-H).

[3] After meeting with Prime Minister Eden and Foreign Minister Lloyd, Dulles told Eisenhower that he could be "subjected to very strong pressure" to head the committee that would negotiate the canal dispute with Nasser. He was not eager to spend the time necessary for such meetings, he said, and he also thought that the United States should "become less conspicuous" if that could be done "without jeopardizing the whole affair" (Dulles to Eisenhower, DULTE 14, Aug. 20, 1956, *ibid.*; see also State, *Foreign Relations, 1955–1957*, vol. XVI, *Suez Crisis July 26–December 31, 1956*, pp. 248–50, 259).

[4] Eighteen out of the twenty-two countries attending the London conference would support the declaration and agree to submit the proposal to Egypt as a basis for negotiation; the Soviet Union, India, Indonesia, and Ceylon would withhold approval. Australian Prime Minister Robert Menzies would head the Suez Committee (with representatives from Australia, Ethiopia, Iran, Sweden, and the United States) in its mission to the Egyptian government (Dulles to Eisenhower, DULTE 19 and 22, Aug. 21, 22, 1956, AWF/D-H; see also State, *Foreign Relations, 1955–1957*, vol. XVI, *Suez Crisis July 26–December 31, 1956*, pp. 249–85; NSC meeting minutes, Aug. 31, 1956, AWF/NSC; Eisenhower, *Waging Peace*, pp. 46–48; Eden, *Full Circle*, pp. 502–6; and Lloyd, *Suez 1956*, pp. 117–19). The State Department sent this message to Dulles as TEDUL 15 on this same date (AWF/D-H). For developments see no. 1972.

1963   *EM, AWF, Name Series*

To EDWARD EVERETT HAZLETT, JR.   *August 20, 1956*
Personal and confidential

Dear Swede: The probable explanation for the simultaneous arrival in New York of your two letters, one bearing three cents and the other six cents postage, is the institution of a new policy on the part of the Postmaster General.[1] Where a subsidized air line is not involved, and a three cent letter can be carried on a plane without extra cost—and space is available—the policy is to pick up the letter and carry it exactly as if it were bearing a six cent stamp.

Not long ago you expressed some of your irritation that anyone should even dream of putting the Services into the same uniform. I won't quarrel with the idea, but I will attempt to give you a slightly different viewpoint toward the Services than you probably have.[2]

So far as I am personally concerned, I should say that my most frustrating domestic problem is that of attempting to achieve any real coordination among the Services. Time and again I have had the high Defense officials in conference—with all the senior military and their civilian bosses present—and have achieved what has seemed to me general agreement on policy and function—but there always comes the break-up.[3] The kindest interpretation that can be put on some of these developments is that each service is so utterly confident that it alone can assure the nation's security, that it feels justified in going before the Congress or the public and urging fantastic programs. Sometimes it is by no means the heads of the Services that start these things. Some subordinate gets to going, and then a demagogue gets into the act and the Chief of the Service finds it rather difficult to say, "No, we could not profitably use another billion dollars."[4]

What I have tried to tell the Chiefs of Staff is that their most important function is their corporate work as a body of advisors to the Secretary of Defense and to me. We now have four-star men acting as their deputies, and those men are either capable of running the day-to-day work in the Services or they should not be wearing that kind of insignia. Yet I have made little or no progress in developing real corporate thinking.

I patiently explain over and over again that American strength is a combination of its economic, moral and military force. If we demand too much in taxes in order to build planes and ships, we will tend to dry up the accumulations of capital that are necessary to provide jobs for the million or more new workers that we must absorb each year. Behind each worker there is an average of about $15,000 in invested capital. His job depends upon this investment at a yearly rate of not less than fifteen to twenty billions. If taxes become so burdensome that investment loses its attractiveness for capital, there will finally be nobody but government to build the facilities. This is one form of Socialism.

Let us not forget that the Armed Services are to defend a "way of life," not merely land, property or lives. So what I try to make the Chiefs realize is that they are men of sufficient stature, training and intelligence to think of this balance—the balance between minimum requirements in the costly implements of war and the health of our economy.[5]

Based on this kind of thinking, they habitually, when with me, give the impression that they are going to work out arrangements that will keep the military appropriations within manageable proportions and do it in a spirit of good will and of give and take.

Yet when each Service puts down its minimum requirments for its own military budget for the following year, and I add up the total, I find that they mount at a fantastic rate. There is seemingly no end to all of this. Yet merely "getting tough" on my part is not an answer. I simply must find men who have the breadth of understanding and devotion to their country rather than to a single Service that will bring about better solutions than I get now.

Strangely enough, the one man who sees this clearly is a Navy man who at one time was an uncompromising exponent of Naval power and its superiority over any other kind of strength. That is Radford.[6]

I do not maintain that putting all of these people in one uniform would cure this difficulty—at least not quickly. But some day there is going to be a man sitting in my present chair who has not been raised in the military services and who will have little understanding of where slashes in their estimates can be made with little or no damage. If that should happen while we still have the state of tension that now exists in the world, I shudder to think of what could happen in this country.

*   *   *   *   *

Tomorrow Mamie and I leave for San Francisco and what promises to be, for us at least, a hectic and tumultuous two days there.[7] Then Cypress Point—and I *hope* some rest.[8]

Give my love to Ibby. *As ever*

[1] Eisenhower's close friend Hazlett had written on August 10 (AWF/N), complaining that it had taken four days to receive the President's letter of August 3 (see no. 1936). He recalled that as an experiment he had once mailed two letters—one airmail and one surface—from North Carolina to New York at the same time. They had arrived at their destination simultaneously, thereby confirming his belief that "up and down this coast first class mail goes quicker by regular than by air" (see no. 1130).

[2] For Hazlett's response to this letter see Hazlett to Eisenhower, Sept. 12, 1956, AWF/N; for more on unification of the armed services see Chandler and Galambos, *Occupation, 1945*, no. 206. In these volumes see no. 207.

[3] Eisenhower had met with the Secretary of Defense on July 31, and with Wilson and Chairman of the Joint Chiefs of Staff Radford on August 17, to begin discussion of the defense budget for fiscal year 1958. Faced with a proposed budget of $48.5 billion, Eisenhower had stated that it was "up to the civilian authorities in Defense to investigate every nickel proposed for expenditure." The President expressed disappointment in the performance of the service chiefs, who did "not seem to be able to rise above a service approach" (see Goodpaster memorandums, July 31 and Aug. 17, 1956, AWF/D; see also Eisenhower, *Mandate for Change*, pp. 454–55).

[4] Growing concern over Soviet air power had led to a debate in Congress regarding the adequacy of the 1957 Air Force budget submitted by the White House. On June 11 General Curtis E. LeMay, Commander of the Strategic Air Command (SAC), had testified in closed session in the Senate that he did not believe that the over-all 1957 Air Force budget would produce the force that the United States needed. He said that "'I support (the 1957 budget for SAC) because that is the way my boss wants it done. My original requirement was for a much higher figure. . . .'" (For background on LeMay, see Galambos, *Columbia University*, no. 389.) On June 29 Congress had appropriated $800 million more than originally requested (see *Congressional Quarterly Almanac*, vol. XII, *1956*, pp. 609–16).

[5] For further background see nos. 727 and 1233. See also Condit, *History of the Joint Chiefs of Staff*, vol. VI, *1955–1956*, pp. 50–55, and Kinnard, *President Eisenhower and Strategy Management*, pp. 21–36, 51–58.

[6] For Eisenhower's evaluation of Radford see no. 194.

[7] Eisenhower would depart for the Republican Convention in San Francisco on August 21. See Eisenhower, *Waging Peace*, pp. 12–13. See also no. 1916.

1964   *EM, AWF, Dulles-Herter Series*

To Robert Daniel Murphy   *August 21, 1956*

Memorandum for the Acting Secretary of State: I concur in the summary of answers that the Department of State has prepared in reply to the questionnaire sent by the NATO "Committee of Three" to all NATO governments.[1]

Colonel Goodpaster will tell you about one phrase concerning which I have a slight question—but it is not important.[2]

I think it is an excellent paper.

[1] For background on the Committee of Three see no. 1930. The American reply to the committee's questionaire, forwarded to the President by Deputy Under Secretary Murphy at Dulles's request, committed the United States to closer cooperation, with the reservation that it could not be diverted from meeting its responsibilities outside the Atlantic area. The United States promised to engage in closer consultation with its allies on a wider range of topics and recommended that NATO develop ways of resolving disputes between member nations " 'within the family.' "

The State Department wanted to avoid turning NATO into an agency for economic and cultural cooperation, but would support better coordination of NATO information and propaganda policies, including improved public relations, increased efforts to counter Communist propaganda, and more effective information programs directed at the Eastern bloc (Murphy to Eisenhower, Aug. 20, 1956, AWF/D-H). For background see no. 1872; for developments see no. 2122.

[2] We were unable to find a record of this conversation in AWF.

1965   *EM, AWF, International Series: Nehru*

To Jawaharlal Nehru   *August 25, 1956*
Secret

Dear Mr. Prime Minister:[1] I recall your letter to me of August tenth in which you expressed your anxiety about the recent developments in regard to the Suez Canal and your hope that the United States would help in arriving at a peaceful settlement of this difficult and intricate problem.[2] We have indeed sought to exert our influence in this direction. It is largely as a result of this that the London Conference was held; and while at that conference our two delegations did not see eye-to-eye as to just what proposals should be made to President Nasser, there was, I believe, a harmony of purpose.[3]

As you know, the overwhelming majority of the nations at the conference felt that certain conditions were needed in order to insure that this great international waterway would not hereafter become an instrument of the national policy of any nation. I believe that these conditions, when explained and broken down into their constituent practical elements, will be seen to be entirely compatible with the sovereignty of Egypt.

I earnestly hope that your personal influence will be exerted in favor of practical talks which, once they are engaged, will, I think, hold out good hope of a settlement, which on the one hand is fully consistent with every Egyptian interest and on the other hand gives the confidence needed by many nations that the canal will be a dependable and secure agency for linking the East and the West.[4]

With assurances of my highest esteem, *Sincerely*[5]

---

[1] Secretary Dulles drafted this letter after Eisenhower had asked if a direct appeal to the Indian Prime Minister would further the London negotiations (State, *Foreign Relations, 1955–1957*, vol. XVI, *Suez Crisis July 26–December 31, 1956*, pp. 257–58, 280). For background on the London Conference see no. 1962.

[2] See Eisenhower to Nehru, August 16, 1956, AWF/I: Nehru, for an earlier response to the Indian leader's letter. Nehru's letter is not in AWF.

[3] India was one of four nations which had refused to support the document establishing a basis for negotiations with the Egyptian president.

[4] Discussions with Nasser would begin on September 3; for developments see no. 1972 and 1985.

[5] Eisenhower added this complimentary close to Dulles's draft.

1966

EM, AWF,
International Series: Burma

To HERBERT CLARK HOOVER, JR.   *August 29, 1956*

Memorandum for the Under Secretary of State (through the Secretary of State): I think you are correct in your belief that I should ask you and some representative of the Defense Department to a conference where we might discuss our future action with respect to Burma.[1]

I shall leave it to you to arrange with Mr. Shanley the date and the hour, after you have ascertained that a representative of the Defense Department can be available at the same time.[2]

---

[1] Prime Minister U Nu of Burma had requested aid from the United States, stipulating that Burma would have to maintain its neutrality by making at least a token reimbursment in rice. On June 15 Eisenhower had sent a reply drafted by the State Department

stating that U Nu's requests merited "sympathetic consideration" (U Nu to Eisenhower, May 22, 1956; Dulles to Eisenhower, n.d.; Eisenhower to U Nu, June 15, 1956, AWF/I: Burma). For Eisenhower's comments on Soviet aid to Burma see no. 1652.

According to Acting Secretary Hoover, aid to Burma had been held up because of opposition from Defense Department officials who believed that Burma was of little military importance. Defense argued that aid should be provided only on a reimbursable basis. The State Department thought that aid was a crucial means of encouraging anticommunism in Burma (Hoover to Eisenhower, Aug. 24, 1956, AWF/I: Burma).
[2] The dispute would be resolved at the August 30 meeting of the National Security Council, where Eisenhower ordered that military aid be provided on the basis of loans, for which no actual repayment would be expected (NSC meeting minutes, Aug. 31, 1956, AWF/NSC; see also State, *Foreign Relations, 1955–1957*, vol. XXII, *Southeast Asia*, pp. 72–85).

1967   *EM, AWF, Administration Series*

To Nelson Aldrich Rockefeller   *August 29, 1956*

Dear Nelson: If I am elected and if the acceptance speech should be by any chance "the charter of the future" (and do you mind if I sometimes steal that phrase?), I am content.[1] And if the next four years can make our hopes a reality, then any personal sacrifice is forgotten.

I shall need your help in the coming months—and I know that, as always, it is there for the asking.[2]

With warm regard, *As ever*

[1] A former assistant to the President, Rockefeller had written (Aug. 25, 1956, AWF/A) to congratulate Eisenhower on his convention performance. Rockefeller used this phrase to describe the enunciation of beliefs and party goals set forth in Eisenhower's acceptance speech of August 23 (*Public Papers of the Presidents: Eisenhower, 1956*, pp. 702–15).
[2] At this time Rockefeller was chairman of Rockefeller Center, Inc.; on his resignation from the President's staff see no. 1671.

1968   *EM, AWF,*
Administration Series: AEC

To Lewis Lichtenstein Strauss   *August 30, 1956*
Personal and confidential

Dear Lewis: I have spoken to you several times about my hope that the need for atomic tests would gradually lift and possibly soon disappear.[1] Yesterday I learned indirectly that Dr. Rabi—for whom I have the greatest respect—entertains such a belief.[2]

I should like to talk to you about this when you have an opportunity.[3] *As ever*

[1] In light of public concern over the dangers of nuclear fallout, the Joint Chiefs had reconsidered the necessity for thermonuclear testing (Twining to Wilson, Apr. 23, 1956, WHO/OSS: [DOD], JCS). In their report to Secretary of Defense Wilson, the JCS had stated that the objectives of the spring 1956 REDWING tests—a series of more than one dozen tests that included the first dropping of a hydrogen bomb from an airplane—were to control radioactive fallout, and second, to improve the quality and effectiveness of American air defense; the tests were not intended "specifically for the purpose of producing bigger 'bangs.'" The JCS concluded that nuclear testing was "essential to the security of the United States and the free world." Any moratorium on testing would be dangerous to Western security unless preceded by "universal acceptance of a comprehensive disarmament system which would provide effective safeguards to insure compliance by all nations." For background on the efforts to ban nuclear testing see nos. 726, 873, and 1317; see also Divine, *Blowing on the Wind*, pp. 18–22, 36–47 and 63–83.

[2] On Columbia University physicist Isidor I. Rabi see Galambos, *Columbia University*, nos. 269 and 325. The concern over nuclear fallout from weapons testing had continued to mount throughout the spring of 1956. In April Democratic presidential candidate Adlai Stevenson had called for a unilateral end to H-bomb testing. The test ban issue continued to be hotly debated throughout the campaign. See Hewlett and Holl, *Atoms for Peace and War*, pp. 326–50, 361–74.

[3] Eisenhower would meet with Strauss on September 4 and September 11. Dissatisfied with the lack of agreement among his principal advisors, Eisenhower would direct Strauss, Stassen, Dulles and Wilson "to work on this problem and not come back until they had a common position to present" (see Goodpaster memorandum, September 14, 1956, AWF/A). On October 23 Eisenhower would issue a comprehensive statement reviewing American policy towards the development and testing of nuclear weapons (see *New York Times*, Oct. 24, 1956). For developments see no. 2041.

1969   *EM, AWF, Name Series*

To Isaac Jack Martin   *August 31, 1956*

Dear Jack: I believe every word of the first page of your memorandum.[1] But there is a problem inherent in the effort you suggest for which you do not suggest a solution.[2] That problem is this: the people that we want to register comprise the great group you talk about as being unaroused and really not interested in government except when they have to be. Now to get these people to register, it would have to be done on a partisan basis—that is, we would have to reach for them in the same way that we reach for a vote. This makes the matter a partisan one—and so makes the work separate and distinct from the non-partisan efforts of organizations like the American Heritage Association, the Boy Scouts, and so on.

Since our political "campaign" is scheduled to start about the middle of the month, a date subsequent to the date that the registration period expires in many states, just how do we go about getting registered the particular people we want?

Now with respect to the final statement you make that "you are the only one who can convince this great segment of our population," if this is true, this puts me in the position of making a speech requesting people to register so that they can vote for *me*.[3] So far as I have come in this political business, I have never yet asked a person to vote for me, and it comes pretty hard to think that I must begin now. However, I would like to have this whole subject thoroughly studied by the staff and see whether we can't come up with some new ideas.[4]

[1] Martin's memorandum of August 31, 1956, regarding voters' indifference to politics is in AWF/N.

[2] Martin had warned Eisenhower that satisfied supporters might not vote in the upcoming elections. As he had noted, this could pose serious problems for Republicans, given the enthusiastic participation of those voters who had a different philosophy and who increasingly voted Democratic. Martin had suggested that Eisenhower actively encourage his supporters to register and vote.

[3] Martin had written that only Eisenhower could convince supporters that "this Administration with which they are so pleased is in danger of being liquidated by their own indifference and negligence . . ." (*ibid.*).

[4] In a memorandum to Eisenhower of September 3, 1956, Martin would suggest that the President make short radio and television speeches reminding voters to register (AWF/N).

1970   *EM, AWF, Administration Series*

To John Hay Whitney   *August 31, 1956*

Dear Jock: I wish that all written reports from Presidential representatives were as interesting, colorful and downright informative as is yours.[1] You make me feel almost as if I had been with you and Betsey throughout the trip. I am grateful to you both for undertaking it.

Your comment on the "segregated" character of the Cypress Point stay is just a bit hazy to me.[2] Of course I knew little of what was going on, except as I could get hold of my friends in turn and set up a golf date. Actually Mamie was the most segregated of anyone I knew; she didn't get out of bed for the first forty-eight hours she was at the Club. Except for Sunday, when she went to church and riding, and Monday afternoon, when she had in a group of old Army friends, she was very secret, though possibly not a weapon.

I wish you could have stayed to play on Monday. That was my best day and, except for three holes, I could not expect to do much better. I birdied #5; I messed up #7 badly and took a bogie on #8, after I had driven over the sand heap well into the middle of the fairway. However, I then started in a streak and was one over par from #9 to #12 inclusive. After that it was a case of "dropping your voice," particularly on the two par threes, #15 and #16, where I took double bogies.

When you come down this way, give me a ring. There is no couple we look forward to seeing with greater pleasure than you and Betsey.[3] Give her my love, and, of course, all the best to yourself. *As ever*

[1] The Whitneys had traveled to Japan and Korea. The August 27 report is in AWF/A (see also Eisenhower to Whitney, Aug. 8, 1956). In December Whitney would become Ambassador to Great Britain (see no. 2161).

[2] Whitney had written: "We wished we could have joined more at Cypress, but it was too 'segregated'!" Following the Republican National Convention, the Eisenhowers, the Whitneys and other close friends had vacationed at the Cypress Point Club in Monterey, California (see no. 1916).

[3] Whitney would visit the White House on November 23 and 24. He and his wife would accompany the Eisenhowers to Augusta, Georgia, November 27–29.

1971   *EM, AWF, DDE Diaries Series*

To Mrs. George D. Jones   *August 31, 1956*

Dear Mrs. Jones: Thank you so much for the note that you sent to me when I was recently at Pebble Beach.[1] Yours was a heartwarming letter. I received it just before returning from Cypress Point and I want, promptly, to thank you for the compliment you paid Mrs. Eisenhower and me by standing along the right of way to see our train pass. I am delighted I had the opportunity to wave to you.

I was struck by the sentence in your note that referred to you as "just an ordinary housewife, mother, school teacher, wife and citizen." When you think of all the work and dedication required for the successful discharge of the responsibilities involved in all those callings, I am quite certain the word "ordinary" cannot be properly applied.

In any event, because you are all of those people, I particularly appreciate the more than generous sentiments you express with respect to my qualifications as a public servant. I can only say that such letters as yours keep Mrs. Eisenhower and me striving to do our duty by this great country.

May the richest blessings of life be granted to you by the Almighty. *Sincerely*

[1] We have been unable to find the note from Mrs. Jones of San Carlos, California, in AWF. Following the Republican National Convention, the Eisenhowers had vacationed at the Cypress Point Club in Monterey, California (see no. 1916).

To Robert Anthony Eden   *September 2, 1956*
Top secret

Dear Anthony:[1] I am grateful for your recent letter, and especially for your kind words on the role of the United States during the London Conference on the Suez Canal. I share your satisfaction at the large number of nations which thought as we do about the future operation of the Canal.[2] In achieving this result we have set in motion a force which I feel will be very useful to us—the united and clearly expressed opinion of the majority users of the Suez waterway and of those nations most dependent upon it. This will exert a pressure which Nasser can scarcely ignore. From Foster I know that this accomplishment is due in no small measure to the expert leadership exhibited by Selwyn Lloyd as Chairman of the Conference, and to the guidance which he received from you.

As for the Russians, it is clear that they sought, at London, to impede the consolidation of a majority point of view, and to generate an atmosphere in the Near East which would make it impossible for Nasser to accept our proposals. I entirely agree with you that the underlying purpose of their policy in this problem is to undermine the Western position in the Near East and Africa, and to weaken the Western nations at home. We must never lose sight of this point.[3]

Now that the London Conference is over, our efforts must be concentrated on the successful outcome of the conversations with Nasser.[4] This delicate situation is going to require the highest skill, not only on the part of the five-nation Committee but also on the part of our Governments. I share your view that it is important that Nasser be under no misapprehension as to the firm interest of the nations primarily concerned with the Canal in safeguarding their rights in that waterway.

As to the possibility of later appeal to the United Nations, we can envisage a situation which would require UN consideration and of course there should be no thought of military action before the influences of the UN are fully explored.[5] However, and most important, we believe that, before going to the UN, the Suez Committee of Five should first be given full opportunity to carry out the course of action agreed upon in London, and to gauge Nasser's intentions.

If the diplomatic front we present is united and is backed by the overwhelming sentiment of our several peoples, the chances should be greater that Nasser will give way without the need for any resort to force. This belief explains our policy at the Conference and also explains the statement which I gave out through Foster after I got back from San Francisco and had a chance to talk fully with him.[6]

I am afraid, Anthony, that from this point onward our views on this situation diverge. As to the use of force or the threat of force at this juncture, I continue to feel as I expressed myself in the letter Foster carried to you some weeks ago.[7] Even now military preparations and civilian evacuation exposed to public view seem to be solidifying support for Nasser which has been shaky in many important quarters.[8] I regard it as indispensable that if we are to proceed solidly together to the solution of this problem, public opinion in our several countries must be overwhelming in its support. I must tell you frankly that American public opinion flatly rejects the thought of using force, particularly when it does not seem that every possible peaceful means of protecting our vital interests has been exhausted without result.[9] Moreover, I gravely doubt we could here secure Congressional authority even for the lesser support measures for which you might have to look to us.

I really do not see how a successful result could be achieved by forcible means. The use of force would, it seems to me, vastly increase the area of jeopardy. I do not see how the economy of Western Europe can long survive the burden of prolonged military operations, as well as the denial of Near East oil. Also the peoples of the Near East and of North Africa and, to some extent, of all of Asia and all of Africa, would be consolidated against the West to a degree which, I fear, could not be overcome in a generation and, perhaps, not even in a century particularly having in mind the capacity of the Russians to make mischief. Before such action were undertaken, all our peoples should unitedly understand that there were no other means available to protect our vital rights and interests.

We have two problems, the first of which is the assurance of permanent and efficient operation of the Suez Canal with justice to all concerned. The second is to see that Nasser shall not grow as a menace to the peace and vital interests of the West. In my view, these two problems need not and possibly cannot be solved simultaneously and by the same methods, although we are exploring further means to this end. The first is the most important for the moment and must be solved in such a way as not to make the second more difficult. Above all, there must be no grounds for our several peoples to believe that anyone is using the Canal difficulty as an excuse to proceed forcibly against Nasser.[10] And we have friends in the Middle East who tell us they would like to see Nasser's deflation brought about. But they seem unanimous in feeling that the Suez is not the issue on which to attempt to do this by force. Under those circumstances, because of the temper of their populations, they say they would have to support Nasser even against their better judgment.

Seldom, I think, have we been faced by so grave a problem. For the time being we must, I think, put our faith in the processes already at work to bring Nasser peacefully to accept the solution along the lines of the 18-nation proposal. I believe that even though this procedure may fail to give the setback to Nasser that he so much deserves, we can better retrieve our position subsequently than if military force were hastily invoked.[11]

Of course, our departments are looking into the implications of all future developments. In this they will keep in close touch with appropriate officials of your Government, as is my wish.[12]

With warm regard, *As ever*

[1] A draft of this letter, written by Secretary Dulles and bearing Eisenhower's extensive handwritten changes, is in AWF/D-H (see also Memorandum of Conversation, Aug. 29, 1956, Dulles Papers, White House Memoranda Series; Hoover to Eisenhower, Aug. 31, 1956, AWF/D-H; State, *Foreign Relations, 1955–1957*, vol. XVI, *Suez Crisis July 26– December 31, 1956*, pp. 355–58; and Eisenhower, *Waging Peace*, p. 49).

[2] For background on the conference, which had ended four days earlier, see no. 1962. Eden had praised Secretary Dulles for his speeches and his constructive leadership. "It was, I think, a remarkable achievement to unite eighteen nations on an agreed statement of this clarity and force" (Eden to Eisenhower, Aug. 27, 1956, AWF/I: Eden).

[3] On August 21 Soviet Foreign Minister Dimitri Shepilov had charged that the proposal agreed upon among eighteen of the twenty-two participating nations was a maneuver of colonialism, designed to reimpose Western rule on Egypt (Dulles to Eisenhower, DULTE 19, Aug. 21, 1956, AWF/D-H; and State, *Foreign Relations, 1955– 1957*, vol. XVI, *Suez Crisis July 26–December 31, 1956*, pp. 237–40, 245–46).

At this point in the letter Eisenhower added, and subsequently deleted, the following passage: "Moreover, while the Soviets are using Nasser it seems clear that he is foolishly assuming that he can use Soviet support to gain his own ends in the Arab World and against the West without eventually paying a fearful price."

[4] The Suez Committee (with representatives from Australia, Ethiopia, Iran, Sweden, and the United States) would meet with the Egyptian president on September 3 (for background see no. 1962; see also State, *Foreign Relations, 1955–1957*, vol. XVI, *Suez Canal July 26–December 31, 1956*, pp. 305–8, 312–13).

[5] Eden had told Eisenhower that British Foreign Secretary Selwyn Lloyd would contact Dulles regarding United Nations intervention (*ibid.*, p. 305; see also Lloyd, *Suez 1956*, pp. 122–23).

[6] Eisenhower had returned from the Republican National Convention and a short vacation on August 28. On the following day he cited the "atmosphere of friendly conciliation" exhibited at the conference. He gave the complete support of the U.S. government and, he believed, the American people to the proposal, which, he said, would respect the sovereignty of Egypt and assure a peaceful solution of the problem (*Public Papers of the Presidents: Eisenhower, 1956*, pp. 716–17).

[7] See no. 1935.

[8] Immediately after the canal seizure Eden had asked his chiefs of staff to prepare a military plan and had begun mobilization of both ground and naval forces. On August 29 the British government had announced that it had given the French permission to station a contingent of troops on Cyprus. British diplomatic missions throughout the Middle East had been instructed to persuade as many British subjects as possible to leave the area (State, *Foreign Relations, 1955–1957*, vol. XVI, *Suez Crisis July 26–December 31, 1956*, pp. 10, 40, 60–61, 171, 342, 350–51, 359–60; see also

Hoover to Chiefs of Mission, Sept. 2, 1956, AWF/I: Eden; and Eisenhower, *Waging Peace*, p. 48).

[9] Eisenhower added the preceding portion of this paragraph to Dulles's draft.

[10] Eisenhower added to the draft the preceding section of this paragraph and the concluding sentence of the previous paragraph.

[11] The President added the words, "fail to give the setback to Nasser that he so much deserves" to the draft; Dulles had originally written, "this procedure may seem to give Nasser a partial victory. . . ."

[12] For developments see no. 1982.

1973   *EM, AWF, Name Series*

To John Reagan McCrary   *September 3, 1956*
Personal

Dear Tex: Thank you both for the telegram that reached me in San Francisco, and the letter that greeted me when I returned to my desk. Only Jinx could, I think, get away with the decoration on the little puppet![1]

I am glad that my television appearance the night of the acceptance speech found favor in your expert eyes.[2] I suppose there is something about the excitement generated by such an affair that emphasizes the inevitable feeling of gratification that comes just from knowing that so many people are willing to work so hard for the principles in which we jointly believe.

Today—Labor Day—we are hard at work on plans for the next months. As to the New York campaign, I can only say that those more familiar with the problem than I will make the best possible decision.[3]

I, too, hope that I shall see you and Jinx sometime, somewhere, during the campaign.[4] As always, I am grateful for your friendship and support.

With warm regard, *As ever*

[1] The telegram and the letter sent August 22 and 24, respectively, had expressed support for Eisenhower (AWF/N). McCrary had enclosed in his letter a photograph taken of some puppeteers who had appeared on Jinx Falkenberg McCrary's television program that aired during the convention. The photo showed a puppet of Harry Truman with a sign hung around its neck reading "I Like Ike."

[2] McCrary had written: "There has never been more vitality, more sheer joy in a job than glowed in your face and movements last night. I know it warmed the nation, too." On the speech, broadcast over radio and television, see *Public Papers of the Presidents: Eisenhower, 1956*, pp. 702–15.

[3] McCrary had complained about the course that the New York Senate race was taking.

[4] McCrary said he and his wife would be campaigning in New York.

To John J. Butkus   *September 5, 1956*

Dear Mr. Butkus: Mr. Hagerty has allowed me to read your very forth-right letter concerning your refusal to allow anyone else to speak for you in the exercise of your indestructible American right of political freedom. I respect you for your pronouncement of union loyalty and all those things for which unions are organized—the betterment of the individual worker's lot through the right and power of organization and collective bargaining.[1]

At the same time I most sincerely hope—and believe—that your determination to express your own political decisions in your own way is shared by the great bulk of Americans, including those who form our trade unions.

I also express the hope that you will never find it necessary, in your support of your elected leaders, to carry out that part of your pledge which says "I will go hungry, as I did many times." It seems to me that this country of ours is producing quality goods at such a rate that it should never again be necessary for a qualified worker to go hungry—even if he should find it upon rare occasions necessary to strike.[2]

With renewed assurances of my respect for your position, and with best wishes,[3] *Sincerely*

[1] John J. Butkus, a truck driver for General Electric Company, and a member of the AFL–CIO, had written White House Press Secretary James Hagerty on September 1, 1956. Butkus said that while he supported his union leaders completely in labor dis-putes, he would not "be a part of their political views." "As far as I am concerned," he said, "they are thinking and speaking for themselves and nobody else" (AWF/N: Famous Letters). On August 28 the executive council of the AFL–CIO had endorsed the Stevenson–Kefauver ticket (see *New York Times*, Aug. 29, 1956).

[2] Butkus had written: "I respect my District Union President and all the high ranking union officials, I will support my respected officers in any labor dispute regardless of what the outcome may be, I will walk picket lines as I have in the past, I will go hungry as I did many times, I will go on strike whenever they say."

[3] In response to a question concerning AFL–CIO support for the Democratic ticket, Eisenhower would quote Butkus's letter at his news conference of September 5 (see *Public Papers of the Presidents: Eisenhower, 1956*, p. 743).

To Ezra Taft Benson   *September 5, 1956*

Dear Ezra: I have had complaints concerning the present situation in agriculture, about as follows:[1]

   a. The allegation has been made that the Commodity Credit Corporation has dumped several million bushels of corn and depressed the price 10 to 15 cents.[2]

b. That the soy bean market has fallen off badly.[3]

c. The same applies to dairy products and potatoes, which are alleged to be down 30 to 40 percent.[4]

Will you give me a report on these matters, and, if there is any ground whatsoever for the statements made, will you tell me what you are doing about it? *As ever*

---

[1] During his visit to the President's office earlier this same day, the Postmaster General had passed on what he had heard from the farming community (Eisenhower to Thornton, Sept. 6, 1956, AWF/D).

[2] In his September 5 reply to Eisenhower (AWF/A), Benson would deny these allegations, explaining that only "out-of-condition" corn from stockpiles was being sold for export and that these sales affected the market negligibly. He maintained that the recent drop to ten cents per bushel was a seasonal fluctuation reflecting the prospect of a large harvest.

[3] Benson would agree that soybean prices were low. Still, he would maintain, growers should profit "pretty well per acre," given the record crop and the current market price, and efforts to stabilize the market through removal of surplus soybean oil and lard were under way. For background on the Administration's efforts to expand domestic and export channels for surplus commodities see no. 652; U.S., *Statutes at Large*, vol. 68, pt. 1, pp. 454–59; Schapsmeier and Schapsmeier, *Ezra Taft Benson and the Politics of Agriculture*, pp. 97–124; Trudy Huskamp Peterson, *Agricultural Exports, Farm Income, and the Eisenhower Administration* [Lincoln, Neb., 1979], pp. 47–69; and on soybean programs, Willard W. Cochrane and Mary E. Ryan, *American Farm Policy, 1948–1973* [Minneapolis, 1976], pp. 77, 248–50, 269–74).

[4] Benson would assert that dairy prices were in good shape, and as of August 15, they had increased to 89 percent of parity (AWF/A). Supplies would continue to exceed demand substantially, however, and the Administration's policy of keeping dairy price supports near the legal minimum (75%) would remain intact. For background see no. 787, and Cochrane and Ryan, *American Farm Policy*, pp. 234–40.

Benson would also explain that since potato prices had been abnormally high the previous July, a decline to market prices currently near 91 percent of parity indicated that there was no depression. If potato prices were to fall, he would be prepared to provide payments from the discretionary funds allocated to the Secretary to cover the losses of producers who diverted surplus commodities from normal to secondary markets. In 1956 the Administration would spend 4.3 million dollars of these funds in programs for potatoes, a commodity for which price supports were optional (U.S., *Statutes at Large*, vol. 49, pt. 1, pp. 774–75 and vol. 68, pt. 1, p. 899; Cochrane and Ryan, *American Farm Policy*, pp. 145, 264–66).

1976   *EM, AWF, Dulles-Herter Series*

To John Foster Dulles   *September 6, 1956*

Dear Foster: This letter looks to me as though it might be of sufficient importance that your staff should have it at once; I have not even taken time to read it carefully.[1]

One point that is not mentioned at all by the Egyptian character is that the Egyptian government had initially placed such a series of conditions upon their acceptance of our offer to help in the financing of the High Dam that we lost interest.[2]

Nevertheless, this Egyptian individual seems so close to Nasser that I assume this letter can be taken as representing his attitude. *As ever*

[1] Richfield Oil Company President Charles Jones had sent Eisenhower a letter he had received from Nils E. Lind, a British subject living in Beirut (see Jones to Eisenhower, Aug. 30, 1956; and Eisenhower to Jones, Sept. 6, 1956, AWF/N). Lind had met with Ali Sabri, Egyptian cabinet chief under President Nasser, who was in London as an observer to the conference on the nationalization of the Suez Canal (see nos. 1932 and 1948 for background). Sabri had told Lind that the Egyptians could not understand the sudden withdrawal by the United States of its offer of aid to construct the Aswan Dam. "Neither intimidation nor physical force will succeed in making us back down from our stand against internationalization of the Suez Canal," Sabri said. "We have not succeeded in getting the British to evacuate their forces from the Canal zone only to make room for forced internationalization of the Canal itself." Sabri assured Lind that the Egyptians would give their "wholehearted co-operation" to a peaceful settlement of the matter (Lind to Jones, Aug. 25, 1956, AWF/N, Jones Corr. and Dulles Papers, White House Memoranda Series).

[2] See nos. 1859 and 1946.

1977   *EM, AWF, Name Series*

To Clifford Roberts   *September 6, 1956*

Dear Cliff: Someone has a new suggestion each day to submit for helping in the job of getting people registered and inducing them to vote.[1] I am sure that every possible angle should be explored, but of course none of our efforts should be such as to make the public feel resentful rather than cooperative.

One thing that has been suggested is that the President of the U.S.G.A. should write to every recognized golf club in the United States, suggesting that immediately there be put up a sign in the golf club stating that the board of directors strongly urged that every member and their families should register immediately and should vote in November. The appeal should include some statement to the effect that the board of directors could point out that one of the great privileges of America is the opportunity to participate in such recreational activities and sports as we please. This is one of our freedoms—and that freedom is strengthened when everybody performs his civic responsibility of registering and voting in every election, local and national.

I do not know the new President of the U.S.G.A.[2] If you think well of this idea, I suggest that you might write to him (I assume that you know him because you know every other figure in golfdom) and lay out the idea.[3] You might even go so far as to suggest a kind of sign that might be persuasive. I would not even object if they wanted to quote me in some such language as "The President has said that every eligible voter owes it to himself and to his country to exercise the priceless privilege and discharge the important duty of voting on Election Day."[4]

Anyhow I shall pursue this matter no further; you may use your own judgment and it will not even be necessary to tell me what you did. If anything happens about it, I shall see the sign at Burning Tree.[5]

I trust you are picking up a bit of weight. While you seemed thin when I saw you at Cypress Point, I thought that otherwise you looked in splendid health. I certainly hope that your improvement continues.[6] *As ever*

[1] See, for example, no. 1969.

[2] Richard Tufts of Pinehurst, North Carolina, was president of the United States Golf Association.

[3] Roberts would wire a copy of this document to Tufts, and would report back to Eisenhower that Tufts had liked the suggestions (Roberts to Tufts, Sept. 10, 1956; Roberts to Whitman, Sept. 10, 1956; Telephone conversation, Roberts and Eisenhower, Sept. 11, 1956, all in AWF/N, Roberts Corr.).

[4] The Executive Committee of the U.S. Golf Association would send a letter to golf clubs asking for assistance in this "non-partisan campaign" to get people to register and vote. Although the committee would not refer to Eisenhower, they would restate his ideas by suggesting that clubs post a notice which read "Vote Before You Play On Election Day–A free democracy can be maintained only by full use of the right to vote" (Sept. 24, 1956, AWF/N, Roberts Corr.).

[5] The President played golf at the Burning Tree Country Club, Bethesda, Maryland.

[6] Roberts had suffered a heart attack in January (see no. 1730).

1978   *EM, AWF, Gettysburg Series*

TO MARSHALL F. NORLING   *September 6, 1956*
Personal

Dear Marshall: I have been embarrassed to learn that some of your salesmen have made a sales argument out of the fact that I have in my home Red Comet extinguishers.[1] In at least one instance—and I enclose the letter—a prospective purchaser called on me for confirmation or denial of the allegation that the gas used is harmful to humans.[2]

I am sure you agree that no salesman should be guilty of the kind of thing that this particular one obviously was. I am sure, also, that you will want to write directly to this lady to give her the facts in the matter. I will appreciate your prompt attention so that her apprehensions are resolved.[3]

With warm regard, *Sincerely*

[1] Norling, of Littleton, Colorado, was president of Red Comet, Incorporated, makers of the fire safety equipment installed in May at the Eisenhowers' Gettysburg, Pennsylvania, home.

[2] Mrs. Shirley Norman of Hamilton, Ohio, had written regarding "alarming reports" of deaths caused by fire-system equipment containing toxic gases ([Aug. 29, 1956], AWF/Gettysburg; see also Whitman to Norman, Sept. 7, 1956, *ibid.*).

In August, at the direction of the chief of the U.S. Secret Service, the U.S. Chemical Warfare Center, at Edgewood, Maryland, had conducted toxicity tests on the Red Comet extinguishers (see Berkey to Anderson, May 31; Anderson to Baughman, Aug. 3; Whitman to Norling, Aug. 6; Norling to Whitman, Aug. 21; Norling to Baughman, Aug. 21, 31; Eisenhower to Norling, Aug. 29; Norling to Eisenhower, Aug. 31; and Anderson to Baughman, Sept. 6, all in AWF/Gettysburg). Following an extensive investigation, it was recommended that some fifty-three Red Comet fire extinguishers be removed from the Gettysburg home and replaced with automatic fire alarm buttons (see Berkey to Whitman, Sept. 6; and Anderson to Baughman, Sept. 4, 6, 27, 1956, all in AWF/Gettysburg).

[3] Norling would enclose with his letter of apology to Eisenhower a copy of his reply to Mrs. Norman (both dated Sept. 10, 1956, AWF/Gettysburg). On September 15 Ann Whitman would write Norling that the President had directed him "'not to worry about the matter'" (*ibid.*). See also Eisenhower to Norling, September 22, 1956, and other correspondence in WHCF/PPF 1128.

1979   *EM, WHCF, President's Personal File 20-AA*

To Pauline Thornton   *September 7, 1956*

Dear Mrs. Thornton: Thank you for your letter and for your good wishes on my renomination.[1]

I was touched by the story of your young daughter. I am glad that she understands I like her—as indeed I like all children and all loyal, law abiding Americans.[2]

In the years ahead, I am convinced that this nation will continue to make great strides toward the realization of our goal, equal respect and opportunity for all Americans. Certainly I shall never cease, regardless of the position I may hold, to work for the coming of the day when every American can hold up his head in pride and dignity— regardless of race or religion.[3]

With best wishes, *Sincerely*

[1] Mrs. Thornton, from Pacoima, California, had written on August 24 (same file as document). A draft of this letter showing Eisenhower's extensive handwritten emendations is in AWF/Drafts.

[2] The five-year-old child had seen Eisenhower on television, and exclaimed, " 'He likes me.' "

[3] The Thorntons feared that their child would suffer from racial prejudice. "We are confident," Mrs. Thornton wrote, "that you will not rest until you have restored at least a portion of the human dignity to which our children are entitled, no matter how dark or fair their skin."

1980   *EM, AWF, Name Series*

To Robert Tyre Jones, Jr.   *September 7, 1956*

Dear Bob: I cannot tell you how pleased I am that you are going to send me one of the first sets of your new clubs. So far as I am concerned, each new addition of the "Jones" clubs has been an improvement over the preceding one.[1] *See P.S.

As to the difficulty with the new "Spalding Dot" ball that you mention, I had not noticed it.[2] While I did not examine them closely at the end of the game, I played with them day before yesterday—incidentally, my best game since I became ill last year.[3]

I am astonished to learn that the sports magazine knew the name of the ball I played with at Cypress Point.[4] Either the professional or the caddy must have talked to a reporter. I had not even known, before I went to Cypress Point, that there was a ball bearing Hogan's name! I thought his activities in the manufacturing field were confined to clubs. But as I started out to play the first day, with my regular supply of "Dots" in my bag, my host came along and handed me a dozen balls. That accounts for the Hogans.

Now, as to club specifications. My present ones seem ideal to me as to length. I think they are also correct as to weight, even though I have been told that as one gets older (and presumably feebler) he should use somewhat lighter clubs. You said that the factory has complete data on the clubs I now have, but on the attached sheet you will find the appropriate information, at least as measured by the pro at the Burning Tree Club.[5]

As for a putter, I believe I do best with the bull's-eye type with a fairly upright stance.[6] Actually, in my case, I think it is the stance more than the exact type of putter. In the last year or so, during which time I have been putting very badly I have tried every kind I can think of.

Of course I am most deeply appreciative of your continued interest in my "hacking," and of your thoughtfulness in seeing that I have the very best equipment—which is exactly the way I regard the Jones clubs. If any of your friends or associates at the factory are especially helpful to you in getting the set fixed up, won't you give me their names so that I can also write to them to express my thanks?[7]

Give my love to Mary, and take care of yourself. I am looking forward to an Augusta trip, regardless of the election outcome, somewhere around November fifteenth.[8] Such plans, of course, presuppose that Nasser and a few other like individuals in the world don't get too obstreperous.[9]

With warm personal regard, *As ever*

P.S. But always I am amazed to realize that there can be any improvement.

---

[1] Jones had written on September 4 that he had "assisted in producing some new model woods and irons to be put out late this Fall" under his name. The new clubs, he thought, would be "a considerable improvement" over Eisenhower's current set (AWF/N; on the current set of clubs see no. 1664).

[2] Jones had said that Spalding was correcting the problem as "the trademark tends to smear if you hit the ball on the pole."

[3] See no. 1595.

[4] Jones had read in *Sports Illustrated* that the President had used a Hogan ball (named for professional golfer Ben Hogan) while golfing at Cypress Point (on the Eisenhowers' post-Republican National Convention vacation see no. 1916). "If you insist on handicapping yourself in this way," Jones had written, "I will no longer be able to sympathize with you when you lose your money."

[5] The specifications regarding swing weight are in AWF/N; see also no. 1492.

[6] Jones had asked for the President's preference.

[7] The new clubs would arrive at the White House on November 20 (see Jones to Whitman, Nov. 7, 1956; Whitman to Jones, Nov. 9, 1956; Jones to Tait, Nov. 9, 1956; and related correspondence, all in AWF/N, Jones Corr.). On November 28 Jones would report that he had sent a copy of Eisenhower's November 20 thank-you letter to the "man especially in charge of producing your clubs" (both in AWF/N; see also Eisenhower to Jones, Nov. 21, 1956, *ibid.*).

[8] Eisenhower would play golf with Jones while vacationing in Augusta, Georgia, from November 27 to December 13.

[9] The President was referring to the Suez Crisis; see no. 1972.

1981   *EM, AWF, Dulles-Herter Series*

To John Foster Dulles   *September 8, 1956*

Dear Foster: Here is a draft in reply to Anthony's letter that I have been preparing. The only usefulness it might have is in its attempt to destroy Anthony's apparent fixation that delay or long drawn out negotiations might result in catastrophe for Great Britain and the West.[1]

I am not even sure that it is worth while sending the document, but won't you look it over and send it back to me with any comments you may care to make?[2] *As ever*

[1] Eden had told Eisenhower that if the Suez committee failed to persuade Nasser to accept the London proposals, "and if the only alternative is to allow Nasser's plans quietly to develop until this country and all Western Europe are held at ransom by Egypt acting at Russia's behest it seems to us that our duty is plain. We have many times led Europe in the fight for freedom. It would be an ignoble end to our long history if we tamely accepted to perish by degrees" (Eden to Eisenhower, Sept. 6, 1956, AWF/I: Eden; see nos. 1932 and 1962 for background).

[2] In the evening of this same day Dulles would discuss the draft with Eisenhower. To give the British and French "a stronger case for not resorting to force" Dulles suggested promoting the idea of an organization of canal users (later to be called the Suez Canal Users' Association) that would employ their own pilots and would allocate to Egypt a portion of the collected fees on a cost basis. He also proposed the announcement of alternative routes for moving oil to Western Europe and of the continuation of some economic measures against Egypt. Although Eisenhower agreed with Dulles, he believed "that world opinion inclined to side with Nasser . . . that since the Canal went through their territory, he was entitled to direct the operations" (Memorandum of Conversation, Sept. 8, 1956, Dulles Papers, White House Memoranda Series; see also Eisenhower, *Waging Peace*, pp. 49–51; and Telephone conversation, Eisenhower and Dulles, Sept. 7, 1956, Dulles Papers, Telephone Conversations; for Dulles's first thoughts on an association of canal users see State, *Foreign Relations, 1955–1957*, vol. XVI, *Suez Crisis July 26–December 31, 1956*, pp. 351–52, 365; see also Eden, *Full Circle*, pp. 515–19; and Lloyd, *Suez*, pp. 125–26). Eisenhower agreed to Dulles's suggestions, and the revised message, incorporating further changes by the President, was given to the British ambassador on this day for delivery to Prime Minister Eden (see the following document).

1982   *EM, AWF, International Series: Eden*

To Robert Anthony Eden   *September 8, 1956*
Secret

Dear Anthony:[1] Whenever, on any international question, I find myself differing even slightly from you, I feel a deep compulsion to reexamine my position instantly and carefully. But permit me to suggest that when you use phrases in connection with the Suez affair, like "ignoble end to our long history" in describing the possible future of your great country, you are making of Nasser a much more important figure than he is.[2]

We have a grave problem confronting us in Nasser's reckless adventure with the Canal, and I do *not* differ from you in your estimate of his intentions and purposes.[3] The place where we apparently do not agree is on the probable effects in the Arab world of the various possible reactions by the Western world.

You seem to believe that any long, drawn-out controversy either within the 18-nation group or in the United Nations will inevitably make Nasser an Arab hero and seriously damage the prestige of Western Europe, including the United Kingdom, and that of the United

States.[4] Further you apparently believe that there would soon result an upheaval in the Arab nations out of which Nasser would emerge as the acknowledged leader of Islam. This, I think, is a picture too dark and is severely distorted.[5]

I shall try to give you a somewhat different appraisal of the situation. First, let me say that my own conclusions are based to some degree upon an understanding of current Arab feeling that differs somewhat from yours. I believe that as this quarrel now stands before the world, we can expect the Arabs to rally firmly to Nasser's support in either of two eventualities.

The first of these is that there should be a resort to force without thoroughly exploring and exhausting every possible peaceful means of settling the issue, regardless of the time consumed, and when there is no evidence before the world that Nasser intends to do more than to nationalize the Canal Company. Unless it can be shown to the world that he is an actual aggressor, then I think all Arabs would be forced to support him, even though some of the ruling monarchs might very much like to see him toppled.

The second would be what seemed like a capitulation to Nasser and complete acceptance of his rule of the Canal traffic.

The use of military force against Egypt under present circumstances might have consequences even more serious than causing the Arabs to support Nasser. It might cause a serious misunderstanding between our two countries because I must say frankly that there is as yet no public opinion in this country which is prepared to support such a move, and the most significant public opinion that there is seems to think that the United Nations was formed to prevent this very thing.

It is for reasons such as these that we have viewed with some misgivings your preparations for mounting a military expedition against Egypt. We believe that Nasser may try to go before the United Nations claiming that these actions imply a rejection of the peaceful machinery of settling the dispute, and therefore may ask the United Nations to brand these operations as aggression.

At the same time, we do not want any capitulation to Nasser. We want to stand firmly with you to deflate the ambitious pretensions of Nasser and to assure permanent free and effective use of the Suez waterway under the terms of the 1888 Treaty.

It seems to Foster and to me that the result that you and I both want can best be assured by slower and less dramatic processes than military force. There are many areas of endeavor which are not yet fully explored because exploration takes time.

We can, for example, promote a semi-permanent organization of the user governments to take over the greatest practical amount of the technical problems of the Canal, such as pilotage, the organization of the traffic pattern, and the collection of dues to cover actual expenses. This organization would be on the spot and in constant contact with Egypt and might work out a *de facto* "coexistence" which would give the users the rights which we want.

There are economic pressures which, if continued, will cause distress in Egypt.

There are Arab rivalries to be exploited and which can be exploited if we do not make Nasser an Arab hero.

There are alternatives to the present dependence upon the Canal and pipelines which should be developed perhaps by more tankers, a possible new pipeline to Turkey and some possible rerouting of oil, including perhaps more from this hemisphere, particularly to European countries which can afford to pay for it in dollars.

Nasser thrives on drama. If we let some of the drama go out of the situation and concentrate upon the task of deflating him through slower but sure processes such as I described, I believe the desired results can more probably be obtained.

Gradually it seems to me we could isolate Nasser and gain a victory which would not only be bloodless, but would be more far-reaching in its ultimate consequences than could be anything brought about by force of arms. In addition, it would be less costly both now and in the future.

Of course, if during this process Nasser himself resorts to violence in clear disregard of the 1888 Treaty, then that would create a new situation and one in which he and not we would be violating the United Nations Charter.

I assure you we are not blind to the fact that eventually there may be no escape from the use of force. Our resolute purpose must be to create conditions of operation in which all users can have confidence. But to resort to military action when the world believes there are other means available for resolving the dispute would set in motion forces that could lead, in the years to come, to the most distressing results.

Obviously there are large areas of agreement between us. But in these exchanges directed toward differing methods I gain some clarification of the confusing and conflicting considerations that apply to this problem.[6]

With warmest regard, *As ever your friend*

---

[1] Eisenhower's original draft of this letter and a draft with Secretary Dulles's suggested changes and the President's subsequent handwritten emendations are in AWF/I: Eden.

[2] See the preceding document.

[3] Eden had compared Nasser to Hitler, whose actions in the 1930s "were tolerated and excused by the majority of the population of Western Europe." The seizure of the Suez Canal, he said, was "the opening gambit in a planned campaign designed by Nasser to expel all Western influence and interests from Arab countries." He could then mount

revolutions in these countries, make them Egyptian satellites, and place their oil resources under Egypt's control (Eden to Eisenhower, Sept. 6, 1956, AWF/I: Eden).

[4] For background on the eighteen-nation group that emerged from the Suez Canal Conference see no. 1948.

[5] At this point in his original draft Eisenhower had included the following paragraph: "It took your nation some eighteen years to put the original Napoleon in his proper place, but you did it. You have dealt more rapidly with his modern imitators." Dulles had argued that Napoleon and his successors "had been dealt with by force and it might be inappropriate to suggest that analogy." The President laughed, according to Dulles, "and said he guessed I was right and struck out the paragraph" (Memorandum of Conversation, Sept. 8, 1956, Dulles Papers, White House Memoranda Series; and Eisenhower, *Waging Peace*, p. 50).

[6] Before Eisenhower made his changes to Dulles's revision, this paragraph had read: "I know, of course, that in our general philosophy we are as one. These letters are confined to the discussion of differing methods and for me, at least, serve the purpose of clarifying the confusing and conflicting considerations that obviously apply to this problem. As it now stands, our main difference seems to be largely the result of differing conclusions as to the probable reaction of the Arab world to the various lines of action open to us." For further developments see no. 1985.

1983   *EM, AWF, Name Series*

TO LOUIS MARX   *September 10, 1956*

Dear Louis: I am always at a loss for words to thank you and David for the many evidences of your friendship and support.[1] At this particular moment I am struggling with the problem of how to tell you how much I appreciate your efforts with the trial unit of CLub.[2] I do congratulate you on the amazing results which, incidentally, I think are more of a tribute to you than to anything else! However, from evidence such as you give me of the interest of so many wonderful people, I derive probably my greatest incentive to continue to do the best I can.

The copy you enclosed has gone over to Len Hall, as you suggested.[3]

I hope both you and Dave, and Idella and Charlene, will be with us on Wednesday, though there isn't going to be, I am afraid, any opportunity for a personal chat.[4]

With warm regard, *Sincerely*

[1] Toy manufacturer Louis Marx was, like his brother David H. Marx, an old friend.
[2] Concerned with voter participation, Marx had previously caught Eisenhower's interest with an idea for a "grassroots" fundraising campaign organization which would have types of memberships and dues organized around the number "150"; the capitals "C" and "L" in "CLub" stood for the Roman numerals 100 and 50 (Marx to Eisenhower, Dec. 29, 1954, and Eisenhower to Marx, Jan. 7, 1955, both in AWF/N).
[3] Marx had reported that the trial unit was successful in both encouraging people to

participate in the election and in raising funds to be used for radio and television spots for Eisenhower's campaign (Marx to Eisenhower, Sept. 5, 1956, AWF/N, and Marx to Whitman, Sept. 5, 1956, AWF/N, Marx Corr.). Eisenhower would later thank Marx for the recordings that he had sent of radio advertisements which were to be broadcast in several cities beginning October 22 and which, Marx had written, were bought with CLub subscriptions and directed by Young & Rubicam without charge (Marx to Whitman, Oct. 22, 1956, and Eisenhower to Marx, Oct. 30, 1956, both in WHCF/OF 138-C-4).

[4] Idella Ruth (Blackadder) Marx, Louis's wife (for background see *Eisenhower Papers*, vols. VIII, IX, and XI) and Charlene Marx, David's wife, would attend with their husbands the "Republican Kick-off campaign activities" held at the Gettysburg farm on September 12 (President's daily appointments).

1984

EM, AWF, Administration Series

TO EZRA TAFT BENSON

September 10, 1956

Dear Ezra: When I was in Front Royal a year or so ago (the day you and I visited Mr. Marriott), I found that your Agricultural Station was doing a lot of work in studying beef cattle.[1] Among other things, one of the principal subjects in which they were interested was dwarfism.

If there has been anything yet published on this subject, I should very much like to have a copy of any paper that has been circulated.

Some people tell me that the risk of dwarfism is very much exaggerated, others seem to talk about it all the time. I am very much interested in seeing whatever we have that is factual.[2] *As ever*

[1] Eisenhower, Benson, and restauranteur J. Willard Marriott had inspected the beef cattle experiment station on December 21, 1954. The research center was operated jointly by the federal government, the State of Virginia, and Virginia Polytechnic Institute (see Benson, *Cross Fire*, pp. 137–38, 221–22, and *New York Times*, Dec. 22, 1954).

[2] On Eisenhower's interest in dwarfism in his Black Angus herd see no. 1608. Benson's reply is not in AWF. For developments see no. 2017.

1985

EM, AWF, International Series: Nehru

TO JAWAHARLAL NEHRU

September 15, 1956

Cable. Secret

Dear Mr. Prime Minister: I have read with interest and appreciation your messages of September 8 and 11 on the Suez Canal situation.[1] I have also had the opportunity to study the text of the statement you made on September 13 in Lok Sabha.[2]

I consider it a privilege to receive the benefit of your views on this important and difficult problem, the satisfactory solution of which is so vital to the peace and well-being of the nations of the world. I am in complete agreement with you that a peaceful approach must be made to this issue, and I have so indicated in several public statements recently.[3] You may be certain that the United States Government will not abandon its belief that, given good will and the realization of the vast implications of the matter, a peaceful solution can be achieved.

I shall not conceal from you my deep disappointment that President Nasser saw fit to reject the proposals of the 18 nations which were so ably set before him by Prime Minister Menzies and the members of the 5-nation committee which went to Cairo.[4] I believed, and continue to believe, that these proposals show the way to a peaceful and constructive arrangement which would benefit all parties concerned.

You have mentioned the Egyptian memorandum of September 10 setting forth a proposal for the formation of a negotiating body to consider the solution of questions involving the Canal and to review the Constantinople Convention of 1888. My preliminary reaction to this runs along the following lines:

It is doubtful that it would be practical to negotiate simultaneously with all countries which are parties to and beneficiaries of the Suez Canal. Such a group would embrace practically all nations of the world and, it seems to me, could not be an effective negotiating body. It is also doubtful that these nations would delegate discretionary negotiating authority to a small group, as such delegation of authority would not be compatible with the normal exercise of sovereign rights.

The procedure followed at the London Conference seems to me the only practical one. That conference drew together all indisputably surviving parties of the 1888 Convention, the nations representing over ninety percent of the traffic through the Canal and also those nations whose pattern of foreign trade has shown significant dependence upon the Canal.[5] To my great regret the Government of Egypt was not represented, but that was entirely due to its own preference to be absent.

At the London Conference there was found to be a large measure of agreement with regard to the conditions necessary to assure that the Canal would be operated in accordance with the principles of the 1888 Convention. This judgment, shared by 18 nations, was carried to Cairo and carefully explained to the Government of Egypt which unfortunately did not accept the viewpoint thus expressed even as a basis for negotiation.

It is my belief at the moment that the views of the 18 nations as presented and explained to the Government of Egypt by the 5-nation Committee furnished the basis for further discussions and negotiations looking toward a fair and equitable settlement of the Suez Canal problem, and that the convening of a new conference on the basis suggested by the Government of Egypt would not be a development helpful in the solution of this difficult issue.

A conference is planned for September 19 in London to enable the 18 nations which joined in the proposals to President Nasser to discuss the Menzies report and various other matters relating to the Suez question. It is planned that this group will discuss the response to the Egyptian memorandum. The final position of the United States on this particular point will not be determined until after the consultation afforded by the new London meeting.[6]

Another subject which will be discussed at London is the proposed association of Canal users, to which the United States has given its support. This step, while it can only be an interim measure might, I think, if accepted by Egypt in the spirit in which we join in it, permit of some practical progress toward an acceptable operation of the Canal.

Please allow me to say how much I appreciate receiving your views. Your messages have given me a clear understanding of the position of the Indian Government, and convince me all the more that there is harmony of purpose in this matter between our two countries.

With kind regard, *Sincerely*

[1] For background see no. 1965. Indian Prime Minister Nehru had told Eisenhower in his September 8 message that negotiations in the Suez controversy must include Egypt and that he hoped the United States would use its great influence toward a peaceful settlement. On September 11 he had expressed his support of the Egyptian proposal to convene a meeting of the canal user representatives to review the Convention of 1888. The Egyptian government had also indicated that solutions could be found to questions regarding freedom and safety of canal navigation, development of the waterway for future requirements, and the establishment of equitable tolls and charges (State, *Foreign Relations, 1955–1957*, vol. XVI, *Suez Crisis, July 26–December 31, 1956*, pp. 459, 502).

[2] Nehru had told India's lower house of Parliament, the Lok Sabha, that the West was risking war with its "imposed" plan to have a users' association assume responsibility for traffic in the canal. Such action, he said, closed the door to further negotiations (*New York Times*, Sept. 14, 1956; for background on the users' association see no. 1981).

[3] See no. 1972; see also *Public Papers of the Presidents: Eisenhower, 1956*, p. 737.

[4] See no. 1962. On September 9 President Nasser had given Menzies his formal rejection of the eighteen-nation proposal for international control of the canal. He said that Egypt was exercising its sovereign right to nationalize the canal and guaranteed freedom of passage through that waterway as provided by the Convention of 1888. Nasser expressed willingness to negotiate a peaceful solution that would respect Egyptian rights of ownership and ensure dependable and efficient operation and development of the canal (State, *Foreign Relations, 1955–1957*, vol. XVI, *Suez Crisis, July 26–December 31, 1956*, pp. 375–76, 393–94, 406, 409, 415–18, 441–43; see also Eisenhower, *Waging Peace*, p. 49; Lloyd, *Suez*, pp. 129–30; Eden, *Full Circle*, pp. 523–28).

[5] See no. 1948.

[6] For developments see no. 1993.

To Reinold Melberg   *September 15, 1956*

Dear Reinold: Of course I am in complete agreement with your basic thesis that we *must* reach people on a door-to-door level, and I think your idea of barbecue or picnic get-togethers has much merit.[1] I shall pass along your suggestion to the people directly concerned with campaign activities of this type.[2]

Incidentally, the Citizens for Eisenhower in Southern California developed an idea of beef stew parties in various communities. I understand their success with them has led other communities in various parts of the country to adopt a similar plan.

My cooking, my so-called "painting," and a lot of other things I like to do have at least temporarily been shelved.[3] I find that official duties and campaign activities[4] more than fill the hours of every day in the week.

With warm regard, *Sincerely*

[1] Melberg was a former West Point classmate of the President (see Galambos, *Chief of Staff*, no. 659). His September 7 letter is in the same file as this document.

[2] On September 12 several hundred Republican leaders had joined Eisenhower at his Gettysburg farm for a picnic-style rally to open his reelection campaign. For some of the campaign activities planned by the National Citizens for Eisenhower see, for example, *New York Times*, Sept. 5, 13, 15, 30, 1956.

[3] Melberg said that while his wife was in Europe he was learning to cook. He never expected to "catch up" with Eisenhower's expertise, he wrote, "but by liberal consultation with cook books I've progressed a little beyond camp style variety."

[4] Eisenhower penned an asterisk here and added a handwritten footnote: "plus the exercise I necessarily must have."

To Edgar Newton Eisenhower   *September 17, 1956*
Personal

Dear Ed: Thank you very much for writing me about the general political situation in your area.[1] To take up your points in order:

(1). So far as I know, Eastvold has not been mentioned for a Federal job since the very early days of 1953. I can assure you that, in view of what you say, he will get no Federal position that calls for Presidential approval.[2]

(2). I was seized almost with a sense of frustration by what you had to say of the difficulties of the "Citizens for Eisenhower" in Pierce County.[3] I have already called up everyone that I believe can do something about it; if you don't get some rapid action, please send me a wire.

(3). As to the people who feel that they should not vote for me because of the added risks this job imposes upon my life, I have no real answer. I have tried, so far as possible, to throw such thoughts out of my mind. The only reason I got into politics in the first place was to attempt to bring the United States around to understand the virtues of progress along a straight, clearly-defined road, rather than one that veered constantly and always to the left. If Americans believe that centralization of power in Washington, inflation with rising living costs, and Federal ownership of an increasing number of types of utilities, would best serve their own interests, then those are the people that should vote against me.[4] As we see it, our main trouble is that while a majority of the United States records itself as on our side so far as a choice between these two positions is concerned, far too many of them feel no compulsion to register and vote. Their attitude is "Things are all right, why worry?"

(4). The political *experts* have, it is true, been advocating that I make the trip to the Northwest to make one major speech, then stay over for a day or so on a personal basis. I think they have been considering a speech in Oregon, and then my coming on to Tacoma for a day of golf with you and Arthur Langlie, and then on my way again. At least I heard this suggested once when two or three of the politicos were talking. I have already passed on to them your idea that such a trip might do more harm than good.[5]

(5). There is one statement you make that illustrates again how easy it is for misapprehensions and misunderstandings to gain great credibility in the United States. You say, "Republicans in that state resent the fact that the national Administration required Doug McKay to resign . . . and run for United States Senator." Nothing could be further from the truth. Doug McKay received a number of suggestions from Oregon that he run for the Senate against Morse on the theory that he (McKay) was the only one who could probably beat Morse.[6] He thought that he was assured that in the event he would resign and declare for the Senate, all other Republican candidates would promptly withdraw from the race and there would be no primary campaign. Quite a number of people around here believed that on the record of past elections, Doug should be able to defeat Morse. I presume that they advised Doug to make the decision to that effect.

In any event, when McKay came to me to announce his intention to resign, he was so certain that he would have no opposition in the primary that I gave him quite a long letter expressing my satisfaction that he was going to carry the banner of the Administration against Morse, who, as you may suspect, ranks quite low in my opinion.

As it turned out, the Oregonian enthusiasts who had been communicating with Doug had not secured the concurrence of Mr. Hitchcock, the most formidable contender in the Republican ranks. But since McKay had already resigned and announced his candidacy, there was little he could do but to go ahead. In any event, after the primary was over, Mr. Hitchcock visited me here in my office and expressed himself to the effect that the race had been a good, hard and clean one, and that he was now prepared to support McKay to the limit of his ability. He stated that in certain sections of Oregon he had a better organization than McKay did, and was perfectly ready to turn it over to McKay's use.[7] I assumed, therefore, that there was no intra-family quarrel in the Republican campaign and that they were all working together.

I have asked some of our people to see what there is to do about it.

Give my love to Lucy, and write to me again when you think there is something I might help straighten out. *As ever*

[1] Edgar Eisenhower's letter of September 13, 1956, could not be located, but see n. 3 below.

[2] For Edgar's earlier criticism of the Attorney General of Washington, Donald W. Eastvold, see no. 75.

[3] From an excerpt of the September 13 letter (enclosure, Whitman to Roberts, Sept. 17, 1956, AWF/D), we know that Edgar hadwritten that his personal friends manning the local Washington organization felt they received no assistance from the state and national offices. Edgar had implied there were problems between the Citizens group and the Washington Republican Committee and had also predicted that if the citizens' organization became "tainted with Republicanism," difficulties would arise as the group was "appealing to the independent voter and the dissatisfied Democrat." An analysis of the tension between the grass-roots citizens organization and the centralized Republican National Committee during the 1956 campaign can be found in Allen, *Eisenhower and the Mass Media*, pp. 77–81, 209–10.

[4] On Eisenhower's middle-of-the-road philosophy see nos. 986 and 998; for more on his views on inflation see no. 1578; on federal power development as a campaign issue see no. 1861.

[5] Eisenhower would visit Portland, Oregon, and Seattle and Tacoma, Washington (President's daily appointments, Oct. 16–20), where he would stay one night with his brother and sister-in-law (see no. 2028). The speeches made on this trip, which included stops in Minneapolis, Los Angeles, and Denver, are in *Public Papers of the Presidents: Eisenhower, 1956*, pp. 931–81.

[6] For background on McKay's campaign against the incumbent Democratic Senator Wayne Morse see nos. 1882 and 1886, and Adams, *Firsthand Report*, pp. 235–37.

[7] On this meeting after Philip S. Hitchcock's loss in the primary see no. 1882.

1988 *Gruenther Papers*

To Alfred Maximilian Gruenther *September 17, 1956*

Dear Al: You will be even more dismayed to learn that on Saturday I shot a 79 or 80.[1] The reason I put it in that indecisive way is that I thought I shot—and was paid off on the basis of—a 79. But the papers say that the score kept by my caddy gave me an 80. I am afraid George has a refund coming to him.[2]

As to the thin-skinned business, you know how I am apt to talk in a fairly urgent tone about anything when I take a real interest. So, for example, when I begin to question the right of anyone to make some of the extraordinary statements that are made, involving distortions and even disregard of fact, I am apt to get very heated. It never occurred to me, though, that anyone thought that I was personally hurt or irritated by those things. I would say it is rather an inability to understand the standards of some people.

However, reports made to you by a couple of my friends point to one conclusion—namely, that I should not miss so many opportunities to keep my mouth shut.[3] I hope to be a little more choosey in selecting those to whom I talk without fear of being misinterpreted. In the meantime I assure you it is not criticism that keeps me awake at night—it is the Suez.

During your farewell trip you will see many of my old friends.[4] Where you can identify them, remember me to them warmly.

Love to Grace and all the best to yourself. *As ever*

[1] Gruenther had written (Sept. 16, 1956, AWF/A) that he was "rather dismayed" to read that recently Eisenhower had shot an eighty-three in a golf game at the Gettysburg Country Club. Claiming that he had inspired Eisenhower's eighty-six (at the Burning Tree Country Club in Washington, D.C.) over the Labor Day weekend, Gruenther said: "Since I was not present for the 83 my argument is that my inspiration stimulated you to even greater heights."
[2] This was George E. Allen.
[3] Gruenther had written that two of Eisenhower's "very close friends" had remarked about his political "sensitivity to criticism."
[4] The NATO Supreme Commander would begin his farewell tour on this same day. For background on Gruenther's retirement see no. 1832; for developments see no. 2121.

1989   *EM, AWF, Name Series*

To Edward Everett Hazlett, Jr.   *September 17, 1956*

Dear Swede: I shall follow your advice and at this moment shall attempt no lengthy answer to your fine letter of the twelfth.[1] I give you merely my own personal report on my health, which is that I really do feel splendid.

On Wednesday evening I am to make about a twenty minute talk on the Columbia Broadcasting System,[2] and the following day I go out to Iowa where I will attend informally (and *without* a major address) the plowing contest at Newton, Iowa.[3] Then, after returning here, I shall go out to Illinois only three or four days later to deliver a major farm speech.[4]

Give my love to Ibby and the children, and again my thanks for your note.[5]

With warm regard, *As ever*

[1] Hazlett, in a lengthy reply (AWF/N) to Eisenhower's August 20 letter (no. 1963), had congratulated Eisenhower on his renomination and advised the President to relax and not answer until after the election.

[2] On the President's address of September 19, the first of a series of television campaign speeches, see *Public Papers of the Presidents: Eisenhower, 1956*, pp. 779–88.

[3] The Eisenhowers would visit Mrs. Eisenhower's birthplace in Boone, Iowa, and attend the National Field Days and Plowing Matches near Des Moines on September 20 and 21 (President's daily appointments). On the President's remarks while in Iowa see *ibid.*, pp. 702–15.

[4] The Eisenhowers would travel on September 25 to Peoria, Illinois (President's daily appointments). Discontent with farm prices had caused concern within the Administration (as early as 1955) about the farm vote (Eisenhower, *Waging Peace*, pp. 15–16; Schapsmeier and Schapsmeier, *The Politics of Agriculture*, pp. 150–54). The sharpness of this speech would be interpreted as reflecting fresh concern for the midwestern farm vote (*New York Times*, Sept. 25, 26, 1956), and there is some evidence to support that analysis (see, for example, no. 1975). But the President's outline of the Administration's farm program would not diverge from his previous policy statements. He would again score the Democratic program of rigid price supports (see *Public Papers of the Presidents: Eisenhower, 1956*, pp. 796–804); for background on price-support policy see no. 1841. The farm vote would not threaten Eisenhower's reelection, but it may have contributed to local Republican losses (Adams, *Firsthand Report*, pp. 218–19; *Congressional Quarterly Almanac*, vol. XIII, *1957*, pp. 803–4; and Edward L. Schapsmeier and Frederick H. Schapsmeier, "Eisenhower and Ezra Taft Benson: Farm Policy in the 1950s," *Agricultural History* 44, no. 4 [1970], 376). For a description of the Administration's campaign strategy and the farm vote see Schapsmeier and Schapsmeier, *The Politics of Agriculture*, pp. 170–79.

[5] The references are to Elizabeth Hazlett and to the Hazletts' two married daughters, Mary Elizabeth Scott and Alice Kessing.

1990   *EM, AWF, International Series:*
Saudi Arabia

TO IBN ABD AL-AZIZ SAUD   *September 18, 1956*
Secret

Your Majesty:[1] I have received with deep appreciation Your Majesty's further message on the Suez Canal problem, referring especially to the proposal for establishment of an association of users of the Canal.[2]

I assure Your Majesty that the vital necessity of preserving peace in the Near East is constantly in our minds. In the Suez Canal issue I have been devoting my best efforts to measures which would strengthen the possibilities of peace and reduce the likelihood of hostilities. I believe that chances for a peaceful solution have been increased, rather than diminished, by recent developments as between the British, French and ourselves.[3] As you know from my public statements and those of the Secretary of State, the United States believes a peaceful solution to this grave problem should be attainable, and is determined to offer its full assistance and cooperation in seeking it. I now reaffirm this to Your Majesty.

It is precisely within this framework that the United States has offered its support to the proposed association of Canal users, and I do not feel that this plan is a basis for apprehension. Certainly, so far as the United States is concerned, there is no purpose to impose forcibly upon Egypt any international regime. The United Nations may, of course, be asked to assume responsibility for the matter in the future. However, in our opinion, nations with deep interests in the Canal need reassurances against the possibility of covert, as well as overt, violation of the 1888 Convention. Moreover, and very important, the user nations badly need some mechanism through which they would be enabled to negotiate with President Nasser. This need would be fulfilled by an ad hoc association.[4] The proposed users' association would fulfill these purposes, and also provide the possibility of working out practical dispositions at the operating level which might be easier than to negotiate in terms of a treaty which would involve national prestige to a greater extent.

I cannot refrain from remarking that the conduct of Egypt throughout this affair has not been such as to inspire confidence. First, by nationalizing the Suez Canal Company Egypt violated a contract which was impressed with a large measure of international interest. Subsequently Egypt refused to attend the London Conference, and later rejected the proposals which an eighteen-nation majority of that Conference put before it.[5] Furthermore, before being possessed of full information concerning the proposed users' association, the Government of Egypt denounced it as an "act of war."[6]

At this point I should like to observe that Your Majesty states that the users' association would operate the Suez Canal. The association would not be set up to carry out so wide a responsibility. It would merely provide a means, consonant with the provisions of the Constantinople Convention, of regulating passage through the Canal of the ships of member nations, in cooperation with the Government of Egypt.

With regard to the possibility of future negotiations, I believed, and still most earnestly do believe, that the proposals formulated in London by the eighteen nations provide the best basis for negotiations aimed at guaranteeing freedom of passage through the Canal. The new proposal of Egypt is in our opinion unconstructive.[7] The important thing is not to get the variety of views which doubtless could be obtained from a meeting of seventy or more nations but to get the views which count, namely those of the countries which rely most upon the Canal. Furthermore, I am sure it will not have escaped Your Majesty's attention that the present proposal of President Nasser is in substance the proposal which was made by the Soviet Delegation at London and which was not there supported by any other Delegation.[8]

I hope that the foregoing will clarify for you the position of the United States on this issue, and will reveal the determination of this Government to achieve a solution of the Canal problem by peaceful means.

Your Majesty's efforts in this situation will continue to be invaluable, and I have welcomed most heartily the steps which you have already taken.[9] I earnestly hope that Your Majesty will use your great influence to bring about some action on the part of the Egyptian Government to restore confidence which has been so badly shaken by the recent Egyptian action. So far, it seems to me that any conciliatory move by President Nasser has been conspicuously lacking.

May God have Your Majesty in his safe keeping.[10] *Your sincere friend*

[1] The State Department drafted this letter to the Saudi Arabian monarch.

[2] King Saud told Eisenhower that he was opposed to the establishment of an international group that would operate the canal. "If this decision is to be carried out, as threatened with the use of force by Britain and France," he said, "it will lead to the most grievous consequences and to 'loss of the reins' (of control) in this part of the world, the result of which cannot (repeat not) be predicted" (Sept. 15, 1956, AWF/I: Saudi Arabia).

[3] British and French acceptance of Secretary Dulles's plan for a Suez Canal Users Association (SCUA) had strengthened Western solidarity, and Prime Minister Eden had agreed to take the Suez matter to the Security Council before resorting to military action. On September 19 the eighteen nations which had supported internationalization of the canal—the plan presented to President Nasser—would meet in London to consider appropriate action in view of his rejection of the proposal (see no. 1993; State, *Foreign Relations, 1955–1957*, vol. XVI, *Suez Crisis July 26–December 31, 1956*, pp. 495–97, 513–16; and Memorandum of Conversation, Sept. 17, 1956, Dulles Papers, White House Memoranda Series).

[4] Eisenhower added the preceding two sentences to the State Department draft.

[5] See nos. 1948 and 1985.

[6] See State, *Foreign Relations, 1955–1957*, vol. XVI, *Suez Crisis July 26–December 31, 1956*, pp. 399, 491–92.

[7] On September 10 Egypt had proposed the establishment of a new negotiating group representing the different views expressed by the various users of the canal (see *ibid.*, p. 459; and no. 1985).

[8] See Dulles to Eisenhower, DULTE 19, Aug. 21, 1956, AWF/D-H; and State, *Foreign Relations, 1955–1957*, vol. XVI, *Suez Crisis July 26–December 31, 1956*, pp. 238–40, 270–73.

[9] King Saud had agreed to meet with Special Emissary Robert Anderson on August 23 (*ibid.*, pp. 220, 230, 246–47, 273–75, 282–83, 287–97).

[10] The text of this message was cabled to King Saud on this same day (Hoover to American Embassy, Jidda, Sept. 18, 1956, AWF/I: Saudi Arabia).

To Robert Anthony Eden

Dear Anthony:[1] You may remember raising with me early this year the question of medium tanks for Germany.[2] As you know, our policy was and is to encourage the Germans to satisfy their armament requirements, insofar as possible, from United Kingdom and European sources. Since the time of our discussion, we have continued to stress this policy with the Germans. We have particularly urged upon them the advantages of purchasing tanks in the United Kingdom, making specific reference to your Centurions.

Despite these efforts, we received a short time ago an official request from the Germans that the United States sell them a sufficient number of our M-47 tanks to meet their medium tank needs. The study I mentioned to you in my letter of March sixth has meanwhile been completed and it is clear that we are able to supply M-47s in the number the Germans want.[3]

I believe we will have to accede to the German request as I can see no alternative for us short of refusing to sell them United States tanks, which I do not believe we can do.

We will be informing them of our decision in a few days, but before doing this I did want you to know the background which surrounded it.[4]

I know this creates difficulties for you and I regret that this matter has turned out as it has.[5]

With warm regard, *As ever*

---

[1] This letter, drafted by State Department officials, was cabled to Dulles in London for personal delivery to Eden (Howe to Goodpaster, Sept. 17, 1956, AWF/I: Eden).

[2] See no. 1771. For background see no. 1521.

[3] Secretary Dulles had informed Eisenhower on August 14 of the West Germans' wish to buy used American M-47 tanks, available for $88,185 each, rather than new British Centurion tanks, which cost $98,000 each. The President had said that he "strongly favored a greater dependence of Europe upon its own production facilities and not dependence upon the United States which might be very difficult to satisfy in time of war because of the transportation problem." Dulles had suggested that if the Germans bought Centurion tanks, the British might be induced not to sell to Latin America (Memorandum of Conversation, Aug. 14, 1956, Dulles Papers, White House Memoranda Series; Dulles to Eisenhower, Sept. 17, 1956, AWF/D-H).

[4] Eisenhower had directed that the State Department delay approval of the tank purchase "until at least Anthony has had a chance to reply. He may perhaps want to appeal to the Germans direct" (Whitman to Goodpaster, Sept. 16, 1956, AWF/I: Eden).

[5] Eden would reply that the British would "surmount" the difficulties "as best we can" and that he was "most grateful" to Eisenhower "for going into this matter personally on our behalf" (Eden to Eisenhower, Sept. 29, 1956, AWF/I: Eden).

In the first week of October the United States would officially approve the tank sale.

A few days later, the West German defense ministry would present its plans to purchase 2,500 M-47 tanks to meet their requirements through 1956. The Bundestag finance and defense committees would reduce the order to 1,400 tanks through 1958 and request the defense ministry to look into purchase of the M-48 tank. This tank, however, cost twice as much as the M-47, was less suited to their purposes, and could not be produced fast enough to meet their proposed schedule. There were also rumors that the new defense minister might reduce the order for the M-47s to 1,100, hoping "to buy Centurions or Conqueror tanks from the British later" (Dulles to Eisenhower, Oct. 29, 1956, AWF/D-H).

1992   *EM, AWF, Admininistration Series*

To Isidore Schwaner Ravdin   *September 18, 1956*

Dear Rav: There seems to be so much political and medical argument about the wisdom of publishing the case history at this moment that I hope you can agree to withhold the report, at least for the time being. It would seem to me that the minute the election was over, there would be no objection to the report coming out. The feeling now seems to be that the results of the operation are evident in my obvious state of good health.[1]

As for myself, I had no strong opinion one way or the other. Consequently, when you felt it would be a good thing to do, I certainly offered no objection—but now with both Howard and Leonard showing an adverse feeling in the matter, and even Jim Hagerty seeming to think that it would probably now bring to the layman more confusion than information, I am disposed toward the line of action I have indicated above.

Of course I realize that you are motivated wholly by your own unselfish interest in me, and I am sorry that you have undertaken a lot of work only to have it all go for naught.[2]

Please give Betty my love, and of course warmest regard to yourself. *As ever*

---

[1] Dr. Ravdin had written September 14 (AWF/A) that he had been notified of the decision not to publish his report on the President's health (see also Snyder to Whitman, Sept. 18, 1956, AWF/A, Ravdin Corr.). He had agreed to "drop the matter," he wrote, but he was not in agreement with doctors Howard Snyder and Leonard Heaton. A published case history, he argued, would have "given an immeasurable amount of confidence" to voters "who wish to be reassured." See also Gilbert, *The Mortal Presidency*, pp. 104–6.

[2] "Any word from you is a command to me," Ravdin would reply on September 26 (AWF/A). He would add that "under no circumstances" would he submit for publication to the *Journal of the American Medical Association* "without the permission of you, Howard, and Leonard."

To John Foster Dulles   *September 19, 1956*

Dear Foster: Thank you for your cable and for your good wishes. I can see from your report that there is much confusion, anxiety and hesitation present at the Conference. It is indeed a difficult situation.[1]

According to the press, Bulganin used one of our press associations again to make a suggestion that so far as I can see has purely propaganda objectives. However, some of the nations may be affected by it, even though it carries the curious thought of calling a "Summit Meeting" in which Egypt would apparently be the equal of any of the Big Four or India, and Nasser would hold the key of success or failure. He does not explain how any of the Big Four have the right to speak for all the user nations in the world—another example of Soviet imperialistic thinking, even while they cry out against "colonialism."

Anyhow, our thoughts are with you always. *As ever*

[1] Dulles was in London for the second Suez Canal conference, called by Great Britain after President Nasser of Egypt rejected the eighteen-nation proposal for an international body to operate the canal (see no. 1985). Dulles had told Eisenhower that the British and French had isolated themselves from countries which were usually their closest friends. "The fact is," he said, "that the United States is the only bridge between the British and the French and the rest of the countries here. I do not yet know whether that bridge is going to hold. The Egyptians are making an enormous effort to make it appear that the users' association is a device to lead the members down the path to war for which the British and the French are preparing, and Egyptian propaganda in this sense is having a definite impact." Dulles had also wished Eisenhower good luck on his initial campaign speech, which the President would deliver to the nation later this same day (Dulles to Eisenhower, DULTE 2, Sept. 19, 1956, AWF/D-H; on the Suez Canal Users' Association see no. 1981; see State, *Foreign Relations, 1955–1957*, vol. XVI, *Suez Crisis July 26–December 31, 1956*, pp. 528–38, 544–50, 552–58; also *U.S. Department of State Bulletin* 35, no. 901 [October 1, 1956], 503–6; and *Public Papers of the Presidents: Eisenhower, 1956*, pp. 779–88).

To Edna Alice Shade Eisenhower   *September 22, 1956*

Dear Edna: Please don't worry about "causing any trouble."[1] Actually, Louise had me in her "doghouse" for a long time because of that Family Chart.[2] I never have been able to understand why people should be so disturbed by the truth.

It was fun to see young Bud and his wife in San Francisco.[3] I wish we could have had more time to visit with them.

Give my best to all your youngsters when you write. Mamie joins me in much love to you. *As ever*

¹ The wife of the President's late brother Roy had apologized for the family chart's appearance in Bela Kornitzer's book, *The Great American Heritage*. Kornitzer, she explained, did not "keep his word" with her (Sept. 19, 1956, AWF/N). For background on the Eisenhower brothers' interviews with Kornitzer see no. 288; on other problems with the chart see no. 400.
² Louise was Arthur Eisenhower's wife.
³ Roy and Edna Eisenhower's youngest child, Lloyd Edgar ("Bud") and his wife, the former Doris Jean Hootman, had attended the Republican National Convention.

1995   *EM, WHCF, Official File 116-H-4*

To John William Bricker   *September 25, 1956*

Dear John: Jack Martin has told me of your misgiving about the provision in the Republican Platform on the subject of the proposed amendment to the Constitution which bears your name.¹

I know of the letter which Sherman Adams sent to Mr. Loyd Wright in May.² Many times I have stated that if an amendment to the Constitution is proposed, I would not object to it provided it squared with the following principles:

(1) No treaty or executive agreement shall be valid if it conflicts with the Constitution.

(2) Treaties and executive agreements are intended to be used in the conduct of our foreign relations, and not as a subterfuge to enact domestic law.

(3) No amendment should change our traditional treaty-making power or hamper the President in his Constitutional authority to conduct foreign affairs.

If before the next session of Congress it is desired to try to find language to express the foregoing principles, you can be assured that we shall try to be helpful.

With warm regard. *Sincerely*

¹ The final text of the Republican party platform regarding the Bricker amendment read "We maintain that no treaty or international agreement can deprive any of our citizens of Constitutional rights. We shall see to it that no treaty or agreement with other countries attempts to deprive our citizens of the rights guaranteed them by the Federal Constitution" (Schlesinger, ed., *History of American Presidential Elections*, vol. IV, *1940–1968*, p. 3387. See also nos. 1820 and 1824).
² Adams's letter of May 29 is in the same file as the document. It had avowed the Administration's willingness to "find the language to clearly express" the principles listed in this letter to Bricker. See also Bricker to Eisenhower, June 4, 1956, and other correspondence in *ibid.*

To Philip Young   *September 25, 1956*

Dear Phil: Thank you for your letter.[1] Before the delivery of that particular speech I felt about it somewhat as you did after hearing it.[2] However, since this was the first talk of the campaign and was designed for delivery in the quiet of a studio, I came to the conclusion that for that special purpose and under those special conditions, the style was probably appropriate.

With warm regard, *As ever*

[1] Young had written that Eisenhower's September 19 campaign kick-off speech: "was almost too perfect as a speech, and not quite enough, for me, characteristic of Ike" (Sept. 20, 1956, AWF/N).

[2] For the text of the televised speech see *Public Papers of the Presidents: Eisenhower, 1956,* pp. 779–88.

To John Alex McCone   *September 26, 1956*

Dear John: Many thanks for sending me so quickly the information on the tank ships on order. It is exactly what I wanted.[1]

It was nice to see you—though I would profoundly wish we did not always have to talk about the troubles in the Suez![2]

With warm regard to you and Rosemary,[3] *As ever*

[1] McCone had been president of the California Shipbuilding Corporation from 1941 until 1946; at this time he was president of the Joshua Hendy Corporation. In 1961 he would become director of the Central Intelligence Agency. After a September 18 meeting with Eisenhower he had sent the President a summary of the tankers under construction or on order in the shipyards of the world on June 30, 1956. The total of 631 ships would be delivered, McCone believed, at a rate of 4,500,000 deadweight tons per year (McCone to Eisenhower, Sept. 20, 1956, AWF/A).

[2] Eisenhower had suggested to McCone that a group of ship operators might negotiate with Egyptian President Nasser. "This might be a very good move," McCone said. "Such a group might develop a formula to finance the deepening and double tracking of the Canal—as a consideration for a long-range and I would hope, irrevocable operating contract with the Users Association now being established in London" (for background see nos. 1981 and 1993).

[3] McCone's wife was the former Rosemary Cooper.

To Ezra Taft Benson   *September 26, 1956*

Dear Ezra: In Peoria yesterday I learned that the only thing our Party leaders in that state seem to fear during the next six weeks is a sharp fall-off in the hog market.[1] They thought this danger was increased by the fact that in one of the big packing companies they have had a serious strike.[2] This now seems to be settled and probably there will be avoided any "rush to the market" that would cause prices to collapse.[3]

I know that you are watching the situation closely and will be ready to take practical steps in the event there should be any unnecessary hardship imposed upon the hog growers. *As ever*

[1] On this campaign stop see no. 1989.

[2] Twenty-five thousand workers affiliated with two AFL–CIO unions had been on strike against the meat-packing operations of Swift & Company since September 20. Labor contracts with all the major meat-packing houses had simultaneously expired on September 1 (*New York Times*, Sept. 15, 1956). Eisenhower had also written Illinois Governor William G. Stratton on September 26 to follow up on their conversation of the previous evening about the strike: "If there is anything we can do I will get the proper people on the job" (AWF/A, Benson Corr.).

[3] Benson would agree that the impending settlement should stabilize the market and comment that he was pleased with the rise in hog prices that had prevailed during the past week. As he would note, programs were being implemented to remove soybean oil and lard from the market, which would probably help sustain live hog prices (Benson to Eisenhower, Sept. 27, 1956, AWF/A; see also no. 1975). Contract agreements with the major packing houses would be announced September 27, but the strikers would hold out until September 30 (*New York Times*, Sept. 27, 30, 1956).

To Arthur Larson   *September 26, 1956*

Dear Arthur:[1] Possibly one of the things that bothers me about the early part of this talk is that we have grouped together both specific goals for 1960 (for example, 70 million workers on the job), along with things that are accomplished and realized in day by day planning and effort. (For example, a 1960 in which long and costly strikes will be rare. This is something that we work for all the time. Or a 1960 which will see the working out of special measures to insure the competitive position of small business.)[2]

Furthermore, I think it is undoubtedly true that the average human would rather have his today's problems solved tomorrow than to be told that his problems will be solved much better in 1960. Take disease— it would be small comfort to a cancer patient today if he knew that by 1960, nobody else was going to die of cancer. However, I am still sure that we should outline the things that we know can be done during the next Administration if we follow the course already charted.

I think this talk has really great possibilities. If I am to put it over, it must be succinct, hard-hitting and logically arranged.

In any event, I send you herewith two sentences I scrawled—one to go at the top of the page and one in the introduction to the three questions. Mrs. Whitman has typed them out and appended them hereto.[3]

I hope that I shall be free by four o'clock tomorrow afternoon, but even if I am delayed a little bit, I will see you after the NSC so that we may try to agree on further developments.[4] *Sincerely*

[1] Larson (B.A. Augustana 1931) had served as Under Secretary of Labor since 1954. He had joined the faculty of Cornell Law School in 1944 and in 1953 had become dean of the University of Pittsburgh Law School.

[2] Larson was assisting with a campaign speech the President would deliver in Lexington, Kentucky, on October 1, 1956. The final version of the speech listed goals, but eliminated any specific reference to their achievement by the year 1960. For the text of the televised speech see *Public Papers of the Presidents: Eisenhower, 1956*, pp. 838–47; see also *New York Times*, October 2, 1956.

[3] We were unable to find the attachments in AWF.

[4] Larson would meet with the President as planned. For Eisenhower's further comments on the draft see no. 2004.

2000   *EM, AWF, Administration Series*

To Henry Cabot Lodge, Jr.   *September 26, 1956*

Dear Cabot: Thank you very much for sending me the pamphlet that was published on the occasion of the memorial plaque dedication at the United Nations Headquarters in June.[1]

Offhand, I must say I like your suggestion for a statement regarding our dependent territories, even though I think there might be difficulties involved. Of course I'll have to check it out with State and Defense.[2]

With warm regard, *As ever*

[1] Lodge had sent Eisenhower a pamphlet published on the occasion of the dedication of a memorial to United Nations soldiers who died in Korea (Lodge to Eisenhower, Sept. 18, 1956, AWF/A).

[2] Lodge had proposed that Eisenhower state that if he were reelected, he would recommend a "study of the rate of progress towards self-government or independence" for American territories such as the Virgin Islands, Guam, Samoa and for the trusteeship

islands in the Pacific (Lodge to Eisenhower, Sept. 19, 1956, AWF/A). Eisenhower would not make the statement Lodge had recommended.

2001   *EM, WHCF,*
President's Personal File 272

To John Reagan McCrary   *September 26, 1956*

Dear Tex: To take up your non-political subjects seriatim:

1. Somewhere I read about the trip that Michael and Kate Roosevelt took to Russia, and I was extremely interested in the photographs that they brought back. I am afraid that I disagree somewhat with your statement that it is "disquieting" that no fear shows in the faces of the young Russians—but maybe we can talk this over when we meet.[1]

2. Bernie Baruch did write me about seeing Billy Rose, and I replied that though it was not easy to find a spot on my schedule these days, I would try to work it in. Since then I have heard nothing more.[2]

3. After November sixth (which is rapidly becoming my slogan these days), I would like very much to have your progress report on the Southwest Washington project.[3]

With warm regard to you and Jinx, *As ever*

[1] McCrary had written (Sept. 26, same file as document) that his son, Michael Brisbane McCrary, and Kate Roosevelt Whitney had visited the Soviet Union to study the cultural and sports activities of students there. After studying the pictures they had taken, McCrary noted: "The disquieting fact is that in the faces of every young Russian in all the pictures, from kindergarten to college, you find no hate and no fear. There *must* be some way to get through to them without war."

[2] McCrary had suggested that Eisenhower meet with theatrical producer Billy Rose, who had traveled to the Soviet Union to promote an artist exchange project. Baruch's September 3 letter is in AWF/A (see also Rose's reports, Sept. 17, 1956, same file as document). Eisenhower's September 7 reply to Baruch is in AWF/A. The President would meet briefly with Rose on October 10.

[3] November sixth was election day. McCrary had offered to come to Washington, with the architects, to present to the President the "final rendering of the plan" to rehabilitate Southwest Washington, D.C.

2002   *EM, AWF, Administration Series*

To Lorraine P. Knox   *September 27, 1956*

Dear Lorraine: Monday proved to be a particularly busy day here in Washington, but I was not for a moment unaware that it marked the "anniversary" of my arrival at Fitzsimons.[1] Many times during the day I wanted to put everything else aside and write you a note, but there seemed to be a never-ending round of decisions to be made, speeches to be redrafted, people to be seen. The usual ingredients of a normal day are intensified two-fold right now with the demand of the unceasing official work and campaign activity.

At any rate, I do want you to know that I was thinking of you, and remembering how kind and reassuring you were one year ago to a bewildered patient. I shall be everlastingly grateful to you.

I enjoyed your letter of the nineteenth of August, and especially the description of your trials with your camera.[2] Some time I would like to see just what you managed to get with your double exposures.

As I just wrote Colonel Pollock, it doesn't look as though I am going to manage even a stop-off in Denver this fall, much as I would like to do so.[3] I'd like to demonstrate to you in person how robust I have really gotten to be. But I am afraid I shall have to postpone any such thoughts for the time being.

With affectionate regard, *Sincerely*

[1] On Eisenhower's September 24, 1955, heart attack see no. 1595.

[2] Knox had written (AWF/A) that after "snapping pictures like mad" of the "Great West," she found out that she had reused a roll of film taken when she left Europe. Consequently, she said, she had "beautiful pictures of a ship in the middle of the desert . . . a waterfall in the middle of the desert etc."

[3] Eisenhower's letter to Pollock explaining that campaign obligations would preclude a trip to Denver is in AWF/A: Fitzsimons (see also Pollock to Eisenhower, Sept. 24, 1956, *ibid.*).

2003

EM, AWF, International Series:
Panama

To John Foster Dulles

September 28, 1956

Approved.[1]

We should be generous in all small adm details. Our firmness should be in holding fast to basic principles and purposes of treaty.

[1] Eisenhower was approving a report that advocated continuing United States policies regarding the interpretation of the Panama Canal Treaty of 1955 (Dulles to Eisenhower, Sept. 28, 1956, AWF/I: Panama). The Panamanian delegate to the Conference of Inter-American Presidential Representatives (formed following Eisenhower's visit to Panama) had raised these questions of interpretation in a memorandum (State, *Foreign Relations, 1955–1957*, vol. VII, *American Republics: Central and South America*, pp. 307–17; see also nos. 1925 and 1926). The Panamanians had demanded that Panamanian workers who were being deprived of the right to purchase deeply discounted goods

in the Canal Zone commissary be given a wage increase in compensation. The State Department responded that their wages would go up only as part of their regular cost-of-living pay increases.

The Panamanian delegate also complained that the Americans were reneging on a treaty commitment to maintain the same "basic wage rate" for Americans and Panamanians. Under the American interpretation, only employees from the United States could receive special allowances in addition to their basic wages (Report to the President on the Memorandum of the Government of Panama Dated Sept., 1956, AWF/I: Panama; see also Coniff, *Panama and the United States*, p. 111).

The third point raised by the Panamanian delegate had to do with a treaty provision limiting the importation of merchandise for resale to items from either United States or Panamanian sources, unless it was not "feasible" to find goods from those two countries. The Panamanians interpreted "feasible" to mean "possible." The Americans insisted that feasibility included the reasonableness of the price (*ibid.*).

2004   *EM, AWF, Administration Series*

To Arthur Larson   *September 28, 1956*

Dear Arthur: As you are editing the Lexington talk, please note the following:[1]

The first paragraph is "Four years ago you gave me a job to do. That job was to give America a new direction." The second paragraph continues "The job was to turn a corner . . ."

In the third paragraph you say "The corner has been turned. The new direction has been taken." This implies quite decidedly that the job has been completed.

The next to last sentence of the talk is "My job is only half done."

On the draft I am sending back I give a suggestion as to how I think this seeming paradox can be cleared up. Please note the first page and last page.[2] *Sincerely*

[1] Under Secretary of Labor Larson was assisting Eisenhower in the preparation of a speech he would deliver in Lexington, Kentucky, on October 1. See no. 1999.
[2] We have not found a copy of Larson's draft in AWF, but see the text of the speech in *Public Papers of the Presidents: Eisenhower, 1956*, pp. 838–47.

2005   *EM, AWF, Administration Series*

To Lewis Williams Douglas   *September 30, 1956*

Dear Lew:[1] The intelligence about the effects of current Federal Reserve System policy contained in your last letter fits with certain other reports that have come to me.[2]

We are, of course, suffering some of the pains of prosperity. The supply of savings and money generally has never been greater but the demand is greater still. The confidence people have in the future has produced plans in a surging volume and the result is so-called "tight money."[3]

While the System's policy of restraint has been rightly directed toward the goal of stability at these high levels of activity, among us here we have had for some time certain reservations about the timing and extent of the policy. These opinions have been made clear to the Federal Reserve Board Chairman and I am sure he has accorded them full weight.[4] But he feels strongly about his responsibility under the law, as he should. The general public, of course, makes no differentiation between the Administration and the fully independent Federal Reserve Board.[5]

We are continuing to explore ways both of making this fact clear and of securing further provision for the legitimate credit needs of small business and agriculture, and I have some reason for hope that the Federal Reserve Board will loosen some of their restrictions within the next few weeks.[6]

We must find a way to foster a healthily growing, high-employment, peacetime economy while containing inflation. It is a new and challenging task.[7]

I am always grateful to have the benefit of your thinking. Thanks again for writing.

With warm regard, *As ever*

[1] Gabriel Hauge drafted this letter for Eisenhower.

[2] Douglas had written the President on September 24 to criticize the Federal Reserve Board's "hard money policy (so called)," which he said was creating a shortage of credit for small businessmen; harming construction; and restricting the amount of credit available to agriculture (AWF/A). Douglas had charged that the Fed, having failed to understand the dynamics of the current inflation, was now applying inappropriate remedies. Douglas feared that the Fed's policy would be "one of the factors which would probably throw Texas in the Democratic column" in the November election. In handwritten comments on Douglas's letter, Treasury Secretary Humphrey had noted that the distinctions Douglas made were correct "but the results can be equally bad unless restrained. I fully share his political fears but think a soaring cost of living would be far worse politically than [a] rise in the cost of money."

[3] On August 24 the Federal Reserve Board had raised the discount rate a quarter point in a move to curb inflationary forces (see no. 1956).

[4] On the Administration's differences with the Federal Reserve Board see no. 1877; see also Kettl, *Leadership at the Fed*, pp. 88–91.

[5] See A. Jerome Clifford, *The Independence of the Federal Reserve System* (Philadelphia, 1965), pp. 229–72, 318–21.

[6] The latter half of this sentence was added to the original draft (in AWF/A). The Board would, however, make no move to ease credit in October 1956.

[7] On Eisenhower's appeal to labor and business leaders for "responsibility" in setting wage increases and in thus curbing inflation see Saulnier, *Constructive Years*, pp. 92–97.

The free world's "sad mess"

OCTOBER 1956 TO JANUARY 1957

22

On Suez "we do not see eye to eye"

To Harry Amos Bullis   *October 2, 1956*
Personal

Dear Harry: A campaign trip is a far cry from establishing a summer headquarters somewhere away from Washington. On a campaign trip a man literally has almost no chance to conduct government business; because of that it is simply impossible to be away from Washington— or from government contacts and advisers—for longer than two or three days at a time.[1]

About "tight" money—Of course you realize that the Federal Reserve Board is a fully independent agency and that the Administration can only make its opinions known to the Chairman of the Board. I know that the general public unfortunately makes no differentiation between the Administration and the Board. We are exploring ways of making this fact clear and of securing further provision for the legitimate credit needs of small business and agriculture, and I have some reason for hope that the Board will loosen some of their restrictions within the next few weeks.[2]

As for your other suggestions, again I say they will be carefully considered by all of us.[3]

One final word, Mamie is a wonderful campaigner and, I truly believe, the best vote-getter of the family.

With warm regard, *As ever*

[1] General Mills Chairman Harry Bullis had written Eisenhower on September 27 (same file as document) to congratulate the President on his September 25 farm speech, delivered at Peoria, Illinois (see no. 1989; see also *Public Papers of the Presidents: Eisenhower, 1956*, pp. 796–804). Bullis had said: "It is the consensus of many of your friends in this upper Middle West area that the best single strategy during the remaining weeks of the campaign is for you and your charming First Lady to be seen by as many people as possible in as many locales. The most effective pre-election statement these days is—'I saw Ike and he looks fine!'"

[2] Bullis had suggested that Eisenhower "Ease the money situation right away, swing it around a bit before election, and overcome the objections of all of these pressure groups." (See the preceding document.)

[3] Bullis's other suggestions had included increasing the criticism of Stevenson, since voters would "like to see you cut him down to size," and forcing "Stevenson to discuss the various Cabinet members that he might appoint. That might prove to be embarrassing to him."

President's Personal File 686

To Hubert Reilly Harmon   *October 2, 1956*

Dear Doodle: This note is really just to say that though I may seem to be preoccupied with campaign business, I nevertheless have you much on my mind. I do hope that by now you have recovered from the shock that inevitably follows any operation, and that it proved beneficial.[1]

Everybody admits that the pressures and duties of a modern-day President are almost too great for any one man to handle. Many believe that something must be done by legislation or otherwise to lighten the burden. When you take that job and add to it the campaigning that by tradition seems inevitable in our political setup, you have really a job that takes twelve hours a day seven days a week (with some twenty-hour days thrown in for good measure). This is not all in the nature of a complaint, since I knew that it would happen, but the point I am trying to make is that I would hope that eventually our people would make it mandatory that an incumbent President, if he seeks reelection, rests his case on the record and takes no active part in the campaign activities. I realize, of course, that this is probably but a dream.

Of course there is another aspect to the business of these jaunts I have been making to various parts of the country. Inescapably both Mamie and I get charged with the enthusiastic and warm welcome we have so far received, and come home exhilarated rather than tired. The coin *does* have two sides after all. But enough of that.

I do want you to know that I am keeping in touch with you through Howard Snyder—and that you and Rosa Maye are always in my thoughts.

With warm regard, *Affectionately*

[1] Lieutenant General Harmon had undergone brain surgery on September 5 and was recuperating at Lackland Air Force Base Hospital in San Antonio, Texas (see Eisenhower to Mrs. Harmon, Sept. 4, 1956; and Mrs. Harmon to Eisenhower, Sept. 6, 1956, both in AWF/N). Earlier this year Harmon had undergone radiation treatments for lung cancer (see Mrs. Harmon to Eisenhower, May 23, 1956; Eisenhower to Griffin, May 24, 1956; Griffin to Eisenhower, May 28, 1956; and Eisenhower to Harmon, June 1, 1956, all in same file as document). For developments see no. 2143.

2008   *Gruenther Papers*

To Alfred Maximilian Gruenther   *October 4, 1956*

Dear Al: I have your two notes of the thirtieth. As to the Italian post, I am glad to have the warning about our friend from New York. Actually, the job has been offered to someone from the West Coast, who is still considering the matter.[1]

Please keep me posted on your personal plans; you know that I have more than a passing interest in your location after you return to this country![2]

Between official work, campaign trips, speeches—and my first world series game—I haven't stopped revolving in weeks. However, I am happy to report that Jim Hagerty paid me off as a result of his ill-advised and completely biased support of the Yankees![3]

Give my love to Grace and, as always, the best to yourself, *As ever*

[1] U.S. Ambassador to Italy Clare Boothe Luce had asked Gruenther to report to Eisenhower her reservations regarding Peter Grimm, a New York real estate executive and Luce's Chief of Economic Mission, as a candidate for the ambassadorship upon her resignation. Grimm had "lost his zip," according to Luce, and was not the best choice for the job (Gruenther to Eisenhower, Sept. 30, 1956, AWF/A; on Luce's resignation see Memorandum of Conversation, July 13, 1956, Dulles Papers, White House Memoranda Series). Californian James D. Zellerbach, president of the Crown Zellerbach Paper Manufacturing Corporation and formerly head of the Economic Cooperation Administration in Rome, would be named to succeed Luce on November 23.

[2] "The outlook for the Red Cross set up appears to be improving," Gruenther had written. "Meanwhile new business offers have been made, and old ones improved" (Gruenther to Eisenhower, Sept. 30, 1956, AWF/A). Gruenther would become president of the American Red Cross on January 1, 1957.

[3] See no. 2030.

2009   *EM, WHCF, Official File 100-A*

To Marcellus Hartley Dodge   *October 4, 1956*

Dear Marcy: I am delighted that you approve of the appointment of Judge Brennan to the Supreme Court. Not only was I impressed with his qualifications for the job, but when I met him I was immediately taken with his warm personality and his genuine understanding of people and problems.[1]

With personal regard, *As ever*

[1] For background on Remington Arms Company Chairman of the Board Marcellus Hartley Dodge see Galambos, *Chief of Staff*, no. 1640. Writing on October 2, Dodge said of Brennan: "He not only has the reputation among my friends of being a top jurist, but he has many other qualifications which make his appointment very important just at this time in nearby New York as well as in New Jersey." The White House had announced the nomination of William Joseph Brennan, Jr., a Catholic and a lifelong Democrat, as an Associate Justice of the Supreme Court on September 29 (see *New York Times*, Sept. 30, 1956). For further background see no. 1334 and Eisenhower, *Mandate for Change*, p. 230.

2010   *EM, AWF, Name Series*

To John Shively Knight   *October 6, 1956*
Personal

Dear Jack: There has just come to my desk your editorial of September thirtieth entitled "With No Party Differences, Ike is the Better

Choice." Naturally I am flattered by your opinion that in the comparison of the two candidates, I should stand above my rival. I am gratified that you have stated this opinion publicly.[1]

However, there is another part of your editorial that I would like to discuss for a moment. I think there is far more difference between the Republican and Democrat philosophies, as indicated by both words and actions, than you seem to believe.

The Republican program aims at a sound dollar, fiscal integrity and the greatest possible decentralization of power to states and communities.[2]

By the record the Democrats believe in almost exactly the opposite.[3]

I cannot, of course, write an essay on the matter in a letter such as this, but I wonder whether you would do me the favor of getting a copy of the October eighth issue of LIFE, and reading the article on pages 36 and 37.[4]

With warm regard, *Sincerely*

[1] Knight had written an editorial entitled "When Abilities Are Weighed, Eisenhower Comes Out Ahead," in which he said "the choice at the November election is between men rather than political philosophies" (*Akron Beacon-Journal*, Sept. 30, 1956).
[2] On the 1956 Republican party platform see no. 1922.
[3] For the text of the Democratic party platform see Schlesinger, ed., *History of American Presidential Elections*, vol. IV, *1940–1968*, pp. 3355–85.
[4] See no. 2016.

2011   *EM, WHCF, Official File 122-0*

TO MARY MCCLURE   *October 6, 1956*

Dear Mrs. McClure: You are perfectly right in thinking that I am delighted to hear from persons like yourself and to have the little conversation that goes on with an exchange of letters. Of course I can read and respond only to a selection from the very large number of letters that are sent me. But a letter like yours, containing so much careful thought, deserves at least this little acknowledgment.[1]

I could scarcely begin to comment on the many matters that you discuss. But it is possible to say that the small business problems that you mention are the subject of constant attention by my economic advisers, by the Small Business Administration and by the Department of Commerce. I am certain that you realize these are not problems capable of any simple solution. Rather they are subjects that require continuing effort over a period of time. I can assure you that we are making that effort.[2]

Thank you again for writing me. I am especially grateful for your prayers.

With best wishes, *Sincerely*

¹ Mary (Mrs. LaVere) McClure, the co-owner with her husband of a small grocery store in Council Bluffs, Iowa, had written the President on September 13 (same file as document). In a four-page typed letter Mrs. McClure had said that she "got to wonder-ing the other day while preoccupied with the family ironing if you aren't sometimes wishing you could talk down to earth with peoples in this great country of ours and learn what is in their hearts and minds, especially men and their families who've been in their country's service, and have positive ideas on health, education, small business, and farming as major issues in the coming election."

² Mrs. McClure had described in detail the problems she and her husband faced in running their small market due to competition with large national chains. She also described their difficulties in obtaining financing from banks; some bankers had told her that "it would be easier to finance us for an investment of $150,000 than the $15,000 we wanted." For background on small business and the Eisenhower Administration see no. 1957. During the campaign the Eisenhower Administration would describe in detail the Administration's accomplishments, which included the creation of the Small Busi-ness Administration; the establishment of the Cabinet Committee on Small Business; adjustments in the tax laws; the reduction of federal competition with business; the increase in federal contracts awarded to small businesses; the extension of the govern-ment "set-aside" policy for small business; an attack on unfair competition; an increase in financial assistance, and the dissemination of management expertise. There were numerous ongoing efforts to aid small business (Herman to Eisenhower, Oct. 14, 1956, and Eisenhower to Herman, Oct. 22, 1956, same file as document).

2012   *EM, AWF, Name Series*

To Milton Stover Eisenhower   *October 7, 1956*

Dear Milton: I have read the front page editorial in the Sunday Sun, as you suggested.[1] If I knew him and should meet him, I would like to say this to the writer:

"I am grateful for the keen perception you have brought to the analysis of my hopes and efforts in the management of national affairs. From the words, 'So we come to the real issue . . .' midway of the first column of your editorial, to the sentence ending '. . . with equal op-portunity under the law' in the second, you have more clearly dis-cerned and more accurately than any one else outlined my philosophy of our government's proper relationship to the individual and to the nation's economy.[2]

"If anything at all is omitted, it is the added truth that the middle way is often difficult to maintain; that a turn to moderation and enduring principles can in itself be a revolution inciting the hatred and enmity of both extremes. You hinted at this when you said that this Administration flipped a page of history.[3] What you did not say was that an extremist frequently attacks the moderate more savagely than he does his opposing extremist; he seemingly is afraid of any effort to incite the good common sense of the public.

"Despite this one, unimportant, observation, your editorial did more to give me the feeling of worthwhileness in the work I've personally undertaken than has anything else I've read. Thank you, from my heart."

So, of course, I thank you for bringing the piece to my attention.[4]

As ever

[1] The President had spoken with Milton on October 7 (Telephone conversation, Oct. 7, 1956, AWF/D) to discuss the campaign speech planned for Pittsburgh on October 9 (see *Public Papers of the Presidents: Eisenhower, 1956*, pp. 872–80). On the seventh the *Baltimore Sun* had published an editorial, entitled "The Case for Mr. Eisenhower," endorsing the President.

[2] The *Sun* editorial commended the Administration for its "sharp break with its predecessor" in domestic policy. The *Sun* praised Eisenhower's "restraint, his fair-mindedness," and "his essentially nonpolitical attitude toward politics." The editorial lauded the manner in which Eisenhower had cleaned house in the federal government and the Republican party, and repaired relations between the executive and legislature. The *Sun* approved the President's fiscal and monetary policies and the manner in which the Administration had strengthened American capitalism. Eisenhower deserved the *Sun*'s support because "Above all, he has tried to redefine that much-abused term 'the people'—and restore its original meaning of a nation of individuals with equal opportunity under the law."

[3] "What the Eisenhower Administration did," the editorial said, "was to flip a page of history—bring an era to an end. It did so against the will of an important element of the Republican Party that wanted to flip the page back the other way to 1929 and before. It did so against the objections of those who had acquired a vested interest in Big Government."

[4] On the following day Eisenhower would again discuss the *Sun* editorial with his brother (Telephone conversation, Oct. 8, 1956, AWF/D). The President would tell Milton that Hagerty had suggested Eisenhower send a copy of his letter to the editor of the *Baltimore Sun*. The President would do so, sending to William F. Schmick, Sr., president and director of the A. S. Abell Company, publisher of the *Baltimore Sun*, a shortened version of his letter to his brother. This version would omit Eisenhower's discussion of the difficulties of the "middle way." The President would agree with the *Sun* that "foreign policy should in no sense be a party issue, and I deplore the fact that, despite my personal desires, certain aspects of it have become so" (AWF/Drafts).

2013   *EM, AWF, DDE Diaries Series*

To Harold Potter Rodes   *October 7, 1956*

Dear Dr. Rodes: Of course I am very highly complimented by the proposal to confer on me in absentia an honorary Doctor of Humanities degree from Bradley University.[1]

It has always been my thought that the conferring of a degree by a University bestows on the recipient a very significant honor which, to be fully meaningful, practically compels his presence at the moment. While I concede that there might be exceptions to a rule of this sort, I truly would prefer to hope that I may one day be present to accept personally Bradley's honorary Doctorate than to receive it in absentia. If perhaps the Faculty and Board of Trustees of the University would wish at some future opportunity to renew their very kind invitation, I would be glad to consider it again.[2]

I cannot close without repeating to you my deep appreciation both of the honor you have suggested and of your courtesy in allowing me to speak at the Bradley University Field House last month.[3]

With warm regard, *Sincerely*

P.S. Thank you for sending me the current issue of "The Bradley Scout." The President of Bradley need in no way be ashamed of his abilities as a reporter—on the contrary, I thought the article was excellent.[4]

[1] Rodes (Ph.D. Yale 1948), president of Bradley University in Peoria, Illinois, since 1954, had proposed that the honorary degree be conferred on the President at the school's annual Founder's Day, October 12 (Oct. 1, 1956, WHCF/PPF 1-P). Eisenhower had earlier declined Rodes's invitation to receive the award when he spoke at the university on September 25 (Sept. 20, 1956, *ibid.*); see n. 3 below.

[2] Rodes would renew the invitation on January 3. Eisenhower would decline again, explaining that "the existence of other long-standing invitations—precludes any possibility of acceptance" (Jan. 11, 1957, both in WHCF/PPF 1-P). Apparently, the basketball scandals at Bradley were considerations in the decision to decline Rodes's several invitations (see Whitman to Adams, n.d., *ibid.*; see also "Mary" to Minnich, Jan. 9, 1956, *ibid.*).

[3] On September 25 Eisenhower had addressed the nation via television and radio from Robinson Memorial Field House at Bradley University (see *Public Papers of the Presidents: Eisenhower, 1956*, pp. 796–804; and *New York Times*, Sept. 26, 1956).

[4] Rodes's article on Eisenhower's visit to the university had appeared in the September 28 issue of the student newspaper (copy in WHCF/PPF 1-P). In his cover letter Rodes had referred to himself as a "neophyte reporter" (Oct. 1, 1956, WHCF/PPF 1-P).

2014   *EM, AWF, Dulles-Herter Series*

To Herbert Clark Hoover, Jr.   *October 8, 1956*
Secret

Dear Herbert: As you could tell from my telephone conversation, I have not any very definite views of what I might do either now or in the future in order to prevent the Suez business from getting out of hand.[1] Some thoughts such as the following occur to me:

(*a*) Assuming that Foster finds the going very sticky at the UN, he might think it helpful if I should issue a White House statement outlining our position and detailing our step-by-step moves to keep the peace.[2] The statement might also contain a frank warning that the United States will not support a war or warlike moves in the Suez area. It would insist that negotiations must be continued until a peaceful but just solution is reached—regardless of how long it takes.

(*b*) Without direct reference to the Suez, we might make public some of the results of studies conducted under the leadership of ODM concerning the world's future need for big tankers. If we should conclude to go ahead with the construction of some of these (approximately sixty thousand tons) regardless of the Suez affair, the announcement of our intention might have a calming effect.[3]

(*c*) Of course the British and the French are bitterly against building up Nasser. This concern has been rather overtaken by events since he has already become, mostly as a result of this quarrel, a world figure. If therefore, we can think of any plan that we could accept, even though it falls somewhat short of the detailed requirements listed by Britain and France, we might through some clandestine means urge Nasser to make an appropriate public offer. Such action ought to start negotiations toward a peaceful settlement.[4]

(*d*) Should we be any more specific in our communications with Nehru in the hope that he could influence Nasser into negotiations?[5]

(*e*) Could the Organization of American States serve any useful purpose now or in the future—such as a joint resolution or the like?[6]

(*f*) I assume that we are secretly keeping our communications with the oil-producing Arab States, in order to get their influence somewhat on our side.[7]

(*g*) A more spectacular thing might be for me to invite a number of nations to a conference, including most of the eighteen who agreed upon the "London Plan" as well as India, Egypt, Israel and possibly Saudi Arabia.

As you know, I am immersed in the sum total of affairs necessitated by governmental and political work. None of the items in this list has been deeply studied; I send it to you more as a clear indication of my readiness to participate in any way in which I can be helpful than as a series of suggestions. However, if you see any virtue in any one of these possibilities, please have it studied, but only by your most trusted and reliable staff officers—those that surely will not leak.[8]

With warm regard, *Sincerely*

[1] Detailed notes on Eisenhower's conversation with Under Secretary of State Hoover are in AWF/D.

[2] Secretary Dulles had arrived in New York on October 5 to attend Security Council deliberations on the Suez crisis. For background on the Anglo-French initiative in bringing the issue to the United Nations see State, *Foreign Relations, 1955–1957*, vol.

XVI, *Suez Crisis July 26–December 31, 1956*, pp. 560–62, 564–65, 581–82, 600–603, 634–39.

³ ODM Director Arthur Flemming had told Eisenhower that 300 sixty-thousand ton tankers would be necessary (by 1960) if Middle Eastern oil were to be shipped around the Cape of Good Hope instead of through the Suez Canal. Approximately half that number, Flemming calculated, could be constructed in the United States in existing private yards, reactivated yards, and two new shipyards (Memorandum, Oct. 6, 1956, AWF/A; see also nos. 1997 and 2027; and State, *Foreign Relations, 1955–1957*, vol. XVI, *Suez Crisis July 26–December 31, 1956*, pp. 192–93). Hoover would tell Eisenhower that the State Department was in close contact with Flemming and Sherman Adams "on the desirability of appointing an advisory group to study this matter" (Hoover to Eisenhower, Oct. 10, 1956; and Memorandum, Oct. 10, 1956, both in AWF/D-H).

⁴ See n. 8, below.

⁵ Although India had "tended to support" Egyptian foreign policy during recent years, Hoover said, India remained dependent upon the canal. Nehru and his representatives had been active in "making suggestions to Nasser for a solution" to the problem, and Hoover opposed additional communication regarding the issue (Memorandum, Oct. 10, 1956, AWF/D-H).

⁶ "Effective action through the OAS at this stage would not be useful," Hoover answered: not all Latin American countries supported the Western position, he said, the principle of nationalization was popular in Latin America, and intervention by the OAS could precipitate a debate over the status of the Panama Canal (*ibid.*).

⁷ Hoover assured Eisenhower that the United States had "continued in close touch," particularly with the countries of Saudi Arabia, Iran, and Iraq (*ibid.*; see also State, *Foreign Relations, 1955–1957*, vol. XVI, *Suez Crisis July 26–December 31, 1956*, p. 686).

⁸ Hoover would tell Eisenhower that Dulles would discuss with him personally the possibility of a White House statement, a plan for Nasser to make a public offer, and a call for another conference (Hoover to Eisenhower, Oct. 10, 1956, AWF/D-H). In forwarding this letter to Dulles, Hoover would tell the Secretary that "as a result of the political situation the President may feel under some pressure to take a more direct part in the proceedings" (Hoover to Dulles, Oct. 8, 1956, Dulles Papers, White House Memoranda Series). Dulles would return briefly to Washington and at a meeting with Eisenhower on October 11 would tell the President "that if things got into a real crisis, we might want to call on him [Eisenhower] to make some move" (State, *Foreign Relations, 1955–1957*, vol. XVI, *Suez Crisis July 26–December 31, 1956*, p. 693).

2015
EM, WHCF, Confidential File:
Suez Canal Crisis

To Ibn Abd al-Aziz Saud
October 8, 1956
Secret

*Your Majesty:*¹ I have read with pleasure Your Majesty's message of September twenty-fifth, which once more eloquently reveals the deep concern of Your Majesty for the preservation of peace in the Near East and for the improvement of the grave situation which has arisen as a result of the action taken by Egypt with respect to the Suez Canal.²

I am interested in what Your Majesty was pleased to tell me of the discussions with President Nasser. Insofar as the general relations between the United States and Egypt are concerned, it is my genuine desire, and that of my Government, that progress be made toward the strengthening of these on a basis of mutual understanding and trust.

With regard to the Suez problem, Your Majesty mentions the possibility of bilateral or multilateral discussions with Egypt. It is my hope that the discussions of the Suez issue in the United Nations, together with the occasions for co-operation with Egypt which the existence of the Suez Canal Users' Association provides, will result in progress toward a satisfactory solution.[3] In both of these instances opportunities for fruitful exchanges of views between representatives of Egypt and those of interested nations will not be lacking.

Your Majesty may rest assured of my continuing deep interest in a peaceful and equitable solution of the Suez problem. I shall not relax my efforts to this end, and I am sure I can count on Your Majesty to do the same.

May God have Your Majesty in his safe keeping. *Your sincere friend*

[1] State Department officials drafted this letter to the Saudi Arabian monarch. Acting Secretary Hoover said: "The message does not encourage the King to believe we favor his suggestion that the United States negotiate with Nasser more or less on the latter's terms, and reveals our determination not to desert our associates in this problem" (see Hoover to Eisenhower, Oct. 6, 1956, AWF/I: Saudi Arabia).

[2] King Saud's letter, in response to Eisenhower's message of September 18, remains classified (see no. 1990; see also Wadsworth to Dulles, Oct. 16, 1956, same file as document).

[3] On the U.N. discussions see the preceding document; on the users' association see no. 1981. The State Department would cable the text of this message to King Saud on October 9.

2016   *EM, AWF, Administration Series*

To Henry Robinson Luce   *October 8, 1956*
Personal

Dear Harry: I can't tell you what a warm and worthwhile feeling the two-page editorial in the current LIFE gave me. The perception in the analysis of the hopes and efforts of this Administration in the management of national affairs was, incidentally, so outstanding that I recommended it to a colleague of yours (who, of course, shall be nameless). In powerful and persuasive terms, the editorial clearly discerns and outlines what we have been trying to do these last four years.[1]

My appreciation of the friendship of Clare and yourself has been of long-standing.[2] While I trust that the LIFE editorial stems from facts, not from friendship, I am aware that my indebtedness to you has been increased.

Give my warm regard to C. D. when you see him.[3]
With personal regard to yourself, *As ever*

[1] Luce's editorial "Why Independents Should Vote Republican," appeared in *Life* on October 8, 1956. The editorial described the Democrats as a party of interest groups and the Republicans as the only party with a coherent program. The editorial offered an extensive description of what Luce called the "New Republican" philosophy.
[2] The reference is to Ambassador Clare Boothe Luce.
[3] C. D. Jackson was a former Special Assistant to the President.

2017   *EM, AWF, Gettysburg Series*

To BILLY G. BYARS   *October 8, 1956*

Dear Billy: I am delighted to know that one of my "discerning Democrat" friends has taken another step—and that you are in the fund raising business for the Republican Party and have decided to vote for the straight Republican ticket. I can't think of a better salesman for some of my other Texas friends.[1]

At the moment there are no definite plans for a trip to Texas, but the matter is under serious consideration and I know that if we do decide it can be done, you will be notified at the earliest possible moment.[2]

Incidentally, I have gotten about half way through that pamphlet on dwarfism, which I find extremely interesting.[3]

With warm regard, *As ever*

[1] Byars had written that he was "having a dinner . . . to raise some funds for the Republican party" (Oct. 2, 1956, AWF/Gettysburg).
[2] Byars had suggested that if the President would make two or three talks in the state, he would "carry Texas." On Eisenhower's campaign itinerary see no. 2028. On November 12 and again on December 23 Eisenhower would thank Byars for his efforts during the campaign (both letters are in AWF/Gettysburg).
[3] The pamphlet on dwarfism in cattle had been sent by Byars under separate cover (for background see no. 1984; see also Bratcher to Stuart, Oct. 29, 1956, AWF/Gettysburg).

2018   *EM, AWF, DDE Diaries Series*

To HENRY KNOX SHERRILL   *October 8, 1956*

My dear Bishop Sherrill: I appreciate very much your personal letter of October fifth.[1]

Actually, not being a communicant of the Episcopal Church, I was in some doubt as to the appropriateness of my participating in Communion, even though the Church is an All-Faith Chapel and the University Chaplain, who assisted, is not an Episcopalian. However, my own doubts in this regard were set at rest by the Episcopal Minister who presided.[2] He personally invited the participation of all present who were communicants of any Christian faith. Further, I was told that the majority of the congregation, that morning, was non-Episcopalian.

Nevertheless, if my action should have offended any member of your Church, I naturally regret it. But I am reassured by the views which you express and am grateful that you wanted to write as you did. *Sincerely*

[1] We could not locate the letter from Sherrill, Presiding Bishop of the Protestant Episcopal Church in the United States. Eisenhower had attended (September 9, 1956) a family service dedicating a chapel at Pennsylvania State University to the memory of Milton Eisenhower's late wife, Helen Eakin Eisenhower. An editorial, which had later appeared in an Episcopalian weekly magazine, strongly criticized the President, a Presbyterian, for receiving Holy Communion in an Episcopalian church. The editorial also acknowledged there was some dissension within the Episcopal Church regarding participation by non-Episcopalians in communion rites (see "Not a Good Precedent" in *Living Church*, Sept. 23, 1956, p. 10). Several Episcopalian clergy had written to the President expressing different views on this subject (see Martin to Eisenhower, Sept. 26, 1956, WHCF/PPF 53-B-1; Kean to Eisenhower, Sept. 26, 1956, and Gary to Eisenhower, Sept. 21, 1956, both in WHCF/PPF 1-A-9.
[2] Chaplain Dr. Luther H. Harshbarger had given the sermon. The Reverend Jones B. Shannon, rector of St. Andrew's Protestant Episcopal Church in adjacent State College, had been celebrant at the communion service (*New York Times*, Sept. 10, 1956).

2019   *EM, AWF, Administration Series*

To Nelson Aldrich Rockefeller   *October 10, 1956*
Personal

Dear Nelson: Thank you for your report on your impressions during the Inauguration of President de la Guardia of Panama. I regret particularly that the attitude of the Arias Government toward the United States seemed to you to verge on the unfriendly.[1] We have certainly tried to be generous and understanding in every way with them—from expediting shipments of Salk vaccine to the ever present and annoying problems of Canal cooperation.[2]

I personally shall do everything in my power to see that President de la Guardia's intrinsic respect for the "fair play" policies of our country is maintained and strengthened.

I hope I shall see you soon. Meantime, my gratitude to you for representing me at the Inauguration, and warm personal regard.[3]
As ever

[1] Rockefeller had represented Eisenhower at de la Guardia's inauguration. He reported that the outgoing President had given a speech attacking the United States for failing to keep its treaty promises and for excluding it from the London Suez Conference (Oct. 5, 1956, AWF/A). Arias's speech prompted the State Department to propose a delay in accepting him as the Panamanian ambassador to the United States "to make plain that his remarks have not gone unnoticed" (Dulles to Eisenhower, Oct. 17, 1956, AWF/I: Panamanian). See also State, *Foreign Relations*, vol. VII, *American Republics: Central and South America*, pp. 318–21. De la Guardia, whom Rockefeller described as "an outstanding friend" of the United States, was considerably more conciliatory. For background see no. 2003; for developments see the following document.
[2] For background on the expedited shipment of Salk vaccine to Panama see no. 1950. On the Salk vaccine see nos. 1401 and 1414.
[3] Rockefeller had also reported that Mrs. Cecilia de Remon, widow of a former president of Panama and minister of labor in the new cabinet, had said "she only wished that she could campaign for [Eisenhower] during this coming month." Rockefeller gave her his Ike button, which she wore throughout the inauguration ceremonies.

2020   *EM, AWF, Dulles-Herter Series*

To HERBERT CLARK HOOVER, JR.   *October 10, 1956*

Memorandum for the Acting Secretary of State: Herewith is a copy of a note from the President of Panama that I should like for you to read.

As you know, I have in the past been completely sympathetic with some of Panama's complaints as to our methods and practices of operation in the Canal Zone.

Just what President de la Guardia had in mind when he said that he had "almost despaired as to the present and future of our relations," I do not know.[1] I just think there is possibly here a problem with which the State Department should keep continuous and intimate touch.

P.S. Please send me a draft of a possible reply to President de la Guardia.[2]

[1] President de la Guardia's note, which praised Nelson Rockefeller's "talents" as a representative, indicated that the Panamanian's "despair" about relations with the United States had "turned into a fresh hope" (Oct. 4, 1956, AWF/I: Panamanian). See also the preceding document.
[2] Dulles would send the President two documents. The first, dated October 16, was drafted by the officer in charge of Panamanian affairs. It accused the Panamanians of attempting to "expand" the meaning of some of the treaty provisions in order to make it appear that the United States was not acting in good faith. At the same time, the memo argued, Panama had not lived up to its agreements by refusing the United States

additional land for two radar sites to protect the canal. Panama was also charged with openly displaying sympathy for the Egyptians in the Suez Canal crisis "in the obvious hope of establishing precedents."

The second document was Dulles's draft reply to de la Guardia (which Eisenhower would approve); this message took the position that the 1955 treaty revision had "eliminated or established the basis for eventual elimination of many of the problems" between the two nations (Dulles to Eisenhower, Oct. 17, 1956, and Eisenhower to de la Guardia, Oct. 22, 1956, AWF/I: Panamanian). See also no. 2003, and State, *Foreign Relations*, vol. VII, *American Republics: Central and South America*, pp. 316–17.

2021   *EM, AWF, Administration Series*

To Paul Dudley White   *October 10, 1956*

Dear Dr. White: Thank you for your long and interesting letter. I shall answer your points seriatim.[1]

One, as to my health. I feel very well—a fact that sometimes seems surprising even to me in view of the trials and tribulations that political activities add to my never-ending official work.[2] The doctors seem satisfied with my condition.

Secondly, I was gratified by the cordial reception you received in Russia, and the evident cooperation extended to you. It is encouraging that in professional matters of this kind there can be a free interchange of information and ideas. I am sure that you and the people travelling with you proved the best kind of Ambassadors, and I hope that eventually we can widen the sphere of the exchange of such representatives.[3]

And, as for your third point, don't worry about any interpretation the press puts upon any remarks. I have been too often misquoted and too often quoted out of context to pay the slightest attention to such things.[4]

With warm regard, *Sincerely*

P.S. I shall, of course, be highly interested in your article in the current issue of the Journal of Chronic Disease.[5]

[1] White had written on October 3 (AWF/A).

[2] Eisenhower's performance during the campaigning of the last few months had "surprised and delighted everyone," White said.

[3] White and five other American heart specialists had traveled to the Soviet Union to "reestablish a satisfactory contact between the medical professions of our two countries . . . and . . . to discuss in some detail . . . research with particular reference to heart disease . . . ." See also "A Statement by Professor Paul D. White and his Colleagues to the Minister of Health of the USSR for the Press Conference in Moscow on September 6, 1956," AWF/A, White Corr.

[4] In a recent interview a reporter had asked White how he would vote. He explained that he had jokingly replied that he "wasn't so sure." And this, he said, was taken out of context.

[5] White had promised to send a reprint to the President. The article presented statistics based on a twenty-five year follow-up on two hundred cases seen by White between 1920 and 1930 (see David W. Richards, Edward F. Bland, and Paul D. White, "A Completed Twenty-Five-Year Follow-up Study of Patients with Myocardial Infarction," *Journal of Chronic Diseases*, 4, no. 4, October 1956, 415–22).

2022   *EM, AWF, Administration Series*

To Howard Pyle   *October 10, 1956*
Memorandum

If, at any time, you want me to write a note to former President Hoover to ask him to make a speech, I shall be glad to do so. Just let me know.[1]

[1] Administrative Assistant to the President Pyle had recommended to Eisenhower that he ask former President Hoover to speak on behalf of the Republican ticket (Oct. 8, 1956, AWF/A). We cannot locate a written request to Hoover in AWF, but Hoover would give a televised speech on behalf of the Republican party candidates on October 29 (*New York Times*, Oct. 30, 1956).

2023   *EM, AWF, Administration Series,*
                                                          C. D. Jackson Corr.

To Frederick Huff Payne   *October 10, 1956*

Dear Mr. Payne: Word of your approaching eightieth birthday has just reached me and I am happy indeed to join your family and friends in warm felicitations on the occasion.[1]

Our association goes back a great many years, almost more than I care to remember. I remember very well the difficulty I had—and the seriousness with which I took my task—when I was assigned to draft speeches for you, when you were then the Assistant Secretary of War.[2] (Incidentally, I am still taking speeches just as seriously— unfortunately, they are my own, these days).

Of late I have seen far too little of you, but I have kept in touch with our occasional correspondence, or through reports I have from friends of your sons.[3] I am happy that such an event as your eightieth anniversary gives me a chance once again to send you my best wishes and affectionate regard, in which I know Mrs. Eisenhower joins. *Sincerely*

[1] C. D. Jackson had written Ann Whitman to say that Payne's son-in-law, his colleague at Time Inc., was gathering congratulatory notes. Jackson had asked if the President

might send one to Payne, a dedicated "Ike" supporter (Oct. 6, 1956, AWF/A, C. D. Jackson Corr.).

[2] Eisenhower, as a major, had been assigned as personal assistant to Payne's predecessor in 1929 and later became assistant to Payne, Assistant Secretary of War, 1930–1933 (Eisenhower, *Waging Peace*, p. 29; Chandler and Galambos, *Occupation, 1945*, no. 181).

[3] Payne's sons were Groverman Blake Payne and Frederick Blake Payne.

2024   *EM, AWF, Dulles-Herter Series*

To ROBERT ANTHONY EDEN   *October 11, 1956*
Top secret

Dear Anthony:[1] Let me acknowledge the note from you which transmitted a copy of Bulganin's letter to you.[2] Truly, this is a rather forbidding letter, and it is scarcely couched in the terms which one would expect in a communication from one Head of Government to another.[3] Also, Foster tells me that Shepilov made a quite nasty speech at the United Nations Council last Monday.[4]

It is clear that the Soviets are playing hard to gain a dominant position in the Near East area, and it is likely they have developed quite a hold on Nasser.[5] This problem will probably remain with us whatever may be the results of the talks in New York. I know that Foster is working there closely with Selwyn Lloyd, and I deeply deplore the suggestions of the press both here and abroad that you and we are at cross purposes.

With warm regard, *As ever*

P.S. I got a chance, at this morning's Press Conference, to say something on how much Britain & the British mean to us.[6]

[1] The State Department drafted this message to Prime Minister Eden. Eisenhower's handwritten changes appear on the October 10 draft.

[2] Eden's October 1 letter is in State, *Foreign Relations, 1955–1957*, vol. XVI, *Suez Crisis July 26–December 31, 1956*, pp. 618–19; see also Eisenhower, *Waging Peace*, pp. 53–54.

[3] According to Eden, Bulganin had "objected to every action upon the Suez problem that the maritime powers had ever proposed or taken. The future of the canal was of little practical concern to Russia, but the Soviet Government saw an opportunity to fish in troubled waters and fish they did" (Eden, *Full Circle*, p. 555).

[4] On October 8 the Soviet Foreign Minister had accused Britain and France of "playing with fire" and said their only reason for bringing the issue before the Security Council was to obtain an excuse for subsequent action outside the United Nations. "American monopolists," Shepilov asserted, planned to take the canal away from Britain and France as well as from Egypt (*New York Times*, Oct. 9, 1956).

[5] "There is no doubt in our minds," Eden told Eisenhower, "that Nasser, whether he likes it or not, is now effectively in Russian hands, just as Mussolini was in Hitler's."

[6] Eisenhower added this postscript to the State Department draft. For the statement see *Public Papers of the Presidents: Eisenhower, 1956*, pp. 882–83. The State Department cabled this message to Eden on this same day.

To Walter Hoving   *October 11, 1956*

Dear Walter: Thanks for your suggestion.[1] Actually, I think it is traditional for the candidates of both parties to make their final appeal to
the voters, on the night before election, not on a partisan basis, but as
an appeal to the voters to get out the vote, regardless of party.[2]

With affectionate regard to Pauline, and all the best to yourself,[3] *As
ever*

P.S. In 1952 I appeared on television twice. Once was a typical
political speech in the Boston Garden. The other was the last several
minutes just before midnight when I appeared, together with Mamie
and the Nixons. At that time I contented myself merely with asking
people to vote and reminding them that they had serious questions to
answer.[4]

[1] We could not find a letter from Tiffany and Company board chairman Hoving to
Eisenhower in AWF.
[2] Eisenhower's televised election-eve speech is in *Public Papers of the Presidents: Eisenhower,
1956*, pp. 1085–89.
[3] Mrs. Hoving, the former Pauline V. Rogers.
[4] See Eisenhower, *Mandate for Change*, p. 73.

2026   *EM, AWF, Dulles-Herter Series*

To Robert Anthony Eden   *October 12, 1956*
Top secret

Dear Anthony: I was very much interested in the thoughts expressed in
your letter of October 5 and wanted to tell you promptly of my views
on the announcement you have proposed.[1]

In the first place I am in hearty agreement on the desirability of
keeping before the world the high degree of cooperation and mutual
confidence in United States-United Kingdom relations which is typ-
ified by our joint efforts in the military atomic field; this is valuable
evidence of the continuing strength of a relationship which lies at the
heart of the defense efforts of the free world.[2]

On the other hand I am sure that you are aware of a number of
sensitive issues, both in our domestic political situation and in our
relations with our other allies, which the proposed announcement
might raise. In particular I have reservations about the desirability of
such an announcement at this moment. It would seem unwise to
invite speculation and debate at this time on the delicate matters

which are the subject of your letter and risk the freezing of attitudes and positions in a way which might well impede further fruitful progress in this field.

Therefore I wonder whether you would agree to holding in abeyance the proposal which was the subject of your letter with the understanding that we would continue our study of the question and that at a later date we might again examine the advisability of proceeding.[3] *With warm regard*

---

[1] Eisenhower's letter to Eden is reprinted in State, *Foreign Relations, 1955–1957*, vol. XX, *Regulation of Armaments; Atomic Energy*, p. 435. We were unable to find Eden's letter in AWF.

[2] Eisenhower wanted to keep secret the retrofitting of Royal Air Force (RAF) planes with atomic capabilities. Acting Secretary of State Hoover had advised him that an announcement so close to the election might lead to further congressional restrictions on atomic cooperation with the British. Hoover also feared that publicity would harm relations with Canada, "where we have treated similar types of cooperation as a highly confidential matter," and with other NATO allies "who are increasingly concerned about being put in a second-class status from a military point of view as compared with their Anglo-Saxon allies" (Hoover to Eisenhower, Oct. 12, 1956, AWF/D-H).

[3] Eisenhower changed "Sincerely" to "With warm regard" but made no other changes in the State Department draft of this letter (Hoover to Eisenhower, Oct. 12, 1956, AWF/D-H). The State Department would cable this message to London on October 15 (Howe to Goodpaster, Oct. 15, 1956, AWF/I: Eden). Eden would reply, "In view of what you say, I accept that we should leave this in abeyance for the time being" (Oct. 29, 1956, AWF/I: Eden).

2027   *EM, AWF, Administration Series*

To Arthur Sherwood Flemming   *October 12, 1956*
Memorandum

I appreciate receiving a report from you stating that it would be possible under the authority of the Defense Production Act for the Government to enter into contractual arrangements with United States ship yard owners for the construction of large tankers—up to the total called for by the Government's full emergency requirements —with the understanding that the Government would acquire these tankers in those cases where private ship owners did not purchase them.[1]

I am directing, therefore, that you take steps immediately to bring together representatives of the National Petroleum Council to meet with the Secretary of State, the Secretary of the Treasury, the Secretary of Defense, the Secretary of the Interior, and the Secretary of Commerce, to consider plans that will be helpful in assuring the efficiency and adequacy of the distribution of petroleum supplies in the foreseeable future in the free world.[2]

These plans should, so far as the interests of the United States are thereby served, provide for the building in United States ship yards of a sufficient number of large tankers to help supplement existing means of distribution and, if necessary, to help serve as an alternative in the transportation of oil in the free world, particularly from the Middle East.[3] The Government's commitments in these regards should be limited as indicated in the first paragraph above. In addition, the Federal Government might, whenever necessary, provide funds for rehabilitation and modification of American ship yards so long as these projects can be undertaken on a self-liquidating basis.

The study should proceed, of course, on the assumption that plans which are developed are to be consistent with the requests that you have made to oil importers to voluntarily keep imports of crude oil into this country at a level where they do not exceed significantly the proportion that imports bore to the production of domestic crude oil in 1954.[4]

The results of these deliberations should be reported to me as soon as practicable.[5]

[1] Defense Mobilization Director Flemming's memo of October 6 is in AWF/A, along with a note from Eisenhower to the effect that he had redictated the memo "hurriedly" and that it was not in final form (Eisenhower to Flemming, Oct. 12, 1956, AWF/A). See also no. 834.

[2] The National Petroleum Council was the industry advisory group appointed by the government.

[3] See no. 2014.

[4] Flemming had previously met with the President and an industry representative to discuss the decline in domestic oil exploration (Goodpaster, Memorandum of Conference, Sept. 12, 1956, AWF/D).

[5] There is no record of a written report in AWF.

2028   *EM, AWF, Name Series*

To Edgar Newton Eisenhower   *October 12, 1956*
Personal

Dear Ed: It occurs to me that my trip to the Northwest could possibly create some embarrassing moments growing out of the possibility that you still hold a grudge against Governor Langlie with respect to the nomination of Mr. Hamley to the Federal Court.[1] Of course if you bear a grudge, it should be against me—no one else.

Under present plans I shall meet and talk with Governor Langlie while I am in Seattle. I understand he is not coming to Tacoma. However, while we are in Seattle, it is altogether likely that you, the Governor and I may be together either in private or in public. Should you feel any embarrassment about this possibility, I can of course arrange that it does not happen. However, I do hope that you have no really strong personal feelings in this matter and that you will find no difficulty being cordial to the Governor while he is with us.[2]

I write you thus frankly because, if you have any reservations about it, I should carefully lay out plans so that the two of you do not meet.

I trust that the addition of Mamie and her companion to the party will not inconvenience you and Lucy materially.[3] As to the sergeant who looks after my things, if he could stay in the apartment over the garage, as you mentioned to Tom Stephens, that would be wonderful.[4] However, if you need that space, Sergeant Woodward can always room downtown for the night and be back early in the morning.[5] I am anxious to cause you the least possible bother.

My love to Lucy, and to Janis and her family.[6] *As ever*

[1] Eisenhower was referring to Governor Arthur Langlie of Washington and to Judge Frederick G. Hamley. For background on Edgar Eisenhower's opposition to the nomination of Hamley to the U.S. Court of Appeals for the Ninth Circuit—a nomination which was apparently sponsored by Langlie—see nos. 1807 and 1812.

[2] Edgar would telegraph Eisenhower on October 15 that the "Seattle meeting will not be embarassing because I have learned that in politics you sleep with a lot of different characters" (AWF/N). Edgar would meet Langlie at the airport when the President arrived in Seattle on October 16, and again on October 18, when the President spoke in Tacoma with Langlie on the platform (President's daily appointments). For the text of Eisenhower's campaign speeches while in Washington from October 16–18 see *Public Papers of the Presidents: Eisenhower, 1956*, pp. 940–48, 950–55.

[3] Dwight and Mamie Eisenhower would stay at the house of Edgar and Lucy Eisenhower on the night of October 17 (President's daily appointments; Eisenhower to Edgar and Lucy Eisenhower, Oct. 20, 1956, AWF/D).

[4] Thomas Edwin Stephens, the President's appointments secretary.

[5] Sergeant Woodward was a White House aide.

[6] Janis Eisenhower Causin, the President's niece.

2029 EM, AWF, Name Series

To Dan Hendrickson *October 12, 1956*
Personal

Dear Mr. Hendrickson: I have read with interest your long letter of October second.[1] I read with special attention your comments on the political situation both in Ohio and New Jersey.[2]

As you say, the "political bug" seems to be an indestructible thing once it really gets into a man's blood. While I feel certain that I have never fallen a victim to this particular germ, I do realize that it is very prevalent among most people who started their political careers younger than I did.

However, you yourself pointed out how satisfied Tom Dewey seems to be in his present work in civil life.[3] Beyond this, he is still doing very valuable and interesting work in the political field. I am quite sure we have no more effective political speaker in the Republican stable than he is. In addition, he retains a very great influence in the state and national circles of the Party. I merely point this out so that no matter what your brother finally decides to do, he does not need to desert completely political activities.

With warm regard, *Sincerely*

[1] Dan Hendrickson was the brother of Robert Hendrickson, who had served as U.S. Ambassador to New Zealand since 1955. A financial scandal had destroyed Robert Hendrickson's chances of reelection to the Senate from New Jersey.

[2] Dan Hendrickson had written of his brother's continuing ambition to run for governor or senator from New Jersey and of the apparent success of the Republican gubernatorial campaign on themes calculated to appeal to independent voters and Democrats (Oct. 2, 1956, AWF/N).

[3] Hendrickson had also suggested that Eisenhower might want to appoint his brother to some other diplomatic or judicial post; if he did not get an appointment, he would return to private law practice, as did former New York Governor Thomas E. Dewey. Eisenhower had already decided not to appoint Hendrickson (see no. 1242).

2030   *EM, AWF, Name Series, Newcombe Corr.*

To WALTER F. O'MALLEY   *October 12, 1956*
Personal

Dear Mr. O'Malley:[1] I must say that the way the Yankee pitchers were going the last four days, it didn't seem that they could have been beaten by a team made up of all the "immortals" of the game.[2] Nevertheless, I was hopeful up to the very last that the Dodgers would rally.

One of the men that I felt really badly about was Don Newcombe.[3] With a record of twenty-seven wins in the season—a record that did so much to bring your team into the Series, it was a pity that he could not come through with a sparkling game during those seven days.

I have written him a little note, which I enclose herewith in an unsealed envelope.[4] It is just possible that he might be the kind that does not like an expression of friendly interest in such circumstances. Consequently, I request that you read the enclosed note and then use your own judgment as to whether or not to deliver it. By no means would I want to remind him of something that he possibly may be trying to forget.

With warm regard, *Sincerely*

[1] O'Malley (LL.B. Fordham University 1930) was president of the Brooklyn Dodgers National League Baseball Club. On October 3 Eisenhower and members of the Cabinet and White House staff had been O'Malley's guests at the opening game of the World Series at Ebbets Field in Brooklyn (see Eisenhower to O'Malley, Oct. 4, 1956, AWF/D; and *New York Times*, Oct. 4, 1956). O'Malley's reply of December 12 is in AWF/N, Newcombe Corr.

[2] The Yankees won the series, four games to three, on October 11. See the President's congratulatory letter (Oct. 10) to Yankee pitcher Don Larsen, who had pitched a perfect game (no opposing batter reached base) in game five (AWF/D).

[3] Newcombe led all National League pitchers with a record of 27–7 in the regular season. In the World Series, however, he pitched in two games, had an earned run average of 21.21, and was credited with one loss—the seventh and deciding game.

[4] The message of this same date is in AWF/N. Newcombe's thank-you letter (Oct. 11) is in *ibid*. On December 12 O'Malley would write Eisenhower that the note to Newcombe "made all the difference in the world in his attitude" (AWF/N, Newcombe Corr.).

2031   *EM, AWF, Name Series*

To Sigurd Stanton Larmon   *October 13, 1956*

Dear Sig: From the tenor of the telegrams and messages we have received here this morning, your idea about "Citizens Ask the President" was a terrific success.[1] I send you herewith copies of the telegrams that we received early this morning—I know you will be pleased.

It occurs to me that such a program might be a very fine thing for Dick Nixon, since one of the criticisms about him is that he does not like and understand people. The very mechanics of such a program ought to correct this impression.[2]

Won't you please congratulate all your people who worked on the program?

With warm regard, *As ever*

[1] Larmon, the chairman and president of Young and Rubicam, a major advertising agency, was one of Eisenhower's media advisers. "The People Ask the President," a show in which Eisenhower was questioned by supporters, aired on October 12, 1956 (*Public Papers of the Presidents: Eisenhower, 1956*, pp. 903–21; *New York Times*, Oct. 13, 1956). On the role of television in the 1956 campaign see Allen, *Eisenhower and the Mass Media*, pp. 86–149. See also the following document.

[2] Larmon would reply that the President "seemed to enjoy every minute" and deserved

credit for the program's success. Larmon would mention that Nixon had answered questions from a group of college editors later that week at Cornell and that "he did a fine job" (Larmon to Eisenhower, Oct. 19, 1956, AWF/N). After that session, however, according to some writers, Nixon had complained to a member of his staff that "you put me on with those shitty-ass liberal sons of bitches, you tried to destroy me in front of thirty million people" (Ambrose, *Nixon*, p. 418; Fawn M. Brodie, *Richard Nixon, the Shaping of His Character* [New York, 1981], p. 425; David Halberstam, *The Powers That Be* [New York, 1979], p. 332).

2032   *EM, WHCF, Official File 6*

To Leonard Wood Hall   *October 13, 1956*

Dear Len: Herewith copies of telegrams received this morning. Careful reading indicates that the *type* of program we put on last evening has a great appeal. It might be a good idea to use another half hour of your television time in the same way. For example, Nixon might do a lot of good for us on such a program.[1]

Everyone who heard the first part of Larson's speech last night was absolutely enthusiastic about it and was bitterly disappointed that it was cut off the air in the middle.[2] I do not see how the "Citizens" group made the mistake of inviting me in at a time when it was bound to interfere with that talk on television. It was a bad waste of money.

I suggest that we have Larson give the identical speech again before some meeting where he can get it all off. I have already had one Democrat for Eisenhower write in and ask me for a number of copies of the talk, which he wants to distribute. You might think of doing this also. *As ever*

[1] See the preceding document.
[2] Under Secretary of Labor Arthur Larson. On November 9 Eisenhower would appoint Larson Director of the United States Information Agency.

2033   *EM, AWF, Name Series*

To Virgil M. Pinkley   *October 13, 1956*

Dear Virgil: I am delighted that you liked the Pittsburgh speech—and in general the way the campaign is going.[1] Actually, I find this business of relying on the record of the Administration much less distasteful (and I am speaking purely personally) than I did the type of campaign we had to wage in 1952.[2] I am proud of what we have done, while at the same time I am the first to admit there are a great many problems still to be tackled.

Thank you for all your suggestions. I have gotten a copy of General Kuter's talk—it is good for the public to hear from someone else, other than me, the real facts.[3]

With warm regard, *As ever*

[1] The reference is to the "Address at the Hunt Armory," *Public Papers of the Presidents: Eisenhower, 1956*, pp. 872–80.

[2] On the 1952 campaign see Galambos, *NATO and the Campaign of 1952*.

[3] Pinkley had quoted a speech given on October 10 by General Laurence Sherman Kuter (Commander, Far Eastern Air Force) before the World Affairs Council. Kuter contrasted the buildup of Communist air forces with Communist calls for disarmament (Oct. 10, AWF/N, Pinkley Corr. An excerpt of Kuter's speech is also in *ibid.*).

2034   *EM, AWF, Dulles-Herter Series*

To JOHN FOSTER DULLES   *October 13, 1956*

Dear Foster: Thank you for your note. Perhaps it is just as well that when we are together our talk must be of Suez or Morocco or South Vietnam. Because I assure you that I am even more tongue-tied than you (and sometimes I blame my inadequacy on my Germanic origin) in trying to tell *you* the rewards I have received from our association.[1]

At any rate, much appreciation and warm personal regard, *As ever*

[1] In a birthday letter (dated October 14, but mailed early) Dulles had written: "I can never adequately express the measure of deep satisfaction which I have had from working so intimately with and under you during these past four years" (AWF/D-H).

2035   *EM, AWF, International Series: Eden*

To ROBERT ANTHONY EDEN   *October 14, 1956*

Dear Anthony: I am more than grateful for the good wishes for my birthday that you extend on behalf of Clarissa and yourself.[1] These "milestones" seem to creep up with ever-increasing frequency.

All you say about our friendship is heartily reciprocated by me.[2] I am always grateful for the understanding you have of our problems— and I know that nothing can ever seriously mar either our personal friendship or the respect that our government and peoples have for each other.

With all your knowledge of our American customs, I venture that you are still constantly amazed by some of the activities.[3] I am.

With warm personal regard, and again my thanks, *As ever*

[1] Eden's handwritten message is in AWF/I: Eden. Mrs. Eden was the former Clarissa Spencer.
[2] "Our friendship remains one of my greatest rewards," Eden had written.
[3] Eden said he did not "envy" Eisenhower the campaign. And, he added, "it is good to kick off the days on the calendar!"

2036   *EM, AWF, Name Series*

To ROBERT WINSHIP WOODRUFF   *October 14, 1956*

Dear Bob: This morning (we work on Sundays *and* birthday now) I found on my breakfast tray the one perfect rose that Ann tells me you specifically requested, together with your greeting.[1] It started the day off cheerfully and I have managed not to lose my temper once—and in view of the forthcoming speeches, that, I insist, is an accomplishment that does credit to all my sixty-six years and to your thoughtfulness.[2]

My birthday always reminds me of *your* wedding aniversary.[3] I know Mamie joins me in all the congratulations in the world, and in affectionate regard to you and Nell. *As ever*

[1] We have been unable to find a written greeting or request in EM.
[2] On the President's activities during the final weeks of the campaign see the President's daily appointments.
[3] The Woodruffs would celebrate their forty-fourth wedding anniversary on October 17.

2037   *Smith Papers*

To WALTER BEDELL SMITH   *October 14, 1956*

Dear Bedell: Last night "Old Yeller" (that I found on my bedside table) engrossed me so that I stayed up long past my normal bedtime. As you well know, I am a real fan of stories of those days and that part of our country.[1]

I don't know how you always seem to find just the thing that pleases me—and since I have long ago given up trying to get people to *forget* my birthdays I can only say "thank you" for the book, and, particularly, for your accompanying note.[2]

With warm regard, *As ever*

1 The book (written by Fred Gipson) had been so placed at Smith's request. The setting of the story stretched from Texas to Abilene, and from the days following the Civil War through the early days of the cattle drives (Schulz to Weaver, Oct. 12, 1956, WHCF/PPF 1-L). When Eisenhower had finished reading the book, he would thank Smith again (Oct. 25, 1956, *ibid.*).
2 We have been unable to find Smith's note in EM.

2038

EM, AWF,
Ann Whitman Diary Series

MEMORANDUM FOR THE RECORD

October 15, 1956

Top secret

The Secretary of State, accompanied by Mr. Hoover and Mr. Rountree of his office, came to see me about the deteriorating situation in the Israel-Jordan area.[1]

It seems to be taken internationally as a foregone conclusion that Jordan is breaking up, and of course all the surrounding countries will be anxious to get their share of the wreckage, including Israel. In fact, there is some suspicion that the recent savage blows of the Israel border armies against the strong points within Jordan territory are intended to hasten this process of dissolution.[2]

On the other side of the picture, there is some indication that Britain is really serious in her announced intention of honoring her Pact with Jordan, which requires her to help defend Jordan in the case of outside invasion.[3]

Should this occur, we would have Britain in the curious position of helping to defend one of the Arab countries, while at the same time she is engaged in a quarrel—which sometimes threatens to break out into war—with Egypt over the Suez question.

All this brings to the fore one particular thing we must bear in mind. It is this: As of this moment we are dealing with the existing situation—that is, with Jordan enjoying the rights of a sovereign country. At the same time, in view of the possible disintegration of the Jordanian government, we must be ready to deal with the situation in which the people and territory of that country would be absorbed by others.

For the moment we can deal only with the first problem.

The Secretary of State is having a long conference with the Israeli Ambassador to this country, Mr. Eban. The Ambassador is about to return to his own country and is visiting Foster to discuss some of the factors in the above problem.[4]

I have told the Secretary of State that he should make very clear to the Israelis that they must stop these attacks against the borders of Jordan. If they continue them, and particularly if they carry them on to the point of trying to take over and hold the territory west of the Jordan River, they will certainly be condemned by the United Nations, and not only Arab opinion but all world opinion will be brought to bear against this little country. Moreover, should there be a United Nations Resolution condemning Israel, there will be no brake or deterrent possible against any Soviet move into the area to help the Arab countries. They could bring considerable forces in under the guise that they were carrying out a United Nations mandate, the ultimate effect of which would be to Sovietize the whole region, including Israel.

There has been some disposition to believe that Ben Gurion's obviously aggressive attitude is inspired, at this moment, by three things:

(*a*). His desire to take advantage of the gradual deterioration in Jordan and to be ready to occupy and lay claim to a goodly portion of the area of that nation;

(*b*). The preoccupation of Egypt and the Western powers in the Suez question, which would tend both to minimize the possibility that Egypt would enter a war against him promptly, while at the same time it would impede Britain's capability of reinforcing Jordan.[5]

(*c*). His belief that the current political campaign in the United States will keep this government from taking a strong stand against any aggressive move he might make.[6]

Secretary Dulles will warn the Ambassador that while, of course, we would hate to create misunderstandings and needless passion in this country over this question, at this moment he should inform his government that no considerations of partisan politics will keep this government from pursuing a course dictated by justice and international decency in the circumstances, and that it will remain true to its pledges under the United Nations.

Ben Gurion should not make any grave mistakes based upon his belief that winning a domestic election is as important to us as preserving and protecting the interests of the United Nations and other nations of the free world in that region. The Secretary is to point out, moreover, that even if Ben Gurion, in an aggressive move, should get an immediate advantage in the region, that on a long term basis aggression on his part cannot fail to bring catastrophe and such friends as he would have left in the world, no matter how powerful, could not do anything about it.

Foster will make this attitude clear and unmistakable to Mr. Eban.

At the same time I have Foster's promise to have ready a policy or plan that would guide our action in the event that the dissolution of Jordan would actually take place and thus create a new situation in the world.[7]

Appendix: It is believed that one of the recent Israeli raids against Jordan involved two or three battalions of infantry, artillery, and jet airplanes. Incidentally, our high-flying reconnaisance planes have shown that Israel has obtained some 60 of the French Mystere pursuit planes, when there had been reported the transfer of only 24. Jordan has no aviation.[8]

[1] This memorandum, along with Assistant Secretary of State William M. Rountree's minutes of the meeting, is reprinted in State, *Foreign Relations, 1955–1957*, vol. XVI, *Suez Crisis July 26–December 31, 1956*, pp. 722–26; see also Eisenhower, *Waging Peace*, pp. 676–77.

[2] See *ibid.*, p. 56. Eisenhower was probably referring to the political turmoil in Jordan following the December 1955 riots and the dismissal of British officers from the Arab Legion (see no. 1681). The Israeli threat to Jordan was "a masterful plan of deception" to draw attention from Egypt, the real object of the attack. On October 10 Israel had launched a large scale raid on Jordan and reportedly had inflicted one hundred Jordanian casualties (Issac Alteras, *Eisenhower and Israel: U.S.-Israeli Relations 1953–1960* [Gainesville, Fla., 1993], p. 212; see also Moshe Dayan, *Diary of the Sinai Campaign* [London, 1966], pp. 43–57).

[3] The "pact" was the Anglo-Jordanian treaty of 1948.

[4] See no. 2046. One hour after this meeting with the President, Dulles would meet with Israeli Ambassador Abba Eban (State, *Foreign Relations, 1955–1957*, vol. XVI, *Suez Crisis July 26–December 31, 1956*, pp. 727–33).

[5] For developments see nos. 2048 and 2068.

[6] For Eisenhower's determination to ignore domestic political pressures in his policy towards Israel see no. 2063.

[7] On October 21 Jordanian voters would give pro-Nasser Arab nationalists a parliamentary majority. The new government would soon announce its intention of abrogating the Anglo-Jordanian defense treaty and would sign a defense pact with Egypt and Syria on October 24 (State, *Foreign Relations, 1955–1957*, vol. XIII, *Near East: Jordan-Yemen*, pp. 57–58, 593–94). For background see Uriel Dann, *King Hussein and the Challenge of Arab Radicalism, Jordan, 1955–1967* (Oxford, 1989), pp. 21–38; Kamal Salibi, *The Modern History of Jordan* (London, 1993), pp. 185–92; Alteras, *Eisenhower and Israel*, pp. 207–12.

[8] The French had agreed as early as June 1956 to supply the Israelis with seventy-two Mystere fighters and forty Super Sherman tanks. The first fighter arrived in Israel on August 18 (Kunz, *The Economic Diplomacy of the Suez Crisis*, p. 163). For the French representations regarding the sale of the Mystere jets see State, *Foreign Relations, 1955–1957*, vol. XVI, *Suez Crisis July 26–December 31, 1956*, pp. 7–8.

2039   *EM, AWF, Name Series*

TO JAMES FREDERICK GAULT   *October 15, 1956*

Dear Jimmy: I am grateful to you for never forgetting one of my anniversaries, even when it comes to a sixty-sixth birthday![1] Despite my personal belief that there is no "celebration" on such an occasion, I must say that people everywhere combined to make the occasion one of the happiest I can remember.

As far as my health is concerned, I truly feel as well as I have in a long time. Despite the trials and tribulations of the political campaign—and the never-ending official work—I seem astonishingly free of fatigue these days.[2]

With warm regard, *As ever*

---

[1] Gault's October 10 letter is in AWF/N.
[2] Eisenhower's longtime friend had remarked on the "heartwarming" reports of the President's good health.

2040   EM, WHCF,
                                                        Official File 138 New York

To ARTHUR HAYS SULZBERGER   *October 16, 1956*
Personal

Dear Arthur: Of course I am glad that, after weighing available evidence, you could point a finger at this Administration.[1]

I was up early enough this morning to read your article carefully before I start off on my Western trip, leaving here at 8:40.[2] In listing some of the things on which you disagreed with me, I have the feeling that one of us is laboring under some misunderstanding.[3]

When this campaign is out of the way—and especially if I am to continue in this position—I hope you will come down some day before the first of the year and spend a couple hours with me. I should like to get the reasons lying behind some of your judgments.[4] In the meantime, I am grateful.

With warm regard, *As ever*

---

[1] The *New York Times* had endorsed Eisenhower for president on October 16, stating that "despite disappointments, there is much in the record of the Eisenhower Administration that is of real and lasting value to the country." Sulzberger was president and publisher of the *Times*.
[2] The President would start a five-day campaign trip on this date.
[3] The *Times* (Oct. 16) had criticized Eisenhower for his "failure to support some of his own measures more vigorously," for his failure to "stand up to Mr. McCarthy," and for his "handling of the security issue in the civil service." The *Times* also disagreed with the President on TVA, on the appointment of Wilson as Secretary of Defense, and on some of the actions of Secretary of State Dulles. The paper was, moreover, sharply critical of Richard Nixon.
[4] Eisenhower would meet with Sulzberger on January 3, 1957.

To NIKOLAI ALEKSANDROVICH BULGANIN   *October 21, 1956*

Dear Mr. Chairman: I have the letter which your Embassy handed me through Secretary Dulles on October nineteenth. I regret to find that this letter departs from accepted international practice in a number of respects.[1]

First, the sending of your note in the midst of a national election campaign of which you take cognizance expressing the support of "certain prominent public figures in the United States" constitutes an interference by a foreign nation in our internal affairs of a kind which, if indulged in by an Ambassador, would lead to his being declared persona non grata in accordance with long-established custom.[2]

Second, having delivered a lengthy communication in the Russian language, you have published it before it could be carefully translated and delivered to me. Because of this, and of the necessity of placing the facts accurately before the public, I am compelled to release this reply immediately.[3]

Third, your statement with respect to the Secretary of State is not only unwarranted, but is personally offensive to me.[4]

Fourth, you seem to impugn my own sincerity.

However, I am not instructing the Department of State to return your letter to your Embassy. This is not because I am tolerant of these departures from accepted international practice, but because I still entertain the hope that direct communications between us may serve the cause of peace.

You and I have exchanged a number of letters since our meeting in Geneva on the reduction of armaments and related matters in our effort to make progress toward the goal of peace. I hope that that practice may be resumed in accordance with accepted standards.[5]

The United States has for a long time been intensively examining, evaluating and planning dependable means of stopping the arms race and reducing and controlling armaments.[6] These explorations include the constant examination and evaluation of nuclear tests.

To be effective, and not simply a mirage, all these plans require systems of inspection and control, both of which your government has steadfastly refused to accept. Even my "Open Skies" proposal of mutual aerial inspection, suggested as a first step, you rejected.[7]

However, though disappointed, we are not discouraged. We will continue unrelenting in our efforts to attain these goals. We will close no doors which might open a secure way to serve humanity.

We shall entertain and seriously evaluate all proposals from any source which seem to have merit, and we shall constantly seek for ourselves formulations which might dependably remove the atomic menace. *Sincerely*

[1] Bulganin had written a public letter supporting Democratic nominee Adlai E. Stevenson's proposals for a ban on nuclear testing. Though he did not name Stevenson, he did allude to the election campaign and reiterated the Soviet government's support for an "unconditional prohibition" of nuclear weapons. He argued, as Stevenson had, that concealment of nuclear testing would have been virtually impossible and that limits on nuclear testing should be separated from other disarmament issues (Bulganin to Eisenhower, Oct. 17, 1956, AWF/I: Bulganin). For background see Hewlett and Holl, *Atoms for Peace and War*, pp. 371–73. Dulles had told Ambassador Walter Bedell Smith that the letter, which implied Communist support for the Democrats, was the "kiss of death" for Stevenson (Telephone conversation, Smith and Dulles, Oct. 21, 1956, Dulles Papers, Telephone Conversations).

[2] Stevenson's call for a test ban had become the centerpiece of his presidential campaign and had been attacked by Vice-President Nixon as "catastrophic nonsense" (*New York Times*, Oct. 17, 1956). A draft of this letter (Oct. 21), with Eisenhower's handwritten emendations, is in AWF/Drafts. Eisenhower had substituted the words "internal" for "international" and "custom" for "American tradition" (*ibid.*).

[3] This paragraph was added after the earlier draft.

[4] Bulganin had specifically accused Secretary Dulles of distortions and "direct attacks against the Soviet Union and its peace-loving foreign policy" (Bulganin to Eisenhower, Oct. 17, 1956, AWF/I: Bulganin). Eisenhower had added to his earlier draft the word "completely" before "unwarranted."

[5] See nos. 1744, 1760, and 1765.

[6] Eisenhower's earlier draft had referred to "realistic" means. Eisenhower substituted the word "dependable."

[7] On Eisenhower's "Open Skies" proposal see no. 1523; Eisenhower, *Mandate for Change*, pp. 520–22; State, *Foreign Relations, 1955–1957*, vol. XX, *Regulation of Armaments; Atomic Energy*, pp. 162–64.

2042   *EM, AWF, Drafts Series*

To Edwin Palmer Hoyt   *October 22, 1956*
Personal

Dear Ep:[1] Mamie and I were delighted to see you and Mrs. Hoyt at Stapleton on Saturday.[2] I am grateful, if I have not mentioned it before, for the support accorded in this campaign by the Denver Post. Someday, when we both have time, I'd like to discuss with you the reasons why so many of the so-called "intellectual" magazines find so little merit in what we are trying to do.[3]

With warm regard, *Sincerely*

[1] Eisenhower made extensive deletions on the original draft of this letter to *Denver Post* publisher Hoyt (AWF/Drafts).

[2] The President had been at Stapleton Airport in Denver on October 20 as part of a Western campaign trip (see no. 2040).

[3] On October 21 the *Denver Post* had reprinted an article by Palmer Hoyt ("My Choice Is Mr. Eisenhower!") from the October 20, 1956, issue of *The Nation*. On October 28 the *Denver Post* would publish an editorial supporting Eisenhower for president: "But we believe that when the heat of this campaign has cooled, most Americans will recognize that Dwight David Eisenhower has been good for America during the last four years. And they will be grateful that he has the restored health and the sustained devotion to serve for four years more."

2043   *EM, AWF, Name Series*

To George Catlett Marshall   *October 25, 1956*

I am delighted to learn that you are today receiving the Woodrow Wilson Award.[1] It gives me another opportunity to reaffirm the admiration, respect and esteem that I have always held for you. In 1948 I tried to express my feelings, thinking of you mainly as an outstanding war leader.[2] But I could well have added what I then felt and feel now, that though I have met all or most of the so-called prominent and great in the world, you head my list of those who, I believe, deserve the most from their country and from the free world, and who have provided the rest of us with an exemplary standard of service.

Mamie joins me in warmest felicitations to you and Mrs. Marshall on this day, and in best wishes for continued health and happiness.

[1] General Marshall, who was approaching his seventy-sixth birthday, accepted the citation at his office in the Pentagon (*New York Times*, Oct. 26, 1956). Marshall's October 27 thank-you letter to Eisenhower is in AWF/N.

[2] Eisenhower may have been referring to the letter (accompanying a limited edition of *Crusade in Europe*) he had sent Marshall in November 1948 (see Galambos, *Columbia University*, no. 246).

2044   *EM, AWF, Ann Whitman Diary Series*

Diary   *October 26, 1956*

Warned both the Chairman of the Chiefs of Staff and the Director of the Central Intelligence Agency to be unusually watchful and alert during the crisis occasioned by the Hungarian revolt.[1]

[1] Eisenhower had anticipated the possibility of unrest in Eastern Europe in the wake of Soviet Communist Party First Secretary Nikita Khrushchev's de-Stalinization cam-

paign; see no. 1813. On October 19 the Polish government had successfully defied Soviet threats to invade its territory and to crush a reformist movement there. The Polish success had encouraged dissidents in neighboring Hungary, where on October 23 Hungarian police had fired on a large crowd demanding the selection of the former premier and liberal reformer Imre Nagy as head of a new government. The protesters also called for the withdrawal of Soviet troops from Hungary and the enactment of political and economic changes that would have reversed many of the agricultural and social policies imposed by the Stalinist-dominated Hungarian Communist party (see State, *Foreign Relations, 1955–1957,* vol. XXV, *Eastern Europe* [1990], pp. 198–209, 263–64, 272–73, 280–86, 295–99; Eisenhower, *Waging Peace,* pp. 58–60, 62–64; Ferenc A. Vali, *Rift and Revolt in Hungary* [Cambridge, Mass., 1961], pp. 266–70, 281–82; and *New York Times,* Oct. 24, 1956). On that night Soviet troops entered Budapest, where they attempted to suppress the insurrection. As street fighting escalated on October 24, the Central Committee appointed Nagy as Premier.

On October 25 Eisenhower had issued a statement deploring the intervention of the Soviet military as "an occupation of Hungary by the forces of an alien government for its own purposes." "The heart of America," he said, "goes out to the people of Hungary" (see *Public Papers of The Presidents: Eisenhower, 1956,* pp. 1018–19). On October 26, after meeting with the National Security Council to review events in Hungary, the President directed the NSC to prepare a comprehensive analysis of the developments in East Europe and the possible courses of action that the United States should consider. Eisenhower also discussed with Dulles the possibility of calling for United Nations action. The President told Dulles that he did "not think we should walk in this alone" as it would appear that the United States was acting for internal political reasons (see Dulles and Lodge, Telephone conversation, Oct. 24, 1956, Dulles to Eisenhower, and Allen Dulles to Dulles, Telephone conversations, Oct. 25, 1956, Dulles Papers, Telephone Conversations; Condit, *History of the Joint Chiefs of Staff,* vol. VI, *1955–1956,* pp. 122–29, 298, n. 56; and NSC meeting minutes, Oct. 26, 1956, AWF/NSC). On October 27 the United States, in conjunction with Britain and France, would request the Security Council to place the Hungarian situation on its agenda (see Condit, *History of the Joint Chiefs of Staff,* vol. VI, *1955–1956,* p. 125; see also Eisenhower, *Waging Peace,* pp. 58–70). For developments see nos. 2055 and 2067.

2045

EM, AWF, Name Series

To Francis Joseph Spellman

October 26, 1956

Your Eminence: Recently Dick Nixon told me of the very cordial reception he had at the annual Alfred E. Smith Dinner.[1] He spoke with particular gratification of your great courtesy to him.

I write this note, firstly, to thank you for the honor you did to a young man whom I consider to be a very splendid American. Secondly, I want to felicitate you on the great success of your Dinner, which seems each year to be a more notable event. Finally, it just seemed to me that it had been such a long time since I had communicated with you directly (I do hear of you often from Bernard Shanley) that I wanted to send along my very best wishes and warm greetings.[2]

When I told Mamie of my intention to drop you a note this morning, she was insistent that I include her affectionate regard along with my own. *Sincerely*

P.S. I most deeply regret the attempt to drag the name of His Holiness the Pope into our political campaign.[3] I assure you that in my own public utterances no reference whatsoever will be made to this.

[1] At Cardinal Spellman's invitation, Nixon had spoken on the subject of civil rights to a $100-a-plate dinner to raise money for the Alfred E. Smith Memorial Hospital. Nixon told the group that "the greatness of America lies in the fact that the nation as a whole has fought to eliminate these injustices and to seek ever more forcefully our ideal of equality." The full text of Nixon's speech is reprinted in the *New York Times*, Oct. 19, 1956.

[2] Bernard Shanley was Special Counsel to the President.

[3] On October 20, in an appeal for a world agreement on the cessation of H-bomb tests, Democratic vice-presidential candidate Estes Kefauver had invoked the name of Pope Pius XII, saying that the Pope had called an international agreement on a test ban "an obligation of nations and their leaders" (*New York Times*, Oct. 21, 1956). In his 1955 Christmas Day message the Pope had called for the renunciation of experimentation and use of nuclear weapons, and control of armaments in general (*ibid.*, Dec. 25, 1955; see also no. 1968).

2046   *EM, AWF, International Series: Israel*

To David Ben Gurion   *October 27, 1956*
Cable. Secret

Dear Mr. Prime Minister: I received your message dated October 20.[1] I have taken very careful note of the reasons you advance against the movement of Iraqi troops into Jordan which you had initially thought would be a constructive step.[2] I am not sure that I agree with your present position but in any event and so far as I am informed there has been no entry of Iraqi troops into Jordan. I hope that you look upon the suspense of that movement as a contribution to peace in the area. I must frankly express my concern at reports of heavy mobilization on your side, a move which I fear will only increase the tension which you indicate you would like to see reduced.[3]

These are days of great strain. Only statesmanship of a high order and self-restraint by all parties can assure that the tensions in the Middle East can be controlled and prevented from becoming a cause for a breach of the peace in that area and in others affected by the ramifications of those tensions.

I remain confident that only a peaceful and moderate approach will genuinely improve the situation and I renew the plea which was communicated to you through Secretary Dulles that there be no forcible initiative on the part of your Government which would endanger the peace and the growing friendship between our two countries. *Sincerely*

¹ In his letter of October 20 Ben Gurion had urged Eisenhower to approach other nations to forestall the entry of Iraqi troops into Jordan. Such a deployment, he said, "would be the first stage in the disruption of the status quo" and might start a war (Ben Gurion to Eisenhower, Oct. 20, 1956, AWF/I: Israel; State, *Foreign Relations, 1955–1957*, vol. XVI, *Suez Crisis July 26–December 31, 1956*, p. 763). Eisenhower had assumed the note needed no reply but asked Dulles to draft one if necessary (Dulles to Eisenhower, n.d., AWF/I: Israel; Eisenhower to Dulles, Oct. 22, 1956, AWF/D-H). After Dulles and Assistant Secretary Rountree informed Eisenhower of a possible Israeli move against Jordan, the President approved this message for dispatch (Goodpaster, Memorandum of Conference, Oct. 27, 1956, Dulles Papers, White House Memoranda Series). For background see no. 2038.
² The alleged Iraqi deployment may have been a rumor concocted by Israeli intelligence (see Dayan, *Diary of the Sinai Campaign*, p. 70). Israeli Ambassador Abba Eban has written that he was "puzzled" at instructions to play up the conflict on Israel's eastern frontier in his talks with Dulles (Abba Solomon Eban, *Abba Eban: An Autobiography* [New York, 1977], p. 210; State, *Foreign Relations, 1955–1957*, vol. XVI, *Suez Crisis July 26–December 31, 1956*, pp. 808, 814; Alteras, *Eisenhower and Israel*, p. 218).
³ For developments see no. 2048.

2047   *EM, AWF, DDE Diaries Series*

To Ray Charles Bliss   *October 27, 1956*

Dear Ray: As we enter the last days of the 1956 campaign, I want to emphasize again the tremendously important part our precinct workers will play in the coming election.¹

Ohio, with more than nine thousand good citizens working for our party at the precinct level, can be an inspiration to every State in the nation. It is my earnest hope that these dedicated men and women will maintain their energy and vigilance right through election day. I know that with a clear understanding of Administration accomplishments, and with our citizens going to the polls in great numbers, there can be no doubt about the decision in Ohio and in the nation on November sixth.²

I wish it were possible for me to express personally my admiration and my gratitude to each one of those who work with you in seeing that the voters in every Ohio precinct go to the polls. But since I cannot possibly contact the more than nine thousand of your associates, may I convey to them through you my heartfelt thanks for their work, and my very best wishes for their success?

With warm regard, *Sincerely*

¹ Bliss was Chairman of the Ohio Republican State Committee.
² Eisenhower would carry Ohio 2,262,610 to 1,439,655 (Schlesinger, *History of American Presidential Elections*, vol. IV, *1940–1968*, p. 3445).

To David Ben Gurion   *October 28, 1956*
Cable. Secret

Dear Mr. Ben Gurion: Yesterday I forwarded to you a personal message expressing my grave concern regarding reports of mobilization in Israel and renewing my previous plea, which had been transmitted to you by the Secretary of State, that no forcible initiative be taken by Israel which would endanger peace in the Middle East.[1]

This morning I have received additional reports which indicate that mobilization of Israel's armed forces is continuing and has become almost complete. This further message is prompted by the gravity of the situation as I see it.[2]

Because of the wide repercussions which might result in the present high state of tension in the Middle East and because of the intentions which the United States expressed in the Tripartite Declaration of May 25, 1950, I have given instructions that this situation be discussed with the United Kingdom and France, which are parties to the Declaration, requesting them to exert all possible efforts to ameliorate the situation.[3] I have also directed that my concern be communicated to other Middle Eastern countries, urgently requesting that they refrain from any action which could lead to hostilities.[4]

Again, Mr. Prime Minister, I feel compelled to emphasize the dangers inherent in the present situation and to urge your government to do nothing which would endanger the peace.[5]

---

[1] Eisenhower dictated this message from Walter Reed Army Hospital, where he had undergone a pre-election physical examination (Eisenhower, *Waging Peace*, p. 70). U.S. Ambassador Edward B. Lawson delivered both this cable and the message of October 27 (no. 2046) to Ben Gurion at 8 P.M. (Israel time). For Lawson's account of his meeting with Ben Gurion see State, *Foreign Relations, 1955–1957*, vol. XVI, *Suez Crisis July 26–December 31, 1956*, pp. 811–12. Eisenhower also publicly warned the Israelis not to use force (*Public Papers of the Presidents: Eisenhower, 1956*, pp. 1034–35).

[2] Eisenhower may have been referring to the Special Watch Report of the Intelligence Advisory Committee, which noted a heavy mobilization of Israeli reserves, suggesting an attack on either Egypt or Jordan (see State, *Foreign Relations, 1955–1957*, vol. XVI, *Suez Crisis July 26–December 31, 1956*, pp. 798–800).

[3] The Tripartite Declaration Regarding Security in the Near East—signed by the United Kingdom, France, and the United States—outlined principles for the sale of arms to Middle East states. According to the declaration, the three governments were obligated to take action to prevent any violation of borders or armistice lines in the region ("Tripartite Declaration Regarding Security in the Near East," *U.S. Department of State Bulletin* 22, no. 570 [June 5, 1950], 886; see also nos. 2051, 2052 and 2053).

Secretary Dulles met with the French ambassador and the British chargé d'affairs this same day and urged their governments to appeal to the Israelis not to initiate military action. Dulles would meet with Israeli Ambassador Abba Eban at 6 P.M. When Eban insisted that the Israeli mobilization was for defensive purposes, Dulles replied that Israel had nothing to worry about: "Egypt is living in constant fear of a British and

French attack. Jordan is weak. It is now clear that the Iraqis are not going to enter Jordan" (Eban, *Autobiography*, p. 211; State, *Foreign Relations, 1955–1957*, vol. XVI, *Suez Crisis July 26–December 31, 1956*, pp. 805–6, 809–10).

[4] Dulles would cable several Arab governments, warning them against military action and arguing that the situation did not justify hostilities (Eisenhower, *Waging Peace*, p. 74; Herman Finer, *Dulles Over Suez: The Theory and Practice of His Diplomacy* [Chicago, 1964], pp. 352–53).

[5] Ben Gurion would reply that Nasser had surrounded Israel with a "ring of steel" and that mobilization was necessary to "ensure that the declared Arab aim of eliminating Israel by force should not come about" (Ben Gurion to Eisenhower, Oct. 29, 1956, AWF/I: Israel; State, *Foreign Relations, 1955–1957*, vol. XVI, *Suez Canal July 26–December 31, 1956*, pp. 843–44). See also Eisenhower, *Waging Peace*, pp. 74–75 and Alteras, *Eisenhower and Israel*, p. 219. For developments see nos. 2051 and 2077.

2049   *EM, AWF, Gettysburg Series*

To Floyd Bostwick Odlum   *October 28, 1956*

Dear Floyd: Art Nevins tells me that Janessa has arrived in Gettysburg—and that she is in excellent condition and appearance. I wish I could run up there immediately for a look at her, but I shall have to wait until November sixth for the opportunity.[1] I shall write you later, but, meantime, once again my grateful thanks for her, and for everything you did to avoid any possible embarrassment in connection with her delivery.[2]

With warm regard to you and Jackie, *As ever*

[1] Odlum had written Nevins on September 28. Janessa, an Aberdeen Angus heifer, had been shipped from Scotland through Canada to Eisenhower's farm (for background see no. 1898; see also Edwards to Whitman, Sept. 28, 1956, and related correspondence). On November 10 Eisenhower would fly to Gettysburg to look over his herd and pay a "special visit to Janessa" (Eisenhower to the Odlums, Nov. 11, 1956).

[2] To avoid publicity, the heifer had been purchased for Eisenhower's partner George E. Allen (see Odlum to Nevins, and Odlum to Miller, Sept. 28, 1956). All papers are in AWF/Gettysburg.

2050   *EM, AWF, Dulles-Herter Series*

To John Foster Dulles   *October 29, 1956*
Secret

Dear Foster: For some days I have been wondering whether the present situations in Eastern Europe and in the Mid East might not be creating in Nehru the feeling that he might, very wisely, begin to strengthen his ties with the West and separate himself more distinctly from the Communists.[1] If he has any such feeling, of course, we would want to nurture and promote it. Incidentally, we should be anxious, also, to find him some face-saving device.

It just might be possible that by writing to him a very serious letter speaking of our deep regret that so many innocent people had to suffer at the hands of Russian imperialism and so forth, and without asking him to do anything except to counsel with us, we might make some advances in this direction.

I assume you have been thinking of these things also, but if we do have any belief that we can do anything at all, we probably should move rapidly.[2] *As ever*

---

[1] For background on the Hungarian uprising and Soviet retaliation see no. 2044; on the Middle East see the preceding document.

[2] In a telephone conversation held a few minutes after Eisenhower had dictated this message, he told the Secretary of State that he wanted "to try to draw Nehru into it." Dulles told the President that he had been thinking along the same lines (Telephone conversation, Eisenhower and Dulles, AWF/D-H). For developments see no. 2070.

2051   *EM, AWF, International Series: Eden*

To ROBERT ANTHONY EDEN   *October 30, 1956*
Cable. Top secret

Dear Anthony: I address you in this note not only as head of Her Majesty's Government but as my long time friend who has, with me, believed in and worked for real Anglo-American understanding.[1]

Last night I invited Mr. Coulson, currently your Washington representative, to come to my house to talk over the worsening situation in the Mid East.[2] I have no doubt that the gist of our conversation has already been communicated to you. But it seemed to me desirable that I should give you my impressions concerning certain phases of this whole affair that are disturbing me very much.

Without bothering here to discuss the military movements themselves and their possible grave consequences, I should like to ask your help in clearing up my understanding as to exactly what is happening between us and our European allies—especially between us, the French and yourselves.

We have learned that the French had provided Israel with a considerable amount of equipment, including airplanes, in excess of the amounts of which we were officially informed. This action was, as you know, in violation of agreements now existing between our three countries. We know also that this process has continued in other items of equipment.[3]

Quite naturally we began watching with increased interest the affairs in the Eastern Mediterranean. Late last week we became convinced that the Israel mobilization was proceeding to a point where something more than mere defense was contemplated, and found the situation serious enough to send a precautionary note to Ben Gurion.[4] On Sunday we repeated this note of caution and made a public statement of our actions, informing both you and the French of our concern.[5] On that day we discovered that the volume of communication traffic between Paris and Tel Aviv jumped enormously; alerting us to the probability that France and Israel were concerting detailed plans of some kind.

When on Monday actual military moves began, we quickly decided that the matter had to go immediately to the United Nations, in view of our Agreement of May, 1950, subscribed to by our three governments.

Last evening our Ambassador to the United Nations met with your Ambassador, Pierson Dixon, to request him to join us in presenting the case to the United Nations this morning. We were astonished to find that he was completely unsympathetic, stating frankly that his government would not agree to any action whatsoever to be taken against Israel. He further argued that the tri-partite statement of May, 1950, was ancient history and without current validity.[6]

Without arguing the point as to whether or not the tri-partite statement is or should be outmoded, I feel very seriously that whenever any agreement or pact of this kind is in spirit renounced by one of its signatories, it is only fair that the other signatories should be notified. Since the United States has continued to look upon that statement as representing the policies and determination of our three governments, I have not only public[ly] announced several times that it represents our policy, but many of our actions in the Mid East have been based upon it. For example, we have in the past denied arms both to Egypt and to Israel on the ground that the 1950 statement was their surest guarantee of national security. We have had no thought of repudiating that statement and we have none now.

All of this development, with its possible consequences, including the possible involvement of you and the French in a general Arab war, seems to me to leave your government and ours in a very sad state of confusion, so far as any possibility of unified understanding and action are concerned. It is true that Egypt has not yet formally asked this government for aid. But the fact is that if the United Nations finds Israel to be an aggressor, Egypt could very well ask the Soviets for help—and then the Mid East fat would really be in the fire. It is this latter possibility that has led us to insist that the West must ask for a United Nations' examination and possible intervention, for we may shortly find ourselves not only at odds concerning what we should do, but confronted with a de facto situation that would make all our present troubles look puny indeed.

Because of all these possibilities, it seems to me of first importance that the UK and the US quickly and clearly lay out their present views and intentions before each other, and that, come what may, we find some way of concerting our ideas and plans so that we may not, in any real crisis, be powerless to act in concert because of misunderstanding of each other. I think it important that our two peoples, as well as the French, have this clear understanding of our common or several viewpoints.[7]

With warm personal regard. *As ever*

[1] A draft of this cable, with Eisenhower's handwritten emendations, is in AWF/I: Eden. The State Department sent this message at 10:50 A.M. EST (see State, *Foreign Relations, 1955–1957*, vol. XVI, *Suez Crisis July 26–December 31, 1956*, pp. 848–50.

[2] On October 29 the Israeli Army had attacked the Gaza Strip and the Sinai Penninsula. The U.S. Joint Chiefs of Staff responded by ordering a concentration of naval forces in the Eastern Mediterranean and placing on alert one regimental combat team and one wing of C-124 transport planes. After a meeting with several advisers, Eisenhower met with Sir John E. Coulson, the British chargé d'affairs, and told him that the United States considered itself pledged to prevent any aggression by either Egypt or Israel. The President added that he was concerned about the obvious French connection to the Israeli military action. He did not know what Eden was thinking, but he urged the British to help stop the Israelis, telling the British diplomat that "it was important that we stick together." Coulson replied that "it should be easy to agree in the Security Council," but he admitted that the French might be involved. Implying that he might take military action against the Israelis, Eisenhower informed Coulson that he was willing to call Congress into session "if necessary in order to redeem our pledge" (*ibid.*, pp. 833–40; see also Eisenhower, *Waging Peace*, p. 75).

[3] See no. 2038.

[4] See no. 2046.

[5] See no. 2048. Eisenhower added the words "informing both you and the French of our concern."

[6] Lodge had reported to Dulles that his conversation with Dixon "was one of the most disagreable and unpleasant experiences that he had ever had," and that Dixon had been "virtually snarling" (Telephone conversation, Lodge and Dulles, Oct. 29, 1956, Dulles Papers, Telephone Conversations; State, *Foreign Relations, 1955–1957*, vol. XVI, *Suez Crisis July 26–December 31, 1956*, pp. 840–42). Dulles would relate the substance of this conversation to the President (Telephone conversation, Eisenhower and Dulles, Oct. 30, 1956, AWF/D).

[7] For developments see nos. 2052, 2053, and 2054.

2052   *EM, AWF, Dulles-Herter Series*

To JOHN FOSTER DULLES   *October 30, 1956*
Top secret

Dear Foster: In view of the fact that one motivation of my earlier cable to Anthony was my astonishment that he should avoid giving us any needed information, I have put together the attached, which I request that you send off to him.[1] If you should see any reason for revision, won't you please give me a ring?[2] *As ever*

[1] For Eisenhower's earlier cable see the preceding document. This note was attached to the following document.

[2] Dulles was not sure that the proposed message would be relevant, because there would be "a shift from the Declaration of 1950," but Eisenhower replied that he wanted Eden to know "that we are a Government of honor, & we stick by it" (Telephone conversation, Eisenhower and Dulles, Oct. 30, 1956, AWF/D).

2053   *EM, AWF, International Series: Eden*

To Robert Anthony Eden   *October 30, 1956*
Cable. Top secret

Dear Anthony: This morning I sent you a long cable to say that we here felt very much in the dark as to your attitude and intentions with respect to the Mid East situation.[1] I have just now received your cable on this subject for which I thank you very much.[2] I shall be awaiting the further message to which you refer.[3]

It seems obvious that your Government and ours hold somewhat different attitudes toward the Tripartite Declaration of 1950. Since you have never publicly announced any modification of the Declaration or any limitations upon its interpretation, we find it difficult at this moment to see how we can violate our pledged word.

In any event, I shall earnestly and even anxiously watch the unfolding situation.

With warm regard, *As ever*

[1] See no. 2051 and the preceding document. The U.S. Embassy in London received this cable at 5:35 P.M. London time and immediately transmitted it to Eden at the House of Commons. See also Eden, *Full Circle*, pp. 586–92.

[2] Eden had written Eisenhower that "we cannot afford to see the Canal closed or to lose the shipping which is daily on passage through it." "We feel that decisive action should be taken at once to stop hostilities." Though willing to refer the matter to the Security Council, Eden felt that the Council's procedure was "unlikely to be either rapid or effective" (Eden to Eisenhower, Oct. 30, 1956, AWF/I: Eden; State, *Foreign Relations, 1955–1957*, vol. XVI, *Suez Crisis July 26–December 31, 1956*, pp. 856–57).

[3] See no. 2055.

2054   *EM, AWF, International Series: Mollet*

To Guy Mollet   *October 30, 1956*

Dear Mr. Prime Minister: I have just learned from the press of the 12-hour ultimatum which you and the French Government have delivered to the Government of Egypt requiring, under threat of forceful intervention, the temporary occupation by Anglo-French forces of key positions at Port Said, Ismailia and Suez in the Suez Canal Zone.[1] I feel I must urgently express to you my deep concern at the prospect of this drastic action even at the very time when the matter is under consideration as it is today by the United Nations Security Council.[2] It is my sincere belief that peaceful processes can and should prevail to secure a solution which will restore the armistice condition as between Israel and Egypt and also justly settle the controversy with Egypt about the Suez Canal. *Sincerely*

[1] An identical message was sent to Eden and is in AWF/I: Eden. Both messages were sent by telephone to the American embassies in Paris and London, respectively. The American ambassador was officially informed of the ultimatum by the British Foreign Office at 11:45 A.M. Washington time. According to a conversation noted by Ann Whitman, Eisenhower commented "I think we almost have to (send the message). At least it establishes us before the Arab world as being no part of it (the invasion)" (Telephone conversation, Eisenhower and Dulles, Oct. 30, 1956, AWF/D).

[2] The American armistice initiative, placed before the Security Council at 4:00 P.M. on October 30, would be vetoed by Britain and France (see State, *Foreign Relations, 1955–1957*, vol. XVI, *Suez Crisis July 26–December 31, 1956*, pp. 881–82).

2055   *EM, AWF, International Series: Eden*

To Robert Anthony Eden   *October 30, 1956*
Top secret

Dear Anthony: Thank you very much for your second explanatory cable which reached me shortly after I had dispatched one to you urging caution and moderation with full opportunity for the United Nations to do its best on this difficult problem.[1]

I must say that it is hard for me to see any good final result emerging from a scheme that seems certain to antagonize the entire Moslem world. Indeed I have difficulty seeing any end whatsoever if all the Arabs should begin reacting somewhat as the North Africans have been operating against the French.[2] Assuredly I hope, as I know you do, that we shall not witness any such spectacle as the Soviets have on their hands in Hungary.[3] However, I assume that you have your plan all worked out and that you foresee no such dreary and unending prospect stretching out ahead.[4]

I think I faintly understand and certainly I deeply sympathize with you in the problem you have to solve. Now we must pray that everything comes out both justly and peacefully.[5]

With warm regard, *As ever*

¹ This draft message is marked "not sent"; see State, *Foreign Relations, 1955–1957,* vol. XVI, *Suez Crisis July 26–December 31, 1956,* pp. 874–75. An attached memorandum informed Dulles's secretary that Eisenhower wanted Dulles to approve the message before it was sent (Whitman to Bernau, Oct. 30, 1956, AWF/D-H). Eisenhower wrote on a subsequent draft (dated October 31) "Do *not* send. Eden and I exchanged short cables last night, late. Be sure our file has copy of all incoming & outgoing messages" (AWF/I: Eden).

Eden's second message defended the Israeli invasion and set forth Anglo-French demands for control of the canal. Eden attempted to assure Eisenhower that the Anglo-French action was "not part of a harking back to the old Colonial and occupational concepts" (Eden to Eisenhower, Oct. 30, 1956, AWF/I: Eden); see also State, *Foreign Relations, 1955–1957,* vol. XVI, *Suez Crisis July 26–December 31, 1956,* pp. 871–72. After receiving this telegram, Eisenhower read this draft reply to Dulles, remarking, "This is getting to be a sort of trans-Atlantic essay contest" (Telephone conversation, Eisenhower and Dulles, Oct. 30, 1956, AWF/D). Dulles, after reading the letter from Eden, remarked that he was "not impressed by its sincerity" (Telephone conversation, Eisenhower and Dulles, Oct. 30, 1956, Dulles Papers, Telephone Conversations; State, *Foreign Relations, 1955–1957,* vol. XVI, *Suez Crisis July 26–December 31, 1956,* pp. 870–71).
² On the difficulties of the French in North Africa see no. 1792.
³ For background see no. 2044. As the Hungarian revolt spread to the countryside, negotiations which would lead to the temporary withdrawal of Soviet troops from Budapest had begun in the capital on October 28. The U.N. Security Council had agreed on the same day to place the Hungarian situation on its agenda but had set no date to begin debate. The United States, Britain, and France had stated that they preferred to "wait and see" what effect the United Nations action would have on the Soviet Union (*New York Times,* Oct. 28, 29, 1956). For developments see no. 2067.
⁴ Eisenhower would change this sentence to read "I assume, however, that you have gone too far to reconsider so I must further assume your plan is all so worked out that you foresee no dreary and unending prospect stretching out ahead."
⁵ Eisenhower would add "reasonably" before "peacefully."

2056   *EM, AWF, Name Series*

To Frank M. Wood   *October 31, 1956*

Dear Frank: It just struck me that it has been a long time since I have had direct word from you—or about your health and doings. I hope everything goes splendidly with you.¹

As you may know, I was counting on being in Texas today, but due to the tense situation in the Mid East I found it necessary to cancel the trip.² Since my scheduled meeting was at the Dallas Airport, I was hopeful of seeing most of my Texas friends as I thought it would be rather easy for most of them to concentrate on that place.

In any event, best of wishes and warm regard to you and yours.
As ever

¹ In his response, which would be initialed by the President, Wood would mention that he had talked with "hundreds of women" in Texas and that all were going to vote for Eisenhower (Nov. 1, 1956, AWF/N). For developments see no. 2081.

[2] Eisenhower later noted that "October 20, 1956 was the start of the most crowded and demanding three weeks of my entire Presidency" (Eisenhower, *Waging Peace*, p. 58). He also wrote Leonard Finder that "in view of the grave crisis now confronting me, I doubt if I shall do much, if any, more of the ordinary type of campaigning" (Oct. 31, AWF/N; see also no. 2063).

2057   *EM, AWF, International Series: Eden*

To John Foster Dulles[1]   *November 1, 1956*

The first objective of the United Nations should be to achieve a cease-fire because this will:

(*a*) Keep the war from spreading.[2]

(*b*) Give time to find out what each side is trying to gain.

(*c*) Develop a final resolution that will represent the considered judgment of the United Nations respecting past blame and future action.[3]

The United States must lead because:

(*a*) While we want to do all the things in 1 above, we want to prevent immediate issuance by the United Nations of a harshly worded resolution that would put us in an acutely embarrassing position, either with France and Britain or with all the rest of the world.

(*b*) At all costs the Soviets must be prevented from seizing a mantle of world leadership through a false but convincing exhibition of concern for smaller nations. Since Africa and Asia almost unanimously hate one of the three nations, Britain, France and Israel, the Soviets need only to propose severe and immediate punishment of these three to have the whole of two continents on their side; unless a good many of the United Nations nations are already committed to something more moderate that we might immediately formulate. We should act speedily so as to have our forces in good order by 5:00 p.m. today.

(*c*) We provide the West's only hope that some vestige of real political and economic union can be preserved with the Moslem world, indeed, possibly also with India.

Unilateral actions now taken by the United States must *not* single out and condemn *any one nation*—but should serve to emphasize to the world our hope for a quick cease-fire to be followed by sane and deliberate action on the part of the United Nations, resulting, hopefully, in a solution to which all parties would adhere by each conceding something.[4]

We should be expected, I think, to suspend governmental shipments, now, to countries in battle areas and be prepared to agree, in concert with others, to later additional action.[5]

[1] This document was attached to a note to Secretary Dulles: "Just some simple thoughts that I have jotted down since our meeting this morning" (Nov. 1, 1956, AWF/D-H; see also State, *Foreign Relations, 1955–1957*, vol. XVI, *Suez Crisis July 26–December 31, 1956*, pp. 924–25). Another copy of the same note to Dulles (AWF/I: Eden) indicates that neither document was sent. The President had met with Dulles at 12:50 P.M.

[2] On October 31 Anglo-French air forces had bombed Egyptian airfields. In retaliation, on the following day the Egyptians sank a ship filled with concrete in the Suez Canal, thus halting canal traffic. Israeli forces continued to advance toward El Arish in north central Sinai (State, *Foreign Relations, 1955–1957*, vol. XVI, *Suez Crisis July 26–December 31, 1956*, p. 900).

[3] On November 2 the United Nations General Assembly would adopt an American-sponsored, cease-fire resolution substantially along the lines proposed by Eisenhower in this document. In a statement to the House of Commons on November 3, Eden would maintain that despite the General Assembly call for a cease-fire, "the police action must be carried through urgently to stop the hostilities" (State, *Foreign Relations, 1955–1957*, vol. XVI, *Suez Crisis July 26–December 31, 1956*, pp. 932–33, 946; see also Eden, *Full Circle*, p. 605; and the following document.

[4] For additional comments by Eisenhower see NSC meeting minutes, Nov. 1, 1956, AWF/NSC; State, *Foreign Relations, 1955–1957*, vol. XVI, *Suez Crisis July 26–December 31, 1956*, pp. 902–18).

[5] Eisenhower would slow shipments of petroleum to Western Europe, allowing only the minimum to maintain NATO reserves. When Under Secretary Hoover commented that in the event of a cutoff of oil from the Middle East, "the British may be estimating that we would have no choice but to take extraordinary means to get oil to them," Eisenhower had replied that "he did not see much value in an unworthy and unreliable ally and that the necessity to support them might not be as great as they believed" (Goodpaster, Memorandum of Conversation, Oct. 30, 1956, AWF/D; Peter L. Hahn, *The United States, Great Britain and Egypt, 1945–1956: Strategy and Diplomacy in the Early Cold War* [Chapel Hill, N.C., 1991], pp. 231–34).

2058   *EM, AWF, International Series: Eden*

To ROBERT ANTHONY EDEN   *November 1, 1956*

Dear Anthony: I am sending you by mail a copy of a fifteen-minute talk I made to the American nation last evening.[1] Its principal point with respect to Britain and France is that these two nations have long been our friends and, although in this particular instance we believe that they have made a serious error, we certainly shall do our best to sustain those friendships. I do not feel it necessary to provide to you any additional evidence of my own sincere desire to bring your nation and ours ever closer together.

If I may, in the circumstances, comment further on the unfolding situation, I should like to make some observations on possible eventualities involving the Soviets and submit a suggestion for your consideration concerning the Mid-East operations.

With respect to the first point, I have seen a press notice that Bulganin has dispatched to me a letter on the Mid-East difficulty.[2] It will probably be very tough. I think the first action we may expect from them is the introduction of a stringent Resolution before the General Assembly this afternoon.

Possibly they will seek some kind of a Resolution that will commit the United Nations to call upon its members for forces with which to intervene in this affair.[3] The reason I suspect something of this sort is because I could not imagine anything more embarrassing for our country. It is possible that even, unilaterally, the Russians may assert the right and attempt to send equipment and "volunteers" to Egypt. Of course this would not be possible if you are quickly successful in establishing an effective blockade.[4]

With respect to my suggestion, I am, of course, ignorant of your minimum objectives and what you expect to do after you attain them. But I am struck by the emphasis you placed in your announcement, as well as in your message to me, on the word "temporary" in your occupation.

As of this moment, I have very sketchy information of actual military developments in Egypt and it appears that you and the French have not yet placed any land forces in the region.[5] If, however, the very second you attain your minumum objectives with such forces, I think you could probably ease tension greatly by doing the following: One—instantly call for a cease fire in the area; two, clearly state the reasons why you entered the Canal Zone; three, announce your intention to resume negotiations concerning the operation of the Canal, on the basis of the 6 principles agreed by the United Nations; four, state your intention to evacuate as quickly as the Israelites return to their own national territory, and Egypt had announced her readiness to negotiate in good faith on the basis of the six principles.[6] In this way I think the almost universal resentment now apparently and the possibility of long drawn out, dreary guerilla operations would diminish.

This, of course, is gratuitous advice, but it springs from my very great desire to see the United Nations preserved, to keep in proper perspective before all of us the fact that the Soviet Communists are still the greatest menace of the free nations and to start restoring that feeling of confidence and trust between your nation and ours that I believe to be vital to the interests of a just world peace.

Just now I was notified that Nehru has dispatched to me a long communication.[7] What he will propose of course is anybody's guess, but it does illustrate how far-reaching may be the reverberations from an act that is intended to be fairly local. I have already had direct and indirect communications from a score of other nations.[8]

[1] For Eisenhower's "Radio and Television Report to the American People on the Developments in Eastern Europe and the Middle East" see *Public Papers of the Presidents:*

Eisenhower, 1956, pp. 1060–66. Eisenhower discussed revisions of this draft with Acting Secretary Hoover. It was not sent to Eden (Telephone conversation, Eisenhower and Hoover, Nov. 2, 1956, AWF/D; see also State, *Foreign Relations, 1955–1957*, vol. XVI, *Suez Crisis July 26–December 31, 1956*, p. 922).

[2] See *New York Times* November 2, 1956. Eisenhower would not actually receive Bulganin's proposal until November 5. See no. 2084.

[3] The Soviets did not introduce such a resolution at the First Emergency Special Session of the General Assembly (United Nations, *General Assembly Official Reports*, Emergency Special Session, Nov. 1–10, 1956, Annex, pp. 1–35).

[4] A proposed insert read "To forestall this, this Government hopes to take a position before the United Nations this afternoon that will be moderate in tone, but for which we might gain a sufficient support, before the meeting, to block any Soviet attempt of the kind I have described above. We would propose (*a*) disapproval of forceful action in the settlement of this dispute; (*b*) an immediate cease fire; (*c*) a statement by each government of its intentions and objectives in the area and (*d*), the purpose of the United Nations to effect a return of all forces to their own borders at the earliest possible moment (AWF/I: Eden).

[5] See the preceding document.

[6] In the six points of Resolution 997 (ES-I), adopted on November 1, the General Assembly urged (1) an immediate cease-fire and an immediate halt to the movement of military forces in the area; (2) withdrawal of all parties behind the armistice lines and scrupulous observation of the armistice agreement; (3) a refusal by member states to send arms into the area or take any action that might impede the cease-fire; (4) reopening of the canal as soon as possible after the cease-fire. The fifth and sixth points requested the Secretary-General to observe and report promptly to the Assembly on the compliance of all parties and kept the Assembly in emergency session until the resolution had been obeyed (State, *Foreign Relations, 1955–1957*, vol. XVI, *Suez Crisis July 26–December 31, 1956*, pp. 932–33).

[7] See no. 2062.

[8] These communications are not in AWF. See, however, Sastroamidjojo to Eisenhower, November 5, 1956, AWF/I: Indonesia; and Telephone conversation, Eisenhower and Hoover, November 2, 1956, AWF/D.

2059   *EM, AWF, Name Series*

To Romona Frates Seeligson   *November 2, 1956*
Personal

Dear Romona: It was fine to have your letter—I was especially intrigued by your observations on the "Woman Power for Eisenhower."[1] Whenever I have a moment of fatigue or discouragement on this job, my supply of energy and enthusiasm is always brought back in a hurry by the knowledge that so many fine Americans are working just as hard—though in a different way—for good government in this country.

The twenty-four-year-old serviceman who signed himself "Jerry" really let himself go when he wrote his letter. It would be fun to meet him sometime.[2]

While I have passed some of his ideas on to one or two of my good friends who are making speeches this evening or tomorrow, I have been careful not to quote any part of this letter verbatim because its publication would be very much against existing law and regulations. Consequently, if some Congressman would want to conduct an investigation, the lad's identity would be discovered and he might be embarrassed.

We are having our troubles in the Mid East, but I most earnestly hope that Mamie and I can run up to the farm or go down to Augusta (only an hour and a half away) for a period of time after election.[3]

The job of carrying on the government and a political campaign at the same time has been very wearing. It has been just about as tough on Mamie as on me because her schedule of activities and her volume of mail are both way up.[4]

My warm greetings to Arthur and the family, and of course best love to yourself, *Sincerely*

[1] Seeligson had written Eisenhower that "If the response to our 'Woman Power for Eisenhower' here is indicative of other parts of the country, everything should go right on election day" (Oct. 29, 1956, AWF/N).

[2] Seeligson had enclosed a letter from a twenty-four-year-old serviceman, "Jerry," to his mother, an Eisenhower campaign worker. He wrote: "I don't have to ask you what you think of Stevenson's proposal on the H-bomb. He is the perfect symbol of his party—a 'Jack-ass.'" "I am neither Democrat nor Republican," "Jerry" continued, "but, by God, I am an American which is more than I can say for that bald-headed snake from Illinois" (n.d., AWF/N, Seeligson Corr.).

[3] The President would not go to Augusta until November 26 (President's daily appointments).

[4] On Mamie's campaign letters see, for example, no. 1867; see also no. 2063.

2060   *EM, WHCF, Official File 115-E*

To Rose Richards   *November 2, 1956*

Dear Mrs. Richards: Thank you for your letter inquiring about the fight against inflation.[1] This problem is one that has given me very real concern. It affects all Americans, but particularly people such as yourself and your husband who either are now retired or are about to retire and must plan to live on limited savings or a fixed pension.

The starting place in this fight to keep down the cost of living and to curb inflation is to regard it as an important matter. This we do. I regret that the platform and campaign speeches of the opposition give it such low priority.[2]

The success of our efforts is best demonstrated by the results. Since this Administration took office, the rise in the consumer's cost of living has been held down to less than three percent. This remarkable stability in the cost of living, in a peacetime economy operating at high levels, is a record to be thankful for and one that we seek to maintain. These results are in sharp contrast with the record of the preceding Administration, during which the cost of living rose almost fifty percent.[3]

This fight we will continue by keeping a close check on government spending, avoiding going into the red year after year, watching credit and fiscal controls carefully to keep inflation from breaking loose once again, and in many other ways keeping a sensitive watch of the kind that has been so successful these past four years. This is a never-ending struggle, but I am sure we can keep on winning.[4]

For the wage earner whose pay increases should purchase more and not less for himself and his family, for the retired person whose savings and pensions must be protected and for all Americans, we will continue our battle to secure a stable dollar.

Again, I thank you for taking the time to write to me. *Sincerely*

[1] Rose Richards of Greenwich, Connecticut, had written the President on October 2 (same file as document) to ask about the Administration's plans "to curb inflation in the next four years." She added that her husband was soon to retire on a fixed pension.
[2] The 1956 Democratic party platform did not mention inflation. The Republican party platform stated: "we endorse the present policy of freedom for the Federal Reserve System to combat both inflation and deflation by wise fiscal policy. The Republican party believes that sound money, which retains its buying power, is an essential foundation for new jobs, a higher standard of living, protection of savings, a secure national defense, and the general economic growth of the country" (Porter and Johnson, *National Party Platforms*, pp. 547–48, 523–42).
[3] See no. 1959.
[4] On Eisenhower's efforts to control inflation see nos. 1578, 1956, and 2005; see also Saulnier, *Constructive Years*, pp. 235–36.

2061   *EM, AWF, International Series:*
                                                         Saudi Arabia

To Ibn Abd al-Aziz Saud   *November 2, 1956*
Cable. Secret

Your Majesty: Thank you for your messages of October 30 and November 1.[1] It is heartening to receive your support of the United States efforts to bring to an end the grave crisis in the Near East. Your Majesty knows of the messages sent by this government to the governments of Israel, the United Kingdom and France in an endeavor to forestall the use of force.[2] We are now exerting every effort through the United Nations to effect a cease-fire and the early withdrawal of forces.[3] The United States first referred the question of the Israeli action to the Security Council. The resolution the US put forward to end the hostilities was not adopted although seven Council members supported it. The US then proposed in a special session of the General Assembly a resolution calling for a cease fire, the halting of the movement of military forces into the area, and the withdrawal of the forces of the parties to the armistice agreements behind the armistice lines. This resolution was adopted by an overwhelming majority of the members of the General Assembly, revealing the deep concern of the world community over the situation in Egypt. I assure Your Majesty that the United States will continue its efforts to resolve the present grave threat to world peace.

Your Majesty knows from my statements of October 31 and November 1 that the United States believes the actions in Egypt to have been taken in error and that we do not accept the use of force as a wise or proper instrument for the settlement of international disputes.[4] Now that these grave steps have been taken we must all work to end the conflict and see that it does not spread. To this end I count on the cooperation of Your Majesty, who shares my deep interest in the preservation of the peace and security of the Near East.[5]

May God have Your Majesty in His safe keeping. *Your sincere friend*

---

[1] King Saud's message of October 30 praised the President's opposition to the threat to Egypt by Israeli and Anglo-French forces and criticized "Zionist aggression" (AWF/I: Saudi Arabia; see also papers in WHCF/OF 116-LL). We were unable to locate King Saud's November 1 message.

[2] See nos. 2048 and 2054.

[3] See no. 2057.

[4] For Eisenhower's statement of October 31 see no. 2058; for his speech of November 1 see *Public Papers of the Presidents: Eisenhower, 1956*, pp. 1066–74.

[5] Eisenhower would send similar messages to Dr. Nazem al Koudsi, Acting President of Syria (Nov. 4, 1956, AWF/I: Syria); King Hussein of Jordan (Nov. 4, 1956, AWF/I: Jordan); and Libyan Prime Minister Mustafa Ben Halim (Nov. 2, 1956, AWF/I: Libya).

2062   *EM, AWF, International Series: Nehru*

To Jawaharlal Nehru   *November 2, 1956*
Cable. Secret

Dear Mr. Prime Minister: I have been deeply touched by your letter of November first in which you expressed your gravest concern at the tragic events in the Middle East, and conveyed to me your great appreciation of the attitude of the United States Government in this matter.[1] We too were shocked by these developments, and distressed that the efforts that we took in the Security Council did not bring about a cessation of hostilities or the withdrawal of forces. We hope that the resolution adopted by the General Assembly with Indian support last night will have this result.[2] I share your fear that this situation might well lead to a widening of the conflict, and destroy the very foundation of the United Nations whose function has been to promote peace and prevent war.[3]

I can well understand that memories of colonialism linger in some countries, but we do have assurances from the Government of Britain that they have no intention of trying to revive this practice, regardless of appearances.[4]

You have my assurance, Mr. Prime Minister, that the fullest efforts of the Government and people of the United States are dedicated to finding a solution to this crisis based on justice and the principles of the United Nations. I am happy to know that we are both considering this matter earnestly and that our efforts are mutually supporting.[5]

With best wishes, *Sincerely*

---

[1] Nehru's November 1 letter remains classified (AWF/I: Nehru). Secretary Dulles had commented that the letter "was said to be cast in very general terms" (NSC meeting minutes, Nov. 1, 1956, AWF/NSC; see also State, *Foreign Relations, 1955–1957*, vol. XVI, *Suez Crisis July 26–December 31, 1956*, p. 924).

[2] See no. 2057.

[3] See no. 2058. Eisenhower told Acting Secretary Hoover that the United States might propose an arbitration commission to settle the entire Middle East situation. If the United Nations should want him to meet with Nehru, he was ready to go anywhere to do so because "he thought they came closer to commanding the respect of the world and it would make it difficult for the world to turn down our proposal." Hoover wrote Secretary Dulles that "The President feels we are on the right track. Therefore, he is willing to do anything. He thinks we have got to keep up the momentum . . . " (Hoover to Dulles, Nov. 2, 1956, Dulles Papers, White House Memoranda Series; see also Telephone conversation, Eisenhower and Hoover, Nov. 2, 1956, AWF/D). Later that afternoon, Dulles, Hoover, and the President discussed the possibility of setting up what Dulles called an "elder statesman 'board of appeals'" composed of Eisenhower and Nehru to "develop a solution to the Middle East dispute." Hoover worried, however, that the United Kingdom or the Pakistanis might object (Goodpaster, Memorandum of Conversation, Nov. 5, 1956, AWF/D).

[4] See no. 2055.

[5] For developments see nos. 2070, 2072, and 2085.

2063 *EM, AWF, Name Series*

To Edward Everett Hazlett, Jr.   *November 2, 1956*
Personal

Dear Swede: Except for an informal appearance on a "Round-up" telecast from 11 to 12 o'clock on Election Eve, I have finished my campaigning.[1] It became too difficult for me to keep in touch with the various items of information that pour constantly into Washington from Europe and the Mid East and at the same time carry on the hectic activities of actual campaigning.

It is not difficult at all to operate efficiently in carrying on Presidential functions from any other point in the United States, if there is opportunity to set up the kind of communications required. But when I am gone from here for a period of eight to twelve hours, or up to two to three days, with no communications available other than commercial telephone, it becomes much more difficult, especially so with a world situation such as now exists.

But there is another reason that I decided to do no more in this campaign. Up until a few months ago, I had set my face determinedly against any campaigning except for three or four television speeches to be given in a Washington studio. Some weeks back, however, a lot of people in the Administration came to believe that the distortions and half truths peddled by Stevenson and Kefauver had to be answered— and that no speaker of ours, other than myself, could gain a sufficient audience to answer them effectively.[2]

So I took to the speaking trail, first to call the hand of the opponents on some of the wild things they were saying, and secondly, to awaken the American people to the importance of the contest and to the realization that each of them should record his own decision.[3]

This I think has been done. So in my last evening's talk, in Philadelphia, I confined myself to laying out the approach I have employed since 1952 to the whole problem of foreign relations and how I would approach it in the future if the American people want me to continue.[4]

Actually, unless I win by a comfortable majority (one that could not be significantly increased or decreased in the next few days by any amount of speaking on either side), I would not want to be elected at all. This is for a few simple reasons, even though I believe that the Stevenson-Kefauver combination is, in some ways, about the sorriest and weakest we have ever had run for the two top offices in the land.[5]

My first reason is that I still have a job of re-forming and revamping the Republican Party. Since by the Constitution this is my final term, my influence in these next four years with my own party is going to be determined by their feeling as to how popular I am with the multitudes. If they feel that my support will be a real asset in the next election they, individually and as a party, will be disposed to go in the direction that I advocate. If, on the contrary, they think that politically I am a rapidly "waning" star, then they would be disposed to take the bit in their teeth regardless of my opinions.

My second reason is that in any event, whether or not we win control of one or both Houses of the Congress, the division is certain to be very close. In almost every project some Democratic help will be absolutely necessary to get it accomplished. Again this strength can be marshalled, on both sides of the aisle, *only* if it is generally believed that I am in a position to go to the people over the heads of the Congressmen—and either help them or cause them trouble in their districts.[6]

For these two reasons I think that my only opportunity for doing anything really worthwhile is to win by a comfortable majority. This belief, incidentally, was an additional reason for my deciding to do a bit of travelling in the campaign. It also offered me a chance to prove to the American people that I am a rather healthy individual.

I had planned two more trips—one for last Wednesday when I was going to stop at the airfields in Dallas, Oklahoma City and Memphis, and the other for the last day of the campaign when I expected to stop in Hartford, Connecticut, and Boston, Massachusetts. These I cancelled, mostly because of preoccupation with official business.[7]

The Mid East thing is a terrible mess. Ever since July twenty-sixth, when Nasser took over the Canal, I have argued for a negotiated settlement.[8] It does not seem to me that there is present in the case anything that justifies the action that Britain, France and Israel apparently concerted among themselves and have initiated.

The 1888 Treaty says nothing at all as to how the Canal is to be operated, although it did recognize the existence of the "Concession" dating, I believe, from 1868. I think, therefore, that no one could question the legal right of Egypt to nationalize the Canal *Company*. And what really became the apparent or legal bone of contention was, "Shall the world's users of the Canal, which is guaranteed as an international waterway in perpetuity, be privileged to use the Canal only on the sufferance of a single nation?"[9] Even this, in my opinion, is not the real heart of the matter.

The real point is that Britain, France and Israel had come to believe—probably correctly—that Nasser was their worst enemy in the Mid East and that until he was removed or deflated, they would have no peace. I do not quarrel with the idea that there is justification for such fears, but I have insisted long and earnestly that you cannot resort to force in international relationships because of your fear of what might happen in the future. In short, I think the British and French seized upon a very poor vehicle to use in bringing Nasser to terms.

Of course, nothing in the region would be so difficult to solve except for the underlying cause of the unrest and dissension that exists there—that is, the Arab-Israel quarrel. This quarrel seems to have no limit in either intensity or in scope. Everybody in the Moslem and Jewish worlds is affected by it. It is so intense that the second any action is taken against one Arab state, by an outsider, all the other Arab and Moslem states seem to regard it as a Jewish plot and react violently. All this complicates the situation enormously.

As we began to uncover evidence that something was building up in Israel, we demanded pledges from Ben-Gurion that he would keep the peace.[10] We realized that he might think he could take advantage of this country because of the approaching election and because of the importance that so many politicians in the past have attached to our Jewish vote. I gave strict orders to the State Department that they should inform Israel that we would handle our affairs exactly as though we didn't have a Jew in America. The welfare and best interests of our own country were to be the sole criteria on which we operated.[11]

I think that France and Britain have made a terrible mistake. Because they had such a poor case, they have isolated themselves from the good opinion of the world and it will take them many years to recover. France was perfectly cold-blooded about the matter. She has a war on her hands in Algeria, and she was anxious to get someone else fighting the Arabs on her Eastern flank so she was ready to do anything to get England and Israel in that affair. But I think the other two countries have hurt themselves immeasurably and this is something of a sad blow because, quite naturally, Britain not only has been, but must be, our best friend in the world.

Only a star-gazer could tell how the whole thing is going to come out.[12] But I can tell you one thing. The existence of this problem does not make sleeping any easier—not merely because of the things I recite above, but because of the opportunities that we have handed to the Russians.[13] I don't know what the final action of the United Nations on this matter will be. We are struggling to get a simple cease-fire and, with it, compulsion on both sides to start negotiations regarding the Canal, withdrawal of troops, and even proper reparations. But the possibility that both sides will accept some compromise solution does not look very bright, and every day the hostilities continue the Soviets have an additional chance to embarrass the Western world beyond measure.

All these thoughts I communicated to Eden time and again. It was undoubtedly because of his knowledge of our bitter opposition to using force in the matter that when he finally decided to undertake the plan, he just went completely silent.[14] Actually, the British had partially dispersed some of their concentrations in the Mid East and, while we knew the trouble was not over, we did think that, so far as Britain and France were concerned, there was some easing of the situation.

Just one more thought before I close this long letter. There is some reason to believe that the plan, when actually put into effect, was not well coordinated. It looks as if the Israeli mobilized pretty rapidly and apparently got ready to attack before the others were immediately ready to follow up, using the Israeli attack as an excuse to "protect" the Canal. In any event, British and French troops, so far as I know, have not yet landed in Egypt. Apparently there has been bombing of airfields, nothing else.

If you have any bright ideas for settling the dispute, I, of course, would be delighted to have them. From what I am told, Walter Lippmann and the Alsops have lots of ideas, but they are far from good—about what you would expect from your youngest grandchild.[15]

Give my love to Ibby and the family. *As ever*

[1] For Eisenhower's election eve speeches see *Public Papers of the Presidents: Eisenhower, 1956*, pp. 1082–89. A draft of this letter with Eisenhower's handwritten emendations is in AWF/Drafts.

[2] On Eisenhower's intention to avoid strenuous campaiging see Eisenhower, *Waging Peace*, pp. 4, 85. See also no. 2025.

[3] In Eisenhower's draft this sentence originally read "secondly, to convince the American people that there is a contest and that it was important for each of them to record their own decision."

[4] Eisenhower's November 1 address in Philadelphia is in *Public Papers of the Presidents: Eisenhower, 1956*, pp. 1066–74. See also the following document.

[5] Eisenhower had originally said that Stevenson and Kefauver were "in many ways about the sorriest pair we have ever had. . . ."

[6] For the election results see nos. 2074 and 2075.

[7] On the cancellation of the Texas trip see no. 2056.

[8] See no. 1932.

[9] Eisenhower added the words "apparent or legal" to the preceding sentence.

[10] See nos. 2038, 2046, and 2048.

[11] At this point in the original draft Eisenhower deleted this sentence: "The trouble is to say this is easy enough, but if we are really trying to get the world accustomed to foregoing [giving up] the use of force in the settlement of quarrels, it takes almost more patience than I possess."

[12] For developments see nos. 2070, 2071, and 2072.

[13] In the first draft Eisenhower had written "potentiality for evil" instead of "opportunities."

[14] See no. 2053.

[15] Joseph and Stuart Alsop would later describe the Administration's Suez policy as "a positive orgy of smarmy self-righteousness." More specifically, the Alsops believed that the American policy should have been more sympathetic to Britain, France and Israel's attempt to topple Nasser, an action they likened to "the slap on the face that doctors recommend as a cure for hysteria" (Alsop and Alsop, *The Reporter's Trade*, pp. 309–13). Lippmann believed that Great Britain should have first delivered an ultimatum to the United Nations, that "if the United Nations did not do something serious about the canal and Palestine, it would be necessary to act outside the United Nations" (John Morton Blum, ed., *Public Philosopher: Selected Letters of Walter Lippmann* [New York, 1985], pp. 587–88).

2064   *Gruenther Papers*

To Alfred Maximilian Gruenther   *November 2, 1956*
Personal

Dear Al: Life gets more difficult by the minute. I really could use a good bridge game.[1]

I am not going to bore you with reciting all of our Mid East troubles; in many ways you know just as much about them as I do. At least I am certain that you are acquainted with the British and French side of the story.

Strangely enough, I have seen some of my old British friends in the last few days and most of them are truly bitter about the action taken by their Government. One man said, "This is nothing except Eden trying to be bigger than he is." I do not dismiss it that lightly. I believe that Eden and his associates have become convinced that this is the last straw and Britain simply *had* to react in the manner of the Victorian period.

If one has to have a fight, then that is that. But I don't see the point in getting into a fight to which there can be no satisfactory end, and in which the whole world believes you are playing the part of the bully and you do not even have the firm backing of your entire people.[2]

But the only further remark I want to make on that is that sleep has been a little slower to come than usual. I seem to go to bed later and wake up earlier—which bores me. Of course in some ways the situation in the satellites calls for just as much concern, but in a far different way. I most prayerfully hope that the Russians are sincere in saying that they are going to withdraw their troops from those areas, although I notice that they didn't say anything about Czechoslovakia in making this offer.[3]

I have finished campaigning. Last night in Philadelphia I made a speech that dealt largely with foreign relations and which had almost no allusions in it whatsoever to the political campaign.[4] My reasons for stopping active campaigning were principally two. My whole chance for doing something constructive for the United States is to have a good, comfortable *popular plurality*. If I have not that "comfortable plurality" now, nothing I can say in the next four days will change the thing significantly. If I do not have that, I would rather not be elected. If I could get only 50.1 percent of the vote, then I would feel that the American people have gone so far away from my philosophy of government that nothing I could do thereafter would be of any real help. This I think in spite of the fact that Stevenson and Kefauver, as a combination, are the sorriest and weakest pair that ever aspired to the highest offices in the land.[5]

George told me the other day that he was going to write to you and give you a state-by-state analysis of election results—one on which you could depend absolutely!! I merely advised him that if he did that, he was not, in the next few days, to send you a frantic telegram and ask you to disregard the whole thing.[6]

I notice that as election day approaches, everybody gets the jitters. You meet a man and he is practically hysterical with the confidence of overwhelming victory, and sometimes you see that same man that evening and his face is a foot long with fright.

Respecting the election, I have one comment only for my good friends. If the American people decide that on the record they don't want me—that they think I have made too many mistakes to be trusted again—then you can be sorry for anyone you want in this world *except me*!!

I have heard many people say a fellow would go crazy doing nothing. But I think a life of raising prize cattle, going shooting two or three times a year, fishing in the summer, and interspersing the whole thing with some golf and bridge—and whenever I felt like talking or writing, doing it with abandon and with no sense of responsibility whatsoever—maybe such a life wouldn't be so bad. A man could pretend to have an office, establish his hours as twelve to one—and take one hour off for lunch!

In any event, America will return somewhat to normal about next Wednesday evening. Until then, I shall hunt a cyclone cellar!

Love to Grace. *As ever*

---

[1] General Gruenther had written Eisenhower on this same day that "My heart has been bleeding for you, especially during the past week." He reported that Eisenhower's address to the nation on October 31 had made "a very favorable impact, even on European audiences," and that his "stature in the Free World has risen tremendously" as a result of his position on Suez—despite the fact that most Europeans were "fed up with Nasser." Even German Chancellor Konrad Adenauer was "secretly praying that Nasser would have his throat cut" (Gruenther to Eisenhower, Nov. 2, 1956; Whitman to Gruenther, Nov. 5, 1956, AWF/A, Gruenther Corr.). Gruenther also informed Eisenhower that he had tentatively accepted the presidency of the American Red Cross, which would give him an office close to the White House. He would, however, delay his final answer until after Eisenhower had been reelected. Gruenther planned to return to Washington on November 23, for his last five weeks in the Army. For background on Gruenther's retirement see nos. 1832 and 1837. Eisenhower would reply on November 11 that even though he regretted Gruenther's decision to leave NATO, he realized "that there will be great advantage to me in having you close by" (Eisenhower to Gruenther, Nov. 11, 1956, Gruenther Papers).

[2] On November 1, when the Labor party had moved to censure the government, the commotion on the floor of the House of Commons forced the speaker to suspend the proceedings for one half hour. Eden's government would survive a vote of confidence on November 8, but the vote made evident the dissatisfaction within the ranks of his own Conservative party (David Carlton, *Britain and the Suez Crisis* [London, 1988], pp. 72, 83; and Eden, *Full Circle*, pp. 600, 623–24).

[3] See no. 2067.

[4] Eisenhower's November 1 address in Philadelphia is in *Public Papers of the Presidents: Eisenhower, 1956*, pp. 1066–74. See also the preceding document.

[5] For similar comments see the preceding document.

[6] George Allen would send his election predictions to Gruenther on November 3 (Allen to Gruenther, AWF/A, Gruenther Corr.). Allen would predict that Eisenhower would win 403 electoral votes to 128 for Stevenson. The President actually won by a vote of 457 to 73, and Eisenhower later wrote Gruenther that "George is a little upset that your

grandson did, or could have, outsmarted him on his political predictions" (Eisenhower to Gruenther, Nov. 11, 1956, Gruenther Papers). Gruenther's telegram of November 7, congratulating the President on his reelection is in AWF/A.

2065   *EM, AWF, Administration Series*

To LEWIS WILLIAMS DOUGLAS   *November 3, 1956*
Personal

Dear Lew: Thank you for your letter, which quite accurately expresses the feelings I have toward our British friends.[1] We must remember, of course, that in spite of all that has happened, Britain must continue to be our best friend—so I have no intention of using the British Government as a whipping boy.

The worst thing about it all, you didn't mention—namely, that they have been stupid. At least that is my firm conviction. Among other things they have allowed their distrust and hatred of Nasser to blind their judgment and they have used the wrong vehicle for carrying on their fight to deflate him.

Since last July I have constantly kept Anthony informed on the temper of this country, the way the people as well as the Government would look upon their venture, and the disastrous effect that such a move might have on the United Nations and particularly on world opinion.[2]

The evidence seems clear that France and Israel were parties to concocting a crisis so that there would be a real excuse for Western intervention to save the Canal. The evidence that Britain was a party to this hoax is less persuasive, but certainly they had to know something of what was going on.

In any event, the British and French timing was such as to destroy any contention that they had to move in to protect Canal traffic; the Israeli were turning back to the North and attacking the Gaza Strip before the British and the French could even make a move toward Egypt.

I do hope now that we can start working together effectively.

With renewed thanks for your letter and, as always, warm personal regard, *As ever*

P.S. I greatly appreciate, too, your telegram of the second.[3]

[1] Douglas had written that he had never thought that he could have been so "angry with the British." He thought they had "tricked us and deceived us in a way which is reminiscent of the 18th century." Referring to Eisenhower's pressure on the British in 1953 to withdraw its troops from Egypt, Douglas said that he had "no doubt" that "we

made mistakes in the early stages, commencing a couple of years ago, when we urged the British to withdraw."Although "we messed up the Middle East," Douglas believed that was no excuse for the British to take action "flaunting" both the United Nations and the principles the United States and Great Britain had both firmly supported (Douglas to Eisenhower, Nov. 1, 1956, AWF/A; see no. 622). On November 6 Douglas would send a telegram to Eisenhower suggesting that Britain and France publicly propose to withdraw from Suez if the Soviets would withdraw from Hungary (WHCF/OF 116-LL).

[2] See nos. 2055 and 2058.

[3] Douglas's telegram praising the President's November 1 address in Philadelphia is in AWF/A. See also no. 2063.

2066   *EM, AWF, Administration Series*

To HENRY ROBINSON LUCE   *November 3, 1956*

Dear Harry: Yours is the kind of note that picks me up on those rare occasions when I allow fatigue to bring me a fleeting sense of frustration.[1] Thank you very much indeed.

With warm regard, *As ever*

[1] Luce had written a "fan-note" (Nov. 1, 1956, AWF/A) commending Eisenhower for his "superb" conduct in the midst of the "'sickening'" Middle East crisis (see no. 2086).

2067   *EM, AWF,*
                              International Series:
                                  Bulganin

To NIKOLAI ALEKSANDROVICH BULGANIN   *November 4, 1956*
Cable. Secret

I have noted with profound distress the reports which have reached me today from Hungary.[1]

The Declaration of the Soviet Government of October 30, 1956, which restated the policy of non-intervention in internal affairs of other states, was generally understood as promising the early withdrawal of Soviet forces from Hungary. Indeed, in that statement, the Soviet Union said that "it considered the further presence of Soviet Army units in Hungary can serve as a cause for an even greater deterioration of the situation." This pronouncement was regarded by the United States Government and myself as an act of high statesmanship. It was followed by the express request of the Hungarian Government for the withdrawal of Soviet forces.[2]

Consequently, we have been inexpressibly shocked by the apparent reversal of this policy. It is especially shocking that this renewed application of force against the Hungarian Government and people took place while negotiations were going on between your representatives and those of the Hungarian Government for the withdrawal of Soviet forces.[3]

As you know, the Security Council of the United Nations has been engaged in an emergency examination of this problem. As late as yesterday afternoon the Council was led to believe by your representative that the negotiations then in progress in Budapest were leading to agreement which would result in the withdrawal of Soviet forces from Hungary as requested by the government of that country. It was on that basis that the Security Council recessed its consideration of this matter.[4]

I urge in the name of humanity and in the cause of peace that the Soviet Union take action to withdraw Soviet forces from Hungary immediately and to permit the Hungarian people to enjoy and exercise the human rights and fundamental freedoms affirmed for all peoples in the United Nations Charter.

The General Assembly of the United Nations is meeting in emergency session this afternoon in New York to consider this tragic situation.[5] It is my hope that your representative will be in a position to announce at the Session today that the Soviet Union is preparing to withdraw its forces from that country and to allow the Hungarian people to enjoy the right to a government of their own choice.[6]

---

[1] For background see nos. 2044 and 2055. On this day Soviet troops had attacked cities, towns, and military installations in an effort to crush the Hungarian uprising. The Soviet action followed the announcement by Premier Imre Nagy that Hungary would immediately repudiate the Warsaw Pact, declare its neutrality, and take Hungary's case before the General Assembly at the United Nations (*Foreign Relations, 1955–1957*, vol. XXV, *Eastern Europe*, pp. 375–86; Vali, *Rift and Revolt in Hungary*, pp. 295–305, 364–77).

[2] The Soviet invasion marked an apparent reversal of policy. Following the Nagy government's October 30 promise to establish a multiparty system and hold free elections, the Soviet government stated that "socialist nations can build their relations only on the principle of full equality, respect of territorial integrity, state independence and sovereignty, and noninterference in one another's domestic affairs." Recognizing that mistakes had been made in its relations with other socialist states, the Soviet Union announced that instructions had been given "to its military command to withdraw the Soviet Army units from Budapest as soon as this is recognized as necessary by the Hungarian government" (*U.S. Department of State Bulletin* 35, no. 907 [November 12, 1956], 745–46; State, *Foreign Relations, 1955–1957*, vol. XXV, *Eastern Europe*, pp. 342–43). In a speech on October 31 Eisenhower had celebrated the Soviet pronouncement and stated that the Administration had "sought clearly to remove any false fears that we would look upon new governments in these Eastern European countries as potential military allies" (*Public Papers of the Presidents: Eisenhower, 1956*, pp. 1060–62, Telephone

conversation, Dulles and Eisenhower, and Draft Cable, Dulles to Bohlen, Oct. 29, 1956, Dulles Papers, Telephone Conversations, Hughes, *Ordeal of Power*, pp. 218–22, and Bohlen, *Witness to History*, pp. 415–19).

[3] On November 1, 1956, Nagy had sent a telegram to the Soviets requesting immediate negotiations regarding the withdrawal of Soviet troops from Hungary. Nagy had also informed the U.N. Secretary General of his decisions and asked for major power protection of Hungarian neutrality (State, *Foreign Relations, 1955–1957*, vol. XXV, *Eastern Europe*, pp. 368–69; see also Paul E. Zinner, ed., *National Communism and Popular Revolt in Eastern Europe* [New York, 1956], p. 462).

[4] Negotiations between the Soviet Union and Hungary on the removal of Soviet troops had begun in Budapest on November 3; Security Council debate on Hungary had begun on the same day. Debate on the U.S. resolution, which had called upon the Soviet Union to withdraw its forces and cease interference in Hungarian internal affairs, had begun in midafternoon but had been suspended when the council was informed that Soviet-Hungarian military negotiations were scheduled to resume (State, *Foreign Relations, 1955–1957*, vol. XXV, *Eastern Europe*, pp. 370–71; *New York Times*, Nov. 3, 1956; see also Goodpaster, Memorandum of Conference, Nov. 3, 1956, AWF/D).

[5] Following the Soviet veto of the United States resolution on November 4, the General Assembly would adopt a resolution calling upon the Soviet Union to withdraw its forces from Hungary and requesting the Secretary General to investigate the situation (State, *Foreign Relations, 1955–1957*, vol. XXV, *Eastern Europe*, pp. 392–93; *New York Times*, Nov. 4, 1956). Recognizing that Hungary was entirely surrounded by Communist or neutral nations, Eisenhower would write: "I still wonder what would have been my recommendation to the Congress and the American people had Hungary been accessible by sea or through the territory of allies who might have agreed to react positively to the tragic fate of the Hungarian people" (Eisenhower, *Waging Peace*, pp. 88–89).

[6] By November 7 fighting in Budapest had ended (although mopping up operations would continue for several more days). The Soviets installed a new regime under the leadership of Janos Kadar and would subsequently execute Nagy. For developments see no. 2082. For Bulganin's response to Eisenhower see no. 2084.

2068   *EM, AWF, International Series: Eden*

To ROBERT ANTHONY EDEN   *November 5, 1956*
Top secret

Dear Anthony: I have both your cables.[1] First off, let me assure you that you cannot possibly feel more saddened than I about the temporary but admittedly deep rift that has occurred in our thinking as respect of the Mid East situation. It cannot fail to have some harmful effect upon our joint efforts as we pursue the great objective of a peaceful world.

This morning I have news that your troops have begun landing.[2] In a sense this creates a new problem, but I believe that the peace plans under development in the United Nations are sufficiently flexible so that this incident will not completely defeat them.

The big thing now is to prevent the situation from becoming more tense and difficult. It is possible that Nasser, knowing the United

Nations is working on a peaceful solution might take the "cease fire" very seriously and temporarily accept the landings without opposition. Thus he would avoid actual military contact until he could see what might develop. It would appear that the basic objective of your own military action would be largely accomplished by the landings themselves, providing no serious fighting or disorder ensues. If no serious fighting came out, I think your position in the area and before world opinion would be tremendously eased.

One way in which serious disorders might be avoided would be keeping troops out of contact with any heavy concentrations of the civil population. In this way you would not get a great police function on your hands which you might not be able to drop easily.

If we could have for the next two or three days a period of relative calm while your troops did nothing but land, we might much more swiftly develop a solution that would be acceptable to both sides and to the world.

I have no doubt that you have thought over all these things most carefully and prayerfully, but I think at the same time that the French, in what has seemed to me to be a rather irrational approach to this whole matter, could be far less restrained and therefore make greater difficulties for all of us.[3]

As you say, Harold's financial problem is going to be a serious one, and this itself I think would dictate a policy of the least possible provocation.[4]

In the meantime, no matter what our differences in the approach to this problem, please remember that my personal regard and friendship for you, Harold, Winston and so many others is unaffected.[5] On top of this, I assure you I shall do all in my power to restore to their full strength our accustomed practices of cooperation just as quickly as it can be done.

New subject. Since dictating the above, I have been informed that the Soviets have made the move that from the first I feared would be their reaction. I am told that in Moscow they have released a statement to the effect that they are demanding that the United States join them in an immediate military move into the Mid East to stop the fighting. I understand that aside from making the proposal directly to us, they are placing it before the United Nations in the alleged hope that that body will give its sanction to this preposterous proposition.[6]

I have not yet seen the text of the message so I cannot comment on it in detail.

With warm regard, *As ever*

---

[1] At the top of this document Ann Whitman wrote "Pres. said events had gone too swiftly. Letter was outdated not to be sent." Eden's cable of November 4 had warned the President that the United Kingdom would not comply with General Assembly

Resolution 999. This "Afro-Asian" resolution, which had passed with American support, called upon the Secretary-General to implement an immediate cease-fire in the Sinai and report back within twelve hours. The Prime Minister could accept, however, the Canadian-sponsored resolution (998) passed by the General Assembly at the same meeting. This had set up an emergency United Nations force to be deployed in the area of the canal within forty-eight hours.

Eden's second telegram was a lengthy explanation of the British position. It stressed the temporary nature of any breach between the Americans and British and attempted to justify the Anglo-French military action. Eden claimed that "if we had allowed things to drift, everything would have gone from bad to worse. Nasser would have become a kind of Moslem Mussolini" (Eden to Eisenhower, Nov. 4, 1956; Eden to Eisenhower, Nov. 5, 1956, AWF/I: Eden; for the text of Eden's letters and background on the U.N. resolutions see also State, *Foreign Relations, 1955–1957*, vol. XVI, *Suez Crisis July 26–December 31, 1956*, pp. 960–64, 980, 984–86).

[2] On November 5 British and French airborne troops had begun landing at Port Said.

[3] At the Bermuda Conference in 1953 Eisenhower had remarked that French sensitivity bordered on "an inferiority complex" (no. 597). He had, however, a well-developed theory about the strategic motives behind French policy; see no. 2063.

[4] Harold Macmillan was Chancellor of the Exchequer. Eden had written (November 5 cable) that the British would be "happy to hand over" their military position. "No one feels more strongly about this than Harold who has to provide the money" (Eden to Eisenhower, Nov. 5, 1956; AWF/I: Eden). On Macmillan's role see Kunz, *The Economic Diplomacy of the Suez Crisis*, pp. 131–33; and Macmillan, *Riding the Storm*, pp. 163–65. For developments see no. 2106.

[5] Former Prime Minister Winston S. Churchill.

[6] Bulganin had proposed that if "Govts of USSR and USA firmly announce their will to guarantee peace and will condemn aggression," war could be avoided. The joint use of American and Soviet air and naval power under U.N. auspices would provide a "reliable guarantee of termination of aggression" against Egypt (State, *Foreign Relations, 1955–1957*, vol. XVI, *Suez Crisis July 26–December 31, 1956*, pp. 993–96. For developments see nos. 2070, 2071, and 2073).

2069   *EM, AWF, Name Series*

To ELI GINZBERG   *November 5, 1956*
Personal

Dear Eli: I cannot tell you how deeply I appreciate your note of the second.[1] The times are indeed difficult—and I am quite certain that justice will not return to the Mid East until all of us show more patience, more understanding and somewhat more wisdom than has yet been brought to bear in that troubled area.

You might be interested in a telegram I got from a man who signs himself "Bibo," who stated that he was leading a part of the Hungarian revolt.[2] He thought that they were winning and that the future was bright with promise until the Mid East flared up. This he thought encouraged the Russians to come in and batter down the insurgents.

I quote this only to show that the influence of none of these violent incidents is ever confined to the exact area in which it physically is located. It is apparent that, rightly or wrongly, certain of the Hungarians will always feel that the Mid East venture denied to them, the Hungarians, their freedom.[3]

With personal regard, *Sincerely*

[1] Ginzberg, a professor at Columbia University and a governor of the Hebrew University in Jerusalem (see Galambos, *Columbia University*, no. 155), had written Eisenhower praising his policy in the Middle East as "evidence of very great leadership" (AWF/N).
[2] We were unable to find this telegram in AWF.
[3] Ginzberg would later send Eisenhower reports on various bits of information he had picked up regarding the relation between Soviet actions in Hungary and in the Middle East. He would advise Eisenhower that "In Formosa you were able to set a geographic line; in the Middle East it will probably be necessary to broaden and specify the kinds of actions by the Russians that the U.S. will not tolerate" (Ginzberg to Eisenhower, Nov. 15, 1956; and other correspondence in AWF/N).

2070   *EM, AWF, International Series: Nehru*

To Jawaharlal Nehru   *November 5, 1956*
Secret

Dear Mr. Prime Minister: We have in the recent past exchanged views concerning the unfortunate situation in the Middle East.[1] The anxiety which we share over these developments has been clearly reflected in the positions which our two Governments have explained publicly on many occasions, and in the attitudes which our representatives have taken in the United Nations.

You may have already seen press reports of the message sent to me today by Premier Bulganin, but in order for you to have the full text as sent, I am enclosing a copy with this message. So far I have not had an opportunity to reply to Premier Bulganin, but I did issue a public statement on this matter which I hope will have beneficial effect. A copy of that statement is also enclosed.[2]

There is in my opinion a need to exert the greatest possible restraint lest this situation radically deteriorate. I hope you will add your powerful voice to those counselling restraint with regard to this proposal for expanded military action.

The United States has only one purpose in this matter—to support the United Nations in removing the threat to peace, and to restore peace and justice in the area.

If you have any suggestions for additional action which might assist in this situation, I would be most appreciative to you for letting me have them.

I have not heretofore communicated with you directly on another situation of critical importance concerning which I wish in this message to emphasize my profound concern, that is, the situation regarding recent events in Eastern Europe and particularly in Hungary.

I have read with interest press reports of the comments which you made at the opening session of the General Conference of UNESCO with respect to Hungary. I have no doubt that you fully share our revulsion at the ruthlessness used in crushing the efforts of the Hungarian people to achieve their independence and in keeping them under the yoke of foreign domination.[3]

It is our duty to mankind not only to bring before world opinion the facts with respect to the deplorable situation in Hungary, but to make it clear that the leaders of free and democratic countries cannot remain silent in the face of such terrifying pressures upon our fellow beings. We can in this way contribute much, I feel sure, toward the ultimate attainment of the goals which we seek for a better future in which men can live in peace under governments of their own choosing.

With kindest personal regards, *Sincerely*

[1] See nos. 2062 and 2072.

[2] For a summary of Bulganin's message see no. 2068. Eisenhower was probably referring to a White House press release announcing that Bulganin had made the "unthinkable suggestion" of joint U.S.-Soviet military action to stop the fighting in Egypt and warning that "neither Soviet nor any other military forces should now enter the Middle East area except under United Nations mandate." The statement pointed out that the Soviets had not supported the resolutions establishing peacekeeping forces and that they themselves were engaged in "brutally repressing the human rights of the Hungarian people" (*New York Times*, Nov. 6, 1956).

[3] In the address delivered to a UNESCO meeting in New Delhi on November 5 Nehru had declared that "We see today in Egypt, as well as in Hungary, that human dignity and freedom outraged and the force of modern arms used to suppress peoples and to gain political objectives" (*New York Times*, Nov. 6, 1956).

2071   *EM, AWF, International Series: Eden*

To ROBERT ANTHONY EDEN   *November 6, 1956*
Cable. Secret

Dear Anthony: I was delighted at the opportunity to talk with you on the telephone and to hear that the U.K. will order a cease-fire this evening.[1] On thinking over our talk I wish to emphasize my urgent view *a)* that the UN Resolution on cease-fire and entry of a UN force be accepted without condition so as not to give Egypt with Soviet backing an opportunity to quibble or start negotiations; items such as [the] use [of] technical troops to clear canal can be handled later; *b)* that it is vital no excuse be given for Soviet participation in UN force, therefore all big five should be excluded from force as UN proposes. Any attack on UN force would meet immediate reaction from all UN; c) I think immediate consummation UN plan of greatest importance otherwise there might be invitation to developments of greatest gravity.[2]

Sincerely hope you find it possible to agree with these views and can so inform Hammarskjold before tonight's meeting.[3]

Let me say again that I will be delighted to have you call me at any time. The telephone connection seemed very satisfactory. *Warmest regard*

---

[1] A draft with Eisenhower's handwritten emendations is in AWF/I: Eden. In his conversation with Eden, Eisenhower had emphasized the need to achieve a cease-fire as quickly as possible. He told the Prime Minister "I don't want to give Egypt an opportunity to begin to quibble so that this thing can be drawn out for a week." The President wanted to keep the troops of the big five powers out of the area because he was "afraid the Red boy is going to demand the lion's share" (State, *Foreign Relations, 1955–1957*, vol. XVI, *Suez Crisis July 26–December 31, 1956*, pp. 1025–27).

[2] On the U.N. cease-fire resolutions see no. 2068. Eden would reply that he believed the British troops should be allowed to clear the canal, because, he claimed, they were on the spot and could do so most speedily. He was inclined to agree with Eisenhower that the Security Council's permanent members should be excluded from the United Nations force, but he could not formally consent to the U.N. cease-fire resolutions without consulting his cabinet (Eden to Eisenhower, Nov. 7, 1956, AWF/I: Eden; State, *Foreign Relations, 1955–1957*, vol. XVI, *Suez Crisis July 26–December 31, 1956*, p. 1039).

[3] Eisenhower added the words after "views" to the State Department draft.

2072   *EM, AWF, International Series: Nehru*

To Jawaharlal Nehru   *November 6, 1956*
Cable. Top secret

Dear Mr. Prime Minister: I feel certain that the world can count upon your hearty cooperation in the cease fire plan developed by the Secretary General of the United Nations.[1] I venture to suggest that it would be most helpful at this juncture if you could personally use your great influence with the British Government to urge that they accept that plan without qualification. Additionally, I feel that if you find it possible to accept the Secretary General's invitation for your country to furnish some part of the United Nations force, your action would have a most calming and beneficial effect upon the entire situation.[2]

I am emboldened to send you these suggestions merely because I know that you share my deep and continuing concern that this situation be composed forthwith.

With warm regard, *Sincerely*

[1] See nos. 2068, 2070, 2071, and 2085.

[2] India would become a principal contributor to the United Nations Emergency Force, sending an infantry battalion and supporting troops. Other nations contributing to the U.N. force, which would eventually total 6,000 troops, included Brazil, Canada, Colombia, Denmark, Finland, Indonesia, Norway, Sweden, and Yugoslavia (Rosalyn Higgins, *United Nations Peacekeeping 1946–1967: Documents and Commentary*, 4 vols. [Oxford, 1969–1981], vol. I, *The Middle East* [1969], pp. 302–3).

2073   *EM, AWF, International Series: Mollet*

To Guy Mollet   *November 6, 1956*
Cable. Secret

Dear Mr. Prime Minister: I have just talked with Prime Minister Eden who has told me of your decision to join in the cease fire proposed by the U.N.[1] This is a notable contribution to peace and an act of high statesmanship. As I told Prime Minister Eden I sincerely hope that the U.N. proposals for the cease fire and the entry of U.N. troops are being accepted without conditions because I fear that if they are not, Egypt with Soviet backing may attempt to start negotiations and introduce conditions that would be unacceptable.[2] Such problems as the use of specialists to reestablish navigation on the canal can be arranged later.[3] I consider it vital that there should be no excuse for any Soviet claim to participate in the U.N. forces, and that therefore none of the big five should be included, which conforms to the U.N. proposal. Should there be any attack on the forces of the United Nations, this would be met by an immediate reaction from the whole of the U.N. I attach the greatest importance to the immediate execution of the U.N. plan since any delay might precipitate the gravest developments. I hope sincerely that you will find it possible to agree with my views and that you can tell Hammarskjold this before tonight's meeting. *With best wishes*

[1] See no. 2071.

[2] Ambassador C. Douglas Dillon would report from Paris that he had met with Mollet and Foreign Minister Christian Pineau. Neither had clearly understood that Eisenhower meant to insist on immediate evacuation of Anglo-French and Israeli forces from Sinai. Mollet would write Eisenhower accepting the idea of a U.N. force which excluded the permanant members of the Security Council, but he insisted that French troops could not be withdrawn until the U.N. force was operational (Dillon to Dulles, Nov. 7, 1956; Mollet to Eisenhower, Nov. 6, 1956, AWF/I: Mollet; see also State, *Foreign Relations, 1955–1957*, vol. XVI, *Suez Crisis July 26–December 31, 1956*, pp. 1033–35).

[3] The Suez Canal would reopen on April 8, 1957 (see Kunz, *Economic Diplomacy of the Suez Crisis*, p. 186).

2074   *EM, AWF, Name Series*

To ADLAI EWING STEVENSON   *November 7, 1956*

I am grateful for your message of good wishes.[1] In these difficult and uncertain days it is heartening to have your affirmation of the fact that the people of our country are united. I appreciate greatly your pledge of cooperation for the immediate future and for the four years that lie ahead.

[1] Eisenhower won the 1956 presidential election by a popular vote of 35,581,003 to 26,031,322, and an electoral vote of 457 to 73 (Schlesinger, ed., *History of American Presidential Elections*, vol. IV, *1940–1968*, p. 3445). The text of Stevenson's telegram to Eisenhower is in Adlai Ewing Stevenson, *The Papers of Adlai E. Stevenson*, Walter Johnson, ed., 8 vols. (Boston 1972–1979), vol. VI, *Toward a New America, 1955–1957* (1976), pp. 325–27.

2075   *EM, AWF, Administration Series*

To LEONARD WOOD HALL   *November 7, 1956*

Dear Len: Before you leave on that much-needed vacation trip to Florida, I want to send you a brief note to express my appreciation of your intensive efforts during the campaign. I know that the job of the Republican National Committee Chairman is difficult and exacting, and one that requires balance, judgment and experience—and in all particulars you performed admirably.

While I am, as you are, disappointed that the Republicans did not carry the Senate and the House, I cannot help but feel a personal sense of gratification at the plurality accorded the Vice President and me.[1]

I want also to tell you that my staff reported nothing but the finest cooperation from all the members of the National Commitee in the political activity that has absorbed so much of the time of all of us for the last weeks.

With affectionate regard to Gladys, and all the best to yourself,[2] *As ever*

[1] The first session of the Eighty-fifth Congress would convene on January 3, 1957, with a Democratic Senate majority of 49 to 47. In the House of Representatives, the Democrats would hold a majority of 233 to 200 (*Congressional Quarterly Almanac*, vol. XIII, *1957*, p. 13).
[2] Hall's wife, Gladys Dowsey Hall.

President Eisenhower coaches his grandson, Dwight D. Eisenhower II, on the proper way to hold the reins during summer vacation in Fraser, Colorado, August 1955.

Indian Prime Minister Jawaharlal
Nehru was the President's guest at
the Eisenhower Gettysburg farm
in December 1956.

Secretary of the Treasury
George M. Humphrey arrives
at Camp David, Maryland,
for a Cabinet meeting,
December 9, 1955.

President Eisenhower and Secretary of State Dulles discuss
the Suez Canal crisis, August 1956.

Sherman Adams congratulates Raymond J. Saulnier, newly named Chairman of the President's Council of Economic Advisers, December 3, 1956.

The President receives last-minute tips from Robert Montgomery and Press Secretary James C. Hagerty before delivering a televised address opening his campaign for reelection, September 19, 1956.

President and Mrs. Eisenhower and Vice-President and Mrs. Nixon at the Republican National Convention, August 1956, in San Francisco, California, where President Eisenhower won the nomination for a second term.

President and Mrs. Eisenhower wave from their campaign train en route to
Philadelphia for President Eisenhower's last formal campaign speech,
November 1, 1956.

President Eisenhower holds his granddaughter Mary Jean Eisenhower
on Christmas Day, 1956.

To Robert Anthony Eden   *November 7, 1956*

Dear Anthony:[1] I want you to know that I welcome the suggestion you made in our telephone conversation today regarding early consultation on many of our mutual problems, and that I agree we should meet at an early date.[2] Now that the election is over, I find it most necessary to consult urgently the leaders of both Houses of the Congress. As you can understand, it will take some days to accomplish this. Furthermore, after a thorough study of all the factors and after talking to various branches of the government here, I feel that while such a meeting should take place quickly, we must be sure that its purpose and aims are not misunderstood in other countries. This would be the case if the U.N. Resolutions had not yet been carried out.[3]

I am heartened by the news that there is a cease-fire in Egypt and sincerely hope that the U.N. Force will promptly begin its work and that the Anglo-French Forces will be withdrawn from Egypt without delay.[4] Once these things are done, the ground will be prepared for our meeting. I would hope that this would permit us to meet here by the end of next week. As I suggested by telephone I would hope that Al Gruenther might meet with you or your people shortly to get your evaluation of the matter you mentioned to me this morning.[5]

With warm regard, *As ever*

[1] The State Department drafted this message, confirming the details of Eisenhower's third telephone conversation with Prime Minister Eden on the morning of this same day; see State, *Foreign Relations, 1955–1957*, vol. XVI, *Suez Crisis July 26–December 31, 1956*, pp. 1047–48, 1052.

[2] Eisenhower had asked Eden to call French Prime Minister Mollet "and assure him that the meeting would not be complete without him." Eisenhower told Eden that "after all, it is like a family spat" (Telephone conversation, Eisenhower and Eden, Nov. 7, 1956, AWF/D).

[3] After agreeing to meet with Eden and Mollet, Eisenhower had conferred with Sherman Adams and Colonel Andrew Goodpaster. The three men discussed the possibility that such a meeting would give the appearance that the United States was "now concerting action in the Middle East independently of the UN action" (Goodpaster, Memorandum for the Record, Nov. 7, 1956, AWF/D; see also Adams, *Firsthand Report*, pp. 259–60). In a second telephone call Eisenhower told Eden that the United States was "very definitely" committed to Secretary-General Hammarskjöld's plan to restore peace to the area (see nos. 2068 and 2071). "If the purpose of the visit would be to concert ourselves in NATO & what we are going to do in the future, then we have nothing to fear. If we are going to discuss this plan & your people would find it necessary to disagree with us, then the resulting divided communique would be unfortunate."

Although Eden would agree to Eisenhower's terms, Acting Secretary of State Hoover would tell the President that the United States should "be very careful not to give the impression that we are teaming with the British and French." Secretary Dulles (recuperating from abdominal surgery) was "very much opposed to the visit at this time," Hoover stated. Eisenhower would agree to call Eden again and postpone the meeting. He would also explain the situation to Mollet. When the Anglo-French forces were withdrawn from Egypt, he told the French Prime Minister, "the circumstances will then be favorable for us to meet" (Goodpaster, Memorandum for the Record, Nov. 7, 1956, AWF/D; Telephone conversation, Eisenhower and Eden, Nov. 7, 1956, AWF/D; State, *Foreign Relations, 1955–1957*, vol. XVI, *Suez Crisis July 26–December 31, 1956*, pp. 1042–43, 1045–46; Eisenhower to Mollet, Nov. 7, 1956, AWF/I: Mollet; see also Eisenhower, *Waging Peace*, pp. 93–94; and Eden, *Full Circle*, pp. 629–31; on Dulles's illness see no. 2126).

[4] See no. 2057 for background.

[5] Eden may have told Eisenhower of intelligence reports concerning the possibility of future Soviet military action in the Middle East. "You have given us something on the military side I didn't know," Eisenhower told Eden. "First, we have got to get quickly in some way a coordinated military intelligence view" (Telephone conversation, Eisenhower and Eden, Nov. 7, 1956, AWF/D; see also Goodpaster, Memorandum for the Record, Nov. 7, 1956, AWF/D; and State, *Foreign Relations, 1955–1957*, vol. XVI, *Suez Crisis July 26–December 31, 1956*, p. 1049). For developments see no. 2086.

2077   *EM, AWF, International Series: Israel*

To David Ben Gurion   *November 7, 1956*
Confidential

Dear Mr. Prime Minister: As you know, the General Assembly of the United Nations has arranged a cease-fire in Egypt to which Egypt, France, the United Kingdom and Israel have agreed.[1] There is being dispatched to Egypt a United Nations force in accordance with pertinent resolutions of the General Assembly. That body has urged that all other foreign forces be withdrawn from Egyptian territory, and specifically, that Israeli forces be withdrawn to the General Armistice line. The resolution covering the cease-fire and withdrawal was introduced by the United States and received the overwhelming vote of the Assembly.

Statements attributed to your Government to the effect that Israel does not intend to withdraw from Egyptian territory, as requested by the United Nations, have been called to my attention.[2] I must say frankly, Mr. Prime Minister, that the United States views these reports, if true, with deep concern. Any such decision by the Government of Israel would seriously undermine the urgent efforts being made by the United Nations to restore peace in the Middle East, and could not but bring about the condemnation of Israel as a violator of the principles as well as the directives of the United Nations.

It is our belief that as a matter of highest priority peace should be restored and foreign troops, except for United Nations forces, withdrawn from Egypt, after which new and energetic steps should be undertaken within the framework of the United Nations to solve the basic problems which have given rise to the present difficulty. The United States has tabled in the General Assembly two resolutions designed to accomplish the latter purposes, and hopes that they will be acted upon favorably as soon as the present emergency has been dealt with.[3]

I need not assure you of the deep interest which the United States has in your country, nor recall the various elements of our policy of support to Israel in so many ways. It is in this context that I urge you to comply with the resolutions of the United Nations General Assembly dealing with the current crisis and to make your decision known immediately. It would be a matter of the greatest regret to all my countrymen if Israeli policy on a matter of such grave concern to the world should in any way impair the friendly cooperation between our two countries.[4]

With best wishes, *Sincerely*

---

[1] See no. 2057; and State, *Foreign Relations, 1955–1957*, vol. XVI, *Suez Crisis July 26–December 31, 1956*, pp. 932–33, 960–64, 980–81, 1010–11, 1016, 1025–26.

[2] Eisenhower may have been referring to reports that Israeli Foreign Minister Golda Meir had told the British ambassador that Israel would not withdraw from the Sinai peninsula (*New York Times*, Nov. 7, 1956).

[3] See State, *Foreign Relations, 1955–1957*, vol. XVI, *Suez Crisis July 26–December 31, 1956*, pp. 960–64.

[4] Eisenhower had directed Acting Secretary Hoover to change the last part of this sentence, which had originally read "impair the friendship and cooperation between our two countries" (Telephone conversation, Eisenhower and Hoover, Nov. 7, 1956, AWF/D). The State Department draft of the cable with Eisenhower's handwritten changes is in AWF/I: Israel.

Ben Gurion would reply that Israel had never planned to annex the Sinai Desert. After concluding satisfactory arrangements with the United Nations regarding the international force, he said, Israel would willingly withdraw its forces (Ben Gurion to Eisenhower, Nov. 8, 1956, *ibid.*; see also Eisenhower to Ben Gurion, Nov. 9, 1956, *ibid.*). For developments see the following document.

2078   *EM, AWF, Dulles-Herter Series*

Memorandum[1]   *November 8, 1956*

(1) Information, not yet official, indicates that both Israel and Egypt have now fully accepted the terms of the United Nations cease-fire plan, and that peaceful conditions should prevail soon in the Mid East.

(2) If the above hope is borne out by events of the next day or so, we should be promptly ready to take any kind of action that will

minimize the effects of the recent difficulties and will exclude from the area Soviet influence.

(3) Measures to be taken under these elements, would be:

    (a) Rapid restoration of pipe line and Canal operation.[2] This might have to be done almost wholly by American technical groups, but I should think that we might also mobilize some people from Germany and Italy. This work should begin instantly.

    (b) Push negotiations under the United Nations so as to prevent renewed outbreak of difficulty.

    (c) Provide to the area, wherever necessary, surplus foods, and so on, to prevent suffering.

(4) Simultaneously we must lay before the several governments information and proposals that will establish real peace in the area and, above all, to exclude Communist influence from making any headway therein. There are a number of things to do.

One of the first is to make certain that none of these governments fails to understand all the details and the full implications of the Soviet suppression of the Hungarian revolt. We should, I think, get all the proof that there is available, including moving pictures taken of the slaughter in Budapest.[3]

We must make certain that every weak country understands what can be in store for it once it falls under the domination of the Soviets.

And beyond this, however, are the constructive things that we can do once these nations understand the truth of the immediately preceding paragraph.

For example, we can provide Egypt with an agreed-upon amount of arms—sufficient to maintain internal order and a reasonable defense of its borders, in return for an agreement that it will never accept any Soviet offer.

We should likewise provide training missions.

We can make arrangements for starting the Aswan Dam on a basis where interest costs would be no higher than the money costs ourselves.[4] This, of course, would be contingent upon Egypt negotiating faithfully on the Suez Canal matter and in accordance with the six principles laid down by the United Nations.

We could assist with technicians in the repair of damage done in Egypt in the late unpleasantness and could even make an economic loan to help out.

In Israel we could renew the compact (Eric Johnston plan) and take up again the 75 million dollar economic loan that they desire.[5]

We could possibly translate the tripartite statement of May 1950 into a bilateral treaty with each of the countries in this area.

We could make some kind of arms agreement—particularly maintenance and training—with Israel of exactly the same type we could make with Egypt.

We could explore other means of assisting the Arab States of Iraq, Jordan, Saudi Arabia and Lebanon, and develop ways and means of strengthening our economic and friendly ties with each of these countries, either on a bilateral or group basis.

[1] Eisenhower dictated this memorandum after the NSC had discussed the current situation in the Middle East and possible future developments (NSC meeting minutes, Nov. 9, 1956, AWF/NSC; see also Eisenhower, *Waging Peace*, pp. 95–97).

[2] As a result of the crisis, the canal had been blocked with sunken ships and the British pipeline from Iraq had been sabotoged, destroying three of its pumping stations (NSC meeting minutes, Nov. 9, 1956, AWF/NSC).

[3] See no. 2067.

[4] On the original proposal for financing the Aswan Dam see no. 1946.

[5] On the Jordan River Development Plan see no. 457; State, *Foreign Relations, 1955–1957*, vol. XIV, *Arab-Israeli Dispute 1955*, pp. 21–23, 109–12, 197–98; and State, *Foreign Relations, 1955–1957*, vol. XV, *Arab-Israeli Dispute January 1–July 26, 1956*, pp. 161–62, 470–73.

2079   *EM, AWF, Name Series*

To Lessing Julius Rosenwald   *November 8, 1956*

Dear Mr. Rosenwald: I have just had the privilege of reading the thoughts you so eloquently express on the explosive and deplorable situation in the Mid East.[1] As I am sure you know, I firmly believe that the only way to "win" the war that sometimes seems so threateningly close is to prevent it. I pledge again every resource at my command to that end, and I share your prayer that we in the family of nations can prove ourselves spiritually and intellectually strong enough to find the true way to peace.

I rather hate to intrude upon this letter another subject, but Sidney Weinberg has told me of the contribution you and Mrs. Rosenwald made to the recent political campaign.[2] I assure you that I am more than grateful for your confidence and support.

With warm regard, *Sincerely*

P.S. Your presentation of the case for decency versus extinction is so moving that I should not be surprised if you find portions of it quoted or paraphrased in a forthcoming Inauguration Address.[3]

[1] For background on Rosenwald, former chairman of the board of Sears, Roebuck and Company, see Galambos, *Columbia University*, no. 98. Rosenwald feared that the world was on a course leading to suicide and questioned whether the "awesome factors of atomic self-destruction" could be controlled. "Partisanship has no place when such a vital question confronts us," he said. "Mothers in Israel and Egypt, sons in England and France, Fathers and husbands in the United States and in Russia are all potential victims and sufferers." He called for men of courage who were "willing to immolate themselves to prevent this Armageddon." Rosenwald had written these thoughts to his wife, who sent them to Ann Whitman for Eisenhower (Rosenwald to Whitman, Nov. 5, 1956, AWF/N, Rosenwald Corr.).

[2] Weinberg, an investment banker and a partner in the firm of Goldman, Sachs and Company, had been very active in Eisenhower's campaign for reelection (see Eisenhower to Weinberg, Nov. 11, 1956; and Weinberg to Eisenhower, Nov. 14, 1956, AWF/N).

[3] Eisenhower would refer to the unity of all nations in the search for peace in his second inaugural address (*Public Papers of the Presidents: Eisenhower, 1957*, pp. 60–65; see also Eisenhower, *Waging Peace*, p. 103).

2080
EM, AWF, Administration Series:
Republican National Committee

To Bertha Sheppard Adkins   *November 8, 1956*

Dear Bertha: The political analysts haven't yet gotten around to their verdict on the weight of the "women's vote" in this 1956 election campaign. I am bold enough to believe that the impressive total rolled up in the Presidential and Vice Presidential race reflects an even greater percentage of that vote than was true in 1952.[1] At any rate, I do *know* that enormous credit is due to your efforts, to the work of the Women's Division of the Republican National Committee, and, of course, to similar women's organizations throughout the country.[2]

For your hard work, your capable leadership and your devotion to the Party, I am deeply grateful.

And now—I hope you have a good rest and that vacation that you so greatly deserve.

With affectionate regard, in which Mamie joins, *Sincerely*

[1] A Gallup poll taken October 31 showed Eisenhower with a decisive margin among women voters of 54 percent to 38 percent; his margin among male voters in the same poll was 48 percent to 44 percent. In contrast, a Gallup poll of September 27, 1952, had shown Eisenhower leading Stevenson among women voters by 55.5 percent to 39 percent, and among men by 54.5 percent to 41.5 percent (George Horace Gallup, *The Gallup Poll: Public Opinion 1935–1971*, 3 vols. [New York, 1972], vol. II, *1949–1958*, pp. 1091, 1452).

[2] In her letter of November 9 Adkins would ask to meet with Eisenhower after his post-election vacation to discuss her plans to increase the effectiveness of women in the Republican party (AWF/A: Republican National Committee).

2081
EM, AWF, Name Series

To Sid Williams Richardson   *November 8, 1956*

Dear Sid: Thank you so much for your "before" and "after" telephone calls. You—and your good friend—did accurately predict the outcome in Texas. I am, of course, deeply grateful for his pledge of renewed cooperation.[1]

You won't get this until after your trip to Mexico—which, incidentally, ought to be a wonderful vacation. And I certainly hope that before too long you will make that promised visit up here and that we can have one of our good chats.

With warm personal regard, *As ever*

[1] Richardson had called the White House on November 6 to report a conversation he had had with Senator Lyndon Baines Johnson, who had said " 'The President is going to carry Texas.' " " 'I have always enjoyed working with him. I am going to continue to work with him' " (Memorandum, AWF/N, Richardson Corr.). Eisenhower carried Texas by a vote of 1,080,619 to 859,958 (Schlesinger, *History of American Presidential Elections*, vol. IV, *1940–1968*, p. 3445).

2082

EM, AWF,
International Series:
Bulganin

To Nikolai Aleksandrovich Bulganin   *November 9, 1956*

Dear Mr. Chairman: Permit me first to thank you for your message of felicitations upon my re-election as President of the United States.[1]

I should like also to bring to your attention again my great concern respecting the Hungarian situation.[2] I am informed that this evening the United Nations is once more addressing itself to a Resolution concerning Hungary. The Resolution will urge the withdrawal from that country of Soviet troops, and will request permission to send a United Nations observers team to Hungary in order to determine needs for food, medicine and to help the wounded.[3] The United States would be glad to cooperate with others in providing the needed supplies. I urge again that the Soviet Government support the provisions of this Resolution because I believe there is nothing else today that could contribute more to quieting fears and to restore hope to a world that is so earnestly seeking peace.[4]

[1] Bulganin had also commended the President for "striving for the relaxation of the international situation and the establishment of peaceful and fruitful relations among all nations and peoples. . ." (Bulganin to Eisenhower, Nov. 8, 1956, AWF/I: Bulganin; see also 2041).

[2] For background see nos. 2044, 2055, and 2067.

[3] For the text of the resolution see State, *Foreign Relations, 1955–1957*, vol. XXV, *Eastern Europe*, p. 427.

[4] U.N. Ambassador Lodge had urged Eisenhower to "find his way clear to sending Bulganin another message" urging consideration of the U.N. resolution. (For back-

ground see nos. 2067 and 2078.) Lodge stated that there was a feeling at the United Nations that "for 10 years we have been exciting the Hungarians through our Radio Free Europe, and now that they are in trouble, we turn our backs on them." Eisenhower demurred, telling Lodge that "we have never excited anyone to rebel" and suggesting that Lodge confirm this with the State Department and the USIA (Telephone conversation, Lodge and Eisenhower, Nov. 9, 1956, AWF/D; for another view see William E. Colby and Peter Forbath, *Honorable Men: My Life in the CIA* [New York, 1978], pp. 134–35).

Eisenhower would discuss this response to Bulganin in a telephone conversation with Dulles (Telephone conversation, Eisenhower and Dulles, Nov. 9, 1956, AWF/D). The Secretary of State would express his lack of enthusiasm for another letter to Bulganin, and the President would agree that he "hated to send messages back and forth, when we know they won't pay any attention to them." Eisenhower, however, wanted to put the "same pressure" on the Soviets that he had been applying to the Israelis in the Suez crisis. He would finally decide to "dictate a short message," pointing out "the great feeling of relief" that would exist if Bulganin would support the U.N. resolution. After discussing the matter with Acting Secretary of State Herbert Hoover, Jr., the President would send him a draft of the letter for State Department consideration (Telephone conversation, Eisenhower and Hoover, Nov. 9, 1956, AWF/D). The State Department would send this letter on November 12. U.S. Ambassador to the Soviet Union Charles Bohlen would later protest Eisenhower's acceptance of Bulganin's congratulations, which he felt would be interpreted as a sign that normal relations with the United States would continue (Bohlen, *Witness to History*, p. 419). For developments see no. 2084.

2083 *EM, AWF, Administration Series*

To Henry Cabot Lodge, Jr. *November 10, 1956*
Personal

Dear Cabot: I am grateful for your congratulations both on the campaign and on the victory.

As I think you know, I want very much to see the Republican Party become, as I said on Tuesday night, the Party of Modern Republicanism.[1] To this end we must lay plans now, I know. The difficulties you know as well as do I, especially when our days are so consumed by crises of one sort or another.

But if I did not believe in my heart that such a thing would be possible, I doubt if I could have gone into the campaign at all.

You cannot imagine what a lift your final paragraph gives me.[2]

With warm regard, *As ever*

[1] For Eisenhower's televised remarks following his election victory see *Public Papers of the Presidents: Eisenhower, 1956*, pp. 1089–91.
[2] Lodge's letter of November 7 congratulating the President on his reelection is in AWF/A. His final paragraph read: "For the rest of the world there is delight—except behind the Iron Curtain where there is respect and relief. There was many an Ike

button among the Ambassadors at the United Nations—and many were the congratulations I received in the General Assembly this morning."

2084

EM, AWF,
International Series:
Bulganin

To Nikolai Aleksandrovich Bulganin   *November 11, 1956*
Cable. Secret

I refer to your message to me of November 5.[1] The fighting in the Near East has now been brought to an end through the efforts of the United Nations, the body properly responsible for accomplishing this.[2] It is essential that peace be totally restored to the area and that no action be taken which would in any way exacerbate the situation there.

With respect to your suggestion that the United States join with the Soviet Union in a bi-partite employment of their military forces to stop the fighting in Egypt, it is our view that neither Soviet nor any other military forces should now enter the Middle East area except under United Nations mandate. Any such action would be directly contrary to resolutions of the General Assembly of the United Nations which have called for the withdrawal of those foreign forces which are now in Egypt. The introduction of new forces under these circumstances would violate the United Nations Charter, and it would be the duty of all United Nations members, including the United States, to oppose any such effort.

It is difficult to reconcile your expressed concern for the principles of morality and the objectives of the United Nations with the action taken by Soviet military units against the people of Hungary. Your letter to me of November 7 concerning this tragic situation was deeply disappointing.[3] Were the Soviet Government now able to comply with the Resolutions of the U.N. on the subject of Hungary, it would be a great and notable contribution to the cause of peace.[4]

[1] After giving Eisenhower his estimate of the destruction that had resulted from Anglo-French and Israeli military moves in Egypt, Bulganin had asked for "united and urgent use" of a combined U.S.-Soviet air and naval force to guarantee peace in the Middle East. "We are convinced," he said, that if both governments "firmly announce their will to guarantee peace and will condemn aggression then aggression will be terminated and there will be no war" (AWF/I: Bulganin; see also Eisenhower, *Waging Peace*, p. 97).
[2] See no. 2078.
[3] In answer to Eisenhower's November 4 letter (no. 2067), Bulganin had told the President that the situation in Hungary was entirely a matter between the Soviet and Hungarian governments (Bohlen to Dulles, Nov. 8, 1956, AWF/I: Bulganin).
[4] See no. 2082.

To Jawaharlal Nehru
Cable. Secret

Dear Mr. Prime Minister: I am grateful for your message of November 7.[1] You were indeed kind to congratulate me upon my re-election. This renewed evidence of the support of the American people for the policy of the Administration was, of course, very welcome to me.

Recent developments in the Near East have improved the atmosphere, although the situation remains critical. The decision of the United Kingdom, France and Israel to cease fire and to withdraw their forces have been significant steps forward. We must all do everything possible to assist in the total restoration of peace and the installation of the UN Force in the area. A renewal or enlargement of hostilities could have most serious consequences.

I have learned with gratification of your decision to provide troops for the United Nations Force in Egypt, a matter concerning which I communicated with you earlier.[2] It is of vital importance that no foreign forces be introduced into the area, whether on a "volunteer" basis or otherwise, except under United Nations auspices. To introduce such forces would be a disservice to the cause of peace and would place in real jeopardy the progress we are making in the United Nations. It was in this vein that I replied to Prime Minister Bulganin's suggestion that the United States join with the Soviet Union in bi-partite employment of their military forces to stop the fighting in Egypt.[3]

Meanwhile, the position of Hungary remains most depressing to all persons anxious to preserve human freedom and national dignity. I hope that your Government will find it possible to join in supporting proposed United Nations actions to deal with the situation in Hungary and to contribute to United Nations efforts to relieve the suffering of the people there.[4]

I appreciate your having asked Ambassador Mehta to pass to me, as he did on November 9, excerpts from Mr. Bulganin's letter to you regarding Hungary. Bulganin's reply does not overcome the stark fact that a foreign power is intervening militarily to repress brutally the desire of the Hungarian people to exercise their fundamental rights to freedom and independence.

I am extraordinarily pleased that final arrangements for your visit here in December are beginning to crystalize. I am looking forward very much to seeing you.[5]

With warm regard, *Sincerely*

---

[1] Nehru's letter remains classified.

[2] See no. 2072.

[3] See the preceeding document.

5 For background on Nehru's visit to the United States see nos. 1533, 1561, 1731, and 1793. For developments see no. 2138. For Eisenhower's discussions with Nehru regarding Hungary and the Suez crisis see no. 2139.

2086   *EM, AWF, International Series: Eden*

To ROBERT ANTHONY EDEN   *November 11, 1956*
Cable. Top secret

Dear Anthony: I am in full agreement with the objectives set forth in your message of November 7 which crossed mine of that same day.[1] We have the problems you describe very much in mind and I, too, hope that we could meet in the near future. Meanwhile, I feel we must continue to push forward on the introduction of the UN Force and the withdrawal of Anglo-French forces, and that these things should be done with the utmost speed. We should then be in a position to consider arranging a meeting. I have sent similar word to Prime Minister Mollet.[2]

My preliminary reports from Al Gruenther indicate that it would not seem necessary for him to come to London to see you.[3]

With warm regard. *As ever*

[1] Eden had stressed the importance of an early meeting with Eisenhower and Mollet. "I should feel much more confidence about the decisions and actions which we shall have to take in the short term," he said, "if we had first reached some common understanding about the attitide which we each intended to take towards a long-term settlement of the outstanding issues in the Middle East." Eden was increasingly concerned that the Soviets, by giving Nasser substantial support, could "precipitate a really grave situation" (AWF/I: Eden; and State, *Foreign Relations, 1955–1957,* vol. XVI, *Suez Crisis July 26–December 31, 1956.* pp. 1061–62). Eisenhower's letter is no. 2076.
[2] See Eisenhower to Mollet and Hoover to Dillon, Nov. 11, 1956, AWF/I: Mollet.
[3] For background see no. 2076. General Gruenther had written Colonel Andrew Goodpaster to say that a proposed visit to London could not be hidden from the press and that his position as NATO commander made his actions sensitive. The British defense minister had suggested that a Royal Air Force marshal visit Gruenther in Paris and that Gruenther could visit Eden later if necessary (State, *Foreign Relations, 1955–1957,* vol. XVI, *Suez Crisis July 26–December 31, 1956,* p. 1111).

2087   *EM, AWF, Name Series*

To BENJAMIN FRANKLIN CAFFEY, JR.   *November 11, 1956*

Dear Frank: One of the most heartwarming aspects of the campaign was indeed the plurality the people of Florida gave me.[1] I am grateful for your efforts, and congratulate you on the result in your district.[2]

I have written to Mr. Anderson, but sometime when you see him, I wish you would again express my appreciation of his energetic support.[3]

At the moment I dare make no firm commitments of any kind because of the acute international situation, but if I am in town I shall, of course, make every effort to see you and discuss your plan with you. I think also that it would be well if you went over the details with Tom Stephens, who will be here at the White House during December.[4]

With warm regard to you and Louise, and again my thanks for all you did, *As ever*[5]

[1] Eisenhower had carried Florida by a vote of 643,849 to 480,371 (Schlesinger, *History of American Presidential Elections*, vol. IV, *1940–1968*, p. 3445).

[2] Caffey had written that Eisenhower had carried his fifth congressional district with 64.44 percent of the vote, up from 57 percent in 1952 (Nov. 8, 1956, AWF/N).

[3] We have been unable to identify Mr. Anderson.

[4] Caffey, who would not meet with the President, sent a detailed memorandum on the future of the Republican party in the South (Caffey to Eisenhower, Dec. 4, 1956, and Eisenhower to Caffey, Dec. 8, 1956, AWF/N). Thomas Edwin Stephens had been Appointments Secretary to the President before leaving the White House to work on Eisenhower's campaign. He would return to his post for most of Eisenhower's second term.

[5] General Caffey's wife, Louise Battle Caffey.

2088

EM, AWF, International Series: Yugoslavia

To Josip Broz Tito
Secret

November 12, 1956

Dear Mr. President: I am indeed grateful for your message of August twenty-sixth expressing your views on various questions which directly concern both of our countries.[1] Events have moved rapidly since then and it does not seem appropriate to discuss in detail the concrete problems of our bilateral relations in the economic and military fields about which you wrote me. This is not because these matters are not important to both our countries, but because I think they are, or soon will be, on their way to a mutually satisfactory solution through negotiations or conversations in regular channels between our Governments.[2]

I am sure we can agree that the cordial relations between our two countries are due, above all else, to our common stand in favor of national sovereignty, independence and non-interference in the internal affairs of other nations. Our two countries have also supported international cooperation in an increasingly interdependent world. Because we both adhere to these principles, we have seen that our relations can serve as proof that dissimilar governments can not only respect each other but also work together.[3]

With respect to the dramatic yet tragic events in Eastern Europe, I am reminded of what Secretary of State Dulles told me of his conversations with you a year ago and I have observed how well those discussions anticipated current trends.[4] Many of the favorable developments can be credited, I am sure, to the personal efforts which I understand you made in Belgrade in 1955 and in Moscow in 1956 to persuade the Soviet leaders to engage themselves not to interfere in the internal affairs of other countries.[5]

Until set back by ruthless full-scale Soviet intervention in Hungary, this trend seemed to open up the possibility of creating better conditions in Eastern Europe. Much now depends on the course of action adopted by the Soviet Union. Our concern at conditions in Eastern Europe in the last decade has been caused not alone by social and economic conditions there or by ideological practices. Our greatest concern has arisen from the Soviet domination exercised over most of the area and from the totalitarian rule of suppression of freedom which has accompanied it. This extension of Soviet power into the heart of Europe poses a grave threat to the security of the whole world.

Tensions in Europe cannot really and permanently be relaxed until the Soviet Union has retired to its frontiers and released Eastern Europe from its grip. The events in Hungary show that desperation may lead a defenseless people to rebel against an oppressive regime which they know has the means for forceful suppression. But I want to assure you that our policy has never been to encourage or induce such revolt by any people.[6] Independence for these nations does not preclude the Soviet Union's having friendly neighbors on its frontiers, but should facilitate this result. It seems to me inevitable that the area will develop into one of hatred for Russia instead of one of peace unless the Soviet Union makes a constructive contribution conforming with the true desires of the people.

You may be assured that the United States does not seek to derive any special benefit or to impose its concepts on these lands. As I announced in my broadcast to the American Nation on October thirty-first, we have, with respect to the Soviet Union, sought to remove any fears that we would look upon any government in the Eastern Europe countries as potential military allies. I said that we had no such ulterior purpose and that we see these people as friends and wish simply that they be friends who are free. I have also made it clear, with the Yugoslav example in mind, that the United States stands ready to furnish assistance without political conditions to those people in Eastern Europe who have started on the path to true national independence.[7]

I believe these views accord with your own. While very much regretting that Yugoslavia in the United Nations was unable to take a stand on some phases involved in Soviet repression of the Hungarian people, we welcome your Government's support for the United Nations' action requesting immediate withdrawal of Soviet troops from Hungary.[8] I also think you can take satisfaction from the fact that your efforts have consistently been in the direction of greater independence for the Eastern European countries. Efforts of this kind will be needed all the more because of the consequences produced in Hungary by a reversal of this trend and because of Soviet pressures being exerted on the new Polish Government. I believe I appreciate something at least of the difficulties the current situation has created for your Government.

I have been happy to note the appreciation shown by your Delegation at the United Nations of the role the United States has been playing with respect to the Middle East crisis. I hope we may be able to count upon your country's support of action by the United Nations which will restore peace to the area.[9]

It has occurred to me that although we have exchanged views on developments on a number of occasions through letters between us, this has hardly been an adequate substitute for a personal contact. It would give me great pleasure if you could find it convenient and agreeable to visit me in Washington sometime during the coming year. I would suggest that a suitable date could be arranged by our respective ambassadors through diplomatic channels.[10]

With every good wish, *Sincerely*

[1] Tito's August 26 letter is in AWF/I: Yugoslavia. The initial delay in replying to his letter was due to State Department and White House efforts to determine Yugoslavia's compliance with the terms of the Mutual Security Act of 1956. The Act required termination of aid to Yugoslavia unless the President decided that continued assistance was in the American interest and that Yugoslavia remained independent of the Soviet Union (State, *Foreign Relations, 1955–1957*, vol. XXVI, *Central and Southeastern Europe*, pp. 737–57; *Congressional Quarterly Almanac*, vol. XII, *1956*, pp. 418–27). Improvement in relations between the Soviet Union and Yugoslavia in 1955 and 1956 had led the White House to reassess American-Yugoslav relations (see no. 1128). Eisenhower had sent an interim reply to Tito on September 14 (see Dulles memorandum, Sept. 13, 1956, and Eisenhower to Tito, Sept. 14, 1956, AWF/I: Yugoslavia).

[2] Major concerns involving U.S.-Yugoslav relations included Tito's requests for 300,000 tons of wheat, major military supplies, and a $10 million loan to assist the development of a copper mining facility. On October 15 Eisenhower had announced the decision to allow economic aid to Yugoslavia; the United States would, however, continue to refuse to supply jet planes and other heavy equipment pending the further clarification of Yugoslav policies (see *Public Papers of the Presidents: Eisenhower, 1956*, pp. 928–30).

[3] See nos. 1593 and 1601.

[4] On the Soviet actions in Hungary see nos. 2044, 2055, and 2067. On November 6, 1955, Tito had explained to Dulles his belief that Soviet policy makers were divided between those who wanted to continue Stalin's policies in both the domestic and foreign fields, and those who held that Stalin's policies had led the Soviet Union into a blind alley. Bulganin, Khrushchev, and Mikoyan, who held this latter view, realized that to get out of the blind alley they needed to change policies, including policy toward the satellites. Dulles reported to Eisenhower that Tito thought there was "a definite new concept which did not involve a renuciation by the Soviets of the desire to have influence in the satellites, but was a change from the previous policy of iron control." Tito believed that independence for the satellite states would happen gradually as the views and policies of the present Soviet leadership became stronger and the elements of Stalinism weaker (State, *Foreign Relations, 1955–1957*, vol. XXVI, *Central and Southeastern Europe*, pp. 680–701; see also no. 1622, and John C. Campbell, *Tito's Separate Road: America and Yugoslavia in World Politics* [New York, 1967], pp. 33–36).

[5] On May 26, 1955, Khrushchev and Bulganin had met with Tito in Belgrade, where they issued an apology for the grave "accusations and offenses" against Yugoslavia. A joint Belgrade Declaration issued on June 2 recognized that "different forms of Socialist development are solely the concern of the individual countries" and condemned aggression and "all attempts to subject countries to political and economic domination." During Tito's June 1956 visit to Moscow, Yugoslavia and the Soviet Union formally reestablished government and party relations (see State, *Foreign Relations, 1955–1957*, vol. XXVI, *Central and Southeastern Europe*, pp. 728–30; see also Duncan Wilson, *Tito's Yugoslavia* [Cambridge, 1979], pp. 95–101; *New York Times*, May 27, June 3, 1955, and *New York Times*, June 19–21, 1956).

[6] The preceding two sentences were added to Acting Secretary of State Hoover's original draft after the Hungarian revolt (see no. 2082, and drafts in AWF/I: Yugoslavia).

[7] See no. 2067, and *Public Papers of the Presidents: Eisenhower, 1956*, pp. 1060–62.

[8] Yugoslavia had abstained several times from voting on U.N. resolutions regarding Soviet actions in Hungary (see Zinner, *National Communism*, pp. 516–41).

[9] See State, *Foreign Relations, 1955–1957*, vol. XVI, *Suez Crisis July 26–December 31, 1956*, pp. 895–96.

[10] In his November 20 response to Eisenhower, Tito would thank the President for his invitation to visit the United States and express hope that he would be able to come in 1957 (AWF/I: Yugoslavia). On the controversy aroused by Tito's impending visit and its ultimate cancellation see State, *Foreign Relations, 1955–1957*, vol. XXVI, *Central and Southeastern Europe*, pp. 757–65.

2089   *EM, AWF, International Series: Indonesia*

To Ali Sastroamidjojo   *November 12, 1956*
Cable. Confidential

Dear Mr. Prime Minister:[1] I was most pleased to receive the assurances contained in your letter of November 3, 1956, of Indonesian support for efforts to bring an end to hostilities in the Middle East and to obtain the withdrawal of foreign forces from Egypt.[2]

As you know, the United States has not wavered in its opposition to the use of force to obtain political objectives and in its faith in the United Nations as an appropriate agency for peaceful settlement of disputes. It was with considerable satisfaction that I noted Indonesia's support for the resolution which we introduced in the United Nations General Assembly on November 1 calling for an immediate cease fire and a halt to the movement of military force and arms into the area of hostilities.[3]

The reported statement from the Soviet Union about "volunteer forces" for the Middle East greatly disturbs me.[4] It is of vital importance that no foreign forces be introduced into the area, whether on a "volunteer" basis or otherwise, except under United Nations auspices. To introduce such forces would be a disservice to the cause of peace and would place in real jeopardy the progress we are making in the United Nations.

On November 3 the United States supported a resolution sponsored by the Asian-African powers again calling for an immediate cease fire.[5] I am sure that you will understand that for the United States to take the lead in this matter in opposition to two of our principal European allies was possible only because of the deep conviction of the American people that the use of force between nations is wrong.

It is this same principle that has guided us in seeking, through the United Nations, to enlist the support of world opinion in halting Soviet armed intervention in the internal affairs of Hungary.[6]

The American people were inexpressibly shocked by the Soviet Union's cynical use of naked force in Hungary. On November 4, 1956, I wrote to Marshal Nikolai A. Bulganin, Chairman of the Council of Ministers of the USSR, to urge in the name of humanity and in the cause of peace that the Soviet Union withdraw its forces from Hungary immediately and permit the Hungarian people to enjoy and exercise the human rights and fundamental freedoms affirmed for all peoples in the United Nations Charter. I am enclosing for your information a copy of my letter to Marshal Bulganin.[7]

I have been informed that your government, by its action of November 8, has now joined with the majority of the Free World in expressing its regret concerning Soviet military action.[8] I welcome this move, regretting only that Indonesia, with some other nations of Asia when this issue was first presented to the United Nations, did not contribute the support of a people that has sacrificed much during recent years to win its own freedom and independence.

There are heartening signs that our mutual effort to restore peace in the Middle East is bearing fruit. There is every reason to believe that the force of a united world opinion could be equally effective in bringing an end to the brutal suppressions of the liberties of the Hungarian people. I am sure you will agree that on a matter of fundamental moral principle, a double standard cannot be applied.

The United States would welcome from Indonesia the same stalwart opposition to the use of force in Hungary as it provided in the case of Egypt. I am hopeful that our two nations will work together in the United Nations for a just solution to the grave problems now confronting us.[9]

[1] Ali Sastroamidjojo, former Indonesian Minister of Education and Culture, had been ambassador to the United States before becoming prime minister in March 1956. The State Department drafted this letter.

[2] Ali had asked Eisenhower to exert all his efforts "to stop aggression towards Egypt" and told the President that the Middle Eastern situation was not "a matter of peace and war any more" but the "feeling of security of small nations towards the big powers" (Nov. 5, 1956, AWF/I: Indonesia). Under Secretary Hoover had told the U.S. ambassador in Indonesia that he was disturbed by the tone of the Prime Minister's letter (State, *Foreign Relations, 1955–1957*, vol. XXII, *Southeast Asia*, p. 328).

[3] See no. 2058.

[4] On the Soviet foreign minister's proposal on November 5 see State, *Foreign Relations, 1955–1957*, vol. XVI, *Suez Crisis July 26–December 31, 1956*, p. 992.

[5] See *ibid.*, pp. 959–60, 963, 978; and Goodpaster, Memorandum of Conference, Nov. 5, 1956, AWF/D.

[6] For the U.N. resolutions see State, *Foreign Relations, 1955–1957*, vol. XXV, *Eastern Europe*, pp. 307–10, 368–69, 371–73, 388–93, 422–23, 427–29.

[7] See no. 2067.

[8] A communiqué issued by the Indonesian government disapproved the Soviet action (see State, *Foreign Relations, 1955–1957*, vol. XXII, *Southeast Asia*, p. 328).

[9] On November 19 Indonesia, with India and Ceylon, would introduce a resolution at the General Assembly urging Hungary to allow observers to enter that country to report on the issue of forcible deportation (State, *Foreign Relations, 1955–1957*, vol. XXV, *Eastern Europe*, pp. 460–61).

2090   *EM, AWF, Dulles-Herter Series*

To HERBERT CLARK HOOVER, JR.   *November 12, 1956*

Memorandum for the Acting Secretary of State: Senator Green came to my office this morning to report on an audience he had been granted by the Emperor of Ethiopia.[1] The substance of the conversation that Senator Green had with the Emperor is reported in the attached aide memoire.[2] Senator Green told me that the only real difference between the aide memoire and the conversation was the fact that in the conversation the Emperor was obviously much more disturbed than would be apparent in the aide memoire and that he used language of a very strong character in expressing his dissatisfaction.

One of the points that the Emperor seemed to make was that the United States had violated an "agreement." He emphasized this point several times. I should like to know whether we have actually been guilty of violating an agreement, no matter whether such agreement was executed before or after this Administration was inaugurated in January 1953.

I promised Senator Green that the State Department would notify our Ambassador in Ethiopia that the Senator had actually delivered his personal message to me. Will you please instruct your Ambassador to suitably inform the Ethiopian Government?

P.S. The friendship of Ethiopia I consider of great importance.[3]

[1] Eighty-eight-year-old Senator Theodore Francis Green, Democrat of Rhode Island, had recently returned from Addis Ababa. Green would become Chairman of the Senate Committee on Foreign Relations at the start of the new session of Congress in 1957.
[2] The aide-memoire is not in AWF. See State, *Foreign Relations, 1955–1957*, vol. XVIII, *Africa*, pp. 329–30, n. 3.
[3] In a telephone conversation later that day, Secretary Hoover would tell the President that he had turned down a request from Ethiopia for an airplane for the Emperor because he "could not give one man, for his personal use, one airplane for $2 million, when we had [a] total program in that country of $5 [million] in one year." Eisenhower, who had been previously informed of the Emperor's request, replied that "you have your 'best drag' in that country when you do something for the Emperor" (Telephone conversation, Eisenhower and Hoover, Nov. 12, 1956, AWF/D; Staff Notes No. 17, Sept. 14, 1956, AWF/D). On November 15 the National Security Council formulated guidelines for military aid to Ethiopia. Under these guidelines the United States would endeavor to give the Ethiopian armed forces the capability to maintain internal security and resist the threat of local aggression by Somalia while making "every effort to avoid a military build-up which would seriously strain the Ethiopian economy or lead to commitments for indefinite U.S. support" (NSC meeting minutes, Nov. 16, 1956, AWF/NSC; State, *Foreign Relations, 1955–1957*, vol. XVIII, *Africa*, pp. 331–39). At that same meeting Eisenhower directed the Department of Defense to make a Constellation available to the Emperor, at a price of only $700,000, far below market value. On January 28, 1957, the Emperor, who had financed the purchase of the plane out of aid funds intended for civil aviation development, thanked the American government for delivering the plane (which crashed and burned about two weeks later) (*ibid.*, pp. 332–33).

2091   *EM, WHCF, Confidential File: Trade Agreements and Tariffs—Cerium Alloys*

To Jere Cooper   *November 12, 1956*

Dear Mr. Chairman: As you know, in its report to me on its escape clause investigation relating to imports of ferrocerium (lighter flints) and all other cerium alloys, the United States Tariff Commission found (1) that such imports were causing serious injury to the domestic industry producing like or directly competitive products and (2) that this injury resulted in part from a tariff concession, effective January 1, 1948, which reduced the duty on such imports by 50 percent. The Tariff Commission in its report recommended that the mentioned concession be withdrawn in full.[1]

During intensive study of this matter within the Executive Branch a question relating to the legal aspects of the competitive situation in the domestic industry emerged. Accordingly, I asked the Attorney General to undertake a thorough exploration of this legal question and to advise me definitively with respect thereto.[2]

I have now heard from the Attorney General and he has advised me that the facts developed in his inquiry do not warrant the filing of any proceeding by the Department of Justice.[3]

After consulting with interested departments and agencies of the Executive Branch, and after reviewing this case again in the light of latest available information, I have decided, on the facts and the law, that this case does not present sufficient grounds for escape clause relief.[4]

When an industry is apparently in straitened circumstances due to a variety of causes it is almost always difficult to assess the degree to which imports may have contributed, if at all, to the industry's problems. Mindful of this consideration and of the Commission's findings in this case, it nevertheless does not appear to me that imports of lighter flints have, as the law provides, "contributed substantially towards causing or threatening serious injury" to the domestic industry. Such difficulties as the United States industry has encountered appear to me to be due rather to an approximately 40 percent decline in United States consumption of lighter flints, from 138,000 pounds in 1951 to 83,400 pounds in 1954, and to a sharp decline of about 90 percent in United States exports, from 86,100 pounds in 1951 to 8,000 pounds in 1954. Imports on the other hand in 1954 were only slightly more than 5,000 pounds and represented only 6.8% of the domestic consumption of lighter flints. Imports have increased since the Commission filed its report but they still represent a relatively small proportion of domestic consumption.

It is the firm policy of the United States to seek continuously expanding levels of world trade and investment. Any departure from this established policy must of course, therefore, be taken only if predicated upon sound evidence and reason.[5] In my judgment such sound evidence and reason are lacking in this case for there is a very serious question that increased imports are contributing substantially towards causing or threatening serious injury. *Sincerely*

[1] Cooper was Chairman of the House Ways and Means Committee. The report is United States Tariff Commission, *Ferrocerium (Lighter Flints) and All Other Cerium Alloys Report to the President on Escape Clause Investigation No. 41 Under the Provisions of Section 7 of the Trade Agreements Extension Act of 1951 as Amended*, 1955. On the escape clause provision of the Trade Agreements Extension Act see nos. 908 and 1004; see also *Congressional Quarterly Almanac*, vol. IX, *1953*, pp. 210–11. Eisenhower would subsequently release the

text of this letter to the press. He would also send a copy to the Chairman of the Senate Committee on Finance (Press release, Nov. 13, 1956, same file as document).

[2] The President had deferred his decision on the Tariff Commission report, submitted to him in December 1955, until after the completion of an antitrust investigation (McPhee memorandum, Mar. 20, 1956, same file as document; see also "Decision on Lighter-Flints Escape-Clause Case Deferred," *U.S. Department of State Bulletin* 34, no. 870 [February 27, 1956], p. 353).

[3] For this response see Brownell to Eisenhower, Sept. 26. 1956, same file as document.

[4] The Department of Labor had concurred with the Tariff Commission's recommendations on special grounds relating to the level of employment in the domestic industry. All of the other interested agencies and departments had disagreed with the commission's findings and recommendations (McPhee memorandum, Nov. 10, 1956, same file as document).

[5] For background on Eisenhower's tariff policies see, for example, nos. 985, 1590, and 1936.

2092   *EM, AWF, Name Series*

To EDGAR NEWTON EISENHOWER   *November 12, 1956*

Dear Ed: I was alarmed by the first paragraph of your letter. I am quite certain of one thing: in view of all you say, a good long rest is clearly indicated. You and Lucy had better take off for Southern California and stay there for a month.[1]

As for myself, my great personal disappointment is that our problem in the Mid East continues at such a critical stage that I cannot contemplate leaving Washington at this time.[2] Since I shall be very busy indeed from December fifteenth onward through the next six months, it seems clear that unless the situation is markedly improved within a few days I am going to get no rest at all before I am in the middle of another session of Congress.

So far as I know, I am in remarkably good health for my age, but at 66 I am sure that no man can continue to take the steady daily beatings, worries and exhausting hours without finally showing some effects.[3] But I am doing my best to get a short period each evening when I can swing my golf clubs for 10 or 15 minutes, and then go the pool for another 10 or 15 minutes' swim. In this way I seem to be getting along very well.

Give my love to Lucy, and do take care of yourself. *As ever*

P.S. Of course when you come back this way I will be glad to have that long talk.[4]

[1] Edgar had written that he had experienced a collapse, apparently brought on by nervous tension (Nov. 9, 1956, AWF/N). In his December 3 (AWF/N) reply to the President's second suggestion of a trip to Southern California (Dec. 1, 1956, *ibid.*),

Edgar would explain that he was suffering from a slipped disc which was impinging on the nerve; see also Lucy Eisenhower to Eisenhower, Dec. 3, 1956, *ibid.* On December 7 Eisenhower would remind Edgar that their brother, Milton, "has had the trouble for some time" (*ibid.*). For developments see no. 2137.

[2] Edgar's letter indicated that he thought the President was going to take a few weeks relaxation in Augusta, Georgia. As it turned out, the forces in the Suez Canal zone would withdraw by mid-November (see no. 2086) and the Eisenhowers would be able to vacation in Augusta from November 26 to December 13.

[3] While the President had "looked strong and appeared quite vigorous" at their last meeting and on television, Edgar had written, he hoped that Eisenhower had not exhausted himself.

[4] Edgar wrote that he wanted to "explore," when they next met, "some phases of our public life" (Nov. 9, 1956).

2093   *EM, WHCF,*
President's Personal File 1092

To Maud Rogers Hurd   *November 12, 1956*

Dear Maud: Mamie shared with me your good letter of the Sunday before the election.[1] While I could not find in my heart any room for a special elation over the outcome of the election—principally because of the tensions and difficulties of the international situation—I was, of course, highly gratified by the vote of confidence given to me by so many of the American people. Incidentally, I quite agree with you that Mamie could have won the election on her own—just by smiling![2] She has turned out to be the star campaigner of the family.

I was, of course, surprised that Kansas—good Republican State that it has always been—chose this year a Democrat Governor, but I am too far from the actual scene really to know the true story there. I suppose the drought had a great deal to do with it, as did the primary fight in the Republican ranks.[3]

I wish that I had known that Myra was with Bill Kent when we were in Minneapolis; I would have liked nothing better than at least to say hello to her.[4]

Incidentally, perhaps you know that I have been recently in touch with Katherine Haughey, and that her husband sent me a painting.[5] The picture is hanging just outside the door of my office.

Mamie and I hope that your health will steadily improve, and want you to know that you are constantly in our thoughts and prayers.[6]

With affectionate regard, *As ever*

[1] Mrs. Hurd, one of Eisenhower's oldest friends from Abilene (see *Eisenhower Papers,* vols. I–XIII), had sent best wishes for his reelection (Nov. 4, 1956, same file as document).

[2] Mrs. Hurd had said, "for it was and is Mamie just sitting there with her graciousness and smile that made the votes! Of course you are sorta nice too Dwight."

[3] George Docking (A.B. University of Kansas 1925), a Lawrence, Kansas, banker, would become the first Democratic governor of Kansas since 1936. The Republican gubernatorial primary had been bitter. Kansas Governor Frederick L. Hall (LL.B. University of Southern California 1941) had been opposed and denied a second term by Warren W. Shaw, a Topeka attorney and state legislator (see *New York Times*, Nov. 7, 1956).

[4] Myra was Mrs. Hurd's daughter. We have been unable to identify Kent. The Eisenhowers had campaigned in Minneapolis on October 16.

[5] We have been unable to identify the Haugheys.

[6] The sixty-eight-year-old Mrs. Hurd had been hospitalized for ten weeks and currently was being cared for by nurses.

2094   *EM, AWF, Name Series*

To Bernard Law Montgomery   *November 13, 1956*

Dear Monty: I'm delighted to receive your enthusiastic note about the results of the political election. I didn't realize you were quite as partisan as you seem to be—but I'm glad your sympathies are all Republican.[1]

With warm regard, *As ever*

[1] The Deputy Commander at SHAPE had sent a handwritten congratulatory message on November 7 (AWF/N). "Hurrah! Hurrah! Hurrah!" he had written, "You definitely hit the Democrats right out of the ground."

2095   *EM, AWF, Name Series*

To William Samuel Paley   *November 14, 1956*
Personal

Dear Bill: My grateful thanks for the compliment you pay me in your letter of the ninth.[1] I agree thoroughly with your thesis that if the Republican Party is to establish itself as a dominant influence in American life, it must do two things.[2] First, it must adopt and live by a philosophy of government that I call "Modern Republicanism" and it must convince all America that it does live and act by this philosophy.[3] Secondly, it must organize itself far better than it has in the past, particularly at the precinct, district and county levels. We have had a Party that I am afraid wanted to have too many generals and too few fighting men.

One part of the first job is gradually going forward, that is the conversion of most Republicans in public life to the need for making their creed modern and suited to the conditions of the day. The selling to the American people of this conversion has not been so well done, as the late election proves.[4] Because of my special responsibility for getting the kind of legislation the country needs, and the fact that the Congress is in the hands of the Democrats, I cannot, of course, be too partisan, but in my appearances before the public, I can preach political philosophy—the kind that America seems to approve. This ought to increase the fertility of the field in which the more partisan politicians can work fruitfully.

It was wonderful to hear from you.

With warm greetings to Mrs. Paley and, of course, personal regard to yourself, *As ever*

[1] Paley had written Eisenhower on November 9, 1956 (AWF/N) to congratulate him on his presidential victory of November 6 (see no. 2074).

[2] Paley believed that in emphasizing Eisenhower's personal popularity as one of the most important factors in the size of his victory, political commentators overlooked the facts that Eisenhower had "made the people aware of the kind of America" he wanted and that "the people want that kind of America too." Paley stated that the American people did "not feel that the Republican party wants it as much as" Eisenhower does.

[3] Eisenhower had outlined his concept of "modern republicanism" in his remarks following the election (see *Public Papers of the Presidents: Eisenhower, 1956*, pp. 1089–91). See also nos. 2083, 2112, and Eisenhower, *Waging Peace*, p. 375.

[4] On the election of a Democratic Congress see no. 2075. Eisenhower was one of only four Presidents, and the first since Zachary Taylor in 1848, to begin a term with both houses of Congress in the hands of the opposition party (see Malcom Moos, "Election of 1956," in Schlesinger, *History of American Presidential Elections*, vol. IV, *1940–1968*, p. 3353.

2096   *EM, AWF, Administration Series*

To Oveta Culp Hobby   *November 15, 1956*

Dear Oveta: You know how hectic things usually are in this office, and I can assure you that since the election the pressures—because of the Mid East situation—have seemingly increased ten-fold. I say all this by way of an explanation why I have not, long before this, thanked you for all you did to be helpful during the campaign.[1] Particularly I was delighted that Texas again reaffirmed its confidence in the principles for which I stand. Although I would not like to be quoted, Texas was one state that in my heart I really wanted to carry.[2]

At any rate, I do assure you of my lasting appreciation for your many contributions to the effort.

With affectionate regard, *As ever*

[1] Hobby had written Eisenhower a letter of congratulations on November 13 (AWF/A). This letter apparently crossed Eisenhower's November 15 letter in the mail (Eisenhower to Hobby, Nov. 19, 1956, AWF/A).
[2] See no. 2081.

2097   *EM, AWF, International Series:*
                                                    Saudi Arabia

To Ibn Abd al-Aziz Saud   *November 16, 1956*
Secret

Your Majesty: I was pleased to receive Your Majesty's two latest messages, through Prince Faisal and the Foreign Office on November 4, and through our Ambassador on November 11.[1]

I am confident that you will continue to support measures such as those referred to in resolutions of the United Nations General Assembly which will restore peace to the area of hostilities.[2] Beyond this, I sincerely hope that you may be able to encourage Egyptian cooperation to achieve solutions for some of the fundamental problems which gave rise to the current crisis.

I deeply appreciate the thanks which you have conveyed for the stand of the United States Government in the recent sessions of the General Assembly dealing with Near Eastern matters.[3] I can assure you that the United States is trying strenuously to bring peace to the area and to work out solutions based on justice and equity for all. We will continue to use our influence to secure compliance with the United Nations resolutions and, thereafter, to encourage actions which will establish lasting peace and stability in the area.

We share with you the concern at the shadow cast, not only over the Near East, but over the whole world, by recent events. Our hearts are made heavy by the shadows cast by the ruthless suppression of the people of Hungary in their quest for freedom.[4] I know that you will share our concern in this, as the events in Hungary may well be indicative of the fate of any who become dominated by the Soviet Union. We would hope that you will see your way clear to support us in our efforts in the United Nations to meet this crisis.

I have read Your Majesty's suggestion regarding Egypt.[5] I share with you the deep regret at the suffering which may have been caused by these recent events. I am hopeful, however, that, when the United Nations forces enter and General Burns has had an opportunity to assess the situation, we may find that the damage was not as extensive or as great as was, at first, believed.[6] Meanwhile, humanitarian agencies in this country and elsewhere are active in the provision of emergency relief.

I am pleased to have these opportunities to exchange views with Your Majesty. I hope that in the months ahead these exchanges may continue, and that perhaps at some stage we will have an opportunity to meet for a general review of problems of common interest.[7]

May God have you in his safe keeping. *Your sincere friend*

[1] Faisal ibn Abdul Aziz, King Saud's brother was Foreign Minister of Saudi Arabia; George E. Wadsworth was the American Ambassador to that country. The State Department drafted this letter to King Saud.

[2] See no. 2071.

[3] See Memorandum, Message of November 5, 1956, from King Saud, AWF/I: Saudi Arabia.

[4] See no. 2067.

[5] King Saud had suggested that the United States use its influence to guarantee that Egypt would be compensated for material losses sustained as a result of the fighting (State, *Foreign Relations, 1955–1957*, vol. XVI, *Suez Crisis July 26–December 31, 1956*, p. 1138).

[6] Major General Eedson L. M. Burns, a Canadian Army officer, was Commander of the United Nations Emergency Force.

[7] King Saud would tell the U.S. ambassador that he welcomed the prospect of such a meeting (Wadsworth to Dulles, Nov. 26, 1956, AWF/D-H). The King would see Eisenhower in January 1957 (see Diary, Jan. 31, 1957, AWF/D; see also no. 2147).

2098   *EM, AWF, Name Series*

To ANTHONY R. PARSHLEY   *November 16, 1956*
Personal

Dear Canon Parshley: Thank you very much for your letter of the seventh. I am, of course, highly gratified by your complimentary references to myself, but I think that some of your conclusions have been reached without a clear appreciation of the facts, as I see them.[1]

I did not say that the victory of last Tuesday was one for the "Republican Party" as you state in your letter. I said it was clear evidence that America approves of "modern Republicanism." This is a term that I used for want of a better one to describe the philosophy, principles and proper functions of government as I understand them, and which I try to promote in all that I say and all that I do.[2]

To me it would be fantastic to believe that the United States elected an individual—or two individuals—merely because of a very great liking for one or both as personalities, or even solely because of a belief in their integrity and purity of purpose. It seems to me that it is belittling the intelligence and judgment of the American people to conclude that they cross party lines in voting unless there is basic similarity between their own convictions and those of the person for whom they are voting.

Now on your side of this argument, I readily admit that the public in general does *not* believe that my own convictions are yet largely characteristic of the Republican Party as a whole. While I know that these convictions are shared by the great majority of the Party, this is not yet true for the whole.

The Republican, or any other, Party aspiring to be an instrumentality for serving well the interests of the United States, must be bound together by principles that appeal to the vast bulk of our citizens.[3]

As to your hope that I will not become too intensely partisan, I submit, in all modesty, that this implied charge cannot, in my opinion, be properly levelled against me in anything I've ever said or done.[4]

I do believe in the two-party system, and I have always held that if I were to be elected President, I would prefer a Republican Congress because then the American people could more accurately determine and fix responsibility for success or for failure.[5]

But before all else, I am an American, just as is any other member of either Party. I conduct this office in that attitude, and certainly I have never used it merely to promote the interests of my own political Party. But I still maintain that it is my duty as leader of the Party to make it a better instrumentality for serving the United States. I shall continue to keep so trying.

With best wishes, *Sincerely*

---

[1] The Reverend Canon Anthony R. Parshley of the Episcopal Diocese of Rhode Island had written the President on November 7, 1956 (same file as document). Parshley, a Stevenson supporter, said that many lifelong Democrats had crossed party lines to vote for Eisenhower on a personal basis: "Please do not let your modesty lead you into the mistake of believing that you were given this evidence of approbation for any impersonal reasons."

A draft of this letter, showing Eisenhower's extensive handwritten changes, is in AWF/Drafts.

[2] Eisenhower was referring to his televised victory speech on modern Republicanism (see *Public Papers of the Presidents: Eisenhower, 1956*, pp. 1989–91; see also no. 2095).

[3] The draft of this letter had read "One of my tasks, as I see it, is to see that the Republican Party, if it aspires to be an instrumentality for serving properly the political interests of the United States, comes to mean exactly this to the American people."

[4] Parshley had written, "I think it would be tragic if you were, in the face of the facts, to permit partisan political considerations to becloud the fact that you are the President whom the people elected because they trusted you more than they trusted any political party."

[5] See also Eisenhower, *Mandate for Change*, pp. 435–36.

EM, AWF,
Administration Series

To SHERMAN ADAMS *November 17, 1956*
Memorandum. Personal and confidential

When Senator Wylie visited me this morning, he spoke to me again about that man _____ that he was so anxious to have appointed to a Federal job several years ago.[1] Herewith a memorandum that tells about all the wonderful characteristics of Mr. _____.[2]

Senator Wylie remarked "I am not trying to get rid of the man. It would be like losing my right arm. So while I do not throw him at you, yet I assure you that if you fail to put him in a responsible position in the Executive Department, you are losing the services of one of the most brilliant men in government."

I remember the case as it came up two or three years ago. The Secretary of State was anxious to get this particular man out of Senator Wylie's office since he considered him a bad influence there, but we could find no job we felt we could in good conscience give the man and that he would take.[3]

---

[1] For background see nos. 356 and 1254.

[2] This memorandum is not in AWF.

[3] For more on Eisenhower's relationship with Wisconsin Senator Alexander Wiley see nos. 114, 806, 1254, and Eisenhower, *Mandate for Change*, p. 301. The person involved would remain in his position with the Senate Foreign Relations Committee until 1958 and would hold a similar post with the Government Operations Subcommittee until 1964.

EM, AWF, Administration Series: Fitzsimons

To EDYTHE P. TURNER *November 17, 1956*

Dear Colonel Turner: Of course I am delighted that you are now assured of that Hawaiian assignment, though I know you will leave Denver with regret both because of your associations there and that cabin up in the hills.[1] I sincerely hope that Mrs. Eisenhower and I will see you here before your departure.[2]

Don't worry about my weight—my problem now is not to *gain*.[3] General Snyder still insists on a liberal daily ration of yogurt and carrots, but even so I have to be very careful lest the scales go up.

I am sorry that you did not get in touch with Mrs. Whitman while you were here, because we wanted you to be with us up at the Sheraton Park the night of the election. But I daresay that you probably saw more of the actual returns on television than did any of us in our crowded suite.[4]

With warm personal regard, *Sincerely*

[1] Lieutenant Colonel Turner had reported the new assignment in a November 13 letter (AWF/A: Fitzsimons; see also Turner to Whitman, Nov. 13, 1956, *ibid.*). Earlier this year, through Presidential Secretary Ann Whitman, Eisenhower had offered to help secure the assignment for Turner, but she had declined (see the related correspondence in *ibid.*).

[2] On January 21 Turner would be among the "Fitzsimons contingent" attending the Inauguration (see Eisenhower to Turner, Dec. 19, 1956, AWF/D).

[3] The President's former nurse had commented on how "wonderful" he looked, and added "Do not lose any more weight. . . ."

[4] Turner said she had been in Washington, D.C., on November 6, but had been unable to reach Ann Whitman. "Needless to say," she wrote, she "stayed up most of the night avidly watching TV" (see also Turner to Whitman, Nov. 13, 1956, AWF/A: Fitzsimons).

2101   *EM, AWF, Drafts Series*

To Winston Spencer Churchill   *November 17, 1956*

Dear Winston: As the end of November approaches, I am reminded that on the 30th you will celebrate your eighty-second birthday. I join the tribute the world will accord you on this milestone.

With affectionate regard to you and Clemmie, in which Mamie joins, *As ever*[1]

[1] An unsigned typewritten note attached to this message reads: "I deliberately made this shorter than usual since I thought his telegram of congratulations was pretty abrupt." Churchill's telegram, conveyed to the President on November 8 via the British Embassy in Washington, D.C., and Eisenhower's November 9 reply are in AWF/I: Churchill.

2102   *EM, AWF, Drafts Series*

To Henry Robinson Luce   *November 19, 1956*
Personal and confidential

Dear Harry: This letter is for your *eyes only.*

This morning Clare came to my office and we had quite a long talk, concerning the critical international situation, on which she has some positive ideas.

Frankly, she has a set of logical reasons for some of the conclusions she has reached concerning the need for drastic American decisions at this point in the world's history.[1] I think, however, that she feels in her heart that we here in Washington, and indeed in other capitals, have been somewhat blind to the developing situation and have not thoroughly studied the various factors in the situation that she rightly deems to be so important.

In essence, she believes, as you undoubtedly know, that the time has come to challenge Russia openly, with force of arms. While I have no doubt that as of this moment we are in as good a relative position of power as we ever will be, to undertake such an adventure, I am quite certain that the implications and inescapable results of an all-out war have not sufficiently impressed themselves upon her as to make her realize that such a war must be a decision *in extremis* and not one to adopt as long as there remains the faintest possibility of reaching a solution by some other method.

She seems convinced that all these other methods have been tried and have failed. But she possibly forgets that these other methods depend upon patience, steadiness, firmness and *time*.

Actually, I have no trouble understanding her forebodings, and the convictions she holds.[2] As I told her, I have stayed awake many nights pondering these things in the hope of finding some way of improving the methods we are now using to maintain and make progress toward better arrangements in the existing world. Moreover, I feel that if the time ever comes when I am convinced that the final and ultimate decision must be made, I will have the fortitude to do it. But I repeat—the inescapable results on the civilization of the northern hemisphere would be something almost beyond the comprehension of the normal individual.

I write this letter only because you know of my affection for you both and of my hope that by quietly contemplating methods other than war, she will finally come to see that as *of this moment* neither "limited" war nor a hydrogen bomb war could really settle anything either in the Mid East or in our relationships with the Kremlin.

When next you are in Washington, please call up to see whether we could not have a bit of a chat. I think there is much more hope in the world situation today than Clare seems to believe truly exists.

Since this letter deals exclusively with my conversation with your wife, you will understand my reason for asking that no one in the world know of it except yourself. I should feel better if you will destroy it after reading it.[3]

With warm regard, *As ever*

---

[1] In this sentence Eisenhower had deleted the words "very fine" before the words "set of logical reasons."

[2] Eisenhower deleted the words "with every word she said I have a great amount of sympathy" after the word "actually" at the beginning of this sentence.

[3] "When Clare was telling me Monday afternoon about her Washington visit she said that she had never had a conversation which so changed her opinion as the one she had had that morning," Luce would tell Eisenhower. "My own estimate as to 'hope in the world situation' runs with yours" (Luce to Eisenhower, Nov. 20, 1956, AWF/A). Luce would meet with Eisenhower on January 19, 1957 (President's daily appointments).

2103 *EM, AWF, Administration Series*

To CHARLES DOUGLAS JACKSON *November 19, 1956*
Personal

Dear C. D.: It has been too long since I have written personally to acknowledge various of your recent communications. I suspect that my neglect has been based upon the definite knowledge that you, of all people, would understand the pressures of the last weeks.[1]

First, but most unimportant, is my appreciation of your telegram of November seventh.[2] In addition to the two ingredients you mention, there is a terrific job ahead in the political arena, for every one of us— and I am hopeful that you will, with your usual enthusiasm and energy, take an active part in it.

Now about your suggestions concerning Hungary.[3] Bill Jackson and I have talked them over, and at least some of Colonel Sarrazac-Soulage's ideas have already been put into effect.[4] I know that your whole being cries out for "action" on the Hungarian problem. I assure you that the measures taken there by the Soviets are just as distressing to me as they are to you. But to annihilate Hungary, should it become the scene of a bitter conflict, is in no way to help her. At the same time, if the United Nations is to work, Mr. Hammarskjold must act as he, and the United Nations, see fit.[5]

One of my friends sent me a particularly moving document on the case of decency versus extinction. I quote from it two or three sentences:

"Partisanship has no place when such a vital question (as atomic self-destruction) confronts us. Mothers in Israel and Egypt, sons in England and France, fathers and husbands in the United States and in Russia are all potential victims and sufferers. *After* the event, all of them, regardless of nationality, will be disinterested in the petty arguments as to who was responsible—or even the niceties of procedure . . . That War (would be) so terrible that the human mind cannot comprehend it."[6]

I realize that this letter in no sense answers your urgent suggestions. Someday perhaps you will be down here and we can talk matters over.[7]

With warm regard, *As ever*

[1] On November 8, 1956, Jackson had sent Ann Whitman a copy of a cable he had wired to White House Special Assistant William Jackson regarding the Soviet suppression of the Hungarian uprising (AWF/A, C.D. Jackson Corr.). For background on the Hungarian situation see nos. 2044, 2055, and 2067. On the Suez crisis see nos. 2068, 2071, and 2073.

[2] In his telegram of November 7 Jackson had written "You have the mandate and we have the man, an unbeatable combination for America" (AWF/A). For more on Eisenhower's victory over Stevenson see no. 2074.

[3] Jackson had written that "under cover of United Nations total preoccupation with Middle Eastern problems and the new general war threat, the Russians are getting away with murder in Hungary." Jackson believed that if the United States were to give Hammarskjöld a "firm prod," he would "get cracking" on appointing and sending an inspection team to the Hungarian border. Jackson stated that those who argued that there was no point in sending a U.N. team because they would be denied admission, missed the "moral pressure point" completely (Jackson to Whitman, Nov. 8, 1956, AWF/A, C. D. Jackson Corr.).

[4] In a November 12 letter to William Jackson, C. D. Jackson had forwarded a letter from Colonel Robert Sarrazac-Soulage, who had fought with the French Resistance during World War II. Sarrazac-Soulage had suggested exploiting "the tremendous psychological trend which is awaiting" and had proposed that members of the Security Council immediately go by special plane to Budapest to study the question of genocide and to obtain from the Soviet Union a corridor for the free passage of medical and relief supplies. Publicizing this trip in a dramatic fashion would, Sarrazac-Soulage hoped, influence world opinion against the Soviet Union (Sarrazac-Soulage to C. D. Jackson, Nov. 9, 1956, AWF/A, C. D. Jackson Corr.).

[5] See no. 2082. On November 12 the Hungarian government had informed the Secretary General that sending United Nations representatives to Budapest was "not warranted," but that Hungary would cooperate with the International Red Cross. United Nations resolutions on November 15 urged Hungary and the Soviet Union to cease deportation of Hungarian nationals and to allow U.N. observers to enter Hungary to report on deportations (State, *Foreign Relations, 1955–1957*, vol. XXV, *Eastern Europe*, pp. 434, 460–61).

[6] The quotation is from Lessing Julius Rosenwald's letter to Eisenhower; see no. 2079.

[7] For developments see no. 2116.

2104   *EM, WHCF, Official File 116-R*

To David William Brooks   *November 19, 1956*
Personal

Dear Mr. Brooks: I am deeply grateful to you for your interesting and thoughtful letter, dealing with the impressions you gained during your recent trip to the Mid East. Your report on the general consensus of the less prejudiced Arab people coincides with my own impression, though of course I have not had the benefit of as many direct contacts as have you.[1]

Whatever the reasons that have brought the situation to the critical stage, our present problem, if matters, militarily speaking, can be stabilized, is to determine how we are going to proceed in the best interests of the peoples of the United States and of all these countries.[2]

This country wants nothing for itself, as you know, but we do want to provide assistance to these nations to enable them to maintain their own independence and to establish themselves economically so that they can provide for their peoples a rising standard of living, of health and of education. If they can foresee a brighter horizon, I am hopeful that much of the bitterness will be relegated to a less important place in their thinking, though at the same time I realize that an imbedded feeling of injustice is probably the most difficult thing in the world to eradicate. The United States stands ready at all times to be of assistance in the providing of technical know-how and tools to bring about a better future for these peoples.

At any rate, I do want you to know that your letter has been helpful in many ways, and I am grateful to you for taking the trouble to write me at such length. *Sincerely*

[1] David William Brooks (M.S. University of Georgia 1923) was general manager of the Cotton Producers Association in Atlanta, Georgia. He had told Eisenhower "the higher type, more stable Arab people" were not fanatical supporters of Nasser. They were sympathetic with the problems of the Jewish people, he said, but they believed that the Jewish side of the problem was usually presented more effectively in the United States than the Arab side. This group of Arabs, Brooks believed, would accept a settlement reducing Israeli territory to that area originally established by the United Nations while compensating those Arabs who had been displaced (Brooks to Eisenhower, Nov. 15, 1956, same file as document).

[2] For Eisenhower's proposals regarding future U.S. policy in the Middle East see no. 2078.

2105   *EM, AWF, DDE Diaries Series*

To Edgar Newton Eisenhower   *November 19, 1956*
Personal and confidential

Dear Ed: It frequently occurs to me that the further removed an area is from this city, the more prolific are the rumors as to what is going to happen here. If I were you, I would stop worrying about the subject you mentioned in your note of the fifteenth. While I do not know who could have been considering the employment of Pearl Wanamaker, I assure you that no one could ever do it with my consent. I have known her for many years, and I have neither liked what she had to say in public or her mannerisms. My refusal to approve any appointment for her has nothing whatever to do with politics.[1] *As ever*

[1] Edgar had heard that the Administration was considering appointing former Washington State legislator and educator Pearl Anderson Wanamaker (A.B. University of Washington 1922). Recently, Mrs. Wanamaker had lost her position as superintendent of public instruction in Washington. Such an appointment, Edgar had written, "would be interpreted as a slap in the face" by Eisenhower supporters "who were so anxious to rid her of her authority" (AWF/N).

2106   *EM, AWF, Dulles-Herter Series*

DIARY   *November 20, 1956*

I called Winthrop Aldrich and told him to let Butler and Macmillan know simultaneously that we are sympathetic with their troubles and interested in helping them out.[1]

[1] For background see nos. 2057 and 2068. Eisenhower had dictated these words after a meeting with Treasury Secretary Humphrey and Acting Secretary of State Hoover regarding Great Britain's request for assistance from the United States. Chancellor of the Exchecquer Harold Macmillan had told Ambassador Aldrich, on the preceding day, of Prime Minister Eden's deteriorating physical condition and his impending three-week vacation. During Eden's absence a triumvirate of Macmillan, Richard A. Butler, leader of the House of Commons, and Lord Salisbury, leader of the House of Lords and senior cabinet minister, would run the government. The first act after Eden's departure, Macmillan said, would be the withdrawal of British troops from Egypt. He asked Aldrich for "a fig leaf to cover our nakedness," one that would persuade the Cabinet to vote for unconditional withdrawal (State, *Foreign Relations, 1955–1957*, vol. XVI, *Suez Crisis July 26–December 31, 1956*, pp. 1150–52, 1163; see also Telephone conversation, Eisenhower and Aldrich, Nov. 19, 1956, AWF/D; Macmillan, *Riding the Storm*, pp. 173–74; and Richard Austen Butler, *The Art of the Possible: The Memoirs of Lord Butler* [London, 1971], pp. 194–95; on Eden's condition see no. 2124).

At the meeting on this day Secretary Humphrey told Eisenhower that financial assistance was available to Great Britain through the World Bank and the Export-Import Bank and that the United States could provide aid to meet stringent needs. The President said that when the British and French had withdrawn their troops, the United States "would talk to the Arabs to obtain the removal of any objections they may have regarding the provision of oil to Western Europe" (Goodpaster, Memorandum of Conference, Nov. 21, 1956, AWF/D).

Eisenhower had then requested Ambassador Aldrich to discuss the situation with Butler and Macmillan together, without embarrassment, if possible, and tell both men that "as soon as things happen that we anticipate, we can furnish 'a lot of fig leaves'" (Telephone conversation, Eisenhower and Aldrich, Nov. 20, 1956, *ibid.*; see also Telephone conversation, Eisenhower and Humphrey, Nov. 21, 1956, *ibid.*). For developments see no. 2123.

2107   *EM, AWF, Name Series*

To Charles S. Jones   *November 20, 1956*

Dear Charlie: Whenever I have had time for casual conversation with
my friends since November sixth, almost invariably the details of the
campaign will come up for discussion. Time and again someone will
remark—about a matter which I had previously not known—
"Charlie Jones took care of that." I realize now a little more than in
the past what a gigantic chore you undertook and how very helpful
you were in a thousand and one phases of the entire operation. For
everything you did, including the things I know and do not know
about, my lasting appreciation.

I had hoped that you would make your way East sometime soon,
but I now hear that you have decided that bears in Utah are more
exciting game than is provided by the social life of these parts. I don't
blame you in the slightest; as a matter of strict honesty, I envy you
greatly.

Until I see you, once again my gratitude for your friendship as I
add this latest business to my long list of indebtedness to you.[1]

With warm personal regard, *As ever*

[1] Jones, of Los Angeles, California, was president of the Richfield Oil Corporation. He
had served Eisenhower as a political adviser and sometimes joined him as a golf
partner. See nos. 1033 and 1180.

2108   *EM, AWF, Ann Whitman Diary Series*

Diary   *November 21, 1956*

I just finished a conversation with the Tunisian Prime Minister,
Mr. Habib Bourguiba.[1]

I was struck by his sincerity, his intelligence and his friendliness. He
is grateful for the help we have given him from surplus foods, particularly wheat. He says that, in addition, his country needs of course a
great deal of technical assistance.[2]

He gave as his biggest problem the existence of the French-Algerian
war. He came back again and again to the expressed hope that the
United States could find some way to mediate in that useless struggle.
He claimed that France would have to concede very little in order to
settle the proposition; on questioning, he expressed the belief that an
arrangement like the British Commonwealth of Nations between
France and Algeria, to become effective within a given number of
years, would be most acceptable to the Algerians.[3]

He says that if we could get this war settled, all the Western World would have a very much finer relationship with North Africa and indeed with the Arab world.

He said that the Jewish-Arab quarrel was no concern of theirs—they are not affected by it.

I assured him of America's friendliness, and particularly of its desire to deal directly with each one of the Moslem countries in the effort to promote our common interests.

---

[1] The United States had recognized the new nation of Tunisia on March 22 (State, *Foreign Relations, 1955–1957*, vol. XVIII, *Africa*, p. 650; Hoover to Eisenhower, Nov. 20, 1956, AWF/D).

[2] Bourguiba had thanked the President for the 45,000 tons of wheat the United States had contributed to relieve famine in Tunisia. See also State, *Foreign Relations, 1955–1957*, vol. XVIII, *Africa*, pp. 656–58.

American aid programs to the region had continued to increase. On September 27 the National Security Council had advocated "reasonable economic and technical aid" for Morocco and Tunisia "when required by our direct interests." Responding to Secretary Humphrey's objections to such aid on fiscal grounds, the President had stated that "it seemed to him a very good investment of fifty million dollars if as a result of the investment we succeeded in keeping the Communists out of this vast and very important strategic area." He approved a military aid program for Tunisia, subject to the normal budgetary review process (NSC meeting minutes, Sept. 28, 1956, AWF/NSC; State, *Foreign Relations, 1955–1957*, vol. XVIII, *Africa*, pp. 130–37). As it turned out, however, the United States would earmark only five million dollars for Tunisia in FY 1957, in accordance with American policy of allowing the French to remain Tunisia's primary aid donor (*ibid.*, pp. 654–55).

[3] See no. 1792; see also Frank Costigliola, *France and the United States: The Cold Alliance Since World War II* [New York, 1992], pp. 111–12.

2109

DIARY

Top secret

I approved today the Joint Chief of Staff's plan for the disposal to bases, fields and ships afloat all the present atomic stock pile, nuclear and fission.[1]

I informed the Chairman of the Chiefs of Staff that (*a*) the State Department should be in agreement with all disposal involving overseas bases, and (*b*) today's dispersal should mark the approximate number of those to be maintained permanently in the field. The bulk of those manufactured hereafter (except for air defense types) should be kept in United States reserve stocks.

---

[1] Colonel Goodpaster noted that the President had approved the JCS plan after he read and discussed a JCS memo that stressed "the desirability of having a considerable

number of weapons in 'safe reserve'" (Goodpaster, Memorandum of Conference, Nov. 21, 1956, AWF/D. See also State, *Foreign Relations, 1955–1957*, vol. XIX, *National Security Policy*, p. 376).

2110

EM, AWF, Name Series

To Aksel Nielsen

November 22, 1956

Dear Aks: I suspect you have come as close as possible to identifying the reasons for Dan's defeat—though the whole thing still leaves me a little puzzled, in view of his previous record, as does Don Brotzman's similar failure.[1] However, what is done is done.

Since November sixth, I have been trying to express my appreciation to people and groups who worked hard during the campaign (in the spare time I have had away from the international situation and official routine, that is). I am afraid that just because you are such a steadfast friend, I have neglected at least a "simple thank you" for all you did to be helpful. I know I don't have ever to tell you of my gratitude for everything you do, in so many ways, for the Eisenhower-Doud family—but once in a while I ought to mind my manners. However, as always, I shall in the end have to rely on your intuitive knowledge of how I feel!

Mamie and I were delighted that you and Helen were with us election night, and are counting on seeing you long before the inauguration.

With warm regard, *As ever*

[1] Former Colorado Governor Dan Thornton had been defeated in the Senate race by a Democrat. Colorado State Senator Donald G. Brotzman had also lost the gubernatorial race to a Democrat. In a November 16 letter Nielsen had suggested that Thornton "got entirely too cocky towards the last" and that there had been a concerted effort by pensioners to defeat him (AWF/N; see also Pexton to Thornton, Aug. 1, 1956; and Hoyt to Eisenhower, Aug. 3, 1956, AWF/N, Hoyt Corr.).

2111

EM, AWF, International Series: Korea

To Syngman Rhee
Confidential

November 23, 1956

Dear Mr. President: I have read with great interest your letter of November 16, 1956, and have considered most carefully the suggestions you have made. I share your views on the importance of international justice for all states, large and small, and the right of self-determination.

It is impossible for me to accept, however, the thesis that because grave violations of these principles have occurred we should now abandon the position that outlawing the use of force is a means of bringing about world peace.[1]

On the contrary, this is the very moment when the potential of the United Nations as an instrument of world opinion has been demonstrated.

In the recent developments in Eastern Europe we now see cracks in the Soviet Empire. The gallant Hungarian people have shown that the spirit of freedom is still alive, despite years of Communist oppression. I am convinced that moral force brought to bear on the Soviet Union through the United Nations will assist to an ever increasing degree in moderating and ultimately bringing to an end Soviet oppression. I believe that these moral forces can bring nearer the day of unification and freedom in Korea also.

In the present crises, there have been terrible injustices and sufferings. War, which is itself an instrument of injustice, is not the remedy. We continue to look to the United Nations as providing the best alternative to global war and the disaster to victor and vanquished alike which would follow in this day of modern weapons. The actions which the free world must, therefore, pursue should be directed toward supporting and strengthening the United Nations so that it may secure justice and peace through law.

May I take up, now, with the utmost frankness your views on expelling the Soviet Union from the United Nations and then reorganizing that body. This course of action has been suggested by others during the past few weeks and has been thoroughly considered.

Although I fully recognize that on numerous occasions the Soviet Union has been guilty of defying every principle of the Charter of the United Nations, we must realize that as a practical matter, the veto power of the Soviet Union would prevent its expulsion. Instead of a new organization, I believe the world should work to strengthen the United Nations so that it can effectively impose its collective will for peace.

Let me assure you that neither the United States Government nor the American people have any illusions whatsoever regarding the nature and objectives of Communist imperialism. The United States has assisted the free countries in developing and maintaining their political, economic and military strength to thwart the Communist objective of world domination. We have clearly demonstrated our willingness to make use of force as a last resort in individual and collective self-defense against aggression. These are times of grave world tension, in which we in the free world must act with calmness and high principle. I have, therefore, welcomed the manner in which you have encouraged a calm resoluteness on the part of your people and your military establishment.

I am pleased that you have felt free to write to me on a confidential and personal basis, and I do not plan to give any publicity to our correspondence. I would like to suggest that you treat our communications in the same way so that we may be at liberty to exchange views from time to time with complete frankness. *Sincerely*

[1] President Syngman Rhee of the Republic of Korea had written Eisenhower on November 16 advocating military and economic assistance to the Hungarians, coupled with a demand that the Soviets withdraw their forces. If they refused, they should be expelled from the United Nations. Rhee also suggested that the United Nations should be replaced by a new organization which would achieve peace with justice by forceful means. Rhee's letter in AWF/I: Korea remains classified. The draft reply suggested by the State Department, with Eisenhower's handwritten emendations, is in AWF/I: Korea (see Hoover to Eisenhower, Nov. 21, 1956, AWF/I: Korea).

2112
EM, AWF, Name Series: "Modern Republicanism"

To Mrs. A. Crocker Landers
November 23, 1956

Dear Mrs. Landers: I was glad to have your provocative and interesting letter, and wish I had time to answer it as fully as it deserves.[1] I agree that there must be leadership in the revitalization of the Republican Party, which means, first of all, that every one of us—and especially those who presume to speak for the Party—must be ready to face the facts set forth in your letter.

While volumes could be written, I content myself here with two observations. We should preach "Modern Republicanism" rather than merely a "New Party."[2] Also we must build from both top and bottom.

I firmly believe that to have a strong basis for the Modern Republicanism that will best represent the interests of all the people, the Party must build upward from the precinct, to the district, to the county and to the state level. Only on such a firm foundation can there be a permanent change. If people will work together, at all levels, the job can be done.

I shall share your letter with those who, with their full energies, deal with the problem; I am hopeful that you will continue your active interest and that you will want to work toward the ends we both seek for the Republican Party.

With best wishes, *Sincerely*

[1] A copy of this letter, with Eisenhower's substantial handwritten changes, is in AWF/Drafts. There is no copy of Mrs. Landers's letter in AWF.
[2] On "Modern Republicanism" see no. 2095; see also the President's remarks in *Public Papers of the Presidents: Eisenhower, 1956*, pp. 1089–91.

To Allen Welsh Dulles   *November 23, 1956*

Dear Allen: Recently Cardinal Mooney, while in my office, made the statement that in certain parts of Czechoslovakia the persecution of citizens based upon religious belief—actually in the hope of stamping out religion itself—is as cruel as anywhere in the world.[1] What do your reports on this matter indicate?[2] *As ever*

[1] Edward Cardinal Mooney had met with the President on November 15.

[2] Director of Central Intelligence Dulles would inform Eisenhower that prior to 1953 the Czech regime had "waged an overt and brutal campaign against the churches" and the Archbishop of Prague still remained under house arrest. Since that time, however, in part because of the success of the campaign to eliminate the church's political influence, "church officials have been allowed to conduct religious services with a minimum of interference." When queried as to whether this information should be reported to Cardinal Mooney, Eisenhower responded "no" (Allen Dulles to Eisenhower, Nov. 29, 1956; [Ann Whitman] to Eisenhower, n.d., AWF/A, Allen Dulles Corr.).

To William Harding Jackson   *November 23, 1956*

Dear Bill: I thoroughly enjoyed your paper "The Fourth Area of the National Effort in Foreign Affairs."[1] On one part only do I have any criticism. This criticism applies to the first three paragraphs under Section IV. Those three paragraphs seem to me to be a little bit fuzzy and are unnecessary to your main theme. If this criticism is valid, then it would probably eliminate also the very short first paragraph in Section V.[2]

In any event, I found your paper both interesting and, I thought, correct. *As ever*

[1] Jackson had become Special Assistant to the President in March 1956; his paper (in AWF/A) was a twelve-page report on psychological warfare (see no. 481). Jackson had defined his subject—the "fourth area" of foreign affairs—as "the area of effort remaining after you have dealt with the diplomatic, economic, and military means of promoting national objectives." Jackson had argued that this was mostly a matter of recognizing the importance of public opinion, even in "totalitarian" countries, and tailoring government actions toward influencing it. He criticized efforts to "rationalize" psychological warfare by the Truman Administration, which had "made the error of attributing unlimited and independent capabilities to psychological warfare."

[2] The first paragraphs of Section IV attempted "to analyze the difference between considering the effect on public opinion of governmental plans, policies, and operations

and considering the psychological implications of such plans, policies and operations."
In the report's fifth section Jackson began his discussion by stating: "In the organization of government it does not seem important to me whether or not a difference can be found between consideration of effect on public opinion and consideration of psychological implications in the proposed actions of government in the field of foreign affairs" (W. H. Jackson, "The Fourth Area of the National Effort in Foreign Affairs," AWF/A).

2115   *EM, AWF, Name Series*

To George Catlett Marshall   *November 23, 1956*

Dear General Marshall: I am more than grateful for your longhand note of felicitations on my re-election.[1] Quite naturally, the confidence of the American people gratified and reassured me, particularly in these troubled days.

Actually, I found the campaign this year fairly easy—at least by comparison with the '52 effort.[2] I tried to make most of the trips one-day affairs, which, while temporarily exhausting, did give me time both to catch my breath and to keep up with the necessary official business.[3]

Mrs. Eisenhower joins me in affectionate regard to you and Mrs. Marshall. *As ever*

[1] Marshall's November 18 note explained that he had waited until after the "flood" of congratulations subsided before writing (AWF/N). He said that Eisenhower's reelection indicated an "unprecedented vote of approval, affection and encouragement in a turbulent world."

[2] On the 1952 campaign see Galambos, *NATO and the Campaign of 1952.*

[3] Between August and November the Suez and Hungarian crises had overshadowed the elections. See nos. 2056, 2063, and 2064 for Eisenhower's attitude toward campaigning and for the impact of the international crises on his campaign style. See no. 2033 for another comparison with the 1952 campaign.

2116   *EM, AWF, Administration Series*

To Charles Douglas Jackson   *November 24, 1956*

Dear C. D.: By coincidence, an hour before the receipt of your letter, I telephoned Foster Dulles to ask what more we can do in the way of helping out the Hungarian refugees.[1]

As far as my going to Kilmer is concerned—and I considered going when the first refugees arrived—my reaction is, "How much can one individual do?"

Since early September I have been battling to obtain something on the order of ten days when I could really have a rest. Every engagement I make merely constitutes another nail in the coffin of my hopes.[2]

Nevertheless, your letter does give me a series of ideas that I shall follow.[3]

My profound thanks for the trouble you took in writing. *As ever*

---

[1] Jackson had written on November 23 (AWF/A) to express his agreement with Eisenhower's view that U.S. action in the Hungarian situation "should not be of such a nature as to trigger a larger conflict." Jackson had suggested four steps that he believed Eisenhower should take: the President should speak out personally on the mass deportations of Hungarian youth by the Communists; he should personally visit refugees at Camp Kilmer in New Jersey; he should use the President of the Hungarian National Council in Exile as an interpreter during this visit, or at least receive him at the White House; and he should reassure the Austrians that the United States was prepared to help with the refugee problem. For background see no. 2103.

[2] Eisenhower would leave Washington for a vacation in Augusta, Georgia, on November 26, after first receiving and posing for pictures with several Hungarian refugees at the White House. The President would remain in Augusta until December 13 (see Goodpaster memorandum, Nov. 25, 1956, AWF/D; and Visit of Hungarian refugees, Nov. 26, 1956, AWF/I: Hungarian).

[3] In addition to welcoming the refugees from Camp Kilmer, Eisenhower would also adapt several of Jackson's other recommendations. During the first week of December the White House would issue statements offering asylum to an additional 21,500 Hungarian refugees and authorizing the relevant executive departments to make the necessary expenditures to fund Hungarian relief efforts (see no. 2131). On December 10 the President would issue a statement on Human Rights Day: "The recent outbreak of brutality in Hungary has moved free peoples everywhere to reactions of horror and revulsion. Our hearts are filled with sorrow. Our deepest sympathy goes out to the courageous, liberty-loving people of Hungary" (*Public Papers of the Presidents: Eisenhower, 1956*, pp. 1114–21; see also Eisenhower, *Waging Peace*, pp. 97–98).

2117

EM, AWF, Administration Series, Hauge Corr.

To Edgar Newton Eisenhower

November 24, 1956

Dear Ed: The Wall Street Journal editorial apparently refers to questionable administration by certain States of relief distribution of Federally-supplied surplus food.[1]

The Department of Agriculture has been under great pressure from the Congress, as you know, to dispose of these surpluses. The story suggests that there are doubtful practices going on in some of the

States. I know something of the strenuous effort made to keep Governor Williams of Michigan from completely destroying the integrity of this program.[2]

On the basis of the clipping you sent me, I am asking Ezra Benson for a report, which I shall see that you get.[3]

With warm regard, *As ever*

[1] On November 20 Edgar Eisenhower had sent his brother clippings of articles from the *Wall Street Journal* that sharply criticized the government's surplus food donations (AWF/A, Hauge Corr.). The *Journal* had criticized the overall structure of the Farm Commodity Distribution Program and its administration by local agencies; had suggested that it competed with grocers unfairly; and had questioned the adequacy of federal supervision over eligibility requirements (Cochrane and Ryan, *American Farm Policy*, pp. 280–83).

[2] Gerhard Mennen "Soapy" Williams (Michigan Law School 1936) was a Democrat. He had been governor since 1949. The *Journal* article implied that as a result of donations being distributed through grocers rather than the normal welfare agency channels in Wayne County and Detroit, Michigan, undeserving recipients were added to the rolls.

[3] Upon sending this request to the Secretary of Agriculture, the President said, "Tell Ezra we don't want to be made monkeys of" (Memorandum, Hauge to Benson, Nov. 26, 1956, AWF/A, Hauge Corr.). The Department of Agriculture would prepare a "Report on the Surplus Food Donations to the Needy" that would conclude that some adverse impact on regular food sales was an inherent problem in donations (Dec. 7, 1956, AWF/A, Hauge Corr.). The report would maintain that since 1954 the Department had attempted to limit the program while Congress had been under pressure to do otherwise; it also concluded that alternatives such as the food stamp plan advocated by food industry interest groups would be more expensive for the federal government (for background see Schapsmeir and Schapsmeir, *Ezra Taft Benson and the Politics of Agriculture*, pp. 118–19; *Congressional Quarterly Almanac*, vol. XI, *1955*, pp. 185–86, and vol. XII, *1956*, pp. 375–76, 489–90; *Wall Street Journal*, Sept. 20, 1956; and Department of Agriculture, Supplementary Report on Surplus Farm Commodity Distribution to Needy Families, Feb. 15, 1955, AWF/Cabinet). According to Colonel Goodpaster's handwritten note on the summary page, the President would be briefed on the report and his brother would receive a copy (Memorandum, Hauge to Goodpaster, and Hauge to Edgar Eisenhower, both dated Dec. 8, 1956, AWF/A, Hauge Corr.; see also correspondence in WHCF/OF 106-I).

2118   *EM, AWF, International Series: Churchill*

To Winston Spencer Churchill   *November 27, 1956*
Cable. Top secret

Dear Winston:[1] I agree fully with the implication of your letter that Nasser is a tool, possibly unwittingly, of the Soviets, and back of the difficulties that the free world is now experiencing lies one principal fact that none of us can afford to forget.[2] The Soviets are the real enemy of the Western World, implacably hostile and seeking our destruction.

Many months ago it became clear that the Soviets were convinced that the mere building of mighty military machines would not necessarily accomplish their purposes, while at the same time their military effort was severely limiting their capacity for conquering the world by other means, especially economic. Unquestionably the greatest factor in turning their minds away from general war as a means of world conquest was their knowledge of America's and Britain's large and growing strength in nuclear and fission weapons.

Starting almost at the instant that Nasser took his high-handed action with respect to the Canal, I tried earnestly to keep Anthony informed of public opinion in this country and of the course that we would feel compelled to follow if there was any attempt to solve by force the problem presented to the free world through Nasser's action. I told him that we were committed to the United Nations and I particularly urged him, in a letter of July thirty-first, to avoid the use of force, at least until it had been proved to the world that the United Nations was incapable of handling the problem.[3] My point was that since the struggle with Russia had obviously taken on a new tactical form, we had to be especially careful that any course of action we adopted should by its logic and justice command world respect, if not sympathy. I argued that to invade Egypt merely because that country had chosen to nationalize a company would be interpreted by the world as power politics and would raise a storm of resentment that, within the Arab States, would result in a long and dreary guerilla warfare; something on the order that the French are now experiencing in Algeria.[4]

I have tried to make it clear that we share the opinion of the British as well as of many others that Nasser has probably begun to see himself as an Egyptian Mussolini and that we would have to concert our actions in making certain that he did not grow to be a danger to our welfare.[5] But for the reasons I have given above, I urged that the nationalization of the Canal Company was not the vehicle to choose for bringing about correction in this matter.

Sometime in the early part of October, all communication between ourselves on the one hand and the British and the French on the other suddenly ceased. Our intelligence showed the gradual buildup of Israeli military strength, finally reaching such a state of completion that I felt compelled on two successive days to warn that country that the United States would honor its part in the Tri-Partite Declaration of May, 1950—in short, that we would oppose clear aggression by any power in the Mid-East.[6]

But so far as Britain and France were concerned, we felt that they had deliberately excluded us from their thinking; we had no choice but to do our best to be prepared for whatever might happen.

The first news we had of the attack and of British-French plans was gained from the newspapers and we had no recourse except to assert our readiness to support the United Nations, before which body, incidentally, the British Government had itself placed the whole Suez controversy.[7]

Now I still believe that we must keep several facts clearly before us, the first one always being that the Soviets are the real enemy and all else must be viewed against the background of that truth. The second fact is that nothing would please this country more nor, in fact, could help us more, than to see British prestige and strength renewed and rejuvenated in the Mid-East. We want those countries to trust and lean toward the Western World, not Russia. A third fact is that we want to help Britain right now, particularly in its difficult fuel and financial situation, daily growing more serious.[8]

All we have asked in order to come out openly has been a British statement that it would conform to the resolutions of the United Nations. The United Nations troops do not, in our opinion, have to be as strong as those of an invading force because any attack upon them will be an attack upon the whole United Nations and if such an act of folly were committed, I think that we could quickly settle the whole affair.

This message does not purport to say that we have set up our judgment against that of our friends in England. I am merely trying to show that in this country there is a very strong public opinion upon these matters that has, I believe, paralleled my own thinking. I continue to believe that the safety of the western world depends in the final analysis upon the closest possible ties between Western Europe, the American hemisphere, and as many allies as we can induce to stand with us. If this incident has proved nothing else, it must have forcefully brought this truth home to us again. A chief factor in the union of the free world must be indestructible ties between the British Commonwealth and ourselves.

The only difficulty I have had in the particular instance is the fact that to me it seemed the action of the British Government was not only in violation of the basic principles by which this great combination of nations can be held together, but that even by the doctrine of expediency the invasion could not be judged as soundly conceived and skillfully executed.

So I hope that this one may be washed off the slate as soon as possible and that we can then together adopt other means of achieving our legitimate objectives in the Mid-East. Nothing saddens me more than the thought that I and my old friends of years have met a problem concerning which we do not see eye to eye. I shall never be happy until our old time closeness has been restored.

With warm regard and best wishes for your continued health, *As ever*

[1] The State Department cabled this Eyes Only message to Ambassador Aldrich in London for delivery to Churchill "on [a] most secret basis."

[2] Churchill had written that "the theme of the Anglo-American alliance is more important today than at any time since the war." "To let events in the Middle East become a gulf between us," Churchill continued, "would be an act of folly, on which our whole civilisation may founder." He warned Eisenhower, "If we do not take immediate action in harmony, it is no exaggeration to say that we must expect to see the Middle East and the North African coastline under Soviet control and Western Europe placed at the mercy of the Russians." Churchill concluded: "I write this letter because I know where your heart lies. You are now the only one who can so influence events both in UNO and the free world as to ensure that the great essentials are not lost in bickerings and pettiness among the nations" (Churchill to Eisenhower, Nov. 23, 1956, AWF/I: Churchill; see also Eisenhower to Churchill, Nov. 25, 1956, *ibid.*; and Minnich to Hoover, Nov. 27, 1956, WHCF/CF: Suez Canal Crisis).

[3] See nos. 1935 and 1972.

[4] See nos. 1792 and 1793.

[5] Prime Minister Eden had told Eisenhower that he believed Nasser was in Russian hands "just as Mussolini was in Hitler's" (see no. 2024).

[6] See nos. 2048 and 2055.

[7] See nos. 2071, 2072, and 2073.

[8] For background on Britain's financial problems see no. 2068. On the petroleum shortage see nos. 2057 and 2123.

2119   *EM, WHCF, Confidential File: Suez Canal Crisis*

To Hastings Lionel Ismay   *November 27, 1956*

Dear Pug: First of all, let me express my profound appreciation that you unburdened yourself to me concerning the sad mess in which the free world has become involved.[1] I shall not attempt to recite the long series of events extending back over many months that have contributed to some of our misunderstanding, but I do assure you that I have never lost sight of the importance of Anglo-American friendship and the absolute necessity of keeping it strong and healthy in the face of the continuing Soviet threat.[2]

I should like at once to give you one or two categorical assurances. The first is that NATO remains the chief cornerstone of America's security alliances. I as earnestly believe in NATO and as earnestly support it as I ever did. Secondly, far from being indifferent to the fuel and financial plight of Western Europe, I have been meeting daily with my staunchest and most trusted advisers to determine how we can be most speedily and effectively helpful.[3] A prime need in any such cooperation is an adequate permanent source of oil and an adequate and permanent supply of oil can come only from the Mid East region. Consequently, it has been vital that our public moves be so timed that they do not irrevocably antagonize the Arab world. This is an extremely delicate matter and one that cannot be publicly talked about.

I realize that because we have adopted as a matter of continuing policy the unequivocable support of the United Nations, our attitude has been misinterpreted by the European public and of course in some cases this has led to unfortunate misunderstandings even among people who know a considerable part of the background of this whole affair. But just as we must make certain of a continuing oil supply, we cannot and will not be in the position of coercing or pressuring our friends, all of which has compelled us to be extremely guarded and almost secret in our actions.

Nevertheless we realize that there is no time to waste and even today I am making an occasion to reassert our support of NATO and as soon as the situation permits, will say even more.[4]

I cannot close without urging that you continue on your present job in the same faith and conviction that have sustained you heretofore. There has been no change in my basic policies and purposes, and I am hopeful that within a very short time all of these things of which I speak so guardedly can be brought out into the open.

With warm personal regard, *As ever*

[1] Lord Ismay, Secretary-General of NATO, had spoken to Ambassador Dillon, who had conveyed his remarks by telegram. The telegram is still classified (State, *Foreign Relations, 1955–1957*, vol. XVI, *Suez Crisis July 26–December 31, 1956*, p. 1202, n. 2). Eisenhower would describe Ismay's message, however, as "very desperate in tone." According to Eisenhower, Ismay had adopted "the European conviction that we deserted our two friends in their hour of trial, and now won't even help them out with oil and gas" (Telephone conversation, Eisenhower and Dulles, Nov. 27, 1956, AWF/D).
[2] For background see the preceding document.
[3] For Eisenhower's earlier attitude on petroleum deliveries see no. 2057. For developments see no. 2123.
[4] Eisenhower would issue a statement denying that the Suez crisis had weakened NATO and announcing that Secretary Dulles, who had been convalescing in Key West, would personally attend the next NATO council meeting (*New York Times*, Nov. 28, 1956).

2120   *EM, WHCF, Official File 116*

To George P. Skouras   *November 27, 1956*
Personal

Dear Mr. Skouras: Thank you for your note of the twenty-third.[1] While I deplore, along with you, the fact that at times our foreign policy does seem to become a "political football," yet I am afraid that the suggestion in your letter would not serve to prevent such a thing. I am heartily in favor of a bipartisan foreign policy, but I do not believe that a Secretary of State of the opposition party would automatically assure that fact, nor, in my opinion, would such an appointment obviate an attack by a political candidate seeking political expediency. Nonetheless I shall pass along your interesting thought to others in the Administration for their consideration.

With my thanks to you and Mrs. Skouras for your prayers, and best wishes, *Sincerely*

---

[1] Skouras was president and chairman of United Artists Theater Circuit, Incorporated. He had suggested that Eisenhower appoint a Secretary of State from the opposite party in order to take foreign policy out of politics "with the hope that such a precedent will be followed by our future Presidents" (Skouras to Eisenhower, Nov. 23, 1956, same file as document).

2121   *EM, AWF, Name Series*

To MALCOLM MUIR   *November 28, 1956*
Personal

Dear Malcolm:[1] I have read with interest your recent letter.[2] Of course I agree that our friendship with the people of Great Britain and Western Europe must be maintained and must be strengthened. It represents a priceless asset of which I have never, for one moment, lost sight. We may among ourselves have occasional difficulties—all "families" do—but I assure you that I cannot and shall not, if I have the power, permit anything in the nature of a permanent rift to develop. You understand, I am sure, that I must be guarded in my statements, even to someone I know as well as I know you. I can only say that we *are* doing everything possible to restore our former good relationships with our friends.[3]

In much the same spirit I view the NATO alliance. That organization must continue to function and to grow; any other possibility is unthinkable.

It is not even necessary for me to comment on your paragraph regarding General Gruenther. My regard for his ability and perception—and his talent for doing a difficult job with tact and skill—is second to none. I have had several talks with him since his return to this country, and I know he continues to stand ready to serve his nation and the cause of peace in any way he can. If necessary, he can take on specific assignments while still acting as President of The American Red Cross.[4]

I have written you fully and as frankly as possible. Again let me thank you for your letter and for your confidence.

With warm regard, *Sincerely*

¹ Malcolm Muir, Sr., president of *Newsweek*, had been editor-in-chief since 1937. He had been the president of the McGraw-Hill Publishing Co. and had served as deputy administrator of the National Recovery Administration during the New Deal.

² Muir had written expressing his hope that Eisenhower would be able to rebuild the NATO alliance which had been "so tragically shattered in recent weeks" (Muir to Eisenhower, Nov. 20, 1956, AWF/N).

³ See nos. 2118, 2119, and 2123.

⁴ Muir had suggested that Gruenther was "the man best equipped to assist you in guiding the world to a durable peace" because he had the confidence of European leaders. For background on Gruenther's appointment at the Red Cross see no. 2064.

2122   *EM, AWF, International Series: Adenauer*

To Konrad Adenauer   *November 29, 1956*
Cable. Secret

Dear Mr. Chancellor: I was very much interested in the views which you recently sent me through General Gruenther.¹ I agree with you that it is of the greatest importance and urgency that full unity be restored in the Western camp. It is most urgent that we bring to an end the threat of hostilities in the Middle East and move in the direction of an overall settlement in the area. The most immediate problems are to secure the withdrawal of armed forces in accordance with the United Nations resolution, keyed to the entry of the United Nations Emergency Force; implementation of the United Nations injunction against the intro- duction of new forces and military materiel in the area of conflict; and clearance of the Suez Canal.² Beyond this, a basis must be found for solving the fundamental Arab-Israeli conflict and reaching agreement on a future regime for the Suez Canal. I welcome your thoughts on the subject and am certain you will agree with me on the necessity of working through the United Nations to find solutions to these prob- lems.

I agree also that there must be improved understanding regarding political consultation among the NATO Governments. You have no doubt by this time seen the report of the Three Wise Men. Although we have not yet had a chance to study this report in detail, it seems to us to provide a sound basis for dealing with this problem. However, methods of consultation are not enough. They must be used. While we must work toward harmonization of policies among the NATO coun- tries, I am sure you will agree that it would be unrealistic to expect that we will be able always to achieve identity of viewpoint with regard to matters outside the NATO area.[3]

Improvement of the economic conditions of the peoples of the Middle East is certainly an essential aspect of the problem of our relations with that area. This problem must be worked out with them on a cooperative basis. However, I doubt whether any general approach can be effectively undertaken until progress has been made toward solving the two basic problems of the Arab-Israeli conflict and of the Suez Canal.[4]

One of our greatest hopes in this direction is the clear and continuing evidence of basic differences in the thinking of some of the Heads of State in the Mideast. Some of these are deeply disturbed over recent developments and have a clear understanding of the dangers inherent in the policies pursued by their more reckless and irresponsible allies.[5]

I appreciate the difficulties which have confronted the Federal Republic in making progress in the buildup of its military forces to which you referred in your message. I hope that the Federal Government will soon be able to give NATO a firm statement of its plans. In our view, the need for the forces which Germany has undertaken to contribute to NATO continues to be as great as ever. I am sure you will agree that the urgency for such a contribution has been made all the more apparent by recent events in Eastern Europe.[6]

While additional forces are needed to provide an effective NATO defense in Europe, it would be difficult to increase the American share. As you are aware, a good portion of our combat-ready ground forces is already stationed in Germany. Furthermore, an increase in our forces at this time would give rise to misunderstanding both here at home and abroad.

I should very much welcome an opportunity to discuss these matters with you and would be glad if you could come to Washington some time in the New Year. I will communicate with you again as to when we might arrange to see one another.[7] *Sincerely*

---

[1] A draft of this letter with Eisenhower's handwritten emendations is in AWF/I: Adenauer. Adenauer had sent a representative to tell Gruenther what to say to the President. Gruenther had written that he was "considerably embarassed to be the medium for the transmission of this message because of the obvious by-passing" of the American Ambassador (Gruenther to Goodpaster, Nov. 19, 1956, AWF/I: Adenauer; see also State, *Foreign Relations, 1955–1957*, vol. XXVI, *Central and Southeastern Europe*, pp. 174–77).

[2] For background see nos. 2058 and 2119.

[3] For background on the so-called "Wise Men" see nos. 1930 and 1964. Their report laid out a new and explicit framework for cooperation in the political, economic, and cultural spheres within the existing NATO structure. True consultation, they stressed, requires "the discussion of problems collectively, in the early stages of policy formation," not merely "letting the NATO Council know about national decisions that have already been taken" ("Report of the Committee of Three on Non-Military Co-

operation in NATO," *U.S. Department of State Bulletin* 36, no. 915 [January 7, 1957], 18–28). See also State, *Foreign Relations, 1955–1957,* vol. IV, *Western European Security and Integration,* pp. 137–49 for an account of the Wise Men's oral report to the NATO Council of Ministers.

[4] Adenauer had suggested that the best solution to the problems of the Middle East might be a multilateral plan for economic development of the region modeled on the Colombo Plan for Cooperative Economic Development in Southeast Asia (Gruenther to Goodpaster, Nov. 19, 1956, AWF/I: Adenauer).

[5] Eisenhower added this paragraph to the State Department draft.

[6] Adenauer had apologized for the Federal Republic's slow military progress. By the end of 1956 the Federal Republic had only 70,000 men under arms, instead of the 96,000 promised, and it contemplated an increase to only 135,000 by the end of 1957, instead of the 270,000 planned. Adenauer promised Eisenhower that the Germans would have a "reasonably effective fighting force" before the end of 1957. He said that "the political situation has been such that he has had to move more slowly than he had originally hoped" and that he was dissatisfied with the German generals who had not "shown enough imagination and push and pull." But he told the President that "he now has a good Defense Minister" (Gruenther to Goodpaster, Nov. 19, 1956, AWF/I: Adenauer; State, *Foreign Relations, 1955–1957,* vol. XXVI, *Central and Southeastern Europe,* p. 195).

[7] Adenauer would write to thank the President for the "extensive consideration" which Eisenhower had given the Chancellor's message (see State, *Foreign Relations, 1955–1957,* vol. XXVI, *Central and Southeastern Europe,* pp. 180, 187). Chancellor Adenauer would visit the United States on May 26–28, 1957.

2123   *EM, AWF, International Series: Mollet*

To Guy Mollet   *November 29, 1956*
Cable. Secret

My dear Mr. Prime Minister: I want you to know that General Gruenther delivered to me the letter which you entrusted to him.[1] He also gave me a full account of his conversation with you, and I thank you for the frankness and friendliness with which you have expressed your views.[2]

As you are doubtless aware, I have, since the very beginning of the present crisis, said that although we felt that the decision to take up arms against Egypt was an error, we were determined to heal the breach and repair as rapidly as possible the temporary damage caused to the Western alliance by recent events. Obviously compliance with the Resolutions of the United Nations is of the essence.[3]

I wish to take this opportunity to assure you that this is still the firm intention of my Government. The importance of the Atlantic community to us all is undiminished. Indeed, events in Eastern Europe reveal more vividly than could any words of mine, how essential it is, now and for the future, that our association and common purpose be maintained and strengthened. In this respect, the views expressed by General Gruenther, in his last major speech before leaving Europe, correspond entirely with mine.[4] We cannot, however, expect all this to happen by itself. The task calls for all our mutual effort and resolve, on both sides of the Atlantic. I have no doubt whatever that we will succeed and that we will continue to follow steadfastly, all together, the road we have traveled since the end of the war, in quest of peace, justice and security in the world.

I feel that we must now look toward the future in order to start moving forward again. I am aware of the heavy strain imposed on Europe's economy by the dislocation of the traditional sources of supply of oil, and I realize that the inevitable shortage will cause hardship through lack of adequate heating and unemployment at the start of a winter.

Our companies are doing their best to mitigate the effects of this shortage. We have been planning urgently in the hope it will be possible soon to take more coordinated actions to alleviate the situation. In the meantime, we will cooperate with the OEEC to the fullest extent possible in its efforts to cope with the problem so that as much oil as possible can be shipped to the countries of Europe by alternative routes. When it is possible to reactivate our Middle East Emergency Committee, it too will work closely with the OEEC on the problem.[5]

And, of course, none of us can afford to forget that any permanent solution to the fuel problems of Western Europe requires access to the Mid East oil supplies. In turn this means that we must not create such resentments among Mid East governments that they will be unwilling, even at great cost to themselves, to supply Western European markets.[6]

It is my hope that the situation in the Middle East can rapidly be stabilized, thanks to the efforts of the United Nations in Egypt which you know we are backing in every way. We have been guided throughout this period only by the urgent desire to limit and stop the fighting, and to establish the basis for permanent and just solutions of the problems of the Suez Canal and of Israeli-Arab relations. I feel we must be in a position to exploit to the full the opportunities, which the heroism of the peoples of Poland and Hungary have given us all, and to expose the brutality and vulnerability of the Communist system.[7] Soviet imperialism is moving on several fronts and we must mobilize in the United Nations the conscience of the whole world, and not merely of the West, against this imperialism.

I, too, look forward to seeing you again, and will welcome the chance of discussing with you and our British friends many matters of common concern. Much as I would have liked to be able to do this sooner, it was my personal judgment, on reflection, that the best interests of us all required that our meeting be postponed until the circumstances were more propitious. I believe that our talks when they take place will be more productive than they could have been earlier.[8]

In conclusion, let me say again that I greatly appreciate the spirit in which you have written to me. I am confident that the way will be found to press forward all together with renewed vigor and resolve for the triumph of those values to which our two countries have for so long been dedicated.

With kindest regards, *Sincerely yours*

[1] A State Department draft of this message is in AWF/I: Mollet. Secretary Hoover commented that "The draft seeks to reassure the Prime Minister of our determination to repair as rapidly as possible the damage caused the Western Alliance by recent events" (Hoover to Eisenhower, Nov. 27, 1956, AWF/I:Mollet). Mollet had earlier notified the President that Gruenther would arrive bearing a letter from him (Mollet to Eisenhower, Nov. 19, 1956, AWF/I: Mollet). Gruenther had written the President that he was "embarrassed to serve as a messenger on this level and especially so twice in the same day." (See the preceding document.) "For this extra curricular service by me I trust that you will require all Governmental hot shots to contribute an extra amount to the Red Cross when it conducts its campaign fund next March" (Gruenther to Goodpaster, Nov. 19, 1956, AWF/I: Mollet).

[2] Most of the cable containing Mollet's remarks to Gruenther remains classified (Gruenther to Goodpaster, Nov. 19, 1956, AWF/I: Mollet).

[3] For background on the U.N. resolutions demanding the withdrawal of British and French forces from Egypt see nos. 2057, 2068, and 2073. On November 7 the General Assembly passed Resolutions 1001 and 1002 creating the United Nations peacekeeping force. On November 24 the Assembly adopted resolution 1120 (XI), which remonstrated against Britain and France for failing to withdraw fully from Egypt and reiterated previous resolutions calling for their immediate withdrawal (State, *Foreign Relations, 1955–1957*, vol. XVI, *Suez Crisis July 26–December 31, 1956*, pp. 1053–54, 1192–93).

[4] In his last speech as NATO commander Gruenther had warned that the Soviets would be "destroyed" if they attacked the West. But he also noted that the possibility of Western military intervention behind the Iron Curtain was "slight" (*New York Times*, Nov. 14, 1956). On Gruenther's retirement from NATO see no. 2064.

[5] The Middle East Emergency Committee (MEEC) was a cartel of American oil companies given temporary immunity from antitrust laws. The immunity made it legal for them to pool their transportation resources to get the maximum possible amount of oil to Europe to alleviate shortages caused by the closing of the Suez Canal. The OEEC was the Organization for European Economic Cooperation. As late as November 23 Eisenhower had been delaying emergency measures to supply Europe with oil until Britain and France withdrew their troops from Egypt. On that date, when Secretary Hoover informed him that the oil situation in Europe was getting critical, he deferred action on the emergency plans, instructing Hoover to tell the British Ambassador that "the first thing we must all give our attention to is helping out on oil." "But in order to do that," Eisenhower continued, "we must stay 4-square with the UN, so Britain must take some preliminary actions" (Goodpaster memorandum, Nov. 23, 1956, AWF/D).

Three days later, however, the President had decided that the emergency committee should be activated in order to alleviate any shortages before the advent of winter (Goodpaster, Memorandum of Conference, Nov. 26, 1956, AWF/D; see also State, *Foreign Relations, 1955–1957*, vol. XVI, *Suez Crisis July 26–December 31, 1956*, pp. 1194–95. By November 28 the United States Maritime Administration, at the request of the Office of Defense Management, had taken eighteen tankers from the reserve fleet for use in ferrying additional oil to Europe (Staff Notes No. 46, Nov. 28, 1956, AWF/D). For background on Eisenhower's actions during the oil shortage see nos. 2057 and 2119. See also Kaufman, *Trade and Aid*, pp. 87–88.

[6] This paragraph was inserted into the State Department draft, presumably at the White House.

[7] On the Hungarian uprising and events in Poland see nos. 2044 and 2055.

[8] Mollet would visit Washington on February 26–28, 1957. Eisenhower had postponed an earlier summit with Eden and Mollet (see no. 2076).

2124   *EM, AWF, International Series: Eden*

To ROBERT ANTHONY EDEN   *November 29, 1956*
Cable

My dear Friend: I understand you are recuperating in Jamaica. This short note brings you my very best wishes for an enjoyable and restful vacation, and a complete return to health.[1] *As ever*

[1] Eden had been suffering from recurring fevers and on the advice of his physicians had flown to Jamaica on November 23 for a three-week rest at the home of his friend, author Ian Fleming. Eden would tender his resignation to Queen Elizabeth on January 9, 1957 (see no. 2163; see also Eden, *Full Circle*, pp. 637, 650–52).

2124A   *EM, AWF, Administration Series*

To LEWIS WILLIAMS DOUGLAS   *November 30, 1956*
Top secret

Dear Lew: You over-estimate, I think, the severity of our present policy as it affects our British and French friends. The fact is we have not only done a lot of work in preparing to help them solve their problems, but are merely awaiting a sensible move on their part to make the cooperative program public.[1]

A bit of past history would help you to understand some important factors in the situation.

Beginning last July I was in frequent communication with Anthony Eden, constantly urging him to avoid force in the Suez, at least until there could be brought about a situation where intervention of that kind would be approved, or at least understood, by the world in general and particularly by the populations of the free world.[2]

After innumerable conferences and communications, we thought we had made him understand that the oil supply of Western Europe, a vital necessity, depended in the long run upon the *readiness of the Arab world to sell to Western Europe* and upon transportation facilities developed to the point where requirements could be met.

We have been convinced, beyond any doubt, that the one thing that would unite all the Arab populations—even against the official desires of such individuals as King Saud, Nuri[3] and the King of Libya—would be the employment of force in the Suez and under a situation where the Arab populations would support Nasser fanatically.

Paranthetically I should remark that we have very strong Arab friends in high places who are just as sick of Nasser as are Britain, France and ourselves.

During Foster's last visit to London the matter was discussed of putting the Suez issue before the United Nations, and Foster came home with the understanding that there would be further conversations on the matter to decide exactly how this should be done.[4] Nevertheless *before he could reach Washington*, the British had inscribed the matter on the United Nations agenda.

Very shortly thereafter there began a complete blackout of news. We had no idea what France and Britain were doing, and this at a time when our intelligence showed that Israel was completing a very extensive mobilization. This latter fact brought about my protests to Ben Gurion, which protests, being public, were naturally known by our British and French friends.[5]

Nevertheless, invasion occurred and we were forced to do one of two things. Either we had to adhere to our obligations under the United Nations Charter, or we had to destroy that organization. As a matter of principle, only one decision was possible. But there was a concomitant consideration which had entered into all of our presentations to the British from the very beginning of the difficulty. This factor was that in the long run Western Europe's economy could be sustained *only by Mid East oil*. Consequently, some member of the West had to preserve the kind of relations with the Arabs that would not encourage that emotional people, even though cutting off their own noses to spite their own faces, to destroy the oil industry. In such a procedure they would have been, of course, enthusiastically supported by the Kremlin which, although unable to use the oil itself at this time, would pay a very fine price to see it denied to the West.

That this feeling was not in any sense theoretical or hypothetical is evidenced by the fact that immediately after the invasion and when the the larger pipelines were destroyed, we were able to keep operating the Tapline—with a capacity of 330,000 barrels a day—only on the promise that, for the moment, none of that oil should go to the British and the French.[6] Since other allies in Western Europe use much more oil than this, we could make that promise and so do something toward evaluating the situation. In the meantime, we began working here at home and conferring with the controlling officials in the Mid East (and talking behind the scenes with our British friends) to see under what conditions we could openly help them in Europe's fuel and financial difficulties.

Because our first decision to support the United Nations was taken on a matter of principle, we could not abandon that stand. Moreover, we felt that if the British would make some general statement to the effect that "so long as the United Nations is entering the Canal Zone to take control until the Canal can be again operating and a settlement properly negotiated, we are ready to comply with the United Nations on the subject," then we could convince the principal Arab officials that we had stood by principle and were now moving rapidly and with their cooperation to preserve *their* markets and to prevent suffering in all Western Europe.

In presenting this to the Arabs we felt we had the long-range factor in our favor; namely, that we should avoid forcing the world's oil supply and distribution into new channels, which would tend to become permanent and so damage, for years to come, the oil sales of the Mid East.

We have studied the financial needs of our Western European allies growing out of this crisis and have been exploring methods designed to allow us to move effectively and openly without making us appear hypocritical in Arab eyes, or giving Soviet propaganda the opportunity of saying we were false to our own convictions and beliefs.

At this moment political leaders in Britain understand all this, and are moving as rapidly as they may—in view of the extreme attitude of some of the backbench Conservatives—to bring about cooperative opportunity for us that I have described above.

In the meantime I have publicly announced several times—the most recent one just two days ago—that though we have differed with our friends over a *particular* international incident, they are *still our friends* and we are going to help them.

You are quite right in all you say about certain possible results of this whole miserable affair being contrary to our national interest. Of course they are. If not, I should never have worked as hard as I did to prevent them from arising in the first place. But I am quite certain that unless we can restore very soon the Mid East as the principal source of oil supply, there is nothing we can do that will save Western Europe. *The fuel requirements of the entire Western world cannot possibly be permanently supplied from North America and Venezuela.* Even if we should succeed in keeping Iran on our side but with the remaining Mid East hostile, and should build the great tankers necessary to bring the oil around the Cape of Good Hope, there would elapse a long period during which Western Europe would undergo great privation. When, finally, requirements could be met as to amount, costs would have gone up tremendously.

I have no quarrel whatsoever with the generalities of your telegram.

But in a situation such as I describe, the answer can scarcely be found by any one nation, even one so powerful as ourselves, unless there is some readiness on each side of the quarrel to conciliate. We must remain true to our friends, but we must likewise remain on a friendly status with the Mid East oil suppliers. The only other alternative would be a gigantic occupation of the Mid East by military force; in view of France's experience in North Africa and the prior British experience in the Suez Canal Zone, no one in the world could contemplate such a venture with complacency. And I repeat—all of these considerations were called to the attention of the British long before they undertook the invasion that was supposed to stabilize the situation.

Having said all this, I am hopeful that the next two or three days will bring a further *public* reconciliation of a break which, as between this government and *some* of our best friends in the British government, has never even occurred.[7]

So to sum up the matter: if it were merely a question of financing and re-routing of oil supplies that would meet Western European requirements, you would find we are working just as hard and openly as we did to preserve Western Europe under the Marshall Plan. But it is a question also of preserving the cheapest and most plentiful oil supplies that can be obtained in the world.

Incidentally and parenthetically, I should remark that there has been no incident in recent years that has more underlined the necessity of uniting Western Europe into one Federated nation than has this one.

I have written to you very frankly and fully—not only because I respect your judgment highly but because if you have any ideas to communicate to me after reading this letter, I would certainly be pleased to receive them.[8]

By the very nature of the whole affair, everything in this letter must be regarded as top secret and for your eyes only.

Again my thanks for your wire, and with warm regard, *As ever*[9]

---

[1] Douglas was concerned that American policy in the Suez Canal crisis required unconditional surrender of the British and French in Egypt before the United States would talk with them "regarding desperately and urgently needed supplies of oil." The consequences of such a policy, he said, could reduce Europe to conditions existing immediately after World War II and could "well create in the Middle East a void into which only the Soviet will move." Although Douglas believed that the British and French had "made a grievous error" and that the U.S. position had been "generally correct," he asked Eisenhower to review immediately Administration policy (Douglas to Eisenhower, Nov. 27, 1956, AWF/A). Douglas had followed his telegram with a letter on November 29, apologizing to Eisenhower "for invading an area" in which he did not belong. "Please believe that I communicated with you as I did because of my very deep concern for the success of your regime and the preservation, if not indeed the advancement, of the things which it seemed to me you believed in so deeply" (*ibid.*; see also

Robert Paul Browder and Thomas G. Smith, *Independent: A Biography of Lewis W. Douglas* [New York, 1986], pp. 385–88). For background on Egypt's nationalization of the canal see no. 1932.

[2] See nos. 1935 and 1972.

[3] General Nuri Pasha al-Said, Iraq's Prime Minister and Minister of Defense.

[4] The second Suez Conference was held in London from September 19–21 (see no. 1993; and State, *Foreign Relations, 1955–1957*, vol. XVI, *Suez Crisis July 26–December 31, 1956*, pp. 556–57).

[5] See no. 2048.

[6] The Trans-Arabian Pipeline (TAPLINE) ran from Saudi Arabia through Syria to the Mediterranean. See State, *Foreign Relations, 1955–1957*, vol. XVI, *Suez Crisis July 26–December 31, 1956*, pp. 389, 1147–48, 1166.

[7] On this same day the Office of Defense Mobilization would issue a statement authorizing fifteen U.S. oil companies to coordinate efforts that would supply oil to Western Europe and Great Britain. On December 3 British Foreign Secretary Selwyn Lloyd would announce the withdrawal of British troops from the Suez (*ibid.*, pp. 1214–15, 1232–33, 1238–39; see also Adams, *Firsthand Report*, pp. 261–70).

[8] Douglas would applaud Eisenhower's decision to provide additional oil to Great Britain as a unilateral action not contingent upon British actions. Douglas said that the decision would allow the British "with good grace" to accelerate the withdrawal of their forces (Douglas to Eisenhower, Dec. 3, 1956, AWF/A).

[9] Eisenhower would later discuss with Secretary Dulles the possible appointment of Douglas to a government position (see Eisenhower to Dulles, Dec. 26, 1956; and Memorandum of Conversation, Dec. 26, 1956, both in AWF/D-H).

23

What is needed is "a calming influence"

To Henry Agard Wallace   *December 1, 1956*

Dear Mr. Secretary: I am grateful for the trouble you took to give me your thinking about Nehru, his place in the world, and his capacity for needed leadership in that region in the years to come.[1]

To me the crux of your letter appears in the paragraph which begins, "The altogether serious long-time problem . . . ."[2] There is no question that the refusal of the world's populations to accept sharply increasing differences in living standards will give rise to increasingly violent rejection of color inferiority, as well as hatreds and envies based on resentments, some of them founded in the imagination rather than in fact. The West must without fail get itself into position that there is no just cause for these resentments and hatreds being directed toward the free nations and, in addition, must work at the job of convincing others that we have no ambitions except to see all share the freedom that we so highly prize. Obviously the material factors that must underlie a sustained national and individual freedom achieve, in this context, an importance that we will neglect at our peril. That is one fact that seems difficult for our own people to grasp.

Again my thanks for your letter, and with personal regard, *Sincerely*

[1] The former Secretary of Agriculture, Secretary of Commerce, and Vice-President of the United States had written Eisenhower in anticipation of Indian Prime Minister Nehru's visit to the United States (see no. 1794). Nehru, he said, was "a very intelligent, self-contained person who, in spite of his western education is sufficiently oriental to go two directions at the same time very politely" (Wallace to Eisenhower, Nov. 27, 1956, AWF/N).

[2] Wallace had written that "modern sanitation has suddenly caused an already over-crowded population greatly and continuously to out-run food supply. If something is not done about this there will be an inevitable decline in living standards coinciding with rising nationalism, increasingly violent rejection of color inferiority, hatred for colonial powers, and growing envy and hatred of the western powers blessed with ten to thirty times the good things of life. . . ." These conditions would lead to hostilities, Wallace said, that would "imperil the very life of Britain and France and finally our own."

2126   *EM, AWF,*
                                              Administration Series

To Arthur Ellsworth Summerfield   *December 3, 1956*

Dear Arthur: Mamie and I were delighted to hear from you, particularly because your letter gave us definite indication that you are indeed much better.[1] I know only too well how slow recovery from an operation can sometimes seem—but I am certain that one of these days you will, overnight, suddenly find that you are again feeling entirely like yourself. Incidentally, Foster has made a remarkable recovery and looks—and says he feels—fine.[2]

We have had rather erratic weather here, a bit on the cold side.[3] My golf, as usual, has displeased me. But the place is entirely restful, with just enough company at all times to ward off boredom.

I cannot tell you how much I appreciate all you say in your final paragraph of your letter.[4] There is much to be done in the next four years, and I am eager to see an overall plan formulated and work underway. My mail gives me evidence that there is still a great deal of momentum left from the 1956 election, which I am anxious not be lost.

With affectionate regard to Miriam and all the best to yourself, *As ever*

[1] Summerfield's December 1 letter thanking the Eisenhowers for a get-well bouquet is in AWF/A. The Postmaster General had had surgery to correct a diverticulum of the esophagus on November 12 (see *New York Times*, Nov. 13, Dec. 6, 1956).
[2] The President had met with Secretary of State Dulles on December 2—one month following Dulles's emergency surgery for cancer (see *New York Times*, Nov. 4, Dec. 3, 1956).
[3] The Eisenhowers were vacationing in Augusta, Georgia.
[4] Summerfield had been inspired by "the tremendous vote of confidence and affection" Americans gave Eisenhower on election day. And he was "confident," he said, that the future "will be productive in the building of a better America and a peaceful world community."

2127   *EM, AWF, Name Series*

TO ELLIS DWINNELL SLATER   *December 3, 1956*

Dear Slats: Our telegram of the other evening was merely to try to tell you how much the "old gang" miss you and Priscilla.[1] I don't want to make you more unhappy by reciting some of the fun we have had here, so I shall concentrate instead on my golf game, which is anything but good. I find that the two or three months in which I did not play increased my difficulties in every department. Ed Dudley has been patient, as usual, but I am going to need a lot of practice before I feel in the slightest satisfied with my score.[2]

Most of our mutual friends have been here, except Pete Jones, who seems to be away again doing some fishing. Even he is expected soon.[3] We have had a lot of good bridge and good conversation, and all in all, this "vacation" is just what I needed. I only wish I could stay a month or longer and completely relax. But for the next four years I see no possibility ever to be out of sound of the telephone or out of reach of the staff people.

I am dreadfully sorry that you must have all the pain and discomfort of a long hospitalization; but please be as philosophic about it as possible. We will have to have a special celebration when once you are up and about.

With affectionate regard to Priscilla and all the best to yourself, *As ever*

---

[1] While commuting to jury duty on November 14 Slater had slipped on subway stairs and was admitted to Beekman Street Hospital in New York City. He had undergone surgery for a broken right arm and a fracture of the right foot and was expected to be hospitalized for several weeks (see Larmon to Whitman, Nov. 14, 1956, and Slater to Whitman, Nov. 29, both in AWF/N, Slater Corr.; and Eisenhower to Slater, Nov. 15, 16, 1956, and Slater to Eisenhower, Nov. 29, 1956, all in AWF/N). The Eisenhowers had been vacationing in Augusta, Georgia, since November 26. They would return to the White House on December 13.

[2] This was professional golfer Edward Bishop Dudley, Jr. (for background see *Eisenhower Papers*, vols. X–XIII).

[3] W. Alton ("Pete") Jones would not visit in Augusta due to his wife's illness (see Eisenhower to Slater, Dec. 12, 1956, AWF/N; and Eisenhower to Nettie Jones, Dec. 12, 1956, AWF/D).

2128

To Margaret Winchester Patterson   *December 4, 1956*
Personal

Dear Margaret: I am, as always, glad to have your viewpoint on current international—and domestic—matters.[1] (I realize of course that your letter was written before the announcement of our plans for the transport of oil to Europe).[2]

That step, and others which I cannot discuss, are all planned in an effort to help our friends of the free world. But the entire matter is delicate and difficult. For example, you realize that if we are to give our European friends help that will be of permanent value to them, the first thing that we must assure them is a durable source of oil. That source can be only the Middle East; consequently, you must see the need for proceeding cautiously at this moment in order that the entire Arab world, highly emotional by nature, does not become so incensed as to refuse to sell the needed oil.

As often as seems practical, I shall give what reassurance I can personally to the people of America and of the world.

With warm regard, *Sincerely*

¹ Mrs. Patterson, the widow of former Secretary of War Robert Porter Patterson, had written Eisenhower about her concern that a possible oil shortage in Europe, resulting from the Suez Canal crisis, would make Europe "a soft spot—and the Soviet Union takes over soft spots." She continued, "Today shows the usual symptoms of a Soviet 'putsch.'" She noted the harmful effects of strikes which would aid the Soviets' "military and economic goal of the moment. . . ." "To starve Europe of oil seems morally indefensible," she concluded, "while we do not dare punish Soviet Russia for mass murders and deportations" (Nov. 29, 1956, same file as document).
² See no. 2123.

2128A   *EM, AWF, Name Series*

To Arthur William Tedder   *December 5, 1956*
Top secret

Dear Arthur: I am sending you on a highly secret basis a letter that I wrote recently to Pug.¹ This letter does not answer, of course, all of the questions that plague your mind and as outlined in the long paragraph on the second page of your letter.²

The only thing I can assure you is this: We on this side of the water have not been insensible to these very same factors and considerations. As I see it, the project undertaken by Britain, France and Israel was not well thought through before the plunge. Many of the consequences that now puzzle you were mentioned as possibilities to Anthony and others very early in the game.³

I have constantly agreed with many of my friends in the Atlantic Community that Nasser was trying to be a new Mussolini and would have to be curbed. But such a thing cannot be done in this day and time when the world believes that *for once* Nasser was within his rights. He did not seize the Canal, he did not stop its operation. He nationalized the Company owning the Canal and then proceeded to operate it fully as efficiently as it had ever been operated in its long history.

So if Nasser was to be punished or brought to task in any way for all the long list of indictments included in your letter, it was up to us to find the proper time and vehicle on which to do it.

In the meantime and on the more hopeful side, you will have learned by now that we are moving as rapidly as is possible to help Western Europe out of the economic mess into which it has fallen as a result of this affair.⁴ We could not move earlier because to do so would have seemingly made us an outright supporter of the venture and would have probably cut off the one thing that *must* be maintained—and that is Western access to Mid East oil.

The measures already taken and announced are going to cost us a very huge sum during the coming two years; I think that gradually it will be understood in Western Europe that we have been a *true* friend throughout. I do not conceive it to be the function of a friend to encourage action that he believes in his heart to be unwise and even inexpedient. This does not mean that friendship is so cheap that sacrifice to preserve such friendship is unjustified. Far from it.

Thank you very much for your letter. It was by no means an impertinence—you should know better than even to think such a thing.

Give my love to Toppy and to Richard, and of course all the best to yourself.[5] *As ever*

[1] Eisenhower's letter to NATO Secretary-General Hastings Lionel ("Pug") Ismay is no. 2119.

[2] At the beginning of the Suez crisis, Tedder had written, the public "was very strongly opposed to armed intervention and consequently was all the more shocked when the ultimatum was issued." Labor Party attacks on Eden, however, had solidified support for the Prime Minister, and many in Great Britain objected to the conditions placed on the United Nations by Egyptian President Nasser. "One accepts the point that on this particular issue Nasser is the 'victim of aggression,' but is it to be forgotten or ignored that for years the same man has blatantly defied U.N.O., preached and practised war against the Jews, stocked himself with Russian arms, [fomented] strife throughout the Middle East and Africa under the guise of supporting nationalism?" Was Nasser's "deliberate and wholesale sabotage" of the canal justified? Tedder asked (Tedder to Eisenhower, Nov. 30, 1956, AWF/N).

[3] See, for example, no. 1935. The "tragedy of the widening rift" between the United States and Great Britain particularly concerned Tedder.

[4] See no. 2123.

[5] Tedder's wife, the former Marie de Seton Black, and his son.

2129   *EM, AWF, Administration Series*

To James Bryant Conant   *December 5, 1956*

Dear Jim: I was deeply interested in the attitudes and the thinking of German university students as reported in your excellent letter.[1] There is much that is truly heartening in your account—particularly the evidence of a strongly-held attachment to a moral basis for the conduct of international affairs. After reading your letter, I sent it on to Secretary Hoover so that he might also have the benefit of your observations.[2]

With warm regard, *As ever*

[1] Conant, U.S. Ambassador to the Federal Republic of Germany, had written the President on November 21 (AWF/A) to report on the sentiment among German students in the wake of the Soviet invasion of Hungary (see nos. 2044, 2055, and 2067). Conant had reported that while the wrath of German students against the Russians was to be expected, what was surprising was the "equal indignation" directed against the British and the French. The Ambassador stated that he believed student sentiment arose from "a deep-seated moral conviction." "It is evident," he wrote, "that the lessons of history had made a deep impression on them and the knowledge of the Nazi atrocities, the Hitler aggression, and the results of this aggression as seen by their ruined cities, had turned them into idealists in regard to a moral basis for international order." On British and French action in Suez see nos. 2068, 2071, and 2073.

[2] The State Department prepared a draft reply to Conant; it was later redrafted in the White House (Howe to Goodpaster, Dec. 3, 1956, AWF/A, Conant Corr.).

2130   *EM, AWF, Administration Series*

To Henry Robinson Luce   *December 5, 1956*
Personal

Dear Harry: Jim Hagerty just showed me a copy of the special pictorial report on "Hungary's Fight for Freedom." It seems to me that it should be very effective in helping Americans understand exactly what price people place upon the freedom of which they have been robbed.[1]

Because of this I should like to send copies to a few of my friends. Jim tells me the price is 50¢—I am enclosing a check for $10 and if you will send me twenty copies I will mail them out.[2]

With warm regard, *As ever*

[1] Eisenhower was referring to an article, "A Desperate Fight for Freedom," in the November 5, 1956 *Life*. For background on the Hungarian revolution see nos. 2044, 2055, and 2067.

[2] Luce would reply on December 8, saying that "It meant a whole lot to the people here who put out the Hungary book to get the message from you via Jim Hagerty. It was a labor of love—the love of freedom" (AWF/A).

2131   *EM, WHCF,*
                                                          Official File 3

To Heads of Executive Departments   *December 6, 1956*
and Establishments
Memorandum

SUBJECT: Hungarian Refugees

Pursuant to the authority vested in me by Section 401 of the Mutual Security Act of 1954, As Amended, it is hereby determined that the

2436

use of funds, available under said Act, for the purpose of carrying out the program of asylum for refugees from Hungary which was announced by my statement of December 1, 1956, is important to the security of the United States and that assistance to such refugees will contribute to the security of the United States.[1]

The Department of State, the Department of Defense, the International Cooperation Administration, and any other Executive Agencies which may participate in this program are authorized and directed to take such action and make such expenditures as may be necessary to perform such services and carry out such activities as are requested by my Representative for Hungarian Refugee Relief,[2] and to be reimbursed from funds available under said Section for additional costs incurred and not otherwise provided for, to the extent agreed upon between such Agencies and ICA and approved by the Director of the Bureau of the Budget. It is my desire that the program be carried out forthwith and without awaiting completion of arrangements for reimbursements.[3]

The Director of the International Cooperation Administration is requested on my behalf to give appropriate notices, pursuant to Section 513 of the Mutual Security Act of 1954, As Amended, to the Chairman of the Senate Committee on Foreign Relations, the Chairman of the House Committee on Foreign Affairs, and the respective Chairmen of the Senate and House Committees on Armed Services.[4]

[1] On December 1 the President had announced that the United States would offer asylum to an additional 21,500 Hungarian refugees (see no. 2116). Eisenhower had emphasized that "the flight of refugees into Austria had created an emergency problem which the United States should share with the other countries of the free world" (*Public Papers of the Presidents: Eisenhower, 1956*, pp. 1116–18).

[2] The White House had announced on November 30 the appointment of Tracy Stebbins Voorhees (LL.B. Columbia University 1915) to serve as Eisenhower's personal representative to coordinate Hungarian refugee problems. Voorhees, a former Under Secretary of the Army under Truman, had served as defense adviser to the United States mission to NATO from 1953–1954, and continued to serve as consultant to Defense Secretary Wilson. In announcing the appointment, Press Secretary Hagerty had stated that Voorhees's task was to assure full coordination of the various voluntary and government agencies and to make sure that everything possible was being done to help the refugees obtain employment and housing (*New York Times*, Nov. 30, 1956).

[3] In his December 1 statement Eisenhower had directed the Secretary of Defense to work out arrangements for the transportation of the refugees to the United States. On December 6 the White House had announced the completion of arrangements for transporting the refugees by air and sea.

[4] For background on John Baker Hollister and the International Cooperation Administration see no. 1402. On the Mutual Security Act of 1954 see *Congressional Quarterly Almanac*, vol. X, *1954*, pp. 275–81. Section 513 required the President to notify Congress of a decision to make use of funds available under Section 401 (Special Funds) in the security interests of the United States (see *United States Statutes at Large*, 1954, vol. 68, pt. 1, pp. 832–64).

To Edward John Bermingham and *December 7, 1956*
Katherine Carpenter Bermingham

Dear Ed and Kay: For a long time I have wanted to write a joint note to the two of you in an attempt to express my appreciation of your efforts in connection with the refurbishing of the Eisenhower home in Abilene.[1]

I realize that you contributed largely to the project and that you—especially Kay—spent a lot of time supervising the actual work.[2] Of course I am eager personally to see the result, but meantime Milton and Earl have told me what a fine job it is, and how pleased they are.[3] I assure you that I am more than grateful to you for your interest and assistance in a matter that is very close to my heart.

With affectionate regard—and many thanks, *Sincerely*

[1] On December 3 Milton Eisenhower had written that the Berminghams had contributed money "to finance the refurbishing of the Eisenhower" boyhood home (AWF/N, Bermingham Corr.; see also Eisenhower to Dillon, Dec. 7, 1956, *ibid.*). On the house, located at the Eisenhower Center and open to the public since June 1947, see Galambos, *The Chief of Staff*, no. 1602; and *Eisenhower Papers*, vols. X–XIII.

[2] Milton had reported that Mrs. Bermingham had been one of five women who supervised the plans and work.

[3] Milton and Earl Eisenhower had attended the dedication and the unveiling ceremonies on November 24 (see *New York Times*, Nov. 25, 1956).

To Mohammad Reza Pahlavi *December 10, 1956*

Your Imperial Majesty: Thank you most sincerely for your letter of November twentieth and for your kind words about my re-election.[1]

Your views regarding recent events in Europe and in the Middle East I have read with care and with great interest. As we face the dangers of which you speak, there can be no doubt in our minds that the free world must base its hopes for peace more and more upon the joint efforts of free nations and upon their regional associations.

Iran can indeed be proud of the part it is playing, along with its neighbors, in the efforts to restore peace and to maintain security in the Middle East. Given close cooperation between free nations in collective efforts to maintain peace, even the largest nations cannot act with impunity and the nations that may be exposed to danger are not alone. The validity of this principle was clearly demonstrated in

1946, when Iran regained sovereign control over its northwest territories.[2]

I have especially noted Your Majesty's words about the lack of preparation to face a sudden emergency. This is, indeed, a problem of mutual concern. The United States has in recent years attempted to assist Iran in strengthening its economy and its armed forces. Such assistance will, of course, continue, insofar as our capabilities and the requirements of the rest of the free world will permit. I am confident that with continued close cooperation between the Government of Iran and the various United States Missions in Iran this aid will produce even more important gains for Iran than have been registered in the past.

The needs of Iran and the demands of her unique position in the Middle East are being given our constant attention. Our Ambassador and the members of our missions have reported fully on the requirements of Iran and the problems with which it is faced. Moreover, the Congress is soon to have the benefit of Mr. Armour's special study of conditions.[3] In the circumstances, I do not believe a special representative is required for further study at this time.

The causes of the dangers which have threatened the Middle East and the means of dealing with them are being given the most careful and urgent consideration by the United States Government. The firm and helpful position adopted by Iran is one of the very reassuring elements in the present situation. I continue to regard any threats to Iran's territorial integrity and political independence as a matter of the utmost gravity.[4]

With best wishes and warmest regard, *Sincerely*

---

[1] A State Department draft of this letter is in AWF/I: Iran. Pahlavi, the Shah of Iran, had written an urgent message to Eisenhower requesting more aid and a personal representative to evaluate the aid programs (Pahlavi to Eisenhower, Nov. 20, 1956, AWF/I: Iran). Despite the suggestion of the American Ambassador to Iran that a special representative be designated, Secretary Dulles had recommended against both steps (Chapin to Dulles, Nov. 22, 1956; Dulles to Eisenhower, Dec. 7, 1956, AWF/I: Iran). Dulles would, however, order the Director of the International Cooperation Administration to make a public announcement of $45 million in aid to Iran in order "to obtain the maximum poltical effect" (State, *Foreign Relations, 1955–1957*, vol. XII, *Near East Region; Iran; Iraq*, pp. 859–60).

[2] Eisenhower is referring to the dispute over the Soviet military occupation of parts of Iran. See Galambos, *Chief of Staff*, no. 809.

[3] For background see no. 1774. Norman Armour, Sr., former U.S. Ambassador to Guatemala, was Consultant to the Senate Special Committee Studying the Mutual Security Program, a special subcommittee of the Senate Committee on Foreign Relations. He would find that the defense of Iran was "of paramount importance to the United States strategic objectives in the Middle East of maintaining free and independent prowestern governments, limiting the expansion of Communist-dominated areas and insuring Western access to strategic raw materials of the area."

While Armour recognized Iran's importance to American strategy, he would have serious doubts about the ability of Iran's main development planning organization "to carry out its program and to make the most effective use of the very considerable funds available to it." Due to steadily increasing oil revenues, Armour would recommend that "leveling off and reducing funds for technical assistance would be more than fully justified," that budgetary aid should be discontinued, and that the non-military aid program in Iran should generally be "in the form of loans."

Armour would support continued grants of military aid to Iran. In order to stem criticism from Iranian officials over delays in delivery of planes and in military construction, he would suggest that the Administration speed up these programs. He would oppose an increase in military aid, however, noting that "there is some doubt as to whether Iran could absorb very much of an increase in the level of military assistance over what is already being furnished" (U.S., Congress, Senate, Special Committee to Study the Foreign Aid Program, *Greece, Turkey, and Iran: Report on United States Foreign Assistance Programs*, committee print, 85th Cong., 1st sess., 1957, esp. pp. 8–11).

[4] An earlier State Department draft had read "The firm and helpful position adopted by Iran is one of the very reassuring elements in the present situation and, for this reason, I continue to regard any threats to Iran's territorial integrity and political independence as a matter of the utmost gravity." At the American Ambassador's suggestion, and with the President's approval, the words "for this reason" were deleted from the final text (see State, *Foreign Relations, 1955–1957*, vol. XII, *Near East Region; Iran; Iraq*, p. 863, n. 6).

2134   *EM, AWF, Dulles-Herter Series*

To John Foster Dulles   *December 12, 1956*
Cablegram to the Secretary of State

Dear Foster: Thank you very much for your cable report that I received yesterday morning. I am of course delighted that our friends seemed to accept our conviction that bilateral are preferable to tripartite talks and conferences.[1]

I hope that our NATO friends will understand clearly that we have no intention of standing idly by to see the southern flank of NATO completely collapse through Communist penetration and success in the Mid East while we do nothing about it. I am sure that they know that we regard Nasser as an evil influence. I think also we have made it abundantly clear that while we share in general the British and French opinions of Nasser, we insisted that they chose a bad time and incident on which to launch corrective measures.

Most important of all, I hope that our friends in Europe will see the necessity, as we see it, of beginning confidentially and on a staff level to develop policies and plans whereby the West can work together in making the Mid East secure from Communist penetration. I have no doubt that for some time to come we would have to be, at least in the public eye, the spearhead of any such movement. But it does seem that at long last we could get a pretty good general understanding among us as to what must be done and how we should go about doing it.

I continue to believe, as I think you do, that one of the measures that we must take is to build up an Arab rival of Nasser, and the natural choice would seem to be the man you and I have often talked about. If we could build him up as the individual to capture the imagination of the Arab world, Nasser would not last long.[2]

A couple of days ago I received a message signed by General Weygand and Marshal Juin sent to me, they said, on the basis of our former association as comrades-in-arms. I think the State Department will probably cable to you certain extracts from the letter. It may not be too important, but it does show at least one kind of thinking that is prevalent in Western Europe, especially in France.[3]

New subject. Yesterday Prime Minister St. Laurent stopped at Augusta to visit with me. While the visit was largely social, he had some ideas about the forthcoming visit of our Asiatic friend.[4] There was nothing particularly new in them, so I do not bother you here with their repetition. I shall probably see you Saturday.

With very warmest regard and the hope that you are suffering no ill effects about going back to work so soon after your recent illness.[5] *As ever*

[1] Eisenhower sent the text of this cable to Acting Secretary of State Hoover, telling him to "look this message over, and if okay, send on to Secretary Dulles at once" (Goodpaster to Minnich, Dec. 12, 1956, WHO/OSS: Subject [State], State Dept.). Dulles was attending the NATO Council of Ministers and had cabled Eisenhower that the "meetings were cordial and the strain has, I think, been ended." The Secretary had also noted that neither France nor Britain had asked for a tripartite (U.S.-British-French) meeting (Dulles to Eisenhower, DULTE 7, Dec. 10, 1956, AWF/D-H). For background on the Council of Ministers see State, *Foreign Relations, 1955–1957*, vol. IV, *Western European Security and Integration*, pp. 103–65.

[2] On Nasser see no. 2141. Eisenhower and Dulles had previously discussed promoting King Saud as an Arab leader; see nos. 1811 and 2155.

[3] Alphonse-Pierre Juin, Marshal of France, and General Maxime Weygand had written Eisenhower expressing their concern about the damage done to NATO by Eisenhower's failure to comment promptly on Soviet threats to bombard Western Europe with missiles. Eisenhower's silence, they said, had created a "psychological crisis" in France. (On November 5, in separate messages to the French and British, the Soviets had compared the invasion of Egypt to hypothetical rocket attacks against France and Britain "by more powerful states possessing every kind of modern destructive weapon" [State, *Foreign Relations, 1955–1957*, vol. XVI, *Suez Crisis July 26–December 31, 1956*, pp. 1003–7, 1018–20, and 1023–25; *New York Times*, Nov. 6, 1956].) Weygand and Juin also criticized American policy in North Africa for failing to support France against Soviet subversion in the French colonies. It was "a snare and a delusion to believe in the possibility of an Arab bloc on the southern and eastern shores of the Mediterranean that would serve the interests of the West" (Juin and Weygand to Eisenhower, Nov. 30, 1956, AWF/I: France).

After his return from Paris Secretary Dulles sent Eisenhower a draft reply, noting that few people knew that the letter had been sent, but that those few included "Mollet, as well as de Gaulle, and both may have approved its contents" (Dulles to Eisenhower, Dec. 22, 1956, AWF/I: France). "It seems to us," Eisenhower's reply read, "that the fact that the United States, despite its deep sympathy for France and Britain, lived up to Article I [of the North Atlantic Treaty] (renunciation of force) provides added assurance, not less assurance, that we shall live up to Article V (resistance to armed attack)." On the question of North Africa, Eisenhower pointed out "we may not always be in complete agreement," but the two nations needed consultation to "seek jointly the solutions which are in the long-term interests of NATO and of our two countries" (Eisenhower to Juin and Weygand, Dec. 26, 1956, AWF/I: France). When presented with the letter by an American embassy officer, Juin commented "Très bien!" He later said that "the President's message had cleared up any doubts on the United States position which he may have had" (Dorman to Department of State, Jan. 2, 1957, WHO/OSS: Subject [State], State Dept.).

[4] Prime Minister Louis St. Laurent of Canada had seen the President in Augusta, Georgia. The "Asiatic friend" was Jawaharlal Nehru, Prime Minister of India. On the Nehru visit see nos. 2138 and 2139.

[5] Secretary Dulles had been hospitalized on November 3 to undergo surgery for cancer. He had resumed his official duties on December 3.

2135   *EM, AWF, Administration Series*

To Herbert Clark Hoover   *December 12, 1956*

Dear Mr. Hoover: Many thanks for your letter suggesting means of strengthening the organization for Hungarian refugee relief.[1] As you know, we are at this moment hard at work on various phases of just this problem. I expect to announce later today the formation of a citizens' committee designed to serve as a focal point for receiving offers of assistance and supporting voluntary groups engaged in work for the refugees.[2]

From Tracy Voorhees, I know something of the help you have already given him, and how valuable it has been. He tells me that he is continuing his efforts to strengthen the government organization for carrying out the program, and I expect to be conferring with him soon after my return to Washington.[3]

We all heartily welcome and appreciate your advice and assistance, based on such great experience.[4]

With warm regard, *Sincerely*

[1] Hoover had written on December 8, 1956 (AWF/A) to suggest that although "There are a host of good people and much efficient work being done" by the Hungarian refugee relief agencies, "it seems to me there must be a much stronger line-up of organizations." He suggested that Eisenhower establish two parallel administrative agencies. The first, to comprise representatives of the government agencies involved, including the Departments of Defense, State, Agriculture, Labor and Justice, might be administered by Eisenhower's personal representative for Hungarian Refugee Relief, Tracy Voorhees. The second would be an independent, non-official council created of eligible voluntary agencies headed by the Chairman of the American Red Cross (for background see no. 2131).

[2] The White House would release an announcement that Eisenhower was establishing a fifteen-member "President's Committee for Hungarian Refugee Relief," to coordinate the work of government and voluntary agencies. Voorhees was named as acting chairman, and Lewis W. Douglas was to serve as the honorary chairperson (*New York Times*, Nov. 13, 1956).

[3] Hoover had written, "Mr. Tracy Voorhees is doing a good job struggling to get coordination." Eisenhower would return to Washington from his "working vacation" in Augusta on December 13 (see no. 2116) and would meet with Voorhees on December 26.

[4] The former President had directed various Allied relief efforts during and after World War I. He had served as Director General of the Commission on the Relief and Reconstruction of Europe.

2136   *EM, AWF, Administration Series:*
                                                          Hauge Corr.

To Ann Cook Whitman   *December 13, 1956*

Mrs. W.: Send these to Sec. Treas. when he returns from London. (Send a doctor along)[1]

[1] Eisenhower's note to Ann Whitman was in response to two memorandums of the same date from Gabriel Hauge (AWF/A, Hauge Corr.). In the first, Hauge had forwarded to the President a quote from Standard and Poor's 1956 fourth quarter report. Based on interviews with more than five hundred corporate executives, the report had concluded that there was an "increasing number of executives who believe a little, continuing inflation is essential to full employment." It also said that "If a popular election were held between an ardent inflationist and an ardent anti-inflationist, we are not at all sure who would win." Eisenhower had underlined the above quoted sentences.

Treasury Secretary Humphrey would respond on December 18: "The doctor has just revived me so that I am now able to acknowledge your note of the 17th with the enclosures from Gabe" (AWF/A). "I am sure there is quite a lot of truth in this report of easy acceptance of creeping inflation," he would note. "There are a lot of business people who are not too thoughtful about the future so long as their current quarterly statements look good. We are sort of in the position of evangelists to get the more thoughtful sufficiently vocal to carry the crowd."

In the second memorandum Hauge had informed the President that "A newspaper in one of our large cities ran a contest to get suggestions on how to finance a particular local improvement program." One of the contestants had written, "Let the Federal Government do it; then it won't cost anybody anything." This notion, Humphrey replied, was "all too prevalent. We have just got to beat it down some way." For more on the President's concerns about inflation see nos. 1578, 1956, and 2060; see also Howard, ed., *The Basic Papers of George M. Humphrey*, pp. 168–73.

2137   *EM, AWF, Name Series*

To Edgar Newton Eisenhower   *December 14, 1956*

Dear Edgar: Before I received your note about Jack we had a short letter from Nina, apparently his wife. I wrote her at once extending the sympathy of Mamie and myself.[1]

It is, of course, difficult to understand why so often the oldsters go on and on into the eighties and nineties, while the younger, more vigorous men are cut down in their youth.[2] There is no way to explain it except that it is one of the accidents of living. It happens with the trees and the birds and everything that grows. No individual can have any possible explanation, and therefore it is one of those things which must be accepted and absorbed into the philosophy that a man develops as he goes along.

In spite of all this—and anything that may have happened in the past—I know that it is hard for you to take. Yet you owe it to those still around you—your wife, your daughter and your grandchildren—to provide an example that is not characterized by pessimism, cynicism and defeat.

This sounds like preaching—and possibly it is. My justification is that I lost a son of my own many years ago—the only one we then had.[3] To this date it is not an easy thing to deal with when it comes fresh to my memory, but it is something that I had to learn to accept or to go crazy.

With love to Lucy, and warm regard to yourself, *As ever*

P.S. I hope the doctors are beginning to decide exactly what is wrong and to do something effective about it.[4]

---

[1] Edgar had written on December 8 that his estranged son Jack had passed away the preceding evening (AWF/N; for background on Jack Eisenhower see Galambos, *Chief of Staff*, no. 754). "In spite of our differences," Edgar wrote, "he was still my son. . . . I sorta feel the world is crumbling" (See also correspondence between the President and Lucy Eisenhower, Dec. 14 and 24, in *ibid.*). We have been unable to find the letter from Nina or Eisenhower's reply in AWF.

[2] Jack Eisenhower had been born on May 30, 1916.

[3] Doud Dwight ("Icky") Eisenhower had died at the age of four (see no. 1014).

[4] See no. 2092. On this same day Mrs. Lucy Eisenhower would report that Edgar did not suffer from a slipped disc. He had "a severe case of neuritis." Edgar was feeling much better, she said, due to strong medication that was helping him sleep through the night (AWF/N). For developments see no. 2159.

2138   *EM, AWF, International Series: Nehru Visit*

Diary   *December 16, 1956*

Luncheon was purely social. No political problems were brought up. Nehru seemed very pleasant and interested in the history of various items about the White House as told to him by Mrs. Eisenhower. Both Nehru and his daughter, Mrs. Gandhi, wore native costumes.[1]

¹ For background on Indian Prime Minister Nehru's visit to Washington and Gettysburg see no. 1794; see also Eisenhower to Nehru, August 16 and November 27, 1956, AWF/I: Nehru. Also present at lunch were Mrs. Eisenhower's mother, Mrs. John Sheldon Doud, and Major and Mrs. John S. D. Eisenhower.

2139   *EM, AWF, International Series:*
                                                              Nehru Visit

Memorandum. Top secret   *[December 18, 1956]*

*Memorandum of Conversations with Prime Minister Nehru of India, December 17–18, 1956.*¹

I.

The conversation was general insofar as it affected common problems of India and the United States. It was often specific insofar as it applied to expositions by the Prime Minister of India's problems involving Pakistan, economic development, and so on. It was conducted on a very friendly basis; there were no arguments or even informal debates of any kind.

II. THE MID-EAST

The Prime Minister gave his impressions of the Mid East difficulties, their causes and consequences, and made certain suggestions of what might be done to improve matters.

According to him, the causes of the recent acute disturbances in the Mid East are those as generally accepted by the public and discussed in the newspapers. This applied both to the Canal stoppage and to the Israeli attack.

He seemingly disagrees with most others as to the degree of guilt that rests upon Nasser. At least he said, "Nasser is the best of the group of Egyptian Army officers and others for whom he is the spokesman. Under present conditions, if Nasser were removed there would come into power someone who would be more inimical to the West and more unreasonable in his actions than is Nasser." He agreed that Nasser was immature when he came to power, but he thinks he has come quite a way in the last two or three years.

He understands the provocations under which the French and British reacted, but he thinks their invasion was stupid and cost them much, particularly in the world opinion and prestige. He thinks that a Pan-Arab Confederation, responding to the whims of a Nasser, would constitute an increased danger for all users of the Canal and for all who are interested in keeping Russia out of the Mid East.

He believes that King Saud probably offers the best counter for Nasser if the latter really pushes any attempt to become head of an Arab Confederation.

The non-operation of the Canal is costing India and other Asiatic users more than they can afford and they are anxious to see the Canal again in operation.

I pointed out to him that this would be easily accomplished had Nasser contented himself with blocking the Canal at one point. I quoted as an example of Nasser's instability and impulsiveness his action in sinking some 39 or more vessels in the Canal. The Prime Minister agreed that this was a foolish act, but he repeated that in his opinion Nasser was more of a brake on what the Egyptian junta really wanted to do than he was a spur to drive them on to even more ill-considered activity.

I gave the Prime Minister the complete story of the Aswan Dam negotiations that were finally used as an excuse by Nasser for seizing the Canal Company in late July. He seemed astonished to learn that our original offer had in effect been rejected by Egypt and that the Egyptians had no right to be surprised when our own announcement of loss of interest in the project was made public.[2]

I told the Prime Minister that I thought he should exert his fullest influence on the Egyptians to make certain that moderation and common sense were substituted for impulsiveness and antagonism so that all of us might cooperate in getting the Canal again in operation. I told him that we had used our influence to temper the British and French and Israeli attitude and would continue to do so.

He agreed that we must make an earnest attempt to settle the underlying grievances in the region.

He spoke disparagingly of Nuri of Iraq, but did not mention the Baghdad Pact as such.[3]

He brought me a letter from the President of Syria. He did not give me the transmittal note, but made the following statement, "This letter was handed to our Ambassador by the Foreign Minister of Syria, who said that it was sent by the President's direction (or approval)" to Nehru for delivery to me. A copy of the letter is attached to this memorandum.[4]

While Nehru said he had not read it carefully, he did agree when I spoke to him about it that it is mere repetition of the Arab complaint as voiced by Nasser in some of his speeches. Incidentally, Nehru attempted to absolve the Arab speakers by saying their public figures seemed to get excited when they addressed a crowd and always talked in extravagant terms under such circumstances.

III. HUNGARY

He expressed a considerable sense of horror and shock about the Hungarian situation and said that India had sent at least token help by shipping certain cargoes of food and other supplies to the Hungarian refugees. I told him that his stock had gone up in the United States when he finally made a very positive statement of protest in regard to this tragedy and advised him to repeat that statement either in his television address to the people of the United States or in his press conference, which is to take place on the 19th.[5] In addition, I told him that I thought it would be helpful if India would make an offer to take at least a token number of the refugees.

Nehru made some observations concerning the results of the Hungarian affair. He said that it spelled the death knell of International Communism. Hungary, he pointed out, was a State that had been under complete dominion of the International Communists for a period of ten years. Yet in all that time they had made so little progress in converting the people to real Communism that we had the spectacle of an uprising in which people were perfectly ready to be killed rather than submit again to their Communist overlords. He felt this was a terrible shock to the men in the Kremlin and that they would likely have to make a reappraisal of their plans. He seemed to feel that the Communist appeal from now on would be clothed in words and language more likely to appeal to the dissatisfied and needy of the world, while threats and the effort to dominate by force would become less and less.

He felt that by this same action, the standing of Communist parties in every country where they are located would be badly damaged. He said that in many cases prominent men had resigned from the party and others were attempting to apologize with very little success.

He believes that this is a propitious moment, because of this great blunder of the Soviets, for the free world to move in by strengthening the faith and hope of those who would naturally like to live in independence and freedom, but who have been at least partially misled by the Communists' doctrine. He said that there was great significance that Poland was continuing to win, step by step, greater independence from their Moscow overlords.

He summed up his opinion by saying, "Nationalism is stronger than Communism."

IV. COMMUNIST CHINA

He talked about Communist China. He felt that logic demanded that any government controlling six hundred million people would sooner or later have to be brought into the Council of nations. He felt that Chiang Kai-shek and his Army on Formosa were showing the ravages of time and that eventually Formosa would be a weakened area which, almost by force of circumstances, would fall into the hands of the Communists. He asked me how I felt about that region.

I told him that the bill of particulars that the American people held against the Red Chinese included the following:

(a) They were branded by the United Nations as an aggressor because of their invasion of North Korea and the fact that they had never done anything to clear themselves of this stain;

(b) They still hold ten American prisoners in China in spite of their repeated promises to release them. This, I pointed out, was a very sensitive point in America;

(c) They had supported and probably provided part of the forces for the invasion in Northern Indo China in defiance of all international law. In addition, they had operated aggressively against both Laos and Burma. * * * * *[6] I told him further that America was disgusted with people who broke their pledged word, as the Chinese had with respect to our prisoners, and that we were very tired of the kind of diplomatic deportment and manner that the Chinese had exhibited over the past several years.

With respect to the Chinese prisoners in our country, I gave him the facts and found that he was aware that the Chinese had refused to allow the Indian Ambassador to inspect our jails to see whether any of the Chinese prisoners incarcerated there for crimes wanted to return to China. I told him we were perfectly ready to send any back that wanted to go.

I told him that, if there was to be any break in the log jam at this moment, I thought the first thing necessary was the release of our prisoners and the next would be the withdrawal of Chinese forces from Korea. I thought a third and very useful thing would be renunciation of force by the Red Chinese in accomplishing any further objectives in that region.

V. INDIA—HER ATTITUDES AND RELATIONS WITH OTHERS

(a) *Policy on neutrality.* Nehru went to considerable trouble to explain the reasons why India pursued a policy of "neutrality." First he said that he used the word neutrality in its traditional sense as meaning a position of aloofness from power combinations, particularly power combinations that were at war or threatening war between themselves. He made clear that he did not use the word to distinguish between concepts of government based on the dignity of man and those based on dictatorships.

He spoke about as follows: India might, logically, fear attack from two countries only—the USSR and China. Concerning such a possibility it is apparent that either one of these countries would have great difficulty in conducting large conventional operations against India, because of the fortunate location of the Himalayan mountain chain.

He next pointed out that both these countries had vast internal problems and if they attacked anyone, it would logically be a nation that posed either a threat to them or the possession of which would provide great advantage. India fulfills neither of these conditions. He said that if a world war eventuated finally, Russia would be too busy in other areas to attack India.

His next point was that he had with China 1800 miles of common border. He said that if he were to attempt the defense of this border by armed force, it would be such an expensive proposition that India would necessarily fail in its purpose of raising the standards of living and so saving India from [Communism] through internal collapse.

Finally he said if a country is to be an ally of any other in a defensive organization, it must do its military part. He said that India was in no position whatsoever to attempt to arm in proportion to its population and geographical size and therefore *any definite alignment by India with the free world would serve only to weaken rather than to strengthen the combination.*

(b) *Attitude toward socialism.* Nehru's attitude is that all countries are a "little bit socialistic"—that there is no such thing as pure free enterprise practiced in any country. On the other hand, we do have the extreme of Communism as practiced in the Soviet Union—and we have the practice of some degree of socialism in all countries. This degree or level of state management in operation is often determined by the conditions prevailing. One of the conditions is that capital must be acquired for industrial development and at times only the government can do this.

In India they do not refer to these two phases of economic development as "socialism and free enterprise." They call them the private sector and the public sector. He said that in his case the public sector was necessarily larger than in the United States and he gave me some books which present in some detail what they consider to be the logical division between these two sectors. However, they overlap. But he did stress the point that they are not necessarily mutually antagonistic. On the contrary he felt that they were mutually helpful. He specifically stated that land ownership and small business would remain in the private sector.

(c) Nehru talked to me a considerable time about *Pakistan.* He reviewed the historical development that led to partition and is unquestionably bitter at the British for what he believes is their part in promoting the anomalous position of two nations in the Indian subcontinent. He is particularly resentful of the fact that the Pakistani did *not* obtain independence by their own efforts; they obtained it through the success of Indian nationalism. He described in detail the terrible administrative job that was brought about by partition and particularly emphasized the difficulties that arose out of the migrations of people between the two countries—Hindus moving from Pakistan into India, and Moslems from India into Pakistan.

In spite of this great movement, he said that India never accepted the theory of the organization of states along religious lines. As a proof of this he cited the fact that there are 40 million Moslems in India today and Moslems are represented in his Cabinet. He said these great migrations ceased for a while, but now they have been renewed, not by any movement of people from India into Pakistan, but by the anxiety of the Indians in East Pakistan to leave that country. He says that India is having to absorb these people at the rate of 1,000 a day.

All this creates unrest as well as economic dislocation.

Nehru made a great point of the fact that the Moslems in the Indian sub-continent are not the descendants of invaders. They are merely Indians who were converted to the Moslem faith. He said, "We speak the same language, often we are of the same families, and in nearly all cases we are good friends." He pointed out that when any question except political ones arose, the Pakistani and the Indians appeared to be one and the same people—which he says they really are. But when political questions come up, they are bitter opponents.

He said that there are four outstanding problems between the two states, none of which is considered insuperable:

(1) the division of river waters between Pakistan and India;

(2) the settlement of property claims arising out of the migrations back and forth across the border;

(3) Kashmir;

(4) (the fourth has slipped my mind, but I have the impression that it had to do with the continuing migration of the Hindus from East Pakistan into India.)

The only one of these questions that he thought would cause any real difficulty in settling (and he indicated India was ready to take a very tolerant attitude toward the others) was Kashmir. He talked about Kashmir at length.

His first contention is that the people of Kashmir want to belong to India, although unfortunately I failed to ask him why he had always opposed a plebiscite in the region. He reviewed in detail the original tribal invasions of Kashmir (following upon partition)—the employment of Indian troops to stop the invasions, the establishment of armistice lines—and pointed out that economic and political life has now become crystallized around the existence of this armistice line. The armistice line gives Pakistan one-third the territory and one-fourth the population of Kashmir. He believes that if the United Nations would approve of the status quo as a basis for permanent settlement, both sides would approve, although there would be some grumbling.

Finally, he pointed out, with respect to Pakistan, that the Indians have a popular belief that the Pakistani are ready to launch an attack against India. He cited the newspapers of the area and the work of what he calls fanatics in trying to promote this idea. This is one reason why the supply of arms to Pakistan aroused so much apprehension and even resentment in India.

(*d*) *Goa.* Nehru next described the Goa situation.[7] He maintained that India would *not* use force to settle this matter, but he did feel that if Portugal would cease creating new irritations and resentments in India, the thing would work out in the long run on a peaceful basis. He particularly referred to what he called the unjust long-term imprisonment of Indians who simply walked into Goa to protest. He insisted that Goa was of no economic value to Portugal and existed merely to satisfy the Portuguese feeling that it helped to make them an "empire." Here again Nehru's intense reactions to the word "colonialism" were quite evident.

(*e*) Nehru thought we could be of some help both in the Goa and in Pakistan problems. He thought we should urge Portugal to release the Indian prisoners, one of whom is a member of the Indian Parliament. This he said would be only a gesture, but it would at least show some respect for India. He thought we could help in the Pakistan problem by urging Pakistan to cease using its newspapers (which he says are really state-controlled) to incite the fears of the Indians. They are, apparently, intensively jingoistic. He said that if Pakistan's newspaper propaganda would talk peace instead of war the whole situation would be greatly ameliorated.

VI. SECOND FIVE-YEAR PLAN

Mr. Nehru outlined in considerable detail his aims and objectives in India's Second Five-Year Plan. The First Five-Year Plan was devoted almost exclusively to increasing agricultural productivity; the Second leans more toward industrialization. However, the chief objectives of the First Plan have become sufficiently understood by the Indian people, he hopes, that progress along agricultural lines will continue automatically.

He is particularly interested in a sort of rural "self help" plan. This plan organizes villages into groups for every kind of improvement— health, education, agriculture and general welfare. The reason for the organization is the paucity of instructors. To each village is assigned a young man who has normally had only one year of training. To each ten villages a supervisor with somewhat more training is allocated, and to each hundred a man who is much more advanced in all of these matters. To this latter man is assigned also a staff of specialists in the things they are trying to accomplish. He gave me the number of these organizations that had developed; while I have forgotten the number, I do recall that it was astonishing in its size.

Mr. Nehru sees as his only difficulty in achieving the objectives of the Second Five-Year Plan the shortage of capital. The Plan itself has a "private" and "public" sector, and he feels that capital will be short in both these. He did not hint to me that he was looking for help from the United States, but of course his failure to do so did not mean that he would be disappointed to have long-term, low-interest loans. Attached to this memorandum is one of the three books Mr. Nehru gave me on the Five-Year Plan. This particular pamphlet is a summary of the others.[8]

VII. SOUTHEAST ASIAN STATES AND INDONESIAN AFFAIRS

We talked at considerable length about this particular subject, but nothing especially new was brought out during the conversations. The one point he made was that he believed we were making a mistake in Laos by demanding that the Government exclude any Communists or Communist sympathizers from the Cabinet as the price of securing from us financial assistance that Laos needs. He pointed out that Laos was in a rather desperate situation. That Government had even inquired from India whether it would supply the money Laos previously expected from the United States, provided Laos should feel forced to go ahead with the plan and include a Laotian from the Communist sector in the Government. He remarked, "Of course we have no money to help them so they will go to one place only, the Communists."

I mentioned Diem (of Viet-Nam) to him several times and remarked that we felt he was doing a good job.[9] On this subject Mr. Nehru merely said nothing. I have no idea whether he approves or disapproves of Diem.

He seemed to think that there would be no great, aggressive efforts, within the near future, of the Communists to take over more territory. He rather felt they would move in where opportunities were good and not too costly, but that both China and Russia now had many problems of their own at home and would probably be somewhat less aggressive in efforts toward expansion.

In talking about Indonesian affairs, he had little to say except that he seemed to doubt the formation of a really stable government for a long time to come. This is not so much because of the diverse interests of the various sections of Indonesia—as I understood him—but rather because of some of the animosities arising out of differing religions.

VIII. GERMAN REUNIFICATION

Mr. Nehru emphasized the fear that Russia has of a rejuvenated Germany and expressed the view that the matter would be settled only if a European organization was set up that to the Russian mind would be a guarantee of their own safety. For example, he talked about the establishment of a great neutral belt reaching down through Europe into the Mediterranean. This would include all the present satellite states, as well as Germany. All of this, together with the "officially neutral" states—namely, Sweden, Austria and Switzerland—would, he thinks, possibly be the best answer to the whole works.

I expressed to Nehru my grave doubts that a people as strong and virile as the Germans could ever be successfully treated as neutrals, particularly in view of their long history in Europe and the fact that they are the most dynamic people of the region. He agreed that this might present some difficulty, but he did repeat—and I agreed—that the Russians are honestly fearful of a German resurgence to great power.

IX. INDIAN-AMERICAN RELATIONS

The subject of Indian-American relations was not discussed at great length, but Mr. Nehru expressed the hope that our personal meeting and conversations would open up an additional channel of communication which would, he hoped, make the occurrence of misunderstandings and mutual suspicion less common than heretofore.

While talking on this particular subject, I gave him every chance to bring up the name of Krishna Menon.[10] For example, I mentioned that our Ambassador in Moscow, Mr. Bohlen, had spoken in the highest terms of his Ambassador in that city, a man whose name I understood was Menon. He merely said it was gratifying to hear such a good report, but still avoided any mention of the other Menon.

I did get the very definite impression that he was sincere in his hope that understanding between our two peoples and governments would improve. Naturally I expressed the same kind of hope, and tried to show him by every courtesy I could think of that we appreciated the effort he had made in coming to visit us. For example, I directed that he be transported back to London in the Presidential plane—and I had delivered to him in New York the day after he left Washington a farewell letter thanking him again for his courtesy.[11]

I particularly asked him to do his best to see that his people and his government did not become too excited by the speeches and statements of some of our more irresponsible people who pose as statesmen. He was quite clear in his own mind as to the divisions of authority in our form of government and stated that he himself paid little attention to what some of our more ambitious politicians sometimes said. On the other hand, I gathered that whenever anyone criticized his pet policies (of neutralism, standing-between-the-two-great-power-blocs, Five-Year Plans, violent anti-colonialism), he would always react quickly and in rather extravagant terms.

[1] These conversations took place at Eisenhower's Gettysburg farm. He recorded these recollections sometime between December 18 and January 4, when he sent a copy to Secretary Dulles (see no. 2156). Ann Whitman had noted on the preceding document that Eisenhower had told her the State Department was "afraid he would say or do the wrong thing." Another rationale for this unusually detailed document was probably

provided by the President's guest. Nehru was "in the habit of dictating long memoranda each night," the President said, "which are then circulated to his people in all parts of the world." For more on Nehru's visit see the preceding document; State, *Foreign Relations, 1955–1957*, vol. VIII, *South Asia*, pp. 327–40; and Eisenhower, *Waging Peace*, pp. 106–13. For Eisenhower's discussions with Secretary Dulles regarding these conversations see Telephone conversations, Dec. 18, 19, 1956, AWF/D. For developments see the following document.

[2] See no. 1946 for background.

[3] General Nuri Pasha al-Said was Iraqi prime minister and minister of defense.

[4] This letter is not in AWF.

[5] On the press conference and address see *New York Times*, December 19 and 20, 1956.

[6] A portion of this paragraph remains classified.

[7] Located on the west coast of India, Goa had been a colony of Portugal since 1510. After the establishment of the Republic of India in 1950, the new government had worked toward the absorption of all European possessions in India.

[8] This pamphlet is not in AWF.

[9] Ngo Dinh Diem was president and chief of state of the Republic of Vietnam.

[10] V. K. Krishna Menon was the chairman of the Indian delegation to the United Nations General Assembly.

[11] See Eisenhower to Nehru, December 20, 1956; and Nehru to Eisenhower, December 26, 1956, both in AWF/I: Nehru.

2140   *EM, AWF, Gettysburg Series*

To Arthur Seymour Nevins   *December 18, 1956*

Dear Arthur: This letter is your written authority for the following:

(*a*). To dispose of the Bandolier bull on January second, or the first day thereafter that you can get him to the butcher. Since the herdsman of Admiral Strauss advises this course of action, I am certain that Admiral Strauss would have no interest in a proferred return of the bull to him.

(*b*). To steer all bull calves sired by Bandolier of Brandy Rock and to throw them in with the steer herd as quickly as they have been weaned from their mothers. (If you prefer to sell them as veal, I would have no objection—but please do not do this until after January first.)

(*c*). To have the herdsman watch very closely over the heifers sired by Bandolier, and if they show signs of developing his weaknesses, particularly in the hind quarters, to dispose of them to the butcher as quickly as he has made up his mind as to their unsuitability for our purpose.

I am very sorry we wasted a year with him, but at the time we got him I had hopes that, because of his breeding, he would develop into a much better bull.[1]

It was good to see you yesterday, but I regret that I did not have the entire day to spend with you around the farm. However, as you know, I was fairly busy![2] *As ever*

[1] On the bull, a gift from Lewis L. Strauss's Brandy Rock Farm, see no. 1516 (see also Nevins, *Five-Star Farmer*, p. 125).
[2] Indian Prime Minister Nehru had accompanied the President to Gettysburg to inspect the farm (on Nehru's visit see nos. 2138 and the preceding document).

2141   *EM, AWF, Dulles-Herter Series*

To JOHN FOSTER DULLES   *December 19, 1956*

Dear Foster: I read the long report by Ambassador Hare on his conversations with Nasser.[1]

I think we should give the Ambassador something that he could convey to Nasser, even if nothing more than an expression of our great satisfaction (yours and mine) that Nasser has spoken so frankly and fully of the matter with which he is now concerned.[2]

My point is that the more we can encourage bilateral confidence and confidences, the better informed we should be as to the problems in the whole region.

As of this moment I have communications from the President of Syria, the King of Saudi Arabia, and now this long report to you from the Ambassador. It seems to me we have here an opportunity.[3]

New subject. Attached hereto is a letter I have just received from Paul Hoffman. His ideas are based upon his experience as a member of our United Nations Delegation. I think you will find it interesting reading.[4]

After the presentation he makes in the first two pages, I was rather astonished at the meagerness of the plan suggested in his three points on page three. Possibly he considers point number one a very important one at this moment.[5] *As ever*

[1] Raymond Arthur Hare (B.A. Grinnell 1924), former Director General of the United States Foreign Service, was Ambassador to Egypt. He had spoken privately with Nasser for three hours on December 15. Dulles had sent the President a copy of Hare's cabled report (Greene to Goodpaster, Dec. 18, 1956, AWF/D-H). In the discussion, Nasser had adopted a conciliatory position toward the United States, emphasizing that his most pressing need was to raise Egyptian living standards. Preoccupation with foreign crises, he said, detracted from that goal. He was looking for a period of "trust and confidence" in his relations with the United States, a trust the Eisenhower Administration had begun to build by its actions during the Suez crisis. It was now time, said Nasser, for the United States to "consolidate" that position.

Nasser had also explained that his foreign policy was basically one of nonalignment. Discounting the importance of his relations with the Soviet Union, he told Hare that "Egypt has no secret agreement with it and never even asked what it would do if Egypt were attacked for fear Soviets would impose conditions." There was no mutual policy with the Soviets regarding the Near East, he said, because Egypt desired to "maintain its complete independence of action." Nasser denied charges that he was trying to export the Egyptian revolution to other Arab states and pointed out that most Egyptians had been indifferent about the existence of Israel until 1955, when Ben Gurion's policies had incited their hatred. He was inclined to believe that a settlement was now out of the question, but he would cooperate to reduce tension. Nasser warned, however, that any nation that tried to force peace would "end up by losing out" with both the Arabs and the Israelis.

As Hare was leaving, Nasser had told him that someone had recommended reading Washington's Farewell Address. Hare observed that the address made reference to no "entangling alliances." Hare recounted that Nasser then "laughed (not his chronic nervous giggle) and said 'Yes, that is the one'" (Hare to Dulles, Dec. 17, 1956, AWF/D-H).

[2] Dulles sent the President (on Dec. 19, 1956) a draft cable to Hare, instructing the Ambassador to "inform Nasser that [the] Department takes satisfaction that he has spoken so fully and, we like to believe, so frankly with respect to the matters you raised with him." Dulles did not mention the President's involvement. The telegram seemed to suggest, however, that Nasser would have to abandon nonalignment as the price for an accomodation with the United States. "The bad turn of events can be dated from the active intervention of the Soviet Union in the area," Dulles wrote (Dulles to Hare, Dec. 20, 1956, AWF/D-H). Dulles informed the President that he had attributed these views to the Department, instead of to the President, "as I doubt it is wise at the present juncture to give Nasser the impression that he is in direct negotiation with you" (Dulles to Eisenhower, Dec. 19, 1956, AWF/D-H).

[3] For the letter from King Saud see no. 2147. Eisenhower had exchanged letters with the President of Syria (al-Quwatli to Eisenhower, Nov. 8, 1956; Eisenhower to al-Quwatli, Nov. 12, 1956, AWF/I: Syria; see also State, *Foreign Relations, 1955–1957*, vol. XIII, *Near East: Jordan-Yemen*, pp. 594–97).

[4] Encouraged by information that Eisenhower was planning to discuss U.S. development programs for underdeveloped nations in his inaugural address, U.N. General Assembly delegate Hoffman had written to advocate a worldwide "Eisenhower Plan" similar to the Marshall Plan (Dec. 17, 1956, AWF/A).

[5] Hoffman's letter was most concerned with a proposal for an "inventory" of the needs and resources of the developing world. His point two called for a "modest participation" in a multilateral aid program. In point three, which was not extensively discussed in the letter, Hoffman suggested continuing support for U.N. Technical Assistance Programs (*ibid.*; see also "Statement by Henry Cabot Lodge, Jr., to the President's Citizen Advisers on the Mutual Security Program," Nov. 30, 1956, AWF/A, Hoffman Corr.).

2142   *EM, AWF, International Series: Pakistan*

To Huseyn Shaheed Suhrawardy   *December 19, 1956*
Cable. Secret

Dear Mr. Prime Minister:[1] Thank you for your message of December 11 transmitted to me by Ambassador Hildreth.[2]

I share your strong desire to bring about harmony among nations and contribute to a lasting peace. It was in this spirit that in mid-1955 we undertook conversations with the Chinese Communists at Geneva. Although those talks have not borne out our hopes, they are continuing and we intend to persevere. Under present circumstances we are convinced that the Ambassadorial level is more appropriate than the Foreign Minister level for this limited negotiation with the Chinese Communists. The matters under discussion can be dealt with adequately by the fully empowered Ambassadors who are meeting regularly at Geneva, if the Chinese Communists have any desire to reach a reasonable agreement on these matters. Since they have so far not demonstrated such a desire we do not consider that raising the level of the talks would improve the prospects of agreement.

We cannot alter our opposition to Chinese Communist entry into the United Nations simply on the basis of Chinese Communist pretenses of good will and in the absence of concrete actions which would demonstrate without question that their policies and practices have changed since the United Nations declared them aggressors in Korea. The seating of Communist China in the United Nations under present circumstances, would, in my opinion, gravely imperil the progress which has been made in strengthening the independence of the free countries of Asia, violate the provisions of the Charter as to membership, and strike a serious blow at the vital interests of our ally, the Government of the Republic of China on Taiwan.

With regard to the ten American civilians (all reputable persons held on political charges) who are still wrongfully imprisoned in Communist China, we consider that they should all have been released long ago.[3] The Chinese Communists declared in the Agreed Announcement of September 10, 1955 that "Americans in the People's Republic of China who desire to return to the United States are entitled to do so" and further promised to "adopt appropriate measures so that they can expeditiously exercise their right to return." This pledge was not qualified in any way and was clearly understood to apply to the Americans in jail, for these were the very persons on whose behalf we were negotiating. We have never been concerned in the Geneva talks with Chinese Communist legal processes and the question of whether or not some of the Americans had been "convicted." Our concern—referred to by Chou En-lai as "haggling" and "dragging out the talks"—was and continues to be to bring the Chinese Communists to fulfill their public commitment to free all of the imprisoned Americans.

With respect to Chinese in the United States, I can assure you that no Chinese is prevented from leaving this country. We issued a public appeal for anyone who knew of a Chinese being prevented from leaving to bring it to the Government's attention. No one has done so. Moreover, we made arrangements for the American National Red Cross to interview personally all Chinese aliens in Federal and state prisons in this country in order to ascertain which of them desired to go to Communist China. There were some thirty such prisoners, all common criminals serving terms for various crimes such as traffic in narcotics or homicide. Only one chose to go to Communist China in preference to completing his sentence. He was deported there through Hong Kong on October 29.

Our experience with the Chinese Communist refusal to fulfill their pledge to release American civilians does not encourage us to rely on any other pledges they might give in the future. Nevertheless, we are pressing them at Geneva to recognize that the serious issue with us regarding the Taiwan area should not lead to armed conflict. We seek an unqualified renunciation of the use of force, which they adamantly refused to give. The continued assertion by the Chinese Communists that they are entitled to attack Taiwan if it is not surrendered to them, coupled with the standing Chinese Communist threat to the Republic of Korea and all Southeast Asia, is a continuing source of instability in the area and a chronic threat to the peace. The disturbing Chinese Communist buildup of its aggressive capabilities in the South China area is a cause for grave concern. Were the Chinese Communist threat of force demonstrably removed, the conferees at Geneva could proceed to the discussion of other practical matters at issue.

I wish to thank you for your interest and to utilize this opportunity to convey to you personally my appreciation for the constructive actions which you and your government have taken in connection with this and other critical international problems which have arisen during recent months. We are aware of your staunch defense of free world interests during your visit to Peiping. Your position on the Hungarian and Middle Eastern crises again demonstrated the adherence of Pakistan to the principles of freedom and justice.[4] Pakistan's posture in foreign affairs, like that of the United States, is independently established in consideration of its own interests. We Americans are proud that Pakistan has determined that its interests and our own lie in the same direction, so that we may pursue parallel courses in so many important fields toward the achievement of our goals. *Sincerely*

[1] The State Department drafted this message to the Pakistani prime minister. The signed original was destroyed in a Military Air Transport Service (MATS) plane crash in Saudi Arabia on December 30; a new letter was sent to Karachi on January 25, 1957 (Howe to Goodpaster, Jan. 23, 1957, AWF/I: Pakistan; see also State, *Foreign Relations, 1955–1957*, vol. III, *China*, pp. 450–51).

[2] Suhrawardy had written Eisenhower after meetings in Peking with Premier Chou En-lai and Chairman Mao Tse-tung in November. Suhrawardy presented the Chinese position on the Geneva discussions between the United States and China, the alleged detention of Chinese nationals in the United States, and other aspects of U.S. policy in Asia. The Chinese premier had asked Suhrawardy to "bring about an understanding" between his country and the United States. The Pakistani leader also told Eisenhower that Pakistan believed that the Peoples' Republic of China was entitled to represent that nation in the United Nations (AWF/I: Pakistan). Horace A. Hildreth (A.B. Bowdoin 1925) had been U.S. Ambassador to Pakistan since May 1953. He had served as governor of Maine from 1945 until 1949 and had been president of Bucknell University from 1949 until 1953.

[3] See no. 1200 for background.

2143   *EM, AWF, Name Series*

To Hubert Reilly Harmon   *December 19, 1956*

Dear Doodle: Yesterday Howard Snyder told me he had seen one of your doctor friends, who reported that you were coming along splendidly.[1] I am delighted. Normally I don't like to talk about my illnesses and operations, but if I could have an hour with you, I think it would be great fun to have a contest in telling of all the things we have been through during this past year.[2]

I understand your son is to graduate from West Point this June. My guess is that he will go in the Air Force and so one of these days he will probably be an instructor in the school you founded in Colorado.[3] I know that he will get great satisfaction out of the sentiment in that connection. My own son, John, is still an instructor at Fort Belvoir. I am hopeful that his next assignment will be here in Washington, of sufficient duration to carry him through my own second tour in this position.[4]

Give my love to Rosa Maye and above all things take good care of yourself, which normally is another way of saying "Do what the doctors tell you."

With affectionate regard to you both, *As ever*

[1] For background on Harmon's health see no. 2007.

[2] On Eisenhower's surgery for ileitis see no. 1894.

[3] In July 1954 Harmon had become the first superintendent of the Air Force General Academy (see no. 980). Harmon's son, Kendrick, would serve in the air force as a first lieutenant until 1960.

[4] In July 1957 John Eisenhower would be assigned to the Pentagon office of the Deputy Chief of Staff of Military Operations. He would be assigned to the White House as Assistant Staff Secretary on October 20, 1958 (see Eisenhower, *Waging Peace*, p. 319; and John Eisenhower, *Strictly Personal*, pp. 193–95, 202).

2144   *EM, AWF, Administration Series*

To Sherman Adams   *December 21, 1956*

Dear Sherman: Spectacular tales of your new and improved golf game have been reaching me with such regularity that, when I was down at Augusta, I went shopping for a bag that I thought might match such excellence. It comes to you with the hope that you and Rachel have, this Christmas, the finest and happiest possible time.[1]

Of course the gift is but a small token of my lasting appreciation of the extraordinary contribution, in your unique post, you are making to the progress of the Administration. I shall be always grateful, as will most Americans, that in the position of trust that you hold, all of us are served by a man whose integrity, competence and selflessness cannot be questioned. And, every day, I am conscious of the many things you do to make my own burden lighter.

Though this note is much too long—it, and the golf bag, bring you my warm personal regard. *As ever*

[1] The Eisenhowers had vacationed in Augusta, Georgia, from November 26 until December 13. Adams's wife was the former Rachel Leona White.

2145   *EM, AWF, Administration Series*

To Jessie Curtis Wilson and   *December 22, 1956*
Charles Erwin Wilson

Dear Jessie and Charlie: The two of you have a remarkably unique ability to choose gifts that delight Mamie and me. The handsome rocking chair that you sent me not only fits perfectly into a spot on the second floor that has long needed a comfortable chair, but it is fast becoming my favorite place to sit for a quiet chat morning and evening with Mamie.[1] My thanks for your thoughtfulness seem entirely inadequate, but are all I am able to muster at the moment.

I hope that you have a wonderful holiday season with those nice grandchildren.

With warm regard, *Sincerely*

[1] In the note that had accompanied the gift the Wilsons said they hoped that it would "provide a bit of relaxation, when needed" (Christmas 1956, AWF/A).

2146   *EM, AWF, Name Series*

To Francis Wilfred de Guingand   *December 23, 1956*
Personal and confidential

Dear Freddie: I assure you that I am as much concerned as are you about the seeming lack of understanding displayed by some people both in Great Britain and in France during the recent crisis; but never for one moment have I wavered in my feeling of friendship for our traditional allies or in my search for ways and means to help them out of the difficulties that, in my opinion, they brought upon themselves by their hasty and ill-considered action.[1]

The measures we have already taken and which are contemplated are going to cost us a huge sum during the coming two years; I think it will gradually be understood in Western Europe that we have been a *true* friend throughout this entire affair. I do not conceive it to be the function of a friend to encourage action that he believes in his heart to be unwise and even [in]expedient. I know, from your letter and from the article that you enclosed, that we think along the same lines—and I am gratified that this is so.[2]

Let us pray that this thing will work out as well as we can possibly expect; meantime, let me wish for you a happy holiday season.

With warm regard, *Sincerely*

[1] For background on the Suez crisis see nos. 2118 and 2119.
[2] De Guingand had written Eisenhower from South Africa that he believed that "the British Government very stupidly did not worry about the consequences of their action" in the Suez crisis. He also said that he had publicly defended the American position in speeches and enclosed a copy of an article he had written on the subject (De Guingand to Eisenhower, Dec. 8, 1956, AWF/N).

2147   *EM, AWF, International Series:*
                                                              Saudi Arabia

To Ibn Abd al-Aziz Saud   *December 24, 1956*
Cable. Secret

Your Majesty:[1] I most deeply regret that Mr. Anderson, who had hoped to visit Riyadh again during these past weeks for another profitable exchange of views with Your Majesty, was obliged to defer his trip.[2] Because of this I all the more appreciate Your Majesty's letter of December 13 on some of the matters which are of mutual concern to us.[3] Moreover, the frankness and comprehension of your message appeal strongly to my sentiments because they so clearly evidence your friendship for this country; good friends are always able to speak and write frankly and fully to each other.

Ambassador Wadsworth has also sent me Your Majesty's very welcome indication that we might meet. I am gratified that you may be willing to come to visit us and have asked Ambassador Wadsworth to discuss this with you further.[4]

In our view, recent days have seen a definite improvement in the Middle Eastern situation. The hopes which you and I have expressed for a lessening of the severe tension created by the events in Egypt are gradually being realized, although, admittedly, important obstacles remain.

The Egyptian Government could be helpful in this respect by taking steps to prevent further fedayeen activity, which was an important underlying cause for the recent hostilities. The Government of Egypt could also assist constructively by moving toward a practical arrangement with the international community relating to the Suez Canal.[5]

I appreciated the commendatory statement which the Saudi Arabian Government issued on December 15 on the role of the United States during the recent crisis.[6] I am particularly gratified that it evidences so clearly Your Majesty's understanding of our nation's purposes. I am sure that you agree that those of us who seek a more stable and peaceful world cannot be content merely with the successful implementation of emergency steps. We, too, have been looking beyond this immediate crisis to those problems that will remain with us when the present crisis has been dealt with.

I value the opportunity to clarify our attitude with respect to a Palestine settlement. First let me say that I agree with your wise observation that progress along this line can scarcely be expected until tension has somewhat subsided.

Earlier on November 3 the United States submitted to the General Assembly a draft resolution calling for the establishment of a commission to seek a just and equitable solution to this question.[7] This resolution has not yet been adopted by the General Assembly, and we shall not press it at this time. While the present situation, as a result of recent events in the Middle East, does not seem conducive to bringing about a Palestine settlement at this moment, we believe that it would be in the interests of the world community to move forward on the basic problems as quickly as the moment seems propitious. I hope that you and I may find ourselves in complete agreement when the time comes to identify that moment.

I assure you that it was not our intention in the resolution we presented to discard or ignore actions which the United Nations has taken in connection with the Palestine problem in recent years. We had in mind that the proposed commission would study carefully all of the pertinent United Nations resolutions. Our purpose in the pending United States resolution was to seek a new framework within which we might find an answer to this critical problem; we have completely open minds as to what that answer might be and will look forward to discussions of this matter with you. I am sure Your Majesty would agree, however, that we should not suspend our search for a solution until we meet but that should an opportunity arise we should take prompt action.

The Syrian problem continues to give us particular cause for concern. We are disturbed by reports that have come to us regarding certain attitudes and certain policies which can be found today among many Syrian officials.[8]

We do not believe that Syria is at the moment in danger of aggression. Our attitude toward aggression is well known to Your Majesty, and was demonstrated again with respect to the Egyptian incident. Furthermore, I assure Your Majesty that the Syrian Government made no serious attempt to purchase arms in the United States. That Government was fully aware that we were prepared to make available certain military items, subject only to the usual agreement applicable in the case of all nations buying arms in this country and similar to the agreement concluded between Saudi Arabia and the United States.

I will be frank to say to Your Majesty that our fear is that the Syrian Government does not fully realize the grave danger of becoming entangled with the Soviet Union. When Mr. Murphy spoke to Ambassador al-Khayyal about the problems of Syrian and Iraq that conversation reflected Mr. Murphy's long experience with the manner and purposes of international Communism operations.[9] All of us who have participated in conferences with the Soviet Union over these past few years and have watched the machinations of Communism in other countries have become acutely conscious of the symptoms of Communist infiltration. I would be less than frank with Your Majesty if I did not state that we see evidences of the pattern developing in Syria. We watch these events, too, with the echoes in our ears of statements of patriotic civilian leaders in nations of Eastern Europe who once assured us that their countries were in no danger of Communism. The tragic fate of the people of Hungary is clear evidence of what could happen in Syria or in other countries unless the leaders understand fully the grave dangers inherent in Communist penetration, and show themselves to be unresponsive to Communist blandishments. [10]

Our attitude toward the Baghdad Pact is governed by this same consciousness of a Soviet pattern designed ultimately to encompass the whole Middle Eastern area.[11] We have long felt the need for an effective defense arrangement to which we could lend support. While we have not joined the Pact, we have supported it because it does, in our minds, represent a practicable arrangement, among the countries which wished to adhere, for area defense. We will, at all times, welcome Your Majesty's comments on this problem.

I have been giving careful thought to how the United States, in the light of recent developments, can make even more evident in our relationships with the countries of the Middle East, our vital concern for their security and permanent independence. I hope shortly to be in a position to communicate to Your Majesty how I feel the United States executive and legislative branches can best demonstrate the determination of this country to cooperate with the Middle Eastern states in protecting themselves against Communist imperialism.

Your Majesty's needs have been always in our mind. A further message will be sent shortly to our Ambassador on the questions of the Dhahran Airfield and of arms.[12] We hope that Your Majesty may find in our proposals another step toward meeting the basic requirements of your nation's defense.

May God have you in His safekeeping. *Sincerely*

[1] The President made minor changes on a State Department draft of this letter after discussion with the Secretary of State (Memorandum of Conversation, Dec. 22, 1956, Dulles Papers, White House Memoranda Series). Eisenhower had "suggested the draft express some satisfaction that we can communicate on so friendly terms." The President wanted the draft to "be prepared quickly and by someone with a flair for writing" who would see that it was not "too matter of fact" (Telephone conversation, Eisenhower and Dulles, Dec. 18, 1956, AWF/D; Dulles to Eisenhower, Dec. 21, 1956, AWF/I: Saudi Arabia). On December 29 the cable was read to King Saud, who exclaimed "It is a good message" (Wadsworth to Dulles, Dec. 30, 1956, WHO/OSS: Subject [State], State Visits).

[2] Robert B. Anderson, as Special Emissary of the President to the Middle East, had previously visited King Saud in August (see no. 1990). There is no record of a subsequent visit by Anderson to Saudi Arabia prior to King Saud's visit.

[3] King Saud's December 13 letter to the President, which remains classified, addressed the Suez crisis, the Palestine problem, the situation in Syria and the Baghdad Pact (see State, *Foreign Relations, 1955–1957*, vol. XIII, *Near East: Jordan-Yemen*, p. 407, n. 3).

[4] For Ambassador George E. Wadsworth's additional conversations with the King see *ibid.*, pp. 408–9. King Saud would visit the United States from January 29 until February 8 (see Eisenhower, *Waging Peace*, pp. 114–20). For developments see no. 2155.

The King's visit would create significant protocol and domestic political problems. While discussing the King's proposed visit, Eisenhower asked Dulles "Will he bring his harem?" (Telephone conversation, Dec. 18, 1956, AWF/D). Despite concerns about the President's health conveyed by the State Department, Saud insisted that as a matter of personal prestige the President must meet him at the airport in Washington. Saud threatened to cancel the visit if Eisenhower did not show up. The President expressed his annoyance about this demand, but ultimately agreed to it (Memorandum of Conversation, Jan. 11, 1957, Dulles Papers, White House Memoranda Series; Eisenhower, *Waging Peace*, pp. 114–16; see also *Public Papers of the Presidents: Eisenhower, 1957*, pp. 108–9).

Saud's visit would arouse opposition in New York. Some Jewish groups had long protested a provision in the lease on Dhahran Air Force Base which prohibited the U.S. Air Force from using Jewish personnel. The Democratic party platform of 1956 carried a plank implicitly criticizing the discriminatory lease agreement (Porter and Johnson, eds., *National Party Platforms 1840–1968*, p. 527). When Saud arrived in New York, Mayor Robert F. Wagner would refuse to welcome him to the city (*New York Times*, Jan. 29, 1957). The State Department was apprised of Wagner's intentions ahead of time and arranged a "program of full military honors" for King Saud to substitute for the usual city ceremony (NSC meeting minutes, Jan. 29, 1957, AWF/NSC; State, *Foreign Relations, 1955–1957*, vol. XIII, *Near East: Jordan-Yemen*, pp. 413–14).

Eisenhower would comment on Wagner's actions at a January 30 press conference, declaring that "You don't promote the cause of peace by talking only to people with whom you agree. That is merely yes-man performance." While he would "deplore any discourtesy shown to a visitor" whose purpose was to ameliorate international difficulties, Eisenhower said, that did not necessarily "imply any approval of any internal actions in such countries" (*Public Papers of the Presidents: Eisenhower, 1957*, pp. 97–98). The State Department had made efforts to end the ban on Jewish personnel (see State, *Foreign Relations, 1955–1957*, vol. XIII, *Near East: Jordan-Yemen*, pp. 393–94).

[5] See no. 2141. Fedayeen were Arab commandos operating against Israel.

[6] The cables from Saud to Eisenhower dated December 15 and 17, 1956 (AWF/I: Saudi Arabia), remain classified.

[7] For the text of the November 3 resolution, which sought to establish a three-member commission to settle the Arab-Israeli dispute, see State, *Foreign Relations, 1955–1957*, vol. XVI, *Suez Crisis July 26–December 31, 1956*, pp. 960–61. On Eisenhower's idea for an arbitration commission see no. 2062.

[8] Secretary Dulles was greatly concerned about increasing Soviet arms aid to Syria (State, *Foreign Relations, 1955–1957*, vol. XIII, *Near East: Jordan-Yemen*, pp. 606–7). For background on increasing American concerns about Soviet influence in Syria see *ibid.*, pp. 575–78, 601–12.

[9] Shaykh 'Abdullah al-Khayyal had been Saudi Arabian ambassador to the United States since August 3, 1955. On Deputy Under Secretary of State for Political Affairs Robert D. Murphy's role in the Suez Crisis see Murphy, *Diplomat Among Warriors*, pp. 375–93.

[10] On the Hungarian Revolt see nos. 2044, 2067, and 2139.

[11] See no. 1811.

[12] The Saudis had permitted the Americans to remain in the base at Dhahran past the expiration date of the original base agreement, pending negotiation of a new understanding. The State Department had proposed separating the military aid question from the issue of renewal of the Dhahran lease; State suggested offering a military training program of $25 million over five years, along with generous offers of military equipment (State, *Foreign Relations, 1955–1957*, vol. XIII, *Near East: Jordan-Yemen*, pp. 410–11). For developments see no. 2155.

2148   *EM, AWF, International Series: Formosa (China)*

To Chiang Kai-shek   *December 26, 1956*
Secret

Dear Mr. President:[1] I appreciate very much your generous expressions of congratulations on my re-election extended to me in your letter of December eleventh, which was brought by Foreign Minister Yeh.[2] It is gratifying to know that in carrying out my responsibilities in the difficult years ahead I can rely not only on support at home, but also on the understanding cooperation of staunch allies abroad.

I believe we are in agreement that the world situation today, and for the next few years, presents both serious dangers and challenging opportunities.[3] Recent developments in the European Soviet bloc afford ample evidence that the oppressed peoples are beginning, little by little, to shake loose the iron control of their Communist rulers.[4] Once started, such a popular movement is extremely difficult to halt or reverse.

The present difficulties in the Communist world demonstrate the weaknesses of the Communist system. In these weaknesses lies the hope that the people now suffering under Communist dominion can eventually gain their freedom without direct military action by the free world. We must recognize, of course, that the portentous changes taking place in the Soviet bloc, and indeed within the Soviet Union itself, while giving cause for hope, do carry risks of erratic communist ventures. Therefore, during this critical period it is necessary for the countries of the free world to remain calm, but steadfast in their dedication to the principles of the United Nations Charter, which we all uphold.

The free countries must maintain their military strength, encourage healthy economic development and fortify their will to remain independent. It is important also to minimize differences between them which frequently tend to serve Communist ends. With greater progress toward these objectives, we can, I believe, face the future with confidence.

We do not yet see within the Communist-dominated parts of Asia the same degree of unrest apparent in Eastern Europe. Yet, I believe that if we persevere in our present firm policy, particularly with respect to the Chinese Communists, we can confidently expect to see in the Far Eastern area also a growing rebelliousness among the captive peoples which their Communist rulers will, in the end, be unable to contain. We must be prepared to take advantage of any such developments in an appropriate manner when the time arrives. I am confident that the continued close cooperation of our two countries will contribute to this end.

In order to develop effective policies in the countries of the free world, it is of the greatest importance that we understand fully each other's viewpoints. It is particularly helpful to know how Asian leaders themselves view developments in that area of rapid change. I appreciate, therefore, receiving your frank assessment of the Far Eastern situation and I hope that we can continue, from time to time, to exchange ideas on this subject.

Mrs. Eisenhower and I extend to you and Madame Chiang our best wishes for a happy and successful New Year. *Sincerely*

[1] The State Department drafted this letter (Dulles to Eisenhower, Dec. 22, 1956, AWF/I: Formosa [China]; see also Rankin to Dulles, Dec. 28, 1956, WHO/OSS: Subject [State], State Dept.). Eisenhower changed only the complimentary close.
[2] Chiang's letter is in AWF/I: Formosa (China). George Kung-chao Yeh, China's Minister of Foreign Affairs since October 1949, had been educated at Amherst College

and Cambridge University. After service in China's Information Ministry during World War II, Yeh had entered the Ministry of Foreign Affairs in 1946.

³ Chiang had written of the "mounting influence of neutralism, particularly in Asia. Disguised as a movement for peace," he said, "its evil influence does not seem to have been fully realized by the world at large." The Soviet Union had successfully manuevered the free world "into a passive position," Chiang continued, and had created "situations in times and places of its own choice and to its own advantage." He referred to the "serious upheaval and unrest" that was widespread behind the Iron Curtain and maintained that the United States, "as the leader of the free nations, should assume the role of a world arsenal for the democracies in combatting Communism" (AWF/I: Formosa [China]).

⁴ For background on the Hungarian uprising see no. 2067.

2149   *EM, AWF, DDE Diaries Series*

To Kenneth Claiborne Royall   *December 27, 1956*

Dear Ken: I have kept hopefully in mind the invitation to address the Southern Society concerning which you spoke to me some weeks back. Since receiving your letter of the fifteenth I have studied the prospects even more earnestly.¹

The upshot is that I cannot be as optimistic as I was when I talked to you. Mamie and I have decided to revive a considerable portion of the traditional social events that take place between the opening of Congress and the beginning of Lent, which is March sixth. This means some half-dozen burdensome engagements.

Added to this, there is a piece of more confidential information that makes the matter much worse. I have a whole list of names of Heads of State and Heads of Government who want to pay a call on me at an early date. This normally means a dinner for the guest and a return dinner at his Embassy.²

Also, I am committed to a trip to the drought area that must take place some time in January.³

When on top of this is piled all the critical problems of an ordinary day, plus speeches that must be delivered to the Congress at the Inauguration and over television, I have a dismaying winter and early spring ahead of me.⁴

Much as I appreciate the force of all you say about reaching a fine sector of the Southern population through an address at the New York Southern Society, I truly feel that the circumstances leave me little recourse except to decline. As you know, I am simply forced to take a certain amount of time for rest and recreation, and to add an engagement which I would deem as important as the one you suggest seems to me to be most unwise. I truly regret that I have to give you a negative answer as it is the kind of thing, as I explained to you when we talked about it, that I really would like to do.

If by chance you would like to have a message from me to read at the dinner, I shall of course be more than glad to send one.[5]

With warm regard, *Sincerely*

P.S. Many thanks for the wire from you and Margaret that reached us on schedule yesterday. I assure you that Mamie and I heartily reciprocate the sentiments you express.[6]

[1] Royall, former Secretary of the Army, had asked the President to speak at the society's annual dinner, tentatively scheduled for February 1, 1957. Royall had suggested that a message given on that occasion would reach the South "more directly and effectively than could any single appearance" (Dec. 15, 1956, WHCF/PPF 47). The New York Southern Society—composed primarily of business and professional leaders—was a fraternal organization for New Yorkers with Southern roots (Donald E. Sutherland, "Southern Fraternal Organizations in the North," *Journal of Southern History* 53, no. 4 [1987], pp. 587–612).

[2] On the President's schedule see the chronology.

[3] Eisenhower would visit drought-stricken areas in Texas, Oklahoma, New Mexico, Arizona, Kansas, and Colorado on January 13–15, 1957 (President's daily appointments).

[4] The Inauguration would be held on January 20, 1957 (*Congressional Quarterly Almanac*, vol. XIII, *1957*, p. 43).

[5] Eisenhower would send Royall a message on January 25 (AWF/D).

[6] General and Mrs. Royall had wired a rhyming poem expressing Christmas greetings (Dec. 21, 1956, WHCF/Alpha).

2150   *EM, AWF, DDE Diaries Series*

To Herbert Brownell, Jr.   *December 27, 1956*

Dear Herb: Herewith the letter from Senator Bricker of which I spoke to you.[1] I hope that the necessary analyses by interested agencies of government will not consume too much time.[2]

Senator Bricker asked me whether I would not call in Judge Orie Phillips to talk about Bricker's latest proposals; he stated that Judge Phillips was in accord with them.[3] I mention this merely because I thought you might want to talk to Judge Phillips either in conference or on the telephone. *Sincerely*

[1] Eisenhower had spoken with Brownell earlier that day about Bricker's revisions to his controversial amendment (Bricker to Eisenhower, Dec. 10, 1956, AWF/D). According to Ann Whitman, Eisenhower had told Brownell that he thought that Bricker's letter was "really an answer to [Eisenhower's] own letter of last fall" (see no. 1995), and that the Administration had to be prepared for more activity on this front (Telephone conversation, Eisenhower and Brownell, Dec. 27, 1956, AWF/D). Bricker had indeed

stressed in his letter and at his meeting with Eisenhower that most of his revisions conformed to Eisenhower's earlier statement of "principles" (President's daily appointments, Dec. 27, 1956; Martin, Memorandum of meeting, Dec. 27, 1956, AWF/D; on Eisenhower's statement see no. 1995; for background on this issue see nos. 59 and 119).

[2] On this same day Eisenhower wrote Bricker that he would have the revisions studied (AWF/D; on the Administration's reaction see Tananbaum, *Bricker Amendment Controversy*, pp. 206–7).

[3] According to I. Jack Martin, Bricker had told Eisenhower that morning that the judge served on the American Bar Association committee which had helped Bricker revise the amendment in accordance with Eisenhower's standards (Martin, Memorandum of Meeting, Dec. 27, 1956, AWF/D). For Phillips's earlier role see nos. 1537 and 1725. This issue would continue to plague the President well into his next Administration (see Tananbaum, *Bricker Amendment Controversy*, pp. 214–15).

2151

EM, AWF,
International Series:
Bulganin

To Nikolai Aleksandrovich Bulganin   *December 31, 1956*

Dear Mr. Chairman: I have given careful consideration to the declaration by the Soviet Government to which you had invited my attention in your letter of November 17, 1956, but find myself in basic disagreement with the analysis of your government as it relates to the source of international tension.[1]

The people of the United States cannot accept the declaration's attempt to dismiss as "a slanderous campaign" the world's indignant reaction to the Soviet armed actions against the people of Hungary.[2] While the Soviet Government has not responded to the constructive recommendations of the United Nations with respect to Hungary, the parties at dispute in the Middle East have accepted the assistance of the United Nations.[3] A similar response by the Soviet Union to the resolutions of the United Nations concerning Hungary would constitute a significant step toward the reduction of the tensions to which the Soviet declaration addresses itself.

Your government's statement suggests that the strategic situation in Western Europe is now advantageous to the armed forces of the Soviet Union.[4] This statement does not seem calculated to relieve international tensions. Moreover, I am convinced in the light of my long association with the North Atlantic Treaty Organization that it is fully capable of carrying out its mission of collective defense.

You suggest further meetings of heads of government. I could agree to a meeting whenever circumstances would make it seem likely to accomplish a significant result. But, in my opinion, deliberations within the framework of the United Nations seem most likely to produce a step forward in the highly complicated matter of disarmament.[5] Accordingly the United States will make further proposals there.

I take hope from your apparent willingness to consider aerial inspection as a positive factor in the problem of armaments. Much to my regret, however, your government's declaration does not signify willingness to seek agreement on the basic element of my Geneva proposal of averting surprise attack through aerial inspection of the centers of our military power.[6]

The United States is giving this and your other disarmament proposals careful study. We are prepared to discuss them, as well as the further United States proposals, in forthcoming meetings of the Disarmament Subcommittee.[7]

You may be sure that our government will continue its efforts in behalf of effective control and reduction of all armaments. It will be my never-ending purpose to seek a stable foundation for a just and durable peace in the mutual interest of all nations. *Sincerely*

[1] On November 17 Bulganin had forwarded to the United States, Britain, France and India a seven-point disarmament plan aimed at averting another world war by planning large-scale reductions in armaments. In a separate cover letter to Eisenhower, Bulganin stated that the "military attack on Egypt has brought on a serious aggravation of the international situation" and that he hoped Eisenhower would "personally" examine the proposals of the Soviet government (AWF/I: Bulganin; *U.S. Department of State Bulletin* 36, no. 917 [January 21, 1957], pp. 89–93; *New York Times*, Nov. 18, 1956. For background on Suez see no. 2068. See also no. 1765). Dulles and Stassen drafted this letter for Eisenhower; see Dulles to Eisenhower, December 29, 1956, AWF/D-H.

[2] The Soviet Declaration had charged the West with attempting to whip up a "slanderous campaign" against the Soviet Union in connection with the failure of the "counter-revolutionary military plot" in Hungary (see no. 2044). The Hungarian rebellion, Bulganin stated, was part of the "general plot of the imperialists against peace and security" in the Middle East and in Europe.

[3] On the U.N. role in resolving the Suez crisis see no. 2057. For further background on the General Assembly condemnation of Soviet violations of the U.N. Charter see *U.S. Department of State Bulletin* 35, nos. 913–14 (December 24, 31, 1956), pp. 975–79.

[4] The Declaration stated that if the Soviets actually had the "aggressive intentions" attributed to them, they could have used the current situation for an "attack against the armed forces of the Atlantic bloc" and achieved their military objectives "even without the use of modern nuclear weapons and rockets."

[5] Bulganin had proposed a conference on disarmament of the heads of the governments of the Soviet Union, the United States, England, France, and India. For Eisenhower's rejection of a similar proposal—presented by Switzerland and accepted by the Soviet Union—see *U.S. Department of State Bulletin* 35, no. 909 (November 26, 1956), p. 839. See also no. 1723.

[6] After having reiterated in their Declaration their objections to Eisenhower's Geneva summit proposal for an "Open Skies" aerial inspection program (see no. 1523), the Soviets stated for the first time their willingness to "consider" aerial photography in a zone eight hundred kilometers to the east and west of the line of demarcation between the NATO and Warsaw Pact forces (see Lincoln P. Bloomfield, Walter C. Clemens, Jr.,

and Franklyn Griffiths, *Khrushchev and the Arms Race: Soviet Interests in Arms Control and Disarmament 1954–1964* [Cambridge, Mass., 1966], pp. 27–30).

[7] The debate over disarmament talks would continue; see U.S. Department of State, *Documents on Disarmament, 1945–1959*, 2 vols. (Washington, D.C., 1960), vol. II, *1957–1959*, pp. 757–62.

2152   *EM, AWF, Name Series:*
                                                               Appreciation Letters

To ANDREW JACKSON GOODPASTER, JR.   *December 31, 1956*

Dear Andy: As perhaps you know, I have these last few days attempted to express to various governmental officials my appreciation of their work.[1] But when I come to your name, I realize that here indeed any words of mine are totally inadequate. Daily—hourly—I realize my good fortune in having you in your particular assignment.

At the same time, since official word of your promotion has just reached my desk, I again congratulate you.[2] General Gruenther won't mind if I repeat myself and say that there could be no one more deserving.[3]

With warm personal regard, *As ever*

[1] See, for example, correspondence in AWF/N: Appreciation Letters.

[2] On December 14 Eisenhower had nominated Goodpaster for promotion from the rank of colonel to the temporary grade of brigadier general. The Senate would confirm the nomination, effective January 1, 1957 (*New York Times*, Dec. 15, 1956, Jan. 14, 1957).

[3] Goodpaster had been Gruenther's assistant at SHAPE from 1950 until 1954.

2153   *EM, AWF, Ann Whitman Diary Series*

DIARY   *[January 1, 1957]*

During my term of office, unless there is some technical or political development that I do not foresee—or a marked inflationary trend in the economy (which I will battle to the death)—I will not approve any obligational or expenditure authorities for the Defense Department that exceed something on the order of 38.5 billion dollar mark.[1] Consequently when yearly obligational authority exceeds the new obligational authority or the expenditure program, this must invariably be made up from "carry-over" and not by a mortgage on future appropriations.[2]

[1] Eisenhower had held intense defense budget discussions during the past month with his Cabinet and the National Security Council in preparation for the January sixteenth submission of the FY 1958 budget to Congress. On Eisenhower's efforts to keep the defense budget within limits see no. 1963; Eisenhower, *Mandate for Change*, pp. 454–55; Kinnard, *President Eisenhower and Strategy Management*, pp. 57–62; Adams, *Firsthand Report*, pp. 360–69. Eisenhower had requested that the Defense Department prepare a budget based on 38 billion dollars for expenditures and 38.5 billion dollars for new obligational authority. He had made a statement similar to this diary entry at a National Security Council meeting (Goodpaster, Memorandum of Conference, Dec. 15, 1956, AWF/D; State, *Foreign Relations*, vol. XIX, *National Security Policy*, p. 394; for background see Condit, *History of the Joint Chiefs of Staff*, vol. VI, *1955–1956*, pp. 50–53). At a December 19 meeting the President had explained that he had aimed at a figure which would provide good defense without causing an economic debacle. He also indicated that he knew that in some instances individual JCS members might feel doubtful concerning the budget, but the final decision had to be made by the President (Goodpaster Memorandum of Conference, Dec. 20, 1956, AWF/D; see also Ann Whitman memorandum, Jan. 1, 1957, AWF/AWD). Each of the Chiefs of Staff and the defense secretaries had later—after expressing qualifications—initialed a memorandum stating their approval of the budget that had been prepared for the President's January 1 remarks to congressional leaders (Ann Whitman memorandum, Jan. 1, 1957, AWF/AWD and State, *Foreign Relations*, vol. XIX, *National Security Policy*, pp. 393–96).
[2] On Eisenhower's proposal for a balanced budget see *Public Papers of the Presidents: Eisenhower, 1955*, pp. 38–58. Later this month the President would approve several directives designed to hold the budget line, indicating that he would reject any proposals for new obligational authority and expenditures which could not be met within the budget limits (Record of Action, Jan. 9, 1957, AWF/Cabinet). According to the Cabinet minutes, he would explain that he felt no need to sell this program to his Cabinet members (Jan. 9, 1957, AWF/Cabinet).

2154   *EM, AWF, Administration Series*

To Arthur Frank Burns   *January 3, 1957*

Dear Arthur: Thank you for your letter of the thirty-first. I agree with you that during the campaign we did make commitments about tax reductions. However, in the Platform there is a qualifying phrase "when budgetary conditions permit."[1]

I am having another conference on the matter very soon.[2] As you well know, I cannot completely still the fears of those who believe any proposed tax reduction will start a flood that we cannot stop.

But I shall do the best I can. *As ever*

P.S. More than 70 bills for tax reductions have already been prepared for submission.[3]

[1] Burns, who had resigned as Chairman of the Council of Economic Advisors in December and returned to the National Bureau of Economic Research, had written Eisenhower about his concern that the Administration would not recommend a tax

reduction for small businesses in the budget for FY 1958 (AWF/A; for background see nos. 1957 and 2011). Burns had reminded Eisenhower that he had given strong indications during the campaign that he would make such a recommendation to Congress and that the Republican platform had endorsed the tax cut (see Eisenhower to Burns, Aug. 9, 1956, AWF/Cabinet). Burns also had warned that the Republican party might suffer politically if people believed that the Administration had not "kept the faith." As a compromise, Burns had proposed a smaller cut than the Cabinet Committee on Small Business originally had recommended.

A memorandum prepared at the President's request in response to Burns's letter outlined the several public occasions on which Eisenhower had referred to this particular tax reduction (Hagerty memorandum, Jan. 1, 1956, AWF/A, Burns Corr.). Concerned with inflationary pressures and national debt reduction, Eisenhower would recommend in his budget message that Congress consider some tax relief for small business but delay substantial tax cuts until a time when a general reduction would be possible (*Public Papers of the Presidents: Eisenhower, 1957*, p. 13; see also Saulnier, *Constructive Years*, pp. 90–103; and Sloan, *Eisenhower and the Management of Prosperity*, pp. 99–101).
² This meeting (Apr. 2, 1957) would focus on the small business program (supplementary notes, Apr. 2, 1957, AWF/LM).
³ For developments see Legislative Leadership meeting notes, April 2, May 28, June 4, and supplementary notes, April 2, June 4, 1957, AWF/LM; *Public Papers of the Presidents: Eisenhower, 1957*, pp. 538–40; and *Congressional Quarterly Almanac*, vol. XIII, *1957*, pp. 613–14, 678–79, and vol. XIV, *1958*, pp. 262–63. Both Republicans and Democrats would introduce tax revisions (many of them minor), but Eisenhower would be successful in extending the existing corporate tax provisions.

2155   *EM, AWF, International Series:*
                                                                Saudi Arabia

To Ibn Abd al-Aziz Saud   *January 3, 1957*
Cable. Secret

Your Majesty: In my letter of December 24, 1956, I indicated that I would soon be in communication with Your Majesty to set forth further ideas as to how the executive and legislative branches of the United States Government might best demonstrate the determination of this country to cooperate with the Middle Eastern states in protecting themselves against communist imperialism.[1]

This matter has occupied our thoughts for some time, and the dangers inherent in the present situation are such, we believe, as to call for early action on our part. One of the elements of this danger is the possibility of a miscalculation on the part of communist leaders as to the reaction by the Free World to new acts of communist aggression in the area which they have long coveted.

As you know the United States, in support of the right of nations to independence, has encouraged the principle of collective security. For this reason it has supported the members of the Baghdad Pact in their cooperative efforts designed to meet the communist threat.[2] A further means which might have been employed by the United States to implement its policy of assisting countries of the area to develop their defense might have been American adherence to the Baghdad Pact.[3] I have, however, been disinclined to recommend this course, my primary reason being Your Majesty's own attitude toward the Pact. In this and in other matters of common interest I have endeavored to take fully into account the views which you have expressed to me.

The program which I have decided to recommend to the Congress involves a joint Congressional resolution which would state clearly and firmly our belief that the imposition by international communism of totalitarian regimes upon the free nations in the general area of the Middle East, by direct or indirect aggression, would undermine the foundations of international peace and hence the security of the United States. The resolution would, at the same time, provide additional Congressional authority for economic assistance to nations in the area for the development of economic strength dedicated to the maintenance of national independence, and for military assistance and cooperation in support of the inherent right of self-defense recognized in Article 51 of the Charter of the United Nations. The latter assistance and cooperation might include the use of the armed forces of the United States in taking measures, consonant with the Charter of the United Nations, to assist in protecting the territorial integrity and political independence of the nations concerned against communist armed aggression.[4]

I am convinced that the best insurance against the dangerous contingency of communist aggression is to make it clear that we are ready to cooperate fully and freely with our friends in the area if, but only if, that be their desire. It is my belief that the measures we are considering will provide a basis for strengthening the mutually beneficial relationships that we now have with the Middle East countries, and will establish a framework for expanding them in ways that will enhance peace and stability.

I shall ask Ambassador Wadsworth to deliver to you as quickly as possible, after their presentation to the Congress, the texts of my message to the legislature and of the proposed resolution. I hope that when you are in the United States, we can discuss this program as it may apply to the area generally and to Saudi Arabia in particular.[5] In the meanwhile, any comments which you might care to make would be most welcome.

May God grant you His safekeeping. *Yours sincerely*

---

[1] Eisenhower's December 24 cable to the Saudi Arabian king is no. 2147. The President made several changes in this letter (AWF/I: Saudi Arabia). Secretary Dulles had also deleted a reference to the rights of people to choose their own government "because they don't have [a democratic government]—they have a monarchy" (Telephone conversations, Eisenhower and Dulles, Jan. 3, 4, 1957, both in Dulles Papers, Telephone Conversations).

[2] This sentence originally read "As you know the United States, in encouraging the principle of collective security, has supported the members of the Baghdad Pact in their cooperative efforts designed to meet the communist threat."

[3] For background on the American relationship to the Baghdad Pact see no. 1811.

[4] For the January 5 message to Congress announcing the "Eisenhower Doctrine"— Eisenhower's program for increasing American involvement in the Middle East—see *Public Papers of the Presidents: Eisenhower, 1957*, pp. 6–16. In that message Eisenhower asked Congress to give advance approval for the use of American forces in the Middle East if necessary "to secure and protect the territorial integrity and political independence" of nations requesting such aid "against overt armed aggression" by the Soviet Union. He asked Congress for authority to grant up to $200 million in economic and military aid to Middle Eastern nations (*ibid.*, p. 13). The President had previously briefed legislative leaders on his proposals (Legislative Leadership meeting notes, Jan. 1, 1957, AWF/LM). After minor amendments, both houses of Congress would pass the President's proposals on March 7 (*Congressional Quarterly Weekly Report* 15 [Mar. 8, 1957], 297; see also Kaufman, *Trade and Aid*, p. 101).

[5] For additional background on the protocol and the domestic political implications of King Saud's visit see no. 2147.

2156   *EM, AWF, Dulles-Herter Series*

To JOHN FOSTER DULLES   *January 4, 1957*
Personal and confidential

Dear Foster: Finally I had an opportunity to set down my recollection of the substance of the talks I had with the Prime Minister of India. A copy of the notes is enclosed for your personal information.[1]

Because of the always present danger of a leak if a document such as this is given any sort of circulation, may I request that you limit its reading to a very few individuals only. When you've finished with it, would you please return to my files? *As ever*

[1] Prime Minister Nehru had visited Washington and Gettysburg in December; see no. 2139 for Eisenhower's notes of the conversations; see also State, *Foreign Relations, 1955–1957*, vol. VIII, *South Asia*, pp. 327–40.

2157   *EM, AWF, International Series: Nehru*

To JAWAHARLAL NEHRU   *January 7, 1957*
Cable. Secret

Dear Mr. Prime Minister:[1] Since our Washington talks, I have continued to give intensive thought to the situation in the Middle East and to how the United States might most effectively cooperate with the countries of the area in the maintenance of peace and stability.[2]

I asked our Charge d'Affaires in New Delhi to provide to you the text of the message which I delivered to the Congress on January 5 with respect to the Middle East. I endeavored in that message to set forth the reasons for our deep concern as well as our views on the policy which we should pursue in providing economic and military assistance to those countries of the area who need and desire such assistance.[3] I would like to add here a few comments.

We have naturally considered a number of alternative courses of action, including adherence to the Baghdad Pact. As you know, we have been under great pressure to join the Pact, but decided against it because of the views of several of our friends, including yourself.

On the other hand, we do need to be in a position to come to the aid of those in the area who might want our help if and when they should be attacked. My constitutional position in this regard is different from that of the chief executives in most other countries. It is necessary for me to have the consent of Congress in advance, if I am to be in a position to act without procedural delays. The fact that we are seeking this authority does not mean that we expect to have to use it. Indeed, it is our belief that a forthright statement of our policy with respect to aggression in the area should serve greatly to diminish the threat of aggression, and thus the possibility that force might have to be employed.

I regret that our thinking in this matter had not at the time you were here developed to the point where you and I could discuss it. I am pleased, however, that we did have the chance to talk of the situation generally so that you know of the general philosophies and evaluations which have led me to recommend this program to the Congress.

With kindest personal regard, *Sincerely*

[1] The State Department drafted this letter to Prime Minister Nehru (Dulles to Eisenhower, Jan. 7, 1957, AWF/I: Nehru).

[2] On Nehru's visit to Washington and Gettysburg see no. 2139.

[3] Eisenhower had proposed the provision of economic and military assistance to the countries in the Middle East. Congress would pass the "Eisenhower Doctrine" proposals, and the President would sign them on March 9. See no. 2155.

2158
EM, AWF, Administration Series,
Jackson Corr.

To Sherman Adams
January 7, 1957
Memorandum

I have just read the memorandum submitted by Mr. Jackson on the organization of the Operations Coordinating Board.[1] I understand that he gave to you a copy of the same memo.[2]

I think it would be well for you to ask Secretary Dulles to read the report, but on a Personal and Confidential basis.[3] Please request him, in my name, not to show the paper to anyone else at the moment.

The reason I should like him to read it is to have his personal thinking on the subject; Jackson's letter makes a lot of sense to me, and it presents the whole idea of coordination in a very logical and philosophical way. This the Secretary of State will readily understand, and I believe it will do much to clarify the thinking of all of us on this most important subject.

[1] William H. Jackson, Special Assistant to the President, had sent Eisenhower a report that advocated giving more power to the Operations Coordinating Board (OCB). Jackson had wanted to integrate the board into the structure of the National Security Council and to give the board broad powers to coordinate the foreign policy activities of the executive agencies and departments. He also suggested appointing the Vice-President as chairman in order to enhance the Board's prestige. In his report, Jackson said that "there must be insistence in the President's name or by the President himself that in such cases there is proper coordination, and no department or agency should be permitted to evade or to stall the process" (Jackson to Eisenhower, Jan. 3, 1957; Memorandum for the President, Dec. 31, 1956, AWF/A). For background see no. 2114.
[2] See Jackson to Adams, January 3, 1957, WHCF/CF: Operations Coordinating Board.
[3] Dulles would vigorously protest the report. He would argue that Jackson's proposals were a departure from "the OCB concept of voluntary cooperation, that one department cannot order another department to do anything—nor should it attempt to do so." He also took exception to the idea of appointing the Vice-President to chair the board, declaring: "I believe that the relations of the Secretary and the Under Secretary of State to the President in regard to foreign affairs are and should be more intimate than those of the Vice President. If the time comes when the Vice President more authoritatively expresses the President's views on these matters than the Secretary of State, then a revolution will indeed have been effected in our form of government." The President would note on his copy of the letter that "So far as objection to V.P. is concerned I agree with Sec. State. But his ideas of true coordination are completely undeveloped—he seems to fear something of a Gestapo kind of activity. D." (Dulles to Eisenhower, Jan. 14, 1957, AWF/D-H). Executive Order 10700, effective on July 1, 1957, would integrate the OCB into the structure of the National Security Council, but the Under Secretary of State would remain chairman of the board.

2159   *EM, AWF, Name Series*

To LUCILLE DAWSON EISENHOWER   *January 7, 1957*

Dear Lucy: Recently I have had no word from you about Ed's condition and so I have been assuming that he was improving.[1] This morning I feel even more sure of this possibility for the reason that I had a short note from Edgar and he said nothing at all about his health.[2] Nevertheless, I should very much like to know whether he feels that he is really recovered. So one of these days when you get a chance, I would be deeply grateful if you would write to me about it.[3]

Please tell Edgar that so far as I know there have been no recommendations received here concerning the man in whom he was interested. However, I will make sure that if his name ever comes up to me, Ed's recommendation will be brought again to my attention.

With affectionate regard, *As ever*

[1] For background see no. 2092.

[2] Edgar had written on January 4 to recommend a man who he thought was being considered for an appointment as ambassador to Mexico (AWF/N).

[3] On January 10 Lucy Eisenhower would apologize for failing to report on Edgar's health (AWF/N). "Ed has progressed tremendously in the last two weeks," she wrote, "and I assumed he was in touch with you. . . ." For developments see no. 2169.

2160   *EM, AWF, Name Series*

To Floyd Bostwick Odlum   *January 8, 1957*
and Jacqueline Cochran Odlum

Dear Jackie and Floyd: At this precise moment nothing appeals to me quite as much as a visit to Southern California, and nothing appears quite as remote as even the possibility of considering such a trip seriously.[1]

The business of getting along with a new Congress, the messages that must be worked over endlessly, the still troubling international situation, the "social" season that I find alarmingly upon me, the visits from foreign dignitaries that have been scheduled (and which I fear I have pushed conveniently into the back of my mind)—all these and many others combine to make the trip we would like to take almost an impossibility.[2] May I beg your indulgence once more and ask for another raincheck for some future day?[3]

With much appreciation and warm personal regard, *As ever*

[1] The Odlums had invited the Eisenhowers and their choice of companions to vacation at their ranch in Indio, California (Jan. 1, 1957, AWF/N).

[2] See no. 2165 and the Chronology for the President's schedule.

[3] The Eisenhowers would not visit the ranch in 1957, but in January the Edgar Eisenhowers would be guests of these old friends (see no. 2169).

2161   *EM, WHCF, President's Personal File 266*

To John Hay Whitney   *January 8, 1957*

Dear Jock: This letter, as I understand it, will be read to you toward the close of a stag dinner at which friends—at least until now you thought they were friends—addressed themselves on the subject of your appointment as Ambassador.[1]

Their remarks, I suspect, were intended to deflate any possible feeling of self-satisfaction rather than to exalt you in your own and in public opinion. Occasionally you may have felt, as each speaker attempted to out-demagogue his predecessor, that it was their combined opinion that you were a better choice for Saint Elizabeth's than for the Court of Saint James.[2] And the question may have entered your mind: "Why did I come here tonight when there were so many other places I could have gone?"

Be of good cheer. Soon, very soon, your friends will be writing you that they plan a brief visit to the United Kingdom and will you help them do this and that and thus. Then you can measure your ability to aid them in the light of the judgment they pronounced on you tonight. It occurs to me that sleeping in a London street on a foggy winter night might be a deserved experience for some of your "well wishers."

With warm personal regard, *As ever*

[1] A mutual friend had asked Eisenhower to contribute a "rude note" to be read to Whitney at a January 11 dinner celebrating Whitney's appointment as U.S. Ambassador to Great Britain (McCrary to Whitman, Jan. 3, 1957, AWF/A). Whitney's January 16 reply is in *ibid.* Whitney would be formally nominated on January 30, and confirmed by the Senate on February 12. He would hold this position until 1961 (*New York Times*, Dec. 28, 1956, Jan. 30, and Feb. 12, 1957).

[2] The reference is to St. Elizabeth's Hospital in Washington, D.C., a psychiatric institution.

2162   *EM, AWF, Administration Series*

To Emmet John Hughes   *January 9, 1957*

Dear Emmet: In the last couple hours, I have had some time to go over your latest draft, and have made some changes—mostly editorial—which are included in the draft I return to you herewith.[1] Please call Mrs. Whitman if there are any to which you object or that may have inadvertently presented what you may believe to be a false picture.

As soon as possible, I shall get Foster Dulles in to read the draft.[2] His criticisms on a paper of this character are always valuable.

You know I am grateful. *As ever*

[1] Hughes had been preparing the inaugural address for the President (Hughes to Eisenhower, Dec. 27, 1956, and Hughes to Whitman, Jan. 8, 1957, AWF/A, Hughes Corr.). After receiving the President's changes, Hughes would send another draft with additional modifications, particularly concerning part III, which addressed the U.S. role in striving for peace and its price (Hughes to Eisenhower, Jan. 16, 1957, AWF/A). For the Second Inaugural Address see *Public Papers of the Presidents: Eisenhower, 1957*, pp. 60–65; see also Hughes, *Ordeal of Power*, pp. 231–32.

2163
              EM, AWF, International Series: Eden

To ROBERT ANTHONY EDEN
              January 10, 1957

Dear Anthony: I cannot tell you how deeply I regret that the strains and stresses of these times finally wore you down physically until you felt it necessary to retire.¹ To me it seems only yesterday that you and I and others were meeting with Winston almost daily—or nightly—to discuss the next logical move of our forces in the war.²

Now you have retired, I have had a heart attack as well as a major operation, and many others of our colleagues of that era are either gone or no longer active.³ The only reason for recalling those days is to assure you that my admiration and affection for you have never diminished; I am truly sorry that you had to quit the office of Her Majesty's First Minister.

Yesterday I issued a short public statement expressing my regret and my good wishes for your future.⁴ But I wanted to tell you in a personal note how sincerely Mamie and I pray that you and Lady Eden will have a long, busy and happy life ahead.⁵

With personal regard, *As ever*

¹ British Prime Minister Eden had announced his retirement on January 9 (*New York Times,* Jan. 10, 1957). On Eden's poor health see no. 136, and his memoir, *Full Circle,* pp. 56–57, 636. For his account of the decision to retire see *ibid.,* p. 651; see also Eisenhower, *Waging Peace,* pp. 88, 120.
² During World War II Eden had been Britain's Secretary of State for Foreign Affairs and Winston Churchill had been Prime Minister (see Chandler, *War Years,* vols. I–V).
³ On the President's heart attack see no. 1595; on his ileotransverse colostomy see no. 1894.
⁴ See *Public Papers of the Presidents: Eisenhower, 1957,* p. 17.
⁵ Eden's January 17 thank-you letter is in AWF/I: Eden.

2164
              EM, AWF, International Series: Macmillan

To HAROLD MACMILLAN
              January 10, 1957

Dear Harold: This morning, upon learning of your designation by Her Majesty as the new Prime Minister, I sent you a formal message of congratulations, the kind that is approved even by State Departments.[1] The purpose of this note is to welcome you to your new headaches. Of course you have had your share in the past, but I assure you that the new ones will be to the old like a broken leg is to a scratched finger. The only real fun you will have is to see just how far you can keep on going with everybody chopping at you with every conceivable kind of weapon.

Knowing you so long and well I predict that your journey will be a great one. But you must remember the old adage, "Now abideth faith, hope and charity—and greater than these is a sense of humor."[2]

With warm regard, *As ever*

---

[1] For background on Anthony Eden's resignation see no. 2124. Eisenhower's formal message to Macmillan would be sent on January 12, after the official installation of Macmillan's cabinet (see Dulles to Eisenhower, Jan. 11, 1957, AWF/I: Macmillan; Aldrich to Eisenhower and Dulles, Jan. 11, 1957, AWF/D-H; see also Telephone conversation, Eisenhower and Dulles, Jan. 10, 1957, Dulles Papers, Telephone Conversations; Macmillan, *Riding the Storm*, pp. 180–85, 194–95; and Alistair Horne, *Harold Macmillan*, 2 vols. [New York, 1988–1989], vol. II, *1957–1986* [1989], pp. 2–6).

[2] "I have no illusions about the headaches in store for me," Macmillan would answer, "but thirty-three years of parliamentary life have left me pretty tough, without, I hope, atrophying my sense of humour" (Macmillan to Eisenhower, Jan. 16, 1957, AWF/I: Macmillan; see also Macmillan to Eisenhower, Jan. 14, 1957, *ibid.*).

2165   *EM, AWF, Name Series*

To James Frederick Gault   *January 10, 1957*

Dear Jimmy: I am gradually getting a number of speaking engagements out of the way and feel as though I will soon be coming up for a breath of fresh air.[1] One of my regrets of recent weeks is that during your visit to Augusta, we did not have any really good chance for a long talk.[2] Not that I had anything in particular on my mind, except reminiscences of the war days and our experiences in SHAPE. But I did have a feeling of loss in my failure to make a better opportunity for a real talk.

The papers have just announced that our old friend Harold Macmillan is to be the new Prime Minister.[3] I suppose if anyone had told the two of us in Algiers in '43 that one day he was to be Prime Minister of Britain and I the President of this country, we would have thought such a prophet to be completely mad. The Wheels of the Gods apparently not only grind slowly, but they grind along unexpected and wholly astonishing courses.

When I saw you there was a possibility, I believe, that you would go back to duty at SHAPE. Please let me know if you do.[4]

With warm regard, *As ever*

[1] Gault's December 8 letter is in AWF/N. On January 5 the President had delivered a special message to Congress on the situation in the Middle East; on this same day he would deliver his State of the Union address; and he was preparing his annual budget message to the Congress (see *Public Papers of the Presidents: Eisenhower, 1957*, pp. 6–16, 17–30, 38–59).

[2] Gault had thanked Eisenhower for "the privilege of playing" golf with him at Augusta National Golf Course on December 3 and 4 (Dec. 8, 1956, AWF/N). The Eisenhowers had vacationed at Augusta from November 26 to December 13.

[3] See the preceding document.

[4] Gault would write on January 30 (AWF/N), explaining that he would not take the position at SHAPE.

2166

EM, AWF, Name Series

To CLIFFORD ROBERTS

January 10, 1957

Dear Cliff: I am sorry about the tooth, but it does establish another link between us.[1] I have been making periodic trips to the dentist for the past two or three weeks. I have one—or several—teeth that begin to ache like fury when anything cold touches them. Having given up on the dentist, I have simply taken ice cream off my diet.

As to the possibility of going West this summer, my own feeling is one of grave doubt. While I have not talked to Mamie about the prospect, the fact is that Congress, in non-election years, usually does not adjourn until some time in mid August. Then if I go away to stay any appreciable time, a very elaborate system of signal communications is necessarily set up. The farther the spot from Washington, the more expensive and elaborate this must be. So as of this moment I do not feel hopeful.[2]

Mr. Jorgensen dropped in to see me the other day.[3] I was highly impressed and upon meeting him, realized that I had talked to him once or twice before, back in 1953. Actually the corps of governmental advisers with whom I normally consult seem to be fixing upon an Easterner as top man. They point out that from California we now have Nixon, Warren and Knowland in very high positions.[4] Possibly they feel that to take another Californian and put him in such a vital post would be regarded by others as an attempt of California to take over the Republican Party. On the other hand, it is possible that they merely think that they have a somewhat more experienced man, more nationally known and more readily acceptable to all sections.

A final decision has not been made.

When I found I could spend a weekend at Augusta, I immediately wrote you—but we found you were in Cuba.[5] Since we went down on Friday and had to return Sunday, I thought it was not worth while trying to notify you. Bill went along, as did George Allen and my son John. Tom Bright was staying there, and Al Gruenther came down on Saturday afternoon to ride back with us on Sunday.[6] Just as we were on the last nine on Sunday and within an hour of starting home, the weather turned beautiful. Up to that time it had not been too pleasant, especially Saturday when it was very windy and quite cool. But we had fun.

With all the best, *As ever*

[1] Roberts had mentioned an ailing tooth in his letter to the President (Jan. 8, 1957, AWF/N).

[2] Roberts had passed on an inquiry made by Charles S. Jones, president of Richfield Oil Company, concerning the President's summer vacation plans. Jones had suggested that Eisenhower might wish to return to the Cypress Point Club on the Monterey Peninsula, California, where he had played golf after the Republican National Convention (Jones to Roberts, Dec. 18, 1956; Roberts to Jones, Jan. 8, 1957, AWF/N, Roberts Corr.; see also no. 1970).

[3] Roberts had given the President information supplied by Jones (see Jones to Roberts, Dec. 18, 1956, AWF/N, Roberts Corr.) on Frank E. Jorgenson (B.A. Drake University), of the Metropolitan Life Insurance Company in San Francisco. Jorgenson was being considered for one of the top Republican National Committee positions (Roberts to Eisenhower, Dec. 14, 1956, AWF/N; Roberts to Jones, Jan. 8, 1957, AWF/N, Roberts Corr.). The President had met with Jorgenson at the White House on January 7, 1957 (President's daily appointments). Jorgenson, an experienced organization man who had held several party committee positions in Los Angeles, would also leave a favorable impression with Roberts (see Ann Whitman memorandum, n.d., *ibid.*).

[4] As Roberts would later write Jorgenson had not been appointed, in part because he was from the same state as Vice-President Richard Nixon, Chief Justice Earl Warren, and Senate Minority Leader William Knowland (May 28, 1957, AWF/N, Roberts Corr.).

[5] This letter to Roberts, dated December 26, 1956, is in AWF/N.

[6] Eisenhower had traveled to Augusta, Georgia, for a golfing weekend with William Robinson and others (listed in President's daily appointments, Dec. 28–30, 1956). Tom Bright could not be identified.

2167   *EM, AWF, DDE Diaries Series*

To ARTHUR GARDNER   *January 11, 1957*
Personal

Dear Arthur: As I told you when you were in my office, I had not checked with the State Department about their Ambassadorial plans for the next four years.[1] The Secretary of State tells me now that he wants to make quite a number of changes and I believe (although my memory of course is not perfect) that all non-career Ambassadors are to be relieved and changed.[2] I am told that the State Department makes it almost an inflexible rule to allow no one to stay in a post more than four years.

I know this is disappointing to you in view of your hope of remaining in Havana as long as President Batista is at the head of that nation. However, there is nothing personal in the matter at all—of that I assure you.[3]

With best wishes and regard, *Sincerely*

[1] Gardner, American Ambassador to Cuba since 1953, had met with the President on January 8. For background on Gardner see Galambos, *Columbia University*, no. 638.

[2] For a list of suggested ambassadorial appointees see Memorandum for the President [1/6/57], and "Matters to Discuss with the President," January 18, 1957, AWF/D-H.

[3] Eisenhower would accept Gardner's resignation on May 14, thanking him for his distinguished service and complimenting his abilities and active interest in the economic development of Cuba (*New York Times*, May 15, 1957). The appointment of a new ambassador would, however, signal a shift of American policy: Gardner's friendship with Batista had become embarrassing to the Administration, and the American public had been impressed by the image of Castro portrayed in a series of interviews published by the *New York Times*. The new American Ambassador to Cuba, Earl E. T. Smith, would be instructed to "alter the prevailing notion in Cuba that the American Ambassador was intervening on behalf of the government of Cuba to perpetuate the Batista dictatorship" (Earl E. T. Smith, *The Fourth Floor: An Account of the Castro Communist Revolution* [New York, 1962], pp. 3–23; see also Rabe, *Eisenhower and Latin America*, pp. 117–22).

2168   *EM, AWF,*
Administration Series: AEC

To Lewis Lichtenstein Strauss   *January 11, 1957*

Dear Lewis: I am intrigued about your idea of a conference of our top men in the social sciences and humanities.[1] You may recall that for a somewhat different purpose I organized an ad hoc commission of my own this last year of this type of person.[2]

Sometime when you are in the office I should like your ideas on how and where this should be done. (But please don't include in it a speech from yours truly!).[3] *As ever*

[1] Inspired by the President's 1955 call for professionals other than scientists to find peaceful uses for atomic energy (see *Public Papers of the Presidents: Eisenhower, 1955*, pp. 593–600), Strauss had sent Eisenhower a proposal for a conference that would consider the problem of "how man is to be kept ahead (or at least abreast) of his scientific discoveries so that he may make use of them." Strauss emphasized that this was not a problem resulting from the development of nuclear weapons alone; it was related to advances in other fields as well (Jan. 9, 1957, AWF/A: AEC). For Eisenhower's views on peaceful uses for atomic energy see no. 598; and *Mandate for Change*, pp. 251–55.

[2] Eisenhower was probably referrring to the Panel on the Human Effects of Nuclear Weapon Development (State, *Foreign Relations*, vol. XIX, *National Security Policy*, pp. 374–75, 413–17, 462–63).

[3] Eisenhower would continue to discuss the possibility of organizing this type of conference (*New York Times*, May 27, 1957; Wilson to Eisenhower, June 6, 1957; Eisenhower to Strauss, June 11, 12, 1957; Strauss to Eisenhower, June 11, 1957; Eisenhower to Wilson, June 12, 1957; all in AWF/A: AEC).

2169   *EM, AWF, Name Series*

To Edgar Newton Eisenhower   *January 11, 1957*

Dear Edgar: Your letter distresses me greatly. Of course you should not attempt the trip East for the Inauguration (and, privately, I think your decision is a wise one regardless of the state of your health).[1] But I am tremendously concerned that you have suffered such pain in the last few months, and that even now you do not feel up to a trip even to Southern California. The only encouragement I find is that you report one good night; I pray that means a real improvement.[2]

As far as the Inaugural ceremonies are concerned, the whole business, from my point of view, is too much of a "show" to have real meaning. I am sorry that we are not going to have a full family reunion, but even that would be difficult under the schedule that has been laid out for Mamie and me.[3]

Don't worry about what the press may say; it never bothers me and it never should you.[4]

The important thing is that the doctors find a way to alleviate your pain and that you and Lucy get away for the rest I know you both need.[5]

With warm regard, *As ever*

P.S. I understand Janis and Bill are coming; you better charge them with the job of a complete report![6]

[1] In his letter of January 7 (AWF/N) Edgar had written that he was "suffering from neuritis of the brachial-plexus. And even though I have doubled up on my medication, my recovery is not sufficient to justify my continuing with my reservations." For background see no. 2092.

[2] Edgar had reported that he had "slept through the entire night" the evening of January 6.

[3] The President's brother had apologized for his inability to join his brothers and their families at the Inauguration.

[4] "I would like the world to know that my absence from your Inauguration is not to be interpreted as a disagreement between you and me, over policy or anything else," Edgar had written.

[5] On January 21 the Edgar Eisenhowers would visit friends in Indio, California (see no. 2160), and then travel to Phoenix, Arizona, "for an indefinite time" (see Lucy

Eisenhower to Eisenhower, Jan. 19, 1957; and Eisenhower to Edgar Eisenhower, Jan. 23, 1957, both in AWF/N; see also *New York Times*, Jan. 19, 1957).

[6] These were Edgar's daughter and son-in-law, the William Oliver Causins.

2170   *EM, AWF, Dulles-Herter Series*

TO JOHN FOSTER DULLES   *January 12, 1957*

Dear Foster: Referring to your memorandum on Pan American Week, I suppose that I will have to appear to make a little talk, although I am getting jumpy about the number of talks I am making—and I was disappointed to find that you wanted one of these fifteen-minute affairs. However, I guess I can manage to get enough stuff together to fill up the time, even if I don't feel particularly inspirational.[1]

With respect to the Radio-Television-Newsreel statement, such things I ordinarily make in the broadcasting room of the White House with no one present. By doing it in this way I can use aids, such as cards and so on, to help in keeping me on the right track. However, if the thing you have in mind is only a brief informal talk expressing satisfaction over the receipt of the medal and a word or two about the value of the Pan American organization, then I would have no objection to doing it in connection with the receipt of the medal.[2]

I should like any appearance I might make to be near the end of the Conference, since I am hopeful of my usual mid-April vacation.[3]

I think we had better talk about this when you are next in my office.

As ever

[1] Dulles had sent Eisenhower a memorandum (Jan. 11, 1957, AWF/D-H), reminding the President that April 14–21 had been designated as "Pan American Week" in the United States and the other twenty American republics. The Secretary of State had recommended that Eisenhower speak for about fifteen minutes at a ceremonial meeting of the Council of the Organization of American States. Dulles said that Eisenhower had last addressed the Council of the OAS in April 1953, so "it would therefore appear appropriate for you to appear before them once again at the beginning of your second term" (see no. 89). The President would not, however, address the Council.

[2] Dulles had recommended that the President make a brief newsreel statement for use in connection with the Pan American Week celebration. The statement, he said, could be made "as part of a brief ceremony at which you would receive the Medal of the Pan-American Society of the United States." On February 21 Eisenhower would proclaim April 14 as Pan-American Day, and April 8–14 (rather than April 14–21) as Pan American Week (*U.S. Department of State Bulletin* 36, no. 925 [March 18, 1957], p. 443). Eisenhower would receive the "Golden Insignia" on April 3 for his "distinguished contributions to inter-American solidarity" (see *Public Papers of the Presidents: Eisenhower, 1957*, pp. 259–60).

[3] Eisenhower would vacation in Augusta, Georgia, from April 18–30.

2171 *EM, AWF, International Series: India*

To John Foster Dulles *January 12, 1957*

Dear Foster: I have dashed off a draft of a reply that might be suitable to Nehru. I do this only because I want to reassure him instantly as to the completely peaceful character of our intentions.[1]

As you know I leave tomorrow to be gone until Wednesday morning.[2] So if you have no changes in this except of an editorial character, please dispatch it under my name.

On the other hand, if you have some important substantive criticism, you might call me at the White House before 3:30 tomorrow afternoon—or merely wait until we can see each other on Wednesday.

I recognize the possibility that you may think it would be better to wait a little while before answering. If so, then we shall have plenty of time to talk it over.[3] *As ever*

[1] The Indian Prime Minister had written Eisenhower regarding the President's message to Congress asking for authorization to employ U.S. forces to protect Middle Eastern countries from armed aggression (see no. 2157). Nehru's letter (January 11) remains classified; Secretary Dulles would tell Eisenhower that the letter was "very mild" and that Nehru did not think there was any chance of aggression in the Middle East by the Soviet Union (Telephone conversation, Eisenhower and Dulles, Jan. 12, 1956, AWF/D).

[2] Eisenhower would tour drought areas in six midwestern states.

[3] Dulles would respond (January 14) that he thought Eisenhower's message was excellent and had dispatched it through the U.S. embassy in New Delhi (AWF/I: India). The President's letter to Prime Minister Nehru is the following document.

2172 *EM, AWF, International Series: Nehru*

To Jawaharlal Nehru *January 14, 1957*
Secret

Dear Mr. Prime Minister: Thank you very much for your fine letter replying to mine of the seventh.[1] I quite agree with you that what is needed in the Mid-East is a calming influence and the pursuit of United States policies and plans that will assist each nation there that may so desire to develop its economy so as to raise standards of living and achieve greater opportunities for individual citizens.

For many years the people of some of these nations have been fearful of possible aggression and have built up an emotionalism that at times borders on the hysterical. This government earnestly seeks to help repair this situation. We have no thought that any country in the group would want, or indeed could afford, great armaments. When we speak of assisting in a military way, we mean only to help each nation achieve that degree of strength that can give it reasonable assurance of protection against any internal rebellion or subversion and make certain that any external aggression would meet resistance. That part of my message which seeks Congressional authority to assist any of these countries in repelling Communistic aggression is merely to reassure them and to place ourselves on record as being ready and most serious about helping defend the independence of the several nations of the region.

Moreover, it is my belief that this announcement will tend to diminish, if not eliminate, any chance of this kind of aggression.

Incidentally, you may be aware of the fact that every nation in the area has, at one time or another, earnestly requested us to assist it in obtaining arms and military equipment.

Again I assure you that this country would never knowingly help any other if we believed that such a nation was preparing aggressive operations against a third power. Moreover, in the event that such unwarranted aggression did occur, we would oppose it in whatever way seemed most appropriate at the moment.

It might be pertinent to point out here that any serious campaign undertaken with weapons of American type would be largely dependent upon this country for ammunition, spare parts, maintenance and replacements. All this would be denied them the instant they made any unjustified use of the weapons.

But we are far more interested in bringing about conditions that will tend to lessen tensions and provide a climate that will bring about the possibility for conciliation even among the Israeli and the Arabs. We stand ready to make considerable sacrifices to bring this about, and in return we want nothing whatsoever except the confidence that these nations are gradually developing their economic strength and living standards and are achieving the ability to live more happily and peacefully among themselves and with the world.

With warm personal regard, *Sincerely*

---

[1] Eisenhower's letter is no. 2157. Nehru's letter of January 11 remains classified; see the preceding document for background.

2173　　　　　　　　　　　　　　　　　　　　　　　　　　*EM, AWF,*
　　　　　　　　　　　　　　　　　　　　　　　　DDE Diaries Series

To John Sheldon Doud Eisenhower　　　　　　　　*January 16, 1957*

Dear John: Your discussion of the binomial theorem gave me the missing clue I needed to figure out what the "quiz lad" actually did in his simplified system of determining the coefficient of each term in any algebraic expression resulting from raising any simple binomial to any power.[1]

I told you he developed a pyramid-like structure of numbers, each row corresponding to the coefficients applicable to that particular exponent of the binomial.

First, the explanation:
(a + b) to the first power—
coefficients are 1, 1.

For each power we have an expression of *one more term* than the exponent itself; i.e., (a + b) has three terms. Now the building of the pyramid becomes easy according to the following rule. After placing the single digit, 1, at beginning and end of the expression, each coefficient of the intermediate terms is found by merely adding each consecutive *pair* of coefficients from the line above.

Here they are:

$(a + b)^1 =$ 1, 1
$(a + b)^2 =$ 1, 2, 1
$(a + b)^3 =$ 1, 3, 3, 1
$(a + b)^4 =$ 1, 4, 6, 4, 1
$(a + b)^5 =$ 1, 5, 10, 10, 5, 1
$(a + b)^6 =$ 1, 6, 15, 20, 15, 6, 1
$(a + b)^7 =$ 1, 7, 21, 35, 35, 21, 7, 1
                   etc.

Example:

Take $(a + b)^6$—place 1 at beginning and end. There are five coefficients left to find. So examine the numbers in the fifth line. The first two add to 6. The second and third, add to 15. The third and fourth, add to 20—etc.

Simple![2] *As ever*

---

[1] On January 14 John had sent his father the results of his inquiry into the binomial theorem (AWF/M: OF). This question had apparently arisen following a television quiz show viewed by the President and his son. "If the boy on the quiz program knew the power of the number and the number of the term," John had written, "he could figure out the coefficient."

[2] According to Professor John C. Wierman, Chairman of the Department of Mathematical Sciences, The Johns Hopkins University, Eisenhower's triangular arrangement of numbers is known in Western societies as "Pascal's Triangle" (found in Blaise Pascal's *Traité du Triangle Arithmétique* [1653]). Pascal's Triangle is part of combinatorial or discrete mathematics and the numbers being calculated are binomial coefficients. The "quiz lad" was probably constructing Pascal's Triangle, "thus calculating a complete set of binomial coefficients for the given power of the binomial" (Memorandum, February 27, 1995, EP).

Bibliography:
Note on Primary Sources

Scholars working on the First Eisenhower Administration have an abundance of source materials on which to base their studies. Many large collections housed in the Dwight D. Eisenhower Presidential Library in Abilene, Kansas, and elsewhere contain a wealth of information on both the man and the government he presided over. The difficulty for researchers lies in the bewildering number of collections, series, subseries, and files that must be examined. This brief essay is intended as a guide to the most useful sources; it also seeks to explain the many file citations that we have used in the source headings and in the annotations to the selected Eisenhower documents.

Most of the documents that appear in these volumes come from the Eisenhower Manuscripts (cited as EM in these volumes), now located in the Eisenhower Library at Abilene. Included in EM are Eisenhower's prepresidential and postpresidential papers, as well as a separate file of financial records and a set of bound volumes containing the President's Daily Appointments. Also included is a group of miscellaneous memorandums and intermittent journal entries known as the Eisenhower Diaries. This collection, which we cite as EM, Diaries, has only a few items from the first half of 1953. It should not be confused with the DDE Diaries series of the Ann Whitman File, described below.

Eisenhower's presidential manuscripts are divided into two parts. The smaller, and richer, of the two EM collections is the Ann Whitman File (Eisenhower's Papers as President), which we abbreviate as AWF. Ann Cook Whitman, Eisenhower's personal secretary, compiled and maintained these files in the President's office in order to have readily available and close at hand the important and personal documents that he might need. She kept her records with an eye toward present and future requirements for a relatively concise body of materials from which histories might be written. Archivists have divided the 270,000 pages (122 linear feet) of records in the Whitman File into eighteen separate series.

The largest and one of the most important collections in AWF is the DDE Diaries Series (AWF/D). This series is something of a distillation of the other series in AWF, and here may be found many duplicates of items located elsewhere. AWF/D is, however, the best source for a few types of records that are difficult to find in other parts of AWF. Foremost among these are the many revealing diary entries and memorandums that Eisenhower dictated in order to clarify issues in his mind and to record his own version of meetings and events. There is also a substantial file of papers relating to the Bricker Amendment controversy that bedeviled Eisenhower for most of his first term. Most of the DDE Diaries Series, however, is arranged chronologically by type of record. Among these records are Eisenhower's personal and official letters, Ann Whitman's memorandums recording the President's telephone calls, memorandums of conversation written by General Andrew J. Goodpaster (Eisenhower's White House Staff Secretary), records of cabinet meetings and conferences with legislative leaders, memorandums of briefings held before presidential press conferences, summaries of Congressional mail and executive office activities ("Toner Notes"), lists of items that Eisenhower signed, appointment calendars, and summaries of intelligence briefings. For the most part there are few incoming letters in the DDE Diaries Series; such letters to Eisenhower will normally be found elsewhere in AWF or in other collections.

The Ann Whitman File contains several series relating to national security matters and the conduct of foreign relations. The most valuable of these, although relatively small, is the Dulles-Herter Series (AWF/D-H). This series, which is arranged chronologically, contains Eisenhower's correspondence with his two secretaries of state (John Foster Dulles and Christian A. Herter) and with their principal deputies. AWF/D-H also contains State Department cables and memorandums of conversation. The International Series (AWF/I), arranged alphabetically by country, region, or U.S. territory, has the President's correspondence with foreign leaders. This series also contains correspondence, briefing papers, drafts of messages, memorandums of conversation, biographical sketches of foreign dignitaries, and a few files containing records of international conferences. More information on such gatherings may be gleaned from files in the small International Meetings Series (AWF/IM); separate subject files relating to conferences held at Bermuda and Geneva (1953, 1955) include cables, position papers, memorandums of conversation, and communiqués. The

NSC Series (AWF/NSC) contains detailed records of the discussions in National Security Council meetings. While these records are not, strictly speaking, verbatim transcripts, we have quoted freely from these "NSC meeting minutes" and believe that they provide an accurate account of Eisenhower's words and thoughts. The date given in each citation is the date on which the record was generated, rather than the date of the meeting itself.

A number of Ann Whitman File series contain material relating to domestic and national security affairs. The Administration Series (AWF/A) contains correspondence—both incoming and outgoing letters and memorandums—with political figures, Cabinet members, government officials, and a few Congressional leaders. Arranged alphabetically by name and subject, AWF/A is also a rich source for reports and other background materials. Researchers should note that correspondence with some individuals may be filed under the name of the organization with which he or she was affiliated. The Cabinet Series (AWF/Cabinet) comprises minutes, agendas, records of action, and other Cabinet papers. The Legislative Meetings Series (AWF/LM) contains records of Eisenhower's frequent consultations with members of Congress. Some of these meetings were with Republican leaders; others included Democrats as well. All papers in both AWF/Cabinet and AWF/LM are arranged chronologically by date of the particular meeting to which the documents pertain. The Ann Whitman Diary Series (AWF/AWD), which should not be confused with the larger DDE Diaries Series, contains a variety of materials, arranged chronologically by month. The most important of these are diary entries dictated by the President (often duplicates of those found in AWF/D), together with the daily observations written by his personal secretary. Whitman's AWF/AWD memorandums contain descriptions of the flow of Eisenhower's Oval Office business, as well as the President's candid observations on the issues and personalities of the day. This series also contains memorandums of conversation, appointment lists, Congressional mail summaries, and other records resembling those found in the DDE Diaries Series.

Two other Whitman File series reveal Eisenhower's private life and correspondence. Most of the files in the Name Series (AWF/N) are composed of Eisenhower's letters to and from friends and family members. (This series does, however, include many files of correspondence with members of Eisenhower's White House staff, prominent Democrats, and public figures who did not hold any official position in the Eisenhower Administration.) AWF/N is arranged alphabetically by name or subject. The Gettysburg Series (AWF/Gettysburg) contains documents relating to the President's Pennsylvania farm. It is arranged alphabetically by subject or, in the case of pedigreed Angus cattle, by name. Separate file folders hold letters to and from General

Arthur S. Nevins, Eisenhower's farm manager; these letters deal with a variety of farm subjects.

A few other AWF collections have also yielded items published or summarized in these volumes. The Drafts Series (AWF/Drafts) contains early versions of letters Eisenhower dictated or altered between 1953 and 1956; often these drafts bear the President's extensive handwritten emendations. The Miscellaneous Series (AWF/Misc.), true to its name, constitutes an odd assortment of subject files gathered together after the other AWF series had been formed. Among the subjects covered in this series are government reorganization, the 1956 Panama meeting of American presidents, and the Palm Springs Golf Classic. The Microfilm Series (AWF/M), which is not yet open to researchers, comprises copies of Ann Whitman's files as they were microfilmed in the White House periodically between 1955 and 1960. For the 1953–57 period covered in these volumes the relevant subsections of AWF/M were the Official Files (AWF/M: OF); the Personal Files (AWF/M: Pers); the Geographic Files (AWF/M: G); and the Administrative and Personal Files (AWF/M: AP). Nearly all of the Microfilm Series files are reproductions of original papers located in other portions of the Ann Whitman File.

Most of the documents generated or retained in the Eisenhower White House eventually made their way into the White House Central Files (WHCF). The permanent staff organized and maintained this vast collection of Eisenhower's presidential records, which, at 3,241 linear feet, is over twenty-five times as large as the Ann Whitman File. It is, in fact, the largest collection in the Eisenhower Library. Except for a small segment of records generated before January 20, 1953—the Pre-Inaugural File—the White House Central Files cover the period of the Eisenhower presidency.

While most important security-classified documents in EM are to be found in the Ann Whitman File, the White House Central Files also contain a significant number of sensitive materials. Most of these are in the Confidential File (WHCF/CF), which is divided into two sections. The first, the Name Series, is a small file arranged alphabetically by name. It contains documents relating to individuals—correspondence and reports deemed too sensitive to be placed in the open White House files. The much larger Subject Series, also arranged alphabetically, is a good place to find both classified and unclassified materials relating to international trade, import tariffs, civil aviation, diplomatic relations, psychological warfare, and foreign aid. Few documents in the Confidential File bear evidence of Eisenhower's direct, personal involvement. As of this writing, large portions of WHCF/CF remain closed to researchers.

The Official File (WHCF/OF) is a prime source for materials relating to politics, domestic policy formulation, and the operations of the federal government. It contains 766,000 pages of records (approximately 380 linear feet). Although there are a number of letters and memos to and from Eisenhower here, the core of this collection seems to consist of papers that passed through the office of Sherman Adams, The Assistant to the President. The Official File is a likely place to locate incoming letters to Eisenhower missing from the DDE Diaries Series. WHCF/OF is arranged by organization and subject, according to an alpha-numeric filing system in which each topic and sub-topic bears its own numeric designation. Researchers interested in the Tennessee Valley Authority, for example, would examine the OF 51 file; those looking for material on the Taft-Hartley Act would request folders bearing the label OF 124-G.

The three remaining portions of the White House Central Files proved to be less valuable for our purposes. Although the Name Series of the Ann Whitman File is the best source for Eisenhower's purely personal correspondence, the President's Personal File (WHCF/PPF) contains many items written by or to the President and not located elsewhere. Here one may find letters from Eisenhower's less frequent correspondents, as well as birthday and anniversary greetings not filed in AWF/N. The most useful section of this large file (approximately 790,000 pages) is arranged by name; each individual correspondent has been given a code number. The remainder of WHCF/PPF is arranged by the subject matter of the materials (invitations, gifts, congratulatory letters, etc.). The General File (WHCF/GF) contains a large body of material relating to recommendations for would-be federal office holders and expressions of opinion on public issues. The Alphabetical File, abbreviated as WHCF/Alpha, is the largest segment of WHCF (approximately 3,000,000 pages). It is for the most part limited to routine letters, cross reference sheets, and forms indicating that correspondence has been referred to other government agencies for disposition and reply.

While the Eisenhower manuscripts are the best sources for the documents and background information contained in these volumes, a number of collateral collections in Abilene also help to fill out the historical record. Foremost among these are the papers of John Foster Dulles, Eisenhower's Secretary of State. The portion of the Dulles Papers most useful to us was the White House Memoranda Series, which includes general correspondence files and records of Dulles's meetings with Eisenhower. Other valuable sections contain memorandums of Dulles's telephone conversations as well as separate chronological and subject series. Also important to our efforts were the Edward J. Bermingham Papers, the John Stewart Bragdon Records, the Alfred M. Gruenther Papers, the James C. Hagerty Papers, the C. D. Jackson Papers, the William E. Robinson Papers, the Bernard Shanley Diaries, and the Walter Bedell Smith Papers.

The records of the White House Office, also in the Eisenhower Presidential Library, were maintained by some of Eisenhower's closest assistants: Paul T. Carroll, Andrew J. Goodpaster, L. Arthur Minnich, Robert Cutler, and Dillon Anderson. These files, which are valuable for foreign, domestic, and national security matters, include the records of the Office of the Special Assistant for National Security Affairs (WHO/OSANSA) and those of the Office of the Staff Secretary (WHO/OSS). We have cited a few items from the White House Social Office (WHO/SO).

A few collections not in Abilene also yielded items useful to us. At the Library of Congress in Washington, D.C., we were able to gather material from the papers of Robert A. Taft and Earl Warren. In the National Archives the most useful documents came from the files of the Joint Chiefs of Staff—the "CCS" file—in Record Group 218. The records of the Federal Bureau of Investigation, housed in the J. Edgar Hoover Building, contained some items that shed light on Eisenhower's involvement with the controversy over J. Robert Oppenheimer. Finally, the Massachusetts Historical Society generously provided us with microfilm copies of the Henry Cabot Lodge Papers.

There are extensive finding aids available to most of the collections listed in this essay. Interested researchers should contact the custodians of the manuscripts for information on security classification, donor-imposed restrictions, and copyright regulations.

Daun van Ee

Bibliography:
Secondary Sources Cited

Acheson, Dean. *Present at the Creation: My Years in the State Department*. New York, 1969.

Adams, Sherman. *Firsthand Report: The Story of the Eisenhower Administration*. New York, 1961.

Alexander, Charles C. *Holding the Line: The Eisenhower Era, 1952–1961*. Bloomington, Ind., 1975.

Alexander, Yonah, and Names, Allan, eds. *The United States and Iran: A Documentary History*. Frederick, Md., 1980.

Allen, Craig. *Eisenhower and the Mass Media: Peace, Prosperity, and Prime–Time TV*. Chapel Hill, 1993.

Alsop, Joseph, and Alsop, Stewart. *The Reporter's Trade*. New York, 1958.

Alteras, Isaac. *Eisenhower and Israel: U. S.–Israeli Relations 1953–1960*. Gainesville, Fla., 1993.

Ambrose, Stephen E. *Eisenhower*. 2 vols. New York, 1983–84. Vol. I, *Soldier, General of the Army, President-Elect, 1890–1952* (1983); vol. II, *The President* (1984).

———. *Nixon: The Education of a Politician, 1913–1962*. New York, 1987.

Ambrose, Stephen E., and Immerman, Richard H. *Milton S. Eisenhower: Educational Statesman*. Baltimore, 1983.

American Assembly. *Economic Security for Americans: An Appraisal of the Progress Made During the Last 50 Years. What Have We Paid For? What Security Have We Got? Can We Do Better?* New York, 1954.

Anderson, David L. *Trapped by Success: The Eisenhower Administration and Vietnam, 1953–1961*. New York, 1991.

———. "J. Lawton Collins, John Foster Dulles and the Eisenhower Administration's Point of No Return in Vietnam." *Diplomatic History* 12, no. 2 (1988).

Anderson, Dillon. "The President and National Security." *Atlantic* 197 (January 1956).

"Armistice in Korea." *U.S. Department of State Bulletin* 29, no. 736 (August 3, 1953).

Arnold, James R. *The First Domino: Eisenhower, the Military, and America's Intervention in Vietnam*. New York, 1991.

Arnold, Peri. *Making the Managerial Presidency: Comprehensive Reorganization Planning, 1905–1980*. Princeton, 1986.

Attorney General of the United States, U.S. District Court, S.D., New York. *Federal Rules Decisions*. Vol. 13 (1953).

Attwood, William. *The Twilight Struggle: Tales of the Cold War.* New York, 1987.

Auerbach, Frank L. "The Refugee Relief Act of 1953." *U.S. Department of State Bulletin* 29, no. 739 (August 24, 1953).

Automobile Manufacturers Association. *Automobile Facts and Figures.* New York, 1957.

Bacevich, A. J. *The Pentomic Era: The U.S. Army Between Korea and Vietnam.* Washington, D.C., 1986.

Bader, Robert Smith. *Prohibition in Kansas: A History.* Lawrence, Kans., 1986.

Bailey, Sydney Dawson. *The Korean Armistice.* London, 1992.

Balogh, Brian. *Chain Reaction: Expert Debate and Public Participation in American Commercial Nuclear Power, 1945-1975.* Cambridge and New York, 1991.

Banks, Arthur C. "International Law Governing Prisoners of War during the Second World War." Ph.D. dissertation, The Johns Hopkins University, 1955.

Barck, Oscar Theodore, Jr., and Lefler, Hugh Talmage. *Colonial America.* New York, 1958.

Barclay, Thomas. "The 1954 Election in California." *The Western Political Quarterly* 7, no. 4 (1954).

Baruch, Bernard. *Baruch: The Public Years.* New York, 1960.

Bayley, Edwin R. *Joe McCarthy and the Press.* Madison, Wis., 1981.

Beard, Edmund. *Developing the ICBM: A Study in Bureaucratic Politics.* New York, 1976.

Beers, Paul B. *Pennsylvania Politics Today and Yesterday.* University Park, Pa., 1980.

Bemis, Samuel Flagg. *A Diplomatic History of the United States,* 4th ed. New York, 1955.

Bender, Marylin, and Altschul, Selig. *The Chosen Instrument.* New York, 1981.

Benet, Stephen Vincent. *John Brown's Body.* 27th ed. New York, 1937.

Benson, Ezra Taft. *Cross Fire: The Eight Years with Eisenhower.* Garden City, N.Y., 1962.

Berger, Raoul. *Executive Privilege: A Constitutional Myth.* Cambridge, Mass., 1974.

Bernstein, Barton J. "Election of 1952." In *History of American Presidential Elections, 1789-1968,* vol. IV. *See* Schlesinger.

———. "Ike and Hiroshima: Did He Oppose It?" *Journal of Strategic Studies* 10, no. 3 (1987).

Bernstein, Merton C., and Bernstein, Joan Brodshaug. *Social Security: The System That Works.* New York, 1988.

Beschloss, Michael R. *Mayday: The U-2 Affair.* New York, 1986.

Best, Gary Dean. *Herbert Hoover: The Postpresidential Years, 1933-1964.* 2 vols. Stanford, 1983. Vol. II, *1946-64.*

Bill, James A., and Louis, William Roger. *Musaddig, Iranian Nationalism, and Oil.* Austin, 1988.

Billings-Yun, Melanie. *Decision Against War: Eisenhower and Dien Bien Phu.* New York, 1988.

Blanksten, George I. *Peron's Argentina.* Chicago, 1953.

Bliss, Edward, Jr., ed. *In Search of Light: The Broadcasts of Edward R. Murrow, 1938-1961.* New York, 1967.

Bloomfield, Lincoln P.; Clemens, Walter C., Jr.; and Griffiths, Franklyn. *Khrushchev and the Arms Race: Soviet Interests in Arms Control and Disarmament 1954-1964.* Cambridge, Mass., 1966.

Blumenson, Martin. *The Patton Papers: 1885-1940.* Boston, 1972.

Bodnar, John. "Power and Memory in Oral History: Workers and Managers at Studebaker." *Journal of American History* 75, no. 4 (1989).

Bohlen, Charles E. *Witness to History, 1929-1969.* New York, 1973.

Boyer, Paul. *By the Bomb's Early Light: American Thought and Culture at the Dawn of the Atomic Age.* New York, 1985.

Boyle, Peter G., ed. *The Churchill-Eisenhower Correspondence, 1953-1955.* Chapel Hill, 1990.

Bradley, Omar N., and Blair, Clay. *A General's Life: An Autobiography by General of the Army Omar N. Bradley.* New York, 1983.

Branyan, Robert L., and Larsen, Lawrence H., eds. *The Eisenhower Administration 1953–1961: A Documentary History*. 2 vols. Vol. II. New York, 1971.

Briggs, B. Bruce. *The Shield of Faith: Strategic Defense from Zeppelins to Star Wars*. New York, 1988.

Brodie, Fawn M. *Richard Nixon: The Shaping of His Character*. New York, 1981.

Brooks, Glenn E. *When Governors Convene: The Governors' Conference and National Politics*. Baltimore, 1961.

Brown, Anthony Cave. *The Last Hero: Wild Bill Donovan*. New York, 1982.

Brown, JoAnne. "'A is for *Atom*, B is for *Bomb*': Civil Defense in American Public Education, 1948–1963." *Journal of American History* 75, no. 1 (1988).

Brownell, Herbert, with Burke, John P. *Advising Ike: The Memoirs of Attorney General Herbert Brownell*. Lawrence, Kans., 1993.

Burk, Robert Frederick. *The Eisenhower Administration and Black Civil Rights*. Knoxville, Tenn., 1984.

Burke, John P. and Greenstein, Fred I. *How Presidents Test Reality: Decisions on Vietnam, 1954 and 1965*. New York, 1989.

Burley, Anne Marie. "Restoration and Reunification: Eisenhower's German Policy." In *Reevaluating Eisenhower: American Foreign Policy in the 1950s*. Edited by Richard A. Melanson and David Mayers. Urbana and Chicago, Ill., 1986.

Burner, David. *Herbert Hoover: A Public Life*. New York, 1979.

Burns, Arthur F. *Prosperity Without Inflation*. New York, 1957.

Butler, Richard Austen. *The Art of the Possible: The Memoirs of Lord Butler*. London, 1971.

Byrnes, James. *All in One Lifetime*. New York, 1958.

Cabot, John M. "Inter-American Cooperation and Hemisphere Solidarity." *U.S. Department of State Bulletin* 29, no. 748 (October 26, 1953).

Campbell, John C. *Tito's Separate Road: America and Yugoslavia in World Politics*. New York, 1967.

———., ed. *Successful Negotiation: Trieste 1954*. Princeton, 1976.

Caraley, Demetrios. *The Politics of Military Unification: A Study of Conflict and the Policy Process*. New York, 1966.

Carleton, William G. "Liberal Swing." *The Nation*, May 22, 1954.

Carlton, David. *Britain and the Suez Crisis*. London, 1988.

Carter, Hodding. "The Republicans Muffed the Ball in Dixie." *Saturday Evening Post*, August 21, 1954.

Castaneda, Christopher J., and Pratt, Joseph A. *From Texas to the East: A Strategic History of Texas Eastern Corporation*. College Station, Tex., 1993.

Champagne, Anthony. *Congressman Sam Rayburn*. New Bruswick, N.J., 1984.

Cherne, Leo M. "Harry A. Bullis: Portrait of the New Businessman." *The Saturday Review*, January 23, 1954.

Churchill, Randolph Spencer, and Gilbert, Martin. *Winston S. Churchill*. 8 vols. Boston, 1966–88. Vol. VIII, *Never Despair, 1945–1965* (1988).

Churchill, Winston S. *A History of the English Speaking Peoples*. 4 vols. London, 1956–58. Vol. I, *The Birth of Britain* (1956).

———. *The Second World War*. 6 vols. Boston, 1948–53. Vol. II, *Their Finest Hour* (1949); vol. VI, *Triumph and Tragedy* (1953).

———. *The Unrelenting Struggle: War Speeches*. Compiled by Charles Eade. Boston, 1942.

Clark, Grenville, and Sohn, Louis Bruno. *Peace Through Disarmament and Charter Revision: Detailed Proposals for Revision of the U.N. Charter*. Dublin, N.H., 1953.

Clark, Keith C., and Legere, Laurence J., eds. *The President and the Management of National Security*. New York, 1969.

Clark, Mark W. *From the Danube to the Yalu*. New York, 1954.

Clemens, Diane Shaver. *Yalta*. New York, 1970.

Clifford, A. Jerome. *The Independence of the Federal Reserve System*. Philadelphia, 1965.

Colby, William E., and Forbath, Peter. *Honorable Men: My Life in the CIA*. New York, 1978.

Cole, Alice C.; Goldberg, Alfred; Tucker, Samuel A.; and Winnacker, Rudolph A., eds. *The Department of Defense: Documents on Establishment and Organization, 1944–1978*. Washington, D.C., 1979.

Coles, Harry L., and Weinberg, Albert K. *Civil Affairs: Soldiers Become Governors*. In *The U.S. Army in World War II, Special Studies*, edited by Stetson Conn. Washington, D.C., 1964.

Collins, J. Lawton. *Lightning Joe: An Autobiography*. Baton Rouge, 1979.

Collins, Robert M. *The Business Response to Keynes, 1929–1964*. New York, 1981.

Columbia University Bicentennial Commission. *Columbia University: An Account of the Planning and Execution of a World-Wide Program of Observance Centering on the Theme: "Man's Right to Knowledge and the Free Use Thereof."* New York, 1956.

Colville, John R. *The Fringes of Power: 10 Downing Street Diaries, 1939–1955*. New York, 1985.

Commission on Foreign Economic Policy. *Report to the President and the Congress*. Washington, D.C., 1954.

Conant, James Bryant. *My Several Lives: Memoirs of a Social Inventor*. New York, 1970.

Condit, Doris. *The Test of War: 1950–1953*. 2 vols. to date. Washington, D.C., 1984–. Vol. II, *History of the Office of the Secretary of Defense*, edited by Alfred Goldberg (1988).

Condit, Kenneth W. *History of the Joint Chiefs of Staff and National Policy 1955–1956*. Washington, D.C., 1992.

Conliffe, Christopher. "The Permanent Joint Board on Defense, 1940–1988." In *The U.S.–Canada Security Relationship: The Politics, Strategy, and Technology of Defense*. Edited by David G. Haglund and Joel L. Sokolsky. Boulder, Colo., 1989.

Conniff, Michael L. *Panama and the United States: The Forced Alliance*. Athens, Ga., 1992.

Cook, Blanche Wiesen. *The Declassified Eisenhower: A Divided Legacy of Peace and Political Warfare*. Garden City, N.Y., 1981.

Costigliola, Frank. *France and the United States: The Cold Alliance Since World War II*. New York, 1992.

Cowles, Gardner. "What the Public Thinks About Big Business." *Look*, February 8, 1955.

Crasweller, Robert D. *Trujillo: The Life and Times of a Caribbean Dictator*. New York, 1966.

Crozier, Brian. *De Gaulle*. New York, 1973.

Cutler, Robert. *No Time for Rest*. Boston, 1966.

———. "The Development of the National Security Council." *Foreign Affairs* 34 (1956).

Dann, Uriel. *King Hussein and the Challenge of Arab Radicalism*. Oxford, 1989.

David, Paul T.; Moos, Malcolm; and Goldman, Ralph M., eds. *Presidential Nominating Politics in 1952*. 5 vols., Baltimore, 1954. Vol. III, *The South*.

Davidson, Phillip B. *Vietnam At War: The History, 1946–1975*. Novato, Calif., 1988.

Davis, Kenneth S. *Soldier of Democracy: A Biography of Dwight Eisenhower*. Garden City, N.Y., 1945.

Dayan, Moshe. *Diary of the Sinai Campaign [by] Major-General Moshe Dayan*. Jerusalem, 1966.

"Decision on Lighter Flints Escape-Clause Case Deferred." *U.S. Department of State Bulletin* 34, no. 870 (February 27, 1956).

The Declassified Documents Quarterly Catalog 2, no. 3 (1976).

De Gaulle, Charles. *The Complete Memoirs of Charles De Gaulle*. New York, 1968.

De Guingand, Francis Wilfred. *Operation Victory*. 3d ed., rev. London, 1963.

Derthick, Martha and Quirk, Paul J. *The Politics of Deregulation*. Washington, D.C., 1985.

De Voto, Bernard A. "The Easy Chair: Let's Close the National Parks." *Harper's*, October 1953.

Dick, Jane. *Volunteers and the Making of Presidents*. New York, 1980.

Divine, Robert A. *Blowing on the Wind: The Nuclear Test Ban Debate, 1954–1960*. New York, 1978.

Donovan, Robert J. *Confidential Secretary: Ann Whitman's 20 Years with Eisenhower and Rockefeller*. New York, 1988.

————. *Conflict and Crisis: The Presidency of Harry S Truman, 1945–1948*. New York, 1977.

————. *Eisenhower: The Inside Story*. New York, 1956.

Dorough, C. Dwight. *Mr. Sam*. New York, 1962.

Drummond, Roscoe. "*Washington:* The President Takes on Senator Bricker." *New York Herald-Tribune*, January 17, 1954.

Duchin, Brian R. "The 'Agonizing Reappraisal': Eisenhower, Dulles, and the EDC." *Diplomatic History* 16, no. 2 (1992).

Dulaney, H. G.; Phillips, Edward Hake; and Reese, MacPhelen, eds. *"Speak, Mr. Speaker."* Bonham, Tex., 1978.

Dulles, Allen. *The Craft of Intelligence*. New York, 1968.

Duram, James C. *A Moderate Among Extremists: Dwight D. Eisenhower and the School Desegregation Crisis*. Chicago, 1981.

Eban, Abba Solomon. *Abba Eban: An Autobiography*. New York, 1977.

Eckes, Alfred E. *A Search for Solvency: Bretton Woods and the International Monetary System, 1941–1971*. Austin, 1975.

————. *The United States and the Global Struggle for Minerals*. Austin, 1979.

Eden, Anthony. *Full Circle: The Memoirs of Anthony Eden*. Boston, 1960.

Eisenhower, Dwight D. *At Ease: Stories I Tell to Friends*. Garden City, N.Y., 1967.

————. *Crusade in Europe*. Garden City, N.Y., 1948.

————. *The Economic Report of the President, 1955*. Washington, D.C., 1955.

————. *The Eisenhower Diaries*. Edited by Robert H. Ferrell. New York, 1981.

————. *Ike's Letters to A Friend: 1941–1958*. Edited by Robert W. Griffith. Lawrence, Kans., 1984.

————. *Letters to Mamie*. Edited by John S. D. Eisenhower. Garden City, N.Y., 1978.

————. *Mandate for Change, 1953–1956*. Garden City, N.Y., 1963.

————. *The Papers of Dwight David Eisenhower*. Baltimore, 1970–. Vols. I–V, *The War Years*, edited by Alfred D. Chandler, Jr. (1970); vol. VI, *Occupation, 1945*, edited by Alfred D. Chandler, Jr., and Louis Galambos (1978); vols. VII–IX, *The Chief of Staff*, edited by Louis Galambos (1978); vols. X–XI, *Columbia University*, edited by Louis Galambos (1983); vols. XII–XIII, *NATO and the Campaign of 1952*, edited by Louis Galambos (1989).

————. *The White House Years: Waging Peace, 1956–1961*. Garden City, N.Y., 1965.

————. "The Middle Way: All Our Freedoms Are a Single Bundle." *Vital Speeches of the Day* 15, no. 23 (1949).

Eisenhower, John S. D. *Strictly Personal*. New York, 1974.

Eisenhower, Milton S. *The President is Calling*. New York, 1974.

————. *The Wine Is Bitter: The United States and Latin America*. Garden City, N.Y., 1963.

Ellis, Clyde T. *A Giant Step*. New York, 1966.

Evangelista, Matthew A. "Stalin's Postwar Army Reappraised." *International Security* 7 (Winter 1982–1983).

Ewald, William Bragg, Jr. *Eisenhower the President: Crucial Days, 1951–1960*. Englewood Cliffs, N.J., 1981.

————. *Who Killed Joe McCarthy?* New York, 1984.

Falcone, Nicholas S. *Labor Law.* New York, 1962.

Fall, Bernard B. *Hell in a Very Small Place: The Siege of Dien Bien Phu.* Philadelphia and New York, 1967.

Fall, Frieda Kay. *The Eisenhower College Collection: The Paintings of Dwight D. Eisenhower.* Los Angeles, 1972.

"Fall of the Hall." *Time,* May 10, 1954.

Farago, Ladislas. *The Last Days of Patton.* New York, 1981.

Fausold, Martin L. *The Presidency of Herbert Hoover.* Lawrence, Kans., 1985.

Feis, Herbert. *From Trust to Terror: The Onset of the Cold War, 1945–1950.* New York, 1970.

Fenno, Richard F., Jr. *The President's Cabinet.* New York, 1959.

Finder, Leonard V. "Ike Will Not Run in '56." *Look,* October 18, 1955.

Fineberg, S. Andhil. *The Rosenberg Case: Fact and Fiction.* New York, 1953.

Finer, Herman. *Dulles Over Suez: The Theory and Practice of His Diplomacy.* Chicago, 1964.

Finkle, Jason "The President Makes a Decision: A Study of Dixon-Yates." *Michigan Governmental Studies* no. 39. Ann Arbor, 1960.

Flynn, John Thomas. "Twenty-four Steps to Communism." *American Mercury* 77 (December 1953).

Folloit, Denise, ed. *Documents on International Affairs 1954.* London, 1957.

"For Democrats, It's '52 Again." *U.S. News and World Report,* September 11, 1953.

Ford, Corey. *Donovan of OSS.* Boston, 1970.

Førland, Tor Egil. "'Selling Firearms to the Indians': Eisenhower's Export Control Policy, 1953–54." *Diplomatic History* 15, no. 2 (1991).

Forrestal, James V. *The Forrestal Diaries.* Edited by Walter Millis. New York, 1951.

Freeman, Douglas Southall. *Lee.* New York, 1991. An abridgement in one volume by Richard Harwell of the four-volume *R. E. Lee.*

Freiberger, Steven Z. *Dawn Over Suez: The Rise of American Power in the Middle East, 1953–1957.* Chicago, 1992.

Frier, David A. *Conflict of Interest in the Eisenhower Administration.* 2d ed. Baltimore, 1970.

Gabrielson, Ira N. *The Fisherman's Encyclopedia.* Harrisburg, Pa., 1954.

Gaddis, John Lewis. *Strategies of Containment: A Critical Appraisal of Postwar American National Security Policy.* New York, 1982.

————. "The Unexpected John Foster Dulles: Nuclear Weapons, Communism, and the Russians." In *John Foster Dulles and the Diplomacy of the Cold War,* edited by Richard H. Immerman. Princeton, 1990.

Galambos, Louis, and Pratt, Joseph A. *The Rise of the Corporate Commonwealth: U.S. Business and Public Policy in the Twentieth Century.* New York, 1988.

Gallup, George Horace. *The Gallup Poll: Public Opinion, 1935–1971.* 3 vols. New York, 1972. Vol. II. *1949–1958.*

Gardner, Lloyd C. *Approaching Vietnam: From World War II Through Dienbienphu, 1941–1954.* New York, 1988.

Garrow, David J., ed. *The Montgomery Bus Boycott and the Women Who Started It: The Memoir of Jo Ann Gibson Robinson.* Knoxville, Tenn., 1987.

————. "The Origins of the Montgomery Bus Boycott." In *The Walking City: The Montgomery Bus Boycott, 1955–1956.* Brooklyn, N.Y., 1989.

George, Alexander L. *Presidential Decisionmaking in Foreign Policy: The Effective Use of Information and Advice.* Boulder, Colo., 1980.

————. "American Policy-Making and the North Korean Aggression." *World Politics* 7 (1955).

Gervasi, Frank H. *Big Government: The Meaning and Purpose of the Hoover Commission Report.* New York, 1949.

Gilbert, Robert E. *The Mortal Presidency: Illness and Anguish in the White House.* New York, 1992.

Gleijeses, Piero. *Shattered Hope: The Guatemalan Revolution and the United States, 1944–1954.* Princeton, 1991.

"GOP Must Be a Team." *Newsweek,* July 13, 1953.

Gordon, Leonard H. D. "United States Opposition to Use of Force in the Taiwan Strait, 1954–1955." *Journal of American History* 87, no. 3 (1985).

Gotham, Frank. "The Inconsistency of John Foster Dulles." *The Nation,* October 18, 1952.

———. "John Foster Dulles: The Cartel's Choice." *The Nation,* October 11, 1952.

Graham, Margaret B. W. *RCA and the VideoDisc: The Business of Research.* New York, 1986.

Great Britain. Parliament. *The Parliamentary Debates.* 5th ser., vol. 514. London, 1953.

Greenstein, Fred I. *The Hidden-Hand Presidency: Eisenhower as Leader.* New York, 1982.

Gregory, Charles O. *Labor and the Law.* New York, 1958.

Griffith, Robert. *The Politics of Fear: Joseph R. McCarthy and the Senate.* Lexington, Ky., 1970.

Griffith, Robert W. "Dwight D. Eisenhower and the Corporate Commonwealth." *American Historical Review* 87, no. 1 (1982).

Hagan, Kenneth J., and Roberts, William R. *Against All Enemies: Interpretations of American Military History.* Westport, Conn., 1986.

Hagerty, James C. *The Diary of James C. Hagerty: Eisenhower in Mid-Course, 1954–1955.* Edited by Robert H. Ferrell. Bloomington, Ind., 1983.

Haglund, David G., and Sokolsky, Joel J., eds. *The U.S.–Canada Security Relationship: The Politics, Strategy, and Technology of Defense.* Boulder, Colo., 1989.

Hahn, Peter L. *The United States, Great Britain and Egypt 1945–1956: Strategy and Diplomacy in the Early Cold War.* Chapel Hill, 1991.

Halberstam, David. *The Powers That Be.* New York, 1979.

Hamilton, Alexander. No. 15. In *The Federalist Papers: A Collection of Essays Written in Support of the Constitution of the United States,* edited by Roy P. Fairfield. Baltimore, 1981.

Hamilton, Charles V. *Adam Clayton Powell, Jr.: The Political Biography of an American Dilemma.* New York, 1991.

Harbaugh, William H. *Lawyer's Lawyer: The Life of John W. Davis.* New York, 1973.

Harrington, Michael. *The Other America: Poverty in the United States.* New York, 1962.

Hatch, Alden. *Red Carpet for Mamie.* New York, 1954.

Hawke, David. *The Colonial Experience.* Indianapolis, 1966.

Hays, Samuel P. *Beauty, Health, and Permanence: Environmental Politics in the United States, 1955–1985.* Cambridge, 1987.

Hazlitt, Henry. "The Return to Gold." *Newsweek,* July 6, 1953.

"H-Bomb in South Carolina: The Road Ahead is Clear." Special Report. *Newsweek,* February 15, 1953.

Heard-Bey, Frauke. *From Trucial States to United Arab Emirates.* London, 1982.

Henderson, Phillip G. *Managing the Presidency: The Eisenhower Legacy—From Kennedy to Reagan.* Boulder, Colo., 1988.

Herring, George C. *America's Longest War: The United States and Vietnam, 1950–1975.* New York, 1979.

Herring, George C., and Immerman, Richard H. "Eisenhower, Dulles, and Dienbienphu: 'The Day We Didn't Go to War' Revisited." *Journal of American History* 71, no. 2 (1984).

Hess, Stephen. *Organizing the Presidency.* Washington, D.C., 1976.

Hewes, James E., Jr. *From Root to McNamara: Army Organization and Administration, 1900–1963.* Washington, D.C., 1975.

Hewlett, Richard G., and Anderson, Oscar E. *The New World, 1939–1946.* Vol. I in *A History of the United States Atomic Energy Commission.* University Park, Pa., 1962.

Hewlett, Richard G., and Duncan, Francis. *Atomic Shield, 1947–1952.* Vol. II in *A History of the United States Atomic Energy Commission.* University Park, Pa., 1969.

Hewlett, Richard G., and Holl, Jack M. *Atoms for Peace and War, 1953–1961.* Berkeley and Los Angeles, 1989.

Hickey, Neil, and Edwin, Ed. *Adam Clayton Powell and the Politics of Race.* New York, 1965.

Hickman, Bert G. *Growth and Stability of the Postwar Economy.* Washington, D.C., 1960.

Higgins, Rosalyn. *United Nations Peacekeeping 1946–1947: Documents and Commentary.* 4 vols. Oxford, 1969–1981. Vol. I, *The Middle East* (1969).

Hogan, Michael J. *The Marshall Plan: America, Britain and the Reconstruction of Western Europe, 1947–1952.* Cambridge, 1987.

Holloway, Rachel L. *In the Matter of J. Robert Oppenheimer: Politics, Rhetoric, and Self-Defense.* Westport, Conn., 1993.

Holman, Frank E. *The Life and Career of a Western Lawyer: 1886–1961.* Baltimore, 1963.

Hoopes, Townsend. *The Devil and John Foster Dulles.* Boston, 1973.

Horne, Alistair. *Harold Macmillan.* 2 vols. New York, 1988–1989. Vol. II, *1957–1986* (1989).

Howard, Kathleen Graham. "Peace Through Strength: A Look at the North Atlantic Treaty Organization." *U.S. Department of State Bulletin* 34, no. 871 (March 5, 1956).

Hoxie, R. Gordon. "Eisenhower and Presidential Leadership." *Presidential Studies Quarterly* 13, no. 4 (1983).

Hughes, Emmet John. *The Ordeal of Power: A Political Memoir of the Eisenhower Years.* New York, 1963.

———. "Collective Rule: Kremlin Takes a Big Gamble." *Life*, February 15, 1954.

———. "A Perceptive Reporter in a Changing Russia." *Life*, February 8, 1954.

Humphrey, George M. *The Basic Papers of George M. Humphrey as Secretary of the Treasury, 1953–1957.* Edited by Nathanial R. Howard. Cleveland, 1965.

Immerman, Richard H. *The CIA in Guatemala: The Foreign Policy of Intervention.* Austin, Tex., 1982.

———. "Eisenhower and Dulles: Who Made the Decisions?" *Political Psychology* 1, no. 2 (1979).

———. "The United States and the Geneva Conference of 1954: A New Look." *Diplomatic History* 14, no. 1 (1990).

Inter-Parliamentary Union. *Parliaments.* New York, 1963.

"International Development of Atomic Energy." *U.S. Department of State Bulletin* 29, no. 741 (September 7, 1953).

Iserman, Theodore R. *Changes to Make in Taft-Hartley.* New York, 1953.

Ismay, Hastings Lionel. *NATO: The First Five Years, 1949–1954.* Netherlands, 1954.

James, D. Clayton. *The Years of MacArthur.* 3 vols. Boston, 1970–85. Vol. I, *1880–1941* (1970); vol. III, *Triumph and Disaster, 1945–1964* (1985).

Jantscher, Gerald R. *Bread Upon the Waters: Federal Aids to the Maritime Industries.* Washington, D.C., 1975.

Jeffreys-Jones, Rhodri. *The CIA and American Democracy.* New Haven, 1989.

Joint Secretariat. *The History of the Joint Chiefs of Staff: The Joint Chiefs of Staff and the War in Vietnam.* 1 vol. to date. Wilmington, Del., 1982–. Vol. I, *History of the Indochina Incident, 1940–1954* (1982).

Jurika, Stephen, Jr., ed., *From Pearl Harbor to Vietnam: The Memoirs of Admiral Arthur W. Radford*. Stanford, 1980.

Kahin, George McTurnan. *Intervention: How America Became Involved in Vietnam*. Garden City, N.Y., 1987.

Karnow, Stanley. *Vietnam: A History*. New York, 1984.

Katcher, Leo. *Earl Warren: A Political Biography*. New York, 1967.

Kaufman, Burton I. *The Oil Cartel Case: A Documentary Study of Antitrust Activity in the Cold War Era*. Westport, Conn., 1978.

———. *Trade and Aid: Eisenhower's Foreign Economic Policy, 1953–1961*. Baltimore, 1982.

Keefer, Edward C. "President Dwight D. Eisenhower and the End of the Korean War." *Diplomatic History* 10, no. 3 (1986).

Kerr, Catherine E. "Incorporating the Star: The Intersection of Business and Aesthetic Strategies in Early American Film." *Business History Review* 64 (Autumn 1990).

Kettl, Donald F. *Leadership at the Fed*. New Haven, Conn., 1986.

Kinnard, Douglas. *The Certain Trumpet: Maxwell Taylor and the American Experience in Vietnam*. Washington, D.C., 1991.

———. *President Eisenhower and Strategy Management: A Study in Defense Politics*. Lexington, Ky., 1977.

Kirkpatrick, Lyman B., Jr. *The Real CIA*. New York, 1968.

Kluger, Richard. *The Paper: The Life and Death of the New York Herald Tribune*. New York, 1986.

———. *Simple Justice: The History of Brown v. Board of Education and Black America's Struggle for Equality*. New York, 1976.

Kolko, Joyce, and Kolko, Gabriel. *The Limits of Power: The World and United States Foreign Policy, 1945–1954*. New York, 1972.

Kornitzer, Bela. *The Great American Heritage: The Story of the Five Eisenhower Brothers*. New York, 1955.

———. "The Eisenhowers: A Story of an American Family," pt. 1, "Where Does Courage Come From?" *Women's Home Companion*, July 1954.

———. "The Great Heritage," pt. 2, "Where Does Courage Come From?" *Women's Home Companion*, August 1954.

Kouwenhoven, John Atlee. *The Columbia Historic Portrait of New York: An Essay in Graphic History in Honor of the Tricentennial of New York City and the Bicentennial of Columbia University*. New York, 1953.

Kovaleff, Theodore Philip. *Business and Government during the Eisenhower Administration: A Study of the Antitrust Policy of the Justice Department*. Athens, Ohio, 1980.

Krock, Arthur. "Will Liberals Take Over Southern Democracy?" *Time*, August 23, 1954.

Kunz, Diane B. *The Economic Diplomacy of the Suez Crisis*. Chapel Hill, 1991.

Kyle, Keith. *Suez*. New York, 1991.

Lacouture, Jean. *De Gaulle*. New York, 1965.

LaFeber, Walter. *America, Russia, and the Cold War, 1945–1992*. New York, 1993.

———. *The Panama Canal: The Crisis in Historical Perspective*. Updated ed. New York, 1989.

Lawrence, Samuel E. *United States Shipping Policies and Politics*. Washington, D.C., 1966.

League of Women Voters of Pennsylvania. *Key to the Keystone State*. University Park, Pa., 1989.

Leary, William M., ed. *The Central Intelligence Agency: History and Documents*. University, Ala., 1984.

Lewis, Anthony, and *The New York Times*. *Portrait of a Decade: The Second American Revolution*. New York, 1964.

Lewy, Guenter. *America in Vietnam*. New York, 1978.

Lilienthal, David E. *The Journals of David E. Lilienthal*. 4 vols. New York, 1964–69. Vol. I, *The TVA Years, 1939–1945* (1964).

Lincoln, Abraham. *The Collected Works of Abraham Lincoln*. Edited by Roy P. Basler. 8 vols. New Brunswick, N.J., 1953. Vol. II, *1848–1858*.

Lipartito, Kenneth J., and Pratt, Joseph A. *Baker and Botts in the Development of Modern Houston*. Austin, 1991.

Lippmann, Walter. *Public Philosopher: Selected Letters of Walter Lippmann*. Edited by John Morton Blum. New York, 1985.

Lloyd, Selwyn. *Suez 1956: A Personal Account*. New York, 1978.

Lodge, Henry Cabot, Jr. *As It Was: An Inside View of Politics and Power in the '50s and '60s*. New York, 1976.

Lowi, Theodore J. "Bases in Spain." In *American Civil-Military Decisions: A Book of Case Studies*. Edited by Harold Stein. Birmingham, Ala., 1963.

Lubell, Samuel. *The Future of American Politics*. New York, 1952.

Lyon, Peter. *Eisenhower: Portrait of the Hero*. Boston, 1974.

McAuliffe, Mary S. "Dwight D. Eisenhower and Wolf Ladejinsky: The Politics of the Declining Red Scare, 1954–55." *Prologue* 14, no. 3 (1982).

McCann, Kevin C. *Man from Abilene*. Garden City, N.Y., 1952.

McEntire, Davis. *Residence and Race*. Berkeley, 1960.

McMahon, Robert J. "The Cold War in Asia: Toward a New Synthesis?" *Diplomatic History* 12, no. 3 (1988).

———. "United States Cold War Strategy and South Asia: Making a Military Commitment to Pakistan, 1947–1954." *Journal of American History* 75, no. 3 (1988).

MacNeil, Neil. *Dirksen: Portrait of a Public Man*. New York, 1970.

MacNeil, Neil, and Metz, Harold W. *The Hoover Report: 1953–1955*. New York, 1956.

Macmillan, Harold. *Riding the Storm, 1956–1959*. London, 1971.

Major, John. *The Oppenheimer Hearing*. London, 1971.

Mansfield, Harvey C. "Federal Executive Reorganization: Thirty Years of Experience." *Public Administration Review* 29 (July–August 1969).

Marks, Frederick W. III. "The United States and Castillo Armas in Guatemala 1954." *Diplomatic History* 14, no. 1 (1990).

Maroger, Jacques. *The Secret Formulas and Techniques of the Masters*. New York, 1948.

Martin, Joseph William, Jr. *My First Fifty Years in Politics*. As told to Robert J. Donovan. New York, 1960.

Martin, Roscoe C., ed. *TVA, The First Twenty Years: A Staff Report*. University, Ala., 1956.

Mayer, Michael S. "The Eisenhower Administration and the Desegregation of Washington, D.C." *Journal of Policy History* 3, no. 1 (1991).

Mayle, Paul D. *Eureka Summit: Agreement in Principle and the Big Three at Tehran*. Newark, Del., 1987.

Mazuzan, George T. *Warren R. Austin at the U.N.: 1946–1953*. Kent, Ohio, 1977.

Mazuzan, George T., and Walker, J. Samuel. *Controlling the Atom: The Beginning of Nuclear Regulation, 1946–1962*. Berkeley, 1984.

Meeropol, Robert, and Meeropol, Michael. *We Are Your Sons*. Boston, 1975.

Merson, Martin. *The Private Diary of a Public Servant*. New York, 1955.

Millikan, Max F., and Rostow, W. W. *A Proposal: Key to an Effective Foreign Policy*. New York, 1957.

Mitgang, Herbert. "Annals of Government: Policing America's Writers." *New Yorker*, October 5, 1987.

Moe, Ronald C. "The Two Hoover Commissions in Retrospect." *Congressional Research Service Report*, 82–14 Gov (March 12, 1982).

Mollenhoff, Clark R. *The Pentagon: Politics, Profit and Plunder*. New York, 1967.

Monroe, Joseph Elmer. *Railroad Men and Wages*. Washington, D.C., 1947.

Montgomery, Bernard Law. *The Memoirs of Field-Marshal the Viscount Montgomery of Alamein, K.G.* Cleveland and New York, 1958.

Moore, Thomas Gale. *Uranium Enrichment and Public Policy*. Washington, D.C., 1978.

Moran, Lord Charles. *Churchill: Taken From the Diaries of Lord Moran*. Boston, 1966.

Moreell, Ben. *Our Nation's Water Resources—Policies and Politics*. Chicago, 1956.

Morgan, Roger P. *The United States and West Germany, 1945–1973: A Study in Alliance Politics*. London, 1974.

Morrow, E. Frederic. *Black Man in the White House*. New York, 1963.

Murphy, Paul L. *The Constitution in Crisis Times, 1918–1969*. New York, 1972.

Murphy, Robert D. *Diplomat Among Warriors*. Garden City, N.Y., 1964.

"Mutual Defense Treaty with Korea Signed." *U.S. Department of State Bulletin* 29, no. 746 (October 12, 1953).

"The Nation's Worst Boss." *Nation's Business* 41, no. 8 (August 1953).

Neal, Steve. *The Eisenhowers: Reluctant Dynasty*. New York, 1978.

Neu, Charles E. "The Rise of the National Security Bureaucracy." In *The New American State: Bureaucracies and Policies Since World War II*, edited by Louis Galambos. Baltimore, 1987.

Neustadt, Richard E. *Presidential Power: The Politics of Leadership*. New York, 1960.

Nevins, Arthur S. *Gettysburg's Five-Star Farmer*. New York, 1977.

Nixon, Richard Milhous. *RN: The Memoirs of Richard Nixon*. New York, 1978.

———. *Six Crises*. Garden City, N.Y., 1962.

Norton-Taylor, Duncan. "The Controversial Mr. Strauss." *Fortune*, January 1955.

Official Report of the Proceedings of the Twenty-sixth Republican National Convention. Washington, D.C., 1956.

Oliver, John. "Administrative Foundations." In *TVA, The First Twenty Years: A Staff Report*, edited by Roscoe C. Martin. University, Ala., 1956.

Owen, Wilfred, and Dearing, Charles L. *Toll Roads and the Problem of Highway Modernization*. Washington, D.C., 1951.

Paddock, Alfred H. *U.S. Army Special Warfare: Its Origins; Psychological and Unconventional Warfare, 1941–1952*. Washington, D.C., 1982.

Paleck, Marvin Andrew. "The United Defense Fund: A Study of the Coordination of Voluntary Welfare Services During Wartime." Ph.D. dissertation, University of Minnesota, 1969.

Paley, William S. *As It Happened: A Memoir*. Garden City, N.Y., 1979.

Parmet, Herbert S. *Eisenhower and the American Crusades*. New York, 1972.

Patterson, Bradley H., Jr. *The Ring of Power: The White House Staff and its Expanding Role in Government*. New York, 1988.

Patterson, James T. *Mr. Republican: A Biography of Robert A. Taft*. Boston, 1972.

Patton, Robert H. *The Pattons: A Personal History of an American Family*. New York, 1994.

Peck, Merton J. *Competition in the Aluminum Industry: 1945–1953*. Cambridge, Mass., 1961.

Peet, Stephen D. *Myths and Symbols: or, Aboriginal Religions in America*. Portland, Maine, 1976.

Pegrum, Dudley F. *Transportation: Economics and Public Policy*. Homewood, Ill., 1963.

Peltason, Jack W. *Fifty-Eight Lonely Men: Southern Federal Judges and School Desegregation*. New York, 1961.

Pemberton, Gregory James. "Australia, the United States, and the Indochina Crisis of 1954." *Diplomatic History* 13, no. 1 (1989).

Pemberton, William E. *Bureaucratic Politics: Executive Reorganization During the Truman Administration.* Columbia, Mo., 1979.

Peterson, Elmer T. *Big Dam Foolishness: The Problem of Modern Flood Control and Water Storage.* New York, 1954.

Pfau, Richard. *No Sacrifice Too Great: The Life of Lewis L. Strauss.* Charlottesville, Va., 1984.

Pickett, William B. *Homer E. Capehart: A Senator's Life 1897–1979.* Indianapolis, 1990.

Pinkley, Virgil, with Scheer, James F. *Eisenhower Declassified.* Old Tappan, N.J., 1979.

Pogue, Forrest C. *George C. Marshall.* 4 vols., New York, 1963–87. Vol. IV, *Statesman, 1945–1959* (1987).

"Politics: New Shoots in the Old South." *Time,* September 7, 1953.

Pollack, Jack Harrison. *Earl Warren: The Judge Who Changed America.* Englewood Cliffs, N.J., 1979.

Pollock, John. *Billy Graham: Evangelist to the World.* New York, 1979.

Porter, Kirk H., and Johnson, Donald Bruce. *National Party Platforms, 1840–1968.* Urbana, Ill., 1970.

Powell, Adam Clayton, Jr. "The President and the Negro." *Reader's Digest,* October 1954.

President's Advisory Committee on Government Housing Policies and Programs: A Report. Washington, D.C., 1953.

"Prices and Cost of Living." *Monthly Labor Review* 76, no. 4 (April 1953).

Priest, Ivy Maude Baker. *Green Grows the Ivy.* New York, 1958.

Public Papers of the Presidents of the United States: Dwight D. Eisenhower, January 20 to December 31, 1953. Washington, D.C., 1960.

Public Papers of the Presidents of the United States: Dwight D. Eisenhower, January 1 to December 31, 1954. Washington, D.C., 1960.

Public Papers of the Presidents of the United States: Dwight D. Eisenhower, January 1 to December 31, 1955. Washington, D.C., 1959.

Public Papers of the Presidents of the United States: Dwight D. Eisenhower, January 1 to December 31, 1956. Washington, D.C., 1958.

Public Papers of the Presidents of the United States: Dwight D. Eisenhower, January 1 to December 31, 1957. Washington, D.C., 1958.

Public Papers of the Presidents of the United States: Dwight D. Eisenhower, January 1 to December 31, 1958. Washington, D.C., 1959.

Public Papers of the Presidents of the United States: Dwight D. Eisenhower, January 1 to December 31, 1959. Washington, D.C., 1960.

Quick, John. *Dictionary of Weapons and Military Terms.* New York, 1973.

Rabe, Stephen G. *Eisenhower and Latin America: The Foreign Policy in Anticommunism.* Chapel Hill, 1988.

———. "The Clues Didn't Check Out: Commentary on 'The CIA and Castillo Armas.'" *Diplomatic History* 14, no. 1 (1990).

Rabel, Roberto G. *Between East and West: Trieste, the United States, and the Cold War, 1941–1954.* Durham, N.C., 1988.

"The Race for the 5,000-Mile Missile." *Fortune,* December 1955.

Radford, Arthur W. *From Pearl Harbor to Vietnam: The Memoirs of Admiral Arthur W. Radford.* Edited by Stephen Jurika, Jr. Stanford, 1980.

Ransom, Harry H. *Central Intelligence and National Security.* Cambridge, 1958.

Raucher, Alan R. *Paul G. Hoffman: Architect of Foreign Aid.* Lexington, Ky., 1985.

Rearden, Steven L. *The Formative Years, 1947–50.* Vol. I of *History of the Office of the Secretary of Defense,* edited by Alfred Goldberg. 2 vols. to date. Washington, D.C., 1984–.

Rees, David. *Korea: The Limited War.* Baltimore, 1964.

Reichard, Gary W. *The Reaffirmation of Republicanism: Eisenhower and the Eighty-third Congress.* Knoxville, Tenn., 1975.

Reston, James. "Choice of New Chief Justice Could Hinge on Many Tests." *New York Times,* September 10, 1953.

"Review of U.N. Charter." *U.S. Department of State Bulletin* 29, no. 741 (September 7, 1953).

Reynolds, Clark G. "American Maritime Power since World War II." In *America's Maritime Legacy: A History of the U.S. Merchant Marine and Shipbuilding Industry Since Colonial Times,* edited by Robert A. Kilmarx. Boulder, Colo., 1979.

Richards, David W.; Bland, Edward F.; and White, Paul D. "A Completed Twenty-five Year Follow-up Study of Patients with Myocardial Infarction." *Journal of Chronic Diseases* 4, no. 4 (October 1956).

Richardson, James D., ed. *A Compilation of the Messages and Papers of the Presidents, 1789–1902.* 10 vols. Washington, D.C., 1896–1903. *Supplement* (1903).

Rickenbacker, Edward Vernon. *Rickenbacker.* Englewood Cliffs, N.J., 1967.

Rose, Mark H. *Interstate: Express Highway Politics, 1941–1956.* Lawrence, Kans., 1979.

Rose, Mark H., and Seely, Bruce E. "Getting the Interstate System Built: Road Engineers and the Implementation of Public Policy." *Journal of Policy History* 2, no. 1 (1990).

Rostow, W. W. *The Diffusion of Power: An Essay in Recent History.* New York, 1972.

———. *Open Skies: Eisenhower's Proposal, July 21, 1955.* Austin, Tex., 1982.

Rothschild, Alonzo. *Lincoln, Master of Men: A Study in Character.* Boston and New York, 1906.

Rovere, Richard H. *Affairs of State: The Eisenhower Years.* New York, 1956.

"Rumanian Diplomat Declared Persona Non Grata." *U.S. Department of State Bulletin* 28, no. 727 (June 8, 1953).

Rushkoff, Bennett. "Eisenhower, Dulles, and the Quemoy–Matsu Crisis, 1954–55." *Political Science Quarterly* 96 (1981).

Salibi, Kamal. *The Modern History of Jordan.* London, 1993.

Saloutos, Theodore. *The American Farmer and the New Deal.* Ames, Iowa, 1982.

Sanders, M. Elizabeth. *The Regulation of Natural Gas: Policy and Politics, 1938–1978.* Philadelphia, 1981.

Saulnier, Raymond J. *Constructive Years: The U.S. Economy Under Eisenhower.* Lanham, Md., 1991.

Scarne, John. *Scarne's Encyclopedia of Games.* New York, 1973.

Schaller, Michael. "Securing the Great Crescent: Occupied Japan and the Origins of Containment in Southeast Asia." *Journal of American History* 69, no. 2 (1982).

Schapsmeier, Edward L., and Schapsmeier, Frederick H. *Dirksen of Illinois: Senatorial Statesman.* Urbana, Ill., 1985.

———. *Ezra Taft Benson and the Politics of Agriculture: The Eisenhower Years, 1953–1964.* Danville, Ill., 1975.

———. "Eisenhower and Agricultural Reform: Ike's Farm Policy Legacy Appraised." *American Journal of Economics and Sociology* 51 (April 1992).

———. "Eisenhower and Ezra Taft Benson: Farm Policy in the 1950s." *Agricultural History* 44, no. 4 (1970).

Scheele, Henry Z. *Charlie Halleck: A Political Biography.* New York, 1966.

Schilling, Warner R.; Hammond, Paul Y.; and Snyder, Glenn H. *Strategy, Politics and Defense Budgets.* New York, 1962.

Schlesinger, Arthur M., ed. *History of American Presidential Elections, 1789–1968*. 4 vols. New York, 1971. Vol. IV. *1940–1968*.

Schoenbrun, David. *The Three Lives of Charles De Gaulle*. New York, 1966.

Schwietert, Arthur H., and Lyon, Leverett S. *The Great Lakes–St. Lawrence Seaway Power Project*. Chicago, 1951.

Sears, Harry. "The Conspiracy Against Gold." *Vital Speeches of the Day* 20, no. 13 (1954).

Seidman, Harold. *Politics, Position and Power*. London, 1975.

Seligman, Lester G. "Developments in the Presidency and the Conception of Political Leadership." *American Sociological Review* 20 (1955).

"Senator Knowland Asks: Will Ike Be a Reluctant Candidate?" *U.S. News and World Report*, January 21, 1955.

Sennholz, Hans F. *Gold I$ Money*. Westport, Conn., 1975.

Severn, William. *Mr. Chief Justice: Earl Warren*. New York, 1968.

Shalom, Stephen Rosskamm. *The United States and the Philippines*. Philadelphia, 1981.

Sheridan, Walter. *The Fall and Rise of Jimmy Hoffa*. New York, 1972.

Sherwood, Robert E. "The Big Stone Book." *American Heritage* 5, no. 2 (1953).

Shuckburgh, Evelyn. *Descent to Suez: Diaries 1951–56*. London, 1986.

Silver, James Wesley. *Mississippi: The Closed Society*. New York, 1963.

Sindler, Allan P. *Huey Long's Louisiana: State Politics, 1920–1952*. Baltimore, 1956.

Slater, Ellis D. *The Ike I Knew*. Baltimore, 1980.

Sloan, Alfred Pritchard, Jr. *My Years With General Motors*. Garden City, N.Y., 1963.

Sloan, John W. *Eisenhower and the Management of Prosperity*. Lawrence, Kans., 1991.

Smith, Alice Kimball, and Weiner, Charles, eds. *Robert Oppenheimer: Letters and Recollections*. Cambridge, Mass., 1980.

Smith, Earl E. T. *The Fourth Floor: An Account of the Castro Communist Revolution*. New York, 1962.

Smith, George David. *From Monopoly to Competition: The Transformation of Alcoa, 1888–1986*. Cambridge, 1988.

Smith, Jane S. *Patenting the Sun: Polio and the Salk Vaccine*. New York, 1990.

Smith, Paul H. *Loyalists and Redcoats: A Study in British Revolutionary Policy*. Chapel Hill, 1964.

Smith, R. B. *An International History of the Vietnam War*. 3 vols. New York, 1983–1991. Vol. I, *Revolution versus Containment* (1983).

Smith, Richard Norton. *Thomas E. Dewey and His Times*. New York, 1982.

Smith, Wayne S. "Critical Junctures in U.S.-Cuban Relations: The Diplomatic Record." *Diplomatic History* 12, no. 4 (1988).

Soffer, Jonathan. "Matthew Bunker Ridgway: Postwar Warrior." Ph.D. dissertation, Columbia University, 1992.

Sproul, Allan. "The Gold Question: The Place of the Federal Reserve System in the Monetary and Economic Life of the Country." *Vital Speeches of the Day* 16, no. 4 (1949).

Stassen, Harold, and Houts, Marshall. *Eisenhower: Turning the World Toward Peace*. St. Paul, Minn., 1990.

Stern, Philip M. *The Oppenheimer Case: Security on Trial*. New York, 1969.

Stevenson, Adlai Ewing. *The Papers of Adlai E. Stevenson*. Edited by Walter Johnson. 8 vols. Boston, 1972–79. Vol. VI, *Toward a New America, 1955–1957* (1976).

Stouffer, Samuel A. *Communism, Conformity and Civil Liberties: A Cross-section of the Nation Speaks Its Mind*. Garden City, N.Y., 1955.

Stover, John F. *The Life and Decline of the American Railroad*. New York, 1970.

Strauss, Lewis L. *Men and Decisions*. Garden City, N.Y., 1962.

Strong, Robert A. "Eisenhower and Arms Control." In *Reevaluating Eisenhower: American*

Foreign Policy in the 1950s, edited by Richard A. Melanson and David Mayers. Urbana, Ill., 1986.

Sufrin, Sidney C., and Sedgwick, Robert C. *Labor Law: Development, Administration, Cases.* New York, 1954.

Sulzberger, C. L. *A Long Row of Candles: Memoirs and Diaries [1934–1954].* New York, 1969.

Sussman, Gennifer. *The St. Lawrence Seaway: History and Analysis of a Joint Water Highway.* Washington, D.C., 1978.

Sutherland, Daniel E. "Southern Fraternal Organizations in the North." *Journal of Southern History* 53, no. 4 (1987).

Tananbaum, Duane. *The Bricker Amendment Controversy: A Test of Eisenhower's Political Leadership.* Ithaca, N.Y., 1988.

Taryam, Abdullah Omran. *The Establishment of the United Arab Emirates 1950–85.* London, 1987.

Taylor, Maxwell D. *Swords and Plowshares.* New York, 1972.

"Text of Draft U.S.–R.O.K. Mutual Defense Treaty." *U.S. Department of State Bulletin* 29, no. 738 (August 17, 1953).

Tiffany, Paul A. *The Decline of American Steel: How Management, Labor, and Government Went Wrong.* New York, 1988.

Tomajan, John S. "The Test: Obedience to the Unenforceable." *New York Times Magazine,* July 3, 1955.

Tomlins, Christopher L. *The State and the Unions: Labor Relations, Law, and the Organized Labor Movement, 1880–1960.* Cambridge, 1985.

Treuenfels, Rudolph L., ed. *Eisenhower Speaks: Dwight D. Eishenhower in His Messages and Speeches.* New York, 1948.

Truman, Harry S. *Memoirs by Harry S. Truman.* 2 vols. New York, 1955–56. Vol. II, *Years of Trial and Hope* (1956).

———. *Mr. Citizen.* New York, 1953.

Ulam, Adam B. *The Rivals: America and Russia Since World War II.* New York, 1971.

U.S., Joint Chiefs of Staff. *The History of the Joint Chiefs of Staff.* 5 vols. to date. Wilmington, Del., 1979–80; Washington, D.C., 1986–. Vol. V, *The Joint Chiefs of Staff and National Policy, 1953–1954*, by Robert J. Watson (1986).

U.S. Army Center of Military History. *Highlights in the History of the Army Nurse Corps*, edited by Robert V. Piemonte and Cindy Gurney. Washington, D.C., 1987.

U.S. Atomic Energy Commission. *In the Matter of J. Robert Oppenheimer, Transcript of Hearing Before Personnel Security Board.* Washington, D.C., 1954.

U.S. Bureau of the Budget. *The Budget of the United States Government for the Fiscal Year Ending June 30, 1955.* Washington, D.C., 1954.

U.S. Bureau of the Budget. *The Budget of the United States Government for the Fiscal Year Ending June 30, 1960.* Washington, D.C., 1959.

U.S. Bureau of the Census. *The Statistical History of the United States.* Stamford, Conn., 1965.

U.S. Commission on Organization of the Executive Branch of the Government. *The Hoover Commission Report on Organization of the Executive Branch of the Government.* New York, 1949.

U.S. Commission on Organization of the Executive Branch of the Government. *Final Report to the Congress.* Washington, D.C., 1955.

U.S. Commission on Organization of the Executive Branch of the Government. *A Task Force Report on Water Resources and Power.* 3 vols. Washington, D.C., 1955.

U.S. Congress. House. *Highway Needs of the National Defense.* 81st Cong., 1st sess., 1949. H. Doc. 249.

———. *House Reports.* 83d Cong., 1st. sess., 1953. Vol. 3, Miscellaneous III, H. Rept. 680.

————. *Interior Department Appropriation Bill, 1954: Conference Report to Accompany H.R. 4828.* 83d Cong., 1st sess., 1953. H. Rept. 947.

————. *Interregional Highways.* 78th Cong., 2d sess., 1944. H. Doc. 379.

————. Committee on Appropriations. *Interior Department Appropriation Bill, 1954: Report to Accompany H.R. 4828.* 83d Cong., 1st sess., 1953. H. Rept. 314.

————. Committee on Foreign Affairs. *Selected Executive Session Hearings of the Committee, 1951–1956.* Vol. X, *Mutual Security Program, Part 2: Mutual Security Act of 1953, Mutual Security Act of 1954.* Washington, D.C., 1980.

————. Committee on Foreign Affairs. *Selected Executive Session Hearings of the Committee, 1951–1956.* Vol. XVI, *The Middle East, Africa, and Inter-American Affairs.* Washington, 1980.

————. Committee on Merchant Marine and Fisheries. *A Review of Maritime Subsidy Policy in the Light of Present National Requirements for a Merchant Marine and a Shipbuilding Industry.* 83d Cong., 2d sess., 1954.

————. Committee on Public Works, Subcommittee on Public Buildings and Grounds. *Rincon Annex Murals San Francisco: Hearings on H.J.R. 211.* 83d Cong., 1st sess., 1953.

U.S. Congress. Senate. *Joint Resolution to Impose Limitations with Regard to Executive Agreements.* 83d Cong., 1st sess., 1953. S.J. Res. 2.

————. *Journal of the Senate of the United States of America.* 83d Cong., 1st sess., 1953.

————. *Senate Reports.* 83d Cong., 1st sess., 1953. Vol. 3, *Miscellaneous III*, S. Rept. 601.

————. Committee on Appropriations. *Agricultural Appropriation Bill, 1955.* 83d Cong., 2d sess., 1954. S. Rept. 1429.

————. Committee on Appropriations. *Interior Department Appropriation Bill, 1954: Report to Accompany H.R. 4828.* 83d Cong., 1st sess., S. Rept. 445.

————. Committe on Appropriations. *Mutual Security Appropriations for 1955: Hearings on H.R. 10051.* 83d Cong., 1st sess., 1953.

————. Committee on Banking and Currency. *Report on FHA Investigation Under Senate Resolution 229.* 84th Cong., 1st sess., 1955.

————. Committee on Finance. *Establishment of Veterans' Administration Domiciliary Facility at Fort Logan, Colo.* 83d Cong., 1st sess., 1953. Rept. 29.

————. Committee on Government Operations. Special Subcommittee on Investigations. *Hearings on Special Senate Investigations on Charges and Countercharges Involving Secretary of the Army Robert T. Stevens, John G. Adams, H. Struve Hensel and Senator Joe McCarthy, Roy M. Cohn, and Francis P. Corr.* 83d Cong., 2d sess., 1954.

————. Committee on the Judiciary. *Treaties and Executive Agreements, Hearings before a Subcommittee on the Judiciary.* 83d Cong., 1st sess., 1953.

————. Committee on Labor and Public Welfare, *Labor-Management Relations Act 1947, as Amended: Report to Accompany S. 2650,* 83d Cong., 2d sess., 1954. S. Rept. 1217.

————. Committee on Retirement Policy for Federal Personnel. *Report Pursuant to P.L. 555, 1952.* 83d Cong., 2d sess., 1954. S. Doc. 89.

————. Resettlement Administration Program. *Letter from the Administrator,* 74th Cong., 2d sess., 1936. Doc. 213.

————. Special Committee to Study the Foreign Aid Program. *Greece, Turkey, and Iran: Report on United States Foreign Assistance Programs,* 85th Cong., 1st sess., 1957.

————. Subcommittee of the Committee on Appropriations on Interior Department Appropriations. *Interior Department Appropriations for 1954: Hearings on H.R. 4828.* 83d Cong., 1st sess., 1953, pts. 1–2.

U.S. Department of Commerce. Bureau of Public Roads. *The Administration of Federal Aid for Highways and Other Activities of the Bureau of Public Roads.* Washington, D.C., 1957.

U.S. Department of State. *Documents on Disarmament, 1945–1959.* 2 vols. Washington, D.C., 1960. Vol. II, *1957–1959.*

———. *Foreign Relations: The Conference at Washington and Quebec, 1943.* Washington, D.C., 1970.

———. *Foreign Relations of the United States, 1946.* 11 vols. Washington, D.C., 1969–72. Vol. XI, *The American Republics* (1969).

———. *Foreign Relations of the United States, 1947.* 8 vols. Washington, D.C., 1972–73. Vol. VIII, *The American Republics* (1972).

———. *Foreign Relations of the United States, 1950.* 7 vols. Washington, D.C., 1976–80. Vol. V, *The Near East, South Asia, and Africa* (1978).

———. *Foreign Relations of the United States, 1951.* 7 vols. Washington, D.C., 1979–82. Vol. I, *National Security Affairs; Foreign Economic Policy* (1980).

———. *Foreign Relations of the United States, 1952–1954.* 16 vols. Washington, D.C., 1979–89. Vol. I, *General: Economic and Political Matters,* pt. 2 (1983); vol. II, *National Security Affairs,* pt. 1 (1981); vol. III, *United Nations Affairs* (1979); vol. IV, *The American Republics* (1983); vol. V, *Western European Security,* pts. 1 and 2 (1983); vol. VI, *Western Europe and Canada,* pt. 1 (1986); vol. VIII, *Eastern Europe; The Soviet Union; Eastern Mediterranean* (1988); vol. IX, *The Near East and Middle East,* pt. 2 (1986); vol. XI, *Africa and South Asia,* pt. 2 (1981); vol. XII, *East Asia and the Pacific,* pt. 1 (1984); vol. XIII, *Indochina,* pt. 1 (1982); vol. XIV, *China and Japan,* pt. 1 (1985); vol. XV, *Korea,* pt. 1 (1984); vol. XVI, *The Geneva Conference* (1981).

———. *Foreign Relations of the United States, 1955–1957.* 27 vols. Washington, D.C., 1985–92. Vol. I, *Vietnam* (1985); vol. II, *China* (1986); vol. III, *China* (1986); vol. IV, *Western European Security and Integration* (1986); vol. V, *Austrian State Treaty: Summit and Foreign Ministers Meetings, 1955* (1988); vol. VI, *American Republics: Multilateral; Mexico; Caribbean* (1987); vol. VII, *American Republics: Central and South America* (1987); vol. VIII, *South Asia* (1987); vol. IX, *Foreign Economic Policy; Foreign Information Program* (1987); vol. X, *Foreign Aid and Economic Defense Policy* (1989); vol. XI, *United Nations and General International Matters* (1988); vol. XII, *Near East Region; Iran; Iraq* (1991); vol. XIII, *Near East: Jordan–Yemen* (1988); vol. XIV, *Arab-Israeli-Dispute, 1955* (1989); vol. XVI, *Suez Canal Crisis, July 27–December 31, 1956* (1990); vol. XVIII, *Africa* (1989); vol. XIX, *National Security Policy* (1990); vol. XX, *Regulation of Armaments; Atomic Energy* (1990); vol. XXI, *East Asian Security; Laos; Cambodia* (1990); vol. XXII, *Southeast Asia* (1989); vol. XXIV, *Soviet Union: Eastern Mediterranean* (1989); vol. XXV, *Eastern Europe* (1990); vol. XXVI, *Central and Southeastern Europe* (1992); vol. XXVII, *Western Europe and Canada* (1992).

———. *General Foreign Policy Series,* no. 117. 2 vols. Washington, D.C., 1957. Vol. II, *American Foreign Policy, 1950–1955.*

———. *United States Treaties and Other International Agreements.* Vol. 4, Pt. 3, *1953.* Washington, D.C., 1955.

U.S. Library of Congress, Legislative Reference Service. *Digest of Public General Bills.* 83d Cong., 1st sess., 1953.

U.S. Office of Management and Budget. *Budget of the United States.* Executive Branch Version. Washington, D.C., 1923–1954.

U.S. Postal Service. *Postage Stamps of the United States.* Washington, D.C., 1970.

"U.S.S.R. Asked to Participate in Foreign Ministers Conference." *U.S. Department of State Bulletin* 29, no. 735 (July 27, 1953).

U.S. Tariff Commission, *Ferrocerium (Lighter Flints) and All Other Cerium Alloys Report to The President on Escape Clause Investigation No. 41 Under the Provisions of Section 7 of the Trade Agreements Extension Act of 1951 as Amended.* Washington, D.C., 1955.

Vali, Ferenc A. *Rift and Revolt in Hungary.* Cambridge, Mass., 1961.

Van Der Beugel, Ernst H. *From Marshall Aid to Atlantic Partnership: European Integration as a Concern of American Foreign Policy.* Amsterdam, 1966.

van Ee, Daun. "From the New Look to Flexible Response." In *Against All Enemies: Interpretations of American Military History From Colonial Times to the Present*, edited by Kenneth J. Hagan and William R. Roberts. Westport, Conn., 1986.

Van Fleet, James A. "Twenty-Five Divisions for the Cost of One." *Reader's Digest*, no. 382 (February 1954).

Vatter, Harold C. *The U.S. Economy in the 1950s: An Economic History.* New York, 1963.

Vietor, Richard H. K. *Energy Policy in America Since 1945: A Study of Business-Government Relations.* Cambridge, 1984.

Vigneras, Marcel. *Rearming the French.* U.S. Army in World War II, edited by Kent Roberts Greenfield. Washington, D.C., 1957.

Vose, Clement E. *Caucasians Only: The Supreme Court, the NAACP and the Restrictive Covenant Cases.* Berkeley, 1959.

Walters, Vernon A. *Silent Missions.* New York, 1978.

Warren, Earl. *The Memoirs of Earl Warren.* New York, 1977.

Washington, George. *The Papers of George Washington.* Charlottesville, Va., 1983–93. 19 vols. Edited by W. W. Abbot and Dorothy Twohig. Presidential Series. Vol. 1, *September 1788–March 1789*; vol. 2, *April–June 1789* (1987).

———. *The Writings of George Washington.* Edited by John C. Fitzpatrick. 39 vols. Washington, D.C., 1931–44. Vol. 35, *March 30, 1796–July 31, 1797* (1940).

Watson, Robert J. *The Joint Chiefs of Staff and National Policy, 1953–1954. See* U.S., Joint Chiefs of Staff.

"We Aren't All Like Ike." *New York Daily News*, January 18, 1954.

Weaver, Carolyn L. "The Social Security Bureaucracy in Triumph and in Crisis." In *The New American State: Bureaucracies and Policies Since World War II*, edited by Louis Galambos. Baltimore, 1987.

Weaver, John D. *Warren: The Man, the Court, the Era.* Boston, 1967.

Weigold, Marilyn E. *The American Mediterranean: An Environmental, Economic and Social History of Long Island Sound.* Port Washington, N.Y., 1974.

Wexley, John. *The Judgment of Julius and Ethel Rosenberg.* New York, 1955.

White, Paul Dudley. *My Life and Medicine: An Autobiographical Memoir.* Boston, 1971.

Whiting, J. S. *Forts of the State of Washington: A Record of the Military and Semi-military Establishments Designated as Forts from May 29, 1792 to November 15, 1951.* Seattle, 1951.

"Why U.S. Is Losing Gold: Aid Abroad Big Reason." *U.S. News & World Report.* August 28, 1953.

Wiarda, Howard J. *Dictatorship and Development: The Methods of Control in Trujillo's Dominican Republic.* Gainesville, Fla., 1968.

Wildavsky, Aaron. *Dixon-Yates: A Study in Power Politics.* New Haven, Conn., 1962.

Williams, T. Harry. *Huey Long.* New York, 1969.

Wilson, Duncan. *Tito's Yugoslavia.* Cambridge, 1979.

Wolbert, George S., Jr. *U.S. Oil Pipe Lines: An Examination of How Oil Pipe Lines Operate and the Current Public Policy Issues Concerning Their Ownership.* Washington, D.C., 1979.

Wolkinson, Herman. "Demands of Congressional Committees for Executive Papers." *Federal Bar Journal* X, April, July, October, 1949, pp. 103–50.

Yanarella, Ernest J. *The Missile Defense Controversy: Strategy, Technology, and Politics, 1955–1972.* Lexington, Ky., 1977.

York, Herbert F. *The Advisors: Oppenheimer, Teller, and the Superbomb.* Stanford, 1989.

Zinner, Paul E., ed. *National Communism and Popular Revolt in Eastern Europe.* New York, 1956.

Glossary

ABA	American Bar Association
ADA	Americans for Democratic Action
AEC	Atomic Energy Commission
AFBF	American Farm Bureau Federation
AHEPA	American Hellenic Educational Progressive Association
AIOC	Anglo-Iranian Oil Company
AF of L	American Federation of Labor
AMA	American Medical Association
ANZUS	Australia, New Zealand, United States
AP	Associated Press
AWF	Ann Whitman File (Eisenhower's presidential papers)
Benelu, Benelux	Belgium, Netherlands, and Luxembourg
BLE	Brotherhood of Locomotive Engineers
BMT	Brooklyn-Manhattan Transit System
CA	Heavy Cruiser
CAB	Civil Aeronautics Board
CARE	Cooperative for American Relief Everywhere, Inc.
CBS	Columbia Broadcasting System
CCC	Commodity Credit Corporation
CCRAK	Covert, Clandestine and Related Activities in Korea
CDU	Christian Democratic Union
CEA	Council of Economic Advisers
CFR	Council of Foreign Relations
Chicoms	Chinese Communists
Chinats	Nationalist Chinese
CIA	Central Intelligence Agency
CINCPAC	Commander in Chief, Pacific Command

CINCUNC	Commander in Chief, United Nations Command
CIO	Congress of Industrial Organizations
CNO	Chief of Naval Operations
COCOM	Coordinating Committee of the Paris Consultation Group
CPX	Command Post Exercise
CRALOG	Council of Registered Relief Agencies Licensed for Operation in Germany
DEW	Distant Early Warning line
DNC	Democratic National Committee
DOD	Department of Defense
ECA	Economic Cooperation Administration
ECSC	European Coal and Steel Community
EDC	European Defense Community
EM	Eisenhower Manuscripts
EPC	European Political Community
EURATOM	European Atomic Energy Community
EVEREADY	U.S. military contingency plan in event Rhee pulled ROK troops out of U.N. command.
FAO	Food and Agriculture Organization
FBI	Federal Bureau of Investigation
FCC	Federal Communications Commission
FDA	Food and Drug Administration
FEPC	Fair Employment Practices Commission
FHA	Federal Housing Administration
FHA	Farmers Home Administration
FOA	Foreign Operations Administration
FPC	Federal Power Commission
FSA	Federal Security Administration
FTC	Federal Trade Commission
GAO	General Accounting Office
GATT	General Agreement on Tariffs and Trade
GDR	German Democratic Republic (Communist Germany)
GE	General Electric
G–4	Logistics section of divisional or higher staff
GOP	Grand Old Party (Republican Party)
GSA	General Services Administration
HEW	Department of Health, Education, and Welfare
HUAC	House Un-American Activities Committee
IBM	International Business Machines
IBRD	International Bank for Reconstruction and Development (World Bank)

ICA	International Cooperation Administration
ICBM	Intercontinental Ballistic Missile
ICC	Interstate Commerce Commission
IIA	International Information Administration
ILA	International Longshoremen's Association
ILO	International Labor Organization
IRBM	Intermediate Range Ballistic Missile
JCS	Joint Chiefs of Staff
MAAG	Military Assistance Advisory Group
MAC	Military Armistice Committee
MATS	Military Air Transport Service
MDAP	Mutual Defense Assistance Program
MEDO	Middle East Defense Organization
MRP	Movement Republicain Populaire
MSA	Mutual Security Administration
NAACP	National Association for the Advancement of Colored People
NAC	North Atlantic Council
NADA	National Automobile Dealers Association
NAM	National Association of Manufacturers
NATO	North Atlantic Treaty Organization
NBC	National Broadcasting Company
NCFE	National Committee for a Free Europe
NLRB	National Labor Relations Board
NNRC	Neutral Nations Repatriation Commission
NNSC	Neutral Nations Supervisory Commission
NRA	National Recovery Administration
NSC	National Security Council
OAS	Organization of American States
OCB	Operations Coordinating Board
ODM	Office of Defense Mobilization
OEEC	Organization for European Economic Cooperation
OPD	Operations Division
OTC	Organization for Trade Cooperation
OVERLORD	Code name for the cross-Channel Allied invasion of northwest Europe in the spring of 1944.
PJBD	Permanent Joint Board on Defense
PMA	Production and Marketing Administration
Point Four	International technical and capital assistance program initiated by the Truman Administration; *see also* Technical Cooperation Administration (TCA)

POL	Petroleum, Oil, Lubricants
POW	Prisoner of war
RAF	Royal Air Force
RCA	Radio Corporation of America
REA	Rural Electrification Administration
RNC	Republican National Committee
ROK	Republic of Korea
ROKA	Republic of Korea Army
SAC	Strategic Air Command
SACEUR	Supreme Allied Commander, Europe
SCUA	Suez Canal Users' Association
SEATO	Southeast Asia Treaty Organization
SEC	Securities and Exchange Commission
SED	Sozialistische Einheitspartei Deutschland
SHAEF	Supreme Headquarters, Allied Expeditionary Force
SHAPE	Supreme Headquarters Allied Powers, Europe
SPA	Southwestern Power Administration
SUNFED	Special United Nations Fund for Economic Development
TCA	Technical Cooperative Administration
TVA	Tennessee Valley Authority
UDF	United Defense Fund
U.K.	United Kingdom
UMT	Universal Military Training
U.N.	United Nations
UNC	United Nations Command
UNESCO	United Nations Educational, Scientific, and Cultural Organization
UNRWA	United Nations Relief and Works Agency
USIA	United States Information Agency
USIS	United States Information Service
USMA	United States Military Academy
USNA	United States Naval Academy
USO	United Service Organizations
USSR	Union of Soviet Socialist Republics
VA	Veterans Administration
VFC	Volunteer Freedom Corps
WAC	Women's Army Corps
WEU	Western European Union
WHCF	White House Central Files (Eisenhower's presidential records)

Chronology

1953

January 21 Washington. Appointments with Attorney General Brownell; U. E. Baughman (Chief, U.S. Secret Service—off the record). Receives Junior Police Boys Club of Denver, Colorado; Mr. and Mrs. J. B. Mintener. Lunch with Governors Thornton and Kohler, and S. Adams. Witnesses swearing-in of presidential appointees to White House staff and Cabinet members.

22 Washington. Appointments with White House staff; Colonel Carroll; Secretary Wilson (off the record); Sam Stern (Elks Club) and S. Adams; Major and Mrs. J. S. D. Eisenhower; F. Joseph Donohue. Witnesses swearing-in of Budget Director Dodge. Other appointments with E. J. Hughes (off the record); E. D. Eisenhower and E. N. Eisenhower; Attorney General Brownell and Secretary Humphrey; Colonel Cannon; General Collins and E. D. Johnson; Colonel and Mrs. Stack; Secretary Dulles; Senator H. A. Smith, Governor Driscoll, and S. Adams; General Cutler; Attorney General Brownell, Secretary Wilson, and Secretary Humphrey (off the record); G. Hauge.

23 Washington. Morning appointment with G. Hauge. Cabinet meeting. Lunch with Secretary Dulles, H. E. Stassen, Ambassador Lodge, and General Cutler.

Witnesses swearing-in of U.N. Ambassador Lodge. Afternoon appointments with Senator H. A. Smith, Secretary Durkin, and E. J. Hughes; Harold S. Vance, President of Studebaker Corporation; General Smith; Postmaster General Summerfield and John C. Allen (Traffic Manager, Sears Roebuck); H. J. Porter (RNC); Colonel Schulz.

24 Washington. Inspects White House dining room. Appointments with J. C. Hagerty (Press Secretary); A. W. Dulles; E. Doud and friends (off the record); Lieutenant General Taylor; Secretary Wilson; Commander Beach; Dr. Elson; C. D. Jackson (Publisher, *Fortune* Magazine), W. H. Jackson, and General Cutler; Budget Director Dodge.

25 Washington. Attends services at National Presbyterian Church.

26 Washington. Appointments with Legislative Leaders; H. E. Stassen and General Persons. Feeling cold symptoms, cancels appointments. Works on State of the Union Address.

27 Washington. Late morning appointment with H. E. Stassen. Afternoon reception at White House for Chiefs of Diplomatic Missions with Mrs. Eisenhower, Vice-President and Mrs. Nixon, and Secretary and Mrs. Dulles.

28 Washington. Witnesses swearing-in of Defense Secretary Wilson, Mutual Security Agency Director H. E. Stassen, and V. E. Peterson as Administrative Assistant to the President.

29 Washington. Morning appointments with Colonel Carroll; Commander Rigdon (Naval Aides' Office); Congressmen Van Zandt and Kearney, Frank Hilton (VFW), and Omar B. Ketchum (VFW). Receives invitation to University of Florida centennial celebration from University of Florida President J. Hillis Miller and the Florida congressional delegation. Appointment with General Cutler and J. S. Lay. National Security Council session. Afternoon appointment with Secretary McKay and Randolph Crossley. Works on State of the Union Address.

30 Washington. Breakfast with Secretary Dulles and H. E. Stassen. Morning appointment with Judge Web-

ster J. Oliver (Chief Judge, U.S. Customs Court). General Berry (Adjutant General, Texas) presents cowbell from Governor Shriver followed by appointments with Ambassador Lodge and J. A. McCone; Budget Director Dodge and G. Hauge. Cabinet meeting. Lunch with Senators Duff and Carlson, and Congressman Judd. Afternoon appointments with Robert McLean (President, Associated Press); David Beck, Roy Fruehauf, B. M. Seymour, and Arthur D. Condon to discuss problems in the trucking industry; Mrs. Emma Michie, Mrs. Clara Gebson, and Congressman Brooks; R. W. Ratton and State Senator Fleeman. Witnesses swearing-in of B. M. Shanley as Acting Special Counsel to the President. Appointments with Reverend Reuben K. Youngdahl; Dr. M. S. Eisenhower; Colonel Carroll; Secretary Durkin, Budget Director Dodge, G. Hauge, and S. Adams. To Broadcasting Room to make kinescope for American Legion Nationwide Spiritual Reawakening Program. Early evening appointment with Ambassador Allen.

31   Washington. Morning appointments with G. Hauge; General Persons; Congresswoman Rogers; Senator Capehart, Congressman Wolcott, S. Adams, G. Hauge, and General Persons; Don Mahon, Roger Rettig, Sam Powers, and Paul Frangen from National Independent Unions Council; Admiral Leahy; Governor Fine; W. Roberts (off the record); Colonel Schulz; Senator Taft (off the record). Lunch with W. E. Robinson.

February   1   Washington. Attends services at National Presbyterian Church with Mrs. Eisenhower. Visits National Gallery of Art with Japanese Ambassador Araki and D. E. Finley to view Japanese exhibition.

2   Washington. Appointments with General Persons (off the record); Admiral Radford. To Capitol with Mrs. Eisenhower and E. Doud to deliver State of the Union Address before Congress. Off-the-record appointment with Secretary McKay and Senators Cordon, Butler, Watkins, and Knowland. Witnesses swearing-in of Deputy Secretary of Defense Kyes. Other appointments with Budget Director Dodge, G. Hauge, A. S. Flemming, and H. S. Vance (ODM); General Bradley.

3   Washington. Morning appointments with Senator Daniel and Robert Storey (President, ABA); General Horkan; Secretary Durkin. Off-the-record appointments with E. D. Slater; J. Jackson and Colonel Schulz; U. E. Baughman. Appointment with Budget Director Dodge. Hosts stag luncheon for Senate leaders. Afternoon appointments with Senator Carlson and Future Farmers of America officers; General Collins; P. G. Hoffman; General Cutler.

4   Washington. Appointments with L. V. Finder; L. M. Pexton; Walker Buckner. National Security Council session followed by appointments with General Persons and Governor and Mrs. Persons; Budget Director Dodge and S. Adams; Chan Gurney (CAB).

5   Washington. Attends International Council for Christian Leadership prayer breakfast with Senator Carlson at the Mayflower Hotel. Appointments with Senators Knowland and Kuchel; General Persons and officers of the American Medical Association; Ambassador Aldrich; Admiral Hewitt; Ambassador Wiley; Harry Lundeberg (Union Leader). Hosts luncheon for House of Representatives leaders. Afternoon appointments with Melvyn Pitzele (N.Y. State Board of Mediation); Senator Mundt, Pastor Poling, and Paul Walmsey. Congressman Scudder presents a redwood gavel. Appointment with Postmaster General Summerfield.

6   Washington. Morning appointments with S. Adams, Budget Director Dodge, A. S. Flemming, General Persons, G. Hauge, and V. E. Peterson; Ambassador Lodge; General Hurley. Cabinet meeting. Hosts stag luncheon for Supreme Court Justices. Afternoon appointments with High Commissioner Conant (Germany); W. Reuther and D. J. McDonald; Secretary Talbott and Robert C. Sprague (RNC, New York).

7   Washington. Morning appointments with American Society of Newspaper Editors delegation; Mr. and Mrs. Tex McCrary. Poses for photographs in Fish Room. Appointments with Jack Benny and Earl H. Gammons (Vice-President, CBS); James Csatari (artist).

8   Washington. Attends services with Mrs. Eisenhower and Colonel Schulz at New York Avenue Presby-

terian Church. Unveils original first draft of Emancipation Proclamation in Lincoln Parlor of church.

9   Washington. Morning appointments with Legislative Leaders; Secretary Dulles and H. E. Stassen; Boy Scouts of America officials and members; American Municipal Association delegation. Afternoon appointments with Louisiana Purchase Sesquicentennial Commission officials; Secretary Weeks; Mutual Security Evaluation Project Group.

10 Washington. Appointment with John H. Whitney. Congressmen Ayres and Bolton and Lyle O. Snader present model sailing boat. Appointments with General Persons and Maine congressional delegation; American Farm Bureau Federation Board of Directors; S. Adams, J. C. Hagerty, and General Persons; Governor Martin; Methodist Committee for Overseas Relief members; Secretary Wilson. Lunch with Eugene Black (President, International Bank). Afternoon appointments with R. P. Burrows; Dr. Robert F. Chandler, Jr., John Elliott, and S. Adams. Attends advance screening of film on Mahatma Gandhi with Mrs. Eisenhower and Commander Beach.

11 Washington. Receives miniature dictating machine to commemorate Thomas A. Edison's birthday. Appointments with General Persons; Lincoln Day Committee representatives; John Carroll Society members; Admiral Leahy. National Security Council session. Hosts luncheon for senators. Afternoon appointments with General Smith, Secretaries Durkin, Weeks, and Humphrey, Senators Taft and Millikin, Congressman Reed, H. Linder, P. Arnow, H. E. Stassen, T. D. Morse, S. W. Anderson, and Budget Director Dodge; Governor Shivers, Weldon Hart, and S. Adams; Attorney General Brownell; Budget Director Dodge, A. S. Flemming, H. S. Vance, J. Brownley, G. Hauge, and S. Adams.

12 Washington. Delegates from Rutgers University and Abraham Lincoln Association present collection of Abraham Lincoln's work. Appointments with Association of American Railroads committee; Bishop Decatur Ward Nichols; Secretary Wilson, Attorney General Brownell, Postmaster General Summerfield, and General Bradley. Cabinet meeting. Appoint-

ments with General Persons and Mr. Alfred Strelsin. To Lincoln Memorial with Mrs. Eisenhower for wreath-laying ceremony. Appointment with Secretary Humphrey. Lunch with W. S. Gifford.

13 Washington. Late morning appointment with Secretary Dulles. Hosts luncheon for congressional members.

14 Washington. Morning appointments with Secretary Benson; Advisory Committee on Government Organization; Edgar Bergen. To Burning Tree Country Club for golf with Colonel Belshe, General Bradley, and R. V. Fleming.

15 Washington. Attends services at National Presbyterian Church with Dr. M. S. Eisenhower. Afternoon appointment and dinner with Secretary Humphrey.

16 Washington. Appointments with Legislative Leaders, Senator H. A. Smith, and Congressman Chiperfield; Secretary Weeks. Witnesses swearing-in of C. D. Jackson as Administrative Assistant to the President. Off-the-record appointment with General Cutler and J. S. Lay. Telephone conversation with Louis Bauer. Off-the-record appointment with Secretary Benson and Senator Carlson. Hosts luncheon for congressional members. Afternoon appointments with Atomic Energy Commission members G. Dean, Thomas E. Murray, Eugene M. Zuckert, and Henry Dewolf Smyth; Special Committee of National Security Council on Atomic Energy. To Congressional Club with Mrs. Eisenhower and Colonel Schulz for early evening reception.

17 Washington. Morning appointments with Senator Hickenlooper and Congressman Cole (off the record); Secretary Benson, General Persons, and Senators Aiken and Carlson. News and radio conference. Receives commemoration medal from Inaugural Committee. Late morning appointments with Dr. Caradine R. Hooton (Executive Secretary, Methodist Church Board of Temperance); Secretary Wilson; A. E. Stevenson and S. Adams. Hosts luncheon for congressional members. Receives delegation representing National Council of Chief State School Officers. Afternoon appointment with General Prentiss. Off-the-record appointments with A. S. Flemming and O. C. Hobby; General Truscott; Secretary

Weeks and B. M. Shanley; G. Hauge and A. Nielson; General Persons; Postmaster General Summerfield. Walks to White House with A. Nielson.

18 Washington. Appointments with Secretary Dulles (off the record); D. K. E. Bruce; General Carl R. Gray (VA Administrator); O. Ryan; National Security Council session. Hosts luncheon for senators. Afternoon appointments with Senator George; Senators Hoey and H. A. Smith, and Congressman Alexander; General Bradley (off the record).

19 Washington. Appointments with Legislative Leaders; J. A. McCone and S. Adams (off the record); Ambassador Whelan; H. Wendell Endicott. Receives delegation from Illinois Bankers Association and G. Hauge. Appointments with H. E. Stassen and William McNeal Rand; Budget Director Dodge (off the record). Hosts luncheon for senators.

20 Washington. Morning appointments with Senator Malone, Harmar D. Denny and S. Adams; N. A. Rockefeller, S. Adams, and Dr. M. S. Eisenhower; Secretary Benson, General Persons, and Dr. M. S. Eisenhower; Ambassador Leslie Knox Munro (New Zealand) and Raymond D. Muir (Division of Protocol). Cabinet meeting. Lunch with N. A. Rockefeller and Dr. M. S. Eisenhower. Afternoon appointments with congressional members of Missouri Basin Commission; J. C. Hagerty and Colonel Schulz. Receives winners of 6th annual Voice of Democracy Contest; Governor McKeldin and Judge S. E. Sobeloff. Off-the-record appointments with Admiral Strauss and S. Adams; B. M. Shanley and General Persons; Colonel Carroll; S. Adams.

21 Washington. Appointment with Congressman Brown. Off-the-record appointments with S. Adams, Secretary Dulles, S. Adams, C. F. Willis, Donald Lourie, and E. J. Hughes; R. Steffan and H. G. Crim; General Sturgis; Secretary Dulles, Secretary Humphrey, W. M. Martin, General Cutler, and C. D. Jackson. To Burning Tree Country Club for golf.

22 Washington. Attends services at Christ Church in Alexandria, Virginia, with Mrs. Eisenhower and Senator Byrd. Dinner at White House with General Cutler.

23   Washington. To Burning Tree Country Club for golf. Evening visit at with R. L. Johnson.

24   Washington. Morning appointments with National Symphony Orchestra representatives Howard Mitchell, Carson G. Frailey, and Gregory Carmichael; W. M. Canady; Helen Waller, Doris Friedman, O. M. and H. R. Reid, and delegates of the New York Herald Tribune High School Forum; Donald C. Cook (Chairman, Securities and Exchange Commission); Ambassador Anibal Jara (Chile) and J. F. Simmons; C. L. Draper; John W. Snyder. Hosts luncheon for congressional members. Afternoon appointments with G. Hauge and A. S. Flemming; General Shanker Shum Shere Jung Bahadur Rana (Nepal Ambassador) and J. F. Simmons. Receives invitation to a dinner from Gridiron Club members. Off-the-record appointment with Attorney General Brownell and E. Lombard.

25   Washington. Appointment with N. A. Rockefeller, Dr. M. S. Eisenhower, and A. S. Flemming. Poses for photographs with Congressman Keating and M. B. Folsom. Meeting to discuss soil conservation and flood control. Appointments with General Cutler and J. S. Lay; New Jersey congressional delegation and General Persons; Cabinet meeting. News conference. Hosts luncheon for senators. Afternoon appointments with General Covell and Bernard McKenna (off the record); Frank Holman and Alfred Schweppe. National Security Council session. Off-the-record appointments with Roger Lewis; Attorney General Brownell.

26   Washington. Morning appointments with H. E. Stassen; Dr. R. C. Hutchinson; Ambassador and Mrs. Dillon; Congressman McGregor. Hosts conference and luncheon to discuss federal-state relations. To MATS terminal with Mrs. Eisenhower en route to Augusta, Georgia. To Augusta National Golf Club.

27   Augusta, Georgia. To Augusta National Golf Club.

28   Augusta, Georgia. To Augusta National Golf Club with E. Dudley, E. D. Slater, and John Budinger. Presents portrait of R. T. Jones (by Eisenhower) to Jones.

| March | 1 | Augusta, Georgia. Attends services at Reid Memorial Presbyterian Church with Mrs. Eisenhower. To MATS terminal with Mrs. Eisenhower and party. |

March   1   Augusta, Georgia. Attends services at Reid Memorial Presbyterian Church with Mrs. Eisenhower. To MATS terminal with Mrs. Eisenhower and party.

2   Washington. Appointments with Legislative Leaders; staff meeting; General Cutler and J. S. Lay; Admiral Strauss; delegation from Saudi Arabia, including Prince Faisal. Hosts luncheon for congressional members. Receives Supreme Lodge, Order of Ahepa, officers, followed by appointment with H. Darby. Off-the-record appointments with Secretary Humphrey and Secretary Weeks; J. F. Simmons; G. Hauge.

3   Washington. Appointment with Admiral Lynde D. McCormick (Supreme Allied Commander, Atlantic). Receives Advisory Commission on Independence Historical Park. Other appointments with Daniel Bell (H. E. Stassen and G. Hauge—off the record); Mayor Joseph S. Clark and H. E. Stassen; Major Draper; William Archer; General Van Fleet. Awards General Van Fleet Oak Leaf Cluster and hosts luncheon in his honor. Receives officers of National Association of State Directors of Veterans Affairs followed by appointments with Foreign Minister of Norway Halvard Lange, Ambassador of Norway Wilhelm Munthe de Morgenstierne, and Secretary Dulles; Secretary Wilson. To home of General and Mrs. Collins with Mrs. Eisenhower for dinner honoring the Van Fleets.

4   Washington. Morning appointments with Senator Goldwater; Governor Kennon; Edward F. Howrey (Federal Trade Commissioner appointee), S. Adams, and B. M. Shanley (off the record); Edgar B. Brossard (U.S. Tariff Commission member); National Security Council session. Witnesses swearing-in of Federal Civil Defense Administrator V. E. Peterson. Appointment with E. Lansing Ray. Hosts luncheon for congressional members. Afternoon appointments with Secretary Dulles; Minister of War Cyro Espirto Santo Cardozo (Brazil), Ambassador Walther Moreira Salles (Brazil), J. M. Cabot; Senator Neely and Congressman Mollohan; Postmaster General Summerfield, Albert J. Robertson, and Ormonde A. Kieb; A. Eden, R. A. Butler, and Secretary Dulles.

5 Washington. Appointments with Norris E. Dodd (Director General, U.N. Food and Agriculture Organization); F. Lazarus, Jr.; Jess Moss (National Commander, Jewish War Veterans) and Bernard Weitzer (National Legislative Director); J. C. Hagerty (off the record). News conference. Off-the-record appointment with Robert L. Garner (Vice-President, International Bank for Reconstruction and Development), followed by appointment with General Crittenberger. Lunch with B. M. Shanley. To Statler Hotel to address American Retail Federation luncheon.

6 Washington. Off-the-record appointments with C. D. Jackson and General Cutler; Adrian C. Tolley; G. Hauge. Appointments with Senator Knowland and E. D. Coblendz (Publisher, *San Francisco Call-Bulletin*); receives illuminated scroll from Senators Ferguson and Potter and Michigan delegation from Americans of Polish Descent; Budget Director Dodge (off the record); R. H. Hyde and S. Adams. Off-the-record appointments with General Vandenberg; Secretary Wilson; O. C. Hobby. Cabinet meeting followed by appointment with A. Eden, Ambassador Makins, Ambassador Aldrich, and Secretary Dulles. Hosts stag luncheon in honor of A. Eden, followed by conference. Afternoon appointments with General Rafael L. Trujillo (Foreign Minister, Dominican Republic), Ambassador Luis F. Thomen (Dominican Republic), and J. F. Simmons; Dr. Roy A. Burkhart (President, World Neighbors, Inc.) and Senator Bricker; H. E. Stassen; dentist.

7 Washington. Morning appointments with Congressman Judd; William Heilprin and James A. Carr (Franklin & Co., Opticians—off the record); S. Adams and John Steelman (off the record); General Van Fleet; C. D. Jackson and Elliott Newcomb (Secretary-General, World Veterans Federation); Dr. Elson.

8 Washington. Attends services with Mrs. Eisenhower at National Presbyterian Church.

9 Washington. Appointments with Legislative Leaders; A. Eden, Ambassador Makins, and General Smith; General Cutler and J. S. Lay; Ambassador Dunn; John L. Sullivan (former Secretary of the Navy); Congressman Trimble, F. A. Teague, Ruth T.

Skewes, and S. Adams. Hosts luncheon for congressional members. Afternoon appointments with Secretary Wilson; representatives from American Bankers Association; Attorney General Brownell, John B. Stoddart, and Edward W. Scruggs (off the record); L. W. Douglas. Late afternoon tea with Mrs. Eisenhower in honor of Madame Chaing Kai-shek.

10   Washington. Receives golf glasses from W. A. Heilprin and J. A. Carr; Congressman Bennett; Dr. Wendell Phillips (President, American Foundation for the Study of Man) and J. F. Simmons; 4-H Club national award winners; H. Ford II; Foreign Affairs Minister Joseph M. A. H. Luns (Netherlands), Ambassador D. H. van Roijen (Netherlands), and General Smith; Senator Capehart, G. Hauge, and General Persons; Ted Eckles (Chairman, Colorado Game and Fish Commission), T. L. Kimball, and S. Adams; Ambassador Aldrich (off the record). Hosts luncheon for congressional members.

11   Washington. Witnesses swearing-in of Housing and Home Finance Agency Administrator A. M. Cole. Appointments with Foreign Minister Pyun Yung Tai (Korea), Ambassador You Chan Yang (Korea), and J. F. Simmons; Captain Burke and Colonel Charles Boyer (Reserve Officers Association); General Hull and H. A. Byroade; National Security Council session; civilian consultants to National Security Council.

12   Washington. Appointments with Budget Director Dodge, S. Adams, and General Persons (off the record); Ralph Rose (American Friends' Service Committee); Harry McDonald (Chairman, Reconstruction Finance Corporation); Congressman Andresen and Alfred Larson (Chairman, Plowing Contest); L. M. Pexton; O. F. Clarke and S. Adams; Felix E. Wormser (Vice-President, St. Joseph Lead Co.). Presents Congressional Medal of Honor to Corporal Duane E. Dewey. Hosts luncheon for congressional members. Appointments with Attorney General Brownell and Vernon Thompson (Wisconsin Attorney General); Lord Ismay and Secretary Dulles; A. S. Flemming, G. Hauge, J. Brownlee, H. S. Vance, and C. Kendall.

13   Washington. Appointments with H. E. Stassen (off the record); James Kemper (President, Lumberman's Mutual Insurance Co.). Witnesses swearing-in of Assistant Federal Civil Defense Administrator K. Howard, followed by appointment with H. J. Porter. Shakes hands with Mrs. Max Freedman and Mr. and Mrs. Seymour Freedman. Cabinet meeting, followed by appointments with E. A. Johnston; Charles R. Sligh, Jr. (President, National Association of Manufacturers); Attorney General Brownell and L. A. Rover. Hosts luncheon for congressional members. Hosts dinner with Mrs. Eisenhower in honor of Lord and Lady Ismay.

14   Washington. Morning appointment with Secretary Weeks. Receives Advisory Committee on Government Organization, joined by Secretaries McKay, Weeks, and Humphrey, W. P. Rogers, Ybgvar Brynildssen (Acting Administrator, Small Defense Plants Administration), and Edward T. Dickinson (Vice-Chairman, N. S. R. B.). Departs with O. C. Hobby for Statler Hotel to address AMA House of Delegates members. Appointment with Colonel Carroll. To Burning Tree Country Club for golf.

15   Washington. No official appointments.

16   Washington. Morning appointments with Vice-President Nixon, Senators Taft, Bridges, Knowland, and Millikin, S. Adams, General Persons, and Congressmen Martin, Halleck, Arends, and Wolcott; Secretary Dulles; General Gruenther; General Cutler and J. S. Lay. Hosts luncheon for congressional members. Afternoon appointments with General Pierre Louis Bodet (Assistant Chief of Staff, Supreme Headquarters Allied Powers Europe); Foreign Minister Paul Van Zeeland (Belgium), Ambassador Silvercruys, Secretary Dulles, and L. Merchant.

17   Washington. Appointments with H. E. Stassen and Reverend C. O. Johnson; Ambassador John Joseph Hearne (Ireland). Receives invitation to Young Republican National Convention in South Dakota. Receives members of Players, Inc. of Catholic University of America followed by appointments with Secretary Dulles, A. W. Dulles, E. J. Hughes, and C. D. Jackson; William Randolph Hearst and his

mother; Senators Butler and Beall. Signs Armed Forces Day Proclamation. Appointments with Secretary Wilson; Secretary Dulles. Hosts luncheon for congressional members. Appointments with General Cutler; T. E. Stephens, J. Rowley, and Major Draper (off the record).

18   Washington. Appointments with R. P. Burroughs; Senator Ives and Italian American representatives; Senator Bricker; Reverend Charles W. Lowrey and Father Joseph E. Gedra; Ambassador Manuel J. Tello Baurraud (Mexico) and J. F. Simmons; Reverend P. B. (Tubby) Clayton, Boulton Smith, and J. F. Simmons; National Security Council session. To Mayflower Hotel with Secretary Weeks to address members of Business Advisory Council. Hosts luncheon for congressional members. Appointments with S. Adams and J. C. Doerfer (off the record); A. B. Kline.

19   Washington. Appointments with Preston Hotchkis (President, Founders Insurance Co.); W. S. Paley; Senator Carlson and Congressman Hope; J. C. Hagerty (off the record). News conference followed by appointments with Mrs. Oswald B. Lord (U.N. Representative, Human Rights Commission) and Herman Phleger (Legal Advisor, Department of State); Lord James Milner and Ambassador Makins; Harold S. Vance; Ambassador White; General Clay. Hosts luncheon for congressional members. Witnesses swearing-in of CEA member A. F. Burns. Appointments with Attorney General Brownell, Senator Cordon, John F. Raper, and Lloyd H. Burke; Colonel Carroll (off the record).

20   Washington. Breakfast with National Security Council consultants. Appointments with Congressman Rivers and General Persons; North Dakota Republican State Senators; Cabinet meeting; Dr. Ernst Reuter, H. Freeman Matthews, Dr. Heinz L. Krekeler (German Diplomat), and Leo M. Cherne to discuss Berlin refugee problem; Ambassador Lodge. Hosts stag luncheon for Special Committee on Organization to the Secretary of Defense. Appointments with H. E. Stassen; General Cristóbel Guzman Cardenas (Mexican Embassy Military Attaché); Congresswo-

man Bolton. Off-the-record appointments with A. S. Flemming; Dr. M. S. Eisenhower; and S. H. High.

21 Washington. Off-the-record appointment with C. D. Jackson. Appointments with Secretary Weeks and his staff; High Commissioner Frank E. Midkiff (Trust Territory, Pacific Islands). Receives Bible from Bible Committee, St. John's lodge. To Burning Tree Country Club for golf. Receives Ambassador Silvercruys, Mrs. Brian McMahon, and Mrs. Georgette Pisart (off the record).

22 Washington. Off-the-record appointment with Secretary Dulles and Attorney General Brownell. Attends services at National Presbyterian Church with Mrs. Eisenhower. Off-the-record lunch with W. E. Robinson and P. G. Hoffman.

23 Washington. Off-the-record appointment with Attorney General Brownell. Appointments with Legislative Leaders; Prince Faisal, Ambassador al-Faquih, Shiekh Ibrahim Suleiman (Assistant to Prince Faisal), Sheikh Ali Reza (U.N. Interpreter), and J. F. Simmons. Witnesses swearing-in of Civil Service Commission Chairman P. Young followed by appointments with General Cutler and J. S. Lay; Zionist leaders to discuss U.S.-Israeli affairs; Ambassador Schoenfeld. Hosts luncheon for congressional members. Afternoon appointments with Generals Bradley and Vandenberg; Madame Vijaya Laksmi Pandit (U.N. Representative from India) and Secretary Dulles; Secretary Dulles. Hosts informal dinner with Mrs. Eisenhower for General and Mrs. Van Fleet.

24 Washington. Breakfast with Secretaries Dulles, Wilson, and Humphrey, and H. E. Stassen. Appointments with F. K. White; U.S. UNESCO members. To old State Department building to open Advertising Council's White House conference. Afternoon appointments with Christian M. Ravndal (American Minister to Hungary); Ambassador Ras Imru Haile Sellassie (Ethiopia), R. D. Muir, and Addimau Tesemma (Ethiopian Embassy); Congressman Celler; Mr. and Mrs. Reno Odlin, Mr. and Mrs. Henry Gonyea, and Mr. and Mrs. Frank Inglis; Mr. and Mrs. Aaron W. Berg; H. E. Stassen and Walter M. Ringer (Denmark Evaluation Team); Mutual Securi-

ty Evaluation Team members. Hosts luncheon for congressional member. Appointments with Vegetable Growers Association of America; Secretary Wilson; J. Rowley, T. E. Stephens, Commander Beach, and Major Draper (off the record).

25 Washington. Breakfast with freshman Republican congressmen. Appointments with Marshall E. Miller, Rufus H. Wilson, Alvin M. Keller, and David F. Schlothauer to discuss veterans' problems; National Security Council session; Mr. and Mrs. William Groat (off the record); R. McLean. Off-the-record appointment with S. Adams and S. Spencer. To home of Senator and Mrs. Taft for reception in honor of Mrs. Eisenhower.

26 Washington. Breakfast with freshman Republican congressmen. Receives invitation to Armed Forces Day dinner. Appointments with Lithuanian American Council; J. C. Hagerty (off the record). News conference. To USS *Williamsburg* for French-American talks. Hosts luncheon in honor of Prime Minister René Mayer (France). Appointments with Attorney General Brownell, Clifford Raemer, and Ed Scheuffler (off the record); H. Gibson and Abba Schwartz; Senator Ferguson; Air Force Marshal Arthur T. Harris (RAF) and family.

27 Washington. Appointments with Paul M. Herzog (NLRB Chairman) and S. Adams; Raymond Blattenberger and S. Adams (off the record); Oklahoma delegation to discuss Foss and Cobb Creek Dams; Secretary Humphrey (off the record); Cabinet meeting; Raymond Loewy; David M. Proctor and Charles S. Rhyne; Ambassador Johnson; Prince Bernhard and Dr. J. H. van Roijen of Netherlands and General Smith. Hosts luncheon for congressional members. Afternoon appointments with C. N. Hilton, Admiral Ross T. McIntire (President, President's Committee on Employment of the Physically Handicapped); Senator Carlson and William Thatcher; Joseph Campbell (Treasurer, Columbia University); General Snyder and H. A. Rusk; C. W. Roberts, S. Adams, and J. C. Hagerty (off the record).

28 Washington. General Willard Paul; General Clark; Frontiers of America members. Attends French-

American talks. To Burning Tree Country Club for golf with Senators Symington and Fulbright and Congressman Westland. Receives Columbia University Club and Glee Club members with Mrs. Eisenhower.

29 Washington. Attends services at Georgetown Presbyterian Church with Mrs. Eisenhower. Off-the-record appointments with Secretary Dulles; W. T. Faricy, W. S. Franklin, and F. G. Gurley; Attorney General Brownell. Hosts dinner for Field Marshal Viscount Montgomery of Alamein.

30 Washington. Morning appointments with Legislative Leaders; General Bradley; General Cutler and J. S. Lay; Senator Johnson and Colonel and Mrs. Royal N. Baker; Clark M. Eichelberger (Executive Director, American Association for the United Nations, Inc.); Jacob Blaustein; Mr. and Mrs. Robert Cromwell. Hosts luncheon for congressional members. Afternoon appointments with Attorney General Brownell and Judge Lester L. Cecil (off the record); David Morse (Director General, ILO) and Secretary Durkin; Senator Thye, A. Nelson, Secretary Benson, and S. Adams; General John S. Seybold (Governor, Panama Canal Zone); S. Adams and G. Hauge (off the record); P. G. Hoffman.

31 Washington. Appointments with C. D. Jackson (off the record); A. F. Burns, S. Adams, and G. Hauge; National Security Council session. Speaks in Rose Garden to planning committee on Governmental Functions and Fiscal Resources. Appointment with Admiral Nimitz. Hosts luncheon for congressional members. National Security Council session.

April 1 Washington. Breakfast with Congressmen Taber and Wigglesworth. Appointments with Mayor and representatives of Industrial Development Committee of Lawrence, Massachusetts; C. A. Herter, Edmund V. Keville, and Frederick M. Dearborn, Jr.; Attorney General Brownell and Judge Stanley Barnes (off the record). Photographs with Mary Pickford. Appointments with Veterans of Foreign Wars members; Malcolm Muir (Publisher, *Newsweek*) and S. Adams. To Burning Tree Country Club for golf with J. E. McClure, General Parks, and Senator Bush. Off-the-record appointments with Attorney General Brownell; A. S. Flemming. Hosts dinner with Mrs. Eisenhower for Mr. and Mrs. Samuel Goldwyn.

2   Washington. Receives members from German Bundestag. Appointments with Senator Taft; Irving Brown (European Representative, AFL); Ralph Cake (former RNC member) (off the record); Congressman Hillings and Frank Jorgenson (Chairman, Los Angeles Republican Committee); E. J. Bermingham; Clark Griffith; Duke Shoop. Lunch with Congressmen Simpson and Reed and G. D. Morgan. Afternoon appointments with H. E. Stassen (off the record); Secretary Dulles, Bishop G. Bromley Oxnam, Dr. O. Frederick Nolde, Dr. Franklin Fry, and Reverend Bilheimer; Ambassador Bohlen and Secretary Dulles; J. C. Hagerty (off the record). News conference.

3   Washington. Appointments with C. D. Jackson (off the record); David L. Cole (Director, Federal Mediation and Conciliation Service); Ambassador Luce; Cabinet meeting. Attends Good Friday services with Mrs. Eisenhower at National Presbyterian Church.

4   Washington. Appointments with Admiral Jerauld Wright; I. Geist; Judge Hall and Mrs. Richard Derby; Governor Langlie; Secretary Wilson. To Burning Tree Country Club for golf with Stanley Rowe, Senator Taft, and J. E. McClure.

5   Washington. Attends services at National Presbyterian Church with Mrs. Eisenhower, E. Doud, and B. T. Eisenhower.

6   Washington. Appointments with General Bradley; Secretary Dulles; N. A. Rockefeller and A. S. Flemming. Attends Easter egg rolling with Mrs. Eisenhower, B. T. Eisenhower, D. D. Eisenhower II, and B. A. Eisenhower. Appointment with Attorney General Brownell and Dallas S. Townsend (off the record). Off-the-record luncheon at Army-Navy Club. To General Bradley's home with Mrs. Eisenhower.

7   Washington. Breakfast with Senator Bridges. Receives United Defense Fund members. Appointments with Keith Funston and Richard M. Crooks to

discuss New York Stock Exchange; Senator Fulbright. To Statler Hotel to address United Defense Fund meeting. Attends German-American talks. Lunch with General Cutler and J. S. Lay. Afternoon appointments with H. E. Stassen (off the record); Postmaster General Summerfield (off the record); Secretary Wilson and N. A. Rockefeller; Senator Wiley and Dr. N. R. Danielien; Secretary Humphrey and General Burgess; Louis Marx; A. Nielson.

8   Washington. Appointments with W. H. Jackson; W. H. Draper; Warren C. Giles (President, National Baseball League); L. J. Rosenwald; National Security Council session. To Burning Tree Country Club for golf with Jim Black, Ned Burnham, and Herb Blunck.

9   Washington. Morning appointments with H. E. Stassen (off the record); Secretary Stevens; Associated Church Press editors; General Cutler, S. Adams, and G. D. Morgan (off the record); General Cutler and Henry J. Tasca (Special Representative, Korean Economic Affairs); members of committee to replace RNC Chairman; Del E. Webb (Owner, NY Yankees); Foreign Minister Moshe Sharret, Ambassador Eban, and R. D. Muir; High Commissioner Conant; Secretary Dulles, Chancellor Konrad Adenauer (West Germany), Dr. Walter Hallstein, and High Commissioner Conant. Attends German-American talks. Hosts luncheon for Chancellor Adenauer. Afternoon appointments with Senator Millikin, Congressman Chenoweth, and Leon Snyder; Advisory Committee on Government Organization; Spyros P. Skouras (President, Twentieth Century-Fox); Senator Knowland; J. B. Mintener; John J. McCloy and General Clay.

10   Washington. Appointments with Eugene C. Pulliam (Publisher, *Indianapolis Star and News*); Secretary Dulles and S. Adams (off the record); Cabinet meeting; Warren L. Pierson (U.S. Representative, Tripartite Commission on German Debts) and B. M. Shanley; Dr. Fahrettin Kerim Gokay (Mayor, Istanbul, Turkey), Ambassador Feridun C. Erkin (Turkey), and R. D. Muir; Thomas Herbert, Harry Cain, and S. Adams. Hosts luncheon in honor of New York Governor Thomas E. Dewey. Appointments with At-

torney General Brownell, Walter Brauckhausen, John O. Henderson, James W. Dorsey, Hartwell Davis, Sherman F. Furey, A. Pratt Kessler, and Charles Rugg (off the record); Michiko Murayama, Tomiko Murayama, Mr. and Mrs. Shinichi Kamimura (Minister, Japanese Embassy), Isami Suzukawa, and R. D. Muir; Foreign Minister Ato Aklilou (Ethiopia), A. Tesemma, and R. D. Muir; H. R. Reid; General George Erskine (Commander in Chief, Eastern Command, U.K.); RNC members; Judge Jacques Rueff; General Norstad; R. A. Roberts; S. W. Richardson (off the record).

11   Washington. Morning appointments with Senators Holland and Smathers; Advisory Committee on Government Organization. Witnesses swearing-in of Secretary of Health, Education, and Welfare Hobby, followed by appointments with Ambassador White; J. A. Farley; Darryl Zanuck (Vice-President, Twentieth Century-Fox); R. H. Demmler and S. Adams (off the record); Secretary Wilson; General Smith, Dr. M. S. Eisenhower, and E. J. Hughes; Budget Director Dodge and S. Adams. To Burning Tree Country Club for golf with Roger Whiteford, W. T. Faricy, and General Twining. Attends Gridiron Dinner at Statler Hotel.

12   Washington. Appointments with E. J. Hughes (off the record); Advisory Committee on Government Organization. Attends services at National Presbyterian Church with Mrs. Eisenhower and B. T. Eisenhower. Addresses Organization of the American States Council. Off-the-record appointment with General Smith, E. J. Hughes, and Paul Nitze (State Department). To Statler Hotel with Mrs. Eisenhower for reception in honor of Gridiron Club President and Mrs. Duke Shoop.

13   Washington. Appointment with National Defense Minister René Jean Pleven (French Republic) and Ambassador Henri Bonnet (French Republic). To MATS terminal with Mrs. Eisenhower en route to Augusta, Georgia.

14   Augusta, Georgia. No official appointments.

15   Augusta, Georgia. No official appointments.

16   Washington. Arrives at White House from Augusta, Georgia. Off-the-record appointment with Secretary Hobby. To Statler Hotel for American Society of Newspaper Editors luncheon. Delivers nationwide radio and television broadcast. Attends baseball season opener at Griffith Stadium. To MATS terminal en route to Salisbury, North Carolina. Speaks at Rowan County Bicentennial Celebration. Enplanes for Augusta, Georgia.

17   Augusta, Georgia. No official appointments.

18   Augusta, Georgia. No official appointments.

19   Augusta, Georgia. No official appointments.

20   Augusta, Georgia. No official appointments.

21   Augusta, Georgia. No official appointments. Departs for Washington, D.C.

22   Washington. Appointments with General Cutler and J. S. Lay; E. R. Black; Charles A. Case and Mr. and Mrs. Kenneth Smith; Postmaster General Summerfield and Colonel Harold Riegelman; N. A. Rockefeller; National Security Council session; Senator Watkins and General Persons (off the record); Vice-President Nixon and General Cutler (off the record); G. Hauge; Congressman Harvey; Senators Carlson and Schoeppel and H. Darby; General Smith. Hosts dinner for Professor and Mrs. Milton S. Osborne.

23   Washington. Breakfast with Congressman Martin, Senator Taft, N. A. Rockefeller, R. M. Kyes, and General Persons. Appointments with Legislative Leaders; J. C. Hagerty (off the record). News conference, followed by appointments with P. Young; Ambassador Fernando Berckemeyer (Peru), Admiral Contra Almirante Roque Saldias, and J. F. Simmons. Presents Citation for Outstanding Service to Secretary McKay, followed by appointments with L. O. Douglas; D. Beck, R. Fruehauf, B. M. Seymour, and A. D. Condon; Congressman Jensen and A. M. Piper; Congressman Hagen and his brothers.

24   Washington. Appointments with Secretary Talbott; Congressman Howell, Beverly L. Carson and Joyce Carson. Witnesses swearing-in of Assistant Secretary of the Interior F. E. Wormser. Appointments with

C. S. Thomas; Cabinet meeting; Ambassador Lodge (off the record); Attorney General Brownell; A. W. Dulles. Addresses Republican Women's Spring Conference at Statler Hotel. Afternoon appointments with Senator Carlson; Attorney General Brownell and Judges Julius J. Hoffman and Win G. Knoch (off the record); Senator Flanders; Secretary Benson.

25   Washington. Appointments with General Cutler (off the record); J. S. Copley and William Shea (Vice-President, Copley Press); Ambassador Taft; Ralph Bard. To Burning Tree Country Club for golf with Senator Bridges and Congressmen Arends and Simpson. Hosts dinner with Mrs. Eisenhower for Admiral and Señora Ernani do Amaral Peixoto (Governor, Rio de Janeiro, Brazil).

26   Washington. Attends services at National Presbyterian Church with Mrs. Eisenhower. Attends brunch at Mayflower Hotel in honor of San Jacinto. Off-the-record appointment with P. G. Hoffman. Off-the-record dinner with P. G. Hoffman, Mr. and Mrs. G. E. Allen, and James Lemon.

27   Washington. Morning appointments with Legislative Leaders; E. A. Johnston; M. C. Taylor; Frank Hecht (President, Navy League); Nathan Cummings and Roland Tognazzini (Consolidated Grocers Corporation). Lunch with Judge Hall, followed by appointments with Judge Hall, S. Adams, General Persons, and C. F. Willis (off the record); Senator Carlson and Mr. and Mrs. Henry Blake; Secretaries Dulles and Humphrey, and H. E. Stassen; A. C. Jacobs. To Capitol Theater with Mrs. Eisenhower for a performance of *La Boheme*.

28   Washington. Receives Washington Ministerial Union of Washington, D.C. members. Off-the-record appointment with Walter Schreiber and S. Adams. Receives representatives of national conservation and natural resource management organizations, followed by appointments with Dr. Israel Goldstein (President, American Jewish Congress); Secretary Dulles (off the record); National Security Council session; Senator Duff, P. T. Sharples, and M. H. Taylor; Attorney General Brownell, Joseph Lesh, Francis Van Alstine, Raleigh Stevenson, and Fred Kaess

(off the record); Mrs. Walter F. Dillingham; Congressman Arends and Dave Merwin. Off-the-record appointments with B. M. Shanley; S. Adams, Generals Cutler and Persons, C. D. Jackson, and J. C. Hagerty; G. Hauge; E. J. Hughes.

29   Washington. Appointments with Senator Ferguson, Harvey Cambell, and Harry Scherer; Congressmen Fulton and Corbett; National Academy of Sciences members; Ralph D. Pittman (President, Washington, D.C., Metropolitan Police Boys' Club), Major Robert V. Murray, and R. V. Fleming to present life membership in Boys' Club of Metropolitan Police, D.C.; A. F. Burns and G. Hauge; Senator Capehart and Maple T. Harl (Chairman, Federal Deposit Insurance Corporation). Receives map cases from National Geographic Society representatives. Receives group of Latin American women who have been studying Home Economics Extension. To Burning Tree Country Club for golf with R. V. Fleming, J. Black, and Arthur Stoddard. Returns to White House for off-the-record appointment with Secretary Humphrey, Generals Cutler and Persons, and C. D. Jackson. To Georgetown University Auditorium to address U.S. Chamber of Commerce banquet.

30   Washington. Breakfast with Secretary Humphrey and Congressmen Taber and Wigglesworth. Appointments with Legislative Leaders; National Security Council session; Dr. Kenneth Wells (President, Freedom Foundation); Trygve Lie (former U.N. Secretary-General) and J. F. Simmons. Receives first American Legion Poppy from American Legion group. Off-the-record appointments with Robert Saunders and S. Adams; C. D. Jackson, General Cutler, and J. C. Hagerty; J. C. Hagerty. News conference followed by appointments with Colonel Schulz (off the record); American Dental Association representatives; General Thomas North (Secretary, American Battle Monuments Commission). To Burning Tree Country Club with Senators Purtell and Griswold for dinner in honor of Senators Bridges and Taft.

May   1   Washington. Morning appointments with Colonel Carroll (off the record); General Persons (off the record); Congressman Judd; group from National

Council of the Churches of Christ; Mr. and Mrs. Patrick Breslin (off the record); Senator H. A. Smith; Vice-President Nixon and John Butler (Mayor, San Diego); Cabinet meeting; Congressmen Auchincloss and McGregor; Governor Thornton (off the record); Ellsworth Bunker; S. Adams, General Gray; General Burgess, G. Hauge, and G. D. Morgan (off the record); H. McDonald; K. C. Royall. Off-the-record appointments with Dr. M. S. Eisenhower; Secretaries Dulles and Kyes and General Vandenberg; Dr. M. S. Eisenhower.

2   Washington. Morning appointments with General Edgerton; Congressmen Bishop and Harris; Ambassador Allison. Shakes hands with friends of Secretary Weeks. Witnesses swearing-in of Administrator of General Services E. F. Mansure. To Burning Tree Country Club for golf with Bob Hope and Senators Bush and Symington. To Statler Hotel for Women's National Press Club dinner with Mrs. Eisenhower.

3   Washington. Attends services at National Presbyterian Church with Mrs. Eisenhower. Lays wreath at statue of John Witherspoon. Early afternoon appointment with General Cutler (off the record).

4   Washington. Opens Governors' Conference in the Executive Office Building. Appointments with T. E. Murray, H. D. Smyth, Admiral Strauss, and General Cutler; Robert Johnston (NATO staff); Minister Florea Ionsescu (Rumania), Corneliu Bogdan (Rumanian interpreter), Stephen A. Fisher (Interpreter, State Department), and J. F. Simmons; Ambassador Malik (Lebanon) and J. F. Simmons; Ambassador Ahmed Hussein (Egypt) and J. F. Simmons. Receives governors with Mrs. Eisenhower. Hosts luncheon for all attending the Governors' Conference. Afternoon appointments with Leonard G. Hagner, James M. Baley, and Wendell A. Miles (U.S. Attorney appointees), and Attorney General Brownell (off the record); Governor Kennon and Committee of Laymens' Association of the Presbyterian Church.

5   Washington. Morning appointments with H. E. Stassen (off the record); E. R. Harriman; W. T. Faricy; American-Korean Foundation committee; A. H.

Sulzberger (off the record); General Jean Etienne Valluy (French Army) and Colonel Walters; Ambassador Alberto Tarchiani (Italy) and J. F. Simmons; B'nai B'rith officers. Closes the Governors' Conference. Lunch with General Cutler and J. S. Lay. Afternoon appointments with F. A. Seaton and Secretary Hobby; Secretary Wilson; Colonel Carroll and Colonel Walters. Witnesses swearing-in of Assistant Director of the Bureau of the Budget R. R. Hughes. Late afternoon tea with Mrs. Eisenhower and General and Mrs. Joyce.

6   Washington. Appointments with General O. N. Bradley; Congressman Cannon; Disabled American Veterans members; Mr. and Mrs. Ray Moore, Mr. and Mrs. James Greene; Nagataka Murayama (President, *Asahi Shimbun*), Ambassador Araki, and J. F. Simmons. National Security Council session. To Burning Tree Country Club for golf with Governors Thornton and Shivers, and Senator Ferguson.

7   Washington. Morning appointments with F. Peavey Heffelfinger (Finance Chairman, RNC); Senator Flanders; Governor Luis Muñoz-Marín (Puerto Rico); Secretary Benson; Admiral Conrad E. L. Helfrich (Holland); Secretary Humphrey; Spyros Markezinis (Minister of Coordination, Greece), Ambassador Athanase G. Politis (Greece), and H. A. Byroade; Prime Minister St. Laurent (Canada), Lester B. Pearson (Secretary of State, External Affairs, Canada), Ambassador Hume Wrong (Canada), Secretary Dulles, Secretary Wilson, and L. J. Merchant. Hosts luncheon in honor of Prime Minister St. Laurent. Afternoon appointments with A. F. Burns, A. S. Flemming, Budget Director Dodge, G. Hauge, and S. Adams; Admiral and Señora Peixoto, Ambassador Salles, and J. M. Cabot; Secretaries Dulles and Wilson, General Smith, F. C. Nash, General Hull, U. A. Johnson, and W. S. Robertson. To Union Station en route to New York, New York. Arrives at Pennsylvania Station and motors directly to Astor Hotel. Addresses New York Republican State Committee dinner at Astor Hotel. Also addresses New York Republican State Committee dinner at Waldorf-Astoria Hotel. Departs from Pennsylvania Station via train for Washington, D.C.

8   Washington. Morning appointments with R. P. Burroughs; Senator Stennis, Congressman Williams, and group of constituents from Tylertown, Mississippi; Carl F. Wente (President, Bank of America); Secretary Dulles, Dag Hammarskjold (Secretary General, U.N.), and Ambassador Lodge. Cabinet meeting. Lunch with Secretary Dulles and General Smith. Afternoon appointments with Budget Director Dodge and General Persons; Secretary Wilson and General Bradley. Receives Ladies' Auxiliary of the Ancient Order of Hibernians in America national leaders. Late afternoon appointments with Prime Minister St. Laurent, L. B. Pearson, Ambassador Wrong, L. T. Merchant, and Secretaries Dulles, Wilson, and Humphrey; Secretaries Dulles and Humphrey, A. W. Dulles, Generals Smith and Cutler, and C. D. Jackson (off the record). To Statler Hotel with J. C. Hagerty for White House Correspondents Association dinner. To White House and then Union Station with Mrs. Eisenhower, E. Doud, Mrs. G. G. Moore, and Mrs. Miller. Departs from Union Station for Pennsylvania.

9   State College, Pennsylvania. Spends weekend at the home of Dr. and Mrs. M. S. Eisenhower, Pennsylvania State College.

10   State College, Pennsylvania. Attends church services at Pennsylvania State College Chapel with Mrs. Eisenhower, E. Doud, and Dr. and Mrs. M. S. Eisenhower. Early evening returns alone to Washington, D.C., via plane.

11   Washington. Morning appointments with C. Bowles and S. Adams; C. R. Sligh and S. Adams; General Bradley; Secretary Hobby (off the record); Secretary McKay, F. E. Wormser, and S. Adams; Budget Director Dodge and S. Adams; Mrs. L. Eakins, Mrs. L. Eakins, Jr., and Mrs. Curtis; K. McCann (off the record). Lunch with General Cutler and J. S. Lay. Off-the-record appointment with Senator Taft.

12   Washington. Breakfast with Senator Cooper, Congressman Short, and General Persons. Morning appointments with the Legislative Leaders; Thomas C. Buchanan (Chairman, Federal Power Commission) and S. Adams (off the record); William M. Rand

(Deputy Director, Mutual Security) (off the record); Congressman Trimble and representatives from Berryville, Arkansas; General Gray, and S. Adams; Hugh Baillie; Senator Thye, Congressmen Hagen and Judd, and residents of Funkley, Minnesota; Secretary Wilson. Hosts luncheon for congressional members. Off-the-record meeting with Frank O. Evans, Frank D. McSherry, Clinton G. Richards, and Lester S. Parsons (Assistant District Attorney appointees), and Attorney General Brownell. To Camp David, Maryland, with Mrs. G. G. Moore and Commander Beach to meet Mrs. Eisenhower. To Floyd D. Akers's lodge at Catoctin Furnace, Maryland, and then to Washington.

13   Washington. Morning appointments with General Crawford; S. Adams, Budget Director Dodge, C. D. Jackson, General Cutler, and E. J. Hughes (off the record); Mrs. H. Rohrer and Mrs. C. Philips (off the record). National Security Council session. To Burning Tree Country Club for golf with Congressman Herlong, Senator Malone, and J. E. McClure. Off-the-record appointment with P. G. Hoffman.

14   Washington. Breakfast with Secretary Humphrey, I. J. Martin, and Congressman Halleck. Morning appointments with Commander and Mrs. C. Black and daughter; J. C. Hagerty (off the record). News conference, followed by appointments with Tom Campbell; Mr. and Mrs. E. Q. Oliphant. Lunch with Budget Director Dodge and Congressmen Taber and Phillips. Afternoon appointments with Postmaster General Summerfield; Ambassador Heath; J. A. McCone. To USS *Williamsburg* for cruise to Yorktown, en route to William and Mary College, Williamsburg, Virginia.

15   Yorktown, Virginia. Delivers brief address in Chamber of Burgesses after welcoming at Colonial Capital in Williamsburg. Meets with Dr. and Mrs. Chandler and trustees of the college. Proceeds to Great Hall for commencement exercises and receiving line with Mrs. Eisenhower. To USS *Williamsburg*.

16   Norfolk, Virginia. Morning fishing and cruising. Arrives at Naval Operating Base. Golf with Admirals McCormick and Huffman, and Colonel G. G.

Moore. Early evening cocktails for golfing party, Mrs. Eisenhower, and Mrs. McCormick.

17 Annapolis, Maryland. Attends services at Naval Academy Chapel. Receives top-ranking midshipmen. Watches Noon Meal Formation at Bancroft Hall. To Midshipmen Mess Hall with Admiral Joy, Captain Buchanan, Dr. M. S. Eisenhower, Commander Beach, T. E. Stephens, and J. C. Hagerty. Addresses Midshipmen Brigade. Golf with Admiral Joy and Captains Buchanan and Flaherty. Cocktails with Mrs. Eisenhower, Mrs. Joy, Mrs. Buchanan, and golf party. Returns to Washington, D.C.

18 [Page missing.]

19 Washington. Morning appointments with Legislative Leaders; Richard Mellon. Receives American Bar Association Board of Governors. Appointment with Secretary Wilson and Secretary Talbott. Addresses United Negro College Fund luncheon at National Press Club. Lunch with General Persons, G. Hauge, and E. J. Hughes (off the record). Late afternoon appointment with Budget Director Dodge. Tea with Mr. and Mrs. Thomas J. Watson (International Business Machines) and Mrs. Eisenhower. Late evening radio speech.

20 Washington. Breakfast with General Ridgway. Morning appointments with General Cutler and J. S. Lay (off the record); National Security Council session; Secretary Wilson, Attorney General Brownell, and Generals Smith and Cutler (off the record); C. R. Hook; S. Adams, G. Hauge, C. D. Jackson, E. J. Hughes, B. C. Duffy, Jock Elliott, and Steve Benedict (off the record). Places wreath at statue of General Lafayette in Lafayette Square. To Burning Tree Country Club for golf with Senator Schoeppel, J. E. McClure, and John Brooks. Delivers message via television to opening ceremonies at the new Research and Engineering Center of the Ford Motor Co.

21 Washington. Breakfast with S. Adams, Attorney General Brownell, Postmaster General Summerfield, L. W. Hall, and T. E. Stephens. Appointments with Jacob S. Temkin, John W. McIlvaine, J. Julius Levy, James L. Guilmartin, and George H. Carswell (District Attorney appointees) and Attorney General

Brownell (off the record); Congressman Reece; Senator H. A. Smith; S. Adams and William D. Mitchell (off the record); Ralph Musser; S. R. Burkholder (Trucking Industry's Driver of the Year); Committee from the American Law Institute; Sarvepalli Radhakrishnan (Vice-President, India), Ambassador Gaganvihari Lallubhai Mehta, and J. F. Simmons. Receives National Conference of Business Paper Editors members. Attends luncheon at Industrial College of the Armed Forces at Fort McNair. Senator Payne, Congressman McIntire, Leo Gorman, and Walter Dickson present first salmon of the season followed by appointments with Congressman Judd; R. P. Burroughs and R. Cake (off the record).

22 Washington. Morning appointments with Senator Ives, Secretary Durkin, and L. A. Mashburn; Vice-President Nixon and Herman Perry (off the record). Cabinet meeting. Signs H. R. 4198. Receives National Spelling Bee winners. Photograph session with White House Photographers Award Contest winners. Lunch with B. M. Baruch. Afternoon appointments with Mrs. John H. Amen; Senator Bennett, Dr. and Mrs. Howard Driggs (President, American Pioneer Trails Association), Camille Driggs, and Dr. Harry Bowlby; Dr. Oppenheimer; Jack Warner (Vice-President, Warner Brothers), Mr. and Mrs. William T. Orr, and George Dorsey. Attends White House Photographers' dinner at Statler Hotel.

23 Washington. To Camp David, Maryland, with S. Adams, General Snyder, and B. M. Shanley. To estate of F. D. Akers at Catoctin Furnace, Maryland, for trout fishing. Early evening, returns to White House.

24 Washington. Morning appointment with General Cutler (off the record). Attends services at National Presbyterian Church with Mrs. Eisenhower. Afternoon bridge and dinner with P. G. Hoffman, Secretary Humphrey, and Secretary Talbott.

25 Washington. Morning appointments with Legislative Leaders; General Bradley; William L. Hutcheson (President Emeritus, United Brotherhood of Carpenters and Joiners of America); A. F. Burns and G. Hauge; Lewis K. Gough (Commander, American Legion). Hosts luncheon for West Point classmates,

class of 1915. Receives Washington Ministerial Union members. Appointments with John E. Babb (Sheriff, Cook County, Illinois) and S. Adams; R. L. Johnson; Admiral Strauss. Tea with Mrs. Eisenhower and Mr. and Mrs. E. J. Bermingham (off the record).

26 Washington. Breakfast with General Cutler and J. S. Lay. Morning appointments with Jeff Speck, Fred Taylor, and Vern Tindall; Congressman Westland; J. J. McCloy. To Beltsville, Maryland, to visit Plant Industry and Research Center, USDA, with Secretary Benson, Dr. W. T. Shaw, and Dr. A. H. Moseman. Tours dairy barns and Research Center grounds. Meets Dr. Hazel Stiebeling at Log Lodge, then proceeds to luncheon. To Burning Tree Country Club for golf with J. E. McClure, Pardee Erdman, and General Parks (off the record).

27 Washington. Morning appointments with J. Townsend (off the record); A. S. Flemming; Congressman Sadlak, General Persons and Polish-American representatives; Hamilton F. Armstrong (Editor, *Foreign Affairs*); Attorney General Brownell and District Attorney appointees Laughton Waters, William C. Calhoun, Edwin R. Denney, William F. Tompkins, and John Sprickler. National Security Council session, followed by appointments with Secretary Wilson; Sarah A. Ferguson. To Pentagon for luncheon in honor of the new and old Joint Chiefs of Staff. Afternoon appointments with W. E. Robinson; Senator Johnson; C. Vardaman; Captain McConnell, Captain Fernandez, Major Draper, and Mrs. J. McConnell. Hosts garden party with Mrs. Eisenhower for veterans.

28 Washington. Morning appointments with Congressman and Mrs. Auchincloss and Charles Auchincloss; Congressman Holt and General Persons; G. Hauge, E. J. Hughes, C. D. Jackson, and B. C. Duffy (off the record); J. C. Hagerty. News conference, followed by appointments with Dr. I. I. Rabi (off the record). Shakes hands with leaders of National Civil Service League. Appointment with E. H. Gammons. Lunch with S. S. Larmon (off the record). To Burning Tree Country Club for golf with J. Black, R.V. Fleming, and Congressman Arends.

29 Washington. Morning appointments with Congressman Hiestand and General Persons. Off-the-record appointments with G. Hauge, Secretary Humphrey, W. M. Martin, A. F. Burns, and A. S. Flemming. Cabinet meeting. Off-the-record appointments with M. Sears and Ambassador Lodge; Justice W. J. Fulton (Illinois Supreme Court); Secretary Hobby. Late morning appointments with Cadets J. G. Donahue, R. P. Ellman, and D. D. Horner; George Murphy; R. Uihlein and General Immell. Lunch with N. A. Rockefeller, A. S. Flemming, Congressman Vorys, and General Persons. Afternoon appointments with Owen R. Cheatham; Colonel Maxwell; Secretary Weeks (off the record); Secretary Dulles and H. E. Stassen; General Spaatz.

30 Washington. Off-the-record appointments with General Cutler; G. Hauge; Budget Director Dodge and G. Hauge. Receives title of Honorary Commander in Chief from Military Order of the World Wars Commanders. To Arlington Cemetery for wreath-laying ceremony with Mrs. Eisenhower, Major Draper, Colonel Schulz, and Commander Beach. Appointments with Secretaries Dulles and Wilson, F. C. Nash, W. S. Robertson, U. A. Johnson, and Generals Collins and Farrell; Budget Director Dodge, A. S. Flemming, H. E. Stassen, General Persons, and G. D. Morgan. To Burning Tree Country Club for golf with R. V. Fleming, General Burgess, and Ray M. Gidney. Visits J. M. Cabot (off the record).

31 Washington. Attends Memorial Services at National Presbyterian Church with Mrs. Eisenhower.

June 1 Washington. Morning appointments with Henry Taylor (radio commentator); Mr. and Mrs. H. K. Bagley; Ahmed Abboud (Cairo, Egypt), Ambassador Mohammed Kamil Abdul Rahim (Egypt), and J. F. Simmons; A. F. Burns; General Collins; Ambassador Rankin. Receives group of supporters from Florida. National Security Council session. To White House projection room for atomic energy movie (off the record).

2 Washington. Morning appointments with H. E. Stassen (off the record); Tom Pappas (RNC money raiser); L. W. Douglas; officers of the National Flying

Farmers Association; Admiral Cooke. Rehearsal for television broadcast. Special appointment with Legislative Leaders. Lunch with General Cutler and J. S. Lay. Makes film for aid to Korea. Afternoon appointments with Senator Carlson and Dr. Franklin D. Murphy (Chancellor, University of Kansas); E. J. Hughes (off the record); Ambassador Duke; Richard C. Patterson, Jr. (American Minister to Switzerland); G. Hauge (off the record); G. Dean (off the record); Secretary Wilson; Lou Kelly and Robert Matthews (American Express) (off the record). Dinner with W. E. Robinson, J. H. Burke, and Mrs. Eisenhower (off the record).

3   Washington. Morning appointments with Doug Black (Doubleday Publishing Co.); Jean Monnet, Franz Etzel, and Dirk Spierenburg (High Authority of the European Coal and Steel Community) and Secretary Dulles, W. Rand, D. K. E. Bruce; E. J. Hughes (off the record); Attorney General Brownell, George R. Blue, and William M. Steger (off the record). Television rehearsal. Appointments with Secretary Dulles and General Smith; Senator Daniel; Chester Davis, Secretary Humphrey, and S. Adams (off the record). To Burning Tree Country Club for golf with Ned Foot, Dr. Charles Hall, and J. Black (off the record). Delivers television speech.

4   Washington. Morning appointments with Legislative Leaders; Attorney General Brownell, and Judges Boldt and Wilson (off the record); National Security Council session; General Cutler, C. D. Jackson, J. Patrick Coyne (NSC Representative), Colonel Carroll, J. S. Lay, S. Everett Gleason, and Admiral Strauss; E. A. Johnston (off the record); group of Republican women from western Massachusetts. Afternoon appointments with C. D. Jackson (off the record); Mrs. Donald Wetzel and Mrs. William Moyer (off the record); John Riley (President, Todd Ship Building Co.); General Gruenther, Chief Justice Vinson, and G. E. Allen (off the record).

5   Washington. Morning appointments with Congressman Bolton; Anna Rosenberg; Congressman Bender and S. Adams; Archibald J. Carey and family. Cabinet meeting, followed by appointments with Ambassador McDermott; Congressman Younger and Frank

Belcher; Congressman Miller. Hosts luncheon with Mrs. Eisenhower for Congressional Baseball Game players. Afternoon appointments with S. Adams and Charles Slusser (off the record); Congressman Andresen and W. Marion Roberts (Area Soil Conservation Service Department); Ambassador Henderson; T. D. Morse, Romeo Short, and G. Hauge (off the record). Attends Congressional Baseball Game with Mrs. Eisenhower at Griffin Stadium.

6 Washington. Morning appointments with H. E. Stassen (off the record); Secretary Dulles, F. C. Nash, General Collins, W. S. Robertson, and U. A. Johnson. To Burning Tree Country Club for golf with Thomas Braniff, General Allen, and Gene Sarazen.

7 Washington. Attends morning services at National Presbyterian Church. Afternoon off-the-record appointment with Colonel Carroll.

8 Washington. Morning appointments with General Cutler and S. E. Gleason; Postmaster General Summerfield (off the record); G. Dean (off the record); A. F. Burns and G. Hauge; Secretary Weeks and Louis Rothschild (off the record); Budget Director Dodge, P. Young, and B. M. Shanley (off the record); General Collins; Ambassador Pfeiffer. Afternoon appointments with Senators Carlson and Schoeppel, Congressmen Scrivner and Miller, and citizens from Kansas; Secretary Dulles (off the record); H. E. Stassen (off the record). Hosts small, off-the-record stag dinner.

9 Washington. Breakfast with Secretary Dulles, H. E. Stassen, General Persons, and Congressmen Chiperfield, Richards, and Vorys. Appointments with Senator Knowland; Osrow Cobb (off the record); National Press Club representatives; Secretaries Dulles and Wilson, and A. W. Dulles (off the record); A. M. Cole. National Security Council session. Afternoon appointments with High Commissioner Conant (off the record); Senator Kerr with constituents from Muskogee and Tulsa, Oklahoma; Attorney General Brownell and U.S. Attorney appointees Sim A. Delapp, John F. Raper, Jr., Edward L. Scheufler, John C. Crawford, Millsap Fitzhugh, and Hugh K. Martin (off the record); Ambassador Hughes and L. T. Mer-

chant; Congressman McConnell, S. Adams, and B. M. Shanley; Secretary Humphrey, I. J. Martin, Congressman Halleck, M. B. Folsom, General Persons, and S. Adams.

10 Washington. Morning off-the-record appointments with Secretary Dulles; General Cutler. To MATS terminal with official party for Minneapolis, Minnesota. Receives welcome. To American Swedish Institute. Proceeds to Minneapolis Auditorium to meet Jaycee members. Speaks via live radio and local television. Visits Ebenezer Home for the Aged. To Clarence Parker Hotel in Minot, North Dakota. Dinner with Governor Brunsdale and Republican party leaders, followed by short reception in Gold Saddle Room.

11 North Dakota. To Garrison Dam with Governor Brunsdale for inspection tour and ceremony. Receives gift from Tribal Council of Indians from Fort Berthold Reservation. To Rapid City, South Dakota. Visits Mt. Rushmore Memorial. Speaks to National Young Republican Convention. Dinner at State Game Lodge with Governor Anderson and guests. Proceeds to Coolidge Inn to meet South Dakota Republican county officials.

12 Custer State Park, South Dakota. Golf at Lead Country Club and fishing at French Creek.

13 Rapid City, South Dakota. Renames Rapid City Air Force Base as Ellsworth Air Force Base. Flies over Flint, Michigan, to view tornado damage en route to Lebanon, New Hampshire. To home of Dartmouth President John Dickey.

14 Dartmouth, New Hampshire. Morning reception, followed by commencement exercises and luncheon. To Mitchel Air Force Base, New York. Delivers speech at Sagamore Hill and receives gifts. Presidential motorcade to Mitchell Air Force Base en route to Washington, D.C.

15 Washington. Morning appointments with Legislative Leaders; Admirals William M. Fechteler and Donald B. Duncan; Admiral Leahy; Ambassador Aldrich; Budget Director Dodge and D. R. Belcher; General Gray. Afternoon appointments with Secretary Dulles;

Secretary Dulles and Attorney General Brownell; Attorney General Brownell, B. M. Shanley, S. Adams, and General Persons; B. M. Shanley, General Persons, and G. D. Morgan (off the record); Admiral Strauss (off the record); U. E. Baughman (Chief, U.S. Secret Service) (off the record); D. MacArthur II (off the record).

16 Washington. Presents diplomas to Capitol Page School graduates. Appointments with Mrs. Thomas H. Powel (Mount Vernon Ladies Association) and Congresswoman Bolton; Harry Anholt and T. E. Stephens (off the record); Senator Bricker; Dr. M. S. Eisenhower, A. S. Flemming, and N. A. Rockefeller; Ambassador Politis; Secretary Wilson. Lunch with Secretary Wilson and K. T. Keller. Afternoon appointments with High Commissioner Conant; Attorney General Brownell and U.S. Attorneys Charles W. Atkinson, and Harry Richards (off the record); Dr. Bernard D. Loomer, Dr. Charles Stewart, Reverends Daniel Rideout and Bruce Dahlberg, and Rabbi Adam Cronback to discuss Rosenberg case.

17 Washington. Breakfast with General Cutler and J. S. Lay. Morning appointments with Congressman Ragan; Congressman Thompson; Maurice Katz and family; Gene Autry and E. H. Gammons; J. C. Hagerty (off the record). News conference, followed by appointments with Prime Minister Paik Doo Jin (Korea), Ambassador Youchan Yang (Korea) and W. S. Robertson; P. Young. To Burning Tree Country Club for golf with Congressman Simpson, H. Anholt, and J. Black (off the record).

18 Washington. Breakfast with Senators Dirksen, Magnuson, and Bridges, Budget Director Dodge, and General Persons; Senator Dirksen; Benjamin F. Fairless (Board Chairman, U.S. Steel); American Political Science Association leaders; Secretaries Dulles and Wilson, and Admiral Fechteler (off the record). National Security Council session. Greets group of handicapped and underprivileged school children. Lunch with Congressman Rayburn. Appointment with General Cutler and Henry J. Tasca (Special Representative, Korean Economic Affairs). Receives participants in the nationwide Cooperative Forest Fire Prevention Program. Appointments with Con-

gressman Rodino, Jr., and B. M. Shanley; J. Sinclair Armstrong, A. Jack Goodwin, and C. F. Willis, Jr. (off the record); General George A. Horkan and D. Gregory Volkert. Hosts reception with Mrs. Eisenhower for members of the 8th Pan American Railway Congress.

19 Washington. Morning appointments with Congressman Jackson, and Robert H. McClure (Editor, *Santa Monica Evening Outlook*) and son; Edward D. Nicholson (United Air Lines) (off the record); Ambassador Lodge and Massachusetts State Senator S. H. Phillips (off the record). Cabinet meeting, followed by appointments with Senators H. A. Smith and Taft, Congressman McConnell, L. A. Mashburn, S. F. Dunn, S. Adams, B. M. Shanley, and G. D. Morgan (off the record); General Julius O. Adler. Lunch with S. W. Richardson. Afternoon appointments with Arthur M. Hill (Greyhound Corporation) and Thomas E. Millsop (President, Weirton Steel Co.); Secretary Humphrey, General Persons, and G. D. Morgan (off the record).

20 Washington. Morning appointments with H. E. Stassen; Congressman Hope (S. Adams—off the record); Congressman Frazier and Lou Williams; Dr. John A. Krout (Provost, Columbia University); Congressman Reed. Signs H. R. 3795.

21 Washington. Attends services at Metropolitan Memorial Methodist Church with Colonel Schulz. Off-the-record appointment with Colonel Carroll.

22 Washington. Breakfast with Secretary Dulles, General Smith, General Van Fleet, and W. S. Robertson (off the record). Off-the-record staff meeting, followed by appointments with Senator Carlson (off the record); Drew Middleton (Chief Correspondent, *New York Times*); General Curtis; General Collins. Receives Optimist International Oratorical Contest winner; members of National 4-H Club Camp. Appointments with Secretaries Dulles and Humphrey, Budget Director Dodge, A. S. Flemming, J. M. Cabot, and Dr. M. S. Eisenhower; Secretary Dulles (off the record); Ambassador Alger. Lunch with D. Wallace (off the record). Afternoon appointments with Mrs. O. B. Lord; A. F. Burns and G. Hauge; Senator

Knowland; General Leroy H. Watson (Chief, Safety Advanced Group) and Colonel Carroll (off the record). Hosts stag dinner (off the record).

23   Washington. Off-the-record appointment with A. S. Flemming. Receives Pennsylvania Association of First Class Townships delegation, followed by appointments with Secretary Humphrey, General Persons, and G. D. Morgan (off the record); Benjamin A. Javits; General Cutler and J. S. Lay; Lansdell Christie and S. Adams (off the record); Senator Cooper and mother (off the record). Lunch with J. E. McClure, John Lambert, Senator Cooper, C. D. Jackson, and A. F. Burns. Off-the-record meeting in Solarium with Secretary Dulles, General Smith, Robert R. Bowie, D. MacArthur II, F. C. Nash, C. D. Jackson, J. C. Hagerty, and T. E. Stephens. Tea with General Robert M. Littlejohn.

24   Washington. Appointments with Legislative Leaders; C. E. Wilson and S. Adams (off the record); Ambassador Silvercruys and Secretary Dulles; Secretary Wilson; Attorney General Brownell and A. W. Dulles; Attorney General Brownell and U.S. Attorneys Clyde Palmer and Edward Beard. To Burning Tree Country Club for golf with P. G. Hoffman, J. H. Whitney, and B. S. Carter. To Constitution Hall closing of American Red Cross Annual Convention.

25   Washington. Receives the Committee from United Church Women, National Council of Churches. Appointment with Congressman Laird. Witnesses the swearing-in of A. S. Flemming as Director of Office of Defense Mobilization. National Security Council session. To Naval Gun Factory to greet veterans making final trip on USS *Williamsburg*. Lunch with Vice-President Nixon, S. Adams, General Persons, and Senators Taft, Bridges, Knowland, Millikin, Saltonstall, Johnson, George, Russell, Hayden, and Clements. Afternoon appointment with Secretary Benson. Signs S. 2112, followed by appointments with Senator Butler, General Persons, and M. M. Rabb (off the record); Secretary Humphrey, Budget Director Dodge, and General Cutler; Senator H. A. Smith, Lester Titus, and Joseph J. Masiello; Mrs. Walton Walker.

26 Washington. Breakfast with Congressmen Taber and Scrivner, Budget Director Dodge, and General Persons. Morning appointments with James Melton; group of cattlemen; members of Washington Student Citizenship Seminar. Cabinet meeting, followed by appointments with S. W. Richardson; Foster Furcolo (Massachusetts State Treasurer) and Ambassador Lodge; Ambassador Stuart; Secretary Dulles (off the record). To Camp David, Maryland, with Mrs. Eisenhower, E. Doud, and Commander Beach.

27 Camp David, Maryland. No official appointments.

28 Camp David, Maryland. Visits Camp Greentop and the Eisenhower farm near Gettysburg, Pennsylvania. Returns to White House in early evening.

29 Washington. Morning appointments with Legislative Leaders; General Bradley and Admiral Fechteler; A. F. Burns and G. Hauge; Bishop Hans Lilje (President, Lutheran World Federation), Dr. Krekeler, J. F. Simmons, Rev. Robert E. Van Deusen (Secretary, National Lutheran Council), and G. Hauge; John M. Wisdom (off the record). Witnesses swearing-in of Katherine G. Howard as Deputy Administrator of the Federal Civil Defense Administration. Afternoon appointments with General Smith, R. M. Kyes, Secretary Stevens, Admiral Fechteler, U. A. Johnson, and Charles Sullivan (Office of Secretary of Defense); Secretary Benson, V. E. Peterson, Robert Farrington (Governor, Farm Credit Administration), and S. Adams; William Schloss and family; A. W. Dulles; C. L. Burgess (off the record).

30 Washington. Breakfast with A. Nielsen, Secretary Humphrey, Budget Director Dodge, and S. Adams (off the record). Signs H. R. 4233. Appointments with H. E. Stassen (off the record); Carlos P. Romulo (former Philippine Ambassador to U.S.) and Temple Wanamaker (State Department); Ben Richards (off the record); C. D. Jackson, General Cutler, W. H. Jackson, and A. M. Washburn (off the record). Presents Young American Medals for Bravery and Service. Appointments with Attorney General Brownell and U.S. Attorneys Paul F. Lavzavola, Charles K. Cyr, Jack C. Brown, Simon S. Cohen, and Thomas F. Wilson (off the record); Ambassador Thompson;

General Twining; L. W. Douglas. Lunch with General Cutler and S. E. Gleason. Afternoon appointments with Postmaster General Summerfield, Senator Dirksen, and Carl Schroeder; R. McLean; Guy Farmer and S. Adams (off the record); S. H. High (off the record).

July 1 Washington. Morning appointments with Budget Director Dodge and C. D. Jackson; Walter S. Lemmon (President, World Wide Broadcasting System) and Leonard Marx; Paul M. Herzog; Major Draper; J. C. Hagerty (off the record). News conference, followed by appointments with Sullivan Barnes (Chairman, Young Republican National Federation) and Marian Smith (Co-Chairman); G. Hauge, S. C. Waugh, John Letty (State Department), John H. Davis (Agriculture Department), and G. D. Morgan; Agriculture Advisory Committee; General Harmon. To Burning Tree Country Club for golf with Colonel Belshe and Congressmen Rogers and Johnson (off the record).

2 Washington. Early morning meeting in H. E. Stassen's office. Receives group from the National Association of Evangelicals. Appointments with Fleur Cowles (*Look* Magazine); National Security Council session; Lindsey C. Warren (U.S. Comptroller General) and S. Adams; Ambassador van Roijen (Netherlands). Signs H. R. 4654. Witnesses the swearing-in of Admiral Strauss as Chairman of the Atomic Energy Commission. Lunch with L. W. Hall. Afternoon appointments with A. S. Flemming, Secretary Humphrey, Budget Director Dodge, K. R. Craven (Administrator, Reconstruction Finance Corporation), and S. C. Waugh; J. Budinger (Bankers Trust Co.); Ambassador Dudley; Warren L. Pierson (Chairman, U.S. Council, International Chamber of Commerce); Dr. Spencer Miller and S. Adams (off the record).

3 Washington. Hosts breakfast for Cabinet members. Morning appointments with Senator Carlson and General Persons (off the record); Colonel George C. Diamantopoulos (Military Attaché, Greek Embassy) and Colonel Carroll (off the record); Secretary Hobby, N. A. Rockefeller, B. M. Shanley, and General Persons. To Camp David, Maryland, with Mrs.

Eisenhower, E. Doud, Commander Beach, and guests C. Roberts, W. E. Robinson, and Mr. and Mrs. E. D. Slater.

4 Camp David, Maryland. No official appointments.

5 Camp David, Maryland. Returns to Washington in early evening.

6 Washington. Morning appointments with H. E. Stassen; Colonel Carroll; C. D. Jackson; Senator Duff; Congressman Wilson and Paul Sutherland (San Diego Young Republican Club); A. C. Tolley. Afternoon appointments with G. Farmer and S. Adams; Ambassador Percy C. Spender (Australia) and Dr. Herbert Evatt (Australia). Off-the-record appointment with G. Whitney. Hosts off-the-record dinner.

7 Washington. Morning appointments with Legislative Leaders; Senator Thye; Secretary Hobby, N. A. Rockefeller, and General Persons; Senator Griswold; General Collins; C. R. Sligh; Admiral Strauss and J. Campbell (off the record). Witnesses swearing-in of Charles E. Slusser as Commissioner of the Public Housing Administration. Makes recording for Boy Scout Jamboree and film for National Vegetable Week. Lunch with Philip Reid (Chairman, General Electric), S. Adams, and C. D. Jackson (off the record). Afternoon appointments with Postmaster General Summerfield and Budget Director Dodge; Secretaries Wilson and Talbott; Stuart Rothman and S. Adams (off the record); General Cutler and S. E. Gleason; C. D. Jackson, General Persons, G. D. Morgan, and M. M. Rabb (off the record); H. Darby.

8 Washington. Breakfast with Secretary Dulles and D. MacArthur II. Morning appointments with Alfred A. Binkerd and family; A. F. Burns and G. Hauge; J. C. Hagerty. News conference, followed by appointments with Attorney General Brownell and potential appointees George C. Doub, William B. Bantz, H. H. Groomes, Ben C. Dawkins, and Floyd McMahon (off the record); Mr. and Mrs. James Guilmartin; Rabbi Abba H. Silver. To Burning Tree Country Club for golf with R. D. Pittman, Senator Bush, and Colonel Belshe. Returns to White House for appointments with Secretaries Dulles and Wil-

son, General Smith, General Collins, F. C. Nash, C. Sullivan, and U. A. Johnson; Secretary Dulles and Senator Knowland; Secretary Wilson, Mr. Floaty, Dr. Casberg, and Colonel Rockwell; Governor Dewey and Secretary Humphrey.

9 Washington. Morning appointments with Philip Willkie; M. Muir, and S. Adams (off the record); Congresswoman Bolton; Vice-President Nixon and I. J. Martin; National Security Council session; William D. Pawley. Lunch with Dr. Samuel Bronfman and E. D. Slater (off the record). Afternoon off-the-record appointments with Harrison Hobart and S. Adams; Howard Freas and S. Adams; L. W. Hall; dentist; P. G. Hoffman.

10 Washington. Cabinet meeting. Signs S. 1514 and S. 106. To MATS terminal en route to Amarillo, Texas. Delivers speech at Municipal Auditorium and returns to Washington, D.C.

11 Washington. Morning appointments with Jack Solomon; C. D. Jackson (off the record); Secretary Dulles (off the record); Secretary Dulles, Lord Salisbury, Ambassador Makins, Georges Bidault (Minister of Foreign Affairs, France), and Ambassador Bonnet (France); A. W. Dulles (off the record); R. Cake and Secretary McKay (off the record). Attends luncheon in the Caucus Room. To Burning Tree Country Club for golf with Congressmen Halleck, Arends, and Bolton (off the record). Returns to White House with congressmen (off the record).

12 Washington. Attends services at National Presbyterian Church with Mrs. Eisenhower.

13 Washington. Morning appointments with Archbishop Michael (Greek Orthodox Church); Attorney General Brownell (off the record); Ambassador Peaslee; General Bradley; A. F. Burns and G. Hauge; Secretary Wilson; Ourot Souvannavong (Minister, Laos) and R. D. Muir; Secretary McKay and Wilbur A. Dexheimer; Governor Warren and Attorney General Brownell (off the record). Receives Maryland congressional delegation. Appointments with Ambassador Kemper; Congressman Taber, H. E. Stassen, General Gruenther, Budget Director Dodge, and B. N. Harlow. Off-the-record appointments with

Secretary Humphrey, General Gruenther, and J. Lemmon; Senator Potter.

14 Washington. Breakfast with Senator Bridges, Budget Director Dodge, and Generals Gruenther and Persons; Legislative Leaders. Receives groups from the National Defense Transportation Association; American Association of Workers for the Blind. Appointment with Secretary Wilson, R. M. Kyes, Admiral Radford, General Ridgway, Admiral Carney, and General Twining (off the record); Senators Watkins and McCarran. National Security Council session. Hosts stag luncheon. Afternoon appointments with General James B. Cress; George L. Warren (State Department) (off the record); Senator Martin and Congressman Dondero. To Hotel Congressional for dinner with members of the "83rd Club."

15 Washington. Breakfast with congressional members. Receives National League of Masonic Clubs delegation. Appointments with Congressman Meader; J. Earl Coke (Assistant Secretary of Agriculture), Knowles Ryerson (Dean, University of California), and S. Adams (off the record); Ambassador Hildreth; Ambassador Aldrich; Ralph T. Reed (President, American Express); Glenn Emmons and S. Adams (off the record); Secretary Dulles and W. S. Robertson. Hosts luncheon for Senate Appropriations Committee. To Burning Tree Country Club for golf with R. T. Reed, R. D. Pittman, and Colonel Belshe. To Statler Hotel for cocktail party for workers of the Commodore Hotel, New York.

16 Washington. Morning appointments with Generals Lowry and Persons (off the record); Harold E. Holt (Minister of Labor, Australia), Australian Ambassador Spender, and Ambassador Peaslee. Off-the-record National Security Council session. Lunch with Cabinet members and military personnel. Off-the-record appointments with James Murphy and C. F. Willis; National Security Council session.

17 Washington. Off-the-record appointments with H. E. Stassen; R. Cake; R. D. Brophy and S. Adams; Attorney General Brownell and U.S. Attorney candidates Anthony Julian, Frank M. Johnson, Charles T. Moriarty, and George Templar; Ambassador Lodge;

Harvey Higley and S. Adams; Captain George Anderson and Helen Weaver. Cabinet meeting. Appointments with Congressman Short; Secretary Hobby. Receives Federal home loan and finance officials. Signs S. 2199. Appointment with J. B. Mintener. To Camp David, Maryland, with Mrs. Eisenhower.

18   Camp David, Maryland. No official appointments.

19   Camp David, Maryland. Returns early evening to White House.

20   Washington. Appointments with Legislative Leaders; Secretary Dulles; General Bradley; Budget Director Dodge and H. E. Stassen; Secretary Wilson and H. Struve Hensel (Defense Department); Congressman Busbey and Blazina family. Off-the-record lunch with Governor Byrnes. Afternoon appointments with V. E. Peterson, Budget Director Dodge, S. Adams, and General Gruenther; S. Adams, Arthur Page, G. Hauge, C. D. Jackson, General Persons, Colonel Carroll, and E. J. Hughes (off the record); A. Nielsen. Signs S. 971. Hosts off-the-record stag dinner.

21   Washington. Receives group of American Civil Air Patrol Cadets. Morning appointments with S. H. High and A. M. Cole (off the record). Presents Freedoms Foundation's George Washington Honor Medals, followed by appointments with Senator Capehart and leaders of Jeffersonian Democrats for Eisenhower; Thomas J. Cuite (National Commander, Catholic War Veterans), Father John J. Wallace, and William L. Nemick; Ambassador Cowen; Ambassador Jaramillo Cipriano Restrepo (Columbia); Ambassador Crowe; Ambassador Hare; Ambassador Strong; Attorney General Brownell and U.S. Attorneys Heard Floore, William W. White, L. H. Burke, and Peter Mills, Jr. (off the record); Senator H. A. Smith; Secretary Dulles, W. S. Robertson, and U. A. Johnson. Luncheon with H. Hoover, S. Adams, L. W. Hall, N. A. Rockefeller, A. S. Flemming, P. Young, Congressman Brown, and Senator Ferguson. Afternoon appointments with A. S. Flemming; Secretary Hobby and Dr. Chester Keefer (Special Assistant) (off the record).

22   Washington. Breakfast with General Cutler and J. S. Lay. Receives officers of the Italian-American World War Veterans. Witnesses swearing-in of Harvey V. Higley as Administrator of Veterans Affairs. Appointment with J. C. Hagerty (off the record). News conference, followed by off-the-record appointments with Admiral Strauss; Secretaries Dulles and Wilson, W. S. Robertson, U. A. Johnson, F. C. Nash; Attorney General Brownell, and Senator Bricker; Attorney General Brownell and Judge O. D. Hamlin; H. E. Stassen, Budget Director Dodge, and General Persons. To Burning Tree Country Club for golf with General Bradley, Senator Bush, and Chuck Spofford (off the record).

23   Washington. Morning appointments with Senator Dirksen; Senator McCarran; Senator Kerr (G. D. Morgan—off the record); Senators and cattlemen from West; H. Hoover. National Security Council session. Lunch with General Clark (off the record). Afternoon appointments with C. D. Jackson (off the record); E. N. Eisenhower and F. S. Bellis; Budget Director Dodge and General Cutler (off the record); Secretary Humphrey, Budget Director Dodge, General Persons, and G. D. Morgan (off the record); General Bradley; General and Mrs. Thomas B. Catron and Mrs. Eisenhower.

24   Washington. Breakfast with senators, congressmen, and officials. Morning appointments with Congressmen Anderson, Horan, Hope, Hill, Hoeven, Harvey, Lovre, and Andresen and L. W. Hall; Ambassador Pote Sarasin (Thailand), Minister of Communications Fuen Ronaphakas Riddhagani (Thailand), Thai Prime Minister's children Chirabat Panyarachun, Pacharabul Pbibulsonggram, Nitya Pbibulsonggram, and J. F. Simmons; Ambassador Wrong; Senator Stennis and Congressman Colmer; B. M. Shanley, G. Hauge, Secretary Weeks and Department of Commerce staff to discuss Inland Waterways (off the record); Secretary Dulles, W. S. Robertson, U. A. Johnson, and General Farrell (off the record). To Quantico, Virginia, for meeting with Chiefs of Staff and Defense Department civilian heads.

25   Quantico, Virginia. No official appointments.

26   Quantico, Virginia. Returns to White House. Addresses the nation regarding Korean truce.

27   Washington. Morning appointments with H. E. Stassen, General Persons, and B. N. Harlow (off the record); Senator Ives; Congressmen Keating and Bennett; Dr. Phillips (off the record); Red Cross delegation; General Bradley; A. F. Burns and G. Hauge; Secretary Wilson; Budget Director Dodge (off the record); Ambassador Guggenheim; Ambassador José R. Chiriboga Villagómez (Ecuador). Signs S. 2342. Appointments with publishers of foreign language newspapers; Secretary Dulles; T. C. Streibert, S. Adams, and C. D. Jackson (off the record); M. B. Folsom and B. M. Shanley (off the record). Hosts off-the-record stag dinner.

28   Washington. Morning appointments with H. E. Stassen (off the record); Postmaster General Summerfield and Congressman Rees (off the record); Congressman C. Hinshaw and General Persons; P. G. Hoffman and R. B. Murray (off the record); Traffic Safety Conference; Congressman Harrison; Secretary Benson. Receives American Dairy Association committee. Lunch with General Cutler and J. S. Lay followed by appointments with Secretary Dulles and D. MacArthur II; Senator Potter and Lew Berry. Off-the-record appointments with Attorney General Brownell; Secretary Wilson and C. S. Thomas; F. A. Seaton; R. W. Woodruff.

29   Washington. Appointment with L. W. Hall (off the record). Receives Boys' Nation members followed by appointments with Dr. M. S. Eisenhower, J. M. Cabot, S. W. Anderson, Andrew N. Overby (Assistant Secretary of Treasury), and W. Tapley Bennett, Jr. (Deputy Director, State Department, Bureau of Inter-American Affairs); R. L. Johnson and new members of the State Department International Information Administration; A. S. Flemming and Victor Cooley; S. Adams and Kenneth Tuggle (off the record). Signs H. R. 5238. To Woodmont Country Club for golf with Colonel Belshe, J. E. McClure, General Bradley, Sam Schwartz, Robert Phillipson, Leo Freidburg, and Allen Miller (off the record).

30 Washington. Breakfast with congressional members. National Security Council session. Luncheon with Secretaries Dulles, Humphrey, and Weeks, and H. E. Stassen, Colonel Randall, S. Adams, and G. Hauge. Afternoon appointments with Congressman Rogers; Senators Martin and Duff, Congressman Simpson, and Republican leaders; Senator Carlson and Council of Motion Picture Association members; Secretary Humphrey, Budget Director Dodge, J. C. Hagerty, and G. Hauge (off the record); Secretary McKay, R. A. Tudor, S. Adams, and G. Hauge. Signs H. R. 5141. Receives White House staff with Mrs. Eisenhower.

31 Washington. Cabinet meeting. Appointments with Secretary Wilson and Frank Newberry; General Cutler (off the record). Reads resolution of thanks from Congress to General March. To home of Mrs. R. A. Taft with Mrs. Eisenhower to pay respects (off the record followed by off-the-record appointment with General Cutler). Lunch with General Snyder and H. A. Rusk. Afternoon appointments with Secretary Dulles (off the record); Secretaries Dulles and Wilson, and H. E. Stassen; E. J. Hughes and A. Page (off the record).

August 1 Washington. Morning appointments with Congressman McConnell and Fred C. Peters; Senator Malone; Ambassador Tello, General Abelardo L. Rodriguez (former President, Mexico), and J. F. Simmons; H. E. Stassen (off the record). Witnesses swearing-in of General Adler, Warren H. Atherton, and Karl D. Compton as National Security Training Commission Commissioners. Receives Girls' Nation members.

2 Washington. Attends services at National Presbyterian Church with Mrs. Eisenhower.

3 Washington. Breakfast with Senators Knowland and Millikin, Budget Director Dodge, Secretary Humphrey, and General Persons; Ambassador Eduardo Zuleta-Angel (Columbia); Ambassador Arnold D. P. Heeney (Canada); General Smith and D. MacArthur II; Vice-President Nixon. Attends memorial services with Mrs. Eisenhower for Robert A. Taft.

Afternoon off-the-record meeting with Secretary Humphrey, Attorney General Brownell, Postmaster General Summerfield, L. W. Hall, Senator Bricker, and Ray Bliss. To MATS terminal en route to Seattle, Washington.

4 Seattle, Washington. Attends Governors' Conference.

5 Washington. Early morning arrival in Washington, D.C. Breakfast with Senator Knowland. Morning appointments with Secretary Hobby and Richard Jones (President, Southern Publishers Association); General Smith, A. W. Dulles, and H. E. Stassen (off the record); Ambassador Stanton. Presents Distinguished Service Medals to recipients. Witnesses swearing-in of T. C. Streibert as Director, U.S. Information Agency. Lunch with S. W. Richardson. Afternoon appointments with General Clark; General Cutler and J. S. Lay. Off-the-record tea with Mrs. Eisenhower and Dr. and Mrs. Evans, Reverend and Mrs. Meyers, and Dr. and Mrs. Hetzel.

6 Washington. Morning appointments with Senator Ferguson; National Security Council session. Witnesses swearing-in of H. E. Stassen as Director, Foreign Operations Administration. Appointments with H. E. Stassen and Webster Todd (off the record); Ambassador Ali Sastroamidjojo (Indonesia). Lunch with General Vandenberg, C. D. Jackson, E. J. Hughes, L. A. Minnich, A. M. Washburn, G. Hauge, General Snyder, T. E. Stephens, and R. R. Mathews (off the record). Afternoon appointments with Senator Purtell and Graham Anthony (Colt Manufacturing); Senator Dworshak; General Vandenburg; General Smith; General Snyder (off the record). Signs H. R. 4353. Delivers "Report to the Nation" on radio.

7 Washington. Breakfast with Cabinet members. Morning appointments with P. Young; G. Hauge and R. F. C. administrators; Ambassador Warren; Ambassador Cannon; Ambassador Coe; L. W. Hall, H. F. Guggenheim, and Bertha S. Adkins. Signs H. R. 6481 and H. R. 121. Lunch with Ambassador Makins, Lord Brabazon, Robert L. Williams, and Congressman Scrivner. Afternoon meeting with Gen-

eral Cutler and civilian consultants to the National Security Council (off the record).

8   Washington. Morning appointments with Ben and Mrs. Hogan; I. J. Martin and General Persons (off the record); Sam Swartz (Woodmont Country Club) (off the record). To MATS terminal with Mrs. Eisenhower en route to Denver, Colorado.

9   Denver, Colorado. Attends services at Corona Presbyterian Church with Mrs. Eisenhower.

10   Lowry Air Force Base. Appointments with Secretary Dulles, Ambassador Lodge, W. S. Robertson, Carl McCardle (Assistant Secretary of State), and Kenneth Young (State Department, Office of North Asian Affairs). Golf at Cherry Hills Country Club with R. Arnold, E. B. Dudley, and Governor Thornton.

11   Lowry Air Force Base. Appointment with Admiral Radford. Golf at Cherry Hills Country Club with E. D. Slater, C. Roberts, and M. Moncrief.

12   Lowry Air Force Base. To Buffalo Creek, Colorado, with A. Nielsen for fishing at B. F. Swan's ranch. Returns to Denver.

13   Lowry Air Force Base. Appointment with H. Darby. Golf at Cherry Hills Country Club with L. M. Pexton, Governor Thornton, J. Murphy, P. Hoyt, W. E. Robinson, W. A. Jones, F. F. Gosden, and C. S. Jones.

14   Lowry Air Force Base. Appointments with Mr. and Mrs. Ralph Farley (off the record); Pierre Belasco (Chef, Brown Palace Hotel); General Burgess (off the record); W. Bannister, and J. Foster. Golf at Cherry Hills Country Club with R. Arnold and E. Dudley.

15   Lowry Air Force Base. Appointments with General Burgess; Sharon D. Pack. Golf at Cherry Hills Country Club with W. E. Robinson, F. F. Gosden, and W. A. Jones.

16   Denver, Colorado. Attends services at Corona Presbyterian Church. To Lakewood to visit sick child, Paul H. Haley.

17   Lowry Air Force Base. Morning appointments with Major Anastacio Quevedo Ver; General Charles S.

Shadle; WAVE representatives; General Burgess, Congressmen Walcott and Hill, Robert Maheu, and Small Defense Plants Administration representatives; Attorney General Brownell.

18 Lowry Air Force Base. Morning appointment with Clarence E. Manion (Chairman, Commission on Intergovernmental Relations). To Fitzsimons General Hospital for golf with General Robinson, Colonel Dierdorf, and F. D. Akers. Departs for New York, New York, aboard *Columbine*.

19 New York, New York. Breakfast with Admiral Strauss and C. D. Jackson at Waldorf-Astoria Hotel. Appointments with Ambassador Lodge; President's Committee on Government Contracts; O. M. Reid; Major Curtis R. Kirkland; William L. Pfeiffer (New York State Republican Chairman) and R. C. Sprague; Harold Reigelman (Mayoral candidate). Receives members of American Committee on Italian Migration. Lunch at Waldorf-Astoria Hotel with Vice-President Nixon, Secretary Durkin, General Clay, A. H. Sulzberger, D. Black, and Governor Dewey. Registers to vote at Board of Elections and proceeds to Baruch Houses for monument unveiling. To Denver, Colorado, aboard the *Columbine*.

20 Lowry Air Force Base. Morning appointments with Congressman Arends; Congressman Chenoweth and State Republican committee; Drought Disaster Program officials; H. C. Butcher and P. Hoyt; Secretary Hobby and N. A. Rockefeller. To Cherry Hills Country Club to watch Hillsdilly Golf Tournament.

21 Denver, Colorado. Breakfast with G. Hauge followed by appointment with Dean Neil Jacoby. Fishing at B. F. Swan's ranch.

22 Denver, Colorado. Morning appointments with L. M. Pexton; H. E. Stassen; Senator and Mrs. Griswold, Congressman Hruska, and Omaha business leaders; P. Young; Mr. and Mrs. James Calder and Leonard Kaplan (Stereo Realist Camera). To Cherry Hills Country Club for golf with E. Dudley, J. E. Davis, and B. W. Vinson.

23 Denver, Colorado. Attends services at Corona Presbyterian Church with F. D. Akers.

24   Lowry Air Force Base. Morning appointments with F. A. Seaton; Senator Carlson. To Fitzsimons General Hospital for medical check-up. Afternoon appointment with General Burgess (off the record). To Gordon Lake in Denver for fishing, dinner, and bridge.

25   Lowry Air Force Base. Morning appointment with Denver Mayor Newton; F. A. Seaton. To Fitzsimons General Hospital for golf with General Robinson, Colonel S. Smith, and Colonel Waltrip.

26   Lowry Air Force Base. To Cherry Hills Country Club for golf with R. Arnold.

27   Denver, Colorado. To A. Nielsen's ranch near Fraser, Colorado.

28   Fraser, Colorado. No official appointments.

29   Fraser, Colorado. Appointments with Carl Norgren; Mr. and Mrs. Richard M. Andrews (Colorado State Fish and Game); Fraser Mayor Clayton and daughter. Hosts party for press.

30   Fraser, Colorado. Lunch with Robert Alexander, Bert Godell, George Hardy, and Andrew J. O'Mailia at Forest Experimentation Headquarters.

31   Fraser, Colorado. No official appointments.

September 1   Fraser, Colorado. No official appointments.

2   Fraser and Denver, Colorado. Morning appointment with Senator Carlson and family. Returns to Doud residence, Denver. Off-the-record appointment with General Cutler.

3   Lowry Air Force Base. Morning appointments with General Burgess (off the record); Ed Lane; Norris W. Cochran and family; H. Darby. To Cherry Hills Country Club for lunch and golf with L. H. Pexton, Mayor Nicholson, Joseph G. Dyer, R. Arnold, and Gordon Williams.

4   Lowry Air Force Base. Morning appointments with General McNarney; Senator Millikin; General Sprague. To Cherry Hills Country Club for luncheon followed by golf with J. Culbreath, J. Black, Mayor Nicholson, and N. Burnham.

5   Lowry Air Force Base. Morning appointments with

Ambassador Dunn; William Henry and Murray Snyder. To Cherry Hills Country Club for lunch and golf with G. Gregory and R. Arnold.

6   Lowry Air Force Base. Attends church services with Mrs. Eisenhower and Colonels Schulz and Draper. Tours base, followed by brunch with Colonel and Mrs. Cavenah.

7   Lowry Air Force Base. Morning appointments with Secretary Dulles; Secretary Stevens; C. Reid. To Cherry Hills Country Club for lunch with R. Arnold, General Snyder, F. Newton, and J. Culbreath. Golf with R. Arnold, F. Newton, and J. Culbreath.

8   Lowry Air Force Base. Morning appointment with H. J. Porter followed by haircut.

9   Lowry Air Force Base. Morning appointments with Alma Schneider; State Senator Nicholson; General Burgess (off the record). Visits Fitzsimons General Hospital. Evening departure for Washington, D.C., for funeral of Chief Justice Vinson.

10 Washington. Morning appointments with General Cutler; Secretary Dulles, H. E. Stassen, and D. Mac-Arthur II; A. S. Flemming; Vice-President Nixon, Attorney General Brownell, S. Adams, B. M. Shanley, and G. D. Morgan; Japanese Prince Akihito, Ambassador Araki, and J. F. Simmons; Secretary Durkin. Witnesses swearing-in of G. D. Morgan as Administrative Assistant to the President. Lunch with Secretary Wilson. Attends memorial services for Chief Justice Vinson. Afternoon departure for Denver, Colorado.

11 Lowry Air Force Base. Morning appointment with Vice-President Nixon. To Cherry Hills Country Club for golf.

12 Lowry Air Force Base. Morning appointments with P. G. Hoffman; Vice-President Nixon. To Cherry Hills Golf Club for golf.

13 Denver, Colorado. Attends services at Corona Presbyterian Church. To Cherry Hills Country Club for lunch with Mrs. Eisenhower, Major and Mrs. J. S. D. Eisenhower, General Snyder, and Leonard Kroenendock. To Brown Palace Hotel for dinner.

14   Denver, Colorado. Morning appointments with Ol-
      iver J. Bryan and family; Senator Johnson and
      Congressman Rogers; Thomas Campbell; Mason
      Knuckles (President, Republican Club), Milton J.
      Blake (President, Citizens for Eisenhower-Nixon),
      and James A. Gaynor (President, J. A. Gaynor and
      Co.); Admiral Leggett; E. J. Bermingham. To Denver
      Federal Center with General Snyder and A. Nielsen.
      Proceeds to A. Nielsen's ranch.

15   Lowry Air Force Base. Morning appointments with
      Senators Millikin, Butler, and Barrett; Congressmen
      Simpson and Chenoweth; B. S. Adkins and Ann
      Wheaton; John C. Cornelius. To Cherry Hills Coun-
      try Club for golf with R. Arnold, W. W. Flenniken,
      and R. Warren. Attends luncheon in his honor at
      country club.

16   Lowry Air Force Base. Morning appointment with
      State Senator McNichols; Secretary Benson; Chan-
      cellor Chester Alter (University of Denver). Receives
      Board of Directors, Uranium Ore Producers Asso-
      ciation of the Western States. To Cherry Hills Coun-
      try Club for golf with M. Knuckles, A. Schrepfer-
      man, and C. W. Allen.

17   Denver, Colorado. Fishing at B. F. Swan's ranch
      with Judge Phillips and A. Nielsen.

18   Lowry Air Force Base. Morning appointments with
      Kathleen Wortz; Carolyn Greene and Mrs. Thomas
      L. Pelican and family; General Henry L. Larsen (Di-
      rector, Colorado Civil Defense Agency); General
      Burgess; P. Hoyt. To Cherry Hills Country Club.

19   Denver, Colorado. To Chicago with Mrs. Eisenhower
      aboard the *Columbine*. Addresses Republican wom-
      en's meeting. To Washington, D.C.

20   Washington. Off-the-record appointments with Gen-
      eral Cutler; S. Adams, T. E. Stephens, and Attorney
      General Brownell; G. E. Allen.

21   Washington. Airborne for Westover Air Force Base,
      Chicopee, Massachusetts. Visits Eastern States Ex-
      position. Luncheon at Massachusetts Building. Pro-
      ceeds to Coliseum to deliver address. To Logan In-
      ternational Airport, East Boston, Massachusetts.
      Meets with publishers at Algonquin Club; R.

Choate. To Boston Garden to speak. Airborne for Washington, D.C.

22 Washington. Extends greetings to 79th Annual Convention of the American Bankers Association at Constitution Hall. Appointment with Ambassador Willis. Presents President's Cup to Lou Fageol. Witnesses swearing-in of I. J. Martin as Administrative Assistant to the President. Appointments with Senator H. A. Smith; C. L. Burgess (off the record). Visits initial meeting of the Commission on Foreign Economic Policy. Afternoon appointments with Secretary Wilson; P. Hotchkis (off the record); R. D. Muir and T. E. Stephens.

23 Washington. Breakfast with General Cutler and J. S. Lay. Off-the-record appointments with James F. Bell and G. Hauge; Secretaries Wilson and Talbott, and Admiral Radford. Receives United States Committee for United Nations Day. Speaks at meeting of President's Committee on Employment of the Physically Handicapped. Receives foreign delegates attending colloquium on Islamic culture. Appointments with A. W. Dulles; General Persons and VFW leaders; Postmaster General Summerfield; Secretary Dulles. Makes two films (for Community Chests and Councils of America and Ernie Pyle Testimonial Celebration). Hosts stag dinner for businessmen and government officials.

24 Washington. Breakfast with General Hull, followed by appointments with H. R. Reid (and General Persons—off the record); Admiral Strauss (off the record); National Security Council session; A. F. Burns (off the record); L. M. Pexton (off the record). Afternoon appointments with A. F. Burns and G. Hauge; S. Adams, G. Hauge, J. C. Hagerty, C. D. Jackson, E. J. Hughes, and B. N. Harlow; F. G. Gurley. Tea with U.S. Judicial Conference members.

25 Washington. Morning appointments with Ambassador Stuart and S. Adams (off the record); Secretary Benson; W. M. Canaday. Cabinet meeting. Afternoon appointments with J. B. Mintener (off the record); Senator Cordon; Foreign Minister Sunario (Indonesia) and Charge d'affaires Zairin Zain (Indonesian Embassy); Governor Shivers.

26   Washington. Morning appointments with Ambassador Gardner (off the record); Colonel Thomas Erie St. Johnston (Chief Constable, Lancashire, England); Ambassador Cumming; Ambassador Károly Szarka (Hungary) and R. D. Muir; Ambassador Syed Amjad Ali (Pakistan) and R. D. Muir; Ambassador Yilma Deressa (Ethiopia) and R. D. Muir; Ambassador Moussa Al-Shabandar (Iraq) and R. D. Muir; Edward Heath (Deputy Conservative Whip, Parliament) and B. M. Shanley; Ambassador Nufer and Dr. M. S. Eisenhower; K. McCann and Dr. M. S. Eisenhower (off the record).

27   Washington. Attends services at National Presbyterian Church with Mrs. Eisenhower.

28   Washington. Staff meeting followed by appointments with General Ian Jacob (BBC); Daniel Moorman (B&O Railroad); International Development Advisory Board; Admiral Leahy; Admiral Radford; G. Hauge and A. F. Burns; Secretary Wilson; Attorney General Brownell (off the record); Thai Prince Wan Waithayakon, Ambassador Sarasin, and R. D. Muir. Afternoon appointments with Judge Evan Howell (U.S. Court of Claims); Secretary Humphrey (off the record); H. E. Stassen (off the record). Hosts dinner for President and Senora de Remon (Panama) with Mrs. Eisenhower and members of the Cabinet and their wives.

29   Washington. Morning appointments with Colonel Randall and S. Adams (off the record); Commission on Organization of the Executive Branch of the Government; Foreign Minister Paul Van Zeeland (Belgium), Ambassador Silvercruys, Secretary Dulles, and Colonel Carroll. Opens Disabled American Veterans annual drive. Presents United States Treasury Distinguished Service Awards. Afternoon off-the-record appointments with Senator H. A. Smith, John V. Rife (Executive Vice-President, CIO), and M. M. Rabb; Ambassador V. K. Wellington Koo (China), General Chiang Ching-kuo, R. D. Muir, and General Carroll; G. Hauge (off the record); Secretary Anderson and Thomas S. Gates (Navy Under Secretary).

30   Washington. Off-the-record briefing by General Cutler and J. S. Lay. Witnesses swearing-in of Louis B.

Toomer as Treasury Registrar. Receives National Fisheries Institute representatives. Appointments with H. E. Stassen and Morris Wolf; Commission on Intergovernmental Relations; J. C. Hagerty and General Persons (off the record). News conference, followed by appointments with P. T. Sharples, Walter H. Annenberg (Publisher, *Philadelphia Enquirer*), Ward Wheelock, T. B. McCabe, Dr. M. S. Eisenhower, and General Carroll (off the record); Secretary Dulles (and General Carroll—off the record). Hosts stag luncheon in honor of Norwegian Prince Olav. Receives members of President's Advisory Committee on Housing. Appointments with H. Hoover (and S. Adams—off the record); Charles Geddes (President, Postal Telegraph and Telephone International) and William C. Doherty (President, National Association of Letter Carriers); Judge and Mrs. Frank Parent, Helen S. Bender, and Beverly Bender. To Sheraton-Carlton Hotel with Mrs. Eisenhower for dinner in their honor.

October   1   Washington. Morning appointments with Attorney General Brownell and Judge John J. Danaher (off the record); Richard J. Gray and Maurice A. Hutcheson (President, United Brotherhood of Carpenters and Joiners of America) to discuss labor situation; National Security Council session; Secretary Dulles and A. E. Stevenson. To Red Cross Chapter House for dedication ceremonies. Hosts stag luncheon in honor of A. E. Stevenson. Appointments with Ambassador Hearne (Ireland), Deputy Prime Minister Seán Lemass (Ireland), and Secretary Shean Leydon (Ireland), and R. D. Muir; Reverend William C. Martin (Resident Bishop) and Dr. Earl F. Adams (Secretary, National Council of Churches of Christ, USA); civil defense state directors; R. P. Burroughs and R. Cake.

            2   Washington. Morning appointments with A. S. Flemming (off the record); General Ely. Cabinet meeting followed by appointments with Attorney General Brownell and appointees Carroll Hinks and Hunter (off the record).

            3   Washington. Off-the-record breakfast with Secretary Dulles, C. D. Jackson, Admirals Strauss and Radford, H. E. Stassen, A. W. Dulles, E. J. Hughes, and Major J. S. D. Eisenhower. Morning off-the-record

appointments with H. C. Butcher; H. E. Stassen; Attorney General Brownell, S. Adams, and General Persons; J. P. Mitchell and M. M. Rabb. Appointments with D. MacArthur II, Antoine Pinay (former Prime Minister, France), and Ambassador Bonnet; P. G. Hoffman; Senator Knowland.

4 Washington. Attends services at National Presbyterian Church with Mrs. Eisenhower.

5 Washington. Breakfast with S. Adams, V. E. Peterson, and Paul Wagner (FCDA). Morning appointments with E. J. Hughes and B. N. Harlow (off the record); Senators H. A. Smith and Ives, and M. M. Rabb (off the record); Secretary Dulles and Foreign Affairs Minister Pyun Yung Tai (Korea); American Legion members; G. Hauge and A. F. Burns; Secretary Wilson. Receives "Junior Ambassadors" from Republics of Panama, Ecuador, Colombia, Peru, Bolivia, Chile, and Argentina. Witnesses swearing-in of E. Warren as Chief Justice at the Supreme Court Building. Afternoon appointments with Board of Inquiry members; American Veterans' Committee; Attorney General Brownell and L. A. Mashburn; General Leslie B. Nicholls (Chairman, Cable and Wireless, England); Ambassador Luce; Vice-President Nixon; H. E. Stassen; Postmaster General Summerfield.

6 Washington. Off-the-record appointments with B. N. Harlow; S. Adams and Robert E. Lee (off the record). To MATS terminal en route to Atlantic City, New Jersey, aboard *Columbine*. Delivers invocation at Convention Hall. Appointments with 6th National Assembly of United Church Women; New Jersey leaders, Operation Building Patio. Returns to Washington, D.C. Afternoon appointments with Secretary Dulles; E. N. Eisenhower. Receives boys of Saint Paul's Cathedral Choir, London, England.

7 Washington. Breakfast with S. Adams and W. W. Williams (off the record). Morning appointments with Secretary Benson, T. D. Morse, Budget Director Dodge, and S. Adams (off the record); F. Cowles; A. B. Kline, G. Hauge, and B. N. Harlow (off the record); C. R. Sligh, Jr.; Admiral Strauss. National Security Council session. Receives American Hungarian Federation delegation. Off-the-record lun-

cheon with E. N. Eisenhower and Richard Auerbach. Afternoon appointments with Colonel Schulz and Robert L. Biggers (Chrysler Corporation) (off the record); Admiral Stark; Budget Director Dodge.

8   Washington. Breakfast with S. Adams and L. W. Hall. To Statler Hotel to speak at the annual meeting of the American Council on Education. Appointments with R. M. Kyes; H. E. Stassen and representatives of British aircraft industry; Senator Ellender and I. J. Martin (off the record); Ambassador McIntosh; Governor Clement and family; E. A. Johnston (off the record); Ambassador Moose; Ambassador Mallory. Hosts luncheon in honor of Mr. and Mrs. E. J. Hughes. Afternoon appointment with J. C. Hagerty. News conference. Tea with Mr. and Mrs. J. A. McCone (off the record).

9   Washington. Witnesses swearing-in of J. P. Mitchell as Secretary of Labor. Off-the-record appointment with Secretary Dulles. Cabinet meeting. To Capitol to greet delegates to the 42nd Conference of the Inter-Parliamentary Union. Early afternoon appointments with Luther Evans (Director General, UNESCO); Mrs. W. G. Kreps (off the record); A. S. Flemming (off the record); Ambassador Bonnet, R. D. Muir, and French Watchmakers. Lunch with General Gruenther, D. MacArthur II, G. D. Morgan, I. J. Martin, and General Gruenther. Receives delegates and wives of Inter-Parliamentary Union with Mrs. Eisenhower.

10   Washington. Morning appointments with Attorney General Brownell; L. F. McCollum; W. C. Doherty and S. Adams (off the record); Mr. and Mrs. T. J. Watson. Off-the-record appointments with General Cutler and C. D. Jackson; S. Adams, G. Hauge, J. C. Hagerty, and B. N. Harlow; C. Roberts.

11   Washington. No official appointments.

12   Washington. Morning appointments with Congressman Broyhill and General Persons; V. L. Pandit and Secretary Dulles; Henry Mahady (National Commander, AMVETS), Rufus Wilson, Alvin Keller, David Schlothauer, and General Carroll; Admiral Radford; A. F. Burns and G. Hauge; Secretary Wilson; General Carroll and Knights of Columbus lead-

ers; N. Cummings and G. Hauge. Lunch with Senator Goldwater, Congressman Halleck, S. Adams, General Persons, I. J. Martin, and G. D. Morgan. Off-the-record afternoon appointment with Secretary Dulles.

13   Washington. Off-the-record appointment with General Cutler and J. S. Lay. National Security Council session. To Hershey Hotel in Hershey, Pennsylvania. Appointment with John Sollenberger (General Manager, Hershey Estates). Evening birthday celebration at Hershey Arena. Returns to Washington, D.C.

14   Washington. Morning appointments with Father Paul A. McNally (Dean, Georgetown Medical School); Secretary Dulles and D. MacArthur II; Senators Case, Duff, and Stennis, and General Persons (off the record); Congressman Thompson, General Persons, and Rural Electrification Officials; Ambassador Spruance; Ambassador Victor Andrade and J. M. Cabot; Ambassador Makins and Lord Cherwell. Receives Executive Committee of International Air Pioneers. To Union Station en route to Defiance, Ohio.

15   Defiance, Ohio. Addresses audience at Defiance College and attends cornerstone-laying ceremony. To Toledo, Ohio, and then Kansas City, Missouri. Motors to Muehlebach Hotel. Appointments with Perry Compton, H. Darby, L. C. Davis, Pearl Josserand, C. I. Noyer, G. Y. Cemple, Estelle Tanner, Prentice Townsend, and A. D. Welsh; John M. Olin (President, Olin Industries, Inc.). Dinner with Governors Arn, Donnelly, Shivers, and Thornton, Senators Carlson and Schoeppel, H. Darby, J. C. Hall, and Roy Roberts. Evening appointment with A. B. and Mrs. Eisenhower. Addresses Future Farmers of America in Municipal Auditorium.

16   Kansas City, Missouri. Attends Governors' Breakfast. To airport en route to Smoky Hill Air Force Base, Salina, Kansas. Proceeds to Eisenhower home near Abilene. Tours house and continues to residence of S. Heller for informal luncheon. Returns by plane to Kansas City. Attends Royal Dinner at Muehlebach Hotel. Attends dedication ceremonies at American Hereford Building and continues to American Royal Building before returning to hotel.

17   Kansas City. To New Orleans, Louisiana. Participates in parade to Jackson Square. Delivers short address. Departs in *Columbine* for Texas. Early evening reception at Governor's home, followed by dinner.

18   Mission, Texas. Attends church. Lunch with Governor Shivers's family and friends. Informal buffet supper at Governor Shivers's Ranch.

19   Texas. Morning departure for Falcon Dam, followed by journey to the international boundary. Receives Mexican and American officials at the Municipal Palace. Witnesses Mexican fiesta. Meets with Mexican President Adolfo Ruíz Cortinez and proceeds to dedication of the dam. To Laredo Air Force Base. Airborne for Washington, D.C.

20   Washington. Morning appointments with Secretary Dulles; General Cutler and National Catholic Community Service executives (off the record); General Daniel C. Spry (Head, Boy Scouts International Bureau); Milton Katz (Ford Foundation); Senator Flanders; Ambassador João Carlos Muñiz (Brazil) and J. F. Simmons; C. D. Jackson (off the record); Clarence Dillon, Sr.; Secretary Wilson.

21   Washington. Breakfast with General William Dean. Morning appointments with General Cutler and J. S. Lay (off the record); Michigan Republican leaders; J. C. Hagerty. News conference, followed by appointments with Congressman Taber; H. E. Stassen (off the record); Admiral Strauss. To Burning Tree Country Club for golf with J. Black (off the record). To Mayflower Hotel with C. D. Jackson for American Heritage Foundation reception. Attends National Symphony Orchestra at Constitution Hall with Mrs. Eisenhower, Chief Justice Warren, and Mr. and Mrs. S. Adams.

22   Washington. Morning appointments with E. J. Hughes and General Carroll; Ambassador Krekeler, State Secretary for Foreign Affairs Walter Hallstein (Germany), and Geoffrey W. Lewis (State Department); General Valluy (French NATO representative), Colonel Phillip Cocke (NATO), and General Carroll; Congressman Judd and group against China's admission to U.N.; National Security Council

session; Secretary Dulles, L. T. Merchant, and Homer M. Byington (Director, Office of Western European Affairs). Receives Advisory Council of Home Bank Loan Board. Records program for Committee on Religion in American Life. Afternoon appointments with L. W. Hall; P. G. Hoffman; Arthur K. Watson (Export Manager, IBM); Jesse Gard (Oregon RNC).

23   Washington. Morning appointments with Ambassador Lodge; Cabinet meeting; Secretary Dulles; Ambassador Riddleberger. Lunch with Secretary Benson, S. Adams, General Persons, G. Hauge, and D. Paarlberg. Afternoon appointment with C. D. Jackson.

24   Washington. Witnesses swearing-in of B. N. Harlow as Administrative Assistant to the President. Morning appointments with Secretary Talbott; E. T. Weir; Ambassador Moekarto Notowidigdo (Indonesia); Ambassador Manuel de Moya Alonzo (Dominican Republic) and J. F. Simmons; National Agricultural Advisory Commission; Attorney General Brownell. Luncheon with National Agricultural Advisory Commission members. To Camp David in afternoon with Mrs. Eisenhower and Commander Beach.

25   Camp David, Maryland. Meets with General and Mrs. Snyder. Visits with Mr. and Mrs. Lawrence Hansen. Returns to White House with Mrs. Eisenhower.

26   Washington. Early morning appointment with doctor and assistant for blood samples. Morning appointments with H. G. Crim; A. M. Cole, S. Adams, and G. Hauge; A. F. Burns and G. Hauge; Secretary Wilson; Secretary Dulles; Ambassador Matthews. Lunch with General Smith, K. McCann, S. Adams, and B. N. Harlow. Afternoon appointments with H. S. Vanderbilt, Dr. H. Branscomb, and General Cutler; Abdel Khalek Hassouna (Secretary General, League of Arab States), General Smith, and John D. Jernegan (Deputy Assistant Secretary of State); Secretary Humphrey. Hosts stag dinner.

27   Washington. Morning appointments with N. Thomas and S. Adams; Colonel Thomas H. King, Colonel Charles Boyer, and General Carroll; T. E. Stephens

and leaders of the United Spanish War Veterans; Foreign Minister Abdullah Bekir (Iraq), Ambassador Moussa Al-Shabandar (Iraq), and J. F. Simmons; Dr. Alberto Dominguez Campora (Uruguay, U.N. Delegate), Ambassador José A. Mora (Uruguay), and J. F. Simmons. Presents Congressional Medal of Honor to recipients.

28   Washington. Morning appointments with Senator Knowland; R. E. McConnell; General Cutler and J. S. Lay; J. C. Hagerty. News conference, followed by appointments with E. D. Eisenhower; Walter Stewart, S. Adams, A. F. Burns, and G. Hauge (off the record); James H. Douglas (Under Secretary, Air Force), General T. D. White (Deputy Chief of Staff), and General Carroll; General Carl H. Seals (off the record). Lunch with Admiral Samuel E. Morison (USNR), General Smith, General R. McClain, Commander Roger Pineau (USNR), and Commander Beach. Afternoon appointment with B. M. Shanley. Hosts dinner with Mrs. Eisenhower for King and Queen of Greece.

29   Washington. Delivers message to opening session of 4th American Forest Congress at Statler Hotel. National Security Council session. Appointment with Governor Lodge. Lunch with General Clark. Receives members of Federal Trade Commission and others.

30   Washington. Off-the-record breakfast with L. W. Hall, S. Adams, General Persons, J. C. Hagerty, and T. E. Stephens. Morning appointment with Ambassador Hill. Cabinet meeting, followed by appointments with Secretary Weeks; Admiral Leahy and Dr. Russell D. Cole (President, Cornell College); Ambassador Davis; Paul Hawkins and American Retail Federation leaders. Lunch with A. Nielsen. Afternoon appointments with Ambassador Makins and Lord Hives (Rolls Royce); Forest Farmers Association Cooperative representatives; Senator Carlson. To Greek Embassy with Mrs. Eisenhower for dinner in their honor.

31   Washington. No official appointments.

November 1   Washington. Attends services at National Presbyterian Church with Mrs. Eisenhower.

2   Washington. Morning appointments with H. E. Stassen; A. S. Flemming; Ambassador Nasrollah Entezam (Iran); G. Hauge and A. F. Burns; Secretary Wilson. Receives French singers with Mrs. Eisenhower.

3   Washington. Morning appointments with Secretaries Dulles and Wilson, and Admiral Duncan; Reverend B. Graham; Ambassador Buchanan; Attorney General Brownell and newly appointed U.S. Attorneys Edward Day, Donald E. Kelley, Louis G. Whitcomb, Theodore F. Bowes, William T. Plumer, and Jack D. H. Hays (off the record); G. Brown and B. M. Shanley; Frank Wood and Toddy L. Wynn (off the record); A. H. Sulzberger; Dr. Grayson Kirk (President, Columbia University), Douglas M. Black (Doubleday), A. H. Sulzberger, and J. A. Kouvenhoven (author); Governor Craig and Elmer "Doc" Sherwood; Hellen Keller and Polly Thompson. Makes television recording for dinner honoring Secretary Humphrey. Hosts State Dinner with Mrs. Eisenhower for Cabinet members and their wives.

4   Washington. Morning appointments with General Cutler and J. S. Lay; G. Hauge, Henry Chalmers (Department of Commerce), and S. Benedict (off the record); Dr. José Antonio Eguiguren (Peru, Supreme Court), Ambassador Berckemeyer, and J. F. Simmons; Congressman Miller and General Persons; Budget Director Dodge; Postmaster General Summerfield and Postal Transportation Service Superintendents. Receives group from American Bible Society with Mrs. Eisenhower. Luncheon with L. W. Douglas, Secretary Humphrey, General Burgess, G. Hauge, and A. F. Burns. Appointment with J. C. Hagerty. News conference.

5   Washington. Breakfast with Congressman Reed and I. J. Martin. Morning appointments with H. E. Stassen; Wesley Powell and E. J. Hopley (off the record); National Security Council session; Senator Upton and General Persons. Receives American Stock Yards Association Board of Directors. Off-the-record lunch with Mr. and Mrs. M. Katz, and Mr. and Mrs. L. M. Pexton. Off-the-record appointments with Robert W. Minor (Acting Deputy Attorney General) and new judges Elmer J. Schnackenberg

and Vernon Forbes; Attorney General Brownell; R. E. McConnell; C. Roberts.

6 Washington. Late morning appointments with Admiral Strauss, Ambassador Lodge, and C. D. Jackson (off the record); Ambassador Lodge; E. J. Bermingham (off the record); E. F. Mansure, S. Adams, and ten General Services Administration regional directors (off the record). Receives National Rural Electrification Cooperative Association members. Lunch with General Clark, Ome Loupart (Chairman, Phillips Electric), General Smith, Secretary Weeks, Ambassador Lodge, and R. M. Kyes (off the record). Hosts stag dinner.

7 Washington. Off-the-record appointments with Secretary Weeks; Murray Chotiner. Attends annual dinner at Burning Tree Country Club.

8 Washington. Attends services at the National Presbyterian Church with Mrs. Eisenhower.

9 Washington. Morning appointments with Secretary Dulles; W. F. Morrow and General Smith; Philip L. Graham (Publisher, *Washington Post*); G. Hauge and A. F. Burns; Secretary Wilson; Postmaster General Summerfield. Receives foreign delegates of U.S. Association of Military Surgeons Convention. Lunch with Secretary Dulles, General Smith, S. Adams, T. E. Stephens, and B. N. Harlow. Afternoon appointments with General M. G. Baker (off the record); General W. E. R. Covell and Bernard J. McKenna; members of the Supreme Court.

10 Washington. Morning appointments with Senator Cooper; Jewish War Veterans' leaders; A. S. Barnes and Co., Inc. representatives. Delivers greetings to delegates of United Daughters of the Confederacy convention at Shoreham Hotel. Presents Harmon International Trophies. Receives delegation from American Booksellers Association. Hosts luncheon with Mrs. Eisenhower in honor of USO-Pal Week. Records short film for larger film on the Boy Scout Jamboree. Delivers greeting to United States Information Agency staff. Off-the-record appointment with Admiral Strauss. Evening diplomatic reception.

11 Washington. Morning appointments with General

Cutler and J. S. Lay (off the record); Congressman Blatnik and General Persons; J. C. Hagerty. News conference. To Arlington National Cemetery to lay wreath on Tomb of the Unknown Soldier. Off-the-record appointment with Secretaries Dulles, Humphrey, and Wilson.

12   Washington. National Security Council session. Cabinet meeting. Late morning appointments with J. B. Mintener (off the record); Budget Director Dodge and R. R. Hughes (off the record); Governor-General Ghulam Mohammed (Pakistan), Ambassador Syed Amjad Ali (Pakistan), and Secretary Dulles. Hosts stag luncheon in honor of Governor-General Mohammed. Opens annual Christmas Seal sale. Afternoon appointments with Camille Gutt (International Chamber of Commerce) and W. L. Pierson; Senator Ferguson and General Persons. To Union Station with Mrs. Eisenhower. Departs by train for Ottawa, Canada.

13   Ottawa, Canada. Arrives in Ottawa in late morning. Visits National War Memorial and lays wreath. To Government House. Plants two trees with Mrs. Eisenhower on Government House grounds. Attends dinner and reception in their honor.

14   Ottawa, Canada. To Parliament Building to address Senate and House of Commons. Proceeds to Speaker's Chambers and then Room Sixteen to meet Cabinet members. Attends luncheon at Prime Minister's residence and visits the Embassy. Hosts dinner in honor of Governor General of Canada at Embassy. Late train departure from Ottawa.

15   Washington. Arrives in Washington, D.C.

16   Washington. Late morning appointments with G. Hauge and A. F. Burns; Senator Monroney and General Persons. Receives turkey from Poultry and Egg National Board and National Turkey Federation. Lunch with Senators Knowland and Dirksen, and General Persons. Afternoon appointment with Budget Director Dodge and G. D. Morgan. Hosts tea with Mrs. Eisenhower for Ambassador and Mrs. Zuleta-Angel, Foreign Minister Ezaristo Sourdis (Columbia), Dr. and Mrs. M. S. Eisenhower, General and Mrs. Littlejohn, and Mr. and Mrs. L. Eakin.

17   Washington. Morning appointments with Congress-
      man Wainwright and I. J. Martin; Congressman
      Becker and I. J. Martin; Secretary Dulles and E. A.
      Johnston; Postmaster General Summerfield, C. R.
      Hook, Eugene Lyons (Post Office Department), S.
      Adams, and General Persons; Secretary Weeks, Sec-
      retary Mitchell, and S. Adams (off the record); Sec-
      retary Humphrey (off the record); Professor James T.
      Shotwell (Columbia University), Dr. Samuel Lind-
      say, and B. M. Shanley. Meets with Trustees of
      Eisenhower Exchange Fellowships, Inc. Lunch with
      A. B. Kline and G. Hauge (and Dr. M. S. Eisenhower,
      Secretary Benson, and B. N. Harlow—off the record).
      Off-the-record meeting to discuss Bermuda Confer-
      ence. Hosts dinner in honor of Supreme Court of the
      United States.

18   Washington. Morning appointments with General
      Cutler and J. S. Lay (off the record); Congressman
      Taber; J. C. Hagerty. News conference. Receives the
      fifty-millionth telephone. Appointments with Secre-
      tary Humphrey, M. B. Folsom, Ken Campbell (Trea-
      sury Department), Dan Smith (Treasury Depart-
      ment), S. Adams, General Persons, G. Hauge, and
      A. F. Burns (off the record). To Statler Hotel for
      luncheon meeting of General Board of the National
      Council of the Churches of Christ. Briefly visits Na-
      tional Association of Ice Industries annual conven-
      tion. To Burning Tree Country Club for golf with N.
      Burnham, E. LeBaron, and M. Elbin.

19   Washington. Breakfast with Congressman Brown
      and I. J. Martin. Morning appointments with Mr.
      and Mrs. Jules Moch (off the record); Ambassador
      Mohammed Kabir Ludin (Afghanistan) (and J. F.
      Simmons—off the record); Bishop Oxnam and Dr.
      W. A. Visser't Hooft (General Secretary, World
      Council of Churches); National Security Council ses-
      sion; Secretary Dulles; Senator Butler (and General
      Persons—off the record); Secretary Wilson. After-
      noon appointments with Federal Power Commission
      members; Clayton E. Whipple (Agriculture Depart-
      ment), Ray A. Ioanes (Agriculture Department), and
      Thorsten Kalijare; Henry Chalmers (Department of
      Commerce), S. Adams, G. Hauge, and S. Benedict.

To Catholic University to receive honorary degree. Hosts stag dinner.

20 Washington. Off-the-record breakfast with L. W. Hall, Secretary Humphrey, Postmaster General Summerfield, Ambassador Lodge, S. Adams, and T. E. Stephens. Appointment with E. A. Johnston. Cabinet meeting, followed by appointments with Congressmen Sadlak and Sealy-Brown, and Senator Purtell. Witnesses swearing-in of C. F. Willis, as Assistant to the Assistant to the President and General Gruenther as Assistant to the Special Assistant to the President. Off-the-record luncheon with Dr. V. Bush, Admiral Strauss, and C. D. Jackson. Off-the-record appointments with Sister Joachim and Sister Cornelia; Attorney General Brownell and J. L. Rankin.

21 Washington. Morning appointments with H. E. Stassen (off the record); O. R. Cheatham; A. W. Havela (President, Midwest Finnish Publishing Co.) and G. Hauge; Admiral Radford (off the record); Judge Irving Kaufman and family (off the record); Secretary Humphrey, Congressmen Reed and Curtis, I. J. Martin, and General Persons; Secretary Dulles and H. Hoover, Jr. (off the record); C. D. Jackson; Secretary Talbott (off the record); B. N. Harlow.

22 Washington. Attends services at the National Presbyterian Church with Mrs. Eisenhower.

23 Washington. Breakfast with General Cutler and J. S. Lay. Morning appointments with National Security Council session; I. J. Martin; Budget Director Dodge and R. R. Hughes; Secretary Benson and G. Hauge; Mr. and Mrs. J. W. Perry (off the record); E. R. Irwin and S. Mudden (off the record). Lunch with B. M. Baruch. Afternoon appointments with Congressman Fenton and General Persons; L. Finder; A. S. Flemming; C. L. Sulzberger and General Carroll (off the record); E. Goldman (off the record). To Mayflower Hotel with Mrs. Eisenhower for B'nai B'rith Dinner.

24 Washington. To MATS terminal with Mrs. Eisenhower. Airborne for Fort Benning and Augusta, Georgia.

25 Augusta, Georgia. No official appointments.

26 Augusta, Georgia. No official appointments.

27 Augusta, Georgia. No official appointments.

28 Augusta, Georgia. No official appointments.

29 Augusta, Georgia. Late evening, arrives in Washington, D.C.

30 Washington. Morning appointment with Secretary Dulles. To Department of Agriculture to view the soil and water conservation display. Appointments with Admiral Radford; A. F. Burns and G. Hauge; Secretary Wilson; leaders of Variety Clubs International. Afternoon appointments with Ambassador Wadsworth; A. J. Robertson (off the record); Secretary Dulles, A. W. Dulles, Admirals Radford and Strauss, R. M. Kyes, and C. D. Jackson (off the record).

December 1 Washington. Off-the-record appointments with Secretary Dulles; Bela Kornitzer and Murray Snyder; C. D. Jackson; Senator Watkins and G. D. Morgan; Attorney General Brownell; H. E. Stassen; Generals Swing and Carroll. Receives Retired Officers Association officers. Afternoon off-the-record appointments with Senator Bridges and G. D. Morgan; Attorney General Brownell and new District Attorneys Osrow Cobb, Duncan W. Daugherty, Julian P. Gaskill, George E. Rapp, and N. Welch Morrissette, Jr. Attends Judicial reception.

2 Washington. Breakfast with General Cutler and J. S. Lay (off the record). Morning appointment with Murray Snyder. News conference, followed by appointments with Secretary Dulles, D. MacArthur II, D. K. E. Bruce, and F. C. Nash. To Shoreham Hotel to extend greetings to Mid-Century Conference on Resources for the Future. Afternoon off-the-record appointments with Budget Director Dodge; R. B. Stearns. Hosts off-the-record dinner for Secretary Benson, T. D. Morse, Dr. W. I. Myers, D. Paarlberg, I. J. Martin, and G. D. Morgan.

3 Washington. Breakfast with L. W. Hall. Morning appointments with Secretaries Dulles and Wilson, R. M. Kyes, and C. D. Jackson (off the record). National Security Council session, followed by appointments with L. W. Douglas; Congressman Reed and

I. J. Martin. Afternoon appointments with W. W. Flenniken (off the record); Budget Director Dodge. Hosts stag dinner at White House.

4 Washington. To MATS terminal en route to Bermuda. To Mid-Ocean Club with Prime Minister Churchill. Attends Heads of State meeting, followed by dinner hosted by Governor General Hood (Bermuda).

5 Bermuda. Late morning appointment with Prime Minister Churchill, Lord Cherwell, and Admiral Strauss. Hosts luncheon in honor of the French President of the Council of Ministers. Attends Heads of State meeting. Dinner with Prime Minister Churchill, A. Eden, and Secretary Dulles.

6 Bermuda. To Kindley Air Force Base for tour and church services. Appointment with Prime Minister Churchill at the Mid-Ocean Club. Hosts luncheon in honor of the British. Attends Heads of State meeting. Hosts dinner in honor of Governor General Hood.

7 Bermuda. Morning appointments with Prime Minister Churchill. Attends Heads of State meeting followed by luncheon hosted by French. Heads of State meeting. Hosts dinner for American officials. Returns to Heads of State meeting.

8 Bermuda. Early afternoon departs for New York, New York. Addresses United Nations Assembly, followed by a reception hosted by United Nations Secretary General Hammarskjöld. Departs for Washington, D.C.

9 Washington. Morning appointments with Secretary Wilson; Ambassador Johnson. Cabinet meeting. Afternoon off-the-record appointments with Admiral Radford; General Cutler and S. E. Gleason; S. Adams and G. Hauge. Attends diplomatic dinner.

10 Washington. Morning appointments with Ambassador Chapin; J. Melton and family; National Security Council session; R. L. Johnson, Dr. Martin Merson, and General Carroll. Lunch with Senator Duff (off the record). Afternoon appointments with C. E. Anderson; R. T. Reed; Senator Potter and General Persons; Secretary Humphrey and Budget Director Dodge. Hosts stag dinner at White House.

11   Washington. Morning appointments with Roy Roberts (off the record); Ambassador Claude Corea (Ceylon) and R. D. Muir; Mrs. O. B. Lord, Mrs. R. Harris, and S. Adams. Cabinet meeting, followed by appointments with H. S. Cullman and T. E. Stephens; Secretary Hobby (off the record); P. Hoyt and S. Adams (off the record); John Campbell (off the record). Afternoon appointments with T. J. Watson (off the record); Governor Dewey and Budget Director Dodge.

12   Washington. Breakfast with S. Adams, C. D. Jackson, J. C. Hagerty, General Persons, B. N. Harlow, K. McCann, Charles Moore, and R. Montgomery (off the record). Morning appointments with Budget Director Dodge, William F. Schaub (Budget Bureau), Ellis H. Veach (Budget Bureau), R. M. Kyes, W. J. McNeil, Lyle S. Garlock (Defense Department), Admiral Radford, Generals Persons and Cutler; V. E. Peterson. Receives Pan American Medical Association officers. Attends Gridiron Dinner at Statler Hotel.

13   Washington. No official appointments.

14   Washington. Breakfast with Secretaries Weeks and Mitchell, S. Adams, B. M. Shanley, I. J. Martin, and G. D. Morgan. Speaks at White House Conference of Mayors opening session. Appointments with G. Hauge and A. F. Burns; Quetico-Superior Committee members; James Petrillo (President, American Federation of Musicians); Ambassador Abdul Munim Rifai (Jordan) and J. F. Simmons; National Security Training Commission. Afternoon appointments with General Cutler and J. S. Lay; Ambassador Lodge. Greets Vice-President and Mrs. Nixon. Hosts reception for the delegates to White House Conference of Mayors.

15   Washington. Morning off-the-record appointments with H. C. Butcher; Attorney General Brownell, J. E. Hoover, Admiral Strauss, A. S. Flemming, and General Cutler; Budget Director Dodge. National Security Council session. Cabinet meeting. Afternoon appointments with Secretary Weeks, R. B. Murray, and Charles L. Dearing (Deputy Under Secretary of Commerce, Transportation); Mayor Robinson, T. A.

Burke, and S. Adams (off the record); C. E. Manion. Attends diplomatic dinner.

16 Washington. Breakfast with L. W. Hall and T. E. Stephens (off the record). Morning appointments with A. S. Flemming; G. Hauge and members of Citizens Committee for the Hoover Report; General Persons and J. C. Hagerty (off the record); News conference, followed by meeting to discuss the St. Lawrence Seaway. Appointments with National Sheriffs' Association representatives; Congressman Ayres and G. D. Morgan. Receives RNC Nationality Groups Advisory Committee. Afternoon appointments with Anna Rosenberg; Senator Smith and B. M. Shanley; B. N. Harlow (off the record). National Security Council session.

17 Washington. Breakfast with S. Adams, General Persons, G. D. Morgan, J. C. Hagerty, and I. J. Martin. Legislative meetings. Luncheon with various legislative officers. Continuation of legislative meetings. To Statler Hotel for Golden Jubilee of Powered Flight dinner.

18 Washington. Legislative Meetings. Luncheon with various legislative officers. Continuation of legislative meetings.

19 Washington. Morning off-the-record appointments with Governor Thornton and S. Adams; H. E. Stassen. Legislative Meetings. Luncheon with various legislative officers. Continuation of Legislative Meetings.

20 Washington. Attends morning services at the National Presbyterian Church. Off-the-record appointments with Secretary Dulles; K. C. Royall.

21 Washington. Morning appointments with Admiral Strauss and General Cutler (off the record); A. W. Dulles and General John Russell Dean; P. Young; G. Hauge and A. F. Burns; Secretaries Wilson, Dulles, and Anderson, and Drs. Melvin A. Casberg and Frank B. Berry; Secretary Dulles and A. Dean; Secretary Mitchell, B. M. Shanley, S. Adams, A. F. Burns, G. D. Morgan, and I. J. Martin; Dr. Snyder and children (off the record). To home of B. M. Shanley with Mrs. Eisenhower for Christmas party (off the record).

22   Washington. Morning appointments with General Cutler and J. S. Lay (off the record); Ambassador Aldrich; Congressmen pledging their support; Secretaries Dulles and Wilson, R. M. Kyes, Admiral Strauss, R. R. Bowie, J. S. Lay, S. E. Gleason, and Generals Smith, Luedecke, Cutler, and Ridgway; Mrs. Eugene Meyer; Secretaries Wilson and Stevens. Afternoon appointments with Secretary Benson and Dr. William I. Myers (Chairman, National Agricultural Advisory Commission); Frank Donahue and Colonel Schulz (off the record); J. C. Hagerty, K. McCann, C. Moore, and R. Montgomery (off the record); Secretary Humphrey (off the record); Budget Director Dodge (off the record).

23   Washington. Morning appointments with General Collins; Postmaster General Summerfield, Charles Folger (American Red Cross), and P. L. Graham; American Medical Association members. National Security Council session. Afternoon rehearsal in Broadcasting Room. Off-the-record appointment with Postmaster General Summerfield.

24   Washington. Morning appointments with H. E. Stassen (off the record); Attorney General Brownell (off the record); Alfalfa Club members; American Newspaper Publishers' Association members; Secretary Dulles; H. E. Stassen and Raymond Sheppard (FOA Technician). Greets White House staff at Annual Christmas Reception with Mrs. Eisenhower. Afternoon appointments with A. M. Cole, R. R. Hughes, G. Hauge, G. D. Morgan, and S. Benedict. Late afternoon, speaks to the nation, and then participates in lighting of the National Community Christmas Tree.

25   Washington. To MATS terminal en route to Augusta, Georgia.

26   Augusta, Georgia. No official appointments.

27   Augusta, Georgia. Attends services at the Reid Memorial Presbyterian Church with Mrs. Eisenhower.

28   Augusta, Georgia. Morning appointment with J. C. Hagerty, K. McCann, and C. Moore.

29   Augusta, Georgia. Morning appointments with J. C.

Hagerty, K. McCann, and C. Moore; General Van Fleet; A. F. Burns and G. Hauge.

30 Augusta, Georgia. No official appointments.

31 Augusta, Georgia. No official appointments.

1954

January 1 Augusta, Georgia. Morning meeting with Ambassador Lodge, Budget Director Dodge, A. S. Flemming, S. Adams, General Persons, B. N. Harlow, G. D. Morgan, I. J. Martin, and J. Jessup.

2 Augusta, Georgia. Morning appointments with General Cutler; Ambassador Lodge, Budget Director Dodge, A. S. Flemming, S. Adams, General Persons, B. N. Harlow, G. D. Morgan, I. J. Martin, and J. Jessup.

3 Augusta, Georgia. Attends services at St. James Methodist Church with Mrs. Eisenhower. Late afternoon departure for Washington, D.C. Early evening, arrives at White House.

4 Washington. Cabinet meeting followed by appointments with Ambassador Donovan; Secretary Benson; Albert C. Beeson (Candidate, NLRB) and S. Adams (off the record); S. Adams and National Security Training Commission members (off the record). Addresses nation on radio and television.

5 Washington. Morning appointments with Postmaster General Summerfield (off the record); Secretary Dulles; Secretaries Dulles and Wilson, H. E. Stassen, Ambassador Lodge, and R. M. Kyes. Presents National Achievement Award to Senator M. C. Smith. Legislative meeting. Hosts luncheon for congressional members. Afternoon appointments with Secretary Wilson; Attorney General Brownell and J. M. Harlan (off the record); B. N. Harlow (off the record).

6 Washington. Attends services at National Presbyterian Church. Morning appointments with G. Hauge, A. F. Burns, Neil H. Jacoby (CEA), and Walter W. Stewart (CEA); B. N. Harlow (off the record); Presbyterian Church leaders; Ambassador Luce. Hosts luncheon with Mrs. Eisenhower for Secretary

and Mrs. Dulles, Congresswoman Bolton, Ambassador and Mrs. Aldrich, Ambassador Luce, C. D. Jackson, and General Cutler. Receives Virginsville Grange members with Mrs. Eisenhower.

7 Washington. Morning off-the-record appointment with Senator Dirksen. Delivers State of the Union Address to Joint Session of Congress. To Burning Tree Country Club for golf with J. Black and J. E. McClure (off the record). Off-the-record appointments with H. Darby and Ray Firestone; General Cutler; Secretary Dulles, Attorney General Brownell, Senators Bricker, Ferguson, Wiley, and Knowland, H. Phleger, J. L. Rankin, Charles Webb (Assistant, Senator Bricker), Dr. Francis O. Wilcox (Foreign Relations Committee), S. Adams, General Persons, and I. J. Martin.

8 Washington. National Security Council session. Appointments with H. E. Stassen and C. Tyler Wood (Economic Coordinator, Korea, FOA); Ambassador Krekeler, Jacob Altmeier (German Parliament), and J. F. Simmons; Senator Thye and S. Adams. Lunch with Ambassador Lodge (off the record). Afternoon off-the-record appointment with W. E. Robinson, L. W. Hall, Attorney General Brownell, Postmaster General Summerfield, and T. E. Stephens.

9 Washington. Morning appointments with L. W. Bentley (off the record); A. S. Flemming, Commander Beach, and General Paul; Budget Director Dodge, Secretary Benson, John H. Davis (Assistant Secretary, Agriculture), and G. Hauge (off the record). Receives Delbert Daines, March of Dimes Poster Boy. Afternoon appointment with Secretary Humphrey, G. E. Allen, and J. Lemmon (off the record).

10 Washington. Afternoon off-the-record meeting with Secretary Weeks, Secretary Mitchell, Budget Director Dodge, S. Adams, I. J. Martin, and C. Moore.

11 Washington. Morning appointments with Legislative Leaders; Admiral Radford; G. Hauge and A. F. Burns; Secretary Wilson; Senator Lehman, Julius Edelstein (Assistant, Senator Lehman), and I. J. Martin; Frank J. Sulloway (RNC, New Hampshire) and S. Adams (off the record). Lunch with General

Smith. Afternoon appointments with H. E. Stassen and Secretary McKay; dentist. Hosts stag dinner.

12 Washington. Morning appointments with Congressman Staggers and I. J. Martin; P. G. Hoffman; Secretary Wilson. Addresses opening of Tenth Annual White House Conference of Business and Industry Associates of the Advertising Council. Presents Congressional Medal of Honor to recipients. Presents Big Brother of the Year award to Captain E. V. Rickenbacker, followed by appointments with J. V. Moon; Morris Snyder (off the record). Evening Departmental reception.

13 Washington. Morning off-the-record appointments with F. A. Seaton; Secretary Stevens; J. C. Hagerty. News conference, followed by appointments with Lord Wakehurst (Governor General, Northern Ireland), Ambassador Makins, and J. F. Simmons; NAACP leaders; S. W. Richardson. Off-the-record appointment with Budget Director Dodge and G. Hauge.

14 Washington. Off-the-record breakfast with Secretary Dulles and Attorney General Brownell. Morning appointments with General Cutler and J. S. Lay; General John W. O'Daniel. National Security Council session. Makes recording for Red Cross Drive. Appointments with Congressman Rayburn, Ralph Porter, E. B. Chapman, J. "Lip" Newell, and Freeman Carney; Secretary Dulles, Admiral Arthur C. Davis (Defense Department), and H. A. Byroade.

15 Washington. Receives members of Commission on Judicial and Congressional Salaries. Cabinet meeting, followed by appointments with Senator Flanders; Senator Case and Paul Bellamy.

16 Washington. Morning appointments with Budget Director Dodge and J. C. Hagerty (off the record); Secretary Dulles, R. M. Kyes, Admiral Strauss, General Smith, Admiral Davis, and C. D. Jackson; Ambassador Guillermo Toriello and J. M. Cabot; S. Adams, General Persons, B. N. Harlow, and J. Jessup (off the record); General Persons.

17 Washington. Attends services at National Presbyterian Church with Mrs. Eisenhower.

18   Washington. Morning appointments with Secretary Mitchell, S. Adams, and General Persons (off the record); Legislative Leaders; G. Hauge and A. F. Burns; Secretary Wilson, Admiral Radford, and A. S. Flemming; L. M. Pexton and Ray Willoughby. Lunch with L. F. McCollum. Rehearses film for Lincoln Day dinners. Visits reception in honor of Washington Press Corps.

19   Washington. Receives international art museum directors, followed by appointments with Ambassador Schoenfeld; General Cutler and J. S. Lay (off the record); A. W. Dulles, General Smith, Admiral Radford, and General Cutler. Makes film for Lincoln Day dinners. Afternoon appointments with Secretary Humphrey; B. M. Shanley; Ambassador Lodge. Hosts dinner with Mrs. Eisenhower for Vice-President Nixon.

20   Washington. Breakfast with Secretary Dulles. Cabinet meeting. Receives Cabinet members, RNC leaders, Citizens for Eisenhower Committee leaders, and White House staff. Morning appointments with Senator Knowland and Harry Lundberg (AFL); Vice-President Nixon and General Persons; W. M. Martin and G. Hauge; Thomas Bolack (off the record). To Fort Leslie J. McNair with Colonel Schulz for National War College Alumni Association luncheon.

21   Washington. Breakfast with Ambassador Lodge, L. W. Hall, and S. Adams (off the record). Off-the-record appointments with L. W. Hall; Colonel Randall, S. Adams, and G. Hauge; T. D. Morse. National Security Council session. Receives National Grange leaders. Lunch with Dr. M. S. Eisenhower. Afternoon appointments with Dr. M. S. Eisenhower, General Smith, J. M. Cabot, S. C. Waugh, Secretaries Humphrey and Weeks, Andrew N. Overby (Assistant Secretary of Treasury), S. W. Anderson, and Glen Edgerton (Import-Export Bank); W. P. Rogers, Senators Butler and Beall, and Judge S. E. Sobeloff; Senator Knowland and National Federation of Republican Women representatives; Mrs. R. B. Murray, Mrs. Henry S. Jones, Mrs. Lewis Borker, and I. J. Martin to discuss Bricker amendment. Hosts stag dinner at White House.

22 Washington. Morning appointments with Harry D. Collier (Standard Oil); J. D. Simmons; A. F. Burns.

23 Washington. To Statler Hotel for 41st Annual Alfalfa Club dinner.

24 Washington. Attends services at National Presbyterian Church with Mrs. Eisenhower.

25 Washington. Morning appointments with Legislative Leaders; A. F. Burns, N. H. Jacoby, W. W. Stewart, and G. Hauge; A. S. Flemming; Ambassador Warren. Signs Armed Forces Day Proclamation. Appointments with Secretary Wilson; Senator George.

26 Washington. Off-the-record breakfast with Senators Knowland and Dworshak. Morning appointments with Oliver C. Carmichael (President, University of Alabama) and General Persons; Dr. Philip V. Cardon (Director General, U.N. Food and Agriculture Organization), Secretary Benson, and J. H. Davis; Secretary McKay; Harold Russell (WVF) and Jeremiah Sundel (WVF); National Association of Manufacturers leaders; Secretary Anderson and Admiral Carney; Ambassador Don Luis Oscar Boettner (Paraguay), Luis Maria Ramirez Boettner (Minister, Paraguay), and R. D. Muir; H. E. Stassen (off the record). Afternoon appointment with General Smith.

27 Washington. Receives National Council of Catholic Women Board of Directors. Appointments with Secretary Humphrey (off the record); J. C. Hagerty. News conference, followed by appointment with Congressman Kersten (off the record). Receives RNC Jewish Advisory Committee. Luncheon with Ambassador Makins, General John Whiteley (British Joint Services Mission), and Air Chief Marshal William Elliot. Appointments with Republican group from Pennsylvania; A. F. Burns. Receives and hosts dinner for President and Mrs. Celal Bayar (Turkey).

28 Washington. Morning appointment with Vice-President Nixon, Senators Knowland, Ferguson, and Millikin, W. P. Rogers, S. Adams, General Persons, and I. J. Martin; National Security Council session; Thomas Mahaffey and Elmer Sherwood from Indiana; Mrs. Douglas Chandor (artist's wife). Afternoon

appointments with Senator Mundt and Kiwanis International leaders; General and Mrs. Joyce (off the record).

29 Washington. Morning appointments with NSF Governing Board and G. Hauge; Secretary McKay and C. Petrus Peterson (President, National Reclamation Association) (off the record); General Smith, Attorney General Brownell, and H. Phleger (off the record); Mr. and Mrs. Robert W. Gunderson (RNC, South Dakota) (off the record); Cabinet meeting; Secretary Benson and I. J. Martin (off the record); Henry Steeger (Publisher, Popular Publications, Inc.) and Noel B. Gerson; H. A. Rusk and S. Adams. Lunch with Dr. M. S. Eisenhower (off the record). To Walter Reed Hospital to visit Generals Snyder, Vandenberg, Carroll, George A. Horkan, and Reuben Jenkins. Afternoon appointment with J. B. Mintener (off the record). To Turkish Embassy with Mrs. Eisenhower for dinner in their honor.

30 Washington. Signs H. R. 6665. Morning meeting with Secretary Weeks, R. B. Murray, M. Brenner (Assistant Secretary of Commerce), V. E. Peterson, S. Adams, B. M. Shanley, and Civil Aeronautics Board members Chan Gurney, Oswald Ryan, and Harmar D. Denny (off the record); Congressman Chenoweth and Leo R. Gottlieb. Afternoon off-the-record appointment with Attorney General Brownell.

31 Washington. Attends special mass at Saint Matthew's Cathedral. Late afternoon appointment with Attorney General Brownell (off the record).

February 1 Washington. Morning appointments with Legislative Leaders; Admiral Radford; A. F. Burns and G. Hauge; Secretary Benson. Receives winner of National Negro Elks oratorical contest. Off-the-record lunch with C. S. Jones. Afternoon off-the-record appointments with Secretary Anderson and S. Adams; Attorney General Brownell and Senators Knowland, Ferguson, and Millikin.

2 Washington. Morning appointments with Attorney General Brownell (off the record); Senator Knowland and Attorney General Brownell (off the record); Congressman Hiestand and Mr. and Mrs. L. I. Mc-

Clellan (President, California Real Estate Association). Receives businessmen to discuss Randall Commission. Appointments with Ambassador Peurifoy; Senator Byrd and Admiral Byrd. Evening Army and Navy reception.

3   Washington. Off-the-record appointments with General Cutler and J. S. Lay; J. C. Hagerty. News conference, followed by appointments with Ambassador Mora and Rotary International officials; Secretary Wilson. Receives winner of National Association of Real Estate Boards nationwide essay contest. Lunch with Congressman Hope and G. D. Morgan (off the record). Receives National Milk Producers Federation Executive Committee. Afternoon off-the-record appointments with Ambassador Rafael de la Colina (Mexico), J. M. Cabot, and J. L. Rankin; Attorney General Brownell, Postmaster General Summerfield, L. W. Hall, W. E. Robinson, B. C. Duffy, and T. E. Stephens.

4   Washington. To Mayflower Hotel for Prayer Breakfast by International Council for Christian Leadership. Morning appointments with Herbert Blunck (Manager, Statler Hotel), Mr. and Mrs. Max Blouet (Manager, George V Hotel); National Security Council session; H. E. Stassen (off the record). Presents Medal of Freedom to General Robert G. Woodside. Lunch with Walker G. Buckner. Afternoon off-the-record appointments with Admiral Strauss; J. L. Murphy and Jacqueline Hume; General Smith; J. C. Hagerty. Hosts stag dinner.

5   Washington. Cabinet meeting. Photographs with the Postmaster General for National Geographic Society. Receives Young Republican National Federation Executive Committee. Afternoon appointment with Secretaries Talbott and Wilson (off the record). Hosts tea with Mrs. Eisenhower for RNC Finance Committee and State Finance Chairmen. Visits Lincoln Day dinner at Uline Arena with Mrs. Eisenhower.

6   Washington. Off-the-record breakfast with C. Roberts. Morning appointments with Ford C. Frick (Baseball Commissioner, NYC) and Horace Stoneham (President, NY Giants); Sylvester Weaver

(President, NBC), General Sarnoff and son, and Ray Scherer; Donald B. Lourie (Under Secretary of State); Admirals Radford and Strauss, Budget Director Dodge, and General Cutler (off the record); B. C. Duffy, and J. Bassett. To Shoreham Hotel with Dr. M. S. Eisenhower for All Pennsylvania College Alumni Association of Washington, D.C. luncheon. To Statler Hotel for Washington Radio and Television Correspondents Association dinner.

7　Washington. Attends services at New York Avenue Presbyterian Church with Mrs. Eisenhower. Broadcasts live for American Legion program, *Back to God*.

8　Washington. Morning appointments with Legislative Leaders; Congressman Angell; A. F. Burns and G. Hauge; Secretary Wilson; Republicans from Indiana; Sir Alfred Robens (Parliament member), Sir Archibald Gordon (Labor Counselor, British Embassy), and B. M. Shanley. Hosts luncheon with Mrs. Eisenhower for FOA Public Advisory Board. Hosts stag dinner. Throws switch to open Third International Trade Fair in Seattle, Washington.

9　Washington. Breakfast with Vice-President Nixon. Morning appointments with Senator Byrd and Kenneth Chorley; Admiral H. Kent Hewitt; Ambassador Antonio Facio (Costa Rica) and R. D. Muir; J. E. Hoover (off the record). Receives Boy Scouts' "Report to the Nation." Off-the-record luncheon with J. E. Hoover, Secretary Humphrey, R. W. Woodruff, and General Persons.

10　Washington. Morning off-the-record appointments with General Cutler and S. E. Gleason; C. L. Burgess and D. Russell; J. C. Hagerty. News conference. Receives United Defense Fund Campaign leaders followed by appointments with Secretary Stevens; Ambassador Kemper. Lunch with Ambassador Lodge. Hosts stag dinner.

11　Washington. Breakfast with Congressmen Wolcott and Phillips, S. Adams, and G. D. Morgan. Receives Cordell Hull Foundation for International Education Board of Trustees. Appointments with Postmaster General Summerfield (off the record); National Security Council session; General Hull. Presents National Geographic Society Hubbard Medal to Mount

Everest Expedition. Lunch with S. S. Larmon. Afternoon appointment with H. E. Stassen.

12   Washington. Breakfast with General Curtis. Morn-
      ing appointments with Senator Hickenlooper; Con-
      gressman Young; Allen C. McIntosh and Don Eck
      (National Editorial Association); S. Adams, Secre-
      tary Benson, J. H. McConnell, and R. Rizley (off the
      record); H. C. Butcher (off the record). To Lincoln
      Memorial for wreath-laying ceremonies. To MATS
      terminal en route to Spencer Air Base, Moultrie,
      Georgia. Motors directly to plantation of Secretary
      Humphrey.

13   Thomasville, Georgia. Hunts quail with Secretary
      Humphrey.

14   Washington. Returns via *Columbine* to Washington.

15   Washington. Morning appointments with Legislative
      Leaders; Admiral Radford; A. F. Burns and G.
      Hauge; R. M. Kyes and W. M. Rand; Congressman
      Hiestand and V. John Krehbiel (RNC, Los Angeles).
      Afternoon appointments with Ambassador Willauer;
      Senator H. A. Smith; General Smith. Receives Veter-
      ans of Foreign Wars national leaders in Rose Garden.

16   Washington. Morning appointments with Elmer
      Staatz (Operations Coordinating Board) and G.
      Hauge (off the record); General Cutler and J. S. Lay
      (off the record); Cabinet meeting, followed by ap-
      pointments with Senators Dworshak, Malone, An-
      derson, and Hayden and G. Hauge; Senator Ander-
      son (off the record). Receives overseas students
      sponsored by *New York Herald Tribune*. Afternoon ap-
      pointments with A. S. Flemming; Senators Watkins
      and Bennett, Congressmen Stringfellow and Daw-
      son, and I. J. Martin; Secretary Mitchell and E. J.
      Wilkins (off the record); Colonel Lee V. Harris; Ad-
      miral Strauss and B. N. Harlow (off the record).
      Hosts dinner with Mrs. Eisenhower for Speaker of
      the House.

17   Washington. National Security Council session. Ad-
      dresses opening session of White House Conference
      on Traffic Safety. Morning appointments with Timo-
      thy J. O'Connor (Police Commissioner, Chicago) and
      son; Governor Lausche (off the record); Congressmen

Arends and Short, and John Blandford (Special Counsel, HASC); Ambassador Allison; Ambassador van Roijen, Cornelis Staf (Minister of Defense, Netherlands), and R. M. Kyes. Afternoon appointment with J. C. Hagerty, followed by News conference. To MATS terminal with Mrs. Eisenhower and E. Doud en route to California. Arrives in Palm Springs, California, and motors directly to Smoke Tree Ranch of P. H. Helms.

18   Palm Springs, California. Golf at Tamarisk Country Club with B. Hogan, P. G. Hoffman, and P. H. Helms. Luncheon with F. F. Gosden, G. E. Allen, P. G. Hoffman, P. H. Helms, B. Hogan, R. Fleet, and F. Turner.

19   Palm Springs, California. Golf at Thunderbolt Club with L. K. Firestone, H. T. Dent, and J. Dawson. Luncheon with partners as well as P. G. Hoffman, C. Garfield, G. E. Allen, D. Zanuck, and P. H. Helms. Visits Jacqueline Cochran in Indio, G. E. Allen in La Quinta, and returns to Smoke Tree Ranch.

20   Palm Springs, California. Golf at Thunderbolt Club with P. G. Hoffman, P. H. Helms, and G. E. Allen. Luncheon with partners as well as P. Helms, Jr., E. Conley, K. B. Norris, H. M. Leisure, S. Goldwyn, J. Dawson, and H. Hazelthime. Returns to Smoke Tree Ranch. Late evening visits dentist in Palm Springs for broken cap of front tooth.

21   Palm Springs, California. Attends services at Palm Springs Community Church with Mrs. Eisenhower. Hosts evening reception at Smoke Tree Ranch.

22   Palm Springs, California. Golf at Tamarisk Country Club with P. G. Hoffman, P. H. Helms, and B. Hogan. Luncheon with partners as well as B. Dean, R. Cobert, J. Ballinger, S. Whitworth, J. G. Dyer, R. Arnold, R. Scott, and B. Littler.

23   Palm Springs, California. Morning appointment with Mr. and Mrs. Latham Castle (Illinois State Attorney General). To Tamarisk Country Club for golf with B. Hogan, F. F. Gosden, P. G. Hoffman, P. H. Helms, F. W. Leahy, P. H. Helms, Jr., G. E. Allen, J. G. Dyer, R. Scott, R. Arnold, and B. Littler. Evening departure for Washington, D.C.

24   Washington. Arrives in Washington. Morning appointment with Legislative Leaders; W. M. Rand; A. F. Burns, G. Hauge, and Secretary Humphrey. Receives National Conference on Labor Legislation members. Lunch with Secretary Dulles. Afternoon appointments with J. S. Lay (off the record); G. Meany.

25   Washington. Receives the winners of 7th annual Voice of Democracy Contest. Witnesses swearing-in of Solicitor General S. E. Sobeloff. Receives winners of Freedom Foundation Association essay contest. Appointment with Vice-President Nixon, S. Adams, and General Persons (off the record). Hosts stag luncheon for congressional members. Afternoon appointment with Secretary Humphrey, M. B. Folsom, A. F. Burns, and G. Hauge.

26   Washington. National Security Council session. Cabinet meeting. Appointments with Ambassador Max Loewenthal (Austria); Congressman Wampler; Ambassador Dillon and Secretary Dulles. Afternoon appointments with Vice-President Nixon, S. Adams, and General Persons; Colonel Stack and Mr. Zimmerman (off the record).

27   Washington. Morning appointments with Secretary McKay, R. A. Tudor, L. Smyth, T. E. Stephens, and Murray Snyder; T. C. Streibert and A. M. Washburn; W. T. Faricy, W. S. Franklin, F. G. Gurley, and H. A. DeButte; Secretary Weeks and S. Adams; Secretary Dulles, R. M. Kyes, Admiral Davis, and H. F. Holland. To Burning Tree Country Club for golf with J. E. McClure, General Twining, and Congressman Bates.

28   Washington. Attends services at National Presbyterian Church with Mrs. Eisenhower. Afternoon off-the-record appointments with Secretary Stevens; R. Montgomery.

March   1   Washington. Morning appointments with Legislative Leaders; Admiral Radford; A. F. Burns and G. Hauge; R. M. Kyes; H. E. Stassen. Afternoon appointments with Admiral Strauss; Secretary Humphrey, M. B. Folsom, General Persons, and G. Hauge; C. Francis, S. Adams, and G. Hauge. Hosts stag dinner.

2   Washington. Morning appointments with R. D. Pittman; L. W. Hall; Jovino S. Lorenzo (businessman,
Philippines) and Aurelio Periquet (businessman,
Philippines); R. A. Tudor, Congressman Johnson,
and H. H. Gruenther; Budget Director Dodge, Secretary McKay, Orme Lewis, S. Adams, General Persons, and H. H. Gruenther (off the record); Ambassador Lodge (off the record); Secretary Stevens (off
the record); Governor King. Off-the-record luncheon
with Vice-President Nixon, S. Adams, General Persons, and J. C. Hagerty. Afternoon appointments
with General Oscar Abbott and F. G. Lippitt, Jr.
(Secretary-Treasurer, Contex Construction Co.);
F. A. Seaton; Postmaster General Summerfield; Governor Muños-Marín and Resident Commissioner
Ferros-Isern; Senator Knowland (off the record).

3   Washington. Off-the-record breakfast with Senator
H. A. Smith, Congressman McConnell, S. Adams,
B. M. Shanley, and G. D. Morgan; J. C. Hagerty.
News conference. Receives first poppy from Ameri-
can Legion Auxiliary leaders, followed by appoint-
ments with General Cutler; W. W. Flenniken and W.
Tomberlin; Budget Director Dodge.

4   Washington. Breakfast with Senator Dirksen followed by appointments with Secretary Weeks; Senator Mundt, Dr. Daniel A. Poling (Editor, *Christian
Herald*), and Joseph Wilson (Freedoms Foundation);
National Security Council session; General Ed Clark
(off the record). Afternoon appointments with Secretary McKay, F. E. Wormser, and William E.
Wrather (Director, Geological Survey); Secretary
Weeks, Roy Williams (Head, Associated Industries
of Massachusetts), and S. Adams. Hosts stag dinner.

5   Washington. Cabinet meeting. Receives American
Jewish Tercentenary Committee. Off-the-record
lunch with Dr. M. S. Eisenhower and Mac Lowry.
Afternoon appointments with P. Young; Senator
Cooper and S. Adams.

6   Washington. Morning appointments with L. W. Bent-
ley (off the record); General LeRoy Lutee; Sergeants
Ellis Humphrey and Earl Davis; General Collins;
Prince Bernhard. Hosts stag luncheon for Prince

Bernhard. To Statler Hotel for White House Correspondents Association dinner.

7 Washington. Attends services at National Presbyterian Church with General Nevins.

8 Washington. Morning appointments with Legislative Leaders; Admiral Radford; A. F. Burns and G. Hauge; Secretary Wilson; Lester Markel (*New York Times*) and J. C. Hagerty. Luncheon with General Kenneth Strong (Director, Joint Intelligence Bureau), General Smith, and A. W. Dulles. Afternoon appointments with A. W. Dulles, General Smith, and C. D. Jackson; L. W. Hall and J. Bassett (off the record).

9 Washington. Breakfast with H. E. Stassen. Morning appointments with Secretary Weeks, Congressman Halleck, and S. Adams (off the record); Secretary Hobby; Congressmen Saylor and Bolton, and I. J. Martin. Receives National 4-H Club award winners, followed by appointments with Secretary Benson and Congressman Belcher; Attorney General Brownell (off the record); Admiral Strauss (off the record); T. B. Morton, S. Adams, and I. J. Martin (off the record). To Burning Tree Country Club for golf with J. E. McClure and Senators Griswold and Bush.

10 Washington. Breakfast with Congressman Taber. Morning appointments with Senator Kerr, Congressman Steed, Earl James (Ruler, Elks), and Ambrose Durkin (Elks); General Cutler and J. S. Lay; J. C. Hagerty. News conference, followed by off-the-record appointments with Secretary Humphrey and B. N. Harlow; S. Adams, J. C. Hagerty, and B. N. Harlow. To Departmental Auditorium to greet NAACP meeting. Afternoon appointments with Ambassador R. S. S. Gunewardene (Ceylon) and J. F. Simmons; Ambassador Karl Gruber (Austria) and J. F. Simmons. To Sulgrave Club for dinner in honor of Senators Knowland and Ferguson.

11 Washington. Hosts breakfast for congressional members. Morning appointments with Colonel James K. Tully; National Security Council session; Jay Taylor. Afternoon appointments with Ambassador Vladimir Popovic (Yugoslavia); Chester Barnard (former President, Rockefeller Foundation). Hosts stag dinner.

12   Washington. Morning appointments with Vernon Smith (off the record); Secretary Humphrey, M. B. Folsom, Dr. M. S. Eisenhower, S. Adams, General Persons, R. Montgomery, K. McCann, G. Hauge, B. N. Harlow, and J. C. Hagerty (off the record); Senator Cooper and F. D. Sampson (former Governor, Kentucky); Cabinet meeting; Vice-President Nixon (off the record). To Camp David with Mrs. Eisenhower, E. Doud, Colonel and Mrs. G. G. Moore, G. E. Allen, and C. H. Tompkins.

13   Camp David, Maryland. No official appointments.

14   Camp David, Maryland. Returns to White House in early evening.

15   Washington. Morning appointments with Legislative Leaders; Dr. Elson (off the record). Receives Western Union Telegraph Co. officials and telegraph key. Attends ceremony to release first power at Fort Randall Dam, South Dakota. Lunch with Secretary Dulles. Afternoon appointments with F. Wood and son (off the record); A. S. Flemming; A. F. Burns; R. Montgomery. Addresses nation on radio and television.

16   Washington. Morning appointments with Citizens for TVA, Inc.; Senator Butler. Receives Rubber Producing Facilities Disposal Commission; R. P. Burroughs; Ambassador Sadao Iguchi (Japan) and J. F. Simmons; General Cutler and J. S. Lay (off the record); G. Hauge (off the record). Hosts luncheon for Joint United States-Canada Committee on Trade and Economic Affairs. Afternoon appointment with Secretary Wilson. Hosts stag dinner.

17   Washington. Morning appointments with Secretary Weeks, S. Adams, G. Hauge, G. D. Morgan, and Colonel Randall (off the record); L. W. Hall and S. Adams (off the record); J. C. Hagerty. News conference, followed by appointments with Hugh J. McCann (Counsellor, Irish Embassy); S. Adams and H. C. Carbaugh (off the record); Congressmen Rogers and Sikes and Florida constituents. To Burning Tree Country Club for golf with Colonel Belshe, J. Black, and Bill Moschie. To Mayflower Hotel for Society of the Friendly Sons of St. Patrick, Washington, dinner. Visits Ancient Order of Hibernians and

Ladies Auxiliary meeting; Business Advisory Council.

18 Washington. Morning appointments with P. Young and M. M. Rabb (off the record); G. Hauge (off the record); Congressman Andresen, G. Hauge, and G. D. Morgan; National Security Council session; General MacArthur. Hosts luncheon in honor of General MacArthur. Receives White House News Photographers Association contest winner. Afternoon appointments with Ambassador Politis, Panayotis Canellopoulos (Minister of Defense, Greece), and J. F. Simmons; Henry Ringling (RNC, Wisconsin) (off the record).

19 Washington. Morning appointments with Secretary Hobby and Roswell B. Perkins (Assistant Secretary, HEW) (off the record). Cabinet meeting, followed by appointments with Congressman Engle; J. J. McCloy. Hosts small stag luncheon. Afternoon off-the-record appointments with L. W. Hall and Postmaster General Summerfield; Attorney General Brownell.

20 Washington. Receives Supreme Lodge, Order of Ahepa, officers. Witnesses swearing-in of Assistant to Deputy Assistant to the President Earle D. Chesney. Morning appointments with H. A. Rusk; Secretaries Dulles and Wilson, A. W. Dulles, Admiral Radford, and D. MacArthur II (off the record); Secretary Hobby, L. Scheele, Budget Director Dodge, R. W. Jones, Frank B. Berry (Assistant Secretary of Defense), General Persons, and B. N. Harlow (off the record). Receives China-Burma-India Veterans Association officers. To Burning Tree Country Club for golf with T. C. Andrews, J. L. Sullivan, and Gene Tunney. To Statler Hotel for White House Photographers Association annual dinner. Lights "Freedom's Flame" in Ripon, Wisconsin, from Hotel and returns to dinner.

21 Washington. Attends services at National Presbyterian Church with Mrs. Eisenhower. Off-the-record appointment with Secretaries Dulles and Wilson, Postmaster General Summerfield, A. W. Dulles, Admiral Radford, and D. MacArthur II.

22 Washington. Morning appointments with Legislative

Leaders; Admiral Radford and General Ely; A. F. Burns and G. Hauge; Secretary Wilson; Harry Precourt and C. D. Jackson (off the record). Receives Ambassador Iguchi and Asuma Kabuki Troupe, Japanese Theater. Hosts luncheon for Secretary Dulles's Committee on Personnel. Afternoon appointments with General Crittenberger; W. A. Moncrief and Arch Rowan (National Petroleum Institute), and J. C. Hagerty (off the record); A. F. Burns; Secretary Mitchell and A. Larson (off the record).

23   Washington. Morning appointments with L. V. Finder; the Archbishop Michael; Erwin D. Canham (Chairman, U.S. Advisory Commission on Information) and William H. Stringer (*Christian Science Monitor*); Senator Kuchel and Congressman Moss; King Hostick and Jack W. Laemmar (off the record); Ambassador Makins and Alexander Fleming (discovered penicillin). Receives Board of Governors, Capitol Hill Club; Post Office Department Advisory Board. Hosts off-the-record luncheon. Afternoon appointments with A. F. Burns, G. Hauge, and General Bragdon (off the record); Secretary Benson, T. D. Morse, J. H. Davis, D. Paarlberg, General Persons, G. Hauge, G. D. Morgan, and I. J. Martin (off the record); S. W. Richardson (off the record). Hosts stag dinner.

24   Washington. Morning appointments with General Cutler and J. S. Lay (off the record); Dartmouth Glee Club (off the record); J. C. Hagerty. News conference, followed by appointments with Captain John Bennett (off the record); P. G. Hoffman. To Burning Tree Country Club for golf with E. Dudley, R. Arnold, Congressman Arends, J. E. McClure, W. K. Warren, J. Black, and W. W. Flenniken.

25   Washington. Morning appointments with J. S. Coleman, J. J. McCloy, H. A. Bullis, E. R. Cook, and G. Hauge; Senators H. A. Smith and Goldwater, G. D. Morgan, and I. J. Martin; Admiral Radford; National Security Council session. Receives Program Committee, Annual Convention of the National Negro Insurance Association. Lunch with Attorney General Brownell and J. E. Hoover. Afternoon appointments with A. S. Flemming, Senator Capehart, F. E.

Wormser, and General Persons (off the record); F. Stanton; H. C. Butcher. Hosts stag dinner.

26 Washington. Morning appointments with Secretary Benson (off the record); Attorney General Brownell and U.S. Attorney appointees Thomas R. Ethridge, Joseph E. Hines, and E. M. Stanley (off the record); Cabinet meeting, followed by appointments with A. S. Flemming, F. E. Wormser, J. C. Hagerty, and I. J. Martin (off the record); B. S. Adkins, Dr. Susan Riley (President, American Association of University Women), and Dorothy Leet (President, International Federation of University Women); Ambassador Guillermo Enciso Velloso (Paraguay) and J. F. Simmons. Off-the-record luncheon with S. W. Richardson, Amon Carter, and F. G. Gurley. Afternoon off-the-record appointments with Colonel Randall, G. Hauge, and G. D. Morgan; H. E. Stassen.

27 Washington. Morning appointments with General Thomas North (Secretary, American Battle Monuments Commission); R. W. Jones and B. M. Shanley (off the record); E. Johnston; Secretary Dulles; K. McCann (off the record). Receives Science Advisory Committee, Office of Defense Mobilization. To Burning Tree Country Club for golf with C. Roberts, F. F. Gosden, Sam Sneed, Colonel Belshe, and J. E. McClure.

28 Washington. Attends services at National Presbyterian Church with Mrs. Eisenhower.

29 Washington. Morning appointments with Legislative Leaders; Vice-President Nixon, L. W. Hall, and J. Bassett; Admiral Radford; A. F. Burns and G. Hauge; Secretary Wilson; Irene S. Gaul and family (off the record). Hosts stag luncheon. Afternoon off-the-record appointments with K. McCann; Postmaster General Summerfield; Secretary Humphrey, M. B. Folsom, W. M. Martin, A. F. Burns, and G. Hauge; B. M. Shanley; Mr. and Mrs. Charles Claunch; H. R. Reid.

30 Washington. Morning appointments with T. C. Streibert and Andrew H. Berding (Assistant Director, USIA); Paul C. French (CARE), General Carroll, and S. Benedict. VFW representatives present first poppy, followed by appointments with General

Cutler, Senator Saltonstall, and R. C. Sprague (off the record); Mr. and Mrs. Jouett Shouse and Hans Ude; Admiral Strauss; L. W. Hall and S. Adams (off the record). Receives International Organizations Employees Loyalty Board. Hosts stag luncheon in honor of General John K. Cannon (Commander, USAF). Afternoon off-the-record appointment with Secretary Dulles and Ambassador Makins.

31 Washington. Breakfast with C. D. Jackson (off the record). Morning appointments with Congressmen Martin, Halleck, Taber, Philips, and Wolcott, A. M. Cole, and G. D. Morgan (off the record); Idaho Attorney General Robert E. Smiley; J. C. Hagerty. News conference, followed by appointments with L. C. Warren (off the record); S. W. Richardson (off the record); Congressman Jenkins; General Cutler and J. S. Lay; S. Adams, J. C. Hagerty, C. D. Jackson, R. Montgomery, K. McCann, G. D. Morgan, B. N. Harlow, and I. J. Martin (off the record). To Library of Congress for White House Photographers' Association exhibit. Afternoon off-the-record appointments with R. Montgomery; Secretary Humphrey; Kenton R. Cravens (Administrator, RFC) and S. Adams; H. E. Stassen; R. W. Woodruff, Dr. M. S. Eisenhower, and W. Cox.

April 1 Washington. Breakfast with Senators Knowland, Ferguson, and Millikin, S. Adams, and General Persons. Morning appointments with Congressmen Brooks, Short, and Simpson, and Senator McClellan; American Foundation for the Blind representatives (off the record); National Security Council session. Lunch with R. Howard, W. Stone, and J. C. Hagerty. Signs H. R. 5337. Afternoon appointments with Governor Heintzleman and Secretary McKay; T. Pappas (off the record); Attorney General Brownell (off the record); R. W. Woodruff (off the record); J. Murphy, S. T. Olin, and S. Adams; M. Kestnbaum (off the record). Attends ceremony to launch American Cancer Society Cancer Crusade.

2 Washington. Morning appointments with Secretaries Dulles and Wilson, Admiral Radford, and General Cutler (off the record); Secretary McKay, Governor Alexander (Virgin Islands), and Val Washington (RNC); Admiral Strauss (off the record); Cabinet

meeting. To Camp David with Mrs. Eisenhower, E. Doud, Mrs. G. G. Moore, and Mrs. Walker.

3   Camp David, Maryland. No official appointments.

4   Camp David, Maryland. Returns to White House in the evening. Off-the-record meeting with Secretary Dulles, General Smith, D. MacArthur II, Admiral Radford, and R. M. Kyes.

5   Washington. Morning appointments with Legislative Leaders; Congressmen Martin, Halleck, and Arends (off the record); Admiral Radford and Carney, and Generals Twining and Ridgway; Washington Baseball Club representatives; A. S. Flemming. To Washington National Cathedral for funeral services of the late General Vandenberg. Late afternoon appointment with General Norstad. Hosts stag dinner.

6   Washington. Breakfast with Senators Knowland, Butler, and Cordon, and General Persons. Morning appointments with Secretary Wilson; Defense Appropriations Committee (off the record). Meeting with sole survivor of Admiral Peary's expedition to North Pole and others. Receives National Conference of Police Associations delegates. Appointments with Congressman Bolton and B. N. Harlow; General Cutler and J. S. Lay (off the record). Off-the-record lunch with Attorney General Brownell and Robert U. Brown (President, *Editor and Publisher*). National Security Council session.

7   Washington. Morning appointments with Senator Carlson; Senator Hickenlooper, Congressmen Talle and Martin, and American Dental Association leaders; J. C. Hagerty. News conference, followed by appointments with Ambassador José Félix de Lequerica (Spain), Señor Manuel Arburua (Minister of Commerce, Spain), Señor Arguelles (Under Secretary of Commerce, Spain), Señor Fernandez Suarez (Under Secretary of Industry, Spain), Edward Williams (Chief, FOA Mission, Madrid), and J. F. Simmons; Senator Aiken and Vermont dairy farmers. To Burning Tree Country Club for golf with Senator Symington, J. H. Whitney, and N. Burnham.

8   Washington. Morning appointments with Congressman Small and leaders of Lions International; Attor-

ney General Brownell and newly appointed federal judges; Mrs. John G. Lee (President, National League of Women Voters) and Miss Ferris; Congressman Cole; Ambassador Percy Spender (Australia), Laurie Short (Secretary, Federal Iron Workers' Association, Australia), Russell L. Riley (State Department), and J. F. Simmons. To Post Office Department for stamp ceremony. Greets National Conference of Republican Women at Statler Hotel. Lunch with L. M. Pexton. Receives Agricultural Trade Missions members. Afternoon appointments with A. F. Burns, S. Adams, and Steel Workers of America leaders; R. M. Kyes, Senators Knowland and Saltonstall. Hosts stag dinner.

9   Washington. Breakfast with Senator Bridges and General Persons. Morning appointments with Secretary Dulles and H. F. Holland; Cabinet meeting; Governor Thornton; Republican Women's Conference attendees; Governor McKeldin, Richard D. Weigle (President, St. John's College), Richard Cleveland (Chairman, St. John's College), S. Adams, and Murray Snyder; Pat Loomis (off the record). Off-the-record lunch with Governor Thornton. Participates in ceremony to launch Help Korea Trains project. Afternoon appointment with Secretary Mitchell.

10   Washington. Off-the-record appointments with H. E. Stassen; H. C. Butcher. Receives Executive Advisory Board and Finance Committee of the National Citizens for Eisenhower Congressional Committee. Off-the-record appointments with Secretary Dulles; Secretaries Weeks and Mitchell, Congressmen Halleck, McConnell, and Arends, S. Adams, B. M. Shanley, and G. D. Morgan; Admiral Strauss, S. Adams, General Persons, J. C. Hagerty, and Murray Snyder. To Burning Tree Country Club for golf with Colonel Belshe, J. S. Brooks, Jr., and F. T. Marshall. Evening appointment with Mr. and Mrs. E. N. Eisenhower (off the record).

11   Washington. Attends services at National Presbyterian Church with Mrs. Eisenhower. Afternoon appointment with Secretary Humphrey, J. H. Whitney, and G. E. Allen (off the record).

12   Washington. Breakfast with B. N. Harlow (off the

record). Morning appointments with Legislative Leaders; General Bragdon (off the record); Admiral Radford; A. F. Burns; R. H. Coffee and Captain Charles M. Whitley (Office of the Secretary of the Navy); Secretary Wilson; Ambassador Cabot; Budget Director Dodge, A. M. Cole, S. Adams, General Persons, and B. M. Shanley (off the record). Lunch with J. A. McCone (off the record). Afternoon appointments with representatives from United States Olympic Committee and *Life* Magazine; J. Monnet and J. F. Simmons; Admiral Wright. Hosts stag dinner.

13   Washington. Morning appointments with General Cutler and J. C. Hagerty; National Security Council session; Senator Hill and S. Adams; General and Mrs. Leonard; Ambassador Leo Mates (Yugoslavia) and J. F. Simmons; Congressman Gubser and daughter. To Griffith Stadium with Mrs. Eisenhower for opening baseball game. To MATS terminal en route to Augusta, Georgia.

14   Augusta, Georgia. Golf with F. Willard, W. E. Robinson, and L. F. McCollum. Late afternoon fishing.

15   Augusta, Georgia. Bill signing ceremony. Golf with J. Budinger, A. Bradley, and C. J. Schoo. Late afternoon fishing.

16   Augusta, Georgia. Plays nine holes with Major and Mrs. J. S. D. Eisenhower, followed by golf with E. Dudley, C. Roberts, and R. W. Woodruff.

17   Augusta, Georgia. Golf with W. E. Robinson, R. W. Woodruff, and A. Bradley. Informal photo session, followed by golf with Major J. S. D. Eisenhower, B. J. Patton, and W. H. Zimmerman.

18   Augusta, Georgia. Attends services at Reid Memorial Presbyterian Church with Mrs. Eisenhower, E. Doud, and Major and Mrs. J. S. D. Eisenhower. Lays cornerstone for new church. Golf with Major J. S. D. Eisenhower, B. J. Patton, and W. H. Zimmerman. Afternoon fishing with D. D. Eisenhower II.

19   Augusta, Georgia. Visits office. Newsreel and still photograph session. Lunch with Secretary Dulles. Golf with E. N. Eisenhower, J. H. Whitney, and W. E. Robinson.

20 Augusta, Georgia. Visits office. Golf with E. N. Eisenhower and E. Dudley. Afternoon golf with E. N. Eisenhower, C. Roberts, and E. Dudley. Evening fishing with D. D. Eisenhower II.

21 Augusta, Georgia. Visits office. Golf with E. Dudley, followed by golf with J. Franklin, J. Roberts, and C. Roberts. Evening fishing with General Carroll.

22 Augusta, Georgia. Visits office. Golf with E. N. Eisenhower, E. Dudley, and B. Christy. Early afternoon departure to Washington, D.C. Greets Daughters of the American Revolution annual convention. Witnesses the swearing-in of Inter-Governmental Relations Commission member M. Kestnbaum. To MATS terminal en route to New York, New York. Meets with representative of the New York Republican Club and receives the Club's War Memorial Award. Addresses American Newspaper Publishers Association annual dinner. Returns to Washington, D.C.

23 Washington. To MATS terminal en route to Louisville, Kentucky. Presents Boy Scout Medal. Lays wreath at Abraham Lincoln Monument, Hodgenville. To Lexington, Kentucky, to present gifts at Transylvania College. Delivers greetings in convocation ceremony and attends reception. Airborne for Augusta, Georgia.

24 Augusta, Georgia. Golf with W. E. Robinson, E. Peabody, and C. Roberts.

25 Augusta, Georgia. Golf with C. Roberts, W. E. Robinson, and R. Taylor. Appointment with E. Elkins. Departs for Washington, D.C.

26 Washington. Morning appointments with Legislative Leaders; Senator Dirksen, Congressman Arends, and S. Adams (off the record); A. F. Burns and G. Hauge; W. J. Donovan. Addresses 42nd Annual Meeting of the Chamber of Commerce opening session. Appointments with C. Francis and W. Wright (off the record); Secretary Wilson. Luncheon with J. Murray, E. L. Mecham, E. F. Arn, S. Adams, General Persons, V. E. Peterson, H. H. Gruenther, and Governors Shivers and Thornton. Attends meeting to discuss drought situation. Afternoon appoint-

ments with High Commissioner Conant; W. Bannister (off the record); General Smith (off the record); Congressmen Taber and Wigglesworth. Hosts dinner for governors of states and territories attending Governors' Conference.

27 Washington. Morning appointments with Admiral Strauss (off the record); Senator Williams, S. Adams, General Persons, and B. M. Shanley; Governor Knight, State Senator Gibson, and Mayor Demon; Secretary Hobby and S. M. Brownell; Rochester Centennial Association representatives; North Carolina delegation; Mr. and Mrs. Ronald W. Welch (off the record). Receives teen-age Republicans from New Jersey. Afternoon appointments with G. Hauge, T. D. Morse, J. H. Davis, H. F. Holland, S. C. Waugh, and S. Benedict; General Van Fleet, Secretary Wilson, and W. J. McNeil; General Garrison Davidson and S. Adams (off the record); Governor Stratton. Attends congressional reception.

28 Washington. Morning appointments with General Cutler and J. S. Lay; Senator Saltonstall and C. A. Herter; Senator Dirksen and J. T. Meek (off the record); Congressman Thompson; Congressman Ostertag and high school essay winners; Governor Anderson, Senator Thye, K. V. Bjornson, and General Carroll; Dr. William Russell (President, Teachers' College). Receives National Committee for Traffic Safety steering committee followed by appointments with Dr. Frederick D. Patterson (Director, Phelps-Stokes Fund); Senator Ferguson, Foster Winter (Chairman, St. Lawrence Waterway Committee), Gerald Warren (Board of Commerce, Detroit), and W. M. Brucker; H. E. Stassen (off the record); Generals Smith and Cutler, and Admiral Radford (off the record). To Burning Tree Country Club for golf with C. E. Anderson, Senator Thye, and V. Bjornson.

29 Washington. Morning appointment with J. C. Hagerty, followed by news conference. Receives United Defense Fund leaders. National Security Council session. Appointment with Admiral Leahy (off the record). Discusses foreign and economic policy proposals with business leaders. Afternoon appointments with Senator Watkins; Congressmen Bishop and Harris, and E. D. Chesney; R. T. Reed (off the

record); Secretary Benson, J. H. Davis, Senator Aiken, Congressman Hope, and G. D. Morgan. Views President's Committee on the Employment of the Physically Handicapped exhibit and presents awards to essay winners.

30   Washington. Off-the-record breakfast with Vice-President Nixon, H. R. Luce, General Persons, G. Hauge, and B. N. Harlow. Morning appointments with General Joseph W. Beacham and grandnieces and nephews (off the record). Cabinet meeting, followed by appointments with C. P. Romulo (Personal Representative, Philippine President) and J. F. Simmons; Edward T. Dicker; K. C. Royall. Receives National American Korean Foundation Veterans' Committee. Attends luncheon in honor of R. M. Kyes, followed by appointment with Defense Advisory Committee on Women in the Services.

May   1   Washington. Morning appointments with General Clark (off the record); Senator Bowring; Congresswoman Bolton and family of Rumanian hostages; Generals Cutler and Carroll (off the record); Robert Atwood (Publisher, *Anchorage Daily*) and J. C. Hagerty (off the record). To Burning Tree Country Club for golf with General Bradley and Governors Thornton and Langlie. Returns to White House with General Bradley, J. Black, and Governors Thornton and Langlie.

2   Washington. Attends morning services at National Presbyterian Church with Mrs. Eisenhower. To Eisenhower farm near Gettysburg, Pennsylvania. After lunch, proceeds to Camp David. Late afternoon returns to White House.

3   Washington. Morning appointments with Legislative Leaders; Admiral Radford; A. F. Burns and G. Hauge; Secretary Wilson. Witnesses swearing-in of Deputy Secretary of Defense R. B. Anderson, Secretary of the Navy C. S. Thomas, and Assistant Secretary of Defense Thomas P. Pike. Presents President's Cup to National Capital Sports Car Race winner. Luncheon with N. A. Rockefeller, Dr. M. S. Eisenhower, A. S. Flemming, R. R. Hughes, and S. Adams. Afternoon appointments with H. Hoover; E. D.

Eisenhower. Receives Governor General Vincent Massey (Canada) and hosts dinner in his honor.

4   Washington. Morning appointments with H. J. Porter (off the record); Union Chamber of Commerce representatives; Warren C. Giles (President, National League of Professional Baseball Clubs); Generals Cutler and Crittenberger; Senator Flanders; Secretary Benson and C. Francis. Greets President's Conference on Occupational Safety opening session. Off-the-record luncheon with Colonel Randall, S. Adams, G. Hauge, General Persons, and G. D. Morgan. Afternoon appointments with A. S. Flemming; L. W. Douglas. Receives congressmen from Tennessee Valley area. To Canadian Embassy with Mrs. Eisenhower for dinner in their honor hosted by Governor General of Canada.

5   Washington. Breakfast with Secretary Dulles and General Cutler. Morning appointments with Attorney General Brownell (off the record); Murray Snyder. News conference, followed by appointments with Ambassador van Roijen, Dr. L. G. Kortenhorst (Chairman, States General, Netherlands), and J. F. Simmons; Congresswoman Rogers and Congressman Radwan. To Burning Tree Country Club for golf with Congressmen Arends, Mahon, and Scrivner.

6   Washington. Morning appointments with Joseph E. Zimet (Hamilton Import Corporation); Secretary Hobby, N. A. Rockefeller, Budget Director Hughes, W. A. Purtell, Senator H. A. Smith, and R. E. James; Attorney General Brownell (off the record); National Security Council session. Signs H. R. 8127. To Sheraton-Park Hotel to greet 22nd Annual Convention of the Military Chaplains Association luncheon. Afternoon appointments with B. M. Shanley (off the record); Ambassador Aldrich; Albert C. Jacobs (President, Trinity College); Secretary Weeks; A. Nielsen and K. McCann (off the record).

7   Washington. Morning appointments with T. C. Streibert and USIA Chiefs; Secretary Dulles and General Cutler; Postmaster General Summerfield (off the record); General Swing and M. M. Rabb; Ambassador J. P. Jooste and General Carroll; O. Lewis and

G. D. Morgan (off the record); General A. C. Smith, Dr. Forrest C. Pogue, and Dr. Kent Greenfield; Budget Director Hughes and P. F. Brundage; Robert H. Cromwell (off the record); Mr. and Mrs. H. L. Emerson (off the record). Presents Gold Lifesaver Medal to School Safety Patrol Boys and Girls.

8   Washington. Morning appointment with E. R. Black; National Security Council session; Dr. John H. Hunt and Nishuane School students (off the record); S. Adams, L. W. Hall, T. E. Stephens, Generals Persons and Carroll, B. M. Shanley, G. D. Morgan, and H. H. Gruenther (off the record); Governor Thornton (off the record); General Auby C. Strickland and Lakemont Academy boys (off the record). To Burning Tree Country Club for golf with Governor Thornton, J. E. McClure, and Judge Whitaker. Returns to White House with Governor Thornton.

9   Washington. To MATS terminal with Mrs. Eisenhower en route to Richmond, Virginia. Attends services at St. Paul's Church with Mrs. Eisenhower. Attends luncheon for vestrymen and their wives at Virginia House. To Fredericksburg, Virginia, for Mothers' Day program at Washington Monument. Returns to Washington, D.C.

10   Washington. Morning appointments with Legislative Leaders; Senator Saltonstall, T. E. Stephens, and Murray Snyder; Admiral Radford; A. F. Burns and G. Hauge; Secretary Wilson; Hawaiian delegation. Luncheon with Senators Duff and Cordon. Afternoon appointments with H. E. Stassen; Utah congressional delegation; Secretaries Dulles and Wilson, Admiral Radford, R. B. Anderson, D. MacArthur II, and R. R. Bowie. Receives European Travel Commission. Hosts stag dinner.

11   Washington. Morning appointments with Secretary Humphrey, Budget Director Hughes, and General Cutler; P. Young and Civil Service Assembly leaders. Attends ceremonies for completion of Rotunda. Receives RNC Advisory Committee, Veterans' Division. Lunch with Secretary Dulles. Afternoon appointments with Attorney General Brownell and Judges Waldo Rogers and John R. Rose (off the record); Attorney General Brownell, S. Adams, and

General Persons (off the record); Jacob Blaustein and M. M. Rabb. Receives Pennsylvania Congressional Delegation and Northeast Pennsylvania Industrial Development Commission.

12   Washington. Morning appointments with General Cutler and J. S. Lay (off the record); California Republican congressmen; National Symphony Orchestra representatives; J. C. Hagerty. News conference. To Statler Hotel to greet Society for Personnel Administration annual conference. To Burning Tree Country Club for golf with W. W. Flenniken, H. Blunck, and Congressman Westland. Afternoon off-the-record appointments with Maude Purcell-Driver; Thomas B. Fegan.

13   Washington. Breakfast with Secretary Talbott (off the record). Signs S. 2150 followed by appointments with Governor Heintzleman and Alaskan delegation; H. E. Stassen; National Security Council session; S. P. Skouras; Congressman Cotton and Sandra Miskelly; Congressman Bentley. Afternoon appointments with L. W. Hall; William W. Chapin; Myron Taylor; R. P. Burroughs (off the record).

14   Washington. Breakfast with H. Darby, J. C. Hall, Carl Byoir, Horace Loomis, K. McCann, and T. E. Stephens. Morning appointment with Secretary Benson. Cabinet meeting, followed by appointments with Postmaster General Summerfield, Congressmen Halleck and Harrison, Robert V. New, and Senator Barrett (off the record); Attorney General Brownell and Congressman Halleck; Senator Martin and Legion of Valor representatives. Afternoon meeting with Office of Defense Mobilization members. To Burning Tree Country Club for golf with J. C. Hagerty and Colonel Belshe. To Statler Hotel for 5th Annual Armed Forces Day dinner.

15   Washington. Breakfast with Secretary Dulles, Admiral Radford, and D. MacArthur II. To Gettysburg to inspect remodeling of home. To Camp David. Fishing with Dr. M. S. Eisenhower at Catoctin, Maryland.

16   Camp David, Maryland. No official appointments.

17   Washington. Off-the-record breakfast with Attorney

General Brownell, J. L. Rankin, S. Adams, General Persons, J. C. Hagerty, B. M. Shanley, G. D. Morgan, and I. J. Martin. Morning appointments with Ambassador Allen; Legislative Leaders; Admiral Radford; A. F. Burns and G. Hauge; General H. J. Kruls (off the record); Secretary Hobby and N. A. Rockefeller (off the record). Hosts luncheon for life insurance executives. Receives American Bar Association Board of Governors. Off-the-record afternoon appointments with Admirals Radford and Carney, and Generals Twining, Ridgway, and Shepherd; G. Hauge, G. D. Morgan, and I. J. Martin.

18　Washington. Breakfast with Congressman Reed, G. Hauge, and I. J. Martin. Receives National Association of Home Builders essay contest winners. Signs H. R. 8097. Morning appointments with Congressmen McDonough and Holt, and E. D. Chesney. To Charlotte, North Carolina, for ceremonies celebrating signing of Mecklenburg Declaration of Independence. Returns to Washington, D.C.

19　Washington. Hosts breakfast for Marching and Chowder Club members. Morning appointments with Secretary Dulles; Robert H. Groz (President, Advertising Association of the West); J. C. Hagerty, followed by News conference. To Burning Tree Country Club for golf with W. Farley, R. V. Fleming, and Senator Bush. Hosts stag dinner.

20　Washington. Morning appointments with General Cutler and J. S. Lay (off the record); Secretary McKay and Texas congressional delegation; Ambassador Simonson; National Security Council session. To Shoreham Hotel to greet Committee for Economic Development members. Afternoon appointments with General Gray; Secretary Dulles, Ambassador Leslie K. Munroe, and T. Clifton Webb (Minister, External Affairs, New Zealand).

21　Washington. Cabinet meeting, followed by appointments with H. E. Stassen, M. Wolf, and G. Lloyd. Receives Teacher of the Year. Afternoon appointment with Budget Director Hughes.

22　Washington. Off-the-record morning appointments with L. W. Hall, S. Adams, General Persons, and T. E. Stephens; F. Waring, General Persons, and

T. E. Stephens; Secretary Dulles; Secretary Dulles, Admiral Radford, R. B. Anderson, A. W. Dulles, and General Cutler; H. E. Stassen; Mr. and Mrs. Meredith C. Lents; P. G. Hoffman. To Fort Meade for lunch and golf with Generals Parks and Harris, and Colonel Chard. To Statler Hotel with Mrs. Eisenhower for dinner in their honor hosted by Women's National Press Club.

23 Washington. Attends services at National Presbyterian Church with Mrs. Eisenhower. Afternoon appointment with Secretary and Mrs. Humphrey, Mr. and Mrs. G. E. Allen, and P. G. Hoffman.

24 Washington. Morning appointments with the Legislative Leaders; Admiral Radford; A. F. Burns and G. Hauge; R. B. Anderson; Major Robert L. Williams (West Point, class of 1915) (off the record).

25 Washington. Morning appointments with Dr. Nathan N. Pusey (President, Harvard University), Secretary Weeks, and General Cutler; National Council of Churches leaders; Reverend E. J. O'Donnell; A. S. Flemming; Ambassador Spruance; Attorney General Brownell and newly appointed judges (off the record); Ambassador Sparks. To Mayflower Hotel to greet National Rivers and Harbors Congress. To Burning Tree Country Club for lunch and golf with J. Black, E. Dudley, and M. Elbin. Late afternoon appointment with Secretary Dulles and R. B. Anderson (off the record).

26 Washington. Breakfast with Secretary Benson, R. Rizley, G. Hauge, G. D. Morgan, and Congressmen Hope, Hill, Moeven, and Andresen; General Cutler and J. S. Lay; Secretary Benson; Congressman Bender and I. J. Martin; Lou Golan (Tamarisk Club) (off the record); M. Hartley Dodge (Trustee, Columbia University); Dr. and Mrs. Leslie Hinkle (off the record); Secretary Weeks and C. F. Willis. (off the record); Budget Director Hughes. Hosts dinner in honor of Emperor Haile Selassie (Ethiopia).

27 Washington. Morning appointments with Ambassador Makins, Admiral J. F. Stevens, and Admiral Cecil Charles Hughes-Hallet (British Joint Services Mission); Admiral Radford, A. S. Flemming, R. B. Anderson, and General Cutler (off the record). Na-

tional Security Council session, followed by appointments with Congressman Reed and G. D. Morgan (off the record); Indiana Republicans. Lunch with R. W. Woodruff. Attends baseball game for Mickey Vernon—Red Cross Day. Afternoon off-the-record appointment with Senator Millikin, General Persons, and T. E. Stephens.

28 Washington. Morning appointment with H. E. Stassen. Receives Federation of the Lutheran Church Board of Governors, followed by appointments with Secretary Dulles, R. B. Anderson, Admiral Radford, and General Cutler (off the record). To the Ethiopian Embassy with Mrs. Eisenhower for dinner in their honor.

29 Washington. To Statler Hotel for National Council, Boy Scouts of America luncheon. To Burning Tree Country Club for lunch and golf with R. V. Fleming, J. E. McClure, and Senator Smathers.

30 Washington. Attends services at National Presbyterian Church with Mrs. Eisenhower and Secretary and Mrs. McKay.

31 Washington. To Arlington National Cemetery for Memorial Day services. To MATS terminal. To New York, New York, and Waldorf-Astoria Hotel. Poses for photographs. Attends reception and dinner for Columbia University Bicentennial. Addresses nation on radio and television. Returns to Washington, D.C.

June 1 Washington. Morning appointments with Senator Ferguson and Michigan delegation; Secretary Talbott (off the record). Receives American Trucking Industry's Driver of the Year; Connecticut Republican congressional delegation; millionth piece of Ethan Allen furniture. Appointments with R. B. Anderson; A. W. Dulles. Hosts luncheon for veterans' group leaders. Signs H. R. 7786.

2 Washington. Off-the-record breakfast with Senator Knowland. Morning appointments with General Cutler and J. S. Lay (off the record); Prime Minister Adnan Menderes (Turkey), Ambassador Erkin, and Ambassador Warren; J. C. Hagerty. News conference, followed by appointments with Secretary Dulles, R. B. Anderson, Admiral Radford, and D.

MacArthur II. Receives former war correspondents who covered Normandy invasion. Off-the-record lunch with R. V. Fleming, J. E. McClure, and Senator Smathers. To Burning Tree Country Club for golf with luncheon guests.

3   Washington. Morning appointment with Colonel Draper. Participates in ceremonies commemorating Allied Invasion of Normandy, followed by appointments with A. F. Burns; Fortuna Pope (Publisher, *Il Progresso*); National Security Council session; Phy Srivisan (Privy Council member, Thailand), M. R. Thuaithep Devakul (Charge d'affaires, Thailand Embassy), and Charles Spruke (Protocol Division). Lunch with Governor Dewey, followed by appointments with Minister Contra Almirante Anibal Olivieri (Navy, Argentina), Ambassador Hipólito Jesús Paz (Argentina), and Secretary Thomas; General Bradley; S. H. High (off the record).

4   Washington. Morning appointments with Secretary Benson; Cabinet meeting; E. Johnston; Ambassador van Roijen, General Marshall, Minister J. G. deBeus (Netherlands Embassy), L. T. Merchant, and D. A. Fitzgerald (Deputy Director for Operations, FOA). Receives National Council of Catholic Nurses leaders; Mr. and Mrs. Alvin Gish and Mr. and Mrs. Clarence Herr (off the record). Hosts stag luncheon in honor of Prime Minister Menderes. Off-the-record appointment with Secretary Dulles. To Camp David with Mrs. Eisenhower.

5   Camp David, Maryland. No official appointments.

6   Camp David, Maryland. No official appointments. To Washington, D.C.

7   Washington. Morning appointments with Legislative Leaders; barber (off the record); Admiral Radford and General Van Fleet; A. F. Burns. To MATS terminal en route to Dover Air Force Base, Delaware. Motors to Chestertown, Maryland, for commencement exercises at Washington College. Returns to Washington, D.C.

8   Washington. Morning appointments with A. W. Dulles, Senator Knowland, S. Adams, and General Persons; National Republican Club leaders; Industry

representatives to discuss tariff and trade issues; Dr. Elton Trueblood (Chief, Religious Information, USIA); General Clark (off the record); Secretary Wilson; Ambassador Allison; Ambassador Aurelio F. Concheso (Cuba) and H. F. Holland. Lunch with S. Adams, General Persons, J. C. Hagerty, G. Hauge, B. N. Harlow, G. D. Morgan, Murray Snyder, and R. Montgomery. Afternoon appointments with Secretary Hobby, Budget Director Hughes, N. A. Rockefeller, S. M. Brownell, General Persons, and I. J. Martin (off the record); General Cutler and J. S. Lay (off the record); Attorney General Brownell, Senator Ferguson, and S. Adams (off the record). To Congressional Hotel Republican 82nd and 83rd Clubs of the House of Representatives dinner.

9   Washington. Morning appointments with Congressmen Arends, Busbey, Kluczunski, McVey and O'Hara, and I. J. Martin; H. F. Armstrong and A. W. Dulles; General Taylor (off the record); Homes Bannard (Freight Traffic Manager, Pennsylvania Railroad) (off the record). National Security Council session. To Burning Tree Country Club for golf with Vice-President Nixon, Senator Butler, and R. Reed.

10 Washington. Morning appointments with G. Hauge; J. C. Hagerty. News conference, followed by appointments with Captain Howard T. Orville (Chairman, Advisory Committee on Weather Control), Lewis W. Douglas, Allan T. Waterman (Director, NSF), and D. A. Quarles; Bob Considine and J. C. Hagerty (off the record); Secretary Humphrey, Generals Burgess and Edgerton, R. Murphy, T. B. Morton, Senators Capehart and Maybank, Congressmen Wolcott and Spence, G. Hauge, and E. D. Chesney. Receives AMVETS Memorial Scholarship winners; World Veterans' Federation, Governing Council. Hosts stag luncheon. Afternoon off-the-record appointment with A. F. Burns. To Statler Hotel for District Chairman, National Citizens for Eisenhower Congressional Committee dinner with Mrs. Eisenhower. Addresses meeting and nation on radio and television.

11 Washington. Off-the-record appointments with Budget Director Hughes, S. Adams, and General Persons; Secretary Benson; H. E. Stassen and W. M. Rand. Cabinet meeting, followed by appointments

with Dr. J. Roscoe Miller (President, Northwestern University) and W. T. Faricy; Ambassador Makins and Duncan Sandys (British Minister of Supply); Governor Kennon and S. Adams (off the record). To Camp David with Mrs. Eisenhower, General and Mrs. Gruenther, Mrs. W. Walker, and W. E. Robinson.

12 Camp David, Maryland. No official appointments.

13 Camp David, Maryland. No official appointments. To Washington, D.C.

14 Washington. Off-the-record breakfast with Ambassador Lodge. Morning appointment with Legislative Leaders; Secretary Dulles; A. F. Burns and G. Hauge; W. P. Rogers and J. M. Swing (off the record); Tom McCall, Roland Morsereau, and Larry Smith. Air raid drill. Luncheon and golf at Burning Tree Country Club with Generals Harmon, Parks, Allen, Conklin, and Gasser, J. Black, J. E. McClure, R. V. Fleming, G. E. Allen, and Colonel Belshe.

15 Washington. Breakfast with Secretary Mitchell. Morning appointments with General Twining; Senator Carlson, Dr. Frank Murphy (Chancellor, Kansas University), Dr. Robert Taft (President, Kansas Centennial Committee), Congressman Rees, and T. E. Stephens; Senator Payne and Congressmen Hale, Nelson, and McIntire; D. A. Poling. Receives Alliance of Croatian Catholic Priests delegation, followed by appointments with H. F. Holland; Mr. and Mrs. Calvin Verity and grandchildren (off the record); Congresswoman Bolton; John H. Winchell and S. Adams (off the record); Attorney General Brownell (off the record); E. S. Graham and Colonel Schulz (off the record). Off-the-record lunch with H. E. Stassen. Hosts stag dinner.

16 Washington. Breakfast with Senator Schoeppel. Morning appointments with General Cutler and J. S. Lay; Congressman Meader and G. D. Morgan; Captain Leo S. Moore (photographer) and T. E. Stephens (off the record); J. C. Hagerty. News conference, followed by appointments with G. Hauge; Governor Craig, Elmer W. Sherwood, Tom Mahaffey, and T. E. Stephens; M. Kestnbaum and K. McCann. To National Guard Armory for National

Association of Retail Grocers convention. Afternoon appointments with Ambassador Donovan and Charles Corell and family (off the record); Secretary Dulles (off the record); B. M. Shanley.

17 Washington. Breakfast with freshman congressmen. Morning appointments with F. Cowles; National Security Council session. Receives National 4-H Club members. Luncheon with Senator Thye, Secretary Benson, and G. D. Morgan (off the record). Presents Father-of-the-Year award to P. G. Hoffman. Afternoon appointments with P. G. Hoffman (off the record); Admiral Morsell and S. Adams; A. M. Cole, W. McKenna, S. Adams, B. M. Shanley, and J. W. Barba (off the record); A. Nielsen (off the record). Signs H. R. 2828.

18 Washington. To Arlington National Cemetery for funeral services for General C. Thompson. Appointments with Secretary Dulles (off the record); Dr. Allen B. DuMont (President, DuMont Laboratories), Keaton Arnet (DuMont's Assistant), and S. Adams (off the record); Joseph Welch and James Sinclair; Ambassador Berckemeyer, Foreign Minister Ricardo R. Schreiber (Peru), and J. F. Simmons. Lunch with H. Hoover. Receives Future Teachers of America state leaders.

19 Washington. Receives Nassau County Republicans. To Quantico, Virginia, for ceremony and luncheon. Golf with Generals Collins, Twining, and Parks. Returns to White House.

20 Washington. Attends services at National Presbyterian Church with Mrs. Eisenhower and Mrs. G. G. Moore. Afternoon off-the-record appointment with Secretary Humphrey.

21 Washington. Morning appointments with Legislative Leaders; Admiral Radford; G. Hauge and A. F. Burns; Secretary Wilson, General Loper, S. Adams, A. S. Flemming, and General Cutler. Lunch with Governor Thornton. Afternoon appointments with Truman Johnson and family (off the record); Attorney General Brownell and Judge George T. Mickelson (off the record); A. S. Flemming; Senator Potter; Congressman Scott; Budget Director Hughes, S. Adams, and General Persons (off the record).

22 Washington. Off-the-record breakfast with H. E. Stassen. Morning appointments with Senators Jenner and Capehart, Attorney General Brownell, and I. J. Martin (off the record); Congressman Sadlak and Polish Legion of American Veterans leaders; Mr. and Mrs. Frank Danihelka, George Danihelka, and E. Dulles; Charles J. Block and son (off the record); Minister Mansour Fethi El-Kekhia (Libya) and J. F. Simmons; Ambassador Hildreth; T. C. Streibert, W. L. Clark, and G. H. Damon. Sits for portrait. Signs Executive Order. Lunch with General Cutler and J. S. Lay. Off-the-record afternoon appointments with Earl Katz and children; Senator Cooper, Congressman Robsion, Graham Brown, Barney Burnett, and General Loper; Secretary Dulles, A. W. Dulles, and H. F. Holland. To Shoreham Hotel for National Editorial Association dinner.

23 Washington. Morning appointments with H. J. Porter (off the record); bipartisan congressional delegation; A. B. Kline. National Security Council session, followed by appointments with R. B. Anderson and Lewis Castle (off the record); Secretary Dulles, General Smith, L. T. Merchant, and D. MacArthur II. To Burning Tree Country Club for lunch and golf with W. W. Flenniken and Congressmen Simpson and Reece.

24 Washington. Attends National Cartoonist Society breakfast. Morning appointments with S. Adams and General Carroll; National Security Council session; Lucius Talley and daughter. Cabinet meeting. Signs S. 2225, followed by appointments with American Veterans' Committee leaders; Secretary Dulles, General Smith, W. S. Robertson, L. T. Merchant, and D. MacArthur II; Admiral William M. Hague and S. Adams (off the record); Attorney General Brownell (off the record). Hosts stag dinner.

25 Washington. Morning appointments with Congressmen Taber and Clevenger; Congressman Judd and G. D. Morgan (off the record). Receives National Association of Radio and Television Broadcasters Board of Directors. Greets Prime Minister Churchill and A. Eden upon their arrival. Luncheon with Prime Minister Churchill, A. Eden, Harold Caccia (Deputy Under Secretary of State), Secretary Dulles,

and L. T. Merchant. Hosts dinner in honor of Prime Minister Churchill.

26 Washington. Morning appointment with Ambassador Aldrich. Luncheon with Prime Minister Churchill, A. Eden, H. Caccia and congressional members. Dinner with Prime Minister Churchill and officials.

27 Washington. Attends services at National Presbyterian Church with Mrs. Eisenhower, and Secretary and Mrs. Dulles. Hosts dinner for Prime Minister Churchill.

28 Washington. Morning appointments with Secretary Dulles and T. B. Morton; Legislative Leaders; Attorney General Brownell (off the record); Frank Kemp (President, Great Western Sugar) and Senators Ferguson and Barrett. British-American talks. Afternoon off-the-record appointment with Frederick Steuck and S. Adams.

29 Washington. Morning appointments with H. E. Stassen (off the record); K. G. Howard; R. Roberts; Florence B. Kane (sculptress), Lillian E. McKay, and J. Harlin O'Connell; Soft-Coal Industry Committee; Ambassador Barry; Prime Minister Churchill. Hosts stag luncheon for American Korean Foundation members. Afternoon appointments with Budget Director Hughes; Dr. William I. Myers; L. W. Hall, S. Adams, T. E. Stephens, K. McCann, and B. N. Harlow (off the record); Vice-President Nixon (off the record).

30 Washington. Breakfast with C. D. Jackson. Morning appointments with General Cutler and J. S. Lay (off the record); J. C. Hagerty. News conference, followed by appointments with Ambassador Gaganvihari Lallabhai Mehta (India) and J. F. Simmons; Senators Crippa and Barrett, General Persons, and H. H. Gruenther; Bernice Woodard and M. M. Rabb (off the record). To Burning Tree Country Club for golf with N. Burnham, Colonel Belshe, and W. J. Mougey. Hosts dinner for West Point Class of 1915.

July 1 Washington. Off-the-record breakfast with Attorney General Brownell, L. W. Hall, and S. Adams. Morning appointments with Secretary Wilson; National

Security Council session; Senator Bowring; Congressman Short and Robert Smart (Clerk, Armed Services Committee). Signs S. 2802. Afternoon appointments with A. S. Flemming, Secretary Humphrey, Budget Director Hughes, A. F. Burns, G. Hauge, Secretary McKay, and F. E. Wormser (off the record); A. F. Burns and G. Hauge; Admiral Strauss; K. McCann. Photo session with Mrs. Eisenhower for wedding anniversary. Late afternoon appointment with Mr. and Mrs. W. D. Pawley.

2   Washington. Morning appointment with Secretary McKay (off the record). Cabinet meeting, followed by appointments with Ambassador Heath; Generals Cutler and Carroll; Senator Butler, S. Adams, and G. Hauge; Harold C. McClellan (President, National Association of Manufacturers). Afternoon departure to Camp David, Maryland, with Mrs. Eisenhower and Mr. and Mrs. G. E. Allen.

3   Camp David, Maryland. No official appointments.

4   Camp David, Maryland. No official appointments.

5   Camp David, Maryland. No official appointments.

6   Washington. Returns to White House. Receives Association of American Colleges committee. Morning appointments with Senator Mundt, Dr. and Mrs. D. K. Baillie, and Vern Jennings (State Legislature, South Dakota); General Srisdi Thanarat (Deputy Minister of Defense, Thailand), General Jira Vichitsonggram (Chief of Defense, Thailand), Ambassador Sarasin, and J. F. Simmons. Receives young people from Sterling, Colorado. Lunch with Secretary Humphrey and George Whitney. Afternoon appointments with E. Johnston; K. C. Royall; S. Adams, Generals Persons and Carroll, G. D. Morgan, I. J. Martin, and Murray Snyder (off the record); Senator Knowland; Secretary Dulles.

7   Washington. Morning appointments with Senators Millikin and Johnson; Legislative Leaders; J. C. Hagerty. News conference, followed by appointments with Senator H. A. Smith and Secretary Mitchell; E. J. Bermingham (off the record); General Doolittle and S. Adams (off the record); Ambassador Makins, Peter Thorneycroft (President, Board of Trade,

Great Britian), and Admiral Walter S. Delaney (Deputy, East-West Trade, FOA). Afternoon appointment with Secretary Dulles. Hosts stag dinner.

8   Washington. Morning appointments with M. M. Rabb (off the record); J. A. Hannah; Governor Langlie, Secretary Mitchell, J. E. Wilkins, and S. Adams; A. F. Burns, N. H. Jacoby, and G. Hauge; Minna Una Tedder; William Zeckendorf, Ieoh M. Pei, and John R. McCrary to discuss slum clearance; Admiral Strauss (off the record); Reverend B. Graham and T. E. Stephens. Lunch with Senator Knowland (off the record). Afternoon appointments with R. Taft, Jr., S. Adams, and I. J. Martin (off the record); Congressman Brown and Springfield, Ohio, business leaders. Receives international attendees of International Conference of Social Work, Toronto, Canada. Hosts tea in honor of Carmen Franco and Dr. Cristobal Martines Bordiu and Ambassador de Lequerica.

9   Washington. Breakfast with P. Hoyt. Morning appointments with J. J. McCloy (off the record); Attorney General Brownell and district judges (off the record); Ambassador Luce; Governor Thornton and J. S. Fine. Cabinet meeting. To Burning Tree Country Club for lunch and golf with Congressman Arends, General Parks, B. J. Patton, and J. E. McClure.

10 Washington. Morning appointments with H. E. Stassen (off the record); Senators Bowring and Reynolds; high school bands from Ottawa, Kansas, and Gladewater, Texas (off the record); General Cortland V. R. Schuyler (Chief of Staff, Allied Powers, Europe); Vice-President Carlos P. Garcia (Philippines), C. P. Romulo, Minister Raul Leuterio (Philippines), and J. F. Simmons; National Grange representatives; W. D. Pawley and S. Adams; T. E. Stephens and Bulova Watch Co. representatives (off the record); Secretary Dulles; S. Adams, General Carroll, and K. McCann (off the record); Board of Inquiry, Atomic Energy Facilities; Governor Russell and M. M. Rabb. To Burning Tree Country Club for lunch with S. Snead, J. E. McClure, J. E. McClure, Jr., B. J. Patton, and Congressman Halleck. Golf with S. Snead, B. J. Patton, and Congressman Halleck.

11   Washington. Attends services with Mrs. Eisenhower at National Presbyterian Church.

12   Washington. Morning off-the-record appointments with Secretary Dulles; A. F. Burns and G. Hauge; Admiral Radford; Secretary Wilson; Attorney General Brownell, Budget Director Hughes, and General Persons. Afternoon appointments with Generals Lanham and Persons (off the record); B. M. Shanley; N. A. Rockefeller, Budget Director Hughes, and G. Hauge (off the record); General Paul (off the record).

13   Washington. Airborne for Blair County Airport, en route to Dr. M. S. Eisenhower's home, State College, Pennsylvania. Attends funeral services for H. E. Eisenhower at St. Andrew's Episcopal Church. Returns to Washington. Afternoon off-the-record appointments with F. A. Seaton and R. B. Crosby; General Vogel and S. Adams; W. D. Pawley, Bruce Brownley, Mr. Franke, Pat Coyne, S. Adams, and Generals Doolittle and Carroll.

14   Washington. Off-the-record breakfast with R. Howard. Morning appointments with the Legislative Leaders; J. C. Hagerty. News conference, followed by appointments with A. S. Flemming and G. D. Morgan (off the record); Admiral Leahy (off the record); Andrew Holmstoon and S. Adams (off the record); Governor Stratton. Discusses lead and zinc issue with bipartisan Senate group. Lunch with P. G. Hoffman. Afternoon appointments with J. S. Lay and S. E. Gleason (off the record); George A. Sloan (President, American Society of French Legion of Honor); Postmaster General Summerfield (off the record); A. S. Flemming; A. S. Flemming and S. Benedict (off the record).

15   Washington. Morning appointments with Senator Daniel and G. D. Morgan; Secretary Dulles and General Smith; Prime Minister Sayyid Mustafa ben Halim (Libya), Minister El-Kekhia, Finance Minister Ali Aneizi (Libya), and H. A. Byroade. National Security Council session. Hosts small stag luncheon in honor of Prime Minister ben Halim. Afternoon appointments with R. Reed (off the record); Foreign Minister Muhammed Fadil Jamali (Iraq), Ambassador Al-Shabandar, and H. A. Byroade; Congress-

man Halleck, Budget Director Hughes, and General Persons; Reserve Officers Association leaders; Attorney General Brownell, R. B. Anderson, and S. Adams (off the record); C. Moore (off the record); Senator Potter.

16 Washington. Breakfast with Senator Knowland. Receives Farm Credit Administration Governor and Federal Farm Credit Board members. Cabinet meeting, followed by appointment with Budget Director Hughes and P. F. Brundage. Signs S. 3291. Afternoon appointments with Secretary Thomas and S. Adams (off the record); Congressional members. To Congressional Country Club for lunch and golf.

17 Washington. Morning off-the-record appointments with Secretary Hobby and N. A. Rockefeller; J. B. Mintener; S. Adams and T. E. Stephens; S. W. Richardson. Off-the-record lunch with G. E. Allen. To Burning Tree Country Club for golf with G. E. Allen.

18 Washington. Off-the-record afternoon appointments with S. W. Richardson; Secretary Dulles.

19 Washington. Morning appointments with Secretary Dulles, H. E. Stassen, Admiral Radford, and Budget Director Hughes (off the record); Legislative Leaders; Congressmen Taber and Wigglesworth, Admiral Radford, H. E. Stassen, Budget Director Hughes, S. Adams, General Persons, and G. D. Morgan; Admiral Radford and General Twining; G. Hauge and A. F. Burns; Secretary Wilson; Secretaries Wilson and Humphrey, and Attorney General Brownell (off the record). Afternoon appointments with E. Johnston (off the record); A. S. Flemming.

20 Washington. Receives Washington and Oregon congressional delegations. Morning appointments with B. S. Adkins; Senator Malone, F. E. Wormser, and G. Hauge; Vernon Bradley and S. Adams; Ambassador Mills; Ambassador Rankin; Field Marshal Earl Alexander (Tunis), Ambassador Makins, General Collins, John E. Graf (Smithsonian), and J. F. Simmons. Lunch with Field Marshal Alexander. Afternoon appointments with Secretary Dulles; General Bryan.

21 Washington. Morning appointments with J. S. Lay and S. E. Gleason (off the record); G. L. Brown and

B. M. Shanley; Congressman Simpson and daughter and State Senator Schlagenhauf (off the record); Senators Butler and Saltonstall, Congressman Tollefson, L. R. Sanford (President, Shipbuilders Council of America), Andrew A. Pettis (Vice-President, CIO), and James A. Brownlow (President, AFL Metal Trades); J. C. Hagerty. News conference, followed by appointment to discuss land clearance and the University of Chicago. To Burning Tree Country Club for golf with Colonel Belshe, E. Wheeler, and R. T. Jones.

22 Washington. Morning appointments with Generals Adler and McClean, S. Adams, and B. N. Harlow; Mrs. J. H. Wallace and John Ashton and family (off the record); National Security Council session; Dr. Alberto Lleras (former Security General, OAS), H. F. Holland, and J. F. Simmons. Presentation of drum by Noble and Cooley Co. Lunch with B. M. Baruch. Afternoon appointments with M. Muir; Major William D. Shearer and family; General Hull; Vice-President Nixon, Postmaster General Summerfield, L. W. Hall, J. Bassett, B. C. Duffy, T. Rogers, C. Newton, and T. E. Stephens (off the record).

23 Washington. Off-the-record breakfast with Senator Dirksen. Cabinet meeting, followed by appointments with Generals Van Fleet and Persons (off the record); Ambassador Lodge (off the record); H. J. Heinz (FOA) and Norman Paul (FOA); Generals Heaton and Snyder (off the record); General Curtis (off the record); Secretary Hobby, Senators Knowland, Purtell, and H. A. Smith; Cardinal Spellman, B. M. Shanley, and General Carroll. Signs H. R. 8247. Afternoon off-the-record appointments with Glen Sutton, S. Adams, and G. Hauge; Postmaster General Summerfield; Budget Director Hughes, R. B. Anderson, R. A. Tudor, J. E. Coke, and General Robinson; James Howard and G. Hauge; Bud Sprague.

24 Washington. To Camp David, Maryland, with Mrs. Eisenhower and Major and Mrs. J. S. D. Eisenhower and children.

25 Camp David, Maryland. Returns to White House in afternoon. To Mayflower Hotel for Twelfth World's Christian Endeavor Convention.

26   Washington. Morning appointments with Budget Director Hughes and General Persons (off the record); Legislative Leaders; Horace Hadley and S. Adams (off the record); A. F. Burns and G. Hauge; J. O. Henderson, R. Bliss, and I. J. Martin; Secretary Wilson and Admiral Radford; Secretary Wilson, A. S. Flemming, Admiral Radford, J. A. Hannah, Colonel Randall, and General Cutler. Luncheon with Secretaries Dulles and Wilson, General Van Fleet, and Admiral Radford. Afternoon appointments with Secretary Dulles (off the record); W. M. Martin, P. E. Miller, and G. Hauge. Hosts dinner in honor of President and Mrs. Syngman Rhee (Korea).

27   Washington. Morning appointments with Governor Kennon and S. Adams (off the record); Joint Mexican-- United States Defense Commission; Korean-American Talks; R. Reid; Republican Congressmen; General Persons and brothers. Signs H. R. 4854. Receives Boys' Nation members. Lunch with Secretary Dulles. Afternoon off-the-record appointments with Admiral Strauss; Secretary Humphrey and T. E. Stephens; H. Hoover, Jr.; Attorney General Brownell; Secretary Humphrey, A. S. Flemming, and R. B. Anderson.

28   Washington. Morning appointments with General Cutler and J. S. Lay (off the record); E. B. Brossard and G. Hauge (off the record); J. C. Hagerty. News conference, followed by appointments with General John H. Michaelis; A. Nielsen (off the record). Signs H. R. 5731. To Burning Tree Country Club for lunch and golf with Major J. S. D. Eisenhower, Senator Reynolds, and B. T. Leithead. To Mayflower Hotel with Mrs. Eisenhower for dinner hosted by President and Mrs. Rhee.

29   Washington. National Security Council session, followed by morning appointments with Secretary Weeks and S. F. Dunn (off the record); Cabinet meeting. Awards Medal of Freedom to Mademoiselle de Galard-Terraube. Afternoon appointments with Congressman Martin and E. D. Chesney (off the record); Korean-American talks; off-the-record meeting in motion picture theater. Receives R. L. Biggers (off the record).

	30	Washington. To Camp David with Mrs. Eisenhower and grandchildren.
	31	Camp David, Maryland. No official appointments.
August	1	Camp David, Maryland. No official appointments.
	2	Washington. Returns to White House in morning. Appointments with Attorney General Brownell, S. Adams, General Persons, G. D. Morgan, and I. J. Martin; Senator Duff. Signs H. R. 7839. Witnesses swearing-in of Commissioner of Federal Housing Administration Norman P. Mason. Afternoon appointments with General W. H. Wilbur; C. Canby Balderston, W. M. Martin, S. Adams, and G. Hauge (off the record); A. F. Burns and G. Hauge; Secretary Dulles (off the record); Postmaster General Summerfield (off the record).
	3	Washington. Morning appointments with Legislative Leaders; C. L. Burgess, B. Patterson, S. Adams, General Persons, General Cutler, General Carroll, M. M. Rabb, B. N. Harlow, and G. D. Morgan (off the record); C. T. Wood; Dr. Geza Kapus and family. Signs S. 2759. Receives Girls' Nation members. Afternoon off-the-record appointment with B. N. Harlow.
	4	Washington. Morning appointments with General Cutler and J. S. Lay (off the record); Reverend J. Waskom Pickett (Senior Bishop, Methodist Church, Southern Asia) and G. Hauge; National Officers, New Farmers of America; H. E. Stassen (off the record); J. C. Hagerty. News conference, followed by appointment with Ambassador Ageton. Hosts stag dinner.
	5	Washington. National Security Council session, followed by appointments with Senator Watkins and Robert Stillmore (off the record); Senator Ellender; H. E. Stassen and Dr. William F. Russell (Deputy of Technical Services, FOA) (off the record); Congressmen Simpson, Hillelson, Cole, and Short; Congressman Lucas; Attorney General Brownell and R. B. Anderson (off the record). Afternoon off-the-record appointments with Budget Director Hughes and General Persons; Generals Ridgway and L. E. Simon; A. W. Dulles; Secretary Humphrey, J. M.

Dodge, A. F. Burns, G. Hauge, General Persons, and G. D. Morgan.

6　Washington. Morning appointments with Admiral Strauss and General Cutler (off the record); Health Resources Advisory Committee; Cabinet meeting; Dr. M. S. Eisenhower. Off-the-record lunch with Dr. M. S. Eisenhower, Budget Director Hughes, N. A. Rockefeller, A. S. Flemming, and J. M. Dodge. To Burning Tree Country Club with Major J. S. D. Eisenhower for golf with Congressman Bishop and Colonel Belshe.

7　Washington. Morning appointments with Senators Ferguson and Potter and Republican candidates; Hawaiian delegate Elizabeth Pruett Farrington. Receives American Field Service international students. Appointments with Rene Dijoud, Charge d'affaires Gontran de Junia (French Embassy), Victor Purse (Acting Chief of Protocol), Captain John W. McElroy (Navy), and Professor Robert M. Langdon (U.S. Naval Academy); Secretary Dulles. To Burning Tree Country Club with Major J. S. D. Eisenhower for golf with Congressman Arends and Colonel Belshe.

8　Washington. Attends services at National Presbyterian Church with Mrs. Eisenhower.

9　Washington. Off-the-record morning appointments with Congressman Rees and G. D. Morgan; William V. Moscatelli; Joe Morris (*Saturday Evening Post*) and J. C. Hagerty; N. A. Rockefeller, Budget Director Hughes, A. S. Flemming, and B. M. Shanley. Appointments with A. F. Burns, G. Hauge, and General Bragdon; Secretary Wilson. Luncheon with Vice-President Nixon, Clifford Cass, L. W. Hall, J. Murphy, B. M. Shanley and Senators H. A. Smith, Hendrickson, and Dirksen; A. S. Flemming. To Naval Gun Factory with family for cruise on Potomac.

10　Washington. Morning appointments with Legislative Leaders; T. C. Streibert, A. M. Washburn, and General Carroll; Ambassador Peurifoy and General Carroll; Budget Director Hughes; S. Adams and T. E. Stephens; Republican congressional delegation; American Museum of Immigration committee; S. P. Skouras, J. Murphy, and L. Washburn (off the record). Luncheon with individuals from Special Committee on Highway Problems, Governors' Conference, and others. Afternoon appointment with P. G. Hoffman.

11 Washington. Morning appointments with Senator Bennett (off the record); General Cutler and J. S. Lay (off the record); James Rhodes (Auditor, Ohio) and family, R. Bliss, and I. J. Martin; D. Beck; J. C. Hagerty. News conference, followed by appointment with C. D. Jackson, S. Adams, and General Carroll (off the record). To Burning Tree Country Club. Signs Justice Department papers. Golf with Generals Horkan and Snyder, and Major J. S. D. Eisenhower. Tea with Ambassador Luce and Mrs. Eisenhower (off the record).

12 Washington. Morning appointment with Senator H. A. Smith (off the record). National Security Council session, followed by appointments with Secretary Dulles; Secretary Benson, Irving Reynolds (Consultant to Secretary Benson), and K. McCann; Postmaster General Summerfield (off the record). Afternoon appointments with Merton B. Tice (National Commander, VFW) and O. B. Ketchum; A. S. Flemming, Budget Director Hughes, Merrill Collett, and Generals Paul and Hurley. Receives Republican congressional candidates. To Camp David, Maryland, with family.

13 Camp David, Maryland. Cabinet meeting.

14 Camp David, Maryland. No official appointments.

15 Camp David, Maryland. Returns to Washington, D.C.

16 Washington. Morning appointments with Legislative Leaders; Republican congressional candidates; A. F. Burns and G. Hauge; A. F. Burns, Secretary Wilson, R. B. Anderson, F. A. Seaton, and Budget Director Hughes (off the record); Secretary Wilson; Ambassador Tran Van Kan (Viet Nam), Robert McClinnick (interpreter), and V. Purse; Ambassador José Luis Cruz-Salazar and V. Purse. Signs H. R. 8300. Afternoon off-the-record appointments with Senator Duff; Congressman Judd; Secretary Stevens, Generals L. L. Lemnitzer, Gavin, and Carroll, and Colonel

Kapp; Congressman Judd and General Carroll; Senator Carlson and General Persons. To Statler Hotel for film, *The Year of the Big Decision.*

17 Washington. Airborne for New York, New York, for voter registration. Returns to Washington. Morning appointments with Secretary Benson and family; H. E. Stassen (off the record). Makes short film for American-Korean Foundation. Afternoon appointment with J. C. Hagerty. News conference, followed by appointments with General Cutler and J. S. Lay (off the record); Secretary Dulles; A. S. Flemming and G. Hauge; Mr. and Mrs. L. F. McCollum (off the record).

18 Washington. Morning appointment with Congressman Davis (off the record). Cabinet meeting; National Security Council session; Senator Bowring; J. E. McClure and Bus Ham (Director, National Celebrities Tournament). To Burning Tree Country Club for lunch and golf with J. E. McClure, Colonel Belshe, and R. Brown.

19 Washington. To MATS terminal en route to Springfield, Illinois. Lays wreath at Lincoln's tomb. Proceeds to Governor's mansion for luncheon. Photo session with 4-H winners. Delivers address at State Fair. To Northwestern University via Glenview Naval Air Station, Evanston, Illinois. Addresses ceremony at Northwestern. Returns to Washington, D.C.

20 Washington. Breakfast with Senator Knowland. Morning appointments with Attorney General Brownell (off the record); Congressman Kersten and L. A. Minnich; air policy meeting (off the record); E. T. Weir; F. Cowles; Secretary General Carlos Davila (Organization of American States) and H. F. Holland; Congressman Martin, S. Adams, Senator Mundt and Iowa constituents. Signs S. J. Res. 140 (off the record). Appointments with National Advisory Committee for Aeronautics leaders; Congressman Keating (off the record); Major Anthony Mrous (off the record). Lunch with Congressman Martin. Afternoon appointments with B. M. Shanley (off the record); General White (off the record); J. S. Lay (off the record); Congressman Bender; Secretary Dulles; P. Young. Reads for Congressional film, *The Year of the*

Big Decision. Lead and Zinc talks. Departs with T. E. Stephens for unknown destination (off the record). Evening appointment with Congressman Halleck (off the record).

21 Washington. Breakfast with Vice-President Nixon (off the record). Receives Republican congressional candidates; Republican congressional delegation. Morning appointments with Congressman Gavin; Ambassador de Lequerica and V. Purse; J. Lyles and D. Lyles. To MATS terminal with Mrs. Eisenhower en route to Denver, Colorado. Motors to Doud residence. To Cherry Hills Country Club for golf with Governor Thornton, R. Arnold, and M. Luxford.

22 Denver, Colorado. To Lowry Air Force Base. No official appointments.

23 Denver, Colorado. To Lowry Air Force Base. Morning appointments with Senator Smith and family. To Cherry Hills Country Club for golf with R. Arnold. Delivers nationwide address from KHZ radio and television station.

24 Denver, Colorado. To Lowry Air Force Base. Morning appointments with General Corlett (off the record); Fred Hall (Lt. Governor, Kansas) and family; Governor Thornton. To Cherry Hills Country Club for golf with Governor Thornton, F. W. Leahy, R. Goldwater, and E. Conley. Lunch with D. G. Gordon, Mark Kramer, L. M. Pexton, Ed Nichols, R. Arnold, Jay L. Beecroft, Governor Thornton, F. W. Leahy, Robert Goldwater, and E. Conley.

25 Denver, Colorado. To Lowry Air Force Base. Morning appointments with Bureau of Reclamation member (off the record); Mrs. T. A. Stockton (RNC) and daughter; B. Farrington; F. W. Leahy; Generals Sprague and E. L. Eubanks; A. Nielsen. To Cherry Hills Country Club with A. Nielsen. Lunch with H. Anholt, R. Arnold, R. W. Braun, and D. G. Gordon and son. Golf with H. Anholt, R. Arnold, and R. W. Braun.

26 Denver, Colorado. To Lowry Air Force Base. Morning appointments with B. M. Shanley; Congressman Scrivner. To Cherry Hills Country Club for golf and lunch with L. C. Fulenwider, H. C. Van Schaack,

and W. K. Koch. Dinner at the Gordon private lake with Mrs. Eisenhower, E. Doud, Governor and Mrs. Thornton, and Mr. and Mrs. D. G. Gordon.

27   Denver, Colorado. To B. F. Swan's ranch for fishing with A. Nielsen, J. C. Hagerty, and U. E. Baughman.

28   Denver, Colorado. To Lowry Air Force Base. Morning appointments with Gordon Callbeck and family; E. R. Harriman. To Cherry Hills Country Club for golf with J. Black, Art Adkinson, and George Hannaway. Lunch with R. Arnold, J. Black, A. Adkinson, G. Hannaway, H. Anholt, Secretary Talbott, F. Waring, and W. W. Flenniken. Golf with Secretary Talbott, W. W. Flenniken, and F. Waring.

29   Denver, Colorado. Attends services with Mrs. Eisenhower at Corona Presbyterian Church. Boards *Columbine* for return to Washington.

30   Washington. To MATS terminal en route to Des Moines, Iowa. To Denver, Colorado, with H. Hoover.

31   Denver, Colorado. To Lowry Air Force Base. Departs for A. Nielsen's ranch with H. Hoover, Dr. M. S. Eisenhower, J. C. Hagerty, and A. Nielsen.

September 1   Fraser, Colorado. A. Nielsen's ranch. No official appointments.

2   Denver, Colorado. Hosts dinner for H. Hoover at Brown Palace Hotel.

3   Denver, Colorado. To Lowry Air Force Base. No official appointments.

4   Denver, Colorado. Departs Lowry Field aboard *Columbine* for air survey of reclamation projects. Lands at Grand Junction, Colorado, and McCook, Nebraska. Returns to Lowry Field.

5   Denver, Colorado. Attends services with Mrs. Eisenhower at Corona Presbyterian Church.

6   Denver, Colorado. Addresses nation from KOA-TV. To Lowry Air Force Base for morning appointments with Congressman Belcher; General Harmon; Fred Mock and Mrs. Mock. Annual checkup at Fitzsimons Army Hospital. Remains overnight.

7   Denver, Colorado. To Lowry Air Force Base. Awards

Congressional Medal of Honor. Morning appointment with L. H. Snyder. To Cherry Hills Country Club for golf with C. Roberts, General Harmon, and L. M. Pexton.

8 Denver, Colorado. To Lowry Air Force Base for morning appointments with Jack Foster (Editor, *Rocky Mountain News*) (off the record); Jock Lawrence. To Cherry Hills Country Club for luncheon followed by golf with F. F. Gosden, D. Garlington, and E. D. Slater. Hosts buffet dinner at Brown Palace Hotel.

9 Denver, Colorado. To Lowry Air Force Base for morning appointments with J. Murphy and Barbara Gunderson; Republican candidates. To Cherry Hills Country Club for luncheon followed by golf with W. A. Jones, W. E. Robinson, and B. T. Leithead. To Brown Palace Hotel for dinner with friends from Augusta National Golf Club. Remains overnight.

10 Denver, Colorado. Breakfast at Brown Palace Hotel with midwestern Republican leaders. To Lowry Air Force Base for morning appointments with General Cutler; General Cutler and Dillon Anderson (off the record); General Cutler, William Francis, Karl Bendetson, and John Blaffer (off the record); John Feikens (Republican State Chairman, Michigan) (off the record). To Cherry Hills Country Club for luncheon followed by golf with C. S. Jones, R. W. Woodruff, and E. Dudley.

11 Denver, Colorado. To Lowry Air Force Base for morning appointment with J. H. Whitney (off the record). To Cherry Hills Country Club for lunch, golf, and bridge with P. Reed, C. Roberts, and J. H. Whitney. Dinner with Governor and Mrs. Thornton and guests from Augusta National Golf Club.

12 Denver, Colorado. To Lowry Air Force Base for afternoon appointments with Attorney General Brownell, Secretary Wilson, Admiral Radford, Secretary Humphrey, and J. E. Hoover; Mrs. Eisenhower, Mrs. Dulles, Mrs. H. A. Smith, and Mrs. Mike Mansfield; Attorney General Brownell, A. Nielsen, and S. N. Barnes; Secretary Dulles; National Security Council session. Dinner at Officers' Club with National Security Council members.

13   Denver, Colorado. To Lowry Air Force Base for pho-
      to session with Republican candidates. News confer-
      ence. To Cherry Hills Country Club for golf with
      Governor Thornton, A. R. Phipps, J. Culbreath, and
      R. Arnold. Luncheon with golf partners, D. Dunbar,
      and C. Shumate.

14   Denver, Colorado. To Lowry Air Force Base for
      meeting with American Retail Federation Executive
      Committee. Attends dedication of National Bureau
      of Standards Laboratory, Boulder, Colorado. Unveils
      Radio Building plaque. Tours the Great Western
      Sugar Co. in Brighton, Colorado. Brief tour of the
      Louie J. Ehlen farm. Returns to Cherry Hills Coun-
      try Club for golf with Governor Thornton, M. Mon-
      crief, and L. M. Pexton.

15   Denver, Colorado. To Lowry Air Force Base for
      morning appointment with General Burgess. To By-
      ers Peak Ranch, Fraser, Colorado, with A. Nielsen
      and J. C. Hagerty.

16   Fraser, Colorado. No official appointments.

17   Fraser, Colorado. No official appointments.

18   Fraser, Colorado. No official appointments.

19   Fraser, Colorado. No official appointments.

20   Denver, Colorado. To Lowry Air Force Base. To
      Cherry Hills Country Club for golf with R. Arnold.
      Dinner at Brown Palace Hotel.

21   Denver, Colorado. To Lowry Air Force Base for
      morning appointments with L. W. Hall, J. Bassett, V.
      Washington, R. Humphrey, S. Adams, General Per-
      sons, I. J. Martin, G. D. Morgan, J. C. Hagerty, and
      Murray Snyder; H. E. Stassen; General Francis de
      Guingand; General Raymond McLain. Luncheon at
      Cherry Hills Country Club with Mayor Nicholson,
      M. Kramer, R. Arnold, J. G. Dyer, L. Skutt, Gover-
      nor Thornton, H. Anholt, H. D. Writer, General
      McLain, C. E. Anderson, D. Kennedy, and R. V.
      Rodman. Golf with General McLain, R. V. Rodman,
      and C. E. Anderson.

22   Denver, Colorado. Attends services with Mrs.
      Eisenhower for National Day of Prayer. Morning ap-
      pointments with W. W. Flenniken and Wyoming rep-

resentatives; A. Nielsen and Shell Oil Co. leaders (off the record); Irving Geist and Arthur Rydstrom (off the record). Airborne for Missoula, Montana, for dedication of new Forest Service Smokejumpers Center. Proceeds to Walla Walla, Washington.

23 Walla Walla, Washington. Breakfast with guests at Marcus Whitman Hotel. To McNary Dam for inspection speech. Airborne for Los Angeles, California. Evening address to National Federation of Republican Women and Citizens for Eisenhower of Southern California.

24 Los Angeles, California. Morning address to AFL 73rd Convention. Returns to Denver, Colorado. To Cherry Hills Country Club for golf with J. Dier and R. Arnold.

25 Denver, Colorado. To Lowry Air Force Base for morning appointments with General Burgess (off the record); General Cutler; Governor Arn and Kansas representatives. To Cherry Hills Country Club for interview with Charles Lucey followed by golf with R. Arnold, F. Manning, Jr., and J. C. Hagerty.

26 Denver, Colorado. Attends services at Corona Presbyterian Church with Mrs. Eisenhower.

27 Denver, Colorado. To Lowry Air Force Base for morning appointments with Congressman Chenoweth; H. Lutcher Brown; filmmakers (off the record); Ellen Harris (congressional candidate). To Cherry Hills Country Club with Secretary Benson. Hosts Luncheon in honor of Secretary Benson followed by golf with E. Dudley, R. Arnold, and B. Maytag.

28 Denver, Colorado. To Lowry Air Force Base for morning appointments with Secretary Stevens and General Ridgway; A. F. Burns; H. T. Shadford. To Cherry Hills Country Club for luncheon followed by golf with Governor Thornton, H. R. Berglund, and D. E. Webb. Gives autograph to Ann and Susan Mack. Attends dinner with General Sprague, Mrs. Eisenhower, and E. Doud.

29 Denver, Colorado. To Lowry Air Force Base. To Cherry Hills Country Club for golf with Governor

Thornton, R. Arnold, and P. Hoyt. Attends luncheon.

30   Denver, Colorado. To Lowry Air Force Base for morning appointments with O. A. Lamoreux (off the record); Colonel Schulz, and John Jackson and son (off the record); Secretary Benson. To Cherry Hills Country Club for golf practice and lunch. Golf with R. Arnold, J. Jackson, Sr., and J. Jackson, Jr. Becomes honorary member of Brownie Troop 643.

October   1   Denver, Colorado. To Lowry Air Force Base for morning appointment with Charles P. White (President, Republic Steel Co.). Sightseeing tour of A. Nielsen's farm with C. P. White, G. E. Allen, and A. Nielsen. To Cherry Hills Country Club for luncheon given by W. W. Flenniken and golf with C. P. White, D. Kelly, and J. Beardwood.

2   Denver, Colorado. To Lowry Air Force Base for morning appointments with Colonel John H. McCann (off the record); General Gruenther. To Cherry Hills Country Club for golf with L. Mangrum, R. Arnold, and W. E. Robinson. Lunch with golf partners and A. Nielsen, Generals Snyder and Gruenther, and G. E. Allen.

3   Denver, Colorado. To Lowry Air Force Base. Attends services at Corona Presbyterian Church with Mrs. Eisenhower. Lunch at Brown Palace Hotel with Congressman Halleck and John Colbourne. Afternoon appointment with General Gruenther, G. E. Allen, and W. E. Robinson. Dinner with General Gruenther, Mr. and Mrs. G. E. Allen, W. E. Robinson, Mrs. Eisenhower, E. Doud, Governor and Mrs. Thornton, Mr. and Mrs. H. Anholt, and General and Mrs. Snyder.

4   Denver, Colorado. To Lowry Air Force Base for morning appointments with Secretary Wilson; S. Adams, General Persons, I. J. Martin, B. N. Harlow, G. D. Morgan, and G. Hauge. To Cherry Hills Country Club for luncheon followed by golf with M. Norling, J. Campbell, and R. McIlvaine. Makes film for commemoration of incandescent light bulb (off the record).

5   Denver, Colorado. To Lowry Air Force Base for

morning appointments with W. H. Jackson; Captain Mario Lopez (Guatemala); Congressman Simpson. To Cherry Hills Country Club for luncheon, followed by golf with Governor Thornton, R. Arnold, and R. Manning. Dinner at Brown Palace Hotel.

6   Denver, Colorado. To Lowry Air Force Base for morning appointment with Republican congressional candidates. To B. F. Swan's ranch with G. E. Allen and A. Nielsen.

7   Denver, Colorado. To Lowry Air Force Base for morning appointments with General Cutler; General Cutler and National Security Council members (off the record); Vice-President Nixon. To Cherry Hills Country Club for luncheon with Vice-President Nixon, R. Arnold, L. W. Hall, Donald Nixon, R. Aberthnot, A. Rydstrom, G. E. Allen, and D. G. Gordon.

8   Denver, Colorado. To Lowry Air Force Base. Signs proclamation for National Nurse Week. Morning appointments with Bishop Ralph A. Ward; Mr. Shadford; Vice-President Nixon. To Brown Palace Hotel for appointment with Legislative Leaders. Addresses Republican rally at Denver City Auditorium. Hosts dinner at Brown Palace Hotel for Legislative Leaders.

9   Denver, Colorado. To Lowry Air Force Base for morning appointment with General Parks. To Cherry Hills Country Club for lunch with Generals Parks and Harmon, and A. S. Flemming. Meets Illinois-California Express Co. employees.

10   Denver, Colorado. To Lowry Air Force Base. Attends services at Corona Presbyterian Church with Mrs. Eisenhower. Visits home of P. H. Dominick with Mrs. Eisenhower and E. Doud.

11   Denver, Colorado. Lowry Air Force Base. Morning appointments with W. P. Wells; F. A. Barrett; Mr. and Mrs. Robert Six; F. Wood (off the record). To Cherry Hills Country Club for lunch with E. Dudley, A. Schrepferman, and Golding Fairchild.

12   Denver, Colorado. To Lowry Air Force Base for morning appointments with C. Walter Allen, Tomoshige Arashi (painter), and Hirotoshi Tagashira (in-

terpreter); Gridiron Club delegation. Makes short film to promote national support for American participation in 1954-55 Olympics. To Cherry Hills Country Club for golf with W. W. Flenniken, B. Warren, and R. Arnold, followed by luncheon.

13   Denver, Colorado. To Lowry Air Force Base for morning appointments with W. Tomberlin; H. W. Scatterday; LeRoy Powelka and Robert S. Lawrence; Senator Watkins; A. Nielsen (off the record). Luncheon at Cherry Hills Country Club with Republican Financial Campaign workers. Evening visit to Brown Palace Hotel.

14   Denver, Colorado. To Lowry Air Force Base for morning appointments with Major and Mrs. Charles J. Pinto; young Republicans. To Windsor Hotel, then to U.S. Mint for tour and inspection. Luncheon at Cherry Hills Country Club. Golf with Governor Thornton and R. Arnold. To Brown Palace Hotel for presidential birthday party.

15   Denver, Colorado. Airborne for Indianapolis, Indiana, en route to Washington, D.C.

16   Washington. Morning appointments with Postmaster General Summerfield (off the record); General Cutler; Bill Bangert (Republican congressional candidate) (off the record); S. P. Skouras and Italian film star; General Bradley; Ambassador Makins and Lord Baillieu; Prime Minister Mohammed Ali (Pakistan), Ambassador Syed Amjad Ali (Pakistan), H. A. Byroade, and Ambassador Hildreth. Hosts stag luncheon for Prime Minister Ali.

17   Washington. Attends services at National Presbyterian Church with Mrs. Eisenhower. Appointments with V. E. Peterson, C. L. Burgess, S. Adams, J. C. Hagerty, and William J. Hopkins (Executive Clerk). Returns to White House with W. E. Robinson.

18   Washington. Morning appointments with Secretary Dulles; Ambassador Peurifoy; Ambassador John E. Holloway (South Africa); G. Hauge; Admiral Radford; Secretaries Dulles and Wilson, Admirals Radford and Carney, and Generals Twining, Ridgway, and Cutler; Secretary Wilson. Receives first "Forget-Me-Not" Disabled American Veterans representa-

tives. Lunch with Attorney General Brownell (off the record), followed by appointments with Vice-President Nixon; President William V. S. Tubman (Liberia). Hosts dinner for President Tubman.

19   Washington. Cabinet meeting. Opens exhibit at Veterans Memorial building by telephone. Appointments with Generals Doolittle and Cutler, J. Patrick Coyne, S. P. Johnston, W. D. Pawley, William D. Franks, and M. Hadley (off the record); Ambassador Makins, Herbert Morrison, and C. Burke Elbrick (Deputy Assistant, Secretary of State). Afternoon appointment with Ambassador Kemper. Participates in the 1954 Department of State Honor Award Ceremony. Afternoon appointment with C. L. Sulzberger (off the record). Attends dinner hosted by President Tubman at the Liberian Embassy with Mrs. Eisenhower.

20   Washington. To MATS terminal en route to Hartford, Connecticut. Receives honorary degree and delivers address at Trinity College. To Bushnell Park for birthday celebration of Governor Lodge. To Bradley Airport en route to New York, New York. To Hotel Astor for New York West Point Society luncheon. Attends dinner hosted by American Jewish Tercentenary Committee.

21   New York, New York. To Roosevelt Hotel to receive finance group and Senator Ives's staff. Visits local sights of interest. To Waldorf-Astoria for afternoon appointments with General Augustín Muñoz-Grandes and Colonel Lyman D. Bothwell (U.S. Army); Lights' Diamond Jubilee committee; Morris Snyder; Republican congressional candidates; Cardinal Spellman. Attends dinner and delivers address in Grand Ballroom.

22   Washington. Returns to Washington, D.C., in the morning. National Security Council session, followed by appointments with A. W. Dulles (off the record); A. S. Flemming; Postmaster General Summerfield and C. R. Hook (off the record). Off-the-record lunch with P. G. Hoffman. Afternoon appointment with J. M. Dodge.

23   Washington. Morning appointments with H. Hoover, Jr., James R. Gardner (Intelligence, State Department), T. Achilles Polyzoides (Intelligence, State De-

partment), and S. Adams (off the record); Walter Sundlun and I. J. Martin. Receives U.S. Committee for U.N. To Eisenhower farm at Gettysburg, Pennsylvania. Stops en route to greet people at Gettysburg Battlefield. Hosts outdoor luncheon for Lloyd H. Wood and other Republican candidates. To Camp David.

24 Camp David, Maryland. No official appointments.

25 Washington. Morning appointments with A. Nielsen (off the record); Ambassador Tappin; Earl of Wemyss and March and Ambassador Makins; Secretary Wilson; Republican congressional candidates. Afternoon appointments with John Pillsbury; A. F. Burns and G. Hauge; Cabinet meeting. To Mayflower Hotel for 11th annual National Security Industrial Association dinner. Receives James Forrestal Memorial Award.

26 Washington. Morning appointments with T. C. Streibert and A. M. Washburn; Dr. Elmer Hess (President-elect, AMA); Polish veteran leaders; Senator Potter; G. Hauge, C. Francis, and J. M. Lambie; General Cutler. Greets National Women's Advisory Committee conference. Afternoon appointments with Mr. and Mrs. Alexander Frieder (off the record); A. W. Dulles (off the record); National Security Council session.

27 Washington. Morning appointments with N. Cummings and G. Hauge; J. C. Hagerty. News conference, followed by appointments with F. G. Gurley, and W. T. Faricy (off the record); L. W. Hall; Secretaries Dulles and Humphrey, and H. Hoover, Jr.; Ambassador Wailes. Off-the-record lunch with W. S. Paley. Afternoon off-the-record appointments with Admiral Strauss; Harlow H. Curtice (President, General Motors) and B. N. Harlow. Hosts stag dinner for businessmen and government officials to discuss Heritage Foundation's campaign, Crusade for Freedom.

28 Washington. National Security Council session, followed by appointments with President's National Highway Program Advisory Committee; Admiral Fechteler; William Aiken and J. F. Simmons; Chancellor Adenauer, Secretary Dulles, Ambassador

Krekeler, Hans von Herwarth (Chief, Protocol, Germany), Walter Hallstein (State Secretary, Foreign Affairs, Germany), and High Commissioner Conant. Hosts stag luncheon for Chancellor Adenauer. Attends Eisenhower Day dinner given by Citizens for Eisenhower Congressional Committee with Mrs. Eisenhower. Addresses nation over radio and television.

29 Washington. To Washington National Airport en route to Cleveland, Ohio; Detroit, Michigan; and Louisville, Kentucky. Meets with members of West Point class of 1915. Airborne for Wilmington, Delaware; Washington, D.C.

30 Washington. Morning appointments with Ambassador Henderson; J. Black (off the record); Eclat Club members; A. S. Flemming and Budget Director Hughes; Circuit Judge Walter N. Bastian; young farmers from India and Pakistan; Secretary Dulles, H. Hoover, Jr., and L. T. Merchant. Makes long distance phone calls to start phone tree.

31 Washington. Attends services at St. John's Episcopal Church with Mrs. Eisenhower.

November 1 Washington. Morning appointments with H. E. Stassen (off the record); Alex Makinsky (off the record); A. F. Burns and G. Hauge; Secretary Wilson, R. B. Anderson, and C. L. Burgess (joined by Secretary Dulles, Admirals Radford and Carney, and General Cutler). Afternoon appointment with Budget Director Hughes, N. A. Rockefeller, and S. Adams. To CBS Station for election-eve radio and television program.

2 Washington. Morning appointments with General Cutler and J. S. Lay; W. M. Canaday; Secretary Weeks and S. Adams (off the record). National Security Council session. Afternoon appointments with Secretaries Dulles and Wilson, and Admirals Radford and Carney. Visits RNC Headquarters in Cafritz building. Dinner at residence of Secretary and Mrs. Humphrey with Mrs. Eisenhower. To Mayflower Hotel for Citizens for Eisenhower Congressional Committee meeting. To Sheraton-Park Hotel to visit Secretary and Mrs. Wilson.

3   Washington. Morning appointments with Ambassador Jacques Léger (Haiti) and J. F. Simmons; Ambassador Drew; J. C. Hagerty. News conference, followed by appointments with Senator Laurel (Philippines) and J. F. Simmons; Secretary Dulles, H. Hoover, Jr., and S. Adams; General Collins; Secretaries Dulles and Wilson, Admiral Radford, and General Collins. Afternoon appointments with A. W. Dulles, General Cutler, S. Adams, and Colonel Goodpaster.

4   Washington. Morning appointments with Postmaster General Summerfield; Ambassador Sarasin, General Phao Siyanon (Director, Police Force, Thailand), Siddi Sawet Sila (Aide, General Phao), and H. Charles Spruks (Protocol); National Security Council session. Afternoon appointments with M. Patterson, Gerard Smith (Consultant, Secretary of State), and S. Adams; J. Murphy and B. Gunderson; R. Guggenheim. Hosts dinner with Mrs. Eisenhower for Elizabeth, Queen Mother of England.

5   Washington. Breakfast with Senator Knowland and General Persons. Morning appointment with Secretary Humphrey (off the record). Cabinet meeting. Signs Instrument of Ratification, Universal Copyright Convention. Afternoon appointments with Senator Ferguson; E. Johnston, C. D. Jackson, and Colonel Goodpaster; Senator Bricker and I. J. Martin; L. W. Hall, R. Humphreys, J. Bassett, and S. Adams. Informal dinner with Elizabeth, Queen Mother of England.

6   Washington. Breakfast with Senator Payne and S. Adams; Ambassador Woodward; H. Hoover, Jr., R. B. Anderson, A. W. Dulles, S. Adams, General Cutler, and Colonel Goodpaster; Ambassador José Maria de Areilza (Spain).

7   Washington. Attends services with Mrs. Eisenhower at National Presbyterian Church.

8   Washington. To MATS terminal en route to Boston, Massachusetts. Photos for Greater Boston Community Fund. Meets Catholic bishops and National Council of Catholic Women officers at Boston Symphony Hall. Addresses ceremony. Returns to Washington, D.C. Witnesses unveiling of Theodore Roose-

velt portrait, Fort McNair. Afternoon appointment with H. E. Stassen, E. Johnston, and J. P. Grace. Attends dinner with Mrs. Eisenhower hosted by Elizabeth, Queen Mother of England.

9 Washington. National Security Council session. Receives naturalization candidates. To Sheraton-Carlton Hotel to greet National Conference on Spiritual Foundations of American Democracy. Appointments with Ambassador Allison and W. S. Robertson (off the record); Prime Minister Shigeru Yoshida (Japan), Ambassador Iguchi, Ambassador Allison, and W. S. Robertson. Hosts stag luncheon in honor of Prime Minister Yoshida. Receives National Milk Producers Federation officers. Appointment with Secretaries Wilson and Humphrey, Attorney General Brownell, and S. N. Barnes (off the record). Makes brief film for Safe Driving Day. Late afternoon appointment with Foreign Minister Paul Henri (Belgium) and Mrs. Spaak (off the record).

10 Washington. Off-the-record breakfast with Senator Hickenlooper, Congressman Cole, Budget Director Hughes, General Persons, and G. D. Morgan; Ambassador Hector David Castro and J. F. Simmons; B. M. Birla (Industrialist, India) and G. Hauge; Dr. Harmodio Arias (former President, Panama) and H. F. Holland; J. C. Hagerty. News conference. Attends dedication ceremonies of Iwo Jima statue. Appointments with Secretary Humphrey, H. Hoover, Jr., General Burgess, Colonel Randall, and G. Hauge; National Conference of Christians and Jews members. To MATS terminal en route to Kansas City, Kansas, and Salina, Kansas. Arrives at Sunflower Hotel with presidential party and visits Eisenhower home and museum.

11 Abilene, Kansas. Visits Abilene Cemetery with Major J. S. D. and D. D. Eisenhower II. Witnesses parade with family. Addresses ceremonies and inspects museum. Departs for Toledo, Ohio, Cedar Point Club.

12 Toledo, Ohio. No official appointments.

13 Toledo, Ohio. Returns to Washington, D.C.

14 Washington. Attends services at National Presbyterian Church with Mrs. Eisenhower.

15   Washington. Morning appointments with General Cutler (off the record); National Security Council session; A. F. Burns and G. Hauge; Admiral Strauss (off the record); Ambassador Cummings. To Mayflower Hotel to greet American Council to Improve our Neighborhoods luncheon. Afternoon appointments with Senator Duff; bipartisan congressional delegation; Secretary Wilson, R. B. Anderson, A. S. Flemming, and Colonel Goodpaster; friends of Mr. and Mrs. H. E. Stassen.

16   Washington. Breakfast with I. J. Martin and G. D. Morgan. Receives National Fund for Medical Education delegation. To Statler Hotel to address meeting of Association of Land-Grant Colleges and Universities. Appointments with K. C. Royall; David Calhoun and James W. McAfee (off the record); Secretary Dulles; National Historical Publications Commission. Receives turkey from Poultry and Egg National Board and National Turkey Federation. Lunch with Ambassador A. D. P. Heeney (Canada), Trade and Commerce Minister Clarence D. Howe (Canada), Defense Minister R. O. Campney (Canada), S. Adams, and Secretaries Humphrey and Wilson. Afternoon appointment with Cardinal Spellman. Hosts dinner for half Diplomatic Corps Mission Chiefs.

17   Washington. Morning appointments with General Cutler (off the record); Ambassador Leo Mates (Yugoslavia), General Svetozar Vukmanovic (Vice-President, Federal Executive Council, Yugoslavia), and V. Purse; bipartisan congressional delegation. Presents Golf President's Cup to 1954 Cup Regatta winner. Presents Harmon International Trophies. Lunch with Dr. M. S. Eisenhower, N. A. Rockefeller, A. A. Kimball, Budget Director Hughes, S. Adams, and G. Hauge. Afternoon appointments with General Bradley; J. Jackson (off the record). Hosts dinner for half Diplomatic Corps Mission Chiefs.

18   Washington. Morning appointments with S. Radhakrishnan, Ambassador Mehta, and H. A. Byroade; Congressman Bonin; Secretary Hobby, N. A. Rockefeller, Generals Snyder and Persons, S. Adams, B. M. Shanley, and G. D. Morgan; J. Campbell; Secretary Humphrey, Budget Director Hughes, and P. F. Brundage; Secretary Dulles; Pierre Mendès-France (Presi-

dent, Council of Ministers, France) and Secretary Dulles; French-American talks. Hosts stag luncheon in honor of P. Mendés-France. Afternoon appointments with General Adler and B. N. Harlow; J. Jackson and Colonel Schulz (off the record); General Clay (off the record).

19 Washington. Breakfast with Vice-President Nixon, S. Adams, and General Persons. Receives United States Junior Chamber of Commerce executive committee and Directors of Canadian and United States Chambers of Commerce. Morning appointments with Charles Gombault and S. Adams; A. S. Flemming and S. Benedict. Cabinet meeting, followed by appointments with Secretary Hobby (off the record); Secretary Mitchell. To Burning Tree Country Club for golf with Colonel Belshe, J. Brooks, and J. W. Harron.

20 Washington. Morning appointments with General Clarke (off the record); W. P. Rogers, S. E. Sobeloff, and M. M. Rabb to discuss segregation; Dr. E. R. Long (Christmas Seals); T. C. Streibert and S. Adams; Dr. Elson; Senator H. A. Smith and B. M. Shanley; Senator-elect Allott; P. Young, Pierce J. Gerety (Civil Service Commission), B. M. Shanley, and J. C. Hagerty; relocation test; S. E. Sobeloff and M. M. Rabb (off the record).

21 Washington. Attends services at National Presbyterian Church with Mrs. Eisenhower.

22 Washington. H. E. Stassen, M. Wolf, and C. A. Herter; A. F. Burns; Secretary Wilson and F. A. Seaton; Secretary Wilson, F. A. Seaton, A. S. Flemming, General Cutler, and B. N. Harlow; Chancellor Julius Rabb (Austria), Ambassador Karl Gruber (Austria), Josef Schoener (Director, Political Department, Austrian Foreign Office), Ambassador Thompson, L. T. Merchant, and Hans Imhof (interpreter). Hosts stag luncheon for Chancellor Rabb. Afternoon appointments with A. W. Dulles; General Georges Catroux (French Army) and J. F. Simmons; U. E. Baughman, J. Rowley, and Murray Snyder (off the record). Hosts stag dinner.

23 Washington. Breakfast with L. W. Hall, S. Adams,

and General Persons. Morning appointments with General Cutler; Admiral Radford; J. C. Hagerty. News conference, followed by appointments with James Linen (Publisher, *Time* Magazine); Budget Director Hughes and P. F. Brundage.

24   Washington. Breakfast with J. M. Dodge. Morning appointments with Secretaries Dulles, Wilson, and Talbott, A. W. Dulles, Generals Twining, Cabell, and Putt, and Colonel Goodpaster (off the record); National Security Council session; Senator Knowland; W. P. McCoy and S. Adams. Hosts stag luncheon in honor of Scandinavian prime ministers. To MATS terminal for christening of *Columbine III* by Mrs. Eisenhower. Airborne for Augusta, Georgia. Motors to Augusta National Golf Club.

25   Augusta, Georgia. To office, followed by afternoon golf with C. Roberts, E. D. Slater, and E. Dudley. Photo session with Mrs. Eisenhower.

26   Augusta, Georgia. To office, followed by afternoon golf with R. Reed, D. Casey, and C. T. Wood.

27   Augusta, Georgia. To office, followed by golf with E. Dudley, W. E. Robinson, and R. W. Woodruff.

28   Augusta, Georgia. Attends services at Reid Memorial Presbyterian Church with Mrs. Eisenhower. Afternoon golf with J. C. Hagerty, W. E. Robinson, and E. Dudley.

29   Augusta, Georgia. To office, followed by golf with W. E. Robinson and E. Dudley. To Bush Field en route to Washington, D.C.

30   Washington. Morning appointments with General Cutler; T. C. Streibert and A. H. Berding; High Commissioner Conant and Colonel Goodpaster; G. Hauge; Budget Director Hughes, P. F. Brundage, and S. Adams; Mrs. O. B. Lord; A. S. Flemming. Lunch with Secretary Dulles. Afternoon appointments with William W. Spear (Republican State Committee, Nebraska); F. A. Seaton, S. Adams, G. D. Morgan, and Colonel Goodpaster (off the record).

December 1   Washington. Breakfast with Congressman Reed and G. D. Morgan. Morning appointments with Secretary Wilson, and Admirals Radford and Strauss; National Security Council session; Secretary Humphrey and P. G. Hoffman. Hosts Cabinet dinner with Mrs. Eisenhower.

2 Washington. Morning appointments with Attorney General Brownell; General Cutler (off the record). Greets Washington Conference of Mayors opening session. Appointments with Defense Mobilization Board; Ambassador Bohlen; Webster Todd (former head, OEA, Paris) and B. M. Shanley; General George Kenny (off the record). Receives White House Conference on Education members. Afternoon appointment with J. C. Hagerty. News conference, followed by appointments with Columbia University Alumni Association of D.C., Maryland, and Virginia; J. M. Dodge. Hosts Military and Departmental Reception at White House with Mrs. Eisenhower.

3 Washington. Morning appointments with General Cutler; National Security Council session; Cabinet meeting. Hosts stag luncheon regarding need for greater milk consumption. Afternoon appointments with Stanley Rumbough (off the record); Thomas Murray (AEC) (off the record); Governor Kennon, General Clay, S. Adams, and I. J. Martin.

4 Washington. Morning appointments with Senator Abel and E. D. Chesney; L. E. Berkey (Charles Tompkins Construction Co.); Senator Watkins and G. D. Morgan. Off-the-record appointments with S. Adams and General Cutler; General Cutler; Samuel Lubell and S. Adams; B. M. Shanley; General Snyder.

5 Washington. No official appointments.

6 Washington. Off-the-record breakfast with Senator Knowland, Congressman Martin, S. Adams, General Persons, G. D. Morgan, and I. J. Martin. Morning appointments with J. P. Grace; A. F. Burns and G. Hauge; Admiral Radford, Secretary Wilson, R. B. Anderson, C. L. Burgess, General Persons, Colonels Stevens, Randall, and Goodpaster, and Commander Beach; Secretary Wilson; Prime Minister John Kotelawala (Ceylon), Ambassador Gunewardene, Gunasena de Soyza (Minister of External Affairs, Ceylon), Ambassador Crowe, and J. D. Jernegan.

Hosts stag luncheon in honor of Prime Minister Kotelawala. Off-the-record appointment with A. Vandenberg, Jr. Hosts stag dinner.

7   Washington. Morning appointments with Pocket Testament League leaders; St. Louis University representatives; Minister Anton Moisescu (Rumania), Mr. Dumitrachescu (interpreter), and J. F. Simmons; Morris Snyder (off the record); Senator Cordon.

8   Washington. Morning appointments with General Cutler; National Automobile Dealers Association officers; J. C. Hagerty. News conference, followed by appointments with Budget Director Hughes, P. F. Brundage, and G. Hauge; L. V. Finder (off the record). Afternoon appointments with Secretaries Dulles and Wilson, Admiral Radford, R. B. Anderson, and L. T. Merchant (off the record); Secretaries Dulles, Wilson, and Humphrey, Budget Director Hughes, A. F. Burns, General Cutler, and S. Adams (off the record). Hosts Supreme Court dinner with Mrs. Eisenhower.

9   Washington. Breakfast with Colonel Randall, S. Adams, and G. Hauge. Morning appointments with General Prentiss and Colonel Lane; Secretary Hobby, N. A. Rockefeller, Budget Director Hughes, R. B. Perkins, C. I. Schottland, S. Adams, and General Persons; American Legion leaders; Governor Hoegh and B. M. Shanley. National Security Council session. Makes Safe Driving recording. Lunch with A. Nielsen. Afternoon appointment with Ambassador Willis and G. Hauge; Ambassador George V. Melas (Greece) and J. F. Simmons; R. Roberts (off the record); I. Geist (off the record). Hosts Judicial Reception with Mrs. Eisenhower.

10 Washington. Off-the-record breakfast with C. D. Jackson. Cabinet meeting. Makes recording for Overseas Press Club Memorial dedication. To Camp David.

11 Camp David, Maryland. To Gettysburg to inspect farm. Returns to Washington, D.C. Attends Gridiron Dinner at Statler Hotel.

12 Washington. Attends services at National Presbyterian Church with Mrs. Eisenhower.

13 Washington. Off-the-record breakfast with H. Hoover, Jr., and Kermit Roosevelt. Legislative Leaders. Iranian-American talks. Hosts luncheon for Shah Muhammed Reza Pahlevi and Empress Soraya (Iran). Legislative Leaders. Hosts stag dinner.

14 Washington. Bipartisan leadership meeting. Appointments with Senator Daniel and H. H. Gruenther; P. Young. Lunch with Secretary Dulles. Presents Young American Medals for Bravery and Service. Witnesses swearing-in of Special Assistant to the President J. M. Dodge and Comptroller General Campbell.

15 Washington. Off-the-record breakfast with L. W. Hall, S. Adams, and T. E. Stephens. Morning appointments with A. S. Flemming; Mrs. Raymond Clapper (CARE); G. L. Brown and Daniel Hornbeck; J. C. Hagerty. News conference, followed by appointments with Senator-elect Bender; Admiral Strauss (off the record); Secretary Hobby (off the record); Congressman Graham and G. D. Morgan. Receives AMVET seals from Pamela Brown.

16 Washington. Morning appointments with C. Davis and Harland Bartholomew (Chairman, National Capital Planning Commission); Budget Director Hughes, P. F. Brundage, and Admiral Strauss; A. F. Burns and G. Hauge; Alfalfa Club officers; Secretary Talbott; P. G. Hoffman; Columbia Interstate Compact Commission executive committee. Afternoon appointments with Attorney General Brownell (off the record); Secretary Mitchell and A. F. Burns.

17 Washington. Cabinet meeting, followed by appointments with Senator Goldwater and G. D. Morgan; Reverend Canon J. Malinkowski and Polish-American group. Presents Collier Trophy. Afternoon appointment with General Cutler and J. S. Lay. Signs World Good Will Book with Mrs. Eisenhower. Opens "Christmas Pageant of Peace."

18 Washington. Morning appointments with Secretary Mitchell and S. Adams; Congressman Rogers and G. D. Morgan.

19 Washington. Attends services at National Presbyterian Church with Mrs. Eisenhower.

20 Washington. Morning appointments with Ambassador Aldrich; Elks leaders and Murray Snyder; Foreign Affairs Minister George K. C. Yeh (China), Ambassador Koo, W. S. Robertson, and Colonel Goodpaster; A. F. Burns and G. Hauge; Secretary Wilson; R. McLean. Lunch with J. K. Javits (off the record). Afternoon appointments with P. Young and W. B. Irons (off the record); M. Katz; Dr. W. F. Russell; Ambassador Lodge and J. Wadsworth (Deputy U.S. Representative to U.N.) (off the record). Hosts stag dinner.

21 Washington. Morning appointment with B. N. Harlow. Signs letter supporting 1955 Red Cross Drive. National Security Council session, followed by off-the-record appointments with H. E. Stassen; J. M. Dodge. To Fiery Run Ranch near Marshall, Virginia. Proceeds to Front Royal Beef-Cattle Research Station. Returns to Washington, D.C.

22 Washington. Morning appointments with General Clark (off the record); National Manpower Council; Attorney General Brownell, Admiral Strauss, A. S. Flemming, Generals Cutler and Loper, J. R. Killian, and R. C. Sprague (off the record); Ambassador Bonnet and J. F. Simmons; H. C. Butcher (off the record); Secretary Wilson, Admirals Radford and Carney, and Generals Ridgway, Twining, and Shepherd; Senator Cooper (off the record). Witnesses swearing-in of Special Assistant to the President N. A. Rockefeller. Afternoon appointments with G. Hauge (off the record); Secretary Dulles; Harry Machette (White House clerk, retiring) and A. C. Tolley.

23 Washington. Greets White House staff at annual Christmas reception with Mrs. Eisenhower. To MATS terminal en route to Augusta, Georgia. Motors to Augusta National Golf Club for golf with E. Dudley and W. E. Robinson.

24 Augusta, Georgia. To Augusta National Golf Club for golf with E. Dudley, W. E. Robinson, and E. P. Peabody.

25 Augusta, Georgia. To Augusta National Golf Club for golf with F. Waring, W. E. Robinson, and C. Roberts.

26   Augusta, Georgia. Attends services at Reid Memorial Presbyterian Church with Mrs. Eisenhower. Afternoon golf with E. Dudley, J. Franklin, and C. Roberts.

27   Augusta, Georgia. Morning appointments with A. F. Burns and G. Hauge. Quail shooting with C. Roberts, J. Franklin, J. Roberts, and J. Bailey. Afternoon practice and golf with J. O. Childs, R. Quinn, and E. Dudley.

28   Augusta, Georgia. To office, followed by golf with J. Roberts, C. Yates, E. Dudley, and G. E. Allen. Afternoon quail shooting with J. Roberts, G. E. Allen, J. Franklin, and J. Bailey.

29   Augusta, Georgia. To office, followed by golf with H. Hurst, C. Chisholm, and E. Dudley. Late afternoon appointment with E. D. Slater.

30   Augusta, Georgia. To office, followed by golf with C. Roberts, D. Carlington, and G. Stout. Late afternoon practice with E. Dudley.

31   Augusta, Georgia. To office, followed by golf with E. Dudley. Afternoon golf with F. F. Gosden, C. Roberts, and E. Dudley.

1955

January   1   Augusta, Georgia. Visits C. Roberts.

2   Washington. Attends services at Reid Memorial Presbyterian Church with Mrs. Eisenhower. Golf with S. S. Larmon, F. Willard, and E. Dudley. To Bush Airfield with Mrs. Eisenhower, and E. Doud en route to Washington, D.C.

3   Washington. Morning appointments with Congressman Reed; H. Pyle, W. E. Robinson, and S. Adams (off the record); Secretary Hobby and B. N. Harlow; A. F. Burns and G. Hauge; Secretary Mitchell, B. N. Harlow, and G. D. Morgan; Secretary Wilson. Luncheon with Cabinet members and others. Cabinet-Congressional leadership meeting.

4   Washington. Morning appointments with T. C. Streibert, A. M. Washburn, and Leland S. Briggs (Chief, Press Section, USIA); Dr. Elson and Presby-

terian leaders; National Cartoonist Society members; E. D. Chesney and Jewish War Veterans' leaders; Ambassador Alberto Tarchiani (Italy) and J. F. Simmons. Off-the-record appointments with A. S. Flemming; General Humfrey Gale; L. W. Hall; General Cutler, J. C. Hagerty, and Colonel Goodpaster; H. Pyle and S. Adams; General Cutler. Appointment with Secretary Weeks and R. B. Murray.

5   Washington. Attends services at National Presbyterian Church. Appointments with Senator Knowland; National Security Council session; J. H. Burke, Bob Leeds, and Robert Brockhurst (RNC photographer); Claude O. Vardaman (RNC, Alabama); B. N. Harlow and S. Adams.

6   Washington. Morning appointment with H. E. Stassen (off the record). Delivers State of the Union Address before Joint Session of Congress. Returns to White House. To Burning Tree Country Club for lunch and golf with Colonel Belshe. Hosts stag dinner.

7   Washington. Morning appointments with Charles E. Saltzman (Under Secretary of State); Ambassador Luce; Senator George. Cabinet meeting. Receives Mary Kosloski, 1955 March of Dimes poster girl. Lunch with Secretary Humphrey. To Camp David, Maryland, with Mrs. Eisenhower and Mrs. J. S. D. Eisenhower.

8   Camp David, Maryland. To Eisenhower farm in Gettysburg, Pennsylvania. Returns to Camp David.

9   Camp David, Maryland. Returns to Washington, D.C., with Mrs. Eisenhower.

10 Washington. Breakfast with Dr. M. S. Eisenhower. Appointments with A. F. Burns and G. Hauge; Senator Flanders; Secretary Dulles; L. Wright and B. M. Shanley. Off-the-record appointment with Joseph Finnegan and S. Adams. Lunch with Senator Duff, followed by appointments with Congressman Horan and Dr. Frank Warren (Whitworth College) (off the record); A. S. Flemming and S. Benedict; R. B. Anderson and Secretary Talbott; Postmaster General Summerfield and I. J. Martin. Receives Secretary Benson and Citrus Merchandising Committee, who

present crystal bowl filled with fruit. Hosts stag dinner.

11 Washington. Appointments with Legislative Leaders; Advisory Committee, National Highway Program; Eisenhower Exchange Fellowships, Inc., fellows and trustees; Harold W. Dodds (President, Princeton University) and S. Adams. Presents Big Brother of the Year Award to C. S. Mott. Afternoon off-the-record appointment with Daniel Parker (Parker Pen Co.) and Bruce Jeffrin. Lunch with Admiral Radford, followed by appointments with Admiral Radford and General Cutler (off the record); L. W. Hall.

12 Washington. Breakfast with Vice-President Nixon. Appointments with D. K. E. Bruce; Senator Thurmond, Major MacArthur Manchester (Reserve Officers Association), and Colonel Goodpaster; J. C. Hagerty. News conference, followed by appointment with M. M. Rabb. To Burning Tree Country Club for golf with Colonel Belshe, L. J. Bernard, and H. C. Stuart. Evening off-the-record appointment with General Cutler and J. S. Lay.

13 Washington. Morning appointments with C. H. Tompkins (off the record); Postmaster General Summerfield; B. S. Adkins and T. E. Stephens. National Security Council session. To Statler Hotel for Association of American Colleges luncheon. Afternoon appointments with Secretary Humphrey and B. F. Fairless (off the record); Dr. I. Lynd Esch (President, Indiana Central College).

14 Washington. Cabinet meeting, followed by appointments with Postmaster General Summerfield; Gardner Cowles (Editor, *Look* Magazine); Duke of Windsor, Ambassador Makins, and J. F. Simmons; Admiral Strauss; W. Harold Brenton (Treasurer, RNC); J. M. Dodge; Mr. and Mrs. B. S. Carter (off the record). Hosts reception with Mrs. Eisenhower for congressional members and their spouses.

15 Washington. Appointments with Secretary Talbott (off the record); J. C. Hagerty; General Cutler; S. Adams; B. M. Shanley; W. J. Hopkins; Colonel Goodpaster; G. Hauge; A. C. Whitman; Mrs. Gerde Kraft and son (off the record); B. M. Shanley.

16   Washington. Attends services at National Presbyterian Church with Mrs. Eisenhower.

17   Washington. Appointments with Attorney General Brownell; A. F. Burns and G. Hauge; E. Johnston; H. Brinkley. Afternoon off-the-record appointments with A. S. Flemming and R. B. Anderson; Secretary Dulles.

18   Washington. Appointments with Legislative Leaders; Disabled American Veterans representatives. Receives Committee for Adequate Overseas Information Program; American Farm Bureau Federation leaders. Greets first 1955 Sub-cabinet meeting. Afternoon appointments with Admiral Radford (off the record); General Cutler. Hosts dinner in honor of Vice-President and Mrs. Nixon.

19   Washington. Breakfast with Senator Knowland. Appointments with Ambassador Dillon; Congresswoman Bolton; J. C. Hagerty. News conference. Receives Committee for Exhibition of 19th Century French Paintings from American Collections, followed by off-the-record appointment with Bishop Ray Witter and family. Off-the-record lunch with Secretary Dulles and Admiral Radford. Hosts dinner with Mrs. Eisenhower in honor of Congressman Martin.

20   Washington. Off-the-record breakfast with S. Adams, L. W. Hall, T. E. Stephens, and General Persons. National Security Council session, followed by off-the-record appointment with F. Cowles and Bertha S. Vester. Off-the-record lunch with General Curtis. Afternoon appointment with A. S. Flemming, S. Adams, and M. M. Rabb.

21   Washington. Breakfast with Governor Craig and T. E. Stephens. National Security Council session. Cabinet meeting followed by appointments with Prime Minister Sidney G. Holland (New Zealand), Ambassador Leslie Knox Monro (New Zealand), L. T. Merchant, and J. F. Simmons; Senator Allott; Secretaries Dulles and Wilson, R. B. Anderson, R. R. Bowie, Admirals Radford and Carney, and Generals Twining and Bolte. Hosts reception with Mrs. Eisenhower in honor of diplomatic corps members.

22   Washington. Breakfast with Congressman Martin; Congressman Kean and Foreign Trade Education Committee; Congressman Wilson; Mrs. E. Meyer, Senator Ives, S. Adams, G. D. Morgan, and Congressman Kearns; L. E. Berkey (off the record); Secretary Dulles, R. R. Bowie, General Cutler, and J. C. Hagerty (joined by Senator Knowland); General Lionel J. Cross. To Statler Hotel for Alfalfa Club dinner.

23   Washington. Attends services at National Presbyterian Church with Mrs. Eisenhower.

24   Washington. Appointments with Howard L. Roach (Chairman, Republican Farm Council), Rod Kreger, and T. E. Stephens; Rubber Producing Facilities Disposal Commission; A. F. Burns and G. Hauge; Secretaries Wilson and Stevens, and Charles C. Finucane (Under Secretary of Army); General Walter Krueger. Off-the-record lunch with S. W. Richardson and John Connally, followed by appointments with N. Burnham and Ralph Follis (Standard Oil) and son (off the record); H. Hoover, Jr., W. S. Robertson, and Generals Collins and Cutler. Hosts stag dinner.

25   Washington. Appointments with Legislative Leaders; Secretary Humphrey; Joseph Ely (former Governor, Massachusetts) and S. Adams; P. Young. To National History Museum, Smithsonian Institute, to receive statue from Ambassador Krekeler. Lunch with Governor Shivers, W. A. Blakley, and S. Adams. Afternoon appointments with Congressman Westlant and Charles Hunter; Ambassador Dunn; General Cutler.

26   Washington. To Sulgrave Club for RNC Women's Division breakfast. Receives National Association of Postmasters, executive committee. Appointments with Ambassador Johan Albert Nykoff (Finland); Ambassador Rafael Heliodoro Valle (Honduras) and V. Purse; Charles A. Thomas; J. M. Dodge (off the record); N. A. Rockefeller (off the record); W. W. Flenniken and T. E. Stephens (off the record); Secretary Dulles and N. A. Rockefeller. Hosts dinner with Mrs. Eisenhower in honor of President and Mrs. Paul E. Magloire (Haiti).

27   Washington. Receives congressional delegation. Appointments with H. A. Rusk; National Security Council session; Secretaries Dulles, Wilson, Stevens, Thomas, and Talbott, Admirals Radford and Carney, Generals Ridgway, Twining, Shepherd, and Cutler, and D. MacArthur II (off the record); Admiral Radford; Secretary Weeks, R. B. Murray, A. Page, S. Adams, and M. M. Rabb (off the record); General Persons; G. Hauge; J. C. Hagerty; General Cutler and Colonel Goodpaster; T. E. Stephens.

28   Washington. Cabinet meeting, followed by morning appointments with Secretary Dulles; Governor Lausche and J. C. Hagerty; R. B. Anderson and Edward J. Noble (Advisory Board, St. Lawrence Seaway); Ambassador Bonbright. Makes recording for United Defense Fund dinner. Appointments with Minister of Legation Henry de Torrente (Switzerland) and V. Purse; Congressman Thompson and Texas businessmen; Admiral Radford. To Sheraton-Park Hotel with Mrs. Eisenhower for dinner in their honor given by President and Mrs. Magloire.

29   Washington. Breakfast with Governors Langlie and Patterson, and S. Adams. Signs H. J. 159. To MATS terminal en route to Augusta, Georgia, with General Snyder, J. C. Hagerty, and C. Roberts. To Augusta National Golf Club for practice with G. Stout and golf with C. Roberts, D. R. Calhoun, and C. A. Thomas. More practice with G. Stout.

30   Augusta, Georgia. To Augusta National Golf Club for practice with G. Stout and golf with W. McAfee, J. Wilson, and W. E. Robinson. To Bush Field, airborne for Washington, D.C., with General Snyder, C. Roberts, and J. C. Hagerty. Returns to White House for off-the-record appointment with H. Hoover, Jr., L. T. Merchant, W. S. Robertson, Ambassador Lodge, D. MacArthur II, Admiral Radford, and Colonel Goodpaster.

31   Washington. Appointments with A. S. Flemming; Secretary Hobby, Budget Director Hughes, S. M. Brownell, R. B. Perkins, and S. Adams; Ambassador Maurice Couve de Murville (France) and V. Purse; Ambassador Cruz-Salazar and V. Purse. Lunch with

L. E. Berkey followed by appointments with General Cutler and G. D. Morgan. Hosts stag dinner.

February 1   Washington. Breakfast with Senator Knowland. Appointment with Legislative Leaders; The Flying Wheels; General Twining; Nettie Moulden, Edna Gaither and son, and Stanley O'Donnell; N. H. Jacoby; Ambassador de Murville, Georges Remy-Neris, General Vincent Saubestre, and V. Purse; Admiral Radford; K. McCann and J. A. Krout. Lunch with General Bradley. Witnesses swearing-in of Administrative Assistant to the President H. Pyle. Afternoon appointments with General Cutler; Budget Director Hughes and S. Adams. Receives Supreme Court members.

2   Washington. Breakfast with Vice-President Nixon, followed by appointments with E. D. Chesney and AMVETS representatives; J. C. Hagerty. News conference. Appointments with H. E. Stassen, H. Struve Hensel (General Counsel, Defense Department), Dr. Raymond Moyer (Regional Director, Far East, FOA), and Colonel Goodpaster; Secretary Hobby (off the record). Receives newly elected national officials of Future Farmers of America. Afternoon appointments with General Collins; Admiral Strauss (off the record). To Congressional Club with Mrs. Eisenhower for reception in their honor.

3   Washington. Breakfast with N. A. Rockefeller. Receives Ann Turner (essay contest winner, National Association of Real Estate Boards). Appointments with Congressmen Hiestand, Teague, and Younger. National Security Council session, followed by off-the-record appointments with A. W. Dulles; H. E. Stassen; Secretaries Talbott and Wilson; Joseph Thorsen. Afternoon appointments with Colonel Walter Bowman and E. D. Chesney; Ambassador Manlio Brosio (Italy) and V. Purse. Hosts stag dinner.

4   Washington. Cabinet meeting, followed by appointments with Lady Astor and S. Adams; Ambassador Hendrickson.

5   Washington. Breakfast with Ambassador Lodge. Off-the-record appointments with Furman J. Finck (artist); Nelson L. Smith (Member, Federal Power Com-

mission); H. E. Stassen. Receives winner of Congressman Wainwright's essay contest. Appointments with General Hurley; Secretary Weeks, R. B. Murray, C. Gurney, E. T. Nunneley, and S. Adams (joined by Senator Thye and Congressman Judd) (off the record); H. Hoover, Jr., Admiral Radford, Colonel Goodpaster, and General Cutler. To Statler Hotel for Washington Radio and Television Correspondents Association dinner.

6   Washington. Attends services at National Presbyterian Church with Mrs. Eisenhower.

7   Washington. Appointments with Secretary Dulles; A. F. Burns and G. Hauge; Ambassador Alonzo and V. Purse. Witnesses swearing-in of Director of the Federal Mediation and Conciliation Service Joseph F. Finnegan. Afternoon appointments with Ambassador Byroade; Senator Kuchel; K. McCann and Murray Snyder (off the record); Admiral Strauss (off the record); Budget Director Hughes and General Persons. Hosts stag dinner.

8   Washington. Appointments with Legislative Leaders; R. L. Biggers; Senators Carlson, Duff, and Case; Walter H. Annenberg (Publisher, *Philadelphia Enquirer*) and J. C. Hagerty. Receives boy scouts and leaders from twelve U.S. regions; Heart of Ohio Aberdeen Angus Breeders' Association. Lunch with Henry Ford II. Afternoon appointments with General Cutler; Attorney General Brownell and A. S. Flemming (off the record); G. L. Murphy (off the record). Makes closed-circuit broadcast for Crusade for Freedom.

9   Washington. To Sulgrave Club for RNC Women's Division breakfast. Appointments with Ambassador Heath; Admiral Radford; J. C. Hagerty. News conference, followed by appointments with Senator Daniel, Everett Hutchinson, and Mr. and Mrs. Gene Kirkly; Congressman Tollefson and Frank Meecham. To Burning Tree Country Club for lunch with Congressmen Arends and Westland, Colonel Belshe, J. Brooks, and Dr. Burt Hagen. Golf with Congressmen Arends and Westland, and Colonel Belshe. Off-the-record appointment with Secretary Dulles. Par-

ticipates by closed circuit in program for American Medical Association.

10 Washington. Breakfast with Secretary Benson and T. D. Morse. Appointments with H. E. Stassen; National Security Council session. To MATS terminal with Mrs. Eisenhower, E. Doud, C. Roberts, and Secretary and Mrs. Humphrey. Airborne for Spence Airfield, Moultrie, Georgia. To Milestone Plantation for quail hunting with Secretary Humphrey and C. Roberts.

11 Thomasville, Georgia. Quail hunting with Secretary Humphrey and C. Roberts.

12 Thomasville, Georgia. Autographs picture of Georgia state police.

13 Thomasville, Georgia. Visits with Mr. and Mrs. R. B. Perkins. To home of Mr. and Mrs. J. H. Whitney in Greenwood. Returns to Washington, D.C.

14 Washington. Morning appointments with L. W. Hall, Attorney General Brownell, Postmaster General Summerfield, R. Humphreys, and Chauncey Robbins (RNC); Admiral Radford; G. Hauge; Secretary Wilson and General Burgess; A. S. Flemming, S. Adams, and S. Benedict. Lunch with Secretary Dulles.

15 Washington. Off-the-record appointment with S. C. Waugh, S. Adams, General Persons, and Senators George, Ellender, Long, Ervin, and Thurmond. Receives foreign delegates from New York *Herald Tribune*'s high school forum. Appointments with Senator Marshall and American Society of Mechanical Engineers representatives; Public Works Projects presentation. Receives American Society of Composers, Authors, and Publishers. Makes film for American Legion program, *Back to God* (off the record); American National Red Cross.

16 Washington. Breakfast with Senator Knowland. Appointments with Legislative Leaders; Budget Director Hughes and S. Adams (off the record); Budget Director Hughes, N. A. Rockefeller, and J. M. Dodge. Off-the-record appointments with General Clark; General Cutler; General Persons, Judge

Whitaker, and Congressman Chatham. Hosts luncheon in honor of T. E. Stephens.

17 Washington. Breakfast with General Clay. Receives Kiwanis International Board of Trustees. Appointments with G. Gray; National Security Council session. To Statler Hotel for RNC. Off-the-record appointments with Carl Corsa (Agriculture Department, Trade Agreements), G. D. Morgan, and H. R. McPhee; Secretary Dulles and H. Hoover, Jr.

18 Washington. Breakfast with Ambassador Conant. Cabinet meeting, followed by appointments with Cape Girardeau, Missouri, leaders; Senator Thye and Mr. and Mrs. Matt Mattson. Presents gold medal to Irving Berlin. Accepts Gold Heart Award from American Heart Association. To Burning Tree Country Club for lunch and golf with Colonel Belshe.

19 Washington. Off-the-record breakfast with E. J. Hughes. Appointments with L. E. Berkey (off the record); A. F. Burns and G. Hauge; Ambassador Concheso; Admiral Radford, General Twining, and Colonel Goodpaster; W. R. Hearst, Jr., Kingsbury Smith, Frank Conniff, and Murray Snyder; H. Darby (off the record).

20 Washington. Attends services at National Presbyterian Church with Mrs. Eisenhower. Speaks at Inter-American Investment Conference.

21 Washington. Witnesses swearing-in of F. A. Seaton as Administrative Assistant to the President. Signs Armed Forces Day Proclamation with Secretary Wilson. Appointments with Secretary Wilson; Ambassador Don Joaquin Eduardo Salazar and J. F. Simmons. Makes film for Inter-American Investment Conference. Lunch with General Smith. Afternoon appointments with Budget Director Hughes, S. Adams, J. C. Hagerty, I. J. Martin, and General Clay; Senators Case, Chaves, Gore, George, and Martin, Congressmen Buckley, Dondero, and Fallen, General Clay, Budget Director Hughes, S. Adams, J. C. Hagerty, and I. J. Martin; H. Hoover, Jr., R. Murphy, Admirals Radford and Duncan, and Colonel Goodpaster.

22 Washington. Appointments with Postmaster General

Summerfield; Legislative Leaders; General Michaelis.

23 Washington. Appointment with Brotherhood Week Campaign representatives, J. C. Hagerty, and M. M. Rabb. Receives 8th annual Voice of Democracy contest winner. Appointment with J. C. Hagerty. News conference, followed by appointment with General Cutler. To Burning Tree Country Club for lunch and golf with S. O'Neil, J. Brooks, and Colonel Belshe.

24 Washington. To Statler Hotel for U.S. Masonic leaders' breakfast in his honor. Appointments with G. Meany, Secretary Mitchell, and G. D. Morgan; J. A. Hannah and Colonel Goodpaster; Judge Boyd S. Leedom (Supreme Court, South Dakota), S. Adams, Bert Tollefson (Secretary, Congressman Berry), Senators Mundt and Case, and Congressman Lovre; National Security Council session; Secretary Wilson, Admiral Radford, and Colonel Goodpaster; General Taylor and Colonel Goodpaster; R. Howard and J. C. Hagerty; Secretary Hobby; Robert Hess (White House photographer); Rotary Club leaders. Hosts stag dinner.

25 Washington. Breakfast with Dr. M. S. Eisenhower, N. A. Rockefeller, A. S. Flemming, Budget Director Hughes, and S. Adams. Receives Grand Councilors, Order of DeMolay. Appointments with W. M. Martin, Charles N. Shepardson (Federal Reserve System), and G. Hauge (off the record); G. Hauge, I. J. Martin, Senators George, Russell, and Byrd, Congressman Abbitt, H. L. Wingate, Stephen Pace, Thomas D. Odom, and J. M. English to discuss peanut imports; doctor. To Eisenhower farm in Gettysburg, Pennsylvania, with Colonel Belshe. Inspects farm and grounds. To Camp David, Maryland, with Mrs. Eisenhower and C. H. Tompkins.

26 Camp David, Maryland. Visits with General and Mrs. Nevins.

27 Camp David, Maryland. Returns to Washington, D.C., with Mrs. Eisenhower and E. Doud.

28 Washington. Off-the-record appointments with Secretary Humphrey, S. Adams, I. J. Martin, and General Persons; Admiral Strauss and General Cutler.

Receives 14th annual science talent search winners; White House photographers' annual awards winners. Appointments with Admiral Radford; A. F. Burns and G. Hauge; T. C. Streibert, A. M. Washburn, and J. R. Poppele (Voice of America); S. Adams, I. J. Martin, and Senator Duff; A. S. Flemming, General Cutler, and Colonel Goodpaster; H. Hoover, Jr. Hosts stag dinner.

March   1   Washington. Appointments with Legislative Leaders; M. M. Rabb. Receives American Legion National Rehabilitation Commission; National Federation of Republican Women, Board of Directors. Appointments with Dr. M. S. Eisenhower; Congressman Broyhill, Mayor Beverley, Robert F. Downhan (Friendship Fire Engine Co.), and Jack Layman (reporter, *Alexandria Gazette*). Hosts stag luncheon for new senators, followed by appointments with A. F. Burns, General Bragdon, and S. Adams; S. Adams, I. J. Martin, H. Pyle, Governors Kennon, Kohler, Boggs, and Hoegh, and General Clay; William S. Campbell (RNC, Idaho) and S. Adams.

   2   Washington. Appointments with General Cutler and J. S. Lay (off the record); Jefferson Caffery (former Ambassador) and Murray Snyder; J. C. Hagerty. News conference, followed by appointments with B. M. Shanley, B. N. Harlow, I. J. Martin, and Senator H. A. Smith (off the record); Attorney General Brownell and General Persons; A. F. Burns, S. Adams, and Professor Joseph S. Davis (Stanford University). To Burning Tree Country Club for lunch and golf with W. W. Flenniken, J. E. McClure, and Senator Bush. Attends dinner given by Secretary and Mrs. McKay with Mrs. Eisenhower.

   3   Washington. Breakfast with Senator Knowland. Appointments with S. Adams and Governor Johnson; Secretary Weeks and S. Adams; Gridiron Club leaders; H. Hoover, Jr. (off the record). National Security Council session. Hosts luncheon for congressional members. To Eisenhower farm in Gettysburg, Pennsylvania, with C. H. Tompkins. Inspects house and grounds. Returns to Washington, D.C.

   4   Washington. Appointments with Budget Director Hughes, N. A. Rockefeller, and S. Adams. Cabinet

meeting, followed by off-the-record appointments with H. Hoover, Jr.; Postmaster General Summerfield; General Twining. Receives Baylor University Choir. Afternoon appointments with A. W. Dulles; James C. Petrillo (President, American Federation of Musicians) and G. D. Morgan; H. Pyle and Senator Goldwater; H. R. Reid (off the record). Hosts off-the-record stag dinner.

5   Washington. Appointments with Senator Capehart, Dr. M. S. Eisenhower, and F. A. Seaton; Bishop Thomas H. Wright (Episcopal Bishop, North Carolina), North Carolina congressional delegation, and B. M. Shanley; E. A. Johnston and Colonel Goodpaster. To Statler Hotel for White House Correspondents Association dinner.

6   Washington. Attends services at National Presbyterian Church with Mrs. Eisenhower.

7   Washington. Appointment with General Spaatz. Receives commanders who participated in Remagen Bridge seizure, World War II; National 4-H Club winners. Appointments with clothing and textile labor leaders, Secretary Mitchell, G. D. Morgan, and M. M. Rabb to discuss minimum wage; Secretary Dulles; A. F. Burns and G. Hauge; Secretary Wilson. Receives officers of Supreme Lodge, Order of Ahepa. Hosts luncheon for congressional members. To Walter Reed Hospital for shoulder x-ray. Visits General Horkan. Evening appointment with Attorney General Brownell, W. P. Rogers, and Judges Joseph C. McGarraghy, Benjamin F. Cameron, and Gilbert H. Jertberg.

8   Washington. Appointments with Legislative Leaders; B. M. Shanley, Father Vernon Gallagher (Duquesne University), and Congressman Fulton; B. M. Shanley and leaders of National Council of U.S. Churches of Christ; Billy Jennings (1955 Easter Seal Child) and Mrs. Jennings, Catherine Bauer (Director of Information, National Society for Crippled Children and Adults, Inc.), and J. C. Hagerty. Lunch with B. M. Baruch.

9   Washington. To Sulgrave Club for RNC Women's Division breakfast. Appointments with H. G. Riter, W. S. Neal, and B. M. Shanley; Secretary Dulles; D.

Thornton and B. M. Shanley. To Burning Tree Country Club for lunch and golf with D. Thornton and Colonel Belshe.

10 Washington. Appointments with General Cutler, J. S. Lay, and D. Anderson (off the record); Murray Snyder, Senators Bridges and Cotton, and Rochester, New Hampshire, representatives; N. A. Rockefeller and Admiral Strauss. Receives foreign students attending Argonne School of Nuclear Science and Engineering. National Security Council session, followed by appointment with Secretary Wilson. Departs for Walter Reed Hospital. Afternoon off-the-record appointment with J. J. McCloy. Hosts off-the-record stag dinner.

11 Washington. Appointments with Congressman Westland and B. M. Shanley; Cabinet meeting; Congresswoman Harden and H. H. Gruenther; Postmaster General Summerfield (off the record); Ambassador Bonsal; W. M. Martin; Secretary Dulles; Senator Bowring and F. A. Seaton; A. F. Burns and R. J. Saulnier (off the record); General Cutler, G. Hauge, and Congressman Judd. Hosts luncheon for congressional members. Afternoon appointment with Secretary Dulles, A. W. Dulles, Generals Twining and Cutler, Admirals Radford and Carney, and Colonel Goodpaster.

12 Washington. Off-the-record appointments with Generals Cutler and George, and D. Anderson; General Cutler and D. Anderson; Secretary Humphrey; Colonel Schulz and businessmen from Haskins and Sells, New York; General Persons, B. N. Harlow, and F. A. Seaton; J. M. Dodge. Appointment with Minister El-Kekhia and J. F. Simmons. To Burning Tree Country Club for lunch and golf with Congressmen Halleck and Simpson, and J. Black. Stops at J. Black's apartment en route to White House. Hosts farewell dinner in honor of General Cutler.

13 Washington. Attends services at National Presbyterian Church.

14 Washington. Breakfast with Senator Knowland. Appointments with H. E. Stassen; A. F. Burns and G. Hauge; Secretary Wilson; Prime Minister Robert G. Menzies (Australia), Ambassador Percy Spender

(Australia), Secretary Dulles, L. T. Merchant, and Admiral Carney. Hosts luncheon in honor of Prime Minister Menzies. Afternoon appointments with Secretary Benson; R. B. Anderson and S. Adams. To Walter Reed Hospital.

15 Washington. Appointments with Legislative Leaders; J. S. Kemper; P. S. Buck, B. L. England (President, Atlantic City Electric Co.), and Governor McKeldin; V. Krishna Menon (Indian delegation, U.N.), Ambassador Mehta, and Secretary Dulles; Secretary Dulles and L. T. Merchant (off the record); J. D. Zellerbach and M. M. Rabb; General Sarnoff and J. C. Hagerty. Afternoon off-the-record appointment with N. A. Rockefeller and Mr. Schreiber to discuss trees. Hosts off-the-record stag dinner.

16 Washington. Appointments with General Cutler and J. S. Lay (off the record); Secretary Stevens and Colonel Goodpaster; F. Lazarus and Colonel Goodpaster; Counselor Joseph D. Brennan (Irish embassy), J. F. Simmons, and B. M. Shanley; J. C. Hagerty. News conference, followed by appointments with General Persons (off the record); G. Hauge, S. C. Waugh, and Winthrop G. Brown (Vice-Chairman, GATT) (off the record); T. E. Dewey; Secretary Dulles. To Burning Tree Country Club for lunch and golf with R. D. Pittman, J. E. McClure, and Congressman Herlong.

17 Washington. Appointments with B. M. Shanley, I. J. Martin, Murray Snyder, and Senator Bender; National Security Council session. Special National Security Council session (off the record), followed by appointments with General Bradley and F. A. Seaton; Governor Dwinell and S. Adams; S. Adams, General Persons, F. A. Seaton, and Senator Case. Hosts luncheon for current and retired congressmen. Afternoon appointments with A. S. Flemming, Budget Director Hughes, Generals George I. Back, Sturgis and Paul, Commander Beach, S. Adams, I. J. Martin, and Colonel Goodpaster (off the record); B. M. Shanley, M. Kramer, Jack Manning, and D. Thornton; W. B. Barnes and F. A. Seaton; Colon Alfaro (Panama) and General Persons. To the 1925 F Street Club for Business Advisory Council dinner.

18   Washington. Appointments with B. M. Shanley and Mrs. O. B. Lord; Cabinet meeting. Receives National Voluntary Mortgage Credit Extension Committee; federal, state, and municipal officials to discuss consumer interest in natural gas. To Eisenhower farm in Gettysburg, Pennsylvania, with General Snyder.

19   Gettysburg, Pennsylvania. Departs for Washington, D.C. To Statler Hotel for White House photographers' dinner.

20   Washington. Attends services at National Presbyterian Church with Mrs. Eisenhower.

21   Washington. Appointments with Admiral Strauss and Colonel Goodpaster; Admiral Radford; A. F. Burns; Secretary Wilson, R. B. Anderson, H. Hoover, Jr., and D. B. Duncan. Off-the-record lunch with B. F. Fairless. Afternoon appointments with R. D. Stuart; W. W. Stewart; Bureau of the Budget presentation on survivorship benefits.

22   Washington. Off-the-record breakfast with N. A. Rockefeller. Appointments with Legislative Leaders; Lee Garlington and Colonel Schulz (off the record); Secretary Dulles; Ambassador and Mrs. Cooper and G. V. Allen; Congresswoman Bolton; S. Adams and William Oates and family (off the record). Greets annual meeting of Advertising Council, Inc. Afternoon appointments with H. E. Stassen; N. A. Rockefeller and Barbara W. Jackson (writer).

23   Washington. To Sulgrave Club for RNC Women's Division breakfast. Appointments with A. W. Cole and Murray Snyder; General Lemnitzer and Colonel Goodpaster; J. C. Hagerty. News conference, followed by appointment with B. M. Shanley and Mr. and Mrs. Alex Jex. To Burning Tree Country Club for lunch and golf with W. W. Flenniken, R. Clark, and J. E. McClure. Hosts off-the-record stag dinner.

24   Washington. Appointments with General Cutler (off the record); B. M. Baruch and G. Hauge; Secretary Weeks and Life and Casualty Insurance Co. officials (off the record). Presents National Security Medal (off the record). National Security Council session, followed by appointments with French Admiral Andre Georges Lemonnier; Secretary Dulles and L. T.

Merchant. Hosts off-the-record luncheon for White House press. Witnesses swearing-in of K. McCann as Special Assistant to the President.

25 Washington. Off-the-record breakfast with Vice-President Nixon, Attorney General Brownell, L. W. Hall, S. Adams, and General Persons. Views oldest known New Testament. Cabinet meeting. Receives United States Escapee Program representatives. Appointments with A. S. Flemming and Commander Beach; B. M. Shanley, E. D. Chesney, and Catholic War Veterans' leaders; Judge Phillips and B. M. Shanley to discuss Bricker amendment. Lunch with Senator Knowland. Afternoon appointments with Lionel Chevrier, Lewis G. Castle, and B. M. Shanley to discuss St. Lawrence seaway; Secretary Humphrey; Len Jordan (Chairman, International Joint Commission) and S. Adams.

26 Washington. Appointments with Secretary Dulles and H. Hoover, Jr. To Eisenhower farm in Gettysburg, Pennsylvania, with Mrs. Eisenhower. Returns to Washington, D.C.

27 Washington. No official appointments.

28 Washington. Off-the-record breakfast with B. N. Harlow and Congressman Taber. Appointments with Admiral Radford; G. Hauge; Secretary Wilson; Prime Minister Mario Scelba (Italy), Foreign Minister Gaetano Martino (Italy), Ambassador Manlio Brosio (Italy), Massimo Magistrati (Chief, Political Affairs, Italian foreign office), Secretary Paolo Canali (Italy), Secretary Dulles, Ambassador Luce, L. T. Merchant, and Colonel Vernon Walters (interpreter). Receives members of Commission on Veterans' Pensions. Hosts luncheon with Mrs. Eisenhower in honor of Prime Minister and Mrs. Scelba. Afternoon appointments with Colonel William F. Santelmann (Leader, U.S. Marine Band), General Lemuel C. Shepherd, and Commander Beach; Governor Simpson, Senator Barrett, Congressman Thompson, and S. Adams.

29 Washington. Appointments with Legislative Leaders; Van Heuven Goedhart (U.N. High Commissioner for Refugees), Christopher H. Phillips, and M. M. Rabb; Admiral Carney (off the record). Re-

ceives first buddy poppy of 1955 VFW sales campaign. Witnesses swearing-in of Theophil C. Kammholz as General Counsel, National Labor Relations Board. Appointments with G. W. Perkins (U.S. representative, NATO) and Colonel Goodpaster; H. E. Stassen (off the record); N. A. Rockefeller, J. M. Dodge, and Stacy May; dentist; Secretary Dulles; Attorney General Brownell, W. P. Rogers, and new judges Warren L. Jones and William E. Miller. Hosts off-the-record dinner.

30   Washington. To Sulgrave Club for RNC Women's Division breakfast. Appointments with Senator Ferguson; John C. Hagan, Jr., L. A. Minnich, and General William H. Milton, Jr., to discuss George C. Marshall research foundation; J. C. Hagerty. News conference, followed by appointments with William V. Griffin (President, English Speaking Union, U.S.) and L. A. Minnich; General Cutler and J. S. Lay. Hosts luncheon for congressional members. Afternoon off-the-record appointment with Allen Hoover and S. Adams. To Burning Tree Country Club for golf with General Milton and Colonel Belshe.

31   Washington. Off-the-record appointments with Congressman Gavin and B. N. Harlow; R. P. Burroughs and R. Cake; American Cancer Society drive representatives; S. Adams and G. Hauge; Governor Stratton and S. Adams. National Security Council session. Hosts luncheon for congressional members. Afternoon appointment with Congressmen Brooks, Martin, Simpson, and F. E. Smith, and B. N. Harlow. To Walter Reed Hospital with General Snyder. Returns to White House. To Secretary and Mrs. Weeks's home for dinner in honor of General Cutler.

April   1   Washington. Appointments with Attorney General Brownell and Senator Wiley (off the record); Secretaries Dulles, Humphrey, and Wilson, H. Hoover, Jr., R. B. Anderson, B. M. Shanley, and Admiral Radford (off the record). Cabinet meeting. Witnesses swearing-in of D. Anderson as Special Assistant to the President for National Security Affairs. Afternoon off-the-record appointment with General Cutler. Receives Railroad Man of the Year. To

Eisenhower farm in Gettysburg, Pennsylvania, with E. Doud and G. E. Allen.

2   Gettysburg, Pennsylvania. Tours grounds with G. E. Allen and General Nevins. To Gettysburg Country Club for golf with G. E. Allen, R. Brown, and General Nevins.

3   Gettysburg, Pennsylvania. Returns to Washington, D.C., with E. Doud.

4   Washington. Appointments with C. R. Hook and A. J. Robertson; A. F. Burns and G. Hauge; Calvin Griffith (President, Washington American League Baseball Club), Howard T. Fox (Publicity Director, Washington Baseball Club), and B. M. Shanley; G. E. Allen; S. Adams and G. D. Morgan; Admiral Radford; Secretary Dulles.

5   Washington. Appointments with Budget Director Hughes, P. F. Brundage, and S. Adams; Secretary McKay and Colonel Goodpaster; Attorney General Brownell; B. N. Harlow and Reserve Officers Association representatives; C. H. Watkins (artist) and M. M. Rabb; Ambassador Satterthwaite. Receives Catholic University Players. Appointments with T. C. Streibert, N. A. Rockefeller, A. M. Washburn, and H. Loomis; Robert Falise and B. M. Shanley (off the record); B. M. Shanley, Murray Snyder, Mr. and Mrs. Francis Worley; H. A. Rusk and American Korean Foundation representatives. Hosts luncheon for American Korean Foundation. Afternoon off-the-record appointment with P. G. Hoffman.

6   Washington. Appointments with D. Anderson (off the record); J. M. Dodge; American Cultural Festival in Paris representatives; Ambassador Jacobs; R. M. Keyes. Hosts luncheon for John Marshall bicentennial commission. To Burning Tree Country Club for golf with E. N. Eisenhower and J. Westland.

7   Washington. Off-the-record closed circuit television test. Appointment with Admiral Strauss and AEC members W. F. Libby and John von Neumann. National Security Council session, followed by appointments with Secretary Dulles and W. J. Hopkins; P. Hotchkiss and L. A. Minnich; Murray Snyder and Knights Templar leaders. Lunch with Secretary Tal-

bott. Afternoon off-the-record appointments with R. B. Anderson, A. S. Flemming, V. E. Peterson, L. A. Minnich, and Admiral Radford; Secretary Dulles, H. E. Stassen, J. M. Dodge, R. B. Anderson, Budget Director Hughes, and N. A. Rockefeller.

8   Washington. Off-the-record appointments with T. E. Stephens. Attends services at National Presbyterian Church with J. C. Hagerty. To Burning Tree Country Club for lunch and golf with J. C. Hagerty, J. E. McClure, and R. V. Fleming.

9   Washington. Off-the-record appointments with D. Anderson; Secretary Mitchell and S. Adams; Secretary Dulles. To Eisenhower farm in Gettysburg, Pennsylvania. Tours ground with Generals Nevins and Snyder. Returns to Washington, D.C.

10   Washington. Attends services at National Presbyterian Church with J. C. Hagerty.

11   Washington. Appointments with A. F. Burns and G. Hauge; Ambassador J. J. Vallarino (Panama) and H. C. Spruks; Secretary Wilson; Admiral Radford. Greets children participating in Easter activities on White House grounds. Appointments with Secretary McKay and family (off the record); Secretary Dulles. Lunch with Secretary Dulles. Throws first ball in season opener at Griffith Stadium. Off-the-record appointment with N. A. Rockefeller, J. C. Hagerty, and K. McCann.

12   Washington. To MATS terminal en route to Charleston, South Carolina. Receives honorary degree at Citadel and reviews graduating class. Attends reception at residence of General Clark. To Charleston Air Force Base en route to Augusta, Georgia. To Augusta National Golf Club for golf with E. Dudley, J. Franklin, and C. Roberts.

13   Augusta, Georgia. To office, practice tee, and back to office. Visits C. Roberts. Golf with E. Dudley, B. Nelson, and C. J. Schoo.

14   Augusta, Georgia. Paints in quarters. Visits C. Roberts en route to office. To practice tee with E. Dudley, followed by golf with E. Dudley, R. Garlington, and W. E. Robinson. Receives guests at cottage.

15   Augusta, Georgia. To office, then practice tee. Golf with W. E. Robinson, R. W. Woodruff, and B. F. Fairless.

16   Augusta, Georgia. Appointment with Admiral Felix Strump. Poses for photographs. Golf with C. Roberts, B. J. Patton, and Mr. Middlecoff.

17   Augusta, Georgia. Attends services at Reid Memorial Presbyterian Church. To practice tee, followed by golf with A. Bradley, L. F. McCollum, and E. Dudley.

18   Augusta, Georgia. To office, followed by golf with E. Dudley, J. H. Whitney, and W. Kerr.

19   Augusta, Georgia. To office, then practice tee. Golf with E. Dudley, W. E. Robinson, and J. Roberts. Fishing with W. E. Robinson.

20   Augusta, Georgia. To office, then practice tee. Golf with E. Dudley, C. Roberts, and J. Franklin. To Bush Airfield en route to Washington, D.C.

21   Washington. To Sulgrave Club for RNC Women's Division breakfast. Off-the-record appointments with H. Hoover, Jr., and J. M. Dodge; D. Anderson; National Security Council session. Greets school superintendents. Afternoon appointments with Ambassador Miguel Angél de la Campa y Caraveda (Cuba) and V. Purse; Judge R. E. Thompson and General Persons (off the record); Colonel Goodpaster; R. Howard and S. Adams (off the record); Generals Smith and Adler, and B. N. Harlow (off the record); G. Hauge, J. C. Hagerty, H. Hoover, Jr., and R. B. Anderson. Hosts off-the-record stag dinner.

22   Washington. Off-the-record breakfast with Ambassador Lodge. Appointment with Ambassador Lacy. Receives Baptist Evangelistic Crusade members; guests of President's Committee on Government Contracts. Cabinet meeting. Appointments with Vice-President Nixon; Congressmen Short and Arends; D. Anderson. Off-the-record lunch with General Collins, H. Hoover, Jr., R. B. Anderson, and D. Anderson. Afternoon appointments with Secretary Hobby; Senator M. C. Smith; Senator Bennett and G. Hauge; H. Hoover, Jr., and Admiral Carney. Pre-

sents citations to Dr. Jonas Salk and Basil O'Conner. To Eisenhower farm in Gettysburg, Pennsylvania.

23   Gettysburg, Pennsylvania. To Gettysburg Country Club for golf with F. Akers, R. Sleichter, and Colonel Belshe.

24   Gettysburg, Pennsylvania. Returns to Washington, D.C., with Mrs. Eisenhower.

25   Washington. Off-the-record appointment with Senator Flanders and General Persons. To MATS terminal en route to New York, New York. To Waldorf-Astoria Hotel with Ambassador Lodge for television and radio luncheon. Receives Associated Press Vice-Presidents. Addresses members of Associated Press at dinner. Returns to Washington, D.C. Receives invitation to U.N. commemorative session, followed by appointment with Secretary Dulles.

26   Washington. Breakfast with Senator Knowland. Appointments with Legislative Leaders; T. C. Streibert, N. A. Rockefeller, A. M. Washburn, and C. DuVal. Receives USO leaders; Lions International officials. Receives Order of Elks national youth leaders. Lunch with G. E. Allen and William Byars. Afternoon appointment with A. F. Burns.

27   Washington. Breakfast with N. A. Rockefeller. Appointments with Attorney General Brownell and General Persons; J. S. Lay and D. Anderson. News conference, followed by appointments with Thomas S. Nichols (President, Olin Matheison Chemical Corporation) and B. M. Shanley; L. M. Pexton and G. Hauge; T. C. Streibert, G. Hauge, Murray Snyder and American Cultural Festival in Paris attendees. To Burning Tree Country Club for lunch and golf with F. Akers, Colonel Belshe, and Congressman Halleck. Hosts off-the-record stag dinner.

28   Washington. Off-the-record breakfast with Vice-President Nixon. Appointments with M. Katz and Colonel Goodpaster; J. S. Lay and D. Anderson; Admiral Cato Glover (Chief, Naval Air Training). National Security Council session, followed by appointments with General Collins; Robert E. Merriam and son, and B. M. Shanley; M. B. Folsom; A. S. Flem-

ming, R. B. Anderson, T. P. Pike, and Robert C. Unkrick. Greets National Trade Policy committee. Afternoon appointments with J. G. Jackson, Jr.; Secretary Humphrey and General Persons.

29 Washington. Appointments with Melvin Maas (Chairman, President's Committee on Employment of the Physically Handicapped) and B. M. Shanley; Governor Muñoz-Marín, Clarence A. Davis (Under Secretary of Interior), and N. A. Rockefeller; Cabinet meeting; H. Hoover, Jr. (off the record); George Strecker (off the record). To Burning Tree Country Club for lunch and golf with Colonels Belshe and Thornquest, and V. Johnson.

30 Washington. Off-the-record appointment with Dr. Ralph W. Sockman (President, Church Peace Union), A. S. Flemming, and Colonel Goodpaster. Lays cornerstone for new AFL Building with Secretary Mitchell. To Burning Tree Country Club for lunch and golf with Congressman Arends, Colonel Belshe, and William McAvoy (Pan American Representative).

May 1 Washington. [Page missing.]

2 Washington. Appointments with G. Hauge and R. J. Saulnier; H. E. Stassen, F. A. Seaton, and General R. W. Porter; receives American Mother of 1955; Tellis F. Aston and H. Sanders Angleo. Greets governors attending Governors' Conference; Chamber of Commerce meeting. Afternoon appointments with Vice-President Nixon, Prime Minister P. Pibulsonggram (Thailand), Ambassador Sarasin, Thai officials, Secretary Dulles, W. S. Robertson, and J. E. Peurifoy. To Burning Tree Country Club with Prime Minister Pibulsonggram for golf with Vice-President Nixon and Colonel Belshe. Attends Governors' Conference dinner at Mayflower Hotel.

3 Washington. Bipartisan meeting. Receives American Agricultural Association; Clarke School for the Deaf students; Donna Marie Crescensci (1955 National Hearing Week Poster Girl). Afternoon appointments with S. P. Skouras and B. M. Shanley (off the record); W. S. Robinson, D. Anderson, and Admiral Radford; Governor Knight (off the record). Initiates

first international agreement on peaceful use of atomic energy. Late-afternoon appointment with Ambassador de Murville, Abbe Henri Groues, and B. M. Shanley.

4   Washington. Appointments with L. Ward Bannister (off the record); Legislative Leaders. News conference, followed by appointments with E. T. Weir (off the record); N. A. Rockefeller, Budget Director Hughes, General Persons, Colonel Goodpaster and Atomic Energy Commission members; J. S. Lay and D. Anderson. To Burning Tree Country Club for lunch and golf with J. E. McClure, W. W. Flenniken, and R. Hatcher.

5   Washington. Off-the-record breakfast with L. W. Hall, Peavey Heffelfinger, J. C. Folger, R. Humphreys, L. Richard Guylay, and S. Adams. Receives Robert S. Abbott Memorial Award. Appointments with Senator Goldwater and I. J. Martin (off the record); Ambassador Romuald Spasowski (Poland) and J. F. Simmons; N. A. Rockefeller. National Security Council session, followed by appointments with Admiral Radford and Secretary Wilson; H. Hoover, Jr., and D. Anderson; General Archibald Nye (Commissioner, United Kingdom), Ambassador Makins, and Colonel Goodpaster; Ambassador Carlos Izaguirre (Honduras) and J. F. Simmons. To Statler Hotel with B. M. Shanley for annual congressional club breakfast. Afternoon appointments with S. Adams, F. A. Seaton, and Governors Anderson, Foss, and Hall; Budget Director Hughes, P. F. Brundage, and S. Adams; G. Hauge. To Walter Reed Hospital with General Snyder.

6   Washington. Appointment with C. P. Peterson and F. A. Seaton. Receives Truck Driver of the Year, Floyd J. Pemberton. Appointments with Secretary McKay, F. A. Seaton, and Governor Elvidge (Guam); Secretaries Wilson and Thomas; Secretaries Dulles and Wilson, H. Hoover, Jr., R. B. Anderson, W. S. Robertson, D. Anderson, Colonel Randall, and Admiral Radford. Receives Operation Brotherhood members. Afternoon appointments with Ambassador Sayyid Saddiq Muntasser (Libya) and Secretary Dulles; Ambassador Krekeler and

J. F. Simmons; J. B. Hollister. Lunch with Secretary Dulles. To Washington Hebrew Congregation Temple with I. J. Martin and Murray Snyder for dedication.

7   Washington. Appointments with N. A. Rockefeller and B. N. Harlow; D. Anderson; A. W. Dulles and Colonel Goodpaster (off the record); L. B. Taft and I. J. Martin. To Congressional Country Club for lunch and golf with General Parks, Colonel G. G. Moore, and W. Cox. To Statler Hotel for annual Gridiron Club dinner.

8   Washington. Attends services at National Presbyterian Church with W. E. Robinson and C. J. Schoo.

9   Washington. Off-the-record breakfast with N. A. Rockefeller, B. N. Harlow, and Congressman Cole. Appointments with Secretary Benson; S. Adams, Budget Director Hughes, P. F. Brundage, and General Vogel; A. F. Burns and G. Hauge; H. Hoover, Jr., and Secretary Wilson. Receives United Cerebral Palsy members; Sault Locks Centennial Commission. Off-the-record lunch with S. W. Richardson. Off-the-record appointment with H. Hoover, Jr. Hosts off-the-record stag dinner.

10   Washington. Legislative Leaders. Receives Organization of World Touring and Automobile Clubs delegates. Greets Republican Women's National Conference at Mayflower Hotel with S. Adams. Off-the-record lunch with Attorney General Brownell, followed by appointments with N. A. Rockefeller (off the record); Secretary Thomas.

11   Washington. Morning appointments with J. S. Lay and D. Anderson; H. Hoover, Jr., R. B. Anderson, D. Anderson, Admiral Radford, General Charles H. Bonesteel III, Carrel I. Tod (Office of Defense Secretary), Harry Schwartz (Department of State), H. Phleger, and Colonel Goodpaster (off the record); N. A. Rockefeller, H. Hoover, Jr., D. Anderson, Secretary Hobby, General Persons, D. Adams, B. M. Shanley, R. B. Anderson, I. J. Martin, Murray Snyder, and Colonel Goodpaster. Receives American Legion Poppy. News conference, followed by appointments with Congressman Powell and M. M.

Rabb; Ambassador White; R. B. Anderson (off the record); Secretary Hobby, S. M. Brownell, N. H. McElroy, R. Larson, and General Persons. To Burning Tree Country Club for lunch and golf with J. Black, W. W. Flenniken, and W. Mangly. Evening appointment with General Howard Smith.

12 Washington. Off-the-record breakfast with Ambassador Lodge. Appointments with Ambassador Hughes; Secretary Stevens and Colonel Goodpaster; Ambassador Briggs. National Security Council session. Receives Congressional Club Cotillion youth group. Afternoon appointments with Senator Mundt and I. J. Martin; Budget Director Hughes, P. F. Brundage, and S. Adams; A. S. Flemming, James Bromley (ODM), S. Adams, General Paul, and Colonel Goodpaster; N. A. Rockefeller and J. C. Hagerty.

13 Washington. Appointments with Colonel Frank Ellis (off the record); Ambassador Reinhardt; Cabinet meeting. To Eisenhower farm in Gettysburg, Pennsylvania.

14 Gettysburg, Pennsylvania. To F. Akers's farm in Thurmont, Maryland, with G. E. Allen. Returns to Gettysburg.

15 Gettysburg, Pennsylvania. Attends services at Presbyterian Church of Gettysburg with Mrs. Eisenhower. Tours Gettysburg Battlefield with G. E. Allen and General H. Smith. Returns to Washington, D.C., with Mrs. Eisenhower.

16 Washington. Appointments with D. Anderson and Colonel Goodpaster; Commander Seaborn Collins (National Commander, American Legion), E. D. Chesney, and B. M. Shanley; Admiral Radford; G. Hauge and A. F. Burns; J. K. Javits and S. Adams. Receives Salk Vaccine report; Virginia constituents. Afternoon appointment with Secretary Dulles and H. Hoover, Jr. Hosts off-the-record stag dinner.

17 Washington. Appointments with Secretary Benson, S. Adams, B. M. Shanley, G. D. Morgan, and I. J. Martin (off the record); Legislative Leaders; H. R. Reid (off the record). Receives Young Republican

National Federation; American Bar Association officers. Appointments with Secretaries Wilson and Thomas, and Admiral Burke; Secretary Wilson and F. A. Seaton; Mayor Otto Sukr (Berlin) and Ambassador Krekeler; W. C. Doherty and G. D. Morgan; Secretary Dulles (off the record); C. R. Hook, E. Lyons, and G. D. Morgan. Makes television broadcast.

18 Washington. To Sulgrave Club with B. M. Shanley and H. Pyle for RNC Women's Division breakfast. Appointments with J. S. Lay, D. Anderson, and Budget Director Hughes; J. C. Hagerty, General Persons, F. A. Seaton, S. Adams, G. D. Morgan, N. A. Rockefeller, and B. M. Shanley. News conference, followed by appointment with M. Muir. To Burning Tree Country Club with B. Hogan and G. Sarazen for lunch with B. Hogan, G. Sarazen, G. K. Nye, J. Ryerson, and Colonel Belshe. "Locker room" appointment with J. Black and R. D. Pittman.

19 Washington. Off-the-record breakfast with General Clay. Receives Teacher of the Year, Miss Margaret Perry. Appointments with S. Adams and Senator Saltonstall (off the record); Budget Director Hughes, S. Adams, and G. D. Morgan; Budget Director Hughes and S. Adams; National Security Council session; General John A. Klein (Adjutant General); H. A. Rusk (off the record). Hosts luncheon for NATO representatives. Afternoon appointments with N. A. Rockefeller; S. Adams and G. Hauge (off the record); military officials to discuss new Army general duty uniform; Secretary Dulles and Senator George (off the record). To Statler Hotel with Mrs. Eisenhower for Women's National Press Club dinner.

20 Washington. Breakfast with General Cutler. Appointments with T. E. Stephens; W. Thacher Longstreth, Congressman Scott, J. M. Pomeroy, Jr., Walter P. Miller, Jr., Stephen E. McLaughlin, B. C. Duffy, Herbert A. Fogel, S. Adams, B. M. Shanley, J. C. Hagerty, Senators Duff and Martin, and Colonel Cooke; Vice-President Nixon and Secretaries Dulles and Wilson; Cabinet meeting. Receives citation for Outstanding Service as Layman. Poses for

photograph with national spelling bee champion. Appointments with W. J. Hopkins; Dr. Robert O. Blood (former Governor, New Hampshire) and S. Adams. To Eisenhower farm in Gettysburg, Pennsylvania, with G. E. Allen.

21 Gettysburg, Pennsylvania. [Page missing.]

22 Gettysburg, Pennsylvania. Returns to Washington, D.C.

23 Washington. Appointments with D. Anderson, J. C. Hagerty, and Colonel Goodpaster; H. E. Stassen. Attends Committee on Employment of the Physically Handicapped annual meeting. Appointments with D. MacArthur II and Colonel Goodpaster; A. F. Burns and G. Hauge; Secretary Wilson, F. A. Seaton, and C. L. Burgess; Alvin C. Cast (Republican Chairman, Indiana), S. Adams, and Governor Craig. Hosts luncheon with Mrs. Eisenhower in honor of former President and Mrs. Vincent Auriol (France). Afternoon appointments with L. E. Berkey (off the record); Ambassador Arielza, Agriculture Minister Rafael Cavestany (Spain), Navy Minister Salvador Moreno (Spain), and J. F. Simmons; N. A. Rockefeller. Hosts off-the-record stag dinner.

24 Washington. Appointments with S. Adams, General Persons, G. D. Morgan, I. J. Martin, and F. A. Seaton; Legislative Leaders; N. A. Rockefeller. Addresses National Association of Radio and Television Broadcasters' convention at Sheraton-Park Hotel. To Burning Tree Country Club for lunch with B. Nelson, C. Middlecoff, J. Black, and Colonel Belshe and golf with B. Nelson, J. Black, and Colonel Belshe (joined by J. E. McClure and F. Akers). Evening appointments with Postmaster General Summerfield; A. Nielsen (off the record). Attends opening ceremonies for Smithsonian Institution's First Ladies' Hall with Mrs. Eisenhower.

25 Washington. To Sulgrave Club for RNC Women's Division breakfast. Appointments with J. S. Lay and D. Anderson; N. A. Rockefeller; Admiral Strauss and Colonel Goodpaster; Secretary Mitchell; Ambassador Beaulac and Colonel Goodpaster (off the record); Secretary Weeks; Ambassador Erkin; S. Adams and G. D. Morgan. Lunch with Secretary

Dulles. Afternoon appointments with A. S. Flemming, Vice-President Nixon, B. M. Shanley, J. C. Hagerty, General Paul, and Commander Beach; N. A. Rockefeller and Admiral Radford; Attorney General Brownell and Judges John K. Brown and William G. East; G. Hauge. Hosts garden party for veterans with Mrs. Eisenhower.

26 Washington. Off-the-record breakfast with Vice-President Nixon. National Security Council session, followed by special National Security Council session (off the record) and appointments with Ambassador Lodge and N. A. Rockefeller. To Walter Reed Hospital for Armed Forces Institute of Pathology dedication. To Burning Tree Country Club for golf with R. Learned, Congressman Halleck, and Colonel Belshe.

27 Washington. Off-the-record breakfast with H. E. Stassen. Appointments with M. M. Rabb; G. Hauge; N. A. Rockefeller; L. W. Douglas; General J. G. Hurley, Sisters M. Henrietta and M. Victorine, and Congressman Bow; Cabinet meeting. Presents National Security Medal to J. Edgar Hoover. Views Library of Congress atomic energy exhibit with Admiral Strauss and N. A. Rockefeller. Afternoon appointments with J. S. Lay; Colonel George Warden (off the record). To Eisenhower farm in Gettysburg, Pennsylvania. Visits with Mr. and Mrs. Sidney Spiegel (former chauffeur).

28 Gettysburg, Pennsylvania. To Gettysburg Country Club for golf with General Nevins and G. E. Allen. To G. E. Allen's home with Generals Nevins and Snyder to inspect well-drilling equipment. To B. Redding's farm to inspect pigs.

29 Gettysburg, Pennsylvania. Attends services at Gettysburg Presbyterian Church with General Nevins. To General Nevins's home.

30 Gettysburg, Pennsylvania. To Gettysburg Country Club for golf with G. E. Allen, R. Sleichter, and General Nevins. To Gettysburg National Cemetery with Mrs. Eisenhower and E. Doud for Memorial Day ceremonies. Tours farm with H. E. Stassen. To B. Redding's farm with G. E. Allen, Secretary Humphrey, and General Nevins.

31 Gettysburg, Pennsylvania. Returns to Washington, D.C. Appointments with Secretaries Humphrey and Weeks, Postmaster General Summerfield, S. Adams, and A. F. Burns; J. C. Hagerty, S. Adams, General Persons, B. M. Shanley, G. D. Morgan, and B. N. Harlow; Secretary Hobby, I. J. Martin, R. B. Perkins, and L. Scheele. News conference, followed by reception for World Health Organization foreign representatives. Receives Securities and Exchange commission officials; U.S. delegation on tariff negotiations; cheese from dairy industry leaders. Off-the-record lunch with S. W. Richardson. Afternoon appointments with Secretary Wilson and Admiral Radford; D. Anderson. Poses for photographs with Ambassador Muñiz honoring Brazilian Reactor Agreement and Ambassador Zuleta-Angel honoring Colombian Reactor Agreement. Appointment with H. Hoover, Jr., and D. MacArthur II. Hosts off-the-record stag dinner.

June 1 Washington. Morning appointments with General Persons, I. J. Martin, and B. N. Harlow; Dr. M. S. Eisenhower and A. B. Eisenhower; Legislative Leaders; B. M. Shanley, G. D. Morgan, and L. Wright; A. F. Burns and G. Hauge; Midshipmen J. B. Perkins, W. A. Kennington and J. W. Allen, and Commanders E. Herron and Beach; Victor Herd (President, National Board of Fire Underwriters) (off the record); Ambassador Makins; S. Adams and G. Hauge. Off-the-record lunch with P. G. Hoffman and A. B. Eisenhower. Afternoon appointment with J. F. Simmons, Senator Reid (Canada), and fishing industry leaders.

2 Washington. Off-the-record breakfast with Senator Knowland. Appointments with Steve Carne, General Persons, B. N. Harlow, and Congressmen Bates, Hardy, Kean, Kilday, and Teague; Attorney General Brownell; Ambassador Fernando Fournier (Costa Rica); D. Anderson; Secretary Weeks, H. Hoover, Jr., A. M. Washburn, S. W. Anderson, R. McIlvaine, General Persons, B. M. Shanley, N. A. Rockefeller, and R. Williams; K. McCann; J. Porter and S. Adams. To Burning Tree Country Club for lunch and golf with C. McAdam, G. Storer, and Colonel Belshe. Hosts off-the-record stag dinner.

3 Washington. Appointments with N. A. Rockefeller, B. M. Shanley, Gilroy Roberts, and William H. Brett (off the record); G. Hauge (off the record); group to discuss National Reserve legislation. Receives United Jewish Appeal humanitarian award. Appointments with I. J. Martin and Senator Dirksen (off the record); O. M. Reid (off the record); D. Anderson; S. Adams, N. A. Rockefeller, and Admiral Strauss. Boards new Aerocommander AF-2 en route to Gettysburg, Pennsylvania. To Eisenhower farm for lunch with J. C. Hagerty, Colonel Belshe, and General Nevins. Receives Aberdeen Angus cow and calf from Brandywine Angus Breeders; Berkshire gilt from National 4-H Club award winner; Angus heifer from Pennick family. Airborne for Washington, D.C.

4 Washington. Appointments with K. McCann; D. MacArthur II and Secretary Dulles.

5 Washington. Attends services at National Presbyterian Church with Mrs. Eisenhower. To MATS terminal with Mrs. Eisenhower en route to West Point, New York. Witnesses retreat review and presents awards. To G. Leone's farm to meet West Point classmates, class of 1915. To Thayer Hotel.

6 West Point, New York. Visits U.S. Military Academy Museum. Attends alumni march, alumni luncheon, and graduation parade. To Old Stone Inn for class of 1915 dinner.

7 West Point, New York. Attends graduation exercises and luncheon. Returns to Washington, D.C., with Mrs. Eisenhower. Late afternoon appointments with Secretary Dulles; Admiral Strauss.

8 Washington. Appointments with H. E. Stassen; Legislative Leaders; J. C. Hagerty, S. Adams, General Persons, B. M. Shanley, N. A. Rockefeller, G. D. Morgan, H. Pyle, F. A. Seaton, B. N. Harlow, I. J. Martin, and Colonel Goodpaster. News conference. Receives National Fraternal Council of Churches; international golfers. Off-the-record appointment with S. Adams, Budget Director Hughes, A. S. Flemming, N. A. Rockefeller, and J. M. Dodge. Lunch with S. Adams, A. S. Flemming, N. A. Rockefeller, Budget Director Hughes, C. Francis, and J. M. Dodge. Af-

ternoon appointments with L. Wright, A. J. Schweppe, B. M. Shanley, G. D. Morgan, and Judge Phillips (off the record); K. McCann; J. S. Lay and D. Anderson; Secretary Humphrey.

9   Washington. Appointments with Commission of Fine Arts members; I. J. Martin and Senator Flanders (off the record); Ambassador Luce; Admiral Radford; Secretary Dulles, Scott McLeod (Administrator, Refugee Relief Program, State Department), and Pierce J. Gerety (Deputy Administrator, Refugee Relief Program, State Department). National Security Council session, followed by appointments with A. F. Burns; Judges Kenneth Grubb, Sterry Waterman, J. Edward Lumbard, and W. P. Rogers. To Burning Tree Country Club for lunch and golf with R. D. Pittman, Senator Bush, and Colonel Belshe.

10   Washington. Appointments with Ambassador Armour; Secretary Wilson; Secretary Dulles. Cabinet meeting. To MATS terminal en route to Pennsylvania State University. Motors to residence of Dr. M. S. Eisenhower.

11   Pennsylvania State University. Tours nuclear reactor. Greets university trustees and wives. Attends commencement exercises and delivers address. Receives honorary degree. To Helen Eisenhower Chapel for cornerstone-laying ceremony. Returns to residence of Dr. M. S. Eisenhower en route to Gettysburg, Pennsylvania, with Walter R. Tkach.

12   Gettysburg, Pennsylvania. Tours grounds on horseback. To Redding farm and G. E. Allen's farm with General Nevins. Returns to Washington, D.C.

13   Washington. Appointments with D. Anderson; Admiral Radford; Dr. Elson; Ambassador Jones; M. Kestnbaum and S. Adams; G. Hauge and A. F. Burns; Secretary Wilson, W. Brucher, and F. A. Seaton; Secretary Wilson and F. A. Seaton. To Burning Tree Country Club for golf with P. D. Reed, C. Roberts, and B. T. Leithead.

14   Washington. Off-the-record breakfast with Secretary Dulles. Appointments with General Persons; Legislative Leaders; Ambassador Mehta, V. K. Menon, and

Secretary Dulles. Receives AMVETS national service foundation memorial scholarship winners. Appointments with C. F. Willis; E. J. Bermingham (off the record); Chancellor Adenauer, Ambassador Krekeler, Herbert Blankenhorn (U.N. Ambassador, Germany), Secretary Dulles, R. Murphy, L. T. Merchant, Nora Lejins (interpreter, State Department), and Heinz Weber (interpreter, Germany). Hosts stag luncheon honoring Chancellor Adenauer. Afternoon off-the-record appointment with Ann Schaeffer and Colonel Henry M. Pendleton. To Walter Reed Hospital for x-ray. Hosts off-the-record stag dinner.

15   Washington. Off-the-record appointments with J. C. Keogh (*Time* Magazine), E. Darby, and J. C. Hagerty; C. F. Willis, and Edward T. Tait. Signs Reactor Agreements with Great Britain, Canada, and Belgium. Appointments with Senator Bush; K. McCann; D. MacArthur II and Secretary Dulles. Participates in relocation exercises and inspects White House relocation site. Attends Interim Assembly Group meeting. To Camp David, Maryland, with D. Anderson and G. D. Morgan.

16   Camp David, Maryland. Poses for photographs. To Fort Richie, Maryland, with General Bonesteel and Colonel Higgins. Joint Chiefs of Staff meeting followed by National Security Council session. Participates in "Telecon" transmission. Returns to Camp David en route to Eisenhower farm in Gettysburg, Pennsylvania. Tours grounds with W. Byars and General Nevins. Returns to Camp David.

17   Camp David, Maryland. To Fort Richie, Maryland. Attends meeting for relocation exercise members. Makes television broadcast. To Eisenhower farm in Gettysburg, Pennsylvania, with W. R. Tkach.

18   Gettysburg, Pennsylvania. To Gettysburg Country Club for golf with General Nevins. Receives lambs from Johnston family.

19   Gettysburg, Pennsylvania. Returns to Washington, D.C., and enplanes for San Francisco, California. To St. Francis Hotel with Governor Knight and Mayor Robinson.

20   San Francisco, California. Breakfast with Arthur

Dolan, Dan London, Joseph Moore, Jr., and Robert Steele. Appointments with J. L. Murphy; General Joyce; Mrs. Alfred Ehrman and Avenali family; General Frank Stoner; General Willard G. Wyman. Receives Citizens Committee. Hosts luncheon. Attends and addresses U.N. meeting at San Francisco Opera House. Returns to St. Francis Hotel. Visits with J. B. Black, H. D. Collier, Theodore Peterson, and Norman L. McLaren. Dinner with D. London, J. C. Hagerty, N. A. Rockefeller, Colonel Draper, and W. R. Tkach. Airborne for Washington, D.C.

21   Washington. Appointments with I. J. Martin, B. N. Harlow, and General Persons; Legislative Leaders; D. Anderson. Appointments with General Collins and Colonel Goodpaster; I. J. Martin; A. F. Burns and G. Hauge. Signs H. R. 1. Receives National Association of Radio and Television Farm Directors; National 4-H Club camp members; International Farm Youth Exchange. Afternoon appointments with Ambassador Haydar Gork (Turkey) and J. F. Simmons; Ambassador Makins and General Ronald Weeks (Chairman, Vickers Ltd.); M. Kestnbaum, S. Adams, B. M. Shanley, and K. McCann; Admiral Radford and D. Anderson; Postmaster General Summerfield.

22   Washington. Appointments with L. E. Berkey (off the record); Budget Director Hughes; Vice-President Nixon, B. M. Shanley, and Young Republican National Federation leaders; Secretary Humphrey; B. F. Fairless (off the record). Poses for photographs with Secretaries Wilson and Stevens, and W. M. Brucker. Airborne for Rutland Municipal Airport, Vermont. Attends luncheon in his honor. Inspects livestock. Address at Rutland Fairgrounds. To Mountain Top Inn, Chittenden, Vermont. Fishing at Furnace Brook with Judge Milford Smith. Returns to Mountain Top Inn for dinner in the President's honor.

23   Rutland, Vermont. Breakfast with women representatives of dairy and agricultural industries. Fishing at Walker Pond with Judge Smith and Ben Schley. To Rutland Municipal Airport en route to Concord Municipal Airport, New Hampshire. Delivers address at

State Capitol. To Laconia Tavern, Laconia, New Hampshire. Motors to Belknap Lodge. Addresses picnickers. Returns to Laconia Tavern.

24 Laconia, New Hampshire. To Lincoln High School en route to Profile Lake for photographs. Addresses ceremony for 150th anniversary of Old Man of the Mountain. To Mountain View Hotel, Whitefield, New Hampshire. Golf with C. Bruno, A. McLaughlin, and R. Cooper. Visits Sports House reception. To Secretary Weeks's home in Lancaster, New Hampshire.

25 Lancaster, New Hampshire. Addresses woodcutting contest at Nansen Ski Jump. Visits Dartmouth College and meets with President John Dickey. To Parmachenee Lake Club, Wilson Mills, Maine, for fishing with Don Cameron (guide).

26 Parmachenee Lake, Maine. Fishing with D. Cameron.

27 Parmachenee Lake, Maine. To Skowhegan, Maine. Address at Skowhegan Fairgrounds and Senator M. C. Smith's home. To Pittsfield, Maine, en route to Dow Air Force Base, Bangor, Maine. Enplanes for Washington, D.C.

28 Washington. Morning appointments with Budget Director Hughes and G. D. Morgan; Legislative Leaders; T. C. Streibert, L. A. Minnich, A. M. Washburn, and A. H. Berding. Presents Distinguished Service Medal to General Ridgway. Receives report from Commission on Intergovernmental Relations, followed by appointments with Secretary Wilson, S. Adams, and F. A. Seaton; A. F. Burns and G. Hauge; General Whiteley, General Gerald Templer (Chief, Imperial General Staff), and Ambassador Makins. Lunch with D. Thornton. Afternoon appointments with Colonels Draper and Goodpaster; H. E. Stassen; G. D. Morgan; Secretary Talbott; L. F. McCollum.

29 Washington. Off-the-record breakfast with Vice-President Nixon, S. Adams, General Persons, Attorney General Brownell, and L. W. Hall. Morning appointments with J. S. Lay and D. Anderson; S. Adams,

General Persons, B. M. Shanley, J. C. Hagerty, G. D. Morgan, B. N. Harlow, H. Pyle, and Murray Snyder. News conference, followed by appointments with Ambassador Lodge; General Taylor and Colonel Goodpaster; Prime Minister U Nu (Burma), Secretary Dulles, J. F. Simmons, W. S. Robertson, William J. Sebald (Deputy Assistant Secretary of State). Hosts luncheon in honor of Prime Minister Nu. Afternoon appointments with Ambassador César Gonzalez (Venezuela) and Cecil Lyon (Deputy Assistant Secretary of State); H. Pyle; Wendall Wyatt (Republican State Chairman) and Congressman Norblad; S. Adams, General Persons, J. C. Hagerty, Budget Director Hughes; J. A. McCone.

30   Washington. Breakfast with A. S. Flemming. Morning appointments with Ambassador Chapin; D. Anderson; Budget Director Hughes, S. Adams, General Persons, and Admiral Strauss; General Bragdon; Admiral Strauss; A. W. Dulles. National Security Council session, followed by appointments with Admiral Radford; Secretary Humphrey; S. Adams, General Persons, and I. J. Martin. Hosts luncheon for Latin American ambassadors. To Burning Tree Country Club with Postmaster General Summerfield for golf with J. Shea, D. O'Connor, and Colonel Belshe.

July   1   Washington. Off-the-record breakfast with Senator Knowland. Appointments with C. P. White (off the record); H. E. Stassen; Ely Culbertson and H. E. Stassen to discuss world disarmament; Secretary Weeks and S. W. Anderson. Witnesses swearing-in of J. B. Hollister as Director of International Cooperation Administration. Cabinet meeting. Receives Boy Scouts. Off-the-record appointments with S. Adams and Congressman Dondero; I. J. Martin and Senator Capehart; S. Adams, A. F. Burns, G. D. Morgan, and Congressman McConnell. Appointment with Holman D. Pettibone (Rubber Producing Facilities Disposal Commission) and S. Adams. To MATS terminal. Airborne for Gettysburg, Pennsylvania. Entertains White House staff, Cabinet members, and wives with Mrs. Eisenhower.

2   Gettysburg, Pennsylvania. To Gettysburg Country Club for golf with G. E. Allen. To Camp David, Maryland, with C. Roberts and W. E. Robinson.

3   Camp David, Maryland. To practice tee with C. Roberts and W. E. Robinson. Visits Attorney General Brownell and G. D. Morgan.

4   Camp David, Maryland. To practice tee with C. Roberts, W. E. Robinson, and G. E. Allen. Departs for Eisenhower farm in Gettysburg, Pennsylvania, with G. E. Allen. To G. E. Allen's farm. Returns to Camp David, Maryland. Attends outdoor movie with Mrs. Eisenhower. Returns to Washington, D.C., with G. E. Allen.

5   Washington. Appointments with General Persons and J. C. Hagerty; J. S. Lay and D. Anderson; G. D. Morgan and Senator Potter; Attorney General Brownell and Secretary Dulles. Views special demonstration. Lunch with S. Adams, I. J. Martin, B. N. Harlow, General Persons, Congressman Martin, and Senator Knowland. Off-the-record appointment with Secretaries Humphrey and Weeks, B. N. Harlow, I. J. Martin, and General Persons. Views *Cinerama* at Warner Theater with White House staff. Evening off-the-record appointment with Secretary Dulles, Ambassador Bohlen, H. Phleger, L. T. Merchant, and Admiral Radford.

6   Washington. Appointments with Legislative Leaders; Budget Director Hughes, S. Adams, and J. C. Hagerty; S. Adams, J. C. Hagerty, G. D. Morgan, I. J. Martin, Murray Snyder, General Persons, and Colonel Goodpaster; N. A. Rockefeller; A. F. Burns and G. Hauge. News conference, followed by NATO standing group luncheon. Afternoon appointments with Secretaries Wilson and Talbott, Admirals Strauss and Radford, Colonel Goodpaster, and Assistant Secretaries of Defense Robert T. Ross and Franklin G. Floete; Secretary Dulles, D. MacArthur II, N. A. Rockefeller, D. Anderson, and L. T. Merchant; V. K. Menon, Ambassador Mehta, and Secretary Dulles.

7   Washington. Off-the-record breakfast with S. S. Larmon. Appointments with H. E. Stassen; A. Z. Baker (new President, Rotary International); General George A. Horkan and Colonel Schulz (off the record). National Security Council session, followed by appointments with Budget Director Hughes, S. Ad-

ams, J. C. Hagerty, and Admiral Strauss; P. G. Hoffman (off the record). To Burning Tree Country Club for lunch and golf with Congressmen Halleck and Frelinghuysen, and S. S. Larmon.

8   Washington. Appointments with Secretary Wilson, R. B. Anderson, and Colonel Goodpaster; Secretary Hobby; H. E. Stassen. Cabinet meeting. To MATS terminal en route to Gettysburg, Pennsylvania. Motors to Eisenhower farm. Takes grandchildren on ride around grounds.

9   Gettysburg, Pennsylvania. Walks around grounds with M. Norling and Ed Barth. To Gettysburg Country Club for golf with E. Barth, M. Norling, and Major J. S. D. Eisenhower. Telephone conversation with R. Thornburg and R. Howard.

10 Gettysburg, Pennsylvania. Attends services at Gettysburg Presbyterian Church and visits home of General Nevins and Gettysburg battlefield and cemetery with Major J. S. D. Eisenhower and D. D. Eisenhower II. Returns to Washington, D.C., with Major and Mrs. J. S. D. Eisenhower and E. Doud.

11 Washington. Appointments with Major J. S. D. Eisenhower; K. McCann; S. Adams and Colonel Goodpaster; General Persons; Senators Dirksen and Clements, and General Persons (off the record); Attorney General Brownell, Budget Director Hughes, and S. Adams; P. Young and General Persons (off the record); D. Anderson; Senator Knowland and General Persons; A. F. Burns and G. Hauge; Congressmen Avery, Curtis, and Frelinghuysen, and B. N. Harlow; H. Hoover, Jr., R. B. Anderson, D. Anderson, and Admiral Radford; Attorney General Brownell. Hosts luncheon for sports representatives. Afternoon off-the-record briefing by State Department officials. Appointments with Senator George; K. McCann. TVA meeting.

12 Washington. Appointments with Secretary Humphrey, Secretary Weeks, I. J. Martin, and General Persons; bipartisan legislative meeting; Senators Clements and Knowland, and Congressmen Rayburn and Martin; Judge Finis J. Garret (off the record); Congressman Bennett and Michigan constituents;

R. B. Anderson, H. Hoover, Jr, and A. S. Flemming. Receives American Field Service students. Afternoon appointments with N. A. Rockefeller; Admiral Radford; S. Adams, Budget Director Hughes, Murray Snyder, and Middle Southern Utilities Co. representatives. To Burning Tree Country Club for lunch and golf with Congressmen Halleck and Arends, and Major J. S. D. Eisenhower.

13 Washington. Morning appointments with S. Adams, G. D. Morgan, I. J. Martin, and General Persons; Legislative Leaders. Addresses resignation ceremony for Secretary of Health, Education, and Welfare Hobby. Appointments with B. M. Baruch and Secretary Dulles; E. J. Sparks; N. A. Rockefeller; J. S. Lay and D. Anderson; state department briefing; R. Reid (off the record); H. E. Stassen; Captain Jack Sayler (off the record); D. Anderson; S. Adams.

14 Washington. Appointments with M. Patterson (off the record); Admiral Strauss. National Security Council session, followed by appointments with Secretary Wilson; A. W. Dulles; H. Hoover, Jr., T. C. Streibert, A. M. Washburn, Admiral Strauss, and Colonel Goodpaster; H. Hoover, Jr.; Postmaster General Summerfield; S. Adams and General Persons; S. Adams and General Persons.

15 Washington. Appointments with G. Hauge; Mrs. Ruth S. Dister and family (off the record); R. Montgomery; H. Hoover, Jr., and Colonel Goodpaster; D. Anderson; Colonel Goodpaster; H. Hoover, Jr., Colonel Goodpaster, and S. Adams. Television broadcast to nation. To MATS terminal with Mrs. Eisenhower and Major J. S. D. Eisenhower. Airborne for Keflavik Air Force Base, Iceland, en route for Geneva, Switzerland.

16 Keflavik Air Force Base, Iceland. Attends luncheon in his honor given by President Asgeir Asgeirsson (Iceland). To Geneva, Switzerland. Motors to Villa Creux de Genthod. Appointment with Secretary Dulles, D. MacArthur II, L. T. Merchant, D. Anderson, and Colonel Goodpaster.

17 Geneva, Switzerland. Attends services at American

Church in Geneva with Mrs. Eisenhower and Major J. S. D. Eisenhower. Appointment with Secretary Dulles, followed by meeting and luncheon with Prime Minister Anthony Eden (Great Britain), Prime Minister Edgar Faure (France), Secretary Dulles, D. MacArthur II, L. T. Merchant, Harold Macmillan (Secretary of State, Foreign Affairs, Great Britain), Ivone Kirkpatrick (Delegate, Great Britian); Norman Brook (Delegate, Great Britian); Antoine Pinay (Foreign Affairs Minister, France), Armand Berard (Diplomatic Counselor, France), M. R. de Margerie (Director General of Political and Economic Affairs, France), and Colonels Goodpaster and Walters. Afternoon off-the-record appointments with General Gault; Prime Minister Eden; Prime Minister Faure, A. Pinay, Secretary Dulles, and Colonel Walters. Off-the-record dinner with General Gault.

18 Geneva, Switzerland. To Palais des Nations for Geneva Summit Conference meeting. Appointment with Secretary General Dag Hammarskjöld (U.N.) and Secretary Dulles. Returns to Villa de Creux for lunch with Secretary General Hammarskjöld, Secretary Dulles, D. Anderson, Colonels Goodpaster and Walters, and Major J. S. D. Eisenhower. Returns to Palais des Nations for Geneva Summit Conference meeting. Hosts dinner for Soviet delegation.

19 Geneva, Switzerland. Appointments with D. Anderson; Colonel Goodpaster. To golf practice tee. Lunch with Major J. S. D. Eisenhower. Buys presents for grandchildren at La Coceinella (novelty shop). Visits American Consul General and American delegation employees; office of White House staff and Secretary Dulles. To Palais des Nations for photographs with Prime Minister Eden, Prime Minister Faure, and Nikolai A. Bulganin. Geneva Summit Conference meeting.

20 Geneva, Switzerland. Breakfast with Prime Minister Eden, H. Macmillan, Secretary Dulles, and D. Anderson. Appointment with H. E. Stassen and N. A. Rockefeller. Lunch with Defense Minister Georgi Konstantinovich Zhukov (U.S.S.R.), O. A. Troyanovsky, and Ambassador Bohlen. Inspects atomic reactor build-

ing en route to Palais des Nations. Geneva Summit Conference meeting. Dinner with Admiral Radford and General Gruenther.

21   Geneva, Switzerland. Walks around grounds. To practice tee. Appointments with H. E. Stassen, R. B. Anderson, Ambassador Bohlen, Admiral Radford, and General Gruenther; Ambassador Bohlen. Lunch with H. E. Stassen, Admiral Radford, and Major J. S. D. Eisenhower. Afternoon appointment with H. E. Stassen, N. A. Rockefeller, D. Anderson, Admiral Radford, and Colonel Goodpaster. To Palais des Nations for Geneva Summit Conference meeting, followed by appointments with Prime Minister Faure, M. Barard, Colonel Walters, and Secretary Dulles; Admiral Radford, H. E. Stassen, General Gruenther, N. A. Rockefeller, and Colonel Goodpaster. To Palais Enyard for dinner given by President Max Petitpierre (Switzerland).

22   Geneva, Switzerland. Goes to office, then practice tee. Appointments with Prime Minister Eden; N. A. Rockefeller. Hosts luncheon in honor of President and Mrs. Petitpierre with Mrs. Eisenhower. Afternoon appointments with D. Anderson; N. A. Rockefeller. To Palais des Nations for Geneva Summit Conference meeting. Hosts reception in honor of Prime Minister and Mrs. Eden, Mrs. Macmillan, and Mrs. Faure. Cabinet meeting.

23   Geneva, Switzerland. Appointments with Secretary Dulles; M. Jeanneret (Rolex Watch Co.); Defense Minister Zhukov, O. A. Troyanovsky, and Ambassador Bohlen. Greets General McAuliffe's staff. To Palais des Nations for appointment with Prime Minister Eden, Prime Minister Faure, H. Macmillan, A. Pinay, D. MacArthur II, and L. T. Merchant, followed by Geneva Summit Conference meeting (restricted session). Lunch with General Gault, Major J. S. D. Eisenhower, and N. A. Rockefeller. Returns to Palais des Nations for Geneva Summit Conference meeting (restricted session) and appointment with Secretary Dulles, H. E. Stassen, and R. B. Anderson. Departs for Cointrin Airport en route to Washington, D.C.

24   Washington. [Page missing.]

25   Washington. Appointments with Secretary Dulles; bipartisan legislative meeting; Congressmen Allen, Arends, and Halleck, I. J. Martin, B. N. Harlow, and General Persons; H. E. Stassen; Secretary Wilson; J. C. Hagerty; T. S. Gates and Commander Beach (off the record); S. Adams; K. McCann and J. C. Hagerty; Secretary Dulles. Makes television broadcast to nation.

26   Washington. Appointments with G. D. Morgan; S. Adams, I. J. Martin, B. N. Harlow, H. C. Rose, and General Persons; Legislative Leaders; Vice-President Nixon and General Persons; T. C. Streibert, R. Cook, and N. A. Rockefeller; A. F. Burns and G. Hauge; Admiral Strauss; S. Adams, Attorney General Brownell, W. P. Rogers, G. D. Morgan, and Admiral Strauss. To Burning Tree Country Club for lunch and golf with H. C. Stuart, J. Sweetser, and Colonel Belshe.

27   Washington. Appointments with S. Adams and J. C. Hagerty; J. S. Lay and D. Anderson; Ambassador White and H. F. Holland; Vice-President Nixon, S. Adams, J. C. Hagerty, N. A. Rockefeller, and General Persons, joined by Murray Snyder, G. D. Morgan, I. J. Martin, H. Pyle, and Colonel Goodpaster (off the record). News conference, followed by appointments with General Carl Spaatz; H. Hoover, Jr., D. A. Quarles, A. T. Waterman, and Colonel Goodpaster; O. C. Hobby and Charles Keefer; Secretary Dulles. Makes film for United Community Campaign.

28   Washington. Greets group from Boys' Nation. Appointments with K. C. Royall; W. P. Rogers and Judge Joe E. Estes. Attends Atoms-for-Peace stamp ceremony. Appointments with Vice-President Nixon, S. Adams, J. C. Hagerty, I. J. Martin, B. N. Harlow, and General Persons; National Security Council session. To Burning Tree Country Club for lunch and golf with L. J. Bernard, Major J. S. D. Eisenhower, and Colonel Belshe.

29   Washington. To Statler Hotel for pre-adjournment congressional breakfast given by L. W. Hall. Appointments with Secretary Dulles, W. S. Robertson,

and U. A. Johnson (off the record); Ambassador Lodge, H. E. Stassen, and Secretary Dulles. Cabinet meeting, followed by appointments with Ambassador Mehta and V. Purse; Postmaster General Summerfield; C. R. Hook. To Eisenhower farm in Gettysburg, Pennsylvania.

30 Gettysburg, Pennsylvania. [Page missing.]

31 Gettysburg, Pennsylvania. [Page missing.]

August 1 Washington. Appointments with D. Anderson; Secretary Benson, J. A. McConnell, G. Hauge, and Senator George. Witnesses swearing-in of M. B. Folsom as Secretary of Health, Education, and Welfare. Appointments with General Twining and Colonel Goodpaster; A. F. Burns and G. Hauge; Secretary Wilson, R. B. Anderson, and Generals Loper and Luedecke; Secretary Wilson, C. L. Burgess, and General Hull; Secretary Humphrey. Off-the-record lunch with S. W. Richardson. Receives car from auto industry leaders. Poses for portrait. To Walter Reed Hospital.

2 Washington. Appointments with Legislative Leaders; Senator Millikin; Senators Millikin and Allott (off the record); S. McLeod, P. J. Gerety, and M. M. Rabb. Greets Governors' Committee for Refugee Relief Program. Greets leaders and members of Bull Elephant Club, Administrative and Secretarial Assistants of Congress. Receives picture from Lawrence F. Whittemore (President, Brown Co.).

3 Washington. Off-the-record breakfast with Vice-President Nixon. Appointments with J. S. Lay and D. Anderson; R. Howard (off the record); Congresswoman Bolton; Secretary Benson and G. Hauge. Presents Medal of Freedom to R. B. Anderson. Appointments with Secretaries Thomas and Wilson, F. A. Seaton, and Admiral Albert Mumma (off the record); D. Anderson; Theodore Repplier (Advertising Council); General Izaak Alphonse Aler (President, K.L.M. Royal Dutch Airlines); Secretary Wilson; Ohio congressional delegation; A. F. Burns and General Persons; Secretary Humphrey, Budget Director Hughes, P. F. Brundage, H. Pyle, and B. N. Harlow (off the record).

4 Washington. Off-the-record breakfast with N. A. Rockefeller. Appointments with Congressman Simpson and T. E. Stephens (off the record); R. B. Anderson; R. B. Anderson and Secretary Dulles. Presents Gold Star to Admiral Carney. Off-the-record lunch with K. C. Royall, followed by afternoon appointments with Dr. and Mrs. Willard Camalier, Nancy Hanks, and N. A. Rockefeller; S. Adams, B. M. Shanley, J. C. Hagerty, Murray Snyder, F. A. Seaton, H. Pyle, N. A. Rockefeller, H. E. Stassen, General Persons, and Colonel Goodpaster. News conference, followed by appointments with Budget Director Hughes; Secretary Wilson (off the record).

5 Washington. Off-the-record breakfast with Senator Knowland. Appointments with Ambassador Aldrich; J. S. Knight (off the record). Witnesses swearing-in of Rueben Robertson as Deputy Secretary of Defense. Cabinet meeting, followed by swearing-in of H. E. Stassen as Deputy Representative on U.N. Disarmament Commission. Appointments with Ambassador Harrington; Secretary Benson; H. E. Stassen, Ambassador Lodge, and Secretary Dulles. Lunch with Secretary Dulles. To MATS terminal en route to Gettysburg, Pennsylvania.

6 Gettysburg, Pennsylvania. To Gettysburg Country Club for golf with J. Rice and General Nevins. Motors around grounds; hunts crows.

7 Gettysburg, Pennsylvania. Attends services at Gettysburg Presbyterian Church with W. R. Tkach. To General Nevins's farm.

8 Gettysburg, Pennsylvania. Lunch and tour of grounds with Reverend B. Graham. Goes crow hunting.

9 Gettysburg, Pennsylvania. To Gettysburg Country Club for golf with General Nevins. Recieves pure bred Holstein calf from Montgomery County Fair Association.

10 Gettysburg, Pennsylvania. Appointment with Secretary Wilson. To Gettysburg Country Club for golf with R. Sleichter.

11 Gettysburg, Pennsylvania. Returns to Washington, D.C., for appointments with Admiral Carney; Secretary Dulles; Attorney General Brownell; J. S. Lay; Secretary Folsom; Ambassador Abdullah Al-Khayall (Saudi Arabia); Ambassador Joaquin E. Salazar (Dominican Republic); A. S. Flemming, Budget Director Hughes, N. A. Rockefeller, Jarold Kieffer, and S. Adams; Judge Ernest H. Van Fossan (U.S. Tax Court); S. Adams and G. Hauge. Off-the-record lunch with A. Vandenberg, Jr., and R. L. Biggers. Afternoon appointments with G. Hauge; General Persons; Colonel Goodpaster; G. D. Morgan.

12 Washington. Off-the-record breakfast with Postmaster General Summerfield. Appointments with P. Young, S. Adams, and N. A. Rockefeller; Cabinet meeting; S. Adams and G. Hauge to discuss bicycle tariffs; G. D. Morgan; K. McCann; I. J. Martin; Secretary Weeks; Secretary Talbott (off the record); Colonel Goodpaster; W. J. Hopkins; G. D. Morgan. To Eisenhower farm in Gettysburg, Pennsylvania.

13 Gettysburg, Pennsylvania. No official appointments.

14 Gettysburg, Pennsylvania. Returns to Washington, D.C. To MATS terminal en route to Denver, Colorado. Motors to summer White House.

15 Denver, Colorado. To office at Lowry Air Force Base for appointments with General Sprague and Colonel Draper; General Harmon; Mayor Nicholson, A. Nielsen, and Harold D. Roberts (joined by D. Thornton); A. Nielsen. To Cherry Hills Country Club for lunch and golf with D. Thornton, R. Arnold, and W. W. Flenniken.

16 Denver, Colorado. To office at Lowry Air Force Base for appointment with General Sprague and Colonel Draper. To Cherry Hills Country Club for lunch and golf with D. Thornton, J. Black, and R. Arnold. To Fraser, Colorado, with J. C. Hagerty and A. Nielsen. Delivers brief speech and receives oil painting. To A. Nielsen's ranch.

17 Fraser, Colorado. Fishing with A. Nielsen. Tours A. Nielsen's grounds with D. D. Eisenhower II and A. Nielsen.

18   Fraser, Colorado. Fishing with A. Nielsen. To practice tee.

19   Fraser, Colorado. News conference followed by photographs with D. D. Eisenhower II. Fishing with A. Nielsen.

20   Fraser, Colorado. Greets boys from Skyline Ranch. Fishing with A. Nielsen.

21   Fraser, Colorado. Fishing with A. Nielsen. To Denver, Colorado, with D. D. Eisenhower II and A. Nielsen.

22   Denver, Colorado. Makes television broadcast regarding disaster relief. To Cherry Hills Country Club for golf with J. G. Dyer, R. Arnold, and Colonel Belshe. Lunch with D. D. Eisenhower II and his friends. Returns to office for appointments with Admirals Strauss and Paul F. Foster, Manuel Dupkin, and Everett Holles; Admiral Strauss. Poses for photographs with Admiral Strauss. To Lowry Air Force Base. Airborne for Hartford, Connecticut.

23   Hartford, Connecticut. Flies over flood-stricken areas. Lands at Bradley Airfield, Hartford, Connecticut. Tours disaster areas in New England. Airborne for Washington, D.C. Appointments with Dr. M. S. Eisenhower; J. C. Hagerty, I. J. Martin, and General Persons (joined by Budget Director Hughes); Secretary Dulles; Dr. M. S. Eisenhower; Admirals Radford and Strauss, Generals Loper and Leudeke, and Major Richard Snyder (Aide, Admiral Radford) (off the record); J. C. Hagerty, I. J. Martin, and Congressman Patterson; J. W. Barba; A. S. Flemming, V. E. Peterson, J. C. Hagerty, I. J. Martin, and Generals Persons and Charles G. Holle (Deputy Chief of Engineers, Army).

24   Washington. Appointment with Secretary Humphrey and General Persons. To MATS terminal with Judge Phillips en route to Philadelphia, Pennsylvania. To Bellevue-Stratford Hotel with E. D. Eisenhower and E. N. Eisenhower. Appointments with Commander Collins; W. T. Longstreth, W. P. Miller, Jr., J. N. Pomeroy, Jr., William H. Gray, Jr., Ephrain R. Gomberg, William B. Kolb, Ray Speiser,

and Congressman Scott. To Independence Mall for luncheon with American Bar Association. Addresses luncheon. To Philadelphia Municipal Airport en route to Washington, D.C. Appointments with A. S. Flemming, V. E. Peterson, J. C. Hagerty, I. J. Martin, and General Persons; General Persons. To MATS terminal with Mrs. Eisenhower en route to Denver, Colorado. Motors to summer White House.

25 Denver, Colorado. To office at Lowry Air Force Base for appointments with L. H. Snyder and Congressman Chenoweth; Secretary McKay, Wilbur A. Dexheimer (Commissioner, Bureau of Reclamation), and Senator Watkins; Senator Watkins; General Bradley. To Cherry Hills Country Club with Ambassador Aldrich. To Lowry Air Force Base officers' club for luncheon with Ambassador Aldrich, P. Hoyt, Colonels Schulz and Draper, and General Sprague. To Fitzsimons Army Hospital for golf with Ambassador Aldrich, P. Hoyt, and Colonel Draper.

26 Denver, Colorado. To B. F. Swan's ranch in Pine, Colorado, with A. Nielsen and Colonel Belshe. Fishing with A. Nielsen, B. F. Swan, and Colonel Belshe.

27 Denver, Colorado. To office at Lowry Air Force Base for appointment with Secretary Mitchell. To Cherry Hills Country Club for golf with E. D. Slater, R. Arnold, and Colonel Belshe. Returns to summer White House en route to Brown Palace Hotel for lunch and bridge with D. Thornton, L. M. Pexton, J. Culbreath, E. D. Slater, P. G. Hoffman, E. Conly, H. Wismer, D. Webb, and Colonel Belshe.

28 Denver, Colorado. Attends services at Corona Presbyterian Church with Mrs. Eisenhower. To Fairmount Cemetery with Mrs. Eisenhower.

29 Denver, Colorado. To office at Lowry Air Force Base. To Cherry Hills Country Club for golf with F. Leahy, R. Arnold, Colonel Belshe. More golf with M. Hicks, R. Arnold, and Colonel Belshe.

30 Denver, Colorado. To office at Lowry Air Force Base for appointment with Julian Wolfson. To Cherry Hills Country Club for golf with J. Culbreath, R. Arnold, and Colonel Belshe, followed by luncheon.

More golf with J. Culbreath, R. Arnold, and Colonel Belshe.

31 Denver, Colorado. Receives boat from people of Denison, Texas. To Cherry Hills Country Club for lunch and golf with J. Black, R. Arnold, and Colonel Belshe.

September 1 Denver, Colorado. To office at Lowry Air Force Base. To Cherry Hills Country Club for lunch and golf with J. C. Hagerty, R. Arnold, and Colonel Belshe. To Brown Palace Hotel with Mrs. Eisenhower.

2 Denver, Colorado. To office at Lowry Air Force Base for off-the-record appointment with Harry Harding, Thomas Lapham, Kenneth Dyke, and T. E. Stephens. Makes television broadcast to nation. To Cherry Hills Country Club for luncheon, followed by golf with C. Roberts, B. T. Leithead, and W. A. Jones. To Brown Palace Hotel for evening.

3 Denver, Colorado. To office at Lowry Air Force Base for appointment with Senator H. A. Smith. To Cherry Hills Country Club for golf with W. E. Robinson, J. H. Whitney, and R. Arnold. Hosts luncheon. To Brown Palace Hotel with W. A. Jones, P. Reed, and S. S. Larmon. Visits Arthur Atkinson, George C. Hannaway, and Mr. Stupp.

4 Denver, Colorado. Attends services at Corona Presbyterian Church with Mrs. Eisenhower. To Brown Palace Hotel with Mrs. Eisenhower for evening.

5 Denver, Colorado. To office at Lowry Air Force Base for appointments with representatives from Vallhaber-Reed; Daniel Gainey; D. Anderson, James Gleason, and Vice-President Nixon; Vice-President Nixon. To Cherry Hills Country Club for golf with L. F. McCollum, F. F. Gosden, and E. Dudley followed by luncheon.

6 Denver, Colorado. To office at Lowry Air Force Base with Colonel Schulz for appointment with T. C. Streibert. To Cherry Hills Country Club for lunch and golf with G. Gregory, R. Manning, and R. Arnold. More golf with R. Arnold.

7 Denver, Colorado. To office at Lowry Air Force Base with Colonel Schulz for appointment with Mr. and Mrs. Donald Brotzman. To Cherry Hills Country

Club for lunch and golf with R. Arnold, A. Schreferman, and Mayor Nicholson (joined by A. Nielsen). To Columbine Country Club for inspection tour. Tours Broomfield Heights with B. F. Swan.

8   Denver, Colorado. To office at Lowry Air Force Base with Colonel Schulz for appointment with L. S. Goodson. To Cherry Hills Country Club for golf with R. Arnold and A. Nielsen, followed by luncheon. Motors with N. Smith and A. Nielsen to N. Smith's ranch in Larkspur, Colorado, for tour. Returns to Cherry Hills Country Club.

9   Denver, Colorado. To office at Lowry Air Force Base with Colonel Schulz for appointment and photographs with Admiral Radford. To Cherry Hills Country Club for golf with E. Dudley, L. B. Maytag, and R. Arnold, followed by luncheon and golf.

10   Denver, Colorado. To Brown Palace Hotel with B. M. Shanley and Murray Snyder to host breakfast for Republican state chairmen. Retires to hotel suite for appointments with B. M. Shanley, Murray Snyder and L. W. Hall (joined by Clarence Adamy and R. Humphreys); John T. Diederich (Republican State Chairman, Kentucky); Samuel Bodine (Republican State Chairman, New Jersey). To Cherry Hills Country Club for lunch and golf with M. Norling, D. Thornton, and R. Arnold. To office at Lowry Air Force Base for appointment with G. Mollet and A. Hubby.

11   Denver, Colorado. To Air Force Academy for ceremonies.

12   Denver, Colorado. To office at Lowry Air Force Base with Colonel Schulz en route to golf at Green Gables Country Club with C. Rosenbaum, J. Schwayder, and D. Thornton. Attends luncheon. Attends dedication of new pulpit at Corona Presbyterian Church with Mrs. Eisenhower and E. Doud.

13   Denver, Colorado. To office at Lowry Air Force Base with Colonel Schulz for appointments with U. E. Baughman (off the record); D. Anderson. To Cherry Hills Country Club for lunch and golf with C. O'Toole, L. Skutt, and R. Arnold.

14 Denver, Colorado. To office at Lowry Air Force Base with Colonel Schulz for appointment with D. Anderson. To Presbyterian Hospital with A. Nielsen to visit E. Houston. To Cherry Hills Country Club for lunch and golf with W. A. Moncrief, W. Flannigan, and R. Arnold (accompanied by General Gruber). To home of P. H. Dominick with Mrs. Eisenhower.

15 Denver, Colorado. To office at Lowry Air Force Base with Colonel Schulz for appointment with Mayor Nicholson. To Cherry Hills Country Club for lunch and golf with F. Manning, Jr., R. Arnold, and J. Novak. More golf with R. Arnold. To Brown Palace Hotel with Mrs. Eisenhower and E. Doud for reception given by F. Manning, Jr.

16 Denver, Colorado. To office at Lowry Air Force Base with Colonel Schulz for appointments with H. E. Stassen; Senator Carlson. To Cherry Hills Country Club for lunch and golf with C. Roberts, C. Yates, and R. Arnold. To Brown Palace Hotel for dinner and bridge.

17 Denver, Colorado. To office at Lowry Air Force Base with Colonel Schulz for appointment with J. A. McCone. To Cherry Hills Country Club for golf with T. R. Garlington, A. Houghton, and F. Ouimet. Lunch with G. E. Allen and General Snyder. To B. Gordon's private lake with G. E. Allen for barbecue dinner.

18 Denver, Colorado. Attends services at Corona Presbyterian Church with Mrs. Eisenhower. To Cherry Hills Country Club with G. E. Allen. To Columbine Country Club with G. E. Allen and A. Nielsen. To Brown Palace Hotel with G. E. Allen and A. Nielsen for dinner with Augusta National Country Club members.

19 Denver, Colorado. To A. Nielsen's ranch in Fraser, Colorado, with A. Nielsen and G. E. Allen. Fishing, followed by lunch and dinner with A. Nielsen, G. E. Allen, Murray Snyder, and General Snyder. Paints.

20 Fraser, Colorado. Breakfast with G. E. Allen, A. Nielsen, Murray Snyder, and General Snyder. Paints. Walks around grounds with A. Nielsen and G. E. Allen. More painting. Dinner with A. Nielsen,

G. E. Allen, Murray Snyder, and General Snyder. Fishing with A. Nielsen.

21 Fraser, Colorado. Breakfast with G. E. Allen, A. Nielsen, Murray Snyder, and General Snyder. Paints. Fishing with A. Nielsen. Visits with C. Norgren, J. Price, and C. Boester. Paints, followed by fishing with A. Nielsen. Speaks to Secretary Dulles by telephone. Prepares dinner for G. E. Allen, R. L. Biggers, A. Nielsen, and General Snyder.

22 Fraser, Colorado. Breakfast with R. L. Biggers, A. Nielsen, and General Snyder. Paints. Fishing with R. L. Biggers, G. E. Allen, and General Snyder. More painting. Dinner with R. L. Biggers, G. E. Allen, A. Nielsen, and General Snyder.

23 Fraser, Colorado. To summer White House with A. Nielsen, G. E. Allen, R. L. Biggers, Murray Snyder, and General Snyder. To office at Lowry Air Force Base for off-the-record appointment with Colonel John H. McCann. To Cherry Hills Country Club for golf with R. Arnold (accompanied by G. E. Allen and J. Culbreath). Lunch with R. Arnold, B. Gordon, and G. E. Allen. Golf with R. Arnold. Speaks with Secretary Dulles by telephone.

24 Denver, Colorado. Suffers heart attack. Admitted to Fitzsimons Army Hospital.

25 Denver, Colorado. Fitzsimons Army Hospital. Visited by immediate family.

26 Denver, Colorado. Fitzsimons Army Hospital. Visited by immediate family.

27 Denver, Colorado. Fitzsimons Army Hospital. Visited by immediate family.

28 Denver, Colorado. Fitzsimons Army Hospital. Visited by immediate family.

29 Denver, Colorado. Fitzsimons Army Hospital. Visited by immediate family.

30 Denver, Colorado. Fitzsimons Army Hospital. Visited by immediate family.

October 1 Denver, Colorado. Fitzsimons Army Hospital. Appointment with S. Adams.

2 Denver, Colorado. Fitzsimons Army Hospital.

3 Denver, Colorado. Fitzsimons Army Hospital. Appointment with S. Adams.

4 Denver, Colorado. Fitzsimons Army Hospital. Appointment with S. Adams.

5 Denver, Colorado. Fitzsimons Army Hospital. Appointment with S. Adams and General Griffin.

6 Denver, Colorado. Fitzsimons Army Hospital.

7 Denver, Colorado. Fitzsimons Army Hospital. Appointment with U. E. Baughman.

8 Denver, Colorado. Fitzsimons Army Hospital.

9 Denver, Colorado. Fitzsimons Army Hospital. Appointment with Vice-President Nixon and S. Adams.

10 Denver, Colorado. Fitzsimons Army Hospital. Appointment with S. Adams and A. C. Whitman.

11 Denver, Colorado. Fitzsimons Army Hospital. Appointments with Secretary Dulles; S. Adams and A. C. Whitman.

12 Denver, Colorado. Fitzsimons Army Hospital. Appointments with Dr. M. S. Eisenhower; S. Adams and A. C. Whitman.

13 Denver, Colorado. Fitzsimons Army Hospital. Appointment with A. Nielsen and General Snyder.

14 Denver, Colorado. Fitzsimons Army Hospital.

15 Denver, Colorado. Fitzsimons Army Hospital. Appointment with Secretary Humphrey and S. Adams.

16 Denver, Colorado. Fitzsimons Army Hospital. Appointments with Secretary Humphrey; S. Adams.

17 Denver, Colorado. Fitzsimons Army Hospital. Appointments with Admiral Radford and Secretary Wilson; S. Adams and A. C. Whitman.

18 Denver, Colorado. Fitzsimons Army Hospital. Appointment with S. Adams and A. C. Whitman.

19 Denver, Colorado. Fitzsimons Army Hospital. Appointments with Secretary Dulles; S. Adams; D. Anderson; S. Adams and A. C. Whitman.

20 Denver, Colorado. Fitzsimons Army Hospital. Appointments with S. Adams; C. Roberts; C. Roberts and Mrs. Eisenhower.

21 Denver, Colorado. Fitzsimons Army Hospital. Appointment with Attorney General Brownell and A. C. Whitman.

22 Denver, Colorado. Fitzsimons Army Hospital. Appointments with B. M. Shanley and Mrs. Eisenhower; S. Adams; S. Adams and A. C. Whitman.

23 Denver, Colorado. Fitzsimons Army Hospital.

24 Denver, Colorado. Fitzsimons Army Hospital. Appointments with Ambassador Lodge and J. C. Hagerty; S. Adams, G. Hauge, and A. F. Burns.

25 Denver, Colorado. Fitzsimons Army Hospital. Appointment with Secretary McKay.

26 Denver, Colorado. Fitzsimons Army Hospital. Appointments with G. E. Allen; S. Adams; G. E. Allen.

27 Denver, Colorado. Fitzsimons Army Hospital. Appointment with S. Adams, K. McCann, and General Persons.

28 Denver, Colorado. Fitzsimons Army Hospital.

29 Denver, Colorado. Fitzsimons Army Hospital. Appointments with S. Adams and A. C. Whitman; Secretary Benson, S. Adams, J. C. Hagerty, and Dr. M. S. Eisenhower.

30 Denver, Colorado. Fitzsimons Army Hospital.

31 Denver, Colorado. Fitzsimons Army Hospital. Appointments with Postmaster General Summerfield; S. Adams; Generals Sprague and Harmon, and Mayor Nicholson.

November 1 Denver, Colorado. Fitzsimons Army Hospital. Appointments with S. Adams and A. C. Whitman; E. Nicholson, J. Foster, and B. F. Swan; R. Braun, G. Campbell, P. Hoyt, and General Snyder.

2 Denver, Colorado. Fitzsimons Army Hospital. Appointments with D. Anderson; General Cutler; S. Adams and A. C. Whitman; Secretary Mitchell and S. Adams; S. Adams.

3   Denver, Colorado. Fitzsimons Army Hospital. Appointments with E. D. Slater; J. C. Hagerty; A. Schrepferman and M. Norling; E. D. Slater.

4   Denver, Colorado. Fitzsimons Army Hospital. Appointments with J. C. Hagerty and Commander Beach; General Taylor.

5   Denver, Colorado. Fitzsimons Army Hospital. Appointment with Field Marshal Montgomery.

6   Denver, Colorado. Fitzsimons Army Hospital. Attends performance of Master Singers at Bushnell Auditorium with Mrs. Eisenhower.

7   Denver, Colorado. Fitzsimons Army Hospital. Appointments with Secretary Folsom; J. H. Whitney.

8   Denver, Colorado. Fitzsimons Army Hospital. Appointments with General Clay; R. Arnold, L. Skutt, W. W. Flenniken, and J. G. Dyer; S. Adams and A. C. Whitman.

9   Denver, Colorado. Fitzsimons Army Hospital. Appointment with President and Mrs. Carlos Castillo-Armas (Guatemala), H. Hoover, Jr., Mr. and Mrs. S. Adams, V. Purse, Frank Madden (State Department), J. C. Hagerty, Louis Malach (State Department), Francisco Linares-Aranda, and Ambassador Cruz-Salazar; H. Hoover, Jr.; S. Adams; R. W. Woodruff.

10 Denver, Colorado. Fitzsimons Army Hospital. Appointments with S. Adams; P. D. White; A. Nielsen.

11 Denver, Colorado. To Lowry Air Force Base with Mrs. Eisenhower. Delivers brief address and enplanes for Washington, D.C. Upon arrival at MATS terminal, delivers brief speech.

12 Washington. Appointment with S. Adams and J. C. Hagerty.

13 Washington. No official appointments.

14 Washington. Appointments with H. Hoover, Jr., S. Adams, and J. C. Hagerty; S. Adams and Colonel Goodpaster; B. M. Shanley. To Eisenhower farm in Gettysburg, Pennsylvania, with Mrs. Eisenhower. Walks around grounds.

15   Gettysburg, Pennsylvania. Walks around grounds with Colonel George McNally and General Snyder. Appointment with S. Adams, J. C. Hagerty, R. Montgomery, and A. C. Whitman.

16   Gettysburg, Pennsylvania. Receives heifer calf from Theodore S. Ryan.

17   Gettysburg, Pennsylvania. Appointments with Secretary Weeks; S. Adams and J. C. Hagerty; Budget Director Hughes; L. E. Oyler (Postmaster, Gettysburg, Pennsylvania); R. J. Byrnes (GSA) and Paul Mish (GSA); Secretary Dulles and H. Hoover, Jr.

18   Gettysburg, Pennsylvania. Appointments with S. Adams and Colonel Goodpaster; D. Anderson; Secretary Dulles (photographs taken); Admiral Strauss. To Feaster farm.

19   Gettysburg, Pennsylvania. No official appointments.

20   Gettysburg, Pennsylvania. No official appointments.

21   Gettysburg, Pennsylvania. Appointments with A. W. Dulles and Colonel Goodpaster. To Camp David, Maryland, for National Security Council session. Evening appointment with Secretary Dulles (joined by Vice-President Nixon, and Secretaries Wilson and Humphrey). Hosts dinner. Plays bridge with Secretaries Humphrey, Dulles, and Wilson.

22   Camp David, Maryland. Breakfast with Vice-President Nixon, General Snyder, and Secretaries Dulles, Humphrey, and Wilson. Appointments with S. Adams, G. D. Morgan, and Colonel Goodpaster; Secretary Weeks (joined by Ambassador Lodge, and Secretaries Dulles, Humphrey, and Wilson). Cabinet meeting. To Gettysburg, Pennsylvania, with H. E. Stassen, J. C. Hagerty, and Colonel Goodpaster.

23   Gettysburg, Pennsylvania. Appointments with Colonel Mattingly and General Snyder; S. Adams, J. C. Hagerty, and R. Montgomery; R. Montgomery. To Gettysburg College with J. C. Hagerty and R. Montgomery to deliver speech to White House Conference on Education.

24   Gettysburg, Pennsylvania. Appointment with General Snyder. To putting green. Poses for photographs with grandchildren. Target practice.

25   Gettysburg, Pennsylvania. Appointments with Murray Snyder and Colonel Goodpaster; Ben Freeman and Archie Mongelli; "Skip" Lambert (Cameraman, United Press-Fox). Lunch with Reverend and Mrs. Brown and Dr. and Mrs. Elson. Afternoon appointments with Mr. and Mrs. G. E. Allen; H. Weaver; General Snyder.

26   Gettysburg, Pennsylvania. Appointments with General Snyder; Murray Snyder and H. Weaver. To putting green. Inspects south pastures with G. E. Allen and General Snyder (joined by General Nevins). To G. E. Allen's farm.

27   Gettysburg, Pennsylvania. Appointments with Mr. and Mrs. G. E. Allen; C. V. McAdam and son; General and Mrs. Nevins.

28   Gettysburg, Pennsylvania. Appointments with Secretary Mitchell; L. W. Hall (photographs taken).

29   Gettysburg, Pennsylvania. Appointments with General Snyder; Colonel Schulz; Colonel Goodpaster and A. C. Whitman.

30   Gettysburg, Pennsylvania. Appointment with Sergeant Elizabeth James (cardiac technician), Private John Douglas (blood technician), and Colonel Mattingly; General Snyder. Walks to Feaster farm with Colonel Schulz and receives tractor from Harold P. Jordan. Appointment with P. G. Hoffman and Colonel Goodpaster. Receives pony from J. R. Lackey. Afternoon appointment with Mr. and Mrs. G. Thompson.

December 1   Gettysburg, Pennsylvania. Appointments with Secretary Folsom, Budget Director Hughes, and S. Adams; D. Anderson. To Camp David, Maryland, with D. Anderson for National Security Council session. Returns to Gettysburg, Pennsylvania, with Attorney General Brownell. Greets Mr. and Mrs. K. C. Royall.

2   Gettysburg, Pennsylvania. Appointments with Secretary Wilson, Admiral Radford, and Colonel Goodpaster; Colonel Goodpaster; G. Hauge.

3   Gettysburg, Pennsylvania. Appointments with Congressman Martin; Colonel Goodpaster; Senator Knowland; Colonel Goodpaster.

4   Gettysburg, Pennsylvania. Visits with Mr. and Mrs. E. D. Slater. Rides around grounds with G. E. Allen and E. D. Slater.

5   Gettysburg, Pennsylvania. Appointments with S. Adams and N. A. Rockefeller; Colonel Goodpaster. Delivers telephone message to AFL-CIO merger convention. Afternoon appointments with R. L. Biggers, W. A. Hagensicker (Chrysler Corporation), Captain Richard W. Streiff (Chrysler Corporation), and General Snyder; Mr. and Mrs. G. E. Allen.

6   Gettysburg, Pennsylvania. Appointments with Secretary Wilson, W. J. McNeill, Budget Director Hughes, P. F. Brundage, and Admiral Radford; Northern Nut Growers Association representatives.

7   Gettysburg, Pennsylvania. Appointment with A. F. Burns and G. Hauge.

8   Gettysburg, Pennsylvania. To Camp David with General Snyder for National Security Council session. Lunch with Vice-President Nixon, Secretaries Dulles, Humphrey, and Wilson, S. Adams, and General Snyder. National Security Council session. Returns with Colonel Goodpaster to Gettysburg, Pennsylvania.

9   Gettysburg, Pennsylvania. To Camp David with General Persons. Appointments with Postmaster General Summerfield, S. Adams, General Persons, and Colonel Goodpaster. Cabinet meeting. Returns with J. C. Hagerty to Gettysburg, Pennsylvania. Afternoon appointment with Mr. and Mrs. W. F. C. Ewing. Rides around grounds with Mr. and Mrs. W. F. C. Ewing.

10 Gettysburg, Pennsylvania. To Walter Reed Hospital in Washington, D.C., with General Snyder for physical examination and visit with Generals Van Voorhis, Sturgis, and Bonesteel, and Mrs. Summerfield. Returns to Gettysburg, Pennsylvania.

11   Gettysburg, Pennsylvania. Lunch with General Cutler and Mrs. Eisenhower. To Fort Belvoir, Virginia, with Mrs. Eisenhower to visit Major J. S. D. Eisenhower and family. To Washington, D.C., for dinner with Mr. and Mrs. G. E. Allen.

12   Washington. Appointments with S. Adams and General Persons; Legislative Leaders; K. McCann; S. Adams; Legislative Leaders. Tea with President and Mrs. Luis Baille Berres (Uruguay) and son, Ambassador and Mrs. Mora, Don Jorge Battle Ibanez, Mrs. Eisenhower, and Secretary and Mrs. Dulles. Afternoon appointment with Legislative Leaders.

13   Washington. Appointments with S. Adams; General Persons and Colonel Goodpaster; bipartisan Legislative Leaders; I. J. Martin and Congressman Reed; D. Anderson; G. D. Morgan and Colonel Goodpaster. To MATS terminal en route to Gettysburg, Pennsylvania.

14   Gettysburg, Pennsylvania. No official appointments.

15   Gettysburg, Pennsylvania. Receives electric golf cart from Cushman Motor Works, Inc. Lunch with C. Roberts and Mrs. Eisenhower. Hosts dinner with Mrs. Eisenhower for General and Mrs. Nevins, Dr. M. S. Eisenhower, J. C. Hagerty, A. C. Whitman, M. J. McCaffree, W. R. Tkach, and Colonel Schulz.

16   Gettysburg, Pennsylvania. Appointment with A. Nielsen. Hunts crows with W. R. Tkach.

17   Gettysburg, Pennsylvania. Lunch with Mrs. Eisenhower and P. D. White.

18   Gettysburg, Pennsylvania. Afternoon departure for Gettysburg College with J. C. Hagerty and Mrs. Eisenhower. Delivers Christmas message to nation and turns on tree lights in Washington, D.C., by remote control.

19   Gettysburg, Pennsylvania. Appointment with Admiral Strauss and Murray Snyder. To old school house for inspection of reconstruction with General Nevins.

20   Gettysburg, Pennsylvania. Appointment with D. Anderson and Colonel Goodpaster. To Gettysburg Airport en route to Washington, D.C. Appointments with General Persons; K. McCann; B. M. Shanley.

To Walter Reed Hospital with Mrs. Eisenhower to visit Mrs. J. S. D. Eisenhower; General Sturgis; General Wood Hess.

21 Washington. Appointments with Colonel Goodpaster; Secretary Humphrey; Secretary Dulles; C. H. Tompkins; R. W. Woodruff.

22 Washington. Appointment with Budget Director Hughes, General Persons, and Colonel Goodpaster. Extends Christmas greetings to White House employees with Mrs. Eisenhower. National Security Council session, followed by appointment with Admiral Strauss and Colonel Goodpaster.

23 Washington. Off-the-record breakfast with S. W. Richardson. Appointments with Attorney General Brownell; J. C. Hagerty; General Persons; K. McCann; Colonel Goodpaster; Ambassador Lodge.

24 Washington. No official appointments.

25 Washington. [Page missing.]

26 Washington. Appointment with Secretary Dulles.

27 Washington. Appointments with J. C. Hagerty, General Persons, and Colonel Goodpaster; G. Hauge and General Persons; Secretary Dulles, T. Gardner, Generals Twining and Cabell, and Colonel Randall (off the record); Vice-President Nixon.

28 Washington. Appointment with General Heaton and Colonel Mattingly. To MATS terminal with J. C. Hagerty en route to United States Naval Base, Key West, Florida. Walks to baseball field with Dr. M. S. Eisenhower and General Snyder. Walks to submarine piers. Attends movie.

29 Key West, Florida. Practices golf on baseball field with J. C. Hagerty, Dr. M. S. Eisenhower, General Snyder, Sergeant Moaney, and Commander Beach. Walks around base with golfing party. Appointment with Admiral Henderson. Attends movie.

30 Key West, Florida. Appointment with K. McCann. Practices golf on baseball field with General Snyder and Commander Beach (joined by K. McCann). Dinner with Mr. and Mrs. J. C. Hagerty. Attends movie.

31   Key West, Florida. Practices golf on baseball field with Sergeant Moaney, General Snyder, and Commander Beach. Greets Mrs. Eisenhower, E. Doud, and Mrs. Snyder. Walks around submarine piers. Attends movie.

1956

January   1   Key West, Florida. Walks to office with Dr. M. S. Eisenhower, General Snyder, and Commander Beach to work on State of the Union Address. Drives around Key West with General and Mrs. Snyder, Commander Beach, Dr. M. S. Eisenhower, E. Doud, and Mrs. Eisenhower. Hosts dinner for driving party.

2   Key West, Florida. Walks to office with Commander Beach en route to golf practice on baseball field (joined by Mrs. Eisenhower). Appointment with Budget Director Hughes, G. Hauge, G. D. Morgan, and Colonel Goodpaster. Hosts dinner with Mrs. Eisenhower for Dr. M. S. Eisenhower, General and Mrs. Snyder, Commander Beach, and E. Doud.

3   Key West, Florida. Walks to office with J. C. Hagerty, G. Hauge, Budget Director Hughes, Commander Beach, and Colonel Goodpaster. Poses for photographs with walking party. Appointments with Colonel Goodpaster; Budget Director Hughes, G. D. Morgan, and G. Hauge; Dr. M. S. Eisenhower. Accompanies Mrs. Eisenhower and E. Doud to Boca Chica Naval Air Station for their flight to Washington, D.C. Tours naval base with Dr. M. S. Eisenhower, General Snyder, and Commander Beach. Dinner with walking party. Attends movie.

4   Key West, Florida. Walks to office en route to golf practice on baseball field with W. E. Robinson and Dr. M. S. Eisenhower. Visits with General Gruenther, J. C. Hagerty, Commander Beach, and Dr. M. S. Eisenhower (joined by W. E. Robinson, E. D. Slater, Captain and Mrs. Burns, and G. E. Allen). Appointment with J. C. Hagerty, Admiral and Mrs. Harry Henderson, and Captain and Mrs. William R. Gleim. Dinner with Generals Gruenther and Snyder, Dr. M. S. Eisenhower, G. E. Allen, and

W. E. Robinson. Plays bridge with E. D. Slater, G. E. Allen, and General Gruenther. Attends movie.

5   Key West, Florida. Greets Juscelino Kubitchek (President-elect, Brazil), Ambassador Dunn, and Ambassador Muñiz. Poses for photographs with Brazilian group. Works on State of the Union Address. Dinner with Generals Snyder and Gruenther, Dr. M. S. Eisenhower, E. D. Slater, W. E. Robinson, and Commander Beach. Plays bridge with G. E. Allen, E. D. Slater, and General Gruenther.

6   Key West, Florida. Walks to office with J. C. Hagerty and Commander Beach. Appointment with Secretary Benson, T. D. Morse, G. Hauge, and F. A. Seaton. Practices golf on baseball field with Generals Gruenther and Snyder, and Dr. M. S. Eisenhower. Attends softball game between Secret Service and White House press at Sonar School. Hosts dinner for Generals Snyder and Gruenther, Dr. M. S. Eisenhower, G. E. Allen, E. D. Slater, W. E. Robinson, and Commander Beach. Plays bridge with G. E. Allen, E. D. Slater, and General Gruenther.

7   Key West, Florida. Walks to baseball field with General Gruenther and Commander Beach (joined by E. D. Slater and G. E. Allen). Plays bridge with E. D. Slater, G. E. Allen, and General Gruenther. Dinner with W. E. Robinson, E. D. Slater, G. E. Allen, Dr. M. S. Eisenhower, Generals Gruenther and Snyder, and Commander Beach. Plays bridge with G. E. Allen, W. E. Robinson, and General Gruenther.

8   Key West, Florida. Appointment with Sheriff John Spottswood (Monroe County, Florida). News conference. To Boca Chica Naval Air Station with Admiral Henderson en route to Washington, D.C.

9   Washington. Appointments with General Persons; A. F. Burns; J. C. Hagerty; Colonel Goodpaster; S. Adams, B. M. Shanley, and Colonel Goodpaster; Colonel Goodpaster.

10 Washington. Appointments with Colonel Goodpaster; Legislative Leaders; S. Adams; J. C. Hagerty; B. M. Shanley and Colonel Goodpaster; Secretary Dulles.

11   Washington. Appointments with J. C. Hagerty; S. Adams; D. Anderson; Colonel Goodpaster; A. S. Flemming and General Persons; Attorney General Brownell and S. Adams. Afternoon appointments with General Persons; Colonel Goodpaster; Secretary Dulles and R. B. Anderson (off the record); S. Adams and J. C. Hagerty; G. D. Morgan and K. McCann; D. Anderson, L. F. McCollum, and W. Francis.

12   Washington. Appointments with Colonel Goodpaster; S. Adams; National Security Council session; A. W. Dulles; H. C. Rose; G. Hauge; S. Adams; Colonel Goodpaster. Greets delegation which represented United States at Liberian presidential inauguration.

13   Washington. Accompanied to office by W. A. Jones. Appointments with Red Cross leaders; Congressmen Reed and Taber, and General Persons (off the record); Secretaries Dulles, Humphrey, and Wilson, Admiral Strauss, D. Anderson, and Colonel Goodpaster; Admiral Strauss.

14   Washington. Appointments with S. Adams, K. McCann, and J. C. Hagerty; Colonel Goodpaster; G. E. Allen.

15   [Page missing.]

16   Washington. Appointments with K. McCann; Colonel Goodpaster; S. Adams and J. C. Hagerty. Cabinet meeting, followed by appointments with Secretary Dulles and S. Adams; Secretary Dulles; Secretary Dulles and J. C. Hagerty; A. F. Burns; D. Anderson; Budget Director Hughes; W. H. Jackson; Secretary Humphrey; G. D. Morgan.

17   Washington. Appointments with H. E. Stassen; Colonel Goodpaster; H. Hoover, C. Francis, M. Kestnbaum, and Colonel Goodpaster; Attorney General Brownell; E. J. Bermingham (off the record); G. Hauge; Attorney General Brownell, S. Adams, and J. C. Hagerty.

18   Washington. Appointments with B. M. Shanley; Colonel Goodpaster. Receives painting of Gettysburg farm by Grandma Moses for inaugural anniversary.

National Security Council session, followed by appointments with Secretary Wilson, R. B. Robertson, A. W. Dulles, General Twining, Admiral Strauss, and Colonel Goodpaster; S. Adams; Walter Ruschmeyer and Colonel Schulz; O. C. Hobby (off the record); R. Montgomery, G. Murphy, and J. C. Hagerty (off the record); S. Adams; R. W. Woodruff.

19 Washington. Appointments with S. Adams and J. C. Hagerty; S. Adams, J. C. Hagerty, F. A. Seaton, H. Pyle, Murray Snyder, General Persons, and Colonel Goodpaster. News conference, followed by appointments with Ambassador Conant; H. S. Cullman; S. Adams and G. Hauge. Off-the-record appointment with Secretaries Dulles and Humphrey, H. Hoover, Jr., J. B. Hollister, J. M. Dodge, S. Adams, and G. Hauge.

20 Washington. Accompanied to office by R. W. Woodruff. Appointments with S. Adams; S. Adams and Colonel Goodpaster; Secretary Dulles and M. Patterson; Colonel Goodpaster. Off-the-record lunch with C. Roberts. Afternoon appointments with R. Montgomery and J. C. Hagerty (off the record); A. F. Burns and G. Hauge. To Sheraton-Park Hotel with Mrs. Eisenhower for Salute to Eisenhower dinner.

21 Washington. Appointments with J. C. Hagerty; S. Adams and Colonel Goodpaster. Off-the-record appointments with R. Montgomery; W. Ruschmeyer, F. J. Donohue, and Colonel Schulz; P. G. Hoffman and S. Adams. To Eisenhower farm in Gettysburg, Pennsylvania, with G. E. Allen. Walks around barns with General Nevins. To old school house en route to G. E. Allen's farm. Returns to Washington, D.C., with G. E. Allen.

22 Washington. Attends services at National Presbyterian Church.

23 Washington. Appointments with National Security Council Net Evaluation Subcommittee; Secretary Dulles; Colonel Goodpaster; Board of Consultants, Foreign Intelligence Activities; L. W. Hall, J. C. Folger, and S. Adams (off the record); Senator George and Secretary Dulles.

24 Washington. Appointments with J. C. Hagerty; General Persons; Colonel Goodpaster; Legislative Leaders; J. C. Hagerty. Afternoon appointments with J. C. Hagerty; J. S. Lay and D. Anderson; T. J. Watson (off the record); General Persons.

25 Washington. Appointments with General Persons; K. McCann; J. C. Hagerty; S. Adams and Colonel Goodpaster; S. Adams, J. C. Hagerty, G. D. Morgan, F. A. Seaton, G. Hauge, Murray Snyder, and General Persons. News conference, followed by appointments with Ambassador Luce and Colonel Goodpaster; Ambassador Georgi N. Zaroubin (USSR), Secretary Dulles, and Alexander Logofet (interpreter); Secretary Dulles and J. C. Hagerty; Secretary Dulles; Colonel Goodpaster. Afternoon appointments with M. Kestnbaum, P. Young, and Colonel Goodpaster; Secretary Dulles, D. MacArthur II, L. T. Merchant, Carl McArdle, J. C. Hagerty, and B. M. Shanley; G. D. Morgan; Prince Bernhard (off the record).

26 Washington. Appointments with J. C. Hagerty; C. L. Burgess; Colonel Goodpaster. National Security Council session, followed by appointments with Secretaries Dulles and Wilson, H. E. Stassen, A. W. Dulles, D. Anderson, and Admiral Radford; General Clark. Off-the-record lunch with S. S. Larmon. Afternoon appointments with S. Adams; Colonel Goodpaster; J. C. Hagerty; P. F. Brundage; Secretary Dulles, D. MacArthur II, L. T. Merchant, Ambassador Allen, and Francis H. Russell; Secretary Dulles; G. D. Morgan; S. Adams.

27 Washington. Appointments with W. J. Hopkins; J. C. Hagerty; S. Adams and G. D. Morgan; Secretary Wilson, Attorney General Brownell, M. Sprague, G. D. Morgan, and Judge Stephen Jackson. Cabinet meeting, followed by appointments with Attorney General Brownell and Secretary Humphrey; Postmaster General Summerfield; S. Adams; J. M. Dodge; Secretary Dulles, W. S. Robertson, L. T. Merchant, D. MacArthur II, and Admiral Radford (off the record) (joined by Gerard C. Smith, W. F. Libby, and General Loper); Secretary Dulles; H. Phleger and L. T. Merchant; W. E. Robinson (off the record); Secretary Dulles (off the record).

28 Washington. Appointments with S. Adams and J. C. Hagerty; Colonel Goodpaster. Receives Ben Hogan Golf Trophy from Congressman Westland. Views exhibit at National Gallery of Art with B. M. Shanley. Appointments with G. D. Morgan; D. Anderson; General Curtis (off the record).

29 Washington. Attends services at National Presbyterian Church with Mrs. Eisenhower. To Fort Belvoir, Virginia, with Mrs. Eisenhower for grandchildren's dance recital. To residence of Major J. S. D. Eisenhower. Returns to Washington.

30 Washington. Appointments with Colonel Goodpaster; J. C. Hagerty; T. Peterson and H. Hoover, Jr. (off the record); Secretary Dulles; Prime Minister Eden and Selwyn Lloyd (Foreign Secretary, Britain). Hosts luncheon for Prime Minister Eden. Afternoon appointments with Colonel Goodpaster; Prime Minister Eden, S. Lloyd, Ambassador Makins, Secretary Dulles, H. Hoover, Jr., L. T. Merchant, Ambassador Aldrich, G. E. Allen, D. MacArthur II, and several advisers.

31 Washington. Appointments with Colonel Goodpaster; J. C. Hagerty; S. Adams, G. D. Morgan, and General Persons; Legislative Leaders; A. F. Burns; G. D. Morgan. Hosts luncheon for Prime Minister Eden. Afternoon appointments with Prime Minister Eden; S. Adams; Governor Craig and son, and S. Adams; British-American talks; Prime Minister Eden.

February 1 Washington. Appointments with D. Anderson, General Persons, A. W. Dulles, and Colonel Goodpaster (off the record); D. Anderson; Colonel Goodpaster; J. C. Hagerty; General Persons; General Henry B. Sayler (off the record); Ambassador Cooper and S. Adams. Afternoon British-American talks followed by appointments with Prime Minister Eden; Ambassador Aldrich; Colonel Goodpaster; Colonel Schulz.

2 Washington. To Mayflower Hotel with B. M. Shanley for International Council of Christian Leadership prayer breakfast. Appointments with S. Adams and G. D. Morgan; S. Adams and H. E. Stassen; S. Adams and General Persons; Congressman Cooper and

General Persons; Admiral Radford; T. E. Dewey; G. D. Morgan; Colonel Goodpaster; General Persons and G. D. Morgan. To Eisenhower farm in Gettysburg, Pennsylvania.

3 Gettysburg, Pennsylvania. To courthouse with Mrs. Eisenhower and J. C. Hagerty for voter registration. Visits General and Mrs. Nevins.

4 Gettysburg, Pennsylvania. Hunts crows and inspects livestock. Visits Secretary and Mrs. Humphrey and Mrs. Gruenther. Goes pheasant hunting with Secretary Humphrey. Visits General and Mrs. Nevins.

5 Gettysburg, Pennsylvania. Tours grounds by foot and car with Secretary Humphrey. Inspects tools and equipment with Secretary Humphrey. Visits General and Mrs. Nevins.

6 Gettysburg, Pennsylvania. To Gettysburg Airport en route to Washington, D.C. Appointments with General Snyder; Commander Beach; S. Adams, G. D. Morgan, and General Persons; S. Adams; General Snyder; Secretary Dulles (joined by Admiral Strauss); Admiral Strauss. Afternoon appointments with J. Rowley; D. Anderson; S. Adams; Commander Beach and Colonel Goodpaster; General Persons.

7 Washington. Appointments with General Persons (joined by G. D. Morgan); Colonel Goodpaster; Legislative Leaders; Secretary Benson, J. Z. Anderson, S. Adams, and General Persons; Vice-President Nixon; Secretary Folsom, Harold C. Hunt (Under Secretary, HEW), Lowell T. Coggeshall (Special Assistant to Secretary Folsom), and S. Adams; General Joyce; M. H. Stans and B. M. Shanley; Cabinet meeting; Ambassador Lodge. Off-the-record National Security Council session.

8 Washington. Appointments with S. Adams; T. C. Streibert and A. M. Washburn; Colonel Goodpaster; S. Adams, J. C. Hagerty, G. D. Morgan, F. A. Seaton, Murray Snyder, General Persons, and Colonel Goodpaster. News conference, followed by appointments with R. Mayer (President, European Coal and Steel Community High Authority), Ambassador Butterworth, L. T. Merchant, and G. Hauge; Colonel Goodpaster. Hosts stag luncheon. Practices golf on White House grounds. Plays bridge.

9   Washington. Accompanied to office by General Gruenther. Appointments with Colonel Goodpaster; B. M. Shanley and M. J. McCaffree; D. Anderson. National Security Council session, followed by appointments with Secretary Dulles and D. Anderson; Admiral Radford. Off-the-record lunch with Dr. M. S. Eisenhower. Afternoon appointments with F. L. Elmendorf (Robert Heller and Associates), Gilman B. Allen (Robert Heller and Associates), F. Moran McConihe, S. Adams, General Persons, and Colonel Goodpaster (off the record) to discuss study of executive office space; S. Adams and K. McCann; L. W. Hall (off the record); J. C. Hagerty.

10   Washington. Appointments with Colonel Goodpaster; Generals Twining, Taylor, and Pate, and Admirals Radford and Burke; P. Young, Budget Director Hughes, and S. Adams; S. Adams; J. C. Hagerty; D. Anderson; Admiral Strauss and H. S. Vance; E. Johnston and Colonel Goodpaster. Afternoon appointments with J. C. Hagerty; B. M. Shanley; Secretary Humphrey; Secretary Dulles, H. E. Stassen, and D. Anderson; S. Adams and Colonel Goodpaster. Off-the-record appointment with R. B. Anderson.

11   Washington. Appointments with J. C. Hagerty; Colonel Goodpaster; S. Adams. To Walter Reed Hospital with Mrs. Eisenhower for examination.

12   Washington. Attends services at National Presbyterian Church with Mrs. Eisenhower.

13   Washington. Appointments with J. C. Hagerty; Attorney General Brownell, S. Adams, and G. D. Morgan. Cabinet meeting, followed by appointments with S. Adams and General Persons; Secretary Mitchell. To Union Station with B. M. Shanley and J. C. Hagerty to view exhibit. Afternoon appointments with D. Anderson; Colonel Russell Reeder (author); Jerome K. Kuykendall (Chairman, Federal Power Commission) and G. D. Morgan (off the record); G. Hauge; C. H. Tompkins; G. D. Morgan, I. J. Martin, and General Persons.

14   Washington. Appointments with B. M. Shanley and Colonel Goodpaster; A. S. Flemming; Colonel Draper; Attorney General Brownell, S. Adams, G. D.

Morgan, and General Persons; Legislative Leaders; Vice-President Nixon, Attorney General Brownell, S. Adams, and General Persons; P. D. White. After-noon appointments with B. M. Shanley; A. F. Burns (joined by G. Hauge); Colonel Goodpaster; J. C. Hagerty (joined by General Persons). Receives physical examination report.

15 Washington. Appointments with Colonel Goodpas-ter and H. G. Crim; Colonel Schulz; G. D. Morgan; Attorney General Brownell, S. Adams, J. C. Hagerty, G. D. Morgan, and General Persons (off the record); Secretary Wilson, Admirals Strauss and Radford, Colonel Goodpaster, H. Hoover, Jr., R. Robertson, H. E. Stassen, and R. R. Bowie; Secretary Wilson and G. D. Morgan. Presents Medal of Freedom to Dr. John von Neumann. Greets foreign student group. To MATS terminal with Mrs. Eisenhower en route to Moultrie, Georgia. To Milestone Plantation in Thomasville, Georgia. Hunts with Secretary Humphrey and General Snyder. Appointment with J. C. Hagerty.

16 Thomasville, Georgia. Hunts quail with Secretary Humphrey and General Snyder. Appointment with J. C. Hagerty. Dinner with Mrs. Eisenhower, Secre-tary and Mrs. Humphrey, Mr. and Mrs. J. H. Whit-ney, W. E. Robinson, and General Snyder. Plays bridge with Secretary Humphrey, J. H. Whitney, and W. E. Robinson.

17 Thomasville, Georgia. To Glen Arven Country Club for golf with J. C. Hagerty, L. H. Magahee, and J. H. Walter. Plays bridge with Secretary Humphrey, J. H. Whitney, and W. E. Robinson. Dinner, followed by more bridge.

18 Thomasville, Georgia. Hunts quail with Secretary Humphrey, R. W. Woodruff, and General Snyder. Dinner with Mrs. Eisenhower, E. Doud, Secretary and Mrs. Humphrey, Mr. and Mrs. J. H. Whitney, W. E. Robinson, and General Snyder. Plays bridge with Secretary Humphrey, J. H. Whitney, and W. E. Robinson.

19 Thomasville, Georgia. Inspects hunting dogs with

Secretary Humphrey. To J. H. Whitney's estate with Mrs. Eisenhower.

20   Thomasville, Georgia. Hunts quail with Secretary Humphrey and General Snyder. Dinner, followed by bridge with Secretary Humphrey, J. H. Whitney, and W. E. Robinson.

21   Thomasville, Georgia. Hunts quail with Secretary Humphrey and General Snyder. Dinner with Mrs. Eisenhower, E. Doud, and Secretary Humphrey.

22   Thomasville, Georgia. To Glen Arven Country Club for golf with J. C. Hagerty, J. H. Whitney, and J. H. Walter. Practices golf at Milestone Plantation. Dinner with Mrs. Eisenhower, E. Doud, Mrs. Humphrey, Mr. and Mrs. J. H. Whitney, and General Snyder. Attends movie.

23   Thomasville, Georgia. To Glen Arven Country Club for golf with J. C. Hagerty, J. H. Whitney, and J. H. Walter. Receives flowers from Mrs. W. B. Cochran, Jr., and Mrs. Pauline Walter. Hunts turkey with Secretary Humphrey and General Snyder. Dinner with Mrs. Eisenhower, E. Doud, Secretary and Mrs. Humphrey, Mr. and Mrs. J. H. Whitney, W. E. Robinson, and General Snyder. Plays bridge with Secretary Humphrey, J. H. Whitney, and W. E. Robinson.

24   Thomasville, Georgia. Hunts quail with Secretary Humphrey and General Snyder (joined by J. H. Whitney). Picnic with Secretary and Mrs. Humphrey, General Snyder, E. Doud, Mr. and Mrs. J. H. Whitney, W. E. Robinson, and Mrs. Eisenhower, followed by quail hunting with Secretary Humphrey, J. H. Whitney, and General Snyder. Listens to St. Thomas Harmony Four. Dinner with Mrs. Eisenhower, E. Doud, Secretary and Mrs. Humphrey, Mr. and Mrs. J. H. Whitney, W. E. Robinson, and General Snyder. Plays bridge with Secretary Humphrey, J. H. Whitney, and W. E. Robinson.

25   Thomasville, Georgia. To home of Rufus Davis (dog keeper) with Secretary Humphrey. Greets cub scouts en route to Moultrie, Georgia. Enplanes with Mrs. Eisenhower for Washington, D.C. Attends birthday party for Secretary Dulles with Mrs. Eisenhower.

26   Washington. Attends services at National Presbyterian Church with Mrs. Eisenhower.

27   Washington. Appointments with Colonel Goodpaster; S. Adams; G. D. Morgan; J. C. Hagerty; National Security Council session. Greets President and Mrs. Giovanni Gronchi (Italy). Afternoon appointments with Generals Taylor, Twining, and Pate, Admirals Burke and Radford, and Colonel Goodpaster; General O'Daniel; Secretary Dulles; Colonel Goodpaster.

28   Washington. Appointments with Colonel Goodpaster; B. M. Shanley; B. N. Harlow, I. J. Martin, and General Persons; S. Adams; Legislative Leaders; Attorney General Brownell, S. Adams, and J. C. Hagerty; President Gronchi, Gaetano Martino (Foreign Affairs Minster, Italy), Ambassador Manlio Brosio (Italy), Mario Luciolli (Chief, Office of International Relations), and Alexandre de Seabra (Interpreter, State Department). Receives bronze statue from President Gronchi. Appointments with S. Adams; President and Mrs. Gronchi. Hosts luncheon in honor of President and Mrs. Gronchi with Mrs. Eisenhower. Afternoon appointments with Vice-President Nixon (off the record); H. Pyle; Secretaries Humphrey and Weeks, I. J. Martin, and General Persons (off the record); Secretary Humphrey and J. C. Hagerty; J. C. Hagerty; S. Adams and J. C. Hagerty; J. C. Hagerty. To swimming pool.

29   Washington. Appointments with J. C. Hagerty and Colonel Goodpaster; G. Hauge; J. C. Hagerty; S. Adams, J. C. Hagerty, G. D. Morgan, F. A. Seaton, H. Pyle, Murray Snyder, and General Persons. News conference, followed by appointments with B. M. Shanley, S. Adams, and J. C. Hagerty; J. C. Hagerty. Prepares speech for television broadcast.

March   1   Washington. Appointments with Colonel Goodpaster; Attorney General Brownell, L. W. Hall, T. E. Stephens, J. C. Hagerty, and General Persons; Dr. M. S. Eisenhower; Secretary Dulles, Ambassador Luce, and Dr. M. S. Eisenhower; President Gronchi, Secretary Dulles, Ambassador Luce, C. B. Elbrick, G. Martino, M. Brosio, M. Luciolli, and A. de-

Seabra. Witnesses swearing-in of W. H. Jackson as Special Assistant to the President. Appointments with G. D. Morgan; J. S. Lay and D. Anderson; D. Anderson; Colonel Goodpaster. Swims. Afternoon appointments with Colonel Goodpaster; Secretary Dulles, R. Robertson, D. Anderson, Ambassador Peaslee, H. E. Stassen, Generals Taylor, Twining, and Pate, and Admirals Burke and Radford (off the record). Witnesses swearing-in of General Curtis as Special Assistant to the President. National Security Council session, followed by appointment with H. E. Stassen.

2   Washington. Appointments with Colonel Goodpaster; Attorney General Brownell and S. Adams (off the record); Secretary Dulles. Cabinet meeting, followed by appointments with Murray Snyder; S. Adams; Attorney General Brownell; A. W. Dulles; A. W. Dulles, Admiral Radford, and Colonel Goodpaster; Colonel Goodpaster; G. D. Morgan; S. Adams; Colonel Goodpaster. To swimming pool. Practices golf on White House grounds. Evening appointment with Colonel Goodpaster.

3   Washington. Appointments with S. Adams and Colonel Goodpaster; S. Adams and B. M. Shanley; Colonel Goodpaster; General Smith. To swimming pool with grandchildren (joined by Mrs. Eisenhower and E. Doud). Lunch with family. To Burning Tree Country Club for golf with Colonel Belshe (accompanied by General Snyder).

4   Washington. Attends services at National Presbyterian Church.

5   Washington. Appointments with S. Adams; General Persons; Colonel Goodpaster; M. Kestnbaum and S. Adams; S. Adams, Daniel W. Turner (former Governor, Iowa), Clifford E. Houck (Head, National Farmers' Organization), and Congressman LeCompte; H. Hoover, Jr., and Colonel Goodpaster (off the record); B. M. Shanley, Murray Snyder, and General John R. Kilpatrick; R. J. Saulnier and G. Hauge; Admiral Strauss and Colonel Goodpaster. To swimming pool. Poses for portrait photographs (off the

record). Afternoon appointment with Colonel Goodpaster.

6   Washington. Appointments with J. A. McCone; I. J. Martin, Colonel Goodpaster, and General Persons; S. Adams; Legislative Leaders. To Statler Hotel with L. W. Hall to address Republican Women's National Conference. Appointment with H. Hoover, Jr., and Colonel Goodpaster. Attends ceremony for signing of Armed Forces Day Proclamation. Appointments with Secretary Wilson, H. Hoover, Jr., and Colonel Goodpaster; Secretary Wilson; Murray Snyder. To swimming pool. Afternoon appointments with S. Adams; G. D. Morgan; B. M. Shanley and Colonel Goodpaster. Practices golf on White House grounds.

7   Washington. Appointments with Colonel Goodpaster; S. Adams; Governor Langlie and S. Adams; S. Adams; Attorney General Brownell and S. Adams; Attorney General Brownell; S. Adams, G. D. Morgan, F. A. Seaton, I. J. Martin, H. Pyle, Colonel Goodpaster, and General Persons. News conference, followed by appointments with Colonel Goodpaster; J. S. Lay and D. Anderson; Lady Astor and son (off the record); G. D. Morgan. Greets 4-H Club winners. To Burning Tree Country Club with W. R. Tkach for golf with Colonel Belshe. Afternoon appointment with S. Adams.

8   Washington. Appointments with Colonel Goodpaster; S. Adams; G. D. Morgan; Admiral Strauss; H. E. Stassen. National Security Council session, followed by appointments with Secretary Humphrey; S. Adams; Secretary McKay; S. Adams; D. Thornton; G. D. Morgan; H. Hoover, Jr.; Colonel Goodpaster; S. Adams and General Persons.

9   Washington. Appointments with W. J. Hopkins; Colonel Goodpaster; S. Adams; Murray Snyder; Secretary Benson. Cabinet meeting, followed by appointments with H. Hoover, Jr.; General Clark; S. Adams; Secretary Folsom and Devereaux Josephs; Colonel Goodpaster. To swimming pool. Afternoon appointments with Secretary Mitchell; D. Anderson; General Persons; S. Adams and Colonel Goodpaster. Practices golf on White House grounds. Evening appointment with General Persons.

10 Washington. Appointments with General Persons; Colonel Stack; Karl Betts. To Burning Tree Country Club with J. E. McClure (accompanied by General Snyder).

11 Washington. Attends services at National Presbyterian Church with Mrs. Eisenhower.

12 Washington. Appointments with Colonel Goodpaster; Commander Beach; B. M. Shanley; A. F. Burns and G. Hauge; H. Hoover, Jr., and Colonel Goodpaster; B. M. Shanley and Murray Snyder. Receives White House Photographers Association contest winners (off the record). To swimming pool. Afternoon appointments with Generals Michaelis and Persons; Colonel Goodpaster; H. Butcher (off the record); L. W. Hall; General Norstad; L. W. Hall, H. Pyle, and Murray Snyder; General Alfred D. Starbird (Atomic Energy Commission) and Colonel Goodpaster; H. Hoover, Jr., and R. B. Anderson (off the record).

13 Washington. Appointments with W. J. Hopkins; Colonel Goodpaster; G. D. Morgan, B. N. Harlow, I. J. Martin, and General Persons; Legislative Leaders; Vice-President Nixon; Colonel Goodpaster. To swimming pool. Afternoon appointments with Secretary Wilson, Admiral Radford, and Colonel Goodpaster; G. D. Morgan; F. A. Seaton; Colonel Goodpaster. To Playhouse Theater for film premiere of *Richard III* sponsored by Ambassador and Lady Makins with Mrs. Eisenhower, E. Doud, Major and Mrs. J. S. D. Eisenhower, and C. H. Tompkins.

14 Washington. Appointments with B. M. Shanley; W. H. Jackson; G. D. Morgan, H. Pyle, F. A. Seaton, Murray Snyder, I. J. Martin, B. N. Harlow, Colonel Goodpaster, and General Persons. News conference, followed by appointments with Colonel Goodpaster; K. McCann; Colonel Goodpaster; N. A. Rockefeller. Greets Prime Minister John A. Costello (Ireland). Hosts luncheon in honor of Prime Minister Costello. Afternoon appointments with General Persons; A. Nielsen (off the record); L. W. Hall; G. D. Morgan and Murray Snyder. Practices golf on White House grounds.

15   Washington. Accompanied to office by A. Nielsen. Appointments with W. J. Hopkins; Colonel Goodpaster; B. M. Shanley; Colonel Goodpaster; D. Anderson (joined by G. D. Morgan, I. J. Martin, and General Persons); Colonels Draper and Goodpaster, and B. M. Shanley; General Persons; John Cowles (President, *Minneapolis Star and Tribune*) (off the record); R. T. B. Stevens; Governor Herter (off the record). Receives 1956 Easter Seal Child, Clara Jo Proudfoot. Appointments with C. L. Burgess, Murray Snyder, and Colonel Goodpaster; Governor Foss and B. M. Shanley; Colonel Schulz. Swims. Afternoon appointments with B. M. Shanley; Colonel Goodpaster; R. Biggers, L. L. Colbert, and Thomas Morrow (off the record); Admirals Radford and Burke, Generals Taylor, Twining, and Pate, and Colonel Goodpaster; M. M. Rabb; Colonel Goodpaster; USO representatives Harvey S. Firestone, Emil Schram, and John L. Sullivan. Greets USO National Council. To Mayflower Hotel with A. Nielsen and General Gruenther for National Business Advisory Council dinner.

16   Washington. Off-the-record breakfast with Ambassador Lodge. Receives bowl of shamrocks from Prime Minister Costello. Sub-cabinet meeting, followed by appointments with H. Hoover, Jr., and Colonel Goodpaster; Colonel Goodpaster; General Persons; G. D. Morgan; W. J. Hopkins. Swims. To Eisenhower farm in Gettysburg, Pennsylvania, with General Gruenther and W. E. Robinson.

17   Gettysburg, Pennsylvania. Tours grounds with Generals Gruenther, Snyder, and Nevins, and G. E. Allen.

18   Gettysburg, Pennsylvania. Tours farm with Mr. and Mrs. A. A. Ryan, G. E. Allen, and General Nevins.

19   Gettysburg, Pennsylvania. Returns to Washington, D.C., with W. E. Robinson, G. E. Allen, and General Gruenther. Appointments with Colonel Schulz; H. Pyle. To swimming pool. Afternoon appointments with J. C. Hagerty; H. Hoover, Jr.; General Bragdon and G. Hauge; S. Adams and G. D. Morgan; G. Hauge; Colonel Goodpaster. Swims.

20   Washington. Appointments with W. J. Hopkins;
      A. C. Whitman; B. N. Harlow, I. J. Martin, and
      General Persons; Legislative Leaders; Vice-President
      Nixon; M. Kestnbaum and S. Adams; J. C. Hagerty
      (off the record); Reverend B. Graham. To swimming
      pool. Lunch with H. Hoover, Jr., and J. J. McCloy.
      Afternoon appointments with J. Bishop and J. C.
      Hagerty; Budget Director Hughes and P. F. Brun-
      dage; Colonel Goodpaster; Attorney General Brown-
      ell and S. Adams. Practices golf on White House
      grounds, followed by appointment with A. C. Whit-
      man.

21   Washington. Appointments with W. J. Hopkins;
      General Persons and Colonel Goodpaster; W. H.
      Jackson, H. Hoover, Jr., Admiral Strauss, and Colo-
      nel Goodpaster; S. Adams, J. C. Hagerty, F. A. Seat-
      on, G. Hauge, G. D. Morgan, I. J. Martin, Murray
      Snyder, and Colonel Goodpaster. News conference,
      followed by off-the-record swearing-in of Peter
      Grimm as Director, United States Operations Mis-
      sion to Italy. Appointments with S. Adams and J. C.
      Hagerty; S. Adams; J. C. Hagerty. To swimming
      pool. Returns to office with B. T. Leithead and son.
      Afternoon appointments with I. J. Martin; J. Durfee
      and S. Adams; Colonel Goodpaster; B. M. Shanley;
      Colonel Goodpaster. Practices golf on White House
      grounds. Evening appointment with H. Hoover, Jr.,
      and Secretary Dulles.

22   Washington. Appointments with General Persons;
      Secretary Dulles and B. M. Shanley; bipartisan legis-
      lative meeting; J. S. Lay and Secretary Dulles; Na-
      tional Security Council session; Colonel Goodpaster
      and A. C. Whitman. Swims. Afternoon appoint-
      ments with S. Adams; H. Hoover, Jr., Dana Latham,
      and S. Adams; B. M. Shanley. Practices golf on
      White House grounds, followed by off-the-record ap-
      pointment with D. J. McDonald and Secretaries
      Humphrey and Mitchell.

23   Washington. Appointments with W. J. Hopkins;
      B. M. Shanley; Colonel Goodpaster; S. Adams; Sec-
      retary Weeks and J. C. Hagerty. Cabinet meeting,
      followed by appointments with General Collins;
      Cabinet meeting; V. E. Peterson, J. S. Lay, and

Ralph E. Spear (Assistant Administrator, Planning, FCDA). To swimming pool. To Burning Tree Country Club for golf with J. E. McClure. Evening appointments with Colonel Goodpaster; Attorney General Brownell, S. Adams, G. D. Morgan, and M. M. Rabb; Attorney General Brownell; Senator George.

24 Washington. Appointments with General Persons; I. J. Martin; H. Hoover, Jr., and S. Adams; Secretary Wilson, H. Hoover, Jr., A. W. Dulles, Secretary Quarles, Admiral Radford, General Twining, and Colonel Goodpaster; Secretary Wilson, H. Hoover, Jr., Admiral Radford, and Colonel Goodpaster; Attorney General Brownell; J. C. Hagerty; G. D. Morgan and Colonel Goodpaster; Colonel Goodpaster. To swimming pool.

25 Washington. To Union Station en route to White Sulphur Springs, West Virginia.

26 White Sulphur Springs, West Virginia. To Greenbrier Hotel with General Snyder and V. Purse. To Greenbrier Golf Course for golf with B. M. Shanley, J. C. Hagerty, and S. Snead. Lunch with B. M. Shanley, J. C. Hagerty, and General Snyder. Appointment with Secretary Dulles, L. T. Merchant, H. F. Holland, and J. C. Hagerty (joined by B. M. Shanley). Greets Prime Minister St. Laurent and President Ruiz Cortines. Hosts dinner in honor of Prime Minister St. Laurent and President Ruiz Cortines.

27 White Sulphur Springs, West Virginia. Breakfast with B. M. Shanley, J. C. Hagerty, Walter J. Tuohy, Cyrus Eaton, E. Truman Wright, Colonels Schulz, Draper, and Walters, Commander Beach, Dr. M. S. Eisenhower, and General Snyder. Appointment with Secretary Dulles. Poses for photographs with Prime Minister St. Laurent and President Ruiz Cortines. Attends Canadian-Mexican-American talks. Lunch with Canadian and Mexican officials. Appointment with President Ruiz Cortines, Minister Luis Padillo Nervo (Mexico), Ambassador Tello, Secretary Dulles, H. F. Holland, J. F. Simmons, and Ambassador White. To Greenbrier Golf Course for golf with B. M. Shanley, S. Snead, and G. Nixon. Hosts dinner

in honor of Prime Minister St. Laurent and President Ruiz Cortines.

28   White Sulphur Springs, West Virginia. Appointments with Secretary Dulles; Ambassador Stuart; L. B. Pearson. Poses for photographs with Canadian and Mexican delegations. Appointment with W. J. Tuohy and E. T. Wright. Returns to Washington, D.C. Afternoon appointments with Dr. M. S. Eisenhower; B. M. Shanley; J. C. Hagerty; Colonel Goodpaster; Secretary Dulles, H. Hoover, Jr., G. E. Allen, W. M. Rountree, Secretary Wilson, R. Robertson, Admiral Radford, and Colonel Goodpaster (off the record).

29   Washington. Appointments with B. M. Shanley and Colonel Goodpaster; W. J. Hopkins; A. C. Whitman; Senators Knowland, Bridges, Saltonstall, Bricker, and Dirksen, General Persons, Secretary Dulles, Attorney General Brownell, G. D. Morgan, and I. J. Martin; Secretary Dulles; J. A. McCone; J. S. Lay, Admiral Radford, and General Gerald C. Thomas. Receives cherry trees from Cherry Blossom Festival Committee. Swims. Afternoon appointments with R. Robertson, W. J. McNeil, Budget Director Hughes, P. F. Brundage, R. Reid, S. Adams, General Persons, and Admiral Radford; B. M. Baruch; J. C. Hagerty; G. D. Morgan; A. C. Whitman; J. Budinger.

30   Washington. Appointments with J. C. Hagerty; S. Adams, J. C. Hagerty, and Colonel Goodpaster; Budget Director Hughes; A. C. Whitman and General Snyder; General Snyder; M. M. Rabb; W. J. Hopkins and Colonel Goodpaster; Colonel Goodpaster; General Persons. Swims. Attends Good Friday services at National Presbyterian Church with Mrs. Eisenhower. Afternoon appointments with J. C. Hagerty; Admirals Radford and Burke, Generals Twining and Taylor, and Colonel Goodpaster (off the record); dentist. Practices golf on White House grounds. Evening appointment with Colonel Goodpaster.

31   Washington. Appointments with S. Adams and Colonel Goodpaster; Colonel Goodpaster. Receives members of President's Commission on Veterans'

Pensions. Appointments with General Bradley; General Persons; W. J. Hopkins; General Persons and Senator Malone; Governor Gordon and Secretary McKay; General Snyder, Major J. S. D. Eisenhower, and Colonel Goodpaster; G. D. Morgan. To Burning Tree Country Club for golf with Major J. S. D. Eisenhower and J. E. McClure. Greets guests at D. D. Eisenhower II's birthday party.

April 1 Washington. Attends Easter services at National Presbyterian Church with Mrs. Eisenhower. Poses for photographs with Roy Rogers and Dale Evans; Mrs. Eisenhower and family.

2 Washington. Appointment with General Valluy, Admiral Radford, and Colonel Walters. Witnesses swearing-in of P. F. Brundage as Director, Bureau of the Budget. Appointments with J. C. Hagerty; G. Hauge. Greets annual Easter Egg Roll guests with Mrs. Eisenhower. Swims. To Army-Navy Club with General Bragdon for luncheon with former West Point classmates. Afternoon appointments with General Taylor and Colonel Goodpaster; G. D. Morgan; R. Reed; General Cutler; B. M. Shanley; K. McCann; S. Adams.

3 Washington. Appointments with S. Adams; G. Hauge; J. C. Hagerty; General Caffey and Colonel Goodpaster; William F. Dickson, General Whiteley, Admiral Radford, and Colonel Goodpaster; General Persons. To District Red Cross Building with B. M. Shanley and J. C. Hagerty. Addresses 12th annual Advertising Council conference. Swims. Afternoon appointments with J. C. Folger, T. B. McCabe, and B. M. Shanley; L. W. Hall; S. Adams; A. R. Jones, Budget Director Brundage, and F. A. Seaton; S. Adams; J. C. Hagerty; Secretary Humphrey, Budget Director Brundage, S. Adams, and General Persons; Secretary Humphrey, Attorney General Brownell, H. Hoover, Jr., R. B. Anderson, and A. S. Flemming (off the record).

4 Washington. Appointments with Colonel Goodpaster; S. Adams and L. Wright (off the record); J. S. Lay; General Persons; S. Adams, J. C. Hagerty, F. A. Seaton, General Persons, and Colonel Goodpaster. News conference. Receives American Cancer Society

Sword of Hope from Colonel Fitzgerald. Appointments with Governor Kohler; General Persons (joined by S. Adams); Colonel Goodpaster. To Burning Tree Country Club for golf with J. Black. Evening appointment with Senators Saltonstall and Duff, and General Persons.

5 Washington. Appointments with Colonel Goodpaster; B. M. Shanley, R. Rizley; Secretary Humphrey and Budget Director Brundage; S. Adams; J. C. Hagerty. National Security Council session, followed by appointments with Secretaries Humphrey and Wilson, R. Robertson, Budget Director Brundage, Admiral Radford, and Colonel Goodpaster; Secretaries Wilson, Humphrey, Quarles, and Thomas, C. Finucane, R. Robertson, Budget Director Brundage, Generals Persons, Pate, and Twining, and Admirals Radford and Burke; S. Adams; General Persons. To swimming pool with Dr. M. S. Eisenhower. Afternoon appointments with Colonels Inez Haynes (Chief, Army Nurse Corps) and E. P. Turner; A. F. Burns; Attorney General Brownell; S. Adams, G. Hauge, F. A. Seaton, Dr. M. S. Eisenhower, and General Persons; T. E. Stephens (off the record). Practices golf on White House grounds.

6 Washington. Appointments with W. J. Hopkins; Colonel Goodpaster; Secretary Dulles; Cabinet meeting. Poses for photographs with Secretary McKay. Presents Young American Medal for Bravery to Patricia A. Strickland. Appointment with H. C. Hunt, N. McElroy, B. M. Shanley, and J. C. Hagerty. Receives report from White House Conference on Education Committee, followed by appointments with O. C. Hobby; Colonel Goodpaster. To swimming pool. Afternoon appointments with Colonel Goodpaster; S. Adams; Secretary Benson; Ambassador Masayuki Tani (Japan); D. Anderson; General Persons (joined by Dr. M. S. Eisenhower); Dr. M. S. Eisenhower (joined by J. C. Hagerty); J. W. Barba; Colonel Goodpaster; Dr. M. S. Eisenhower and A. C. Whitman.

7 Washington. Appointments with S. Adams and B. M. Shanley; W. J. Hopkins; J. S. Lay; Colonel Goodpaster. Receives American League baseball pass from Calvin Griffith. Appointments with Am-

bassador George Arthur Padmore (Liberia); S. Adams; Secretary Benson, T. D. Morse, S. Adams, G. Hauge, and General Persons; R. R. Bowie, K. McCann, and Dr. M. S. Eisenhower; S. Adams, K. McCann, and Governor Aronson. To swimming pool. Motors with Dr. M. S. Eisenhower to Mrs. G. G. Moore's farm in Hillsboro, Virginia. Returns to Washington, D.C.

8   Washington. [Page missing.]

9   Washington. Appointments with Colonel Goodpaster; A. C. Whitman; General Persons; Legislative Leaders; Vice-President Nixon; S. Adams; J. W. Barba; L. W. Hall; Secretary Dulles. To MATS terminal with Mrs. Eisenhower and E. Doud en route to Augusta, Georgia. Golf with E. Dudley, L. K. Firestone, and E. D. Slater.

10   Augusta, Georgia. To practice tee, then golf with J. H. Whitney, W. A. Jones, and E. Dudley.

11   Augusta, Georgia. Signs S. 500.

12   Augusta, Georgia. To practice tee, then pro shop. Visits C. Roberts. Golf with E. Dudley, F. F. Gosden, and Major J. S. D. Eisenhower. Plays catch with D. D. Eisenhower II. Watches D. D. Eisenhower II practice golf.

13   Augusta, Georgia. To office, pro shop, and practice tee. Golf with S. S. Larmon, E. Dudley, and Major J. S. D. Eisenhower. Practice, followed by golf with E. Dudley, G. Stout, and Major J. S. D. Eisenhower. Fishes at 15th hole.

14   Augusta, Georgia. Appointments with J. C. Hagerty and F. A. Seaton; Secretary Benson, T. D. Morse, D. Paarlberg, F. A. Seaton, K. McCann, G. Hauge, and J. C. Hagerty. To practice tee. Golf with F. Willard, E. Dudley, and Major J. S. D. Eisenhower.

15   Augusta, Georgia. Attends services at Reid Memorial Church with Mrs. Eisenhower and Major J. S. D. Eisenhower. Golf with R. W. Woodruff, E. Dudley, and Major J. S. D. Eisenhower. To Bush Field en route to Washington, D.C.

16   Washington. Appointments with Governors Hoegh, Hall, and Foss; Secretary Benson; H. D. Newsom

and S. Adams. Prepares speech. To Statler Hotel with Dr. M. S. Eisenhower to visit E. N. Eisenhower. Delivers speech to nation.

17   Washington. Appointments with J. C. Hagerty; Legislative Leaders; Dr. M. S. Eisenhower; S. Adams. Throws out first ball of season at Griffith Stadium. To Sheraton-Park Hotel to address RNC dinner.

18   Washington. Appointments with Colonel Goodpaster; S. Adams; J. S. Lay; Admiral Radford and Colonel Goodpaster; Foreign Minister and Mrs. Alberto Martin Artajo (Spain), Ambassador and Mrs. de Areilza, Secretary Dulles, L. T. Merchant, Ambassador and Mrs. Lodge, and J. F. Simmons; American Legion representatives; W. J. Hopkins; Colonel Goodpaster; W. J. Hopkins; G. Hauge; G. D. Morgan; A. S. Flemming, F. A. Seaton, General Paul, and Colonel Goodpaster; Budget Director Brundage. Practices golf on White House grounds.

19   Washington. Appointments with B. M. Shanley; S. Adams; General Persons; F. A. Seaton; W. H. Jackson; H. E. Capehart, S. Adams, and General Persons; Colonel Goodpaster; J. Wadsworth. Receives Commission on Veterans' Pensions. To swimming pool. Attends civil defense meeting, followed by afternoon appointment with B. M. Shanley; H. Hoover, Jr., and Secretary Dulles; M. A. Hutcheson, M. C. Raddock (United Brotherhood of Carpenters and Joiners of America), and Secretary Mitchell. Practices golf on White House grounds.

20   Washington. Appointments with W. J. Hopkins; H. Pyle; Colonel Goodpaster; Ambassador Bohlen; S. Adams; Ambassador Lodge; Cabinet meeting; Secretary Dulles, R. R. Bowie, and K. McCann. Swims. Afternoon appointments with J. C. Hagerty; A. F. Burns and G. Hauge; F. J. Donohue, W. Ruschmeyer, and Colonel Schulz (off the record); P. G. Hoffman (off the record); K. McCann. Practices golf on White House grounds.

21   Washington. Appointments with S. Adams and G. D. Morgan; A. C. Whitman; Colonel Goodpaster; R. Montgomery, R. R. Bowie, and K. McCann (off the record); Secretary Benson, G. D. Morgan, G. Hauge, and I. J. Martin. Departs for golf at Burn-

ing Tree Country Club with General Bradley, Major J. S. D. Eisenhower, and Colonel Wyman. To Statler Hotel with Mrs. Eisenhower for televised speech at annual banquet of the American Society of Newspaper Editors. Following television address, makes off-the-record remarks to banquet guests.

22 Washington. [Page missing.]

23 Washington. Appointments with B. M. Shanley; G. D. Morgan; Colonel Goodpaster; H. W. Dodds, L. Carmichael, Budget Director Brundage, S. Adams, and H. Pyle; S. Adams; B. M. Shanley and M. J. McCaffree; R. B. Anderson. Receives American Council on NATO. Appointments with B. M. Shanley and Colonel Draper; A. Nielsen. Receives honorary membership in American Society of Mechanical Engineers. To swimming pool. Afternoon appointments with Colonel Goodpaster; S. Adams; C. L. Burgess, Walter K. Scott (International Cooperation Administration), Robert D. Francis (Assistant Secretary of Defense), S. Adams, General Persons, and Colonel Goodpaster to discuss staff organization; B. M. Shanley, J. C. Hagerty, and Colonel Draper; A. W. Dulles and Colonel Goodpaster; J. C. Hagerty; S. Adams and Colonel Draper. Practices golf on White House grounds. To Eisenhower farm in Gettysburg, Pennsylvania, with J. C. Hagerty and General Snyder.

24 Gettysburg, Pennsylvania. To Cumberland Township Election House with General Snyder to vote. Returns to Washington, D.C. Appointments with S. Adams and General Persons; Legislative Leaders; J. A. Mora (Secretary General, OAS) and H. F. Holland (joined by H. Mitchell); G. Hauge; W. F. Libby and Colonel Goodpaster; J. B. Hollister and General Persons. Receives 100 pound halibut from Neston Hill, accompanied by S. Adams and Congressman Nicholson. To swimming pool. Afternoon appointments with Vice-President Nixon; Vice-President Nixon, Secretary Dulles, J. B. Hollister, H. Hoover, Jr., Budget Director Brundage, J. M. Dodge, William Finan, and General Persons; Postmaster General Summerfield. Evening off-the-record appointment with J. L. Hamon, L. F. McCollum, and R. B. Anderson.

25 Washington. Appointments with K. McCann; Colonel Goodpaster; W. J. Hopkins; J. S. Lay and J. M. Dodge; J. S. Lay; Secretary Wilson and Colonel Goodpaster; J. C. Hagerty, G. D. Morgan, H. Pyle, I. J. Martin, G. Hauge, Murray Snyder, and General Persons. News conference, followed by appointment with Attorney General Brownell. To Burning Tree Country Club with W. R. Tkach for golf with F. Akers, Congressman Halleck, and Colonel Belshe.

26 Washington. Appointments with Colonel Goodpaster; General Persons; Ambassador White. National Security Council session, followed by appointments with Rabbi Silver and Secretary Dulles; B. N. Harlow and General Sarnoff; S. H. High (off the record); Budget Director Brundage and Colonel Goodpaster; Vice-President Nixon (off the record). Practices golf on White House grounds.

27 Washington. Makes traffic safety recording. Appointments with B. M. Shanley; General Persons; Ambassador Lodge; Secretary Wilson. Cabinet meeting, followed by appointments with Secretary Folsom; J. S. Lay; G. D. Morgan; Colonel Goodpaster; M. Katz. Receives Committee on Education Beyond High School. Departs with W. R. Tkach for Eisenhower farm in Gettysburg, Pennsylvania. To F. Akers's estate in Thurmont, Maryland, with W. R. Tkach for fishing.

28 Gettysburg, Pennsylvania. Receives plaque and cherry tree from National Red Cherry Institute. To Gettysburg Country Club for golf with G. E. Allen and General Nevins. Tours farm with Generals Caffey and Nevins, and G. E. Allen.

29 Gettysburg, Pennsylvania. Attends services at Gettysburg Presbyterian Church with Mrs. Eisenhower.

30 Gettysburg, Pennsylvania. Returns to Washington, D.C. Appointments with J. C. Hagerty; General Persons; Colonel Goodpaster. Signs H. R. 9428. Appointments with G. D. Morgan; B. M. Shanley and K. McCann; G. D. Morgan; Secretaries Dulles and Mitchell, H. Phleger, Attorney General Brownell, and G. D. Morgan; Secretary Dulles, Attorney General Brownell, H. Phleger, G. D. Morgan, F. A. Seaton, and General Persons; Attorney General Brown-

ell; Ambassador Krekeler; Ambassador Silviu Brucan (Rumania). Practices golf on White House grounds. Evening appointment with Secretary Dulles, Congressmen Richards and Chiperfield, Senators George and H. A. Smith, and General Persons.

May   1   Washington. Appointments with B. M. Shanley; W. J. Hopkins; A. C. Whitman; General Persons; A. C. Whitman; B. M. Shanley; Colonel Goodpaster; Legislative Leaders; Secretary Dulles and J. C. Hagerty; L. W. Hall. To Burning Tree Country Club with General Snyder and G. E. Allen for golf with G. E. Allen and Colonel Belshe.

2   Washington. Appointments with General Persons; B. M. Shanley, J. C. Hagerty, and General Persons; A. F. Burns and K. McCann; Vice-President João Belchoir Goulart (Brazil), Ambassador Muñiz, Senator João Lima Teixeira (Bahia, Brazil), Governor Roberto Silveira (Rio de Janeiro, Brazil), João Pinheiro (Economic Officer, Brazilian Foreign Office), Geraldo Nascimiento e Silva (interpreter), H. Hoover, Jr., H. F. Holland, J. F. Simmons, and A. de Seabra; H. Hoover, Jr., and Colonel Goodpaster; G. D. Morgan; C. G. Parker and S. Adams; Lord Mayor and Mrs. Cuthbert Akroyd (London), Sheriff and Mrs. Whaley-Cohen (London), W. T. Boston (Sword bearer), Chief Commoner C. F. Glenny, and Robert E. McLaughlin (President, D.C. Board of Commissioners). Attends memorial service for Senator Barkley at Foundry Methodist Church. Appointments with Colonel Goodpaster; General Persons; F. A. Seaton; E. R. Black and Senator Ferguson; L. M. Pexton; W. R. Hearst and J. C. Hagerty; S. Adams; D. Anderson; Colonel Goodpaster.

3   Washington. Appointments with A. F. Burns and G. Hauge; B. M. Shanley, Murray Snyder, Governor Johnson, and Mayor Nicholson. National Security Council session, followed by appointments with General W. Anders and Captain Eugene Lubelirski; Attorney General Brownell and S. Adams; Colonel Goodpaster; W. M. Canaday. To Burning Tree Country Club for golf with A. F. Kroeger and Colonel Belshe. Evening appointment with G. D. Morgan.

4   Washington. Appointments with Colonel Goodpaster; B. M. Shanley; Admiral Strauss; G. Hauge; Public Advisors to Tariff negotiations, Geneva; Colonel Goodpaster; G. Hauge and R. McPhee; S. Adams, J. C. Hagerty, G. D. Morgan, H. Hoover, Jr., F. A. Seaton, G. Hauge, H. Pyle, Murray Snyder, I. J. Martin, and Colonel Goodpaster. News conference, followed by appointments with M. Pusey, J. C. Hagerty, and Murray Snyder; E. T. Weir; A. Nelson and daughter, and S. Adams; L. W. Douglas, S. Adams and G. D. Morgan; Colonel Goodpaster. To Eisenhower farm in Gettysburg, Pennsylvania, with D. D. Eisenhower II and B. A. Eisenhower. To putting green. Walks around main house with D. D. Eisenhower II, B. A. Eisenhower, and Mrs. Eisenhower.

5   Gettysburg, Pennsylvania. To Gettysburg Country Club for golf with G. E. Allen and General Nevins. To F. Akers's estate in Thurmont, Maryland, with G. E. Allen and General Snyder for fishing. Returns to Gettysburg, Pennsylvania. Fishing in duck pond.

6   Gettysburg, Pennsylvania. Attends services at Christ Chapel at Gettysburg College with Mrs. Eisenhower. Tours farm and inspects cattle with H. R. Purdy, Irving Feaster, Generals Snyder and Nevins, and G. E. Allen. To G. E. Allen's farm with touring group.

7   Gettysburg, Pennsylvania. Tours grounds with General Nevins. Visits with General and Mrs. Snyder. Appointment with L. E. Berkey. Returns to Washington, D.C., with Mrs. Eisenhower. Afternoon appointments with Colonel Goodpaster; H. Hoover, Jr., and Secretary Dulles; S. Adams and J. C. Hagerty; A. W. Dulles, Herbert Scoville (Assistant Director, Scientific Intelligence, CIA), and Colonel Goodpaster; Colonel Goodpaster.

8   Washington. Appointments with J. C. Hagerty; W. J. Hopkins; S. Adams, G. D. Morgan, B. N. Harlow, and I. J. Martin; Legislative Leaders; J. C. Hagerty; Ambassador Pinkerton; D. Anderson; Secretary Benson; General Cutler and D. Anderson; H. E. Stassen; General Paul; Postmaster General Summerfield; Ambassador Lawson; J. C. Hagerty. Practices golf on

White House grounds. Evening off-the-record appointment with P. G. Hoffman.

9   Washington. Appointments with S. Adams; Colonel Goodpaster; S. Adams and J. C. Hagerty; Ambassador Wadsworth. Receives National Association of Military Chaplains, followed by appointments with Secretary Dulles and R. C. Hill (joined by S. Adams); S. Adams, G. D. Morgan, G. Hauge, J. C. Hagerty, F. A. Seaton, I. J. Martin, B. N. Harlow, Murray Snyder, and Colonel Goodpaster. News conference, followed by appointments with S. P. Skouras; S. Adams; G. D. Morgan. To Burning Tree Country Club for golf with Congressmen Arends and Halleck, and Colonel Belshe. Evening appointments with Claude Maer and family (off the record); S. Adams and B. M. Shanley. Dinner with General and Mrs. Clyde Beck and Mrs. Eisenhower.

10   Washington. Accompanied to office by Colonel Schulz. Appointments with B. M. Shanley; Secretary Mitchell; R. J. Gray and Secretary Mitchell; B. M. Shanley and Colonel Goodpaster; A. T. Waterman, Budget Director Brundage, and L. A. Minnich; W. J. Hopkins; G. D. Morgan; Secretary Wilson. National Security Council session. Receives medallion commemorating St. Lawrence Seaway Act. Appointments with Senator Wiley; S. Adams. To swimming pool. Poses for photographs in office. Afternoon appointments with B. N. Harlow; G. D. Morgan; Colonel Goodpaster; Congressman Vorys and B. N. Harlow (off the record); B. M. Shanley and Colonel Goodpaster; G. D. Morgan. Practices golf on White House grounds. To Walter Reed Hospital with J. C. Hagerty for two days of extensive examinations.

11   Washington. After examination and tests, visits children's wards; General Frank S. Cochieu; General Carter B. Magruder; C. P. Romulo.

12   Washington. After examination and tests, to Burning Tree Country Club for golf with J. E. McClure, Congressman Halleck, and Colonel Belshe. Returns to White House. To Statler Hotel for Gridiron Club Dinner.

13   Washington. To MATS terminal with Dr. M. S.

Eisenhower en route to Eisenhower farm in Gettysburg, Pennsylvania. Inspects grounds with Dr. M. S. Eisenhower; Colonel and Mrs. G. G. Moore, and Mrs. Eisenhower. To Neuman farm with Colonel and Mrs. G. G. Moore and Mrs. Eisenhower. Tours fields with J. Bernard West (Chief Usher). Tours surrounding farms with W. Byars, G. E. Allen, and General Nevins.

14   Gettysburg, Pennsylvania. Returns to Washington, D.C., with W. R. Tkach. Appointments with G. D. Morgan; Colonel Goodpaster; K. McCann; Secretary Mitchell; Budget Director Brundage; Mayor Christopher and S. Adams; Edwin Plowden (Head, British Atomic Energy Authority), J. E. Coulson, and Admiral Strauss; Colonel Goodpaster; Governor Langlie and S. Adams. To Constitution Hall with Governor Langlie and J. C. Hagerty. Addresses attendees of the Conference on Occupational Safety. Appointments with J. C. Hagerty; S. Adams; G. D. Birla (Birla Brothers, Ltd., India) and S. Adams; J. R. Killian, James B. Fisk (Vice-President, Bell Telephone Laboratories), A. S. Flemming, and Colonel Goodpaster; O. M. Reid; Admiral Radford and Colonel Goodpaster; Ambassador Holmes and F. A. Seaton; Attorney General Brownell; J. C. Hagerty; Secretary Dulles; Senator George and Secretary Dulles.

15   Washington. Appointments with Secretary Mitchell, S. Adams, G. D. Morgan, I. J. Martin, and Frederick H. Mueller (Assistant Secretary of Commerce); S. Adams, G. D. Morgan, B. N. Harlow, and I. J. Martin; S. Adams and B. N. Harlow; G. D. Morgan; W. J. Hopkins; Legislative Leaders; AMVETS leaders; H. E. Stassen; Budget Director Brundage; E. Johnston; S. Adams and Colonel Goodpaster; S. Adams. Hosts luncheon for former West Point classmates. To Burning Tree Country Club for golf with G. Bunker, R. Learned, and Colonel Belshe.

16   Washington. Appointments with R. Montgomery; Colonel Goodpaster; A. C. Whitman; S. Adams; T. C. Streibert, A. M. Washburn, Conger Reynolds (Office of Private Enterprise Cooperation), and J. C. Hagerty. Cabinet meeting, followed by appointments with K. McCann; J. S. Lay and D. Anderson; Colo-

nel Goodpaster. Hosts luncheon in honor of President Ahmed Sukarno (Indonesia). Makes remarks on closed-circuit television regarding dedication of General Motors' technical center. Afternoon appointments with General Curtis; Justus B. L. Lawrence. Practices golf on White House grounds.

17 Washington. Appointments with W. J. Hopkins; S. Adams; B. M. Shanley; B. M. Shanley, Colonel Louis F. Lucas (Deputy Executive Director, NRA), and General Parks. National Security Council session, followed by appointments with Attorney General Brownell and S. Adams; B. M. Shanley; A. W. Dulles; B. M. Shanley; K. McCann and A. C. Whitman; S. Adams and B. N. Harlow. Practices golf on White House grounds. To Statler Hotel with Mrs. Eisenhower for Women's National Press Club annual dinner.

18 Washington. Appointments with S. Adams and B. N. Harlow; Colonel Goodpaster; S. Adams and B. N. Harlow; Congressman Martin; B. N. Harlow; J. C. Hagerty and Colonel Goodpaster; Colonels Randall and Goodpaster, and Secretary Wilson (joined by S. Adams and I. J. Martin); General Bragdon and Colonel Goodpaster. Greets foreign Presbyterian church leaders. Appointments with G. D. Morgan; A. F. Burns; G. D. Morgan; B. M. Shanley and Colonel Goodpaster. To Burning Tree Country Club for golf with J. E. McClure. To Mayflower Hotel with Mrs. Eisenhower for dinner in their honor given by President Sukarno.

19 Washington. Appointments with S. Adams, F. A. Seaton, and General Bragdon; S. Adams; Admirals Radford and Stump; B. M. Shanley and Commander Beach; G. D. Morgan; S. Adams. To Burning Tree Country Club for golf with J. E. McClure, Major J. S. D. Eisenhower, and Colonel Belshe.

20 Washington. Attends services at National Presbyterian Church with Mrs. Eisenhower, D. D. Eisenhower II, B. A. Eisenhower, and S. E. Eisenhower.

21 Washington. Appointments with K. McCann; D. Anderson and Colonel Goodpaster; D. Anderson; Ambassador Muntasser; Ambassador Lyon; Captain Margaret Williams (U.S. Army Nurses Corps);

S. Adams; Colonel Goodpaster; Attorney General Brownell. Receives hospitalized veterans with Mrs. Eisenhower.

22 Washington. Accompanied to office by General Gruenther. Appointments with W. J. Hopkins; S. Adams, P. Young, I. J. Martin, and General Persons; B. M. Shanley and Senator Flanders; Secretary Weeks; A. C. Whitman; Legislative Leaders; Hugh Gaitskell (Leader, British Labor Party), Ambassador Makins, and C. Burke Elbrick (Acting Assistant Secretary, State Department); Secretary Wilson, F. A. Seaton, Colonel Randall, Admiral Radford, and General Persons; Murray Snyder; G. D. Morgan. To swimming pool with A. Nielsen. Returns to office with Mrs. W. A. Jones. Afternoon appointments with S. Adams; G. D. Morgan; W. J. Hopkins; Dr. M. S. Eisenhower. Practices golf on White House grounds.

23 Washington. Accompanied to office by General Gruenther. Receives tickets for annual Republican-Democratic baseball game. Appointments with Colonel Goodpaster; William P. Goldman; Budget Director Brundage; S. Adams, G. D. Morgan, G. Hauge, B. N. Harlow, I. J. Martin, F. A. Seaton, Murray Snyder, General Persons, and Colonel Goodpaster. News conference, followed by appointments with Secretary Weeks; B. M. Shanley. Hosts luncheon for congressional delegation and former congressmen. To Burning Tree Country Club for golf with General Curtis and Colonel Belshe (joined by C. Roberts).

24 Washington. Appointments with Colonel Goodpaster (joined by B. M. Shanley); A. C. Whitman; General Persons. Presents American Legion's Robert L. Hague Maritime Award for 1956 to Senator Butler. Appointments with W. H. Jackson; S. Adams; J. S. Lay and D. Anderson; General Taylor and Admiral Radford (off the record); Congressman Hillings. Receives chickens from 1956 Pennsylvania Junior Chicken-of-Tomorrow contest winners. Afternoon appointments with Colonel Goodpaster; S. Adams and Admiral Byrd; B. M. Shanley; Secretary Dulles; group to discuss water resources. Practices golf on White House grounds. Evening appointments with Colonel Goodpaster; A. C. Whitman. To Sheraton-

Park Hotel for White House Correspondents' Association dinner.

25 Washington. To MATS terminal with Captain Streiff en route to Waco, Texas. Addresses graduates and guests at Baylor University commencement exercises and receives honorary degree. Meets with Texas Republican State Committee. Returns to Washington, D.C., and enplanes for Eisenhower farm in Gettysburg, Pennsylvania.

26 Gettysburg, Pennsylvania. [Page missing.]

27 Gettysburg, Pennsylvania. Visits with Mr. and Mrs. G. E. Allen and Mrs. Cane. Tours grounds in car with General Snyder and G. E. Allen. Tours Feaster farm.

28 Gettysburg, Pennsylvania. To Gettysburg Airport with General Snyder en route to Washington, D.C. Appointments with B. M. Shanley; S. Adams; W. J. Hopkins; P. S. Hitchcock and H. Pyle; A. W. Dulles, H. Hoover, Jr., Admiral Radford, and General Twining; B. M. Shanley; J. C. Hagerty (joined by B. M. Shanley and J. Rowley); Midshipmen R. E. Smith and R. D. Roberts, Commander Beach, and Lieutenant John K. Ryder; S. Adams and General Persons; H. R. Luce; G. D. Morgan; S. Adams; A. Larson and S. Adams; Murray Snyder; J. C. Hagerty. Signs Farm Bill. Practices golf on White House grounds.

29 Washington. Accompanied to office by Captain Streiff. Appointments with Colonel Goodpaster; Secretary Benson and G. Hauge; Admiral Strauss and Colonel Goodpaster; Ambassador Mehta, Rajkumari Amrit Kaur (Minister of Health, India), and J. B. Mintener; Senator H. A. Smith. Receives Teacher of the Year. Appointments with K. McCann; J. C. Hagerty. Receives Board of Directors, Freedom Foundation, Valley Forge. Appointments with G. D. Morgan; Colonel Goodpaster. To MATS terminal en route to Eisenhower farm in Gettysburg, Pennsylvania.

30 Gettysburg, Pennsylvania. To Gettysburg Airport with W. R. Tkach en route to Washington, D.C. Appointments with J. C. Hagerty; J. C. Hagerty and B. M. Shanley; Secretaries Wilson, Humphrey, and

Quarles, and J. C. Hagerty. Walks to St. John's Episcopal Church with Secretaries Wilson, Humphrey, and Quarles. Appointments with Secretaries Wilson and Humphrey; Congressman Osmers and B. N. Harlow; J. S. Lay and D. Anderson; Eleanor Harris (*American Weekly*) and J. C. Hagerty (off the record); A. F. Burns and G. Hauge; Colonel Goodpaster.

31 Washington. Accompanied to office by Captain Streiff. Appointments with K. McCann; B. M. Shanley; G. Hauge; H. C. Rose and S. Adams. Addresses Citizens for Eisenhower Committee at Statler Hotel. Receives copy of 1956 *Howitzer* from West Point Cadets. National Security Council session, followed by appointments with Vice-President Nixon and S. Adams; Postmaster General Summerfield, S. Adams, and General Persons; Postmaster General Summerfield. To Burning Tree Country Club for golf with J. E. McClure, R. Hatcher, and Colonel Belshe. Evening appointment with Secretary Humphrey.

June 1 Washington. Accompanied to office by Captain Streiff. Appointments with Ruth M. Peterson and Senator Thye; Colonel Goodpaster; S. Adams; B. M. Shanley; Ambassador Lodge. Cabinet meeting, followed by appointments with J. C. Hagerty; General Persons; Colonel Randall and S. Adams; Colonel Goodpaster; W. J. Hopkins. To Eisenhower farm in Gettysburg, Pennsylvania, with W. R. Tkach. To F. Akers's estate in Thurmont, Maryland, with W. R. Tkach for fishing. Returns to Gettysburg, Pennsylvania, for walking tour of grounds with Mrs. Eisenhower.

2 Gettysburg, Pennsylvania. To home of General Nevins with Mrs. Eisenhower. Returns to farm. Receives two quarter horses from American Quarter Horse Association.

3 Gettysburg, Pennsylvania. Rides horse. Walks around grounds. Visits with Mrs. Kendall Lynch and Mrs. A. A. Hansen and daughter; Mrs. G. E. Allen, Mrs. Crane, and Mrs. H. Brewer; General and Mrs. Nevins. Inspects barn with General Nevins.

4 Gettysburg, Pennsylvania. To Gettysburg Airport en

route to Washington, D.C. Appointments with General Persons; W. J. Hopkins; S. Adams; J. C. Hagerty; Colonel Goodpaster. Receives birthday cake in recognition of National School Lunch Program. Appointments with Lord Home (Secretary of State, Britain) and Ambassador Makins; Admiral Cope. Addresses guests at dedication ceremony for new AFL-CIO Building. Poses for photographs. Afternoon appointments with J. C. Hagerty; D. Thornton (joined by S. Adams); G. D. Morgan; General Persons. Practices golf on White House grounds.

5   Washington. Appointments with W. J. Hopkins; S. Adams, B. N. Harlow, Postmaster General Summerfield, I. J. Martin, G. D. Morgan, and General Persons; Colonel Goodpaster; Legislative Leaders; T. J. Murphy, O. B. Ketchum, Matthew J. Kane (Personal Representative of T. J. Murphy), and E. D. Chesney; General Persons; J. S. Lay and D. Anderson; Colonel Goodpaster. To Burning Tree Country Club with General Snyder for golf with Congressmen Halleck and Arends, and Colonel Belshe. Meeting to discuss Mutual Security Program.

6   Washington. Accompanied to office by Captain Streiff. Appointments with B. M. Shanley and Murray Snyder; B. M. Shanley; B. M. Shanley and J. C. Hagerty; J. C. Hagerty; D. Anderson; Admiral Radford and Colonel Goodpaster; Ambassador Hollington K. Tong (China) and V. Purse; G. Hauge; Colonel Goodpaster; S. Adams, J. C. Hagerty, G. D. Morgan, G. Hauge, B. N. Harlow, I. J. Martin, Murray Snyder, H. Pyle, and General Persons; G. D. Morgan. News conference, followed by reception for Young Republican Leaders. To MATS terminal with General Snyder en route to Eisenhower farm in Gettysburg, Pennsylvania. Tours farm with A. A. Ryan, L. Leechman, P. H. Bailey, G. Currie, and General Nevins. To Gettysburg Airport with General Snyder en route to Washington, D.C. Afternoon appointment with J. C. Hagerty. Hosts off-the-record dinner with Mrs. Eisenhower for Mr. and Mrs. L. Marx, Mr. and Mrs. D. Marx, and Mr. and Mrs. C. J. Schoo.

7   Washington. Appointments with Colonel Goodpas-

ter; W. J. Hopkins; Attorney General Brownell, S. Adams, and G. D. Morgan. National Security Council session, followed by appointments with R. Robertson; Attorney General Brownell; C. J. Schoo; General Persons. Afternoon appointments with J. C. Hagerty; Colonels Goodpaster and George Lincoln (Professor, U.S. Military Academy); H. E. Stassen and S. Adams; J. C. Hagerty; Dr. Charles Mayo (joined by J. C. Hagerty); H. Cain and G. D. Morgan; Budget Director Brundage and A. R. Jones; J. C. Hagerty; Secretary Dulles; G. D. Morgan. Practices golf on White House grounds with C. J. Schoo. To Sheraton-Park Hotel for White House News Photographers' Association dinner.

8   Washington. Suffers attack of ileitis. Admitted to Walter Reed Hospital.

9   Washington. Walter Reed Hospital.

10 Washington. Walter Reed Hospital.

11 Washington. Walter Reed Hospital.

12 Washington. Walter Reed Hospital. Appointment with S. Adams, General Persons, and Colonel Goodpaster.

13 Washington. Walter Reed Hospital. Appointments with S. Adams, G. D. Morgan, J. C. Hagerty, and Colonel Goodpaster; A. C. Whitman.

14 Washington. Walter Reed Hospital. Appointment with Chancellor Adenauer, Secretary Dulles, Eugene Weber, J. C. Hagerty, and Colonel Schulz.

15 Washington. Walter Reed Hospital. Appointment with S. Adams, J. C. Hagerty, Colonels Goodpaster and Schulz, and General Snyder.

16 Washington. Walter Reed Hospital.

17 Washington. Walter Reed Hospital. Visits with family.

18 Washington. Walter Reed Hospital. Appointments with Vice-President Nixon, Secretary Dulles, S. Adams, J. C. Hagerty, General Snyder, and Colonel Goodpaster; G. D. Morgan; S. Adams; General Persons.

19 Washington. Walter Reed Hospital. Appointments with S. Adams, G. D. Morgan, J. C. Hagerty, and Colonel Goodpaster; U. E. Baughman; D. D. Eisenhower II.

20 Washington. Walter Reed Hospital. Appointments with S. Adams, G. D. Morgan, J. C. Hagerty, Wayne Hawks, and Colonel Goodpaster; J. C. Hagerty and A. C. Whitman; Christian Pineau (Foreign Minister, France), Secretary Dulles, and J. C. Hagerty.

21 Washington. Walter Reed Hospital. Appointments with S. Adams; G. D. Morgan, W. Hawks, and Colonel Goodpaster; A. C. Whitman; General Gruenther; General and Mrs. Heaton, Dr. Blades, General Gruenther, and Mrs. Eisenhower.

22 Washington. Walter Reed Hospital. Appointments with S. Adams, G. D. Morgan, Murray Snyder, W. Hawks, and Colonel Goodpaster; A. C. Whitman; General Persons; Dr. M. S. Eisenhower.

23 Washington. Walter Reed Hospital. Appointment with S. Adams, J. C. Hagerty, Murray Snyder, W. Hawks, A. C. Whitman, and Colonel Goodpaster.

24 Washington. Walter Reed Hospital. Appointments with S. Adams and J. C. Hagerty; Dr. M. S. Eisenhower and General Gruenther.

25 Washington. Walter Reed Hospital. Appointments with S. Adams; General Persons; G. D. Morgan, W. Hawks, and Colonel Goodpaster; A. C. Whitman and G. Hauge.

26 Washington. Walter Reed Hospital.

27 Washington. Walter Reed Hospital. Appointment with S. Adams, G. D. Morgan, J. C. Hagerty, W. Hawks, A. C. Whitman, General Persons, and Colonel Goodpaster.

28 Washington. Walter Reed Hospital. Appointments with A. Nielsen; Secretary Wilson, S. Adams, J. C. Hagerty, and General Persons.

29 Washington. Walter Reed Hospital. Appointments with S. Adams, J. C. Hagerty, G. D. Morgan, A. C. Whitman, and Colonel Goodpaster; Vice-President Nixon and J. C. Hagerty; G. D. Morgan and

W. Hawks; Mrs. Paul A. Hodgson, I. S. and E. G. Ravdin, General and Mrs. Heaton, General and Mrs. Snyder, and Major and Mrs. J. S. D. Eisenhower.

30 Washington. To Eisenhower farm in Gettysburg, Pennsylvania, with Mrs. Eisenhower.

July 1 Gettysburg, Pennsylvania. Celebrates wedding anniversary with Mrs. Eisenhower. Visits with General and Mrs. Heaton, General and Mrs. Nevins, General and Mrs. Snyder, and Mr. and Mrs. G. E. Allen.

2 Gettysburg, Pennsylvania. Appointment with S. Adams, G. D. Morgan, J. C. Hagerty, W. Hawks, and Colonel Goodpaster.

3 Gettysburg, Pennsylvania. Appointment with S. Adams, G. D. Morgan, J. C. Hagerty, W. Hawks, and Colonel Goodpaster.

4 Gettysburg, Pennsylvania. Walks around grounds. Practices golf.

5 Gettysburg, Pennsylvania. Appointment with Secretaries Wilson and Quarles, S. Adams, J. C. Hagerty, Generals Twining, Persons and Everest, Colonels Goodpaster and Randall, and Admiral Radford.

6 Gettysburg, Pennsylvania. Appointment with J. C. Hagerty. Watches Charles Tressler erect playhouse for grandchildren with Generals Heaton and Snyder, and G. E. Allen. To putting green with Generals Heaton and Snyder, and G. E. Allen.

7 Gettysburg, Pennsylvania. No official appointments.

8 Gettysburg, Pennsylvania. Inspects pigs with General Heaton and G. E. Allen at Feaster farm. Walks around grounds.

9 Gettysburg, Pennsylvania. Appointment with S. Adams, G. D. Morgan, D. Anderson, J. C. Hagerty, W. Hawks, General Persons, and Colonel Goodpaster. Inspects cattle with General Heaton and G. E. Allen at Allen's farm.

10 Gettysburg, Pennsylvania. To office at Gettysburg College with J. Rowley and Captain Crittenberger. Appointment with Legislative Leaders. Poses for

photographs. Practices golf with Generals Heaton and Nevins; G. E. Allen and General Heaton.

11 Gettysburg, Pennsylvania. Appointments with S. Adams, J. C. Hagerty, A. S. Flemming, and Colonel Goodpaster; G. D. Morgan, Budget Director Brundage, and W. Hawks. Walks around grounds. Visits with C. W. Tompkins.

12 Gettysburg, Pennsylvania. Appointments with H. E. Stassen, S. Adams, and W. Hawks; L. W. Hall, J. C. Hagerty, and R. Carter.

13 Gettysburg, Pennsylvania. Appointment with Secretary Dulles, S. Adams, and W. Hawks.

14 Gettysburg, Pennsylvania. Appointment with Vice-President Nixon, J. C. Hagerty, G. D. Morgan, W. Hawks, General Persons, and Colonel Goodpaster. Receives World War I Tank Corp Association. Visits with Secretary and Mrs. Humphrey.

15 Gettysburg, Pennsylvania. Walks around grounds with J. C. Hagerty, G. E. Allen, Generals Heaton and Snyder, and I. S. Ravdin. Practices golf. Returns to Washington, D.C.

16 Washington. Accompanied to office by Colonel Schulz. Appointment with General Persons (joined by S. Adams and J. C. Hagerty); S. Adams; Admiral Strauss; B. M. Shanley; G. D. Morgan; Secretary Dulles (photographs taken); Ambassador Chiriboga; General Persons; Colonel Goodpaster; S. Adams; B. M. Shanley. Walks around White House grounds.

17 Washington. Accompanied to office by Colonel Schulz. Appointments with Colonel Goodpaster; W. J. Hopkins; General Persons and I. J. Martin; Legislative Leaders; V. E. Peterson, Colonel Goodpaster, and Commander Beach; Commander Beach; H. Pyle; Ambassador Peter Kós (Hungary); A. Larson; Colonel Goodpaster; G. Hauge; J. C. Hagerty; S. Adams; B. M. Shanley; G. D. Morgan. To swimming pool.

18 Washington. Appointments with General Persons; T. E. Stephens; D. Anderson and S. Adams; Ambassador Peixoto and J. F. Simmons; Admiral Radford and General Persons; Colonel Goodpaster; Secre-

taries Humphrey, Weeks, and Mitchell, J. Finnegan, S. Adams, and A. F. Burns (off the record); S. Adams (off the record); K. McCann; L. W. Hall (off the record); G. D. Morgan and W. J. Hopkins; G. D. Morgan; Colonel Goodpaster; Secretary Dulles; H. F. Holland; Murray Snyder; S. Adams.

19   Washington. Accompanied to office by Colonel Schulz. Appointments with Colonel Goodpaster; W. J. Hopkins; National Security Council session; H. Hoover, Jr., and Secretary Dulles; Secretary Seaton; S. Adams; A. S. Flemming, G. D. Morgan, and Murray Snyder; A. W. Dulles and Colonel Goodpaster; Ambassador Briggs; W. J. Hopkins; B. M. Shanley and General Persons; Postmaster General Summerfield, G. D. Morgan, and General Persons (joined by I. J. Martin); G. D. Morgan.

20   Washington. Accompanied to office by Colonel Schulz. Appointments with W. J. Hopkins; Colonel Goodpaster; A. F. Burns; S. Adams; H. E. Stassen; A. Larson; Captain Streiff (off the record); D. Anderson; G. D. Morgan; General Persons; B. M. Shanley; Colonel Goodpaster. National Security Council session, followed by appointments with J. M. Dodge; H. Hoover, Jr.; S. Adams; Colonel Goodpaster; W. J. Hopkins. To MATS terminal en route to Panama City, Panama.

21   Panama City, Panama. To United States Embassy. To Presidential Palace for Panama Conference. Visits cemetery. Returns to United States Embassy en route to El Panama Hotel for appointment with President Ruiz Cortines and President Castillo-Armas. Receives honorary decoration at Presidential Palace.

22   Panama City, Panama. To Simon Bolivar Salon to sign Declaration of Panama. Addresses members of conference. Returns to United States Embassy en route to El Panama Hotel for appointment with President Kubitchek, President-elect D. Manuel Prade (Peru), and President José Figueres Ferrer (Costa Rica). Attends reception in Balboa Room.

23   Panama City, Panama. Tours canal zone. Returns to United States Embassy for appointments with President Stroessner; President José Maria Lemus (El Salvador); President Hector Bienvenido Trujillo

(Dominican Republic); President Arias Espinosa. To Tocumen International Airport en route to Washington, D.C.

24   Washington. Accompanied to office by Colonel Schulz. Appointments with W. J. Hopkins; A. S. Flemming, V. E. Peterson, Colonel Goodpaster, and Commander Beach; Colonel Goodpaster; B. M. Shanley; S. Adams; G. D. Morgan; Colonel Goodpaster; General Persons; B. M. Shanley. Practices golf on White House grounds.

25   Washington. Appointments with Legislative Leaders; Colonel Goodpaster; J. C. Hagerty; Secretary Folsom and S. Adams; S. Adams, H. Pyle, L. W. Hall, R. Humphreys, T. E. Stephens, B. M. Shanley, R. Montgomery, and General Persons (off the record); S. Adams and R. Montgomery; R. Montgomery; Colonel Goodpaster; Senator Dirksen and General Persons; D. Long; R. McLean, S. Adams, and W. H. Jackson; G. D. Morgan; Postmaster General Summerfield. Cabinet meeting.

26   Washington. Accompanied to office by Colonel Schulz. Appointments with W. J. Hopkins; B. M. Shanley; S. Adams and General Persons; Senator Saltonstall and S. Adams; S. E. Sobeloff; S. Adams; General Persons; Ambassador de Murville. Greets Boys' Nation group. Appointments with W. J. Hopkins; Colonel Goodpaster; Senator H. A. Smith and General Persons; A. Larson; Colonel Goodpaster; S. Adams and B. N. Harlow; J. C. Hagerty; General Persons; G. D. Morgan; Colonel Randall and Mr. and Mrs. Charles Percy; Colonel Goodpaster; B. M. Shanley. Practices golf on White House grounds.

27   Washington. Accompanied to office by Colonel Schulz. Appointments with W. J. Hopkins; B. M. Shanley; A. W. Dulles, H. Hoover, Jr., and Colonel Goodpaster; H. Hoover, Jr., and S. Adams. Cabinet meeting, followed by appointments with H. Hoover, Jr.; Secretary Weeks; Attorney General Brownell; Ambassador Lodge; S. Adams; J. C. Hagerty; W. J. Hopkins; H. Pyle. To swimming pool. Afternoon appointments with Mr. and Mrs. Earl Merrifield; Attorney General Brownell and S. Adams; G. D. Morgan; General Persons; I. J. Martin; General Persons;

B. M. Shanley; H. Pyle; J. Rowley; H. Hoover, Jr. (joined by Colonel Goodpaster).

28 Washington. Accompanied to office by Colonel Schulz. Appointments with Vice-President Nixon (off the record); S. Adams; Colonel Goodpaster; G. D. Morgan; Colonel Goodpaster; H. Hoover, Jr., R. Murphy, and Colonel Goodpaster; S. Adams; Colonel Goodpaster. To MATS terminal en route to Eisenhower farm in Gettysburg, Pennsylvania. Tours farm in car with Dr. M. S. Eisenhower and Robert Weaver. Walks to duck pond.

29 Gettysburg, Pennsylvania. Practices golf. Attends services at Gettysburg Presbyterian Church with Mrs. Eisenhower. Visits with E. D. Slater, W. E. Robinson, and Mr. and Mrs. G. E. Allen.

30 Gettysburg, Pennsylvania. Walks around grounds and practices golf with E. D. Slater and W. E. Robinson. Appointment with H. E. Stassen, G. D. Morgan, and Murray Snyder. Walks around grounds with E. D. Slater.

31 Gettysburg, Pennsylvania. Returns to Washington, D.C. Appointments with General Snyder; Secretary Dulles, H. Hoover, Jr., and H. Phleger (joined by Secretary Humphrey, R. Robertson, A. W. Dulles, G. Gray, and Admiral Burke—off the record); A. F. Burns; Senator Watkins and General Persons; P. Roth and S. Adams; S. Adams; Murray Snyder; Secretary Wilson, R. Robertson, S. Adams, W. J. McNeil, Colonels Goodpaster and Randall, and General Persons; S. Adams and Colonel Goodpaster; H. E. Stassen, Ambassador Peaslee, and S. Adams (joined by Admiral Strauss); Admiral Strauss; L. W. Hall; General Cutler; G. D. Morgan; Colonel Goodpaster; B. M. Shanley.

August 1 Washington. Accompanied to office by Colonel Schulz. Appointments with General Persons; Senator Kuchel and General Persons; Senator Bush and General Persons; G. D. Morgan; S. Adams; Budget Director Brundage; S. Adams, G. D. Morgan, I. J. Martin, B. N. Harlow, H. Pyle, G. Hauge, Murray Snyder, General Persons, and Colonel Goodpaster; José Vallarino (grandson of Ambassador Vallarino). News conference, followed by appointments with

J. B. Mintener; Secretaries Humphrey and Weeks, Attorney General Brownell, Postmaster General Summerfield, G. D. Morgan, F. H. Mueller, and General Persons; S. Adams; Secretary Humphrey. Receives foreign students from National Catholic Welfare Conference. Afternoon appointments with G. D. Morgan; S. Adams; Colonel Goodpaster. Practices golf on White House grounds. Evening appointment with General Persons.

2   Washington. Accompanied to office by Colonel Schulz. Appointments with Norman Rockwell (off the record); W. J. Hopkins; S. Adams; Budget Director Brundage; E. J. Hughes; Governor McKeldin and family; Mr. and Mrs. E. J. Hughes; B. M. Shanley and Colonel Goodpaster. Receives military personnel who aided in Grand Canyon plane crash operation. Appointments with Secretary Brucker, Generals Taylor and Klein, Colonels Schulz, Draper, and H. D. Kight (Department of Army Project Officer), Major Horace E. Beaman (Assistant to Project Officer), Captain Crittenberger, John A. Collings (Executive Vice-President, TWA), and Richard Petty (Vice-President, Flight Operations, United Airlines); G. D. Morgan; Congressman Auchincloss and B. M. Shanley. To swimming pool. Afternoon appointments with A. F. Burns; Colonel Goodpaster.

3   Washington. Appointments with B. M. Shanley; S. Adams; Mr. and Mrs. J. H. Whitney; Cabinet meeting; Secretary Wilson; S. Adams and Murray Snyder; Attorney General Brownell; T. P. Pike; S. Adams; Prime Minister Menzies, Percy Spender, W. J. Sebold, and H. Hoover, Jr.; G. D. Morgan; H. Hoover, Jr., and Secretary Dulles; G. D. Morgan. Addresses nation via television and radio.

4   Washington. To Sheraton-Park Hotel with General Snyder and Major J. S. D. Eisenhower en route to golf at Burning Tree Country Club with G. E. Allen, Major J. S. D. Eisenhower, and Colonel Belshe. To swimming pool.

5   Washington. Attends services at National Presbyterian Church with Mrs. Eisenhower.

6   Washington. Appointments with L. A. Minnich;

G. D. Morgan and General Persons; W. J. Hopkins; D. Anderson; L. A. Minnich, General Loper, and Admiral Strauss; C. L. Sulzberger and Colonel Schulz (off the record); A. Larson; Murray Snyder; H. Pyle and Murray Snyder; Senator Dirksen and General Persons; Murray Snyder and General Persons; G. D. Morgan; Secretary Dulles and D. Anderson; B. M. Shanley. Practices golf on White House grounds.

7   Washington. Appointments with K. McCann; General Curtis; B. M. Shanley and General Persons; K. McCann. Greets legislative liaison officers; National Teenage Road-e-o finalists. Appointments with H. Pyle; G. D. Morgan; K. McCann. Tests teleprompter with K. McCann. Appointments with B. M. Shanley; Dr. M. S. Eisenhower; S. Weinberg; J. A. McCone and B. M. Shanley; A. Larson and Dr. M. S. Eisenhower (off the record); General Persons.

8   Washington. Appointments with G. Hauge; W. J. Hopkins; D. Anderson; G. D. Morgan; S. Adams, G. Hauge, Murray Snyder, H. Pyle, B. N. Harlow, I. J. Martin, G. D. Morgan, and General Persons. News conference, followed by appointments with B. M. Shanley; A. F. Burns and S. Adams; Secretary Dulles; B. M. Shanley. To Burning Tree Country Club for golf with G. E. Allen, General Heaton, and Colonel Belshe.

9   Washington. Appointments with L. A. Minnich; W. J. Hopkins; A. F. Burns; E. J. Bermingham; Secretary Dulles. National Security Council session, followed by appointments with H. E. Talbott; General Persons; B. M. Shanley; S. Adams; B. M. Shanley; A. Larson; S. Adams; G. D. Morgan; General Persons; H. Pyle; I. J. Martin and General Persons; B. M. Shanley; Secretary Humphrey; General Persons; B. M. Shanley. Receives grandmother clock.

10 Washington. Appointments with General Persons; S. Adams; S. Adams and B. M. Shanley; K. McCann; Vice-President Nixon; G. Hauge; Senator Farley and B. M. Shanley; Secretary Benson; Amintore Fanfani (Italian Christian Democratic Party), E. Bunker, C. B. Elbrick, Egidio Ortona (Italian Embassy), Girolamo Messeri, and Colonel Walters

(interpreter); D. Anderson and W. H. Jackson; A. S. Flemming and General Persons; G. D. Morgan; W. J. Hopkins; D. Thornton; F. M. Flynn, S. Adams, and Murray Snyder.

11 Washington. To Burning Tree Country Club for golf with G. E. Allen, W. E. Robinson, and Colonel Belshe. Afternoon appointment with General Persons.

12 Washington. Appointments with Secretary Dulles, A. S. Flemming, Generals Persons and Gruenther, and Admiral Radford (joined by D. Anderson, G. Gray, and A. W. Dulles); Secretary Dulles and Senator George. Attends bi-partisan congressional leadership meeting.

13 Washington. Accompanied to office by General Gruenther and Colonel Schulz. Appointments with General Gruenther; S. Adams and J. C. Hagerty; J. C. Hagerty; Senator Knowland; J. C. Hagerty, I. J. Martin, and General Persons; S. Adams; J. C. Hagerty; T. E. Stephens; I. J. Martin; J. C. Hagerty, I. J. Martin, and Senator Bennett; B. M. Shanley; S. Adams; Postmaster General Summerfield. Practices golf on White House grounds.

14 Washington. Accompanied to office by Colonel Schulz. Appointments with S. Adams; D. Anderson and S. Adams; B. M. Shanley and J. C. Hagerty. Receives group of congressional candidates. Appointments with Secretary Dulles and J. C. Hagerty; David A. Hamil (Administrator, Rural Electrification Administration); A. Larson (off the record); W. J. Hopkins. Practices golf on White House grounds. Returns to office with R. W. Woodruff.

15 Washington. Accompanied to office by Colonel Schulz. Appointments with S. Adams; B. M. Shanley; J. C. Hagerty (joined by T. E. Stephens); S. Adams; G. Hauge and A. F. Burns. Receives President's Cup Regatta swimming and diving champions. Appointments with T. E. Dewey; A. Larson (off the record). To swimming pool. Returns to office with D. D. Eisenhower II and S. E. Eisenhower. Afternoon appointments with J. C. Hagerty; Senator George; S. Adams; Colonel Randall; Secretary Humphrey, H. Hoover, Jr., J. B. Hollister; J. J. McCloy, R.

Robertson, S. Adams, Colonel Randall, and General Persons; P. G. Hoffman (off the record).

16   Washington. Appointments with B. M. Shanley; J. C. Hagerty; General Persons; Attorney General Brownell; tailor (off the record); National Security Council session; D. Anderson and Colonel Goodpaster; H. E. Stassen (off the record); S. Adams. To Burning Tree Country Club for golf with Colonel Belshe. Evening off-the-record appointment with H. Hoover, Jr.

17   Washington. Appointments with J. C. Hagerty. Off-the-record appointments with H. E. Stassen (joined by J. C. Hagerty); Secretary Wilson, Admiral Radford, and Colonel Goodpaster. National Security Council session, followed by appointments with Secretary Wilson, R. Robertson, G. Gray, Admiral Radford, and Colonel Goodpaster; A. W. Dulles and Colonel Goodpaster. Tests teleprompter with J. C. Hagerty. Afternoon appointments with Colonel Goodpaster; General Persons; Colonel Randall; Dr. M. S. Eisenhower; K. McCann; J. C. Hagerty and General Persons.

18   Washington. Accompanied to office by Colonel Schulz. Morning appointments with J. C. Hagerty; Colonel Goodpaster. To Burning Tree Country Club for golf with Colonel Belshe followed by appointments with Colonel Goodpaster; J. C. Hagerty; H. Hoover, Jr.; J. C. Hagerty, K. McCann, General Persons, Major J. S. D. Eisenhower, and Colonel Goodpaster. Works on speech for Republican National Convention with K. McCann. Evening appointment with J. C. Hagerty, General Persons, and Colonel Goodpaster.

19   Washington. Attends services at National Presbyterian Church with Mrs. Eisenhower.

20   Washington. Accompanied to office by Colonel Schulz. Appointment with Colonel Goodpaster. Receives delegates to 55th annual convention of Ancient Egyptian Arabic Order. Visits General Persons's office, followed by appointments with Colonel Goodpaster; J. C. Hagerty and General Persons; Commission on Increased Industrial Use of Agricultural Products; General Persons; Colonel Draper;

G. Hauge; J. C. Hagerty; G. Hauge; Colonel Goodpaster; G. Hauge. Practices golf on White House grounds.

21 Washington. Accompanied to office by Colonel Schulz. Appointments with Colonel Goodpaster; D. Anderson; R. Robertson, Admiral Radford, and Colonel Goodpaster; Budget Director Brundage; G. D. Morgan; W. J. Hopkins; W. R. Tkach; Colonel Goodpaster; General Persons. To MATS terminal with Mrs. Eisenhower en route to Republican National Convention in San Francisco, California. To St. Francis Hotel.

22 San Francisco, California. Breakfast with L. W. Hall. Appointments and photographs with Senator Knowland; Congressman Martin; Senator Bush; A. Nelson; Senator Kuchel; H. E. Stassen; Governor Aronson; John Feihens, Clifford O'Sullivan (National Committeeman), and Mayor Cobo. Appointment with Mr. and Mrs. C. J. Schoo. News conference, followed by appointments with Mickey McKill; Mr. and Mrs. L. Lambert, Mrs. McCammon, and Mrs. Gary; General Clay; Mrs. J. Stack and daughters; H. Hoover and H. Hoover, Jr.; Mr. and Mrs. E. D. Eisenhower and Mr. and Mrs. J. Kubik; Mr. and Mrs. E. N. Eisenhower; R. W. Woodruff; F. Leahy and W. Higgins. To Civic Auditorium for ball.

23 San Francisco, California. Receives congressional candidates. Appointments with United San Francisco Republican Committee; Governor Stratton (pictures taken); Mr. and Mrs. Warren Shaw (Gubernatorial candidate) and Senator Darby (pictures taken); Governor Mechem; D. McKay, Douglas McKeever, T. B. Morton, Chapman Revercomb, Clifton Young, Senators Bender, Butler, Capehart, Dirksen, Duff, Cooper, Welker, and Case, and Governor Langlie; Republican Gubernatorial candidates; Governor Herter (pictures taken). Receives Notification Committee. Appointments with H. D. Collier; Governor Foss and Mr. Barcues; RNC members. Poses for photographs with teenagers. To Cow Palace with Mrs. Eisenhower to deliver acceptance speech. To Bayshore Railroad Station with Mrs. Eisenhower en route to Monterey, California. To Cypress Point Club.

24 Monterey, California. To practice tee. Golf with H. C. Hunt, J. A. McCone, and S. B. Morse. Visits with W. E. Robinson and R. W. Woodruff. Tours golf course with W. E. Robinson, R. W. Woodruff, F. F. Gosden, and P. Reed. Visits with W. E. Robinson, R. W. Woodruff, and E. D. Slater.

25 Monterey, California. Walks around grounds en route to B. M. Shanley's office. Poses for photographs at pro shop. Golf with N. Chandler, C. S. Jones, and B. T. Leithead. To pro shop with J. C. Hagerty. Practices golf and receives visitors.

26 Monterey, California. To Carmel Mission with Mrs. Eisenhower and J. C. Hagerty for tour (joined by Mr. and Mrs. J. A. McCone and Mr. and Mrs. B. M. Shanley). Attends services at Carmel Presbyterian Church with Mrs. Eisenhower. Attends luncheon with Mrs. Eisenhower given in their honor by Mr. and Mrs. J. A. McCone. Golf with E. D. Slater, F. F. Gosden, and P. Pigott. Visits with E. D. Slater, W. E. Robinson, R. W. Woodruff, J. Gould, F. Willard, C. J. Schoo, B. T. Leithead, and F. F. Gosden.

27 Monterey, California. Golf with W. E. Robinson, F. Willard, and J. A. McCone. Attends reception given by Mr. and Mrs. J. A. McCone. Visits with E. D. Slater, W. E. Robinson, and F. Willard.

28 Monterey, California. Poses for photographs at pro shop. To United States Naval Station, Monterey, California, with Mrs. Eisenhower en route to Washington, D.C.

29 Washington. Accompanied to office by Colonel Schulz. Appointments with J. C. Hagerty; Colonel Goodpaster; B. M. Shanley; Secretary Dulles (joined by Admiral Radford and Colonel Goodpaster). Receives Civil Defense Advisory Panel, followed by appointments with B. M. Shanley; J. C. Hagerty; B. M. Shanley, Secretary Mitchell, and General Persons; Senator George; R. McPhee; J. S. Lay, W. H. Jackson, and D. Anderson; Colonel Goodpaster; K. McCann and Colonel Goodpaster; Colonel Goodpaster; J. C. Hagerty, I. S. Ravdin, and Generals Heaton and Snyder.

30 Washington. Accompanied to office by Colonel

Schulz. Appointments with Colonel Goodpaster; K. McCann; A. S. Flemming and B. M. Shanley; National Security Council session; Attorney General Brownell; Ambassador Gonzalo J. Facio (Costa Rica) and V. Purse. Makes broadcast for armed forces. Afternoon appointments with Heinrich Krone (Parliamentary Chairman, Germany), Werner Dollinger (Deputy Chairman, Germany), Albert von Kessel (Minister, German Embassy), Jacob Beam (Acting Assistant Secretary of State, Germany), and N. Lejins; Secretary Benson; Secretary Dulles; Colonel Goodpaster; J. C. Hagerty and Dr. M. S. Eisenhower.

31   Washington. Accompanied to office by Colonel Schulz and Dr. M. S. Eisenhower. Appointments with R. B. Anderson; J. C. Hagerty; T. C. Streibert, A. M. Washburn, C. Reynolds, and L. A. Minnich; B. M. Shanley and Senator Case; Colonel Goodpaster; J. C. Hagerty, I. J. Martin, General Persons, and Colonel Goodpaster. News conference, followed by appointments with B. M. Shanley; D. Anderson; Ambassador Ibrahim Anis (Sudan); Dr. M. S. Eisenhower. To swimming pool with Dr. M. S. Eisenhower. Afternoon appointments with Colonel Goodpaster; G. D. Morgan and General Persons; I. J. Martin; Christopher del Sesto (Republican gubernatorial candidate) and photographer; H. Hoover, Jr., and J. C. Hagerty; Colonel Goodpaster. To Griffith Stadium for baseball game.

September 1   Washington. Appointment with G. D. Morgan. Participates in Labor Day Stamp ceremonies. Receives Kenya senior golf team. Appointments with J. C. Hagerty, General Persons, and Colonel Goodpaster; J. C. Hagerty; Frank Ahern (Police Chief) and family. To Burning Tree Country Club for golf with G. E. Allen, J. E. McClure, and Colonel Belshe.

2   Washington. Attends services at National Presbyterian Church with Mrs. Eisenhower.

3   Washington. To Burning Tree Country Club for golf with G. E. Allen, J. E. McClure, and W. E. Robinson. Afternoon appointments with S. Adams, L. W. Hall, Attorney General Brownell, T. E. Stephens, J. C. Hagerty, and General Persons; K. McCann,

E. J. Hughes, S. Adams, T. E. Stephens, G. D. Morgan, B. N. Harlow, J. C. Hagerty, and General Persons.

4 Washington. Appointments with Colonel Goodpaster; J. C. Hagerty; S. Adams, J. C. Hagerty, and E. J. Hughes; Admiral Strauss; Secretary Thomas. Receives congressional candidates. Afternoon appointments with T. E. Stephens; Ambassadors Allen, Cannon, Hare, and Jones, and Colonel Goodpaster; Colonel Goodpaster; H. Hoover, Jr., and Secretary Dulles; S. Adams; J. C. Hagerty; G. D. Morgan; S. Adams; G. Hauge. Practices golf on White House grounds.

5 Washington. Appointments with Colonel Goodpaster; Ambassador El Mehdi Ben Aboud (Morocco) and J. F. Simmons; J. S. Lay and W. H. Jackson; S. Adams; J. C. Hagerty; S. Adams; S. Adams, Attorney General Brownell, H. Pyle, G. D. Morgan, J. C. Hagerty, B. N. Harlow, I. J. Martin, Murray Snyder, G. Hauge, and General Persons. News conference, followed by appointments with B. F. Fairless, Secretaries Humphrey and Dulles, H. Hoover, Jr., J. B. Hollister, R. Robertson, S. Adams, and Colonel Randall; Joseph A. Rheam (potential Deputy Director, NSA), W. H. Jackson, and R. Robertson (off the record); R. Robertson; Postmaster General Summerfield; Colonel Goodpaster. To Burning Tree Country Club for golf with F. Akers and R. D. Pittman. Evening appointment with J. C. Hagerty and K. McCann.

6 Washington. Appointments with T. E. Stephens; Colonel Goodpaster; Ambassador Mongi Slim (Tunisia); Ambassador Lodge; J. C. Hagerty. National Security Council session, followed by appointments with Secretary Dulles, H. Hoover, Jr., H. E. Stassen, W. H. Jackson, and G. Gray (off the record); Secretary Dulles; K. McCann; Colonel Goodpaster; Murray Snyder. Makes films for Civil Defense Administration and United Community Campaign. Afternoon appointments with Secretary Humphrey; Colonel Schulz; K. McCann; J. C. Hagerty; Colonel Goodpaster.

7 Washington. Appointments with Ambassador

Wentzel Christoffel du Plessis (Union of South Africa); B. M. Shanley; Colonel Goodpaster; Gerard B. Lambert, S. Adams, and T. E. Stephens; T. E. Stephens; J. C. Hagerty; S. Adams; Commander Beach; S. Adams; Ambassador Conant and S. Adams; L. W. Hall and T. E. Stephens; W. P. Rogers; B. M. Shanley; General Cutler. To swimming pool.

8   Washington. Appointment with Colonel Goodpaster. To Burning Tree Country Club for golf with G. E. Allen, J. Lemon, and Major J. S. D. Eisenhower.

9   Washington. To MATS terminal en route to Dr. M. S. Eisenhower's residence in State College, Pennsylvania. Attends services at Pennsylvania State University chapel. Views portrait of late Helen Eakin Eisenhower. Receives guests from memorial service for H. E. Eisenhower. Inspects Chapel of Catholic Faith. To Pennsylvania State University Airport en route to Washington, D.C.

10 Washington. Accompanied to office by Colonel Schulz. Appointments with G. Hauge; S. Adams and T. E. Stephens; S. P. Skouras; Arthur Fiedler (conductor, Boston Pops Orchestra), Robert Rogers (Executive Director, Committee of Arts and Sciences for Eisenhower), Howard Hanson (President, National Music Council), and S. Adams; L. W. Hall. Receives congressional candidates. Appointments with General Norstad; Vice-President Nixon, S. Adams, J. C. Hagerty, and J. Bassett; Attorney General Brownell; Ambassador Hervi Alphand (France); S. Adams; E. J. Hughes; S. Adams. Practices golf on White House grounds.

11 Washington. Accompanied to office by Colonel Schulz. Appointments with W. J. Hopkins; G. Hauge; General Sarnoff; S. Adams; E. J. Hughes. Greets attendees of People-to-People conference at National Red Cross building. Appointments with J. C. Hagerty; Secretary Dulles, G. D. Morgan, W. M. Rountree, H. Phleger, Secretary Humphrey, A. S. Flemming, and Colonel Goodpaster to discuss Suez situation. Receives group presenting John Barry statue to Ireland. Off-the-record appointment with Robert L. Wood (President, Independent Petroleum Association of America), A. S. Flemming, and Colonel

Goodpaster. Afternoon appointments with S. Adams, J. C. Hagerty, G. D. Morgan, I. J. Martin, Murray Snyder, and Colonel Goodpaster; Secretary Dulles and J. C. Hagerty; Secretaries Dulles and Wilson, H. E. Stassen, Ambassador Peaslee, S. Adams, W. H. Jackson, and Admirals Strauss and Radford; Secretary Dulles; S. Adams and J. C. Hagerty. Practices golf on White House grounds.

12   Washington. Accompanied to office by Colonel Schulz. Appointments with B. M. Shanley and Colonel Goodpaster; E. J. Hughes, L. W. Hall, T. E. Stephens, and J. C. Hagerty; S. Adams; K. McCann and E. J. Hughes; E. J. Hughes; A. S. Flemming and Colonel Goodpaster; G. D. Morgan; Colonel Goodpaster. To Eisenhower farm in Gettysburg, Pennsylvania. Delivers opening campaign address on grounds.

13   Gettysburg, Pennsylvania. To Gettysburg Country Club for golf with G. E. Allen and General Nevins. Hunts pigeons at Feaster and pig farms. Visits with Mr. and Mrs. G. E. Allen and General and Mrs. Nevins.

14   Gettysburg, Pennsylvania. To Gettysburg Country Club for golf with G. E. Allen and General Nevins. To Gettysburg Airport en route to Washington, D.C. Afternoon appointments with Secretary Dulles; Prime Minister Menzies and Ambassador Spender; S. Adams and J. C. Hagerty. Receives French Parliament members; foreign delegates attending Ninth World Methodist Conference, followed by appointments with General Jerome D. Fenton; S. Adams, G. D. Morgan, G. Hauge, I. J. Martin, R. McPhee, and Senator Knowland; Colonel Goodpaster; T. D. Morse, S. Adams, H. Pyle, G. Hauge, I. J. Martin, M. M. Rabb, T. E. Stephens, Murray Snyder, and L. A. Minnich; E. J. Hughes. To MATS terminal en route to Eisenhower farm in Gettysburg, Pennsylvania.

15   Gettysburg, Pennsylvania. To Gettysburg Country Club for golf with G. E. Allen and General Nevins. Tours farm with R. W. Woodruff.

16   Gettysburg, Pennsylvania. Walks around grounds

with R. W. Woodruff and General Snyder. Poses for photographs with Mrs. Eisenhower and grandchildren. Returns with General Snyder to Washington, D.C.

17   Washington. Accompanied to office by Colonel Schulz. Appointments with E. J. Hughes; S. Adams; B. M. Shanley and J. C. Hagerty; Dr. M. S. Eisenhower and B. N. Harlow; S. Adams; Dr. M. S. Eisenhower; I. J. Martin, Senator Hickenlooper, and photographer; E. J. Hughes; H. Hoover, Jr., and Secretary Dulles (joined by S. Adams). Hosts luncheon in honor of Inter-American Committee of Presidential Representatives. Afternoon appointments with K. McCann; General Van Fleet; Admiral Radford, General Cabell, and Colonel Goodpaster; W. H. Jackson, H. E. Stassen, and Colonel Goodpaster. Receives President's Cup Regatta winner. Practices golf on White House grounds.

18   Washington. To Washington National Airport for Republican Kick-Off breakfast for Vice-President Nixon. Appointments with W. J. Hopkins; S. Adams and T. E. Stephens; J. C. Hagerty; Colonel Goodpaster; Elder and Mrs. Lightfoot Solomon Michaux and F. Morrow; General Clark; A. F. Burns; A. F. Burns, W. B. Barnes, and Murray Snyder. Makes "Get out the vote" films. Afternoon appointments with R. Montgomery; J. C. Hagerty; B. C. Duffy and S. Adams; E. J. Hughes and R. Montgomery. Practices golf on White House grounds.

19   Washington. Accompanied to office by Colonel Schulz. Appointments with E. J. Hughes; Colonel Goodpaster; E. J. Hughes; S. S. Larmon, H. Harding, Harry Hartwick, David Levy, J. C. Hagerty, and E. J. Hughes (off the record); J. S. Lay and W. H. Jackson; General Valluy and Colonel Walters. Receives advisory group on presidential awards for meritorious civilian service. Appointments with R. Montgomery; T. E. Stephens and J. C. Hagerty; K. McCann and G. Hauge; S. Adams; Colonel Goodpaster; B. N. Harlow. Practices golf on White House grounds. To 40th and Brandywine Streets with Mrs. Eisenhower for television broadcast.

20   Washington. Accompanied to office by Colonel

Schulz. Appointments with Colonel Goodpaster; W. J. Hopkins; P. G. Hoffman; G. D. Morgan; I. J. Martin; L. W. Hall and T. S. Voorhees. National Security Council session, followed by appointments with Secretary Wilson; A. Nielsen; Omer Carmichael (School Superintendent, Louisville, Kentucky) and G. D. Morgan; S. Adams. Receives National Agricultural Advisory Commission. To MATS terminal with Mrs. Eisenhower en route to Des Moines, Iowa. To residence of Mr. and Mrs. Joel Carlson in Boone, Iowa.

21 Boone, Iowa. To Mrs. Eisenhower's birthplace, 718 Carroll Street, with Mrs. Eisenhower en route to National Field Days and Plowing Matches in Des Moines, Iowa. Luncheon in presidential tent. Delivers address via television and radio. Presents scrolls to All-American Plowmen. Addresses Iowa weekly paper editors at Des Moines Airport. Receives Iowa Republican Party officials. Returns to Washington, D.C.

22 Washington. Evening appointment with Secretary Dulles.

23 Washington. Attends services at National Presbyterian Church with Mrs. Eisenhower.

24 Washington. Accompanied to office by Colonel Schulz. Appointments with W. J. Hopkins; Colonel Goodpaster; Attorney General Brownell; General Snyder; S. Adams and T. E. Stephens; Prince Savang Vatthana (Laos); J. C. Hagerty; Cooper T. Holt (Commander-in-Chief, VFW), O. Ketchum, and E. D. Chesney. Poses for photographs with Republican candidates. Appointments with B. N. Harlow; General Cutler; J. D. Zellerbach; S. Adams; Secretary Weeks, Joseph Spang (President, Gillette Co.), and S. Adams; A. Larson and B. N. Harlow; A. Larson (joined by S. Adams and J. C. Hagerty); Colonel Goodpaster; G. Hauge and B. N. Harlow. Practices golf on White House grounds.

25 Washington. Accompanied to office by Colonel Schulz. Appointments with S. Adams; J. C. Hagerty; B. M. Shanley; Colonel Goodpaster; G. Hauge; H. MacMillan and Ambassador Makins (off the record); T. E. Stephens; G. Hauge; B. N. Harlow. To

MATS terminal en route to Peoria, Illinois. To Pere Marquett Hotel for reception. Delivers address at Bradley Field Airport. Greets state candidates, Illinois Citizens' Committee for Eisenhower, and farm leaders at hotel. Greets attendees of Illinois Bankers' Association Convention. Dinner with Governor and Mrs. Stratton, Senator and Mrs. Dirksen, and General Snyder. Addresses audience and nation via television and radio from Bradley University. To Bradley Field Airport with Mrs. Eisenhower en route to Washington, D.C.

26 Washington. Accompanied to office by Colonel Schulz. Appointments with S. Adams; J. C. Hagerty; W. J. Hopkins; J. C. Hagerty; Colonel Goodpaster; W. H. Jackson; Secretary Humphrey, I. J. Martin, and T. E. Stephens; Colonel Goodpaster; American Legion leaders; Colonel Goodpaster; D. Middleton (off the record); J. C. Hagerty, General Persons, and Congressman McConnell; W. M. Canaday; G. D. Morgan; S. Adams; C. G. Parker and S. Adams. Practices golf on White House grounds.

27 Washington. Accompanied to office by Colonel Schulz. Appointment with A. F. Burns, S. Adams, B. M. Shanley, and G. Hauge. Receives Small Business Administration's National Council of Consultants. Appointments with B. M. Shanley; J. C. Hagerty; S. Adams, J. C. Hagerty, Murray Snyder, B. N. Harlow, and General Persons. News conference, followed by appointments with M. M. Rabb; Fairless committee; J. C. Hagerty; T. E. Stephens; Colonel Goodpaster; Betty Correa; A. Larson. National Security Council session.

28 Washington. Appointment with K. McCann and General Persons; Interdepartmental committee to discuss rural development program; Cabinet meeting; Secretary Humphrey; Ambassador Julio A. Lacarte Muro (Uruguay); S. Goldwyn and S. Adams. To Sheraton-Park Hotel with Secretary Humphrey to address delegates attending World Bank and International Monetary Fund meeting. Makes film entitled *Four Full Years*. Afternoon appointments with S. Adams; Charles Rozmarek (President, Polish American Congress), S. Adams, and Ab Hermann;

G. D. Morgan; Attorney General Brownell and S. Adams; E. J. Hughes; S. Adams; Secretary Mitchell and J. C. Hagerty; Secretary Seaton; A. F. Burns; Colonel Goodpaster; K. McCann. Practices golf on White House grounds.

29   Washington. Appointments with J. C. Hagerty; S. Adams; A. Larson and E. J. Hughes; W. J. Brennan, Attorney General Brownell, and S. Adams; Colonel Goodpaster; A. Larson and E. J. Hughes; General Cutler; A. Larson and E. J. Hughes; S. Adams. Swims. Afternoon appointment with W. J. Brennan, Attorney General Brownell, and J. C. Hagerty.

30   Washington. Attends services at St. Sophia's Greek Orthodox Church with Mrs. Eisenhower and M. M. Rabb. Participates in church cornerstone-laying ceremonies. To Union Station with Mrs. Eisenhower en route to Cleveland, Ohio.

October   1   Cleveland, Ohio. To Cleveland Hotel. Greets Ohio officials and dignitaries in hotel dining room. Addresses Sales Executive Group at luncheon. To public square to address Ohio officials and dignitaries. To Cleveland Hopkins Airport with Mrs. Eisenhower en route to Lexington, Kentucky. Addresses audience at airport. To Phoenix Hotel. Addresses Republican county leaders in convention hall. Addresses audience and nation via television and radio from University of Kentucky Coliseum. To Blue Grass Airport en route to Washington, D.C.

2   Washington. Accompanied to office by Colonel Schulz. Appointments with Colonel Goodpaster; W. J. Hopkins; B. M. Shanley; S. Adams and J. C. Hagerty. Receives Nationalities Division, RNC. Appointments with C. D. Jackson; J. K. Javits and General Persons; S. Adams, G. D. Morgan, and Murray Snyder; A. Nielsen; T. E. Stephens and J. Rowley; Colonel Goodpaster; Secretary Dulles (joined by R. Robertson, G. Gray, W. J. McNeil, C. B. Elbrick, D. MacArthur II, Admiral Radford, and Colonel Goodpaster) (off the record); S. Adams and J. C. Hagerty; Senator Welker and General Persons; G. D. Morgan; E. J. Hughes. Practices golf on White House grounds.

3   Washington. Accompanied to office by Colonel Schulz. Appointments with S. Adams and T. E. Stephens; Jewish War Veterans leaders; Colonel Goodpaster; S. Adams; J. S. Lay and W. H. Jackson; B. M. Shanley; Secretary Dulles, Admiral Radford, General Cabell, and Colonel Goodpaster. To MATS terminal en route to New York, New York, for baseball game.

4   Washington. Accompanied to office by Colonel Schulz. Appointments with E. Johnston; B. M. Shanley; Colonel Goodpaster; National Security Council session; Colonel Randall; Portia W. Pittman (President, Booker T. Washington Foundation) and F. Morrow; S. Adams and J. C. Hagerty; F. Morrow; T. P. Pike. Views Twentieth Century Fox film about the President. Afternoon appointments with S. Adams; Senator Bowring; Vice-President Nixon; S. Adams; Colonel Goodpaster; W. J. Hopkins; E. J. Hughes. Practices golf on White House grounds.

5   Washington. Accompanied to office by Colonel Schulz. Receives members of Committee on Governmental Contracts. Appointments with J. C. Hagerty; Colonel Goodpaster; General Cutler, E. J. Hughes, and Admiral Strauss; Admiral Strauss; S. Adams, G. D. Morgan, G. Hauge, I. J. Martin, Murray Snyder, General Persons, and Colonel Goodpaster. News conference, followed by appointments with Ambassador Makins; Disabled American Veterans leaders; William H. White (President, Baylor University), R. D. Pittman, and George Sauer (Athletic Director, Baylor University); B. M. Shanley; J. S. Copley and General Persons; G. D. Morgan and E. J. Hughes; Carl Bendetsen, R. Robertson, G. Gray, W. S. Robertson, Admiral Radford, and Colonel Goodpaster; Attorney General Brownell, S. Adams, and J. C. Hagerty; S. H. High; General Cutler, E. J. Hughes, and Admiral Strauss; Colonel Goodpaster; S. H. High; G. D. Morgan; Colonel Goodpaster. Practices golf on White House grounds.

6   Washington. Accompanied to office by Colonel Schulz. Appointment with J. C. Hagerty. Receives "Typical Newspaper Boy of the Year." Poses for photographs. Appointments with H. Hoover, Jr.; S. Adams; Vice-President Nixon; S. Adams and Congress-

man Halleck; Colonel Goodpaster; Mr. and Mrs. P. H. Helms, Mr. and Mrs. R. B. Anderson, Mr. and Mrs. Harold Anderson, and Mr. and Mrs. Holmes Tuttle; J. C. Hagerty.

7   Washington. Attends services at National Presbyterian Church.

8   Washington. Accompanied to office by Colonel Schulz. Appointments with Colonel Goodpaster; G. Hauge and E. J. Hughes; E. J. Hughes; J. C. Hagerty; S. Adams and A. S. Flemming; H. S. Cullman; Senator Knowland; Frank Moraes (Editor, *India Times*), S. Adams, and J. C. Hagerty; P. Young; E. J. Hughes; Senator H. A. Smith; S. Adams. Practices golf on White House grounds. Evening appointment with S. Adams and T. E. Stephens.

9   Washington. Accompanied to office by Colonel Schulz. Appointments with W. J. Hopkins; E. J. Hughes (joined by G. Hauge); J. C. Hagerty (joined by T. E. Stephens); Colonel Goodpaster; B. N. Harlow (joined by E. J. Hughes); Captain Beach; Colonel Goodpaster; R. Howard; S. Adams; B. M. Shanley. To MATS terminal with Mrs. Eisenhower en route to Pittsburgh, Pennsylvania. To Penn Sheraton Hotel. Greets Allegheny County Republican Finance Committee. Greets Republican county workers. To Hunt Armory to deliver nationally televised campaign speech. To Greater Pittsburgh Airport en route to Washington, D.C.

10   Washington. Accompanied to office by Colonel Schulz. Appointments with R. Cake and R. P. Burroughs; K. McCann (joined by E. J. Hughes); Colonel Goodpaster; W. H. Jackson (joined by J. S. Lay); Colonel Goodpaster; Secretary Mitchell and S. Adams; B. Rose; T. E. Dewey; William Haley (Editor, *London Times*) and J. E. Coulson (off the record). Receives "Vote Getters for Ike." Afternoon appointments with B. N. Harlow; S. Adams. Practices golf on White House grounds.

11   Washington. Accompanied to office by Colonel Schulz. Appointments with Colonel Goodpaster; W. J. Hopkins; B. N. Harlow; Secretaries Wilson and Brucker, Colonels Randall and Goodpaster, and General Taylor; Secretary Dulles and H. Hoover, Jr.;

S. Adams, J. C. Hagerty, G. Hauge, G. D. Morgan, I. J. Martin, Murray Snyder, B. N. Harlow, and Colonel Goodpaster. News conference, followed by appointments with J. C. Hagerty; S. Waugh, S. Adams, and J. C. Hagerty; Attorney General Brownell and S. Adams; R. Reed. To Statler Hotel with P. Young and J. C. Hagerty to address Civil Service Assembly luncheon. Afternoon appointments with Prince Rainier III and Princess Grace (Monaco); B. M. Shanley; Dr. M. S. Eisenhower; V. Washington, J. C. Hagerty, B. M. Shanley, and Congressman Powell; Dr. M. S. Eisenhower; W. T. Faricy and S. Adams; R. Brockhurst, H. H. Gruenther, and Congressman L. H. Smith. Practices golf on White House grounds. Receives Supreme Court Justices and court officers.

12   Washington. Accompanied to office by Colonel Schulz. Appointments with B. M. Shanley; General Persons; S. Adams; R. Hatcher, Coleman Wortham, Jr., and T. E. Stephens; Congressman Martin; W. H. Jackson. National Security Council session, followed by appointments with H. Hoover, Jr.; A. S. Flemming and S. Adams; Colonel Goodpaster; barber; K. McCann and G. Hauge; K. McCann; Committee of Arts and Sciences for Eisenhower; Prem Bhatia (political correspondent, *The Statesman*, India) and S. Adams; D. Levy, R. Montgomery, and J. C. Hagerty; R. Montgomery; A. S. Flemming and S. Adams; O. R. Cheatham and S. Adams; T. E. Stephens; Colonel Goodpaster; D. Zanuck and S. Adams (joined by D. Zanuck's son); G. D. Morgan; T. E. Stephens; Colonel Goodpaster. Practices golf on White House grounds. To Sheraton-Park Hotel to participate in radio and television appearance.

13   Washington. Accompanied to office by Colonel Schulz. Appointments with E. J. Hughes; H. E. Stassen and S. Adams; S. Adams; Charles E. Kelly (Association of Congressional Medal of Honor winners); dentist. Receives birthday card from Joseph Donahue, Jr., and family; birthday present from White House staff; cousins A. M. Cooper and E. S. Bowers. To swimming pool with G. E. Allen. Views birthday parade. To Sheraton-Park Hotel with J. C. Hagerty to participate in television program. To

birthday banquet in hotel given by Citizens for Eisenhower.

14 Washington. Attends services at National Presbyterian Church with Mrs. Eisenhower. Listens to army band play "Happy Birthday." Poses for family photographs.

15 Washington. Accompanied to office by Colonel Schulz. Appointments with W. J. Hopkins; J. C. Hagerty and Colonel Goodpaster; S. Adams and T. E. Stephens; A. F. Burns; B. M. Shanley, Murray Snyder, and H. H. Gruenther; H. Mitchell and C. G. Frailey; Secretary Weeks, Clarence G. Morse (Chairman, Maritime Commission), L. Rothschild, Louis H. Roddis, Jr., (Deputy Director, Reactor Development, AEC), B. M. Shanley, J. C. Hagerty, Admiral Strauss, General K. E. Fields (General Manager, Atomic Energy Commission), Captain Beach, and Colonel Goodpaster; Secretary Wilson and Admiral Strauss; AMVETS representatives. Receives congressional candidates for appointment and photographs. Appointments with Secretary Dulles, H. Hoover, Jr., and W. M. Rountree; Independent Advisory Committee to Trucking Industry. Pushes button from Cabinet room to start Upper Colorado River Project. Afternoon appointments with Peter Tali Coleman (Attorney General, Guam) and Governor Richard B. Lowe (Guam); Ottis Peterson (photographs taken); T. E. Stephens, J. C. Hagerty, J. Rowley, and Colonel Draper; C. Dillon (off the record); T. E. Stephens, J. C. Hagerty, and J. Rowley; B. N. Harlow, G. Hauge, and E. J. Hughes. Practices golf on White House grounds. Evening appointment with L. W. Hall.

16 Washington. Accompanied to office by Colonel Schulz. Appointments with J. C. Hagerty; S. Adams; T. E. Stephens; W. J. Hopkins; B. M. Shanley; Colonel Goodpaster; G. D. Morgan. To MATS terminal with Mrs. Eisenhower en route to Minneapolis, Minnesota. Addresses audience at Rice Park; First National Bank. To Wold-Chamberlain Airport en route to Seattle, Washington. To Olympic Hotel. Greets Washington State Republican Finance Committee.

17   Seattle, Washington. To Civic Auditorium to address audience and nation via television and radio. Motors with Mr. and Mrs. E. N. Eisenhower to their residence in Tacoma, Washington.

18   Tacoma, Washington. To Memorial Field House at College of Puget Sound with Mr. and Mrs. E. N. Eisenhower. Delivers address. To McChord Air Force Base with Mrs. Eisenhower en route to Portland, Oregon. Greets Citizens for Eisenhower workers en route to Hotel Multnomah. Addresses audience and nation via television and radio from Civic Auditorium.

19   Portland, Oregon. To Portland International Airport with Mrs. Eisenhower en route to Los Angeles, California. To Beverly Hilton Hotel. Addresses audience at Hollywood Bowl.

20   Los Angeles, California. To Lockheed Air Terminal with Mrs. Eisenhower en route to Denver, Colorado. Delivers address. Greets citizens; members of Fitzsimons Army Hospital staff. Enplanes with Mrs. Eisenhower for Washington, D.C.

21   Washington. Attends services at National Presbyterian Church.

22   Washington. Morning appointments with E. J. Hughes; J. C. Hagerty; S. Adams, B. M. Shanley, K. McCann, and T. E. Stephens; T. E. Stephens; General Cutler and Admiral Strauss; J. C. Hagerty; Secretary Benson; T. E. Stephens; S. Adams; Colonel Goodpaster; G. D. Morgan. Witnesses swearing-in of Federal Highway Administrator John A. Volpe. Afternoon appointments with Colonel Goodpaster; J. C. Hagerty (joined by T. E. Stephens); S. Adams; L. W. Hall, S. Adams, J. C. Hagerty, B. C. Duffy, and C. Newton; T. E. Stephens and J. Rowley; General Persons; K. McCann; Colonel Goodpaster; General Cutler.

23   Washington. Appointments with General Taylor; L. W. Hall, S. Adams, Attorney General Brownell, J. C. Hagerty, T. E. Stephens, and Generals Clay and Persons; Attorney General Brownell; National Retail Dry Goods Association representatives. Presents 1956 Harmon International Trophies, followed by

appointments with K. McCann; J. C. Hagerty; S. Adams; State Senator Cora M. Brown, Mrs. Robert L. Vann (President, *Pittsburgh Courier*), J. C. Hagerty, and M. M. Rabb; J. C. Hagerty. Greets "Vets for Ike." Afternoon appointments with Secretary Dulles, G. Gray, Ambassador Peaslee, J. C. Hagerty, E. J. Hughes, Generals Cutler and Loper, Admiral Strauss, and Colonel Goodpaster; Secretary Dulles. Practices golf on White House grounds. To Sheraton-Park Hotel with Secretary Mitchell to address guests at United Brotherhood of Carpenters and Joiners of America 75th annual dinner.

24 Washington. Accompanied to office by Colonel Schulz. Appointments with W. J. Hopkins; General Persons; G. D. Morgan; S. Adams, T. E. Stephens, M. M. Rabb, and Ralph J. Bunche; Edward Corsi and M. M. Rabb; J. S. Lay and W. H. Jackson; Budget Director Brundage; Colonel Goodpaster; Catholic War Veterans' representatives; Secretary Dulles. To 40th and Brandywine Streets with Mrs. Eisenhower to address audience and nation via television and radio. Afternoon appointments with Colonels Draper and Goodpaster; B. N. Harlow; I. J. Martin and General Persons; Colonel Goodpaster. Practices golf on White House grounds.

25 Washington. Appointments with Colonel Goodpaster; S. Adams. To Union Station with Mrs. Eisenhower en route to New York, New York. To Commodore Hotel. Greets various ethnic groups. To Madison Square Garden to address audience and nation via television and radio. To La Guardia Airport en route to Washington, D.C.

26 Washington. Accompanied to office by Colonel Schulz. Appointments with W. J. Hopkins; Colonel Goodpaster; B. M. Shanley; Secretary Dulles; National Security Council session. Receives Pennsylvania Council of Republican Women. Appointments with Secretary Dulles; S. Adams; Colonel Goodpaster; G. D. Morgan; Secretary Dulles; Secretary Dulles and Senator George; J. C. Hagerty; S. Adams. Makes campaign recordings. Afternoon appointments with Colonel Goodpaster; G. Hauge; E. J. Hughes; G. D. Morgan; Colonel Goodpaster.

27   Washington. Accompanied to office by Colonel Schulz. Appointments with K. McCann; Colonel Goodpaster; K. McCann; Jackson Wheeler and family; Senator Potter and Minute Men and Women; B. N. Harlow; G. D. Morgan; Secretary Dulles, H. Hoover, Jr., W. M. Rountree, and Colonel Goodpaster; G. E. Allen and B. N. Harlow. To swimming pool. To Walter Reed Hospital with General Snyder for physical examination.

28   Washington. Undergoes examination at Walter Reed Hospital. Appointment with H. Hoover, Jr. Returns to White House with J. C. Hagerty and Colonel Schulz.

29   Washington. Accompanied to office by Colonel Schulz. Appointment with Colonel Goodpaster. To MATS terminal with Mrs. Eisenhower en route to Miami, Florida. Delivers address at airport. Greets Florida Republicans; congressional candidates. Enplanes for Jacksonville, Florida. Addresses group at Imeson Airport. Enplanes for Richmond, Virginia. Addresses gathering. Greets Republican officials and candidates. Enplanes for Washington, D.C. Evening appointment with Secretaries Dulles and Wilson, A. W. Dulles, H. Hoover, Jr., S. Adams, J. C. Hagerty, Admiral Radford, General Persons, and Colonel Goodpaster.

30   Washington. Accompanied to office by Colonel Schulz. Appointments with J. C. Hagerty; Colonel Goodpaster; B. N. Harlow and E. J. Hughes; S. Adams and J. C. Hagerty; S. Adams, J. C. Hagerty, and B. N. Harlow; Edward L. McCarthy (Member, United Steelworkers of America), S. Adams, and Murray Snyder; Secretary Dulles, H. Hoover, Jr., H. Phleger, S. Adams, J. C. Hagerty, and Colonel Goodpaster; Friedhelm Kreis, Ambassador Krekeler, Frederich Dann (Ford Motor Co., Germany), S. Adams, and J. F. Simmons; R. Gray, M. A. Hutcheson, and S. Adams; Secretary Dulles, H. Hoover, Jr., H. Phleger, J. C. Hagerty, and Colonel Goodpaster; Ambassador Walles and Colonel Goodpaster; T. E. Stephens; S. Adams; Colonel Goodpaster; W. J. Hopkins; Colonel Goodpaster; J. C. Hagerty; Colonel Goodpaster; A. S. Flemming and Colonel Goodpaster; E. J. Hughes; S. Adams.

31	Washington. Accompanied to office by Colonel Schulz. Morning appointments with T. E. Stephens; J. S. Lay and W. H. Jackson; Admiral Radford; S. Adams and J. C. Hagerty; Winant Volunteers' leaders; Secretary Dulles and J. C. Hagerty; S. Adams; Army Research and Study fellowship recipients; E. J. Hughes; S. Adams and W. J. Hopkins; S. Adams. Afternoon appointments with John Slesson (former Head, British Air Force) (off the record); S. S. Larmon, D. Levy, T. Lapham, and T. E. Stephens (off the record); S. Adams and R. Montgomery. Practices golf on White House grounds. Addresses nation regarding Middle East and European developments via television and radio.
November 1	Washington. Accompanied to office by Colonel Schulz. Appointments with Secretary Weeks, H. C. McClellan, and B. M. Shanley; J. C. Hagerty; National Security Council session; Colonel Goodpaster; Attorney General Brownell and S. Adams. To George Washington Hospital to visit C. W. Tompkins. Afternoon appointments with H. Hoover, Jr., and Secretary Dulles; E. J. Hughes; G. D. Morgan; S. Adams; Colonel Goodpaster; J. C. Hagerty; E. J. Hughes; S. Adams. To Union Station with Mrs. Eisenhower en route to Philadelphia, Pennsylvania. To Convention Hall to deliver address. To B & O railroad station with Mrs. Eisenhower en route to Washington, D.C.
2	Washington. Accompanied to office by Colonel Schulz. Appointments with J. C. Hagerty; S. Adams; Colonel Goodpaster; General Cutler; group of scientists; Colonel Goodpaster; J. C. Hagerty; H. Hoover, Jr., and Secretary Dulles; G. D. Morgan and General Persons. To swimming pool.
3	Washington. Accompanied to office by Colonel Schulz. Appointments with J. C. Hagerty; Colonel Goodpaster; J. C. Hagerty; Secretary Wilson, Admiral Radford, and Colonel Goodpaster; W. J. Hopkins; Colonel Goodpaster; H. Hoover, Jr., W. M. Rountree, H. Phleger, and Colonel Goodpaster (joined by J. C. Hagerty); W. H. Jackson. To swimming pool.
4	Washington. Attends services at National Presbyterian Church with Major and Mrs. J. S. D.

Eisenhower. To Walter Reed Hospital with Major J. S. D. Eisenhower and J. C. Hagerty to visit Secretary Dulles.

5   Washington. Accompanied to office by Colonel Schulz. Appointments with Colonel Goodpaster; J. C. Hagerty and Colonel Goodpaster; S. Adams; Colonel Goodpaster; Vice-President Nixon (joined by H. Hoover, Jr., H. Phleger, J. C. Hagerty, and Colonel Goodpaster); J. C. Hagerty; L. W. Hall; W. J. Hopkins. To swimming pool. To Republican National Headquarters with J. C. Hagerty. Greets Republican workers. Afternoon appointments with Colonel Goodpaster; S. Adams; H. E. Stassen; R. Montgomery; J. C. Hagerty (joined by S. Adams); Attorney General Brownell; Colonel Goodpaster; H. Hoover, Jr., H. Phleger, S. Adams, and Colonel Goodpaster.

6   Washington. Accompanied to office by Colonel Schulz. Appointments with S. Adams; Colonel Goodpaster; A. W. Dulles, S. Adams, and Colonel Goodpaster (joined by H. Hoover, Jr., A. S. Flemming, and S. Adams) (off the record); Colonel Goodpaster. To Cumberland Township Election House in Gettysburg, Pennsylvania, with Mrs. Eisenhower, G. E. Allen, J. C. Hagerty, Rose Wood, Sergeant and Mrs. John Moaney, and General Snyder. Votes with Mrs. Eisenhower. Poses for photographs. Motors to Eisenhower farm. To Gettysburg Airport with J. C. Hagerty and General Snyder en route to Washington, D.C. Afternoon appointments with H. Hoover, Jr., Vice-President Nixon, A. W. Dulles, R. Robertson, A. S. Flemming, W. H. Jackson, H. Phleger, R. Murphy, S. Adams, J. C. Hagerty, Generals Twining, Palmer, Pate, and Persons, Captain Beach, Admirals Radford and Burke, and Colonel Goodpaster; S. Adams. To Sheraton-Park Hotel with Mrs. Eisenhower, Dr. M. S. Eisenhower, E. Doud, and Major J. S. D. Eisenhower. Awaits election results with family, close friends, and Cabinet members and their spouses. Proceeds with Mrs. Eisenhower and Vice-President and Mrs. Nixon to Sheraton Hall for victory speech to audience and nation.

7   Washington. Appointment with S. Adams, General

Persons, and Colonel Goodpaster. Accompanied to office by Colonel Schulz. Appointments with S. Adams and Colonel Goodpaster; H. Hoover, Jr., S. Adams, and Colonel Goodpaster (joined by Secretary Humphrey). To Walter Reed Hospital with H. Hoover, Jr., to visit Secretary Dulles. Afternoon appointments with A. F. Burns; Colonel Goodpaster; A. Nielsen; Colonel Goodpaster; Postmaster General Summerfield; G. Hauge. Practices golf on White House grounds. Evening appointment with T. E. Stephens, R. W. Woodruff, Murray Snyder, and Colonel Goodpaster.

8   Washington. Accompanied to office by Colonel Schulz. Appointments with Colonel Goodpaster; G. Hauge and B. M. Shanley; G. Hauge, Paul W. McCracken (Consultant, CEA), and R. J. Saulnier (off the record); L. W. Hall and S. Adams. National Security Council session, followed by appointments with Secretary Wilson, H. Hoover, Jr., S. Adams, Colonels Goodpaster and Randall, and Admiral Radford; Colonel Goodpaster; E. J. Hughes; Ambassador H. Alphand, Charles Lucet (Minister, France), J. F. Simmons, and C. B. Elbrick; J. C. Hagerty. Poses for photographs. Afternoon appointments with S. Adams and General Persons; H. Hoover, Jr., A. W. Dulles, H. Phleger, A. S. Flemming, Vice-President Nixon, W. S. Robertson, D. MacArthur II, R. C. Hill, R. R. Bowie, S. Adams, General Persons, and Admiral Radford; H. Hoover, Jr., and D. MacArthur II. Practices golf on White House grounds.

9   Washington. Accompanied to office by Colonel Schulz. Appointments with J. C. Hagerty; Colonel Goodpaster; B. M. Shanley; W. J. Hopkins; Ambassador Harold A. Caccia (Great Britain), J. F. Simmons, and Colonel Goodpaster; General Persons; Colonel Goodpaster; H. Hoover, Jr.; bipartisan legislative meeting; Congressman Halleck; J. C. Hagerty; General Persons; E. Ginzberg; B. M. Shanley; H. E. Stassen; S. Adams and A. Larson. Practices golf on White House grounds. To swimming pool.

10   Washington. Appointments with Colonel Goodpaster; S. Adams; B. M. Shanley. To MATS terminal with G. E. Allen, J. C. Hagerty, and General Snyder en route to Eisenhower farm in Gettysburg, Pennsyl-

vania. To G. E. Allen's farm with G. E. Allen and General Snyder. Returns to Eisenhower farm en route to Gettysburg Airport. Enplanes for Washington, D.C.

11 Washington. Attends services at National Presbyterian Church with Mrs. Eisenhower.

12 Washington. Accompanied to office by Dr. M. S. Eisenhower. Appointments with Captain Crittenberger; General Persons; Colonel Goodpaster; B. M. Shanley; B. M. Shanley and Senator Green; B. M. Shanley; Colonel Goodpaster; S. Adams, General Persons, and Colonel Goodpaster; General Persons and Colonel Goodpaster; R. McPhee; Secretary Wilson. To Walter Reed Hospital to visit Secretary Dulles. Afternoon appointment with Murray Snyder. Practices golf on White House grounds.

13 Washington. Accompanied to office by Colonel Schulz. Appointments with B. M. Shanley; J. C. Hagerty; D. MacArthur II and Colonel Goodpaster; B. M. Shanley; General Persons; S. Adams; Ambassador Mehta, W. M. Rountree, and J. F. Simmons; Colonel Belshe; T. C. Streibert; J. C. Hagerty; W. H. Jackson; Colonel Goodpaster. To Burning Tree Country Club with W. R. Tkach for golf with Colonel Belshe. Practices at driving range with Colonel Belshe. Afternoon appointment with Colonel Goodpaster. To swimming pool.

14 Washington. Accompanied to office by Colonel Schulz. Appointments with D. MacArthur II and Colonel Goodpaster; Admiral Strauss; S. Adams; J. S. Lay and W. H. Jackson. Receives first set of Christmas Seals. Appointments with J. C. Hagerty; S. Adams, J. C. Hagerty, G. D. Morgan, G. Hauge, H. Pyle, I. J. Martin, Murray Snyder, General Persons, and Colonel Goodpaster. News conference, followed by appointments with J. C. Hagerty and Murray Snyder; B. F. Fairless, Howard Mullin, S. Adams, and General Smith (joined by Colonel Goodpaster); B. M. Shanley and Colonel Goodpaster; I. J. Martin and Senator-elect Revercomb; S. Adams; Senator-elect Cooper; J. C. Hagerty; Senator-elect Javits and S. Adams; General Curtis;

Secretary Humphrey; Colonel Goodpaster. To swimming pool.

15   Washington. Accompanied to office by Colonel Schulz. Appointments with D. MacArthur II and Colonel Goodpaster; Attorney General Brownell; National Security Council session; Secretary Humphrey; H. Hoover, Jr., and S. Adams. Hosts stag luncheon in honor of Prime Minister Constantine Karamanlis (Greece). Afternoon appointments with Douglass Fairbanks, Jr.; H. Hoover, Jr., A. W. Dulles, Admiral Radford, and Colonel Goodpaster; R. V. Fleming and S. Adams; General Bragdon and Colonel Goodpaster; B. M. Shanley; Cardinals Mooney, Spellman, and James F. McIntyre, and B. M. Shanley. To swimming pool.

16   Washington. Accompanied to office by Colonel Schulz. Appointments with Colonel Goodpaster; J. C. Hagerty; Attorney General Brownell; B. M. Shanley; Cabinet meeting; M. M. Rabb; A. Krock and J. C. Hagerty; Prime Minister Joseph Bech (Luxembourg); T. E. Dewey (off the record); S. Adams; G. D. Morgan; General Persons; Colonel Goodpaster. To swimming pool.

17   Washington. Accompanied to office by Colonel Schulz. Appointments with S. Adams; Governor-elect Underwood, John P. Hoblitzell (Republican State Chairman, West Virginia), and S. Adams; J. C. Hagerty and Colonel Goodpaster; W. J. Hopkins; F. J. Donohue, W. Ruschmeyer, and Colonel Schulz (off the record); A. S. Flemming (off the record); S. Adams; Senator Wiley; Colonel Goodpaster. To Walter Reed Hospital to visit Secretary Dulles. Afternoon appointments with J. C. Hagerty; Colonel Goodpaster.

18   Washington. [Page missing.]

19   Washington. Accompanied to office by Colonel Schulz. Appointments with S. Adams; Ambassador Luce; Secretary Benson. Receives turkey from National Turkey Federation. Appointments with Budget Director Brundage and A. R. Jones; S. Adams; H. Hoover, Jr., and Colonel Goodpaster; W. J. Hopkins and Colonel Goodpaster; J. C. Hagerty; H. E.

Stassen; Secretary Humphrey; Colonel Goodpaster. Practices golf on White House grounds. To swimming pool.

20　Washington. Accompanied to office by Colonel Schulz. Appointments with B. M. Shanley; D. MacArthur II and Colonel Goodpaster; G. D. Morgan; R. B. Perkins; J. C. Hagerty; K. McCann. To Burning Tree Country Club for golf with J. C. Hagerty and Colonel Belshe. Evening appointments with Colonel Goodpaster; B. M. Shanley; H. Hoover, Jr.; Secretary Humphrey; J. C. Hagerty.

21　Washington. Accompanied to office by Colonel Schulz. Appointments with B. M. Shanley; Colonel Goodpaster; D. MacArthur II; V. E. Peterson, R. E. Spear, Frank Fremont-Smith (Chairman, Panel on Human Effects of Nuclear Weapons), J. S. Lay, W. H. Jackson, and Colonel Goodpaster (off the record); Colonel Goodpaster. Cabinet meeting, followed by appointments with Secretary Wilson and H. Hoover, Jr.; H. Hoover, Jr., Secretary Wilson, W. H. Jackson, H. E. Stassen, Ambassador Peaslee, R. R. Bowie, Admirals Radford and Strauss, and Colonel Goodpaster (off the record); Prime Minister Habib Bourguiba (Tunisia), R. Murphy, and Ambassador Mongi Slim (Tunisia); Colonel Goodpaster. Afternoon appointments with J. C. Hagerty and Colonel Goodpaster; B. M. Shanley; R. Robertson, Generals Luedecke and Loper, and Admiral Radford (off the record); Senator Duff; Colonel Goodpaster; J. C. Hagerty; A. W. Dulles, R. Robertson, J. B. Hollister, Secretary Humphrey, A. S. Flemming, H. Hoover, Jr., Admiral Radford, and Colonel Goodpaster (off the record); Ambassador Lodge; G. D. Morgan.

22　Washington. Attends services at National Presbyterian Church with Mrs. Eisenhower. To home of Major J. S. D. Eisenhower at Fort Belvoir, Virginia, for Thanksgiving dinner. Returns to Washington, D.C., with E. Doud and Mrs. Eisenhower.

23　Washington. Accompanied to office by Captain Crittenberger. Appointments with D. MacArthur II and Colonel Goodpaster; J. C. Hagerty; Colonel Goodpaster; W. H. Jackson; Mr. and Mrs. Carl Brisson; General Cutler (off the record); W. H. Jackson (off the record); Prime Minister Solomon W. R. D. Bandaranaike (Ceylon), G. de Soyza, R. Murphy, Ambassador Crowe, and Ambassador Gunewardene; H. Hoover, Jr., and D. MacArthur II (joined by Colonel Goodpaster); Foreign Minister Jorge Loreto Arismendi (Venezuela), Ambassador Gonzales, H. Hoover, Jr., and Roy R. Rubottom (Acting Secretary, Inter-American Affairs); G. D. Morgan; S. Adams. To swimming pool. Off-the-record appointment with J. H. Whitney.

24 Washington. Accompanied to office by J. H. Whitney. Appointments with J. H. Whitney; G. D. Morgan; D. MacArthur II and Colonel Goodpaster; S. Adams and B. N. Harlow; W. J. Hopkins; Mark Trice, T. E. Stephens, and Senator Bridges; J. B. Hollister; S. Adams; T. E. Stephens, George E. Keneipp (Traffic Director, Washington, D.C.), and General Thomas A. Lane (Engineer Commissioner, Washington, D.C.) (off the record); S. Adams; Colonel Goodpaster; T. E. Stephens. To swimming pool.

25 Washington. Attends services at National Presbyterian Church.

26 Washington. Accompanied to office by Colonel Schulz. Appointments with D. MacArthur II, S. McLeod, B. M. Shanley, J. C. Hagerty, and Colonel Goodpaster; D. MacArthur II and Colonel Goodpaster; Budget Director Brundage and A. R. Jones; J. C. Hagerty. Receives Hungarian refugees, followed by appointments with S. Adams; Attorney General Brownell and S. Adams; W. J. Hopkins; B. M. Shanley. To MATS terminal with Mrs. Eisenhower en route to Augusta, Georgia. Golf with C. Roberts, W. E. Robinson, and E. Dudley. Dinner with E. Doud, General and Mrs. Snyder, G. E. Allen, W. E. Robinson, C. Roberts, and Colonel Schulz.

27 Augusta, Georgia. Walks to C. Roberts's quarters en route to office. To practice tee with E. Dudley and General Snyder, followed by golf with C. Roberts, W. E. Robinson, and E. Dudley. Dinner with E. Doud, Mr. and Mrs. J. H. Whitney, General and Mrs. Snyder, C. Roberts, and W. E. Robinson.

28 Augusta, Georgia. Walks to C. Roberts's quarters en

route to office. Inspects new wine cellar and kitchen with C. Roberts en route to practice tee. Golf with J. H. Whitney, W. E. Robinson, and E. Dudley. Dinner with E. Doud, J. Black, and Colonel Schulz.

29   Augusta, Georgia. Walks to office en route to practice tee. Golf with C. J. Schoo, J. H. Whitney, and E. Dudley. Appointment with Thomas E. Stephens (painter). Dinner with Mr. and Mrs. R. W. Woodruff, Mr. and Mrs. J. H. Whitney, W. E. Robinson, S. S. Larmon, Mr. and Mrs. C. J. Schoo, General and Mrs. Snyder, and Colonel Schulz.

30   Augusta, Georgia. Walks to office with Colonel Schulz en route to practice tee. Golf with S. S. Larmon and E. Dudley.

December   1   Augusta, Georgia. Walks to office en route to practice tee. Golf with F. F. Gosden, R. W. Woodruff, and E. Dudley. Visits W. E. Robinson's quarters.

2   Augusta, Georgia. Walks to office en route to pro shop. Attends services at Reid Presbyterian Church with Mrs. Eisenhower and Secretary Dulles. Lunch with Secretary Dulles. Poses for photographs with Secretary Dulles. Golf with E. Dudley.

3   Augusta, Georgia. Appointment with General Gault. To practice tee, followed by golf with W. E. Robinson, E. Dudley, and General Gault. Lunch with Colonel and Mrs. G. G. Moore, Mr. and Mrs. G. E. Allen, and General Gault. Receives heat treatment. To club house with J. C. Hagerty and G. E. Allen.

4   Augusta, Georgia. Appointment with Budget Director Brundage and Colonel Goodpaster. To practice tee, followed by golf with E. Dudley, Colonel G. G. Moore, and General Gault. Rides around golf course with G. E. Allen.

5   Augusta, Georgia. To office, then practice tee. Golf with C. Jones, W. Allen, and E. Dudley.

6   Augusta, Georgia. Appointment with Ambassador Dillon. To pro shop en route to practice tee. Golf with F. F. Gosden, G. E. Allen, and E. Dudley. Fishes at 16th hole with G. E. Allen.

7   Augusta, Georgia. Appointment with Secretary Wilson, W. J. McNeil, Budget Director Brundage, S.

Adams, and General Persons. Lunch with G. E. Allen, W. Kerr, Pete Kambach, F. F. Gosden, and General Snyder. Golf with P. Kambach, G. E. Allen, and E. Dudley.

8 Augusta, Georgia. Appointments with Budget Director Brundage, A. R. Jones, Don S. Burrows (Controller, AEC), and Admiral Strauss; General Marcel Penette. To Trophy Room for annual meeting of Augusta National Golf Club. To practice tee, followed by golf with C. Roberts, A. Bradley, and E. Dudley.

9 Augusta, Georgia. To office, then practice tee. Golf with P. Reed, T. Butler, and R. McConnell.

10 Augusta, Georgia. Accompanied to office by General Gruenther. To practice tee. Golf with E. Dudley, C. J. Schoo, and R. McConnell. Talks with General Gruenther and G. E. Allen before their departure. To office en route to R. McConnell's quarters.

11 Augusta, Georgia. To office en route to pro shop. To practice tee and putting green. Greets Prime Minister St. Laurent and family. Hosts luncheon in honor of Prime Minister St. Laurent. Golf with Prime Minister St. Laurent, Mrs. Hugh O'Donnell (Prime Minister St. Laurent's daughter), and E. Dudley. Escorts Prime Minister St. Laurent and his party to automobiles. More golf with E. Dudley, followed by dinner with E. Doud, Mrs. Eisenhower, R. McConnell, C. J. Schoo, E. Clark, J. Brownlee, and Colonel Schulz.

12 Augusta, Georgia. To office. To practice tee, followed by golf with C. J. Schoo, R. McConnell, and E. Dudley. Walks to club house.

13 Augusta, Georgia. To office. To practice tee, followed by golf with C. J. Schoo, R. McConnell, and E. Dudley. Returns with Mrs. Eisenhower and E. Doud to Washington, D.C.

14 Washington. Accompanied to office by Colonel Schulz. Appointments with W. J. Hopkins; S. Adams; B. M. Shanley and Colonel Goodpaster; Budget Director Brundage, S. Adams, A. R. Jones, and General Persons; Postmaster General Summerfield; Attorney General Brownell and Vice-President Nixon. Cabinet meeting. Poses for photographs with Vice-

President Nixon. Appointments with B. M. Shanley; Colonel Goodpaster. To St. John's Episcopal Church with Mrs. Eisenhower to attend funeral services for C. W. Tompkins. To swimming pool. Afternoon appointments with Colonel Goodpaster; H. Hoover, Jr., W. M. Rountree, S. Adams, J. C. Hagerty, and Colonel Goodpaster; H. Hoover, Jr., and Colonel Goodpaster; J. C. Hagerty; Senator Cooper; General Cutler; G. D. Morgan, General Persons, and Colonel Goodpaster; Colonel Goodpaster.

15   Washington. Accompanied to office by Colonel Schulz. Appointments with J. C. Hagerty; P. G. Hoffman and S. Adams (off the record); S. Adams, W. H. Jackson, and General Cutler; Budget Director Brundage, S. Adams, G. D. Morgan, I. J. Martin, K. McCann, and General Persons. Witnesses swearing-in of Jack Z. Anderson as Administrative Assistant to the President. Appointments with H. Pyle; S. Adams; Secretary Weeks and P. Ray; Postmaster General Summerfield and M. H. Stans; A. W. Dulles and Colonel Goodpaster; Secretary Dulles, H. Hoover, Jr., J. C. Hagerty, and Colonel Goodpaster; Colonel Goodpaster. To swimming pool.

16   Washington. Attends services at National Presbyterian Church. Appointment with Prime Minister Pandit Jawaharlal Nehru (India), Indira Gandhi, N. R. Pillai (Secretary General, Ministry of External Affairs, India), M. O. Mathai (Special Assistant to Prime Minister Nehru), Vice-President and Mrs. Nixon, Secretary and Mrs. Dulles, and Admiral and Mrs. Radford. Hosts luncheon with Mrs. Eisenhower in honor of Prime Minister Nehru and I. Gandhi.

17   Washington. Accompanied to office by Colonel Schulz. Appointments with Colonel Goodpaster; J. C. Hagerty. To Blair House to pick up Prime Minister Nehru en route to Eisenhower farm in Gettysburg, Pennsylvania. To Feaster farm with Prime Minister Nehru to inspect cows. To Neuman farm en route to memorial statue of Robert E. Lee. Inspects barn with Prime Minister Nehru.

18   Washington. Gettysburg, Pennsylvania. Returns to Washington, D.C., with Prime Minister Nehru. Appointments with Captain Beach; Vice-President Nix-

on; S. Adams; W. J. Hopkins; Colonel Goodpaster. Witnesses swearing-in of A. Larson as Director, United States Information Service. Afternoon appointments with Secretary Dulles; E. J. Hughes; Colonel Goodpaster; K. McCann; S. Adams; dentist.

19   Washington. Accompanied to office by Colonel Schulz. Appointments with B. M. Shanley; J. C. Hagerty; W. H. Jackson; B. M. Shanley; Colonel Goodpaster; J. C. Hagerty; Ambassador José R. Chiriboga (Ecuador); Prime Minister Nehru; B. M. Shanley; S. Adams; Secretary Wilson, W. J. McNeil, S. Adams, Generals Twining, Taylor, and Pate, Admirals Radford and Burke, and Colonels Randall and Goodpaster; Secretary Wilson and S. Adams; Colonel Goodpaster. To Indian Embassy with Mrs. Eisenhower for reception and dinner in their honor.

20   Washington. Accompanied to office by Colonel Schulz. Appointments with J. C. Hagerty; Colonel Goodpaster; Dr. Irving H. Page (President, American Heart Association) and General Clark. National Security Council session, followed by appointments with Secretary Dulles and S. Adams; Governor-elect O'Neill; Secretary Dulles, Secretary Wilson, Admiral Radford, and Colonel Goodpaster; Secretary Dulles; S. Adams. Poses for photographs with Governor-elect O'Neill. Afternoon appointments with Colonel Goodpaster; Secretary Folsom, M. H. Stans, R. C. Siciliano, and B. M. Shanley. Participates in ceremonies for Children's Stamp of 1956, followed by appointments with B. F. Fairless; President's Foreign Intelligence Activities consultants; Governor-elect Handley. Motors with Mrs. Eisenhower and Colonel Schulz to Ellipse for Christmas address to audience and nation via television and radio. Throws switch to light National Community Christmas tree. Hosts Christmas party with Mrs. Eisenhower for White House staff.

21   Washington. Accompanied to office by Colonel Schulz. Appointments with G. Hauge; Colonel Goodpaster; National Security Council session; Secretary Mitchell and G. D. Morgan. Hosts reception with Mrs. Eisenhower for White House staff. Afternoon appointments with Roderigo del Llano (Publisher, *Excelsior*, Mexico City), Justo Sierra (Mexican

Embassy), and J. C. Hagerty; Advisory Committee on Government Organization (off the record); B. M. Shanley; Inaugural Committee; Attorney General Brownell; G. Gray and Colonel Goodpaster; H. E. Stassen; Colonel Goodpaster. To swimming pool.

22 Washington. Accompanied to office by Colonel Schulz. Appointments with General Persons; Colonel Goodpaster; G. D. Morgan; J. C. Hagerty; General Persons and I. J. Martin; Colonel Goodpaster; dentist; G. Hauge; Colonel Goodpaster; General Swing; Colonel Goodpaster.

23 Washington. Attends services at National Presbyterian Church with Mrs. Eisenhower.

24 Washington. Appointments with J. C. Hagerty; Colonel Goodpaster.

25 Washington. [Page missing.]

26 Washington. Accompanied to office by Colonel Schulz. Appointments with Colonel Goodpaster; Ambassador Ricardo M. A. Espinosa (Panama) and J. F. Simmons; A. F. Burns; Ambassador Suleiman Jerbi (Libya); A. S. Flemming, G. Hauge, and General Persons; W. H. Jackson and Don P. Caulkins; Captain Beach; Vice-President Nixon, L. W. Henderson, J. B. Hollister, W. P. Rogers, T. S. Voorhees, Murray Snyder, General Persons, and Colonel Goodpaster; Vice-President Nixon; Colonel Goodpaster; Secretary Dulles, R. Murphy, and Colonel Goodpaster; Vice-President Nixon and Murray Snyder; General Persons and Colonel Goodpaster.

27 Washington. Accompanied to office by Colonel Schulz. Appointments with Colonel Goodpaster; W. J. Hopkins; Colonel Goodpaster; C. A. Davis; Senator Bricker; H. C. Butcher; L. M. Hall; Colonel Goodpaster; Secretary Folsom and I. J. Martin; Colonel Goodpaster; G. D. Morgan. Receives Cordiner Committee report. Afternoon appointments with Colonel Goodpaster; Secretary Dulles, Budget Director Brundage, and Colonel Goodpaster; Dr. M. S. Eisenhower. To swimming pool.

28 Washington. Accompanied to office by Colonel Schulz. Appointments with J. Z. Anderson and General Persons; Colonel Goodpaster; G. D. Morgan,

G. Hauge, and R. J. Saulnier; T. E. Stephens and
B. N. Harlow; Ambassador Osvaldo Chaves (Para-
guay); M. J. McCaffree and Colonel Goodpaster;
Vice-President Nixon and Shane McCarthy; Secre-
tary Benson; Prince Wan Waithayakon (President,
U.N. General Assembly), Ambassador Sarasin,
W. S. Robertson, and F. O. Wilcox; K. McCann;
Congressman Martin; W. J. Hopkins, General Per-
sons, and Colonel Goodpaster. Presents Distin-
guished Service Medal to General Gruenther. To
MATS terminal en route to Augusta, Georgia. To
practice tee, followed by golf with W. E. Robinson,
G. E. Allen, and E. Dudley.

29   Augusta, Georgia. To practice tee, followed by golf
with W. E. Robinson, G. E. Allen, E. Dudley, and
Major J. S. D. Eisenhower (joined by General
Gruenther).

30   Augusta, Georgia. Golf with W. E. Robinson, G. E.
Allen, E. Dudley, and Major J. S. D. Eisenhower. To
Bush Field en route to Washington, D.C.

31   Washington. Accompanied to office by Colonel
Schulz. Appointments with J. C. Hagerty; S. Adams;
I. J. Martin, General Persons, and Colonel Goodpas-
ter; Legislative Leaders; General Persons and Colo-
nel Goodpaster; Colonel Goodpaster; Legislative
Leaders; G. D. Morgan; Colonel Goodpaster.

1957

January   1   Washington. Morning appointments with S. Adams;
Vice-President Nixon and J. C. Hagerty; K. Mc-
Cann; W. J. Hopkins; Secretary Dulles. Afternoon
appointments with I. J. Martin; General Persons;
Secretary Dulles; bipartisan Legislative Leaders.

2   Washington. Morning appointments with General
Persons; J. C. Hagerty and T. E. Stephens; K. Mc-
Cann; J. S. Lay and S. E. Gleason; General Good-
paster and M. M. Rabb; General Goodpaster. After-
noon appointments with General Persons; S. Adams;
W. J. Hopkins. To swimming pool.

3   Washington. Attends Service of Intersession and
Holy Communion at National Presbyterian Church

with S. Adams and J. C. Hagerty. Appointments with General Goodpaster; National Security Council session; Secretary Humphrey, Budget Director Brundage, and S. Adams; Secretary Mitchell and James T. O'Connell; Louis J. Hector and S. Adams; L. T. Coggeshall and General Goodpaster; Secretary Dulles, Budget Director Brundage, and General Persons (joined by J. C. Hagerty). Afternoon appointments with S. Adams; General Persons; G. D. Morgan; A. H. Sulzberger (off the record); General Persons; General Goodpaster and W. J. Hopkins; General Goodpaster. Off-the-record appointment with R. B. Anderson, J. L. Hamon, and L. F. McCollum.

4   Washington. Morning appointments with T. E. Stephens; General Goodpaster; G. D. Morgan; General Goodpaster; R. J. Saulnier and G. Hauge; S. Adams; Dr. Elson and T. E. Stephens; National Church leaders. Receives Touchdown Club gold lifetime membership card. Practices golf on White House grounds. Afternoon appointments with J. C. Hagerty; T. E. Stephens; Secretary Dulles (joined by Senator George); G. D. Morgan. To swimming pool.

5   Washington. Accompanied to office by Colonel Schulz. Morning appointments with B. N. Harlow, T. E. Stephens, and Colonel Draper; L. A. Minnich; M. M. Rabb and L. A. Minnich; Murray Snyder; Attorney General Brownell, A. S. Flemming, S. Adams, and G. D. Morgan; Attorney General Brownell; General Persons; J. C. Hagerty. Receives George Washington Carver Memorial Institute Gold Medal. To 23rd and C Streets, N.W., for cornerstone-laying ceremonies at new State Department building, accompanied by S. Adams, General Persons, J. C. Hagerty, General Goodpaster, M. M. Rabb, and Murray Snyder. To Capitol with Mrs. Eisenhower, S. Adams, General Persons, J. C. Hagerty, General Snyder, and Murray Snyder. Addresses joint session of Congress on Middle East crisis. Attends dinner at home of Secretary and Mrs. Weeks.

6   Washington. Attends services at National Presbyterian Church with Mrs. Eisenhower with Mr. and Mrs. D. McKay.

7   Washington. Accompanied to office by Colonel Schulz. Morning appointments with B. M. Shanley, J. C. Hagerty, General Goodpaster, and M. J. Mc-Caffree; Attorney General Brownell and S. Adams; J. C. Hagerty; H. E. Stassen; General Van Fleet; General Cutler; F. E. Jorgensen and T. E. Stephens. Witnesses swearing-in of General Cutler as Special Assistant to President, National Security Affairs; J. P. Richards as Special Assistant to the President. Afternoon appointments with K. McCann; Ambassador Zellerbach; J. C. Hagerty and General Goodpaster; General Persons; S. Adams; Vice-President Nixon. Receives Electoral College delegation. Appointments with Vice-President Nixon; W. F. Knowland; General Persons and I. J. Martin; S. Adams. To swimming pool.

8   Washington. Morning appointments with General Persons and G. D. Morgan; W. J. Hopkins; Legislative Leaders; General Goodpaster; Secretary Humphrey; Ambassador Gardner (off the record); A. Larson; Price Daniel and S. Adams; S. Adams; Billy Berry (sick child) and family; H. Pyle. Afternoon appointments with B. M. Shanley and General Goodpaster; L. W. Hall. Hosts private dinner with Mrs. Eisenhower for Vice-President and Mrs. Nixon, Mr. and Mrs. S. Adams, Mr. and Mrs. D. McKay, Dr. M. S. Eisenhower, E. Doud, and General Snyder. Attends National Symphony Orchestra concert.

9   Washington. Accompanied to office by Colonel Schulz. Morning appointments with P. Young; S. Adams and K. McCann; Secretary Dulles. Cabinet meeting, followed by appointments with Secretary Benson; S. Adams; Secretary Weeks; President's Committee on Employment of Physically Handicapped; K. McCann. Afternoon appointments with Major J. S. D. Eisenhower; K. McCann; W. J. Hopkins; S. Adams; Hugh Meade Alcorn, Jr., S. Adams, and T. E. Stephens.

10 Washington. Accompanied to office by Colonel Schulz. Morning appointments with Secretary Mitchell; K. McCann; General Goodpaster; J. C. Hagerty; J. C. Hagerty and General Goodpaster. Delivers State of the Union Address before Congress. Afternoon appointments with B. M. Shanley; Attorney

General Brownell; General Cutler; President's Advisory Committee on Government Organization (off the record); Dr. M. S. Eisenhower and Budget Director Brundage; General Goodpaster.

11 Washington. Accompanied to office by Colonel Schulz. Morning appointments with S. Adams; M. J. McCaffree; L. W. Hall and J. C. Hagerty; G. D. Morgan; General Persons and I. J. Martin. National Security Council session, followed by appointments with Secretary Dulles; Secretaries Wilson and Humphrey, Budget Director Brundage, General Cutler, J. S. Lay, and General Goodpaster; Secretary Wilson. Afternoon appointments with J. C. Hagerty; W. J. Hopkins; General Goodpaster; T. E. Stephens.

12 Washington. Accompanied to office by Colonel Schulz. Appointments with General Cutler; General Persons and I. J. Martin; G. D. Morgan; S. Adams; B. M. Shanley; General Goodpaster and W. J. Hopkins.

13 Washington. Attends services at National Presbyterian Church with Mrs. Eisenhower. To MATS terminal en route to San Angelo, Texas.

14 San Angelo, Texas. To Officers' Club for breakfast meeting. Tours drought area. To Woodward, Oklahoma, for tour of drought area. Receives leather fringed coats and tie from Mayor Stark. To Clovis, New Mexico, for tour of drought area. To Tucson, Arizona. Dinner with Senator Goldwater, Secretaries Seaton and Benson, Colonel Draper, H. Pyle, L. O. Douglas, and Generals Snyder, Itchner, and James V. Edmundson.

15 Tucson, Arizona. Breakfast meeting regarding drought situation. Enplanes for Pueblo, Colorado, for tour of drought area. Meets with former Governor Johnson. Enplanes for Garden City, Kansas. Attends conference. Enplanes for Wichita, Kansas. Meets with farmers; Regional Drought Conference delegates. Returns to Washington, D.C.

16 Washington. Accompanied to office by Colonel Schulz. Morning appointments with B. M. Shanley and General Goodpaster; General Goodpaster; Budget Director Brundage and W. J. Hopkins; S. Adams.

Receives Gold Inaugural Medals with Vice-President Nixon. Appointments with J. C. Hagerty; G. D. Morgan; G. Hauge and R. J. Saulnier; B. M. Shanley; S. Adams; General Cutler, S. Adams, and J. S Lay; S. Adams; Secretary Mitchell; Labor Leaders. To swimming pool.

17 Washington. Accompanied to office by Colonel Schulz. Morning appointments with B. M. Shanley, General Goodpaster, and Murray Snyder; Ambassador Bunker; Vice-President Nixon, Secretaries Dulles, Wilson, and Humphrey, A. S. Flemming, A. W. Dulles, Admiral Radford, Budget Director Brundage, J. R. Killian, Generals Cutler and Goodpaster, J. S. Lay, and R. Robertson; Secretary Humphrey; Secretary Wilson; D. Thornton. Afternoon appointments with J. C. Hagerty and T. E. Stephens; W. J. Hopkins; J. H. Whitney (off the record); J. C. Folger; Secretary Dulles.

18 Washington. Accompanied to office by Colonel Schulz. Morning appointments with General Goodpaster; B. M. Shanley and General Goodpaster; Ambassador Ramón Villeda Morales (Honduras) and J. F. Simmons; B. M. Shanley. Cabinet meeting, followed by appointments with Secretary Weeks; Secretary Dulles, S. Adams, and General Goodpaster; General Persons; H. Pyle; President's Committee for Traffic Safety; J. A. McCone (off the record); C. del Sesto and S. Adams; P. Young; S. Adams; General Goodpaster.

19 Washington. Morning appointments with H. R. Luce (off the record); E. J. Hughes; T. E. Stephens; G. Hauge; Secretary Weeks and family; M. J. McCaffree and I. J. Martin; R. W. Woodruff.

20 Washington. Attends services at National Presbyterian Church with Mrs. Eisenhower and Major and Mrs. J. S. D. Eisenhower. Witnesses swearing-in of Vice-President Nixon. Takes Oath of Office. Attends reception at State Dining Room.

Index

Abel, I. W.: background, 1012; meets with E. on economy, 1012

Aberdeen Angus. *See* Gettysburg farm: Aberdeen Angus cattle

Aberdeen Angus Association: makes E. life member, 1559–60; pledges heifer for E., 1560–61; registers E. as "Eisenhower Farms," 1781

Abilene, Kansas: postmaster in, appointment of, 1221–22. *See also* Eisenhower Foundation for the Promotion of Citizenship

Abilene Foundation. *See* Eisenhower Foundation for the Promotion of Citizenship

Abu Dhabi: and Buraimi dispute, 296–97; Sheikh of, 296; and U.K., 296, 297

Acheson, Dean Gooderham, 1223–24, 1425; on China's "loss," Nixon's view, 1155

Acheson-Lilienthal Plan, 90, 91

Adams, John Gibbons: background, 1070; and principle of executive privilege, 1070–71, 1076; refuses to testify, 1070–71, 1076

Adams, John Quincy, on greatness of, 1438

Adams, Rachel Leona (White), 2459–60

Adams, Sherman, 30, 86, 387–88, 446–47, 809, 1777; and AEC on uncleared observers, 800; on aid for Port Townsend, 878, 879; and Allen, 241; on apathy in economic recovery, 1312–13; on appointees for D.C. civic auditorium commission, 1773–74; on appointment for Lucas, 1239–40; on appointment for Mahaffie, 1459; on appointment for Relin, 998; on appointment for Ryan, 1459, 1466; appreciation to, from E., 1941–42, 2459–60; on assignment for Barrows, 1633; as Assistant to the President, 6, 225, 229, 934–35, 1230, 1231, 1330–31; on atomic reactor for New

England, 1872; attends meeting on economic activities, 1963–64; attends stag dinner, 2062–63; background, 6; and Beardwood's view, 762; and Bricker amendment, 75, 2291; and CAB, 725, 1509–10; and Colorado River Storage Project, 1071, 1136–38; and disaster relief legislation, 1650–51; and Donovan's *Inside Story*, 2065–68; drafts letter to Knowland, 1817; and Durkin's resignation, 565–67, 571; on dust bowl problems in Colorado, 1063–64; and E.'s advisory committee, 1422–24; and E.'s candidacy in 1956, 1979; E. endorses Pius XII Memorial Library, 1369–70; E.'s esteem for, 830–31, 832; and E.'s finance committee, 1423; and E.'s heart attack, 1876, 2042; E. recommends Murphy to, 1205–6; on farm issues, 1304–5, 1311–12; and FCC appointment, 1090; and federal appointments, 6–7, 26–27, 329–30, 437, 516, 851–52, 2397; and foreign economic policy study, 1183; and FPC appointment, 2136–37; and Georgia politics, 1029; Gunderson's view, 646–47; on Hughes's address before Republican National Convention, 2247–48; Hughes's esteem for, 1461–62; and investigation of CIA, 1136–38; on Jackson plan on foreign aid policy, 1248–49; and John Marshall Bicentennial, 1280–81, 1290–91; and Johnson's message for E., 1797; on judicial appointments, 1610; Kelland's attack on, 1322; and Knuckles, 580–81; on liaison with Advertising Council, 1570–71; on liaison with Congress, 546; and Martin, 241; meets with Benson on farm message, 801, meets with E., 197, 1924; meets with E., Cole, 607; meets with E. on McCarthy, 1026–27;

memo to, on indexes for Cabinet, legislative meetings, 57; memo to, on India, 56–57; memo to, on mutualization, 2080–81; memo to, on N. Thomas, 612–14; and memo on treatment of government personnel, 930–31; on midterm campaign strategy, 1328–29; on Milton E.'s candidacy, 1878; and Minnesota primary, 2084–85; and Morgan's complaint, 928–29; on Morrow's nomination, 1255; and mutual security legislation, 2187–88; and national highway program, 1067; on organization of Operations Coordinating Board, 2476–77; on political advice for RNC, 1553; as political adviser, 857; on political strategist for E., 1287; on post for Caffey, 286–87; on post for Farley, 1553, 1624; on post for Reid, 1713; on public relations, 686–88; receives golf bag from E., 2459–60; and release of McMahon letters, 1092–93; as Republican leader, 2064–65; on RNC leadership, 1411–12; on secretarial assistance for E., 1571–72, 1633; on stag dinner guests, 1611; on steel strike, 2202–3; as successor to E., 229; and Suez Canal crisis, 2309–11; on Swiss watch tariff issue, 1226; and Taft-Hartley Act revisions, 538–39; on tax reduction proposal, 1943–44; and tripartite meeting on Suez, 2371–72; and TVA appointment, 1001; on U.S. economy, 1011; and use of E.'s name on letterheads, 579–80; and Wilson's peace plan, 1629–30

Adenauer, Konrad: cautious optimism of, 59–60; Churchill's message to, 1281, 1283; on clothing for East Germans, 554–55; on crisis in Middle East, 2418–20; displeasure of, on NATO manpower reductions, 2236; Eden visits, 1298–99; and food shortage in East Germany, 377–78, 399–400; and foreign ministers' meeting in Paris, 1613; and Franco-German discussions on Saar, 740–41, 1445–47; on Geneva Summit Conference, 1801–2; on German military strength, 1283, 2418–20; on German rearmament and reunification, 1375–76, 1801–2; on German unity and EDC, 383–86, 410–13, 1261–62; on greatness of, 1438; health of, 1965; invites Hoover to visit Germany, 1135; and London-Paris Accords, 1487–88, 1613; meets with E., Dulles, 1375–76; meets with George, 2218–19; on Nasser, 2359; and NATO defense policy, 2218–19, 2418–20; and plan for demilitarized zones in Europe, 1740–41, 1742–43; reacts to Soviet note, 707; requests E.'s Lincoln portrait print, 1428; on return of alien properties, 1432–33; sends message to E. by way of Gruenther, 2418–19; on Soviet invitation to Moscow, 1821, 1823; thanks E. for U.S. aid, 525; on uprisings in East Germany, 325–26, 410–13, 524–26; on U.S. presence in Europe, 707, 2418–20; visits U.S., 154–55, 161, 1428,

2227, 2229, 2419–20; voters endorse policies of, 508, 527–28, 569, 572

Adkins, Bertha Sheppard: background, 1128; on Green's cynicism, 1128; meets with Rickard on Oregon politics, 1708–9; praise for, from E., 1727, 2376; praise for, from Gunderson, 1727; on women in Republican party, 2376; on women's vote in presidential elections, 2376

Advertising Council: background, 1570–71; on liaison with White House, 1570–71; plans campaign for NATO, 1757–58; and USIA, 2111–12; and White House Conference of Business and Industry Associates of, 815–16

Advisory Board of Economic Growth and Stability: background, 277; Burns heads, 277–78; and McDonald's recommendations, 1011–13

Advisory Committee on Army Organization, 856

Advisory Committee on Government Organization. See President's Advisory Committee on Government Organization

Afghanistan, Republic of: Soviet aid to, 1922, 1923; and Turkey-Pakistan Alliance, 1114–15

Africa: air routes to, 1385; Asian-African powers call for cease-fire in Middle East, 2385–87; free scriptures for, 1439; on goodwill trips to, 2102; and Suez Canal crisis, 2263–64

African Americans: Byrnes's view, 418; and desegregation in public schools, 418, 421, 480–82; discrimination against, on public conveyances, 2086, 2087–88; E. appoints Wilkins, 934–35; on elections of, 2086; Graham's view on 1956 election, 2189–90; Lodge's view, 934–35; and patronage, 284–85; and Powell's article in Reader's Digest, 1342–43; Powell praises E., 934–35, 1342; as steelworkers in South, 2090, 2091; voting strength of, 284–85, 408–9, 418. See also Civil rights

Ageton, Arthur Ainslee: background, 329–30; as U.S. ambassador to Paraguay, 329–30

Agreed Announcement of September 10, 1955, and American political prisoners in Red China, 2457

Agricultural Act of 1933, and import quotas, 707–8

Agricultural Act of 1948: Kline's view, 554; Truman's criticism of, 563–64

Agricultural Act of 1954: and acreage allotment program, 1304–5, 2126; and flexible price supports, 1304–5, 2017, 2019

Agricultural Act of 1956, 2162–63; provisions of, 2126–27

Agricultural Adjustment Act of 1949: background, 126; and dairy price supports, 967–68; Kline's view, 563–64; and long-staple cotton quotas, 906–8; and mandatory price supports, 152–53; and price supports for oats, 707–8; and price supports for tung imports, 1083; and rye imports from Canada, 990–91; Thye's amendment to, 967–68

Agricultural Adjustment Act of 1954, 563–64, 806–7; assigns agricultural attachés, 1094–95; and price supports for beef cattle, 1297–98; provides flexible support for dairy prices, 967–68

Agricultural Advisory Commission. *See* National Agricultural Advisory Commission

Agricultural Appropriation Bill (1955), 1153

Agricultural Research Act (1954), 985–86

Agricultural Research and Marketing Act of 1946, 351–52

Agricultural Research Service, 985–86

Agricultural Trade Development and Assistance Act of 1954, 806–7

Agriculture: and disaster relief legislation, 1650–51; and effects of drought, 242, 1650–51; and Federal Reserve policy, 2303; and surpluses abroad, 369–70, 495–96, 1094–95; and Wheat Aid Act, 336–37, 369–70. *See also* Agriculture, Department of; Benson, Ezra Taft
—research: Benson's view, 351–52; E. endorses, 351–52, 985–86; and National Land Policy bill, 563–64

Agriculture, Department of: and Administration policy, 242, 423–24, 806–7, 1191–92, 1304–5, 1311–12, 1687, 1730, 1731, 1863–64, 2017, 2019–20; and Advisory Board of Economic Growth and Stability, 277–78; on appointments to, 379–80; and appointments of agricultural attachés, 1094–95; on beef purchasing program, 1603; and Benson's plan to expand agricultural exports, 768–69; and budget, FY 1955, 351–52, 643–44; and Bureau of Land Management, 1339–40; on Canada and oats imports, 707–8; on cattle imports, 1769–70, 1854–55; on conservation issues, 1841, 2019; on Cuba and sugar program, 1554; at Denver Federal Center, 343–44; and development of Washita River basin, 516–17; and disaster relief legislation, 1650–51; E.'s message to trade missions, 1016; and federal surplus food distribution, 2411–12; and funding for research, education, 351–52; and Ladejinsky case, 1494–95; and land purchase program, 1391–92; and land retirement program, 1863–64, 2017, 2019; on liaison with Congress, 546; on long-staple cotton quotas, 906–8; and meat-packers' strike, 2293; and meetings with cattlemen, 588–89; and Milton E.'s report on Latin America, 814–15; and oats imports, 707–8; opposes "time-lag bill," 920–21; on political adviser to RNC, 1424; and psychological warfare, 1812–13; and Randall Commission, 552–53; and REA, 1341–42; and reaction to Benson's plan, 968; recommends higher wool tariffs, 482–83; on rural development program, 2019; soil bank proposal, 1863–64, 2017, 2019, 2117–18, 2126–27, 2162–63; and soybeans for Formosa, 944; and state regulations

on cattle shipments, 1854–55; and sugar import quotas, 1529–30, 1530, 1554; and tung imports, 1083–85; and water resources policy, 689–90; and wool stockpiles, 482–83. *See also* Agriculture; Benson, Ezra Taft; Natural resources: conservation
—dairy products: Benson reduces supports for, 962–63, 964, 967–68, 991–92; and federal purchase of eggs, 1348–49; Kline's protest on butter surplus, 1053–54; margarine *v.* butter, 152–53; and price supports for, 152–53, 1053–54, 2267–68; public reaction to Benson's plan, 991–92
—farm program, 17, 1203, 1204, 1230; and acreage control, 125–26, 468–69, 495–96, 651, 653, 654, 655, 678–79, 1304–5, 1687, 2126; advertising and education, 655; Ayres's view, 764–65; on beef and vegetable consumption, 1297–98; Benson insists on "Eisenhower" plan, 801, 886; and cattle surplus, 1297–98; and chemical industry, 2126; and conservation issues, 1841, 2019; and dairy products, 962–63, 964, 967–68, 991–92, 1348–49; on disposal of surplus commodities, 2267–68, 2411–12; E. campaigns for farm vote, 2284–85; E. favors free-market economy, 393–94; E. speaks to Future Farmers, 558–59, 560–61; extension of farm credit law, 369–70; on farm bill, E.'s view, 2116–18; and farm bill veto, 2118, 2126–27, 2127–28; and farm politics, 423–24; and flexible farm supports, 2017, 2060; in FY 1955, 1841; and grass-roots tour, 423–24, 655; Gunderson's view, 646–47; Hazlitt's plan, 1942–43; and hog market prices, 2293; Kline's protest, 1053–54; and land purchase program, 1391–92; Lodge's proposal, 1858–59, 2162–63; and midterm election, 1348–49; Mintener's view, 664–65; need for gradualism in, 962–63; parity for commodities, 653, 655; as partisan political issue, 2116; and price supports, 125–26, 468–69, 588–89, 653, 655, 806–7, 861–62, 1203, 1204, 1297–98, 1311–12, 1687, 2017, 2019, 2060, 2162–63; and Randall Commission, 552–53; research, 655; reserve supplies of wheat, 495–96, 1391–92; and rigid price supports, 2017, 2019, 2060, 2126–27, 2162–63; and RNC, 1342; Roberts's view, 1304–5, 1311–12, 1342; Scripps-Howard survey on, 899; on stabilizing prices, 825; and storage for farm commodities, 468–69, 806–7; Summerfield's view, 2267–68; support for, in Iowa, 2112–13; on surpluses, 653, 655, 806–7, 1297–98, 1311–12, 2127–28; surpluses as food for POWs, 57–59; Thatcher's view, 125–26; Thornton's view, 861–62; Vermont supports, 923–24; and wheat referendum, 1687
—non-perishable products: price supports for, 393–94, 468–69, 806–7; reserve supplies of, 495–96, 806–7

Agriculture Conservation Program, and wind erosion control, 1650–51

Aiken, George David: background, 1111–12; and federal judgeship in Vermont, 1509; visits E., 1111–12

Air Coordinating Committee, and national aviation policy, 1317

Aircraft: air battle over South China Sea, 1223–24; B-26 bombers to French for Indochina, 887; C-47 transports to Indochina, 742, 746, 887; Constellation for Haile Selassie, 2387–88; on flying to E.'s farm (Aero Commander 560), 1735–36; and Fokker S-14 jet trainers from Holland, 1716–17; France requests C-119 transports to Vietnam, 1041–42; France requests U.S. mechanics for, in Indochina, 887, 892–94; and French Mystere jets for Israel, 2330; helicopters to Indochina, 742; on jet interceptor fighters, 1809; and J-57 jet engine production, 1603–4; and Lockheed T-33 trainers from U.S., 1716–17, 1747–48; and MIG incident, 529–32; on P-40s to France, World War II, 530, 531; on plant dispersal, 1808–9; on production of F-104s, 1809; Soviet jets down Navy P2V bomber, 1283, 1284, 1296–97

Air power: aircraft carrier to Indochina, 742, 746; Baruch's view, 1250; and budget policy for FY 1955, 643–44, 711, 712; E.'s view, 237–38, 341–42; and New Look, 197, 355–57, 589–90, 897, 2113–15; Schaefer's view, 1017–18; Scripps-Howard survey on, 899; Simon's view, 2113–15; Spaatz supports, 237–38; U.S. bases in Morocco, Spain, 583–84. *See also* Aircraft; New Look; Nike program; Strategic Air Command; United States Air Force

Air routes: to Africa, 1385; to Mexico, 1568–70. *See also* Civil Aeronautics Board

Akers, Floyd DeSoto: background, 1875; and Little Hunting Creek Lodge, 1874, 1875; recommends Charlie, 1874

Akers, Mrs. Russell Franklin, Jr., 637

Akers, Russell Franklin ("Red"), Jr., 637

Alabama, 623. *See also* Enon Farm

Alaska: on airlines serving, 1717–18; statehood for, 36

Albania, Republic of: on admission of, to U.N., 1901–2; Armstrong's view, 270

Albany Plan of Union. *See* New York

Albrecht, Henry Richard: on advantages of chisel plow, 1625; background, 1625

Alcoa Aluminum Company: antitrust suit against, 608–9; and third round increases, 608–9. *See also* Raw materials; Strategic materials

Aldrich, Harriet (Alexander), 1141–42

Aldrich, Winthrop Williams, 66, 168, 317–18; on aid to *New York Herald Tribune*, 1622–23; background, 44, 46; and Bermuda Conference, 271–72; and Churchill-Eden visit, 1141–42;

delivers message to Churchill, 2415; E. declines U.K. visit, 1749–50; and E.'s letter to Churchill, 1211; and E.'s letters to foreign friends, 19; and E.'s portrait of Churchill, 1524, 1525; and E.'s proposal for four-power meeting, 1614; on Geneva Summit, 1729; on Great Britain's request for assistance, 2403; on invitation to Cochran, 1728–29; presents medal to Churchill, 1646–47, 1906–7; and regional meetings with ambassadors, 66, 76–77; on Suez Canal base, 304–5; on Trieste negotiations, 1277; as U.S. ambassador to Great Britain, 44, 46, 1848–49; and U.S.-U.K. role in Egypt, 300–303, 304–5

Alexander, Harold Rupert Leofric George: background, 105; Birley's death, 105; Birley's portrait of E., 105

Alexander, Henry Clay: background, 904; meets with Hauge, 903; on statement by son, 904

Alexander, Holmes Moss: background, 1546; esteem of, for E., 1546

Alfred E. Smith Memorial Foundation: E. declines dinner invitation, 431–32; E. speaks at dinner, 517–19, 523–24, 1352–53; Gruenther speaks at dinner, 431–32, 523–24; Nixon addresses, 2335–36; Spellman's unhappiness, 517–19

Alger, Bruce Reynolds: background, 1477–78; wins Texas midterm election, 1477–78, 1637–38

Alger, Frederick Moulton, Jr., background, 129

Algeria: and conflict with French, 2076–77, 2404–5, 2413; Donovan's concern, 2076–77; Hoover's view, 2076–77; and Nasser's intentions, 2077–78; and U.N., 2164

Ali, Mohammed: background, 336–37; on Pakistan, 182–84; thanks E. for wheat, 336–37

Alien Enlistment Act, 79

Alien properties: and Dirksen, 932; return of, 932, 1432–33; Senate investigates Alien Properties Office, 932

Alien Property Custodian, 244

Ali Sastroamidjojo: background, 2385; on support from, in Hungarian crisis, 2386, 2387; on support from, in Middle East crisis, 2385–87

al-Khayyal, Shaykh 'Abdullah: background, 2463, 2465; on communism in Syria, Iraq, 2463, 2465

Allen, George Edward, 2199–2200; and Aberdeen Angus herd, 1486–87, 1496–97, 1546, 1560–61, 1593–94, 1601–2, 1864–65; and Allen-Byars partnership, 1463, 2174, 2175; and Allen-Humphrey bridge team, 1190–91; on aluminum shed at farm, 1619; arrogance of, at bridge, 1375–76; attends stag dinner, 918–19; background, 720–21; and Ballindalloch Jilt, 2197–98; and Barbarosa, 2197–98; and Brandon farm, 1496–97, 1593, 1594; and bridge with E., 1082, 1083, 1091–92,

American Library Association, and library "purges," 321–23

American Meat Institute (AMI), sends steaks to E., 763

American Medical Association (AMA), supports Bricker amendment, 860

American Motors Corporation, and defense procurement contracts, 1603–4

American National Red Cross, 163, 533–34; and aid to East Germans, 554–55; anniversary of, 1802–3; and Chinese aliens in U.S., 2457–58; Foster declines to head, 251; Gruenther heads, 2120, 2124, 2304–5, 2359, 2417–18, 2422; and Harriman, 1802–3. *See also* International Red Cross

American Newspaper Publishers' Association, E. addresses, 667–68

American Pipeline Corporation, 2244

American Public Power Association, opposes Dixon-Yates contract, 1201

American Quarter Horse Association, 1771; on horses for E., David E., 2184–85

American Relief to Korea, 159

American Retail Federation: on sales taxes, 624–25; on Social Security, 624–25; on Taft-Hartley Act, 624–25

American School of Classical Studies, Canaday represents E. at ceremony, 2159–60

Americans for Democratic Action (ADA), 1942; background, 1403, 1405; and Carroll, 1946; E.'s view, 1403; Hoover's view, 2156

American Smoking Tobacco Manufacturers Association, 38

American Society of Newspaper Editors: E. addresses, 32–33, 119–20, 667–68; E. predicts collapse of communism, 1958–59

AmVets, and absentee voting laws for service personnel, 1541

Ancell, Nathan S.: background, 1111–12; visits E., 1111–12

Andersen, A. Bogh: background, 1054; and coat of arms for E., 1054

Andersen, H. Carl, on agricultural price supports, 393–94

Anderson, Andrew, 278

Anderson, Clinton Presba, 37; background, 1853–54; on ICBM program, 1853–54

Anderson, Dillon: background, 807–8, 871–72; on Bricker amendment, 871–72, 882–83; on Holland's appointment, 807–8; and ICBM program, 1853–54; on mobilization stockpile, 1952–53; and study on U.S.-Soviet war, 1973–74

Anderson, Harrison Ray: background, 2105–6; offers benediction at Republican National Convention, 2105–6

Anderson, Marian, 780

Anderson, Mr., 2087

Anderson, Robert Bernerd: announces shipbuilding program, 1344; background, 225, 229; on breaking codes, 1330–31; on defense contracts, 1344; delays visit with Saud, 2461, 2464; as Deputy Secretary of Defense, 229, 941, 1055; directs desegregation at Charleston, S.C., and Norfolk, Va., naval shipyards, 473; on Egypt-Israel conflict, 1952–53, 2029, 2068–69; and E.'s invitation to Baylor, 1738–39; and E.'s New Look defense policy, 1488–89, 1491; on FOA transfer to Defense, State departments, 1660–61; meets with E., Dulles, 2029; meets with Saud, 2287; meets with Taber on defense appropriation reductions, 942; and National Manpower Council, 1474–75; and navy acoustic range on Puget Sound, 230–31, 232; and Oppenheimer case, 718; promotes Weaver, 38–39; on rank of service academy commandants, 1088–89; as Republican leader, 2064–65; as Secretary of Navy, 225, 229; as Secretary of Treasury, 229; and shelling of Quemoy, 1279; as successor to E., 229, 1439, 1953; and vice-presidency, 229, 2074–75; visits Middle East, 1952–53, 2028–29, 2068–69, 2096–97; visits Near East, 2028–29

Anderson, Warren, on son's drowning, 690–92

Andrews, Bert, death of, 595–96

Andrews, Thomas Coleman: background, 65; as Commissioner of Internal Revenue, 65; warns E. about Haskell, 1405–6

Anglo-Iranian Oil Company, nationalization of, 339

Anglo-Jordanian Treaty of 1948, 2328–30

Anschluss, and Austrian State Treaty, 1706–7

Antarctica, Byrd's expedition to, 1659–60

Antiaircraft weaponry, on Nike installation leaks to press, 767–68

Antipodes, 2111–12

Applegate, Rex: background, 1101–2; recommendations on U.S. ambassador to Mexico, 1101–2

Arab-Israeli war (1949), and conflict following, 569–70, 573. *See also* Arab States; Israel, State of

Arab States: and Baghdad Pact, 1948–50, 2055–56; boycott Israel, 573; Brooks's view, 2401–2; conflict with Israel, 165, 178, 569–70, 573, 1020, 1787, 1788, 1949–50, 2054–55, 2355–56, 2412–15, 2418–20, 2420–22, 2465; Dulles's view, 2053–55, 2060, 2338–39; Eden's concern, 1787, 1788, 1899; and Egypt's conflict with Israel, 2028–29, 2055–56, 2096–97; E.'s view, 2068–69, 2355–56; fear Turkey, 303; and Israeli-Jordanian conflict, 2328–30; and Nasser, as leader of Arab States, 2096–97, 2274–77; on "northern tier" of, 1788; oil reserves in, 1787, 2069; on oil for Western Europe, 2423–27, 2433–34; refugees from, 175, 573; Reid's plan, 1845, 1849; and sale of Soviet arms to Egypt, 1877–78; Soviet penetration of, Ben Gurion's view, 2142–43;

and Suez Canal base, 287–89, 569–70, 573; and tanks for Iraq, 2051–52; U.S. aid to, 168, 772–75, 1787–88, 2374; and U.S. economic policy in Mideast, 1966–68
—United Arab States: creation of, 2077–78; Nasser's intentions, 2077–78. *See also* Egypt
Arbenz Guzmán, Jacobo: background, 1168–69; resigns, 1168–69
Arends, Leslie Cornelius: background, 248; golf with E., 180; on military unification, 246–49
Argentina, Republic of, 300; abstains at Caracas Conference, 701; and breeders of Aberdeen Angus, 2012–13; military junta ousts Perón, 1947–49; Milton E.'s visit to, 316–17, 1327–28; and *New York Times* reports on, 514–15; Perón's attitude, 316–17; relations with U.S., 316–17, 514–15; Thomas visits, 1705; and tung imports, 1085
Argentine General Confederation of Labor, 648–49
Arias, Olga de: background, 2243; on pique during U.S. visit, 2242–43; on Salk vaccine for Panama, 2243
Arias Espinosa, Ricardo M.: attacks U.S., 2314–15; foresees trouble in U.S.-Panama relations, 2212–13; invites E. to Panama, 2211–12; and meeting of Presidents of American Republics, 2211–12; as Panamanian ambassador to U.S., 2314–15; as president of Panama, 2211–12; on Suez Conference Committee, 2314–15
Arizona: and Colorado River Storage Project, 901–3; E. visits drought-stricken areas in, 2467, 2468; on Pyle for governor, 2089
Arkansas, 222
Armas, Carlos Castillo. *See* Castillo Armas, Carlos Enrique
Armed forces: in Asia, Hull's view, 1160–61; in Asia, Van Fleet's view, 823, 1160–61; in Europe, 1446, 2204; and Formosa Resolution, 1520–21; in Germany, 2218–19; and JCS on force levels, 589–90, 591–92, 671–72; in Korea, and American women, 465–66; and military-industrial complex, 635–36; and NSC on force levels, 591–92, 611, 1160–61; personnel strength in, 1491; segregation in, 470–73, 698; and UDF, 1623–24; use of, in Korean reconstruction, 462, 639–40; and USO, 1623–24
Armed Forces Nurses and Medical Specialists Incentives Act, passes in 1957, 1887
Armed Forces Policy Council, and rank of service academy commandants, 1088–89
Armed forces reserves: legislation bolsters forces (H.R. 7000), 1757; and reserve mobilization policy, 1222–23; role of, in collective security, 1490–91; segregation in, 1753
Armed services: on absentee voting laws for, 957–58, 1541–44; and Capehart housing, 2056–57; and Career Incentives Act, 1531–32;

Chynoweth's view, 1220; and civilian leadership of, 1196; on common uniform for, 2254–56; Communists in, 951; duplications in, 434–35; housing for, 1885, 1886; interservice rivalries in, 405, 407, 1148–49; on limiting service promotions, 695–96; medical benefits for, 685–86, 1196, 1531–32; on nurses and medical specialists in, 1884–87; personnel policies for, 1196, 1531–32; and reconstruction in Korea, 442–45, 462; retirement and survivor benefits for, 449–50, 1196, 1396–97, 1531–32, 1748–49, 1751–52; roles and missions of, 434–35; salary scales for, 1196, 1200, 1531–32, 1730, 1731; unification of, 246–49, 255–56; and Wherry housing, 2171–72
Armed Services Memorial Museum, establishment of, 2006–7
Armistice Day, 675
Armour, Norman, Sr.: background, 1728; reports to Congress on Iran, 2439–40; resigns as U.S. ambassador to Guatemala, 1728; takes post with U.N., 1728
Armstrong, Hamilton Fish: background, 270–71; on Eastern European countries, 270–71
Army, Department of: at Denver Federal Center, 343–44; and personnel reduction, 1862; puts hold on new construction, 1862; and water resources policy, 689–90. *See also* United States Army
Army Command and General Staff College (Fort Leavenworth): E.'s recollections of, 1307, 1308; John E. attends, 1087, 1307, 1308, 1639
Army-Navy football game, 696–97
Army Nurse Corps. *See* United States Army Nurse Corps
Army Retirement Act (1948), 2094
Arn, Edward F.: background, 1399–1400; on judicial appointment for, 1399–1400
Arnold, Eleanor ("Bea") (Pool), on widow's benefits for, 449–50
Arnold, Henry Harley ("Hap"): background, 449–50; on benefits for widow of, 449–50
Arnold, Ralph ("Rip"), 1836; and "Augusta National Weekend" in Denver, 1300; background, 1300
Arrowsmith, Marvin, E.'s esteem for, 829, 832
Articles of Confederation. *See* Confederation, Articles of
Asia: Asian-African powers call for cease-fire in Middle East, 2385–87; and atom bomb, Cousins's view, 2234; Chiang's view, 2170–71, 2467; Clark's view of U.S. Pacific policy, 1073; communism in, 823, 1178–79, 1180–81, 1504–5, 1563–65, 1575–79, 1639–43, 2170–71, 2466; East Asia defense pacts, 278–82; E. compares with Latin America, 1416–17; foreign forces in, Van Fleet's view, 823; power ratio in, 1002, 1005; on research reactor program in, 1883–84; and SEATO, 1179, 1180–81; and Suez Canal crisis, 2264; U.S.

economic aid to, 1417, 1551; U.S. policy in, Judd's view, 1699–1700; and U.S. policy on Japan, 1535–36

Asian-African Conference, Chou En-lai's view, 1700

Associated Press (AP), 119; E.'s invitation to speak to, 667–68

Associated States of Indochina. *See* Indochina: Associated States of

Aswan Dam: Dulles's view, 2096–97; and High Dam project, 2028–30; and Nasser's attack on U.S., 2239–40; Sabri's view, 2268–69; and Soviet intervention, 2151, 2153; and Sudan, 2153; U.S. aid for, 2151, 2153; U.S. withdraws aid for, 2219–20, 2239–40, 2268–69, 2446. *See also* Egypt

Athletics, on independent athletic association, 1100–1101. *See also* Sports

Atlantic Community, Streit's proposal to strengthen, 2216–17. *See also* NATO

Atlantic Exploratory Convention, 2216–17

Atomic energy, 1240; and agency for international, 822; and Baruch Plan, 842–43, 862, 1617; Cole's concern, 1015–16; commercial development of, 368–69; control of, 487–88, 1059; and data exchange agreement, 764; discussion of, with Churchill, 1074; and Donovan's *Inside Story*, 2065–68; E.'s plan to harness, 825, 1112–13; E. speaks to U.N. on, 652, 655, 743–44, 747, 748, 759–60, 777, 790–91, 793, 798, 799, 822, 965–66, 1015–16, 1731–32; and EURATOM, 1965–66; as a force for peace, 1127–28, 1604–5; and New Look, 897; and nuclear research reactor program, 1883–84; and Oppenheimer case, 716–19, 1026–27; peaceful uses of, 1804, 2484–85; and power reactor for New England, 1870–72; and radiation study, 1589–90; and release of McMahon letters, 1092–93; and Shippingport plant, 1350–51; Soviet-Yugoslav declaration, 1732; on storage of, 1567–68; and U.N. Commission on, 862; and uranium production, 1567–68. *See also* Atomic Energy Commission; Atomic weaponry; Tennessee Valley Authority: Dixon-Yates controversy

Atomic Energy Act of 1946, 303–4, 1092–93; and Chalk River atomic energy plant, 363–64; and Cole, 368–69, 1216; and data exchange agreement, 764, 997–98, 2138–39; and Dixon-Yates controversy, 1197–98, 1200–1202; and protection of official secrets, 368–69

Atomic Energy Act of 1954, 1223–24; amendment to, 2001; authorizes Dixon-Yates contract, 1251–52; background, 1218; Cole supports, 1216; House passes, 1216; on research reactors abroad, 1883–84; Senate passes, 1218, 1231; on sharing naval nuclear secrets with British, 1905–6

Atomic Energy Commission (AEC): and atomic energy legislation, 1216, 1905–6; and Chalk River atomic energy plant, 363–64; on dangers of nuclear fallout, 1545–46; at Denver Federal Center, 343–44; on deployment of atomic weapons, 1417–18; and Dixon-Yates contract, 1443, 1454–55, 1778, 1780–81; and E.'s Atoms for Peace plan, 798–99, 1180; economic operations of, 1147–48; and ICBM program, 1853–54; Murray's proposals, 1426; on nuclear research reactor program, 1883–84; and Oppenheimer case, 716–19, 1026–27, 1036–37, 1133, 1476–77; and power reactor for New England, 1870–72; proposes International Atomic Energy Agency, 965–66; and release of McMahon letters, 1092–93; and restricted data exchange with Canada, 303–4; on sharing nuclear naval secrets with British, 1905–6; and Shippingport plant, 1351; and Strauss, 1476–77; on study of effects of radiation, 1589–90; and TVA, 556, 1197–98, 1200–1202, 1240–41, 1251–52, 1367–68, 1443, 1454–55, 1778, 1780–81, 1784; and uncleared observers at CASTLE tests, 799–800. *See also* Joint Committee on Atomic Energy; Tennessee Valley Authority: Dixon-Yates controversy

Atomic weaponry: air transport of, by British, 732–35; and arms reduction, 487–88, 504–7, 1697–98; ban of, 798–99; Baruch's view, 1018, 1038–39; as campaign issue, 2260, 2332–33; and CASTLE tests at Bikini Atoll, 799–800, 1015–16, 1068–69; Churchill's concern, 1522–25; Cole's concern, 1015–16; as conventional weaponry, 1604–5; Cousins's view, 2233; dangers of, 2101; and data exchange agreement, 764; and defense budget, FY 1955, 1206–7; on deployment of atomic weapons, 1417–18; Dulles speaks on, 1604–5; and E.'s Open Skies proposal, 1790, 1792, 1865–66, 2233; E. speaks to U.N. on, 745–46, 747, 748, 759–60, 798, 799, 965–66, 2041; and Formosa crisis, 1654–59; and H-bomb capabilities, 505, 507; and ICBM program, 1853–54; on increasing divisional firepower, 2236; on increasing production of fissionable material, 2234; on inspections of, 1616–17, 2039; Jackson's view, 798–99; and JCS plan for disposal of, 2405; JCS view on, 355–57, 711, 712; "just another weapon," 733, 735; Kefauver speaks on, 2336; Monty's view, 2154; Murray's proposal on atomic emergency, 1426; Murray's proposal on test limitations of, 896; and national security policy, 589–90, 671–72; and New Look, 897; and nuclear deterrence, Eden's view, 2218–19; and nuclear fallout, 1545–46, 2001, 2260; on nuclear war, Rosenwald's view, 2401; and "policy of candor," 251–52, 487, 504–7; Pope Pius XII speaks on, 2336; and "set-asides" policy, 765–66; on RAF planes, 2319–20; reserves of, for British, 732–35; at Savannah River plant,

303–4; Soviet fear of, 2413; Soviets propose ban of, 793; Stevenson calls for test ban, 2333; on thermonuclear testing, 2259–60; and "tube alloys," 1522, 1524; in U.K., 1522–25; use of, in failed Korean truce, 728, 732, 735; use of, in war, 1488–91; and Western diplomacy in Middle East, 479–80; Wilson's blunder, 1615–16. *See also* Disarmament; Hydrogen bomb; Missiles

AT&T Company, and Doerfer's FCC appointment, 1123–24

Attlee, Clement Richard: as British Labor opposition leader, 275–76; McCarthy's attack on, 275–76

Augusta National Golf Club. *See* Golf

Austin, Mildred Marie (Lucas), 923–24

Austin, Warren Robinson: background, 923–24; surveys Vermont views, 923–24

Australia, Commonwealth of: and communism in Asia, 1002, 1003, 1578; E. proposes coalition on crisis in Indochina, 1003, 1035, 1041–42, 1120; and mutual defense pact with U.S., 280, 282; and SEATO, 1181; and Suez Canal Committee, 2254, 2265; supports British opposition to coalition, 1041–42; and U.K. view on communism in Asia, 1639–43; and U.S. foreign policy, 2111–12; and wool tariffs, 552–53

Australia-New Zealand-U.S. Conference (ANZUS), Dulles discusses with E., 507

Austria, Republic of, 398–99: on admission of, to U.N., 1901–2; and Anschluss, 1706–7; Dulles reports on treaty, 1706–7; Dulles visits state opera, 1888–89; esteem in, for Kaghan, 256–58; France withdraws forces from, 1246–47; Hungarian refugees flee to, 2436–37; liberation of, 1112–13; Molotov's view, 1707; on redeployment of U.S. forces from Trieste, 1236–37, 1246–47; and refugees, 150–52; and Rosenbergs, 291; and State Treaty, 648–49, 658, 741–42, 1178, 1180, 1613, 1614, 1697–98, 1714, 1821, 1823

Automobile industry: and antitrust legislation, 2133–34; on automobile bootlegging, 2133–34; on economic problems of dealers, 2133–34; General Motors, Chrysler close plants, 2128–29; John E. buys Chrysler, 1088; on price-fixing, Baruch's view, 1018; on production in 1955, 2128–29; and Studebaker-Packard contracts, 2128–29; and Summerfields, 2133–34

Avent, Hugh P.: background, 1093–94; and West Point reunion, class of 1915, 1093–94

Ayres, William Hanes: background, 764–65; reports to E., 764–65; as Republican leader, 2064–65

Bachrach, Louis Fabian, background, 316

Baghdad Pact, 1950, 2446, 2459; E.'s concern, 2055–56; and Eisenhower Doctrine, 2473–75;

Nasser's intentions, 2077–78; Saud's view, 2474; Soviet view, 2157–58; and tanks for Iraq, 2051–52, 2055–56; and U.S. view, 2054–55, 2096–97, 2463

Bailey, Judy, 1150–51

Baker, Milton Grafly: background, 1580–81; praises Lodge, 1580–81

Balderson, C. Canby, E. appoints to Federal Reserve Board, 582–83

Balkan Pact, 275; background, 1114–15; discussions with Menderes on, 1114–15; U.S. concerns regarding, 1114–15

Ballistic missiles. *See* Missiles

Baltic Sea, 1609

Bandung Conference, 1763–64

Bankhead-Jones Act of 1935, 351–52

Bankruptcy Act, and Long Island Rail Road, 758–59

Barber, Edward John, 153–54

Barber, Ethel Amweg (Scott), 153

Bard College, 158–59

Barkley, Alben William: background, 1425; defeats Cooper, 1425

Barnard College, 21–22, 1688

Barnes, Stanley M.: on Alcoa antitrust suit, 608–9; background, 608–9; on defense contracts, 1344

Barnes, Sullivan: background, 1516; plans to reshape Republican party, 1516

Barnes, Wendell Burton: background, 1430–31; Collord's concern, 1430–31

Barrows, Roberta: assignment for, 1633; background, 1633

Barton, Bruce: background, 1651; on Formosa crisis, 1651; offers campaign advice to E., 2088

Baruch, Bernard Mannes, 124, 592–93; advises on cold war strategy, 1250; advises on NSC policies, 1148–49; on Armistice Day, 675; on automobile price-fixing, 1018; background, 91; and Baruch Houses, 149, 571; on Billy Rose, 2295; birthday of, 149, 150, 215–16, 237, 374, 395, 396, 402–3, 478–79, 511–12, 564, 571, 1250; and Churchill-Eden visit, 1141–42; on copper industry, 1250; on disarmament, 842–43, 1018, 1038–39, 1616–17; on E.'s Atoms for Peace speech, 753–54; on EDC, 1250; favors trade with Communist nations, 2103, 2104; on gold standard, 1158–59; on ICBM program, 1909–10, 1919, 2021–22, 2102–4; influences nuclear disarmament policy, 862; invites E. to visit, 1407; on lead and zinc issue, 1250; and Lubell's disarmament plan, 90–92, 374; lunches with E., 675; meets with E., 2021–22; memo from, to Roosevelt, 675; on Nike program, 1148–49; represents U.S. on U.N. AEC, 862; sends quail to E., 862; on Social Security, 1401; speaks at Industrial College, 1038–39; on standby mobilization legislation, 1038–39; on unemployment insurance, 1018, 1401; visits E., 2099; visits "Little Hobcaw," 753–54; warns E. on Soviet gold, 675

Baruch, Simon, 149; advice from, on vacations, 1407

Baruch Plan, 90, 91, 759–60, 842–43, 1617

Baseball: on Dodgers loss in World Series, 2323–24; on Larsen, 2324; on Newcombe, 2323–24

Bass, Perry Richardson, 14–15, 467–68

Bassett, James: background, 933; discusses patronage problems with Cabinet, 933; and public relations, 998; as RNC director of public relations, 998

Bataan, 749

Batista y Zaldívar, Fulgencio: background, 1554; E.'s view, 1554; friendship of, with Gardner, 2484; U.S. view, 2484

Battle, Laurie Calvin, on Randall Commission, 201

Battle Act. See Mutual Defense Assistance Control Act of 1951

Bay, C. Ulrick: background, 16; resigns as U.S. ambassador to Norway, 16

Baylor University, 1738–39; E. speaks at commencement, 2185–86

Beach, Edward Latimer: and Armed Services Memorial Museum, 2006–7; and Nimitz's visit, 111

Beardwood, Jack B.: background, 762; on Republican party in California, 762

Beaulac, Willard L.: background, 1949; as U.S. ambassador to Argentina, 1949

Beaulieu, David: background, 1455; on Maryland highway construction, 1455

Beck, David ("Dave"): background, 1245; on communism in labor ranks, 1245; and Eisenhower Fellowships, 1245

Beef. See Livestock

Belcher, Donald Ray, and Advisory Board of Economic Growth and Stability, 278

Belgian FN (Fabrique Nationale) rifle, 888–90

Belgium, Kingdom of: and EDC, 366–67, 1132; and EURATOM, 1965–66; and NATO, 1614; and Rosenbergs, 291; and WEU, 1614

Belgrade Declaration, 2383, 2385

Bellis, Frank S.: background, 459–60; as Earl E.'s business partner, 459–60, 478

Belshe, Thomas M., 1836; advises E. on putting green, 1594–95; background, 1594–95, 2053; E.'s esteem for, 2053; visits E., 1595

Bender, George Harrison: background, 284–85; on midterm election (1954), 284–85; on minorities, 284–85; on patronage, 284–85

Benedict, Stephen Gordon: background, 1312; on farm policy, 1304–5, 1311–12; on limiting E.'s travel, 1502

Benelu, Benelux (Belgium, Netherlands, and Luxembourg): and EDC alternatives, 1276; Eden's tour of, on NATO plan, 1298–99

Benét, Stephen Vincent, and *John Brown's Body*, 2005, 2027

Ben Gurion, David: Anderson meets with, 1953, 2068–69; background, 1953; and Egypt-Israeli conflict, 1952–53, 2068–69, 2142–43, 2336–37, 2338–39, 2355, 2372–73; E.'s message to, 2029, 2142–43; E.'s warning to, 2338–39, 2424; on Hammarskjöld's mission, 2121, 2142–43; on Iraqi troops in Jordan, 2336–37; and Israeli-Jordanian conflict, 2329–30; motivation of, 2329, 2355–56; Nasser's view, 2455–56; seeks arms from U.S., 2142–43; on U.N. cease-fire in Egypt, 2372–73; on withdrawal of Israeli force in Egypt, 2372–73

Ben Halim, Mustafa: background, 2352; and Suez crisis, 2351–52

Benjamin, Curtis G., on publishing E.'s speeches, 597–98

Bennett, Archibald Fowler: background, 846; and E.'s family, 845–46

Bennett, Charles Edward: background, 1604; on paper currency motto, "In God We Trust," 1604

Bennett, Wallace Foster, and Colorado River Storage Project, 902, 1138

Benson, Ezra Taft, 26, 88, 845; on acreage allotment policy, 1304–5, 1687; on appointments, 379–80; background, 5–6; and beef industry, 588–89, 645, 646, 656–57, 678–79, 1297–98, 1603; on bicycle tariffs, 1789, 1828–29; on Bricker amendment, 364; on budget policy for FY 1955, 643–44; on Bureau of Land Management transfer, 1339–40; calls for solutions to farm problem, 1942–43; on cattle imports, 1566, 1769–70, 1854–55; and Clay's farmer opinion poll, 1863–64; on corn market, 2267–68; on Cuba's sugar imports, 1529–30, 1554; and dairy products market, 152–53, 588–89, 962–63, 964, 967–68, 991–92, 2267–68; and death of Senator Taft, 448; and development of Washita River basin, 516–17; and D'Ewart, 1351–52; on disaster relief program, 1650–51; and drought in Southwest, 242, 364; on dwarfism in beef cattle, 2278; and Earl E.'s article, 880; on "Eisenhower" farm program, 801, 806–7; on elections for postmasters, 1400–1401; E. requests farm income forecast from, 991–92; E. supports, 646–47, 962–63, 967–68; fails in principle of gradualism, 962–63, 964, 968; on farm policy, 423–24, 588–89, 1304–5, 1311–12; on federal surplus food distributions, 2411–12; on flexible price supports, 806–7, 1312, 1687, 2017, 2019, 2060, 2267–68; and funding for research, education, 351–52; Gunderson's view, 646–47; on hog market prices, 2293; and Kleberg's plan, 588–89; on Kline and farm program, 563–64; Kline protests butter subsidy, 1053–54; and Ladejinsky case, 1494–95;

on IIA, 1754–55; *Road to Recovery* from Dutch, 1104–5

—Bible, on free scriptures for Africa, 1439; gifts for White House, 642–43; influence of, in family, 845–46. *See also* Eisenhower Administration: legislative program, and "Administration Bible"

Boone, Walter Frederick: background, 1189; heads Naval Academy, 1189

Borden, William Liscum: background, 718; and Oppenheimer, 718, 722–23, 724–25

Bor-Komorowski, Tadeuz, background, 2083–84

Bourguiba, Habib: background, 2405; on French-Algerian war, 2404–5; thanks E. for wheat, 2405; and U.S. aid to Tunisia, 2404–5

Bowie, Robert Richardson: background, 1019–20, 1526; as Assistant Secretary of State for Policy Planning, 1526

Bowles, Chester, 30; background, 52, 2206–7; on India, 53, 56–57; on Korean War, 53; political philosophy of, 2206–7; resigns as U.S. ambassador to India and Nepal, 52–53; sends book to E., 2206–7; suggests Milton E. visit Southeast Asia, 1727

Boyd, D. Rae: background, 681–82; reports scandal to E., 681–82

Boyd, Robert Osborne, heads National Mediation Board, 567, 571

Boye, Frederic William: background, 1093–94; and West Point reunion, class of 1915, 1093–94, 1126–27

Bracero Agreement, and importation of Mexican laborers, 2096

Bradley, Elizabeth Cannell, 469–70

Bradley, Mary Elizabeth (Quayle), 469–70

Bradley, Omar Nelson, 236, 1710; attends Elizabeth II's coronation, 72; attends NAC meeting, 178; background, 40–41; on conflicts between USO and UDF, 1623–24; E. awards fourth DSM, 469–70; favors research and development, 260–61; heads Commission on Veterans' Pensions, 1397; meets with E., 156; on national security policy, 356–57; on reimbursement for U.S. logistical support in Korea, 422–23; retirement of, 189, 469–70; as USO campaign chairman, 1623

Bradley, Vernon: background, 1204–5; loses in midterm election, 1204–5

Bradley University: on basketball scandals at, 2309; E. declines invitation to, 2308–9; E. speaks at, 2308–9

Bragdon, John Stewart: background, 1966; as CAB board member, 1966; death of, 1966

Brandon, Earl, Jones purchases farm of, 1190–91, 1395

Brandon farm: Aberdeen-Angus herd at, 1496–97; and Allen-E. partnership in, 1496–97; boundaries of, 1393; gas pump at, 1619; Nevins's concerns about, 1496–97. *See also* Gettysburg farm

Brandywine Breeders Association, gives heifer to E., 1735

Braniff Airways, and U.S.-Mexico air routes, 1569

Brannan, Charles Franklin: and ADA, 1403, 1405; background, 1405

Branscomb, Harvie: background, 617–18; invites E. to Vanderbilt, 617–18

Brazil, Federative Republic of, 171, 178; coffee prices in, 894–95; Cowles's memo on, 575; Italian immigrants in, 660–61; Kubitschek meets with E., 2211–12; Milton E.'s view, 575; and Rio Conference, 1275–77; sends U.N. force to Brazil, 2368–69; Thomas visits, 1705; U.S. relations with, 575

Brennan, William Joseph, Jr.: background, 1397–98; Dodge's view, 2305; E. appoints to Supreme Court, 1397–98, 1606–7, 2305

Brewer, Michael Joseph, 721

Brice, Arthur H.: background, 657–58; invites E. to hunt, 657–58

Bricker, John William, 282–83, 369–70, 784–85, 2141–42; attacks E., 848–49; calls E. "misled," 849–50; decides not to press amendment, 2111; deliberates on revisions to amendment, 1803–4; and Dulles's view on amendment, 2107–8; and Knowland's letter from E., 849–50; and Knowland's substitute amendment, 419, 421, 848–49; meets with E., 109; obsession with amendment, 136; opposes Bohlen, 137; reintroduces amendment, 75, 1511, 1962–63; and Republican party platform, 850–51, 2291; and Status of Forces Agreement, 386–87; submits further revisions, 2468–69; submits new draft amendment (S.J. Res. 181), 1095–96, 1103–4, 1789–90; urges E.'s candidacy in 1956, 2044

Bricker amendment, 831, 1730, 1731; and AMA, 860; Anderson's view, 871–72, 882–83; background, 75, 76, 140; Benson's view, 364; Brownell opposes new draft, 1095–96; Clay opposes, 834, 875; and Constitution, 784–85, 861–62, 875; Davis opposes, 834; debate on, unresolved in 1955, 1789–90; Dulles opposes new draft, 1095–96; Dulles's view on treaties, 840, 2107–8; E.'s attempts at compromise, 812, 816–17, 833–34, 835–38, 844, 866–67, 1095–96, 1994–95; E. cancels TV talk on, 837, 838, 844; E. critiques Dulles's paper on, 139–40; Edgar E.'s revisions, 812, 1789–90, 1803–4; Edgar E.'s view, 784–85, 1772, 1809–10, 1962–63, 1994–95; E.'s hypothetical question on, 2109–11; E. jokes about, 873–74; E. opposes, 74–76, 126–27, 136, 138, 282–83, 419, 421, 810–12, 833–34, 835–38, 841–43, 870, 871; E. takes stand against, 848–49; E. wearies of, 873–74, 1095–96, 1498–99, 1772; and executive agreements, 162, 282–83, 784–85, 842, 850–51, 861–62, 875, 913, 914, 1511; George's role on, 848–49,

913, 914, 1511, 2092; Griswold opposes, 833–34; Holman's role, 836, 838; Knowland favors, 1470–71; Knowland supports George amendment, 952; and Knowland's substitute, 419, 421, 848–49; Kuchel favors, 1470–71; lacks Senate teamwork, 963, 964; McCloy opposes, 816–17, 835–38; memo to Cabinet on, 74–76; Murphy's view, 860, 866–67; new draft of (S.J. Res. 181), 1095–96, 1103–4; Nixon opposes new draft, 1095–96; on Phleger's role, 1809–10; plagues E., 2468–69; on public power policy, 1570; reports of Edgar E.'s difference with E. on, 952–53; and Republican party platform, 850–51, 2291; and Republican ultra-conservatives, 762; revisions to, 282–83, 2468–69; Schaefer favors, 843; Scripps-Howard survey on, 899–900; Senate defeats Bricker's final effort, 914, 1435, 1439; senators sponsor, 836, 838; and Status of Forces Agreements, 386–87; and treaty obligations, 810–12, 841–43, 844, 848–49, 850–51; and "which clause," 75, 421, 812, 849–50, 850–51; Wriston opposes, 838–39

Bridge: with Allen, 1082, 1083, 1091–92, 1375–76, 1393, 1414, 1415, 1487–88, 1519, 1719–20, 1937, 1998–99, 2050–51; at Camp David, 1161–62, 1177; E. misses Allen's crabbing, 1955–56; E.'s skill in, 223; with Humphrey, 1082, 1083, 2028, 2035; at Palm Springs, Calif., 910–11; and party plans in Denver, 1835–37; with Robinson, 1082, 1092, 1177, 1375–76, 1414, 1415, 1487–88, 1519, 1719–20, 1937, 1955–56, 2034, 2050–51; sends "winnings" to John E., 867; tiresome at times, 2032; with Whitney, 2028, 2034. *See also* Gruenther, Alfred Maximilian

Bridges, H. Styles: background, 27, 29; dinner honoring, with Taft, 197; Edgar E.'s view, 141–42; Edgar E. visits, 2155; E.'s differences with, 826; E.'s view, 27, 29; golfs with E., 180; on judges' salaries, 129; lacks leadership skills, 827; meets with E., 142, 162, 328–29; opposes Bohlen, 138; votes against McCarthy censure, 1429

Brier pipes. *See* United States: foreign trade

Briggs, Ellis O., 281–82; background, 1536; on Rhee's treaty proposal, 1535, 1536; sends Rhee E.'s speech, 172, 174

Bright, Tom, 2483

British Chiefs of Staff: on joint planning, E.'s view, 1993–94; Stirling's appointment, 1993–94

Bromfield, Louis: background, 858; criticizes E.'s advisers, 857–59

Bronfman, Samuel: background, 382–83; and plan for world peace, 382–83

Brook, Norman Craven: background, 271–72; and Bermuda Conference (1953), 271–72

Brooks, David William: background, 2402; view of, on Arabs, 2401–2

Brossard, Edgar Bernard: background, 1084; on price supports for tung imports, 1083–85

Brotherhood of Locomotive Engineers (BLE): Brown heads, 922–23; and St. Lawrence Seaway, 922–23

Brotzman, Donald G.: background, 2406; loses Colorado gubernatorial race, 2406

Brown, Clarence J., background, 67

Brown, Guy Linden: attends stag dinner, 699; background, 699, 922–23; and BLE, 922–23; on labor's role in U.S. politics, 922–23; on publishing E.'s letter, 922–23; on St. Lawrence Seaway, 922–23

Brown, John Robert: background, 1510; federal judgeship for, 1510, 1637–38

Brown, Paul: background, 1365; on Post Office Department and Railway Express Service, 1365

Brown, Richard A.: background, 1268–69; on purchase of adjacent farms, 1483, 1485; and water rights at Gettysburg farm, 1268–69

Brownell, Gilbert Smith: background, 1145–46; illness of, 1152–53, 1192; misses reunion party, 1192; and Zahner case, 1145–46, 1152–53

Brownell, Herbert, Jr., 291, 368–69, 467–68, 1467–68; on absentee voting laws for service personnel, 1543; on AEC-TVA power issue, 1251–52; and Alcoa antitrust suit, 608–9; on antitrust policies, 1023–24; on appointing Catholics to federal bench, 1397–98, 1606–7; on appointment for Arn, 1399–1400; and appointments to Federal Reserve Board, 582–83; and appointments to judiciary, 1, 15, 516, 1507–9, 1610, 1637–38; attends stag dinner, 1986; as Attorney General, 5, 225, 227, 230; on authority of, to conduct investigations, 1045–46; on automobile bootlegging practices, 2133–34; background, 5–6; brief by, on racial segregation, 480–82, 714; Bromfield's attack on, 857–59; on CAB, 1509–10; on Clay's illness, 1876; on condemnation of forced labor, 2141–42; on defense contracts, 1344; and Denver Blue River Project, 1823–25; and Earl E.'s business venture, 478; E.'s esteem for, 1436; on E.'s finance committee, 1423; on E.'s letter to Knowland, 849–50; on emergency evacuation procedures, 1448–49; E. recommends McKeogh to, 1944–45; favors S.J. Res. 44, 1167–68; on financial aid for *New York Herald Tribune*, 1622–23; on honorary citizenship for Churchill, 1646–47; on Hughes's address before Republican National Convention, 2247–48; and immigration legislation, 118; on interstate commerce, 786–87; investigates lighter flints industry, 2389–90; and John Marshall bicentennial, 1280–81, 1290–91, 1555, 1606–7; memo to, on Department of Peace, 813–14; memo to, on Porter's complaints, 96–97; and migratory labor, 915–16; and N. Roosevelt's letter, 578; and

2332–33; on arms for Egypt, 1867, 1877–78; attacks Dulles, 2332, 2333; background, 1794–95; and Belgrade Declaration, 2383, 2385; congratulates E. on 1956 election, 2377–78; considers aerial inspections, 2470; on control of nuclear weapons, 2230–31; on E.'s Open Skies proposal, 1865–66, 2039, 2230, 2332, 2333, 2470; E.'s replies to, 2030, 2039–41, 2229–32; at Geneva Summit, 1794–95, 2230–31; on Hungarian revolt, 2361–63, 2377–78, 2379, 2386, 2469, 2470; meets with Eden in London, 2115–16, 2140–41, 2157–58; meets with Tito, 2383, 2385; and NATO, 2231; proposes conference on disarmament, 2470; proposes control posts, 1865–66; proposes U.S.-Soviet force at Suez, 2366–67, 2379, 2380–81; proposes U.S.-Soviet treaty, 1992, 2030; on reduction of troop levels, 2229, 2231; rejects aerial inspections, 2230; on reunification of Germany, 2230, 2231; sends message to E., 1987–88, 1992; and Soviet Declaration on disarmament, 2470; on Soviet military powers, 2470; on spirit of cooperation, 1794–95, 2231; and Suez crisis, 2232, 2318, 2348, 2470; supports Stevenson for president, 2333; on unconditional prohibition of nuclear weaponry, 2333; on U.N. disarmament subcommittee, 2231; visits Burma, 1923; visits Yugoslavia, 1860–61

Bulgaria, Republic of, on admission of, to U.N., 1901–2

Bullis, Harry Amos, 307; asks E.'s support for Bjornson, 1335; background, 234, 393; and Committee for National Trade Policy, 1226; on E.'s farm speech, 2303; on fight against communism, 233–34; on Judd's case, 233–34; on McCarthy, 233–34, 393, 1059–60; on Stevenson, 2303; on Swiss watch tariff issue, 1226; on tax and fiscal program, 234, 393, 961–62; on wheat stocks, 393, 495–96

Bullis, Maria Robert (Smorczwska), background, 961–62

Bunche, Ralph Johnson, background, 780

Bundestag (Assembly of West Germany). See Germany, Federal Republic of

Buraimi Oasis: and British, 2008, 2011, 2054, 2069, 2167–68; dispute in, with Saudi Arabia, 295–98, 2054, 2069, 2167–68

Bureau of Public Roads, studies nations' highways, 1067

Burgess, Carter L.: and absentee voting laws for service personnel, 1543; background, 1543, 1689; and Nichols's military training plan, 1688–89

Burgess, Warren Randolph, background, 1923

Burke, Arleigh Albert: background, 1705; as CNO, 1705, 1822–23

Burma: Bulganin, Khrushchev visit, 1923; and communism in Asia, 1002, 1416–17; and Communist China, 2448; Nationalist Chinese

irregulars in, 541–42, 1007–8; Soviet aid to, 1923; U Nu aids children of, 1760–61; on U.S. aid to, 2258–59

Burnham, William H.: background, 73; death of, 224; illness of, 72–73, 87–88, 114–15, 148; kindness of, to Min, 73

Burning Tree Country Club. See Golf

Burns, Arthur Frank: and agricultural price supports, 393–94; announces stable economy, 1147–48; background, 393–94; on bankers, 1011–12; on economic effect of government procurement, 1579–80; and economic operations of independent government agencies, 1147–48; and Federal Reserve Board policy, 2169–70, 2248; on FY 1956 revenues, 1831; heads Council of Economic Advisors, 794; and Jackson's world economic plan, 1019–20; on liberal home mortgages, 1579–80, 1696; on national housing surplus, 1696; participates in Republican legislative conference, 794; proposes Area Development Agency, 1847–48; and public works, 867–69; reports on economic welfare, 2249–50; resigns as CEA head, 2472; sees economic downturn, 804–5; and Small Business report, 2248–49; on steel strike, 2202–3; and Studebaker-Packard contracts, 2128–29; submits economic report to E., 1503–4; on tax reductions, 2472–73; thanks to, from E., 794; on unemployment, 1847–48; on U.S. economy, 1011–13, 1147–48, 1959–60

Burns, Eedson Louis Milllard: background, 2394–95; commands U.N. Emergency Force in Egypt, 2394–95

Burroughs, Robert Phillips: background, 129, 956; critiques E.'s TV appearance, 956, 957; on reforms in Italy, 956; on U.S.-Mexican relations, 1101–2

Burton, Courtney, takes Republican Finance Committee post, 852–53

Burton, Harold Hitz: background, 555; on Warren's appointment, 555

Bush, George Herbert Walker: background, 2019; on Keck's reported reprisals, 2071–72

Bush, Jimmie Tull: background, 1935; receives rug from E., 1934–35; remembers school days with E., 1934–35

Bush, Prescott Sheldon: and Harris-Fulbright Bill, 2016, 2018; on Keck's reported reprisals, 2071–72; on Randall Commission, 201

Bush, Vannevar: on atomic threat, 251–52; background, 251–52

Business. See Economy, U.S.

Business Advisory Council, seeks Robinson as member, 2246

Business and Defense Services Administration (Department of Commerce), and decontrol of nickel, 581–82

Business and Industry Associates. See Advertising Council

Butcher, Harry Cecil: on AT&T rate increase, 1123–24; background, 50; displeases E., 50; on E.'s gas act veto, 2071–72; employs McKeogh, 1944–45; meets with E., 2071–72; protests Doerfer's FCC appointment, 1123–24; protests FCC role in KIST litigation, 2071–72; on talk show programming, 2071–72

Butkus, John J.: background, 2267; on trade union politics, 2267

Butler, John Marshall, and Bricker amendment, 76

Butler, Karl Douglas: background, 1246; and Gettysburg farm, 1246

Butler, Paul M.: background, 1587; backs tax reduction bill, 1587

Butler, Richard Austen: background, 2403; on free-world economies, 357–58; and Iran, 216–18; requests U.S. assistance, 2403; on withdrawal of British force in Egypt, 2403

Butler, Thomas: background, 921–22; and E.'s finances, 921–22

Butterfield, Mrs. A. W.: background, 2161–62; Mamie E.'s appreciation to, 2161–62

Buy America Act: and Chief Joseph Dam, 306, 307, 1685–86; need for clarification of, 1081, 1082; and Randall Commission, 552–53; and "unreasonable" foreign bids, 1685–86

Byars, Billy G.: attends stag dinner, 1336–37; background, 1336–37; and Blackcap Bessie 13th of TT 1560–61; on cattle breeding, 1601–2, 2182–83, 2186–87; on dwarfism in cattle, 2313; on fundraising for Republicans, 2313; gives calf to E., 1463, 1496–97; Nevins visits, 1336–37; and partnership with Allen, 1336–37, 1394, 1395, 1463, 1601–2; and Prince 105 TT, 1601–2; on raising Angus cattle, 1336–37; sends chain to E., 1394, 1395; sends heifers to E., 1394, 1395; votes Republican, 2313; and Whitney Jilt 10th, 1560–61

Byrd, Harry Clifton: background, 628; coaches football with E., 628; rumors of candidacy, 628; tribute to, 628

Byrd, Harry Flood: attacks highway program, 1557; background, 1439; E.'s esteem for, 1435; investigates FHA, 1356–57; on Randall Commission, 201

Byrd, Richard Evelyn: background, 1659–60; heads Antarctic expedition, 1659–60; sends medals to E., 1659–60; urges more bipartisan action, 1659–60

Byrnes, James Francis: background, 261–62, 408–9, 1184; on black voters, 408–9; and Citadel head, 261–62; on desegregation in public schools, 418, 421; E. invites to Augusta, 1665; and E.'s view on civil rights, 470–73, 498–99; and federal judgeship in Florida, 1510; on hospital at Fort Jackson, 1862; meets with E., 418, 470, 471, 1665; at Potsdam, 1667–68; and President's Committee on Government

Contracts, 471, 472–73, 498–99; racial segregation ends at Charleston, S.C., and Norfolk, Va., naval shipyards, 471, 473; sends photo to E., 408–9; testimonial dinner for, 1665

Cabinet, U.S., 28, 30, 152; on appointments to, 683–85, 824–26; approves Area Assistance Administration, 1847–48; on Arab-Israeli conflict, 165; attends World Series, 2324; and automobile industry, 2133–34; Benson reports to, on drought in Southwest, 364; on budget figures, 716; Burns reports to, on economy, 1012, 1503–4; celebrates Inaugural anniversary, 839–40; and Committee on Water Resources, 1137, 1138, 1824; concerns of, on Formosa crisis, 1636–37; conference with members of (December 1953), 764–65, 778–79; discusses aid to Bolivia, 375–76; discusses censorship on DOD disclosures, 631–32; discusses E.'s role in labor-management disputes, 754–55; discusses foreign service in Department of Agriculture, 1094–95; discusses goodwill trips to Afro-Asian nations, 2102; discusses housing program, 751, 752, 801–2; discusses internal security program, 1494–95; discusses soil bank initiative, 1863–64; discusses unemployment insurance, 752; and DOD budget, FY 1958, 2472; and Donovan's Inside Story, 2065–68; Dulles reports to, on Communist intentions, 1618; and Durkin's resignation, 565–67, 571, 824; on economic operations of independent government agencies, 1147–48; and education policy, 913–15; E.'s esteem for, 1435–36; E. jokes to, about Bricker, 873–74; E.'s letter to, 1873–74; E. meets with, at Camp David, 1894–95, 1900–1901; favors St. Lawrence Seaway, 132–33; and foreign economic policy, 1182–83, 1244–45; and health reinsurance program, 1460–61; hears report on mutualization, 2080–81; and Hobby, 692–93; on indexes for meetings of, 57; on internal security risks, 897–98; and Italian immigration, 1113–14; on last minute legislative requests, 897, 898; and lead and zinc imports, 1242–43; members of, on TV panel, 278, 684, 685; on New Dealers in federal work force, 108; on treatment of government personnel, 930–31; on U.S.-Latin American relations, 436–37; and Milton E.'s report on Latin America, 670–71; and Mitchell, 673, 674; need for consultation with congressional leadership, 89; Nixon hosts meeting of, 1785; and opening prayer at meetings of, 22; on personnel reductions, 1715–16; and public works planning, 868–69; on reductions in military strength, 897; and Republican legislative conference (December 1953), 791, 793, 794; on return of alien properties, 1432–33; Rockefeller misspeaks on Ad-

ministration split, 1924; on rules of precedence, 666–67; sees Sarnoff's message device, 1825–26; Schaaf's view, 683–85; on selection of members, 1435–36; sends birthday greetings to E., 1872–73; sends E. flowering quince trees, 1872–73; on strains between congressional committees, executive departments, 897, 898; as team of leaders, 751; on U.S. forces abroad, 610–12; on VA, FHA mortgage policies, 1696; White House reception for, 1389–90; Wood's view, 1551–52
—Committee on Energy Supplies and Resources Policy: and Phillips case, 2018, 2033–34; recommends Natural Gas Act amendment, 2018
—Committee on Small Business, 2248–49, 2307; on tax reductions, FY 1958, 2473

Cabot, John Moors, 181, 183, 345; background, 345, 840–41; and Moores' visit to Latin America, 840–41; on relations with Latin America, 436–37, 464; visits Nicaragua, 202

Caffery, Jefferson: as U.S. ambassador to Egypt, 161, 245, 246; and U.S.-U.K. role in Egypt, 391

Caffey, Benjamin Franklin, Jr.: background, 286–87, 429–30; on E.'s election victory in Florida, 2381–82; E. recommends, 286–87; and media reports on Russia, 1216; on planning for disarmament inspections, 2189; on post for, 1737–38; on Republican party in South, 2381–82; on taxation, 429–30, 462–63

Caffey, Louise (Battle), 429–30, 1216

Cake, Ralph Harlan: background, 558, 802; calls housing plan "farce," 802; meets with E., 558; on U.S.-Mexican relations, 1101–2

Calhoun, John Caldwell: background, 1186; on states' rights, 1185

California: Beardwood's report on politics in, 762; Democrats for Eisenhower, 1193; drownings in, 690–92; endorses Knowland, Kuchel, 1606; Helms supports E.-Nixon in, 1606; Lodge reports on public opinion in, 547; midterm elections in, 662, 663–64, 1193; and Nixon, 1606; politics in, 662–64, 1232, 1470–71, 1606; seeks aircraft carrier contract, 1938; and Taft-Hartley Act revisions, 489–90

Cambodia, State of, 373; on admission of, to U.N., 1901–2; Communist aggression in, 1079; and Formosa crisis, 1654–59, 1662–63; and Geneva accords, 1199–1200; independence for, 677–78; and SEATO, 1181; U.S. aid to, 1079, 1310, 1311, 1547–48; U.S. diplomatic representation in, 1079; and U.S. position on, 1068–69, 1079, 1134–35; and Vietminh, 1042

Cameron, Benjamin Franklin: background, 1510; federal judgeship for, 1510

Campbell, Joseph: background, 989–90; as Comptroller General, 989–90

Campbell, Samuel James: advises E. on Angus herd, 1786; attends stag dinner, 1786; background, 1786

Campbell, Thomas Donald: background, 468–69; meets with E., 468–69; on storage for farm commodities, 468–69

Camp David, 369–70, 376–77, 1074; Allen visits, 1091, 1161–62; background, 407; bridge games at, 1091, 1161–62, 1177; E. meets Cabinet, NSC at, 1894–95, 1900–1901; E. visits, 1072–73, 1157–58, 1496–97; Gruenthers visit, 1082, 1083, 1105, 1146–47, 1157–58; Joneses visit, 1130, 1161–62; Nevinses visit, 1362–63; Robinson visits, 1091, 1161–62, 1177; Slaters visit, 1161–62

Camp Kilmer (N.J.), and Hungarian refugees, 2410–11

Canada, 2320; agrees to limit oats imports, 707–8; and Alcoa antitrust suit, 608–9; and Aluminum, Ltd., 608–9; and Chalk River atomic energy plant, 363–64; on diplomatic visits, 1961–62; discussions with, on control of nuclear weapons, 799; Dulles visits, 1627, 1629; E. visits, 593–94, 664–65, 672; fishing industry in, 1138–39; and gold, 1158–59; and lead and zinc imports, 1242–43; on Massey's visit, 973; and NATO, 1614; and Niagara River power development, 758–59; and Passamaquoddy power project, 1234; and restricted data exchange with U.S., 303–4; and rye imports, 990–91; and St. Lawrence Seaway project, 132–33, 146–47, 187–88; and Savannah River plant, 303–4; sends U.N. force to Suez, 2368–69; Stuart retires, 1932; and tripartite meeting with E., 2075; and waterway control legislation, 1278

Canaday, Ward Murphey: background, 2160; represents E. at American School of Classical Studies, 2160

Canal Treaty of 1903. See Panama, Republic of: Canal Zone

Cancer: on cigarettes and lung cancer, 755–56; on research for, and treatment of, 753

Candor. See Atomic weaponry, and "policy of candor"

Cannon, Cavendish Welles: background, 2070; on British role in Cyprus, 2070

Cantera, José Remón Antonio. See Remón Cantera, José Antonio

Cantril, Hadley, background, 1951

Cao Dai, in Vietnam, 1380, 1547–48

Capehart, Homer Earl: background, 27, 29, 1356–57; and Capehart amendment to Wherry Act, 2057; E.'s view, 27, 29; and FHA scandals, 1356–57

Cape Vincent Guides Association, 1154

Capitalism, E.'s view, 359–62

Caracas Conference. See Tenth Inter-American Conference

Ceylon, State of: on admission of, to U.N., 1901–2; supports U.N. action in Hungarian crisis, 2387; and trade with Red China, 2009, 2010; withholds approval on Suez declaration, 2254

Chamber of Commerce, 157

Chandor, Douglas, background, 1982–83

Chapin, Samuel M., 668–69

Chapin, Selden, background, 152

Charette, William R., 815–16

Chase, C. Thurston, Jr., 88

Chase, Jackson B.: background, 1961; on lawnmower for E., 1960–61

Cheatham, Owen Robertson: background, 124; and E.'s portrait, 721–22, 737–38; Roberts's view, 721–22

Cherne, Leo M., background, 961–62

Cherry Hills Country Club. *See* Golf

Cherwell, Frederick Alexander Lindemann: on atomic energy data exchange, 733–35, 764; background, 672; at Bermuda Conference, 672, 764; on reserve atomic weaponry for U.K., 734

Chiang Kai-shek: on collective security for Asian nations, 327–28; on communism in Far East, 2465–67; congratulates E. on reelection, 2465; Dulles meets with, 2170–71; Gruenther's view, 1540; Howard visits, 1708; on influence of neutralism, 2467; on irregulars in Burma, 541–42, 1008; on islands as "outposts," 1575–76, 1683–84; on Korea, 327–28, 340–41; and "loss" of China, 1155; on morale of forces, 1628, 1640, 1654–59, 1662–63, 1787; on moral leadership of U.S., 327–28; and Mutual Defense treaty, 1575, 1579, 1581, 1583; and Nanchi Island, 1581, 1582; Nehru's view, 2447; proposes revolutionary tactics, 2171; protests Outer Mongolia's admission to U.N., 1901–2; and Quemoy and Matsu, 1581, 1583; rejects U.S. proposal on offshore islands, 1683–84; and Soviet "peace offensive," 208–11; and U.S. force on Taiwan, 1581, 1583; and U.S. policy on Formosa, 1563, 1565, 1575–79, 1581, 1583, 1608, 1639–43, 1653–54, 1654–59, 1683–84, 1787. *See also* China, Republic of

Chicago Daily Tribune, and publication of Yalta papers, 1627–29. *See also* Media: press

ChiComs. *See* China, People's Republic of

Chief Joseph Dam: American bids on, 1685–86; British bids on, 306, 307, 1761–62; DOD rejects bids, 214–15; Reed's view, 1684–86; Wilson's view, 307

Chief Justice of the United States. *See* Supreme Court of the United States; Vinson, Frederick Moore; Warren, Earl

Chief of Naval Operations (CNO): and Formosa, 1533; replacement of, 1822–23. *See also* Carney, Robert Bostwick

Chile, Republic of: Ibañez meets with E., 2211–12; sells copper to U.S., 1954

China, People's Republic of (Communist China, Red China, ChiComs): admission of, to U.N., 234, 267–69, 275–76, 745, 773, 775, 796–97, 952, 1171–73, 1180, 1653–54, 2164, 2457, 2459; aggression of, in Burma, 2448; aggression of, in Laos, 2448; air battle over Sea of Japan, 1281, 1283, 1284, 1296–97, 1609; air battle over South China Sea, 1223–24; attacks by, on Tachens, 1520, 1533; attacks by, on U.N., 1172, 1173; attacks by, on U.S., 1172, 1173; on British trade with, 275–76, 773, 775, 2008, 2009, 2010–11; builds up forces, 1582, 1583; can pay any price in manpower, 1445–46; and captured U.S. airmen, 1413, 1449, 1451, 1526, 1576, 1579, 1668–69, 1718–19, 1720–21, 1779, 1781, 1800–1801, 2118–19; Chiang proposes revolutionary tactics, 2170–71; and Chinese aliens in U.S., 2448, 2457, 2458; Churchill's view, 728–29, 1172–73, 1180–81, 1444, 1446, 1522–25, 1577–79; and Collins's mission to Vietnam, 1377–81; controls on strategic trade with, 796–97, 2140–41; Cullen's fears, 627; demands withdrawal of Seventh Fleet, 1565; demands withdrawal of U.S. forces from Japan, 1565; Dulles's view, 1604–5; Eden's view, 1787, 1788; and "emigre" Chinese, 1641; and evacuation of Tachens, 1533, 1576, 1579; E.'s view on admission to U.N., 1178, 1180; and Formosa, 1282–83, 1511, 1533, 1536–40, 1575–79, 1581, 1583, 1654–59, 1662–63, 1692; and Geneva Conference, 952, 963, 964, 1021–23, 1068–69, 1172; and Geneva Summit Conference, 2458; and hatred of West, 1537; holds American political prisoners, 2448, 2457; holds U.S. POWs, 1171, 1173; hopes to break U.S.-U.K. unity, 1563; and invasion of Northern Indochina, 2448; Judd's view, 603–4, 1699–1700; Knowland's concern, 952, 1157–58, 1180; Laotian fear of, 1641; Lee's view, 795–97; Lodge's view, 312–13; McCarthy scores E. on, 1420; masters of surprise attack, 1577; Menon's view, 1779; and MSA bill, 1173; Mundt's view, 1694–95; Nehru's view, 1763–64, 2447; New England's view, in U.N., 923–24; Nixon's view, 1155; and offshore islands, 1519–21, 1533, 1581, 1583, 1608–10, 1644, 1654–59; and power ratio in Asia, 1002, 1005, 1033–36, 1576–79; and Quemoy, 1279, 1284–85, 1300–1301, 1331–32, 1575–79; releases U.S. airmen, 1718–19; and Sino-Soviet Treaty, 1539–40, 1565; Soviets propose "5-power meeting" with, 744, 747; supports Vietminh, 1003, 1005; threatens Korea, 2457; threatens Taiwan, 2457; on trade with Ceylon, 2008, 2010; on trade with Japan, 2009, 2010, 2103, 2104; and U.N. cease-fire proposal, 1520–21; U.S. changes policy toward, 18–19. *See also* Communism; Communists; Geneva Summit Conference

—Indochina: aggression of, in, 1171; E.'s state-

Churchill, Clementine (Hozier): health of, 2138–39; looks forward to Bermuda summit (June 1953), 240

Churchill, Winston Spencer: and American lineage, 1627–28; on atomic warfare, 2138–39; birthday greetings to, 1439, 1906–7, 2398; on Britain's desertion of duty in India, 743, 1134; calls for East-West summit, 216–18; calls for four-power meeting, 365; on cold war, 2099–2101, 2412–15; and colonialism, 1208–11, 1413, 1575, 1627; congratulates E. on reelection, 2398; deafness of, 729, 734; on deterrents to atomic warfare, 1522–25; on East-West trade controls, 958–61, 984; E. compares Mendès-France to, 1413; E.'s concern on Cyprus controversy, 1257–58; E.'s esteem for, 1642, 2364; encourages Luce to paint, 1706; E. proposes speech by, 1209, 1257–58; on E.'s U.N. speech, 734, 735; E.'s view, 734, 741–45, 789, 1436–37, 1626–27; on E.'s world peace speech, 154–55, 168, 181–82; faces House of Commons on atomic energy, 997–98; fears hydrogen bomb, 964–66, 987, 997–98, 1032, 1522–25; and foreign ministers' meeting in Paris, 1613, 1614; on free-world economies, 357–58; on free-world solidarity, 888, 1210–11, 1578, 2100–2101; on "gainsaying," 331; and Geneva Conference, 1002, 1005, 1032, 1074; and Geneva Summit Conference, 1614, 1782; on Germany and London-Paris Accords, 1614; Gifford's view, 43; greatness of, 1436–37; health of, improves, 862, 888–90; hopes E. is not "vexed," 1172; illness of, 331, 365–66, 398–99, 574–75, 592–93, 739, 746, 862, 1154–55; India, on Britain's desertion of duty in, 743, 1134; invitation to, from E., 592–93, 1074, 1099; and London-Paris Accords, 1614; memoir by, *Triumph and Tragedy*, 511–12; a mix of belligerence and caution, 744; Monty's concern, 385; and moratorium on H-bomb tests, 1068–69; on NATO, 60; and Nine-Power Conference, 1320–21; on portrait of, by E., 1446, 1448, 1524, 1525, 1565, 1566, 1628–29, 1706; proposes meeting with E., 574–75; on Queen's invitation to E., 1445–47; receives medal from E., 1646–47, 1906–7; requests visit to U.S., 1030–31, 1031–32, 1037–38, 1068–69, 1074; retirement of, 1614, 1626–28, 1646–47, 1666–67, 2099, 2101; on Saudi Arabia and Buraimi dispute, 296, 297; sends E. *History of English Speaking People*, 2138–39; on sharing atomic data, 1522–25; and Soviet "turn-abouts," 2100, 2101; on his swan song, 1211; tests Belgian FN rifle, 888–90; tests thoughts against E.'s, 921; and tripartite summit, 239–40, 398–99; on "tube alloys," 1522, 1524; on U.K.'s atomic stockpile, 1523, 1525; on U.S.-U.K. policies, 728–31, 741, 744, 1578–79; visits E., 592–93, 1074, 1099, 1132, 1133, 1134, 1140–41, 1154–55, 1165–67, 1183–84, 1207, 1210; on weekend with Luce, Hughes, 1706; on Western European Union, 1628; on World War II nostalgia, 1626; and Yalta papers, 1627–29

—Bermuda Conference (1953), 304–5, 317–18, 1154–55, 1793; agenda, 271–72, 739; appreciation of, from E., 735; and atomic energy data exchange, 764; on atomic weaponry, 732–35, 743–44; attendees, 270, 271–72; and Bidault, 741–42; British dinner at, 732; on burdens of independence, 743; cancellation of, 331; and Egypt, 742–43; final report on, 764; and four-power foreign ministers' meeting, 744, 746; and France's fear of Germany, 741–42; invitation to France, 665–66; invitation to Ismay, 330, 672; invites Baruch to, 694; and "joint ultimatum," 744; planning for, 253–54, 259–60, 270–71; political problems in France, 313–14, 315, 739–42; on postponement of, 292–93, 313–14, 315; purpose of, 738–39; renewed plans for, 648–49, 658, 665–66; takes "paintbox" to, 665–66

—Communist China: on admission of, to U.N., 728–29, 731, 1171–73, 1178, 1180; and Formosa, 1282–83, 1523–24, 1575–79; not a major threat, 1444, 1446; and press reports on U.N. question, 1180; and Quemoy and Matsu, 1575–79; and U.K. recognition of, 1282; on U.S. policy toward, 18–19, 744–45, 1170–73, 1522–25, 1575–79

—EDC, 60, 313–14, 365–68; and Bermuda Conference, 741–42; Bolton's view, 1294–95; and Eden's NATO alternative plan to, 1298–99; and France, 729, 731, 1261–62

—Egypt, 100–102, 216–18, 393; on Anglo-American alliance in, 2415; blunder regarding, at Bermuda Conference, 742–43; on Case A, Case B, 365, 367; hopes for U.S.-U.K. cooperation, 160–61, 742–43; and Suez Canal base, 288–90, 302, 304–5, 775, 782; suggests U.S. military figure at Suez talks, 68–69; and U.S. economic aid to, 773–74, 775, 782; and U.S. role in, 111–13, 160–61, 287–89, 300–303, 304–5, 365, 367

—Formosa: and Red China, 1282–83, 1575–79; and U.S. policy in, 1523–24, 1575–79, 1628

—France: and Bermuda Conference, 741–42; and crisis in Indochina, 1002, 1005; key to EDC, 729, 731, 1261–62; on policies of, in Indochina, 1134–35, 1172–73; in World War II, 1006

—Indochina, 1032: and coalition on crisis in, 1003, 1036, 1134–35; opposes military intervention in, 1042; on policies of France in, 1134–35, 1172–73; and Red China, 1178, 1180

—Korea, 435; opposes atom bomb in, 744; on Panmunjom truce talks, 259–60; and Red China, 1171–73, 1180; and U.S. plan for failed armistice in, 728, 731

—Soviet Union: advice to Molotov, on Korea, 259–60; advises vigilance, 154–55; E. advises patience regarding, 181–82, 206–8; and fisheries treaty, 155; and four-power foreign ministers' meeting, 744–45; on German invasion of, 641–42; on meeting with Soviets, 92–93, 181–82, 206–8, 216–18, 965–66, 1166–67, 1172, 1178, 1179, 1208, 1210, 1445–46, 1628; as real enemy in Middle East, 2413; on Wiley's speech, 366–67

—United States: and Anglo-American relations, 772–75, 782, 1172, 1178–82, 1210–11, 1281–83, 1563, 1565, 1575–79, 1639–40, 1642, 1646–47, 2138–39, 2412–15; on atomic data exchange with U.K., 997–98; and atomic energy, 965–66, 987, 1074; and CASTLE thermonuclear tests, 987, 997–98; and policy in Southeast Asia, 1134–35, 1575–79; on U.S. government, 1183–84

Church World Service, and aid to East Germans, 554–55

Chynoweth, Bradford Grethen: background, 1186; on Bricker amendment, 1220; on Cabinet rank for armed services, 1220; on Congress, 1220–21; on decentralizing industry, 1221; differs with E. on Middle Way, 1185, 1202–4, 1326–27; on economics, 1221; on eighteen-year-old vote, 1220; on Executive Branch, 1220; on farm program, 1220–21; on foreign policy, 1220; on hope, 1221; on military discipline, 1220; on Moses and the Amalekites, 1221; nationalism, 1220; political philosophy of, 1204, 1220–21, 1326–27; on public v. private power, 1221; on reinsurance program, 1221; on secretaries of state, army, 1220; on social security, 1202, 1204; on tax reform, 1221

Chynoweth, Grace (Woodruff), background, 1187

Cigarettes, and lung cancer, 755–56

CINCPAC (Commander in Chief, Pacific Command): and defense of offshore islands, 1581, 1582, 1618; and U.S. policy on Nanchi, 1581, 1582; and U.S. policy in Tachens, 1520, 1533. See also Stump, Felix Budwell

Citadel, The, 261–62; awards E. honorary degree, 1652, 1665, 1675; E. meets Byrnes at, 1665

Citizens for Eisenhower: background, 1328–29; celebrate Inaugural anniversary, 839–40; and Citizens Press Conference, 2084–85; Drummond's view, 1851–52; E. addresses Congressional Committee of, 1335–36, 1368–69; and E.'s nomination (1952), 396–97; and E.'s portrait, 580–81; give beef stew parties, 2281; Lodge's view, 687–88; and midterm elections, 1193, 1314–15, 1328–29, 1335–36, 1368–69; Murphy's view, 1376–77; and Nixon's candidacy in 1956, 2130–31; reprints Powell's article, 1342; Roberts's view, 1328–29, 1770; Willis's role, 1747

Citizenship, importance of, 1238–39

Citizens League of Rockingham and Strafford Counties (N.H.), 467

Civil Aeronautics Board (CAB): and appointments to, 725, 1459; criticisms of, 1464, 1509–10; economic operations of, 1147–48; and Gurney as acting chairman, 1466; and Northwest Airlines, 1317, 1717–18; and Pacific Northern Airlines, 1717–18; and Pan American World Airways, 1317, 1717–18; and recommendations on Pacific Northwest-Hawaii route, 1317; Rizley as chairman, 1466; and Ryan, 51, 1459, 1464–66; and U.S.-Alaska air routes, 1717–18; and U.S.-Mexico air routes, 1569

Civil Defense Administration, 286–87, 1238–39; Caffey takes post with, 1737–38; and defense budget, FY 1955, 1206–7; economic operations of, 1147–48; and emergency evacuation procedures, 1448–49, 1665–66; and "Operation Alert," 1751; Sarnoff's recommendations, 1825–26

Civil liberties: Finder's plan, 978–79, 1693–94; Hobby's plan, 978–79; and McCarthyism, 978–79; Stouffer's study on, 1693. See also Civil rights

Civil rights, 17, 408–9, 1238–39; Byrnes's view, 498–99, 713–14; in Charleston, S.C., 471, 473; and desegregation, E.'s view, 2084–85; on discrimination in labor unions, 2091; E.'s view, 470–73, 712–14, 1752–54, 1986, 2086–88; and Fourteenth Amendment, 421, 713, 714; Graham's advice to E., 2104–5, 2189–90; McCrary's plan on housing, 1690; and Morrow's appointment, 2095; in National Guard, 1753; in Norfolk, Va., 473; in North Carolina, 1355–56; Nixon speaks on, 2335; and Powell's article in Reader's Digest, 1342–43; Powell's view, 1753–43; and President's Committee on Government Contracts, 476–77, 498–99, 698; on progress in Post Office Department, 2095; on public conveyances, 2086, 2087–88; and Rosa Parks, 2087–88; Rummel integrates New Orleans Catholic schools, 2086–87, 2088; and school construction legislation, 1753–54, 1986; in schools and universities, 2086, 2087; and separate-but-equal doctrine, 408–9, 713–14; in South, 2090, 2091; and Supreme Court, 1354–56; Thornton's view, 2271–72; in Washington, D.C., 698. See also Civil liberties

Civil service: E. vetoes pay bill for federal employees, 1286–88; federal aid for, 1586, 1587; and federal personnel programs in D.C., 2122–23; and group insurance law, 1287, 1288; on increase in number of federal civilian employees, 2106–7; and N. Thomas, 612–14; on overseas tours for nurses, 1885, 1887; and patronage in California, 662, 664; proposed reforms in, 1203, 1204; security standards for, 825. *See also* Civil Service Commission

Civil Service Commission: at Denver Federal Center, 343–44; economic operations of, 1147–48; and Employee Security Program, 736; and health insurance program, 1521–22; and internal security program, 1494–95; and job security reforms, 320–21; on personnel reduction in, 1715–16; Schneider's complaint, 509–11; search for director, 28, 30; under Truman, 320–21, 473–74; and Zahner case, 1145–46, 1152–53

Civil War, 220

Clancy, William P., and release of McMahon letters, 1092–93

Clapp, Gordon Rufus: background, 928–29; Cooper's view, 1001; recommends Memphis steam plants, 1188; TVA term expires, 928–29

Clark, Charles Edward, background, 142; and Bricker amendment, 142

Clark, Edwin Norman: background, 927–28; memo by, on U.S. Pacific policy, 1073; on political problems in Italy, 927–28; on U.S. foreign policy, 927–28

Clark, Evans, E.'s esteem for, 829, 832

Clark, Grenville: background, 615–16; on disarmament, 615–16; on U.N. charter review, 615–16

Clark, Mark Wayne: and American-Korean Foundation visit, 159; and ammunition shortage in Korea, 10; awards E. honorary degree, 1652; background, 10, 1652; concern for John E., 10; and food for POWs, 59; heads CIA investigation, 1137, 1213; heads Citadel, 261–62; and Korean reconstruction plan, 462; on Korean truce, thanks to, from E., 425–26; and MIG incident, 531; and prisoner exchange proposal, 135, 146–47; on promotion for John E., 458, 459; on reinforcements in Korea, 397–98; and Rhee, 281–82, 309–10; on truce negotiations, 259–60

Clark, Maurine (Doran), 10; illness of, 425–26

Clarke, Kenneth: background, 1931; on Scottish Angus cattle, 1931; sends Scottish cap to E., 2081–82

Clarke, Owen Frederick, 94–95

Clark Hill Dam, 1511–12, 1515, 1569–70

Classified documents, declassification of, E.'s view, 1627

Clay, Frank B., 396

Clay, Henry: background, 1186; as "The Great Pacificator," 1186

Clay, Lucius Du Bignon, 128, 464; admires Blaik, 983; as adviser to JCS, 635–36; attends stag dinner, 396, 875, 891–92, 1423, 2062–63; on E.'s advisory committee, 1423, 1557; and E.'s candidacy in 1956, 1402–5, 2033; E.'s esteem for, 394–96; and farmer opinion poll, 1863–64; on General Motors expansion plans,

1528, 1556–57; heads national highway advisory committee, 1067, 1557; hospitalized, 1863–64, 1876; meets with E., 1557; offers service to E., 891–92; on Nixon as vice-presidential candidate in 1956, 2130–31; opposes Bricker amendment, 834, 875; serves on West Point board of visitors, 983; shoots hole in one, 1806–7; to visit Alaska, 396; visits E. in Denver, 396, 1876; and Wilson's proposal, 120

Clay, Lucius Du Bignon, Jr., 396

Clay, Marjorie (McKeown): background, 396; illness of, 891–92

Clemenceau, Georges: background, 318–19; E. likens De Gaulle to, 1035, 1036; E. likens Pleven to, 318–19

Clement, Frank Goad: protests E.'s policies, 1368; speaks at Democratic National Convention, 2250–51; and TVA, 557, 1366–68, 1778, 1780

Clement, Martin Withington: background, 1459; recommends Mahaffie, 1459

Clements, Earle C., 328–29

Coal, on aid to depressed anthracite regions in Pennsylvania, 1068

Cobo, Albert Eugene: background, 2065; as Republican leader, 2064–65

Coca-Cola Company: on Robinson as president, 1518–19; Woodruff steps down, 1518–19

Cochran, Jacqueline (Mrs. Floyd Bostwick Odlum): background, 1470–71; campaigns for Congress, 1998–99; E. paints Floyd for, 1652–53; E. sends Washington, Lincoln paintings to, 1652–53; on invitation to Parliament, 1728–29; invites E. to visit, 1470–71, 2478; sends get-well wishes to E., 2191; sends heifer to E., 2191; wins primary, 2191. *See also* Odlum, Floyd Bostwick

Codes: Dulles approves Omega for Middle East policy, 2096–97; on "tube alloys," 1522, 1524

Coffee, prices of, in Brazil, 894–95

Cohn, Roy Marcus: army's charges against, 951–52; investigates Kaghan, 257; and Schine, 951–52

Cold war, 17–18, 195–97, 1238–39; in Asia, 1416–17, 1575–79, 1639–43; and atomic weaponry, 732–35, 747–48, 965–66, 1616–17; Baruch's concerns, 1250, 1616–17; and Bricker amendment, 2111–12; Chiang's view, 2467; and Citizen Advisors on Mutual Security, 2134–35, 2163; Clare Boothe Luce's view, 2398–2400; and Communist China, 1575–79, 1641–42; and debate on admission to U.N., 1901–2; Dulles's view on Molotov's speech, 1889–90; and East-West trade controls, 2140–41; on economic weapons in, 1921–23, 1925; and Eisenhower Doctrine, 2474–75, 2476, 2487, 2487–88; E. proposes Churchill speak to issues of, 1209–11; E. proposes coalition on crisis in Indochina, 1002–

60; in Liberia, 1988–89; Lindtner's view, 1170; Lodge's recommendations, 697–98, 1553; Luce's view, 1520; and McCarthy, 428, 1170, 1420; in Mexico, 1099–1100, 1101–2, 1230; in Middle East, 2421, 2440–41; Nehru's view, 2447; "no haven" for, in Vermont, 923–24; penetrates Western Pacific, 1537–40; in Philippines, 1504–5; Presbyterians on, 667–68; Rhee's fear of, 1534, 1536; Roman Catholics on, 667–68; and SEATO, 1179, 1180–81; Soviet intentions, Monty's view, 2153, 2155; stand against, in Argentina, 316–17; study of, E.'s view, 321–23; on subversive activities, 699–701, 736; in Syria, 2463; and ultranationalism, 627–28, 633–34; and U.N., 2407–8; in U.S., and civil liberties, 1693–94; and U.S. economic policy in Mideast, 1966–68; U.S. fight against, 203, 433, 1574–79; U.S. POWs choose, 886; and U.S.-U.K. unity, 1563, 1565, 1574–79, 1639–40; in Vietnam, 1377–81, 1546–49; on weaknesses in system, 2466. See also China, People's Republic of; China, Republic of; Cold war; Communist party; Communists; Egypt; Hungary, Republic of

Communist China. See China, People's Republic of

Communist party: attacks Stalin at Twentieth Congress, 2101; congressional debates on, in labor unions, 813–14; and Hungarian revolt, 2334–35; influence of, in Guatemala, 1066–67; influence of, in Honduras, 1066–67; and legislation to outlaw, 813–14. See also Communism; Communists

Communists: aggression of, in Korea, 1534–36; in armed services, 951; call for disarmament, Kuter's view, 2326; on coexistence with, Reston's view, 1240; debate on admission to U.N., 1901–2; economic offensives by, in cold war, 1248–49; exploit spirit of nationalism, 372; at Geneva Conference, 1022–23, 1191; investigation of, in CIA, 1136–38; Kaghan's case, 256–58; Knowland's view, 1390–91, 1635–36; in Latin America, 1142–43; Lodge's view, 1635–36; and "loss" of China, 1155; in Malaya, 314, 315; and media reports on way of life, 1216; in Mexico, 1195, 1199, 1230; and MIG incident, 529–32; Murray's view, 1142–43; N. Thomas's protest, 612–14; and Oppenheimer case, 716–19; and Paris Accords, 1469–70; questions on, for Brownell, 974–75; and Radulovich case, 679–80; and riots in East Germany, 325–26, 410–13, 524–26; and Rosenbergs, 290–91, 298–99; and Sulzberger's plan for "political amnesty," 362–63, 559–60, 640–42; and Taft-Hartley Act revisions, 832–33, 872–73; and trade with, 790, 2103, 2104. See also China, People's Republic of; Communism; Communist party; Geneva Summit Conference; McCarthy, Joseph Raymond

Compton, Wilson Martindale, resigns as IIA head, 71

Comptroller General of the United States, Campbell's appointment as, 989–90

Conant, James Bryant: background, 66, 464, 1036–37; and Bernhard's conference, 1061–62; on charges against Oppenheimer, 1036–37; and EURATOM, 1965–66; on food shortage in East Germany, 377–78, 604–5; on four-power meeting, 707; as High Commissioner for Germany, 66, 127, 884; on Hoover's visit to Germany, 1135; on Hungary and Suez, German views, 2435–36; on Lysikov's defection, 1668–69; on meeting with Adenauer, 707, 1965–66; NSC Planning Board hears, 308–9; on problems with British, 604–5; on reducing diplomatic staff in Bonn, 604–5; and regional meetings with ambassadors, 66, 76–77

Confederation, Articles of: and Treaty of 1783, 837, 870; weakness in, and Bricker amendment, 837, 842, 870, 871, 883, 1994–95. See also Bricker amendment

Conference of Egyptian Ambassadors and Ministers to Arab States, 2077–78

Conference of Inter-American Presidential Representatives, on wage discrimination practices, 2296–97

Conference of National Organizations, 1733–34

Conference on Peaceful Uses of Atomic Energy, Strauss delivers message to from E., 1804

Congress, U.S.: on absentee voting laws for service personnel, 1541–44; and Agriculture Adjustment Act, 1297–98; and Air Force budget, FY 1957, 2255–56; on aluminum shortages, 608–9; appropriations for foreign aid, 33, 36, 204–5, 212–13; on appropriations, reduced requests for, 825; on appropriations for VA hospitals, 1805–6; approves home rule in Washington, D.C., (1959), 1176–77; authorizes FDR Memorial Commission, 1869–70; authorizes funds for wind-erosion control, 1063–64; and Battle Act, 959, 960; on bipartisan foreign policy, 1453–54, 1511, 1986; and Bricker amendment, 419, 421, 784–85, 811, 812, 816–17, 835–38, 866–67; Chynoweth's view, 1220; and Clapp's recommendation on TVA, 1188; close political balance in, 275–76; and Collins's mission to Vietnam, 1546–49; and Colorado River Storage Project, 901–3; committees of, scrutinize VOA, 71; condemns McCarthy, 1413, 1422; conference with leaders of (December 1953), 764–65, 778–79; and corporate giving, 533–34; and Customs Simplification Act, 306, 307; cuts navy research request, 260–61; and declaration on Soviet oppression, 63–64; and decontrol of nickel, 581–82; and defense reorganization plan (No. 6), 246–49, 255–56, 666–67; and Delaware River dredging pro-

1807–8; and Harlan's confirmation, 1664–65; on health programs, 1807–8; Martin's role, 1817–18; and natural gas legislation, 2013–16, 2018–19; passes Passamaquoddy power project, 1234; and reciprocal trade program, 1808, 1818; on refugee act amendments, 1808; on salaries for government employees, 1808; on school construction, 1807–8; on strengthening military reserves, 1808
—85th: and Armour's report on Iran, 2439–40; Democratic majority in 1956, 2370, 2392–93
Congress of Industrial Organizations (CIO): chills relations with E., 673–75; "dominant influence" in Democratic party, 1435; Dulles speaks to, 676, 677; E.'s message to, 673–75; esteem of, for E. (1946), 674; merges with AFL, 1584–85; and Mitchell, 673, 674, 1443–44, 1492; reelects Reuther, 558–59; and Taft-Hartley Act, 561–62, 673–75; and World War II, 673, 674
Conn, Fred J., and Eisenhower Birthplace Foundation, Inc., 609–10
Connecticut, federal judgeship in, 1509
Connor, Paul E., 513
Conolly, Richard L.: background, 1137; and investigation of CIA, 1137; member, Foreign Intelligence Activities Board, 1983–84
Conservation. See Natural resources: conservation; Water resources
Constantinople Convention of 1888. See Convention of 1888
Constitution of the United States, 280–81; amendments to, 126–27, 162, 1167–68, 1436, 1439, 2044, 2045; and Committee for the Defense of the Constitution by Preserving the Treaty Power, 834; and condemnation of forced labor, 2141–42; Edgar E.'s view, 1386–88; Fourteenth Amendment to, and segregation, 480–82, 713–14; and interstate commerce, 786–87; and Middle Way, 1185–87, 1386–89; and principle of executive privilege, 1069–71, 1075–76, 1080; and S.J. Res. 44, 1167–68; and Supreme Court, 1386, 1388; and Taft-Hartley Act, Francis's view, 771–72; on treaties, Dulles's view, 840; on treaties, Edgar E.'s view, 873–74; on treaties, E.'s view, 810–12, 835–38, 842–43, 848–49, 870, 871, 1994–95; Twenty-second Amendment to, limits presidential terms, 1436, 1439, 2045; and vote for eighteen-year-olds, 1829–30. See also Bricker amendment; Civil rights
Constitutional Convention of 1787, and Streit's proposal, 2216–17
Construction: air base, 466–67, 500–502, 895–96; for defense, 868–69; highway, 1455; of hospitals, 753, 1286, 1862; housing, 1696; and liberal home mortgage terms, 1579–80; maritime, 868; and public buildings, 868; reduction of, in armed services, 1862; of schools,

1586, 1587, 1753, 1754, 1807–8, 2084–85. See also Education; Highways
Continental Oil Company, and Harris-Fulbright Bill, 2015
Convention of 1888: and Suez Canal Conference, 2241, 2252; and Suez Canal crisis, 2222, 2238–39, 2276, 2279, 2280, 2286, 2355. See also Egypt
Cook, Everett Richard: attends stag dinner, 557; background, 556; on TVA, views of, 555–57
Cooke, Charles M. ("Savvy"), Jr.: background, 55; criticizes National Security Council, 54–55
Cooley, Harold Dunbar, background, 189
Coolidge, Grace Anna (Goodhue), and Young, 1169
Cooney, Mr., 1385
Cooper, Jere: background, 1828; on escape clause relief for lighter flints (ferrocerium), 2388–90; and import duties on bicycles, 1826–29; on Randall Commission, 201
Cooper, John Sherman: background, 286; meets with E., 286; and midterm election, 1001; and Nehru, 1634, 2000; rebukes McCarthy, Dirksen, Jenner, 286; on release of captured U.S. airmen, 1718–19; seeks foreign-policy role, 286; and TVA appointment, 928–29, 1001; as U.S. ambassador to India, 286, 1425–26, 1634, 1719
Cooperative for American Relief Everywhere, Inc. (CARE), and aid to East Germans, 554–55
Coordinating Committee of Paris Consultative Group (COCOM), and East-West trade controls, 959, 960, 984, 2140–41
Cope, Charles West: background, 1932; Whitneys send E. work by, 1932
Cope, Harley Francis: background, 2181–82; on curbing juvenile delinquency, 2181–82; on message to E. from John E., 2181–82
Copper: on copper wire exports, 2158–59, 2162; and East-West trade controls, 2140–41. See also Raw materials; Strategic materials
Cornelius, John Church, 900; background, 521; E. recommends, to Hall, 521
Cornell University, Nixon's complaint, 2324–25
Corps of Engineers. See United States Army Corps of Engineers
Corwin, Edward Samuel: background, 834; opposes Bricker amendment, 833–34, 875
Coty, René: background, 783; chooses Mendès-France as prime minister, 1132; congratulations to, from E., 783–84; E.'s message to, on fall of Dien Bien Phu, 1032–33; E. proposes four-power meeting, 1612–14; as president of France, 782, 789, 793; and ratification of Paris Accords, 1612; and U.S. role in Indochina, 1131–33
Cougar Dam. See Oregon
Coulson, John Eltringham: and Arab-Israeli conflict, 2340; background, 2342; on tripartitie agreement of 1950, 2341

Council of Economic Advisors: background, 277–78, 393–94; Burns heads Advisory Board of Economic Growth and Stability, 277–78; Burns reports to Cabinet on views of, 1011–13, 1503–4; Burns resigns, 2472; and McDonald's recommendations, 1011–13; and maintenance of prosperity, 803

Council of Europe, Consultative Assembly of, 317–18

Council on Foreign Economic Policy: Dodge's role in establishment of, 1244–45; and tariffs on Swiss watch imports, 1227

Council on Foreign Relations (CFR): E. chairs Aid to Europe Study Group, 839; E.'s interest in, 270–71

Council of Registered Relief Agencies Licensed for Operations in Germany (CRALOG), and aid for East Germans, 554–55

Cousins, Norman: background, 2233; calls for disarmament, 2232–34

Covert, Clandestine and Related Activities in Korea (CCRAK), background, 776–77

Cowen, Myron Melvin: background, 403–4; on Philippine elections, 650–51; as U.S. ambassador to Philippines, 403–4; on U.S. prestige abroad, 403–4

Cowles, Fleur (Fenton): attends Elizabeth II's coronation, 72; background, 575, 1128–29; memo to E. on Brazil, 575; on Shah's visit to U.S., 1128–29

Cowles, Gardner ("Mike"), 72; article by, on big business, 1505; background, 1505; on support of E.'s farm program, 2112–13

Cowles, John: background, 615; on disarmament, 615–16; on foreign aid to neutral nations, 2031–32; on support of E.'s farm program, 2112–13; and Toynbee's view of colonialism, foreign aid, 1925–26

Coykendall, Frederick: background, 120; death of, 1457, 1459

Coyne, Robert W., 440, 442

Cox, Willard R.: background, 1218; sends snapshots to E., 1217; vacations with E., 2196–97

Craig, George North: background, 980–81; on McCarthyism, 980–81; and Vogel, 1441–42

Crawford, Frederick Coolidge: background, 852–53; declines Republican Finance Committee post, 852–53

Crim, Howell G.: background, 642, 643; and gift Bibles for White House, 642–43

Crittenberger, Willis Dale ("Critt"): and ambassadorship to Mexico, 1101–2; background, 79; chairs Volunteer Freedom Corps Committee, 78–79

Crusade in Europe. See Eisenhower, Dwight David

Crusade for Freedom, 46; E.'s dinner in support of, 533–34; Holman heads, 2208–9

Cruz Salazar, Jose Luis: background, 1541; on U.S. aid to Guatemala, 1540–41

Cuba, Republic of: and Castro, U.S. view, 2484; communism in, 1553, 1554; Department of Agriculture view, 1554; on Gardner's friendship with Batista, 2484; Gardner resigns, 2484; Hauge visits Guantanamo Bay Naval Base, 1748–49; on Smith as U.S. ambassador to, 2484; State Department view, 1554; and sugar imports to U.S., 1529–30, 1530, 1553, 1554; Thomas visits, 1705

Culbreath, John, 1835; and "Augusta National Weekend" in Denver, 1300; background, 1300

Cullen, Hugh Roy: background, 627; isolationist view of, 627; on Korea, suspects Red Chinese buildup, 627; objects to E.'s gas bill veto, 2033–34

Cullman, Howard Stix: background, 755–56, 1966; on cigarettes and cancer, 755–56; on New York dock strike, 755–56; retires, New York Port Authority, 1966; takes Brussels World's Fair post, 1966

Culzean Castle: background, 1704; on E., as "Laird of Culzean," 1729; Milton E. visits, 1703–4

Currency, and paper currency motto, "In God We Trust," 1604. *See also* Monetary policy

Currie, Ralph W., background, 1637–38

Curtis, Carl Thomas: chairs Social Security study, 562–63; opposes Social Security tax, 692–93

Curtis, Harry Alfred: background, 1240–41; and tensions between TVA and AEC, 1240–41

Customs, Bureau of: personnel reductions in, 1715–16; valuation, pending legislation on, 1081–82, 1109–10

Customs Simplification Act of 1953, 37; becomes law, 306, 307, 369–70; and H.R. 1, 1573

Cutler, Robert ("Bobby"), 30, 78, 103, 308–9, 1559; on absentee voting for service personnel, 957–58, 1543–44; address by, on national security policy, 1972; advises E. on national security affairs, 54–55, 225, 229; and Alcoa antitrust suit, 608–9; on atomic weaponry in defense of Formosa, 1617–18; attends stag dinner, 2062–63; background, 11–12; on breaking codes, 1330–31; and Bricker amendment, 834; briefs E. on China policy, 1300–1301; and Bush-Oppenheimer visit, 251–52; and Clark's memo on U.S. Pacific policy, 1073; directs National Security Council, 225; and disarmament, E.'s view, 487–88; drafts reply to Baruch, 1148–49; E.'s esteem for, 831, 832; on emergency evacuation plans, 1448–49; esteem for Holland, 807–8; and executive branch study, 11; on farewell dinner for Smith, 1302; on FY 1955 budget matters, 589–90; Gruenther's view on France, 891; on invitation to Zhukov, 1583–84; meets with E., 197; on MIG incident, 531; on military retirees as advisers, 620–21, 636; on National Committee for a Free Europe, 533–34; and OCB, 1330–31; and Oppenheimer case, 718, 722–23; and

Denny, Harmar Denny: background, 725; as CAB vice-chairman, 725
Denver Federal Center: motor vehicles at, 343–44; overstaffing at, 343–44; personnel reductions at, 343–44; space needs at, 343–44
Department of Agriculture and Farm Credit Administration Appropriation Act, 1955, 1153
Department of Defense Appropriation Act of 1956, 1772–73
Department of Peace: memo to Brownell on, 813–14; Staggers proposes, 812–13
Depression, McDonald's report on, 1011–13. *See also* Economy, U.S.
Desegregation. *See* Civil rights; Supreme Court of the United States
Deupree, Richard Redwood ("Red"): background, 852–53; recommends Crawford for Republican Finance Committee post, 852–53
Development Assistance Agreement, and U.S. aid to Guatemala, 1541
D'Ewart, Wesley Abner: background, 933, 1351–52; candidacy of, 933–34; loses to Murray in midterm election, 1351–52; takes post with Benson, 1351–52
de Welden, Felix Weihs: background, 258; and bust of E., 258
Dewey, Frances E. (Hutt), background, 1339
Dewey, Thomas Edmund: attends stag dinner, 1467–68, 2062–63; background, 572; Bromfield's view, 857–59; on cigarettes and cancer, 755–56; declines Canadian-American Defense Board, 758–59; on Edwards, 1384; on E.'s midterm campaign role, 1339; endorses flymaster, 1842; E.'s view, 2323; on Long Island Rail Road, 758–59; meets with E., 1383; on midterm election, 1383; on Niagara power development, 758–59; political plans of, 758–59, 1467–68; on Supreme Court, E.'s view, 568
DEW line (Distant Early Warning), and study on U.S.-Soviet war, 1973–74
Dexheimer, Wilbur App: background, 1346; on irrigation plans at Gettysburg farm, 1345–46
Dhahran Airfield. *See* Saudi Arabia
Diem, Ngo Dinh: background, 1310, 1547; and Collins's mission to Vietnam, 1378–80, 1546–49; Collins recommends ouster of, 1548; conflict with Binh Xuyen, 1547–48; esteem of, for O'Daniel, 1929–30; E. supports, 1546–49, 2452, 2454; on free elections in Vietnam, 2006; seeks U.S. aid, 1309–11; as Vietnam's prime minister, 1310
Digby, Seaborn Lee: background, 448–49; E. appoints to FPC, 448–49
Dillon, Clarence: background, 49; on return to gold standard, 1158–59
Dillon, Clarence Douglas: background, 66; and Bermuda Conference (1953), 253–54, 271–72; conveys Ismay's message, 2416; and EDC, 527, 528; on Indochina, E.'s view, 213;

meets with Donovan on Algeria, 2076–77; meets with French leaders, 213; meets with Laniel, 433; meets with Mollet on Suez ceasefire, 2369; and Pleven's view on Indochina, 954; and Pleven's view on Red China, 953–54; and regional meetings with ambassadors, 66, 76–77; seeks E.'s help for Case, 1288–89; speech by, supports France, 2076–77; supports aid to France in Vietnam, 1042; on training Vietnamese troops, 1121; on U.S. aid in Indochina, 433, 1132–33; as U.S. ambassador to France, 65–66
Dina Abdel Hamid, Queen of Jordan, on visit to U.S., 1845, 1849
Dinosaur National Monument, 1071–72, 1194–95, 1198–99. *See also* Colorado
Director of the Budget. *See also* Brundage, Percival Flack; Dodge, Joseph Morrell
Dirksen, Everett McKinley: agrees to assist in McCarthy situation, 932; announces candidacy for second term, 1859–60; and army poultry purchases, 934; background, 27, 29; and Bricker amendment, 76, 140; on Case's candidacy, 933; dinner honoring, 1859–60; discusses patronage problems with Cabinet, 933; E.'s ally in Congress, 827, 832, 1267–68; E.'s view, 27, 29, 333, 413–14, 453, 974, 1859–60; favors Carbaugh for TVA post, 932, 933; on foreign aid in Indochina, 933; on funds for forestry research in Illinois, 1153; and immigration legislation, 333, 413–14; on Korea, 275–76; on Langer, 932, 933; meets with E., 413–14, 921; on mutual security program, 413–14; as political adviser, 858; on Red China's admission to U.N., 267–69, 275–76; repudiates position on foreign aid, 1859–60; and return of alien properties, 932; role of, in midterm campaign, 1313–14; speaks to AHEPA, 974; supports Case, 1289; supports McCarthy, 275–76; supports waterway control legislation, 1267–68, 1278; and Taft isolationists, 1859–60; tours Asia, Middle East, Europe, 1859–60; on trading with Red China, 275–76; and TVA appointment, 928–29; votes against McCarthy censure, 1419
Disarmament: Baruch's view, 862, 1018, 1038–39; Bulganin proposes conference on, 2470; Bulganin's view, 2030, 2231, 2332–33, 2470; Caffey's view, 2189; Clark's view, 615–16; Cousins calls for, 2232–34; Cowles's view, 615–16; discussions of moratorium on weapons testing, 1068–69, 2259–60; Dulles's view, 1974–76; Eden's plan, 1790–92; and E.'s Open Skies proposal, 1790, 1792, 1865–66, 2039, 2041, 2470; E.'s view, 487–88, 615–16, 747–48, 798–99, 1038–39, 1794–95, 2039–41; and inspections, Soviet opposition to, 1947, 1974–76, 2009–10, 2011, 2030, 2230; on inspections violations in Korea, 1790, 1792; Kuter's view, 2326; *London Daily Tele-*

graph's view, 1790, 1791–92; Lubell's plan, 90–92, 374; and nuclear disarmament, 798–99, 2230–31, 2259–60; and revision of U.N. charter, 615–16; and Soviet Declaration on, 2470; and Stassen, as special assistant for, 944–45, 1439, 1590–91, 1621, 2041; Stassen's view, 2189; State-Defense disagree on, 798–99; Stevenson calls for, 2333; and United Nations, 1975–76, 2009–10, 2011; U.S. position on, at Geneva Summit, 1774–75, 1791; and Wilson's peace plan, 1629–30; Zhukov's view, 1741. *See also* Atomic weaponry; Cold war; Hydrogen bomb; Soviet Union

Disaster relief programs, 1650–51; and E.'s disaster relief fund, 1650–51; federal *v.* state issues, 1650–51

Discrimination, and world living standards, 2431. *See also* Civil rights

District of Columbia: on appointees for cultural center commission, 1773–74; discrimination in, 26–27; on emergency evacuation procedures, 1448–49; ending discrimination in, 698; ending segregation in, 698; on federal personnel programs in, 2122–23; and home rule for, 1176–77, 2011–12; housing sales in, 1696; and Maryland-D.C. parkway, 1224–25; new commissioners for, 33, 38; on rehabilitating southwest Washington, 2295; segregation in, 17, 470–72

Dixon, Edgar: background, 1188; and joint contract with Yates, 1188, 1240–41, 1780. *See also* Tennessee Valley Authority: Dixon-Yates controversy

Dixon, Pierson John: on Arab-Israeli conflict, 2341; background, 2342; meets with Lodge, 2341; on tripartite agreement of 1950, 2341

Docking, George: background, 2391–92; as governor of Kansas, 2391–92

Dodge, Joseph Morrell, 164; on abolishing FOA, 1527–28; on absent department heads, concern of, 710, 711–12, 716; on agricultural research, 351–52; attends meeting on economic activities, 1963–64; background, 28, 30, 925; on bipartisan cooperation, 1453–54; on Brennan's appointment to Supreme Court, 2305; on budget policy for FY 1955, 643–44, 710–12, 925; and Citizen Advisors on Mutual Security, 2134–35; and Colorado River Storage Project, 901–3; on conservation projects, 643–44, 901–3; and Council on Foreign Economic Policy, 229, 925, 1244–45; and Denver Federal Center, 343–44; as Director of Budget, 225; and Douglas's plan to aid Mideast economy, 1967–68; E.'s view, 28, 30, 229, 488–89, 925; on FOA transfer to State, Defense departments, 1660–61, 1662, 1677–80; and foreign trade with Red China, 2010; heads study on foreign economic policy, 1183, 1244–45, 1432; and HEW budget, 484–86; on liberal trade policy, 1631; meets with E.,

643–44; midyear budget review by, 488–89; on MSA budget, 204, 205; on national security policy, 355, 711, 712; and power policy, 73–74, 311–12; predicts surplus, 488–89; reimbursement for U.S. logistical support in Korea, 422–23; resigns, 229, 925; revises Truman budget, 925; sees Stephens's portraits of Es., 1982–83; sends E. Western novel, 1595; on support for FAO, 736–37; and Taft's outburst, 196, 197; on TVA, 557, 689–90, 1188, 1201; and U.S. aid to Korea, 445; and water resources debate, 689–90, 766–67, 786

Dodge, Julia Jane (Jeffers), 488–89

Dodge, Marcellus Hartley: background, 1097; and Donovan's resignation, 1097

Doerfer, John Charles: background, 1090; and Butcher's allegations, 1123–24; and FCC post, 1090, 1123–24; Potter's view, 1090

Dominic, Ethel: assists Whitman, 1571–72; background, 1571–72

Dominican Republic: oil and mineral resources in, 1893–94; Pawley's interest in, 1893–94

Donnelly, Howard: background, 988–89; on son's appointment to West Point, 988–89

Donnelly, Howard, Jr.: background, 988–89; and appointment to West Point, 988–89

Donohue, Charles, and Taft-Hartley Act revisions, 538–39

Donovan, Robert John: E.'s esteem for, 829, 832; writes *Inside Story*, 2065–68

Donovan, William Joseph: on Algerian situation, 2076–77; background, 1097; on elections in Vietnam, 2006; resigns as U.S. ambassador to Thailand, 1097; sees Stephens's portraits of Es., 1982–83

Doolittle, James Harold: background, 1214; heads CIA study, 1213–15; member, Foreign Intelligence Activities Board, 1983–84

Doubleday and Company, Inc., on publishing E.'s speeches, 597–99

Doud, Elivera (Carlson) ("Min"), 1772–73, 1836, 2210, 2444–45; at Augusta for Christmas (1953), 787; and Bermuda Conference (1953), 259–60; birthday celebration for, 223; and Burnham's kindness, 73; in Denver, 381–82; E.'s vacation home with, in Denver, 477–78, 482–83, 1259–60; family of, attends Inauguration (1953), 31–32; health of, 1164–65, 1307; in Palm Springs, Calif., 905–6, 910–11; at White House, 179–80

Douglas, James Stuart: background, 1064; father's defense of, 1064

Douglas, Lewis Williams, 464; on anger with British in Suez crisis, 2360–61; on appointment for, 2427; background, 357–58, 1347; declines post on Permanent Joint Board on Defense, 682–83; defends son, 1064; and dollar-sterling relationships, 357–58; on foreign economic policy, 357–58; on gold standard, 1158–59; as honorary chair for Hungarian refugee relief, 2442–43; on interstate commerce, 800–801, 832–33; on Knowland, 1347; meets with E., 1673–74; on Nehru's visit to U.S., 1799, 1800, 1801; on oil for Western Europe, 2423–27; praises E.'s Philadelphia speech, 2360, 2361; on Radford, 1347; on reappraising NATO, 2234–35; on Republican party, 1347; scores Federal Reserve Board's hard money policy, 2297–98; scores U.K.-French role in Mideast, 2426; studies moisture precipitation, 1610; on Taft-Hartley Act revisions, 770–71, 800–801, 832–33, 872–73; undergoes surgery, 1968, 2234; on U.S. economic policy in Mideast, 1967–68; on U.S. policy in Formosa Strait, 1608–10, 1645, 1673–74; on U.S. policy in Mideast, 2426; on wife's illness, 1609, 1610

Douglas, Paul Howard: and ADA, 1405; background, 1122, 1439; wins Illinois midterm election, 1122; woos "leftish" vote, 1435

Douglas, Peggy (Zinsser): background, 1610; illness of, 1609, 1610

Douglas, William Orville, and Rosenbergs, 291

Downs, Robert Bingham: background, 322; commends E. on "book burners" speech, 321–23

Draper, Claude Llewellyn: background, 2136–37; retires from FPC, 2136–37

Draper, William Grafton, 1739–40: background, 1262–63; flight schedule for, 1384; inspects flood control projects with E., 1262–63; takes Stephens to Fort Leavenworth, 1440

Draper, William Henry, Jr.: background, 8; meets with French leaders, 213; on NATO and European unity, 8, 102–3; on U.S. objectives in Europe, 308–9; as U.S. Special Representative in Paris, 8

Drees, Willem: background, 60; and Dutch participation in EDC, 60

Drought. *See* Benson, Ezra Taft; Texas

Drummond, Roscoe: background, 595–96; on Bricker amendment, 843; on E.'s candidacy in 1956, 1851–52; E.'s esteem for, 595–96, 829, 832, 1850–51; and questions on McCarthy by media, 796–97

DuBridge, Lee Alvin: background, 723, 724; and Oppenheimer case, 723, 724

Dudley, Edward Bishop, Jr.: background, 844, 845, 2432–33; on Bermuda grass for Gettysburg farm, 1055; and E.'s golf game, 2432–33

Duff, James Henderson: background, 601, 602, 603; and "Blue Bell Boys," 859–60; on cancer research, 753; and compromise candidate Wood, 859–60; and Delaware River Project, 1714; and Pennsylvania gubernatorial race, 601; as possible Secretary of Labor, 514–15; recommends Thomas, 1493–94; and St. Lawrence Seaway project, 187, 188; and stag dinners, 1467–68

Duffey, Robert, 859–60

Duffy, Bernard Cornelius: background, 687; produces E.'s TV panel program, 687; on public relations, 687

Duffy, James: background, 1714; on Delaware River Project, 1714

Du Flon, Henry A.: and absentee voting laws for service personnel, 1543–44; background, 1543

Dugan, Frank Joseph: background, 1606–7; on John Marshall Bicentennial Commission, 1606–7

Duke, Angier Biddle: background, 590–91; Dulles's view, 590–91

Dulles, Allen Welsh, 927–28; Armstrong's view, 270–71; on atomic weaponry in defense of Formosa, 1617–18; and benefits for Polish veterans, 1361; on breaking codes, 1330–31; and CIA investigation, 1215; denies U.S. role in East German uprisings, 413; Doolittle's view, 1215; drafts message to Holman, 2208–9; E. recommends Howard to, 919–20; E.'s view, 1215; and Foreign Intelligence Activities Board, 1983–84; Gruenther's view on France, 891; and Hungarian revolt, 2334–35; and Koenig's visit, 2129–30; and memo on Arab-Israeli conflict, 165, 2080; and Oppenheimer case, 717, 723–25; on post for Windfohr, 1406–7; on religious persecution in Czechoslovakia, 2409; and Suez crisis, 2219–20

Dulles, Janet Pomeroy (Avery), 157, 1141–42

Dulles, John Foster, 11, 66, 68, 69, 71, 103, 119, 306, 308–9, 317–18, 372; addresses ABA, on treaties, 840; addresses American Legion, 1832–33; addresses Council on Foreign Relations, 805–6; addresses Illinois Manufacturers' Association, 1925; addresses nation on foreign policy, 1604–5, 1610, 1711–12; addresses Overseas Press Club, 1003, 1005; and Adenauer's plan for demilitarized zones in Europe, 1740–41, 1742–43; admires Lloyd, 2138–39; admires Macmillan, 2138–39; advises against message to Churchill, 1283; advises Collins on Diem, 1548; and Anderson's visit to Mideast, 1952–53; on antitrust policies, 1023–24; on appointment of agricultural attachés, 1094–95; on appointment for Douglas, 2427; Armstrong's view, 270–71; and Aswan Dam, 2096–97; on atomic test limitations, 896; on atomic weaponry, 1604–5; attends briefing on meeting with St. Laurent and Ruiz Cortines, 2075; attends meeting of American presidents, 2219–20; attends meeting on economic activities, 1963–64; attends NAC ministerial meeting, 1706–7, 2441; background, 5; and Berlin Conference, 893–94, 1191; and Bermingham's proposal, 554; on bipartisan cooperation in foreign affairs, 1453–54, 1511, 1986; and Bohlen's confirmation, 138; on Bolton's post, 1144–45, 1634–

35; breakfasts with E., 1789–90; and Bricker amendment, 136, 139–40, 142, 282–83, 866–67, 1095–96, 1103–4, 1772, 2107–8, 2111; on Bulganin's support for Stevenson, 2333; at Caracas Conference (March 1954), 926–27; and Citizen Advisors on Mutual Security, 2134–35, 2163; and Clark's memo on U.S. Pacific policy, 1073; on clothing for East Germans, 554–55; on cold war, E.'s view, 1921–23, 1924–25; and colonialism, 1925; compliment to, from *Daily Worker*, 1020; convalesces in Key West, 2416; critiques E.'s second Inaugural Address, 2479–80; on dangers of nuclear fallout, 1545–46; on defense budget FY 1955, 671–72; on deployment of atomic weapons, 1418; on diplomatic dinners, reception, 1291; on diplomatic recognition of Vatican, 1227–28; on disarmament, 1774–75, 1974–76; on disarmament post for Stassen, 1590–91; discusses foreign policy with E., 1947–49; drafts letters for E., 167; and Duck Island, 157, 648–49, 658, 1154; and "Dulles Doldrums," 1223–24; on East-West trade controls, 960, 2140–41; E. attends birthday dinner for, 2030; and educational exchange program, 1732–33; E.'s esteem for, 858, 951–52, 975–76, 1030–31, 1461–62, 1948; and Eisenhower Doctrine, 2474–75; and E.'s letter to Churchill, 1210, 1446, 1574–79; and E.'s letters to foreign friends, 19; Ervin's view, 1353, 1355; and E.'s speech to ABA, 1816; and E.'s speech to U.N., 745, 747, 1713–14; esteem of, for Bruce, 1399; esteem of, for Holland, 807–8; esteem of, for Jackson, 1078; on extension of Trade Agreements Act, 1109–10; and Falcon Dam, 98, 254; and FOA, 1432, 1527–28, 1660–61, 1662, 1677–80; on foreign aid, Cowles's view, 1925–26; on foreign ministers' meetings, 731, 881–82, 888–90, 965–66, 1873–74, 1877; on free-world economies, 357–58; and FY 1955 budget policy, 10, 716; on "gainsaying," 331; and GATT, 1109–10, 1382–83; on Grace Kelly's wedding, 2119–20; on Gruenther's esteem for, 1461–62, 1463–64; and Gruenther's joke message for, 2237; and Gruenther's retirement, 2098–99; on Hoffman at U.N., 2455–56; on ILO's condemnation of forced labor, 2141–42; and immigration legislation, 118, 119, 178–79, 400–401; and International Atomic Energy Agency, 822; invites E. to fish, 1154; on Jackson plan on foreign aid policy, 1248–49; Jackson proposes conference on world economy, 1019–20; journalistic studies of, 975–76; Knowland attacks, 950–51; Knowland scores U.S. foreign policy, 1390–91; and Ladejinsky case, 1494–95; on Latin American relations, 820; on lead and zinc imports, 1242–43; on Legion of Merit awards, 1398; on liaison with Congress, 546; on limiting state visits, 1105–

6, 1128–29; and London-Paris Accords, 1614; on McCarthy and Greek shipowners, 143–44; meets with Adenauer, 154–55; meets with Bidault, Salisbury, 398–99, 592–93; meets with Churchill, 1004, 1006; meets with E., 504–7, 1020; meets with French leaders, 213; and MIG incident, 531; on Milton E. as "Roving Ambassador," 1426; on Milton E.'s trip to Central America, 1363–64; and moratorium on H-bomb tests, 1068–69; and Morrow's nomination, 1255; and MSA bill, 1173; Msgr. McCarthy's view, 1049, 1050; on mutual security legislation, 2187–88; on mutual withdrawal of forces and arms limitation, 504–7; at NAC meeting, Paris, 648–49, 1445, 1447, 2157–58; and national security policy, 671–72; and Nine-Power Conference, 1320–21; and N. Thomas, 614; objects to Duke appointment, 590–91; and Oppenheimer case, 717, 723–25; opposes Department of Peace, 812–13; opposes honorary citizenship for Churchill, 1646–47; opposes Streit's proposal, 2216–17; on organization of Operations Coordinating Board, 2476–77; on Pan American Week, 2486; on post for Ageton, 329–30; on post for Cooper, 1425–26; on post for Delmar, 1187; on posts for Dunn, Kemper, 1275–77; on post for Henderson, 1366; on post for Jacobs, 1334, 1366; on post for Milton E., 1217–18; on post for Reid, 1713; on post for Stassen, 944–45, 1621; and post for Whitney, 1931–32; praises Mendès-France, 1199; praises Wiley, 435–36; and press reports of rift with E., 506–7; on protocol for visiting heads of state, 593–94, 973, 1105–6; on psychological warfare, 600–601; on reconsideration of security policies, 504–5, 507; on relations with Latin America, 436–37, 464, 465, 814–15; on relationship with Eden, 1792–93, 2138–39; reports on Churchill, 592–93; on Reston's article, 1240; and Rio Conference, 1291–92; on Rio Treaty, 1066; on rules of precedence, 666–67; and St. Lawrence Seaway, 147, 188; and SEATO, 1179, 1180–81, 1265–66, 1266, 1582, 1591, 1604–5, 1618, 1641, 2006, 2060, 2077–78, 2080, 2171; as Secretary of State, 5, 224, 228; seen as controversial, 952; sees Howard's message, 2111–12; sends birthday greetings to E., 2326; on Smith's birthday dinner, 1302; speech by, to CIO, 676, 677; speech by, to 4-H Club Congress, 1406; speech by, to U.N., 506–7; on Spruance, Swing posts, 708–9; and Stevenson, 55–56; and SUNFED, 2177; on support of U.N., 269; on thermonuclear testing, 2281; on tung imports, 1085; on U.N. charter review, 615–16; undergoes surgery, 2371–72, 2431–32, 2442; on UNESCO paper, 1833; on U.S. delegation to U.N., 987–88; on U.S. forces abroad, 591–92; on U.S.

foreign policy, 1264–65, 1265–66, 1406, 2111–12; and USIA, 2125, 2183–84; on U.S. and prestige abroad, 403–4; visits E. in Denver, 1266, 1291–92; visits Far East, 2077–78; visits Middle East, 157, 175, 183–84, 216–18, 274; and Wilson's blunders, 1615–16; on winning cold war, Jackson's view, 1758–59; and white wine for White House dinners, 1236–37; and wool tariffs, 552–53; on world peace, Shields's proposal, 1059

—Africa: on goodwill trips to, 2102; on U.S. air routes to, 1385

—Argentina: on Milton E.'s visit to, 316–17; on rapprochement with U.S., 649–50

—Austria: reports to E. on, 1706–7; reports to NSC on treaty with, 1180; on visit to, 1888–89

—Bermuda Conference (1953), 253–54, 270; to attend with E., 271–72, 312–13, 665–66; attends British dinner, 732; cancellation of, 331; invitation to Baruch, 694; invitation to Ismay, 330; on invitations to Strauss, Cherwell, 672; postponement of, 314, 315; renewed plans for, 648–49, 658; reports on Korea, 743–44, 746

—Bolivia, memo to, on aid to, 586

—Brazil, Cowles's memo on, 575

—Cambodia: on diplomatic representation in, 1079; U.S. military aid to, 1079

—Canada: on diplomatic visits, 1961–62; explains U.S. policy on Formosa, 1676; on Massey's visit, 973; meets with Canadian Cabinet, 1627, 1629, 1676; and Permanent Joint Board on Defense, 682–83; plans for E.'s visit, 593–94

—Communist China: attacks Tachens, 1519–21; and E.'s message to Churchill, 1281–83, 1574–79; and Judd's petition on admission of, to U.N., 603–4; opposes admission of, to U.N., 1180; on release of captured U.S. airmen, 1718–19; on report U.K. supports admission of, to U.N., 1180; on shelling of Quemoy, 1300–1301, 1331–32; on U.S. policy toward, 1574–79, 1582, 1583; on U.S. relations with, Nehru's view, 1763–64; on virulent intentions of, 1618

—Cuba: Dulles's view, 1554; and sugar imports to U.S., 1529–30, 1530

—Cyprus: on Eden's proposal, 2192–93; and Skouras's mission, 2166–67

—EDC: Churchill's view, 1261–62; and Eden's plan on alternative to, 1298–99; to Europe on behalf of, 39, 41, 60, 202, 204–5; and France, 893, 927–28, 1261–62; on ratification of, and Mendès-France, 1261–62; statement on, 774, 775

—Egypt, 69; on Anglo-French initiative at U.N., 2318; and Arab-Israeli conflict, 2054–55, 2060; on Aswan Dam project, 2239–40, 2268–69; and canal users' association, 2274,

2285–87; Dulles opposes tripartite meeting on Suez, 2371–72; and economic aid to, 775; and elder statesman board of appeals, 2352–53; on Hammarskjöld's mission to, 2121; on Hare's conversation with Nasser, 2455–56; on negotiations with Nasser, 2274; proposes aid to, 392; on second Suez Canal Conference, 2290, 2427; Shepilov's view, 2318; on Soviet arms for, 1867, 1877–78; and Suez Canal Conference, 2241, 2249, 2251–52, 2253–54, 2263–65; and Suez Canal crisis, 287–89, 300–303, 2220–21, 2352–53; and Suez issue at U.N., 2309–11, 2424; talks with Salisbury, 365, 368; urges flexibility in, 392; and U.S. arms to, 217–18; and U.S. role in, 111–13, 300–303, 304–5, 365, 367, 2080, 2208, 2346–47; visits, with Stassen, 175, 287, 289

—France: and Arab-Israeli conflict, 2338–39; on Coty's election, 783; and EDC, 1261–62; and fall of Dien Bien Phu, 1032–33; and Franco-German agreement on Saar, 740, 746; and Koenig's visit, 2129–30; and Mendès-France, 1415, 1472–73, 1493; and message to Coty from E., 1032–33; and NATO, 927–28, 2441–42; on North Africa, 1415, 2442; talks with Bidault on Vietnam, 1030–31; and U.N. role in Indochina, 1120–21; on U.S. aid to Vietnam, 1311; and U.S. commitment to, in Indochina, 892–94, 1030–31

—Geneva Conference, 1020, 1037–38, 1191; accords at, 1196, 1199–1200; agreement with Rhee on, 970–71, 1022–23; Dulles differs with Eden, 1052; on E.'s statement, misinterpreted, 1051, 1052; invites Rhee to Washington, 1023; returns to U.S., 1052

—Geneva Summit Conference, 1720–21, 1782–83; on E.'s meeting with Eden, 1788

—Germany, 410–13; Dulles meets with E., Adenauer on reunification and rearmament, 1375–76; and EDC, 1261–62; and Franco-German agreement on Saar, 740, 746; on Hoover's visit, 1135; on reply to Monty, 383–86; on return of alien properties, 1432–33; on tanks for, 2288; on unification, Soviet view, 1882–83; and U.S. food for East Germany, 399–400, 604–5

—Greece: and Cyprus, 2166–67; Dulles meets with Markezinis, 273–74; and increase in forces of, in Korea, 274; and royals visit to U.S., 593–94; visit to, 274

—Guatemala: on invitation to Castillo Armas, 1168–69; and reports of Communist influence in, 1066–67

—Haiti: ambassador of, visits U.S., 780; and Magloire's visit to U.S., 1105–6, 1128

—Honduras: and United Fruit Company strike in, 1066–67; on U.S. military aid to, 1066–67

—Hungary: on aid to refugees, 2410–11; on revolt in, 2335, 2377–78; on U.N. resolution to withdraw Soviet force, 2377–78

Eban, Abba Solomon: background, 2328, 2330; on Iraqi troops in Jordan, 2337; meets with Dulles on Israeli-Jordanian conflict, 2328, 2330
Echo Park Dam, 1071, 1194–95, 1198–99. *See also* Colorado
Economic Cooperation Administration (ECA), and Marshall Plan aid for Europe, 504, 507
Economic Defense Advisory Committee, and East-West trade controls, 960
Economy, foreign: and agricultural research, 985–86; and Chief Joseph Dam, 306, 307; and Customs Simplification Act, 306, 307; and East-West trade controls, 960, 985–86; E.'s view, 985–86; and FOA, 1432; in free-world countries, 357–58, 660–61; and GATT, 1381–83; and H.R. 1, 1572–73, 1631; importance of Arab oil to, 2069; and Jackson's proposal, 1019–20, 1248–49; policy study of, 1182–83, 1244–45, 1432; on positive aspects of U.S. aid, 1551; and Randall Commission, 200–202, 552–53, 985–86, 1573; and Reciprocal Trade Agreements Act, extension and amendment of, 200–202, 306, 307, 1057–58, 1109–10, 1573, 1631; tariff legislation, 306, 307, 1109–10; and sterling-dollar relationships, 357–58; and Swiss watch tariff issue, 1225–27; on U.K.'s problems, 1996–97; and U.S. policy, 1057–58, 1499–1500; and U.S. Tariff Commission, 306–7. *See also* General Agreement on Tariffs and Trade; Randall Commission; Trade; United States: foreign trade
Economy, U.S., 17, 1230; Administration policy in 1955, 2128–29; agriculture, and Federal Reserve policy, 2303; on apathy in industrial activity, 1311–12, 1312–13; and automakers, 2128–29; and balancing the budget, 335–36, 429–30, 903, 1586, 1587; Burns reports on, 1503–4, 1960, 2249–50; on deficit spending, 429–30, 1586, 1587; and Democrats, 1585–87; and economic operations of independent government agencies, 1147–48; on economic stability, 903, 1147–48; effect on, of foreign economic policy, 200–202, 203–6, 347–48, 552–53, 1572–73, 1631; and effect of government procurement, 1579–80; E.'s view, 1387; and Federal Reserve policy, 2169–70, 2248, 2297–98; and foreign economic policy study, 1182–83; and gold standard, 323–25, 1158–59; and government controls, 90–92; and H.R. 1, 1572–74, 1631; Humphrey's view, 605–6, 1960; Leffingwell's concern, 903–4; and Liesveld's positive view of, 947–48; McDonald's recommendations on, 1011–13; off-the-record meeting on policies, 1963–64; on price change statistics, 157–58; and Rayburn's political move, 1586, 1587; on removing controls, 825; and responsibilities of labor and management, 2091; on role of fed-eral government in, 903; and "sound dollar," 2090; and tax reform, 963, 964, 2472–73; on transition from wartime to peacetime, 947–48, 1147–48; and U.S. security policy, 589–90; weakening of, 356; Whitney, Humphrey, advise E., 1143–44. *See also* Advisory Board of Economic Growth and Stability; Council of Economic Advisors; Taxation
—big business: Cowles's article on, 1505; and defense contracts, 1343–45; and E.'s policies, Schaaf's view, 683; and GM's industrial expansion plan, 1528, 1556–57; Larmon's concern, 816–17; and midterm election, 1343–44; statesmanship in, 2090
—depression: Ayres's view, 764–65; E.'s view, 903, 947–48, 961–62; on preventing, through public works planning, 867–69
—inflation: and economic operation of independent government agencies, 1147–48; E.'s view, 947–48, 2090, 2350–51; and Federal Reserve policies, 2297–98; Javits's fear of, 1847; and Republican party platform, 2350–51; Standard & Poor's report on, 2443; on trend toward, 1959–60, 2169–70; Vermont's view, 923–24
—recession: Burns's plan, 1147–48; E.'s view, 947–48; government weapons against, 868–69; Leffingwell's concern, 903–4; recovery from (1954), 805, 1312–13; trend toward, 2169–70
—small business: and automobile industry, 2133–34; Burns's view, 2248; and Cabinet Committee on Small Business, 2248–49, 2307; as campaign issue, 2248, 2306–7; Collord's concern, 1430–31; decontrol of nickel, boon to, 581–82; and Federal Reserve policy, 2303; McClure's view, 2306–7; and "set-aside" policy, 2307; on tax reductions in FY 1958, 2473
—unemployment, 1730, 1731; Austin's survey on, 923–24; Ayres's view on, 764–65; Baruch's view, 1018, 1401; Burns proposes Area Development Agency, 1847–48; Burns reports on, 869; in coal communities of Pennsylvania, 1068; and dispersal policy in defense production, 765–66, 1312–13; and economic operation of independent government agencies, 1147–48; Schaefer's view, 1395–97; in Vermont, 923–24
Ecuador, Republic of: and Milton E.'s report on Latin America, 814–15; Murray visits, 1142–43
Eddie, as Young's guide, 2196–97
Eden, Clarissa (Churchill), background, 1666–67, 2327
Eden, Robert Anthony, 93, 146–47; accompanies Churchill to U.S., 1074, 1099, 1132, 1133, 1134, 1140–41, 1141–42, 1154–55; and Alpha Project, 1787, 1788; and alternative to EDC, 1294–95, 1298–99; and Anglo-American

ry, 1077; and Eisenhower Birthplace Foundation, Inc., 609–10; on family genealogy, 221–22, 497–98, 946–47; at Fort Leavenworth, 1307, 1309, 1327; at Fort Lewis, 1717–18; at Fort Logan, 1805–6; at Fort Sam Houston, 1513; on publication of 1929 diary, 1895–96; recalls schooldays with Bush, 1934–35; relationship of, with father, 348–50; on restoration of boyhood home, 2438; at SHAEF, 824; as Supreme Commander, AEF, 750, 752, 824; on virtues of parents, 845–46; with War Department (1941), 749

—candidacy: accepts nomination, 2266; advisory committee, 1422–24, 1557; Allen's view, 1998–99; analysis on, to Hazlett, 1820–21, 2041–45, 2353–55, 2357; analysis on, to Milton E., 1850–51; *Baltimore Sun* editorial on, 2307–8; Barton's advice, 2088; Bullis's view, 2303; as campaigner, 2327, 2345–46, 2353–55, 2357, 2410; and "Citizens Ask the President," 2325; Clay seeks commitment (1956), 1402–5; and Democrats, 826; E. announces, 1996–97, 2024–25, 2034–35, 2041–45, 2061; on E.'s decision to run, 1984–85, 2282, 2283; Edgar's view, 2053; E. ends campaigning, 2358; Emanuel's view, 2005; and Fair Play Amendment (1952), 378; Finder's view, 1784–85; Graham's advice on civil rights, 2104–5; Hazlett's view, 1878–79; and Helms's support, 1606; and "indecent pressures," 2027; kicks off campaign at Gettysburg, 2281; on Lincoln's soliloquy, 2005, 2027; and Lindtner's recollection, 1170; McCrary's view, 1979–80, 2027; Madison Square Garden rally, 1422; and media, 1751; Milton E.'s view, 1851; Nielsen's view, 2049–50; and Nixon, 2061, 2324–25, Pinkley's view, 2325–26; Pollock's view, 1968–69; on press-ganging, Harris's view, 1716; pressures of campaign, 2281, 2303–4, 2345–46; pressure to run in 1948 and 1952, 2155; on publication of health report, 2289; question of stamina, 1976–78; and Republicans, 826, 831, 1851–52; Richberg's interest in, 1978–79; scores Knowland on Eisenhower draft, 1492–93; for second term, 1402–5, 1492–93, 1549–50, 1729–30, 1850–52; "Secret Intentions" (1956), 792; seeks midwestern farm vote, 2284–85; and sense of duty, 1404, 1851, 2005, 2117; "Serenade to Ike" rally, 1422; Sulzberger's view, 2331; takes to campaign trail, 2353–55, 2357; televises campaign speeches, 2284–85, 2354; on thermonuclear testing as campaign issue, 2260; undergoes pre-election physical, 2338; White's view, 1957–58; wins New Hampshire primary, 1965; wins presidential election, 2370; and "Woman Power for E.," 2349–50; Wood's view, 1551–52. *See also* Elections; Republican National Convention; "Salute to Eisenhower" dinners

—health of, 179–80; bout with flu, 13, 23, 30; bursitis in shoulder, 911–12, 1385, 1602–3, 1672–73, 1683, 1697, 1716; and candidacy, 1731, 1979–81; Clay's concern, 1402; convalesces at "Little White House," Key West (1949), 407; on dietary habits, 844–45; food poisoning, 155; injures elbow, 497–98, 526, 527, 599–600, 625–26; keeping public informed on, 1978–79; old shoulder injury, 53; on sensitive teeth, 2482–83; undergoes pre-election physical, 2338; undergoes two tonsillectomies, 2198. *See also* heart attack; ileitis

—heart attack, 1731, 1734, 1738–39, 1764–65, 1786, 1796, 2480; advice to Roberts on, 1999; anniversary of, 2295–96; appreciation to Knox, 1891–92, 1897–98, 1936–37, 2045–47, 2295–96; appreciation to Koger, 1892–93, 1971–72; appreciation to Nixon, 1894; appreciation to Pollock, 1935–36; appreciation to Powell, 1894–95, 1927–28; appreciation to Sheedy, 1910–11; appreciation to Snyder, 2207; appreciation to Turner, 1936–37, 1969–70; appreciation to Williams, 1970–71; book, table from Robinson, 1873; Cabinet sends flowering quince, 1872–73; Castillo Armas visits at Fitzsimons, 1814; convalesces at Gettysburg, 1888–89, 1894–95, 1910–11, 1912, 1928, 1939; daily schedule, 2022–23; on diet and weight, 2144–45; at Doud home in Denver, 1863–64; enjoys comedy film from Skouras, 1879–80; feels better, 1870, 1910–11, 1970–71; feels well as ever, 2049–50, 2138–39; and golf, 1912, 2026–27, 2052–53; Hazlett writes, 1864, 1879–80; Howard's advice on "Rest Regime," 2058–59; lacks zeal, 2138–39; leaves Fitzsimons November 11, 1886, 1888–89, 1890–91; Mattingly's view, 1881, 1896–97, 1935–36; Milton discontinues visits, 1878; needs exercise, 1939, 1976–78; new responsibilities following, 1892–93, 1894–95; Odlum's offer, 1864–65; pain of, 2032; Pawley offers Miami house, 1893–94; Pollock's view on candidacy, 1968–69; questions for White, 1887–88; recuperates at Fitzsimons, 1864, 1876, 1880; on reports of fatigue, 1934; rests in Key West, 1931, 1951, 1977–78; on sleep and nap regimen, 1976–78; Snyder's view, 1896–97, 1912, 1935; on Stephens's portrait of E.'s mother, 1870; takes light exercise, 1951, 1956, 1970–71; takes midday rest, 2138–39; Taylor visits, 1884, 1886; travels to Key West, 1931; travels to Washington, 1888–89, 1890–91, 1894; walks few steps, 1878–79; wears charm on chain, 1936; White accompanies E. to Washington, 1890–91; White advises physicians, 1880, 1881;

expectations, 1233–34; on White House dinners, 451, 2467–68
—religion, 362; Burroughs recommends special prayers at Easter, 956; as Episcopal communicant, 2313–14; on faith among free nations, 889; and free government, 508–9; on Inaugural prayer, 1252–53; influence of, on family, 845–46; joins Presbyterian church, 16–17, 518, 985; on national prayer days, 219–21, 376–77, 1256–57; on spiritualism, 116; supports church expansion fund, 985; on World Day of Prayer for Peace, 1256–57
—speeches, 148–49; on absentee voting for service personnel, 957–58; accepts nomination, 2266; to Administration leaders, 1808, 1818; on Administration progress, 778–79, 1252–53, 1263–64, 1266–67; at Al Smith dinner (1952), 523–24; at Al Smith dinner (1954), 517–19, 1352–53; to American Bar Association, 138, 1186–87, 1347, 1682, 1765–66, 1789–90, 1809–10, 1815–16, 1832–33, 1837, 1856; American Federation of Labor, 1300–1301, 1304, 1314–15, 1322, 1323–24; to American Jewish Tercentenary Dinner, 1339; to American Legion, 1212, 1218, 1235, 1266; to American Newspaper Publishers' Association (1954), 667–68, 1036, 1042–43, 1045; to American Society of Newspaper Editors, 32–33, 119–20, 155, 172, 174, 202, 210–11, 274, 487–88, 667–68, 747–48, 1059, 1959; announces candidacy in 1956, 2044, 2049–50, 2061; on armistice in Korea, 425–26; to Associated Press (April 1955); Atoms for Peace (to U.N., December 1953), 168, 652, 655, 732–35, 745–46, 747–48, 753–54, 759–60, 777, 790–91, 793, 798, 799, 822, 965–66, 1015–16, 1180, 1635–36, 1699, 2041; at Baylor commencement, 2185–86; to B'nai B'rith, 683, 697–98; in Boston, 531, 2319; at Boston Garden, 483–84, 542–43; at Bradley University, 2308–9; campaign speeches, 2290, 2293–94, 2303, 2307–8, 2322, 2325–26, 2353–54, 2357; at Catholic University, 681, 697–98; to Citizens for Eisenhower, 1300–1301, 1304, 1308, 1309, 1313–14, 1314–15, 1322, 1328; to Citizens for Eisenhower Congressional Committee, D.C., 1309, 1335–36; at Columbia (1949), 429–30; at Columbia Bicentennial, 617–18, 818–19, 1059, 1112–13, 1129–30, 1139–40; to Columbia Republican Club, Indianapolis, 1309, 1350; on Communist threat, 1007, 1014–15; to Conference on Highway Safety, 861–62; at Dartmouth, on "book burners," 322–23, 466–67; at dedication of McNary Dam, 1304, 1313–14, 1322, 1328; on defense needs, 237–38; to Democrats for Eisenhower, 1304, 1313–14, 1322, 1328; on disarmament, at Geneva Summit, 1774–75; on disaster relief program, 1650–51; drafts of, on disarmament, 487–88; on the economy,

277–78, 335–36; at Eisenhower Day Dinner, 1309, 1335–36; election night (1952), 2319; on farm bill veto, 2126–27; on farm politics (Plowville, 1952), 423–24, 563–64; on foreign policy, 1711–12, 2358; to Future Farmers, 558–59, 560–61, 563–64; on Geneva Summit Conference, 1794; at Governors' Conference, 433; to Gridiron Club, 1707–8; High recommends Ferguson as speechwriter, 1122, 1256–57; at Illinois State Fair, 1122, 1255; Inaugural Address (1953), 8–9, 220; at Iowa State Fair, 1212, 1235; and John Marshall Bicentennial 1815–16; on legislative record, 387–88; in Lexington, Kentucky, 2293–94; Lodge's advice on, 605–6; McCann's advice on, 1017; to Masons, 1589; on message of hope, 725–26; Milton E.'s advice on, 1017, 1112–13; on modern republicanism, 2392–93, 2395–96; to National Citizens for Eisenhower Congressional Committee, 1126; to National Civil Liberties Clearing House, 978–79, 1694; to National Council of Catholic Women, 1389; to National Federation of Republican Women, 1193, 1300–1301, 1304, 1308, 1322; to National Institute of Animal Agriculture, 1339; to New York Republican State Committee, 1309, 1339; in 1952 campaign, 429–30; on nonsense speech from Robinson, 1427; on Open Skies proposal at Geneva Summit, 1794, 1797, 1865–66; to Organization of American States, 107–8, 202; on parity in marketplace (Kasson, Minnesota, 1952), 2117, 2118; at Penn State, 1735, 1741–42, 1804, 1883–84; in Philadelphia, on foreign policy, 2354, 2357, 2358, 2361; to press, on foreign economic policy, 985–86; on publication of, 597–99; on Puerto Rican independence, 814; to Republican Groups of Southern California, 1304, 1322; to Republican Precinct Day Rally, Denver, 1309, 1335–36, 1339; to Republican Women's National Conference, 1727–28, 1959; and "Salute to Eisenhower" dinners, 1970, 1979–80; on school construction legislation, 1753–54; on Social Security, 562–63, 624–25; State of the Union (1953), 17–18, 20–21, 33, 36, 472, 581–82, 624–25, 697–98; State of the Union (1954), 651–56, 719, 725–26, 753, 760–61, 778–79, 784–85, 786, 787, 805, 870, 957–58, 1829; State of the Union (1955), 1502–3, 1650–51, 1754; State of the Union (1956), 1815, 1943–44, 2011; State of the Union (1957), 2481–82; on Suez crisis, 2347–49; on tax program, 624–25, 947–48, 951–52, 957, 961–62, 966–67, 978, 1943–44; on UMT, 760–61; to U.N., 487–88, 719, 731–32, 759–60, 1713–14, 1731–32, 1750, 1751, 1752, 1774–75; to United Church Women, 518; to U.S. Chamber of Commerce, 1693; on U.S. policy in Eastern Europe, 2382–85; on vote

for eighteen-year-olds, 1829; at Washington College commencement, 617–18, 818–19; on water resources, 786; at West Point, 1712; at West Springfield, Massachusetts (Eastern States Exposition), 531; to World Council of Churches, 617–18, 818–19, 1122, 1256–57, 1630; World Day of Prayer for Peace, 68, 1256–57, 1630
— to Congress: on budget, 947–48, 1475–76, 1856, 1943–44, 2482; on conservation, 1856; on domestic policy, 778–79; economic report, 805, 869; on education, 915; on Eisenhower Doctrine, 2474–75, 2487, 2488; on farm program, 801, 806–7, 1016, 2118; on foreign economic policy, \ 1046–47, 1057–58, 869, 1225–26; on foreign policy, 778–79, 985–86; on foreign trade, 200–201, 553, 1023–24, 1024–25, 1382–83; on highway program, 1557; on home rule for D.C., 2011–12; on labor-management relations, 832–33; on merchant marine, 1024–25; on Middle East, 2482; military reserves, 1425–26; on mutual security program, 1680, 2052; on New Look defense policy, 1490–91; on Passamaquoddy power project, 1234; on public housing, 607–8, 801–2; on tax legislation, 624; on tax relief for small business, 2473; on treaties, 842–43; on tung imports, 1084; on VA hospitals, 1806
— trips, 158, 179–80, 300, 431–32, 617–18; attends Helen E.'s funeral, 1184; to Bermuda Conference, 657–58; to Bohemian Grove (1950), 430–31; to California, 1312–13; campaigns in Illinois, 2284–85; campaigns in Iowa, 2284–85; campaigns in Northwest, 2281–83, 2321–22; campaigns in West, 2331, 2333–34; to Canada, 593–94, 664–65; to Cedar Point Club, Ohio, 1359–60, 1384, 1409; to Charlotte, N.C., 1093–94; to Chestertown, Md., 617–18; to the Dakotas, 465–66; to Eisenhower Museum dedication, 1384, 1389; to Falcon Dam dedication, 574–75, 618–19; to Geneva Summit Conference, 1757–58, 1782–83, 1789–90; to Governors' Conference, Seattle, Wash. (1953), 349–50, 395, 396, 430–31, 453, 454, 455, 456, 457, 459–60, 465–66, 466–67; to Hartford, Conn., 1073; to Illinois, 617–18, 1121–22, 1211, 1255; to Iowa, 1212, 1235; to Kentucky, 1031, 1036; to Larkspur, Colo., 1849–50; limits travel, 1497, 1502, 1513; to Michigan, 535–36; and midterm campaign trips, 1307–9; to Midwestern states, 574–75, 2487; to Minnesota, 465–66; to Montana, 1312–13; at Naval Academy commencement, 243; to New England, 1751; to New Orleans, 618–19; to New York, 402–3, 564–65, 571, 1035, 1036; to Ottawa, 657–58; to Panama, 2196–97, 2199–2200, 2210; to Penn State, 176, 180–81, 184–85, 1735, 1741–42; to

Pennsylvania for Waring birthday party, 524; to Quantico, with JCS, 424–25, 427; to Republican National Convention, 2256–57; to San Francisco, 1731–32, 1750, 1751, 1752, 2256–57; to Southern states, 574–75; to Texas, cities of Mission and Pharr, 618–19; to Texas, on drought, 364; to Vinson's funeral, 567; to Washington, 1312–13; to West, 308–9, 1314–15; to West Point, 1145–46, 1152–53, 1157–58, 1735–36; to West Springfield, Mass. (4-H awards), 483–84, 531. See also Golf
— vacations: and beef stew luncheon at Cherry Hills, 1297–98; criticisms of, 1338, 1339, 1340, 1517; to Cypress Point Club, Monterey, Calif., 2256–57; in Denver, 149, 180, 223–24, 300, 378–79, 395–96, 402–3, 424–25, 451, 457, 458, 462–63, 473–74, 477–78, 727–28, 769, 1086–88, 1112–13, 1160, 1164–65, 1173–74, 1204–5, 1211–12, 1218, 1235, 1256–57, 1257–58, 1260–61, 1262–63, 1263–64, 1266, 1268–69, 1300, 1300–1301, 1318, 1340–41, 1350, 1764–65, 1772–73, 1810–11, 1856; on family vacations, 1086–88; to forget political "yammering," 467–68; in Key West, Fla., 1931, 1937, 1939, 1951, 1955–56, 1977–78; and midterm campaign plans, 1307–9, 1338; to Milestone Plantation, Ga., 1407, 2025, 2026–27, 2032, 2033; to Minnesota and Dakotas, 465–66; on Moisie River (1950), 720; on Nielsen's ranch at Fraser, Colo., 1164–65, 1235, 1772–73, 1834, 1846; at Palm Springs, Calif., 845, 850–51, 861–62, 905–6, 910–11, 911–12, 921–22, 939, 947, 1497, 1513, 1834; on plans for, following heart attack, 2046, 2047; at Thomasville, Ga., 2035. See also Camp David; Gettysburg farm; Golf: esp. Augusta National Golf Club
Eisenhower, Dwight David II (grandson), 23, 165–66, 1126; advice to, from E., 1843–44; birthday gift to, from E., 954–55, 1639; by Byers Peak Ranch, 1843–44, 2203; celebrates Christmas 1955 at White House, 1941; celebrates Easter at White House, 2108–9; E.'s affection for, 2190; with Easter basket, 179; eighth birthday party, 2108–9; fishing with E., 1829, 1834, 1843–44; at Fraser, Colo., with E., 1843–44; and golf, 621–22, 622–23, 1308, 1327, 1350, 1562–63, 1639, 1692, 1843–44; on horseback rides, 1692; keepsakes for, from E., 1350; and Lincoln's bed, 1165; plays with Michael Gilmer, 2190; plays "soldier," 114; progress of, at school, 1350, 1562–63; quarter horse for, 1771; receives polio vaccination, 1692; rides Smokey, 1843–44; at Sky Line Camp, 1843–44; and Sporty Miss, 2184–85, 2203; Stephens's portrait of, 1440; studies Battle of Gettysburg, 2199–2200; swims at White House, 179, 1970, 1984–85; on tumbling skills of, 1941; vacation plans with E., 1843–44

Eisenhower, Earl Dewey (brother): article by, 879–80; attends Eisenhower Museum dedication, 1384; attends Inauguration (1953), 31–32; background, 459–60, 478; business venture, 459–60, 478; on communication with RNC workers, 1837; congratulates Es. on wedding anniversary, 2196; E.'s advice on being "used," 459–60; hears E. address ABA, 1837; media scores, 478; relationship of, with father, 348–50; and restoration of boyhood home, 2438

Eisenhower, Edgar Newton (brother), 1125; and ABA, 148–49, 287, 1347; admires Benson, 2031–32; apologizes to E., 859; article misquote upsets, 2155–57; attends Inauguration (1953), 31–32; background, 32; on being "used," 459–60; and Belshe, 2053; and Bohlen's appointment, 141–42; and Bridges, 141–42; buys new car, 1025–26; cannot attend Inauguration, 2485; and care of parents' graves, 61–62; celebrates birthday, 32; on Citizens for Eisenhower, 2281–83; comments on E.'s tiredness, 1682; on communication with RNC workers, 1837; on death of son Jack, 2443–44; and E.'s address to ABA, 1809–10; on E.'s Administration, 1386–89; and E.'s advisers, 857–59; on E.'s appearance, 953; on Earl E.'s business venture, 459–60; on Eastvold, 94, 2281, 2283; on E.'s "bad advice," 1387–88; and E.'s birthday party, 524; E. campaigns in Washington, 2281–83; on E.'s candidacy in 1956, 2053, 2281–83; on E. at Fort Lewis, 1717–18; and E.'s golf game, 2052–53; and E.'s grandchildren, 1165; and E.'s heart attack, 2052–53; on elephant for E., 211–12; E. recommends vacation for, 2390–91; E. regrets letter to, 1994–95; on E.'s schedule, 625–26; E.'s view of, 457; Es. visit, 2321–22; and family genealogy, 221–22, 497–98; and federal appointments, 94, 520–21; on federal appointment for Wanamaker, 2402–3; on federal surplus food distributions, 2411–12; on Fred Waring, 1902, 1904; and golf, 30–32, 51–52, 124, 850–51, 953, 978, 1025–26, 1607–8, 1682; on Hamley for federal judiciary, 2093–94, 2097–98, 2321–22; on Hazlitt's solution to farm problem, 1942–43; hears E. address ABA, 1837; meets E. in Seattle, 459–60; on Internal Revenue Bureau, 65; irritates E., 141–42, 859, 1962–63; and John Marshall Bicentennial, 1280–81, 1290–91, 1555, 1607–8, 1682, 1765–66; and Kornitzer, 123–24, 348–50; on law career for John E., 457, 458; on McClure's invitation to E., 1607–8; on McKay's Senate race, 2282–83; meets with E., 2052–53; and midterm campaign strategy, 1352; and national air policy, 1318, 1717–18; and navy acoustic range on Puget Sound, 230–31, 232; opposes Warren on High Court,

551–52; on patronage, 2093–94; and pique with Langlie, 2321–22; on politicians, 532; on politics in Washington, 2281–83; relationship of, with father, 348–50; and role of neutral nations, 2031–32; sends cartoon, 287; sends E. Alaska king crabs, 1809–10; Snyder treats, for illness, 2165–66; suffers nervous collapse, 2390–91, 2477–78; suffers neuritis, 2485; suffers slipped disc, 2390–91, 2477–78; on Supreme Court appointment, 520–21, 532, 551–52; and Taft booklet, 348, 350; on tax reform, 978; travels to Arizona and California, 2485; vacations at Augusta, 1025–26; visits Bridges, 2155; visits E., 497–98, 575, 625–26, 1607–8; visits Odlums, 2478; on Washington State politics, 1718, 2281–83

—Bricker amendment: Edgar E. favors, 75, 141–42, 871–72, 1994–95; E. differs with Edgar E. on, 1994–95; and E.'s hypothetical question on, 2109–11; and executive agreements, 126–27, 162, 784–85, 850–51; on Phleger's role, 1809–10; reports of difference with E. on, 952–53; and Republican party platform, 850–51; restates position on, 873–74, 1962–63; revisions to, by, 812, 1772, 1789–90, 1803–4; and substitute amendment, 784–85; takes offense at E.'s letter, 1994–95

Eisenhower, Edna Alice (Shade) (widow of Roy), and family genealogy, 222, 2290–91

Eisenhower, Helen Elsie (Eakin) (wife of Milton), 104, 175–76; death of, 861–62, 1184, 1218; illness of, 180–81, 184–85, 186, 187, 226, 459–60, 514–15, 911–12, 917–18; at Naval Academy commencement, 243; Penn State dedicates chapel to memory of, 2313; visits Latin America, 375–76, 634

Eisenhower, Ida (Stover) (mother), 221; E.'s view, 349; religious influence of, 845–46; and Stephens's portrait of, for E., 1870; virtues of, 845–46

Eisenhower, Jack (son of Edgar), death of, 2443–44

Eisenhower, Jacob (grandfather), 221, 947

Eisenhower, Janis. See Causin, Janis Eisenhower

Eisenhower, John (son of Samuel), 946–47

Eisenhower, John Sheldon Doud (son) 53, 526, 527, 881, 2444–45; at Army Command and General Staff College, 381–82, 1308, 1384, 1639; on assignment at Pentagon, 2459; on assignment at White House, 2459; attends Eisenhower Museum dedication, 1384; attends Inauguration (1953), 9, 23; background, 9; and binomial theorem, 2488–89; birthday of, 410, 457, 458, 1814; and birth of Mary Jean, 1939; buys Chrysler sedan, 1087–88; on David's clothes, 179; and David's golf, 1308; on Denver, 1087; and E.'s golf, 1308; and E.'s heart attack, 1891–92; E. inquires for Anne, 1320; E. offers gun, rod, and reel, 599–600; E. offers to help, 180; and E.'s speech

320–21; clashes with conservationists, 902–3; Clement's protest on TVA, 1366, 1368; concern of, on powers of modern administrative state, 800–801; on conservation issues, support of, 1855–56; and corporate giving, 533–34; and defense contracts, 1343–45; differs with Federal Reserve system, 2297–98, 2303; and Dixon-Yates contract, 1197–98, 1200–1202, 1251–52, 1368, 1454–55; and Donovan's *Inside Story*, 2065–68; economic aid policy, 796–97; on economic program of, 1011–13, 2128–29; and education policy, 913–15; and 84th Congress, 1807-8, 1817–18; and 83d Congress, 1196, 1200, 1217, 1807, 1818; and Eisenhower Doctrine, 2474–75, 2487; endorses Status of Forces Agreements, 386–87; foreign aid, Gruenther testifies on, 2028; and foreign economic policy, 1019–20, 1109–10, 1182–83; E.'s philosophy regarding, 751–52; extremists threaten Middle Way, 561–62; and farm program, 801, 806–7, 1304–5, 1311, 1312, 1858–59, 2267–68; and FY 1955 budget policy, 710–12; and foreign economic policy, 1057–58, 1080–82, 1182–83; on foreign policy in Mideast, Douglas's view, 2426, 2427; on foreign policy and national security, Dulles's view, 805–6; and Herald Tribune Forum, 536–37; High's article on, 206; increases production of fissionable material, 2234; and internal security program, 1494–95; and Korean reconstruction plan, 462; Leviero's report on Formosa, Korea, 185; and medical benefits for uninsured, 1460–61; and Middle Way, 980–81; military aid policy, 796–97; and MSA budget for FY 1954, 426, 427; Msgr. McCarthy's view, 1049–51; and national parks restoration, 808–9; and national security program, 341–43; *New York Times* supports, 2331; policies of, and reactionaries, 576, 577; prestige of, abroad, 403–4; on program to aid small business, 2306–7; and psychological warfare, 1330–31; and public power policy, 1341–42; public relations for, 547, 663, 686–88, 865–66; and railroads, 1332–33; and Republican anxiety, 828; Roberts's advice, 1304–5, 1311, 1312; Rockefeller misspeaks on split in, 1924; and soil conservation issues, 1841; and State of the Union Address (1954), 719; and subversive activities in, 699–701, 1571; and support of NATO, U.N., 627, 2216–17; and Taft-Hartley law, 513; and transition from wartime to peacetime economy, 947–48; on war in Indochina, 1033–36; and water resources policy, 766–67; and wheat surpluses, 495–96
—legislative program: and "Administration Bible," 651, 663, 719; Austin's survey on, 923–24; Cabinet's role in, 825; defense budget, 211, 341–43, 355–57; on departmental liaison with Congress, 546; discussion of, 33–38; and 83d Congress, 1196, 1200; E. meets with legislative leaders on, 1927–28; E. seeks support for, 1125–26; E.'s use of media, 956–57, 1126; E.'s view, 1807–8; on farm bill, E.'s view, 2116–17; Halleck's role, 1807–8; on health, 1217, 1460–61; on housing, 1217; legislative leaders meet with E., 778–79; Lodge's advice, 1450; McCarthy's effect on, 950, 1013–14; and mutual security program, 2187–88, 2194; and need for Democratic support, 275–76; and public power projects, 311–12; Rayburn's blast, 332, 467–68; and Republican reactionary fringe, 950; Sulzberger's view, 1139–40; and tariff legislation, 1057–58; and tax reform, 439–42, 963, 964, 2472–73. *See also* House of Representatives, U.S.; Senate, U.S.
—public opinion: Austin's survey on, 923–24; and deployment of atomic weapons, 1418; and E.'s advisory committee, 1422–24, 1557; and Eden's proposal to meet with Soviets, 1697–98; and Formosa crisis, 1654–59; on indifference of, to small business, 2133–34; Jackson's report on, 2409–10; and McCarthy issue, 949–52; and nuclear fallout, 2260; and public relations program, 686–88; and Republican legislative conference (December 1953), 791–92, 793; and sale of Soviet arms to Egypt, 1877–78; on Suez Canal crisis, 2263–65, 2275, 2413; in Utah, 795, 797; in Vermont, 923–24; in Western states, 547; on White House guests, 809

Eisenhower Birthplace Foundation, Inc., a birthday gift for E., 609–10

Eisenhower brothers: on being "used," 459–60; and care of parents' graves, 61–62; and family genealogy, 221–22, 497–98; public pressures on, 320; relationship of, with father, 348–50

Eisenhower Doctrine, 2474–75, 2476, 2487

Eisenhower Exchange Fellowships: background, 1245; and teamsters, 1245

Eisenhower Foundation for the Promotion of Citizenship, 880; and care of parents' graves, 61–62; cornerstone laying, E.'s address at, 845–46; dedicates library, 935–36; dedicates museum, 935–36; and E.'s portrait, 721–22, 737–38; establishes library, museum, 935–36; Hall's interest in, 846; Milton E.'s role, 935–36; potential contributors to, 117. *See also* Eisenhower Library; Eisenhower Museum

Eisenhower grandchildren, 114, 526, 527; at Augusta, 179–80, 186; David, Anne, visit E., 2199–2200; Easter-egg roll at White House, 147–48; E. doubles guard for, 299; on E. as President, 1165; and family vacation plans, 1086–87; on gifts to, from E., 1639; and golf, 1327; on horseback rides for, 1692; meet Roy Rogers and Dale Evans, 2108–9; Stephens's portrait of, 1440; swim at White House, 179, 186; visit E., 165–66, 179–80, 186, 1971; visit maternal grandparents, 1739–40

Eisenhower Library: dedication of, 935–36; displays bust of E., 258; and Eisenhower Presidential Library Commission, 1709–10; and E.'s scrapbooks, 935–36. *See also* Eisenhower Foundation for the Promotion of Citizenship

Eisenhower Museum: and bust of E., 258; dedication of, 935–36, 1323–24, 1384, 1389, 1399–1400, 1440; and portraits of E.'s mother, 1870; on replacing portrait of E., 1440. *See also* Eisenhower Foundation for the Promotion of Citizenship

Eisenhower Youth Development Program, 1768

Elbin, Max: advises E. on golf clubs, 1759–60; background, 1759–60

Elections: and discrimination in domestic politics, 1230; E.'s plan to get out the vote, 1428–29; and home rule in Washington, D.C., 1176–77; on need for younger candidates, 1549, 2063–65; for postmasters, 1400–1401; on presidential term limits, 2044, 2045; in Vietnam, 2006; on voter registration, 2260–61, 2269–70

—midterm 1954, 828, 832, 1399; and absentee voting for service personnel, 957–58; and African Americans, 1342; Alger wins in Texas, 1477–78, 1637–38; Allott wins in Colorado, 1385; Beardwood's view, in California, 762; Bjornson loses to Humphrey, 1335; Bradley loses, 1204–5; and campaign film, "Year of Big Decision," 1252–53; and Case's campaign, 1288–90; and Citizens for Eisenhower Congressional Committee, 1368–69; and Columbia University alumni poll, 1477–78; and defense contracts, 1344; Democrats attack farm program, 1304–5, 1312; Democrats regain control of Congress, 1373, 1375–76, 1438, 1454; Dewey's view, 1339, 1383; Dirksen's role in, 1313–14; disappoints Republicans, 1428–29; Douglas's view, 1347; E.'s campaign role in, 1193, 1194, 1204–5, 1263–64, 1266, 1268–69, 1302–4, 1307, 1309, 1322, 1328–29, 1335, 1337–39, 1341, 1373; Edgar E.'s view, 1352; and farm crisis, 1349; and Hall's leadership, 1411–12; Harris loses in Colorado, 1362; Hazlett's view, 1354–55; High's advice on Meek, 1121–22; on Illinois politics, 1122; influences on, in the South, 479–80; Lodge's advice, 1328, 1345; Meek loses in Illinois, 1122; Moncrief's contribution to, 1347–48; and "mossbackism," 1313–14; Murphy's view, 1376–77; Murray's tactics, 1351–52; and need for young Republicans, 756–57; Nixon's role in, 1302–4, 1313–14, 1319; on Oklahoma politics, 1302; on patronage, Bender's view, 284–85; on patronage, Dirksen's view, 932; in Pennsylvania, 859–60; and Republican congressional defeats in New Jersey, Wisconsin, 664; and Republican gubernatorial defeats in Virginia, New Jersey, 664; results, 1373, 1375–76,

1381; results surprise E., 1392; RNC reports on, 1381; Roberts's role, 1342–43, 1368–69; Snyder's candidacy, 1325–26; Thornton's predictions, 861–62

—presidential 1948: on E.'s decision not to run, 2045; pressures on E. to run, 2155

—presidential 1952, 378, 762, 2410; and Citizens for Eisenhower, 396–97; and E.'s campaign supporters, 1467–68; E.'s decision to run, 2043, 2045; and GOP split in Georgia, 1029; Morrow supports E. in, 1255; pressures on E. to run, 2155; and problems with McCarthy, 939, 940; and Warren's role in, 461, 568

—presidential 1956: and AFL-CIO, 2267; and Allen's predictions, 2359–60; on Arab-Israeli conflict and Jewish vote, 2356; Bulganin supports Stevenson, 2333; Bullis's view, 2303; campaign kickoff at Gettysburg farm, 2281; Clay seeks commitment, 1402–5; Cochran wins primary, 2191–92; and Defense Department, Lodge's view, 1815; on Democrats in, Lodge's view, 2242; and Democrats' tax proposal, 1585–87; and Donovan's *Inside Story*, 2065–68; and dump Nixon charges, 2061, 2074–75; E. accepts nomination, 2266; E. advises Nixon, 2063–65; E. announces candidacy, 2024–25, 2044, 2061; E. campaigns for farm vote, 2284–85, 2293; E. campaigns in Northwest, 2283; E. carries Florida, 2381–82; E. carries Ohio, 2337; E. carries Texas, 2376–77; E.'s intentions, 1729–30; on Eisenhower draft, Knowland's view, 1492–93; E. leads Stevenson among women voters, 2376; election results, 2359, 2370; E. votes in Pennsylvania primary, 2131–32; E. wins New Hampshire primary, 1965; and farm opinion, 1863–64, 2117; Graham's advice on campaign strategy, 2189–90; Helms's view in California, 1606; Hungarian crisis overshadows, 2410; Kefauver wins Minnesota primary, 2084–85, 2091, 2093; Kefauver wins New Hampshire primary, 1965; on Lodge to review campaign speeches, 2082–83; and Marx brothers fundraising campaign, 2277–78; Melberg suggests campaign picnics, 2281; Nixon agrees to run, 2130–31; on Oregon primary, 2175–76, 2180–81; on party platforms, 2303; on primaries, 1978–79; Roberts's concern, 1770; "Secret Intentions," 792; and small business as campaign issue, 2306–7; Stevenson loses Minnesota primary, 2084–85, 2093; Stevenson's message to E., 2370; Suez crisis overshadows, 2410; and tax reform, 2472–73; on thermonuclear testing as campaign issue, 2260; and U.N. issues, 2164; on voters' indifference, Martin's view, 2260–61; on Warren as candidate, 1995–96; will not run, 792; on winning by "comfortable majority," 2354, 2358. *See also* Eisenhower, Dwight David: candidacy; Nixon, Richard Milhous

post for, 1553, 1624; and Second Hoover Commission, 418

Farm Bureaus: Cooperative Associations of Indiana, Ohio, Pennsylvania present tractor to E., 1913; on farm bill, E.'s view, 2116–17. *See also* American Farm Bureau Federation; Federal Farm Loan Bureau

Farm Commodity Distribution Program, 2411–12

Farm Credit Act of 1953, 2080–81

Farm Credit Act of 1955, 1772–73, 2080–81

Farm Credit Administration, and mutualization, 2080–81

Farm program. *See* Agriculture

Farmers Home Administration (FHA): on loan policies, 1145–46, 1152–53; state directors of, meet with E., 468–69; and Zahner case, 1145–46, 1152–53

Farmers Union, 126; opposes Benson, 665

Farouk I, King of Egypt: in exile, 365, 367; and Nasser's fear, 2068–69

Fawzi Bey, Mahmoud, discussions with, on Suez, 288, 289

Feaster, Ivan, background, 1648–49. *See also* Gettysburg farm

Fedayeen: E.'s view, 2462; in Israel, 2465

Federal-Aid Highway Act of 1954, 1067

Federal Bureau of Investigation (FBI): on Communists in U.S., 974–75; on emergency evacuation procedures, 1448–49; and federal judgeships, 1508; investigates Horton, 283–84; investigates Oppenheimer, 718, 722–23, 723–25; investigates Sherwood, 1026–27; investigates U.S. Mission to U.N., 697–98, 736; and subversives, 1571; and Sulzberger's plan for "political amnesty," 362–63, 559–60; and unauthorized disclosures of classified data, 767–68

Federal Civil Defense Administration. *See* Civil Defense Administration

Federal Communications Commission (FCC): appointments to, 437, 438, 441–42, 1123–24; Butcher asks E.'s intervention against, 2071–72; Butcher recommends Haines, 1124; criticism of, 448–49; and Doerfer, 1090, 1123–24; economic operations of, 1147–48; and Hyde, 1090; McCarthy demands equal time, 938, 939; McConnaughey heads, 1090; Potter's view, 1090; and Pulliam, 438, 441

Federal Crop Insurance Corporation, and appointments to Board of Directors of, 379–80

Federal Emergency Relief Administration, and land purchase program, 1391–92

Federal Fair Employment Practices Commission (FEPC): Byrnes's view, 473; E.'s view, 498–99

Federal Farm Loan Bureau, view of, on price supports, 1687

Federal Government. *See* United States Government

Federal Housing Administration (FHA): authori-

zations for, 606–8; Cole's recommendations, 801–2; economic operations of, 1147–48; E.'s recommendations, 607; and Housing Amendments of 1955, 1579–80; investigation of, 1356–57; mortgage terms, 1696

Federal Housing and Home Finance Agency, 607, 802; and investigation of FHA, 1356–57

Federal Intermediate Credit Banks, and mutualization, 2080–81

Federal Mediation and Conciliation Service, 27; and New York dock strike, 754–55; and steelworkers' strike, 2202–3

Federal National Mortgage Association, E. recommends reorganization of, 607

Federal Power Commission (FPC): appointments to, 448–49, 2136–37; criticism of, 448–49; Draper retires, 2136–37; E. appoints Kline to, 2136–37; economic operations of, 1147–48; and Harris-Fulbright Bill, 2013–16, 2018, 2033–34; and regulations on natural gas sales, 1386, 1388, 1670, 2013–16, 2018, 2033–34; and St. Lawrence Seaway, 132, 187, 188; supports Dixon-Yates Contract, 1779, 1781, 1784; and water resources policy, 689–90

Federal Records Council, 812–13

Federal Reserve System (Fed), 803, 805; and Advisory Board of Economic Growth and Stability, 277–78, 1011–12; and appointments to Board, 582–83, 605–6; boosts discount rate, 2169; concern of, on inflation, 2169–70; and convertibility of currencies, 1081; differs with Administration, 2303; economic operations of, 1147–48; and hard money policy, 2297–98; and liberal mortgage policies, 1696; on loosening credit, 1011; Martin's view, 2248; postpones discount rate raise, 2248; raises discount rate, 2248, 2297–98; and Republican party platform, 2350–51; on tight money policy, 2169, 2303

Federal Security Administration, reorganization of, 83–84

Federal Trade Commission (FTC), 33, 38; economic operations of, 1147–48; investigates Brazilian coffee prices, 895

Federal Voting Assistance Act of 1954, 957–58

Feller, Herman H.: background, 1842; offers E. flymaster control, 1842, 1843

Fenton, Ivor David: background, 1068; on depressed coal regions of Pennsylvania, 1068

Ferguson, Charles W.: background, 1122; as speechwriter for E., 1122, 1256–57

Ferguson, Homer: background, 1095–96; Bricker amendment causes political problems for, 1095–96; drafts compromise Bricker amendment, 866–67; favors Trice for Comptroller General, 989–90; supports Administration in Bricker debate, 1095–96

Ferguson, Sarah: background, 1190; and Finn twins, 1189–90

Ferrocerium (lighter flints), 2388–90

Figl, Leopold: background, 257; commends Kaghan, 257, 262

Finder, Leonard V.: background, 131; and civil liberties commission, 978–79, 1693–94, 1784; on Dixon-Yates controversy, 1783–85; on E.'s 1956 candidacy, 1783, 1784–85, 2346; on McCarthy, 131

Fine, John Sydney: background, 602–3; and gubernatorial race in Pennsylvania, 601–2, 602–3; supports E., 602–3; visits Korea, 1184; and Wood's candidacy, 859–60

Finland, Republic of, 2104; on admission of, to U.N., 1901–2; sends U.N. force to Suez, 2368–69

Finletter, Thomas Knight: and Air Policy Commission, 434–35; background, 434–35

Finley, David Edward: background, 1060–61; and Maroger's book, 1060–61

Finn, Charles, and war surplus airplane, 1190

Finn, George, and war surplus airplane, 1190

Finnegan, Joseph Francis: background, 2202–3; and steel strike, 2202–3

First Boston Corporation, and Wenzell's role in Dixon-Yates debate, 1780–81

Fiscal policy. *See* Economy, U.S.; Federal Reserve System

Fishing: with Allen, 1846; critics of E.'s interest in, 547; with David E., 1829, 1834; Dulles's invitation, 1154; and encyclopedia on, 1696, 1697; and Fisherman's Prayer, 1592; in Georgia, 1624; and groundfish fillets, 1138–39; with Hagerty, 1235; with Hoover in Denver, 1235; with Milton E., 1235; on Moisie River (1950), 720; in New England, 1751; with Nielsen, 1164–65, 1235; with Snyder, 1235; on spinning reels, 1353–54; on Swan's ranch, 477–78; Thornton sends fishing license #1, 769; on vacation in Colorado, 467–68, 477–78, 1164–65, 1846

Fitzsimons Army Hospital: admits E., 1863–64, 1864–65; praise for staff, from E., 1884, 1928, 1935–36; staff of, corresponds with E., 2108–9, 2144–45, 2237–38; staff of, receives painting reproductions from E., 1936–37. *See also* Eisenhower, Dwight David: heart attack

Flanders, Ralph Edward: background, 372; denounces McCarthy, 940; and federal judgeship in Vermont, 1509, 1510; on French foreign policy, 372, 373; speech by, on Korea, 371–73; on U.S. foreign policy, 371–73

Fleck, Jack: background, 1755–56; wins U.S. Open, 1755–56

Fleming, Ian Lancaster, 2423

Fleming, Lamar, Jr., and Randall Commission, 201

Fleming, Robert Vedder: background, 1773–74; on D.C. cultural center commission, 1773–74

Flemming, Arthur Sherwood, 177; on aid for Port Townsend, 877, 878–79; background, 67; on construction of large tankers, 2313; on decon-

trol of nickel, 581–82; and defense budget, FY 1955, 1206–7; on defense contracts, 1343–45; and defense production in depressed areas, 765–66, 1344; as Director of ODM, 67, 1558–59; and duties on watch imports, 1115–17; on emergency evacuation procedures, 1448–49, 1665–66; esteem of, for Jackson, 1078; E.'s view, 28, 30, 226, 227–28, 229, 230; and foreign economic policy study, 1244–45; on future need for big tankers, 2310, 2311; heads HEW, 230, 1559; and Hoover Commission, 66–67; introduces "set-asides" policy, 765–66; on lead and zinc imports, 1242–43; to meet Gruenther, 1499–1500; meets with E., 1344; and memo on treatment of government personnel, 930–31; on Mexican oil production, 2244–45; and Milton E.'s report on Latin America, 814–15; on mobilization stockpile, 1952–53, 1953–54; and New Dealers in federal work force, 108; and Ohio Wesleyan University, 1499–1500, 1558–59; and Oppenheimer case, 723–25; as possible Secretary of Labor, 514–15; on Quemoy, 1300–1301; and railway strike contingency plan, 619–20; on readiness plans in Far East, 1300–1301; resigns, 230; and Second Hoover Commission, 418; on selective service, 583; sends E. flowering quince, 1872–73; on Suez crisis and oil pipeline in U.S., 2243–44; and Sulzberger's plan for "political amnesty," 642; on UMT, 760–61

Flenniken, William W., 1836; background, 727–28; sends photos to E., 727–28

Floberg, John Forrest, background, 141

Flood Control Act of 1944, and public *v.* private power policy, 1511

Florida: Caffey's view, 2381–82; E. carries state in 1956, 2381–82; and federal judgeship in, 1508; on "Little White House" at Key West, 407

Flynn, John Thomas: opposes Conant's appointment, 127; supports Bricker amendment, 126–27

Flynn, Streeter Blanton: attends stag dinner, 933; background, 932–33; E. encourages candidacy of, 932–33

Fodor, M. W. ("Mike"), background, 346–47

Folger, John Clifford ("Cliff"): background, 1986, 2018; and Harris-Fulbright Bill, 2016, 2018; and "Salute to Eisenhower" dinners, 1986

Folsom, Marion Bayard: and Advisory Board of Economic Growth and Stability, 277–78; background, 1776–77; on Cope's plan to curb juvenile delinquency, 2181–82; heads HEW, 1776–77

Food and Agriculture Organization (FAO): U.S. support for, 736–37; world conference of, 736–37

Food and Drug Administration (FDA), 84

For America: background, 1405; opposes E.'s pol-

Fourteenth Amendment, and civil rights, 480–82, 713, 714. *See also* Constitution of the United States

Fourth Extraordinary Meeting of the Inter-American Economic and Social Council. *See* Rio Conference

Fox, Harold C.: background, 1626; offers single-breasted suit, 1625–26

Fox, William Thornton Rickert: background, 1819; and Institute of War and Peace, 1818–19

France, Republic of, 154–55; Adenauer's view, 707; aid to, in World War II, 530, 531; and air bases in Morocco, 583–84; and Austrian State Treaty, 1707; and colonialism, 1413–14; Communists in, 789; and constitution of Fourth Republic, 1473–74; Council of Republic ratifies London-Paris Accords, 1493, 1525; and D-Day commemoration plans, 1076–77; defections in World War II, 530; de Gaullists in, 789, 1473–74, 1498–99; desires to remain world power, 1043; Dulles's view, 783; and East-West trade controls, 959, 961; E. encourages talks with, 574–75; elections in, 648–49, 707; elects Coty, 746, 775, 782, 783–84, 793; E.'s message to Coty, 1032–33; and EURATOM, 1965–66; favors Western European Union, 1466–67, 1469–70, 1472–73; fear of Germany, 741; and five-power summit (Geneva), 893–94; forces of, leave Southeast Asia, 1575; and four-power foreign ministers' meeting, 731, 744–45, 746, 881–82, 1613, 1614, 1698; on Franco-German relations, 1613; Gaullist party votes, 253–54; and Geneva accords, 1196, 1199–1200; and Geneva Summit Conference, 1782–83; Gruenther's view, 41, 318–19, 890–91, 1033–36; Hauge's view, 522; and Hungarian revolt, 2334–35, 2345; "inferiority complex" of, 739, 1033–36, 2365; and Israeli-Arab conflict, 2011; and Koenig as defense minister, 1161–62; and London-Paris Accords, 1446–47, 1469–70, 1525; and Malta Conference, 101–2; Mendès-France as prime minister, 1132, 1196, 1199, 1445–47, 1469–70; Middle of Road group in, 789; and Movement Republican Populaire, 1469–70; and NATO post for Juin, 166–67; and North Africa, 1445, 1447, 2076–77, 2344, 2442; Pleven's role, 318–19; political crisis in, 259–60, 318–19, 729, 746, 1033–36; proposes unilateral U.S. intervention in Vietnam, 1033–36; protests U.S. policy in Vietnam, 1311; and question of Puerto Rican independence, 709–10; and regional meetings with ambassadors, 76–77; and Rosenbergs, 291; and Saar question, 740–41, 746, 1375–76, 1445–47; scores U.S. foreign policy, 2441; and SEATO, 1179, 1180–81; Socialist party in, 161; stations troops on Cyprus, 2265; and tripartite meeting, 239, 240;

and Turkey, 253–54, 259–60; and unification of Germany, 325–26; U.S.-U.K relationship with, 101–2, 207; and Villa St. Pierre, 1393; and Western European Union, 1469–70, 1493; in World War II, 1004, 1006

—Algeria: and Arab-Israeli conflict, 2356; Donovan's view, 2076–77; and French-Algerian War, 2404–5, 2413, 2426; unrest in, 2076–77

—Associated States of Indochina, 433; and French Union, 677, 1132–33; independence for, 676, 677–78, 892, 1033–36, 1132–33; and U.S. efforts to build anti-Communist coalition, 1068–69

—Austria, France withdraws troops from, 1246–47

—Bermuda Conference (1953): and Bidault-Laniel rivalry, 739, 746; and Bidault's monologue, 740–42, 746; cancellation of, 331; Churchill's invitation to, 665–66; and EDC, 740–42, 746; and four-power foreign ministers' meeting, 744–45, 746; Laniel's illness, 732; and NATO, 740–42, 746; political problems at home, 271–72, 313–14, 315, 789–90; on postponement of, 292–93, 313–14, 315; renewed plans for, 648–49, 658, 665–66; and Saar question, 740–41, 746; scheduling of, 253–54, 259–60, 271–72; too many experts at, 739; and U.S.-U.K. ground strength in Europe, 740; and world press, 739

—EDC, 60, 161, 314, 966; assurances from E. on U.S. support, 1131–33; and Bermuda Conference, 739–42, 746; Bidault's view, 527, 528, 740, 1031; Bolton's view, 1294–95; Churchill's view, 1261–62; defeats treaty, 1261–62, 1282, 1285, 1294–95, 1295–96; de Gaulle rejects, 1161–62; Dulles's view, 1261–62; Eden's plan as alternative to, 1298–99; E.'s view, 777, 790, 793, 1161–62, 1261–62; and four-power meeting, 365, 367, 731; Gruenther's view, 890–91, 1161–62; and Indochina, 893; Juin denounces, 1007; Koenig's view, 1161–62; Laniel's view, 527–29; Makinsky's view, 1295–96; on ratification of, 365–68, 527–29, 569, 592, 774, 775; and Saar, 569, 572; U.S. assurances on, 927–28; and U.S. Congress, 366–68

—Egypt, 742–43, 2076–77; Anglo-French forces bomb Egyptian airfields, 2346–47, 2356; Anglo-French force withdraws, 2371–72, 2381; and Anglo-French initiative at U.N., 2310–11, 2318; on Anglo-French invasion of Suez Canal Zone, 2343–44, 2365, 2434–35; communication with U.S. ends, 2413–14, 2424; de Guingand's view, 2460–61; Douglas's view, 2426, 2427; E.'s effort to end hostilities, 2347–49, 2351–52, 2355, 2356, 2358, 2412–15; French motives in, 2355, 2356, 2357, 2365; on German students' attitude, 2435–36; Nehru's view, 2446; Saud's view, 2352; and Suez Canal Conference, 2241,

2249, 2251–52, 2253–54, 2285–87; and Suez Canal crisis, 2219–20, 2220–21, 2227–29, 2239, 2265, 2273–74, 2285–87, 2318; on U.N. cease-fire agreement, 2372–73, 2380–81; U.N. remonstrates on withdrawal of force in, 2420–22

— Geneva Conference: and bargaining position of France at, 1068–69, 1179, 1181; Bidault misinterprets E.'s statement, 1052

— Germany: fear of, and EDC, 528, 741, 746, 774, 775, 1034, 1161–62; and Saar question, 569, 572, 741

— Indochina, 965–66: aggressive strategy in, 887; Bidault's view, 742, 746; Churchill's view, 1134–35, 1172; and EDC, 893; E. proposes coalition on crisis in, 1002–6, 1035, 1036, 1041–42, 1043–44, 1045, 1068–69, 1118–21, 1131–33; E.'s view, 790, 1033–36, 1043–44, 1170–1173; foreign policy in, 212–13, 314, 371–73, 1043–44, 1045, 1171; and Geneva Conference, 1068–69; on Mendès-France's pledge, 1134; names Navarre in, 213; Navarre plan in, 892–93; opposes U.N. role in, 1120–21; and Pleven's view on Red China's power in, 954; and Pleven's view on U.S. aid in, 1118–21; and policy on conscripts, 1119–21; and psychological effect of, 963; a "rathole," 823; U.S. aid in, 433, 570, 573, 886–87, 892–93; and U.S. commitment to France in, 892–94, 1119–21, 1131–33; U.S. technicians in, 886–87, 892–94; weakness of, 1444. *See also* Indochina; Southeast Asia; Vietnam, State of

— Israel: concocts crisis in Suez with France, 2360; sells Mystere jets, Super Sherman tanks for, 2330, 2340; and tripartite agreement of 1950, 2341, 2413

— National Assembly: accepts Laniel, 253–54; accepts Mendès-France, 1134; debates EDC, 740–42, 746; Marie fails, 313–14; no confidence in Mayer, 253–54; ousts Mendès-France, 1415, 1498–99; ratifies London-Paris Accords, 1447, 1469, 1472–73, 1487–88, 1493, 1497, 1498–99; rejects EDC, 573; rejects London-Paris Accords, 1469; and Western European Union, 1469

— Red China, 953–54; on admission to U.N. as peace settlement, 1172; on gains in Indochina, 1444

— Soviet Union: and arms for Egypt, 1867; Bulganin proposes disarmament conference, 2470; fear of, 1034; submits Declaration on disarmament, 2470

— Vietnam: and Collins-Ely agreement, 1380; and Collins's mission to, 1378–81, 1546–49; crisis at Dien Bien Phu, 1002, 1004, 1030–31, 1043–44, 1045; and Ely's despair, 1172; fall of Dien Bien Phu, 1032–33, 1083; on French morale, Gruenther's view, 1082, 1083; French position crumbles, 1179, 1180–81; requests

supplies for Dien Bien Phu, 1041, 1042; requests U.S. air support in, 1030–36; resists internationalization of war in, 1030–31, 1043; and Tonkin Delta, 1171; and U.S. aid to, 1311; U.S.-U.K. talks on, 1134–35. *See also* Indochina; Vietnam, State of

Francis, Bill, 128

Francis, Clarence: advises on selling surplus produce abroad, 1053–54; attends stag dinner, 771–72; background, 771–72, 1053–54; commends Nixon, 1756; heads policy study on agricultural surplus, 1053–54; on Taft-Hartley Act, 771–72

Franco y Bahamonde, Francisco: and agreements on economic and military aid to Spain, 500–502; Dulles meets with, 1882–83; and North African invasion, 604–5

Franke, William Birrell: background, 1215; and CIA study, 1213, 1215

Frankfurter, Felix, 571, 1397–98

Franklin, Benjamin, 1873

Franklin, Jerome A.: background, 388–89; and "Cemetery," 388–89

Franklin, Walter S.: background, 920–21; on railroad rate increases, 920–21

Frederika, Queen of the Hellenes: visits Marshall, 626; visits U.S., 274, 593–94, 626

Frederiksborg Castle Church Museum (Copenhagen, Denmark), 1047–48, 1054

Free, Lloyd, background, 1951

Free Europe Committee, 2208–9

Free Slavic Legion, 79

Free Vietnam. *See* Vietnam, State of

Free world, 244–46, 610–11; and Anglo-American relations, 1282, 1563, 1565, 1574–79, 1627, 1639–40, 2319–20, 2412–15, 2415–16; on Asian peace, E.'s view, 1051; and Bernhard's conference on U.S.-European relations, 1615; challenges for, 293–94, 1208–9; Chiang's view, 2465–67; and cold war, 1921, 2412–15; and conflict with Red China, 1444–46, 1539–40, 1563–66, 1574–79, 1641, 1654–59; and crisis in Iran, 1387, 1389; depends upon Mideast oil, 2100; and differences with nations receiving U.S. aid, 796, 797; on distribution of oil to, 2320–21, 2433–34; Dulles's view, 1463–64, 1711–12; and East-West trade controls, 959, 984, 2010; and EDC, 1523; and Eisenhower Doctrine, 2474–75; E. as leader of, 1979–81; on expansion of trade in, 1109–10; and foreign economic policy, 1057–58, 1080–82, 1572–73; and GATT, 1382–83; and Geneva Conference, 1021–23; and Geneva Summit Conference, 1791, 1793, 1794–95; on German reunification and rearmament, 1375–76; growing strength of, 2171; on international travel in, E.'s view, 1081, 1082; Iran's role in Mideast crisis, 2439–40; Jackson proposes conference on world economy, 1019–20; and Japan's need for world trade, 2047;

sadors, 76–77; reluctant to meet with Eden, 2381; on retirement, 455–56, 1719–20, 1919–20, 2070–71, 2098–99, 2120, 2124, 2283–84; returns to U.S., 59–60, 147–48, 189, 1236–37, 1284–85; sends Chivas Regal to E., 1006, 1007; sends E.'s photo, 1514; sends wine to E., 1236–37, 1285, 1468–69; on Soviet military activity in Mideast, 2371–72; speaks at Alfred E. Smith dinner, 431–32, 523–24; speaks French, 1514; speaks in London, 1007; speaks to National Security Industrial Association, 1236–37, 1285; speaks in Oslo, 1375–76; speaks at St. Thomas College, 1236–37, 1285; and successor at NATO, 1919–20; as Supreme Allied Commander, Europe, 186, 236, 346–47; testifies, 1191, 2026–27, 2028; on Trieste, 549–50, 1236–37, 1246–47; undergoes minor surgery, 1920, 1937; urges Es. visit Paris, 1757–58; on U.S. forces abroad, 610–12; and U.S. policy on Formosa, 1540, 1566; visits Camp David, 1082, 1083, 1105, 1146–47, 1157–58; visits E., 523–24, 575, 586–87, 890–91, 1036, 1083, 1105, 1120, 1121, 1284–85, 1487–88, 1514, 1540, 1591, 1592, 1920, 2124; visits E. at Augusta, 2483; on visits from E.'s friends, 346–47; visits E. at Gettysburg, 2028; visits E. in Key West, 1937; wagers on sex of E.'s grandchild, 1937; on Walters's accident, 1469–70; warns Congress of Soviet power, 1177; warns Soviets, 2421–22; and war in Vietnam, 1033–36, 1118–21; on Western European Union, 1469–70; on White case, 688–89; Wilson's proposal, 120 —bridge, 147, 206, 223, 236, 346–47, 890–91, 1082, 1083, 1091, 1146–47, 1177, 1190–91, 1285, 1414, 1415, 1487–88, 1499–1500, 1514, 1519, 1937, 1955–56, 2026–27, 2028; on Allen's arrogance, 1375–76; on Eisenhower coup, 1146–47; E. longs for, 2357; on joke message for Dulles, 2237; and rivalry with Robinson, 2028; and Robinson's report on victories, 1177

Gruenther, Grace Elizabeth (Crum), 41, 1285; admires Mme. Mendès-France, 1393; E. sends steaks to, 1191; and flea market junkets, 60, 186, 783–84; and flea market photo frame for E., 1514; regrets moving, 236–37; visits E., 1105

Gruenther, Homer H., background, 891

Guam, 2294–95

Guantanamo Bay Naval Base. See Cuba, Republic of

Guatemala, Republic of, 1730, 1731, 1948–49; and Armour's resignation, 1728; and Caracas Conference, 701; and CIA, 1066–67, 1168–69; Communist intervention in, 1066–67, 1099–1100, 1101–2, 1540–41, 1728; Dulles's view, 1168–69; and FOA aid, 1541; and Inter-American Highway, 1728; on invitation to Castillo Armas, 1168–69, 1728; Murray

visits, 1142–43; and Mutual Security Act of 1954, 1541; and overthrow of Arbenz Guzmán, 1168–69; signs Development Assistance Agreement, 1541; signs General Agreement for Technical Cooperation, 1541; Swope's view, 1168; U.S. aid to, 1728

Guerrilla warfare: report of plan for, in Egypt, 301–2; in Vietnam, 1119

Guggenheim, Harry Frank: background, 464; on Latin American relations, 463–64, 820; as U.S. ambassador to Cuba, 463, 464

Guided Missiles. See Missiles

Guillaume, Augustin, background, 213

Gunderson, Barbara (Bates): background, 465–66; and "Carry Nation hatchet" approach, 465–66; commends E., 1727; defends Benson, 646–47; on international affairs, 1223–24; praises Adkins, 1727; praises E.'s Baylor speech, 2185–86; on Republican women, 1223–24, 1727–28; on South Dakota politics, 1223–24; writes speech for E., 465–66

Gunderson, Robert W., background, 1728

Gurley, Fred G.: background, 920–21; discusses railroad issues with E., 1332–33; on Post Office Department and Railway Express Service, 1364–65; protests Mitchell's view on right-to-work laws, 1492; on railroad rate increase delays, 920–21, 1332–33; recommends E. travel by train, 1332–33; supports E., 1466

Gurley, Ruth (Brown), background, 1332–33

Gurney, Chan: background, 725, 1466; as CAB chairman, 725, 1466

Gustaf VI Adolf, King of Sweden, sends greetings to E., 2104

Hadley, Morris: background, 1215; and CIA study, 1213, 1215

Hagerty, James Andrew: background, 1156; retires, 1156

Hagerty, James C., 33, 55, 93, 407–8, 525, 1774–75; advises on reply to Wood, 2003; on assistant for, 1229, 1231; attends briefing on meeting with St. Laurent and Ruiz Cortines, 2075; background, 21; on *Baltimore Sun* editorial, 2307–8; and Berkeley's photograph of E., 580–81; and Bricker amendment controversy, 848–49, 873–74; and Butcher's blunder, 50; and Butkus's letter on union politics, 2267; and Donovan's *Inside Story*, 2067; on Earl E.'s article, 880; and E.'s candidacy in 1956, 1979; on Edwards, 1383–84; E.'s esteem for, 831; and E.'s letter to Knowland, 849–50; and Elson, 20; and E.'s order on executive privilege, 1080; and E.'s TV talk on Bricker amendment, 844; on E.'s vacations, 1517; on father's retirement, 1156; fishing with E., 1235; Gunderson's view, 646–47; on Halleck, 985–86; and Hannah's blunder, 1222; and Hughes's address before Republican National Convention, 2247–48; and *Life* article on

64; and liberal home mortgage terms, 1579–80; on Liesveld's letter, 947–48; on long-staple cotton quotas, 907; on McCarthy, 1322; meets with Alexander, on economy, 903; meets with E. on economic message, 1503–4; meets with Hutton, 562–63; and midterm election, 1322, 1328–29; on military benefits, 1748–49; on need for transportation policy, 972–73; and oats imports, 707–8; and price-change statistics, 156–57; on public works planning, 869; on publishing E.'s speeches, 597–99; and reclamation-multipurpose dam projects policy, 73–74, 98; reports from Paris, 522; on Republican Right Wing, 1322; reviews study on railroad industry, 972–73; on skilled workers in watch industry, 1116–17; and State of the Union speech (1954), 725–26; and Studebaker-Packard contracts, 2128–29; as successor to E., 230; on U.S.-European relations, 1615; visits Cuba, 1748–49; on water resources debate, 689–90; on Zeugen's complaint, 1129–30

Haughey, Katherine, 2391–92
Hawaii: and national aviation policy, 1317; statehood for, 17, 33, 36, 369–70
Hayden, Carl Trumball, 328–29
Hayes, Albert John: background, 1474–75; and National Manpower Council, 1474–75
Hayes, George E. C., 38
Hazlett, Alice, marriage of, 404, 407. *See also* Kessing, Alice (Hazlett)
Hazlett, Edward Everett, Jr. ("Swede"), 307; on aging, 963; on Atoms for Peace speech, E.'s view, 790–91, 793; background, 407; on benefits for service personnel, 1531–32; on Bermuda Conference, E.'s view, 788–89; on British fear of World War III, 1044; on Cabinet, E.'s view, 1435–36; on Churchill, E.'s view, 789, 1436–37; comments on E.'s messages, 855; congratulates E. on nomination, 2284–85; on daughter's marriage, 404, 407; on Democrats, E.'s view, 1435–36, 1439; on Dien Bien Phu, E.'s view, 1043; on disappointing performance of JCS, 2255–56; on E.'s age, 1823; on eating slowly, 1977; and E.'s candidacy in 1956, 792, 1434–35, 1729–30, 1820, 1823, 1977–78, 2044–45, 2227–29; on Echo Park Dam, 1194–95, 1198; on efficiency of postal service, 2254, 2256; on E.'s goals, 2045; on E.'s golf and fishing, 1821, 1823; on E.'s heart attack, 1864, 1878–79, 1976–78, 2044, 2227, 2229; on E.'s ileitis surgery, 2200–2201, 2227, 2229; E. misses Inspector General's service, 1044, 1045; E. reports to, on "State of the Union," 962; on E.'s signature, 404, 407; on E.'s sleep habits, 1976–78; on exercise, 1976–78; favors Milton E.'s candidacy, 1878–79; on "four-headed" foreign policy, 1353, 1355; on France, E.'s view, 789–90, 1043–44,

1045; and friendship with E., 406, 408; on Gettysburg farm, 2200–2201; on greatness, E.'s view, 1437–39; on Indochina, 1353–55; on internationalizing war in Southeast Asia, 1043; on Kefauver, 1821, 1823; on labor unions, E.'s view, 1435, 1438; on McCarthy, 405, 1044, 1045; on the media, 406, 788–89, 793, 1042–43, 1045; on Mendès-France, 1354–55; on Middle Way, E.'s view, 1791; on midterm election, 1353–55, 1435, 1439; opposes second term for E., 1878–79; on pay increase for service personnel, 1531–32; on presidential campaign pressures, E.'s view, 2353–55; receives Lincoln print from E., 855; receives winter scene print from E., 1939; recommends Fahrion to E., 2246; replacing CNO, 1822–23; on Republican legislative conference, E.'s view, 791–92, 793; saves E.'s letters, 963; scores French, 1354–55; on second-term candidacy, 1434–35, 1436, 1438, 1878–79, 2227, 2229; son of, resigns from navy, 1531–32; on Soviet Union, E.'s view, 790–91; on spinning reels, 1353–54; on Stevenson, 1355, 1821; on successors, E.'s view, 793, 1436, 1820–21, 2229; on Suez Canal crisis, E.'s view, 2355–57; suffers coronary thrombosis, 793, 1864; on U.S.S. *Williamsburg*, 406, 407; on world problems, E.'s view, 2227–29
Hazlett, Elizabeth ("Ibby"), 407
Hazlett, Mary Elizabeth. *See* Scott, Mary Elizabeth (Hazlett)
Hazlitt, Henry, article by, on farm problem, 1942–43
Health, Education, and Welfare, Department of (HEW), 803; on age factor in employment, 1401; on cancer research, 753, 755–56; on Cope's plan to curb juvenile delinquency, 2181–82; creation of, 84, 1430–31; at Denver Federal Center, 343–44; and education policy, 915; and federally impacted areas, 2085; Flemming heads, 1559; Folsom heads, 1776–77; Hobby heads, 30; Hobby resigns, 1775–76; Hughes's view on medical benefits, 1460–61; on liaison with Congress, 546; on mental retardation, aid for, 1619–20; 1955 budget of, disappoints E., 484–86; on Office of Education cuts, 485; on reinsurance legislation, 1217, 1460–61, 1466–67; rejects Blaik's youth training plan, 1126–27; on school construction in federally impacted areas, 2084–85; Scripps-Howard survey on, 899; session on, at Republican legislative conference (December 1953), 794; and State of the Union Address, 654, 656
Heath, Donald R.: background, 1380; on plans to aid Diem, 1380
Heaton, Leonard Dudley: background, 1588–89, 2199–2200; as CG, Walter Reed Hospital, 1588; declines Surgeon General post, 1589;

on E.'s diet, 2205–6; as E.'s surgeon, 1589, 2199–2200, 2201–2; opposes publishing report on E.'s health, 2289

Heckett, Eric Harlow: and artificial insemination of E.'s heifers, 1981–82; background, 1560, 1854–55; on cattle imports from Canada, 1769–70, 1854–55; on cattle imports from Scotland, 1566; on cattle imports from U.K., 1769–70, 1854–55; and health regulations for cattle, 1769–70; sends heifer and calf to E., 1560–61, 1875, 1876; sends Horace epodes to E., 1648–49; sends photos, art catalogue to E., 1648–49; and state regulations on cattle shipments, 1854–55; visits E., 1648–49

Heckett, Greta (Shield), 1648–49; background, 1485; on Blithe Miss BB Heckmere and Prince 160th E.F., 1485, 1496–97; on cattle imports from Scotland, 1566

Heilbronn, Kurt, 681–82

Hejaz, 297

Helms, Paul Hoy: background, 905–6; and California politics, 1470–71, 1606; on E.'s Columbia Bicentennial speech, 1112–13; E. visits Smoketree Ranch, 905–6, 939, 1112–13, 1834; on Hoffman, 1834; invites E. to Palm Springs, 1470–71; on Knowland, 1470–71, 1606; on Kuchel, 1470–71, 1606; on leadership, E.'s view, 1112–13; on McCarthy, E.'s view, 937–40; on Nixon, 1471, 1606; on stag dinners for "little people," 1027–28; supports E. in 1956, 1606; undergoes surgery, 1112–13, 1691, 1767, 1834, 1912; vacations in Colorado, 1112–13; and Warren, 1470, 1471

Helms, Pearl E. (Ellis), 1767; background, 940

Henderson, Loy Wesley: as Assistant Secretary of State, 1366; background, 337, 339; and political situation in Iran, 337–40

Hendrickson, Dan: appeals to E. on brother's behalf, 2322–23; background, 1390; sends ties to E., 1390

Hendrickson, Robert Clymer: background, 1499; and financial scandal, 2323; political ambition of, 2323; as U.S. ambassador to New Zealand, 1499

Henry, Barklie McKee: background, 12; and executive branch study, 11

Herald Tribune Forum: Brownell's appearance, 536–37; on visit from Nasser, Hussein, 1845, 1849

Herter, Christian Archibald: background, 1138–39; on groundfish fillets, 1138–39

Hess, Robert: background, 1588; transfers to CBS, 1587–88

Heusinger, Adolf: background, 1740–41; and plan for demilitarized zones in Europe, 1740–41, 1742–43

Hickenlooper, Bourke Blakemore, on Randall Commission, 201

Hiestand, Edgar Willard, 325

Higgins, Frank H.: background, 1500–1501; on Hereford heifer for E., 1500–1501

High, Stanley Hoflund: on advisory panel for E., 128–29; article by, on Administration leadership, 206; background, 42; on Davenport's memo, 127–28; on E.'s support for Meek, 1121–22; on Illinois politics, 1121–22; in Latin America, 380; on need for spiritualism, 116; plans book on E., 100; and Powell's article in *Reader's Digest*, 1342–43; recommends Ferguson as speechwriter, 1122, 1256–57; suggests Stevenson visit E., 42–43, 55

Highways, 868; and Buckner's study, 23–25; Byrd attacks program, 1557; E.'s interest in, 25, 1067; and emergency evacuation procedures, 1448–49; E. proposes self-liquidation plan, 1067, 1184; federal financing for, 1733–34; Gore's plan, 1733–34; Gurley's concern, 1332–33; improvements to, near farm, 83; on Inter-American Highway, 1728; legislation fails on national plan, 1067, 1586, 1587, 1691; and Maryland-D.C. parkway, 1224–25, 1455

Higley, Harvey V.: background, 1361; on benefits for Polish veterans, 1360–61

Hildreth, Horace A.: background, 2456, 2458; on Suhrawardy's message for E., 2456, 2458

Hill, Lister, supports TVA, 1200

Hill, Robert Charles: background, 1600–1601; Nixon's visit to El Salvador, 1600–1601

Hilleboe, Herman Ertresvaag: background, 1442; and Vogel, 1441–42

Hilliard, John F.: background, 879; reports on Port Townsend, 878–79

Hilton, Conrad Nicholson: background, 2119–20; and Grace Kelly's wedding, 2119–20

Hinds, Sidney Rae: background, 1111; Lodge recommends to head TVA, 1111

Hindus, migration of, to India, 2449

Hinh, Nguyen Van: background, 1379; threatens Diem's government, 1379–80

Hinshaw, John Carl Williams: on aviation policy, 434–35; background, 434–35; on duplications in armed services, 434–35; meets with E., 434–35

Hirohito (Emperor of Japan), 1004, 1006

Hirshon, Diana Joy, on mother's death, 396–97

Hirshon, Dorothy Joy (Richards), death of, 396–97

Hirshon, Walter, on wife's death, 396–97

Hitchcock, Philip Stanley: background, 2175–76; cooperates with McKay, 2180–81, 2282–83; loses in Oregon primary, 2175–76, 2180–81, 2282–83; meets with E., 2175–76; on need for youth in Republican party, 2180–81

Hitler, Adolf, 1004, 1538, 1612, 1642; insane determination of, 2138–39; and Mussolini, 2318

Hixon, C. Graham: background, 853; on stocking quail at Gettysburg farm, 853

Hoa Hao, in Vietnam, 1380, 1547–48

standard, 1158–59, 1686–87; and Howard's "Rest Regime" for E., 2058–59; hunts ducks with E., Milton E., 1359–60, 1384, 1409; on inflation, 2443; on Iran, 216–18; on Javits's fear of inflation, 1847; and lead and zinc imports, 1242–43; on McDonald's recommendations, 1011–13; meets with E., McDonald on domestic issues, 2090; meets with Markezinis, 274; meets with Whitney, E., on economy, 1143–44; memo to, on aid to Bolivia, 586; on military budget cuts, 2078–79; on military retirees as consultants, 620–21; on mobilization stockpile, 1953–54; on multilateral economic aid, 2177; on narcotics traffic, 1441–42; on national security policy, 355, 671–72; objects to aid for North Africa, 2404–5; on oil and gas fuel policies, 1670; and Oppenheimer case, 718; opposes individual tax exemptions, 966–67; opposes tax credit bill, 1587, 1595; on paper currency motto, "In God We Trust," 1604; on personal income tax reductions, 1943–44; on personnel reductions, 1715–16; as political adviser, 857; praise for, from E., 65, 224, 228; on public relations, 686–88; and reimbursement for U.S. logistical support in Korea, 422–23; releases midyear budget report, 488–89; reports to E. on FY 1955 budget, economy, 605–6; and Rio Conference, 1358–60, 1408–9; on Ruiz Cortines, 1743–44; on sales taxes, 624–25; on Schneider's complaint, 511; scores Rockefeller, 1924; as Secretary of Treasury, 5, 224, 228; on Social Security program, 624–25; on steel industry price increase, 1831–32; and steel strike, 2202–3; and Studebaker-Packard contracts, 2128–29; supports Case's campaign, 1288, 1289–90; and Taft's outburst, 196, 197; on tax deductions for congressmen, 834–35; on tax exemptions for dependent children, 966–67; on U.S. assistance to Great Britain, 2403; on U.S. policy on Formosa, 1645–46

Humphrey, Hubert Horatio, Jr.: and ADA, 1403, 1405; background, 1405, 1439; on condemnation of forced labor, 2141–42; and Stevenson, 2084–85; woos "leftish" vote, 1435

Humphrey, Pamela (Stark), background, 1290

Hungarian National Council in Exile, 2411

Hungary, Republic of: on admission of, to U.N., 1901–2; on aid to refugees, 2410–11, 2436–37, 2442–43; students hijack airliner, 2208–9 —revolt in: article on, in Life, 2436; Bulganin's view, 2379; E. appeals to Bulganin, 2361–63, 2469; E. appeals to Saud, 2394–95; E. seeks Indonesian support on, 2385–87; Jackson's view, 2400–2401; on Nagy as premier, 2335; Nehru's view, 2366–67, 2446–47; Sarrazac-Soulage's view, 2400–2401; on Soviet deportations, 2401; Soviets execute Nagy, 2363; Soviets install Kadar, 2363; Soviet troops at-

tack, 2335, 2362, 2374, 2421, 2423; Tito's view, 2382–85; U.N. action on, 2345, 2362, 2363, 2469; view of Soviet invasion by German students, 2435–36; on withdrawal of Soviet troops, 2345, 2361–63

Hunt, Haroldson Lafayette: background, 1388; political view of, 1386, 1388

Hunting: Brice's invitation, 657–58; at Cedar Point Club, Ohio, 1359, 1360, 1384, 1409; quail shoot at Milestone Plantation, 2026–27, 2028; thanks from Carter's quail, 1466

Hurd, Maud (Rogers): background, 2391–92; congratulates E. on reelection, 2391–92; illness of, 2391–92; on Mamie E. as campaigner, 2391–92

Hurd, Myra, background, 2391–92

Hurley, Patrick Jay: on ambassadorship to Mexico, 1101–2; background, 1101–2; and Bonus March, 2002

Hussein, Ahmed, background, 211

Hussein ibn Talal, King of Jordan: on invitation to visit U.S., 1845, 1849; and Suez crisis, 2351–52

Hutchison, Ralph Cooper: background, 84; and reorganization of FSA, 83–84

Hutton, Edward F.: background, 562–63; on Social Security, 562–63

Hyde, James F. C., Jr.: on absentee voting laws for service personnel, 1542; background, 957–58

Hyde, Rosel Herschel: background, 1090; Potter's view, 1090

Hydrogen bomb: Churchill's fear of, 964–66, 987, 1525; Cole's concern, 1015–16; debate on, in House of Commons, 997–98, 1007; and E.'s Open Skies proposal, 2039–41; E. opposes moratorium on testing of, 1068–69; E.'s proposal on ban of, 798–99; on fear of fallout, 2260; McCarthy's view, 1026–27; and moratorium on testing of, 1020, 1068–69; and Murray's proposal on test limitations, 896; and Oppenheimer, 716–19, 1026–27, 1036–37; and REDWING, 2260; and thermonuclear testing, 2259–60; and uncleared observers at Bikini Atoll, 799–800. See also Atomic weaponry; CASTLE

Ibáñez, Carlos de Campo: background, 2211–12; E.'s view, 2211–12

Ibn Saud, Abdul Aziz (King of Saudi Arabia until November 1953): background, 297; and Buraimi dispute, 295–98; E. recommends arbitration, 295–98. See also Saud, ibn Abd al-Aziz; Saud Ibn Abdul Aziz Al-Feisal

Iceland, Republic of, and NATO, 1614

Ichiang Island. See China, Republic of

Illinois: Douglas wins midterm election in, 1122; E. campaigns in, 2284–85, 2293, 2303; E. supports Meek, 1121–22; E. visits State Fair, 1122; and funds for forestry research in, 1153;

High's advice on politics in, 1121–22; and hog market prices in, 2293; and waterway control legislation, 1267–68, 1278

Immigration: emergency legislation on, 825; and McCarran-Walter Act, 118, 119, 400–401, 536–37, 1290; NAC endorses legislation, 178–79; and Refugee Relief Act of 1953, 400–401, 577, 578, 659–61. *See also* Refugees

Immigration and Naturalization, Bureau of, and subversives, 1571

Inauguration. *See* Eisenhower, Dwight David: Inauguration

Independent party: and Citizens for Eisenhower Congressional Committee, 1368–69; on E.'s hope to win over, 1429; E. speculates on forming, 568; McCrary's view, 1422; recruits new voters, 1429

India, Republic of: Allen resigns as U.S. ambassador to, 1425; Bowles's view, 53, 56–57; Bulganin proposes disarmament conference, 2470; Churchill's view, 743; Cooper as U.S. ambassador to, 1425, 1634; and Goa, 2451, 2454; and Kashmir, 121, 790, 2450; key to balance in Far East, 1799; and Lok Sabha, 2280; and Menon, 1633–34; and Nehru, 1633–34, 1799–1801; Nehru's view on Pakistan, 675–76, 2450–51; and Nehru's visit to U.S., 1830, 2000, 2078, 2445–54; and Neutral Nations Supervisory Commission, Korea, 281–82, 291–92, 570, 573, 616–17, 905; and Pakistan, 183–84, 216, 218, 790, 908–9, 2449–51; on policy of neutrality, 2448; political and economic situation in, 56–57; praise for, from E., 616–17; Radhakrishnan visits U.S., 1415–16; and release of captured U.S. airmen, 1718–19; on Rhee's objection to troops of, 570, 573, 616–17, 1021, 1022; sends U.N. force to Egypt, 2380–81; and Soviet Declaration on disarmament, 2470; and Suez Canal crisis, 2278–80, 2309–11, 2445–46; and Suez Canal Users' Association, 2280; on support of U.N. action in Hungary, 2387; U.S. aid to, 908–9; on U.S. relations with, 675–76, 1415–16, 1633–34, 1830, 2453; withholds approval of Suez declaration, 2254. *See also* Nehru, Jawaharlal

Indiana, and Mansfield Reservoir project, 1632

Indochina, 886, 1730, 1731, 1948–49; Bidault's view, 742, 746; Churchill's view, 1172; and Collins's mission to Vietnam, 1377–81; and communism in Asia, 1416–17; and Communist China, 744–45, 1171–73, 1444, 2448; Dirksen's proposal on, 933; E. proposes coalition on crisis in, 1002–6, 1035, 1041, 1042, 1118–21, 1171–73; E.'s statement on, misinterpreted, 1051, 1052; E.'s view, 212–13, 963, 964, 1033–36, 1170–73; and France, 648–49, 742, 790, 965–66, 1033–36, 1083, 1118–21, 1172, 1196, 1199–1200, 1498–99; France requests U.S. technicians in, 886–87, 892–93;

and Geneva Conference, 1179, 1181, 1196, 1199–1200; Gruenther's view, 890–91, 1033, 1035, 1083; Hoffman's view, 1556; Laniel's promises, 570; need for French leader in, 212–13; Nixon's view, 1155; partition of, unacceptable, 1051, 1052; and psychological effect on France, 963; security in, 1112–13; on self-rule for, 212–13, 372, 373; on training native forces in, 823, 1119, 1121; U.S. aid in, 433, 573, 742, 746, 892–93, 1033–36, 1118–21; on U.S. intervention in, 1353–55; on U.S. readiness plans in, 1300–1301; war in, and Churchill's view, 773, 775, 1134–35. *See also* France, Republic of; Vietnam, State of

—Associated States of: and conditions for U.S. intervention in Indochina, 1132–33; E. proposes coalition on crisis in Indochina, 1003, 1006, 1035, 1036, 1041, 1042, 1132–33; French domination of, 314, 372, 373; and French Union, 677–78; on independence for, 433, 570, 677–78, 892–93, 1035, 1043

Indonesia, Republic of: and communism in Asia, 1002–6, 1537, 1563; and defense of Formosa, 1644; and "emigre" Chinese, 1641; Nehru's view, 2452; sends U.N. force to Suez, 2368–69; on support of U.N. action in Hungary, 2385–87; on support for U.N. action in Middle East, 2385–87; withholds approval of Suez declaration, 2254

Industrial College of the Armed Forces, Baruch addresses, 1038–39

Industry: and automobiles, 2133–34; and defense contracts, 1311–13; and foreign economic program (H.R. 1), 1572–74, 1631; and GM's industrial expansion plan, 1528, 1556–57; and military-industrial complex, 635–36; on need for stimulation in, 1311, 1312–13; on productive capacity in, 1489. *See also* Manufacturers

Inflation: and deficit spending, 429–30; E.'s view, 204; on halting, 825; Lodge's view, 605–6. *See also* Economy, U.S.

Inglis, John: background, 1039–40; on E.'s portrait of Ouimet, 1039–40

Institute of War and Peace. *See* Columbia University

Insurance: Baruch's view on unemployment, 1018; and Gay's concern, 1521–22; and group insurance law, 1287, 1288; and HEW, 1460–61, 1466–67; and inflation, 825; on insurance for military personnel, 1748–49; and need for sound dollar, 2090; and pensions, 2090; and reinsurance program, 1217, 1219, 1460–61, 1466–67; Scripps-Howard survey on unemployment, 899; and Social Security program, 562–63

Intelligence. *See* Board of Consultants on Foreign Intelligence Activities; CIA; Intelligence Advisory Committee

Intelligence Advisory Committee, and Economic

sory committee, 1423; E.'s appreciation to, on 1956 campaign, 2404; on E.'s Geneva Summit report, 1794; invites E. to California, 2483; and Suez crisis, 2268–69

Jones, Clara (Thomas), and E.'s portrait of son, 115–16

Jones, James Weldon: on appointment to U.S. Tariff Commission, 1857–58; background, 1857–58; on criticism of E.'s vacations, 1857–58

Jones, Mary (Malone), background, 1039–40

Jones, Mrs. George D., background, 2262

Jones, Nettie Marie (Marvin), 1212; background, 1163–64; on Eaton, 1163–64; E. declines and-irons, 1673; on red rug for Gettysburg office, 1672–73; on Scottish Angus cattle, 1926, 2081–82; sends briars to E., 2081–82; sends Scottish cap to E., 2081–82; visits Gettysburg farm, 1926

Jones, Robert ("Bobby") Tyre, Jr.: advises E. on golf game, 1340–41; attends White House luncheon, 1759–60; on E.'s golf clubs, 1759–60, 1934; E.'s portrait of, 115–16; and E.'s portrait of Ouimet, 1039–40, 1341; on golf balls, 2272–73; greetings from Anderson, 278; sends E. Fisherman's Prayer, 1592; sends E. new golf clubs, 2272–73; on U.S. fiscal problems, 278; visits E. at Augusta, 1039–40, 2272–73

Jones, Robert Tyre, Sr.: and Dixon-Yates contract, 1200; and E.'s portrait of son, 115–16; illness of, 115–16, 172

Jones, Roger W., background, 957–58

Jones, Rowland, Jr., meets with E., 624–25

Jones, Ruby (Hackett), background, 1857–58

Jones, Sam Houston: background, 516; and federal appointments, 516

Jones, Warren L.: background, 1510; federal judgeship for, 1510

Jones, William Alton ("Pete"), 1907–8; attends stag dinner, 2062–63; and "Augusta National" weekend in Denver, 1211–12, 1259–60; background, 129, 1130; buys land adjacent to E.'s farm, 1131, 1190–92, 1483, 1485, 1558, 1560–61; buys Redding farm, 1561–62; on Eaton, 1163–64; on E.'s gas bill veto, 2026; on E.'s Geneva Summit report, 1794; and E.'s ileitis surgery, 2191–92; gives E. skeet and trap range, 2191–92; gives watch to E., 1163–64; on pig farming, 1130; and Pitzer schoolhouse, 1561, 1845–46; on red rug for Gettysburg office, 1672–73; visits Camp David, 1130, 1161–62, 1163–64; visits Gettysburg farm, 1926; and wife's illness, 2432–33

Jordan, Kingdom of: on admission of, to U.N., 1901–2; and Anglo-Jordanian treaty, 2328–30; and Arab-Israeli conflict, 570, 573, 2068–69; and Baghdad Pact, 1948, 1950, 2055–56; Ben Gurion's view, 2336–37; crisis in government of, 2328–30; Dulles's recommendation,

2096–97; on Iraqi troops in, 2336–37; Israelis attack Qibya, 709–10; Israeli border armies attack, 2328–30; lacks aviation, 2330; and Nasser's intentions, 2077–78; pro-Nasser forces win election, 2330; Reid's plan, 1845, 1849; relations with U.S., 1948, 1950; riots in, 2330; signs defense pact with Egypt, Syria, 2330; and Suez Canal base, 288; and Suez crisis, 2351–52; and U.K. aid to Iraq, 2055–56; U.K. relations with, 1948–50, 2055–56, 2328–30; U.S. aid to, 168, 2374–75; withdraws from Northern Tier Pact, 1948, 1950

Jordan River Project (Eric Johnston plan), 570, 573, 1845, 2374, 2375; Israel, Jordan reject, 2069–70

Jorgenson, Frank E.: background, 2483; on RNC post for, 2482–83

Joy, Charles Turner: background, 1189; retires, 1189

Joyce, Kenyon Ashe: and Armed Services Memorial Museum, 2006–7; background, 250; and San Francisco murals, 250

Judd, Walter Henry: background, 234; candidacy of, 234; on Chou En-lai, 1699–1700; on foreign policy in Asia, 234, 1699–1700; opposes Communist China in U.N., 234, 603–4; round-the-world trip by, 594–95

Judiciary: on appointing Catholics to federal bench, 1606–7; on appointment for Arn, 1399–1400; appointments to Circuit Court of Appeals, 1508, 1637–38; and civil rights, 2084–85, 2086, 2087; Denman's complaint, 496–97; on federal judgeship in Connecticut, 1509; on federal judgeship in Florida, 1508; on federal judgeship in Mississippi, 1508; on federal judgeship in New York, 1509; on federal judgeship in Texas, 1507–8, 1637–38; federal judgeship in Vermont, 1509; on federal judgeship in Wisconsin, 1508–9; on Hamley's appointment, 2093–94, 2097–98; on recommendations for federal appointments, 1610, 1637–38, 1670–71; and Rubenstein's disbarment proceedings, 1957; and S.J. Res. 44, 1167–68; and State of the Union Address, 652, 655; on technical cases, 558; U.S. Court of Appeals denies Rosenbergs new trial, 289–91. *See also* Supreme Court of the United States; Justice, Department of; United States Government: judicial branch

Juin, Alphonse Pierre: background, 167; and ceremony in Tunis, 223; as C in C, central region, NATO, 166–67; denounces EDC, 1006–7; NATO command structure, 166–67; scores U.S. foreign policy, 2441; supports amended EDC, 890–91

Juliana, Queen of the Netherlands: background, 151; concern of, for refugees from Eastern Europe, 150–52

Justice, Department of: and AEC-TVA power issue, 1251–52; antitrust ruling and auto-

can Week, 2486; and Perón, 649–50; and Rio Conference, 1275–77, 1291–92, 1358–60, 1407–9, 1550, 1599, 1600; Swope's view, 1168; Thomas visits, 1705; on ultranationalism in, 627–28, 633–34; on U.S. economic aid to, 1408–9, 1416–17; U.S. relations with, 436–37, 463–65, 1099–1100, 1101–2, 1275–77, 1599–1600, 1743–44. *See also* Presidents of American Republics, meeting of

Lattimore, Owen, 15

Latvia, 64

Lausche, Frank John: background, 265, 266; as governor of Ohio, 265, 266; as vice-presidential candidate in 1956, 2074–75

Lawrence, David, 32; article by, on role of neutral nations, 2031–32

Lawrence, William Howard: background, 2061; on Nixon candidacy in 1956, 2061

Lawson, Edward Burnett: background, 2338; on meeting with Ben Gurion, 2338

Lawson, Lawrence Milton: background, 98; and Boundary Commission, 98

Lay, James Selden, Jr.: background, 11; and Oppenheimer case, 718; and President's Committee on International Information Activities, 10–11

Lazarus, Fred, Jr., and President's Committee on Government Contracts, 476–77

Leachman, Leland L. ("Lee"), 2197–98; background, 1931; and Scottish Angus breeds, 1930, 1931

Lead. *See* Raw materials

Leader, George Michael: background, 859–60; wins Pennsylvania governorship, 859–60

Leahy, Frank W.: background, 1392; on midterm election results, 1392

Lebanon, Republic of: Dulles's recommendation, 2096–97; U.S. aid to, 168, 2375

Le Compte, Karl Miles: on absentee voting laws for service personnel, 1541–44; background, 1543

Lee, Joseph Bracken: background, 797; on foreign aid, 796–97; on Red China and U.N., 796–97

Lee, Robert Edward: E.'s attempt to paint, 2003–4; on greatness of, 2289; Newton sends photos of, 2003–4; rank of, 2003–4

Leffingwell, Russell Cornell: background, 904; concerns of, on economy, 903–4

Leghorn (Italy). *See* Trieste, redeployment of U.S. troops

Legion of Merit, value of, 1398

Legislative Appropriations Act of 1956, 1772–73

Legislative leaders: on absentee voting laws for service personnel, 1541–44; and Army-McCarthy hearings, 932, 1541; 1059–60; on atomic weaponry, E.'s view, 2104; discuss highway program, 1557; discuss Randall Commission report, 985–86; and Donovan's *Inside Story,* 266–68; and Eisenhower Doctrine, 2475; E.

meets with, 1928; E.'s relationship with, 826–28; and film, "Year of Big Decision," 1252–53; on friction between congressional committees and executive departments, 897, 898; and funding for educational exchange program, 1025–26; and immigration legislation, 400–401; memo to, on St. Lawrence Seaway, 132–33; need indexes for meetings of, 57; oppose E.'s TV talk on Bricker amendment, 844; oppose sending U.S. technicians to Indochina, 886–87; and principle of executive privilege, 1075–76; and Taft's outburst, 196, 197

—Republican conference of (December 1953), 764–65, 770–71, 825–26, 831; Burns's role in, 794; Carroll's contribution, 787; E. assesses, 779–80; praise for Martin from E., 778–79; purpose of, 791

Lei, Trygve, as U.S. Secretary General, 125

Leib, Richard: background, 1558; on insuring heifers, 1557–58

Leibrand, L. W., background, 2136–37

Leithead, Barry T.: and "Augusta National" weekend in Denver, 1212, 1259–60; and "Salute to Eisenhower" dinners, 1911–12

LeMay, Curtis Emerson: on Air Force budget, FY 1957, 2256; background, 2256; and Wilson's proposal, 120

Lenin, Vladimir Ilyich, 1643; on communism, 359–60; on contradictions in capitalism, 359–60

Leviero, Anthony: and charge of indiscrete reporting, 185–86; E.'s esteem for, 829, 832

Levitt, William Jaird: background, 1690; and Levittown, 1690; on segregated housing, 1690–91

Lewis, John Llewellyn: background, 2091; and Citizen Advisors on Mutual Security, 2134–35; and UMW contract, 2091

Liberia, Republic of: on Communist influence in, 1988–89; Tubman's inauguration, 1988–89; Tubman's visit to U.S., 1105–6; on U.S.-Liberian relations, 1988–89

Library of Congress: and appointment of Librarian, 851–52, 989–90; Black proposes Houghton, 851–52; librarian from, catalogues E.'s books, 1711

Libya: on admission of, to U.N., 1901–2; and Arab-Israeli conflict, 2069; Dulles's recommendation, 2096–97; and Nasser's intentions, 2077–78; on sending Libyans to West Point, 1616; and Suez crisis, 2352, 2424; U.S. relations with, 2060, 2069

Liesveld, Alice: background, 948; on U.S. economy, 947–48

Life magazine: article in, on party platforms, 2305–6; E. orders article in, on Hungarian revolution, 2436; on Luce's editorial, 2312–13

Light, Sam R., gives setter puppies to E., 1739

Lincoln, Abraham, 1165, 2058; on "better angels of our nature," 2235; Chynoweth's view, 1186, 1204; E.'s portrait of, 726–27, 727–28, 802,

847, 1428; on function of government, 2157; greatness of, 1438; leadership style of, E.'s view, 131; and the Middle Way, 1185, 1186; on prayer, 220–21; as a "real" Republican, 2157; soliloquy of, in *John Brown's Body*, 2005, 2027

Lincoln, Benjamin, 2000–2001

Lind, Nils E.: background, 2268–69; on Suez crisis, 2268–69

Lindtner, Jere Knight: background, 1170; on McCarthyism, 1170

Links Club, and E.'s portrait, 721–22, 737–38

Lippmann, Walter: background, 2357; on Suez Canal crisis, 2357

Lipscomb, Glenard L., 664

Lithuania, 64

Littlejohn, Robert McGowan: background, 145; E. recommends, for GSA head, 144; recommends Ageton, 329–30

Livestock: and effects of drought, 242; E.'s interest in, 1091. *See also* Agriculture, Department of; Gettysburg farm

—beef, 26; Benson's promotion on consumption of, 1297–98; on cattle imports, 1769–70, 1854–55; cattlemen meet with Benson, 588–89; on declining market prices, 588–89, 645–46, 646–47, 656–57, 678–79, 1297–98, 1603; diseases of, 1566; dwarfism in, 2278, 2313; health regulations on, 1566, 1769–70, 1854–55; and hearty stew by E., 1297–98; Heckett's view, 1854–55; Hough's theory on surplus of, 588–89; and imports from Canada, 1769–70, 1854–55; and imports from Mexico, 1566; and imports from Scotland, 1566; and imports from U.K., 1566, 1769–70, 1854–55; Kleberg's plan, 588–89; McConnell's view, 656–57, 678–79; Pexton's view, 656–57, 678–79, 1603; on purchasing program, 1603; on Scottish Angus, 1930–31

—hogs, and meat-packers' strike, 2293

—poultry, 1091; army purchase of, in Delaware, 934; and egg industry crisis, 1348–49

Livingston, Robert R., 440, 442

Lizee, Miss, background, 1477–78

Lloyd, John Selwyn Brooke: announces withdrawal of British force from Suez, 2427; attends NAC meeting in Paris, 2158–59; background, 2010; on copper wire exports, 2158–59, 2162; as Foreign Minister, 2138–39; on problems in Middle East, 2055–56; on rubber exports to China, 2140–41; and SEATO, 2056; and Suez Canal Conference, 2254, 2263, 2265; and Suez crisis, 2219–20, 2318; visits U.S. with Eden, 2010; works well with Eden, 2138–39

Lobbyists: and Harris-Fulbright Bill, 2015–16; on oil and natural gas interests, 2015–16

Lodge, Emily (Sears), 177–78

Lodge, Henry Cabot, Jr., 731–32; advice for E., 605–6; advises E. to commend Martin, 1754;

advises E. on domestic politics, 780–81, 1328, 1552–53, 2164; advises E. on stag dinner publicity, 1467–68; advises E. on U.N. affairs, 780–81; on AF of L-CIO merger, 1584–85; on appointing Catholics, 1553; assists in drafting 1956 platform, 2082–83, 2102, 2209–10; attends stag dinner, 1424, 1449, 1450, 1467–68; background, 28, 30; on Bermuda Conference, 312–13; birthday note to, 378; on Bricker amendment, 871–72; on captured U.S. airmen, 1449–50, 2118–19; on Chinese Nationalist forces in Burma, 541–42; commends E., 1814–15; on communism in Cuba, 1553; congratulates E. on reelection, 2378–79; at D-Day commemoration, 1076–77; declines, as E.'s adviser, 1288; on Defense Department in 1956 election, 1815; on Democrats in 1956 election, 1814–15; on E.'s appointment of Wilkins, 934–35; on employment statistics, 1848–49; on E.'s nomination (1952), 378; on E.-Truman relationship, 1848–49; E.'s view, 28, 177–78, 205, 225, 226–27, 228, 230, 1436; on federal civilian pay, 1286–88; on Geneva Summit Conference, 1814–15; on goodwill trips to Afro-Asian countries, 2102; on Hammarskjöld's mission to Middle East, 2118–19; on Hungarian revolt, 2377–78; on internal security program, 1553; and January 1954 meeting, 1062–63; and Lincoln Day speech, 1553; on McCarthy, 934–35, 1815; meets with Jebb and Gromyko, 124–25; on midterm campaign strategy, 1313–14, 1328, 1345; on modern Republicanism, 2378–79; on multilateral economic aid, 2102, 2159–60; on need for U.N. troops in Korea, 241, 312–13; on need for young Republicans, 1848–49; note to, from Pandit, 709–10; on Open Skies proposal, 1815; on placing U.S. art at U.N., 936–37; on political strategist, 934–35, 979–80, 1287–88; on politics in Western states, 547; on post for Farley, 1553, 1624; on Powell's praise for E., 934–35; praise from Baker, on speech by, 1580–81; praise from E., on speech by, 1580–81; praises Nutting, 1449, 1450; on principle of executive privilege, 1080; proposes commission on farm problem, 1858–59; on public relations, 686–88; and Puerto Rico, 709–10, 814; recommends Cooper, 286; recommends E. speak on communism, 697–98; recommends four-power conference, 312–13; recommends Hinds to head TVA, 1111; recommends Whitney, 1848–49; and reduction of U.S. forces in Korea, 775–76; refuses to testify at Army-McCarthy hearings, 1062–63, 1080; on reimbursement to U.S. for logistical support in Korea, 422–23; replies to Knowland, 1635–36; as Republican leader, 2064; on Republican National Committee, 780–81; to review campaign speeches, 2082–83; reviews

Dulles's U.N. speech, 506–7; on Rio Conference, 1408–9; on St. Lawrence Seaway, 133; on security risks, 736; sends "cryptic" note to E., 1079–80; on snubbing congressional invitations, 1762–63; speaks to Associated Press, 667–68; speaks to Council Against Discrimination, 934–35; speaks at U.N., 125; on State of the Union message, 1815; as successor to E., 230, 793; suggests statement on dependent territories, 2294–95; and SUNFED, 2177; and Taft-Hartley Act revisions, 770–71; on Talbott's appointment, 1815; on U.N. appropriations, 269; on U.N. issues and 1956 election, 2164; on U.N. memorial plaque to war dead in Korea, 2294–95; on U.N. role in Indochina, 1118–21; on U.N. security clearances, 736; on U.N. as world forum, 1635–36; urges E. to address U.N., 1699, 1713–14, 1731–32; on U.S. delegates to U.N., 987–88, 1010–11; on U.S. forces in Korea, 241, 328–29, 422–23; and Volunteer Freedom Corps, 79; on work with U.N., 177–78, 227, 1218

Lodge, John Davis: background, 129; birthday celebration for, 1073

Lok Sabha. *See* India, Republic of

London Agreements. *See* London-Paris Accords

London Conference. *See* Egypt: Suez Canal Conferences

London Daily-Telegraph, and E.'s Open Skies address, 1790–92

London-Paris Accords, 1730, 1731; background, 1320–21; Churchill favors, 1448; E. proposes four-power meeting on ratification of, 1612, 1614; and Formosa crisis, 1617–18; France ratifies, 1447, 1469–70, 1487–88, 1525; France rejects, 1469–70; Gruenther's prediction, 1487–88; and Mendès-France, 1445–47, 1469–70, 1498–99; Saarlanders reject, 1447; Soviets denounce, 1447, 1469–70, 1821, 1823; and U.S. forces in Europe, 1445, 1447; and Western European Union, 1469–70; West Germany ratifies, 1487–88, 1525. *See also* Brussels Treaty Organization; Foreign Ministers' Meetings: Nine-Power Conference; Western European Union

Long, Huey Pierce: background, 406, 407; dynasty of, 516

Long, Russell Billiu: background, 1569; on U.S.-Mexico air routes, 1569

Long Island Rail Road: bankruptcy of, 758–59; Dewey's view, 758–59; reorganization of, 758–59

Long Island Transit Authority, and bankrupt Long Island Rail Road, 758–59

Longstreet, James, 2003–4

Loper, Herbert Bernard: background, 1418; on dispersal of atomic weapons, 1418

Lord, Mary Pillsbury: to assist Hall, RNC, 1423; background, 1423

Lorenzen, Anton Frederick, background, 508–9

Louisiana: army maneuvers in (1941), 516; E. visits New Orleans, 618–19; on integration of Catholic parochial schools, 2086–87, 2088; and New Orleans bridge, 103–4; on New Orleans-Mexico air routes, 1569

Louisiana Purchase, 618–19

Lovett, Robert Abercrombie: background, 1983–84; member, Foreign Intelligence Activities Board, 1983–84

Low, Merritt B., 115

Lowry Air Force Base (Denver, Colorado): as E.'s vacation office, 473–74, 1339; on Gruenther's arrival, 1285

Lubell, Samuel, proposes disarmament plan, 90–92, 374

Lucas, Wingate Hezekiah: appointment for, 1239–40; background, 1239–40

Luce, Clare Boothe, 2312–13; advice to, from E., 659–61; background, 66; esteem of, for Jacobs, 1334; and Italian immigration, 1113–14; and NATO bases in Italy, 1174–76; on painting, 1706; recommends armed force, 2398–2400; reports crisis in Italy, 659–61; reservations on Grimm, 2304–5; resigns, 2304–5; on Scelba, 1280; on Trieste, 549–50, 1176, 1277, 1280; as U.S. ambassador to Italy, 66, 190, 534–35; on weekend with Churchills, Hughes, 1706; Zellerbach succeeds, 2304–5

Luce, Henry Robinson, 661; background, 66; on Clare's recommendation of armed force, 2398–2400; commends E., 2361; editorial by, in *Life*, 2312–13; E. orders article on Hungarian revolution, 2436; E. praises station KLZ, 1263–64; Hughes returns to Time, Inc., 534–35; on Institute of War and Peace, 1818–19; meets with E., 2400; on Red China's attack on Tachens, 1520; reports on Clare, 190; on winning cold war, Jackson's view, 1758–59

Lucey, Charles Timothy, E.'s esteem for, 829, 832

Lucey, Robert Emmet: background, 915–16; on Mexican nationals working in U.S. agriculture, 915–16

Lucy, Autherine: background, 2087; enrolls at University of Alabama, 2087

Lumbard, J. Edward, Jr.: background, 1510; federal judgeship for, 1510

Luther, Martin, greatness of, 1437

Lutheran World Relief, and aid to East Germans, 554–55

Luxembourg: and EDC, 1132; and EURATOM, 1965–66; Mesta resigns, 167, 763; and NATO, 1614; and WEU, 1613, 1614

Lysikov, Valery Alexandrovich: background, 1668–69; defects, 1668–69; returns to Soviet Union, 1668–69

McAdam, Charles Vincent: background, 1907–8; offers Florida house to E., 1907–8; visits E., 1907–8

Index   2881

McAdam, Charles Vincent, Jr., visits E., 1907–8
McAdam, Marguerite (Wimby), background, 1907–8
McAfee, James W.: background, 1188; recommends Dixon, 1188
MacArthur, Douglas: and Bonus March, 2002; on Hunt's book about, Hodgson's view, 1735–36; and military force in Japan, 570, 573; relief of, McCarran's view, 1353, 1355
MacArthur, Douglas II: to attend Bermuda Conference (1953), 271–72; background, 271–72, 433; coordinates Omega policy, 2096–97; declines Forum speech, 536–37; drafts reply to Monty, 384; on French conscripts in Indochina, 1121; meets with Laniel, 433; and U.S. aid in Indochina, 433
McCabe, Thomas Bayard: background, 1245; on teamsters and Eisenhower Fellowships, 1245
McCaffree, Mary Jane, 2161–62; on dinners, reception for diplomatic corps, 1291; on invitations to Senator George, 1526–27; as Mrs. E.'s personal secretary, 72–73; on party plans in Denver, 1835–37
McCaffrey, John Lawrence, and President's Committee on Government Contracts, 476–77
McCammon, Bess, background, 1521, 1522
McCann, Kevin Coyle: assists E. on speeches, 1017, 1559, 1815, 1816; background, 1017, 2132–33; drafts message to Churchill, 1906–7; on E.'s speech to ABA, 1815, 1816; on E.'s U.N. speech, 1731–32; and Larmon's report on public relations, 865–66; on leave from Defiance College, 1559; and *Man from Abilene*, 96; on news reports regarding, 2132–33; returns to Defiance College, 2132–33
McCardle, Carl W.: background, 1833; on UNESCO paper, 1833
McCarran, Patrick A.: asks increase in wool tariffs, 482–83; background, 1355; cosponsors Bricker amendment, 75; opposes Bohlen, 138; opposes emergency immigration legislation, 400–401; opposes Truman's policies, 1355
McCarran-Walter Immigration and Nationality Act (Refugee Relief Act), 400–401, 659, 661; background, 118, 1113–14; becomes law, 1113–14, 1290; and Italian immigration, 1113–14
McCarthy, Joseph Raymond, 369–70, 667–68, 1124; and Arthur E.'s blunder, 445–46; attacks Zwicker, 913–14; on Attlee, 275–76; and Attwood's diary, 537; belligerence of, 413–14, 949–51; Berg's view, 1010; breaks with E., 1430; captures headlines, 136, 138, 233–34, 275–76, 428, 913–14, 937–40, 950, 976–77, 1010, 1429–30, 1430–31, 1435; and CIA investigation, 1137, 1214–15; Craig's concern, 980–81; on critics of E. regarding, 547; declares self victim of "mudslinging," 939; demands E.'s advisers be subpoenaed, 1076; demands media time, 939; directs fed-

eral employees to defy security rules, 1080; E.'s differences with, 826; E.'s view, 122, 136, 138, 233–34, 305–7, 405–6, 949–51, 962, 963, 980–81; on expenses at CBS, 1098; Finder's view, 131; and Greek shipowners, 138, 143–44; Hall's rebuke, 951; Hazlett's view, 405; humiliates Stevens, 914; insists on right to cross-examine, 977; investigates Kaghan, 256–58, 262; investigates Peress, 914; on Korea, 275–76; Krock's view, 1419; Kuchel opposes censure, 1470–71; Larmon recommends "offensive" against, 865–66; Lodge's view, 1815; McCrary's view, 1420–22; and midterm election, 1322; Msgr. McCarthy's view, 1049, 1050; and Murrow, 940, 1026–27, 1098; and Oppenheimer, 1026–27, 1133; opposes Bohlen, 138, 141–42; opposes Hoffman as U.N. delegate, 2236; questions on, for Brownell, 974–75; questions on, from media, 976–77; Reed's view, 305–7; relinquishes committee chairmanship, 976; and Republican reactionary fringe, 950, 975–76, 1402, 1405, 1429; Robinson's view, 975–76; scrutinizes VOA, 71, 138; on "self-imposed abstention," 1322; Senate condemns, 1413, 1422, 1429; Senate votes to censure, 1429; and split in Republican party, 949, 980–81; tactics of, and congressional committees, 897–98; tactics of, repulse E., 939, 980–81; Vermont's view, 923–24; will contest E., 939; Wilson's retort to, 951. *See also* Eisenhower, Dwight David: McCarthy; McCarthyism
—Army-McCarthy hearings, 1430–31; business community reacts, 1059–60; and Cohn, 951–52; Dirksen agrees to help, 932; effect of, on internal security program, 1494–95; E.'s view, 976–77, 1044–45, 1059–60; and Hall's rebuke, 951; Hoyt's view, 1102–3; Lodge refuses to testify, 1062–63; and memo on treatment of government personnel, 930–31, 1064–66; Mundt as temporary chair, 976, 1064, 1065; and Peress case, 1064–65; and principle of executive privilege, 1069–71, 1075–76, 1080, 1102–3; on requests from investigating committees, 1064–66; Ridgway's objections, 1065; and Schine, 951–52; Somers's view, 1452–53; and Stevens, 914, 1064–66
McCarthy, Thomas J.: background, 1050; on Dulles, 1049, 1050; on E.'s Administration, 1049–51; on foreign policy, 1049–51; on McCarthyism, 1049, 1050
McCarthyism, 122; Ayres's view, 764–65; and East-West trade controls, 2140–41; effect of, on legislative program, 950; Europe reacts to, 537; Katz's concern, 1013–14; Lindtner's view, 1170; N. Thomas's view, 614; and Old Guardism, 950; and Presbyterian Manifesto, 667–68; and press, 950; and Roman Catholics, 667–68; Stevenson's charge, 939; Sulz-

berger strikes at, 362–63; a "wasim," 1769; and White case, 683, 688–89. *See also* McCarthy, Joseph Raymond

McClendon, Sarah Newcomb: appreciation of, to White House staff, 2143–44; background, 2143–44; on E.'s news conferences, 2143–44; on E.'s paintings, 2143–44

McCloy, John Jay, 464; background, 257, 822, 1411; and Bilderberg Club, 1410, 1411; on Communist infiltration of U.S. cultural and informational programs, 262; declines International Atomic Energy Agency post, 822; and D'Ewart's candidacy, 933; on E.'s Atoms for Peace speech, 777; on Kaghan's resignation, 256–58, 262; on McCarthy, 262; on Oppenheimer, 1026–27; opposes Bricker amendment, 816–17, 835–38

McClure, John Elmer: background, 1319; on Mrs. Patton's ashes, 1830; organizes National Celebrities Golf Tournament, 1319; supports eighteen-year-old vote, 1829; travels to Europe, Middle East, 1829

McClure, LaVere, 2306–7

McClure, Mary: background, 2307; and small business problems, 2306–7

McClure, Robert Alexis: background, 1001; and psychological warfare, 999–1001

McClure, Robert Battey: background, 1607–8; invites E. to Monterey, 1607–8

McCollum, Leonard Franklin: attends stag dinner, 2062–63; background, 1252–53; on E.'s gas bill veto, 2026; on E.'s Inaugural prayer, 1252–53

McCone, John Alex: background, 129, 2292; heads CIA, 2292; reports on tanker construction, 2292; on Suez Canal crisis, 2292

McCone, Rosemary (Cooper), background, 2292

McConnaughey, George Carlton: background, 1090; heads FCC, 1090

McConnell, Joseph Howard: background, 451–52; leaves NBC, 451–52, 455

McConnell, Robert Earl: attends stag dinner, 2062–63; background, 242, 446–47; on beef-price problem, 656–57, 678–79; E.'s esteem for, 242; to meet with Benson on cattle situation, 242; on Pexton's view, 656–57

McConnell, Samuel Kerns, Jr.: on House rejection of education bill, 2200; and Pennsylvania gubernatorial race, 859–60; and Taft-Hartley Act revisions, 538–39, 565, 571, 982–83

McCormack, John William: background, 1587; backs tax reduction bill, 1587; opposes OTC bill, 2173

McCormick, Elmer S.: background, 1060

McCormick, Kenneth Dale: background, 598; on publishing E.'s speeches, 598

McCormick, Robert Rutherford: background, 1405; irritates E., 205, 206; and reactionary fringe, 1402, 1405

McCoy, Frank Ross, background, 1011

McCoy, Whitley Peterson, 27

McCrary, Jinx Falkenburg. *See* Falkenburg, Jinx

McCrary, John Reagan, Jr. ("Tex"): attends stag dinner, 1424; background, 1421; on Baruch and Billy Rose, 2295; congratulates E. on acceptance speech, 2266; and E.'s health concerns, 1980; and Einstein's formula, 1980; on ending housing segregation, 1690; establishes public relations firm, 1911–12; on fearless young Russians, 2295; on Madison Square Garden rally, 1422, 1979–80; on New York Senate race, 2266; praises Javits, 1420, 1421–22; on rally for McCarthy, 1422; on rehabilitating southwest Washington, D.C., 2295; on "Salute to Eisenhower" dinners, 1911–12, 1979–80; sees waning support for E., 1420–22; on "Serenade to Ike" rally, 1911–12; urges E.'s candidacy in 1956, 2027; works for Republican party, 1422, 2266

McCrary, Michael Brisbane: background, 2295; visits Russia, 2295

McCullom, Leonard Franklin, background, 49

McDonald, David John: background, 373–74; and Bernhard's conference, 1061–62; and fiscal policy objectives, 373–74, 2090; and gangsterism on New York waterfront, 2090, 2091; on Hoffa, 2090; on labor union issues, 2090; on racial problems in South, 2090; recommendations by, on U.S. economy, 1011–13, 2090; and Tariff Commission, 200

McElroy, Neil H.: background, 1423; on E.'s advisory committee, 1423

McGee, Pat, 440, 442

McGill, Ralph Emerson: background, 128, 1232–33; sends book to E., 1232–33

McGowan, M. M.: on appointment to federal bench, 1424; background, 1424

McGraw-Hill Book Company, on publishing E.'s speeches, 597–99

McGuire, Verona M., background, 2047

McIntosh, Millicent: background, 21–22; E. recommends Horak to, 1688; thanks to, from E., 21–22

McKay, Douglas: announces federal power policy, 311–312; background, 6; on child's drowning, 690–91, 691–92; and Colorado River Storage Project, 902, 1071; Edgar E.'s view, 2282–83; on Forbes's retirement, 514–15; heads policy study on reclamation and multipurpose dam projects, 73–74; and Hitchcock, 2180–81, 2282–83; loses to Morse in Senate race, 2180–81, 2282, 2283; and national park system, 808–9; on need for young Republicans, 2180–81; opposes transfer of Land Management Bureau, 1339–40; requests loan of E.'s painting, 233; resigns, 2175–76, 2283; on St. Lawrence Seaway, 133; as Secretary of Interior, 5; wins Oregon senatorial primary, 2175–76

McKay, Mabel (Hill), background, 2180–81

Index   2883

Mansfield, Michael Joseph: asks increase in wool tariffs, 482–83; and Bricker amendment, 76; and Suez Canal Conference, 2241
Mansfield Reservoir, 1632
Mansure, Edmund F.: background, 145; and contract awards for Nicaro, Cuba, nickel plant, 2016, 2019; and Denver Federal Center, 343–44; favors Republicans, 2016–17, 2019; heads GSA, 145; resigns, 2016, 2017, 2019
Manufacturers: and debate on H.R. 1, 1573–74; of twine and cordage favor H.R. 1, 1574, 1631. *See also* Industry
Mao Tse-tung, background, 1643
Marie, André: background, 292–93; and Bermuda Conference (1953), 292–93; to form cabinet, 292–93; government of, fails, 313–14
Maritime industry, 1230; on atomic ship, 1808; construction of U.S.S. *Kitty Hawk*, 1938; desegregation in, 471, 472–73; and Greek shipowners, 138, 143–44; in Honduran crisis, 1067; McCone's report on tanker construction, 2292; on need for big oil tankers, 2310, 2311, 2320–21; on sale of Panama Canal ships, 1746–47; shipbuilding program, 1344; and trade with North Korea, 796. *See also* Egypt: Suez Canal; Oil; United States: foreign trade
Markezinis, Spyros: background, 274; meets with E., 272, 274
Marnes-La-Coquette, 824; Gruenther as honorary citizen of, 1514
Maroger, Jacques: background, 1060–61; book by, on techniques to preserve paintings, 1060–61, 1456; Morgan takes medium to E., 1456
Marriott, J. Willard: background, 2278; inspects beef cattle station, 2278
Marshall, George Catlett: appreciation to, from Dutch, 1104–5; attends Elizabeth II's coronation, 71–72, 371; and Churchill-Eden visit, 1141–42; congratulates E. on reelection, 2410; and E.'s 1952 campaign speech, 1422; greatness of, 1438, 2334; illness of, 626; misses dinner with Greek royals, 626; opposes Red China in U.N., 603–4; receives Nobel peace prize, 626; receives Woodrow Wilson award, 2334. *See also* Marshall Plan
Marshall, John, 532; background, 1281; and bicentennial plans, 1280–81, 1682; Edgar E.'s role, 1290–91. *See also* John Marshall Bicentennial Commission
Marshall, Katherine Boyce Tupper (Brown), 371, 1141–42
Marshall, Thurgood: background, 1690; on segregated housing, 1690
Marshall Plan, 626, 1417, 2134–35, 2426; appreciation to Marshall from Dutch, 1104–5; Hoffman's view, 504, 507; and Jackson plan on foreign aid policy, 1238–39; and U.S. foreign policy, 2206–7

Martha, Crown Princess of Norway, 16
Martin, Edward: background, 602; and Delaware River Project, 1714; and Pennsylvania gubernatorial race, 601–2, 602–3, 859–60; supports Taft, 602
Martin, Isaac Jack: background, 872–73, 1260–61; and Benson's plan, 968; and Bricker amendment, 1095–96, 2291, 2469; and Colorado River Storage Project, 902; E.'s esteem for, 1260–61; and foreign economic policy, 1057–58; and midterm election, 1328–29; and Taft-Hartley Act revisions, 872–73; on voters' indifference, 2260–61
Martin, John, 97
Martin, Joseph William, Jr., 84, 132, 332; and Adams, 241; background, 27, 29; E.'s view, 27, 453–54, 827, 1754; and excess-profits tax legislation, 335–36; and foreign trade program (H.R. 1), 1573; and immigration legislation, 118; and Massey's visit, 973; and midterm campaign strategies, 1313–14; on mutual security legislation, 2187–88; on OTC legislation, 2172–73; praise for, from E., 1817–18; and resolution on subjugation of free peoples, 63–64; on second term for E., 759–60; and study on foreign economic policy, 200, 202; supports E. at Republican legislative conference, 778–79; supports tax program, 963; and textile manufacturers, 1573–74
Martin, Lawrence C.: apologizes to E., 1102–3; and "appeasement" paper, 1102–3; background, 1102–3
Martin, William McChesney, Jr.: background, 582–83; as chairman, Federal Reserve Board, 357–58; on Federal Reserve System's discount rate, 2248; and Federal Reserve Board vacancies, 582–83; and foreign economic policy, 357–58; Humphrey agrees to pressure, 1012–13
Martino, Gaetano: background, 2216–17; and Committee of Three, 2216–17
Marx, Charlene: attends campaign kickoff, 2278; background, 2278
Marx, David H.: attends campaign kickoff, 2278; background, 2278; on fundraising campaign for E., 2277–78
Marx, Idella Ruth (Blackadder): attends campaign kickoff, 2278; background, 2278
Marx, Karl Heinrich, 1643
Marx, Louis: attends campaign kickoff, 2278; background, 2277; and "CLub" subscriptions, 2277–78; on fundraising campaign for E., 2277–78
Maryland: in Baltimore, a tree in E.'s name, 1647; Brice invites E. to hunt, 657–58; and Maryland-D.C. parkway, 1224–25; University of, honors Byrd, 628
Mashburn, Lloyd A.: E. rejects, as Labor Secretary, 566–67, 571; and Taft-Hartley Act revisions, 538–39

Massachusetts: Bradley loses midterm election in, 1204–5; fishing industry in, 1138–39; and Northampton tercentennial, 1150–51, 1169; as "Old Guard," 858; textile manufacturers oppose H.R. 1, 1573–74; and Yankee Atomic Electric Company, 1871–72

Massey, Vincent, visits U.S., 973

Masten, L. O., 364

Masterson, Charles F.: background, 762; Beardwood's report on California, 762

Mathews, Robert, 117

Matsu; the Matsus. *See* China, Republic of: Matsu

Mattingly, Thomas William: background, 1881; on E.'s heart attack, 1881, 1891–92, 1894–95, 1897–98, 1935; and E.'s surgery for ileitis, 2237

Mayer, Augustus Kiefer: background, 1981–82; on performance tests for livestock, 1981–82

Mayer, Lucy (Barnett), background, 1981–82

Mayer, René: background, 60; and Bermuda Conference (1953), 253–54; and EDC, 60; resigns, 253–54; suggests tripartite summit, 239, 240; visits E., 161

Maytag, Lewis Bergman ("Bud"): background, 1764–65; on Eisenhower Golf Course at Air Force Academy, 1764–65

Meany, George: and Bernhard's conference, 1061–62; on electrical work at Gettysburg farm, 1637; and President's Committee on Government Contracts, 476–77

Medals: for distinguished civilian achievement, 1676–77; of Merit, 1398

Media: on censorship of DOD disclosures, 631–32, 767–68; deals in personalities, 829; on Dulles, 951–52; E.'s advice to, 667–68; and E.'s interest in Europe, 40; on E.'s second-term candidacy, 1434–35, 1751, 1770, 2061; E.'s use of, 956–57, 1126; Larmon as media adviser, 2324–25; and McCarthy, 405–6, 949–50, 975–76, 1419; misquotes by, 2317; no leaks to, on Taft-Hartley Act, 561–62; rebukes Knowland, 950–51; and reports on Russia, 1216; restrictions on, in Argentina, 316–17; speculates on Milton E.'s candidacy, 1878; and stag dinner publicity, 1467–68; Thornton's view, 861–62; in World War II, 750; and USIA, 2183–84

—motion pictures, and "Year of Big Decision," 1252–53

—news conferences, 2118–19; on atomic energy, 1015–16; on Benson, 646–47; on Bricker amendment, 784–85, 2107–8; on candidacy in 1956, 1965, 2024–25, 2042, 2044, 2061; on captured U.S. airmen, 1450; on Carney, 1636–37; on cattlemen's caravan, 588–89; on civil service, 662, 664; on condemnation of forced labor, 2141–42; on constitutional balance of power, 875; on Cyprus situation, 2070; on dangers of, 631–32; on Delaware River

dredging project, 1475–76; on Dixon-Yates debate, 1456–57; Drummond's wish, 976; and dump Nixon charge, 2061, 2074–75; on EDC and German military, 385; E. defends Nixon, 1156, 2061; and E.'s statement on Indochina, misinterpreted, 1051, 1052; on extension of Reciprocal Trade Act, 1057–58; on Flanders's denunciation of McCarthy, 940; on foreign aid, 796, 797; on foreign economic policy study, 1244–45; on FY 1954 budget, 197; on German reunification, 384; on health, 1993–94; on Horton case, 283–84; on McCarthy, 938–40, 976–77, 1059–60; McClendon's appreciation of, 2143–44; on Mitchell, and right-to-work laws, 1492; on mutual security legislation, 2187–88; on natural gas bill veto, 2024–25; on Nixon's candidacy in 1956, 2130–31; on omnibus tax bill, 976; on Oppenheimer, 1026–27; opposes Red China in U.N., 1180; on Peress case, 914; on Philippine elections, 650–51; on prisoner exchange in Korea, 146–47; Reston's view on "good partner" policy, 1240; on right- to-work laws, Mitchell's view, 1443–44; on school construction legislation, 1753–54; on segregation in National Guard, 1753, 1754; on Taft's alarming speech, 275–76; on Talbott's resignation, 1797–98; on TVA, 557; on U.N. appropriations, 268; on UNESCO, 243; on U.S. military aid to Pakistan, 675–76; on Wagner's refusal to greet Saud, 2464; on Warren as candidate in 1956, 1995–96; Wilson's blunder, 1615–16; on world trade, 1226

—press: and Atoms for Peace speech, 759–60; attacks Strauss, 1476–77; *Baltimore Sun* endorses E., 2307–8; and Bermuda Conference (1953), 259–60, 271–72, 738, 746, 790, 793; on *Chicago Daily Tribune*, E.'s view, 203, 206, 287, 445–46, 828–30, 832; on columnists' methods, 275–76, 428, 576, 578, 684, 829–830, 857–58, 859, 1064; on decline of *New York Herald Tribune*, 1622–23; *Denver Post* on subversives, 1571; *Denver Post* supports E., 2334; *Des Moines Register and Tribune* supports E.'s farm program, 2112–13; E. addresses, 985–86, 1042, 1045; E.'s advice to Edgar E. on, 857–58, 859; Earl E.'s article in *American Weekly*, 879–80; and E.'s second-term candidacy, 1751, 1770, 1850–51; on inaccurate reporting, 1194; and McCarthy, 405–6, 428, 938–40, 1065, 1429; McCormick irritates E., 205, 206; Meeman praises E. in *Memphis Press-Scimitar*, 873; *Minneapolis Star and Tribune* supports E.'s farm program, 2112–13; *New Amsterdam News* prints Powell's article, 1342; on "newspaper work," E.'s view, 1156; *New York Daily News* attacks young Douglas, 1064; on *Philadelphia Bulletin*, 829; *Pittsburgh Courier* prints Powell's article, 1342; Pleven meets with, on Indochina, 954; *Pravda* reprints

Weir's pamphlet, 603; reports Dulles-E. rift, 506–7; Reston's view, 1240; scores Earl E., 478; on treatment of government personnel, 1064–66; on TVA and Dixon-Yates contract, 1454–55; on U.S. forces abroad, 591–92, 610–11; and USIA, 2125; and U.S. prestige abroad, 403–4; *Wall Street Journal* on E.'s candidacy, 1550; *Washington Post* prints Foster's letter, 877; Wiggins irritates E., 188, 189; on world trade, 1226. *See also New York Herald Tribune; New York Times*
—radio: and Bermuda Conference, 789, 793; E. praises station KLZ, 1263–64; and midterm election campaign, 1328–29, 1335–36; report on legislative record, 387–88
—television: and Bermuda Conference, 789, 793; on "Citizens Ask the President," 2324; and Citizens Press Conference, 2084–85; critiques on E.'s appearance, 684–85, 956–57; Dulles, E. speak on U.S. foreign policy, 1711–12; E. accepts nomination, 2266; E.'s appearances on (1952), 2319; and Gruenther on "Meet the Press," 586–87; and Knowland on "Meet the Press," 1492–93; Lodge's advice, 605–6; McCarthy demands equal time, 939; and midterm election campaign, 1307, 1309, 1328–29, 1335–36; Murrow and McCarthy, 940, 1013–14, 1026–27, 1098; panel discussion on, 278, 623, 684–85; Swope's advice, 542–43; "What's Your Name" features E.'s family, 846
Medical benefits: for armed services, 685–86; and E.'s reinsurance proposal, 1460–61, 1466–67; and HEW, 1460–61, 1466–67; to uninsured, 1460–61, 1466–67
Medical Facilities Survey and Construction Act of 1954, 753; and federal aid for Presbyterian Hospital, 1286
Medical profession, Scripps-Howard survey on, 899
Mediterranean, and Cyprus, 1948–49
Meek, Joseph T.: background, 1121–22; E. supports, 1121–22; High's advice on, 1121–22; loses to Douglas, 1122
Meeman, Edward John: background, 873; esteem of, for E., 873
Meeting of Ministers of Finance on Economy of the American Republics. *See* Rio Conference
"Meet the Press." *See* Media: television
Mehta, Gaganvihari L., 2380–81; background, 1719; meets with E., 1719; on Nehru's visit to U.S., 2078
Meir, Golda: background, 2372–73; on withdrawal of Israeli force at Sinai, 2372–73
Melberg, Reinold: background, 2281; learns to cook, 2281; suggests campaign picnics, 2281
Melville, Ward: and Attwood's diary, 537; background, 537
Menderes, Adnan: background, 1114–15; on strengthening "Southern Flank Alliance," 1114–15; and U.S. aid to Turkey, 1114–15

Mendès-France, Lily (Cicurel): background, 1393; charms E., 1413; charms Gruenther, 1393, 1413, 1415
Mendès-France, Pierre: background, 1134; Churchill's view, 1134–35, 1261–62; Dulles meets with, 1181; and EDC, 1261–62, 1498–99; and Geneva Conference, 1179, 1181, 1196, 1199; Gruenther's advice, 1393; impressions of, 1354–55, 1413–15, 1461–62, 1498–99; loses election, 1415, 1498–99; lunches with Gruenther, 1391; on North Africa, 1414, 1415, 1445, 1447; and Paris Accords, 1469–70, 1472–73, 1498–99; pledges end to Indochina war, 1134; praise for, 1196; as prime minister, 1132; proposes conference with Soviets, 1472–73, 1493; on Tunisia, 1414, 1415; visits E., 1393, 1413, 1415; and Western European Union, 1469–70, 1472–73
Menoher, Pearson: background, 1093–94; and West Point reunion, class of 1915, 1093–94
Menon, V. K. Krishna, 2453, 2454; background, 1634; a boor and menace, 1779; Dulles's view, 1634; and release of U.S. airmen, 1718–19, 1779, 1781; on U.S. relations with Communist China, 1763–64, 1779; visits E., 1633–34, 1718–19, 1779, 1781
Mental retardation, 1619–20
Menzies, Robert Gordon: background, 2111–12; on British foreign policy, 2111–12; heads Suez Committee, 2254, 2279, 2280; Nasser rejects proposals of, 2280; on U.S. foreign policy, 2111–12
Merchant, Livingston Tallmadge: on Adenauer's plan for demilitarized zones in Europe, 1742–43; attends briefing on meeting with St. Laurent and Ruiz Cortines, 2075; background, 1363; drafts letter to Coty, 1613; on Soviet-Yugoslav relations, 1363
Merchant marine, recommendations on, by Commerce Department, 1024–25
Merson, Martin: background, 1754–55; Johnson's concern, 1754–55
Mesta, Perle Skirvin: reportedly attacks E., 763; resigns as U.S. ambassador to Luxembourg, 167, 763
Mexico: abstains at Caracas Conference, 701; ambassadorship to, 1101–2; Bermingham's concern, 170–71, 345, 1099–1100, 1101–2, 1550, 1599–1600, 1743–44, 1744–45, 1750; and Bermudez, 345, 693–94, 1599; and Bracero Agreement, 2096; Burroughs's view, 1101–2; Cake's view, 902; cattle imports from, 1566; Communist activity in, 1101–2, 1195, 1199, 1230, 1743–44; on diplomatic visits, 1961–62; Dulles advises E. not to invite Ruiz Cortines, 1743–44; Dulles advises E. not to visit, 1472; and Falcon Dam, 98, 254, 300, 431–32, 554, 574–75, 593–94; leaders of, visit Milton E., 1363–64; on lead and zinc imports, 1230, 1231, 1242–43; on loans to,

Monroe Doctrine, and Caracas Conference, 701
Monsanto Chemical Corporation, and krilium, 2072–73
Montana, and D'Ewart's candidacy, 933, 1351–52
Montgomery, Bernard Law ("Monty"): addresses NATO CPX exercises, 2153–55; background, 189–90; congratulates E. on reelection, 2392; and de Guingand, 1324–25; E.'s difficulties with, 1324–25; on EDC, 383–86; on Gruenther, 696–97; on imaginary war with Soviets, 2153–55; on NATO, 383–86, 2154; praise for, from Zhukov, 1077; on reunification of Germany, 383–86; on Soviet intentions, 2153, 2155; visits E., 696–97, 1324–25, 2154, 2155
Montgomery, Robert: background, 957; and Burroughs's recommendations, 956–57; critique of film, "Year of Big Decision," 1252–53; helps rid E.'s farm of crows, 1805; and Larmon's report on public relations, 865–66
Mooney, Edward (Cardinal): background, 681; on E.'s speaking skill, 697–98; on religious persecution in Czechoslovakia, 2409
Moore, Archie: background, 1768; on juvenile delinquency, 1768
Moore, George Gordon, Jr.: background, 840–41; visits Latin America, 840–41
Moore, Mable Frances Doud ("Mike"), 1141–42, 1739–40; background, 840–41; visits Latin America, 840–41
Moore, Maurice Thompson ("Tex"): background, 49; as Columbia board chairman, 1671
Mora, José Antonio: background, 2211–12; on meeting of Presidents of American Republics, 2211–12
Moran, First Baron of Manton (Lord Moran). *See* Wilson, Charles McMoran
Moreell, Ben: as adviser to JCS, 635–36; background, 636; chairs water resources study, 689–90, 821, 1137, 1138; opposes Colorado River Project, 1137
Morgan, Arthur Ernest: background, 928–29; protests TVA appointment, 928–29
Morgan, Gerald Demuth: background, 538–39; and Benson's plan, 967–68; Durkin's attack on, 565, 571; E.'s esteem for, 831; and farm policy, 1304–5; Gunderson's view, 646–47; on Jenner's report, 701; and midterm election, 1328–29; and Taft-Hartley Act revisions, 538–39, 561–62
Morgan, Henry, 2214
Morgan, Justin Colfax: background, 1957; wins federal judicial post, 1957
Morgan, Shirley C.: background, 1456; on Maroger's medium, 1456
Morocco, Kingdom of: and France, 1043, 1119; and Mendès-France, 1445, 1447; and Nasser's intentions, 2077–78; NSC advocates aid

to, 2405; Soviet influence in, 2076–77; strategic air bases in, 583–84
Morris, William Richard (First Viscount of Nuffield), background, 1306, 1307
Morrison, Herbert Stanley, on E.'s world peace speech, 181–82
Morrow, E. Frederick: on appointment of, 2095; background, 2095
Morrow, Wright Francis: background, 1255; controversial nomination of, to U.N., 1254–56, 1268; supports E. in 1952, 1255
Morse, True Delbert: and Advisory Board of Economic Growth and Stability, 277–78; background, 1084; on farm issues, 991–92, 1304–5; on tung imports, 1084–85
Morse, Wayne Lyman: E.'s view, 1435, 1439; and McKay, 2282, 2283; and Oregon senatorial primary, 2175–76; resigns from GOP, 265, 266; wins Oregon Senate race, 2180–81, 2282, 2283
Morton, Alfred Hammond, suspension of, as VOA head, 71
Morton, Thruston Ballard: background, 973, 979–80; Lodge recommends as political strategist, 979–80; on Massey's visit, 973; and Morrow's nomination to U.N., 1255
Moses, and the Amalekites, 1219–21
Moslems: and Anglo-French invasion of Suez Canal Zone, 2344; and impact of Arab-Israeli conflict, 2355; in India, 2449–50; migration of, to Pakistan, 2449; on Nasser, as "Moslem Mussolini," 2365; Nehru's view, 2449–50; on U.S. role on behalf of, in Suez crisis, 2346–47
Moss, 516
Mossadeq, Mohammed: background, 339; government of, overthrown, 340; requests U.S. aid, 337–40; and U.S. role in Iran-U.K. dispute, 337–40
Motion picture industry: and admission tax repeal, 439–42; E. vetoes tax bill, 442; on "stars" of, 439–40
Moulton, John Fletcher, background, 1832
Mountbatten, Edwina Cynthia Annette (Ashley), background, 1905–6
Mountbatten, Louis Francis Albert ("Dickie"): background, 1905–6; on sharing nuclear naval secrets with British, 1905–6; visits U.S., 1905–6
Movement Republican Populaire (MRP), opposes Mendès-France, 1469–70
Moyer, Austin A., 2122–23
Muir, Malcolm, Sr.: on Anglo-American relations, 2417–18; background, 2418; on Gruenther, 2417–18; on Mideast crisis, 2417–18; on NATO alliance, 2417–18
Mumford, Lawrence Quincy: background, 989–90; as Librarian of Congress, 989–90
Mundt, Karl Earl: background, 932; favors rigid price supports, 2017, 2019–20; requests vote on McCarthy hearings, 932; as temporary

chair, McCarthy committee, 976; and U.S. policy on Formosa crisis, 1694–95

Munich, 1576

Munson, Henry Lee, as possible aide to Hagerty, 529

Murphree, Eger Vaughan: background, 2021–22; and ICBM program, 2021–22

Murphy, Frank, 514–15

Murphy, Franklin David: on AMA's support of Bricker amendment, 860, 866–67; background, 860, 866–67; on E.'s candidacy for second term, 1549–50; E.'s esteem for, 1205–6; on E.'s Presidential Library Commission, 1709–10; heads bipartisan security commission, 1205–6; on international educational exchange program, 1732–33

Murphy, George Lloyd: background, 693–94, 853; and California politics, 1232; E. considers as staff adviser, 853; meets with E., 693–94; organizes Inaugural entertainment, 853

Murphy, James L.: background, 1769; chairs Citizens Congressional Committee, 1376–77; on communication with RNC workers, 1837–38; on E.'s advisory committee, 1423; and Larmon's report on public relations, 865–66; on McCarthy, 1769; meets with E., 1769; on midterm election, 1376–77; on Republican county chairmen, 1769; on Wood's attitude, 1551–52

Murphy, James Raymond: background, 1833; and UNESCO paper, 1833

Murphy, John Bartlett: and absentee voting laws for service personnel, 1542; background, 1543

Murphy, Robert Daniel: advises against message to Churchill, 1283; background, 1061–62; on Bernhard's conference, 1061–62; and Committee of Three, 2257; on communism in Syria, Iraq, 2463, 2465; and diplomatic relations with Vatican, 1227–28; encourages Haitian President Magloire's visit, 1105–6; on Mrs. Arias's pique, 2242–43; and NATO, 2257; and Soviet-Yugoslav relations, 1860–61; and Suez Canal crisis, 2219–20, 2222–24; and talks on Trieste, 1277, 1279, 1280, 1293–94; on U.S. military aid to Yugoslavia, 1860–61; visits Yugoslavia, 1860–61; and Wright's offer, 1124–25

Murray, Athol, background, 508–9

Murray, James Edward: background, 1351, 1439; campaign tactics of, irritate E., 1351–52; Nixon chides, 1351–52; wins Montana midterm, 1351–52; woos "leftish" vote, 1435

Murray, Johnston: background, 516–17, 1142–43; and development of Washita River basin, 516–17; visits Latin America, 1142–43

Murray, Philip, 674

Murray, Thomas Edward: on AEC and Dixon-Yates, 1201; background, 799; proposal by, on atomic emergency, 1426; proposes atomic test limitations, 896; proposes moratorium on thermonuclear tests, 1426; on uncleared observers at CASTLE series, 799–800

Murrow, Edward R.: attacks McCarthy, 940, 1013–14; and McCarthy's expenses at CBS, 1098; McCarthy's view, 1026–27; and Murrow's expenses at CBS, 1098; and Radulovich case, 679–80

Muscat and Oman, Sultan of, and Buraimi dispute, 296

Muse, Virginia Elaine (Nielsen), 13–14

Mussolini, Benito, 1004, 1642; on Nasser, as "Egyptian Mussolini," 2413; on Nasser, as "Moslem Mussolini," 2365; on Nasser, as new Mussolini, 2434–35

Mutual Defense Assistance Agreement (1954), with Japan, 1656, 1659

Mutual Defense Assistance Control Act of 1951 (Battle Act): background, 960; and East-West trade controls, 960, 984

Mutual Defense Assistance Program, 207, 208; and agreement with Spain, 500–502; and aid to Iran, 339; and U.S. bases in Philippines, 389–90; U.S. sells jet trainers under, 1716–17

Mutual Defense Treaty: and Korea, 638–40, 969–71, 1534; and Nationalist China, 1520, 1538, 1540, 1565, 1575, 1578, 1653–54; and U.S. force on Taiwan, 1581, 1583

Mutual security. See Collective security; Foreign Ministers' Meetings; Mutual Security Acts; Mutual Security Agency; Mutual Security Program

Mutual Security Act of 1951: and aid to Nicaragua, 202; Flanders opposes amendment to, 372; Lodge defends, 125

Mutual Security Act of 1953: and aid for Bolivia, 585; and assistance to Spain, 502; and foreign-aid appropriations for 1954, 495–96

Mutual Security Act of 1954, 1177; abolishes FOA, 1432, 1527–28, 1677, 1680; and aid to Hungarian refugees, 2436–37; allocates aid to Guatemala, 1541

Mutual Security Act of 1955, on restructuring FOA, 1680

Mutual Security Act of 1956, 2051–52, 2092, 2093; Congress restores funds for, 2187–88; Richards's view, 2194; and SUNFED, 2177; on Yugoslav compliance with, 2382, 2384

Mutual Security Agency (MSA), 374; and aid to Indochina, 314–15; and aid to Iran, 216–18; and aid to Israel, 168; aid to Southeast Asia, 213; budget of, 134, 426–28; on McCarthy and Greek shipowners, 143; and psychological warfare, 1812–13; surveys U.S. foreign-aid program, 134; unexpended funds of, 204–5

Mutual Security Appropriations Act of 1956, Dirksen supports, 1859–60

Mutual Security Authorization for 1955, amendment to, passes, 1173

Mutual Security Program: and aid to Berlin, 526;

and Armour's report on Iran, 2439–40; and
Bernhard's plan for jet trainer sales, 1747–48;
and Citizen Advisors on, 2134–35, 2163;
Congress restores funds for, 2187–88; and
EDC, 365–67; funding for, 346–47, 498–99;
George's view, 2092; and Jackson plan on foreign aid policy, 1248–49; and OTC legislation, 2172–73; reduction of, 796, 797; and reorganization of FOA, 1677–80; and tanks for
Iraq, 2051–52; and U.S.-U.K aid to Iraq,
1787–88. See also Mutual Security Agency

Naguib, Muhammad: and Aswan dam project,
175; background, 68–69; and Egyptian nationalism, 365, 367; E.'s view, 160–61, 365;
and gift pistol to, 211; rebuffs U.S.-U.K. ambassadors, 160–61; sends ibis to E., 211; and
Suez Canal base, 288, 391–93; suspends talks
with U.K. on Suez, 246; and U.S. position,
100–102, 111–13, 216–18, 244–46, 288, 391–
93. See also Egypt
Nagy, Imre: background, 2335; execution of,
2363; and Hungarian revolt, 2335, 2362–63;
as premier, 2335
Namm, Benjamin Harrison: attends stag dinner,
1733–34; background, 1733–34; supports
highway program, 1733–34
Nanchi Island. See China, Republic of: Nanchi
Island
Napoleon I, 2277; on greatness of, 1438
Narcotics, Bureau of, and Vogel, 1441–42
Narcotics, Geist's view, 1441–42
Nash, Frank C. (Francis Carroll), approves
Dulles's reply to Franco, 501
Nasser, Gamal Abdul: ambition of, 2096–97; An-
derson meets with, 1952–53, 2028–29, 2068–
69; as Arab hero, 2274–75, 2424; on Arab-
Israeli quarrel, 2028–29, 2054–55, 2055–56,
2068–69, 2239–40, 2355–57, 2455–56; and
Aswan Dam project, 2446; background on
quarrel with, 2239–40; and Baghdad Pact,
2077–78; Ben Gurion's view, 2142–43, 2339;
builds military force, 2239–40; and Canal
Users' Association, 2280, 2286, 2287; and
Convention of 1888, 2279, 2280; critics of,
2424; destabilization of, 2208; and E.'s concern on Suez, 2227, 2263–65, 2272–73, 2310;
Eden compares to Hitler, 2276–77; Eden
compares to "Moslem Mussolini," 2365; as
"Egyptian Mussolini," 2413; as enemy of
Britain, France, and Israel, 2355; as evil influence, 2440; fears of, 2068; Ginzberg's view,
2208; on Hammarskjöld's mission, 2121; and
High Dam at Aswan, 2028–30, 2268–69; as
leader of Arab world, 2068–69, 2096–97,
2310; meets with Hare, 2455–56; meets with
Suez Canal Committee, 2263, 2265; national-
izes Suez Canal Company, 2219–20, 2222–
24, 2239–40, 2244, 2280, 2286–87, 2355,
2413, 2434–35; Nehru's view, 2445–46, 2455–

56; as new Mussolini, 2434–35; plans creation of United Arab States, 2077–78; rejects
Menzies's report, 2280, 2286, 2287, 2290; on
relations with Soviet Union, 2455–56; on relations with U.S., 2455–56; and Saudi Arabia, 2077–78; on Saud as rival to, 2441;
Saud's view, 2311–12; and second Suez Canal
Conference, 2290; sinks ships in Canal, 2446;
on Soviet arms for Egypt, 1867; Soviet hold
on, 2318; and Soviet Union, 2096, 2219–20;
and Suez Canal Conference, 2251–52, 2253–
54, 2258, 2263, 2265; on Suez Canal crisis,
2318, 2363–64; as tool of Soviets, 2412–13;
U.S. withdraws Aswan Dam offer, 2239–40;
on visit to U.S., 1845, 1849; on Washington's
Farewell Address, 2455–56; within rights at
Suez, 2434–35
Nation, Carry, 465–66
National Academy of Sciences, and study of effects of atomic radiation, 1590
National Advisory Council on International
Monetary and Financial Problems: and convertibility of currencies, 1046–47; and foreign
economic policy, 1182–83
National Agricultural Advisory Commission,
1858–59; appointments to, 379–80; back-
ground, 495–96; Kline's criticism of, 563–64;
and recommendations on acreage control,
1687
National Archives, and presidential libraries,
1710
National Association for the Advancement of
Colored People (NAACP): encourages Mag-
loire's visit, 1105–6; Marshall's view on hous-
ing, 1690; protests segregation at Charleston
Naval Shipyard, 473
National Association of Evangelicals, 364
National Association of Manufacturers (NAM),
and price change statistics, 157–58
National Association of Railroad and Utilities
Commissioners, 1123
National Automobile Dealers Association (NADA),
supports franchise legislation, 2133–34
National Broadcasting Company (NBC), 452
National Capital Park and Planning Commis-
sion, and Maryland-D.C. parkway, 1224–25
National Catholic Welfare Conference, and aid to
East Germans, 554–55
National Citizens Commission for Public
Schools, 955
National Citizens for Eisenhower Congressional
Committee, E. addresses, on legislative pro-
gram, 1126
National Civil Liberties Clearing House, E. ad-
dresses, 978–79, 1694
National Committee for a Free Asia, 531
National Committee for a Free Europe, back-
ground, 533–34
National Committee to Secure Justice in the
Rosenberg Case, 291

National Council of Catholic Women, E. addresses, 1389
National Council for U.S. Art, Inc., 936–37
National Day of Penance and Prayer, 219–21
National defense. *See* Defense, Department of; United States: national security
National Farm Bureau, and farm bill, E.'s view, 2116–17
National Farmers Union: opposes Dixon-Yates contract, 1201; sponsors cattlemen's caravan, 588–89
National Federation of Republican Women, E. addresses, 1193
National Foundation to Honor General Dwight D. Eisenhower and the United States Armed Forces, Inc. *See* Eisenhower Foundation for the Promotion of Citizenship
National Guard: and emergency evacuation procedures, 1665–66; and reserve mobilization policy, 1222–23; segregation in, Powell's view, 1752–54
National Housing Act of 1949, E. recommends amendment to, 607
National Jewish Welfare Board, 2055
National Labor Relations Board (NLRB): and ILA, 754–55; and ILA-AF of L, 754–55; and New York dock strike, 754–55; and Taft-Hartley Act, 489–90, 538–39, 872–73, 982–83
National Live Stock and Meat Board, 1297–98
National Manpower Council: background, 1474–75; E. commends, 1474–75
National Mediation Board, Boyd heads, 567, 571
National Park Service: appropriations in FY 1954, 808–9; appropriations in FY 1955, 808–9; and charges of parks deterioration, 808–9; and Fort Lorenzo, Panama, 2214; and Maryland-D.C. parkway, 1224–25
National Petroleum Council, and distribution of oil to free world, 2320–21
National Press Club, elects Warren president, 1503
National Railway Mediation Board, negotiations with, fail, 619–20
National Recovery Administration (NRA), and land purchase program, 1391–92
National Rural Electric Cooperative Association: opposes Dixon-Yates contract, 1201; scores E.'s public power policy, 1341–42
National security. *See* United States: national security
National Security Act of 1947, 248; amendments to, 255–56
National Security Council (NSC): advocates aid for Morocco, Tunisia, 2405; on aid to Burma, 2259; on air bases in Morocco, Spain, 583–84; on Alcoa antitrust and "round" increases, 608–9; and Arab-Israeli conflict, 573; and Austrian treaty, 1178, 1180; and Baghdad Pact, 1950; on ballistic missile program and

interservice rivalry, 1932–33; Baruch's view, 1148–49; Bush-Oppenheimer visit, 251–52; on censorship of DOD disclosures, 631–32, 767–68; and CIA study, 1213–15; considers defense budget, 342–43, 355–57; considers restricted data exchange with Canada, 303–4; Cooke's view, 54–55; and crisis in Egypt, 246, 2346–47; and Cutler's address on national security policy, 1972; and decline in Anglo-American relations, 244–46; on defense of Nanchi, 1581, 1582; discusses continental defense, 1017–18; on dispersal policy in defense production, 765–66; and DOD budget, FY 1958, 2472; and Donovan's *Inside Story*, 2067; on East-West trade controls, 984, 2140–41; E. meets with, at Camp David, 1894–95, 1900–1901; on emergency evacuation procedures (NSC 5513), 1448–49; endorses U.S. aid to Pakistan, 908–9; E.'s view, 54–55; and FOA policies, 1432; and foreign economic policy, 1182–83; and Formosa, 185, 1283, 1654–59; and Hungarian revolt, 2334–35; and ICBM program, 1853–54, 2021–22; and Killian Committee report, 1909–10; on Latin America, 107, 1276–77; on McClure's assignment in Iran, 1000–1001; on Middle East defense organization, 303; on military aid to Ethiopia, 2387–88; on military budget cuts, 2078–79; on military retirees as advisers to JCS, 620–21, 635–36; and Milton E.'s report on Latin America, 670–71; on MSA budget, 134; on NATO, E.'s view, 1919–20; Nixon reports to, on Asian trip, 761–62; Nixon reports to, on Rhee, 640; on NSC 162, NSC 162/2, 589–90, 733, 735, 1036; on nuclear reactors abroad, 1567–68; opposes moratorium on H-bomb tests, 1068–69; and organization of Operations Coordinating Board, 2476–77; and "policy of candor," 487–88; on post for Stassen, 1621; and Project Solarium, 356; and Quemoy, 1279, 1300–1301; recommends U.S. aid in Indochina, 433; on reorganization of, 1330–31; and reserve mobilization policy, 1222–23; and St. Lawrence Seaway project, 188; and Saudi Arabia, 295–98; and selective service, 583; on Soviet industrial progress, 1963–64; on Soviet sale of arms to Egypt, 1877–78; and stability of U.S. foreign policy, 927–28; on status of EDC, 927–28; supports NATO alternative to EDC, 1298–99; and Taft's outburst, 195–97; on UMT program, 760–61; on U.S. policy on Mexico, 1600; on U.S. troop deployment, 591–92, 611–12; and Volunteer Freedom Corps, 79; and Wilson's blunder, 1615–16. *See also* Operations Coordinating Board
—Egypt, Suez Canal crisis, 2309–11
—France: on retaining U.S. forces in Europe, 927–28; on U.S. participation in NATO, 927–28

—Indochina: approves aid to, 742, 746; discusses situation in, 212–13, 1131–33; E.'s view on U.S. involvement in, 886–87

—Korea, 185; and NSC 118/2, 426–28; on reduction of U.S. forces in, 770, 775–76; on reimbursement for U.S. logistical support in, 241, 422–23; and reinforcements in, 397–98; and postwar relief for, 426–28, 547–49, 1160–61; studies reserve program in, 971; and troop levels in, 241, 328–29, 426–27, 1160–61; and U.S. plan on failed truce in, 728

—Planning Board: hears Draper and Conant, 308–9; and Hull's report on Rhee, 596–97; and NSC 162, 589–90; recommendations by, on East-West trade controls, 960

—Trieste: and decision on redeployment of U.S. troops in, 1246–47; and drought in Yugoslavia, 1292–94

—Vietnam: aid to, 1311; Radford's view, 1311; Ridgway's view, 964; on Vietminh at Dien Bien Phu, 963, 964

—Yugoslavia, discussions on drought in, and Trieste, 1292–94

National Security Training Commission, advocates UMT, 760–61

Native Americans: and Manitou, 1852–53; and Murray's goodwill trips, 1142–43

NATO, 374; Advertising Council campaigns for, 1757–58; on bases in Italy, 1175–76; and Bermuda Conference, 738–47; on Bernhard's plan for jet trainer sales, 1747–48; and Churchill, 1628; and command structure of, 155–56, 166–67; and Committee of Three, 2257, 2418–20; Conference in Paris (April 1953), 203; Conference in Paris (December 1953), 738–47, 783–84; Conference in Paris (April 1954), 1030–31; and Council of Ministers, 155–56, 2419–20, 2441; and Council of Permanent Deputies, 385; and Cyprus, 2192–93; defense policy of, Eden's view, 2218–19; Draper's view, 102–3, 308–9; Dulles addresses, 1704; on Dulles, Gruenther's view, 1461–62, 1463–64; Dulles's view, 805–6; E.'s advice to Gruenther on, 455–56; and East-West trade controls, 959; E.'s confidence in, 2469; and EDC, 366–67, 738–47, 774, 775, 1132, 1261–62, 1275–76, 1285; E.'s view, 1919–20; Flemming meets with Supply Ministers of, 1499–1500; and France, 648–49, 738–47, 927–28, 1261–62, 1275–76, 1285, 2441; George's role, 2164–65; and German sovereignty, 1375–76; on Gruenther's retirement, 1919–20, 2070–71; Hauge's view, 522; and Indochina, 740, 742, 746; Ismay's concern, 2415–16; and Italy, 927–28; and Jackson plan on foreign aid policy, 1248–49; and London-Paris Accords, 1612, 1614; on manpower reductions in Germany, 2236–37; member nations of, 1614; and membership in, for Germany, 1298–99, 1320–21, 1472–73,

1613, 1794–95, 1823; and Mendès-France, 1445, 1447; and Military Standing Group, 155–56, 385; on mobilization stockpile, 1953–54; Monty's concern, 383–86, 2154; on nonmilitary cooperation in, 2164–65; on Norstad as SACEUR, 2070–71, 2120; reappraisal of, 2234–35; on Schuyler's post, 2120; and "Southern Flank Alliance," 1114–15; and Status of Forces Agreement, 386–87; and Streit's proposal, 2216–17; on successor to Gruenther, 1919–20, 2070–71; and Suez crisis, 2219–20, 2346–47, 2415–16; on testimony of leaders, E.'s view, 346–47; and Three Wise Men, 2418–20; and Trieste, 549–50, 568–69, 572, 1175–76, 1246–47; and U.S. base rights in Greece, 272–75; and U.S. forces abroad, 591–92, 2204; on U.S. support of, 627, 1132, 2257, 2415–16, 2417–18; and Vietnam, 1030–31; on Western Europe, Gruenther's view, 2421–22. *See also* North Atlantic Council

Natural gas: and Bermudez, 554; and "Big Inch," 2243–44; and Committee on Energy Supplies and Resources Policy, 1670; congressional legislation on, 1670, 2013–20; and Harris-Fulbright Bill, 2013–16, 2018–19, 2025; and Humphrey's report on fuel policies, 1670; and "most favored nation" contracts, 2015, 2018; on rates, 2131–32; regulations on sales of, 1386, 1388, 2013–20. *See also* Natural Gas Act

Natural Gas Act: on amendment to, 2013–16, 2018–19; Cullen's view, 2033–34; E. vetoes, 2024–25, 2025, 2026, 2062–63

Natural resources, 677, 1136, 1137–38; and Arab boycott of Israel, 570, 573; and commemorative stamps on wildlife, 1855–56; and emergency evacuation procedures, 1448–49; and international oil cartel, 216–18; and oil in Saudi Arabia, 297; and submerged lands, 33, 37, 369–70. *See also* Coal; Natural gas; Oil; Public power policy; Tennessee Valley Authority; Water resources

—conservation, 1230; ABFB view, 563–64; and Agricultural Act of 1948, 563–64; Benson's plan, 113–14; and budget policy for FY 1955, 643–44; and Bureau of Reclamation, 804, 805; and Colorado dust bowl problems, 1063–64; and Colorado River Storage Project, 901–3; and commemorative stamps on, 1855–56; and development of Washita River basin, 516–17; and disaster relief legislation, 1650–51; and flood control, 113–14, 643–44, 1262–63; and Governors' Conference study of, 1063–64; on krilium for soil rehabilitation, 2072–73; and National Land Policy Bill, 563–64; and need for coordination between Agriculture and Reclamation, 804; on soil bank, 1841, 1863–64, 2017, 2019, 2116–17, 2126–27; and soil management, 113–14, 563–64,

Republican Precinct Day Rally, 1319; as successor to E., 225, 229, 793; suggests Milton E. visit Southeast Asia, 1727; supports educational exchange funding, 1025–26; and Tariff Commission, 200–201; travels to Far East, Middle East, 378–79, 596–97, 669–70, 761–62, 1504–5; upsets E., 1155; and U.S. appropriations to U.N., 267–69; on U.S. Embassy party in Moscow, 1785–86; visits El Salvador, 1600–1601; visits India, 1800, 1801; visits Latin America, 1600–1601; visits Korea, 596–97, 968; visits Zahedi, 669–70

Nixon, Thelma Catherine Patricia (Ryan), 761–62, 1141–42, 1303

Norgren, Carl August, 861–62, 1835; background, 477–78; E. visits ranch of, 477–78

Norling, Marshall F., 1836; background, 1412; sends photos to E., 1412; on toxicity of Red Comet extinguishers, 2270–71

Norman, Shirley, on toxicity of Red Comet extinguishers, 2270–71

Normandy: recalls campaign in, 1626; recalls visit to landing beaches, 1820; and tenth anniversary of D-Day, 1076, 1077

Norstad, Lauris, 167, 1747–48; background, 1160; plays golf with Sulzberger, 1160; as SACEUR, 2120; as successor to Gruenther, 1920, 2070–71; Wilson's proposal, 120

North Africa: and France, 2076–77, 2344, 2426; and French-Algerian War, 2404–5; invasion of, 604–5, 749, 1154–55; and Mendès-France, 1413, 1414, 1415, 1445, 1447; nationalists in, 709–10; Soviet subversion in, 2442; and Suez Canal crisis, 2263–64; and U.S. foreign policy, 2442

North Atlantic Council (NAC): and Committee of Three Ministers, 2216–17, 2257, 2419–20; discusses refugee issue, 119; endorses immigration legislation, 178–79; George's role, 2164–65; meets in Paris (April 1953), 156, 178, 189; meets in Paris (December 1953), 648–49, 739–47; meets in Paris (December 1954), 1447, 1461–62; meets in Paris (May 1956), 2157–58; names Norstad as SACEUR, 2070–71; and NATO, 2216–17; and Nine-Power Conference, 1298–99, 1320–21; and problems with Mendès-France, 1445, 1447; and psychological warfare in Europe, 600–601; and Streit's plan, 2216–17. See also NATO

North Atlantic Treaty Organization. See NATO

North Dakota, E. visits, 158

Northern Tier Pact, 1787–88, 1948–50. See also Baghdad Pact

North Korea. See Korea, Democratic People's Republic of

Northwest Airlines: and CAB recommendation, 1317, 1718; and Pacific Northwest-Hawaii route, 1317

Norway, Kingdom of: and Bay's resignation, 16;

and NATO, 1614; sends U.N. force to Suez, 2368–69

Nu, U: aids Burmese children, 1760–61; on Chinese Nationalist forces in Burma, 541–42, 1007–9; E. gives painting to, 1760–61; on U.S. aid to Burma, 2258–59; on U.S. relations with Communist China, 1763–64; visits E., 1760–61

Nuclear energy. See Atomic energy

Nuclear weaponry. See Atomic weaponry

Nufer, Alfred F.: loses favor, 1947, 1949; and Perón's proposals, 649–50; resigns, 1947, 1949; as U.S. ambassador to Argentina, 375–76

Nuffield Foundation, 1306, 1307

Nuri Pasha al-Said. See al-Said, Nuri Pasha

Nutting, Anthony: background, 1450; Lodge's esteem for, 1450

O'Boyle, Patrick A. (Bishop), background, 681

O'Brien, Leo William: and Albany Plan of Union, 1149–50; background, 1149–50

O'Daniel, John Wilson ("Iron Mike"): background, 892–93; Diem's esteem for, 1929–30; meets with E., 1930; on plans to aid Diem, 1380–81; reports on Dien Bien Phu, 892–93; on training Vietnamese troops, 1121; visits Vietnam, 1930

Odell, Joseph Conrad: background, 145; promotion of, 145–46

Odlum, Floyd Bostwick, 1998–99; background, 1472; on commercial uses of uranium, 1567–68; invites E. to visit, 1471–72, 1497, 2478; offers home during E.'s recuperation, 1864–65; sends get-well message to E., 2191; sends heifer (Janessa) to E., 2191, 2339

Odlum, Jacqueline (Cochran). See Cochran, Jacqueline

Office of Defense Mobilization (ODM), 804, 805; and aluminum production, 608–9; and amendment to H.R. 1, 1631; background, 619–20; Baruch's view, 1250; and controlled materials plan, 608–9; and copper industry, 1250; and defense budget, FY 1955, 1206–7; and dispersal policy in defense production, 765–66; and duties on watch imports, 1115–17; on emergency evacuation procedures, 1448–49, 1665–66; and Flemming, 1499–1500, 1558–59; on high precision mechanisms, manpower for, 1116–17; memo to, on U.S.-Latin American relations, 436–37; and military-industrial complex, 635–36; on oil for Great Britain, 2427; on oil for Western Europe, 2422–23, 2427; and Oppenheimer case, 723–25; and psychological warfare, 1812–13; and readiness plans in Far East, 1300–1301; and reserve mobilization policy, 1222–23; and "set-asides" policy, 765–66; staff of, visits Bulova Watch Company, 1117; and standby mobilization legislation, 1038–39; studies need for big tankers, 2310, 2311;

Panama Canal Treaty of 1955: on imports for resale, 2296–97; on interpretation of, 2296–97; on wage discrimination, 2296–97

Panama Line, 1746–47

Pan American Society of the United States, honors E., 2486

Pan American Union. *See* Organization of American States

Pan American Week, 2486; honors E., 2486

Pan American World Airways: and CAB recommendation, 1317, 1718; as "chosen instrument," 1317; and Pacific Northwest-Hawaii route, 1317

Pandit, Vijaya Lakshmi, background, 709–10

Panel on Human Effects of Nuclear Weapon Development, 2484–85

Pantelleria, 750

Papagos, Alexander: offers to increase Greek forces in Korea, 273; on Soviet expansionism, 274; and U.S. base rights in Greece, 272–75

Pappas, Thomas Anthony: attends stag dinner, 1467–68; background, 1467–68

Paraguay, Republic of: Ageton, as U.S. ambassador to, 329–30; Christenberry represents E. at Inaugural, 1327–28; and Delmar, 1187; Stroessner meets with E., 2211–12; and tung imports, 1085; U.S. aid to, 814–15

Paris Accords. *See* London-Paris Accords

Paris Agreements. *See* London-Paris Accords

Paris Consultative Group, coordinating committee of, and East-West trade controls, 959–60, 960–61

Parker, Cola Godden, on Randall Commission, 201

Parker, John Johnston, 567, 572: background, 519–20; Smith's recommendation, 519–20

Parks, Floyd Lavinius: background, 2023–24; retires, 2023–24

Parks, Rosa, and Montgomery, Alabama, bus boycott, 2087

Parshley, Anthony R.: background, 2395–96; on E. as nonpartisan president, 2395–96

Parteet, Willie Frank. *See* "Cemetery"

Passamaquoddy Bay, 1234

Patronage, 332–33; on appointing Democrats, 1424; Bender on, 284–85; Benson on, 379–80; Berg's complaint, 1637–38, 1670–71; Bermingham on, 386–87; in California, 662–64; and cooperation between Executive Branch and RNC, 780–81, 1637–38; Dirksen's view, 933; E.'s view, 751, 752, 1637–38, 1670–71, 2093–94; and Hamley's appointment, 2093–94; and minorities, 284–85, 437; Morgan's protest on TVA post, 928–29; and public relations, 687; and Pulliam, 438, 441–42; RNC and, 284–85

Patterson, Margaret (Winchester), on world affairs, 293–94, 2433–34

Patterson, Morehead: background, 822; and International Atomic Energy Agency, 822

Patterson, Robert Porter, background, 293–94, 2433–34

Patton, Beatrice Banning (Ayer): background, 249; burial of, 1830; criticizes defense budget, 249; death of, 550–51

Patton, Bill Joe: background, 1140–41; on E.'s golf swing, 1905; in U.S. Open, 1140–41

Patton, George Smith, Jr.: background, 249–50; death of, 1830; widow's death, 550–51, 1830

Patton, George Smith, III, 550–51

Patton, James George: background, 1341; scores REA, 1341–42

Paul, Willard Stewart: background, 261–62; and Citadel head, 261–62; heads church expansion fund, 985

Paul I, King of the Hellenes: and U.S. base rights in Greece, 273; visits U.S., 274, 593–94, 626. *See also* Greece

Pawley, Edna Earle (Caldenhead), 454

Pawley, William Douglas: attends stag dinner, 1667–68; background, 454, 1215; and CIA study, 1213, 1215; on Dominican Republic oil and mineral resources, 1893–94; and farm in Virginia, 454; offers Miami house to E., 1893–94; on Russia's entry in Pacific war, 1667–68

Payne, Frederick Blake, 2318

Payne, Frederick Huff: background, 2318; birthday greetings to, from E., 2317–18

Payne, Groverman Blake, 2318

Peace. *See* World peace

Pearl Harbor, 1626

Pearson, Drew, attacks Strauss, 1476–77

Pearson, Lester Bowles: background, 147, 2102; and Committee of Three, 2216–17; and St. Lawrence Seaway, 146–47; speaks on multilateral economic aid, 2102

Peaslee, Horace Whittier: background, 1315–16; on landscaping at farm, 1315–16

Peking. *See* China, People's Republic of

Pella, Guiseppe, on Trieste, 549–50

Pemex (Petroleus Mexicanos): Bermingham's view, 1750; on U.S. loans to, 1550, 1599–1600, 1743–44, 1750

Penick, A. J., Fred, and Herbert, give heifer to E., 1735

Pennsylvania: and Delaware River Project, 1714; Es. register to vote in, 2161–62; E. votes in primary, 2131–32; gubernatorial candidates in, 601–3, 859–60; Leader wins governorship, 859–60; opposes St. Lawrence Seaway project, 187, 188; Pennsylvania Power and Light plant, 1871, 1872; political scandal in, 681–82, 1493–94; and Shippingport plant, 1351, 1870, 1872; and Taft-Hartley Act, 489–90; on unemployment in coal regions of, 1068; Waring's party for E., 524; Weir's concern on politics in, 601–3. *See also* Gettysburg farm

Pennsylvania Fish and Game Department, 854

Pennsylvania Rail Road, and bankrupt Long Island Rail Road, 758–59
Pennsylvania State University, 1192; advises E. on farm, 854, 1130; dedicates chapel to memory of Helen Eisenhower, 2314; E. speaks at centennial commencement, 1735, 1744–45, 1804, 1883–84; and heifers from, for E.'s farm, 2182–83, 2216; on independent athletic association, 1100–1101; Milton E. resigns, 2196–97. *See also* Eisenhower, Milton Stover
Pennsylvania Transformer Company, and Chief Joseph Dam, 306, 307
Pentagon, and censorship of DOD disclosures, 631–32
Percy, Charles Harting: background, 1082; and extension of Reciprocal Trade Agreements Act, 1057–58; supports E.'s foreign economic policy, 1080–82
Peress, Irving: background, 914; and McCarthy, 914; Mundt committee requests data on, 1064–65
Pérez Jiménez, Marcos: background, 1663–64; wishes to visit U.S., 1663–64
Pericles, 274
Permanent Joint Board on Defense: Dewey declines to head, 758–59; Douglas declines to head, 682–83; Hannah heads, 682–83; and U.S.-Canada relations, 682–83
Perón, Juan Domingo: attitude of, toward U.S., 300, 316–17; background, 316–17; military junta ousts, 1947, 1949; and Milton E.'s visit, 316–17, 375–76, 1327–28; praises Milton E., 1327–28; on rapprochement with U.S., 649–50; restricts U.S. press, 649–50
Pershing, Muriel, 396–97
Persia. *See* Iran, Islamic Republic of
Persons, Wilton Burton ("Jerry"), 153, 437, 1439, 1777, 1940–41; advises on REA charges, 1341; background, 30; and Benson's plan, 968; and Citizen Advisors on Mutual Security, 2134–35; and compensation for widows of retired military personnel, 449–50; as congressional liaison, 134, 226, 230, 332–33, 934–35; as counsel to Cabinet, 89; and defense budget, 342; and Dirksen's request on forestry research, 1153; discusses RNC problems with E., 853; and Donovan's *Inside Story*, 2067; drafts reply to Halleck, 1808; on dust bowl problems in Colorado, 1063–64; and E.'s heart attack, 1869–70; E. recommends Fahrion to, 2246; E.'s view, 226, 230, 831; and Kittrell's correspondence, 1433–34; on last minute requests for legislation, 897; on McClure's invitation, 1607–8; memo to, on congressional relations, 109; and midterm election, 1328–29; on military survivor benefits legislation, 1748–49; on MSA appropriations, 205; on reply to Smith, 916–17; and Rubenstein's disbarment proceedings, 1957; on selective service, 583; succeeds Adams, 230

Peru, Republic of: and long-staple cotton quotas, 908; Milton E.'s visit to, 380; Murray visits, 1142–43; Thomas visits, 1705; U.S. aid to, 814–15
Pescadores Islands. *See* China, Republic of
Peters, Frederick C., 859–60
Peterson, Elmer T., writes on chisel plow, 1625
Peterson, Frederick Valdemar Erastus ("Val"): background, 28, 30; and disaster relief legislation, 1650–51; as Federal Civil Defense Administrator, 1737–38; opposed as U.S. ambassador to India, 28, 30; as White House liaison, 30
Pexton, Lawrence McCool, 1835; background, 656–57; on beef-price problem, 656–57, 678–79, 1603; and beef purchasing program, 1603; on McConnell's view, 656–57; sends golf clubs to E., 1385
Phelps, W. H.: background, 1961; offers lawnmower to E., 1960–61
Philadelphia Bulletin. See Media: press
Philadelphia-Delaware-South Jersey Council, and Delaware River dredging project, 1475–76, 1714
Philippines, Republic of: assists evacuation of Tachens, 1577; defense of, 315; and defense of Formosa, 1644, 1656, 1662–63; elections in, 650–51; and "emigre" Chinese, 1641; E. proposes coalition on crisis in Indochina, 1003, 1041, 1042, 1052, 1120; and expansion of U.S. bases in, 389–90; and Magsaysay as president of, 708–9, 1014–15, 1504–5; and mutual defense pact with U.S., 280, 282; Nixon visits, 1504–5; on people of, E.'s view, 650–51; and SEATO, 1179, 1181, 1265–66; and Spruance, 708–9; and Swing, 708–9, 1014–15; and threat of communism, 1537, 1563, 1577, 1641, 1656; on title to U.S. bases in, 2151, 2152
Phillips, Orie Leon, 567, 572: background, 520–21; and Bricker amendment, 1803–4, 1994–95, 2468–69; Edgar E.'s recommendation, 520–21
Phillips, William: background, 275–76; on leadership, 275–76; on McCarthy, 276
Phillips Petroleum Company, and FPC regulations, 1388
Phillips Petroleum Company v. *State of Wisconsin*, Supreme Court ruling on, 2017, 2033–34
Phleger, Herman: background, 1763–64; and Bricker amendment, 1809–10; Edgar E.'s concern, 1809–10
Physical fitness, E.'s interest in, 1796. *See also* Sports
Pierson, Warren Lee, 215
Pike, Thomas Potter: background, 1344; on defense contracts, 1344
Pinay, Antoine: background, 1889–90; on European security and reunification of Germany, 1889–90

President's Advisory Committee on Government Organization: and foreign economic policy study, 1183, 1244–45; recommends Bureau of Land Management transfer, 1339–40; recommends Cabinet Committee on Water Resources, 1137, 1138; and reorganization of FOA, 1679. *See also* Hoover Commission

President's Advisory Committee on a National Highway Program: Clay heads, 1067; reports to E., 1067; reports to legislative leaders, 1557

Presidents of American Republics, meeting of: celebrates signing of Bolivar Agreement, 2211–12; E. attends, 2153, 2196–97, 2199–2200, 2210; E.'s view, 2211–12; Milton E. accompanies E. to, 2196–97

President's Citizen Advisors Commission on Mutual Security Program: Fairless heads, 2134–35; Hoffman's role, 2163; and SUNFED, 2177

President's Commission on Veterans' Pensions. *See* Commission on Veterans' Pensions

President's Committee on Government Contracts: background, 472–73; Nixon chairs, 476–77, 498–99; work of, in Washington, D.C., 698

President's Committee for Hungarian Refugee Relief, 2442–43

President's Committee on International Information Activities, 10–12; Jackson's view on NSC, 1330–31

Press: *See* Media: news conferences; and press

Prettyman, Virgil, Jr.: background, 2000–2001; sends E. quote by Washington, 2000–2001

Priest, Ivy Maude (Baker), 465–66; background, 6; as Treasurer of U.S., 6–7

Prisoners, political: and Agreed Announcement of September 10, 1955, 2457; American, held in Red China, 2448, 2457; on Chinese aliens in U.S., 2448, 2457

Prisoners of war (POW): on feeding of, 57–59; held by Red Chinese, 1171, 1173; and Indian troops, in Korea, 616–17, 905; Korean, and exchange of sick and wounded, 135, 146–47; North Korea captures U.S. airmen, 1413, 1449, 1450, 1451, 1526, 1670; on release of U.S. airmen, 1718–19, 1779, 1781, 1800, 1801, 2118–19; repatriation of, in Korea, 259–60, 279, 281, 291–92, 905; Rhee releases, 309–10, 310–11; U.N., and treatment of, by Red Chinese, 603–4; from U.S., defect, 886

Private enterprise: and TVA's mandate, 1201, 1251–52. *See also* United States Government: federal *v.* state issues

Probasco, Kenneth W.: background, 1913; presents tractor to E., 1913

Production credit corporations, and mutualization, 2080–81

Production and Marketing Administration

(PMA): appointments to, 379–80; background, 379–80

Professional Golfers' Association, gives E. putting green, 1595

Propaganda: Knowland's view, 1635–36; Lodge's view, 1635–36; and MIG incident, 529–32; opportunities for, through multilateral economic aid, 2159–60; on Soviets and atoms for peace plan, 747–48; and U.N. as free-world forum, 1635–36

Psychological warfare: and CCRAK, 776–77; E.'s interest in, 10–12, 1766; as "fourth area" of foreign affairs, 2409–10; and Jackson committee, 71; Jackson resigns, 831, 832; Jackson's report on, 2409–10; and McClure's assignment, 999–1001; and MIG incident, 529–32; misinterpretations of, 600–601; on need for coordination in, 1812–13; Rockefeller succeeds Jackson, 1330–31; on successor to Jackson, 817–18, 988, 1330–31; William Jackson's view, 1330–31

Psychological Warfare Board, and CCRAK, 776–77

Public Health Service, 84

Public Housing Administration: authorizations for (FY 1956), 607; economic operations of, 1147–48

Public power policy, 1230; and Clark Hill Dam, 1511–12, 1514–15, 1569–70; and Denver Blue River policy, 1823–25; and federal funding for, 369–70, 1201–2, 1251–52, 1367–68, 1454–55, 1569–70, 1632; and Hartwell Dam, 1511–12, 1514–15, 1569–70; and Mansfield Dam and Reservoir project, 1632; and Memphis steam plant, 1777–78, 1780; and Niagara River power development, 758–59; and Passamaquoddy power project, 1234; and public power projects, 868–69, 1511–12, 1514–15, 1569–70, 1632; and REA, 1569–70; and St. Lawrence Seaway, 147; and Shippingport power plant, 1351; and Southwestern Power Administration, 311–12; and steam plants, 555–57, 1197, 1198, 1251–52, 1366; strained relations regarding, 1341–42. *See also* Natural gas; Oil; Tennessee Valley Authority; United States Government: federal *v.* state issues; Water resources

Public relations, 547; Bermingham's view, 693–94; E.'s view, 686–88; Gunderson's view, 646–47; Hall's view, 664; Humphrey's view, 605–6; Larmon's view, 865–66; Lodge's view, 605–6; Migel's recommendation, 998; need for, 603, 686–88, 1423; and RNC, 662–64; Robinson's advice, 680, 1231, 1266–67; Robinson writes to John E. on, 1427; and U.S. policy on Nationalist China, 1536–40. *See also* Political strategist

Public utilities, and Harris-Fulbright Bill, 2014

Public works: and budget policy for FY 1955, 643–44; and Colorado River Storage Project,

901–3; need for advance planning in, 803–4, 867–69

Puerto Rico, Commonwealth of: and colonialism, 1414, 1415; on independence for, 709–10; relationship with U.S., 814; and status of, at U.N., 709–10, 814; Thomas visits, 1705

Pulliam, Eugene Collins: background, 438, 441–42; irritates E., 438

Purdy, Herman R.: advises on E.'s Angus herd, 1408, 1409, 1735, 2173–75; background, 1409, 1625; on breeding Angus herd, 2182–83; on E.'s young bulls, 1875, 1876; offers service of O. Bardoliermere 32d, 2216; recommends Hartley, 2216

Putnam, Albert William ("Bert"): background, 1458; on successor to Coykendall, 1457, 1459

Pyle, Howard: and Arizona governorship, 2089; background, 1713; briefs Cabinet on campaign speeches, 2082–83; on communication with RNC workers, 1837–38; on Hoover as campaign speaker, 2317; on Namm's support for highway program, 1733–34; on Oregon primary, 2175–76; on post for Reid, 1713; on Roberts's complaint about Hall, 1770

Quail. See Gettysburg farm

Quantico, Virginia, and conference on national defense, 1140–41

Quantico II Panel: and psychological aspects of U.S. strategy, 1924; and Soviet missile program, 2104

Quantico Vulnerabilities Panel: background, 1745–46; Jackson's view, 1745–46, 1758–59; Rockefeller's role, 1745–46; and U.S. position at Geneva Summit, 1774–75; on winning cold war, 1758–59

Quarles, Donald Aubrey, as Secretary of Air Force, 1797–98, 1809

Quartermaster General: Hastings named, 795; Horkan retires, 795; increases beef reserves, 645–46

Quemoy. See China, Republic of

Quirino, Elpidio: background, 389–90; loses election, 389–90, 650–51; on U.S. bases in Philippines, 389–90; visits U.S., 389–90

Rabb, Maxwell Milton, 13–14; on Byrnes and civil rights, 472; as E.'s aide in minority affairs, 941; Gunderson's view, 646–47; Lodge recommends as political strategist, 979–80; and McCrary's housing plan, 1690; and President's Committee on Government Contracts, 476–77; and Taft-Hartley Act revisions, 561–62

Rabi, Isidor Isaac: background, 2260; on thermonuclear testing, 2260

Racial discrimination. See Civil rights

Radford, Arthur William: and Adenauer's plan for demilitarized zones in Europe, 1740–41, 1742–43; approves letter to Wiltsee, 1297; Ar-

ends endorses, 248; on atomic test limitations, 896; on atomic weaponry in defense of Formosa, 1617–18; background, 235, 434–35; as chairman, JCS, 189, 235–36, 634–36, 1636–37, 2255–56; Chiang rejects U.S. proposal on offshore islands, 1683–84, 1787, 1788; and Chiang's role in Formosa crisis, 1582; and Churchill-Eden visit, 1141–42; criticizes Air Force programs, 235–36; on defense budget, FY 1958, 2255–56; on deployment of atomic weapons, 1418; Douglas's view, 1347; and East-West trade controls, 2140–41; E.'s esteem for, 2255–56; on evacuation of Nanchi, 1583; on Formosa conference, 1532–33; and Gruenther's retirement, 2098–99; and Gruenther's view on France, 890–91; and Hungarian revolt, 2334; and medical care for service dependents, 685–86; meets with Dulles, Eden, on Vietnam, 1031; meets with E. on Middle East, 2096–97; on military retirees as advisers, 636; and mutual security legislation, 2187–88; and NATO command structure, 166–67; opposes sending U.S. technicians to Indochina, 886–87; opposes U.S. aid to Vietnam, 1311; on Quemoy, 1279; receives honorary degree at Harvard, 1740–41; and redeployment of U.S. forces in Trieste, 1236–37, 1237–38, 1246–47; scores Diem, 1311; and study on U.S.-Soviet war, 1973–74; on U.S. forces in Europe, 2204; and U.S. policy in Far East, 2080; Wilson's proposal, 120

Radhakrishnan, Sarvapalli: background, 1416; visits U.S., 1415–16

Radio. See Media

Radio Corporation of America (RCA), 451–52

Radio Free Europe, 2208–9; and Hungarian revolt, 2377–78

Radko, A. M.: advises on Bermuda grass, 1055; background, 1055; builds putting green at White House, 1055

Radulovich, Milo J.: background, 679–80; loyalty of, 679–80

Railroads, 605–6; and bankrupt Long Island Rail Road, 758–59; and Brotherhood of Big Four, 619–20; Brown's view, 699; and government policies, 972–73; Gurley's complaints, 1332–33; Hauge's view, 972–73; on loans for, in Mexico, 1599, 1600; Milton E.'s view, 972–73; and New York Central fight, 917–19; and Pennsylvania Railroad, 758–59; and Post Office Department, 1364–65; and rate increase delays, 920–21; and "time-lag bill," 920–21; workers strike plans, 619–20

Railway Express Service, and parcel post rates, 1364–65

Railway Labor Act of 1926, 619–20

Randall, Clarence Belden: advises E. on H.R. 1 amendment, 1631; background, 201–2, 1023–24; on bipartisan cooperation, 1453–

meets with E., 478–79; seeks aid for *New York Herald Tribune*, 1622–23; and President's Committee on Government Contracts, 476–77; recommends Baruch's view on NSC, 1148–49; reconsiders invitation to Coronation, 71–72; resigns as chairman of *New York Herald Tribune* board, 1623; on visit from Nasser, Hussein, 1845, 1849

Reid, Ogden Rogers, 595–96; as president, publisher, *New York Herald Tribune*, 1623

Reid, Whitelaw, 595–96; as board chairman, *New York Herald Tribune*, 1623; and Citizen Advisors on Mutual Security, 2134–35; on post for, 1713

Reinert, Paul C., S.J.: background, 1439–40; and Pius XII Memorial Library, 1439–40

Reinhardt, George Frederick: background, 1548–49; as U.S. ambassador to Vietnam, 1548–49

Religion: and Al Smith Foundation, 517–19; civil rights and clergy, 2086, 2104–5; on free scriptures for Africa, 1438–39; Graham's view, 2104–5, 2189–90; High on spiritualism, 116; on religious persecution in Czechoslovakia, 2409; and subway message, 2235; and Wilson's peace plan, 1629–30. *See also* Eisenhower, Dwight David: religion

—Catholics: and Al Smith dinner, 517–19; on appointment of, to Supreme Court, 1397–98, 1606–7; in Italy, 659; and John Marshall Bicentennial Commission, 1606–7; and McCarthyism, 667–68; on posts for, 1553, 1606–7

—Episcopalians, on E.'s participation in communion rites, 2313–14

—Jews, 1397–98; and Al Smith Foundation, 518

—Presbyterians: and E., 518; E. supports expansion fund, 985; on McCarthyism, 667–68

Relin, Bernard, background, 998

Remón, Cecilia de: and assassination of husband, 1517–18; background, 1518; supports E.'s candidacy, 2314–15; on U.S. commitments to Panama, 1517–18

Remón Cantera, José Antonio: assassination of, 1518; complains to E., 666, 926–27; on non-American workers' wages, 912–13; on Panama-American relations, 544–45, 926–27; on U.S. commitments to Panama, 1517–18; visits E., 544–45, 593–94, 666

Reorganization Plan: and Advisory Board of Economic Growth and Stability, 277–78; extension of, 369–70. *See also* Government Reorganization Plan; Hoover Commission; President's Advisory Committee on Government Organization; United States Commission on Organization of Executive Branch of Government; United States Government: Executive Branch

Repplier, Theodore Silkman: background, 1813; urges speech by E., 1811–13

Republican National Committee (RNC), 623, 1124; in California, 662, 663–64; celebrates Inaugural anniversary, 839–40; on communi-

cation with party workers, 1837–38; on cooperation with Executive Branch, 780–81; on county chairmen, Murphy's view, 1769, 1837–38; and Delmar, 1187; E. commends, on 1956 campaign, 2370; endorses Hall, 284–85; and farm program, 1343; and federal appointments, 6; and Grace Kelly's wedding, 2119–20; Gunderson's view, 646–47, 1223–24; Hoffman's view, 719; Larmon's view, 865–66; on leadership in, Hoffman's view, 1411–12; Lodge's view, 780–81; on Lord as adviser to, 1423; and Morrow's nomination to U.N., 1255; need for restructuring, 853; and patronage appointments, 284–85, 662, 664, 2093–94; on political adviser to, 1424; problems in Kansas, 93–94, 121–23; problems of leadership in, 853; and public relations, 686–88, 998; reports on midterm election, 1381; and Republican National Convention (1956), 1607–8; and Roberts, 121–23, 134–35, 1770; and Robinson's public relations plan, 680; and Rubenstein's candidacy for judiciary, 1957; sends trees to Gettysburg farm, 1843; on speakers for student political conventions, 2137–38; on subversives, 1571; supports E.'s candidacy in 1956, 2044; Weir's view, on lack of leadership, 602, 603; Willis's report on, 780–81; Wisdom's role, 479–80

—Strategy Committee: Lodge's view, 780–81; and public relations, 680; and Summerfield, 687

Republican National Convention: on Anderson's role at, 2105–6; on clergy's role at, 2105–6; E.'s advice on longwinded speakers, 2250; E. attends, 2265; on E.'s performance at, 2259; on E.'s plans, 2204–5, 2256–57; Halleck nominates E., 2242; Hoover attends, 2195; Hughes addresses, 2247–48; Slater attends, 2204–5

Republican party (GOP), 623; Barnes plans to reshape, 1516; and Bricker amendment, 282–83, 866–67; Byars joins, 2313; in California, 762, 1232, 1470–71; and Case's New Jersey campaign, 1288–90; Clay seeks reforms in, 1402–5; and Cornelius, 521; Douglas's view, 1346–47; Drummond's view on E.'s candidacy in 1956, 1851–52; and effectiveness of women in, 2376; on Eisenhower draft in 1956, Knowland's view, 1492–93; E. means to revamp, 2354; Falkenburg heads Women's Division, New York Finance Committee, 1206; and farm politics, 423–24; favors "time-lag bill," 920–21; and Formosa crisis, Isaacs's view, 1649–50; in Georgia, 1028–30; Graham's view on 1956 election, 2189–90; Hall's view, 662–64; leaders of, at farm rally, 1359, 1360; Hoover campaigns for candidates of, 2317; on leadership in, 1411–12; Lodge calls for unity in, 1580–81; Luce's view, 2313; Mamie E. entertains women of, 2062; on midterm election, Berg's view,

1477–78; and midterm election, Murphy's view, 1376–77; in Mississippi, 97; on Moderate Progressives, 1429, 1470–71, 1549–50; on modern Republicanism, 2378–79, 2395–96, 2408; on mossbacks, Lodge's view, 1450; on Neanderthal Right Wing of, 1322; and need for teamwork in, 109–10, 222, 791; needs "taste appeal," 985–86; needs young leaders, 2063–65, 2137–38, 2180–81; and New York dock strike, 755–56; and *New York Herald Tribune*, 1622–23; on Old Guarders and McCarthyites, 980–81, 1013–14; and Oregon politics, 2282–83; Paley's view, 2392–93; in Pennsylvania, 601–3; platform and Bricker amendment, 850–51, 2291; platform (1952) on Soviet oppression, 64; platform (1956), 2102, 2209–10, 2305–6; platform (1956) and tax reform, 2472–73; and public relations, 686–88; Rayburn's view, 332; and reactionary fringe, 950, 1088, 1402–5; and Robinson's public relations plan, 680; and "Salute to Eisenhower" dinners, 1979–80; in South, 97, 479–80, 2381–82; in South Dakota, 1223–24; on split in, 1435; on split in, and McCarthy, 950; and Stassen, 1436, 1439; and State of the Union Address (1954), 719; in Texas, 96–97, 1637–38; and trade union leaders, 770–71; ultra-conservatives in, attack E., 762; and Waring's party for E., 524; and Washington politics, 2281–83; on Williams as adviser to, 1423; Willis's report on, 780–81. *See also* Elections; Republicans

Republicans, 890–91, 655; and African American view, 408–9; and African American vote, 418; an "anxious period" for, 828; in bipartisan action with Democrats, 89; and Bricker amendment, 282–83, 849–50; and CAB appointments, 725; in California, 1606; Chynoweth's view, 1202–4; conservatives oppose Case, 1288–89; cooperate on tax reform, 963, 966–67; and Dixon-Yates question, 1200, 1368; E.'s differences with, 826–28; E.'s esteem for Anderson, 1436; and E.'s farm bill veto, 2126–27; E. meets with state chairmen, 1851, 1852; E. proposes world event review for, 2070–71; favor Carbaugh for TVA post, 932, 933; favor flexible price supports, 2017; and film, "Year of Big Decision," 1252–53; and foreign trade expansion, 1109–10; on Formosa crisis, conservatives view, 1692; Francis's view, 1756; Gunderson's view, 646–47; and Hoover Commission, 821; Hoover's view, 2156; and housing bill, 13–14; lacks successors to E., 2227, 2229; leaders meet with E. (December 1953), 764–65, 778–79; and legislative program, 33–38, 387–88; margin of, in House, 664, 779–80, 1375–76; margin of, in Senate, 664, 779–80, 1375–76; and midterm election (1954), 479–80, 662–64, 1193, 1322, 1347–48, 1375–76, 1454; and minority appointments, 284–85;

Mintener meets with, 665; and mossbacks, 688, 1313–14, 1756; need for solidarity among, 137, 791; need for young blood, 94, 727–28, 1549, 1848–49, 2063–65, 2137–38, 2180–81; in New York, McCrary's view, 1421–22; Nixon addresses, 1756; and Oklahoma politics, 1302–4; and Old Guard, 64, 578, 950, 975–76, 980–81; in opposition to President, 27–30, 136–39, 275–76, 578; partisan bickering by, 1502–3; and patronage, 284–85, 1637–38; and postmaster in Abilene, 1221–22; protest "chosen instrument" air policy, 1317; and public power policy, 1341–42, 1368; and Randall Commission recommendations, 985–86; reactionary, and McCarthy, 950, 980–81; on "real" Republicans, 2157; on "Rightest" thinking, 1429; on Right Wing, Hauge's view, 1322; Roberts complains about Milton E., 917–18; and "Salute to Eisenhower" dinners, 1970; on snubbing congressional invitations, 1762–63; speculate on Milton E.'s candidacy, 1878; and stag dinners, Lodge's concern, 1467–68; Stevenson's charge, 939; on supporting Administration policy, 1762–63; and Taft's influence on, 265–67; and Tariff Commission, 200–202; and Warren's appointment, E.'s view, 567–68, 571–72; in Washington State, Edgar's view, 1718, 2281–83; Weir's view, 601–3; and Yalta agreements, 1628–29. *See also* Legislative leaders: Republican conference of; Republican party

Republican Women's National Conference: E. addresses, 1717–28; E. predicts collapse of communism, 1958–59

Reserve forces. *See* Armed forces reserves

Reserve Forces Act of 1955, 1757, 1772–73

Resettlement Administration, and land purchase program, 1391–92

Resolution of the German Bundestag, 411, 413

Reston, James Barrett: background, 1240; and Donovan's *Inside Story*, 2067; on "good partner" policy, 1240

Reuter, Ernst: background, 524–25; death of, 525; and food for East Germans, 524–26, 604–5; requests U.S. aid, 525–26

Reuther, Walter Philip: background, 673–75; on E.'s message to CIO, 675; on Middle Way, 674; on Mitchell's appointment, 674; and President's Committee on Government Contracts, 476–77; reelection of, 675; view of, on E., 673–75

Revenue Act of 1926, and percentage depletion allowance for oil and gas well owners, 1670

Revenue Act of 1951, and tax deductions for congressmen, 834–35

Rhee, Syngman, 372, 425–26; agrees to attend Geneva Conference, 1022–23; on aid for Hungarians, 2408; embarrasses U.S., 340–41, 570, 573; on expelling Soviets from U.N.,

meets Anderson, 1055; on post for Jorgenson, 2482–83; suffers ailing tooth, 2482–83; suffers heart attack, 1999, 2008, 2022–23, 2033; in Switzerland, 1212; on TV quiz show, 2008, 2022–23; undergoes tonsillectomy, 2198; visits Cuba, 2483; visits E. at Augusta, 621–22, 1429, 1999, 2008, 2022–23, 2124; visits E. at Gettysburg, 1907–8; on voter registration, 2269–70

Roberts, Dennis Joseph: on atomic plants in New England, 1870–72; background, 1872

Roberts, Harold: background, 1822; meets with E., 1822

Roberts, Roy Allison: background, 756–57; editorial by, 858, 859; and need for young Republicans, 756–57; as political adviser, 857, 1423; on reprints of Powell's article, 1342–43; scores farm program, 1304–5, 1311, 1312; on Taft-Hartley Act, advice to E., 756–57

Robertson, A. Willis: background, 1439; E.'s esteem for, 1435

Robertson, Brian Hubert: background, 302; on Case A, 301–3, 304–5; on U.S.-U.K. role in Egypt, 301–3, 391, 392

Robertson, Walter Spencer: Chiang rejects U.S. proposal on islands, 1683–84, 1787, 1788; drafts letter to Rhee, 970; and message for Rhee, 375; and U.S. aid to Korea, 445, 548

Robinson, John N.: background, 95; plans biography of E., 95–96

Robinson, Marguerite (Luddy), background, 595–96

Robinson, William Edward, 42, 124, 128, 318–19, 1739–40, 1907–8; attends Gridiron Dinner, 1427; attends stag dinner, 1424, 1427, 2062–63; and "Augusta National" weekend in Denver, 1212, 1259–60, 1266–67, 1300; background, 32; bridge with Allen, 2168–69; and bridge with E., 1091–92, 1177, 1236–37, 1375–76, 1414, 1415, 1487–88, 1519, 1719–20, 1955–56, 2028, 2034, 2050–51; brings shirts from McCleod, 478–79; and Business Advisory Council, 2246; and Donovan's book, 2065–68; on Dulles, E.'s view, 951–52, 975–76; on E.'s advisory committee, 1423; on E.'s farm bill veto, 2126–27; on E.'s Presidential Library Commission, 1710; golfs with E., 478–79, 2483; on Gruenther's future, 2124; hires Drummond, 595–96; illness of, 2121–22, 2126–27; on Knowland, E.'s view, 950–52; on McCarthy and Old Guard, 975–76; on McCarthy and press, 428, 950–51, 975–76; praises E.'s speech, 1266–67; as president of Coca-Cola, 1518–19; and public relations program for E., 680, 687, 865–66, 1228–31, 1266–67; and Republican reactionary fringe, 950, 975–76; sends campaign advice from Barton, 2088; sends E. book, photos, vest for Christmas, 1940–41; sends E. book, table, 1873; sends E. nonsense speech, 1427; on

Spellman and Al Smith dinner, 517–18; and tax program, E.'s view, 951–52; undergoes surgery, 2168–69; on U.S. Steel stockholders, E.'s view, 975–76; value of, at stag dinners, 595–96; visits Camp David, 1091, 1161–62, 1163–64, 1177; visits E. at Augusta, 2124, 2126–27; visits E. in Key West, Fla., 1955–56; visits Gettysburg farm, 1719–20; visits Gunnison, Texas, with Moncrief, 478–79; writes Gruenther on bridge victories, 1176–77; writes John E. on public relations, 1427

Robinson, Willma: background, 595–96; marriage of, 1519

Robinson, Wirt: background, 1648; E.'s recollection of, 1648

Robinson, Wirt Russell, background, 1648

Rochefoucauld, Duc de la, 2065

Rockefeller, David: background, 1622; on financial aid for *New York Herald Tribune*, 1622–23

Rockefeller, John Davison: background, 808–9; on parks deterioration, 808–9

Rockefeller, Meile Louise, birth of, 1940

Rockefeller, Nelson Aldrich: attends stag dinner, 2062–63; on bipartisan cooperation, 1453–54; demonstrates Sarnoff's message device, 1826; on economic aid to Asia, 1551; on E.'s convention performance, 2259; finances Tames photo reproductions, 1241–42; on financial aid for *New York Herald Tribune*, 1622–23; on foreign economic policy study, 1182–83, 1244–45; and Gettysburg battlefield print for E., 854–55; gives E. embroidered eagle, 1940; heads government reorganization study, 36, 71, 104, 177, 1183; and HEW budget, 485; as HEW Under Secretary, 172; on honoring Churchill, 1646–47, 1906–7; misspeaks on Administration split, 1924; on paper currency motto, "In God We Trust," 1604; on post for Reid, 1713; and Quantico II Panel, 1924, 2104; and Quantico Vulnerabilities Panel, 1745–46, 1758–59; reports on Foreign Ministers' Conference, 1950–51; reports on inauguration of de la Guardia, 2314–15; reports on U.S. strategies, 1923; on Repplier's proposal, 1811–13; resigns, 171, 176, 1940, 2007; sends table, chairs, rug to E., 1704; sends trees to Gettysburg farm, 1487–88, ships tulips to Gettysburg farm, 1672; as special assistant to E., 1451–52; speech by, praises E., 2007; succeeds Jackson, 1330–31, 1451–52; on USIA and cultural exchange programs, 1766; and U.S. information program, 198–99; on U.S.-Panama relations, 2314–15

Rockefeller, Rodman Clark, background, 1940

Rockefeller Foundation, on study of effects of atomic radiation, 1589–90

Rockwell, Norman, and E.'s portrait, 721–22

Rodes, Harold Potter: background, 2309; proposes honorary degree in absentia for E., 2308–9

Rodgers, Philip R., and Taft-Hartley Act revisions, 538–39

Rodman, Roland Vere: background, 1302, 1303; and Oklahoma politics, 1302, 1303

Rogers, Byron Giles: background, 1362; wins Colorado midterm election, 1362

Rogers, Edith Nourse, background, 2055

Rogers, Roy, visits White House, 2108–9

Rogers, Walter Edward: background, 1771; on quarter horse for David E., 1771

Rogers, William Pierce: background, 65; as successor to E., 793

Roosevelt, Anna Eleanor: and American policy toward Israel, 168; and E.'s joke about Bricker, 873–74

Roosevelt, Franklin Delano, 43, 762, 838; and agreement with Churchill on atomic cooperation (1943), 997–98; appoints Morgan to TVA, 928–29; as leader, 275–76; memo to, from Baruch, 675; and memorial commission for, 1869–70; and public power policy, 1511; role of, as candidate, 1337–38; and Shangri-la, 407; at Teheran, 811, 812, 816–17; and TVA, 1188; and Twenty-second Amendment, 2045; at Yalta, 162, 811, 812, 816–17, 900, 1628–29

Roosevelt, John Aspinwall, and President's Committee on Government Contracts, 476–77

Roosevelt, Nicholas: background, 578; on McCarthy, 577, 578; scores E., 576–79; on Warren's appointment, 576, 578

Roosevelt, Theodore, 1980–81; and physical fitness, 956; as vice-president, 2061

Rose, Billy: meets with E., 2295; visits Russia, 2295

Rose, H. Chapman, and Schneider's complaint, 511

Rosenberg, Ethel and Julius, 330; conviction of, 289–91; E.'s view, 289–91, 298–99; Miller's plea, 289–91

Rosenberg, Michael and Robert, 291

Rosenwald, Lessing Julius: background, 2375–76; on Middle East, 2375–76; on nuclear war, 2401; supports E.'s campaign, 2375–76

Ross, Donald Roe, background, 503

Rostow, Walt W., background, 1019–20; and Jackson plan on foreign aid policy, 1248–49; on winning cold war, 1758–59

Rountree, William Manning: background, 2330; on Iraqi troops in Jordan, 2337; and Israeli-Jordanian conflict, 2328, 2330

Rousseau, Jean Jacques: background, 1202–3, 1204; Chynoweth's view, 1204; E.'s view, 1202–3

Rowe, James Henry: background, 1869–70; on FDR Memorial Commission, 1869–70

Rowley, James: background, 1440; and E.'s visit to Paris, 1757–58; takes Stephens to Abilene, 1440

Royal Air Force (RAF): collects CASTLE debris, 987, 997–98; on retrofitting with atomic weaponry, 2319–20

Royall, Kenneth Claiborne, 104; background, 1796–97; E. declines invitation from, 2467–68; visits E., 1796–97

Royall, Margaret (Best), background, 1796–97

Rubber, and East-West trade controls, 2140–41

Rubenstein, Joseph: background, 1957; as candidate for federal judiciary, 1957; disbarment proceedings against, 1957

Ruiz Cortines, Adolfo: admires Lincoln, 2058; background, 254; and Bermingham, 345, 1750, 2058; Dulles's view, 1743–44; and Falcon Dam, 254, 300, 554, 574–75, 593–94; meets with E., 593–94, 1743–44, 2058, 2075, 2096; takes pro-American view, 1101–2; and U.S.-Mexican relations, 1099–1100, 1472, 1599, 1743–44, 1750, 2096; on value of visit with, 1472, 1743–44, 1750

Rumania, Republic of: on admission of, to U.N., 1901–2; and Georgescu case, 414–16; Moisescu meets with E., 1438, 1440

Rumbough, Stanley Maddox, Jr.: background, 762; and Beardwood's view, 762; and Citizens for Eisenhower, 396–97

Rummel, Joseph Francis: background, 2088; integrates Catholic parochial schools, 2086–87, 2088

Rural Electrification Administration (REA): background, 1570; and Clark Hill and Hartwell dam projects, 1569–70; Patton's charges, 1341–42; Rayburn's dedication to, 311–12

Rusk, Dean: background, 1590; on study of effects of atomic radiation, 1589–90

Rusk, Howard Archibald: background, 159, 462; and Korean reconstruction plan, 462; visits Korea, 159, 462

Russell, Donald Stuart: background, 1137; investigation of CIA, 1137

Russell, Richard Brevard: background, 1439; E.'s esteem for, 1435; opposes vote for eighteen-year-olds, 1829

Rutledge, Edward, 1233–34

Rutledge, Wiley Blount, 514–15

Ryan, Allan A.: on Aberdeen Angus breeds, 2012–13, 2182–83; and Ankonian 3551, 2197–98; background, 2013, 2182–83

Ryan, Grace M. (Amory), background, 2197–98

Ryan, John T., background, 1741–42

Ryan, Oswald: as CAB board member, 725; as CAB chairman, 51; Carter's recommendation, 50–51, 1459, 1464–66

Ryerson, Edward Larned: background, 1423; on E.'s advisory committee, 1423; member, Foreign Intelligence Activities Board, 1983–84

Saar: Bidault's view, 741, 746; and EDC, 569, 572, 741, 742, 746; Franco-German differences, 155, 569, 572, 741–42, 746, 1445–47;

River Project, 1138; and compensation for federal and service personnel, 449–50, 1396, 1397; condemns McCarthy, 1413, 1422, 1429; confirms Campbell, 989–90; confirms Doerfer, 1124; confirms Federal Reserve Board appointments, 582–83; confirms Hamley, 2093–94; confirms Harlan's appointment, 1664–65; confirms Hendrickson, 1499; confirms Holland, 807–8; confirms Kline, 2136–37; confirms McConnaughey, 1090; confirms minister to Laos, 1079; confirms Mumford, 989–90; confirms U.S. ambassador to Cambodia, 1079; confirms Warren, 977; confirms Whitney, 2479; defeats vote for eighteen-year-olds, 1829; Democratic majority in, 1373, 1413, 2370; Democrats delay Harlan's confirmation, 1664–65; disapproves Red China's admission to U.N., 268–69; and disaster relief legislation, 1650–51; and Dixon-Yates question, 1200; and East-West trade controls, 2140–41; and educational exchange program, 1025–26; E. testifies before, on defense program (1946), 249–50; E.'s view, 826–27; favors Trice for Comptroller General, 989–90; Flanders denounces McCarthy, 940; George's role, 2164–65; honors Churchill, 1646–47; and immigration legislation, 400–401; on Knowland's role in, 951–52; Knowland scores U.S. foreign policy, 1390–91; and legislation to outlaw Communist party, 813–14; and McCarthy, E.'s embarrassment for, 1044; and midterm election, 1290, 1351–52, 1375–76, 1454; on military survivor benefits legislation, 1748–49, 1751–52; and MSA bill, 1173; and Mutual Defense Treaty, 638–40, 1538, 1540, 1565; and Old Guarders, 950; opposes Korean reconstruction plan, 462; passes Atomic Energy Act of 1954, 1218, 1231; passes D.C. Home Rule bill, 2012; passes Formosa Resolution, 1520–21; passes Passamaquoddy power project, 1234; political balance in, 275–76; Radhakrishnan's gift to, 1415; and ratification of treaties, 873–74; ratifies Geneva Conventions of 1949, 1802–3; Republicans in, E.'s view, 1413; Republican margin in, 779–80; and return to gold standard, 1158–59; on school construction legislation and segregation, 1752–54; splinter group in, 1429; on sugar import quotas, 1529–30, 1530; supports Resolution 12, 2216–17; and Taft's illness, 446–47; and waterway control legislation, 1278; and wool legislation, 552–53
—Agriculture and Forestry Committee: Benson testifies, 126; and dairy price supports, 967–68; favors rigid price supports, 2017, 2019
—Appropriations Committee: and funds for forestry research in Illinois, 1153; and Gruenther's testimony, 346–47, 1191; and HEW cuts, 484–86; and U.S. appropriation to U.N., 268–69

—Armed Services Committee: and aid for Hungarian refugees, 2436–37; curtails military construction, 466–67; and France's request for technicians in Indochina, 887; and jurisdiction over Communists in armed services, 951–52
—Banking and Currency Committee, and FHA scandals investigation, 1357
—District of Columbia Committee, and home rule, 1176–77
—Elections Committee, sponsors party for Washington Press Corps, 828
—Finance Committee: on amendment to H.R. 1, 1631; and customs valuation legislation, 1081–82; and escape clause relief on lighter flints, 2390
—Foreign Relations Committee: and aid for Hungarian refugees, 2436–37; approves Hoffman as U.N. delegate, 2236; and Bohlen's confirmation, 138; and Bricker amendment, 282–83; considers Status of Forces Agreement, 386–87; Green chairs, 2387–88; Gruenther testifies before, 1177; kills resolution on Soviet oppression, 64; and Morrow's nomination to U.N., 1255; and Passamaquoddy power project, 1234; Streit testifies before, 2216–17; subcommittee of, studies U.N. charter review, 615–16; and Suez Canal Conference, 2241; supports European Coal and Steel Community, 294–95; and U.S. information program, 199
—Government Operations Committee, E.'s directive on executive privilege, 1069–71, 1076, 1080. See also Senate, U.S.: Permanent Subcommittee on Investigations
—Internal Security Committee, and Jenner's report on Soviet Fifth Column, 699–701
—Interstate and Foreign Commerce Committee, and "time-lag bill," 920–21
—Joint Committee on Reduction of Non-Essential Federal Expenditures, and FHA investigation, 1357
—Judiciary Committee: and Bricker amendment, 74, 76, 140, 282–83, 848–49, 2107–8, 2110, 2111; and Dulles's view on treaties, 840; investigates Alien Properties Office, 932; and S.J. Res. 44, 1167–68
—Labor and Public Welfare Committee: debates condemnation of forced labor, 2141–42; and medal for distinguished civilian achievement, 1677; and Taft-Hartley Act revisions, 565, 571, 982–83
—Permanent Subcommittee on Investigations: and army's charges against McCarthy and Cohn, 951–52; and CIA investigation, 1137; Dirksen agrees to help, 932; E. speaks to tactics of, 914; and Greek shipowners, 143; investigates Kaghan, 257–58; investigates Peress, 914; investigates Talbott, 1797–98; McCarthy insists on right to cross-examine,

976–77; McCarthy relinquishes chairmanship of, 976; Mundt takes temporary chairmanship, 976, 1064–65; and principle of executive privilege, 1069–71, 1075–76, 1080; requests Peress data, 1064–65; Ridgway objects to Peress data, 1065; Stevens agrees to provide Peress data, 1065; Wilson's concern, 1064–65. *See also* McCarthy, Joseph Raymond: Army-McCarthy hearings; Senate, U.S.: Government Operations Committee
— Post Office and Civil Service Committee, and parcel post rates and Railway Express Service, 1364–65
— Public Works Committee: Dewey testifies on Niagara River power project, 758–59; highway legislation, 1691; Public Roads subcommittee holds hearings on national highway system, 1067
— Republican Policy Committee: approves rules change for investigations, 951; and Bricker amendment, 812
— Select Committee on Improper Activities in Labor and Management Fields, 2091
Senate Joint Resolution 1 (S.J. Res. 1). *See* Bricker amendment
Seniors Golf Association of Southern California, 522–23
"Serenade to Ike" rally, 1911–12
Sevilla-Sacasa, Guillermo: background, 202; praises E.'s speech, 202–3
SHAEF (Supreme Headquarters, Allied Expeditionary Force): insignia of, in E.'s coat of arms, 1047–48, 1054; a "lonely life," 824
Shah of Iran. *See* Pahlavi, Mohammed Reza
Shakespeare, William, 2246
Shangri-la, E. renames Camp David, 407
Shanley, Bernard Michael, 446–47, 780, 1443; on absentee voting for service personnel, 957–58, 1543; advises E. on chasing crows, 1805; on aid to Burma, 2258; attends briefing on meeting with St. Laurent and Ruiz Cortines, 2075; background, 145; Christmas party at home of (1953), 781–82; and corporate giving, 533–34, 714; Durkin's attack on, 565, 571; E.'s esteem for, 831; Gunderson's view, 646–47; on John Marshall Bicentennial Commission, 1606–7; on Silver's visit, 2123–24; and Spellman, 2335, 2336; on Taft-Hartley Act revisions, 489–90, 538–39, 561–62, 872–73; and USIA, 2183–84
Shannon, Jones B., 2314
SHAPE (Supreme Headquarters Allied Powers, Europe): insignia of, in E.'s coat of arms, 1054; a "lonely life," 824; sends birthday greetings to E., 586–87; staff changes at, 40, 41
Sharples, Phil, 188
Shartzer, William: background, 1029; and Georgia politics, 1029
Shaw, Warren W.: background, 2391–92; wins Kansas gubernatorial primary, 2391–92

Sheedy, John Austin: background, 1910–11; E.'s appreciation to, 1910–11; Masters Singers perform for E., 1910–11
Sheen, Fulton John (Bishop): background, 220; E.'s apology to, 1352–53; on national days of prayer, 219–21
Sheffield, Frederick: background, 579–80; and E. as honorary trustee, New York School of Social Work, 579–80
Sheldon, William Herbert, 106–7
Shenefelt, Arthur B.: background, 922–23; on publishing E.'s letter, 922–23
Shepardson, Whitney Hart: background, 1048–49; message to exiled labor leaders, 1048–49
Shepilov, Dimitri Trofimovich: background, 2265; scores Anglo-French initiative at U.N., 2318; scores Suez Canal Conference, 2265
Sherburne, Edward Gill: background, 1093–94; and West Point reunion, class of 1915, 1093–94
Sherman, Donald Park: background, 1085–86; on E.'s oversight in Richmond, 1085–86
Sherrill, Henry Knox (Bishop): background, 2314; on Episcopalian communion rites, 2313–14
Sherwood, Robert Emmet: background, 1026–27; investigation of, by FBI, 1026–27; on McCarthy, 1026–27; on Oppenheimer, 1026–27
Shields, Murray: background, 1059; proposal by, on world peace, 1059
Shipping. *See* Maritime industry
Shivers, Allan, 861–62; background, 350; E. visits, 618–19; golf with, 350, 1602–3; visits Korea, 1184; wins Texas runoff primary, 1256
Shivers, Marialice (Shary), background, 1602–3
Short, Dewey: background, 1757; supports reserve forces legislation, 1757
Showalter, Edward R., Jr., 815–16
Shuman, Charles B.: background, 2117; urges farm bill veto, 2116, 2117
Siberia, 1283
Siciliano, Rocco Carmine: and Advisory Board of Economic Growth and Stability, 277–78; as Assistant Secretary of Labor, 446–47; background, 446–47
Sicily, 750, 1626
Sihanouk, Norodom: background, 1310; seeks U.S. aid to Cambodia, 1310
Silver, Abba Hillel: asks arms for Israel, 2123–24; background, 2123–24; on E.'s candidacy in 1956, 2123–24; visits E., 2123–24
Silvercruys, Robert (Baron), background, 1092–93
Silvercruys, Rosemary (Turner) McMahon (Baroness): background, 1092–93; and release of McMahon letters, 1092–93
Simon, Richard Leo: background, 2114; and E.'s view on war, 2114; urges air power program, 2114
Simpson, J. E., 222

Simpson, Richard Murray: discusses patronage problems with Cabinet, 933; foe of freer trade, 603; and gubernatorial race in Pennsylvania, 601, 603; on Randall Commission, 201; on tariff legislation, 201, 306, 307

Simpson, Sidney Elmer, and golf with E., 180

Simpson, William Hood: background, 847–48; promotion for, 847–48

Sinai Desert. *See* Egypt; Israel, State of

Sino-Soviet Treaty of Friendship and Alliance, 1539–40; and Outer Mongolia, 1901–2; and U.S. forces in Japan, 1565; and U.S. Seventh fleet, 1565

Sixteen Nation Declaration, and Korea, 969, 971, 1534, 1536

S.J. Res. 1. *See* Bricker amendment

S.J. Res. 181. *See* Bricker amendment

Skinner, Robert P.: background, 130; scores USIS and VOA, 130–31

Skouras, George P.: background, 2417; on bipartisan foreign policy, 2416–17

Skouras, Spyros Panagiotes: background, 1879–80; and mission on Cyprus, 2166–67; provides films for E., Mamie E., 1879–80

Slater, Ellis Dwinnell ("Slats"), 1907–8; and artificial insemination of E.'s heifers, 1981–82, 2125–26; attends Republican National Convention, 2204–5; and "Augusta National" weekend in Denver, 1212; background, 258, 382–83; and Bronfman meet with E., 382–83; and bust of E., 258; and Dark's letter on Milton E., 1025–26; and Eva Bandolier Lad, 2182–83, 2186–87; on fabric from, for vicuña sports coat, 2125–26; golf with E., 2204–5; sends undershorts to E., 1767; undergoes surgery, 2432–33; visits Camp David, 1161–62, 1163–64; visits E. at Augusta, 2125–26

Slater, Priscilla (Allen), 1212

Slim, William Joseph, background, 69

Sloan, George Arthur: background, 47; on coalition in Southeast Asia, 1088; and foreign trade, 47–48, 88, 214–15; reports to E., 133–34; 214–15; on Republican reactionary fringe, 1088

Slum clearance. *See* Public Housing Administration

Small Business Administration: establishment of, 369–70, 2307; and Port Townsend, 879

Smith, Alfred Emanuel. *See* Alfred E. Smith Memorial Foundation

Smith, Charles Henry, Jr.: attends ILO conference, 2141–42; background, 2141–42

Smith, Earl E. T.: and Batista dictatorship, 2484; as U.S. ambassador to Cuba, 2484

Smith, Edith (Branson), 519–20

Smith, H. Alexander: background, 982–83; and Bricker amendment, 76; as delegate to U.N., 1011; introduces bill for civilian achievement medal, 1677; and Taft-Hartley Act revisions, 538–39, 565, 571, 982–83

Smith, James H., Jr., 141

Smith, Lawrence Henry: background, 1267–68; opposes waterway control legislation, 1267–68

Smith, Margaret Chase: background, 916–17; and Passamaquoddy power project, 1234; questions U.S. defense strategy, 916–17

Smith, Mary Eleanor (Cline), background, 1254

Smith, Merriman, E.'s esteem for, 829, 832

Smith, Norman, and weight performance tests on bulls, 1981–82

Smith, Sidney, and letter to Lady Liverpool, 262

Smith, Thor, E.'s esteem for, 830, 832

Smith, Walter Bedell, 181, 182, 389–90, 648–49, 932, 933, 1004; on aid to Ethiopia, 169–70; on Anglo-American relations, 1281–83; on antitrust policies, 1023–24; approves letter to Churchill, 889; approves letter to Luce, 661; approves message to Laniel, 1033; attends Bernhard's conference on U.S.-European relations, 1615; attends stag dinner, 617, 1302; background, 86, 1254, 1411; and Baruch's disarmament plan, 1018; and Bilderberg Club, 1411; birthday dinner for, 1302; Black's memo on Egypt, 174–75; on Bricker amendment, 860; and Bulganin's support for Stevenson, 2333; on Canadian oats imports, 707–8; and Churchill-Eden visit, 1141–42; Churchill's view, 730–31; and Citizen Advisors on Mutual Security, 2134–35; on de Lattre, 1702–3; on diplomatic recognition of Vatican, 1227–28; and Dulles's view on treaties, 840; as E.'s Chief of Staff, 1667–68, 1702–3; and EDC, 1275–77; and E.'s message to Churchill, 1320–21; on E.'s problem with Monty, 1324–25; esteem for Holland, 807–8; and Falcon Dam, 254; farewell dinner for, 1302; and FCC appointment, 437; and French morale, 1035–36; on Geneva Conference and ROK, 1023; at Geneva, reports on Communist position, 1191; and Georgescu case, 415; gives E. Alexandrian coin, 1703; and Gruenther's view on France, 890–91; health of, 1279; on Horton's appointment, 283–84; and Kaghan's resignation, 256–58; on labor policies in Canal Zone, 912–13; on Latin American ambassadorship for Guggenheim, 465; leaves Geneva, 1181; on long-staple cotton quotas, 907; and MIG incident, 529–32; and Milton E.'s report on Latin America, 670–71; and Moores' visit to Latin America, 840–41; and Nine-Power Conference, 1320–21; on Panama-American relations, 545, 666; on Pleven's view of Red Chinese power in Indochina, 954; political problems in Italy, 927–28; on posts for Dunn, Kemper, 1275–76; on psychological warfare misinterpretation, 600–601; on refugees, 151–52; reimbursement for U.S. logistical support in Korea, 422–23; represents U.S. at Geneva, 1052, 1068–69, 1181, 1199;

resigns as Under Secretary of State, 1254, 1302, 1330–31; on Rhee's "insulting" letter to E., 894; and Rio Conference, 1275–77; and SEATO, 1180–81; sends E. birthday book, 2327–28; on supplies for Dien Bien Phu, 1042; and Taber's complaint about Wolfe, 942–43; to talk with French on U.S. aid to Vietnam, Cambodia, 1310; transmits cables to Churchill, 921, 1032; transmits cable to Dulles, 1031; on Trieste, 1277, 1278–79, 1294; and tripartite summit, 239; as Under Secretary of State, 86; on U.S. aid to Cambodia, 1310; on U.S. aid to Vietnam, 1310; on U.S. commitment to France in Indochina, 893, 1132–33; and U.S. intervention in Vietnam, 1035–36; and U.S. military aid to Nicaragua, 202; on U.S. policy in Latin America, 1275–77; and Van Fleet's article, 823; on V-E Day anniversary, 1702–3

Smith, Young Berryman: background, 519–20; and recommendations for Supreme Court appointment, 519–20

Smylie, Robert E.: background, 387–88; on dump Nixon charges, 2074–75; scores Congress, 387–88

Smyth, Henry DeWolf, on AEC and Dixon-Yates, 1201

Snyder, Howard McCrum, Sr., 223, 1836; background, 99; birthday greetings to, from E., 2004–5; Clay's concern, 1402, 1405; E.'s appreciation to, 2207; and E.'s heart attack, 1870, 1876, 1897–98, 1935, 2004–5, 2207; and E.'s ileitis surgery, 2199–2200, 2205–6, 2207; and E.'s injured elbow, 526, 527; fishing with E., 1235; and Forkner's "If I Were President" memo, 2047; on Harmon's illness, 2303–4; on Howard's "Rest Regime," 2058–59; on Mamie E.'s health, 1708; on medical care for service dependents, 685–86; on Milton E.'s bursitis, 1122–23; and National Manpower Council, 1474–75; opposes publishing report on E.'s health, 2289; and Pollock's report on E., 1968–69, 1970; and portraits of E., 737–38; prescribes yogurt, carrots for E., 2221, 2397–98; recuperates from surgery, 845; on Roberts's health, 1999; on Robinson's illness, 2121–22; on Taft's illness, 446–47; treats Carroll, 787; treats Edgar E., 2165–66; visits E. at Augusta, 2121–22; Young dedicates book to, 99. See also Eisenhower, Dwight David: health

Snyder, Morris ("Marty"): background, 1325–26; campaigns for E., 1325–26; candidacy of, 1325–26; registers as Independent, 1325–26; withdraws candidacy, 1325–26

Snyder, Murray: as aide to Hagerty, 1229; background, 1231; on farm policy, 1304–5; on Nixon's attendance at stag dinner, 2062–63

Social Democratic party, loses in West German election, 508

Socialism: Nehru's view, 2449; N. Thomas's protest, 612–14; and Second International (1889), 359–60, 362; in U.S. government, Edgar E.'s view, 2155, 2157

Social security, 1730, 1731; E.'s view, 1323–24; Schaefer's view, 1323–24

Social Security Administration, 17, 84, 803; an American Assembly topic, 647–48; and American Retail Federation, 624–25; Ayres's view, 764–65; and budget policy for FY 1955, 643–44; E.'s recommendations, 624–25; and extension of old age and survivors insurance, 33, 37–38, 369–70, 624–25, 643–44; Hutton's view, 562–63; and Reed-Curtis conferences, 692–93; Republicans oppose programs of, 275–76, 762; Scripps-Howard survey on, 899; session on, at Republican legislative leaders' conference (December 1953), 794; and State of the Union Address, 654, 656

Social Security Amendments Act (1956), and HEW health care program, 1460–61

Social service workers, at White House, Weeks's view, 809

Sohn, Louis Bruno: background, 615–16; on disarmament and U.N. charter review, 615–16

Solomon, Jack, beef for E., 587–88, 1173–74

Somers, Richard Herbert: background, 1453; esteem of, for E., 1453; on McCarthy, 1453

Somoza Garcia, Anastasio: invites Milton E. to Nicaragua, 202; meets with E., 2211–12; requests U.S. military aid, 202

Songgram, P. Pibul: background, 1693; visits E., 1692–93

South (U.S.): E.'s problems in, 1029; George's concern on race relations, 2092; housing construction in, 1696; judiciary in, and civil rights, 2084–85, 2087; and midterm election (1954), 479–80; and President's Committee on Government Contracts, 479–80; racial policies in, 470–73, 498–99, 2090, 2091; Republican party in, Caffey's view, 2381–82; and vice-presidential candidacy in 1956, 2074–75

South Africa: and gold, 1158–59; on U.S. air routes to, 1385

South America. See Latin America

Southard, Frank S., Jr.: background, 1046–47; and convertibility of currencies, 1046–47

South Asia. See Far East; Southeast Asia

South Carolina: Aiken honors Byrnes, 1665; E.'s attitude on, 1862; and hospital at Fort Jackson, 1862; racial discrimination ends in Charleston Naval Shipyard, 471–73; and Savannah River plant in, 303–4

South Dakota: on Benson, Mintener's view, 665; E. visits, 158; farm problems in, Gunderson's view, 646–47; on politics in, Gunderson's view, 1223–24

Southeast Asia, 216, 218; Churchill's view, 1134–35; communism in, 433, 1002–6, 1033–36,

1179, 1180–81, 1618; and defense of Formosa, 1644, 1654–59; Dulles's view, 1618; and emigre Chinese, 1787; E. proposes coalition in, 1041, 1042, 1068–69; on France's purpose in, 1043, 1118–21; on internationalizing war in, 1043; and Mendès-France's pledge, 1134; Milton E. considers trip to, 1727; Nehru's view, 2452; Nixon's view, 761–62; and SEATO, 1179, 1180–81; U.S. aid to, 1118–21; war in, 773, 775, 1030–31. *See also* Far East; France, Republic of; Indochina; SEATO

Soviet bloc: and arms for Saudi Arabia, 2168; unrest in, 2465–66
Soviet Union (USSR, Union of Soviet Socialist Republics): and Adenauer's plan for demilitarized zones in Europe, 1740–41; on agreements with, 604–5; on air strength of, Spaatz's view, 238; and Arab-Israeli conflict, 2054–55, 2069; on arms to Egypt, 1867, 1877–78, 1953, 2054; on arms to Mexico from, 1101–2; and arms reduction declaration, 2470; and Aswan Dam project, 2151, 2153; and atomic energy for peaceful purpose, 487–88, 747–48, 759–60, 791, 793; and atomic warfare, British view, 733, 966, 2218–19; and Austria, 1178, 1180, 1706–7, 1714, 1821, 1823; boasts of military powers, 2470; Bulganin's view on Geneva Summit, 1794–95; Chiang proposes revolutionary tactics, 2170–71; Churchill proposes meeting with, 93, 206–8, 965–66, 1166–67, 1178, 1179, 1208, 1210; Clare Boothe Luce's view, 2398–2400; on Communist penetration in Syria, Iraq, 2463; considers aerial inspections, 2470; on cultural exchange with U.S., 1990; and D-Day commemoration, 1077, 1078; denounces London-Paris Accords, 1447, 1823; denounces Stalin, 2100, 2101, 2108, 2232, 2334–35; detonates thermonuclear device, 589–90; and disarmament, 615–16, 862, 1038–39, 1616–17, 1790–92, 1947, 1974–76, 2039–41, 2233; domination by, in Eastern Europe, 2382–85; and East-West trade controls, 959, 960, 984, 2140–41; and E.'s Atoms for Peace speech, 753–54, 791, 793; economic initiatives of, 1921–23, 1990, 2163, 2171, 2413; and Eisenhower Doctrine, 2475, 2487; and E.'s message on peace, 154–55; and E.'s 1956 candidacy, 1790; and E.'s Open Skies proposal, 1865–66, 2039, 2470; E. proposes meeting with, 1613; E. replies to Bulganin,

1989–93; and European security, 1882–83, 1889–90, 1899; fears Germany, 2452–53; on Fifth Column, Jenner's view, 699–701; and foreign ministers' meetings, 398–99, 648–49, 658, 665–66, 672, 707, 731, 744–45, 746–47, 788–89, 793, 881–82, 888–90, 1882–83, 1888–90, 1899; France's fear of, 1034; at Geneva Conference, 1023, 1199; and Geneva Summit, 1720–21, 1782–83; and Georgescu case, 414–16; and German, Austrian peace treaties, 744, 746; Gruenther's warning, 1177; Hughes's view, 883–84; and ICBMs, 1853–54; influence of, in Mexico, 1743–44; influence of, in Middle East, 2374, 2381, 2412–15; intentions of, in Near East, 2055–56; interest of, in Greek ports, 274; on invitation to Four-Power Summit, 398–99; on invitation to Zhukov, 1583–84; invites Adenauer to Moscow, 1821, 1823; and Israeli-Jordanian conflict, 2329–30; Jackson's view, in cold war, 1248–49; jets of, down navy bomber, 1283, 1284, 1296, 1297, 1609; Khrushchev attends U.S. Embassy party, 1785; land forces in, Spaatz's view, 238; on leadership of, 208–11; and Liberia, 1988–89; Lodge reports on, 177–78; Lodge talks with Gromyko, 124–25; and Lubell's disarmament plan, 90, 92, 374; McCrary-Whitney visit, 2295; Makinsky's view, 2215; may seek to split U.S.-U.K. unity, 1179; and media reports on way of life in, 1216; and Mendès-France, 1199, 1472–73, 1493; military occupation of, in Iran, 2439; on multilateral economic aid through U.N., 2159–60; and mutual withdrawal of forces and arms limitation, 504–7; Nehru visits, 1763–64; and nuclear fallout, 2001; objectives of, in Europe, 600–601; occupies Hobomai, 1609; occupies Kuriles, 1609; offers aid to Egypt, 246; and oil for Western Europe, 2424; and Oppenheimer, 718, 723–25; on opportunities for, in Middle East, 2356; in Pacific war, 1667–68; Patterson's view, 2433–34; and "peace offensive" of 206–8, 208–11, 366–67; pilot's repatriation in World War II, 531; on plan for mutual security in Europe, 1882–83; and plight of captive peoples, E.'s view, 63–64; proposes ban on nuclear weapons, 793; proposes conference on disarmament, 2470; proposes "5-power meeting," 744–45; proposes "volunteer" force in Middle East, 2386, 2387; and Red China, 269; rejects Open Skies concept, 1790–92; and satellites of, 270–71; sells gold, 675; and Sino-Soviet Treaty, 1539–40, 1565; and Soviet-Yugoslav relations, 1363, 1860–61; and spies against U.S., 298–99; and strategic trade controls, 796; supports Arab policies, 2077–78, 2080; threatens Western Europe, 2441; and Trieste, 568–69, 572, 659, 661, 1292–93, 1363; troop cuts after World War II, 2229; and U.S.-China war, E.'s

secretary, 2381–82; on E.'s finance committee, 1423; and E.'s meeting with Strauss, 800; on E.'s Presidential Library Commission, 1710; E.'s view, 226, 230, 831; Hall's interest in E.'s painting, 847; and Harriman on home rule for D.C., 1176–77; on invitation to Vanderbilt, 617–18; and Kline, 563–64; on Kraft's visit, 1512; and Larmon's report on public relations, 865–66; on limiting E.'s travel, 1502; and lunch for E., Baruch, 675; meets with Taber on defense appropriation reductions, 942; on midterm election strategy, 1345; on Oklahoma politics, 1303; on political adviser in agriculture, 1424; on public relations, 686–88; reserves rooms at St. Francis, 2204–5; returns to White House, 1841; as Secretary to President, 111, 286; on soil conservation issues, 1841; and Sulzberger's visit, 1160; on trees for E. from Republicans, 1843; as White House assistant, 7–8

Stevens, Robert Ten Broeck: advice to, from E., on "bungling" Peress case, 1065; agrees to provide data on Peress case, 1065; and cadetships at West Point, 47; and CCRAK, 776–77; E.'s confidence in, 914; E. recommends Howard to, 919–20, 1009; and "fried chicken lunch," 1065; and McCarthy, 229, 914, 1065; and McClure's assignment, 999–1001; and New Orleans bridge, 103–4; offers to resign, 914; and Oppenheimer case, 718; on promotions to rank of general, 847–48; on Quartermaster General post, 795; and request for U.S. troops in Korea, 971; resigns, 229; Ridgway objects on Peress data, 1065; as Secretary of the Army, 29, 225; as successor to E., 793; and West Point superintendency, 909–10, 1088–89, 1189; and Wilson's confirmation, 29

Stevens, Thaddeus, 387–88

Stevenson, Adlai Ewing: and ADA, 1403, 1405; and African American vote, 408–9; and Bullis's advice, 2303; calls for ban on nuclear testing, 2260, 2333, 2349–50; campaigns in Oregon, 2156; Communist support for, "kiss of death," 2333; declines U.N. post, 56; E. leads, among women voters, 2376; E.'s view, 1353, 1821, 2354, 2357, 2358; Hazlett's view, 1355; and Humphrey, 2084–85; John E.'s view, 1984–85; as leader of Democratic party, 1821; loses Minnesota primary, 2084–85, 2093; loses presidential election, 2370; on McCarthyism, 939–40; promotes bipartisanship in foreign affairs, 55–56; scores E., 939–40, 2156, 2157; scores Republicans, 2156; sends message to E., 2370; visits Asia, Middle East, Western Europe, 55, 537; visits E., 42–43, 55–56

Stevenson, Ralph Clarmont Skrine, as British ambassador to Egypt, 161

Stewart, Tommy, on E.'s young bulls, 1875, 1876

Stewart, Walter W., and foreign economic policy, 357–58

Stimson, Henry Lewis: background, 1439; greatness of, 1438; on using atomic bomb, 1667–68

Stirling, Frances Marguerite (Wilson), background, 1993–94

Stirling, William Gurdon: background, 1993–94; new post for, 1993–94

Stone, Harlan Fiske, 532

Stone, Walker, 32

Stouffer, Samuel Andrew: background, 1693; writes on civil liberties, 1693

Stover, Simon, 221

Strategic Air Command: and deployment of atomic weapons, 1418; Schaefer's view, 1017–18

Strategic Air Force, strength requirements of, 711

Strategic materials: and aluminum shortage, 608–9; and atomic weaponry, 747–48; and Bolivian tin industry, 375–76; control of, in trade with Communist China, 796, 797; and copper industry, 1250, 1954, 2158–59, 2162; decontrol of nickel, 581–82; on increased production of fissionable material, 2234; and mobilization stockpile, 1952–54; and national security, 1489, 1491; and titanium, 1954; and uranium, 2039

Strategic planning, and military-industrial complex, 635–36

Stratemeyer, George Edward: background, 1405; and reactionary fringe, 1402, 1405

Stratton, William Grant: background, 1267–68; and meat-packers' strike, 2293; and waterway control legislation, 1267–68

Straughn, Mary, background, 2081–82

Strauss, Lewis Lichtenstein, 368–69; as AEC chairman, 363–64; and AEC decision on observers at Bikini, 799–800; and AEC steam plants, 1188, 1368; and atomic data exchange, 764, 997–98; on atomic test limitations, 896; attends Masonic breakfast with E., 1567–68; background, 363–64; and Baruch's disarmament plan, 1018, 1038–39; at Bermuda Conference, 672, 764; and Chalk River accident, 363–64; on dangers of nuclear fallout, 1545–46; on defense contracts, 1344; delivers message from E. at Geneva Summit, 1804; on deployment of atomic weapons, 1417–18; on disarmament, E.'s view, 487–88; and Dixon-Yates contract, 1201, 1251–52, 1368, 1443, 1454–55, 1476–77; on evaluation of CASTLE tests, 1069; on financial aid for New York Herald Tribune, 1622–23; on inspections of atomic weaponry, 1617; on Iranian oil production, 1567–68; meets with E., 800, 987, 1443; and nuclear disarmament, 798–99; on nuclear fallout, 2001, 2260; on nuclear research reactor program, 1883–84; offers bull to E., 1463, 1560–61, 1601–2, 1781–82, 1804, 1875, 2454–55; and Oppenheimer case, 717–18, 722–25, 1026–27, 1036–37, 1133, 1476–77; and production of fissionable material, 2234; on production of nuclear weaponry, 2039–41; proposes conference on scientific developments, 2484–85; receives unfavorable press, 1476–77; on reserve atomic weaponry for U.K., 733, 735; on sharing atomic data with British, 1905–6; and Shippingport plant, 1351; on storing nuclear energy, 1567–68; on study of effects of atomic radiation, 1589–90; and study on U.S.-Soviet war, 1973–74; and Sulzberger's plan for "political amnesty," 642; and talks with Soviets, 862; on thermonuclear testing, 2260; on U.K. anxiety about CASTLE, 987; on uranium production, 1567–68. *See also* Tennessee Valley Authority

Street, Richard T.: background, 1857; offers E. Weimaraner puppy, 1857, 1875, 1876, 1927

Streibert, Theodore Cuyler: background, 1077; on bipartisan cooperation, 1453–54; and cultural exchange programs, 1766; and D-Day anniversary statement, 1077; E. recommends McKeogh to, 1945; on honorary citizenship for Churchill, 1646–47; Howard's view, 2183–84; meets with E., 2125; on Murray's goodwill trips, 1142–43; and Thomas's report on Latin America, 1705; and USIA, 1766, 2125, 2183–84

Streiff, Richard W.: background, 1672–73; on red rug for Gettysburg office, 1672–73

Streit, Clarence Kirshman: background, 2216–17; on proposal by, to further Atlantic union, 2216–17

Stringfellow, Douglas R., and Colorado River Storage Project, 902

Stroessner, Alfredo: background, 2211–12; E.'s view, 2211–12

Stuart, R. Douglas: background, 1676; on Dulles's visit to Canada, 1676; retires, 1932

Stuart, Tommie: background, 2186–87; on breeding Black Angus, 2186–87

Studebaker Corporation, collective bargaining at, 1259

Studebaker-Packard Corporation: Curtiss-Wright acquires, 2128–29; and defense procurement policy, 1603–4; and J-47 jet engine production, 1603–4; verges on liquidation, 2128–29

Stump, Felix Budwell: background, 1533; briefs Dulles, 1582; as CINCPAC, 1533; and Formosa directive, 1533; and U.S. policy on Nanchi, 1582

Sturzo, Don Luigi: background, 927–28; founds Italian Popular party, 927–28

Submerged lands. *See* Natural resources

Sudan, 175, 217; and Aswan Dam project, 2153; Dulles's recommendation, 2096–97; independence of 68–69, 246

Suez Canal. *See* Egypt: Suez Canal

Suez Canal Conference. *See* Egypt: Suez Canal Conferences

Suez Canal Users' Association (SCUA). *See* Egypt: Suez Canal Users' Association

Sugar: and Cuba, 1529–30, 1530; domestic quotas on, 1529–30, 1530; "sugar states" concerns on imports, 1529–30, 1530

Sugar Act of 1956: and Cuba, 1553, 1554; quota legislation, 1554

Suhrawardy, Huseyn Shaheed: background, 2458; favors Red China's membership in U.N., 2456–58; meets with Red Chinese leaders, 2458

Sullivan, John Lawrence, background, 681

Sulzberger, Arthur Hays: on address by E. to Associated Press, 667–68; background, 49; chairs Columbia Bicentennial Committee, 511–12; on Churchill's memoir, 511–12; and Columbia's Bicentennial commemorative stamp, 87; E. declines dinner honoring, 1459; editorial by, endorses E.'s candidacy, 2331; on E.'s speeches to media, 119; and gift book for E., 636–37; and Leviero's report, 185–86; meets with E., 511–12; and *New York Times* reports on Argentina, 514–15; reports on Columbia projects, 252; and plan for "political amnesty," 362–63, 559–60, 640–42; praises E.'s program, 1139–40; and Presbyterians on McCarthyism, 667–68

Sulzberger, Cyrus Leo: background, 1160; and golf, 884, 1160; on Krock's attempts to see E., 550

Sulzberger, Iphogene B. (Ochs), 119; receives award, 252

Sulzberger, Marina Tatiana (Lada), background, 1160

Summerall, Charles Pelot, Jr.: background, 261–62; retires, 261–62

Summerfield, Arthur Ellsworth, 1467–68; and automobile industry, 2133–34; background, 6; and Columbia's Bicentennial commemorative stamp, 87; and commemorative stamps on conservation, 1855–56; congratulates E. on reelection, 2431–32; on E.'s finance committee, 1423; on elections for postmasters, 1400–1401; on employing African Americans, 2095; on moving mail by air, 1365; and "Operation Tornado," 535–36; as political adviser, 857; on postal workers pay bill, 1287, 1288; and postmaster in Abilene, 1221–22; as Postmaster General, 5, 6; on Post Office Department and Railway Express Service, 1365; and Public Law 199, 1365; on public relations, 686–88, 865–66; and Railway Express Service, 1365; and RNC Board of Strategy, 687; and San Francisco murals, 250; scores Benson's farm program, 2267–68; on Studebaker-Packard contracts, 2128–29; on Taft-Hartley Act, 561–62; undergoes surgery, 2431–32

Thompson, Llewellyn E., Jr.: background, 1117; and talks on Trieste, 1117–18, 1277, 1294
Thompson, Percy Walter, 179–80, 1562–63; and family reunion, 298, 300; grandchildren visit, 1739–40; John E. and family visit, 1087
Thompson, Ruth: background, 118; and immigration legislation, 117, 118
Thone, Charles: background, 503; a controversial appointee, 502–4
Thornt, Major General, 905
Thornton, Daniel I. J., 6, 1835; aids Colorado boy, 1909; attends stag dinner, 1412, 1467–68, 2062–63; and "Augusta National" weekend in Denver, 1300; background, 26; and beef-stew luncheon, 1297–98; as candidate for Senate, 2221; chairs committee on Korean rehabilitation, 1056–57, 1184; chairs Governors' Conference, 861–62, 1063–64; on dust bowl problems in Colorado, 1063–64; on E.'s advisory committee, 1423; E.'s interest in political future of, 1056–57; and E.'s painting, 522–23; golf with, 350, 522–23; on Herefords, 1412; loses Senate race, 2406; meets with E., 1822; and Moncrief's contribution, 1348; Nielsen's view, 2406; as Republican leader, 2064; sends fishing license #1, 769; on vice-presidential candidacy in 1956, 2074–75; visits Korea, 1184; will not run for Senate, 1056–57, 1063–64
Thornton, Jesse (Willock), background, 861–62
Thornton, Pauline, supports E. on civil rights, 2271–72
Three-power summit. See Foreign ministers' meetings
Three Wise Men. See NATO
Thurmond, James Strom: background, 1569; on U.S.-Mexico air routes, 1569
Thye, Edward John: background, 967; favors rigid price supports, 2017, 2019–20; protests Benson's farm plan, 967–68
Tidelands Bill, 33, 37, 2033, 2034
Tilt, Agnes J. (Morgan), background, 2196–97
Tilt, Charles Arthur, background, 2196–97
Time magazine, on E.'s bridge skill, 223
Tin. See Raw materials; Strategic materials
Tisserant, Eugene (Cardinal): background, 2208; meets with Ginzberg, 2208; on Nasser, 2208; on U.S. policy in Middle East, 2208
Titanium. See Raw materials; Strategic materials
Tito, Josip Broz: and Belgrade Declaration, 2383, 2385; and crisis in Middle East, 2382–85; Dulles meets with, 1868–69, 1888–89; and foreign ministers' meeting (October 1955), 1868–69, 1888–89; on Hungarian revolt, 2383, 2385; on military aid to Yugoslavia, 1860–61; on Murphy's visit, 1860–61, 1868–69; on rapprochement with Soviet Union, 1860–61; reacts to U.S.-U.K. plan, 659; requests U.S. aid, 2382, 2384; on Soviet attitude, 270–71, 2383, 2385; on Stalin's death,

112–13; on U.K. support, 270–71; on U.S.-Yugoslav relations, 1363, 1868–69; on visit by, to U.S., 2384, 2385; visits U.S.S.R., 2383, 2385
—Trieste: 568, 572, 1275, 1277, 1279, 1280; E. proposes settlement, 1292–94; and Soviet-Yugoslav relations, 1363; terms of final settlement, 1292–94
Tobruk, 1626
Tomajan, John S., background, 1832
Tompkins, Charles H. Company: and Berkey's advice on fences, 1394; renovates Gettysburg farm, 1773–74
Tompkins, Charles Hook: background, 1773–74; and cornerstone at farmhouse, 1055–56; and D.C. cultural center commission, 1773–74; and Gettysburg farm, 176, 184–85; and outbuildings at farm, 1483, 1485; and trees at farm, 1315–16
TORCH, 1626
Totten, James K., 550–51
Totten, Ruth Ellen (Patton), on mother's death, 550–51
Tourism, 2075–76
Toynbee, Arnold Joseph: background, 1925; on colonialism and U.S. foreign aid, 1925–26
Trade: and Bullis on world trade, 393; with Communists, Baruch's view, 2103–4; and East-West trade controls, 958–61, 984, 985–86, 2140–41; and long-staple cotton quotas, 906–8; and rye imports from Canada, 990–91; and State of the Union Address, 654, 656; and tariff legislation, 1057–58; and watch industry, 1115–17; wool industry's problems, 482–83; on world trade and isolationism, 2228–29. See also Economy, foreign; General Agreement on Tariffs and Trade; Randall Commission; Reciprocal Trade Agreements Act; United States: foreign trade
Trade Agreements Act of 1934, and GATT, 1573–74
Trade Agreements Extension Act of 1951, 33, 37; extension and amendment of, 1081
Trade Agreements Extension Act of 1953, 1057–58; background, 1109–10; Dulles and Reed discuss, 1109–10; escape clause in, 1226, 1574, 2389; and GATT, 1382–83; and lead and zinc imports, 1242–43; and "peril points," 1574; and Tariff Commission, 1574; and watch imports, 1115–17, 1226
Trade Agreements Extension Act of 1955: and duties on bicycle imports, 1827; and GATT, 1573; and H.R. 1, 1631
Trading with the Enemy Act, 244
Trans-Arabian Pipeline. See Oil; Tapline
Transportation, need for policy on, 972–73. See also Railroads
Treasury, Department of the, 715, 1599; and Advisory Board of Economic Growth and Stability, 277–78; and Edgar E.'s query, 65; favors

tax rate reductions over increased exemptions, 966–67; and fiscal policy objectives, 373–74; on gold standard, 1158–59; and liberal mortgage policies, 1696; and midyear budget review, 488–89; and Milton E.'s report on Latin America, 814–15; and report of political scandal, 681–82; and power policy, 311–12; and State of the Union Address, 652, 655

Treaties: and Committee for the Defense of the Constitution by Preserving the Treaty Power, 834; and Constitution of U.S., 848–49, 870–71; Dulles's view, 840, 2107–8; principles of, 810–12. *See also* Bricker amendment; Constitution of the United States

Treaty of Friendship, Commerce, and Navigation (1953), with Japan, 1659, 2049

Treaty of 1783: and Articles of Confederation, 837; and Bricker amendment, 837

Trees, in E.'s name, 1647. *See also* Gettysburg farm: trees and shrubs

Tregor, Nison A.: background, 258; and bust of E., 258

Trice, J. Mark: background, 989–90; as candidate for Comptroller General, 989–90

Trieste, 1948–49; Armstrong's view, 270–71; Dulles discusses, with E., 507, 1175–76; Dulles reports on negotiations, 1117–18; E. appeals to Tito, 1292–94; final settlement, 1294, 1363; Italian, Yugoslav claims to, 549–50, 1277, 1280; Luce's view, 659, 661, 1175, 1176, 1277, 1280; on redeployment of U.S. troops in, 1236–37, 1237–38, 1246–47; refugee problem in, 151; riots in, 659, 661; and Soviet-Yugoslav relations, 1363; on stalemate, E.'s concern, 1275, 1277, 1279; and Tito, 1363; on zones A, B, 1118, 1293. *See also* Italy, Republic of; Yugoslavia, Federal Republic of

Trigger, 2108–9

Trimble, James William, 222

Trinidad, Republic of, Thomas visits, 1705

Trinity College (Hartford, Connecticut): honors E., 1072–73; Jacobs invites E. to, 818–19, 1072–73

Tripartite Agreement of 1950. *See* Tripartite Declaration Regarding Security in the Near East

Tripartite Declaration of 1950. *See* Tripartite Declaration Regarding Security in the Near East

Tripartite Declaration Regarding Security in the Near East: Eden's view, 2343; E. fears U.K. shift from, 2343; E.'s view, 2374; and France, 2341; and sale of arms in Middle East, 2338; U.K., U.S., France sign, 2338; U.S. position on, 2341, 2413; U.S.-U.K. views differ, 2343

Truman, Harry S., 84, 151, 220, 311–12, 407, 762, 838, 1442, 1470; Administration of, E.'s view, 1387; and AEC contracts, 1188; and Agricultural Act of 1948, 563–64; apprecia-

tion to, 9; and assurances to Arab States, 296, 297; attacks E., 2027; authorizes hydrogen bomb project, 1036–37; and automobile industry, 2133–34; barnstorming tactics of, 1337; and civil service, 320–21; and Committee on Government Contract Compliance, 473; and defense of Indochina, 314–15; and diplomatic relations with Vatican, 1227–28; and dispersal policy in defense production, 765–66; establishes Loyalty Review Boards, 1494–95; and Falkenberg's puppet, 2266; fiscal policies of, 335–36; and foreign aid estimates, 206; and FY 1953 budget, 238; and FY 1954 budget, 195, 197, 238, 269; and Gifford's retirement, 46; and guided-missiles program, 232; and Harry Dexter White, 648–49, 688–89; and Hoover Commission, 822; and Korea, troop levels and logistical support in, 241; and Kornitzer, 123–24; and Latin America, 107; McCarran opposes policies of, 1355; mutual security program, 796, 797; opposes invasion of South Korea, 1644; and Panama Canal, 401–2; and Point Four (IV) Program, 2075–76; at Potsdam, 900, 1667–68; and presidential power, 162; public power policy, 1511; and rearmament program, 342–43; relationship with E., 9, 1848–49; and Rickenbacker, 1568–69; and rights to tidelands oil, 37; role of, as candidate, 1337; and Rosenbergs, 291; sends John E. to Inauguration, 9; signs Army Retirement Act, 2094; and steel seizure, 29–30; and TCA, 86–87; TVA appointees oppose Dixon-Yates contract, 1200, 1454–55; and TVA budget, 555–57; and UMT, 583; and U.S.-Mexico air routes, 1568–69; and U.S.S. *Williamsburg*, 163; and year of maximum danger (1954), 342–43

Tube alloys, 1522, 1524

Tubman, William Vavanarat Shadrack: background, 1105–6; inauguration of, 1988–89; on U.S.-Liberian relations, 1988–89; visits U.S., 1105–6

Tufts, Richard: background, 2269–70; on voter registration, 2269–70

Tully, Jasper William: background, 2026; on E.'s gas bill veto, 2026

Tunisia, Republic of: Bourguiba's view, 2404–5; ceremony in, 223; and France, 1043, 1119, 1121; and Mendès-France, 1414, 1415; and Nasser's intentions, 2077–78; NSC advocates aid to, 2405; Soviet influence in, 2076–77; terrorism in, 223; U.S. recognizes, 2405; U.S. sends wheat to, 2404–5

Turkey, Republic of: and Arab States, 303, 1788; and collaboration agreement with Pakistan, 908–9; and Cyprus, 1257–58, 1948–49, 2070, 2166–67; Eden's proposal on, 2192–93; and NATO, 1614; and Northern Tier Pact, 1948–49; and oil for Western Europe, 2276; refugee problem in, 118, 151; signs Baghdad Pact,

Declaration of Washington, 1997–98, 2009; and Democratic Congress, 1511; and deployment of atomic weapons, 1417–18; and disarmament, 1974–76; Douglas's plan to aid Mideast economy, 1967–68; Dulles speaks on, 1406; Eden's view, 1787–89; E. discusses with Dulles, 1947–49; and Egypt, 68–69, 100–102, 111–12, 244–46, 2412–15; and Eisenhower Doctrine, 2474–75, 2476, 2487–88; E. objects to Churchill's view, 729–30; E. proposes coalition on crisis in Indochina, 1002–6, 1033–36, 1118–21; E. replies to Bulganin, 1989–93; E. speaks to editors on, 487; E. speaks to U.N. on, 747–48, 759–60; E. supports H.R. 1, 1572–73, 1631; E.'s view, 1386–89, 1574–79, 2206–7; on foreign economic policy, 1019–20, 1080–82, 1109–10, 1182–83, 1432, 1572–74, 1631; on Formosa, 1654–59; and four-power foreign ministers' meetings, 739–47, 881–82, 1613–14; on furnishing "fig leaves" to Great Britain, 2403; at Geneva Conference, 893–94, 1051–53, 1068–79; and Geneva Summit Conference, 1800, 1801; and German, Austrian peace treaties, 744, 746; Grew's view, 347–48; and Guatemala, 1066–67, 1168–69; on Hammarskjöld's mission to Near East, 2121; Hazlett's view, 1353–55; and Honduras, 1066–67; and Howard's survey on, 871; and Hungarian revolt, 2334–35, 2344, 2345; and immigration, 117–19, 333; and India, 908–9, 2453; initiative in, 825; and Iran-U.K. dispute, 337–40; on Israeli-Jordanian conflict, 2328–30; and Italo-Yugoslav tensions, 659, 661; in Italy, 927–28; Knowland's attack on, 1390–91; and Latin American relations, 820; Leviero's report, 185; Lodge's view, 1580–81; and London-Paris Accords, 1446–48, 1612, 1614; and Lubell's disarmament plan, 374; Makinsky's view, 1264–65; and Mexico, 170–71, 1099–1100; Monty's strategy, 383–86; on moral values in, 372; and MSA bill, 1173; Msgr. McCarthy's view, 1049–51; mutual defense treaty with ROK, 432; and Nationalist China's offshore islands, 1282–83, 1536–40, 1574–79, 1654–59; and national security, 805–6; and NATO, 1298–99, 1614, 2236–37, 2415–16; in Pacific, Clark's view, 1073; and Pakistan, 908–9; in Panama, 543–45, 666; and Perón's proposals, 649–50; in Philippines, 389–90; in postwar Korea, 547–49, 968–71, 1171–72, 1534–36; psychological aspects of, 1923; and Puerto Rico, 814; and Red China, 1171–73, 1519–21, 1533, 1536–40, 1574–79, 1582, 1583; and refugee problem, 150–52; reimbursement policy for logistical support in Korea, 241, 422–23; and relations with India, 1415–16; and Rhee, 172–74, 278–82, 596–97; and Saar question, 741, 746, 1445–47; and St. Lawrence Seaway, 132–33;

and Saudi Arabia, 295–98, 2167–68; Scripps-Howard survey on, 898–900; and SEATO, 1179, 1180–81; shift in, in Cuba, 2483–84; and Soviet Declaration on disarmament, 2470; on Soviet influence in Middle East, 2412–15, 2415–16; and Soviet-Yugoslav relations, 1363; stability of, in Europe, 927–28; and State of the Union Address (1954), 778–79; and Suez crisis, 2219–20, 2241, 2251–52, 2253–54, 2263–65, 2372–73, 2373–75, 2412–15; supports EDC, 527–29, 1261–62; and Trieste, 549–50, 568, 572, 1117–18, 1292–94; and tripartite agreement of 1950, 2343, 2413; tripartite meeting, 239–40; and U.N. appropriations, 267–69; and unification of Germany, 325–26, 383–86, 410–13, 508; and U.S.-European relations, 1615; on U.S. forces abroad, 591–92, 610–12; U.S.-U.K. emergency plan, 732–35; and Vatican, recognition of, 1227–28; in Vietnam, 1118–21, 1171, 1172, 1377–81; view of, as belligerent, 1297; view of, in Europe, 403–4, 688–89; Wilson's blunder on, 1615–16; and Wright's offer, 1124–25. *See also* Atomic weaponry; Cold war; Geneva Summit Conference; Bermuda Conference; European Defense Community; Middle East; Randall Commission; *or under individual nations*

—foreign trade, 18, 200–202, 660–61, 1730, 1731; and agricultural "foreign service," 1094–95; on antitrust policies, 1023–24; and Bolivian tin industry, 375–76; and brier pipe tariffs, 33–38, 47–48; and British bids on Chief Joseph Dam, 214–15, 1761–62, 1788, 1789; with Communist China, 796, 797, 2008, 2009, 2010; and convertibility of currencies, 1046–47; and Cuba's sugar imports, 1529–30, 1530; Draper's view, 308–9; and duties on watch imports, 1115–17; on East-West trade controls, 958–61, 984, 985–86, 2140–41; E.'s message to trade missions, 1016; E.'s philosophy on, 359–62, 1195–96, 2228–29; and extension of Reciprocal Trade Act, 33, 37, 214–15, 1057–58, 1080–82, 1109–10, 1573, 1631, 1857–58; and fishing industry, 1138–39; Ford's view, 106; and foreign economic program (H.R. 1), 1572–74, 1631, 1685; and GATT, 1382–83, 1573–74; and grain imports from Canada, 990–91; Jones's view, 1857–58; importance of, to Japan, 2047; on lead and zinc tariffs, 1230, 1231, 1242–43, 1250; and lighter flints industry, 2388–90; and long-staple cotton quotas, 906–8; with Mexico, 1195, 1230, 1231, 1242–43; and "most favored nation" policy, 1195; and OTC legislation, 2172–73; Percy's support on, 1082; Schnoor supports, 1358; Sloan's view, 214–15; and State of the Union Address, 654, 655; and Swiss watch tariff issue, 1225–27; and tariffs on British-made bicycles, 1761–62,

Index 2933

1788, 1789, 1826–29; tariff debate, 33, 38, 47–48, 360–62, 1195–96; and tung imports, 1083–85; with U.K., Douglas's view, 357–58; and U.S. policy, 1057–58, 1499–1500; and wool industry problems, 482–83, 552–53. *See also* Economy, foreign; Randall Commission; General Agreement on Tariffs and Trade; United States Tariff Commission
—national security, 17–18; and aid to Hungarian refugees, 2436–37; and bipartisan commission to study, 1205–6; and budget planning, 589–90, 671–72; and censorship of DOD disclosures, 631–32, 767–68; and CIA study, 1213–15; clergy's view, 667–68; E.'s plan for, 341–43, 1488–91; and foreign policy, 805–6; on friction between congressional committees, executive departments, 897, 898; and government procurement, Reed's view, 1685; and Harry Dexter White case, 683; and ICBM program, 1853–54; and interlocking subversion, 699–701; and internal security program, 1494–95; on investigations of, 256–58; and Jenner's report, 699–701; Lodge's view, 697–98, 736; McCarran's view, 1353, 1355; and memo on treatment of government personnel, 930–31, 1065–66; misunderstanding of, among Americans, 504–6; and mutual security program, 796, 797; and need for nuclear testing, 2260; and New Look, 356–57, 589–90, 671–72, 1488–91; and Oppenheimer case, 717–19, 722–25, 1026–27; and Panama Canal, 401–2; and principle of executive privilege, 1069–71, 1075–76, 1080; and protection of official secrets, 368–69; and Quantico Vulnerabilities Panel, 1745–46; questions for Brownell on, 974–75; Radulovich case, 679–80; and Rosenbergs, 290–91; and Sherwood, 1026–27; and Socialists in civil service, 612–14; and Soviet Fifth Column, 699–701; and State of the Union Address (1954), 652, 655, 778–79; and study on war with Soviet Union, 1973–74; Sulzberger's plan for "political amnesty," 362–63, 559–60, 640–42; on support of NATO, U.N., 627; and Taft's outburst, 195–97; and unauthorized disclosure of classified data, 767–68; and UNESCO, 243. *See also* Bricker amendment; Internal security; McCarthy, Joseph Raymond; McCarthyism; Wilson, Charles Erwin

United States Academy of Nursing, 1887
United States Advisory Commission on Information: and cultural exchange programs, 1766; Reed's role, 1686, 1766
United States Air Force: announces aircraft production plans, 1808–9; base closings in U.S., 896; base construction in Spain, 500–502, 583–84, 768–69; on base construction in U.S., 895–96; budget, FY 1957, 1155–56; cancels air base construction, 466–67; controversy at Dhahran, Saudi Arabia, 2464, 2465;

controversy at Plattsburgh, N.Y., 466–67; controversy at Portsmouth-Newington, N.H., 466–67; cuts in appropriations for, 341–43; Fifth, relocates in Japan, 1534, 1536; Fifth, withdraws from Korea, 1534, 1536; France requests technicians of, in Indochina, 886–87, 892–93; and FY 1955 budget policy, 711, 712; and ICBM, IRBM program, 1853–54, 1932–33; and New Look, 197, 711, 958; personnel strength in, 1488, 1491; POWs of, in Red China, 1171, 1173; Quarles as Secretary of, 1797–98, 1809; and Radford's view, 235–36; and Radulovich case, 679–80; and retirement legislation for nurses, 1886, 1887; and statement of procurement proposals, 1675; Talbott resigns, 1797–98, 1809; Talbott as Secretary of, 29. *See also* Aircraft; Air power; New Look
United States Air Force Academy: background, 1189; and Eisenhower Golf Course, 1764–65; E. visits, 1852–53; Harmon heads, 1189, 2459–60; and Manitou, 1852–53; on superintendency of, 1189
United States Army: and beef purchasing program, 645–46, 1603; and Bonus March, 2002; charges by, against McCarthy and Cohn, 951–52; and Chief Joseph Dam, 214–15; E. misses Inspector General's service, 1044–45; 45th Division leaves Korea, 775–76; and ICBM, IRBM program, 1932–33; integration in, 2084–85; investigates CCRAK, 776–77; and New Orleans bridge, 103–4; and Peress case, 914, 1064–65; personnel reduction in, 671–72, 711, 712, 1862; and poultry purchases, 934; promotions, 847–48; Ridgway objects to providing Peress data, 1065; and statement of procurement proposals, 1675; 351st Regiment returns to U.S., 1246–47; and TVA, 1251–52. *See also* Armed Forces; Armed Services; McCarthy, Joseph Raymond: Army-McCarthy hearings
United States Army Corps of Engineers: and Chief Joseph Dam, 214–15; and Clark Hill Dam, 1511–12; and Hartwell Dam, 1515; and Mansfield Reservoir project, 1632; and Port Townsend, 878–79; and Passamaquoddy power project, 1234; and water resources policy, 689–90, 766–67, 786; and waterway control legislation, 1267–68, 1278
United States Army Nurse Corps: adequate quarters for, 1885, 1886; celebrates anniversary, 1969–70; field grades in, 1885; Harlow reports on, 1886–87; on overseas tours, 1885, 1887; problems of, E.'s concern, 1884–87, 1936–37; promotions in, 1885; and Reserve program, 1884, 1886–87; retirement policy, 1886, 1887
United States Army Student Nurse Program, 1887
United States-Canada Committee on Trade and

—United Kingdom: on British participation in war, 1034, 1041, 1042; Churchill's view, 1170–73; Eden's view, 1030–31

Vigilant Women for the Bricker Amendment, and Dulles's position, 840

Villach (Austria), 1236–37, 1246–47. *See* Trieste, on redeployment of U.S. troops in

Villa St. Pierre, 1393

Vinson, Frederick Moore, 124; background, 129; death of, 461, 514–15, 532, 567; on overloaded courts, 129; swears in Cabinet, 5–6

Virginia: E. attends Virginia Resolution observance, 163; E. inspects Front Royal beef cattle station in, 2278; E.'s oversight in Richmond, 1085–86; and E.'s stand on Bricker amendment, 871–72; racial discrimination ends at Norfolk Naval Shipyard, 473; Republican midterm election defeat in, 664

Virginia Polytechnic Institute, sponsors beef cattle station, 2278

Virgin Islands, 2294–95

Vogel, Herbert Davis: background, 1111; and Dixon-Yates contract, 1201, 1251–52, 1454; to head TVA, 1111, 1201, 1368

Vogel, Victor H.: background, 1442; Hobby objects to, 1442

Voice of America, 753–54; airs Fred Waring show, 1902, 1904; E.'s support of, 130, 198–99; Knowland's view, 1635–36; misunderstanding with Johnson, 69–71; Skinner's view, 130–31

Volunteer Freedom Corps, 79

von Opel, Fritz, 244

von Opel, Margot, 244

Voorhees, Tracy Stebbins: background, 2436–37; coordinates aid to Hungarian refugees, 2436–37, 2442–43

Vorys, John Martin: background, 270; on Randall Commission, 201

Voting: and absentee laws for service personnel, 957–58, 1541–44; Adkins's interest in, 2376; for eighteen-year-olds, 1219, 1220, 1829–30; E.'s view, 1829–30; Hoving's view, 2319; on voter registration, 2260–61, 2269–70, 2282; on women voters, 2376

Voting Assistance Act of 1942, 1543

Voting Assistance Act of 1955, 1544

Wadmond, Lowell Curtis, 165

Wadsworth, George E.: and Eisenhower Doctrine, 2474; and King Saud, 2167, 2168, 2461, 2464; as U.S. ambassador to Saudi Arabia, 2168, 2394–95

Wadsworth, James J.: background, 328–29; and U.S. forces in Korea, 328–29

Wagenheim, Mr., 2205–6

Wages: E.'s executive order on, 37; on 1955 increases in, 1960; and price controls, 17, 20–21; and rise in steel wages, 1960

Waggoner, Walter H., 185

Wagner, Captain, 1648–49

Wagner, Robert F., Jr.: background, 2464; irritates E., 2464; refuses to greet Saud, 2464

Wainwright, Stuyvesant II: background, 2065; as Republican leader, 2064–65

Wallace, Henry Agard: background, 106, 2431; on Malenkov, 106–7; on Nehru's visit, 2431; praises E., 106; on world living standards, 2431

Wall Street Journal, scores federal surplus food distributions, 2411–12. *See also* Media: press

Walter Reed Army Hospital: E. visits for checkup, 1928, 2338; Heaton as CG, 1588; and Marshall's illness, 626; on painting for, by E., 1835; and Taft's illness, 446–47; and treatments for E.'s bursitis, 1697. *See also* Eisenhower, Dwight David: ileitis

Walters, Vernon A. ("Dick"): background, 1470, 2058; injures leg, 1469–70; as interpreter for E., 2058, 2075, 2096; reports on meeting with Ruiz Cortines, 2096

Wanamaker, Pearl (Anderson): background, 2403; on rumors of federal appointment for, 2402–3

War, U.N. as best alternative to, 2407. *See also* Eisenhower, Dwight David

War Advertising Council, 1570–71

Warburton, Herbert Birchby: background, 2065; as Republican leader, 2064–65

War Department, and media, in World War II, 749, 752

Waring, Fred M.: Edgar E.'s concern, 1904; E.'s view, 1902–3; plans birthday party for E., 497–98, 524

Warner, Harry Morris, 172

Warren, Dorothy, 370–71

Warren, Earl, 2482–83; appoints Kuchel to serve out Nixon's term, 1470–71; Burton's view, 555; as candidate in 1956, 1995–96; as Chief Justice, 461, 551–52, 567, 568, 571, 977, 1354–55; and coronation of Queen Elizabeth II, 72, 370–71, 461; declines California gubernatorial race, 461; and desegregation, 2084–85; on John Marshall Centennial, 1765–66; on Knowland, 1470–71; on Kuchel, 1470–71; medical plan fails, 551–52; Milton E.'s view, 514–15; and 1952 Republican Convention, 568; N. Roosevelt's view, 576, 578; praises brief on segregation, 714; as solicitor general, 461. *See also* Supreme Court of the United States

Warren, George Earle: background, 1982–83; on Eisenhowers' portraits at Columbia, 1982–83

Warren, Lucian Crissey: background, 1503; heads National Press Club, 1503

Warren, Nina Elizabeth, 370–71

Warren, Nina (Palmquist) Meyers, 370–71

Warren, Virginia, 370–71

War Resources Administration: and civil defense policies, 1665–66; and emergency evacuation procedures, 1665–66

Warsaw Pact, 2362
Washburn, Abbott McConnell: background, 12; and executive branch study, 11; on Fred Waring and USIA, 1904
Washington (State): Citizens for Eisenhower in, 2281–83; and deactivation of Fort Worden, 876–79; and dedication of McNary Dam, 1304; and Eastvold, 2281–83; E. campaigns in, 2283; and McKay's Senate race, 2282–83; and navy acoustic range, Puget Sound, 230–31, 232; politics in, 1718, 2281–83; on problems at Port Townsend, 876–79
Washington, D.C. See District of Columbia
Washington, George: biographies of, from Lamoreux, 1318; on election (1789), 378; E.'s portrait of, 1427–28, 1485–86, 2143–44; on expectations as President, 1233–34; on Farewell Address, 2455–56; greatness of, 1437; quotes by, on presidency, 2000–2001, 2027
Washington College, E. speaks at, 818–19
Washington Press Club, and Churchill, 1074
Watches: Benrus opposes duty increase, 1117; duties on imports of, 1115–17, 1225–27; Elgin, Hamilton, Waltham companies seek duty increase, 1116; need for skilled workers in industry, 1115–17; ODM staff visits Bulova, 1117; and Swiss watch tariff issue, 1225–27, 1631; and Watch Industry Advisory Committee, 1226
Waterman, Sterry R.: background, 1510; federal judgeship for, 1510
Water resources: and budget policy for FY 1955, 643–44; and budget policy for FY 1956, 1632; and Cabinet Committee on, 1137, 1138; and Colorado River Storage Project, 901–3, 1136, 1137, 1138; debate, 689–90, 766–67, 786, 901–3; and Denver Blue River project, 1823–25; and Dinosaur National Monument, 1071–72, 1138; and Echo Park Dam, 1071–72, 1138; E.'s interest in, 1858–59; E. recommends funds for, 803, 805; E. vetoes rivers and harbors bill, 1632; and Hoover Commission task force on, 812, 1137, 1138; and Mansfield Reservoir project, 1632; and State of the Union Address, 652, 655; and water rights at Gettysburg farm, 1268–69, 1345–46; and waterway control legislation, 1267–68, 1278. See also Natural resources; Tennessee Valley Authority
Watkins, Arthur Vivian: and Bricker amendment, 140; and Colorado River Storage Project, 902, 1071, 1137, 1138; E. commends, on McCarthy censure, 1430; on lead and zinc imports, 1242–43
Watson, Samuel: background, 1283; on Formosa and Red China, 1283
Waugh, Samuel Clark: background, 1382; heads U.S. GATT delegation, 1382–83
Weaponry. See Ordnance
Weaver, Helen E., 78; receives promotion, 38–39

Wedemeyer, Albert Coady: background, 1588; on Formosan question, 1589; recommends Heaton as Surgeon General, 1588; on Schaefer's stroke, 1588, 1589
Weeks, Jane Tomkins (Rankin), background, 2195
Weeks, Sinclair, 1199; background 6; on decentralization in departments, 546; and decontrol of nickel, 581–82; on defense contracts, 1344; on E.'s finance committee, 1423; E.'s view, 28, 30; invites Robinson on Business Advisory Council, 2246; on liaison with Congress, 546; and Maryland-D.C. parkway, 1224–25; on Morrow's appointment, 2095; on national aviation policy, 1317, 1510; protests air routes to Africa, 1385; on railroad rate increases, 920–21; reports on merchant marine, 1024–25; on St. Lawrence Seaway, 133; as Secretary of Commerce, 5; sends get-well message to E., 2195; and Shields's proposal on world peace, 1059; on social service workers at White House, 809; and steel strike, 2202–3; and Taft-Hartley Act revisions, 538, 872–73; and "time-lag bill," 920–21; and Weather Bureau service, 1320. See also Commerce, Department of
Weems, M. L., 1318
Weimaraner Club of America, and pedigree of E.'s puppy, 1927
Weimar Republic, 527
Weinberg, Sidney James: background, 2375–76; supports E.'s campaign, 2375–76
Weir, Ernest Tener: background, 602; on foreign trade policy, 602, 603; pamphlet by, on foreign affairs, 603; on Pennsylvania politics, 601–2, 602–3; on Republican leadership, 602, 603; on U.S. policy on Formosa, 1662–63; visits Europe, 603
Wenzell, Adolphe: background, 1202, 1780; and Dixon-Yates contract, 1202, 1780–81
Wertenbaker, Charles Christian, E.'s esteem for, 830, 832
West (U.S.): and dump Nixon charges, 2074–75; housing construction in, 1696
West, Ernest E., 815–16
West, Walter A. ("Chief"): background, 1843; on game birds at E.'s farm, 2179–80; on trees for E.'s farm, 1843
West, Warren Reed: background, 989–90; as candidate for Librarian of Congress, 989–90
West Berlin. See Germany, Federal Republic of
Western Air Lines, and U.S.-Mexico air routes, 1569
Western Europe. See Europe: Western Europe
Western European Union (WEU): Churchill's view, 1628; and Formosa crisis, 1618; France favors, 1466–67, 1469–70, 1472–73; and London-Paris Accords, 1320–21, 1355, 1472–73, 1493, 1613, 1614; member nations of, 1614

Index 2939

Williams, George Mertens: background, 1773–74; on D.C. cultural center commission, 1773–74

Williams, Gerhard Mennen ("Soapy"): background, 2412; on distribution of federal surplus food, 2412

Williams, John Henry: and foreign economic policy, 357–58; on Randall Commission, 201

Williams, John James: on army poultry purchases, 934; background, 934

Williams, Margaret, E. reports to, on health, 1970–71

Williams, W. Walter: and Advisory Board of Economic Growth and Stability, 277–78; to assist Hall, RNC, 1423; attends stag dinner, 2062–63; and CAB, 1718; and public relations for Administration, 547

Willis, Charles Fountain, Jr., 387–88; background, 1747; and Butcher's charges, 1123–24; calls Ryan "controversial," 1465–66; and Citizens for Eisenhower, 396–97, 1747; on Georgia politics, 1029; on Republican party, reports to E., 780–81; resigns, 1747; visits Venezuela, 1663–64

Willis, Frances Elizabeth: background, 1116; and duties on Swiss watch imports, 1116–17, 1226

Willkie, Wendell Louis, 43

Wilson, Charles Edward, 128; background, 7; proposes experts panel, 7–8; proposes peace plan, 68, 1629–30; and Stassen, 1629–30

Wilson, Charles Erwin, 103, 169–70, 236, 389–90; on absentee voting laws for service personnel, 957–58, 1541–44; on aid for Hungarian refugees, 2436–37; on aid to Yugoslavia, 583–84; on air base closings, 895–96; on air bases in Morocco, 583–84; on air bases in Spain, 583–84, 768–69; approves army reorganization plan, 857; and Army-McCarthy hearings, 1064–66; and army reorganization, 855–57; attends NAC meeting, 178; background, 10; on ballistic missile program and interservice rivalries, 1932–33; and beef purchasing program, 1603; and Benson's plan to expand agricultural exports, 768–69; on bipartisan cooperation, 1453–54; on Bryan's rank as West Point head, 1088–89, 1189; and captured U.S. airmen, 1451; and Chief Joseph Dam, 306, 307, 1761–62, 1788, 1789; on China policy, Cutler's report, 1300–1301; and Churchill-Eden visit, 1141–42; on contract for U.S.S. *Kitty Hawk*, 1938; and control of nuclear weapons, 798–99; on cuts in DOD civilian personnel, 2078–79; and defense budget, FY 1955, 589–90, 671–72, 711, 712, 1206–7; on defense budget, FY 1958, 2255–56; on defense contracts and procurement, 1344, 1603–4, 1674–76, 1808–9; on deployment of atomic weapons, 1418; dislikes research and development, 260–61; divests self of stock, 29, 228; on DOD

censorship for media, 591–92, 631–32, 767–68; drafts reply to Smith, 916–17; E.'s directive to, on executive privilege, 1069–71, 1075–76; on E.'s New Look defense policy, 1488–91, 1591; E. reprimands, 1615–16; E. retires U.S.S. *Williamsburg*, 163; Es. visit, on midterm election night, 1375–76; favors St. Lawrence Seaway project, 188; on feeding POWs, 57–59; and France's request for technicians in Indochina, 886–87; and Gruenther's view on France, 890–91; and guided-missile program, 232–33, 1919; on head, Permanent Joint Board on Defense, 682–83; and Hinshaw's plan, 434–35; and ICBM program, 1853–54, 1932–33, 2021–22; and IRBM program, 1932–33; and JCS report on thermonuclear testing, 2260; on jet trainer sales to Germany, 1747–48; and Joint Chiefs of Staff, 355–57, 397–98, 635–36, 711, 712; Judd's trip, 594–95; on Korea, memo to, from E., 397–98; on Korean truce, 425–26; on Legion of Merit awards, 1398; on liaison with Congress, 546; on Libyans at West Point, 1616; on medical benefits for armed services, 685–86; meets with E. on Middle East, 2096–97; meets with French leaders, 213; memo to, on declining beef prices, 646, 656–57, 1603; and MIG incident, 529–32; and national security policy, 589–90, 671–72; and NATO command structure, 155–56, 166–67; at NATO ministerial meeting, Paris, 746; and New Look, 356, 589–90, 1488–91; on nuclear disarmament, 2039–41; on objective advice to, from JCS, 141; and Oppenheimer case, 717–19, 722–25; opposes mobilization stockpile, 1953–54; and ordnance production costs, 85; and Pack's device, 474–76; on Panamanian-American relations, 543–45, 912–13, 2213–14; on personnel strength in armed forces, 1488–91; on post for Reid, 1713; and Radford as JCS head, 235; and Radulovich case, 679–80; on rank for service academy superintendents, 1189; on redeployment of U.S. forces in Trieste, 1236–37, 1237–38, 1246–47; on reducing defense appropriations, 941–42; and reduction of U.S. forces in Korea, 770, 775–76; and REDWING, 2260; on reserve mobilization policy, 1222–23; resigns, 228; on Seaton, E.'s view, 486; as Secretary of Defense, 10, 225; on secret report leaks, 583–84, 767–68; sends rocking chair to E., 2460; on service promotions, 695–96; and Studebaker-Packard contracts, 2128–29; and study on U.S.-Soviet war, 1973–74; suggests changes in JCS personnel, 120; suspends military construction, 466–67; on Taber's proposals, 941–42; on U.S. aid to Korea, 427, 428, 442–45, 543, 547–49; on U.S. forces abroad, 591–92, 611–12, 2204; on U.S. policy in Far East, 2080; and Wherry housing, 2171–72

Wilson, Charles McMoran (Lord Moran): on

Churchill's health, 862; on Laniel's illness, 732

Wilson, Jessie Ann (Curtis): background, 2460; sends rocking chair to E., 2460

Wilson, Woodrow, 1318, 1980–81; greatness of, 1438–39; role of, as candidate, 1337–38

Wiltsee, Paul E.: background, 1296–97; Radford approves letter to, 1297; on Soviet aggression, 1296–97

Windfohr, R. W.: background, 1406–7; post for, 1406–7

Windsor, Duke of, 368

Windsor Castle, 1993–94

Wisconsin: censures Wiley, 435–36; congressional elections in, 605–6; federal judgeship in, 1508–9; and McCarthy in 1952 campaign, 939; objects to waterway control legislation, 1278; Republican midterm election defeat, 664

Wisdom, John Minor: background, 97; endorses White, 516; and President's Committee on Government Contracts, 476–77; and Republicans in South, 97, 479–80

Witten, J. H., 618–19

Wolfe, Glenn George: background, 943; Taber's complaint, 942–43

Wolverton, Charles Anderson, 109

Wolverton, Donnell Knox, 109

Women: Adkins's role on, 1727–28, 2376; and army nurse program, 1884–87; E. addresses Republican Women's National Conference, 1727–28; E.'s esteem for, 2262; on Ethel Rosenberg, 290; Falkenburg helps Republicans, 1206; Gunderson's view, 465–66, 1223–24, 1727–28; housing for, in armed services, 1885, 1886; and National Manpower Council, 1474–75; in Republican party, 2376; voting power of, 2376; on WACS, Hobby's role, 1776; and widows of retired service personnel, 1396, 1397; on "Woman Power for E.," 2349–50; in work force, Schaefer's view, 1397

Women's Army Corps (WACS): field grades in, 1885; in World War II, Hobby's role, 1776

Women's Medical Specialist Corps, field grades in, 1885

Wood, Austin Voorhees: background, 2003; esteem of, for E., 2003

Wood, C. Tyler: background, 548; as economic coordinator in Korea, 547–49

Wood, Frank M.: background, 785; on gifts for E., 587–88, 785; on gift knives as mementos, 785; and Mrs. Wood, 1502–3; on partisan bickering, 1502–3; supports E.'s candidacy, 2345; visits E., 587–88

Wood, Lloyd H.: as "compromise" gubernatorial candidate in Pennsylvania, 601–2, 603, 859–60; loses to Leader, 859–60

Wood, Robert Elkington: background, 1365; cochairs For America, 1402, 1405; on E.'s candidacy, 1552; on E.'s policies, 1551–52; on

Post Office Department and Railway Express Service, 1364–65; in reactionary fringe, 1402, 1405

Woodruff, Nell (Hodgson), 617, 1212

Woodruff, Robert Winship, 1956; attends stag dinner, 617; and "Augusta National" weekend in Denver, 1212, 1259–60; background, 617; on Bermingham's illness, 2057–58; birthday wishes to, from E., 1921; celebrates wedding anniversary, 2327; delivers Robinson's letter, 975–76; E.'s appreciation to, 1605–6; on E.'s meeting with George, 2093; and Georgia politics, 1028, 1029, 1968; gift for E., 617; meets with George, 1511, 1605–6; as political adviser to E., 1968; sends birthday greetings to E., 2327; sends socks to E., 1919–20; on stag dinners for "little people," 1026–27; steps down as chairman of Coca-Cola, 1518–19

Woods, Rose Mary: background, 1050; on Msgr. McCarthy, 1050; sends Nixon's speech to Whitman, 1319

Woodward, Robert Forbes: background, 1360; on Rio Conference, 1360

Woodward, Sergeant, 2322

Wool, producers of, oppose H.R. 1, 1573–74. See also Raw materials

World Bank, 1963–64; and Aswan Dam project, 2030, 2153, 2239–40; and Douglas's plan to aid Mideast economy, 1967–68; and Iran-U.K. dispute, 339; and Mexican-Pacific Railroad, 1599, 1600; and multilateral economic aid, 2177; and U.S. aid to Great Britain, 2403. See also International Bank for Reconstruction and Development

World Council of Churches, Assembly of, E. addresses, 818–19, 1122, 1256–57, 1630

World Day of Prayer for Peace, 220, 376–77, 1256–57, 1630

World peace: Bronfman's plan, 382–83; and E.'s Open Skies proposal, 2041; E.'s role in, White's view, 1957–58; on preservation of, 1238–39; on Suez crisis, as threat to, 2351–52; and Wilson's peace plan, 1629–30; and World Day of Prayer for Peace, 1256–57. See also Cold war; Free world

World War I: and France at Verdun, 1034; Tank Corps Association honors Patton, 249; veterans of, and Bonus March, 2002

World War II: and alien properties seized in, 932, 1432–33; and benefits for Polish veterans, 1360–61; and "Big Inch," 2244; and Churchill's memoir, *Triumph and Tragedy,* 511–12; CIO in, 558–59; on Communist sweep since, 1642; and D-Day anniversary statement, 1076–78; E. compares D-day and Korean truce, 458; on E.'s problem with Monty, 1324–25; E.'s role in, and presidency, 824; defections in, 530, 531; and division of Korea, 278–80; E. recalls Churchill during, 1626; on